# Walt Whitman

## COMPLETE POETRY & SELECTED
## PROSE AND LETTERS

EDITED BY EMORY HOLLOWAY

LONDON : THE NONESUCH PRESS
1967

First Published *1938*
Second Impression *1942*
Third Impression *1944*
Fourth Impression *1947*
Fifth Impression *1949*
Sixth Impression *1964*
Seventh Impression *1967*

PRINTED IN GREAT BRITAIN
BY ROBERT MACLEHOSE & CO. LTD, GLASGOW

26168

# Contents

## I. POETRY

### LEAVES OF GRASS

## DRUM-TAPS

## II. PROSE

### III. LETTERS

# Editor's Preface

"I am large: I contain multitudes," wrote Whitman, expressing his disdain for that "foolish consistency" which Emerson had declared to be the bugbear of small minds. His personality was as many-sided as was the American life which he sought to present through the lyric-epic of a representative character. It is because he contained multitudes and was, himself, like his nation, constantly growing, that a "compendious" edition is required adequately to present him as poet, prophet and man. Critics are agreed that his work is, from the artistic point of view, very unequal. But though one should conclude that, like Coleridge, he has but "fifty pages of pure gold" to his credit, the task of his editor yet does not become so simple as the mere winnowing of these pages from the chaff of his hasty compositions in newspapers and diaries. Moreover, readers will never agree as to these pages of gold, although a few of his great poems are praised almost universally. Even those who see him only as a poet entertain divergent views concerning his poetry; some would discard everything save his more "finished specimens", while others praise him for the rude suggestiveness of his poetic pioneering. Then there are readers who, accepting at its face value his own disavowal of purely literary aims, approach him as a spokesman of democracy, a reformatory force, if not as a systematic thinker. Still others discover in him, in an age of increasing regimentation, a refreshing example of sublime self-reliance, a symbol of human brotherhood, a religious mystic without cant. There is likewise a growing tendency to view him in perspective as the personification of a *Zeitgeist*, a composite photograph of nineteenth-century America. He is all these to us, and future readers may choose to see in him a still wider significance. Under these circumstances his editor seeks, in so far as it can be done in one volume, to present, not the "gems from Walt Whitman" which he so abhorred, but enough of his poetry, prose and correspondence to represent fully and fairly the many-sidedness of his nature and achievement. It is hoped that the "gems" are all here, but they require an adequate setting.

Since Whitman's work, both in verse and in prose, constitutes, and was intended to constitute, a sort of growing autobiography, the edition has been planned to facilitate reading in chronological order. Such an arrangement is in itself a commentary upon his unfolding purposes. Paradoxically, however, Whitman did not follow a strict chronological plan in arranging his own poetry or prose. He revised so much, rejecting, adding and recombining, that to present his poetry in strict chronological order could escape confusion only by reprinting at great cost of space the Triggs Variorum Readings, which are already accessible in the standard (Inclusive) edition by the present editor. The date of composition of each poem (if known, otherwise the date of its first known publication) is, however, given below the last line of the poem, to the left. The date of its final revision and inclusion in *Leaves of Grass* is given at the right. To enable the reader to peruse these poems chronologically, the first of these dates is given after the title in the Table of Contents. The letters follow a strict chronological order. The prose selections are arranged in the order of their composition or first known publication, except that autobiographical passages are arranged according to the period of Whitman's life which they describe. In the notes will be found numerous cross-references designed further to assist the reader who wishes to trace, through the inner and outer life of the man, his self-revelation and his growth. Three parallel lines of light are thus being thrown for the first time upon his whole career. The Biographical and Bibliographical Chronology will, it is hoped, prove an added help as a cross-reference index.

Such volumes as this could not have been prepared when the editor began his researches over two decades ago. The so-called *Complete Writings*, issued by Whitman's literary executors in 1902, was far from complete. Since then, however, scholars have unearthed a great mass of poetry and prose important to our present plan of tracing the evolution of America's great poet; they have furthermore discovered facts of chronology and circumstances of publication almost equally essential. There are still many letters of Whitman which have not been published, and many manuscripts. But the editor has examined so large a proportion of these as to be able to say with reasonable certainty that what is now presented is not likely to be seriously qualified by future publication. There are still mysteries of interpretation, and doubtless always will be; but there are no longer significant gaps in the biography of Whitman's adult life, and every type and period of his writing is here represented.

The need for such a compilation is emphasized by the fact that the standard edition of Whitman's *Complete Prose* is out of print, as are *The Wound Dresser, Calamus, With Walt Whitman in Camden, Walt Whitman the Man,* and other volumes in which selections of his letters have appeared. His fugitive writings in prose, if they remain in print, are scattered in a great variety of books, some of which were issued only in limited editions. There is real danger, therefore, that the general reader, lacking the facilities or the habits of the scholar, will form his impression of Whitman almost entirely from the verse, or from the biographies of the poet. But here he is allowed to speak freely for himself both in prose and verse, and what he says may now and then be all the more significant for not having been addressed, in the first instance, to the modern reader.

The notes are, for the most part, intended to clarify rather than to interpret. When possible, facts concerning the date and occasion of first publication have been given for the light they throw on the genesis of poem or prose passage, and to suggest the range of Whitman's reception by the editors of his own day, of which he sometimes complained. Whitman's own comment on his work, or the comment of contemporaries having first-hand information, has been linked with the annotated passages by means of notes or cross-references. Complete annotation, however, would be so voluminous as to require the sacrifice of Whitman's own text.

All selections are given without omissions, unless these omissions appear in the only available source. Interpolated matter, such as known but unexpressed addresses in the correspondence, has been enclosed in brackets. For the sake of uniformity, the arrangement of letter headings has sometimes been shifted on the page. All notes found at the foot of the page are Whitman's own.

The text of the poetry is that of the Inclusive Edition, itself based upon the last edition which Whitman revised. Rejected or uncollected poems are added at the end of the section. All the poetry Whitman published is included, with the exception of a few juvenile verses (represented here) to be found in *Uncollected Poetry and Prose* and a few unimportant fragments in *Complete Prose*. The text of the prose is indicated in the notes in each case. The letters have been collated, where possible, with the manuscripts; but in most cases they have followed the published text. This involves no end of eccentricities but a conventionalized Whitman ceases to be Whitman.

## ACKNOWLEDGMENTS

I am grateful to Doubleday, Doran and Co., and especially to Mr. Harry E. Maule, for permission to include much material from the following books: *Leaves of Grass, Complete Prose, The Wound Dresser, Calamus,* and *The Uncollected Poetry and Prose of Walt Whitman,* of which they hold whatever copyrights are still in force. These selections are found on pages 3-501, 503-05, 506-30, 571-86, 728-36; 533-42, 561-66, 618-24, 628-32, 638-48, 651-56, 657-728, 736-833, 838-58, 874-80, 955-56, 1039-40; 632-37, 888-92, 893-95, 900-13, 936-48; 978-81, 984-85, 990-94, 996, 1007-08, 1011-12, 1013-15, 1018-20, 1034-35, 1044; 502, 505-06, 542-61, 566-71, 834-38, 895-900. Mrs. Horace Traubel has kindly permitted quotation, from her husband's *With Walt Whitman in Camden,* of the letters found on pages 657, 915-25, 928-36, 951-52, 954, 963-71, 973-74, 976-77, 981-83, 986-89, 997-98, 999, 1000-1004, 1009, 1017-18, 1022-23, 1025-27, 1028, 1044. The original manuscript of all the letters to Anne Gilchrist which have been included were graciously placed at my disposal by Mrs. Frank J. Sprague. For permission to use various letters (pages 884-85, 893, 1010-11, 1030-31, 1032, 1045, 1048, 1051) collected by Professor Rollo G. Silver and published in *American Literature,* I am indebted to Professor J. B. Hubbell and his editorial colleagues, who were good enough to make an exception to their rule which forbids republication from the pages of that quarterly. Professor Bliss Perry kindly supplied me with the complete manuscript of Letter XXXIX. I am grateful also to Mr. David Goodale for helpful services in connection therewith. Professor Clifton Joseph Furness and his publisher, the Harvard University Press, have my thanks for permission to reprint, from *Walt Whitman's Workshop*, "*The Eighteenth Presidency*", which was there first printed in America. He has kindly furnished also the text of Letter CLXIV. Selections from Professor Charles I. Glicksberg's *Walt Whitman and the Civil War* (pages 624-28, 649-50, 913-15, 953-54, 1000, 1010) are used by his kind permission and that of the University of Pennsylvania Press. Letter CXXIV is printed through the kindness of Mr. Alfred F. Goldsmith. Houghton Mifflin Co. generously permit me to include many letters from Clara Barrus' *Whitman and Burroughs, Comrades* (found on pages 948-49, 1008-09, 1018, 1020-21, 1029, 1033-34, 1036-37, 1038-39, 1040-42, 1048-49, 1050-51). And Messrs. George Allen & Unwin Ltd. did likewise for the letters on pages 1052-57, 1058. The four selections from *I Sit and Look Out* (pages 612-17) are reprinted with the permission of the Columbia University Press. Mr. Ralph Adimari has been good enough to supply me with information used in several of the notes. Information embodied in many of the notes, especially those concerning Whitman music and Whitman bibliography, has been supplied me during the last twenty years by Mr. Henry S. Saunders, whose carefully made notes on Whitman, now in the Brown University library, are a boon to Whitman scholarship. I thank Captain Frank L. Pleadwell for supplying Letter CXXXVI, and Mr. W. T. H. Howe for a similar privilege concerning letters on pages 983-84, 994, 1015, 1016, 1021, 1027-28, 1035-36, 1038, 1047, 1049-50, which have either not been previously or completely published, and for supplying photostats of many letters in his Whitman collection which have enabled me to detect inaccuracies in their published versions.

EMORY HOLLOWAY

Brooklyn, *January* 25, 1938

# Biographical and Bibliographical Chronology

NOTE.—The purpose of this chronology is to assist the reader who wishes to read Whitman's poetry, prose and letters chronologically and together as a composite autobiography. It is not intended as a complete index to the material in the volume.

The record of publications is extended beyond the date of the poet's death in order to complete the list of Whitman's writings printed to date. An exhaustive bibliography (supplementing those by Frank Shay, Carolyn Wells and Alfred F. Goldsmith, and Emory Holloway and Henry S. Saunders) is about to go to the press of Houghton, Mifflin and Company, Boston, prepared by Clifton Joseph Furness and Henry S. Saunders in collaboration with the present editor.

1819. May 31, born on a farm at West Hills, near Huntington, Long Island.

1823. Moved to Brooklyn, living first in Front Street, near the ferry.

1825-30. Attended public school; office boy to a lawyer and a doctor.

1831-34. In Brooklyn printing offices, learning the trade.

1836. A compositor in New York.

1836-41. Taught schools, "boarding round" in various parts of Long Island.

1838. June 5, started a weekly newspaper, *The Long Islander*, at Huntington.

1839-40. At Jamaica, as compositor on *Long Island Democrat*, in which he published most of his earliest extant verse and prose, 1839-40.
Also electioneering for Van Buren.

1841. May, returned to New York. Worked as compositor and editor and began writing prose and verse for magazines.

1842. His poorly written *Franklin Evans*, a temperance tract, widely read.

1846-48. Edited Brooklyn *Daily Eagle*. Lost position because of liberal (free soil) political principles.

1848. March-May, in New Orleans as an editor of *Daily Crescent*. Accompanied on journey by his brother Jefferson. June 15, back in Brooklyn. Active in "Barnburner" political campaign.
September, began editing Brooklyn *Freeman*.

1849. September, retired from *Freeman* and probably made a second trip to the South.

1850. March 22, publishes first free verse, "Blood Money", on slavery issue.
May-June, anonymously connected with Brooklyn *Daily Advertiser*.

1851-54. Contributor or correspondent for New York *Evening Post*.
Carpentering and house building with his father. At work on *Leaves of Grass*.

1855. July 4, First Edition, *Leaves of Grass*, Brooklyn, no publisher, 4to, 94 pp.
July 11, lost his father by death.
July 21, received Emerson's famous letter praising his book.
September 17, visited by Moncure D. Conway.
November 10, visited by Thoreau and Alcott.
November, published the first of a number of articles in *Life Illustrated*. Connection ended about August, 1856.

1856. Second Edition, *Leaves of Grass*, Brooklyn, printed and sold by Fowler and Wells, 16mo, 384 pp.
Interested in Republican presidential campaign.
Visited by Emerson.

1857-59. Edited Brooklyn *Daily Times*.

1860. Third Edition, *Leaves of Grass*, Boston, Thayer and Eldridge, 12 mo, 456 pp.
*Leaves of Grass. Imprints*, criticisms of Whitman's poetry.
March, in Boston, seeing his poems through the press.
Met William Douglas O'Connor and J. T. Trowbridge.
April, *Atlantic Monthly* published "Bardic Symbols".

1861. June 8, began series of twenty-five *Brooklynia* sketches for Brooklyn weekly *Standard*; ended November, 1862.
Fall, journeyed through Long Island.
Composed some of *Drum-Taps* poems, publishing some to stimulate recruiting.

1862. Wrote articles for New York *Leader*.
December 16, left for Virginia war front, where his brother George had been reported wounded.

1863. January, returned to Washington with the wounded and began volunteer missionary work in the hospitals. Wrote war correspondence of New York and Brooklyn papers and did copying to support himself and to supply funds for his ministrations. Distributed gifts from others to the wounded.
November, met John Burroughs.

1864. June 23, prostrated, returned home, for nearly a half-year in Brooklyn, where he continued to visit hospitals. Planned publication of *Drum-Taps*.

1865. January 24, appointed to clerkship in Indian Bureau, Interior Department, where he worked a few hours a day. Salary, $1200.
May 11, promoted to a clerkship of the second class.
June 30, dismissed by James Harlan, Secretary of Interior.
August, appointed clerk in Attorney General's Office.
September, O'Connor gave Whitman his sobriquet by publishing *The Good Gray Poet*, protesting against his dismissal by Harlan for authorship "of an indecent book".
*Walt Whitman's Drum-Taps*, New York, 1865, no publisher. All but the first few copies contain the *Sequel to Drum-Taps*, which includes "When Lilacs Last in the Dooryard Bloom'd".

1866. Probably met Peter Doyle in this year.

1867. Fourth Edition, *Leaves of Grass*, New York, no publisher, 12mo, 338 pp.
Assisted John Burroughs in writing *Notes on Walt Whitman as Poet and Person*.

1867. October, regularly assigned as recording clerk. Salary, $1600 a year.

1868. William Michael Rossetti's selected *Poems by Walt Whitman*, J. C. Hotten, London.
October, visiting congressman Thomas Davis in Providence, Rhode Island.

1869. June-July, Mrs. Anne Gilchrist read the Rossetti selection and fell in love with the poet.
August-September, in Brooklyn on vacation.

1870. August-September, in Brooklyn on vacation, having his poems electrotyped for the 1871 Edition of *Leaves of Grass*.

1871. Summer in Brooklyn.
July, received cordial letter from Tennyson.
September 7, read "After All, Not to Create Only" at opening of American Institute in New York.
Fifth Edition, *Leaves of Grass*, Washington, no publisher, 8vo, 384 pp., and *Passage to India*, 120 pp., in one volume. Both also published separately.
*After All Not to Create Only*, Washington, no publisher.
*Democratic Vistas*, Washington, no publisher.

1872. February-April, July, in Brooklyn.
June, journeyed to Hanover, Vermont, to read "As a Strong Bird on Pinions Free" at the Dartmouth College Commencement, visiting his sister at Burlington on the return trip.
*Democratic Vistas* translated into Danish by Rudolph Schmidt.
Sixth Edition, *Leaves of Grass*, Washington, 8vo, no publisher. Little change from Fifth Edition.

1873. January 23, suffered an attack of paralysis.
February 19, lost his sister-in-law (Mrs. Jefferson Whitman) by death.
March 10, transferred to the office of the Solicitor of the Treasury.
May 20, started to sea coast in search of health, but got only as far as Camden, New Jersey, where he lived with his brother Col. George Whitman till 1884.

May 23, lost his mother, who died at Camden.

Wrote verse and prose for *Daily Graphic*.

Met Horace Traubel, who was to prove a devoted friend and voluminous biographer.

1874. January-March, wrote six articles on the war for the New York *Weekly Graphic*.

March, published "The Prayer of Columbus", swan song of his greatest poetry, in *Harper's*.

June, wrote "The Song of the Universal", read by proxy at the Tufts College Commencement.

July 1, dismissed from clerkship, which he had held by employing a substitute.

1875. November, visited by Lord Houghton. Visited Washington and Baltimore. Poor health.

*Memoranda During the War*, author's publication, Camden.

1876. Seventh Edition (Author's Centennial), *Leaves of Grass*, Camden, reprint of 1871 Edition.

*Two Rivulets, Prose and Verse*, Camden, containing *Democratic Vistas, Centennial Songs*, and *Passage to India*.

Robert Buchanan's letter about Whitman's need attracted wide attention in England and the new books brought substantial financial returns.

Summer, went, as often later, to Timber Creek, near Whitehorse, for sun and baths, gradually improving in health. Wrote nature notes, later included in *Specimen Days*. Mrs. Gilchrist moved to Philadelphia to be near him.

1877. February, visited J. H. Johnston in New York and John Burroughs in Ulster County.

May 1, visited by Edward Carpenter, and by Dr. R. M. Bucke, in 1883 to become his authorized biographer.

1878. June-July, visited J. H. Johnston and Burroughs.

1879. April 14, delivered the first of his Lincoln lectures at Steck Hall in New York. Afterwards he visited Burroughs at Esopus.

September-December, visited Jefferson Whitman in St. Louis and travelled as far west as Denver.

1880. June-September, visited Dr. Bucke at London, Ontario, and with him visited Montreal, Quebec and the Saguenay River, making notes, to be posthumously published in *Diary in Canada*.

1881. April, delivered Lincoln lecture in Boston; visited Longfellow.

May, visited J. H. Johnston for six weeks at Mott Haven. July, returned to his birthplace.

August, in Boston, reading proofs for Osgood Edition of his poems. Visited Concord as guest of Frank B. Sanborn and was entertained at dinner by Emerson and his family.

Eighth Edition, *Leaves of Grass*, Boston, James R. Osgood and Co., 8vo, 382 pp. London editions issued by Bogue and by Trübner and Co.

1882. Osgood, threatened with prosecution, abandoned the publication of *Leaves of Grass*, and Whitman, with the same plates, issued the Ninth Edition in Camden, as an Author's Edition. Later in the year Rees, Welsh and Company, Philadelphia, published the book. David McKay published various editions from these plates.

*Specimen Days and Collect*, Rees, Welsh and Company, Philadelphia. Issued the next year in Glasgow by Wilson and McCormick.

1883. September, at Ocean Grove, New Jersey, with Burroughs.

1884. March, bought house at 328 Mickle Street, where he was to spend the remaining nine years of his life and where he was visited by a great number of foreign and American admirers.

1885. Too lame to get about; a subscription was taken to buy him a horse and buggy, Mark Twain, Richard Watson Gilder, Oliver Wendel Holmes, Whittier, and others contributing.

1886. Royalties very small, but Talcott Williams arranged for a Lincoln lecture at Chestnut Street Opera House in Philadelphia, which netted $692.

Summer, on a voyage to Montauk Point, Long Island.

December, *Pall Mall Gazette*, printing a rumour that Whitman was starving, raised £125.

An unsuccessful attempt was made to obtain for Whitman a pension for his hospital services.

*The Poems of Walt Whitman*, selection by Ernest Rhys, Walter Scott, London.

1887. April 15, delivered Lincoln lecture in Madison Square Theatre, New York, attended by Mark Twain, John Hay, Lowell, St. Gaudens, Edmund Clarence Stedman, and other prominent persons. Andrew Carnegie paid $350 for a box; proceeds, $600.

Friends in Boston donated $800 to poet.

*Specimen Days in America*, revised, Walter Scott, London.

1888. April, suffered new paralytic attack; near death in November.

*November Boughs*, David McKay, Philadelphia; English Edition, Alexander Gardner, Paisley and London, 1889.

*Democratic Vistas and Other Papers*, Walter Scott, London.

*Complete Poems and Prose of Walt Whitman, Authenticated and Personal. (Handled by Walt Whitman), Portraits from Life. Autograph, Containing Sands at Seventy and November Boughs.*

Regular contributor to New York *Herald*.

1889. May 31, birthday dinner given him by citizens of Camden.

Ninth Edition, *Leaves of Grass*, containing *Sands at Seventy* and "A Backward Glance O'er Travel'd Roads", issued as a birthday souvenir. Later issued by D. Appleton and Company, 1908, and by Mitchell Kennerley, 1914.

1890. April 15, Whitman delivered Lincoln lecture at Contemporary Club.

May 31, attended a public birthday dinner in Philadelphia.

October 21, Robert Ingersoll gave a benefit lecture on "Liberty in Literature" at Horticultural Hall, Philadelphia.

December, ill with pneumonia.

1891. *Good-Bye, My Fancy*, 2d Annex to *Leaves of Grass*, David McKay, Philadelphia.

Tenth Edition, *Leaves of Grass*, containing *Sands at Seventy*, *Good-Bye, My Fancy*, "A Backward Glance O'er Travel'd Roads," and portrait from life, David McKay, the so-called "Deathbed Edition".

1892. March 26, died at Camden.

March 30, buried in a tomb in Harleigh Cemetery designed by himself.

*Complete Prose Works*, David McKay, Philadelphia.

1897. *Calamus*, letters to Peter Doyle, edited by Richard Maurice Bucke, Laurens Maynard, Boston.

Eleventh Edition, *Leaves of Grass*, containing *Old Age Echoes*, Small, Maynard, and Company, Boston. Later reprinted by D. Appleton and Company, 1908; Mitchell Kennerley, 1914, English imprint, G. P. Putnam's Sons.

1898. *Complete Prose Works, Specimen Days and Collect, November Boughs* and *Good-Bye, My Fancy*, Small, Maynard and Company, Boston. Later reprinted by D. Appleton and Company, 1908; Mitchell Kennerley, 1914; and Doubleday, Page & Co.

*The Wound Dresser*, letters from Whitman to his mother during the war, edited by Richard Maurice Bucke, Small, Maynard and Company, Boston.

1899. *Notes and Fragments*, edited by Richard Maurice Bucke, printed for private distribution.

1902. *The Complete Writings of Walt Whitman*, issued under the editorial supervision of his Literary Executors, Richard Maurice Bucke, Thomas B. Harned and Horace L. Traubel, containing biographical and critical material and Trigg's Variorum Readings, 10 volumes, G. P. Putnam's Sons, New York and London. The three volumes of verse were issued in one by Doubleday, Page and Company, Garden City, in 1917.

1920. *The Gathering of the Forces*, Whitman writings in the Brooklyn *Eagle*, edited by Cleveland Rodgers and John Black, G. P. Putnam's Sons, New York and London, 2 volumes.

1921. *The Uncollected Poetry and Prose of Walt Whitman*, 2 volumes, edited by Emory Holloway, Doubleday, Page and Company, Garden City, and William Heinemann, London (1922).

1924. Inclusive Edition, *Leaves of Grass*, including variorum readings, prefaces and rejected poems, edited by Emory Holloway, Doubleday, Page and Company, Garden City.

COME, said my soul,
Such verses for my body let us write, (for we are one,)
That should I after death invisibly return,
Or, long, long hence, in other spheres,
There to some group of mates the chants resuming,
(Tallying earth's soil, trees, winds, tumultuous waves,)
Ever with pleas'd smile I may keep on,
Ever and ever yet the verses owning—as, first, I here and now,
Signing for soul and body, set to them my name,

*Walt Whitman*

# I. Poetry

A

# Leaves of Grass

## Inscriptions

### ONE'S-SELF I SING

ONE'S-SELF I sing, a simple separate person,
Yet utter the word Democratic, the word En-Masse.

Of physiology from top to toe I sing,
Not physiognomy alone nor brain alone is worthy for the
    Muse, I say the Form complete is worthier far,
The Female equally with the Male I sing.

Of Life immense in passion, pulse, and power,
Cheerful, for freest action form'd under the laws divine,
The Modern Man I sing.
1867                                                    1871

### AS I PONDER'D IN SILENCE

As I ponder'd in silence,
Returning upon my poems, considering, lingering long,
A Phantom arose before me with distrustful aspect,
Terrible in beauty, age, and power,
The genius of poets of old lands,
As to me directing like flame its eyes,
With finger pointing to many immortal songs,
And menacing voice, *What singest thou?* it said,
*Know'st thou not there is but one theme for ever-enduring bards?*
*And that is the theme of War, the fortune of battles,*
*The making of perfect soldiers.*

*Be it so,* then I answer'd,
*I too haughty Shade also sing war, and a longer and greater one
    than any,*
*Waged in my book with varying fortune, with flight, advance
    and retreat, victory deferr'd and wavering,*

3

*(Yet methinks certain, or as good as certain, at the last,) the*
   *field the world,*
*For life and death, for the Body and for the eternal Soul,*
*Lo, I too am come, chanting the chant of battles,*
*I above all promote brave soldiers.*
1871                                                    1871


## IN CABIN'D SHIPS AT SEA

In cabin'd ships at sea,
The boundless blue on every side expanding,
With whistling winds and music of the waves, the large im-
        perious waves,
Or some lone bark buoy'd on the dense marine,
Where joyous full of faith, spreading white sails,
She cleaves the ether mid the sparkle and the foam of day, or
        under many a star at night,
By sailors young and old haply will I, a reminiscence of the
        land, be read,
In full rapport at last.

*Here are our thoughts, voyagers' thoughts,*
*Here not the land, firm land, alone appears, may then by them*
        *be said,*
*The sky o'erarches here, we feel the undulating deck beneath*
        *our feet,*
*We feel the long pulsation, ebb and flow of endless motion.*
*The tones of unseen mystery, the vague and vast suggestions of*
        *the briny world, the liquid-flowing syllables,*
*The perfume, the faint creaking of the cordage, the melancholy*
        *rhythm,*
*The boundless vista and the horizon far and dim are all here,*
*And this is ocean's poem.*

Then falter not O book, fulfil your destiny,
You not a reminiscence of the land alone,
You too as a lone bark cleaving the ether, purpos'd I know
        not whither, yet ever full of faith,
Consort to every ship that sails, sail you!
Bear forth to them folded my love, (dear mariners, for you
        I fold it here in every leaf;)

Speed on my book! spread your white sails my little bark
    athwart the imperious waves,
Chant on, sail on, bear o'er the boundless blue from me to
    every sea,
This song for mariners and all their ships.
1871
                                               1881

## TO FOREIGN LANDS

I HEARD that you ask'd for something to prove this puzzle the
    New World,
And to define America, her athletic Democracy,
Therefore I send you my poems that you behold in them
    what you wanted.
1860
                                               1871

## TO A HISTORIAN

YOU who celebrate bygones,
Who have explored the outward, the surfaces of the races,
    the life that has exhibited itself,
Who have treated of man as the creature of politics, aggre-
    gates, rulers and priests,
I, habitan of the Alleghanies, treating of him as he is in him-
    self in his own rights,
Pressing the pulse of the life that has seldom exhibited itself,
    (the great pride of man in himself),
Chanter of Personality, outlining what is yet to be,
I project the history of the future.
1860
                                             1871

## TO THEE OLD CAUSE

To thee old cause!
Thou peerless, passionate, good cause,
Thou stern, remorseless, sweet idea,
Deathless throughout the ages, races, lands,
After a strange sad war, great war for thee,
(I think all war through time was really fought, and ever will
    be really fought, for thee,)
These chants for thee, the eternal march of thee.

(A war O soldiers not for itself alone,
Far, far more stood silently waiting behind, now to advance
   in this book.)

Thou orb of many orbs!
Thou seething principle! thou well-kept, latent germ! thou
   centre!
Around the idea of thee the war revolving,
With all its angry and vehement play of causes,
(With vast results to come for thrice a thousand years,)
These recitatives for thee,—my book and the war are one,
Merged in its spirit I and mine, as the contest hinged on thee,
As a wheel on its axis turns, this book unwitting to itself,
Around the idea of thee.
1871                                                              1881

## EIDÓLONS

     I MET a seer,
Passing the hues and objects of the world,
The fields of art and learning, pleasure, sense,
     To glean eidólons.

     Put in thy chants said he,
No more the puzzling hour nor day, nor segments, parts, put
   in,
Put first before the rest as light for all and entrance-song of all,
     That of eidólons.

     Ever the dim beginning,
Ever the growth, the rounding of the circle,
Ever the summit and the merge at last, (to surely start again,)
     Eidólons! eidólons!

     Ever the mutable,
Ever materials, changing, crumbling, re-cohering,
Ever the ateliers, the factories divine,
     Issuing eidólons.

     Lo, I or you,
Or woman, man, or state, known or unknown,
We seeming solid wealth, strength, beauty build,
     But really build eidólons.

The ostent evanescent,
The substance of an artist's mood or savan's studies long,
Or warrior's, martyr's, hero's toils,
To fashion his eidólon.

Of every human life,
(The units gather'd, posted, not a thought, emotion, deed,
    left out,)
The whole or large or small summ'd, added up,
In its eidólon.

The old, old urge,
Based on the ancient pinnacles, lo, newer, higher pinnacles,
From science and the modern still impell'd,
The old, old urge, eidólons.

The present now and here,
America's busy, teeming, intricate whirl,
Of aggregate and segregate for only thence releasing,
To-day's eidólons.

These with the past,
Of vanish'd lands, of all the reigns of kings across the sea,
Old conquerors, old campaigns, old sailor's voyages,
Joining eidólons.

Densities, growth, façades,
Strata of mountains, soils, rocks, giant trees,
Far-born, far-dying, living long, to leave,
Eidólons everlasting.

Exaltè, rapt, ecstatic,
The visible but their womb of birth,
Of orbic tendencies to shape and shape and shape,
The mighty earth-eidólon.

All space, all time,
(The stars, the terrible perturbations of the suns,
Swelling, collapsing, ending, serving their longer, shorter
    use,)
Fill'd with eidólons only.

The noiseless myriads,
The infinite oceans where the rivers empty,
The separate countless free identities, like eyesight,
      The true realities, eidólons.

Not this the world,
Nor these the universes, they the universes,
Purport and end, ever the permanent life of life,
      Eidólons, eidólons.

Beyond thy lectures learn'd professor,
Beyond thy telescope or spectroscope observer keen, beyond
      all mathematics,
Beyond the doctor's surgery, anatomy, beyond the chemist
      with his chemistry,
      The entities of entities, eidólons.

Unfixed yet fix'd,
Ever shall be, ever have been and are,
Sweeping the present to the infinite future,
      Eidólons, eidólons, eidólons.

The prophet and the bard,
Shall yet maintain themselves, in higher stages yet,
Shall mediate to the Modern, to Democracy, interpret yet to
      them,
      God and eidólons.

And thee my soul,
Joys, ceaseless exercises, exaltations,
Thy yearning amply fed at last, prepared to meet,
      Thy mates, eidólons.

Thy body permanent,
The body lurking there within thy body,
The only purport of the form thou art, the real I myself,
      An image, an eidólon.

Thy very songs not in thy songs,
No special strains to sing, none for itself,
But from the whole resulting, rising at last and floating,
      A round full-orb'd eidólon.

1876                                        1876

## FOR HIM I SING

For him I sing,
I raise the present on the past,
(As some perennial tree out of its roots, the present on the past,)
With time and space I him dilate and fuse the immortal laws,
To make himself by them the law unto himself.
1871                                          1871

## WHEN I READ THE BOOK

When I read the book, the biography famous,
And is this then (said I) what the author calls a man's life?
And so will some one when I am dead and gone write my life?
(As if any man really knew aught of my life,
Why even I myself I often think know little or nothing of my
      real life,
Only a few hints, a few diffused faint clews and indirections
I seek for my own use to trace out here.)
1867                                          1871

## BEGINNING MY STUDIES

Beginning my studies the first step pleas'd me so much,
The mere fact consciousness, these forms, the power of motion,
The least insect or animal, the senses, eyesight, love,
The first step I say awed me and pleas'd me so much,
I have hardly gone and hardly wish'd to go any farther,
But stop and loiter all the time to sing it in ecstatic songs.
1867                                          1871

## BEGINNERS

How they are provided for upon the earth, (appearing at
      intervals,)
How dear and dreadful they are to the earth,
How they inure to themselves as much as to any—what a
      paradox appears their age,
How people respond to them, yet know them not,
How there is something relentless in their fate all times,
How all times mischoose the objects of their adulation and
      reward,
And how the same inexorable price must still be paid for the
      same great purchase.
1860                                          1860

## TO THE STATES

To the States or any one of them, or any city of the States,
  *Resist much, obey little,*
Once unquestioning obedience, once fully enslaved,
Once fully enslaved, no nation, state, city, of this earth, evei
  afterward resumes its liberty.
1860                                                          1881

## ON JOURNEYS THROUGH THE STATES

On journeys through the States we start,
(Ay through the world, urged by these songs,
Sailing henceforth to every land, to every sea,)
We willing learners of all, teachers of all, and lovers of all.

We have watch'd the seasons dispensing themselves and
  passing on,
And have said, Why should not a man or woman do as much
  as the seasons, and effuse as much?

We dwell a while in every city and town,
We pass through Kanada, the North-east, the vast valley of
  the Mississippi, and the Southern States,
We confer on equal terms with each of the States,
We make trial of ourselves and invite men and women to hear,
We say to ourselves, Remember, fear not, be candid, pro-
  mulge the body and the soul,
Dwell a while and pass on, be copious, temperate, chaste,
  magnetic,
And what you effuse may then return as the seasons return,
And may be just as much as the seasons.
1860                                                          1871

## TO A CERTAIN CANTATRICE

Here, take this gift,
I was reserving it for some hero, speaker, or general,
One who should serve the good old cause, the great idea, the
  progress and freedom of the race,
Some brave confronter of despots, some daring rebel;
But I see that what I was reserving belongs to you just as
  much as to any.
1860                                                          1871

## ME IMPERTURBE

Me imperturbe, standing at ease in Nature,
Master of all or mistress of all, aplomb in the midst of irrational things,
Imbued as they, passive, receptive, silent as they,
Finding my occupation, poverty, notoriety, foibles, crimes, less important than I thought,
Me toward the Mexican sea, or in the Mannahatta or the Tennessee, or far north or inland,
A river man, or a man of the woods or of any farm-life of these States or of the coast, or the lakes or Kanada,
Me wherever my life is lived, O to be self-balanced for contingencies,
To confront night, storms, hunger, ridicule, accidents, rebuffs, as the trees and animals do.

1860                                                             1881

## SAVANTISM

Thither as I look I see each result and glory retracing itself and nestling close, always obligated,
Thither hours, months, years—thither trades, compacts, establishments, even the most minute,
Thither every-day life, speech, utensils, politics, persons, estates;
Thither we also, I with my leaves and songs, trustful, admirant,
As a father to his father going takes his children along with him.

1860                                                             1860

## THE SHIP STARTING

Lo, the unbounded sea,
On its breast a ship starting, spreading all sails, carrying even her moonsails,
The pennant is flying aloft as she speeds she speeds so stately —below emulous waves press forward,
They surround the ship with shining curving motions and foam.

1865                                                             1881

## I HEAR AMERICA SINGING

I HEAR America singing, the varied carols I hear,
Those of mechanics, each one singing his as it should be
  blithe and strong,
The carpenter singing his as he measures his plank or beam,
The mason singing his as he makes ready for work, or leaves
  off work,
The boatman singing what belongs to him in his boat, the
  deck-hand singing on the steamboat deck,
The shoemaker singing as he sits on his bench, the hatter
  singing as he stands,
The wood-cutter's song, the ploughboy's on his way in the
  morning, or at noon intermission or at sundown,
The delicious singing of the mother, or of the young wife at
  work, or of the girl sewing or washing,
Each singing what belongs to him or her and to none else,
The day what belongs to the day—at night the party of young
  fellows, robust, friendly,
Singing with open mouths their strong melodious songs.
1860                                                    1867

## WHAT PLACE IS BESIEGED?

WHAT place is besieged, and vainly tries to raise the siege?
Lo, I send to that place a commander, swift, brave, immortal,
And with him horse and foot, and parks of artillery,
And artillery-men, the deadliest that ever fired gun.
1860                                                    1867

## STILL THOUGH THE ONE I SING

STILL though the one I sing,
(One, yet of contradictions made,) I dedicate to Nationality,
I leave in him revolt, (O latent right of insurrection! O
  quenchless, indispensable fire!)
1871                                                    1871

## SHUT NOT YOUR DOORS

SHUT not your doors to me proud libraries,
For that which was lacking on all your well-fill'd shelves, yet
  needed most, I bring,
Forth from the war emerging, a book I have made,

The words of my book nothing, the drift of it every thing,
A book separate, not link'd with the rest nor felt by the intellect,
But you ye untold latencies will thrill to every page.
1865                                                              1881

## POETS TO COME

Poets to come! orators, singers, musicians to come!
Not to-day is to justify me and answer what I am for,
But you, a new brood, native, athletic, continental, greater
than before known,
Arouse! for you must justify me.

I myself but write one or two indicative words for the future,
I but advance a moment only to wheel and hurry back in the
darkness.

I am a man who, sauntering along without fully stopping,
turns a casual look upon you and then averts his face,
Leaving it to you to prove and define it,
Expecting the main things from you.
1860                                                              1867

## TO YOU

Stranger, if you passing meet me and desire to speak to me,
why should you not speak to me?
And why should I not speak to you?
1860                                                              1860

## THOU READER

Thou reader throbbest life and pride and love the same as I,
Therefore for thee the following chants.
1881                                                              1881

# *Starting from Paumanok*

## 1

STARTING from fish-shape Paumanok where I was born,
Well-begotten, and rais'd by a perfect mother,
After roaming many lands, lover of populous pavements,
Dweller in Mannahatta my city, or on southern savannas,
Or a soldier camp'd or carrying my knapsack and gun, or a
    miner in California,
Or rude in my home in Dakota's woods, my diet meat, my
    drink from the spring,
Or withdrawn to muse and meditate in some deep recess,
Far from the clank of crowds intervals passing rapt and
    happy,
Aware of the fresh free giver the flowing Missouri, aware of
    mighty Niagara,
Aware of the buffalo herds grazing the plains, the hirsute and
    strong-breasted bull,
Of earth, rocks, Fifth-month flowers experienced, stars, rain,
    snow, my amaze,
Having studied the mocking-bird's tones and the flight of the
    mountain-hawk,
And heard at dawn the unrivall'd one, the hermit thrush
    from the swamp-cedars,
Solitary, singing in the West, I strike up for a New World.

## 2

Victory, union, faith, identity, time,
The indissoluble compacts, riches, mystery,
Eternal progress, the kosmos, and the modern reports.

This then is life,
Here is what has come to the surface after so many throes
    and convulsions.

How curious! how real!
Underfoot the divine soil, overhead the sun.

See revolving the globe,
The ancestor-continents away group'd together,
The present and future continents north and south, with the
    isthmus between.

See, vast trackless spaces,
As in a dream they change, they swiftly fill,
Countless masses debouch upon them,
They are now cover'd with the foremost people, arts, institu-
    tions, known.

See, projected through time,
For me an audience interminable.

With firm and regular step they wend, they never stop,
Successions of men, Americanos, a hundred millions,
One generation playing its part and passing on,
Another generation playing its part and passing on in its turn,
With faces turn'd sideways or backward towards me to listen,
With eyes retrospective towards me.

### 3

Americanos! conquerors! marches humanitarian!
Foremost! century marches! Libertad! masses!
For you a programme of chants.

Chants of the prairies,
Chants of the long-running Mississippi, and down to the
    Mexican sea,
Chants of Ohio, Indiana, Illinois, Iowa, Wisconsin and Min-
    nesota,
Chants going forth from the centre from Kansas, and thence
    equidistant,
Shooting in pulses of fire ceaseless to vivify all.

### 4

Take my leaves America, take them South and take them
    North,

Make welcome for them everywhere, for they are your own
offspring,
Surround them East and West, for they would surround you,
And you precedents, connect lovingly with them, for they
connect lovingly with you.

I conn'd old times,
I sat studying at the feet of the great masters,
Now if eligible O that the great masters might return and
study me.

In the name of these States shall I scorn the antique?
Why these are the children of the antique to justify it.

### 5

Dead poets, philosophs, priests,
Martyrs, artists, inventors, governments long since,
Language-shapers on other shores,
Nations once powerful, now reduced, withdrawn, or desolate,
I dare not proceed till I respectfully credit what you have left
wafted hither,
I have perused it, own it is admirable, (moving awhile among
it,)
Think nothing can ever be greater, nothing can ever deserve
more than it deserves,
Regarding it all intently a long while, then dismissing it,
I stand in my place with my own day here.

Here lands female and male,
Here the heir-ship and heiress-ship of the world, here the
flame of materials,
Here spirituality the translatress, the openly-avow'd,
The ever-tending, the finalè of visible forms,
The satisfier, after due long-waiting now advancing,
Yes here comes my mistress the soul.

### 6

The soul,
Forever and forever—longer than soil is brown and solid—
longer than water ebbs and flows.

I will make the poems of materials, for I think they are to be
the most spiritual poems,
And I will make the poems of my body and of mortality,
For I think I shall then supply myself with the poems of my
soul and of immortality.

I will make a song for these States that no one State may
under any circumstances be subjected to another State,
And I will make a song that there shall be comity by day and
by night between all the States, and between any two of
them,
And I will make a song for the ears of the President, full of
weapons with menacing points,
And behind the weapons countless dissatisfied faces;
And a song make I of the One form'd out of all,
The fang'd and glittering One whose head is over all,
Resolute warlike One including and over all,
(However high the head of any else that head is over all.)

I will acknowledge contemporary lands,
I will trail the whole geography of the globe and salute courteously every city large and small,
And employments! I will put in my poems that with you is
heroism upon land and sea,
And I will report all heroism from an American point of
view.

I will sing the song of companionship,
I will show what alone must finally compact these,
I believe these are to found their own ideal of manly love,
indicating it in me,
I will therefore let flame from me the burning fires that were
threatening to consume me,
I will lift what has too long kept down those smouldering
fires,
I will give them complete abandonment,
I will write the evangel-poem of comrades and of love,
For who but I should understand love with all its sorrow and
joy?
And who but I should be the poet of comrades?

### 7

I am the credulous man of qualities, ages, races,
I advance from the people in their own spirit,
Here is what sings unrestricted faith.

Omnes! omnes! let others ignore what they may,
I make the poem of evil also, I commemorate that part also,
I am myself just as much evil as good, and my nation is—and
    I say there is in fact no evil,
(Or if there is I say it is just as important to you, to the land
    or to me, as any thing else.)

I too, following many and follow'd by many, inaugurate a
    religion, I descend into the arena,
(It may be I am destin'd to utter the loudest cries there, the
    winner's pealing shouts,
Who knows? they may rise from me yet, and soar above
    every thing.)

Each is not for its own sake,
I say the whole earth and all the stars in the sky are for reli-
    gion's sake.

I say no man has ever yet been half devout enough,
None has ever yet adored or worship'd half enough,
None has begun to think how divine he himself is, and how
    certain the future is.

I say that the real and permanent grandeur of these States
    must be their religion,
Otherwise there is no real and permanent grandeur;
(Nor character nor life worthy the name without religion,
Nor land nor man or woman without religion.)

### 8

What are you doing young man?
Are you so earnest, so given up to literature, science, art,
    amours?
These ostensible realities, politics, points?
Your ambition or business whatever it may be?

It is well—against such I say not a word, I am their poet also,
But behold! such swiftly subside, burnt up for religion's sake,
For not all matter is fuel to heat, impalpable flame, the essen-
    tial life of the earth,
Any more than such are to religion.

### 9

What do you seek so pensive and silent?
What do you need camerado?
Dear son do you think it is love?

Listen dear son—listen America, daughter or son,
It is a painful thing to love a man or woman to excess, and
    yet it satisfies, it is great,
But there is something else very great, it makes the whole
    coincide,
It, magnificent, beyond materials, with continuous hands
    sweeps and provides for all.

### 10

Know you, solely to drop in the earth the germs of a greater
    religion,
The following chants each for its kind I sing.

My comrade!
For you to share with me two greatnesses, and a third one
    rising inclusive and more resplendent,
The greatness of Love and Democracy, and the greatness of
    Religion.

Melange mine own, the unseen and the seen,
Mysterious ocean where the streams empty,
Prophetic spirit of material shifting and flickering around
    me,
Living beings, identities now doubtless near us in the air that
    we know not of,
Contact daily and hourly that will not release me,
These selecting, these in hints demanded of me.

Not he with a daily kiss onward from childhood kissing
    me,

Has winded and twisted around me that which holds me to
     him,
Any more than I am held to the heavens and all the spiritual
     world,
After what they have done to me, suggesting themes.

O such themes—equalities! O divine average!
Warblings under the sun, usher'd as now, or at noon, or
     setting,
Strains musical flowing through ages, now reaching hither,
I take to your reckless and composite chords, add to them,
     and cheerfully pass them forward.

### 11

As I have walk'd in Alabama my morning walk,
I have seen where the she-bird the mocking-bird sat on her
     nest in the briers hatching her brood.

I have seen the he-bird also,
I have paus'd to hear him near at hand inflating his throat
     and joyfully singing.

And while I paus'd it came to me that what he really sang for
     was not there only,
Nor for his mate nor himself only, nor all sent back by the
     echoes,
But subtle, clandestine, away beyond,
A charge transmitted and gift occult for those being born.

### 12

Democracy! near at hand to you a throat is now inflating
     itself and joyfully singing.

Ma femme! for the brood beyond us and of us,
For those who belong here and those to come,
I exultant to be ready for them will now shake out carols
     stronger and haughtier than have ever yet been heard
     upon earth.
I will make the songs of passion to give them their way,
And your songs outlaw'd offenders, for I scan you with kin-
     dred eyes, and carry you with me the same as any.

I will make the true poem of riches,
To earn for the body and the mind whatever adheres and
goes forward and is not dròpt by death;
I will effuse egotism and show it underlying all, and I will be
the bard of personality,
And I will show of male and female that either is but the
equal of the other,
And sexual organs and acts! do you concentrate in me, for I
am determin'd to tell you with courageous clear voice to
prove you illustrious,
And I will show that there is no imperfection in the present,
and can be none in the future,
And I will show that whatever happens to anybody it may be
turn'd to beautiful results,
And I will show that nothing can happen more beautiful than
death,
And I will thread a thread through my poems that time and
events are compact,
And that all the things of the universe are perfect miracles,
each as profound as any.

I will not make poems with reference to parts,
But I will make poems, songs, thoughts, with reference to
ensemble,
And I will not sing with reference to a day, but with reference
to all days,
And I will not make a poem nor the least part of a poem but
has reference to the soul,
Because having look'd at the objects of the universe, I find
there is no one nor any particle of one but has reference
to the soul.

### 13

Was somebody asking to see the soul?
See, your own shape and countenance, persons, substances,
beasts, the trees, the running rivers, the rocks and sands.

All hold spiritual joys and afterwards loosen them;
How can the real body ever die and be buried?

Of your real body and any man's or woman's real body,
Item for item it will elude the hands of the corpse-cleaners
    and pass to fitting spheres,
Carrying what has accrued to it from the moment of birth to
    the moment of death.

Not the types set up by the printer return their impression,
    the meaning, the main concern,
Any more than a man's substance and life or a woman's sub-
    stance and life return in the body and the soul,
Indifferently before death and after death.

Behold, the body includes and is the meaning, the main con-
    cern, and includes and is the soul;
Whoever you are, how superb and how divine is your body,
    or any part of it!

### 14

Whoever you are, to you endless announcements!

Daughter of the lands did you wait for your poet?
Did you wait for one with a flowing mouth and indicative
    hand?
Toward the male of the States, and toward the female of the
    States,
Exulting words, words to Democracy's lands.

Interlink'd, food-yielding lands!
Land of coal and iron! land of gold! land of cotton, sugar,
    rice!
Land of wheat, beef, pork! land of wool and hemp! land of
    the apple and the grape!
Land of the pastoral plains, the grass-fields of the world! land
    of those sweet-air'd interminable plateaus!
Land of the herd, the garden, the healthy house of adobie!
Lands where the north-west Columbia winds, and where the
    south-west Colorado winds!
Land of the eastern Chesapeake! land of the Delaware!
Land of Ontario, Erie, Huron, Michigan!
Land of the Old Thirteen! Massachusetts land! land of Ver-
    mont and Connecticut!

Land of the ocean shores! land of sierras and peaks!
Land of boatmen and sailors! fishermen's land!
Inextricable lands! the clutch'd together! the passionate
    ones!
The side by side! the elder and younger brothers! the bony-
    limb'd!
The great women's land! the feminine! the experienced sisters
    and the inexperienced sisters!
Far breath'd land! Arctic braced! Mexican breez'd! the di-
    verse! the compact!
The Pennsylvanian! the Virginian! the double Carolinian!
O all and each well-loved by me! my intrepid nations! O I at
    any rate include you all with perfect love!
I cannot be discharged from you! not from one any sooner
    than another!
O death! O for all that, I am yet of you unseen this hour with
    irrepressible love,
Walking New England, a friend, a traveler,
Splashing my bare feet in the edge of the summer ripples on
    Paumanok's sands,
Crossing the prairies, dwelling again in Chicago, dwelling in
    every town,
Observing shows, births, improvements, structures, arts,
Listening to orators and oratresses in public halls,
Of and through the States as during life, each man and
    woman my neighbor,
The Louisianian, the Georgian, as near to me, and I as near
    to him and her,
The Mississippian and Arkansian yet with me, and I yet with
    any of them,
Yet upon the plains west of the spinal river, yet in my house
    of adobie,
Yet returning eastward, yet in the Seaside State or in Mary-
    land,
Yet Kanadian cheerily braving the winter, the snow and ice
    welcome to me,
Yet a true son either of Maine or of the Granite State, or the
    Narragansett Bay State, or the Empire State,
Yet sailing to other shores to annex the same, yet welcoming
    every new brother,

Hereby applying these leaves to the new ones from the hour
    they unite with the old ones,
Coming among the new ones myself to be their companion
    and equal, coming personally to you now,
Enjoining you to acts, characters, spectacles, with me.


## 15

With me with firm holding, yet haste, haste on.

For your life adhere to me,
(I may have to be persuaded many times before I consent to
    give myself really to you, but what of that?
Must not Nature be persuaded many times?)

No dainty dolce affettuoso I,
Bearded, sun-burnt, gray-neck'd, forbidding, I have arrived,
To be wrestled with as I pass for the solid prizes of the uni-
    verse,
For such I afford whoever can persevere to win them.


## 16

On my way a moment I pause,
Here for you! and here for America!
Still the present I raise aloft, still the future of the States I
    harbinge glad and sublime,
And for the past I pronounce what the air holds of the red
    aborigines.

The red aborigines,
Leaving natural breaths, sounds of rain and winds, calls as of
    birds and animals in the woods, syllabled, to us for
    names,
Okonee, Koosa, Ottawa, Monongahela, Sauk, Natchez,
    Chattahoochee, Kaqueta, Oronoco,
Wabash, Miami, Saginaw, Chippewa, Oshkosh, Walla-
    Walla,
Leaving such to the States they melt, they depart, charging
    the water and the land with names.

### 17

Expanding and swift, henceforth,
Elements, breeds, adjustments, turbulent, quick and audacious,
A world primal again, vistas of glory incessant and branching,
A new race dominating previous ones and grander far, with
new contests,
New politics, new literatures and religions, new inventions
and arts.

These, my voice announcing—I will sleep no more but arise,
You oceans that have been calm within me! how I feel you,
fathomless, stirring, preparing unprecedented waves and
storms.

### 18

See, steamers steaming through my poems,
See, in my poems immigrants continually coming and landing,
See, in arriere, the wigwam, the trail, the hunter's hut, the
flatboat, the maize-leaf, the claim, the rude fence, and
the backwoods village,
See, on the one side the Western Sea and on the other the
Eastern Sea, how they advance and retreat upon my
poems as upon their own shores,
See, pastures and forests in my poems—see, animals wild and
tame—see, beyond the Kaw, countless herds of buffalo
feeding on short curly grass,
See, in my poems, cities, solid, vast, inland, with paved
streets, with iron and stone edifices, ceaseless vehicles,
and commerce,
See, the many-cylinder'd steam printing-press—see, the
electric telegraph stretching across the continent,
See, through Atlantica's depths pulses American Europe
reaching, pulses of Europe duly return'd,
See, the strong and quick locomotive as it departs, panting,
blowing the steam-whistle,
See, ploughmen ploughing farms—see, miners digging mines
—see, the numberless factories,

See, mechanics busy at their benches with tools—see from
among them superior judges, philosophs, Presidents,
emerge, drest in working dresses,
See, lounging through the shops and fields of the States, me
well-belov'd, close-held by day and night,
Hear the loud echoes of my songs there—read the hints come
at last.

19

O camerado close! O you and me at last, and us two only.
O a word to clear one's path ahead endlessly!
O something ecstatic and undemonstrable! O music wild!
O now I triumph—and you shall also;
O hand in hand—O wholesome pleasure—O one more de-
sirer and lover!
O to haste firm holding—to haste, haste on with me.
1860                                                                    1881

# Song of Myself

1

I CELEBRATE myself, and sing myself,
And what I assume you shall assume,
For every atom belonging to me as good belongs to you.

I loafe and invite my soul,
I lean and loafe at my ease observing a spear of summer grass.

My tongue, every atom of my blood, form'd from this soil,
this air,
Born here of parents born here from parents the same, and
their parents the same,
I, now thirty-seven years old in perfect health begin,
Hoping to cease not till death.

Creeds and schools in abeyance,
Retiring back a while sufficed at what they are, but never forgotten,

I harbor for good or bad, I permit to speak at every hazard,
Nature without check with original energy.

## 2

Houses and rooms are full of perfumes, the shelves are
    crowded with perfumes,
I breathe the fragrance myself and know it and like it,
The distillation would intoxicate me also, but I shall not let it.

The atmosphere is not a perfume, it has no taste of the dis-
    tillation, it is odorless,
It is for my mouth forever, I am in love with it,
I will go to the bank by the wood and become undisguised
    and naked,
I am mad for it to be in contact with me.

The smoke of my own breath,
Echoes, ripples, buzz'd whispers, love-root, silk-thread,
    crotch and vine,
My respiration and inspiration, the beating of my heart, the
    passing of blood and air through my lungs,
The sniff of green leaves and dry leaves, and of the shore and
    dark-color'd sea-rocks, and of hay in the barn,
The sound of the belch'd words of my voice loos'd to the
    eddies of the wind,
A few light kisses, a few embraces, a reaching around of arms,
The play of shine and shade on the trees as the supple boughs
    wag,
The delight alone or in the rush of the streets, or along the
    fields and hill-sides,
The feeling of health, the full-noon trill, the song of me rising
    from bed and meeting the sun.

Have you reckon'd a thousand acres much? have you rec-
    kon'd the earth much?
Have you practis'd so long to learn to read?
Have you felt so proud to get at the meaning of poems?

Stop this day and night with me and you shall possess the
    origin of all poems,

You shall possess the good of the earth and sun, (there are
    millions of suns left,)
You shall no longer take things at second or third hand, nor
    look through the eyes of the dead, nor feed on the
    spectres in books,
You shall not look through my eyes either, nor take things
    from me,
You shall listen to all sides and filter them from your self.

### 3

I have heard what the talkers were talking, the talk of the
    beginning and the end,
But I do not talk of the beginning or the end.

There was never any more inception than there is now,
Nor any more youth or age than there is now,
And will never be any more perfection than there is now,
Nor any more heaven or hell than there is now.

Urge and urge and urge,
Always the procreant urge of the world.
Out of the dimness opposite equals advance, always sub-
    stance and increase, always sex,
Always a knit of identity, always distinction, always a breed
    of life.

To elaborate is no avail, learn'd and unlearn'd feel that it is so.

Sure as the most certain sure, plumb in the uprights, well
    entretied, braced in the beams,
Stout as a horse, affectionate, haughty, electrical,
I and this mystery here we stand.

Clear and sweet is my soul, and clear and sweet is all that is
    not my soul.

Lack one lacks both, and the unseen is proved by the seen,
Till that becomes unseen and receives proof in its turn.

Showing the best and dividing it from the worst age vexes age,
Knowing the perfect fitness and equanimity of things, while
    they discuss I am silent, and go bathe and admire myself.

Welcome is every organ and attribute of me, and of any man
    hearty and clean,
Not an inch nor a particle of an inch is vile, and none shall be
    less familiar than the rest.

I am satisfied—I see, dance, laugh, sing;
As the hugging and loving bed-fellow sleeps at my side
    through the night, and withdraws at the peep of the day
    with stealthy tread,
Leaving me baskets cover'd with white towels swelling the
    house with their plenty,
Shall I postpone my acceptation and realization and scream
    at my eyes,
That they turn from gazing after and down the road,
And forthwith cipher and show me to a cent,
Exactly the value of one and exactly the value of two, and
    which is ahead?


### 4

Trippers and askers surround me,
People I meet, the effect upon me of my early life or the ward
    and city I live in, or the nation,
The latest dates, discoveries, inventions, societies, authors
    old and new,
My dinner, dress, associates, looks, compliments, dues,
The real or fancied indifference of some man or woman I
    love,
The sickness of one of my folks or of myself, or ill-doing or
    loss or lack of money, or depressions or exaltations,
Battles, the horrors of fratricidal war, the fever of doubtful
    news, the fitful events;
These come to me days and nights and go from me again,
But they are not the Me myself.
Apart from the pulling and hauling stands what I am,
Stands amused, complacent, compassionating, idle, uni-
    tary,
Looks down, is erect, or bends an arm on an impalpable cer-
    tain rest,
Looking with side-curved head curious what will come next,

Both in and out of the game and watching and wondering
     at it.

Backward I see in my own days where I sweated through fog
     with linguists and contenders,
I have no mockings or arguments, I witness and wait.

### 5

I believe in you my soul, the other I am must not abase itself
     to you,
And you must not be abased to the other.

Loafe with me on the grass, loose the stop from your throat,
Not words, not music or rhyme I want, not custom or lecture,
     not even the best,
Only the lull I like, the hum of your valvèd voice.

I mind how once we lay such a transparent summer morn-
     ing,
How you settled your head athwart my hips and gently turn'd
     over upon me,
And parted the shirt from my bosom-bone, and plunged your
     tongue to my bare-stript heart,
And reach'd till you felt my beard, and reach'd till you held
     my feet.

Swiftly arose and spread around me the peace and knowledge
     that pass all the argument of the earth,
And I know that the hand of God is the promise of my
     own,
And I know that the spirit of God is the brother of my own,
And that all the men ever born are also my brothers, and the
     women my sisters and lovers,

And that a kelson of the creation is love,
And limitless are leaves stiff or drooping in the fields,
And brown ants in the little wells beneath them,
And mossy scabs of the worm fence, heap'd stones, elder,
     mullein and poke-weed.

6

A child said *What is the grass?* fetching it to me with full
    hands,
How could I answer the child? I do not know what it is any
    more than he.

I guess it must be the flag of my disposition, out of hopeful
    green stuff woven.

Or I guess it is the handkerchief of the Lord,
A scented gift and remembrancer designedly dropt,
Bearing the owner's name someway in the corners, that we
    may see and remark, and say *Whose?*

Or I guess the grass is itself a child, the produced babe of the
    vegetation.

Or I guess it is a uniform hieroglyphic,
And it means, Sprouting alike in broad zones and narrow
    zones,
Growing among black folks as among white,
Kanuck, Tuckahoe, Congressman, Cuff, I give them the
    same, I receive them the same.

And now it seems to me the beautiful uncut hair of graves.

Tenderly will I use you curling grass,
It may be you transpire from the breasts of young men,
It may be if I had known them I would have loved them,
It may be you are from old people, or from offspring taken
    soon out of their mothers' laps,
And here you are the mothers' laps.

This grass is very dark to be from the white heads of old
    mothers,
Darker than the colourless beards of old men,
Dark to come from under the faint red roofs of mouths.

O I perceive after all so many uttering tongues,
And I perceive they do not come from the roofs of mouths
    for nothing.

I wish I could translate the hints about the dead young men
    and women,
And the hints about old men and mothers, and the offspring
    taken soon out of their laps.

What do you think has become of the young and old men?
And what do you think has become of the women and chil-
    dren?

They are alive and well somewhere,
The smallest sprout shows there is really no death,
And if ever there was it led forward life, and does not wait at
    the end to arrest it,
And ceas'd the moment life appear'd.

All goes onward and outward, nothing collapses,
And to die is different from what any one supposed, and
    luckier.

### 7

Has any one supposed it lucky to be born?
I hasten to inform him or her it is just as lucky to die, and I
    know it.

I pass death with the dying and birth with the new-wash'd
    babe, and am not contain'd between my hat and boots,
And peruse manifold objects, no two alike and every one
    good,
The earth good and the stars good, and their adjuncts all
    good.

I am not an earth nor an adjunct of an earth,
I am the mate and companion of people, all just as immortal
    and fathomless as myself,
(They do not know how immortal, but I know.)

Every kind for itself and its own, for me mine male and fe-
    male,
For me those that have been boys and that love women,
For me the man that is proud and feels how it stings to be
    slighted,

For me the sweet-heart and the old maid, for me mothers and
    the mothers of mothers,
For me lips that have smiled, eyes that have shed tears,
For me children and the begetters of children.

Undrape! you are not guilty to me, nor stale nor discarded,
I see through the broadcloth and gingham whether or no,
And am around, tenacious, acquisitive, tireless, and cannot
    be shaken away.

8

The little one sleeps in its cradle,
I lift the gauze and look a long time, and silently brush away
    flies with my hand.

The youngster and the red-faced girl turn aside up the bushy
    hill,
I peeringly view them from the top.

The suicide sprawls on the bloody floor of the bedroom,
I witness the corpse with its dabbled hair, I note where the
    pistol has fallen.

The blab of the pave, tires of carts, sluff of boot-soles, talk of
    the promenaders,
The heavy omnibus, the driver with his interrogating thumb,
    the clank of the shod horses on the granite floor,
The snow-sleighs, clinking, shouted jokes, pelts of snow-balls,
The hurrahs for popular favorites, the fury of rous'd mobs,
The flap of the curtain'd litter, a sick man inside borne to the
    hospital,
The meeting of enemies, the sudden oath, the blows and fall,
The excited crowd, the policeman with his star quickly work-
    ing his passage to the centre of the crowd,
The impassive stones that receive and return so many echoes,
What groans of over-fed or half-starv'd who fall sunstruck or
    in fits,
What exclamations of women taken suddenly who hurry
    home and give birth to babes,

What living and buried speech is always vibrating here, what
    howls restrain'd by decorum,
Arrests of criminals, slights, adulterous offers made, accept-
    ances, rejections with convex lips,
I mind them or the show or resonance of them—I come and I
    depart.

### 9

The big doors of the country barn stand open and ready,
The dried grass of the harvest-time loads the slow-drawn
    wagon,
The clear light plays on the brown gray and green inter-
    tinged,
The armfuls are pack'd to the sagging mow.

I am there, I help, I came stretch'd atop of the load,
I felt its soft jolts, one leg reclined on the other,
I jump from the cross-beams and seize the clover and
    timothy,
And roll head over heels and tangle my hair full of wisps.

### 10

Alone far in the wilds and mountains I hunt,
Wandering amazed at my own lightness and glee,
In the late afternoon choosing a safe spot to pass the night,
Kindling a fire and broiling the fresh-kill'd game,
Falling asleep on the gather'd leaves with my dog and gun by
    my side.

The Yankee clipper is under her sky-sails, she cuts the sparkle
    and scud,
My eyes settle the land, I bend at her prow or shout joyously
    from the deck.

The boatmen and clam-diggers arose early and stopt for
    me,
I tuck'd my trowser-ends in my boots and went and had a
    good time;
You should have been with us that day round the chowder-
    kettle.

I saw the marriage of the trapper in the open air in the far
    west, the bride was a red girl,
Her father and his friends sat near cross-legged and dumbly
    smoking, they had moccasins to their feet and large
    thick blankets hanging from their shoulders,
On a bank lounged the trapper, he was drest mostly in skins,
    his luxuriant beard and curls protected his neck, he held
    his bride by the hand,
She had long eyelashes, her head was bare, her coarse straight
    locks descended upon her voluptuous limbs and reach'd
    to her feet.

The runaway slave came to my house and stopt outside,
I heard his motions crackling the twigs of the woodpile,
Through the swung half-door of the kitchen I saw him limpsy
    and weak,
And went where he sat on a log and led him in and assured
    him,
And brought water and fill'd a tub for his sweated body and
    bruis'd feet,
And gave him a room that enter'd from my own, and gave
    him some coarse clean clothes,
And remember perfectly well his revolving eyes and his awk-
    wardness,
And remember putting plasters on the galls of his neck and
    ankles;
He staid with me a week before he was recuperated and
    pass'd north,
I had him sit next me at table, my fire-lock lean'd in the
    corner.

## 11

Twenty-eight young men bathe by the shore,
Twenty-eight young men and all so friendly;
Twenty-eight years of womanly life and all so lonesome.

She owns the fine house by the rise of the bank,
She hides handsome and richly drest aft the blinds of the
    window.

Which of the young men does she like the best?
Ah the homeliest of them is beautiful to her.

Where are you off to, lady? for I see you,
You splash in the water there, yet stay stock still in your room.

Dancing and laughing along the beach came the twenty-
ninth bather,
The rest did not see her, but she saw them and loved them.

The beards of the young men glisten'd with wet, it ran from
their long hair,
Little streams pass'd all over their bodies.

An unseen hand also pass'd over their bodies,
It descended tremblingly from their temples and ribs.

The young men float on their backs, their white bellies bulge
to the sun, they do not ask who seizes fast to them,
They do not know who puffs and declines with pendant and
bending arch,
They do not think whom they souse with spray.

### 12

The butcher-boy puts off his killing-clothes, or sharpens his
knife at the stall in the market,
I loiter enjoying his repartee and his shuffle and break-
down.

Blacksmiths with grimed and hairy chests environ the anvil,
Each has his main-sledge, they are all out, there is a great
heat in the fire.

From the cinder-strew'd threshold I follow their movements,
The lithe sheer of their waists plays even with their massive
arms,
Overhand the hammers swing, overhand so slow, overhand
so sure,
They do not hasten, each man hits in his place.

13

The negro holds firmly the reins of his four horses, the block
        swags underneath on its tied-over chain,
The negro that drives the long dray of the stone-yard, steady
        and tall he stands pois'd on one leg on the string-
        piece,
His blue shirt exposes his ample neck and breast and loosens
        over his hip-band,
His glance is calm and commanding, he tosses the slouch of
        his hat away from his forehead,
The sun falls on his crispy hair and mustache, falls on the
        black of his polish'd and perfect limbs.

I behold the picturesque giant and love him, and I do not
        stop there,
I go with the team also.

In me the caresser of life wherever moving, backward as well
        as forward sluing,
To niches aside and junior bending, not a person or object
        missing,
Absorbing all to myself and for this song.

Oxen that rattle the yoke and chain or halt in the leafy shade,
        what is that you express in your eyes?
It seems to me more than all the print I have read in my life.

My tread scares the wood-drake and wood-duck on my dis-
        tant and day-long ramble,
They rise together, they slowly circle around.

I believe in those wing'd purposes,
And acknowledge red, yellow, white, playing within me,
And consider green and violet and the tufted crown inten-
        tional,
And do not call the tortoise unworthy because she is not
        something else,
And the jay in the woods never studied the gamut, yet trills
        pretty well to me,
And the look of the bay mare shames silliness out of me.

## 14

The wild gander leads his flock through the cool night,
*Ya-honk* he says, and sounds it down to me like an invitation,
The pert may suppose it meaningless, but I listening close,
Find its purpose and place up there toward the wintry sky.

The sharp-hoof'd moose of the north, the cat on the house-
　　sill, the chickadee, the prairie-dog,
The litter of the grunting sow as they tug at her teats,
The brood of the turkey-hen and she with her half-spread
　　wings,
I see in them and myself the same old law.

The press of my foot to the earth springs a hundred affec-
　　tions,
They scorn the best I can do to relate them.

I am enamour'd of growing out-doors,
Of men that live among cattle or taste of the ocean or woods,
Of the builders and steerers of ships and the wielders of axes
　　and mauls, and the drivers of horses,
I can eat and sleep with them week in and week out.

What is commonest, cheapest, nearest, easiest, is Me,
Me going in for my chances, spending for vast returns,
Adorning myself to bestow myself on the first that will take
　　me,
Not asking the sky to come down to my good will,
Scattering it freely forever.

## 15

The pure contralto sings in the organ loft,
The carpenter dresses his plank, the tongue of his foreplane
　　whistles its wild ascending lisp,
The married and unmarried children ride home to their
　　Thanksgiving dinner,
The pilot seizes the king-pin, he heaves down with a strong
　　arm,
The mate stands braced in the whale-boat, lance and harpoon
　　are ready,

The duck-shooter walks by silent and cautious stretches,
The deacons are ordain'd with cross'd hands at the altar,
The spinning-girl retreats and advances to the hum of the big wheel,
The farmer stops by the bars as he walks on a First-day loafe and looks at the oats and rye,
The lunatic is carried at last to the asylum a confirm'd case,
(He will never sleep any more as he did in the cot in his mother's bedroom;)
The jour printer with gray head and gaunt jaws works at his case,
He turns his quid of tobacco while his eyes blurr with the manuscript;
The malform'd limbs are tied to the surgeon's table,
What is removed drops horribly in a pail;
The quadroon girl is sold at the auction-stand, the drunkard nods by the bar-room stove,
The machinist rolls up his sleeves, the policeman travels his beat, the gate-keeper marks who pass,
The young fellow drives the express-wagon, (I love him, though I do not know him;)
The half-breed straps on his light boots to compete in the race,
The western turkey-shooting draws old and young, some lean on their rifles, some sit on logs,
Out from the crowd steps the marksman, takes his position, levels his piece;
The groups of newly-come immigrants cover the wharf or levee,
As the woolly-pates hoe in the sugar-field, the overseer views them from his saddle,
The bugle calls in the ball-room, the gentlemen run for their partners, the dancers bow to each other,
The youth lies awake in the cedar-roof'd garret and harks to the musical rain,
The Wolverine sets traps on the creek that helps fill the Huron,
The squaw wrapt in her yellow-hemm'd cloth is offering moccasins and bead-bags for sale,
The connoisseur peers along the exhibition-gallery with half-shut eyes bent sideways,

As the deck-hands make fast the steamboat the plank is
    thrown for the shore-going passengers,
The young sister holds out the skein while the elder sister
    winds it off in a ball, and stops now and then for the
    knots,
The one-year wife is recovering and happy having a week ago
    borne her first child,
The clean-hair'd Yankee girl works with her sewing-machine
    or in the factory or mill,
The paving-man leans on his two-handed rammer, the re-
    porter's lead flies swiftly over the note-book, the sign-
    painter is lettering with blue and gold,
The canal boy trots on the tow-path, the book-keeper counts
    at his desk, the shoemaker waxes his thread,
The conductor beats time for the band and all the performers
    follow him,
The child is baptized, the convert is making his first profes-
    sions,
The regatta is spread on the bay, the race is begun, (how the
    white sails sparkle!)
The drover watching his drove sings out to them that would
    stray,
The pedler sweats with his pack on his back, (the purchaser
    higgling about the odd cent;)
The bride unrumples her white dress, the minute-hand of the
    clock moves slowly,
The opium-eater reclines with rigid head and just-open'd lips,
The prostitute draggles her shawl, her bonnet bobs on her
    tipsy and pimpled neck,
The crowd laugh at her blackguard oaths, the men jeer and
    wink to each other,
(Miserable! I do not laugh at your oaths nor jeer you;)
The President holding a cabinet council is surrounded by the
    great Secretaries,
On the piazza walk three matrons stately and friendly with
    twined arms,
The crew of the fish-smack pack repeated layers of halibut in
    the hold,
The Missourian crosses the plains toting his wares and his
    cattle,

As the fare-collector goes through the train he gives notice by
    the jingling of loose change,
The floor-men are laying the floor, the tinners are tinning the
    roof, the masons are calling for mortar,
In single file each shouldering his hod pass onward the
    laborers;
Seasons pursuing each other the indescribable crowd is
    gather'd, it is the fourth of Seventh-month, (what salutes
    of cannon and small arms!)
Seasons pursuing each other the plougher ploughs, the
    mower mows, and the winter-grain falls in the ground;
Off on the lakes the pike-fisher watches and waits by the hole
    in the frozen surface,
The stumps stand thick round the clearing, the squatter
    strikes deep with his axe,
Flatboatmen make fast towards dusk near the cotton-wood
    or pecan-trees,
Coon-seekers go through the regions of the Red river or
    through those drain'd by the Tennessee, or through
    those of the Arkansas,
Torches shine in the dark that hangs on the Chattahooche or
    Altamahaw,
Patriarchs sit at supper with sons and grandsons and great-
    grandsons around them,
In walls of adobie, in canvas tents, rest hunters and trappers
    after their day's sport,
The city sleeps and the country sleeps,
The living sleep for their time, the dead sleep for their time,
The old husband sleeps by his wife and the young husband
    sleeps by his wife;
And these tend inward to me, and I tend outward to them,
And such as it is to be of these more or less I am,
And of these one and all I weave the song of myself.


16

I am of old and young, of the foolish as much as the wise,
Regardless of others, ever regardful of others,
Maternal as well as paternal, a child as well as a man,
Stuff'd with the stuff that is coarse and stuff'd with the stuff
    that is fine,

One of the Nation of many nations, the smallest the same
    and the largest the same,
A Southerner soon as a Northerner, a planter nonchalant
    and hospitable down by the Oconee I live,
A Yankee bound my own way ready for trade, my joints the
    limberest joints on earth and the sternest joints on earth,
A Kentuckian walking the vale of the Elkhorn in my deer-
    skin leggings, a Louisianian or Georgian,
A boatman over lakes or bays or along coasts, a Hoosier,
    Badger, Buck-eye;
At home on Kanadian snow-shoes or up in the bush, or with
    fishermen off Newfoundland,
At home in the fleet of ice-boats, sailing with the rest and
    tacking,
At home on the hills of Vermont or in the woods of Maine,
    or the Texan ranch,
Comrade of Californians, comrade of free North-Westerners,
    (loving their big proportions,)
Comrade of raftsmen and coalmen, comrade of all who shake
    hands and welcome to drink and meat,
A learner with the simplest, a teacher of the thoughtfullest,
A novice beginning yet experient of myriads of seasons,
Of every hue and caste am I, of every rank and religion,
A farmer, mechanic, artist, gentleman, sailor, quaker,
Prisoner, fancy-man, rowdy, lawyer, physician, priest.

I resist any thing better than my own diversity,
Breathe the air but leave plenty after me,
And am not stuck up, and am in my place.

(The moth and the fish-eggs are in their place,
The bright suns I see and the dark suns I cannot see are in
    their place,
The palpable is in its place and the impalpable is in its place.)

## 17

These are really the thoughts of all men in all ages and lands,
    they are not original with me,
If they are not yours as much as mine they are nothing, or
    next to nothing,

If they are not the riddle and the untying of the riddle they
    are nothing,
If they are not just as close as they are distant they are
    nothing.

This is the grass that grows wherever the land is and the
    water is,
This the common air that bathes the globe.

### 18

With music strong I come, with my cornets and my drums,
I play not marches for accepted victors only, I play marches
    for conquer'd and slain persons.

Have you heard that it was good to gain the day?
I also say it is good to fall, battles are lost in the same spirit in
    which they are won.

I beat and pound for the dead,
I blow through my embouchures my loudest and gayest for
    them.

Vivas to those who have fail'd!
And to those whose war-vessels sank in the sea!
And to those themselves who sank in the sea!
And to all generals that lost engagements, and all overcome
    heroes!
And the numberless unknown heroes equal to the greatest
    heroes known!

### 19

This is the meal equally set, this the meat for natural hunger,
It is for the wicked just the same as the righteous, I make
    appointments with all,
I will not have a single person slighted or left away,
The kept-woman, sponger, thief, are hereby invited,
The heavy-lipp'd slave is invited, the venerealee is invited;
There shall be no difference between them and the rest.

This is the press of a bashful hand, this the float and odor of
    hair,

This the touch of my lips to yours, this the murmur of yearning,
This the far-off depth and height reflecting my own face,
This the thoughtful merge of myself, and the outlet again.

Do you guess I have some intricate purpose?
Well I have, for the Fourth-month showers have, and the
  mica on the side of a rock has.

Do you take it I would astonish?
Does the daylight astonish? does the early redstart twittering
  through the woods?
Do I astonish more than they?

This hour I tell things in confidence,
I might not tell everybody, but I will tell you.

## 20

Who goes there? hankering, gross, mystical, nude;
How is it I extract strength from the beef I eat?

What is a man anyhow? what am I? what are you?

All I mark as my own you shall offset it with your own,
Else it were time lost listening to me.

I do not snivel that snivel the world over,
That months are vacuums and the ground but wallow and filth.

Whimpering and truckling fold with powders for invalids,
  conformity goes to the fourth-remov'd,
I wear my hat as I please indoors or out.

Why should I pray? why should I venerate and be ceremoni-
  ous?

Having pried through the strata, analyzed to a hair, counsel'd
  with doctors and calculated close,
I find no sweeter fat than sticks to my own bones.

In all people I see myself, none more and not one a barleycorn less,
And the good or bad I say of myself I say of them.

I know I am solid and sound,
To me the converging objects of the universe perpetually flow,
All are written to me, and I must get what the writing means.

I know I am deathless,
I know this orbit of mine cannot be swept by a carpenter's
    compass,
I know I shall not pass like a child's carlacue cut with a burnt
    stick at night.

I know I am august,
I do not trouble my spirit to vindicate itself or be understood,
I see that the elementary laws never apologize,
(I reckon I behave no prouder than the level I plant my house
    by, after all.)

I exist as I am, that is enough,
If no other in the world be aware I sit content,
And if each and all be aware I sit content.

One world is aware and by far the largest to me, and that is
    myself,
And whether I come to my own to-day or in ten thousand or
    ten million years,
I can cheerfully take it now, or with equal cheerfulness I can
    wait.

My foothold is tenon'd and mortis'd in granite,
I laugh at what you call dissolution,
And I know the amplitude of time.

## 21

I am the poet of the Body and I am the poet of the Soul,
The pleasures of heaven are with me and the pains of hell are
    with me,
The first I graft and increase upon myself, the latter I trans-
    late into a new tongue.

I am the poet of the woman the same as the man,
And I say it is as great to be a woman as to be a man,
And I say there is nothing greater than the mother of men.

I chant the chant of dilation or pride,
We have had ducking and deprecating about enough,
I show that size is only development.

Have you outstript the rest? are you the President?
It is a trifle, they will more than arrive there every one, and
    still pass on.

I am he that walks with the tender and growing night,
I call to the earth and sea half-held by the night.

Press close bare-bosom'd night—press close magnetic nour-
    ishing night!
Night of south winds—night of the large few stars!
Still nodding night—mad naked summer night.

Smile O voluptuous cool-breath'd earth!
Earth of the slumbering and liquid trees!
Earth of departed sunset—earth of the mountains misty-topt!
Earth of the vitreous pour of the full moon just tinged with
    blue!
Earth of shine and dark mottling the tide of the river!
Earth of the limpid gray of clouds brighter and clearer for
    my sake!
Far-swooping elbow'd earth—rich apple-blossom'd earth!
Smile, for your lover comes.

Prodigal, you have given me love—therefore I to you give
    love!
O unspeakable passionate love.

## 22

You sea! I resign myself to you also—I guess what you mean,
I behold from the beach your crooked inviting fingers,
I believe you refuse to go back without feeling of me,
We must have a turn together, I undress, hurry me out of
    sight of the land,
Cushion me soft, rock me in billowy drowse,
Dash me with amorous wet, I can repay you.

Sea of stretch'd ground-swells,
Sea breathing broad and convulsive breaths,
Sea of the brine of life and of unshovell'd yet always-ready
    graves,
Howler and scooper of storms, capricious and dainty sea,
I am integral with you, I too am of one phase and of all
    phases.

Partaker of influx and efflux, I, extoller of hate and concilia-
    tion,
Extoller of amies and those that sleep in each others' arms.

I am he attesting sympathy,
(Shall I make my list of things in the house and skip the house
    that supports them?)

I am not the poet of goodness only, I do not decline to be the
    poet of wickedness also.

What blurt is this about virtue and about vice?
Evil propels me and reform of evil propels me, I stand in-
    different,
My gait is no fault-finder's or rejecter's gait,
I moisten the roots of all that has grown.

Did you fear some scrofula out of the unflagging pregnancy?
Did you guess the celestial laws are yet to be work'd over and
    rectified?

I find one side a balance and the antipodal side a balance,
Soft doctrine as steady help as stable doctrine,
Thoughts and deeds of the present our rouse and early start.

This minute that comes to me over the past decillions,
There is no better than it and now.

What behaved well in the past or behaves well to-day is not
    such a wonder,
The wonder is always and always how there can be a mean
    man or an infidel.

23

Endless unfolding of words of ages!
And mine a word of the modern, the word En-Masse.

A word of the faith that never balks,
Here or henceforward it is all the same to me, I accept Time
    absolutely.

It alone is without flaw, it alone rounds and completes
    all,
That mystic baffling wonder alone completes all.

I accept Reality and dare not question it,
Materialism first and last imbuing.

Hurrah for positive science! long live exact demonstration!
Fetch stonecrop mixt with cedar and branches of lilac,
This is the lexicographer, this the chemist, this made a gram-
    mar of the old cartouches,
These mariners put the ship through dangerous unknown
    seas,
This is the geologist, this works with the scalpel, and this is a
    mathematician.

Gentlemen, to you the first honors always!
Your facts are useful, and yet they are not my dwelling,
I but enter by them to an area of my dwelling.

Less the reminders of properties told my words,
And more the reminders they of life untold, and of freedom
    and extrication,
And make short account of neuters and geldings, and favor
    men and women fully equipt,
And beat the gong of revolt, and stop with fugitives and
    them that plot and conspire.

24

Walt Whitman, a kosmos, of Manhattan the son,
Turbulent, fleshy, sensual, eating, drinking and breeding,

No sentimentalist, no stander above men and women or
    apart from them,
No more modest than immodest.

Unscrew the locks from the doors!
Unscrew the doors themselves from their jambs!

Whoever degrades another degrades me,
And whatever is done or said returns at last to me.

Through me the afflatus surging and surging, through me the
    current and index.

I speak the pass-word primeval, I give the sign of democracy,
By God! I will accept nothing which all cannot have their
    counterpart of on the same terms.

Through me many long dumb voices,
Voices of the interminable generation of prisoners and slaves,
Voices of the diseas'd and despairing and of thieves and
    dwarfs,
Voices of cycles of preparation and accretion,
And of the threads that connect the stars, and of wombs and
    of the father-stuff,
And of the rights of them the others are down upon,
Of the deform'd, trivial, flat, foolish, despised,
Fog in the air, beetles rolling balls of dung.

Through me forbidden voices,
Voices of sexes and lusts, voices veil'd and I remove the veil,
Voices indecent by me clarified and transfigur'd.

I do not press my fingers across my mouth,
I keep as delicate around the bowels as around the head and
    heart,
Copulation is no more rank to me than death is.

I believe in the flesh and the appetites,
Seeing, hearing, feeling, are miracles, and each part and tag
    of me is a miracle.

Divine am I inside and out, and I make holy whatever I touch
    or am touch'd from,
The scent of these arm-pits aroma finer than prayer,
This head more than churches, bibles, and all the creeds.


If I worship one thing more than another it shall be the
    spread of my own body, or any part of it,
Translucent mould of me it shall be you!
Shaded ledges and rests it shall be you!
Firm masculine colter it shall be you!
Whatever goes to the tilth of me it shall be you!
You my rich blood! your milky stream pale strippings of my
    life!
Breast that presses against other breasts it shall be you!
My brain it shall be your occult convolutions!
Root of wash'd sweet-flag! timorous pond-snipe! nest of
    guarded duplicate eggs! it shall be you!
Mix'd tussled hay of head, beard, brawn, it shall be you!
Trickling sap of maple, fibre of manly wheat, it shall be
    you!
Sun so generous it shall be you!
Vapors lighting and shading my face it shall be you!
You sweaty brooks and dews it shall be you!
Winds whose soft-tickling genitals rub against me it shall be
    you!
Broad muscular fields, branches of live oak, loving lounger in
    my winding paths, it shall be you!
Hands I have taken, face I have kiss'd, mortal I have ever
    touch'd, it shall be you.


I dote on myself, there is that lot of me and all so luscious,
Each moment and whatever happens thrills me with joy,
I cannot tell how my ankles bend, nor whence the cause of
    my faintest wish,
Nor the cause of the friendship I emit, nor the cause of the
    friendship I take again.


That I walk up my stoop, I pause to consider if it really be,
A morning-glory at my window satisfies me more than the
    metaphysics of books.

To behold the day-break!
The little light fades the immense and diaphanous shadows,
The air tastes good to my palate.

Hefts of the moving world at innocent gambols silently rising,
        freshly exuding,
Scooting obliquely high and low.

Something I cannot see puts upward libidinous prongs,
Seas of bright juice suffuse heaven.

The earth by the sky staid with, the daily close of their junc-
        tion,
The heav'd challenge from the east that moment over my
        head,
The mocking taunt, See then whether you shall be master!

### 25

Dazzling and tremendous how quick the sun-rise would kill
        me,
If I could not now and always send sun-rise out of me.

We also ascend dazzling and tremendous as the sun,
We found our own O my soul in the calm and cool of the
        day-break.

My voice goes after what my eyes cannot reach,
With the twirl of my tongue I encompass worlds and volumes
        of worlds.

Speech is the twin of my vision, it is unequal to measure itself,
It provokes me forever, it says sarcastically,
*Walt you contain enough, why don't you let it out then?*

Come now I will not be tantalized, you conceive too much of
        articulation,
Do you not know O speech how the buds beneath you are
        folded?
Waiting in gloom, protected by frost,
The dirt receding before my prophetical screams,
I underlying causes to balance them at last,

My knowledge my live parts, it keeping tally with the mear-
ing of all things,
Happiness, (which whoever hears me let him or her set out in
search of this day.)

My final merit I refuse you, I refuse putting from me what I
really am,
Encompass worlds, but never try to encompass me,
I crowd your sleekest and best by simply looking toward
you.

Writing and talk do not prove me,
I carry the plenum of proof and every thing else in my face,
With the hush of my lips I wholly confound the skeptic.

### 26

Now I will do nothing but listen,
To accrue what I hear into this song, to let sounds contribute
toward it.

I hear bravuras of birds, bustle of growing wheat, gossip of
flames, clack of sticks cooking my meals.
I hear the sound I love, the sound of the human voice,
I hear all sounds running together, combined, fused or
following,
Sounds of the city and sounds out of the city, sounds of the
day and night,
Talkative young ones to those that like them, the loud laugh
of work-people at their meals,
The angry base of disjointed friendship, the faint tones of the
sick,
The judge with hands tight to the desk, his pallid lips pro-
nouncing a death-sentence,
The heave'e'yo of stevedores unlading ships by the wharves,
the refrain of the anchor-lifters,
The ring of alarm-bells, the cry of fire, the whirr of swift-
streaking engines and hose-carts with premonitory
tinkles and color'd lights,
The steam-whistle, the solid roll of the train of approaching
cars,

The slow march play'd at the head of the association marching two and two,
(They go to guard some corpse, the flag-tops are draped with
black muslin.)

I hear the violoncello, ('tis the young man's heart's com-
plaint,)
I hear the key'd cornet, it glides quickly in through my ears,
It shakes mad-sweet pangs through my belly and breast.

I hear the chorus, it is a grand opera,
Ah this indeed is music—this suits me.

A tenor large and fresh as the creation fills me,
The orbic flex of his mouth is pouring and filling me full.

I hear the train'd soprano (what work with hers is this?)
The orchestra whirls me wider than Uranus flies,
It wrenches such ardors from me I did not know I possess'd
them,
It sails me, I dab with bare feet, they are lick'd by the indolent
waves,
I am cut by bitter and angry hail, I lose my breath,
Steep'd amid honey'd morphine, my windpipe throttled in
fakes of death,
At length let up again to feel the puzzle of puzzles,
And that we call Being.

## 27

To be in any form, what is that?
(Round and round we go, all of us, and ever come back
thither,)
If nothing lay more develop'd the quahaug in its callous shell
were enough.

Mine is no callous shell,
I have instant conductors all over me whether I pass or stop,
They seize every object and lead it harmlessly through me.

I merely stir, press, feel with my fingers, and am happy,
To touch my person to some one else's is about as much as I
can stand.

## 28

Is this then a touch? quivering me to a new identity,
Flames and ether making a rush for my veins,
Treacherous tip of me reaching and crowding to help them,
My flesh and blood playing out lightning to strike what is
     hardly different from myself,
On all sides prurient provokers stiffening my limbs,
Straining the udder of my heart for its withheld drip,
Behaving licentious toward me, taking no denial,
Depriving me of my best as for a purpose,
Unbuttoning my clothes, holding me by the bare waist,
Deluding my confusion with the calm of the sunlight and
     pasture-fields,
Immodestly sliding the fellow-senses away,
They bribed to swap off with touch and go and graze at the
     edges of me,
No consideration, no regard for my draining strength or my
     anger,
Fetching the rest of the herd around to enjoy them a while,
Then all uniting to stand on a headland and worry me.

The sentries desert every other part of me,
They have left me helpless to a red marauder,
They all come to the headland to witness and assist against
     me.

I am given up by traitors,
I talk wildly, I have lost my wits, I and nobody else am the
     greatest traitor,
I went myself first to the headland, my own hands carried me
     there.

You villain touch! what are you doing? my breath is tight in
     its throat,
Unclench your floodgates, you are too much for me.

## 29

Blind loving wrestling touch, sheath'd hooded sharp-tooth'd
     touch!
Did it make you ache so, leaving me?

Parting track'd by arriving, perpetual payment of perpetual
loan,
Rich showering rain, and recompense richer afterward.

Sprouts take and accumulate, stand by the curb prolific and
vital,
Landscapes projected masculine, full-sized and golden.

### 30

All truths wait in all things,
They neither hasten their own delivery nor resist it,
They do not need the obstetric forceps of the surgeon,
The insignificant is as big to me as any,
(What is less or more than a touch?)

Logic and sermons never convince,
The damp of the night drives deeper into my soul.

(Only what proves itself to every man and woman is so,
Only what nobody denies is so.)

A minute and a drop of me settle my brain,
I believe the soggy clods shall become lovers and lamps,
And a compend of compends is the meat of a man or woman,
And a summit and flower there is the feeling they have for
each other,
And they are to branch boundlessly out of that lesson until it
becomes omnific,
And until one and all shall delight us, and we them.

### 31

I believe a leaf of grass is no less than the journey-work of
the stars,
And the pismire is equally perfect, and a grain of sand, and
the egg of the wren,
And the tree-toad is a chef-d'œuvre for the highest,
And the running blackberry would adorn the parlors of
heaven,
And the narrowest hinge in my hand puts to scorn all
machinery,

And the cow crunching with depress'd head surpasses **any**
　　statue,
And a mouse is miracle enough to stagger sextillions of
　　infidels.

I find I incorporate gneiss, coal, long-threaded moss, fruits,
　　grains, esculent roots,
And am stucco'd with quadrupeds and birds all over,
And have distanced what is behind me for good reasons,
But call any thing back again when I desire it.

In vain the speeding or shyness,
In vain the plutonic rocks send their old heat against my
　　approach,
In vain the mastodon retreats beneath its own powder'd
　　bones,
In vain objects stand leagues off and assume manifold shapes,
In vain the ocean setting in hollows and the great monsters
　　lying low,
In vain the buzzard houses herself with the sky,
In vain the snake slides through the creepers and logs,
In vain the elk takes to the inner passes of the woods,
In vain the razor-bill'd auk sails far north to Labrador,
I follow quickly, I ascend to the nest in the fissure of the
　　cliff.

32

I think I could turn and live with animals, they're so placid
　　and self-contain'd,
I stand and look at them long and long.

They do not sweat and whine about their condition,
They do not lie awake in the dark and weep for their sins,
They do not make me sick discussing their duty to God,
Not one is dissatisfied, not one is demented with the mania of
　　owning things,
Not one kneels to another, nor to his kind that lived thou-
　　sands of years ago,
Not one is respectable or unhappy over the whole earth.

So they show their relations to me and I accept them,
They bring me tokens of myself, they evince them plainly in
    their possession.

I wonder where they get those tokens,
Did I pass that way huge times ago and negligently drop
    them?

Myself moving forward then and now and forever,
Gathering and showing more always and with velocity,
Infinite and omnigenous, and the like of these among them,
Not too exclusive toward the reachers of my remembrancers,
Picking out here one that I love, and now go with him on
    brotherly terms.

A gigantic beauty of a stallion, fresh and responsive to my
    caresses,
Head high in the forehead, wide between the ears,
Limbs glossy and supple, tail dusting the ground,
Eyes full of sparkling wickedness, ears finely cut, flexibly
    moving.

His nostrils dilate as my heels embrace him,
His well-built limbs tremble with pleasure as we race around
    and return.
I but use you a minute, then I resign you, stallion,
Why do I need your paces when I myself out-gallop them?
Even as I stand or sit passing faster than you.

### 33

Space and Time! now I see it is true, what I guess'd at,
What I guess'd when I loaf'd on the grass,
What I guess'd while I lay alone in my bed,
And again as I walk'd the beach under the paling stars of the
    morning.

My ties and ballasts leave me, my elbows rest in sea-gaps,
I skirt sierras, my palms cover continents,
I am afoot with my vision.

By the city's quadrangular houses—in log huts, camping
　　with lumbermen,
Along the ruts of the turnpike, along the dry gulch and rivu-
　　let bed,
Weeding my onion-patch or hoeing rows of carrots and par-
　　snips, crossing savannas, trailing in forests,
Prospecting, gold-digging, girdling the trees of a new pur-
　　chase,
Scorch'd ankle-deep by the hot sand, hauling my boat down
　　the shallow river,
Where the panther walks to and fro on a limb overhead,
　　where the buck turns furiously at the hunter,
Where the rattlesnake suns his flabby length on a rock, where
　　the otter is feeding on fish,
Where the alligator in his tough pimples sleeps by the
　　bayou,
Where the black bear is searching for roots or honey, where
　　the beaver pats the mud with his paddle-shaped tail;
Over the growing sugar, over the yellow-flower'd cotton
　　plant, over the rice in its low moist field,
Over the sharp-peak'd farm house, with its scallop'd scum
　　and slender shoots from the gutters,
Over the western persimmon, over the long-leav'd corn, over
　　the delicate blue-flower flax,
Over the white and brown buckwheat, a hummer and buzzer
　　there with the rest,
Over the dusky green of the rye as it ripples and shades in the
　　breeze;
Scaling mountains, pulling myself cautiously up, holding on
　　by low scragged limbs,
Walking the path worn in the grass and beat through the
　　leaves of the brush,
Where the quail is whistling betwixt the woods and the wheat-
　　lot,
Where the bat flies in the Seventh-month eve, where the great
　　gold-bug drops through the dark,
Where the brook puts out of the roots of the old tree and
　　flows to the meadow,
Where cattle stand and shake away flies with the tremulous
　　shuddering of their hides,

Where the cheese-cloth hangs in the kitchen, where andirons
straddle the hearth-slab, where cobwebs fall in festoons
from the rafters;
Where trip-hammers crash, where the press is whirling its
cylinders,
Where the human heart beats with terrible throes under its
ribs,
Where the pear-shaped balloon is floating aloft, (floating in
it myself and looking composedly down,)
Where the life-car is drawn on the slip-noose, where the heat
hatches pale-green eggs in the dented sand,
Where the she-whale swims with her calf and never forsakes it,
Where the steam-ship trails hind-ways its long pennant of
smoke,
Where the fin of the shark cuts like a black chip out of the
water,
Where the half-burn'd brig is riding on unknown currents,
Where shells grow to her slimy deck, where the dead are
corrupting below;
Where the dense-starr'd flag is borne at the head of the regi-
ments,
Approaching Manhattan up by the long-stretching island,
Under Niagara, the cataract falling like a veil over my coun-
tenance,
Upon a door-step, upon the horse-block of hard wood out-
side,
Upon the race-course, or enjoying picnics or jigs or a good
game of base-ball,
At he-festivals, with blackguard gibes, ironical license, bull-
dances, drinking, laughter,
At the cider-mill tasting the sweets of the brown mash, suck-
ing the juice through a straw,
At apple-peelings wanting kisses for all the red fruit I find,
At musters, beach-parties, friendly bees, huskings, house-
raisings;
Where the mocking-bird sounds his delicious gurgles, cackles,
screams, weeps,
Where the hay-rick stands in the barn-yard, where the dry-
stalks are scatter'd, where the brood-cow waits in the
hovel,

Where the bull advances to do his masculine work, where the
      stud to the mare, where the cock is treading the hen,
Where the heifers browse, where geese nip their food with
      short jerks,
Where sun-down shadows lengthen over the limitless and
      lonesome prairie,
Where herds of buffalo make a crawling spread of the square
      miles far and near,
Where the humming-bird shimmers, where the neck of the
      long-lived swan is curving and winding,
Where the laughing-gull scoots by the shore, where she laughs
      her near-human laugh,
Where bee-hives range on a gray bench in the garden half hid
      by the high weeds,
Where band-neck'd partridges roost in a ring on the ground
      with their heads out,
Where burial coaches enter the arch'd gates of a cemetery,
Where winter wolves bark amid wastes of snow and icicled
      trees,
Where the yellow-crown'd heron comes to the edge of the
      marsh at night and feeds upon small crabs,
Where the splash of swimmers and divers cools the warm
      noon,
Where the katy-did works her chromatic reed on the walnut-
      tree over the wall,
Through patches of citrons and cucumbers with silver-wired
      leaves,
Through the salt-lick or orange glade, or under conical firs,
Through the gymnasium, through the curtain'd saloon,
      through the office or public hall;
Pleas'd with the native and pleas'd with the foreign, pleas'd
      with the new and old,
Pleas'd with the homely woman as well as the handsome,
Pleas'd with the quakeress as she puts off her bonnet and
      talks melodiously,
Pleas'd with the tune of the choir of the whitewash'd church,
Pleas'd with the earnest words of the sweating Methodist
      preacher, impress'd seriously at the camp-meeting;
Looking in at the shop-windows of Broadway the whole fore-
      noon, flatting the flesh of my nose on the thick plate glass,

Wandering the same afternoon with my face turn'd up to the
    clouds, or down a lane or along the beach,
My right and left arms round the sides of two friends, and I
    in the middle;
Coming home with the silent and dark-cheek'd bush-boy,
    (behind me he rides at the drape of the day,)
Far from the settlements studying the print of animals' feet,
    or the moccasin print,
By the cot in the hospital reaching lemonade to a feverish
    patient,
Nigh the coffin'd corpse when all is still, examining with a
    candle;
Voyaging to every port to dicker and adventure,
Hurrying with the modern crowd as eager and flickle as any,
Hot toward one I hate, ready in my madness to knife him,
Solitary at midnight in my back yard, my thoughts gone from
    me a long while,
Walking the old hills of Judæa with the beautiful gentle God
    by my side,
Speeding through space, speeding through heaven and the
    stars,
Speeding amid the seven satellites and the broad ring, and
    the diameter of eighty thousand miles,
Speeding with tail'd meteors, throwing fire-balls like the
    rest,
Carrying the crescent child that carries its own full mother in
    its belly,
Storming, enjoying, planning, loving, cautioning,
Backing and filling, appearing and disappearing,
I tread day and night such roads.

I visit the orchards of spheres and look at the product,
And look at quintillions ripen'd and look at quintillions
    green.

I fly those flights of a fluid and swallowing soul,
My course runs below the soundings of plummets.

I help myself to material and immaterial,
No guard can shut me off, no law prevent me.

I anchor my ship for a little while only,
My messengers continually cruise away or bring their returns
    to me.

I go hunting polar furs and the seal, leaping chasms with a
    pike-pointed staff, clinging to topples of brittle and blue.

I ascend to the foretruck,
I take my place late at night in the crow's-nest,
We sail the arctic sea, it is plenty light enough,
Through the clear atmosphere I stretch around on the won-
    derful beauty,
The enormous masses of ice pass me and I pass them, the
    scenery is plain in all directions,
The white-topt mountains show in the distance, I fling out
    my fancies toward them,
We are approaching some great battle-field in which we are
    soon to be engaged,
We pass the colossal outposts of the encampment, we pass
    with still feet and caution,
Or we are entering by the suburbs some vast and ruin'd city,
The blocks and fallen architecture more than all the living
    cities of the globe.

I am a free companion, I bivouac by invading watchfires,
I turn the bridegroom out of bed and stay with the bride
    myself,
I tighten her all night to my thighs and lips.

My voice is the wife's voice, the screech by the rail of the stairs,
They fetch my man's body up dripping and drown'd.

I understand the large hearts of heroes,
The courage of present times and all times,
How the skipper saw the crowded and rudderless wreck of
    the steamship, and Death chasing it up and down the
    storm,
How he knuckled tight and gave not back an inch, and was
    faithful of days and faithful of nights,
And chalk'd in large letters on a board, *Be of good cheer, we
    will not desert you;*

How he follow'd with them and tack'd with them three days
  and would not give it up,
How he saved the drifting company at last,
How the lank loose-gown'd women look'd when boated
  from the side of their prepared graves,
How the silent old-faced infants and the lifted sick, and the
  sharp-lipp'd unshaved men;
All this I swallow, it tastes good, I like it well, it becomes
  mine,
I am the man, I suffer'd, I was there.

The disdain and calmness of martyrs,
The mother of old, condemn'd for a witch, burnt with dry
  wood, her children gazing on,
The hounded slave that flags in the race, leans by the fence,
  blowing, cover'd with sweat,
The twinges that sting like needles his legs and neck, the
  murderous buckshot and the bullets,
All these I feel or am.

I am the hounded slave, I wince at the bite of the dogs,
Hell and despair are upon me, crack and again crack the
  marksmen,
I clutch the rails of the fence, my gore dribs, thinn'd with the
  ooze of my skin,
I fall on the weeds and stones,
The riders spur their unwilling horses, haul close,
Taunt my dizzy ears and beat me violently over the head with
  whip-stocks.

Agonies are one of my changes of garments,
I do not ask the wounded person how he feels, I myself be-
  come the wounded person,
My hurts turn livid upon me as I lean on a cane and observe.

I am the mash'd fireman with breast-bone broken,
Tumbling walls buried me in their debris,
Heat and smoke I inspired, I heard the yelling shouts of my
  comrades,
I neard the distant click of their picks and shovels,
They have clear'd the beams away, they tenderly lift me forth.

I lie in the night air in my red shirt, the pervading hush is for
    my sake,
Painless after all I lie exhausted but not so unhappy,
White and beautiful are the faces around me, the heads are
    bared of their fire-caps,
The kneeling crowd fades with the light of the torches.

Distant and dead resuscitate,
They show as the dial or move as the hands of me, I am the
    clock myself.

I am an old artillerist, I tell of my fort's bombardment,
I am there again.

Again the long roll of the drummers,
Again the attacking cannon, mortars,
Again to my listening ears the cannon responsive.

I take part, I see and hear the whole,
The cries, curses, roar, the plaudits for well-aim'd shots,
The ambulanza slowly passing trailing its red drip,
Workmen searching after damages, making indispensable
    repairs,
The fall of grenades through the rent roof, the fan-shaped
    explosion,
The whizz of limbs, heads, stone, wood, iron, high in the
    air.

Again gurgles the mouth of my dying general, he furiously
    waves with his hand,
He gasps through the clot *Mind not me—mind—the entrench-*
    *ments.*

## 34

Now I tell what I knew in Texas in my early youth,
(I tell not the fall of Alamo,
Not one escaped to tell the fall of Alamo,
The hundred and fifty are dumb yet at Alamo,)
'Tis the tale of the murder in cold blood of four hundred and
    twelve young men.

Retreating they had form'd in a hollow square with their baggage for breastworks,
Nine hundred lives out of the surrounding enemy's, nine
times their number, was the price they took in advance,
Their colonel was wounded and their ammunition gone,
They treated for an honorable capitulation, receiv'd writing
and seal, gave up their arms and march'd back prisoners
of war.

They were the glory of the race of rangers,
Matchless with horse, rifle, song, supper, courtship,
Large, turbulent, generous, handsome, proud, and affection-
ate,
Bearded, sunburnt, drest in the free costume of hunters,
Not a single one over thirty years of age.

The second First-day morning they were brought out in
squads and massacred, it was beautiful early summer,
The work commenced about five o'clock and was over by
eight.

None obey'd the command to kneel,
Some made a mad and helpless rush, some stood stark and
straight,
A few fell at once, shot in the temple or heart, the living and
dead lay together,
The maim'd and mangled dug in the dirt, the new-comers saw
them there,
Some half-kill'd attempted to crawl away,
These were despatch'd with bayonets or batter'd with the
blunts of muskets.
A youth not seventeen years old seiz'd his assassin till two
more came to release him,
The three were all torn and cover'd with the boy's blood.

At eleven o'clock began the burning of the bodies;
That is the tale of the murder of the four hundred and twelve
young men.

c                                                    H.W.

## 35

Would you hear of an old-time sea-fight?
Would you learn who won by the light of the moon and stars?
List to the yarn, as my grandmother's father the sailor told it
  to me.

Our foe was no skulk in his ship I tell you, (said he,)
His was the surly English pluck, and there is no tougher or
  truer, and never was, and never will be;
Along the lower'd eve he came horribly raking us.

We closed with him, the yards entangled, the cannon touch'd,
My captain lash'd fast with his own hands.

We had receiv'd some eighteen pound shots under the water,
On our lower-gun-deck two large pieces had burst at the first
  fire, killing all around and blowing up overhead.

Fighting at sun-down, fighting at dark,
Ten o'clock at night, the full moon well up, our leaks on the
  gain, and five feet of water reported,
The master-at-arms loosing the prisoners confined in the
  after-hold to give them a chance for themselves.

The transit to and from the magazine is now stopt by the
  sentinels,
They see so many strange faces they do not know whom to trust.

Our frigate takes fire,
The other asks if we demand quarter?
If our colors are struck and the fighting done?

Now I laugh content, for I hear the voice of my little captain,
*We have not struck,* he composedly cries, *we have just begun
  our part of the fighting.*

Only three guns are in use,
One is directed by the captain himself against the enemy's
  main-mast,
Two well serv'd with grape and canister silence his musketry
  and clear his decks.

The tops alone second the fire of this little battery, especially
    the main-top,
They hold out bravely during the whole of the action.

Not a moment's cease,
The leaks gain fast on the pumps, the fire eats toward the
    powder-magazine.

One of the pumps has been shot away, it is generally thought
    we are sinking.

Serene stands the little captain,
He is not hurried, his voice is neither high nor low,
His eyes give more light to us than our battle-lanterns.

Toward twelve there in the beams of the moon they surrender
    to us.

## 36

Stretch'd and still lies the midnight,
Two great hulls motionless on the breast of the darkness,
Our vessel riddled and slowly sinking, preparations to pass
    to the one we have conquer'd,
The captain on the quarter-deck coldly giving his orders
    through a countenance white as a sheet,
Near by the corpse of the child that serv'd in the cabin,
The dead face of an old salt with long white hair and care-
    fully curl'd whiskers,
The flames spite of all that can be done flickering aloft and
    below,
The husky voices of the two or three officers yet fit for duty,
Formless stacks of bodies and bodies by themselves, dabs of
    flesh upon the masts and spars,
Cut of cordage, dangle of rigging, slight shock of the soothe
    of waves,
Black and impassive guns, litter of powder-parcels, strong
    scent,
A few large stars overhead, silent and mournful shining,
Delicate sniffs of sea-breeze, smells of sedgy grass and fields
    by the shore, death-messages given in charge to sur-
    vivors,

The hiss of the surgeon's knife, the gnawing teeth of his
    saw,
Wheeze, cluck, swash of falling blood, short wild scream, and
    long, dull, tapering groan,
These so, these irretrievable.

### 37

You laggards there on guard! look to your arms!
In at the conquer'd doors they crowd! I am possess'd!
Embody all presences outlaw'd or suffering,
See myself in prison shaped like another man,
And feel the dull unintermitted pain,
For me the keepers of convicts shoulder their carbines and
    keep watch,
It is I let out in the morning and barr'd at night.

Not a mutineer walks handcuff'd to jail but I am handcuff'd
    to him and walk by his side,
(I am less the jolly one there, and more the silent one with
    sweat on my twitching lips.)

Not a youngster is taken for larceny but I go up too, and am
    tried and sentenced.

Not a cholera patient lies at the last gasp but I also lie at the
    last gasp,
My face is ash-color'd, my sinews gnarl, away from me
    people retreat.

Askers embody themselves in me and I am embodied in
    them,
I project my hat, sit shame-faced, and beg.

### 38

Enough! enough! enough!
Somehow I have been stunn'd.  Stand back!
Give me a little time beyond my cuff'd head, slumbers,
    dreams, gaping,
I discover myself on the verge of a usual mistake.

That I could forget the mockers and insults!
That I could forget the trickling tears and the blows of the
    bludgeons and hammers!
That I could look with a separate look on my own crucifixion
    and bloody crowning!

I remember now,
I resume the overstaid fraction,
The grave of rock multiplies what has been confided to it, or
    to any graves,
Corpses rise, gashes heal, fastenings roll from me.

I troop forth replenish'd with supreme power, one of an
    average unending procession,
Inland and sea-coast we go, and pass all boundary lines,
Our swift ordinances on their way over the whole earth,
The blossoms we wear in our hats the growth of thousands of
    years.

Eleves, I salute you! come forward!
Continue your annotations, continue your questionings.

### 39

The friendly and flowing savage, who is he?
Is he waiting for civilization, or past it and mastering it?

Is he some Southwesterner rais'd out-doors? is he Kanadian?
Is he from the Mississippi country? Iowa, Oregon, Califor-
    nia?
The mountains? prairie-life, bush-life? or sailor from the sea?

Wherever he goes men and women accept and desire him,
They desire he should like them, touch them, speak to them,
    stay with them.

Behavior lawless as snow-flakes, words simple as grass, un-
    comb'd head, laughter, and naivetè,
Slow-stepping feet, common features, common modes and
    emanations,
They descend in new forms from the tips of his fingers,

They are wafted with the odor of his body or breath, they fly
    out of the glance of his eyes.

### 40

Flaunt of the sunshine I need not your bask—lie over!
You light surfaces only, I force surfaces and depths also.

Earth! you seem to look for something at my hands,
Say, old top-knot, what do you want?

Man or woman, I might tell how I like you, but cannot,
And might tell what it is in me and what it is in you, but
    cannot,
And might tell that pining I have, that pulse of my nights and
    days.

Behold, I do not give lectures or a little charity,
When I give I give myself.

You there, impotent, loose in the knees,
Open your scarf'd chops till I blow grit within you,
Spread your palms and lift the flaps of your pockets,
I am not to be denied, I compel, I have stores plenty and to
    spare,
And any thing I have I bestow.

I do not ask who you are, that is not important to me,
You can do nothing and be nothing but what I will infold
    you.

To cotton-field drudge or cleaner of privies I lean,
On his right cheek I put the family kiss,
And in my soul I swear I never will deny him.

On women fit for conception I start bigger and nimbler
    babes,
(This day I am jetting the stuff of far more arrogant repub-
    lics.)

To any one dying, thither I speed and twist the knob of the
    door,

Turn the bed-clothes toward the foot of the bed,
Let the physician and the priest go home.

I seize the descending man and raise him with resistless will,
O despairer, here is my neck,
By God, you shall not go down! hang your whole weight
    upon me.

I dilate you with tremendous breath, I buoy you up,
Every room of the house do I fill with an arm'd force,
Lovers of me, bafflers of graves.

Sleep—I and they keep guard all night,
Not doubt, not disease shall dare to lay finger upon you,
I have embraced you, and henceforth possess you to myself,
And when you rise in the morning you will find what I tell
    you is so.

### 41

I am he bringing help for the sick as they pant on their backs,
And for strong upright men I bring yet more needed help.

I heard what was said of the universe,
Heard it and heard it of several thousand years;
It is middling well as far as it goes—but is that all?

Magnifying and applying come I,
Outbidding at the start the old cautious hucksters,
Taking myself the exact dimensions of Jehovah,
Lithographing Kronos, Zeus his son, and Hercules his
    grandson,
Buying drafts of Osiris, Isis, Belus, Brahma, Buddha,
In my portfolio placing Manito loose, Allah on a leaf, the
    crucifix engraved,
With Odin and the hideous-faced Mexitli and every idol and
    image,
Taking them all for what they are worth and not a cent more,
Admitting they were alive and did the work of their days,
(They bore mites as for unfledg'd birds who have now to rise
    and fly and sing for themselves,)

Accepting the rough deific sketches to fill out better in myself,
    bestowing them freely on each man and woman I see,
Discovering as much or more in a framer framing a house,
Putting higher claims for him there with his roll'd-up sleeves
    driving the mallet and chisel,
Not objecting to special revelations, considering a curl of
    smoke or a hair on the back of my hand just as curious
    as any revelation,
Lads ahold of fire-engines and hook-and-ladder ropes no less
    to me than the gods of the antique wars,
Minding their voices peal through the crash of destruction,
Their brawny limbs passing safe over charr'd laths, their
    white foreheads whole and unhurt out of the flames;
By the mechanic's wife with her babe at her nipple interced-
    ing for every person born,
Three scythes at harvest whizzing in a row from three lusty
    angels with shirts bagg'd out at their waists,
The snag-tooth'd hostler with red hair redeeming sins past
    and to come,
Selling all he possesses, traveling on foot to fee lawyers for
    his brother and sit by him while he is tried for forgery;
What was strewn in the amplest strewing the square rod
    about me, and not filling the square rod then,
The bull and the bug never worshipp'd half enough,
Dung and dirt more admirable than was dream'd,
The supernatural of no account, myself waiting my time to
    be one of the supremes,
The day getting ready for me when I shall do as much good
    as the best, and be as prodigious;
By my life-lumps! becoming already a creator,
Putting myself here and now to the ambush'd womb of the
    shadows.

### 42

A call in the midst of the crowd,
My own voice, orotund sweeping and final.

Come my children,
Come my boys and girls, my women, household and inti-
    mates,

Now the performer launches his nerve, he has pass'd his prelude on the reeds within.

Easily written loose-finger'd chords—I feel the thrum of your
climax and close.

My head slues round on my neck,
Music rolls, but not from the organ,
Folks are around me, but they are no household of mine.

Ever the hard unsunk ground,
Ever the eaters and drinkers, ever the upward and downward
sun, ever the air and the ceaseless tides,
Ever myself and my neighbors, refreshing, wicked, real,
Ever the old inexplicable query, ever that thorn'd thumb,
that breath of itches and thirsts,
Ever the vexer's *hoot! hoot!* till we find where the sly one
hides and bring him forth,
Ever love, ever the sobbing liquid of life,
Ever the bandage under the chin, ever the trestles of death.

Here and there with dimes on the eyes walking,
To feed the greed of the belly the brains liberally spooning,
Tickets buying, taking, selling, but in to the feast never once
going,
Many sweating, ploughing, thrashing, and then the chaff for
payment receiving,
A few idly owning, and they the wheat continually claiming.

This is the city and I am one of the citizens,
Whatever interests the rest interests me, politics, wars, markets, newspapers, schools,
The mayor and councils, banks, tariffs, steamships, factories,
stocks, stores, real estate and personal estate.

The little plentiful manikins skipping around in collars and
tail'd coats,
I am aware who they are, (they are positively not worms or
fleas,)
I acknowledge the duplicates of myself, the weakest and
shallowest is deathless with me,

What I do and say the same waits for them,
Every thought that flounders in me the same flounders in
  them.

I know perfectly well my own egotism,
Know my omnivorous lines and must not write any less,
And would fetch you whoever you are flush with myself.

Not words of routine this song of mine,
But abruptly to question, to leap beyond yet nearer bring;
This printed and bound book—but the printer and the
  printing-office boy?
The well-taken photographs—but your wife or friend close
  and solid in your arms?
The black ship mail'd with iron, her mighty guns in her
  turrets— but the pluck of the captain and engineers?
In the houses the dishes and fare and furniture—but the host
  and hostess, and the look out of their eyes?
The sky up there—yet here or next door, or across the way?
The saints and sages in history—but you yourself?
Sermons, creeds, theology—but the fathomless human
  brain,
And what is reason? and what is love? and what is life?

### 43

I do not despise you priests, all time, the world over,
My faith is the greatest of faiths and the least of faiths,
Enclosing worship ancient and modern and all between
  ancient and modern,
Believing I shall come again upon the earth after five thou-
  sand years,
Waiting responses from oracles, honoring the gods, saluting
  the sun,
Making a fetich of the first rock or stump, powowing with
  sticks in the circle of obis,
Helping the llama or brahmin as he trims the lamps of the
  idols,
Dancing yet through the streets in a phallic procession, rapt
  and austere in the woods a gymnosophist,
Drinking mead from the skull-cup, to Shastas and Vedas
  admirant, minding the Koran,

Walking the teokallis, spotted with gore from the stone and
    knife, beating the serpent-skin drum,
Accepting the Gospels, accepting him that was crucified,
    knowing assuredly that he is divine,
To the mass kneeling or the puritan's prayer rising, or sitting
    patiently in a pew,
Ranting and frothing in my insane crisis, or waiting dead-like
    till my spirit arouses me,
Looking forth on pavement and land, or outside of pavement
    and land,
Belonging to the winders of the circuit of circuits.

One of that centripetal and centrifugal gang I turn and talk
    like a man leaving charges before a journey.

Down-hearted doubters dull and excluded,
Frivolous, sullen, moping, angry, affected, dishearten'd,
    atheistical,
I know every one of you, I know the sea of torment, doubt,
    despair and unbelief.

How the flukes splash!
How they contort rapid as lightning, with spasms and spouts
    of blood!

Be at peace bloody flukes of doubters and sullen mopers,
I take my place among you as much as among any,
The past is the push of you, me, all, precisely the same,
And what is yet untried and afterward is for you, me, all
    precisely the same.

I do not know what is untried and afterward,
But I know it will in its turn prove sufficient, and cannot fail.

Each who passes is consider'd, each who stops is consider'd,
    not a single one can it fail.

It cannot fail the young man who died and was buried,
Nor the young woman who died and was put by his side,
Nor the little child that peep'd in at the door, and then drew
    back and was never seen again,

Nor the old man who has lived without purpose, and feels it
with bitterness worse than gall,
Nor him in the poor house tubercled by rum and the bad
disorder,
Nor the numberless slaughter'd and wreck'd, nor the brutish
koboo call'd the ordure of humanity,
Nor the sacs merely floating with open mouths for food to
slip in,
Nor any thing in the earth, or down in the oldest graves of
the earth,
Nor any thing in the myriads of spheres, nor the myriads of
myriads that inhabit them,
Nor the present, nor the least wisp that is known.

## 44

It is time to explain myself—let us stand up.

What is known I strip away,
I launch all men and women forward with me into the Unknown.

The clock indicates the moment—but what does eternity
indicate?

We have thus far exhausted trillions of winters and summers,
There are trillions ahead, and trillions ahead of them.

Births have brought us richness and variety,
And other births will bring us richness and variety.

I do not call one greater and one smaller,
That which fills its period and place is equal to any.

Were mankind murderous or jealous upon you, my brother,
my sister?
I am sorry for you, they are not murderous or jealous upon
me,
All has been gentle with me, I keep no account with lamentation,
(What have I to do with lamentation?)

I am an acme of things accomplish'd, and I an encloser of
   things to be.

My feet strike an apex of the apices of the stairs,
On every step bunches of ages, and larger bunches between
   the steps,
All below duly travel'd, and still I mount and mount.

Rise after rise bow the phantoms behind me,
Afar down I see the huge first Nothing, I know I was even
   there,
I waited unseen and always, and slept through the lethargic
   mist,
And took my time, and took no hurt from the fetid carbon.

Long I was hugg'd close—long and long.

Immense have been the preparations for me,
Faithful and friendly the arms that have help'd me.

Cycles ferried my cradle, rowing and rowing like cheerful
   boatmen,
For room to me stars kept aside in their own rings,
They sent influences to look after what was to hold me.

Before I was born out of my mother generations guided me,
My embryo has never been torpid, nothing could overlay it.

For it the nebula cohered to an orb,
The long slow strata piled to rest it on,
Vast vegetables gave it sustenance,
Monstrous sauroids transported it in their mouths and de-
   posited it with care.

All forces have been steadily employ'd to complete and delight me,
Now on this spot I stand with my robust soul.

45

O span of youth! ever-push'd elasticity!
O manhood, balanced, florid and full.

My lovers suffocate me,
Crowding my lips, thick in the pores of my skin,
Jostling me through streets and public halls, coming naked to
    me at night,
Crying by day *Ahoy!* from the rocks of the river, swinging
    and chirping over my head,
Calling my name from flower-beds, vines, tangled under-
    brush,
Lighting on every moment of my life,
Bussing my body with soft balsamic busses,
Noiselessly passing handfuls out of their hearts and giving
    them to be mine.

Old age superbly rising! O welcome, ineffable grace of dying
    days!

Every condition promulges not only itself, it promulges what
    grows after and out of itself,
And the dark hush promulges as much as any.

I open my scuttle at night and see the far-sprinkled systems,
And all I see multiplied as high as I can cipher edge but the
    rim of the farther systems.

Wider and wider they spread, expanding, always expanding,
Outward and outward and forever outward.

My sun has his sun and round him obediently wheels,
He joins with his partners a group of superior circuit,
And greater sets follow, making specks of the greatest inside
    them.

There is no stoppage and never can be stoppage,
If I, you, and the worlds, and all beneath or upon their sur-
    faces, were this moment reduced back to a pallid float,
    it would not avail in the long run,
We should surely bring up again where we now stand,
And surely go as much farther, and then farther and farther.

A few quadrillions of eras, a few octillions of cubic leagues,
    do not hazard the span or make it impatient,
They are but parts, any thing is but a part.

See ever so far, there is limitless space outside of that,
Count ever so much, there is limitless time around that.

My rendezvous is appointed, it is certain,
The Lord will be there and wait till I come on perfect terms,
The great Camerado, the lover true for whom I pine will be
    there.


46

I know I have the best of time and space, and was never
    measured and never will be measured.

I tramp a perpetual journey, (come listen all!)
My signs are a rain-proof coat, good shoes, and a staff cut
    from the woods,
No friend of mine takes his ease in my chair,
I have no chair, no church, no philosophy,
I lead no man to a dinner-table, library, exchange,
But each man and each woman of you I lead upon a knoll,
My left hand hooking you round the waist,
My right hand pointing to landscapes of continents and the
    public road.

Not I, not any one else can travel that road for you,
You must travel it for yourself.

It is not far, it is within reach,
Perhaps you have been on it since you were born and did not
    know,
Perhaps it is everywhere on water and on land.

Shoulder your duds dear son, and I will mine, and let us
    hasten forth,
Wonderful cities and free nations we shall fetch as we go.

If you tire, give me both burdens, and rest the chuff of your
    hand on my hip,
And in due time you shall repay the same service to me,
For after we start we never lie by again.

This day before dawn I ascended a hill and look'd at the
    crowded heaven,
And I said to my spirit *When we become the enfolders of those
    orbs, and the pleasure and knowledge of every thing in
    them, shall we be fill'd and satisfied then?*
And my spirit said *No, we but level that lift to pass and con-
    tinue beyond.*

You are also asking me questions and I hear you,
I answer that I cannot answer, you must find out for yourself.

Sit a while dear son,
Here are biscuits to eat and here is milk to drink,
But as soon as you sleep and renew yourself in sweet clothes,
    I kiss you with a good-by kiss and open the gate for your
    egress hence.

Long enough have you dream'd contemptible dreams,
Now I wash the gum from your eyes,
You must habit yourself to the dazzle of the light and of
    every moment of your life.

Long have you timidly waded holding a plank by the shore,
Now I will you to be a bold swimmer,
To jump off in the midst of the sea, rise again, nod to me,
    shout, and laughingly dash with your hair.

### 47

I am the teacher of athletes,
He that by me spreads a wider breast than my own proves
    the width of my own,
He most honors my style who learns under it to destroy the
    teacher.

The boy I love, the same becomes a man not through derived
    power, but in his own right,
Wicked rather than virtuous out of conformity or fear,
Fond of his sweetheart, relishing well his steak,
Unrequited love or a slight cutting him worse than sharp
    steel cuts,

First-rate to ride, to fight, to hit the bull's eye, to sail a skiff,
    to sing a song or play on the banjo,
Preferring scars and the beard and faces pitted with small-
    pox over all latherers,
And those well-tann'd to those that keep out of the sun.

I teach straying from me, yet who can stray from me?
I follow you whoever you are from the present hour,
My words itch at your ears till you understand them.

I do not say these things for a dollar or to fill up the time
    while I wait for a boat,
(It is you talking just as much as myself, I act as the tongue of
    you,
Tied in your mouth, in mine it begins to be loosen'd.)

I swear I will never again mention love or death inside a
    house,
And I swear I will never translate myself at all, only to him or
    her who privately stays with me in the open air.

If you would understand me go to the heights or water-
    shore,
The nearest gnat is an explanation, and a drop or motion of
    waves a key,
The maul, the oar, the hand-saw, second my words.

No shutter'd room or school can commune with me,
But roughs and little children better than they.

The young mechanic is closest to me, he knows me well,
The woodman that takes his axe and jug with him shall take
    me with him all day,
The farm-boy ploughing in the field feels good at the sound
    of my voice,
In vessels that sail my words sail, I go with fishermen and
    seamen and love them.

The soldier camp'd or upon the march is mine,
On the night ere the pending battle many seek me, and I do
    not fail them.

On that solemn night (it may be their last) those that know
     me seek me.

My face rubs to the hunter's face when he lies down alone in
     his blanket,
The driver thinking of me does not mind the jolt of his
     wagon,
The young mother and old mother comprehend me,
The girl and the wife rest the needle a moment and forget
     where they are,
They and all would resume what I have told them.

### 48

I have said that the soul is not more than the body,
And I have said that the body is not more than the soul,
And nothing, not God, is greater to one than one's self is,
And whoever walks a furlong without sympathy walks to his
     own funeral drest in his shroud,
And I or you pocketless of a dime may purchase the pick of
     the earth,
And to glance with an eye or show a bean in its pod con-
     founds the learning of all times,
And there is no trade or employment but the young man fol-
     lowing it may become a hero,
And there is no object so soft but it makes a hub for the
     wheel'd universe,
And I say to any man or woman, Let your soul stand cool
     and composed before a million universes.

And I say to mankind, Be not curious about God,
For I who am curious about each am not curious about
     God,
(No array of terms can say how much I am at peace about
     God and about death.)

I hear and behold God in every object, yet understand God
     not in the least,
Nor do I understand who there can be more wonderful than
     myself.

Why should I wish to see God better than this day?
I see something of God each hour of the twenty-four, and
    each moment then,
In the faces of men and women I see God, and in my own
    face in the glass,
I find letters from God dropt in the street, and every one is
    sign'd by God's name,
And I leave them where they are, for I know that wheresoe'er
    I go,
Others will punctually come for ever and ever.

49

And as to you Death, and you bitter hug of mortality, it is
    idle to try to alarm me.

To his work without flinching the accoucheur comes,
I see the elder-hand pressing receiving supporting,
I recline by the sills of the exquisite flexible doors,
And mark the outlet, and mark the relief and escape.

And as to you Corpse I think you are good manure, but that
    does not offend me,
I smell the white roses sweet-scented and growing,
I reach to the leafy lips, I reach to the polish'd breasts of
    melons.

And as to you Life I reckon you are the leavings of many
    deaths,
(No doubt I have died myself ten thousand times before.)

I hear you whispering there O stars of heaven,
O suns—O grass of graves—O perpetual transfers and pro-
    motions,
If you do not say any thing how can I say any thing?

Of the turbid pool that lies in the autumn forest,
Of the moon that descends the steeps of the soughing twi-
    light,
Toss, sparkles of day and dusk—toss on the black stems that
    decay in the muck,
Toss to the moaning gibberish of the dry limbs.

I ascend from the moon, I ascend from the night,
I perceive that the ghastly glimmer is noonday sunbeams
   reflected,
And debouch to the steady and central from the offspring
   great or small.

## 50

There is that in me—I do not know what it is—but I know it
   is in me.

Wrench'd and sweaty—calm and cool then my body becomes,
I sleep—I sleep long.

I do not know it—it is without name—it is a word unsaid,
It is not in any dictionary, utterance, symbol.

Something it swings on more than the earth I swing on,
To it the creation is the friend whose embracing awakes me.

Perhaps I might tell more. Outlines! I plead for my brothers
   and sisters.

Do you see O my brothers and sisters?
It is not chaos or death—it is form, union, plan—it is eternal
   life—it is Happiness.

## 51

The past and present wilt—I have fill'd them, emptied them,
And proceed to fill my next fold of the future.

Listener up there! what have you to confide to me?
Look in my face while I snuff the sidle of evening,
(Talk honestly, no one else hears you, and I stay only a
   minute longer.)

Do I contradict myself?
Very well then I contradict myself,
(I am large, I contain multitudes.)

I concentrate toward them that are nigh, I wait on the door-
   slab.

Who has done his day's work? who will soonest be through
    with his supper?
Who wishes to walk with me?

Will you speak before I am gone? will you prove already too
    late?

### 52

The spotted hawk swoops by and accuses me, he complains
    of my gab and my loitering.

I too am not a bit tamed, I too am untranslatable,
I sound my barbaric yawp over the roofs of the world.

The last scud of day holds back for me,
It flings my likeness after the rest and true as any on the
    shadow'd wilds,
It coaxes me to the vapor and the dusk.

I depart as air, I shake my white locks at the runaway sun,
I effuse my flesh in eddies, and drift it in lacy jags.

I bequeath myself to the dirt to grow from the grass I love,
If you want me again look for me under your boot-soles.

You will hardly know who I am or what I mean,
But I shall be good health to you nevertheless,
And filter and fibre your blood.

Failing to fetch me at first keep encouraged,
Missing me one place search another,
I stop somewhere waiting for you.

1855                                      1881

# *Children of Adam*

## TO THE GARDEN THE WORLD

To the garden the world anew ascending,
Potent mates, daughters, sons, preluding,
The love, the life of their bodies, meaning and being,
Curious here behold my resurrection after slumber,
The revolving cycles in their wide sweep having brought me
    again,
Amorous, mature, all beautiful to me, all wondrous,
My limbs and the quivering fire that ever plays through them,
    for reasons, most wondrous,
Existing I peer and penetrate still,
Content with the present, content with the past,
By my side or back of me Eve following,
Or in front, and I following her just the same.
1860                       1867

## FROM PENT-UP ACHING RIVERS

From pent-up aching rivers,
From that of myself without which I were nothing,
From what I am determin'd to make illustrious, even if I
    stand sole among men,
From my own voice resonant, singing the phallus,
Singing the song of procreation,
Singing the need of superb children and therein superb grown
    people,
Singing the muscular urge and the blending,
Singing the bedfellow's song, (O resistless yearning!
O for any and each the body correlative attracting!
O for you whoever you are your correlative body! O it,
    more than all else, you delighting!)
From the hungry gnaw that eats me night and day,

From native moments, from bashful pains, singing them,
Seeking something yet unfound though I have diligently
    sought it many a long year,
Singing the true song of the soul fitful at random,
Renascent with grossest Nature or among animals,
Of that, of them and what goes with them my poems in-
    forming,
Of the smell of apples and lemons, of the pairing of birds,
Of the wet of woods, of the lapping of waves,
Of the mad pushes of waves upon the land, I them chanting,
The overture lightly sounding, the strain anticipating,
The welcome nearness, the sight of the perfect body,
The swimmer swimming naked in the bath, or motionless on
    his back lying and floating,
The female form approaching, I pensive, love-flesh tremulous
    aching,
The divine list for myself or you or for any one making,
The face, the limbs, the index from head to foot, and what it
    arouses,
The mystic deliria, the madness amorous, the utter abandon-
    ment,
(Hark close and still what I now whisper to you,
I love you, O you entirely possess me,
O that you and I escape from the rest and go utterly off, free
    and lawless,
Two hawks in the air, two fishes swimming in the sea not
    more lawless than we;)
The furious storm through me careering, I passionately
    trembling,
The oath of the inseparableness of two together, of the
    woman that loves me and whom I love more than my
    life, that oath swearing,
(O I willingly stake all for you,
O let me be lost if it must be so!
O you and I! what is it to us what the rest do or think?
What is all else to us? only that we enjoy each other and ex-
    haust each other if it must be so;)
From the master, the pilot I yield the vessel to,
The general commanding me, commanding all, from him
    permission taking,

From time the programme hastening, (I have loiter'd too
    long as it is,)
From sex, from the warp and from the woof,
From privacy, from frequent repinings alone,
From plenty of persons near and yet the right person not
    near,
From the soft sliding of hands over me and thrusting of
    fingers through my hair and beard,
From the long sustain'd kiss upon the mouth or bosom,
From the close pressure that makes me or any man drunk,
    fainting with excess,
From what the divine husband knows, from the work of
    fatherhood,
From exultation, victory and relief from the bedfellow's
    embrace in the night,
From the act-poems of eyes, hands, hips and bosoms,
From the cling of the trembling arm,
From the bending curve and the clinch,
From side by side the pliant coverlet off-throwing,
From the one so unwilling to have me leave, and me just as
    unwilling to leave,
(Yet a moment O tender waiter, and I return,)
From the hour of shining stars and dropping dews,
From the night a moment I emerging flitting out,
Celebrate you act divine and you children prepared for,
And you stalwart loins.

1860                                          1881

## I SING THE BODY ELECTRIC

### 1

I SING the body electric,
The armies of those I love engirth me and I engirth them,
They will not let me off till I go with them, respond to
    them,
And discorrupt them, and charge them full with the charge of
    the soul.

Was it doubted that those who corrupt their own bodies con-
    ceal themselves?

And if those who defile the living are as bad as they who de-
file the dead?
And if the body does not do fully as much as the soul?
And if the body were not the soul, what is the soul?

2

The love of the body of man or woman balks account, the
body itself balks account,
That of the male is perfect, and that of the female is perfect.

The expression of the face balks account,
But the expression of a well-made man appears not only in
his face,
It is in his limbs and joints also, it is curiously in the joints of
his hips and wrists,
It is in his walk, the carriage of his neck, the flex of his waist
and knees, dress does not hide him,
The strong sweet quality he has strikes through the cotton
and broad-cloth,
To see him pass conveys as much as the best poem, perhaps
more,
You linger to see his back, and the back of his neck and
shoulder-side.

The sprawl and fulness of babes, the bosoms and heads of
women, the folds of their dress, their style as we pass in
the street, the contour of their shape downwards,
The swimmer naked in the swimming-bath, seen as he
swims through the transparent green-shine, or lies with
his face up and rolls silently to and fro in the heave of
the water,
The bending forward and backward of rowers in row-boats,
the horseman in his saddle,
Girls, mothers, house-keepers, in all their performances,
The group of laborers seated at noon-time with their open
dinner kettles, and their wives waiting,
The female soothing a child, the farmer's daughter in the
garden or cow-yard,
The young fellow hoeing corn, the sleigh-driver driving his
six horses through the crowd,

The wrestle of wrestlers, two apprentice-boys, quite grown,
lusty, good-natured, native-born, out on the vacant lot
at sundown after work,

The coats and caps thrown down, the embrace of love and
resistance,

The upper-hold and under-hold, the hair rumpled over and
blinding the eyes;

The march of firemen in their own costumes, the play of
masculine muscle through clean-setting trowsers and
waist-straps,

The slow return from the fire, the pause when the bell strikes
suddenly again, and the listening on the alert,

The natural, perfect, varied attitudes, the bent head, the
curv'd neck and the counting;

Such-like I love—I loosen myself, pass freely, am at the
mother's breast with the little child,

Swim with the swimmers, wrestle with wrestlers, march in
line with the firemen, and pause, listen, count.

### 3

I knew a man, a common farmer, the father of five sons,
And in them the fathers of sons, and in them the fathers of
sons.

This man was of wonderful vigor, calmness, beauty of person,

The shape of his head, the pale yellow and white of his hair
and beard, the immeasurable meaning of his black eyes,
the richness and breadth of his manners,

These I used to go and visit him to see, he was wise also,

He was six feet tall, he was over eighty years old, his sons
were massive, clean, bearded, tan-faced, handsome,

They and his daughters loved him, all who saw him loved him,

They did not love him by allowance, they loved him with
personal love,

He drank water only, the blood show'd like scarlet through
the clear-brown skin of his face,

He was a frequent gunner and fisher, he sail'd his boat himself, he had a fine one presented to him by a ship-joiner,
he had fowling-pieces presented to him by men that
loved him,

When he went with his five sons and many grand-sons to
    hunt or fish, you would pick him out as the most beauti-
    ful and vigorous of the gang,
You would wish long and long to be with him, you would
    wish to sit by him in the boat that you and he might
    touch each other.


### 4

I have perceiv'd that to be with those I like is enough,
To stop in company with the rest at evening is enough,
To be surrounded by beautiful, curious, breathing, laughing
    flesh is enough,
To pass among them or touch any one, or rest my arm ever
    so lightly round his or her neck for a moment, what is
    this then?
I do not ask any more delight, I swim in it as in a sea.

There is something in staying close to men and women and
    looking on them, and in the contact and odor of them,
    that pleases the soul well,
All things please the soul, but these please the soul well.


### 5

This is the female form,
A divine nimbus exhales from it from head to foot,
It attracts with fierce undeniable attraction,
I am drawn by its breath as if I were no more than a helpless
    vapor, all falls aside but myself and it,
Books, art, religion, time, the visible and solid earth, and
    what was expected of heaven or fear'd of hell, are now
    consumed,
Mad filaments, ungovernable shoots play out of it, the re-
    sponse likewise ungovernable,
Hair, bosom, hips, bend of legs, negligent falling hands all
    diffused, mine too diffused,
Ebb stung by the flow and flow stung by the ebb, love-flesh
    swelling and deliciously aching,
Limitless limpid jets of love hot and enormous, quivering
    jelly of love, white-blow and delirious juice,

Bridegroom night of love working surely and softly into the
    prostrate dawn,
Undulating into the willing and yielding day,
Lost in the cleave of the clasping and sweet-flesh'd day.

This the nucleus—after the child is born of woman, man is
    born of woman,
This the bath of birth, this the merge of small and large, and
    the outlet again.

Be not ashamed women, your privilege encloses the rest, and
    is the exit of the rest,
You are the gates of the body, and you are the gates of the soul.

The female contains all qualities and tempers them,
She is in her place and moves with perfect balance,
She is all things duly veil'd, she is both passive and active,
She is to conceive daughters as well as sons, and sons as well
    as daughters.

As I see my soul reflected in Nature,
As I see through a mist, One with inexpressible completeness,
    sanity, beauty,
See the bent head and arms folded over the breast, the Fe-
    male I see.

### 6

The male is not less the soul nor more, he too is in his place,
He too is all qualities, he is action and power,
The flush of the known universe is in him,
Scorn becomes him well, and appetite and defiance become
    him well,
The wildest largest passions, bliss that is utmost, sorrow that
    is utmost become him well, pride is for him,
The full-spread pride of man is calming and excellent to the
    soul,
Knowledge becomes him, he likes it always, he brings every
    thing to the test of himself,
Whatever the survey, whatever the sea and the sail he strikes
    soundings at last only here,
(Where else does he strike soundings except here?)

The man's body is sacred and the woman's body is sacred,
No matter who it is, it is sacred—is it the meanest one in the
    laborer's gang?
Is it one of the dull-faced immigrants just landed on the
    wharf?
Each belongs here or anywhere just as much as the well-off,
    just as much as you,
Each has his or her place in the procession.

(All is a procession,
The universe is a procession with measured and perfect
    motion.)

Do you know so much yourself that you call the meanest
    ignorant?
Do you suppose you have a right to a good sight, and he or
    she has no right to a sight?
Do you think matter has cohered together from its diffuse
    float, and the soil is on the surface, and water runs and
    vegetation sprouts,
For you only, and not for him and her?

### 7

A man's body at auction,
(For before the war I often go to the slave-mart and watch
    the sale,)
I help the auctioneer, the sloven does not half know his
    business.

Gentlemen look on this wonder,
Whatever the bids of the bidders they cannot be high enough
    for it,
For it the globe lay preparing quintillions of years without
    one animal or plant,
For it the revolving cycles truly and steadily roll'd.

In this head the all-baffling brain,
In it and below it the makings of heroes.

Examine these limbs, red, black, or white, they are cunning in
    tendon and nerve,
They shall be stript that you may see them.

Exquisite senses, life-lit eyes, pluck, volition,
Flakes of breast-muscle, pliant backbone and neck, flesh not
    flabby, good-sized arms and legs,
And wonders within there yet.

Within there runs blood,
The same old blood! the same red-running blood!
There swells and jets a heart, there all passions, desires,
    reachings, aspirations,
(Do you think they are not there because they are not ex-
    press'd in parlors and lecture-rooms?)

This is not only one man, this the father of those who shall
    be fathers in their turns,
In him the start of populous states and rich republics,
Of him countless immortal lives with countless embodiments
    and enjoyments.

How do you know who shall come from the offspring of his
    offspring through the centuries?
(Who might you find you have come from yourself, if you
    could trace back through the centuries?)

## 8

A woman's body at auction,
She too is not only herself, she is the teeming mother of
    mothers,
She is the bearer of them that shall grow and be mates to the
    mothers.

Have you ever loved the body of a woman?
Have you ever loved the body of a man?
Do you not see that these are exactly the same to all in all
    nations and times all over the earth?

If any thing is sacred the human body is sacred,
And the glory and sweat of a man is the token of manhood
    untainted,
And in man or woman a clean, strong, firm-fibred body, is
    more beautiful than the most beautiful face.

Have you seen the fool that corrupted his own live body? or
   the fool that corrupted her own live body?
For they do not conceal themselves, and cannot conceal
   themselves.

### 9

O my body! I dare not desert the likes of you in other men
   and women, nor the likes of the parts of you,
I believe the likes of you are to stand or fall with the likes of
   the soul, (and that they are the soul,)
I believe the likes of you shall stand or fall with my poems,
   and that they are my poems,
Man's, woman's, child's, youth's, wife's, husband's, mother's,
   father's, young man's, young woman's poems,
Head, neck, hair, ears, drop and tympan of the ears,
Eyes, eye-fringes, iris of the eye, eyebrows, and the waking or
   sleeping of the lids,
Mouth, tongue, lips, teeth, roof of the mouth, jaws, and the
   jaw-hinges,
Nose, nostrils of the nose, and the partition,
Cheeks, temples, forehead, chin, throat, back of the neck,
   neck-slue,
Strong shoulders, manly beard, scapula, hind-shoulders, and
   the ample side-round of the chest,
Upper-arm, armpit, elbow-socket, lower-arm, arm-sinews,
   arm-bones,
Wrist and wrist-joints, hand, palm, knuckles, thumb, fore-
   finger, finger-joints, finger-nails,
Broad breast-front, curling hair of the breast, breast-bone,
   breast-side,
Ribs, belly, backbone, joints of the backbone,
Hips, hip-sockets, hip-strength, inward and outward round,
   man-balls, man-root,
Strong set of thighs, well carrying the trunk above,
Leg-fibres, knee, knee-pan, upper-leg, under-leg,
Ankles, instep, foot-ball, toes, toe-joints, the heel;
All attitudes, all the shapeliness, all the belongings of my or
   your body or of any one's body, male or female,
The lung-sponges, the stomach-sac, the bowels sweet and
   clean,

The brain in its folds inside the skull-frame,
Sympathies, heart-valves, palate-valves, sexuality, maternity,
Womanhood and all that is a woman, and the man that
    comes from woman,
The womb, the teats, nipples, breast-milk, tears, laughter,
    weeping, love-looks, love-perturbations and risings,
The voice, articulation, language, whispering, shouting aloud,
Food, drink, pulse, digestion, sweat, sleep, walking, swim-
    ming,
Poise on the hips, leaping, reclining, embracing, arm-curving
    and tightening,
The continual changes of the flex of the mouth, and around
    the eyes,
The skin, the sunburnt shade, freckles, hair,
The curious sympathy one feels when feeling with the hand
    the naked meat of the body,
The circling rivers the breath, and breathing it in and out,
The beauty of the waist, and thence of the hips, and thence
    downward toward the knees,
The thin red jellies within you or within me, the bones and
    the marrow in the bones,
The exquisite realization of health ;
O I say these are not the parts and poems of the body only,
    but of the soul,
O I say now these are the soul!
1855                                                    1881


## A WOMAN WAITS FOR ME

A WOMAN waits for me, she contains all, nothing is lacking,
Yet all were lacking if sex were lacking, or if the moisture of
    the right man were lacking.
Sex contains all, bodies, souls,
Meanings, proofs, purities, delicacies, results, promulgations,
Songs, commands, health, pride, the maternal mystery, the
    seminal milk,
All hopes, benefactions, bestowals, all the passions, loves,
    beauties, delights of the earth,
All the governments, judges, gods, follow'd persons of the
    earth,

These are contain'd in sex as parts of itself and justifications
of itself.

Without shame the man I like knows and avows the deli-
ciousness of his sex,
Without shame the woman I like knows and avows hers.

Now I will dismiss myself from impassive women,
I will go stay with her who waits for me, and with those
women that are warm-blooded and sufficient for me,
I see that they understand me and do not deny me,
I see that they are worthy of me, I will be the robust husband
of those women.

They are not one jot less than I am,
They are tann'd in the face by shining suns and blowing
winds,
Their flesh has the old divine suppleness and strength,
They know how to swim, row, ride, wrestle, shoot, run,
strike, retreat, advance, resist, defend themselves,
They are ultimate in their own right—they are calm, clear,
well-possess'd of themselves.

I draw you close to me, you women,
I cannot let you go, I would do you good,
I am for you, and you are for me, not only for our own sake,
but for others' sakes,
Envelop'd in you sleep greater heroes and bards,
They refuse to awake at the touch of any man but me.

It is I, you women, I make my way,
I am stern, acrid, large, undissuadable, but I love you,
I do not hurt you any more than is necessary for you,
I pour the stuff to start sons and daughters fit for these States,
I press with slow rude muscle,
I brace myself effectually, I listen to no entreaties,
I dare not withdraw till I deposit what has so long accumu-
lated within me.

Through you I drain the pent-up rivers of myself,
In you I wrap a thousand onward years,

D                                                              W.

On you I graft the grafts of the best-beloved of me and
 America,
The drops I distil upon you shall grow fierce and athletic
 girls, new artists, musicians, and singers,
The babes I beget upon you are to beget babes in their turn,
I shall demand perfect men and women out of my love-
 spendings,
I shall expect them to interpenetrate with others, as I and you
 interpenetrate now,
I shall count on the fruits of the gushing showers of them, as
 I count on the fruits of the gushing showers I give now,
I shall look for loving crops from the birth, life, death, im-
 mortality, I plant so lovingly now.

1856                                                        1871


## SPONTANEOUS ME

SPONTANEOUS me, Nature,
The loving day, the mounting sun, the friend I am happy
 with,
The arm of my friend hanging idly over my shoulder,
The hillside whiten'd with blossoms of the mountain ash,
The same late in autumn, the hues of red, yellow, drab,
 purple, and light and dark green,
The rich coverlet of the grass, animals and birds, the private
 untrimm'd bank, the primitive apples, the pebble-stones,
Beautiful dripping fragments, the negligent list of one after
 another as I happen to call them to me or think of them,
The real poems, (what we call poems being merely pictures,)
The poems of the privacy of the night, and of men like me,
This poem drooping shy and unseen that I always carry, and
 that all men carry,
(Know once for all, avow'd on purpose, wherever are men like
 me, are our lusty lurking masculine poems,)
Love-thoughts, love-juice, love-odor, love-yielding, love-
 climbers, and the climbing sap,
Arms and hands of love, lips of love, phallic thumb of love,
 breasts of love, bellies press'd and glued together with
 love,
Earth of chaste love, life that is only life after love,

The body of my love, the body of the woman I love, the body
    of the man, the body of the earth,
Soft forenoon airs that blow from the south-west,
The hairy wild-bee that murmurs and hankers up and down,
    that gripes the full-grown lady-flower, curves upon her
    with amorous firm legs, takes his will of her, and holds
    himself tremulous and tight till he is satisfied;
The wet of woods through the early hours,
Two sleepers at night lying close together as they sleep, one
    with an arm slanting down across and below the waist of
    the other,
The smell of apples, aromas from crush'd sage-plant, mint,
    birch-bark,
The boy's longings, the glow and pressure as he confides to
    me what he was dreaming,
The dead leaf whirling its spiral whirl and falling still and
    content to the ground,
The no-form'd stings that sights, people, objects, sting me
    with,
The hubb'd sting of myself, stinging me as much as it ever
    can any one,
The sensitive, orbic, underlapp'd brothers, that only privi-
    leged feelers may be intimate where they are,
The curious roamer the hand roaming all over the body, the
    bashful withdrawing of flesh where the fingers soothingly
    pause and edge themselves,
The limpid liquid within the young man,
The vex'd corrosion so pensive and so painful,
The torment, the irritable tide that will not be at rest,
The like of the same I feel, the like of the same in others,
The young man that flushes and flushes, and the young
    woman that flushes and flushes,
The young man that wakes deep at night, the hot hand seek-
    ing to repress what would master him,
The mystic amorous night, the strange half-welcome pangs,
    visions, sweats,
The pulse pounding through palms and trembling encircling
    fingers, the young man all color'd, red, ashamed, angry;
The souse upon me of my lover the sea, as I lie willing and
    naked,

The merriment of the twin babies that crawl over the grass in
the sun, the mother never turning her vigilant eyes from
them,
The walnut-trunk, the walnut-husks, and the ripening or
ripen'd long-round walnuts,
The continence of vegetables, birds, animals,
The consequent meanness of me should I skulk or find myself
indecent, while birds and animals never once skulk or
find themselves indecent,
The great chastity of paternity, to match the great chastity of
maternity,
The oath of procreation I have sworn, my Adamic and fresh
daughters,
The greed that eats me day and night with hungry gnaw, till
I saturate what shall produce boys to fill my place when
I am through,
The wholesome relief, repose, content,
And this bunch pluck'd at random from myself,
It has done its work—I toss it carelessly to fall where it may.
1856                                          1867


## ONE HOUR TO MADNESS AND JOY

ONE hour to madness and joy! O furious! O confine me not!
(What is this that frees me so in storms?
What do my shouts amid lightnings and raging winds mean?)

O to drink the mystic deliria deeper than any other man!
O savage and tender achings! (I bequeath them to you, my
children,
I tell them to you, for reasons, O bridegroom and bride.)

O to be yielded to you whoever you are, and you to be yielded
to me in defiance of the world!
O to return to Paradise! O bashful and feminine!
O to draw you to me, to plant on you for the first time the
lips of a determin'd man.

O the puzzle, the thrice-tied knot, the deep and dark pool, all
untied and illumin'd!

O to speed where there is space enough and air enough at
    last!
To be absolv'd from previous ties and conventions, I from
    mine and you from yours!
To find a new unthought-of nonchalance with the best of
    Nature!
To have the gag remov'd from one's mouth!
To have the feeling to-day or any day I am sufficient as I am.

O something unprov'd! something in a trance!
To escape utterly from others' anchors and holds!
To drive free! to love free! to dash reckless and dangerous!
To court destruction with taunts, with invitations!
To ascend, to leap to the heavens of the love indicated to me!
To rise thither with my inebriate soul!
To be lost if it must be so!
To feed the remainder of life with one hour of fulness and
    freedom!
With one brief hour of madness and joy.
1860                                1881

## OUT OF THE ROLLING OCEAN THE CROWD

OUT of the rolling ocean the crowd came a drop gently to me,
Whispering *I love you, before long I die,*
*I have travel'd a long way merely to look on you to touch you,*
*For I could not die till I once look'd on you,*
*For I fear'd I might afterward lose you.*

Now we have met, we have look'd, we are safe,
Return in peace to the ocean my love,
I too am part of that ocean my love, we are not so much
    separated,
Behold the great rondure, the cohesion of all, how perfect!
But as for me, for you, the irresistible sea is to separate us,
As for an hour carrying us diverse, yet cannot carry us di-
    verse forever;
Be not impatient—a little space— know you I salute the air,
    the ocean and the land,
Every day at sundown for your dear sake my love.
1865                                  1867

## AGES AND AGES RETURNING AT INTERVALS

AGES and ages returning at intervals,
Undestroy'd, wandering immortal,
Lusty, phallic, with the potent original loins, perfectly sweet,
I, chanter of Adamic songs,
Through the new garden the West, the great cities calling,
Deliriate, thus prelude what is generated, offering these,
    offering myself,
Bathing myself, bathing my songs in Sex,
Offspring of my loins.
1860                           1867

## WE TWO, HOW LONG WE WERE FOOL'D

WE two, how long we were fool'd,
Now transmuted, we swiftly escape as Nature escapes,
We are Nature, long have we been absent, but now we return,
We become plants, trunks, foliage, roots, bark,
We are bedded in the ground, we are rocks,
We are oaks, we grow in the openings side by side,
We browse, we are two among the wild herds spontaneous as
    any,
We are two fishes swimming in the sea together,
We are what locust blossoms are, we drop scent around lanes
    mornings and evenings,
We are also the coarse smut of beasts, vegetables, minerals,
We are two predatory hawks, we soar above and look down,
We are two resplendent suns, we it is who balance ourselves
    orbic and stellar, we are as two comets,
We prowl fang'd and four-footed in the woods, we spring on
    prey,
We are two clouds forenoons and afternoons driving over-
    head,
We are seas mingling, we are two of those cheerful waves
    rolling over each other and interwetting each other,
We are what the atmosphere is, transparent, receptive, per-
    vious, impervious,
We are snow, rain, cold, darkness, we are each product and
    influence of the globe,

We have circled and circled till we have arrived home again,
    we two,
We have voided all but freedom and all but our own joy.
1860                                                    1881

## O HYMEN! O HYMENEE!

O HYMEN! O hymenee! why do you tantalize me thus?
O why sting me for a swift moment only?
Why can you not continue? O why do you now cease?
Is it because if you continued beyond the swift moment you
    would soon certainly kill me?
1860                                                    1867

## I AM HE THAT ACHES WITH LOVE

I AM he that aches with amorous love;
Does the earth gravitate? does not all matter, aching, attract
    all matter?
So the body of me to all I meet or know.
1860                                                    1867

## NATIVE MOMENTS

NATIVE moments—when you come upon me—ah you are
    here now,
Give me now libidinous joys only,
Give me the drench of my passions, give me life coarse and
    rank,
To-day I go consort with Nature's darlings, to-night too,
I am for those who believe in loose delights, I share the mid-
    night orgies of young men,
I dance with the dancers and drink with the drinkers,
The echoes ring with our indecent calls, I pick out some low
    person for my dearest friend,
He shall be lawless, rude, illiterate, he shall be one con-
    demned by others for deeds done,
I will play a part no longer, why should I exile myself from
    my companions?
O you shunn'd persons, I at least do not shun you,
I come forthwith in your midst, I will be your poet,
I will be more to you than to any of the rest.
1860                                                    1881

## ONCE I PASS'D THROUGH A POPULOUS CITY

ONCE I pass'd through a populous city imprinting my brain
    for future use with its shows, architecture, customs,
    traditions,
Yet now of all that city I remember only a woman I casually
    met there who detain'd me for love of me,
Day by day and night by night we were together—all else has
    long been forgotten by me,
I remember I say only that woman who passionately clung to
    me,
Again we wander, we love, we separate again,
Again she holds me by the hand, I must not go,
I see her close beside me with silent lips sad and tremulous.
1860                               1867

## I HEARD YOU SOLEMN-SWEET PIPES OF THE ORGAN

I HEARD you solemn-sweet pipes of the organ as last Sunday
    morn I pass'd the church,
Winds of autumn, as I walk'd the woods at dusk I heard your
    long-stretch'd sighs up above so mournful,
I heard the perfect Italian tenor singing at the opera, I heard
    the soprano in the midst of the quartet singing;
Heart of my love! you too I heard murmuring low through
    one of the wrists around my head,
Heard the pulse of you when all was still ringing little bells
    last night under my ear.
1861                               1867

## FACING WEST FROM CALIFORNIA'S SHORES

FACING west from California's shores,
Inquiring, tireless, seeking what is yet unfound,
I, a child, very old, over waves, towards the house of mater-
    nity, the land of migrations, look afar,
Look off the shores of my Western sea, the circle almost
    circled;
For starting westward from Hindustan, from the vales of
    Kashmere,

From Asia, from the north, from the God, the sage, and the
    hero,
From the south, from the flowery peninsulas and the spice
    islands,
Long having wander'd since, round the earth having wan-
    der'd,
Now I face home again, very pleas'd and joyous,
(But where is what I started for so long ago?
And why is it yet unfound?)
1860                                                              1867

## AS ADAM EARLY IN THE MORNING

As Adam early in the morning,
Walking forth from the bower refresh'd with sleep,
Behold me where I pass, hear my voice, approach,
Touch me, touch the palm of your hand to my body as I pass,
Be not afraid of my body.
1860                                                              1867

# *Calamus*

## IN PATHS UNTRODDEN

In paths untrodden,
In the growths by margins of pond-waters,
Escaped from the life that exhibits itself,
From all the standards hitherto publish'd, from the pleasures,
        profits, conformities,
Which too long I was offering to feed my soul,
Clear to me now standards not yet publish'd, clear to me that
        my soul,
That the soul of the man I speak for rejoices in comrades,
Here by myself away from the clank of the world,
Tallying and talk'd to here by tongues aromatic,
No longer abash'd, (for in this secluded spot I can respond as
        I would not dare elsewhere,)
Strong upon me the life that does not exhibit itself, yet con-
        tains all the rest,
Resolv'd to sing no songs to-day but those of manly attach-
        ment,
Projecting them along that substantial life,
Bequeathing hence types of athletic love,
Afternoon this delicious Ninth-month in my forty-first year,
I proceed for all who are or have been young men,
To tell the secret of my nights and days,
To celebrate the need of comrades.
1860                                                          1867

## SCENTED HERBAGE OF MY BREAST

Scented herbage of my breast,
Leaves from you I glean, I write, to be perused best after-
        wards,
Tomb-leaves, body-leaves growing up above me above death,

Perennial roots, tall leaves, O the winter shall not freeze you
delicate leaves,

Every year shall you bloom again, out from where you retired
you shall emerge again;

O I do not know whether many passing by will discover you
or inhale your faint odor, but I believe a few will;

O slender leaves! O blossoms of my blood! I permit you to
tell in your own way of the heart that is under you,

O I do not know what you mean there underneath yourselves,
you are not happiness,

You are often more bitter than I can bear, you burn and sting
me,

Yet you are beautiful to me you faint-tinged roots, you make
me think of death,

Death is beautiful from you, (what indeed is finally beautiful
except death and love?)

O I think it is not for life I am chanting here my chant of
lovers, I think it must be for death,

For how calm, how solemn it grows to ascend to the atmosphere of lovers,

Death or life I am then indifferent, my soul declines to prefer,

(I am not sure but the high soul of lovers welcomes death
most,)

Indeed O death, I think now these leaves mean precisely the
same as you mean,

Grow up taller sweet leaves that I may see! grow up out of
my breast!

Spring away from the conceal'd heart there!

Do not fold yourself so in your pink-tinged roots timid leaves!

Do not remain down there so ashamed, herbage of my breast!

Come I am determin'd to unbare this broad breast of mine, I
have long enough stifled and choked;

Emblematic and capricious blades I leave you, now you serve
me not,

I will say what I have to say by itself,

I will sound myself and comrades only, I will never again
utter a call only their call,

I will raise with it immortal reverberations through the States,

I will give an example to lovers to take permanent shape and
will through the States,

Through me shall the words be said to make death exhilarat-
　　ing.
Give me your tone therefore O death, that I may accord with
　　it,
Give me yourself, for I see that you belong to me now above
　　all, and are folded inseparably together, you love and
　　death are,
Nor will I allow you to balk me any more with what I was
　　calling life,
For now it is convey'd to me that you are the purports essen-
　　tial,
That you hide in these shifting forms of life, for reasons, and
　　that they are mainly for you,
That you beyond them come forth to remain, the real reality,
That behind the mask of materials you patiently wait, no
　　matter how long,
That you will one day perhaps take control of all,
That you will perhaps dissipate this entire show of appear-
　　ance,
That may-be you are what it is all for, but it does not last so
　　very long,
But you will last very long.
1860　　　　　　　　　　　　　　　　　　　　　　　　1881


## WHOEVER YOU ARE HOLDING ME NOW IN HAND

WHOEVER you are holding me now in hand,
Without one thing all will be useless,
I give you fair warning before you attempt me further,
I am not what you supposed, but far different.

Who is he that would become my follower?
Who would sign himself a candidate for my affections?

The way is suspicious, the result uncertain, perhaps destruc-
　　tive,
You would have to give up all else, I alone would expect to
　　be your sole and exclusive standard,
Your novitiate would even then be long and exhausting,

The whole past theory of your life and all conformity to the
lives around you would have to be abandon'd,
Therefore release me now before troubling yourself any further, let go your hand from my shoulders,
Put me down and depart on your way.

Or else by stealth in some wood for trial,
Or back of a rock in the open air,
(For in any roof'd room of a house I emerge not, nor in com-
pany,
And in libraries I lie as one dumb, a gawk, or unborn, or
dead,)
But just possibly with you on a high hill, first watching lest
any person for miles around approach unawares,
Or possibly with you sailing at sea, or on the beach of the sea
or some quiet island,
Here to put your lips upon mine I permit you,
With the comrade's long-dwelling kiss or the new husband's
kiss,
For I am the new husband and I am the comrade.

Or if you will, thrusting me beneath your clothing,
Where I may feel the throbs of your heart or rest upon your
hip,
Carry me when you go forth over land or sea;
For thus merely touching you is enough, is best,
And thus touching you would I silently sleep and be carried
eternally.

But these leaves conning you con at peril,
For these leaves and me you will not understand,
They will elude you at first and still more afterward, I will
certainly elude you,
Even while you should think you had unquestionably caught
me, behold!
Already you see I have escaped from you.

For it is not for what I have put into it that I have written
this book,
Nor is it by reading it you will acquire it,

Nor do those know me best who admire me and vauntingly
    praise me,
Nor will the candidates for my love (unless at most a very
    few) prove victorious,
Nor will my poems do good only, they will do just as much
    evil, perhaps more,
For all is useless without that which you may guess at many
    times and not hit, that which I hinted at;
Therefore release me and depart on your way.
1860                         1881

## FOR YOU O DEMOCRACY

COME, I will make the continent indissoluble,
I will make the most splendid race the sun ever shone upon,
I will make divine magnetic lands,
        With the love of comrades,
           With the life-long love of comrades.

I will plant companionship thick as trees along all the rivers
    of America, and along the shores of the great lakes, and
    all over the prairies,
I will make inseparable cities with their arms about each
    other's necks,
        By the love of comrades,
           By the manly love of comrades.

For you these from me, O Democracy, to serve you ma
    femme!
For you, for you I am trilling these songs.
1860                         1881

## THESE I SINGING IN SPRING

THESE I singing in spring collect for lovers,
(For who but I should understand lovers and all their sorrow
    and joy?
And who but I should be the poet of comrades?)
Collecting I traverse the garden the world, but soon I pass
    the gates,
Now along the pond-side, now wading in a little, fearing not
    the wet,

Now by the post-and-rail fences where the old stones thrown
there, pick'd from the fields, have accumulated,
(Wild-flowers and vines and weeds come up through the
stones and partly cover them, beyond these I pass,)
Far, far in the forest, or sauntering later in summer, before I
think where I go,
Solitary, smelling the earthy smell, stopping now and then in
the silence,
Alone I had thought, yet soon a troop gathers around me,
Some walk by my side and some behind, and some embrace
my arms or neck,
They the spirits of dear friends dead or alive, thicker they
come, a great crowd, and I in the middle,
Collecting, dispensing, singing, there I wander with them,
Plucking something for tokens, tossing toward whoever is
near me,
Here, lilac, with a branch of pine,
Here, out of my pocket, some moss which I pull'd off a live-
oak in Florida as it hung trailing down,
Here, some pinks and laurel leaves, and a handful of sage,
And here what I now draw from the water, wading in the
pond-side,
(O here I last saw him that tenderly loves me, and returns
again never to separate from me,
And this, O this shall henceforth be the token of comrades,
this calamus-root shall,
Interchange it youths with each other! let none render it back!)
And twigs of maple and a bunch of wild orange and chestnut,
And stems of currants and plum-blows, and the aromatic
cedar,
These I compass'd around by a thick cloud of spirits,
Wandering, point to or touch as I pass, or throw them loosely
from me,
Indicating to each one what he shall have, giving something
to each;
But what I drew from the water by the pond-side, that I
reserve,
I will give of it, but only to them that love as I myself am
capable of loving.

1860                                                          1867

## NOT HEAVING FROM MY RIBB'D BREAST ONLY

Not heaving from my ribb'd breast only,
Not in sighs at night in rage dissatisfied with myself,
Not in those long-drawn, ill-supprest sighs,
Not in many an oath and promise broken,
Not in my wilful and savage soul's volition,
Not in the subtle nourishment of the air,
Not in this beating and pounding at my temples and wrists,
Not in the curious systole and diastole within which will one
    day cease,
Not in many a hungry wish told to the skies only,
Not in cries, laughter, defiances, thrown from me when alone
    far in the wilds,
Not in husky pantings through clinch'd teeth,
Not in sounded and resounded words, chattering words,
    echoes, dead words,
Not in the murmurs of my dreams while I sleep,
Nor the other murmurs of these incredible dreams of every
    day,
Nor in the limbs and senses of my body that take you and
    dismiss you continually—not there,
Not in any or all of them O adhesiveness! O pulse of my life!
Need I that you exist and show yourself any more than in
    these songs.
1860                                            1867

## OF THE TERRIBLE DOUBT OF APPEARANCES

Of the terrible doubt of appearances,
Of the uncertainty after all, that we may be deluded,
That may-be reliance and hope are but speculations after all,
That may-be identity beyond the grave is a beautiful fable
    only,
May-be the things I perceive, the animals, plants, men, hills,
    shining and flowing waters,
The skies of day and night, colors, densities, forms, may-be
    these are (as doubtless they are) only apparitions, and
    the real something has yet to be known,
(How often they dart out of themselves as if to confound me
    and mock me!

How often I think neither I know, nor any man knows, aught
    of them,)
May-be seeming to me what they are (as doubtless they in-
    deed but seem) as from my present point of view, and
    might prove (as of course they would) nought of what
    they appear, or nought anyhow, from entirely changed
    points of view;
To me these and the like of these are curiously answer'd by
    my lovers, my dear friends,
When he whom I love travels with me or sits a long while
    holding me by the hand,
When the subtle air, the impalpable, the sense that words and
    reason hold not, surround us and pervade us,
Then I am charged with untold and untellable wisdom, I am
    silent, I require nothing further,
I cannot answer the question of appearances or that of iden-
    tity beyond the grave,
But I walk or sit indifferent, I am satisfied,
He ahold of my hand has completely satisfied me.
1860                                1867

## THE BASE OF ALL METAPHYSICS

AND now gentlemen,
A word I give to remain in your memories and minds,
As base and finalè too for all metaphysics.

(So to the students the old professor,
At the close of his crowded course.)

Having studied the new and antique, the Greek and Ger-
    manic systems,
Kant having studied and stated, Fichte and Schelling and
    Hegel,
Stated the lore of Plato, and Socrates greater than Plato,
And greater than Socrates sought and stated, Christ divine
    having studied long,
I see reminiscent to-day those Greek and Germanic systems,
See the philosophies all, Christian churches and tenets see,
Yet underneath Socrates clearly see, and underneath Christ
    the divine I see,

The dear love of man for his comrade, the attraction of
friend to friend,
Of the well-married husband and wife, of children and
parents,
Of city for city and land for land.
1871                                                          1871

## RECORDERS AGES HENCE

RECORDERS ages hence,
Come, I will take you down underneath this impassive ex-
terior, I will tell you what to say of me,
Publish my name and hang up my picture as that of the ten-
derest lover,
The friend the lover's portrait, of whom his friend his lover
was fondest,
Who was not proud of his songs, but of the measureless
ocean of love within him, and freely pour'd it forth,
Who often walk'd lonesome walks thinking of his dear
friends, his lovers,
Who pensive away from one he lov'd often lay sleepless and
dissatisfied at night,
Who knew too well the sick, sick dread lest the one he lov'd
might secretly be indifferent to him,
Whose happiest days were far away through fields, in woods,
on hills, he and another wandering hand in hand, they
twain apart from other men,
Who oft as he saunter'd the streets curv'd with his arm the
shoulder of his friend, while the arm of his friend rested
upon him also.
1860                                                          1867

## WHEN I HEARD AT THE CLOSE OF THE DAY

WHEN I heard at the close of the day how my name had been
receiv'd with plaudits in the capitol, still it was not a
happy night for me that follow'd,
And else when I carous'd, or when my plans were accomplish'd, still I was not happy,
But the day when I rose at dawn from the bed of perfect
health, refresh'd, singing, inhaling the ripe breath of
autumn,

When I saw the full moon in the west grow pale and disap-
    pear in the morning light,
When I wander'd alone over the beach, and undressing
    bathed, laughing with the cool waters, and saw the sun
    rise,
And when I thought how my dear friend my lover was on his
    way coming, O then I was happy,
O then each breath tasted sweeter, and all that day my food
    nourish'd me more, and the beautiful day pass'd well,
And the next came with equal joy, and with the next at even-
    ing came my friend,
And that night while all was still I heard the waters roll slowly
    continually up the shores,
I heard the hissing rustle of the liquid and sands as directed
    to me whispering to congratulate me,
For the one I love most lay sleeping by me under the same
    cover in the cool night,
In the stillness in the autumn moonbeams his face was in-
    clined toward me,
And his arm lay lightly around my breast—and that night I
    was happy.
1860                                   1867

## ARE YOU THE NEW PERSON DRAWN TOWARD ME?

ARE you the new person drawn toward me?
To begin with take warning, I am surely far different from
    what you suppose;
Do you suppose you will find in me your ideal?
Do you think it is so easy to have me become your lover?
Do you think the friendship of me would be unalloy'd satis-
    faction?
Do you think I am trusty and faithful?
Do you see no further than this façade, this smooth and
    tolerant manner of me?
Do you suppose yourself advancing on real ground toward a
    real heroic man?
Have you no thought O dreamer that it may be all maya,
    illusion?
1860                                   1867

## ROOTS AND LEAVES THEMSELVES ALONE

ROOTS and leaves themselves alone are these,
Scents brought to men and women from the wild woods and
    pond-side,
Breast-sorrel and pinks of love, fingers that wind around
    tighter than vines,
Gushes from the throats of birds hid in the foliage of trees as
    the sun is risen,
Breezes of land and love set from living shores to you on the
    living sea, to you O sailors!
Frost-mellow'd berries and Third-month twigs offer'd fresh
    to young persons wandering out in the fields when the
    winter breaks up,
Love-buds put before you and within you whoever you
    are,
Buds to be unfolded on the old terms,
If you bring the warmth of the sun to them they will open
    and bring form, color, perfume, to you,
If you become the aliment and the wet they will become
    flowers, fruits, tall branches and trees.

1860                                              1867


## NOT HEAT FLAMES UP AND CONSUMES

NOT heat flames up and consumes,
Not sea-waves hurry in and out,
Not the air delicious and dry, the air of ripe summer, bears
    lightly along white down-balls of myriads of seeds,
Wafted, sailing gracefully, to drop where they may;
Not these, O none of these more than the flames of me, con-
    suming, burning for his love whom I love,
O none more than I hurrying in and out;
Does the tide hurry, seeking something, and never give up?
    O I the same,
O nor down-balls nor perfumes, nor the high rain-emitting
    clouds, are borne through the open air,
Any more than my soul is borne through the open air,
Wafted in all directions O love, for friendship, for you.

1860                                              1867

## TRICKLE DROPS

TRICKLE drops! my blue veins leaving!
O drops of me! trickle, slow drops,
Candid from me falling, drip, bleeding drops,
From wounds made to free you whence you were prison'd,
From my face, from my forehead and lips,
From my breast, from within where I was conceal'd, press
    forth red drops, confession drops,
Stain every page, stain every song I sing, every word I say,
    bloody drops,
Let them know your scarlet heat, let them glisten,
Saturate them with yourself all ashamed and wet,
Glow upon all I have written or shall write, bleeding drops,
Let it all be seen in your light, blushing drops.
1860                                 1867

## CITY OF ORGIES

CITY of orgies, walks and joys,
City whom that I have lived and sung in your midst will one
    day make you illustrious,
Not the pageants of you, not your shifting tableaus, your
    spectacles, repay me,
Not the interminable rows of your houses, nor the ships at
    the wharves,
Nor the processions in the streets, nor the bright windows
    with goods in them,
Nor to converse with learn'd persons, or bear my share in the
    soiree or feast;
Not those, but as I pass O Manhattan, your frequent and
    swift flash of eyes offering me love,
Offering response to my own—these repay me,
Lovers, continual lovers, only repay me.
1860                                   1867

## BEHOLD THIS SWARTHY FACE

BEHOLD this swarthy face, these gray eyes,
This beard, the white wool unclipt upon my neck,
My brown hands and the silent manner of me without charm;

Yet comes one a Manhattanese and ever at parting kisses me
    lightly on the lips with robust love,
And I on the crossing of the street or on the ship's deck give a
    kiss in return,
We observe that salute of American comrades land and sea,
We are those two natural and nonchalant persons.
1860                                                              1867

## I SAW IN LOUISIANA A LIVE-OAK GROWING

I SAW in Louisiana a live-oak growing,
All alone stood it and the moss hung down from the branches,
Without any companion it grew there uttering joyous leaves
    of dark green,
And its look, rude, unbending, lusty, made me think of my-
    self,
But I wonder'd how it could utter joyous leaves standing
    alone there without its friend near, for I knew I could
    not,
And I broke off a twig with a certain number of leaves upon
    it, and twined around it a little moss,
And brought it away, and I have placed it in sight, in my room,
It is not needed to remind me as of my own dear friends,
(For I believe lately I think of little else than of them,)
Yet it remains to me a curious token, it makes me think of
    manly love;
For all that, and though the live-oak glistens there in Louisi-
    ana solitary in a wide flat space,
Uttering joyous leaves all its life without a friend a lover near,
I know very well I could not.
1860                                                              1867

## TO A STRANGER

PASSING stranger! you do not know how longingly I look
    upon you,
You must be he I was seeking, or she I was seeking, (it comes
    to me as of a dream,)
I have somewhere surely lived a life of joy with you,
All is recall'd as we flit by each other, fluid, affectionate,
    chaste, matured,

You grew up with me, were a boy with me or a girl with
me,
I ate with you and slept with you, your body has become not
yours only nor left my body mine only,
You give me the pleasure of your eyes, face, flesh, as we pass,
you take of my beard, breast, hands, in return,
I am not to speak to you, I am to think of you when I sit
alone or wake at night alone,
I am to wait, I do not doubt I am to meet you again,
I am to see to it that I do not lose you.
1860                                                    1867


## THIS MOMENT YEARNING AND THOUGHTFUL

THIS moment yearning and thoughtful sitting alone,
It seems to me there are other men in other lands yearning
and thoughtful,
It seems to me I can look over and behold them in Germany,
Italy, France, Spain,
Or far, far away, in China, or in Russia or Japan, talking
other dialects,
And it seems to me if I could know those men I should become
attached to them as I do to men in my own lands,
O I know we should be brethren and lovers,
I know I should be happy with them.
1860                                                    1867


## I HEAR IT WAS CHARGED AGAINST ME

I HEAR it was charged against me that I sought to destroy
institutions,
But really I am neither for nor against institutions,
(What indeed have I in common with them? or what with the
destruction of them?)
Only I will establish in the Mannahatta and in every city of
these States inland and seaboard,
And in the fields and woods, and above every keel little or
large that dents the water,
Without edifices or rules or trustees or any argument,
The institution of the dear love of comrades.
1860                                                    1867

## THE PRAIRIE-GRASS DIVIDING

THE prairie-grass dividing, its special odor breathing,
I demand of it the spiritual corresponding,
Demand the most copious and close companionship of men,
Demand the blades to rise of words, acts, beings,
Those of the open atmosphere, coarse, sunlit, fresh, nutri-
    tious,
Those that go their own gait, erect, stepping with freedom
    and command, leading not following,
Those with a never-quell'd audacity, those with sweet and
    lusty flesh clear of taint,
Those that look carelessly in the faces of Presidents and
    governors, as to say *Who are you?*
Those of earth-born passion, simple, never constrain'd, never
    obedient,
Those of inland America.
1860                                                    1867


## WHEN I PERUSE THE CONQUER'D FAME

WHEN I peruse the conquer'd fame of heroes and the victories
    of mighty generals, I do not envy the generals,
Nor the President in his Presidency, nor the rich in his great
    house,
But when I hear of the brotherhood of lovers, how it was
    with them,
How together through life, through dangers, odium, un-
    changing, long and long,
Through youth and through middle and old age, how un-
    faltering, how affectionate and faithful they were,
Then I am pensive—I hastily walk away fill'd with the bitter-
    est envy.
1860                                                    1871


## WE TWO BOYS TOGETHER CLINGING

WE two boys together clinging,
One the other never leaving,
Up and down the roads going, North and South excursions
    making,

Power enjoying, elbows stretching, fingers clutching,
Arm'd and fearless, eating, drinking, sleeping, loving,
No law less than ourselves owning, sailing, soldiering, thiev-
ing, threatening,
Misers, menials, priests alarming, air breathing, water drink-
ing, on the turf or the sea-beach dancing,
Cities wrenching, ease scorning, statutes mocking, feebleness
chasing,
Fulfilling our foray.
1860                                                                    1867

## A PROMISE TO CALIFORNIA

A PROMISE to California,
Or inland to the great pastoral Plains, and on to Puget sound
and Oregon;
Sojourning east a while longer, soon I travel toward you, to
remain, to teach robust American love,
For I know very well that I and robust love belong among
you, inland, and along the Western sea;
For these States tend inland and toward the Western sea, and
I will also.
1860                                                                    1867

## HERE THE FRAILEST LEAVES OF ME

HERE the frailest leaves of me and yet my strongest lasting,
Here I shade and hide my thoughts, I myself do not expose
them,
And yet they expose me more than all my other poems.
1860                                                                    1871

## NO LABOR-SAVING MACHINE

No labor-saving machine,
Nor discovery have I made,
Nor will I be able to leave behind me any wealthy bequest to
found a hospital or library,
Nor reminiscence of any deed of courage for America,
Nor literary success nor intellect, nor book for the book-shelf,
But a few carols vibrating through the air I leave,
For comrades and lovers.
1860                                                                    1881

## A GLIMPSE

A GLIMPSE through an interstice caught,
Of a crowd of workmen and drivers in a bar-room around
the stove late of a winter night, and I unremark'd seated
in a corner,
Of a youth who loves me and whom I love, silently approaching and seating himself near, that he may hold me by the
hand,
A long while amid the noises of coming and going, of drinking and oath and smutty jest,
There we two, content, happy in being together, speaking
little, perhaps not a word.
1860                                                          1867

## A LEAF FOR HAND IN HAND

A LEAF for hand in hand;
You natural persons old and young!
You on the Mississippi and on all the branches and bayous
of the Mississippi!
You friendly boatmen and mechanics! you roughs!
You twain! and all processions moving along the streets!
I wish to infuse myself among you till I see it common for
you to walk hand in hand.
1860                                                          1867

## EARTH, MY LIKENESS

EARTH, my likeness,
Though you look so impassive, ample and spheric there,
I now suspect that is not all;
I now suspect there is something fierce in you eligible to burst
forth,
For an athlete is enamour'd of me, and I of him,
But toward him there is something fierce and terrible in me
eligible to burst forth,
I dare not tell it in words, not even in these songs.
1860                                                          1867

## I DREAM'D IN A DREAM

I DREAM'D in a dream I saw a city invincible to the attacks of
the whole of the rest of the earth,
I dream'd that was the new city of Friends,
Nothing was greater there than the quality of robust love, it
led the rest,
It was seen every hour in the actions of the men of that city,
And in all their looks and words.
1860                                                      1867


## WHAT THINK YOU I TAKE MY PEN IN HAND?

WHAT think you I take my pen in hand to record?
The battle-ship, perfect-model'd, majestic, that I saw pass the
offing to-day under full sail?
The splendors of the past day? or the splendor of the night
that envelops me?
Or the vaunted glory and growth of the great city spread
around me?—no;
But merely of two simple men I saw to-day on the pier in the
midst of the crowd, parting the parting of dear friends,
The one to remain hung on the other's neck and passionately
kiss'd him,
While the one to depart tightly prest the one to remain in his
arms.
1860                                                      1867


## TO THE EAST AND TO THE WEST

To the East and to the West,
To the man of the Seaside State and of Pennsylvania,
To the Kanadian of the north, to the Southerner I love,
These with perfect trust to depict you as myself, the germs
are in all men,
I believe the main purport of these States is to found a superb
friendship, exaltè, previously unknown,
Because I perceive it waits, and has been always waiting,
latent in all men.
1860                                                      1867

## SOMETIMES WITH ONE I LOVE

SOMETIMES with one I love I fill myself with rage for fear I
　　effuse unreturn'd love,
But now I think there is no unreturn'd love, the pay is certain
　　one way or another,
(I loved a certain person ardently and my love was not re-
　　turn'd,
Yet out of that I have written these songs.)
1860　　　　　　　　　　　　　　　　　　　　　　　　1867


## TO A WESTERN BOY

MANY things to absorb I teach to help you become eleve of
　　mine;
Yet if blood like mine circle not in your veins,
If you be not silently selected by lovers and do not silently
　　select lovers,
Of what use is it that you seek to become eleve of mine?
1860　　　　　　　　　　　　　　　　　　　　　　　　1881


## FAST-ANCHOR'D ETERNAL O LOVE!

FAST-ANCHOR'D eternal O love! O woman I love!
O bride! O wife! more resistless than I can tell, the thought
　　of you!
Then separate, as disembodied or another born,
Ethereal, the last athletic reality, my consolation,
I ascend, I float in the regions of your love O man,
O sharer of my roving life.
1860　　　　　　　　　　　　　　　　　　　　　　　　1867


## AMONG THE MULTITUDE

AMONG the men and women the multitude,
I perceive one picking me out by secret and divine signs,
Acknowledging none else, not parent, wife, husband, bro·
　　ther, child, any nearer than I am,
Some are baffled, but that one is not—that one knows me.

Ah lover and perfect equal,
I meant that you should discover me so by faint indirections,
And I when I meet you mean to discover you by the like in
    you.
1860                                        1881

## O YOU WHOM I OFTEN AND SILENTLY COME

O you whom I often and silently come where you are that I
    may be with you,
As I walk by your side or sit near, or remain in the same
    room with you,
Little you know the subtle electric fire that for your sake is
    playing within me.
1860                                          1867

## THAT SHADOW MY LIKENESS

THAT shadow my likeness that goes to and fro seeking a liveli-
    hood, chattering, chaffering,
How often I find myself standing and looking at it where it
    flits,
How often I question and doubt whether that is really me;
But among my lovers and caroling these songs,
O I never doubt whether that is really me.
(1859?)                                      1881

## FULL OF LIFE NOW

FULL of life now, compact, visible,
I, forty years old the eighty-third year of the States,
To one a century hence or any number of centuries hence,
To you yet unborn these, seeking you.

When you read these I that was visible am become invisible,
Now it is you, compact, visible, realizing my poems, seeking
    me,
Fancying how happy you were if I could be with you and
    become your comrade;
Be it as if I were with you. (Be not too certain but I am now
    with you.)
1860                                          1871

# *Salut Au Monde!*

## 1

O TAKE my hand Walt Whitman!
Such gliding wonders! such sights and sounds!
Such join'd unended links, each hook'd to the next,
Each answering all, each sharing the earth with all.

What widens within you Walt Whitman?
What waves and soils exuding?
What climes? what persons and cities are here?
Who are the infants, some playing, some slumbering?
Who are the girls? who are the married women?
Who are the groups of old men going slowly with their arms
    about each other's necks?
What rivers are these? what forests and fruits are these?
What are the mountains call'd that rise so high in the
    mists?
What myriads of dwellings are they fill'd with dwellers?

## 2

Within me latitude widens, longitude lengthens,
Asia, Africa, Europe, are to the east—America is provided
    for in the west,
Banding the bulge of the earth winds the hot equator,
Curiously north and south turn the axis-ends,
Within me is the longest day, the sun wheels in slanting rings,
    it does not set for months,
Stretch'd in due time within me the midnight sun just rises
    above the horizon and sinks again,
Within me zones, seas, cataracts, forests, volcanoes, groups,
Malaysia, Polynesia, and the great West Indian islands.

## 3

What do you hear Walt Whitman?

I hear the workman singing and the farmer's wife singing,
I hear in the distance the sounds of children and of animals
early in the day,
I hear emulous shouts of Australians pursuing the wild horse,
I hear the Spanish dance with castanets in the chestnut shade,
to the rebeck and guitar,
I hear continual echoes from the Thames,
I hear fierce French liberty songs,
I hear of the Italian boat-sculler the musical recitative of old
poems,
I hear the locusts in Syria as they strike the grain and grass
with the showers of their terrible clouds,
I hear the Coptic refrain toward sundown, pensively falling
on the breast of the black venerable vast mother the Nile,
I hear the chirp of the Mexican muleteer, and the bells of the
mule,
I hear the Arab muezzin calling from the top of the mosque,
I hear the Christian priests at the altars of their churches, I
hear the responsive base and soprano,
I hear the cry of the Cossack, and the sailor's voice putting to
sea at Okotsk,
I hear the wheeze of the slave-coffle as the slaves march on, as
the husky gangs pass on by twos and threes, fasten'd
together with wrist-chains and ankle-chains,
I hear the Hebrew reading his records and psalms,
I hear the rhythmic myths of the Greeks, and the strong
legends of the Romans,
I hear the tale of the divine life and bloody death of the beautiful God the Christ,
I hear the Hindoo teaching his favorite pupil the loves, wars,
adages, transmitted safely to this day from poets who
wrote three thousand years ago.

## 4

What do you see Walt Whitman?
Who are they you salute, and that one after another salute you?

I see a great round wonder rolling through space,
I see diminute farms, hamlets, ruins, graveyards, jails, factories, palaces, hovels, huts of barbarians, tents of
 nomads upon the surface,
I see the shaded part on one side where the sleepers are sleeping, and the sunlit part on the other side,
I see the curious rapid change of the light and shade,
I see distant lands, as real and near to the inhabitants of them
 as my land is to me.


I see plenteous waters,
I see mountain peaks, I see the sierras of Andes where they
 range,
I see plainly the Himalayas, Chian Shahs, Altays, Ghauts,
I see the giant pinnacles of Elbruz, Kazbek, Bazardjusi,
I see the Styrian Alps, and the Karnac Alps,
I see the Pyrenees, Balks, Carpathians, and to the north the
 Dofrafields, and off at sea mount Hecla,
I see Vesuvius and Etna, the mountains of the Moon, and the
 Red mountains of Madagascar,
I see the Lybian, Arabian, and Asiatic deserts,
I see huge dreadful Arctic and Antarctic icebergs,
I see the superior oceans and the interior ones, the Atlantic
 and Pacific, the sea of Mexico, the Brazilian sea, and the
 sea of Peru,
The waters of Hindustan, the China sea, and the gulf of
 Guinea,
The Japan waters, the beautiful bay of Nagasaki land-lock'd
 in its mountains,
The spread of the Baltic, Caspian, Bothnia, the British shores,
 and the bay of Biscay,
The clear-sunn'd Mediterranean, and from one to another of
 its islands,
The White sea, and the sea around Greenland.


I behold the mariners of the world,
Some are in storms, some in the night with the watch on the
 lookout,
Some drifting helplessly, some with contagious diseases.

I behold the sail and steamships of the world, some in clus-
ters in port, some on their voyages,
Some double the cape of Storms, some cape Verde, others
capes Guardafui, Bon, or Bajadore,
Others Dondra head, others pass the straits of Sunda, others
cape Lopatka, others Behring's straits,
Others cape Horn, others sail the gulf of Mexico or along
Cuba or Hayti, others Hudson's bay or Baffin's bay,
Others pass the straits of Dover, others enter the Wash,
others the firth of Solway, others round cape Clear,
others the Land's End,
Others traverse the Zuyder Zee or the Scheld,
Others as comers and goers at Gibraltar or the Dardanelles,
Others sternly push their way through the northern winter-
packs,
Others descend or ascend the Obi or the Lena,
Others the Niger or the Congo, others the Indus, the Buram-
pooter and Cambodia,
Others wait steam'd up ready to start in the ports of Aus-
tralia,
Wait at Liverpool, Glasgow, Dublin, Marseilles, Lisbon,
Naples, Hamburg, Bremen, Bordeaux, the Hague,
Copenhagen,
Wait at Valparaiso, Rio Janeiro, Panama.

5

I see the tracks of the railroads of the earth,
I see them in Great Britain, I see them in Europe,
I see them in Asia and in Africa.

I see the electric telegraphs of the earth,
I see the filaments of the news of the wars, deaths, losses,
gains, passions, of my race.

I see the long river-stripes of the earth,
I see the Amazon and the Paraguay,
I see the four great rivers of China, the Amour, the Yellow
River, the Yiang-tse, and the Pearl,
I see where the Seine flows, and where the Danube, the Loire,
the Rhone, and the Guadalquiver flow,

E                                              w.

I see the windings of the Volga, the Dnieper, the Oder,
I see the Tuscan going down the Arno, and the Venetian along the Po,
I see the Greek seaman sailing out of Egina bay.

6

I see the sight of the old empire of Assyria, and that of Persia, and that of India,
I see the falling of the Ganges over the high rim of Saukara.

I see the place of the idea of the Deity incarnated by avatars in human forms,
I see the spots of the successions of priests on the earth, oracles, sacrificers, brahmins, sabians, llamas, monks, muftis, exhorters,
I see where druids walk'd the groves of Mona, I see the mistletoe and vervain,
I see the temples of the deaths of the bodies of Gods, I see the old signifiers.

I see Christ eating the bread of his last supper in the midst of youths and old persons,
I see where the strong divine young man the Hercules toil'd faithfully and long and then died,
I see the place of the innocent rich life and hapless fate of the beautiful nocturnal son, the full-limb'd Bacchus,
I see Kneph, blooming, drest in blue, with the crown of feathers on his head,
I see Hermes, unsuspected, dying, well-belov'd, saying to the people *Do not weep for me,*
*This is not my true country, I have lived banish'd from my true country, I now go back there,*
*I return to the celestial sphere where every one goes in his turn.*

7

I see the battle-fields of the earth, grass grows upon them and blossoms and corn,
I see the tracks of ancient and modern expeditions.

I see the nameless masonries, venerable messages of the un-
    known events, heroes, records of the earth.

I see the places of the sagas,
I see pine-trees and fir-trees torn by northern blasts,
I see granite bowlders and cliffs, I see green meadows and
    lakes,
I see the burial-cairns of Scandinavian warriors,
I see them raised high with stones by the marge of restless
    oceans, that the dead men's spirits when they wearied of
    their quiet graves might rise up through the mounds and
    gaze on the tossing billows, and be refresh'd by storms,
    immensity, liberty, action.

I see the steppes of Asia,
I see the tumuli of Mongolia, I see the tents of Kalmucks
    and Baskirs,
I see the nomadic tribes with herds of oxen and cows,
I see the table-lands notch'd with ravines, I see the jungles
    and deserts,
I see the camel, the wild steed, the bustard, the fat-tail'd
    sheep, the antelope, and the burrowing wolf.

I see the highlands of Abyssinia,
I see flocks of goats feeding, and see the fig-tree, tamarind,
    date,
And see fields of teff-wheat and places of verdure and gold.

I see the Brazilian vaquero,
I see the Bolivian ascending mount Sorata,
I see the Wacho crossing the plains, I see the incomparable
    rider of horses with his lasso on his arm,
I see over the pampas the pursuit of wild cattle for their hides.

8, [9]

I see the regions of snow and ice,
I see the sharp-eyed Samoiede and the Finn,
I see the seal-seeker in his boat poising his lance,
I see the Siberian on his slight-built sledge drawn by dogs,

I see the porpoise-hunters, I see the whale-crews of the south
    Pacific and the north Atlantic,
I see the cliffs, glaciers, torrents, valleys, of Switzerland—I
    mark the long winters and the isolation.

I see the cities of the earth and make myself at random a part
    of them,
I am a real Parisian,
I am a habitan of Vienna, St. Petersburg, Berlin, Constan-
    tinople,
I am of Adelaide, Sidney, Melbourne,
I am of London, Manchester, Bristol, Edinburgh, Limerick,
I am of Madrid, Cadiz, Barcelona, Oporto, Lyons, Brussels,
    Berne, Frankfort, Stuttgart, Turin, Florence,
I belong in Moscow, Cracow, Warsaw, or northward in
    Christiania or Stockholm, or in Siberian Irkutsk, or in
    some street in Iceland,
I descend upon all those cities, and rise from them again.

### 10

I see vapors exhaling from unexplored countries,
I see the savage types, the bow and arrow, the poison'd
    splint, the fetich, and the obi.

I see African and Asiatic towns,
I see Algiers, Tripoli, Derne, Mogadore, Timbuctoo, Mon-
    rovia,
I see the swarms of Pekin, Canton, Benares, Delhi, Calcutta,
    Tokio,
I see the Kruman in his hut, and the Dahoman and Ashantee-
    man in their huts,
I see the Turk smoking opium in Aleppo,
I see the picturesque crowds at the fairs of Khiva and those of
    Herat,
I see Teheran, I see Muscat and Medina and the intervening
    sands, I see the caravans toiling onward,
I see Egypt and the Egyptians, I see the pyramids and obelisks,
I look on chisell'd histories, records of conquering kings,
    dynasties, cut in slabs of sand-stone, or on granite-
    blocks,

I see at Memphis mummy-pits containing mummies embalm'd, swathed in linen-cloth, lying there many centuries,
I look on the fall'n Theban, the large-ball'd eyes, the side-
drooping neck, the hands folded across the breast.

I see all the menials of the earth, laboring,
I see all the prisoners in the prisons,
I see the defective human bodies of the earth,
The blind, the deaf and dumb, idiots, hunchbacks, lunatics,
The pirates, thieves, betrayers, murderers, slave-makers of
the earth,
The helpless infants, and the helpless old men and women.

I see male and female everywhere,
I see the serene brotherhood of philosophs,
I see the constructiveness of my race,
I see the results of the perseverance and industry of my race,
I see ranks, colors, barbarisms, civilizations, I go among
them, I mix indiscriminately,
And I salute all the inhabitants of the earth.

### 11

You whoever you are!
You daughter or son of England!
You of the mighty Slavic tribes and empires! you Russ in
Russia!
You dim-descended, black, divine-soul'd African, large, fine-
headed, nobly-form'd, superbly destin'd, on equal terms
with me!
You Norwegian! Swede! Dane! Icelander! you Prussian!
You Spaniard of Spain! you Portuguese!
You Frenchwoman and Frenchman of France!
You Belge! you liberty-lover of the Netherlands! (you stock
whence I myself have descended;)
You sturdy Austrian! you Lombard! Hun! Bohemian! far-
mer of Styria!
You neighbor of the Danube!
You working-man of the Rhine, the Elbe, or the Weser! you
working-woman too!

You Sardinian! you Bavarian! Swabian! Saxon! Wallachian!
    Bulgarian!

You Roman! Neapolitan! you Greek!

You lithe matador in the arena at Seville!

You mountaineer living lawlessly on the Taurus or Caucasus!

You Bokh horse-herd watching your mares and stallions
    feeding!

You beautiful-bodied Persian at full speed in the saddle
    shooting arrows to the mark!

You Chinaman and Chinawoman of China! you Tartar of
    Tartary!

You women of the earth subordinated at your tasks!

You Jew journeying in your old age through every risk to
    stand once on Syrian ground!

You other Jews waiting in all lands for your Messiah!

You thoughtful Armenian pondering by some stream of the
    Euphrates! you peering amid the ruins of Nineveh! you
    ascending mount Ararat!

You foot-worn pilgrim welcoming the far-away sparkle of
    the minarets of Mecca!

You sheiks along the stretch from Suez to Bab-el-mandeb
    ruling your families and tribes!

You olive-grower tending your fruit on fields of Nazareth,
    Damascus, or lake Tiberias!

You Thibet trader on the wide inland or bargaining in the
    shops of Lassa!

You Japanese man or woman! you liver in Madagascar,
    Ceylon, Sumatra, Borneo!

All you continentals of Asia, Africa, Europe, Australia, in-
    different of place!

All you on the numberless islands of the archipelagoes of the
    sea!

And you of centuries hence when you listen to me!

And you each and everywhere whom I specify not, but in-
    clude just the same!

Health to you! good will to you all, from me and America sent!

Each of us inevitable,

Each of us limitless—each of us with his or her right upon
    the earth,

Each of us allow'd the eternal purports of the earth,
Each of us here as divinely as any is here.


### 12

You Hottentot with clicking palate! you woolly-hair'd
     hordes!
You own'd persons dropping sweat-drops or blood-drops!
You human forms with the fathomless ever-impressive coun-
     tenances of brutes!
You poor koboo whom the meanest of the rest look down
     upon for all your glimmering language and spirituality!
You dwarf'd Kamtschatkan, Greenlander, Lapp!
You Austral negro, naked, red, sooty, with protrusive lip,
     groveling, seeking your food!
You Caffre, Berber, Soudanese!
You haggard, uncouth, untutor'd Bedowee!
You plague-swarms in Madras, Nankin, Kaubul, Cairo!
You benighted roamer of Amazonia! you Patagonian! you
     Feejee-man!
I do not prefer others so very much before you either,
I do not say one word against you, away back there where
     you stand,
(You will come forward in due time to my side.)


### 13

My spirit has pass'd in compassion and determination around
     the whole earth,
I have look'd for equals and lovers and found them ready for
     me in all lands,
I think some divine rapport has equalized me with them.


You vapors, I think I have risen with you, moved away
     to distant continents, and fallen down there, for
     reasons,
I think I have blown with you you winds;
You waters I have finger'd every shore with you,
I have run through what any river or strait of the globe has
     run through,

I have taken my stand on the bases of peninsulas and on the
    high embedded rocks, to cry thence:

*Salut au monde!*
What cities the light or warmth penetrates I penetrate those
    cities myself,
All islands to which birds wing their way I wing my way
    myself.

Toward you all, in America's name,
I raise high the perpendicular hand, I make the signal,
To remain after me in sight forever,
For all the haunts and homes of men.
1856                                                            1881


# Song of the Open Road

## 1

AFOOT and light-hearted I take to the open road,
Healthy, free, the world before me,
The long brown path before me leading wherever I choose.

Henceforth I ask not good-fortune, I myself am good-for-
    tune,
Henceforth I whimper no more, postpone no more, need
    nothing,
Done with indoor complaints, libraries, querulous criticisms,
Strong and content I travel the open road.

The earth, that is sufficient,
I do not want the constellations any nearer,
I know they are very well where they are,
I know they suffice for those who belong to them.

(Still here I carry my old delicious burdens,
I carry them, men and women, I carry them with me wher-
    ever I go,

I swear it is impossible for me to get rid of them,
I am fill'd with them ; and I will fill them in return.)

### 2

You road I enter upon and look around, I believe you are
    not all that is here,
I believe that much unseen is also here.

Here the profound lesson of reception, nor preference nor
    denial,
The black with his woolly head, the felon, the diseas'd, the
    illiterate person, are not denied ;
The birth, the hasting after the physician, the beggar's tramp,
    the drunkard's stagger, the laughing party of mechanics,
The escaped youth, the rich person's carriage, the fop, the
    eloping couple,
The early market-man, the hearse, the moving of furniture
    into the town, the return back from the town,
They pass, I also pass, any thing passes, none can be inter-
    dicted,
None but are accepted, none but shall be dear to me.

### 3

You air that serves me with breath to speak!
You objects that call from diffusion my meanings and give
    them shape!
You light that wraps me and all things in delicate equable
    showers!
You paths worn in the irregular hollows by the roadsides!
I believe you are latent with unseen existences, you are so
    dear to me.

You flagg'd walks of the cities! you strong curbs at the edges!
You ferries! you planks and posts of wharves! you timber-
    lined sides! you distant ships!
You rows of houses! you window-pierc'd façades! you roofs!
You porches and entrances! you copings and iron guards!
You windows whose transparent shells might expose so
    much!

You doors and ascending steps! you arches!

You gray stones of interminable pavements! you trodden
crossings!

From all that has touch'd you I believe you have imparted to
yourselves, and now would impart the same secretly to
me,

From the living and the dead you have peopled your impassive surfaces, and the spirits thereof would be evident
and amicable with me.


## 4

The earth expanding right hand and left hand,

The picture alive, every part in its best light,

The music falling in where it is wanted, and stopping where
it is not wanted,

The cheerful voice of the public road, the gay fresh sentiment
of the road.


O highway I travel, do you say to me *Do not leave me?*

Do you say *Venture not—if you leave me you are lost?*

Do you say *I am already prepared, I am well-beaten and undenied, adhere to me?*


O public road, I say back I am not afraid to leave you, yet I
love you,

You express me better than I can express myself,

You shall be more to me than my poem.


I think heroic deeds were all conceiv'd in the open air, and all
free poems also,

I think I could stop here myself and do miracles,

I think whatever I shall meet on the road I shall like, and
whoever beholds me shall like me,

I think whoever I see must be happy.


## 5

From this hour I ordain myself loos'd of limits and imaginary lines,

Going where I list, my own master total and absolute,

Listening to others, considering well what they say,

Pausing, searching, receiving, contemplating,
Gently, but with undeniable will, divesting myself of the
holds that would hold me.

I inhale great draughts of space,
The east and the west are mine, and the north and the south
are mine.

I am larger, better than I thought,
I did not know I held so much goodness.

All seems beautiful to me,
I can repeat over to men and women You have done such
good to me I would do the same to you,
I will recruit for myself and you as I go,
I will scatter myself among men and women as I go,
I will toss a new gladness and roughness among them,
Whoever denies me it shall not trouble me,
Whoever accepts me he or she shall be blessed and shall bless
me.

### 6

Now if a thousand perfect men were to appear it would not
amaze me,
Now if a thousand beautiful forms of women appear'd it
would not astonish me.

Now I see the secret of the making of the best persons,
It is to grow in the open air and to eat and sleep with the
earth.

Here a great personal deed has room,
(Such a deed seizes upon the hearts of the whole race of men,
Its effusion of strength and will overwhelms law and mocks
all authority and all argument against it.)

Here is the test of wisdom,
Wisdom is not finally tested in schools,
Wisdom cannot be pass'd from one having it to another not
having it,

Wisdom is of the soul, is not susceptible of proof, is its own
  proof,
Applies to all stages and objects and qualities and is content,
Is the certainty of the reality and immortality of things, and
  the excellence of things;
Something there is in the float of the sight of things that provokes it out of the soul.

Now I re-examine philosophies and religions,
They may prove well in lecture-rooms, yet not prove at all
  under the spacious clouds and along the landscape and
  flowing currents.

Here is realization,
Here is a man tallied—he realizes here what he has in him,
The past, the future, majesty, love—if they are vacant of you,
  you are vacant of them.

Only the kernel of every object nourishes;
Where is he who tears off the husks for you and me?
Where is he that undoes stratagems and envelopes for you
  and me?

Here is adhesiveness, it is not previously fashion'd, it is
  apropos;
Do you know what it is as you pass to be loved by strangers?
Do you know the talk of those turning eye-balls?

7

Here is the efflux of the soul,
The efflux of the soul comes from within through embower'd
  gates, ever provoking questions,
These yearnings why are they? these thoughts in the darkness
  why are they?
Why are there men and women that while they are nigh me
  the sunlight expands my blood?
Why when they leave me do my pennants of joy sink flat and
  lank?
Why are there trees I never walk under but large and melodious thoughts descend upon me?

(I think they hang there winter and summer on those trees
    and always drop fruit as I pass;)
What is it I interchange so suddenly with strangers?
What with some driver as I ride on the seat by his side?
What with some fisherman drawing his seine by the shore as
    I walk by and pause?
What gives me to be free to a woman's and man's good-will?
    what gives them to be free to mine?


8

The efflux of the soul is happiness, here is happiness,
I think it pervades the open air, waiting at all times,
Now it flows unto us, we are rightly charged.

Here rises the fluid and attaching character,
The fluid and attaching character is the freshness and sweet-
    ness of man and woman,
(The herbs of the morning sprout no fresher and sweeter
    every day out of the roots of themselves, than it sprouts
    fresh and sweet continually out of itself.)
Toward the fluid and attaching character exudes the sweat of
    the love of young and old,
From it falls distill'd the charm that mocks beauty and
    attainments,
Toward it heaves the shuddering longing ache of con-
    tact.


9

Allons! whoever you are come travel with me!
Traveling with me you find what never tires.

The earth never tires,
The earth is rude, silent, incomprehensible at first, Nature is
    rude and incomprehensible at first,
Be not discouraged, keep on, there are divine things well
    envelop'd,
I swear to you there are divine things more beautiful than
    words can tell.

Allons! we must not stop here,
However sweet these laid-up stores, however convenient this
    dwelling we cannot remain here,
However shelter'd this port and however calm these waters
    we must not anchor here,
However welcome the hospitality that surrounds us we are
    permitted to receive it but a little while.

### 10

Allons! the inducements shall be greater,
We will sail pathless and wild seas,
We will go where winds blow, waves dash, and the Yankee
    clipper speeds by under full sail.

Allons! with power, liberty, the earth, the elements,
Health, defiance, gayety, self-esteem, curiosity;
Allons! from all formules!
From your formules, O bat-eyed and materialistic priests.

The stale cadaver blocks up the passage—the burial waits no
    longer.

Allons! yet take warning!
He traveling with me needs the best blood, thews, endurance,
None may come to the trial till he or she bring courage and
    health,
Come not here if you have already spent the best of yourself,
Only those may come who come in sweet and determin'd
    bodies,
No diseas'd person, no rum-drinker or venereal taint is per-
    mitted here.

(I and mine do not convince by arguments, similes, rhymes,
We convince by our presence.)

### 11

Listen! I will be honest with you,
I do not offer the old smooth prizes, but offer rough new
    prizes,
These are the days that must happen to you:

You shall not heap up what is call'd riches,
You shall scatter with lavish hand all that you earn or
    achieve,
You but arrive at the city to which you were destin'd, you
    hardly settle yourself to satisfaction before you are
    call'd by an irresistible call to depart,
You shall be treated to the ironical smiles and mockings of
    those who remain behind you,
What beckonings of love you receive you shall only answer
    with passionate kisses of parting,
You shall not allow the hold of those who spread their
    reach'd hands toward you.

### 12

Allons! after the great Companions, and to belong to them!
They too are on the road—they are the swift and majestic
    men—they are the greatest women,
Enjoyers of calms of seas and storms of seas,
Sailors of many a ship, walkers of many a mile of land,
Habituès of many distant countries, habituès of far-distant
    dwellings,
Trusters of men and women, observers of cities, solitary
    toilers,
Pausers and contemplators of tufts, blossoms, shells of the
    shore,
Dancers at wedding-dances, kissers of brides, tender helpers
    of children, bearers of children,
Soldiers of revolts, standers by gaping graves, lowerers-down
    of coffins,
Journeyers over consecutive seasons, over the years, the
    curious years each emerging from that which preceded it,
Journeyers as with companions, namely their own diverse
    phases,
Forth-steppers from the latent unrealized baby-days,
Journeyers gayly with their own youth, journeyers with their
    bearded and well-grain'd manhood,
Journeyers with their womanhood, ample, unsurpass'd, con-
    tent,
Journeyers with their own sublime old age of manhood or
    womanhood,

Old age, calm, expanded, broad with the haughty breadth of
the universe,
Old age, flowing free with the delicious near-by freedom of
death.

13

Allons! to that which is endless as it was beginningless,
To undergo much, tramps of days, rests of nights,
To merge all in the travel they tend to, and the days and
nights they tend to,
Again to merge them in the start of superior journeys,
To see nothing anywhere but what you may reach it and pass
it,
To conceive no time, however distant, but what you may
reach it and pass it,
To look up or down no road but it stretches and waits for
you, however long but it stretches and waits for you,
To see no being, not God's or any, but you also go thither,
To see no possession but you may possess it, enjoying all
without labor or purchase, abstracting the feast yet not
abstracting one particle of it,
To take the best of the farmer's farm and the rich man's
elegant villa, and the chaste blessings of the well-married
couple, and the fruits of orchards and flowers of gardens,
To take to your use out of the compact cities as you pass
through,
To carry buildings and streets with you afterward wherever
you go,
To gather the minds of men out of their brains as you en-
counter them, to gather the love out of their hearts,
To take your lovers on the road with you, for all that you
leave them behind you,
To know the universe itself as a road, as many roads, as roads
for traveling souls.

All parts away for the progress of souls,
All religion, all solid things, arts, governments—all that was
or is apparent upon this globe or any globe, falls into
niches and corners before the procession of souls along
the grand roads of the universe.

Of the progress of the souls of men and women along the grand roads of the universe, all other progress is the needed emblem and sustenance.

Forever alive, forever forward,
Stately, solemn, sad, withdrawn, baffled, mad, turbulent, feeble, dissatisfied,
Desperate, proud, fond, sick, accepted by men, rejected by men,
They go! they go! I know that they go, but I know not where they go,
But I know that they go toward the best—toward something great.

Whoever you are, come forth! or man or woman come forth!
You must not stay sleeping and dallying there in the house, though you built it, or though it has been built for you.

Out of the dark confinement! out from behind the screen!
It is useless to protest, I know all and expose it.

Behold through you as bad as the rest,
Through the laughter, dancing, dining, supping, of people,
Inside of dresses and ornaments, inside of those wash'd and trimm'd faces,
Behold a secret silent loathing and despair.

No husband, no wife, no friend, trusted to hear the confession,
Another self, a duplicate of every one, skulking and hiding it goes,
Formless and wordless through the streets of the cities, polite and bland in the parlors,
In the cars of railroads, in steamboats, in the public assembly,
Home to the houses of men and women, at the table, in the bedroom, everywhere,
Smartly attired, countenance smiling, form upright, death under the breast-bones, hell under the skull-bones,
Under the broadcloth and gloves, under the ribbons and artificial flowers,

Keeping fair with the customs, speaking not a syllable of
　　itself,
Speaking of any thing else but never of itself.


### 14

Allons! through struggles and wars!
The goal that was named cannot be countermanded.

Have the past struggles succeeded?
What has succeeded? yourself? your nation? Nature?
Now understand me well—it is provided in the essence of
　　things that from any fruition of success, no matter what,
　　shall come forth something to make a greater struggle
　　necessary.

My call is the call of battle, I nourish active rebellion,
He going with me must go well arm'd,
He going with me goes often with spare diet, poverty, angry
　　enemies, desertions.


### 15

Allons! the road is before us!
It is safe—I have tried it—my own feet have tried it well—be
　　not detain'd!
Let the paper remain on the desk unwritten, and the book on
　　the shelf unopen'd!

Let the tools remain in the workshop! let the money remain
　　unearn'd!
Let the school stand! mind not the cry of the teacher!
Let the preacher preach in his pulpit! let the lawyer plead in
　　the court, and the judge expound the law.

Camerado, I give you my hand!
I give you my love more precise than money,
I give you myself before preaching or law;
Will you give me yourself? will you come travel with me?
Shall we stick by each other as long as we live?
1856　　　　　　　　　　　　　　　　　　　　　1881

# Crossing Brooklyn Ferry

FLOOD-TIDE below me! I see you face to face!
Clouds of the west—sun there half an hour high—I see you
   also face to face.

Crowds of men and women attired in the usual costumes,
   how curious you are to me!
On the ferry-boats the hundreds and hundreds that cross,
   returning home, are more curious to me than you suppose,
And you that shall cross from shore to shore years hence are
   more to me, and more in my meditations, than you
   might suppose.

The impalpable sustenance of me from all things at all hours
   of the day,
The simple, compact, well-join'd scheme, myself disintegrated, every one disintegrated yet part of the scheme,
The similitudes of the past and those of the future,
The glories strung like beads on my smallest sights and
   hearings, on the walk in the street and the passage over
   the river,
The current rushing so swiftly and swimming with me far
   away,
The others that are to follow me, the ties between me and
   them,
The certainty of others, the life, love, sight, hearing of others.

Others will enter the gates of the ferry and cross from shore
   to shore,
Others will watch the run of the flood-tide,
Others will see the shipping of Manhattan north and west,
   and the heights of Brooklyn to the south and east,
Others will see the islands large and small;

Fifty years hence, others will see them as they cross, the sun
    half an hour high,
A hundred years hence, or ever so many hundred years hence,
    others will see them,
Will enjoy the sunset, the pouring-in of the flood-tide, the
    falling-back to the sea of the ebb-tide.

### 3

It avails not, time nor place—distance avails not,
I am with you, you men and women of a generation, or ever
    so many generations hence,
Just as you feel when you look on the river and sky, so I felt,
Just as any of you is one of a living crowd, I was one of a
    crowd,
Just as you are refresh'd by the gladness of the river and the
    bright flow, I was refresh'd,
Just as you stand and lean on the rail, yet hurry with the swift
    current, I stood yet was hurried,
Just as you look on the numberless masts of ships and the
    thick-stemm'd pipes of steamboats, I look'd.

I too many and many a time cross'd the river of old,
Watched the Twelfth-month sea-gulls, saw them high in the
    air floating with motionless wings, oscillating their
    bodies,
Saw how the glistening yellow lit up parts of their bodies and
    left the rest in strong shadow,
Saw the slow-wheeling circles and the gradual edging toward
    the south,
Saw the reflection of the summer sky in the water,
Had my eyes dazzled by the shimmering track of beams,
Look'd at the fine centrifugal spokes of light round the shape
    of my head in the sunlit water,
Look'd on the haze on the hills southward and south-west-
    ward,
Look'd on the vapor as it flew in fleeces tinged with violet,
Look'd toward the lower bay to notice the vessels arriving,
Saw their approach, saw aboard those that were near me,
Saw the white sails of schooners and sloops, saw the ships at
    anchor,

The sailors at work in the rigging or out astride the spars,

The round masts, the swinging motion of the hulls, the slender serpentine pennants,

The large and small steamers in motion, the pilots in their
pilot-houses,

The white wake left by the passage, the quick tremulous whirl
of the wheels,

The flags of all nations, the falling of them at sunset,

The scallop-edged waves in the twilight, the ladled cups, the
frolicsome crests and glistening,

The stretch afar growing dimmer and dimmer, the gray walls
of the granite storehouses by the docks,

On the river the shadowy group, the big steam-tug closely
flank'd on each side by the barges, the hay-boat, the
belated lighter,

On the neighboring shore the fires from the foundry chimneys burning high and glaringly into the night,

Casting their flicker of black contrasted with wild red and
yellow light over the tops of houses, and down into the
clefts of streets.

### 4

These and all else were to me the same as they are to you,

I loved well those cities, loved well the stately and rapid river,

The men and women I saw were all near to me,

Others the same—others who look back on me because I
look'd forward to them,

(The time will come, though I stop here to-day, and to-night.)

### 5

What is it then between us?

What is the count of the scores or hundreds of years between
us?

Whatever it is, it avails not—distance avails not, and place
avails not,

I too lived, Brooklyn of ample hills was mine,

I too walk'd the streets of Manhattan island, and bathed in
the waters around it,

I too felt the curious abrupt questionings stir within me.

In the day among crowds of people sometimes they came
    upon me,
In my walks home late at night or as I lay in my bed they
    came upon me,
I too had been struck from the float forever held in solution,
I too had receiv'd identity by my body,
That I was I knew was of my body, and what I should be I
    knew I should be of my body.

### 6

It is not upon you alone the dark patches fall,
The dark threw its patches down upon me also,
The best I had done seem'd to me blank and suspicious,
My great thoughts as I supposed them, were they not in
    reality meagre?
Nor is it you alone who know what it is to be evil,
I am he who knew what it was to be evil,
I too knitted the old knot of contrariety,
Blabb'd, blush'd, resented, lied, stole, grudg'd,
Had guile, anger, lust, hot wishes I dared not speak,
Was wayward, vain, greedy, shallow, sly, cowardly, malig-
    nant,
The wolf, the snake, the hog, not wanting in me,
The cheating look, the frivolous word, the adulterous wish,
    not wanting,
Refusals, hates, postponements, meanness, laziness, none of
    these wanting,
Was one with the rest, the days and haps of the rest,
Was call'd by my nighest name by clear loud voices of young
    men as they saw me approaching or passing,
Felt their arms on my neck as I stood, or the negligent lean-
    ing of their flesh against me as I sat,
Saw many I loved in the street or ferry-boat or public assem-
    bly, yet never told them a word,
Lived the same life with the rest, the same old laughing,
    gnawing, sleeping,
Play'd the part that still looks back on the actor or actress,
The same old role, the role that is what we make it, as great
    as we like,
Or as small as we like, or both great and small.

## 7

Closer yet I approach you,
What thought you have of me now, I had as much of you—I
    laid in my stores in advance,
I consider'd long and seriously of you before you were born.

Who was to know what should come home to me?
Who knows but I am enjoying this?
Who knows, for all the distance, but I am as good as looking
    at you now, for all you cannot see me?

## 8

Ah, what can ever be more stately and admirable to me than
    mast-hemm'd Manhattan?
River and sunset and scallop-edg'd waves of flood-tide?
The sea-gulls oscillating their bodies, the hay-boat in the
    twilight, and the belated lighter?

What gods can exceed these that clasp me by the hand, and
    with voices I love call me promptly and loudly by my
    nighest name as I approach?

What is more subtle than this which ties me to the woman or
    man that looks in my face?
Which fuses me into you now, and pours my meaning into
    you?

We understand then do we not?
What I promis'd without mentioning it, have you not ac-
    cepted?
What the study could not teach—what the preaching could
    not accomplish is accomplish'd, is it not?

## 9

Flow on, river! flow with the flood-tide, and ebb with the
    ebb-tide!
Frolic on, crested and scallop-edg'd waves!
Gorgeous clouds of the sunset! drench with your splendor
    me, or the men and women generations after me!

Cross from shore to shore, countless crowds of passengers!

Stand up, tall masts of Mannahatta! stand up, beautiful hills of Brooklyn!

Throb, baffled and curious brain! throw out questions and answers!

Suspend here and everywhere, eternal float of solution!

Gaze, loving and thirsting eyes, in the house or street or public assembly!

Sound out, voices of young men! loudly and musically call me by my nighest name!

Live, old life! play the part that looks back on the actor or actress!

Play the old role, the role that is great or small according as one makes it!

Consider, you who peruse me, whether I may not in unknown ways be looking upon you;

Be firm, rail over the river, to support those who lean idly, yet haste with the hasting current;

Fly on, sea-birds! fly sideways, or wheel in large circles high in the air;

Receive the summer sky, you water, and faithfully hold it till all downcast eyes have time to take it from you!

Diverge, fine spokes of light, from the shape of my head, or any one's head, in the sunlit water!

Come on, ships from the lower bay! pass up or down, white-sail'd schooners, sloops, lighters!

Flaunt away, flags of all nations! be duly lower'd at sunset!

Burn high your fires, foundry chimneys! cast black shadows at nightfall! cast red and yellow light over the tops of the houses!

Appearances, now or henceforth, indicate what you are,

You necessary film, continue to envelop the soul,

About my body for me, and your body for you, be hung our divinest aromas,

Thrive, cities—bring your freight, bring your shows, ample and sufficient rivers,

Expand, being than which none else is perhaps more spiritual,

Keep your places, objects than which none else is more lasting.

You have waited, you always wait, you dumb, beautiful
　　ministers,
We receive you with free sense at last, and are insatiate hence-
　　forward,
Not you any more shall be able to foil us, or withhold your-
　　selves from us,
We use you, and do not cast you aside—we plant you per-
　　manently within us,
We fathom you not—we love you—there is perfection in you
　　also,
You furnish your parts toward eternity,
Great or small, you furnish your parts toward the soul.
1856　　　　　　　　　　　　　　　　　　　　　　1881


# *Song of the Answerer*


Now list to my morning's romanza, I tell the signs of the
　　Answerer,
To the cities and farms I sing as they spread in the sunshine
　　before me.

A young man comes to me bearing a message from his brother,
How shall the young man know the whether and when of his
　　brother?
Tell him to send me the signs.

And I stand before the young man face to face, and take his
　　right hand in my left hand and his left hand in my right
　　hand,
And I answer for his brother and for men, and I answer for
　　him that answers for all, and send these signs.

Him all wait for, him all yield up to, his word is decisive and
　　final,
Him they accept, in him lave, in him perceive themselves as
　　amid light,
Him they immerse and he immerses them.

Beautiful women, the haughtiest nations, laws, the landscape, people, animals,
The profound earth and its attributes and the unquiet ocean, (so tell I my morning's romanza,)
All enjoyments and properties and money, and whatever money will buy,
The best farms, others toiling and planting and he unavoidably reaps,
The noblest and costliest cities, others grading and building and he domiciles there,
Nothing for any one but what is for him, near and far are for him, the ships in the offing,
The perpetual shows and marches on land are for him if they are for anybody.

He puts things in their attitudes,
He puts to-day out of himself with plasticity and love,
He places his own times, reminiscences, parents, brothers and sisters, associations, employment, politics, so that the rest never shame them afterward, nor assume to command them.

He is the Answerer,
What can be answer'd he answers, and what cannot be answer'd he shows how it cannot be answer'd.

A man is a summons and challenge,
(It is vain to skulk—do you hear that mocking and laughter? do you hear the ironical echoes?)

Books, friendships, philosophers, priests, action, pleasure, pride, beat up and down seeking to give satisfaction,
He indicates the satisfaction, and indicates them that beat up and down also.

Whichever the sex, whatever the season or place, he may go freshly and gently and safely by day or by night,
He has the pass-key of hearts, to him the response of the prying of hands on the knobs.

His welcome is universal, the flow of beauty is not more welcome or universal than he is,
The person he favors by day or sleeps with at night is blessed.

Every existence has its idiom, every thing has an idiom and
tongue,
He resolves all tongues into his own and bestows it upon
men, and any man translates, and any man translates
himself also,
One part does not counteract another part, he is the joiner,
he sees how they join.

He says indifferently and alike *How are you friend?* to the
President at his levee,
And he says *Good-day my brother*, to Cudge that hoes in the
sugar-field,
And both understand him and know that his speech is right.

He walks with perfect ease in the capitol,
He walks among the Congress, and one Representative says
to another, *Here is our equal appearing and new.*

Then the mechanics take him for a mechanic,
And the soldiers suppose him to be a soldier, and the sailors
that he has follow'd the sea,
And the authors take him for an author, and the artists for
an artist,
And the laborers perceive he could labor with them and love
them,
No matter what the work is, that he is the one to follow it or
has follow'd it,
No matter what the nation, that he might find his brothers
and sisters there.

The English believe he comes of their English stock,
A Jew to the Jew he seems, a Russ to the Russ, usual and
near, removed from none.

Whoever he looks at in the traveler's coffee-house claims him,
The Italian or Frenchman is sure, the German is sure, the
Spaniard is sure, and the island Cuban is sure,

The engineer, the deck-hand on the great lakes, or on the Mississippi or St. Lawrence or Sacramento, or Hudson or Paumanok sound, claims him.

The gentleman of perfect blood acknowledges his perfect blood,
The insulter, the prostitute, the angry person, the beggar, see themselves in the ways of him, he strangely transmutes them,
They are not vile any more, they hardly know themselves they are so grown.

## 2

The indications and tally of time,
Perfect sanity shows the master among philosophs,
Time, always without break, indicates itself in parts,
What always indicates the poet is the crowd of the pleasant company of singers, and their words,
The words of the singers are the hours or minutes of the light or dark, but the words of the maker of poems are the general light and dark,
The maker of poems settles justice, reality, immortality,
His insight and power encircle things and the human race,
He is the glory and extract thus far of things and of the human race.

The singers do not beget, only the Poet begets,
The singers are welcom'd, understood, appear often enough, but rare has the day been, likewise the spot, of the birth of the maker of poems, the Answerer,
(Not every century nor every five centuries has contain'd such a day, for all its names.)

The singers of successive hours of centuries may have ostensible names, but the name of each of them is one of the singers,
The name of each is, eye-singer, ear-singer, head-singer, sweet-singer, night-singer, parlor-singer, love-singer, weird-singer, or something else.

All this time and at all times wait the words of true poems,
The words of true poems do not merely please,
The true poets are not followers of beauty but the august
    masters of beauty;
The greatness of sons is the exuding of the greatness of
    mothers and fathers,
The words of true poems are the tuft and final applause of
    science.

Divine instinct, breadth of vision, the law of reason, health,
    rudeness of body, withdrawnness,
Gayety, sun-tan, air-sweetness, such are some of the words of
    poems.

The sailor and traveler underlie the maker of poems, the
    Answerer,
The builder, geometer, chemist, anatomist, phrenologist,
    artist, all these underlie the maker of poems, the
    Answerer.

The words of the true poems give you more than poems,
They give you to form for yourself poems, religions, politics,
    war, peace, behavior, histories, essays, daily life, and
    every thing else,
They balance ranks, colors, races, creeds, and the sexes,
They do not seek beauty, they are sought,
Forever touching them or close upon them follows beauty,
    longing, fain, love-sick.

They prepare for death, yet they are not the finish, but rather
    the outset,
They bring none to his or her terminus or to be content and
    full,
Whom they take they take into space to behold the birth of
    stars, to learn one of the meanings,
To launch off with absolute faith, to sweep through the cease-
    less rings and never be quiet again.
1855                                                                    1881

# Our Old Feuillage

ALWAYS our old feuillage!

Always Florida's green peninsula—always the priceless delta of Louisiana—always the cotton-fields of Alabama and Texas,

Always California's golden hills and hollows, and the silver mountains of New Mexico—always soft-breath'd Cuba,

Always the vast slope drain'd by the Southern sea, inseparable with the slopes drain'd by the Eastern and Western seas,

The area the eighty-third year of these States, the three and a half millions of square miles,

The eighteen thousand miles of sea-coast and bay-coast on the main, the thirty thousand miles of river navigation,

The seven millions of distinct families and the same number of dwellings—always these, and more, branching forth into numberless branches,

Always the free range and diversity—always the continent of Democracy;

Always the prairies, pastures, forests, vast cities, travelers, Kanada, the snows;

Always these compact lands tied at the hips with the belt stringing the huge oval lakes;

Always the West with strong native persons, the increasing density there, the habitans, friendly, threatening, ironical, scorning invaders;

All sights, South, North, East—all deeds promiscuously done at all times,

All characters, movements, growths, a few noticed, myriads unnoticed,

Through Mannahatta's streets I walking, these things gathering,

On interior rivers by night in the glare of pine knots, steamboats wooding up,

Sunlight by day on the valley of the Susquehanna, and on the valleys of the Potomac and Rappahannock, and the valleys of the Roanoke and Delaware,

158

In their northerly wilds beasts of prey haunting the Adirondacks the hills, or lapping the Saginaw waters to drink,
In a lonesome inlet a sheldrake lost from the flock, sitting on
the water rocking silently,
In farmers' barns oxen in the stable, their harvest labor done,
they rest standing, they are too tired,
Afar on arctic ice the she-walrus lying drowsily while her cubs
play around,
The hawk sailing where men have not yet sail'd, the farthest
polar sea, ripply, crystalline, open, beyond the floes,
White drift spooning ahead where the ship in the tempest
dashes,
On solid land what is done in cities as the bells strike midnight together,
In primitive woods the sounds there also sounding, the howl
of the wolf, the scream of the panther, and the hoarse
bellow of the elk,
In winter beneath the hard blue ice of Moosehead lake, in
summer visible through the clear waters, the great trout
swimming,
In lower latitudes in warmer air in the Carolinas the large
black buzzard floating slowly high beyond the tree
tops,
Below, the red cedar festoon'd with tylandria, the pines and
cypresses growing out of the white sand that spreads far
and flat,
Rude boats descending the big Pedee, climbing plants, para-
sites with color'd flowers and berries enveloping huge
trees,
The waving drapery on the live-oak trailing long and low,
noiselessly waved by the wind,
The camp of Georgia wagoners just after dark, the supper-
fires and the cooking and eating by whites and negroes,
Thirty or forty great wagons, the mules, cattle, horses, feeding from troughs,
The shadows, gleams, up under the leaves of the old syca-
more-trees, the flames with the black smoke from the
pitch-pine curling and rising;
Southern fishermen fishing, the sounds and inlets of North
Carolina's coast, the shad-fishery and the herring-

fishery, the large sweep-seines, the windlasses on shore
work'd by horses, the clearing, curing, and packing-
houses;

Deep in the forest in piney woods turpentine dropping from
the incisions in the trees, there are the turpentine works,

There are the negroes at work in good health, the ground in
all directions is cover'd with pine straw;

In Tennessee and Kentucky slaves busy in the coalings, at
the forge, by the furnace-blaze, or at the corn-shucking,

In Virginia, the planter's son returning after a long absence,
joyfully welcom'd and kiss'd by the aged mulatto nurse,

On rivers boatmen safely moor'd at nightfall in their boats
under shelter of high banks,

Some of the younger men dance to the sound of the banjo or
fiddle, others sit on the gunwale smoking and talking;

Late in the afternoon the mocking-bird, the American mimic,
singing in the Great Dismal Swamp,

There are the greenish waters, the resinous odor, the plenteous moss, the cypress-tree, and the juniper-tree;

Northward, young men of Mannahatta, the target company
from an excursion returning home at evening, the mus-
ket-muzzles all bear bunches of flowers presented by
women;

Children at play, or on his father's lap a young boy fallen
asleep, (how his lips move! how he smiles in his sleep!)

The scout riding on horseback over the plains west of the
Mississippi, he ascends a knoll and sweeps his eyes
around;

California life, the miner, bearded, dress'd in his rude costume, the stanch California friendship, the sweet air, the
graves one in passing meets solitary just aside the horse-
path;

Down in Texas the cotton-field, the negro-cabins, drivers
driving mules or oxen before rude carts, cotton bales
piled on banks and wharves;

Encircling all, vast-darting up and wide, the American Soul,
with equal hemispheres, one Love, one Dilation or Pride;

In arriere the peace-talk with the Iroquois the aborigines, the
calumet, the pipe of good-will, arbitration, and indorsement,

The sachem blowing the smoke first toward the sun and then
toward the earth,

The drama of the scalp-dance enacted with painted faces and
guttural exclamations,

The setting out of the war-party, the long and stealthy march,

The single file, the swinging hatchets, the surprise and
slaughter of enemies;

All the acts, scenes, ways, persons, attitudes of these States,
reminiscences, institutions,

All these States compact, every square mile of these States
without excepting a particle;

Me pleas'd, rambling in lanes and country fields, Paumanok's
fields,

Observing the spiral flight of two little yellow butterflies
shuffling between each other, ascending high in the
air,

The darting swallow, the destroyer of insects, the fall traveler
southward but returning northward early in the spring,

The country boy at the close of the day driving the herd of
cows and shouting to them as they loiter to browse by
the roadside,

The city wharf, Boston, Philadelphia, Baltimore, Charleston,
New Orleans, San Francisco,

The departing ships when the sailors heave at the capstan;

Evening—me in my room—the setting sun,

The setting summer sun shining in my open window, showing
the swarm of flies, suspended, balancing in the air in the
centre of the room, darting athwart, up and down, casting swift shadows in specks on the opposite wall where
the shine is;

The athletic American matron speaking in public to crowds
of listeners,

Males, females, immigrants, combinations, the copiousness,
the individuality of the States, each for itself—the
money-makers,

Factories, machinery, the mechanical forces, the windlass,
lever, pulley, all certainties,

The certainty of space, increase, freedom, futurity,

In space the sporades, the scatter'd islands, the stars—on the
firm earth, the lands, my lands,

F                                                    w.

O lands! all so dear to me—what you are, (whatever it is,) I
      putting it at random in these songs, become a part of
      that, whatever it is,
Southward there, I screaming, with wings slow flapping, with
      the myriads of gulls wintering along the coasts of
      Florida,
Otherways there atwixt the banks of the Arkansas, the Rio
      Grande, the Nueces, the Brazos, the Tombigbee, the
      Red River, the Saskatchewan or the Osage, I with the
      spring waters laughing and skipping and running,
Northward, on the sands, on some shallow bay of Paumanok,
      I with parties of snowy herons wading in the wet to seek
      worms and aquatic plants,
Retreating, triumphantly twittering, the king-bird, from
      piercing the crow with its bill, for amusement—and I
      triumphantly twittering,
The migrating flock of wild geese alighting in autumn to
      refresh themselves, the body of the flock feed, the sen-
      tinels outside move around with erect heads watching,
      and are from time to time reliev'd by other sentinels—
      and I feeding and taking turns with the rest,
In Kanadian forests the moose, large as an ox, corner'd by
      hunters, rising desperately on his hind-feet, and plung-
      ing with his fore-feet, the hoofs as sharp as knives—and
      I, plunging at the hunters, corner'd and desperate,
In the Mannahatta, streets, piers, shipping, store-houses, and
      the countless workmen working in the shops,
And I too of the Mannahatta, singing thereof—and no less in
      myself than the whole of the Mannahatta in itself,
Singing the song of These, my ever-united lands—my body
      no more inevitably united, part to part, and made out of
      a thousand diverse contributions one identity, any more
      than my lands are inevitably united and made ONE
      IDENTITY;
Nativities, climates, the grass of the great pastoral Plains,
Cities, labors, death, animals, products, war, good and evil—
      these me,
These affording, in all their particulars, the old feuillage to
      me and to America, how can I do less than pass the clew
      of the union of them, to afford the like to you?

Whoever you are! how can I but offer you divine leaves, that
    you also be eligible as I am?
How can I but as here chanting, invite you for yourself to
    collect bouquets of the incomparable feuillage of these
    States?

1860                                                    1881


# *A Song of Joys*

O TO make the most jubilant song!
Full of music—full of manhood, womanhood, infancy!
Full of common employments—full of grain and trees.

O for the voices of animals—O for the swiftness and balance
    of fishes!
O for the dropping of raindrops in a song!
O for the sunshine and motion of waves in a song!

O the joy of my spirit—it is uncaged—it darts like lightning!
It is not enough to have this globe or a certain time,
I will have thousands of globes and all time.

O the engineer's joys! to go with a locomotive!
To hear the hiss of steam, the merry shriek, the steam-whistle,
    the laughing locomotive!
To push with resistless way and speed off in the distance.

O the gleesome saunter over fields and hillsides!
The leaves and flowers of the commonest weeds, the moist
    fresh stillness of the woods,
The exquisite smell of the earth at daybreak, and all through
    the forenoon.

O the horseman's and horsewoman's joys!
The saddle, the gallop, the pressure upon the seat, the cool
    gurgling by the ears and hair.

O the fireman's joys!
I hear the alarm at dead of night,
I hear bells, shouts! I pass the crowd, I run!
The sight of the flames maddens me with pleasure.

O the joy of the strong-brawn'd fighter, towering in the arena
in perfect condition, conscious of power, thirsting to
meet his opponent.

O the joy of that vast elemental sympathy which only the
human soul is capable of generating and emitting in
steady and limitless floods.

O the mother's joys!
The watching, the endurance, the precious love, the anguish,
the patiently yielded life.

O the joy of increase, growth, recuperation,
The joy of soothing and pacifying, the joy of concord and
harmony.

O to go back to the place where I was born,
To hear the birds sing once more,
To ramble about the house and barn and over the fields once
more,
And through the orchard and along the old lanes once more.

O to have been brought up on bays, lagoons, creeks, or along
the coast,
To continue and be employ'd there all my life,
The briny and damp smell, the shore, the salt weeds exposed
at low water,
The work of fishermen, the work of the eel-fisher and clam-
fisher;
I come with my clam-rake and spade, I come with my eel-
spear,
Is the tide out? I join the group of clam-diggers on the flats,
I laugh and work with them, I joke at my work like a mettle-
some young man;
In winter I take my eel-basket and eel-spear and travel out on
foot on the ice—I have a small axe to cut holes in the ice,

Behold me well-clothed going gayly or returning in the
    afternoon, my brood of tough boys accompanying
    me,
My brood of grown and part-grown boys, who love to be
    with no one else so well as they love to be with me,
By day to work with me, and by night to sleep with me.

Another time in warm weather out in a boat, to lift the
    lobster-pots where they are sunk with heavy stones, (I
    know the buoys,)
O the sweetness of the Fifth-month morning upon the water
    as I row just before sunrise toward the buoys,
I pull the wicker pots up slantingly, the dark green lobsters
    are desperate with their claws as I take them out, I insert
    wooden pegs in the joints of their pincers,
I go to all the places one after another, and then row back to
    the shore,
There in a huge kettle of boiling water the lobsters shall be
    boil'd till their color becomes scarlet.

Another time mackerel-taking,
Voracious, mad for the hook, near the surface, they seem to
    fill the water for miles;
Another time fishing for rock-fish in Chesapeake Bay, I one
    of the brown-faced crew;
Another time trailing for blue-fish off Paumanok, I stand
    with braced body,
My left foot is on the gunwale, my right arm throws far out
    the coils of slender rope,
In sight around me the quick veering and darting of fifty
    skiffs, my companions.

O boating on the rivers,
The voyage down the St. Lawrence, the superb scenery, the
    steamers,
The ships sailing, the Thousand Islands, the occasional tim-
    ber-raft and the raftsmen with long-reaching sweep-
    oars,
The little huts on the rafts, and the stream of smoke when
    they cook supper at evening.

(O something pernicious and dread!
Something far away from a puny and pious life!
Something unproved! something in a trance!
Something escaped from the anchorage and driving free.)

O to work in mines, or forging iron,
Foundry casting, the foundry itself, the rude high roof, the
    ample and shadow'd space,
The furnace, the hot liquid pour'd out and running.

O to resume the joys of the soldier!
To feel the presence of a brave commanding officer—to feel
    his sympathy!
To behold his calmness—to be warm'd in the rays of his
    smile!
To go to battle—to hear the bugles play and the drums beat!
To hear the crash of artillery—to see the glittering of the
    bayonets and musket-barrels in the sun!
To see men fall and die and not complain!
To taste the savage taste of blood—to be so devilish!
To gloat so over the wounds and deaths of the enemy.

O the whaleman's joys! O I cruise my old cruise again!
I feel the ship's motion under me, I feel the Atlantic breezes
    fanning me,
I hear the cry again sent down from the mast-head, *There—
    she blows!*
Again I spring up the rigging to look with the rest—we de-
    scend, wild with excitement,
I leap in the lower'd boat, we row toward our prey where he
    lies,
We approach stealthy and silent, I see the mountainous mass,
    lethargic, basking,
I see the harpooner standing up, I see the weapon dart from
    his vigorous arm;
O swift again far out in the ocean the wounded whale,
    settling, running to windward, tows me,
Again I see him rise to breathe, we row close again,
I see a lance driven through his side, press'd deep, turn'd in
    the wound,

Again we back off, I see him settle again, the life is leaving
    him fast,
As he rises he spouts blood, I see him swim in circles nar-
    rower and narrower, swiftly cutting the water—I see
    him die,
He gives one convulsive leap in the centre of the circle, and
    then falls flat and still in the bloody foam.

O the old manhood of me, my noblest joy of all!
My children and grand-children, my white hair and beard,
My largeness, calmness, majesty, out of the long stretch of
    my life.

O ripen'd joy of womanhood! O happiness at last!
I am more than eighty years of age, I am the most venerable
    mother,
How clear is my mind—how all people draw nigh to me!
What attractions are these beyond any before? what bloom
    more than the bloom of youth?
What beauty is this that descends upon me and rises out of me?

O the orator's joys!
To inflate the chest, to roll the thunder of the voice out from
    the ribs and throat,
To make the people rage, weep, hate, desire, with yourself,
To lead America—to quell America with a great tongue.

O the joy of my soul leaning pois'd on itself, receiving iden-
    tity through materials and loving them, observing char-
    acters and absorbing them,
My soul vibrated back to me from them, from sight, hearing,
    touch, reason, articulation, comparison, memory, and
    the like,
The real life of my senses and flesh transcending my senses
    and flesh,
My body done with materials, my sight done with my
    material eyes,
Proved to me this day beyond cavil that it is not my material
    eyes which finally see,
Nor my material body which finally loves, walks, laughs,
    shouts, embraces, procreates.

O the farmer's joys!
Ohioan's, Illinoisian's, Wisconsinese', Kanadian's, Iowan's,
    Kansian's, Missourian's, Oregonese' joys!
To rise at peep of day and pass forth nimbly to work,
To plough land in the fall for winter-sown crops,
To plough land in the spring for maize,
To train orchards, to graft the trees, to gather apples in the
    fall.

O to bathe in the swimming-bath, or in a good place along
    shore,
To splash the water! to walk ankle-deep, or race naked along
    the shore.

O to realize space!
The plenteousness of all, that there are no bounds,
To emerge and be of the sky, of the sun and moon and flying
    clouds, as one with them.

O the joy of a manly self-hood!
To be servile to none, to defer to none, not to any tyrant
    known or unknown,
To walk with erect carriage, a step springy and elastic,
To look with calm gaze or with a flashing eye,
To speak with a full and sonorous voice out of a broad chest,
To confront with your personality all the other personalities
    of the earth.

Know'st thou the excellent joys of youth?
Joys of the dear companions and of the merry word and
    laughing face?
Joy of the glad light-beaming day, joy of the wide-breath'd
    games?
Joy of sweet music, joy of the lighted ball-room and the
    dancers?
Joy of the plenteous dinner, strong carouse and drinking?

Yet O my soul supreme!
Know'st thou the joys of pensive thought?
Joys of the free and lonesome heart, the tender, gloomy
    heart?

Joys of the solitary walk, the spirit bow'd yet proud, the
    suffering and the struggle?
The agonistic throes, the ecstasies, joys of the solemn mus-
    ings day or night?
Joys of the thought of Death, the great spheres Time and
    Space?
Prophetic joys of better, loftier love's ideals, the divine wife,
    the sweet, eternal, perfect comrade?
Joys all thine own undying one, joys worthy thee O soul.

O while I live to be the ruler of life, not a slave,
To meet life as a powerful conqueror,
No fumes, no ennui, no more complaints or scornful
    criticisms,
To these proud laws of the air, the water and the ground,
    proving my interior soul impregnable,
And nothing exterior shall ever take command of me.

For not life's joys alone I sing, repeating—the joy of death!
The beautiful touch of Death, soothing and benumbing a
    few moments, for reasons,
Myself discharging my excrementitious body to be burn'd, or
    render'd to powder, or buried,
My real body doubtless left to me for other spheres,
My voided body nothing more to me, returning to the puri-
    fications, further offices, eternal uses of the earth.

O to attract by more than attraction!
How it is I know not—yet behold! the something which
    obeys none of the rest,
It is offensive, never defensive—yet how magnetic it draws.

O to struggle against great odds, to meet enemies undaunted!
To be entirely alone with them, to find how much one can
    stand!
To look strife, torture, prison, popular odium, face to
    face!
To mount the scaffold, to advance to the muzzles of guns
    with perfect nonchalance!
To be indeed a God!

O to sail to sea in a ship!
To leave this steady unendurable land,
To leave the tiresome sameness of the streets, the sidewalks
    and the houses,
To leave you O you solid motionless land, and entering a
    ship,
To sail and sail and sail!

O to have life henceforth a poem of new joys!
To dance, clap hands, exult, shout, skip, leap, roll on, float
    on!
To be a sailor of the world bound for all ports,
A ship itself, (see indeed these sails I spread to the sun and
    air,)
A swift and swelling ship full of rich words, full of joys.
1860                                                 1881

# Song of the Broad-Axe

## 1

WEAPON shapely, naked, wan,
Head from the mother's bowels drawn,
Wooded flesh and metal bone, limb only one and lip only
    one,
Gray-blue leaf by red-heat grown, helve produced from a
    little seed sown,
Resting the grass amid and upon,
To be lean'd and to lean on.

Strong shapes and attributes of strong shapes, masculine
    trades, sights and sounds,
Long varied train of an emblem, dabs of music,
Fingers of the organist skipping staccato over the keys of the
    great organ.

## 2

Welcome are all earth's lands, each for its kind,
Welcome are lands of pine and oak,

Welcome are lands of the lemon and fig,
Welcome are lands of gold,
Welcome are lands of wheat and maize, welcome those of the
    grape,
Welcome are lands of sugar and rice,
Welcome the cotton-lands, welcome those of the white
    potato and sweet potato,
Welcome are mountains, flats, sands, forests, prairies,
Welcome the rich borders of rivers, table-lands, openings,
Welcome the measureless grazing-lands, welcome the teem-
    ing soil of orchards, flax, honey, hemp;
Welcome just as much the other more hard-faced lands,
Lands rich as lands of gold or wheat and fruit lands,
Lands of mines, lands of the manly and rugged ores,
Lands of coal, copper, lead, tin, zinc,
Lands of iron—lands of the make of the axe.


### 3

The log at the wood-pile, the axe supported by it,
The sylvan hut, the vine over the doorway, the space clear'd
    for a garden,
The irregular tapping of rain down on the leaves after the
    storm is lull'd,
The wailing and moaning at intervals, the thought of the sea,
The thought of ships struck in the storm and put on their
    beam ends, and the cutting away of masts,
The sentiment of the huge timbers of old-fashion'd houses
    and barns,
The remember'd print or narrative, the voyage at a venture
    of men, families, goods,
The disembarkation, the founding of a new city,
The voyage of those who sought a New England and found
    it, the outset anywhere,
The settlements of the Arkansas, Colorado, Ottawa, Willa-
    mette,
The slow progress, the scant fare, the axe, rifle, saddle-bags;
The beauty of all adventurous and daring persons,
The beauty of wood-boys and wood-men with their clear
    untrimm'd faces,

The beauty of independence, departure, actions that rely on themselves,

The American contempt for statutes and ceremonies, the boundless impatience of restraint,

The loose drift of character, the inkling through random types, the solidification;

The butcher in the slaughter-house, the hands aboard schooners and sloops, the raftsmen, the pioneer,

Lumbermen in their winter camp, daybreak in the woods, stripes of snow on the limbs of trees, the occasional snapping,

The glad clear sound of one's own voice, the merry song, the natural life of the woods, the strong day's work,

The blazing fire at night, the sweet taste of supper, the talk, the bed of hemlock-boughs and the bear-skin;

The house-builder at work in cities or anywhere,

The preparatory jointing, squaring, sawing, mortising,

The hoist-up of beams, the push of them in their places, laying them regular,

Setting the studs by their tenons in the mortises according as they were prepared,

The blows of mallets and hammers, the attitudes of the men, their curv'd limbs,

Bending, standing, astride the beams, driving in pins, holding on by posts and braces,

The hook'd arm over the plate, the other arm wielding the axe,

The floor-men forcing the planks close to be nail'd,

Their postures bringing their weapons downward on the bearers,

The echoes resounding through the vacant building;

The huge storehouse carried up in the city well under way,

The six framing-men, two in the middle and two at each end, carefully bearing on their shoulders a heavy stick for a cross-beam,

The crowded line of masons with trowels in their right hands rapidly laying the long side-wall, two hundred feet from front to rear,

The flexible rise and fall of backs, the continual click of the trowels striking the bricks,

The bricks one after another each laid so workmanlike in its place, and set with a knock of the trowel-handle,

The piles of materials, the mortar on the mortar-boards, and the steady replenishing by the hod-men;

Spar-makers in the spar-yard, the swarming row of well-grown apprentices,

The swing of their axes on the square-hew'd log shaping it toward the shape of a mast,

The brisk short crackle of the steel driven slantingly into the pine,

The butter-color'd chips flying off in great flakes and slivers,

The limber motion of brawny young arms and hips in easy costumes,

The constructor of wharves, bridges, piers, bulk-heads, floats, stays against the sea;

The city fireman, the fire that suddenly bursts forth in the close-pack'd square,

The arriving engines, the hoarse shouts, the nimble stepping and daring,

The strong command through the fire-trumpets, the falling in line, the rise and fall of the arms forcing the water,

The slender, spasmic, blue-white jets, the bringing to bear of the hooks and ladders and their execution,

The crash and cut away of connecting wood-work, or through floors if the fire smoulders under them,

The crowd with their lit faces watching, the glare and dense shadows;

The forger at his forge-furnace and the user of iron after him,

The maker of the axe large and small, and the welder and temperer,

The chooser breathing his breath on the cold steel and trying the edge with his thumb,

The one who clean-shapes the handle and sets it firmly in the socket;

The shadowy processions of the portraits of the past users also,

The primal patient mechanics, the architects and engineers,

The far-off Assyrian edifice and Mizra edifice,

The Roman lictors preceding the consuls,

The antique European warrior with his axe in combat,

The uplifted arm, the clatter of blows on the helmeted head,
The death-howl, the limpsy tumbling body, the rush of
friend and foe thither,
The siege of revolted lieges determin'd for liberty,
The summons to surrender, the battering at castle gates, the
truce and parley,
The sack of an old city in its time,
The bursting in of mercenaries and bigots tumultuously and
disorderly,
Roar, flames, blood, drunkenness, madness,
Goods freely rifled from houses and temples, screams of
women in the gripe of brigands,
Craft and thievery of camp-followers, men running, old per-
sons despairing,
The hell of war, the cruelties of creeds,
The list of all executive deeds and words just or unjust,
The power of personality just or unjust.

### 4

Muscle and pluck forever!
What invigorates life invigorates death,
And the dead advance as much as the living advance,
And the future is no more uncertain than the present,
For the roughness of the earth and of man encloses as much
as the delicatesse of the earth and of man,
And nothing endures but personal qualities.

What do you think endures?
Do you think a great city endures?
Or a teeming manufacturing state? or a prepared constitu-
tion? or the best built steamships?
Or hotels of granite and iron? or any chef-d'œuvres of en-
gineering, forts, armaments?

Away! these are not to be cherish'd for themselves,
They fill their hour, the dancers dance, the musicians play for
them,
The show passes, all does well enough of course,
All does very well till one flash of defiance.

A great city is that which has the greatest men and women,
If it be a few ragged huts it is still the greatest city in the
whole world.

5

The place where a great city stands is not the place of
stretch'd wharves, docks, manufactures, deposits of
produce merely,
Nor the place of ceaseless salutes of new-comers or the
anchor-lifters of the departing,
Nor the place of the tallest and costliest buildings or shops
selling goods from the rest of the earth,
Nor the place of the best libraries and schools, nor the place
where money is plentiest,
Nor the place of the most numerous population.

Where the city stands with the brawniest breed of orators and
bards,
Where the city stands that is belov'd by these, and loves them
in return and understands them,
Where no monuments exist to heroes but in the common
words and deeds,
Where thrift is in its place, and prudence is in its place,
Where the men and women think lightly of the laws,
Where the slave ceases, and the master of slaves ceases,
Where the populace rise at once against the never-ending
audacity of elected persons,
Where fierce men and women pour forth as the sea to the
whistle of death pours its sweeping and unript waves,
Where outside authority enters always after the precedence
of inside authority,
Where the citizen is always the head and ideal, and Presi-
dent, Mayor, Governor and what not, are agents for
pay,
Where children are taught to be laws to themselves, and to
depend on themselves,
Where equanimity is illustrated in affairs,
Where speculations on the soul are encouraged,
Where women walk in public processions in the streets the
same as the men,

Where they enter the public assembly and take places the
    same as the men;
Where the city of the faithfulest friends stands,
Where the city of the cleanliness of the sexes stands,
Where the city of the healthiest fathers stands,
Where the city of the best-bodied mothers stands,
There the great city stands.

6

How beggarly appear arguments before a defiant deed!
How the floridness of the materials of cities shrivels before a
    man's or woman's look!

All waits or goes by default till a strong being appears;
A strong being is the proof of the race and of the ability of the
    universe,
When he or she appears materials are overaw'd,
The dispute on the soul stops,
The old customs and phrases are confronted, turn'd back, or
    laid away.

What is your money-making now? what can it do now?
What is your respectability now?
What are your theology, tuition, society, traditions, statute-
    books, now?
Where are your jibes of being now?
Where are your cavils about the soul now?

7

A sterile landscape covers the ore, there is as good as the best
    for all the forbidding appearance,
There is the mine, there are the miners,
The forge-furnace is there, the melt is accomplish'd, the
    hammers-men are at hand with their tongs and hammers,
What always served and always serves is at hand.

Than this nothing has better served, it has served all,
Served the fluent-tongued and subtle-sensed Greek, and long
    ere the Greek,
Served in building the buildings that last longer than any,

Served the Hebrew, the Persian, the most ancient Hindu-
    stanee,
Served the mound-raiser on the Mississippi, served those
    whose relics remain in Central America,
Served Albic temples in woods or on plains, with unhewn
    pillars and the druids,
Served the artificial clefts, vast, high, silent, on the snow-
    cover'd hills of Scandinavia,
Served those who time out of mind made on the granite
    walls rough sketches of the sun, moon, stars, ships,
    ocean waves,
Served the paths of the irruptions of the Goths, served the
    pastoral tribes and nomads,
Served the long distant Kelt, served the hardy pirates of the
    Baltic,
Served before any of those the venerable and harmless men
    of Ethiopia,
Served the making of helms for the galleys of pleasure and
    the making of those for war,
Served all great works on land and all great works on the sea,
For the mediæval ages and before the mediæval ages,
Served not the living only then as now, but served the dead.

## 8

I see the European headsman,
He stands mask'd, clothed in red, with huge legs and strong
    naked arms,
And leans on a ponderous axe.

(Whom have you slaughter'd lately European headsman?
Whose is that blood upon you so wet and sticky?)

I see the clear sunsets of the martyrs,
I see from the scaffolds the descending ghosts,
Ghosts of dead lords, uncrown'd ladies, impeach'd ministers,
    rejected kings,
Rivals, traitors, poisoners, disgraced chieftains and the rest.

I see those who in any land have died for the good cause,
The seed is spare, nevertheless the crop shall never run out,

(Mind you O foreign kings, O priests, the crop shall never
    run out.)

I see the blood wash'd entirely away from the axe,
Both blade and helve are clean,
They spirt no more the blood of European nobles, they clasp
    no more the necks of queens.

I see the headsman withdraw and become useless,
I see the scaffold untrodden and mouldy, I see no longer any
    axe upon it,
I see the mighty and friendly emblem of the power of my own
    race, the newest, largest race.

### 9

(America! I do not vaunt my love for you,
I have what I have.)

The axe leaps!
The solid forest gives fluid utterances,
They tumble forth, they rise and form,
Hut, tent, landing, survey,
Flail, plough, pick, crowbar, spade,
Shingle, rail, prop, wainscot, jamb, lath, panel, gable,
Citadel, ceiling, saloon, academy, organ, exhibition-house,
    library,
Cornice, trellis, pilaster, balcony, window, turret, porch,
Hoe, rake, pitchfork, pencil, wagon, staff, saw, jack-plane,
    mallet, wedge, rounce,
Chair, tub, hoop, table, wicket, vane, sash, floor,
Work-box, chest, string'd instrument, boat, frame, and what
    not,
Capitols of States, and capitol of the nation of States,
Long stately rows in avenues, hospitals for orphans or for
    the poor or sick,
Manhattan steamboats and clippers taking the measure of all
    seas.

The shapes arise!
Shapes of the using of axes anyhow, and the users and all that
    neighbors them,

Cutters down of wood and haulers of it to the Penobscot or
    Kennebec,
Dwellers in cabins among the Californian mountains or by
    the little lakes, or on the Columbia,
Dwellers south on the banks of the Gila or Rio Grande,
    friendly gatherings, the characters and fun,
Dwellers along the St. Lawrence, or north in Kanada, or
    down by the Yellowstone, dwellers on coasts and off
    coasts,
Seal-fishers, whalers, arctic seamen breaking passages
    through the ice.

The shapes arise!
Shapes of factories, arsenals, foundries, markets,
Shapes of the two-threaded tracks of railroads,
Shapes of the sleepers of bridges, vast frameworks, girders,
    arches,
Shapes of the fleets of barges, tows, lake and canal craft,
    river craft,
Ship-yards and dry-docks along the Eastern and Western
    seas, and in many a bay and by-place,
The live-oak kelsons, the pine planks, the spars, the hack-
    matack-roots for knees,
The ships themselves on their ways, the tiers of scaffolds, the
    workmen busy outside and inside,
The tools lying around, the great auger and little auger, the
    adze, bolt, line, square, gouge, and bead-plane.

### 10

The shapes arise!
The shape measur'd, saw'd, jack'd, join'd, stain'd,
The coffin-shape for the dead to lie within in his shroud,
The shape got out in posts, in the bedstead posts, in the posts
    of the bride's bed,
The shape of the little trough, the shape of the rockers be-
    neath, the shape of the babe's cradle,
The shape of the floor-planks, the floor-planks for dancer's
    feet,
The shape of the planks of the family home, the home of the
    friendly parents and children,

The shape of the roof of the home of the happy young man
and woman, the roof over the well-married young man
and woman,
The roof over the supper joyously cook'd by the chaste wife,
and joyously eaten by the chaste husband, content after
his day's work.

The shapes arise!
The shape of the prisoner's place in the court-room, and of
him or her seated in the place.
The shape of the liquor-bar lean'd against by the young rum-
drinker and the old rum-drinker,
The shape of the shamed and angry stairs trod by sneaking
footsteps,
The shape of the sly settee, and the adulterous unwholesome
couple,
The shape of the gambling-board with its devilish winnings
and losings,
The shape of the step-ladder for the convicted and sentenced
murderer, the murderer with haggard face and pinion'd
arms,
The sheriff at hand with his deputies, the silent and white-
lipp'd crowd, the dangling of the rope.

The shapes arise!
Shapes of doors giving many exits and entrances,
The door passing the dissever'd friend flush'd and in haste,
The door that admits good news and bad news,
The door whence the son left home confident and puff'd up,
The door he enter'd again from a long and scandaious ab-
sence, diseas'd, broken down, without innocence, with-
out means.

## 11

Her shape arises,
She less guarded than ever, yet more guarded than ever,
The gross and soil'd she moves among do not make her gross
and soil'd,
She knows the thoughts as she passes, nothing is conceal'd
from her,

She is none the less considerate or friendly therefor,
She is the best belov'd, it is without exception, she has no
  reason to fear and she does not fear,
Oaths, quarrels, hiccupp'd songs, smutty expressions are idle
  to her as she passes,
She is silent, she is possess'd of herself, they do not offend
  her,
She receives them as the laws of Nature receive them, she is
  strong,
She too is a law of Nature—there is no law stronger than
  she is.

### 12

The main shapes arise!
Shapes of Democracy total, result of centuries,
Shapes ever projecting other shapes,
Shapes of turbulent manly cities,
Shapes of the friends and home-givers of the whole earth,
Shapes bracing the earth and braced with the whole earth.
1856                                                    1881


# Song of the Exposition

### 1

(Ah little recks the laborer,
How near his work is holding him to God,
The loving Laborer through space and time.)

After all not to create only, or found only,
But to bring perhaps from afar what is already founded,
To give it our own identity, average, limitless, free,
To fill the gross the torpid bulk with vital religious fire,
Not to repel or destroy so much as accept, fuse, rehabilitate,
To obey as well as command, to follow more than to lead,
These also are the lessons of our New World;
While how little the New after all, how much the Old, Old
  World!

Long and long has the grass been growing,
Long and long has the rain been falling,
Long has the globe been rolling round.

### 2

Come Muse migrate from Greece and Ionia,
Cross out please those immensely overpaid accounts,
That matter of Troy and Achilles' wrath, and Æneas', Odys-
    seus' wanderings,
Placard "Removed" and "To Let" on the rocks of your
    snowy Parnassus,
Repeat at Jerusalem, place the notice high on Jaffa's gate and
    on Mount Moriah,
The same on the walls of your German, French and Spanish
    castles, and Italian collections,
For know a better, fresher, busier sphere, a wide, untried
    domain awaits, demands you.

### 3

Responsive to our summons,
Or rather to her long-nurs'd inclination,
Join'd with an irresistible, natural gravitation,
She comes! I hear the rustling of her gown,
I scent the odor of her breath's delicious fragrance,
I mark her step divine, her curious eyes a-turning, rolling,
Upon this very scene.

The dame of dames! can I believe then,
Those ancient temples, sculptures classic, could none of them
    retain her?
Nor shades of Virgil and Dante, nor myriad memories,
    poems, old associations, magnetize and hold on to her?
But that she's left them all—and here?

Yes, if you will allow me to say so,
I, my friends, if you do not, can plainly see her,
The same undying soul of earth's, activity's, beauty's, hero-
    ism's expression,
Out from her evolutions hither come, ended the strata of her
    former themes,

Hidden and cover'd by to-day's, foundation of to-day's,
Ended, deceas'd through time, her voice by Castaly's fountain,
Silent the broken-lipp'd Sphynx in Egypt, silent all those century-baffling tombs,
Ended for aye the epics of Asia's, Europe's helmeted warriors, ended the primitive call of the muses,
Calliope's call forever closed, Clio, Melpomene, Thalia dead,
Ended the stately rhythmus of Una and Oriana, ended the quest of the Holy Graal,
Jerusalem a handful of ashes blown by the wind, extinct,
The Crusaders' streams of shadowy midnight troops sped with the sunrise,
Amadis, Tancred, utterly gone, Charlemagne, Roland, Oliver gone,
Palmerin, ogre, departed, vanish'd the turrets that Usk from its waters reflected,
Arthur vanish'd with all his knights, Merlin and Lancelot and Galahad, all gone, dissolv'd utterly like an exhalation;
Pass'd! pass'd! for us, forever pass'd, that once so mighty world, now void, inanimate, phantom world,
Embroider'd, dazzling, foreign world, with all its gorgeous legends, myths,
Its kings and castles proud, its priests and warlike lords and courtly dames,
Pass'd to its charnel vault, coffin'd with crown and armor on,
Blazon'd with Shakspere's purple page,
And dirged by Tennyson's sweet sad rhyme.

I say I see, my friends, if you do not, the illustrious emigré,
(having it is true in her day, although the same, changed, journey'd considerable,)
Making directly for this rendezvous, vigorously clearing a path for herself, striding through the confusion,
By thud of machinery and shrill steam-whistle undismay'd,
Bluff'd not a bit by drain-pipe, gasometers, artificial fertilizers,
Smiling and pleas'd with palpable intent to stay,
She's here, install'd amid the kitchen ware!

**4**

But hold—don't I forget my manners?
To introduce the stranger, (what else indeed do I live to
  chant for?) to thee Columbia;
In liberty's name welcome immortal! clasp hands,
And ever henceforth sisters dear be both.

Fear not O Muse! truly new ways and days receive, surround
  you,
I candidly confess a queer, queer race, of novel fashion,
And yet the same old human race, the same within, without,
Faces and hearts the same, feelings the same, yearnings the
  same,
The same old love, beauty and use the same.

**5**

We do not blame thee elder World, nor really separate our-
  selves from thee,
(Would the son separate himself from the father?)
Looking back on thee, seeing thee to thy duties, grandeurs,
  through past ages bending, building,
We build to ours to-day.

Mightier than Egypt's tombs,
Fairer than Grecia's, Roma's temples,
Prouder then Milan's statued, spired, cathedral,
More picturesque than Rhenish castle-keeps,
We plan even now to raise, beyond them all,
Thy great cathedral sacred industry, no tomb,
A keep for life for practical invention.

As in a waking vision,
E'en while I chant I see it rise, I scan and prophesy outside
  and in,
Its manifold ensemble.

Around a palace, loftier, fairer, ampler than any yet,
Earth's modern wonder, history's seven outstripping,
High rising tier on tier with glass and iron façades,
Gladdening the sun and sky, enhued in cheerfulest hues,

Bronze, lilac, robin's-egg, marine and crimson,
Over whose golden roof shall flaunt, beneath thy banner
    Freedom,
The banners of the States and flags of every land,
A brood of lofty, fair, but lesser palaces shall cluster.

Somewhere within their walls shall all that forwards perfect
    human life be started,
Tried, taught, advanced, visibly exhibited.

Not only all the world of works, trade, products,
But all the workmen of the world here to be represented.

Here shall you trace in flowing operation,
In every state of practical, busy movement, the rills of civili-
    zation,
Materials here under your eye shall change their shape as if
    by magic,
The cotton shall be pick'd almost in the very field,
Shall be dried, clean'd, ginn'd, baled, spun into thread and
    cloth before you,
You shall see hands at work at all the old processes and all
    the new ones,
You shall see the various grains and how flour is made and
    then bread baked by the bakers,
You shall see the crude ores of California and Nevada pass-
    ing on and on till they become bullion,
You shall watch how the printer sets type, and learn what a
    composing-stick is,
You shall mark in amazement the Hoe press whirling its
    cylinders, shedding the printed leaves steady and fast,
The photograph, model, watch, pin, nail, shall be created
    before you.

In large calm halls, a stately museum shall teach you the
    infinite lessons of minerals,
In another, woods, plants, vegetation shall be illustrated—in
    another animals, animal life and development.

One stately house shall be the music house,
Others for other arts—learning, the sciences, shall all be here,

None shall be slighted, none but shall here be honor'd,
    help'd, exampled.

### 6

(This, this and these, America, shall be *your* pyramids and
    obelisks,
Your Alexandrian Pharos, gardens of Babylon,
Your temple at Olympia.)

The male and female many laboring not,
Shall ever here confront the laboring many,
With precious benefits to both, glory to all,
To thee America, and thee eternal Muse.

And here shall ye inhabit powerful Matrons!
In your vast state vaster than all the old,
Echoed through long, long centuries to come,
To sound of different, prouder songs, with stronger themes,
Practical, peaceful life, the people's life, the People them-
    selves,
Lifted, illumin'd, bathed in peace—elate, secure in peace.

### 7

Away with themes of war! away with war itself!
Hence from my shuddering sight to never more return that
    show of blacken'd, mutilated corpses!
That hell unpent and raid of blood, fit for wild tigers or for
    lop-tongued wolves, not reasoning men,
And in its stead speed industry's campaigns,
With thy undaunted armies, engineering,
Thy pennants labor, loosen'd to the breeze,
Thy bugles sounding loud and clear.

Away with old romance!
Away with novels, plots and plays of foreign courts,
Away with love-verses, sugar'd in rhyme, the intrigues,
    amours of idlers,
Fitted for only banquets of the night where dancers to late
    music slide,
The unhealthy pleasures, extravagant dissipation of the few,

With perfumes, heat and wine, beneath the dazzling chandeliers.

To you ye reverent sane sisters,
I raise a voice for far superber themes for poets and for art,
To exalt the present and the real,
To teach the average man the glory of his daily walk and
   trade,
To sing in songs how exercise and chemical life are never to
   be baffled,
To manual work for each and all, to plough, hoe, dig,
To plant and tend the tree, the berry, vegetables, flowers,
For every man to see to it that he really do something, for
   every woman too;
To use the hammer and the saw, (rip, or cross-cut,)
To cultivate a turn for carpentering, plastering, painting,
To work as tailor, tailoress, nurse, hostler, porter,
To invent a little, something ingenious, to aid the washing,
   cooking, cleaning,
And hold it no disgrace to take a hand at them themselves.

I say I bring thee Muse to-day and here,
All occupations, duties broad and close,
Toil, healthy toil and sweat, endless, without cessation,
The old, old practical burdens, interests, joys,
The family, parentage, childhood, husband and wife,
The house-comforts, the house itself and all its belongings,
Food and its preservation, chemistry applied to it,
Whatever forms the average, strong, complete, sweet-blooded
   man or woman, the perfect longeve personality,
And helps its present life to health and happiness, and shapes
   its soul,
For the eternal real life to come.

With latest connections, works, the inter-transportation of
   the world,
Steam-power, the great express lines, gas, petroleum,
These triumphs of our time, the Atlantic's delicate cable,
The Pacific railroad, the Suez canal, the Mont Cenis and
   Gothard and Hoosac tunnels, the Brooklyn bridge,

This earth all spann'd with iron rails, with lines of steamships
    threading every sea,
Our own rondure, the current globe I bring.

### 8

And thou America,
Thy offspring towering e'er so high, yet higher Thee above all
    towering,
With Victory on thy left, and at thy right hand Law;
Thou Union holding all, fusing, absorbing, tolerating all,
Thee, ever thee, I sing.

Thou, also thou, a World,
With all thy wide geographies, manifold, different, distant,
Rounded by thee in one—one common orbic language,
One common indivisible destiny for All.

And by the spells which ye vouchsafe to those your ministers
    in earnest,
I here personify and call my themes, to make them pass
    before ye.

Behold, America! (and thou, ineffable guest and sister!)
For thee come trooping up thy waters and thy lands;
Behold! thy fields and farms, thy far-off woods and moun-
    tains,
As in procession coming.

Behold, the sea itself,
And on its limitless, heaving breast, the ships;
See, where their white sails, bellying in the wind, speckle the
    green and blue,
See, the steamers coming and going, steaming in or out of
    port,
See, dusky and undulating, the long pennants of smoke.

Behold, in Oregon, far in the north and west,
Or in Maine, far in the north and east, thy cheerful axemen,
Wielding all day their axes.

Behold, on the lakes, thy pilots at their wheels, thy oarsmen,
How the ash writhes under those muscular arms!

There by the furnace, and there by the anvil,
Behold thy sturdy blacksmiths swinging their sledges,
Overhand so steady, overhand they turn and fall with joyous
    clank,
Like a tumult of laughter.

Mark the spirit of invention everywhere, thy rapid patents,
Thy continual workshops, foundries, risen or rising,
See, from their chimneys how the tall flame-fires stream.

Mark, thy interminable farms, North, South,
Thy wealthy daughter-states, Eastern and Western,
The varied products of Ohio, Pennsylvania, Missouri,
    Georgia, Texas, and the rest,
Thy limitless crops, grass, wheat, sugar, oil, corn, rice, hemp,
    hops,
Thy barns all fill'd, the endless freight-train and the bulging
    storehouse,
The grapes that ripen on thy vines, the apples in thy orchards,
Thy incalculable lumber, beef, pork, potatoes, thy coal, thy
    gold and silver,
The inexhaustible iron in thy mines.

All thine, O sacred Union!
Ships, farms, shops, barns, factories, mines,
City and State, North, South, item and aggregate,
We dedicate, dread Mother, all to thee!

Protectress absolute, thou! bulwark of all!
For well we know that while thou givest each and all, (gener-
    ous as God,)
Without thee neither all nor each, nor land, home,
Nor ship, nor mine, nor any here this day secure,
Nor aught, nor any day secure.

9

And thou, the Emblem waving over all!
Delicate beauty, a word to thee, (it may be salutary,)

Remember thou hast not always been as here to-day so com-
 fortably ensovereign'd,
In other scenes than these have I observ'd thee flag,
Not quite so trim and whole and freshly blooming in folds of
 stainless silk,
But I have seen thee bunting, to tatters torn upon thy splin-
 ter'd staff,
Or clutch'd to some young color-bearer's breast with des-
 perate hands,
Savagely struggled for, for life or death, fought over long,
'Mid cannons' thunder-crash and many a curse and groan
 and yell, and rifle-volleys cracking sharp,
And moving masses as wild demons surging, and lives as
 nothing risk'd,
For thy mere remnant grimed with dirt and smoke and
 sopp'd in blood,
For sake of that, my beauty, and that thou might'st dally as
 now secure up there,
Many a good man have I seen go under.


Now here and these and hence in peace, all thine, O flag!
And here and hence for thee, O universal Muse! and thou for
 them!
And here and hence O Union, all the work and workmen
 thine!
None separate from thee—henceforth One only, we and thou,
(For the blood of the children, what is it, only the blood
 maternal?
And lives and works, what are they all at last, except the
 roads to faith and death?)


While we rehearse our measureless wealth, it is for thee, dear
 Mother,
We own it all and several to-day indissoluble in thee;
Think not our chant, our show, merely for products gross or
 lucre—it is for thee, the soul in thee, electric, spiritual!
Our farms, inventions, crops, we own in thee! cities and
 States in thee!
Our freedom all in thee! our very lives in thee!
1871               1881

# Song of the Redwood-Tree

## 1

A CALIFORNIA song,
A prophecy and indirection, a thought impalpable to breathe
    as air,
A chorus of dryads, fading, departing, or hamadryads de-
    parting,
A murmuring, fateful, giant voice, out of the earth and
    sky,
Voice of a mighty dying tree in the redwood forest dense.

*Farewell my brethren,*
*Farewell O earth and sky, farewell ye neighboring waters,*
*My time has ended, my term has come.*

Along the northern coast,
Just back from the rock-bound shore and the caves,
In the saline air from the sea in the Mendocino country,
With the surge for base and accompaniment low and hoarse,
With crackling blows of axes sounding musically driven by
    strong arms,
Riven deep by the sharp tongues of the axes, there in the red-
    wood forest dense,
I heard the mighty tree its death-chant chanting.

The choppers heard not, the camp shanties echoed not,
The quick-ear'd teamsters and chain and jack-screw men
    heard not,
As the wood-spirits came from their haunts of a thousand
    years to join the refrain,
But in my soul I plainly heard.

Murmuring out of its myriad leaves,
Down from its lofty top rising two hundred feet high,
Out of its stalwart trunk and limbs, out of its foot-thick
    bark,

That chant of the seasons and time, chant not of the past
    only but the future.

*You untold life of me,*
*And all you venerable and innocent joys,*
*Perennial hardy life of me with joys 'mid rain and many a*
    *summer sun,*
*And the white snows and night and the wild winds;*
*O the great patient rugged joys, my soul's strong joys unreck'd*
    *by man,*
*(For know I bear the soul befitting me, I too have conscious-*
    *ness, identity,*
*And all the rocks and mountains have, and all the earth,)*
*Joys of the life befitting me and brothers mine,*
*Our time, our term has come.*

*Nor yield we mournfully majestic brothers,*
*We who have grandly fill'd our time;*
*With Nature's calm content, with tacit huge delight,*
*We welcome what we wrought for through the past,*
*And leave the field for them.*
*For them predicted long,*
*For a superber race, they too to grandly fill their time,*
*For them we abdicate, in them ourselves ye forest kings!*
*In them these skies and airs, these mountain peaks, Shasta,*
    *Nevadas,*
*These huge precipitous cliffs, this amplitude, these valleys, far*
    *Yosemite,*
*To be in them absorb'd, assimilated.*

Then to a loftier strain,
Still prouder, more ecstatic rose the chant,
As if the heirs, the deities of the West,
Joining with master-tongue bore part.

*Not wan from Asia's fetiches,*
*Nor red from Europe's old dynastic slaughter-house,*
*(Area of murder-plots of thrones, with scent left yet of wars and*
    *scaffolds everywhere,)*
*But come from Nature's long and harmless throes, peacefully*
    *builded thence,*

*These virgin lands, lands of the Western shore,*
*To the new culminating man, to you, the empire new,*
*You promis'd long, we pledge, we dedicate.*

*You occult deep volitions,*
*You average spiritual manhood, purpose of all, pois'd on your-*
*    self, giving not taking law,*
*You womanhood divine, mistress and source of all, whence life*
*    and love and aught that comes from life and love,*
*You unseen moral essence of all the vast materials of America,*
*    (age upon age working in death the same as life,)*
*You that, sometimes known, oftener unknown, really shape*
*    and mould the New World, adjusting it to Time and*
*    Space,*
*You hidden national will lying in your abysms, conceal'd but*
*    ever alert,*
*You past and present purposes tenaciously pursued, may-be*
*    unconscious of yourselves,*
*Unswerv'd by all the passing errors, perturbations of the sur-*
*    face;*
*You vital, universal, deathless germs, beneath all creeds, arts,*
*    statutes, literatures,*
*Here build your homes for good, establish here, these areas*
*    entire, lands of the Western shore,*
*We pledge, we dedicate to you.*

*For man of you, your characteristic race,*
*Here may he hardy, sweet, gigantic grow, here tower propor-*
*    tionate to Nature,*
*Here climb the vast pure spaces unconfined, uncheck'd by wall*
*    or roof,*
*Here laugh with storm or sun, here joy, here patiently inure,*
*Here heed himself, unfold himself, (not others' formulas heed,)*
*    here fill his time,*
*To duly fall, to aid, unreck'd at last,*
*To disappear, to serve.*

Thus on the northern coast,
In the echo of teamsters' calls and the clinking chains, and
    the music of choppers' axes,

G                                                    W.

The falling trunk and limbs, the crash, the muffled shriek,
    the groan,
Such words combined from the redwood-tree, as of voices
    ecstatic, ancient and rustling,
The century-lasting, unseen dryads, singing, withdrawing,
All their recesses of forests and mountains leaving,
From the Cascade range to the Wasatch, or Idaho far, or
    Utah,
To the deities of the modern henceforth yielding,
The chorus and indications, the vistas of coming humanity,
    the settlements, features all,
In the Mendocino woods I caught.

2

The flashing and golden pageant of California,
The sudden and gorgeous drama, the sunny and ample lands,
The long and varied stretch from Puget sound to Colorado
    south,
Lands bathed in sweeter, rarer, healthier air, valleys and
    mountain cliffs,
The fields of Nature long prepared and fallow, the silent,
    cyclic chemistry,
The slow and steady ages plodding, the unoccupied surface
    ripening, the rich ores forming beneath;
At last the New arriving, assuming, taking possession,
A swarming and busy race settling and organizing every-
    where,
Ships coming in from the whole round world, and going out
    to the whole world,
To India and China and Australia and the thousand island
    paradises of the Pacific,
Populous cities, the latest inventions, the steamers on the
    rivers, the railroads, with many a thrifty farm, with
    machinery,
And wood and wheat and the grape, and diggings of yellow
    gold.

3

But more in you than these, lands of the Western shore,
(These but the means, the implements, the standing-ground,)

I see in you, certain to come, the promise of thousands of
    years, till now deferr'd,
Promis'd to be fulfill'd, our common kind, the race.

The new society at last, proportionate to Nature,
In man of you, more than your mountain peaks or stalwart
    trees imperial,
In woman more, far more, than all your gold or vines, or
    even vital air.

Fresh come, to a new world indeed, yet long prepared,
I see the genius of the modern, child of the real and
    ideal,
Clearing the ground for broad humanity, the true America,
    heir of the past so grand,
To build a grander future.
1874                          1881

# *A Song for Occupations*

## 1

A SONG for occupations!
In the labor of engines and trades and the labor of fields I
    find the developments,
And find the eternal meanings.

Workmen and Workwomen!
Were all educations practical and ornamental well display'd
    out of me, what would it amount to?
Were I as the head teacher, charitable proprietor, wise states-
    man, what would it amount to?
Were I to you as the boss employing and paying you, would
    that satisfy you?

The learn'd, virtuous, benevolent, and the usual terms,
A man like me and never the usual terms.

Neither a servant nor a master I,
I take no sooner a large price than a small price, I will have
    my own whoever enjoys me,
I will be even with you and you shall be even with me.

If you stand at work in a shop I stand as nigh as the nighest
    in the same shop,
If you bestow gifts on your brother or dearest friend I de-
    mand as good as your brother or dearest friend,
If your lover, husband, wife, is welcome by day or night, I
    must be personally as welcome,
If you become degraded, criminal, ill, then I become so for
    your sake,
If you remember your foolish and outlaw'd deeds, do you
    think I cannot remember my own foolish and outlaw'd
    deeds?
If you carouse at the table I carouse at the opposite side of
    the table,
If you meet some stranger in the streets and love him or her,
    why I often meet strangers in the street and love them.

Why what have you thought of yourself?
Is it you then that thought yourself less?
Is it you that thought the President greater than you?
Or the rich better off than you? or the educated wiser than
    you?

(Because you are greasy or pimpled, or were once drunk, or a
    thief,
Or that you are diseas'd, or rheumatic, or a prostitute,
Or from frivolity or impotence, or that you are no scholar
    and never saw your name in print,
Do you give in that you are any less immortal?)

2

Souls of men and women! it is not you I call unseen, un-
    heard, untouchable and untouching,
It is not you I go argue pro and con about, and to settle
    whether you are alive or no,
I own publicly who you are, if nobody else owns.

Grown, half-grown and babe, of this country and every
    country, indoors and out-doors, one just as much as the
    other, I see,
And all else behind or through them.

The wife, and she is not one jot less than the husband,
The daughter, and she is just as good as the son,
The mother, and she is every bit as much as the father.

Offspring of ignorant and poor, boys apprenticed to trades,
Young fellows working on farms and old fellows working on
    farms,
Sailor-men, merchant-men, coasters, immigrants,
All these I see, but nigher and farther the same I see,
None shall escape me and none shall wish to escape me.

I bring what you much need yet always have,
Not money, amours, dress, eating, erudition, but as good,
I send no agent or medium, offer no representative of value,
    but offer the value itself.

There is something that comes to one now and perpetually,
It is not what is printed, preach'd, discussed, it eludes dis-
    cussion and print,
It is not to be put in a book, it is not in this book,
It is for you whoever you are, it is no farther from you than
    your hearing and sight are from you,
It is hinted by nearest, commonest, readiest, it is ever pro-
    voked by them.

You may read in many languages, yet read nothing about it,
You may read the President's message and read nothing
    about it there,
Nothing in the reports from the State department or Trea-
    sury department, or in the daily papers or weekly papers,
Or in the census or revenue returns, prices current, or any
    accounts of stock.

### 3

The sun and stars that float in the open air,
The apple-shaped earth and we upon it, surely the drift of
    them is something grand,

I do not know what it is except that it is grand, and that it is
happiness,

And that the enclosing purport of us here is not a speculation
or bon-mot or reconnoissance,

And that it is not something which by luck may turn out well
for us, and without luck must be a failure for us,

And not something which may yet be retracted in a certain
contingency.


The light and shade, the curious sense of body and identity,
the greed that with perfect complaisance devours all
things,

The endless pride and outstretching of man, unspeakable
joys and sorrows,

The wonder every one sees in every one else he sees, and the
wonders that fill each minute of time forever,

What have you reckon'd them for, camerado?

Have you reckon'd them for your trade or farm-work? or for
the profits of your store?

Or to achieve yourself a position? or to fill a gentleman's
leisure, or a lady's leisure?


Have you reckon'd that the landscape took substance and
form that it might be painted in a picture?

Or men and women that they might be written of, and songs
sung?

Or the attraction of gravity, and the great laws and harmonious combinations and the fluids of the air, as subjects
for the savans?

Or the brown land and the blue sea for maps and charts?

Or the stars to be put in constellations and named fancy
names?

Or that the growth of seeds is for agricultural tables, or
agriculture itself?


Old institutions, these arts, libraries, legends, collections, and
the practice handed along in manufactures, will we rate
them so high?

Will we rate our cash and business high? I have no objection,

I rate them as high as the highest—then a child born of a
woman and man I rate beyond all rate.

We thought our Union grand, and our Constitution grand,
I do not say they are not grand and good, for they are,
I am this day just as much in love with them as you,
Then I am in love with You, and with all my fellows upon the
    earth.

We consider bibles and religions divine—I do not say they
    are not divine,
I say they have all grown out of you, and may grow out of
    you still,
It is not they who give the life, it is you who give the life,
Leaves are not more shed from the trees, or trees from the
    earth, than they are shed out of you.

### 4

The sum of all known reverence I add up in you whoever you
    are,
The President is there in the White House for you, it is not
    you who are here for him,
The Secretaries act in their bureaus for you, not you here for
    them,
The Congress convenes every Twelfth-month for you,
Laws, courts, the forming of States, the charters of cities, the
    going and coming of commerce and mails, are all for
    you.

List close my scholars dear,
Doctrines, politics and civilization exurge from you,
Sculpture and monuments and any thing inscribed anywhere
    are tallied in you,
The gist of histories and statistics as far back as the records
    reach is in you this hour, and myths and tales the same,
If you were not breathing and walking here, where would
    they all be?
The most renown'd poems would be ashes, orations and
    plays would be vacuums.

All architecture is what you do to it when you look upon it,
(Did you think it was in the white or gray stone? or the lines
    of the arches and cornices?)

All music is what awakes from you when you are reminded
    by the instruments,
It is not the violins and the cornets, it is not the oboe nor the
    beating drums, nor the score of the baritone singer sing-
    ing his sweet romanza, nor that of the men's chorus, nor
    that of the women's chorus,
It is nearer and farther than they.

### 5

Will the whole come back then?
Can each see signs of the best by a look in the looking-glass?
    is there nothing greater or more?
Does all sit there with you, with the mystic unseen soul?

Strange and hard that paradox true I give,
Objects gross and the unseen soul are one.

House-building, measuring, sawing the boards,
Blacksmithing, glass-blowing, nail-making, coopering, tin-
    roofing, shingle-dressing,
Ship-joining, dock-building, fish-curing, flagging of side-
    walks by flaggers,
The pump, the pile-driver, the great derrick, the coal-kiln
    and brick-kiln,
Coal-mines and all that is down there, the lamps in the dark-
    ness, echoes, songs, what meditations, what vast native
    thoughts looking through smutch'd faces,
Iron-works, forge-fires in the mountains or by river-banks,
    men around feeling the melt with huge crowbars, lumps
    of ore, the due combining of ore, limestone, coal,
The blast-furnace and the puddling-furnace, the loup-lump
    at the bottom of the melt at last, the rolling-mill, the
    stumpy bars of pig-iron, the strong, clean-shaped T-rail
    for railroads,
Oil-works, silk-works, white-lead-works, the sugar-house,
    steam-saws, the great mills and factories,
Stone-cutting, shapely trimmings for façades or window or
    door-lintels, the mallet, the tooth-chisel, the jib to pro-
    tect the thumb,
The calking-iron, the kettle of boiling vault-cement, and the
    fire under the kettle,

The cotton-bale, the stevedore's hook, the saw and buck of
   the sawyer, the mould of the moulder, the working-knife
   of the butcher, the ice-saw, and all the work with ice,
The work and tools of the rigger, grappler, sail-maker, block-
   maker,
Goods of gutta-percha, papier-maché, colors, brushes, brush-
   making, glazier's implements,
The veneer and glue-pot, the confectioner's ornaments, the
   decanter and glasses, the shears and flat-iron,
The awl and knee-strap, the pint measure and quart measure,
   the counter and stool, the writing-pen of quill or metal,
   the making of all sorts of edged tools,
The brewery, brewing, the malt, the vats, everything that is
   done by brewers, wine-makers, vinegar-makers,
Leather-dressing, coach-making, boiler-making, rope-twist-
   ing, distilling, sign-painting, lime-burning, cotton-pick-
   ing, electroplating, electrotyping, stereotyping,
Stave-machines,     planing-machines,     reaping-machines,
   ploughing-machines, thrashing-machines, steam wagons,
The cart of the carman, the omnibus, the ponderous dray,
Pyrotechny, letting off color'd fireworks at night, fancy
   figures and jets;
Beef on the butcher's stall, the slaughter-house of the butcher,
   the butcher in his killing-clothes,
The pens of live pork, the killing-hammer, the hog-hook, the
   scalder's tub, gutting, the cutter's cleaver, the packer's
   maul, and the plenteous winterwork of pork-packing,
Flour-works, grinding of wheat, rye, maize, rice, the barrels
   and the half and quarter barrels, the loaded barges, the
   high piles on wharves and levees,
The men and the work of the men on ferries, railroad,
   coasters, fish-boats, canals;
The hourly routine of your own or any man's life, the shop,
   yard, store, or factory,
These shows all near you by day and night—workman! whoever you are, your daily life!
In that and them the heft of the heaviest—in that and them
   far more than you estimated, (and far less also,)
In them realities for you and me, in them poems for you and
   me,

In them, not yourself—you and your soul enclose all things,
regardless of estimation,
In them the development good—in them all themes, hints,
possibilities.

I do not affirm that what you see beyond is futile, I do not
advise you to stop,
I do not say leadings you thought great are not great,
But I say that none lead to greater than these lead to.

### 6

Will you seek afar off? you surely come back at last,
In things best known to you finding the best, or as good as
the best,
In folks nearest to you finding the sweetest, strongest,
lovingest,
Happiness, knowledge, not in another place but this place,
not for another hour but this hour,
Man in the first you see or touch, always in friend, brother,
nighest neighbor—woman in mother, sister, wife,
The popular tastes and employments taking precedence in
poems or anywhere,
You workwomen and workmen of these States having your
own divine and strong life,
And all else giving place to men and women like you.

When the psalm sings instead of the singer,
When the script preaches instead of the preacher,
When the pulpit descends and goes instead of the carver that
carved the supporting desk,
When I can touch the body of books by night or by day, and
when they touch my body back again,
When a university course convinces like a slumbering woman
and child convince,
When the minted gold in the vault smiles like the night-
watchman's daughter,
When warrantee deeds loafe in chairs opposite and are my
friendly companions,
I intend to reach them my hand, and make as much of them
as I do of men and women like you.

1855                                    1881

# A Song of the Rolling Earth

A SONG of the rolling earth, and of words according,
Were you thinking that those were the words, those upright
    lines? those curves, angles, dots?
No, those are not the words, the substantial words are in the
    ground and sea,
They are in the air, they are in you.

Were you thinking that those were the words, those delicious
    sounds out of your friends' mouths?
No, the real words are more delicious than they.

Human bodies are words, myriads of words,
(In the best poems re-appears the body, man's or woman's,
    well-shaped, natural, gay,
Every part able, active, receptive, without shame or the need
    of shame.)

Air, soil, water, fire—those are words,
I myself am a word with them—my qualities interpenetrate
    with theirs—my name is nothing to them,
Though it were told in the three thousand languages, what
    would air, soil, water, fire, know of my name?

A healthy presence, a friendly or commanding gesture, are
    words, sayings, meanings,
The charms that go with the mere looks of some men and
    women, are sayings and meanings also.

The workmanship of souls is by those inaudible words of the
    earth,
The masters know the earth's words and use them more than
    audible words.

Amelioration is one of the earth's words,
The earth neither lags nor hastens,

It has all attributes, growths, effects, latent in itself from the
    jump,
It is not half beautiful only, defects and excrescences show
    just as much as perfections show.

The earth does not withhold, it is generous enough,
The truths of the earth continually wait, they are not so con-
    ceal'd either,
They are calm, subtle, untransmissible by print,
They are imbued through all things conveying themselves
    willingly,
Conveying a sentiment and invitation, I utter and utter,
I speak not, yet if you hear me not of what avail am I to you?
To bear, to better, lacking these of what avail am I?

(Accouche! accouchez!
Will you rot your own fruit in yourself there?
Will you squat and stifle there?)

The earth does not argue,
Is not pathetic, has no arrangements,
Does not scream, haste, persuade, threaten, promise,
Makes no discriminations, has no conceivable failures,
Closes nothing, refuses nothing, shuts none out,
Of all the powers, objects, states, it notifies, shuts none out.

The earth does not exhibit itself nor refuse to exhibit itself,
    possesses still underneath,
Underneath the ostensible sounds, the august chorus of
    heroes, the wail of slaves,
Persuasions of lovers, curses, gasps of the dying, laughter of
    young people, accents of bargainers,
Underneath these possessing words that never fail.

To her children the words of the eloquent dumb great mother
    never fail,
The true words do not fail, for motion does not fail and re-
    flection does not fail,
Also the day and night do not fail, and the voyage we pursue
    does not fail.

Of the interminable sisters,
Of the ceaseless cotillions of sisters,
Of the centripetal and centrifugal sisters, the elder and
    younger sisters,
The beautiful sister we know dances on with the rest.

With her ample back towards every beholder,
With the fascinations of youth and the equal fascinations of
    age,
Sits she whom I too love like the rest, sits undisturb'd,
Holding up in her hand what has the character of a mirror,
    while her eyes glance back from it,
Glance as she sits, inviting none, denying none,
Holding a mirror day and night tirelessly before her own face.

Seen at hand or seen at a distance,
Duly the twenty-four appear in public every day,
Duly approach and pass with their companions or a com-
    panion,
Looking from no countenances of their own, but from the
    countenances of those who are with them,
From the countenances of children or women or the manly
    countenance,
From the open countenances of animals or from inanimate
    things,
From the landscape or waters or from the exquisite appari-
    tion of the sky,
From our countenances, mine and yours, faithfully returning
    them,
Every day in public appearing without fail, but never twice
    with the same companions.

Embracing man, embracing all, proceed the three hundred
    and sixty-five resistlessly round the sun;
Embracing all, soothing, supporting, follow close three
    hundred and sixty-five offsets of the first, sure and neces-
    sary as they.

Tumbling on steadily, nothing dreading,
Sunshine, storm, cold, heat, forever withstanding, passing,
    carrying,

The soul's realization and determination still inheriting,
The fluid vacuum around and ahead still entering and divid-
    ing,
No balk retarding, no anchor anchoring, on no rock striking,
Swift, glad, content, unbereav'd, nothing losing,
Of all able and ready at any time to give strict account,
The divine ship sails the divine sea.

2.

Whoever you are! motion and reflection are especially for you,
The divine ship sails the divine sea for you.

Whoever you are! you are he or she for whom the earth is
    solid and liquid,
You are he or she for whom the sun and moon hang in the sky,
For none more than you are the present and the past,
For none more than you is immortality.

Each man to himself and each woman to herself, is the word
    of the past and present, and the true word of immortality;
No one can acquire for another—not one,
Not one can grow for another—not one.

The song is to the singer, and comes back most to him,
The teaching is to the teacher, and comes back most to him,
The murder is to the murderer, and comes back most to him,
The theft is to the thief, and comes back most to him,
The love is to the lover, and comes back most to him,
The gift is to the giver, and comes back most to him—it
    cannot fail,
The oration is to the orator, the acting is to the actor and
    actress not to the audience,
And no man understands any greatness or goodness but his
    own, or the indication of his own.

3

I swear the earth shall surely be complete to him or her who
    shall be complete,
The earth remains jagged and broken only to him or her who
    remains jagged and broken.

I swear there is no greatness or power that does not emulate
    those of the earth,
There can be no theory of any account unless it corroborate
    the theory of the earth,
No politics, song, religion, behavior, or what not, is of
    account, unless it compare with the amplitude of the
    earth,
Unless it face the exactness, vitality, impartiality, rectitude of
    the earth.

I swear I begin to see love with sweeter spasms than that
    which responds love,
It is that which contains itself, which never invites and never
    refuses.

I swear I begin to see little or nothing in audible words,
All merges toward the presentation of the unspoken mean-
    ings of the earth,
Toward him who sings the songs of the body and of the
    truths of the earth,
Toward him who makes the dictionaries of words that print
    cannot touch.

I swear I see what is better than to tell the best,
It is always to leave the best untold.

When I undertake to tell the best I find I cannot,
My tongue is ineffectual on its pivots,
My breath will not be obedient to its organs,
I become a dumb man.

The best of the earth cannot be told anyhow, all or any is
    best,
It is not what you anticipated, it is cheaper, easier, nearer,
Things are not dismiss'd from the places they held before,
The earth is just as positive and direct as it was before,
Facts, religions, improvements, politics, trades, are as real as
    before,
But the soul is also real, it too is positive and direct,
No reasoning, no proof has establish'd it,
Undeniable growth has establish'd it.

4

These to echo the tones of souls and the phrases of souls,
(If they did not echo the phrases of souls what were they
    then?
If they had not reference to you in especial what were they
    then?)

I swear I will never henceforth have to do with the faith that
    tells the best,
I will have to do only with that faith that leaves the best
    untold.

Say on, sayers! sing on, singers!
Delve! mould! pile the words of the earth!
Work on, age after age, nothing is to be lost,
It may have to wait long, but it will certainly come in use,
When the materials are all prepared and ready, the architects
    shall appear.

I swear to you the architects shall appear without fail,
I swear to you they will understand you and justify you,
The greatest among them shall be he who best knows you,
    and encloses all and is faithful to all,
He and the rest shall not forget you, they shall perceive that
    you are not an iota less than they,
You shall be fully glorified in them.
1856                                                        1881


YOUTH, DAY, OLD AGE AND NIGHT

YOUTH, large, lusty, loving—youth full of grace, force,
    fascination,
Do you know that Old Age may come after you with equal
    grace, force, fascination?

Day full-blown and splendid—day of the immense sun,
    action, ambition, laughter,
The Night follows close with millions of suns, and sleep and
    restoring darkness.
1881                                                        1881

# *Birds of Passage*

## SONG OF THE UNIVERSAL

### 1

COME said the Muse,
Sing me a song no poet yet has chanted,
Sing me the universal.

In this broad earth of ours,
Amid the measureless grossness and the slag,
Enclosed and safe within its central heart,
Nestles the seed perfection.

By every life a share or more or less,
None born but it is born, conceal'd or unconceal'd the seed
    is waiting.

### 2

Lo! keen-eyed towering science,
As from tall peaks the modern overlooking,
Successive absolute fiats issuing.

Yet again, lo! the soul, above all science,
For it has history gather'd like husks around the globe,
For it the entire star-myriads roll through the sky.

In spiral routes by long detours,
(As a much-tacking ship upon the sea,)
For it the partial to the permanent flowing,
For it the real to the ideal tends.

For it the mystic evolution,
Not the right only justified, what we call evil also justified.

Forth from their masks, no matter what,
From the huge festering trunk, from craft and guile and tears,
Health to emerge and joy, joy universal.

Out of the bulk, the morbid and the shallow,
Out of the bad majority, the varied countless frauds of men
    and states,
Electric, antiseptic yet, cleaving, suffusing all,
Only the good is universal.

### 3

Over the mountain-growths disease and sorrow,
An uncaught bird is ever hovering, hovering,
High in the purer, happier air.

From imperfection's murkiest cloud,
Darts always forth one ray of perfect light,
One flash of heaven's glory.

To fashion's, custom's discord,
To the mad Babel-din, the deafening orgies,
Soothing each lull a strain is heard, just heard,
From some far shore the final chorus sounding.

O the blest eyes, the happy hearts,
That see, that know the guiding thread so fine,
Along the mighty labyrinth.

### 4

And thou America,
For the scheme's culmination, its thought and its reality,
For these (not for thyself) thou hast arrived.

Thou too surroundest all,
Embracing carrying welcoming all, thou too by pathways
    broad and new,
To the ideal tendest.

The measur'd faiths of other lands, the grandeurs of the past,
Are not for thee, but grandeurs of thine own,
Deific faiths and amplitudes, absorbing, comprehending all,
All eligible to all.

All, all for immortality,
Love like the light silently wrapping all,
Nature's amelioration blessing all,
The blossoms, fruits of ages, orchards divine and certain,
Forms, objects, growths, humanities, to spiritual images
    ripening.

Give me O God to sing that thought,
Give me, give him or her I love this quenchless faith
In Thy ensemble, whatever else withheld withhold not from us,
Belief in plan of Thee enclosed in Time and Space,
Health, peace, salvation universal.

Is it a dream?
Nay but the lack of it the dream,
And failing it life's lore and wealth a dream,
And all the world a dream.
1874                        1881

## PIONEERS! O PIONEERS!

COME my tan-faced children,
Follow well in order, get your weapons ready,
Have you your pistols? have you your sharp-edged axes?
    Pioneers! O pioneers!

For we cannot tarry here,
We must march my darlings, we must bear the brunt of
    danger,
We the youthful sinewy races, all the rest on us depend,
    Pioneers! O pioneers!

O you youths, Western youths,
So impatient, full of action, full of manly pride and friendship,
Plain I see you Western youths, see you tramping with the
    foremost,
    Pioneers! O pioneers!

Have the elder races halted?
Do they droop and end their lesson, wearied over there be-
    yond the seas?

We take up the task eternal, and the burden and the lesson,
   Pioneers! O pioneers!


All the past we leave behind,
We debouch upon a newer mightier world, varied world,
Fresh and strong the world we seize, world of labor and the
  march,
   Pioneers! O pioneers!


We detachments steady throwing,
Down the edges, through the passes, up the mountains steep,
Conquering, holding, daring, venturing as we go the un-
  known ways,
   Pioneers! O pioneers!


We primeval forests felling,
We the rivers stemming, vexing we and piercing deep the
  mines within,
We the surface broad surveying, we the virgin soil upheaving,
   Pioneers! O pioneers!


Colorado men are we,
From the peaks gigantic, from the great sierras and the high
  plateaus,
From the mine and from the gully, from the hunting trail we
  come,
   Pioneers! O pioneers!


From Nebraska, from Arkansas,
Central inland race are we, from Missouri, with the conti-
  nental blood intervein'd,
All the hands of comrades clasping, all the Southern, all the
  Northern,
   Pioneers! O pioneers!


O resistless restless race!
O beloved race in all! O my breast aches with tender love for
  all!
O I mourn and yet exult, I am rapt with love for all,
   Pioneers! O pioneers!

Raise the mighty mother mistress,
Waving high the delicate mistress, over all the starry mistress,
(bend your heads all,)
Raise the fang'd and warlike mistress, stern, impassive,
weapon'd mistress,
Pioneers! O pioneers!

See my children, resolute children,
By those swarms upon our rear we must never yield or falter,
Ages back in ghostly millions frowning there behind us
urging,
Pioneers! O pioneers!

On and on the compact ranks,
With accessions ever waiting, with the places of the dead
quickly fill'd,
Through the battle, through defeat, moving yet and never
stopping,
Pioneers! O pioneers!

O to die advancing on!
Are there some of us to droop and die? has the hour come?
Then upon the march we fittest die, soon and sure the gap is
fill'd,
Pioneers! O pioneers!

All the pulses of the world,
Falling in they beat for us, with the Western movement beat,
Holding single or together, steady moving to the front, all
for us,
Pioneers! O pioneers!

Life's involv'd and varied pageants,
All the forms and shows, all the workmen at their work,
All the seamen and the landsmen, all the masters with their
slaves,
Pioneers! O pioneers!

All the hapless silent lovers,
All the prisoners in the prisons, all the righteous and the
wicked,

All the joyous, all the sorrowing, all the living, all the dying,
        Pioneers! O pioneers!


I too with my soul and body,
We, a curious trio, picking, wandering on our way,
Through these shores amid the shadows, with the apparitions
        pressing,
                Pioneers! O pioneers!


Lo, the darting bowling orb!
Lo, the brother orbs around, all the clustering suns and
        planets,
All the dazzling days, all the mystic nights with dreams,
                Pioneers! O pioneers!


These are of us, they are with us,
All for primal needed work, while the followers there in em-
        bryo wait behind,
We to-day's procession heading, we the route for travel
        clearing,
                Pioneers! O pioneers!


O you daughters of the West!
O you young and elder daughters! O you mothers and you
        wives!
Never must you be divided, in our ranks you move united,
                Pioneers! O pioneers!


Minstrels latent on the prairies!
(Shrouded bards of other lands, you may rest, you have done
        your work,)
Soon I hear you coming warbling, soon you rise and tramp
        amid us,
                Pioneers! O pioneers!


Not for delectations sweet,
Not the cushion and the slipper, not the peaceful and the
        studious,
Not the riches safe and palling, not for us the tame enjoy-
        ment,
                Pioneers! O pioneers!

Do the feasters gluttonous feast?
Do the corpulent sleepers sleep? have they lock'd and bolted
    doors?
Still be ours the diet hard, and the blanket on the ground,
        Pioneers! O pioneers!

Has the night descended?
Was the road of late so toilsome? did we stop discouraged
    nodding on our way?
Yet a passing hour I yield you in your tracks to pause obli-
    vious,
        Pioneers! O pioneers!

Till with sound of trumpet,
Far, far off the daybreak call—hark! how loud and clear I
    hear it wind,
Swift! to the head of the army!—swift! spring to your places,
        Pioneers! O pioneers!
1865                                      1881

## TO YOU

WHOEVER you are, I fear you are walking the walks of dreams,
I fear these supposed realities are to melt from under your
    feet and hands,
Even now your features, joys, speech, house, trade, manners,
    troubles, follies, costume, crimes, dissipate away from
    you,
Your true soul and body appear before me,
They stand forth out of affairs, out of commerce, shops,
    work, farms, clothes, the house, buying, selling, eating,
    drinking, suffering, dying.

Whoever you are, now I place my hand upon you, that you
    be my poem,
I whisper with my lips close to your ear,
I have loved many women and men, but I love none better
    than you.

O I have been dilatory and dumb,
I should have made my way straight to you long ago,

I should have blabb'd nothing but you, I should have chanted
　　nothing but you.

I will leave all and come and make the hymns of you,
None has understood you, but I understand you,
None has done justice to you, you have not done justice to
　　yourself,
None but has found you imperfect, I only find no imperfec-
　　tion in you,
None but would subordinate you, I only am he who will
　　never consent to subordinate you,
I only am he who places over you no master, owner, better,
　　God, beyond what waits intrinsically in yourself.

Painters have painted their swarming groups and the centre-
　　figure of all,
From the head of the centre-figure spreading a nimbus of
　　gold-color'd light,
But I paint myriads of heads, but paint no head without its
　　nimbus of gold-color'd light,
From my hand from the brain of every man and woman it
　　streams, effulgently flowing forever.

O I could sing such grandeurs and glories about you!
You have not known what you are, you have slumber'd upon
　　yourself all your life,
Your eyelids have been the same as closed most of the time,
What you have done returns already in mockeries,
(Your thrift, knowledge, prayers, if they do not return in
　　mockeries, what is their return?)

The mockeries are not you,
Underneath them and within them I see you lurk,
I pursue you where none else has pursued you,
Silence, the desk, the flippant expression, the night, the
　　accustom'd routine, if these conceal you from others or
　　from yourself, they do not conceal you from me,
The shaved face, the unsteady eye, the impure complexion, if
　　these balk others they do not balk me,
The pert apparel, the deform'd attitude, drunkenness, greed,
　　premature death, all these I part aside.

There is no endowment in man or woman that is not tallied
    in you,
There is no virtue, no beauty in man or woman, but as good
    is in you,
No pluck, no endurance in others, but as good is in you,
No pleasure waiting for others, but an equal pleasure waits
    for you.

As for me, I give nothing to any one except I give the like
    carefully to you,
I sing the songs of the glory of none, not God, sooner than I
    sing the songs of the glory of you.

Whoever you are! claim your own at any hazard!
These shows of the East and West are tame compared to you,
These immense meadows, these interminable rivers, you are
    immense and interminable as they,
These furies, elements, storms, motions of Nature, throes of
    apparent dissolution, you are he or she who is master or
    mistress over them,
Master or mistress in your own right over Nature, elements,
    pain, passion, dissolution.

The hopples fall from your ankles, you find an unfailing
    sufficiency,
Old or young, male or female, rude, low, rejected by the rest,
    whatever you are promulges itself,
Through birth, life, death, burial, the means are provided,
    nothing is scanted,
Through angers, losses, ambition, ignorance, ennui, what you
    are picks its way.
1856                             1881

## FRANCE

### *The* 18*th Year of these States*

A GREAT year and place,
A harsh discordant natal scream out-sounding, to touch the
    mother's heart closer than any yet.

I walk'd the shores of my Eastern sea,
Heard over the waves the little voice,
Saw the divine infant where she woke mournfully wailing,
   amid the roar of cannon, curses, shouts, crush of falling
   buildings,
Was not so sick from the blood in the gutters running, nor
   from the single corpses, nor those in heaps, nor those
   borne away in the tumbrils,
Was not so desperate at the battues of death—was not so
   shock'd at the repeated fusillades of the guns.

Pale, silent, stern, what could I say to that long-accrued re-
   tribution?
Could I wish humanity different?
Could I wish the people made of wood and stone?
Or that there be no justice in destiny or time?

O liberty! O mate for me!
Here too the blaze, the grape-shot and the axe, in reserve, to
   fetch them out in case of need,
Here too, though long represt, can never be destroy'd,
Here too could rise at last murdering and ecstatic,
Here too demanding full arrears of vengeance.

Hence I sign this salute over the sea,
And I do not deny that terrible red birth and baptism,
But remember the little voice that I heard wailing, and wait
   with perfect trust, no matter how long,
And from to-day sad and cogent I maintain the bequeath'd
   cause, as for all lands,
And I send these words to Paris with my love,
And I guess some chansonniers there will understand them,
For I guess there is latent music yet in France, floods of it,
O I hear already the bustle of instruments, they will soon be
   drowning all that would interrupt them,
O I think the east wind brings a triumphal and free march,
It reaches hither, it swells me to joyful madness,
I will run transpose it in words, to justify it,
I will yet sing a song for you ma femme.
1860                                                              1871

## MYSELF AND MINE

MYSELF and mine gymnastic ever,
To stand the cold or heat, to make good aim with a gun, to
    sail a boat, to manage horses, to beget superb chil-
    dren,
To speak readily and clearly, to feel at home among common
    people,
And to hold our own in terrible positions on land and sea.

Not for an embroiderer,
(There will always be plenty of embroiderers, I welcome
    them also,)
But for the fibre of things and for inherent men and women.

Not to chisel ornaments,
But to chisel with free stroke the heads and limbs of plen-
    teous supreme Gods, that the States may realize them
    walking and talking.

Let me have my own way,
Let others promulge the laws, I will make no account of the
    laws,
Let others praise eminent men and hold up peace, I hold up
    agitation and conflict,
I praise no eminent man, I rebuke to his face the one that was
    thought most worthy.

(Who are you? and what are you secretly guilty of all your
    life?
Will you turn aside all your life? will you grub and chatter all
    your life?
And who are you, blabbing by rote, years, pages, languages,
    reminiscences,
Unwitting to-day that you do not know how to speak pro-
    perly a single word?)

Let others finish specimens, I never finish specimens,
I start them by exhaustless laws as Nature does, fresh and
    modern continually.

I give nothing as duties,
What others give as duties I give as living impulses,
(Shall I give the heart's action as a duty?)

Let others dispose of questions, I dispose of nothing, I
　　arouse unanswerable questions,
Who are they I see and touch, and what about them?
What about these likes of myself that draw me so close by
　　tender directions and indirections?

I call to the world to distrust the accounts of my friends, but
　　listen to my enemies, as I myself do,
I charge you forever reject those who would expound me, for
　　I cannot expound myself,
I charge that there be no theory or school founded out of
　　me,
I charge you to leave all free, as I have left all free.

After me, vista!
O I see life is not short, but immeasurably long,
I henceforth tread the world chaste, temperate, an early
　　riser, a steady grower,
Every hour the semen of centuries, and still of centuries.

I must follow up these continual lessons of the air, water,
　　earth,
I perceive I have no time to lose.
1860　　　　　　　　　　　　　　　　　　　　　　1881

## YEAR OF METEORS

### (1859-60)

YEAR of meteors! brooding year!
I would bind in words retrospective some of your deeds and
　　signs,
I would sing your contest for the 19th Presidentiad,
I would sing how an old man, tall, with white hair, mounted
　　the scaffold in Virginia,
(I was at hand, silent I stood with teeth shut close, I
　　watch'd,

I stood very near you old man when cool and indifferent, but
    trembling with age and your unheal'd wounds, you
    mounted the scaffold;)
I would sing in my copious song your census returns of the
    States,
The tables of population and products, I would sing of your
    ships and their cargoes,
The proud black ships of Manhattan arriving, some fill'd with
    immigrants, some from the isthmus with cargoes of gold,
Songs thereof would I sing, to all that hitherward comes
    would I welcome give,
And you would I sing, fair stripling! welcome to you from
    me, young prince of England!
(Remember you surging Manhattan's crowds as you pass'd
    with your cortege of nobles?
There in the crowds stood I, and singled you out with
    attachment;)
Nor forget I to sing of the wonder, the ship as she swam up
    my bay,
Well-shaped and stately the Great Eastern swam up my bay,
    she was 600 feet long,
Her moving swiftly surrounded by myriads of small craft I
    forget not to sing;
Nor the comet that came unannounced out of the north
    flaring in heaven,
Nor the strange huge meteor-procession dazzling and clear
    shooting over our heads,
(A moment, a moment long it sail'd its balls of unearthly
    light over our heads,
Then departed, dropt in the night, and was gone;)
Of such, and fitful as they, I sing—with gleams from them
    would I gleam and patch these chants,
Your chants, O year all mottled with evil and good—year of
    forebodings!
Year of comets and meteors transient and strange—lo! even
    here one equally transient and strange!
As I flit through you hastily, soon to fall and be gone, what
    is this chant,
What am I myself but one of your meteors?

(1860?)                          1881

## WITH ANTECEDENTS

### 1

WITH antecedents,
With my fathers and mothers and the accumulations of past
    ages,
With all which, had it not been, I would not now be here, as
    I am,
With Egypt, India, Phenicia, Greece and Rome,
With the Kelt, the Scandinavian, the Alb and the Saxon,
With antique maritime ventures, laws, artisanship, wars and
    journeys,
With the poet, the skald, the saga, the myth, and the oracle,
With the sale of slaves, with enthusiasts, with the troubadour,
    the crusader, and the monk,
With those old continents whence we have come to this new
    continent,
With the fading kingdoms and kings over there,
With the fading religions and priests,
With the small shores we look back to from our own large
    and present shores,
With countless years drawing themselves onward and arrived
    at these years,
You and me arrived—America arrived and making this year,
This year! sending itself ahead countless years to come.

### 2

O but it is not the years—it is I, it is You,
We touch all laws and tally all antecedents,
We are the skald, the oracle, the monk and the knight, we
    easily include them and more,
We stand amid time beginningless and endless, we stand
    amid evil and good,
All swings around us, there is as much darkness as light,
The very sun swings itself and its system of planets around
    us,
Its sun, and its again, all swing around us.

As for me, (torn, stormy, amid these vehement days,)
I have the idea of all, and am all and believe in all,

I believe materialism is true and spiritualism is true, I reject no part.

(Have I forgotten any part? any thing in the past?
Come to me whoever and whatever, till I give you recognition.)

I respect Assyria, China, Teutonia, and the Hebrews,
I adopt each theory, myth, god, and demi-god,
I see that the old accounts, bibles, genealogies, are true, without exception,
I assert that all past days were what they must have been,
And that they could no-how have been better than they were,
And that to-day is what it must be, and that America is,
And that to-day and America could no-how be better than they are.

### 3

In the name of these States and in your and my name, the Past,
And in the name of these States and in your and my name, the Present time.

I know that the past was great and the future will be great,
And I know that both curiously conjoint in the present time,
(For the sake of him I typify, for the common average man's sake, your sake if you are he,)
And that where I am or you are this present day, there is the centre of all days, all races,
And there is the meaning to us of all that has ever come of races and days, or ever will come.

1860                                                                 1881

# *A Broadway Pageant*

## 1

OVER the Western sea hither from Niphon come,
Courteous, the swart-cheek'd two-sworded envoys,
Leaning back in their open barouches, bare-headed, impassive,
Ride to-day through Manhattan.

Libertad! I do not know whether others behold what I behold,
In the procession along with the nobles of Niphon, the errand-bearers,
Bringing up the rear, hovering above, around, or in the ranks marching,
But I will sing you a song of what I behold Libertad.

When million-footed Manhattan unpent descends to her pavements,
When the thunder-cracking guns arouse me with the proud roar I love,
When the round-mouth'd guns out of the smoke and smell I love spit their salutes,
When the fire-flashing guns have fully alerted me, and heaven clouds canopy my city with a delicate thin haze,
When gorgeous the countless straight stems, the forests at the wharves, thicken with colors,
When every ship richly drest carries her flag at the peak,
When pennants trail and street-festoons hang from the windows,
When Broadway is entirely given up to foot-passengers and foot-standers, when the mass is densest,
When the façades of the houses are alive with people, when eyes gaze riveted tens of thousands at a time,

When the guests from the islands advance, when the pageant
 moves forward visible,
When the summons is made, when the answer that waited
 thousands of years answers,
I too arising, answering, descend to the pavements, merge
 with the crowd, and gaze with them.


2

Superb-faced Manhattan!
Comrade Americanos! to us, then at last the Orient comes.

To us, my city,
Where our tall-topt marble and iron beauties range on
 opposite sides, to walk in the space between,
To-day our Antipodes comes.

The Originatress comes,
The nest of languages, the bequeather of poems, the race of
 eld,
Florid with blood, pensive, rapt with musings, hot with
 passion,
Sultry with perfume, with ample and flowing garments,
With sunburnt visage, with intense soul and glittering eyes,
The race of Brahma comes.

See my cantabile! these and more are flashing to us from the
 procession,
As it moves changing, a kaleidoscope divine it moves changing before us.

For not the envoys nor the tann'd Japanee from his island
 only,
Lithe and silent the Hindoo appears, the Asiatic continent
 itself appears, the past, the dead,
The murky night-morning of wonder and fable inscrutable,
The envelop'd mysteries, the old and unknown hive-bees,
The north, the sweltering south, eastern Assyria, the He-
 brews, the ancient of ancients,
Vast desolated cities, the gliding present, all of these and
 more are in the pageant-procession.

H                                                         W.

Geography, the world, is in it,

The Great Sea, the brood of islands, Polynesia, the coast beyond,

The coast you henceforth are facing—you, Libertad! from your Western golden shores,

The countries there with their populations, the millions en-masse are curiously here,

The swarming market-places, the temples with idols ranged along the sides or at the end, bonze, brahmin, and llama,

Mandarin, farmer, merchant, mechanic, and fisherman,

The singing-girl and the dancing-girl, the ecstatic persons, the secluded emperors,

Confucius himself, the great poets and heroes, the warriors, the castes, all,

Trooping up, crowding from all directions, from the Altay mountains,

From Thibet, from the four winding and far-flowing rivers of China,

From the southern peninsulas and the demi-continental islands, from Malaysia,

These and whatever belongs to them palpable show forth to me, and are seiz'd by me,

And I am seiz'd by them, and friendlily held by them,

Till as here them all I chant, Libertad! for themselves and for you.


For I too raising my voice join the ranks of this pageant,

I am the chanter, I chant aloud over the pageant,

I chant the world on my Western sea,

I chant copious the islands beyond, thick as stars in the sky,

I chant the new empire grander than any before, as in a vision it comes to me,

I chant America the mistress, I chant a greater supremacy,

I chant projected a thousand blooming cities yet in time on those groups of sea-islands,

My sail-ships and steam-ships threading the archipelagoes,

My stars and stripes fluttering in the wind,

Commerce opening, the sleep of ages having done its work, races reborn, refresh'd,

Lives, works resumed—the object I know not—but the old,
    the Asiatic renew'd as it must be,
Commencing from this day surrounded by the world.


## 3

And you Libertad of the world!
You shall sit in the middle well-pois'd thousands and thou-
    sands of years,
As to-day from one side the nobles of Asia come to you,
As to-morrow from the other side the queen of England sends
    her eldest son to you.

The sign is reversing, the orb is enclosed,
The ring is circled, the journey is done,
The box-lid is but perceptibly open'd, nevertheless the per-
    fume pours copiously out of the whole box.

Young Libertad! with the venerable Asia, the all-mother,
Be considerate with her now and ever hot Libertad, for you
    are all,
Bend your proud neck to the long-off mother now sending
    messages over the archipelagoes to you,
Bend your proud neck low for once, young Libertad.

Were the children straying westward so long? so wide the
    tramping?
Were the precedent dim ages debouching westward from
    Paradise so long?
Were the centuries steadily footing it that way, all the while
    unknown, for you, for reasons?

They are justified, they are accomplish'd, they shall now be
    turn'd the other way also, to travel toward you thence,
They shall now also march obediently eastward for your
    sake Libertad.
(1860?)                                 1881

# Sea-Drift

## OUT OF THE CRADLE ENDLESSLY ROCKING

Out of the cradle endlessly rocking,
Out of the mocking-bird's throat, the musical shuttle,
Out of the Ninth-month midnight,
Over the sterile sands and the fields beyond, where the child
    leaving his bed wander'd alone, bareheaded, barefoot,
Down from the shower'd halo,
Up from the mystic play of shadows twining and twisting as
    if they were alive,
Out from the patches of briers and blackberries,
From the memories of the bird that chanted to me,
From your memories sad brother, from the fitful risings and
    fallings I heard,
From under that yellow half-moon late-risen and swollen as
    if with tears,
From those beginning notes of yearning and love there in the
    mist,
From the thousand responses of my heart never to cease,
From the myriad thence-arous'd words,
From the word stronger and more delicious than any,
From such as now they start the scene revisiting,
As a flock, twittering, rising, or overhead passing,
Borne hither, ere all eludes me, hurriedly,
A man, yet by these tears a little boy again,
Throwing myself on the sand, confronting the waves,
I, chanter of pains and joys, uniter of here and hereafter,
Taking all hints to use them, but swiftly leaping beyond them,
A reminiscence sing.

Once Paumanok,
When the lilac-scent was in the air and Fifth-month grass
    was growing,

Up this seashore in some briers,
Two feather'd guests from Alabama, two together,
And their nest, and four light-green eggs spotted with brown,
And every day the he-bird to and fro near at hand,
And every day the she-bird crouch'd on her nest, silent, with
    bright eyes,
And every day I, a curious boy, never too close, never dis-
    turbing them,
Cautiously peering, absorbing, translating.

*Shine ! shine ! shine !*
*Pour down your warmth, great sun !*
*While we bask, we two together.*

*Two together !*
*Winds blow south, or winds blow north,*
*Day come white, or night come black,*
*Home, or rivers and mountains from home,*
*Singing all time, minding no time,*
*While we two keep together.*

Till of a sudden,
May-be kill'd, unknown to her mate,
One forenoon the she-bird crouch'd not on the nest,
Nor return'd that afternoon, nor the next,
Nor ever appear'd again.

And thenceforward all summer in the sound of the sea,
And at night under the full of the moon in calmer weather,
Over the hoarse surging of the sea,
Or flitting from brier to brier by day,
I saw, I heard at intervals the remaining one, the he-bird,
The solitary guest from Alabama.

*Blow ! blow ! blow !*
*Blow up sea-winds along Paumanok's shore;*
*I wait and I wait till you blow my mate to me.*

Yes, when the stars glisten'd,
All night long on the prong of a moss-scallop'd stake,

Down almost amid the slapping waves,
Sat the lone singer wonderful causing tears.

He call'd on his mate,
He pour'd forth the meanings which I of all men know.

Yes my brother I know,
The rest might not, but I have treasur'd every note,
For more than once dimly down to the beach gliding,
Silent, avoiding the moonbeams, blending myself with the
    shadows,
Recalling now the obscure shapes, the echoes, the sounds
    and sights after their sorts,
The white arms out in the breakers tirelessly tossing,
I, with bare feet, a child, the wind wafting my hair,
Listen'd long and long.

Listen'd to keep, to sing, now translating the notes,
Following you my brother.

*Soothe ! soothe ! soothe !*
*Close on its wave soothes the wave behind,*
*And again another behind embracing and lapping, every one*
    *close,*
*But my love soothes not me, not me.*

*Low hangs the moon, it rose late,*
*It is lagging—O I think it is heavy with love, with love.*

*O madly the sea pushes upon the land,*
*With love, with love.*

*O night ! do I not see my love fluttering out among the*
    *breakers?*
*What is that little black thing I see there in the white?*

*Loud ! loud ! loud !*
*Loud I call to you, my love !*
*High and clear I shoot my voice over the waves,*
*Surely you must know who is here, is here,*
*You must know who I am, my love.*

*Low-hanging moon!*
*What is that dusky spot in your brown yellow?*
*O it is the shape, the shape of my mate!*
*O moon do not keep her from me any longer.*

*Land! land! O land!*
*Whichever way I turn, O I think you could give me my mate*
   *back again if you only would,*
*For I am almost sure I see her dimly whichever way I look.*

*O rising stars!*
*Perhaps the one I want so much will rise, will rise with some of*
   *you.*

*O throat! O trembling throat!*
*Sound clearer through the atmosphere!*
*Pierce the woods, the earth,*
*Somewhere listening to catch you must be the one I want.*

*Shake out carols!*
*Solitary here, the night's carols!*
*Carols of lonesome love! death's carols!*
*Carols under that lagging, yellow, waning moon!*
*O under that moon where she droops almost down into the sea!*
*O reckless despairing carols.*

*But soft! sink low!*
*Soft! let me just murmur,*
*And do you wait a moment you husky-nois'd sea,*
*For somewhere I believe I heard my mate responding to me,*
*So faint, I must be still, be still to listen,*
*But not altogether still, for then she might not come immediately*
   *to me.*

*Hither my love!*
*Here I am! here!*
*With this just-sustain'd note I announce myself to you,*
*This gentle call is for you my love, for you.*

*Do not be decoy'd elsewhere,*
*That is the whistle of the wind, it is not my voice,*

*That is the fluttering, the fluttering of the spray,*
*Those are the shadows of leaves.*

*O darkness! O in vain!*
*O I am very sick and sorrowful.*

*O brown halo in the sky near the moon, drooping upon the sea!*
*O troubled reflection in the sea!*
*O throat! O throbbing heart!*
*And I singing uselessly, uselessly all the night.*

*O past! O happy life! O songs of joy!*
*In the air, in the woods, over fields,*
*Loved! loved! loved! loved! loved!*
*But my mate no more, no more with me!*
*We two together no more.*

The aria sinking,
All else continuing, the stars shining,
The winds blowing, the notes of the bird continuous echoing,
With angry moans the fierce old mother incessantly moaning,
On the sands of Paumanok's shore gray and rustling,
The yellow half-moon enlarged, sagging down, drooping, the
　　　face of the sea almost touching,
The boy ecstatic, with his bare feet the waves, with his hair
　　　the atmosphere dallying,
The love in the heart long pent, now loose, now at last
　　　tumultuously bursting,
The aria's meaning, the ears, the soul, swiftly depositing,
The strange tears down the cheeks coursing,
The colloquy there, the trio, each uttering,
The undertone, the savage old mother incessantly crying,
To the boy's soul's questions sullenly timing, some drown'd
　　　secret hissing,
To the outsetting bard.

Demon or bird! (said the boy's soul,)
Is it indeed toward your mate you sing? or is it really to me?
For I, that was a child, my tongue's use sleeping, now I have
　　　heard you,
Now in a moment I know what I am for, I awake,

And already a thousand singers, a thousand songs, clearer,
    louder and more sorrowful than yours,
A thousand warbling echoes have started to life within me,
    never to die.

O you singer solitary, singing by yourself, projecting me,
O solitary me listening, never more shall I cease perpetuating
    you,
Never more shall I escape, never more the reverberations,
Never more the cries of unsatisfied love be absent from me,
Never again leave me to be the peaceful child I was before
    what there in the night,
By the sea under the yellow and sagging moon,
The messenger there arous'd, the fire, the sweet hell within,
The unknown want, the destiny of me.

O give me the clew! (it lurks in the night here somewhere,)
O if I am to have so much, let me have more!

A word then, (for I will conquer it,)
The word final, superior to all,
Subtle, sent up—what is it?—I listen;
Are you whispering it, and have been all the time, you sea
    waves?
Is that it from your liquid rims and wet sands?

Whereto answering, the sea,
Delaying not, hurrying not,
Whisper'd me through the night, and very plainly before
    daybreak,
Lisp'd to me the low and delicious word death,
And again death, death, death, death,
Hissing melodious, neither like the bird nor like my arous'd
    child's heart,
But edging near as privately for me rustling at my feet,
Creeping thence steadily up to my ears and laving me softly
    all over,
Death, death, death, death, death.

Which I do not forget,
But fuse the song of my dusky demon and brother,

That he sang to me in the moonlight on Paumanok's gray
    beach,
With the thousand responsive songs at random,
My own songs awaked from that hour,
And with them the key, the word up from the waves,
The word of the sweetest song and all songs,
That strong and delicious word which, creeping to my feet,
(Or like some old crone rocking the cradle, swathed in sweet
    garments, bending aside,)
The sea whisper'd me.
1859                                      1881

## AS I EBB'D WITH THE OCEAN OF LIFE

### 1

As I ebb'd with the ocean of life,
As I wended the shores I know,
As I walk'd where the ripples continually wash you Paumanok,
Where they rustle up hoarse and sibilant,
Where the fierce old mother endlessly cries for her castaways,
I musing late in the autumn day, gazing off southward,
Held by this electric self out of the pride of which I utter
    poems,
Was seiz'd by the spirit that trails in the lines underfoot,
The rim, the sediment that stands for all the water and all the
    land of the globe.

Fascinated, my eyes reverting from the south, dropt, to
    follow those slender windrows,
Chaff, straw, splinters of wood, weeds, and the sea-gluten,
Scum, scales from shining rocks, leaves of salt-lettuce, left by
    the tide,
Miles walking, the sound of breaking waves the other side of
    me,
Paumanok there and then as I thought the old thought of
    likenesses,
These you presented to me you fish-shaped island,
As I wended the shores I know,
As I walk'd with that electric self seeking types.

## 2

As I wend to the shores I know not,
As I list to the dirge, the voices of men and women wreck'd,
As I inhale the impalpable breezes that set in upon me,
As the ocean so mysterious rolls toward me closer and closer,
I too but signify at the utmost a little wash'd-up drift,
A few sands and dead leaves to gather,
Gather, and merge myself as part of the sands and drift.

O baffled, balk'd, bent to the very earth,
Oppress'd with myself that I have dared to open my mouth,
Aware now that amid all that blab whose echoes recoil upon
    me I have not once had the least idea who or what I am,
But that before all my arrogant poems the real Me stands yet
    untouch'd, untold, altogether unreach'd,
Withdrawn far, mocking me with mock-congratulatory signs
    and bows,
With peals of distant ironical laughter at every word I have
    written,
Pointing in silence to these songs, and then to the sand be-
    neath.
I perceive I have not really understood any thing, not a
    single object, and that no man ever can,
Nature here in sight of the sea taking advantage of me to dart
    upon me and sting me,
Because I have dared to open my mouth to sing at all.

## 3

You oceans both, I close with you,
We murmur alike reproachfully rolling sands and drift,
    knowing not why,
These little shreds indeed standing for you and me and all.

You friable shore with trails of debris,
You fish-shaped island, I take what is underfoot,
What is yours is mine my father.

I too Paumanok,
I too have bubbled up, floated the measureless float, and
    been wash'd on your shores,

I too am but a trail of drift and debris,
I too leave little wrecks upon you, you fish-shaped island.

I throw myself upon your breast my father,
I cling to you so that you cannot unloose me,
I hold you so firm till you answer me something.

Kiss me my father,
Touch me with your lips as I touch those I love,
Breathe to me while I hold you close the secret of the mur-
        muring I envy.

4

Ebb, ocean of life, (the flow will return,)
Cease not your moaning you fierce old mother,
Endlessly cry for your castaways, but fear not, deny not me,
Rustle not up so hoarse and angry against my feet as I touch
        you or gather from you.

I mean tenderly by you and all,
I gather for myself and for this phantom looking down where
        we lead, and following me and mine.

Me and mine, loose windrows, little corpses,
Froth, snowy white, and bubbles,
(See, from my dead lips the ooze exuding at last,
See, the prismatic colors glistening and rolling,)
Tufts of straw, sands, fragments,
Buoy'd hither from many moods, one contradicting another,
From the storm, the long calm, the darkness, the swell,
Musing, pondering, a breath, a briny tear, a dab of liquid or
        soil,
Up just as much out of fathomless workings fermented and
        thrown,
A limp blossom or two, torn, just as much over waves float-
        ing, drifted at random,
Just as much for us that sobbing dirge of Nature,
Just as much whence we come that blare of the cloud-trum-
        pets,
We, capricious, brought hither we know not whence, spread
        out before you,

You up there walking or sitting,
Whoever you are, we too lie in drifts at your feet.
1860                                              1881


## TEARS

TEARS! tears! tears!
In the night, in solitude, tears,
On the white shore dripping, dripping, suck'd in by the sand,
Tears, not a star shining, all dark and desolate,
Moist tears from the eyes of a muffled head;
O who is that ghost? that form in the dark, with tears?
What shapeless lump is that, bent, crouch'd there on the
    sand?
Streaming tears, sobbing tears, throes, choked with wild
    cries;
O storm, embodied, rising, careering with swift steps along
    the beach!
O wild and dismal night storm, with wind—O belching and
    desperate!
O shade so sedate and decorous by day, with calm counten-
    ance and regulated pace,
But away at night as you fly, none looking—O then the un-
    loosen'd ocean,
Of tears! tears! tears!
1867                                              1871


## TO THE MAN-OF-WAR-BIRD

THOU who hast slept all night upon the storm,
Waking renew'd on thy prodigious pinions,
(Burst the wild storm? above it thou ascended'st,
And rested on the sky, thy slave that cradled thee,)
Now a blue point, far, far in heaven floating,
As to the light emerging here on deck I watch thee,
(Myself a speck, a point on the world's floating vast.)
Far, far at sea,
After the night's fierce drifts have strewn the shore with
    wrecks,

With re-appearing day as now so happy and serene,
The rosy and elastic dawn, the flashing sun,
The limpid spread of air cerulean,
Thou also re-appearest.

Thou born to match the gale, (thou art all wings,)
To cope with heaven and earth and sea and hurricane,
Thou ship of air that never furl'st thy sails,
Days, even weeks untired and onward, through spaces,
    realms gyrating,
At dusk that look'st on Senegal, at morn America,
That sport'st amid the lightning-flash and thunder-cloud,
In them, in thy experiences, had'st thou my soul,
What joys! what joys were thine!
1876                                                        1881


## ABOARD AT A SHIP'S HELM

ABOARD at a ship's helm,
A young steersman steering with care.

Through fog on a sea-coast dolefully ringing,
An ocean-bell—O a warning bell, rock'd by the waves.

O you give good notice indeed, you bell by the sea-reefs
    ringing,
Ringing, ringing, to warn the ship from its wreck-place.

For as on the alert O steersman, you mind the loud admoni-
    tion,
The bows turn, the freighted ship tacking speeds away under
    her gray sails,
The beautiful and noble ship with all her precious wealth
    speeds away gayly and safe.

But O the ship, the immortal ship! O ship aboard the ship!
Ship of the body, ship of the soul, voyaging, voyaging,
    voyaging.
1867                                                        1871

## ON THE BEACH AT NIGHT

ON the beach at night,
Stands a child with her father,
Watching the east, the autumn sky.


Up through the darkness,
While ravening clouds, the burial clouds, in black masses
spreading,
Lower sullen and fast athwart and down the sky,
Amid a transparent clear belt of ether yet left in the east,
Ascends large and calm the lord-star Jupiter,
And nigh at hand, only a very little above,
Swim the delicate sisters the Pleiades.


From the beach the child holding the hand of her father,
Those burial clouds that lower victorious soon to devour all,
Watching, silently weeps.


Weep not, child,
Weep not, my darling,
With these kisses let me remove your tears,
The ravening clouds shall not long be victorious,
They shall not long possess the sky, they devour the stars
only in apparition,
Jupiter shall emerge, be patient, watch again another night,
the Pleiades shall emerge,
They are immortal, all those stars both silvery and golden
shall shine out again,
The great stars and the little ones shall shine out again, they
endure,
The vast immortal suns and the long-enduring pensive moons
shall again shine.


Then dearest child mournest thou only for Jupiter?
Considerest thou alone the burial of the stars?
Something there is,
(With my lips soothing thee, adding I whisper,
I give thee the first suggestion, the problem and indirection,)
Something there is more immortal even than the stars,

(Many the burials, many the days and nights, passing away,)
Something that shall endure longer even than lustrous
 Jupiter,
Longer than sun or any revolving satellite,
Or the radiant sisters the Pleiades.
1871              1871

## THE WORLD BELOW THE BRINE

THE world below the brine,
Forests at the bottom of the sea, the branches and leaves,
Sea-lettuce, vast lichens, strange flowers and seeds, the thick
 tangle, openings, and pink turf,
Different colors, pale gray and green, purple, white, and gold,
 the play of light through the water,
Dumb swimmers there among the rocks, coral, gluten, grass,
 rushes, and the aliment of the swimmers,
Sluggish existences grazing there suspended, or slowly crawling close to the bottom,
The sperm-whale at the surface blowing air and spray, or
 disporting with his flukes,
The leaden-eyed shark, the walrus, the turtle, the hairy sea-
 leopard, and the sting-ray,
Passions there, wars, pursuits, tribes, sight in those ocean-
 depths, breathing that thick-breathing air, as so many
 do,
The change thence to the sight here, and to the subtle air
 breathed by beings like us who walk this sphere,
The change onward from ours to that of beings who walk
 other spheres.
1860              1871

## ON THE BEACH AT NIGHT ALONE

ON the beach at night alone,
As the old mother sways her to and fro singing her husky
 song,
As I watch the bright stars shining, I think a thought of the
 clef of the universes and of the future.

A vast similitude interlocks all,
All spheres, grown, ungrown, small, large, suns, moons, planets,
All distances of place however wide,
All distances of time, all inanimate forms,
All souls, all living bodies though they be ever so different, or in different worlds,
All gaseous, watery, vegetable, mineral processes, the fishes, the brutes,
All nations, colors, barbarisms, civilizations, languages,
All identities that have existed or may exist on this globe, or any globe,
All lives and deaths, all of the past, present, future,
This vast similitude spans them, and always has spann'd,
And shall forever span them and compactly hold and enclose them.

1856                                                           1881


## SONG FOR ALL SEAS, ALL SHIPS

### 1

To-day a rude brief recitative,
Of ships sailing the seas, each with its special flag or ship-signal,
Of unnamed heroes in the ships—of waves spreading and spreading far as the eye can reach,
Of dashing spray, and the winds piping and blowing,
And out of these a chant for the sailors of all nations,
Fitful, like a surge.

Of sea-captains young or old, and the mates, and of all intrepid sailors,
Of the few, very choice, taciturn, whom fate can never surprise nor death dismay,
Pick'd sparingly without noise by thee old ocean, chosen by thee,
Thou sea that pickest and cullest the race in time, and unitest nations,
Suckled by thee, old husky nurse, embodying thee,
Indomitable, untamed as thee.

(Ever the heroes on water or on land, by ones or twos
   appearing,
Ever the stock preserv'd and never lost, though rare, enough
   for seed preserv'd.)

2

Flaunt out O sea your separate flags of nations!
Flaunt out visible as ever the various ship-signals!
But do you reserve especially for yourself and for the soul of
   man one flag above all the rest,
A spiritual woven signal for all nations, emblem of man elate
   above death,
Token of all brave captains and all intrepid sailors and mates,
And all that went down doing their duty,
Reminiscent of them, twined from all intrepid captains
   young or old,
A pennant universal, subtly waving all time, o'er all brave
   sailors,
All seas, all ships.
1873                                                                     1881

PATROLING BARNEGAT

WILD, wild the storm, and the sea high running,
Steady the roar of the gale, with incessant undertone mutter-
   ing,
Shouts of demoniac laughter fitfully piercing and pealing,
Waves, air, midnight, their savagest trinity lashing,
Out in the shadows there milk-white combs careering,
On beachy slush and sand spirts of snow fierce slanting,
Where through the murk the easterly death-wind breasting,
Through cutting swirl and spray watchful and firm advanc-
   ing,
(That in the distance! is that a wreck? is the red signal
   flaring?)
Slush and sand of the beach tireless till daylight wending,
Steadily, slowly, through hoarse roar never remitting,
Along the midnight edge by those milk-white combs career-
   ing,

A group of dim, weird forms, struggling, the night confronting,
That savage trinity warily watching.
1880                                                          1881


## AFTER THE SEA-SHIP

AFTER the sea-ship, after the whistling winds,
After the white-gray sails taut to their spars and ropes,
Below, a myriad myriad waves hastening, lifting up their
necks,
Tending in ceaseless flow toward the track of the ship,
Waves of the ocean bubbling and gurgling, blithely prying,
Waves, undulating waves, liquid, uneven, emulous waves,
Toward that whirling current, laughing and buoyant, with
curves,
Where the great vessel sailing and tacking displaced the
surface,
Larger and smaller waves in the spread of the ocean yearn-
fully flowing,
The wake of the sea-ship after she passes, flashing and frolic-
some under the sun,
A motley procession with many a fleck of foam and many
fragments,
Following the stately and rapid ship, in the wake following.
1874                                                          1881

# By the Roadside

## A BOSTON BALLAD

### (1854)

To get betimes in Boston town I rose this morning early,
Here's a good place at the corner, I must stand and see the
    show.

Clear the way there Jonathan!
Way for the President's marshal—way for the government
    cannon!
Way for the Federal foot and dragoons, (and the apparitions
    copiously tumbling.)

I love to look on the Stars and Stripes, I hope the fifes will
    play Yankee Doodle.

How bright shine the cutlasses of the foremost troops!
Every man holds his revolver, marching stiff through Boston
    town.

A fog follows, antiques of the same come limping,
Some appear wooden-legged, and some appear bandaged
    and bloodless.

Why this is indeed a show—it has called the dead out of the
    earth!
The old graveyards of the hills have hurried to see!
Phantoms! phantoms countless by flank and rear!
Cock'd hats of mothy mould—crutches made of mist!
Arms in slings—old men leaning on young men's shoulders.

What troubles you Yankee phantoms? what is all this chat-
    tering of bare gums?

244

Does the ague convulse your limbs? do you mistake your crutches for firelocks and level them?

If you blind your eyes with tears you will not see the President's marshal,
If you groan such groans you might balk the government cannon.

For shame old maniacs—bring down those toss'd arms, and let your white hair be,
Here gape your great-grandsons, their wives gaze at them from the windows,
See how well dress'd, see how orderly they conduct themselves.

Worse and worse—can't you stand it? are you retreating?
Is this hour with the living too dead for you?

Retreat then—pell-mell!
To your graves—back—back to the hills old limpers!
I do not think you belong here anyhow.

But there is one thing that belongs here—shall I tell you what it is, gentlemen of Boston?

I will whisper it to the Mayor, he shall send a committee to England,
They shall get a grant from the Parliament, go with a cart to the royal vault,
Dig out King George's coffin, unwrap him quick from the grave-clothes, box up his bones for a journey,
Find a swift Yankee clipper—here is freight for you, black-bellied clipper,
Up with your anchor—shake out your sails—steer straight toward Boston bay.

Now call for the President's marshal again, bring out the government cannon,
Fetch home the roarers from Congress, make another procession, guard it with foot and dragoons.

This centre-piece for them;
Look, all orderly citizens—look from the windows, women!

The committee open the box, set up the regal ribs, glue those
    that will not stay,
Clap the skull on top of the ribs, and clap a crown on top of
    the skull.

You have got your revenge, old buster—the crown is come to
    its own, and more than its own.

Stick your hands in your pockets, Jonathan—you are a made
    man from this day,
You are mighty cute—and here is one of your bargains.
(1854?)                                                            1871

# EUROPE

## *The 72d and 73d Years of These States*

SUDDENLY out of its stale and drowsy lair, the lair of
    slaves,
Like lightning it le'pt forth half startled at itself,
Its feet upon the ashes and the rags, its hand tight to the
    throats of kings.

O hope and faith!
O aching close of exiled patriots' lives!
O many a sicken'd heart!
Turn back unto this day and make yourselves afresh.

And you, paid to defile the People—you liars, mark!
Not for numberless agonies, murders, lusts,
For court thieving in its manifold mean forms, worming
    from his simplicity the poor man's wages,
For many a promise sworn by royal lips and broken and
    laugh'd at in the breaking,
Then in their power not for all these did the blows strike
    revenge, or the heads of the nobles fall;
The People scorn'd the ferocity of kings.

But the sweetness of mercy brew'd bitter destruction, and the
frighten'd monarchs come back,
Each comes in state with his train, hangman, priest, tax-
gatherer,
Soldier, lawyer, lord, jailer, and sycophant.

Yet behind all lowering stealing, lo, a shape,
Vague as the night, draped interminably, head, front and
form, in scarlet folds,
Whose face and eyes none may see,
Out of its robes only this, the red robes lifted by the arm,
One finger crook'd pointed high over the top, like the head of
a snake appears.

Meanwhile corpses lie in new-made graves, bloody corpses of
young men,
The rope of the gibbet hangs heavily, the bullets of princes
are flying, the creatures of power laugh aloud,
And all these things bear fruits, and they are good.

Those corpses of young men,
Those martyrs that hang from the gibbets, those hearts
pierc'd by the gray lead,
Cold and motionless as they seem live elsewhere with un-
slaughter'd vitality.

They live in other young men O kings!
They live in brothers again ready to defy you,
They were purified by death, they were taught and exalted.

Not a grave of the murder'd for freedom but grows seed for
freedom, in its turn to bear seed,
Which the winds carry afar and re-sow, and the rains and the
snows nourish.

Not a disembodied spirit can the weapons of tyrants let loose,
But it stalks invisibly over the earth, whispering, counseling,
cautioning.

Liberty, let others despair of you—I never despair of you.

Is the house shut? is the master away?
Nevertheless, be ready, be not weary of watching,
He will soon return, his messengers come anon.
1850                                                    1860

## A HAND-MIRROR

HOLD it up sternly—see this it sends back, (who is it? is it you?)
Outside fair costume, within ashes and filth,
No more a flashing eye, no more a sonorous voice or springy step,
Now some slave's eye, voice, hands, step,
A drunkard's breath, unwholesome eater's face, venerealee's flesh,
Lungs rotting away piecemeal, stomach sour and cankerous,
Joints rheumatic, bowels clogged with abomination,
Blood circulating dark and poisonous streams,
Words babble, hearing and touch callous,
No brain, no heart left, no magnetism of sex ;
Such from one look in this looking-glass ere you go hence,
Such a result so soon—and from such a beginning!
1860                                                    1860

## GODS

LOVER divine and perfect Comrade,
Waiting content, invisible yet, but certain,
Be thou my God.

Thou, thou, the Ideal Man,
Fair, able, beautiful, content, and loving,
Complete in body and dilate in spirit,
Be thou my God.

O Death, (for Life has served its turn,)
Opener and usher to the heavenly mansion,
Be thou my God.

Aught, aught of mightiest, best I see, conceive, or know,
(To break the stagnant tie—thee, thee to free, O soul,)
Be thou my God.

All great ideas, the races' aspirations,
All heroisms, deeds of rapt enthusiasts,
Be ye my Gods.

Or Time and Space,
Or shape of Earth divine and wondrous,
Or some fair shape I viewing, worship,
Or lustrous orb of sun or star by night,
Be ye my Gods.

1870                                                                    1881

## GERMS

FORMS, qualities, lives, humanity, language, thoughts,
The ones known, and the ones unknown, the ones on the stars,
The stars themselves, some shaped, others unshaped,
Wonders as of those countries, the soil, trees, cities, inhabi-
    tants, whatever they may be,
Splendid suns, the moons and rings, the countless combina-
    tions and effects,
Such-like, and as good as such-like, visible here or anywhere,
    stand provided for in a handful of space, which I extend
    my arm and half enclose with my hand,
That containing the start of each and all, the virtue, the
    germs of all.

1860                                                                    1871

## THOUGHTS

OF ownership—as if one fit to own things could not at
    pleasure enter upon all, and incorporate them into him-
    self or herself;
Of vista—suppose some sight in arriere through the forma-
    tive chaos, presuming the growth, fulness, life, now
    attain'd on the journey,
(But I see the road continued, and the journey ever con-
    tinued;)
Of what was once lacking on earth, and in due time has be-
    come supplied—and of what will yet be supplied,
Because all I see and know I believe to have its main purport
    in what will yet be supplied.

1860                                                                    1881

## WHEN I HEARD THE LEARN'D ASTRONOMER

WHEN I heard the learn'd astronomer,
When the proofs, the figures, were ranged in columns before
    me,
When I was shown the charts and diagrams, to add, divide,
    and measure them,
When I sitting heard the astronomer where he lectured with
    much applause in the lecture-room,
How soon unaccountable I became tired and sick,
Till rising and gliding out I wander'd off by myself,
In the mystical moist night-air, and from time to time,
Look'd up in perfect silence at the stars.
1865                                                    1867

## PERFECTIONS

ONLY themselves understand themselves and the like of
    themselves,
As souls only understand souls.
1860                                                    1860

## O ME! O LIFE!

O ME! O life! of the questions of these recurring,
Of the endless trains of the faithless, of cities fill'd with the
    foolish,
Of myself forever reproaching myself, (for who more foolish
    than I, and who more faithless?)
Of eyes that vainly crave the light, of the objects mean, of the
    struggle ever renew'd,
Of the poor results of all, of the plodding and sordid crowds
    I see around me,
Of the empty and useless years of the rest, with the rest me
    intertwined,
The question, O me! so sad, recurring—What good amid
    these, O me, O life?

### Answer

That you are here—that life exists and identity,
That the powerful play goes on, and you may contribute a
    verse.
1865–6                                                 1867

## TO A PRESIDENT

ALL you are doing and saying is to America dangled mirages,
You have not learn'd of Nature—of the politics of Nature
    you have not learn'd the great amplitude, rectitude,
    impartiality,
You have not seen that only such as they are for these States,
And that what is less than they must sooner or later lift off
    from these States.
1860                                                    1860

## I SIT AND LOOK OUT

I SIT and look out upon all the sorrows of the world, and
    upon all oppression and shame,
I hear secret convulsive sobs from young men at anguish
    with themselves, remorseful after deeds done,
I see in low life the mother misused by her children, dying,
    neglected, gaunt, desperate,
I see the wife misused by her husband, I see the treacherous
    seducer of young women,
I mark the ranklings of jealousy and unrequited love at-
    tempted to be hid, I see these sights on the earth,
I see the workings of battle, pestilence, tyranny, I see martyrs
    and prisoners,
I observe a famine at sea, I observe the sailors casting lots
    who shall be kill'd to preserve the lives of the rest,
I observe the slights and degradations cast by arrogant per-
    sons upon laborers, the poor, and upon negroes, and the
    like;
All these—all the meanness and agony without end I sitting
    look out upon,
See, hear, and am silent.
1860                                                    1860

## TO RICH GIVERS                                        •

WHAT you give me I cheerfully accept,
A little sustenance, a hut and garden, a little money, as I
    rendezvous with my poems,

A traveler's lodging and breakfast as I journey through the
    States,—why should I be ashamed to own such gifts?
    why to advertise for them?
For I myself am not one who bestows nothing upon man and
    woman,
For I bestow upon any man or woman the entrance to all the
    gifts of the universe.
1860                                             1867

## THE DALLIANCE OF THE EAGLES

SKIRTING the river road, (my forenoon walk, my rest,)
Skyward in air a sudden muffled sound, the dalliance of the
    eagles,
The rushing amorous contact high in space together,
The clinching interlocking claws, a living, fierce, gyrating
    wheel,
Four beating wings, two beaks, a swirling mass tight grappling,
In tumbling turning clustering loops, straight downward
    falling,
Till o'er the river pois'd, the twain yet one, a moment's lull,
A motionless still balance in the air, then parting, talons
    loosing,
Upward again on slow-firm pinions slanting, their separate
    diverse flight,
She hers, he his, pursuing.
1880                                             1881

## ROAMING IN THOUGHT

### (*After reading* HEGEL)

ROAMING in thought over the Universe, I saw the little that is
    Good steadily hastening towards immortality,
And the vast all that is call'd Evil I saw hastening to merge
    itself and become lost and dead.
1881                                             1881

## A FARM PICTURE

THROUGH the ample open door of the peaceful country barn,
A sunlit pasture field with cattle and horses feeding,
And haze and vista, and the far horizon fading away.
1865                                             1871

## A CHILD'S AMAZE

SILENT and amazed even when a little boy,
I remember I heard the preacher every Sunday put God in
    his statements,
As contending against some being or influence.
1865                                   1867

## THE RUNNER

ON a flat road runs the well-train'd runner,
He is lean and sinewy with muscular legs,
He is thinly clothed, he leans forward as he runs,
With lightly closed fists and arms partially rais'd.
1867                                   1867

## BEAUTIFUL WOMEN

WOMEN sit or move to and fro, some old, some young,
The young are beautiful—but the old are more beautiful than
    the young.
1860                                   1860

## MOTHER AND BABE

I SEE the sleeping babe nestling the breast of its mother,
The sleeping mother and babe—hush'd, I study them long
    and long.
1865                                   1867

## THOUGHT

OF obedience, faith, adhesiveness;
As I stand aloof and look there is to me something profoundly
    affecting in large masses of men following the lead of
    those who do not believe in men.
1860                                   1860

## VISOR'D

A MASK, a perpetual natural disguiser of herself,
Concealing her face, concealing her form,
Changes and transformations every hour, every moment,
Falling upon her even when she sleeps.
1860                                   1867

## THOUGHT

OF Justice—as if Justice could be any thing but the same
    ample law, expounded by natural judges and saviors,
As if it might be this thing or that thing, according to decisions.
1860                                            1860

## GLIDING O'ER ALL

GLIDING o'er all, through all,
Through Nature, Time, and Space,
As a ship on the waters advancing,
The voyage of the soul—not life alone,
Death, many deaths I'll sing.

1871                                            1871

## HAST NEVER COME TO THEE AN HOUR

HAST never come to thee an hour,
A sudden gleam divine, precipitating, bursting all these
    bubbles, fashions, wealth?
These eager business aims—books, politics, art, amours,
To utter nothingness?
1881                                           1881

## THOUGHT

OF Equality—as if it harm'd me, giving others the same
    chances and rights as myself—as if it were not indis-
    pensable to my own rights that others possess the same.
1860                                            1860

## TO OLD AGE

I SEE in you the estuary that enlarges and spreads itself
    grandly as it pours in the great sea.
1860                                            1860

## LOCATIONS AND TIMES

LOCATIONS and times—what is it in me that meets them all,
    whenever and wherever, and makes me at home?
Forms, colors, densities, odors—what is it in me that cor-
    responds with them?
1860                                            1871

## OFFERINGS

A THOUSAND perfect men and women appear,
Around each gathers a cluster of friends, and gay children
    and youths, with offerings.

1860                                                          1871

## TO THE STATES

### *To Identify the 16th, 17th, or 18th Presidentiad*

WHY reclining, interrogating? why myself and all drowsing?
What deepening twilight—scum floating atop of the waters,
Who are they as bats and night-dogs askant in the capitol?
What a filthy Presidentiad! (O South, your torrid suns! O
    North, your arctic freezings!)
Are those really Congressmen? are those the great Judges? is
    that the President?
Then I will sleep awhile yet, for I see that these States sleep,
    for reasons;
(With gathering murk, with muttering thunder and lambent
    shoots we all duly awake,
South, North, East, West, inland and seaboard, we will surely
    awake.)

1860                                                          1860

# *Drum-Taps*

## FIRST O SONGS FOR A PRELUDE

FIRST O songs for a prelude,
Lightly strike on the stretch'd tympanum pride and joy in
my city,
How she led the rest to arms, how she gave the cue,
How at once with lithe limbs unwaiting a moment she sprang,
(O superb! O Manhattan, my own, my peerless!
O strongest you in the hour of danger, in crisis! O truer than
steel!)
How you sprang—how you threw off the costumes of peace
with indifferent hand,
How your soft opera-music changed, and the drum and fife
were heard in their stead,
How you led to the war, (that shall serve for our prelude,
songs of soldiers,)
How Manhattan drum-taps led.

Forty years had I in my city seen soldiers parading,
Forty years as a pageant, till unawares the lady of this teem-
ing and turbulent city,
Sleepless amid her ships, her houses, her incalculable wealth,
With her million children around her, suddenly,
At dead of night, at news from the south,
Incens'd struck with clinch'd hand the pavement.

A shock electric, the night sustain'd it,
Till with ominous hum our hive at daybreak pour'd out its
myriads.

From the houses then and the workshops, and through all
the doorways,
Leapt they tumultuous, and lo! Manhattan arming.

To the drum-taps prompt,

The young men falling in and arming,

The mechanics arming, (the trowel, the jack-plane, the blacksmith's hammer, tost aside with precipitation,)

The lawyer leaving his office and arming, the judge leaving
the court,

The driver deserting his wagon in the street, jumping down,
throwing the reins abruptly down on the horses' backs,

The salesman leaving the store, the boss, book-keeper, porter, all leaving;

Squads gather everywhere by common consent and arm,

The new recruits, even boys, the old men show them how to
wear their accoutrements, they buckle the straps carefully,

Outdoors, arming, indoors arming, the flash of the musket-
barrels,

The white tents cluster in camps, the arm'd sentries around,
the sunrise cannon and again at sunset,

Arm'd regiments arrive every day, pass through the city, and
embark from the wharves,

(How good they look as they tramp down to the river, sweaty,
with their guns on their shoulders!

How I love them! how I could hug them, with their brown
faces and their clothes and knapsacks cover'd with
dust!)

The blood of the city up—arm'd! arm'd! the cry everywhere,

The flags flung out from the steeples of churches and from all
the public buildings and stores,

The tearful parting, the mother kisses her son, the son kisses
his mother,

(Loth is the mother to part, yet not a word does she speak to
detain him,)

The tumultuous escort, the ranks of policemen preceding,
clearing the way,

The unpent enthusiasm, the wild cheers of the crowd for
their favorites,

The artillery, the silent cannons bright as gold, drawn along,
rumble lightly over the stones,

(Silent cannons, soon to cease your silence,

Soon unlimber'd to begin the red business;)

I                                                        **W.**

All the mutter of preparation, all the determin'd arming,
The hospital service, the lint, bandages and medicines,
The women volunteering for nurses, the work begun for in
　　　earnest, no mere parade now;
War! an arm'd race is advancing! the welcome for battle, no
　　　turning away;
War! be it weeks, months, or years, an arm'd race is advanc-
　　　ing to welcome it.

Mannahatta a-march—and it's O to sing it well!
It's O for a manly life in the camp.

And the sturdy artillery,
The guns bright as gold, the work for giants, to serve well the
　　　guns,
Unlimber them! (no more as the past forty years for salute or
　　　courtesies merely,
Put in something now besides powder and wadding.)

And you lady of ships, you Mannahatta,
Old matron of this proud, friendly, turbulent city,
Often in peace and wealth you were pensive or covertly
　　　frown'd amid all your children,
But now you smile with joy exulting old Mannahatta.
1865                                                                           1867


## EIGHTEEN SIXTY-ONE

Arm'd year—year of the struggle,
No dainty rhymes or sentimental love verses for you terrible
　　　year,
Not you as some pale poetling seated at a desk lisping
　　　cadenzas piano,
But as a strong man erect, clothed in blue clothes, advancing,
　　　carrying a rifle on your shoulder,
With well-gristled body and sunburnt face and hands, with a
　　　knife in the belt at your side,
As I heard you shouting loud, your sonorous voice ringing
　　　across the continent,
Your masculine voice O year, as rising amid the great cities,

Amid the men of Manhattan I saw you as one of the workmen, the dwellers in Manhattan,

Or with large steps crossing the prairies out of Illinois and
Indiana,

Rapidly crossing the West with springy gait and descending
the Alleghanies,

Or down from the great lakes or in Pennsylvania, or on deck
along the Ohio river,

Or southward along the Tennessee or Cumberland rivers, or
at Chattanooga on the mountain top,

Saw I your gait and saw I your sinewy limbs clothed in blue,
bearing weapons, robust year,

Heard your determin'd voice launch'd forth again and again,

Year that suddenly sang by the mouths of the round-lipp'd
cannon,

I repeat you, hurrying, crashing, sad, distracted year.
(1861?)                                                1867

## BEAT! BEAT! DRUMS!

BEAT! beat! drums!—blow! bugles! blow!

Through the windows—through doors—burst like a ruthless
force,

Into the solemn church, and scatter the congregation,

Into the school where the scholar is studying;

Leave not the bridegroom quiet—no happiness must he have
now with his bride,

Nor the peaceful farmer any peace, ploughing his field or
gathering his grain,

So fierce you whirr and pound you drums—so shrill you
bugles blow.

Beat! beat! drums!—blow! bugles! blow!

Over the traffic of cities—over the rumble of wheels in the
streets;

Are beds prepared for sleepers at night in the houses? no
sleepers must sleep in those beds,

No bargainers' bargains by day—no brokers or speculators
—would they continue?

Would the talkers be talking? would the singer attempt to
sing?

Would the lawyer rise in the court to state his case before the
judge?
Then rattle quicker, heavier drums—you bugles wilder blow.

Beat! beat! drums!—blow! bugles! blow!
Make no parley—stop for no expostulation,
Mind not the timid—mind not the weeper or prayer,
Mind not the old man beseeching the young man,
Let not the child's voice be heard, nor the mother's entreaties,
Make even the trestles to shake the dead where they lie
awaiting the hearses,
So strong you thump O terrible drums—so loud you bugles
blow.
1861                                                                  1867

## FROM PAUMANOK STARTING I FLY LIKE A BIRD

From Paumanok starting I fly like a bird,
Around and around to soar to sing the idea of all,
To the north betaking myself to sing there arctic songs,
To Kanada till I absorb Kanada in myself, to Michigan then,
To Wisconsin, Iowa, Minnesota, to sing their songs, (they
are inimitable;)
Then to Ohio and Indiana to sing theirs, to Missouri and
Kansas and Arkansas to sing theirs,
To Tennessee and Kentucky, to the Carolinas and Georgia
to sing theirs,
To Texas and so along up toward California, to roam
accepted everywhere;
To sing first, (to the tap of the war-drum if need be,)
The idea of all, of the Western world one and inseparable,
And then the song of each member of these States.
1865                                                                  1867

## SONG OF THE BANNER AT DAYBREAK

*Poet*

O a new song, a free song,
Flapping, flapping, flapping, flapping, by sounds, by voices
clearer,

By the wind's voice and that of the drum,
By the banner's voice and child's voice and sea's voice and
    father's voice,
Low on the ground and high in the air,
On the ground where father and child stand,
In the upward air where their eyes turn,
Where the banner at daybreak is flapping.


Words! book-words! what are you?
Words no more, for hearken and see,
My song is there in the open air, and I must sing,
With the banner and pennant a-flapping.


I'll weave the chord and twine in,
Man's desire and babe's desire, I'll twine them in, I'll put in
    life,
I'll put the bayonet's flashing point, I'll let bullets and slugs
    whizz,
(As one carrying a symbol and menace far into the
    future,
Crying with trumpet voice, *Arouse and beware! Beware and
    arouse!*)
I'll pour the verse with streams of blood, full of volition, full
    of joy,
Then loosen, launch forth, to go and compete,
With the banner and pennant a-flapping.


### Pennant

Come up here, bard, bard,
Come up here, soul, soul,
Come up here, dear little child,
To fly in the clouds and winds with me, and play with the
    measureless light.


### Child

Father what is that in the sky beckoning to me with long
    finger?
And what does it say to me all the while?

### Father

Nothing my babe you see in the sky,
And nothing at all to you it says—but look you my babe,
Look at these dazzling things in the houses, and see you the
    money-shops opening,
And see you the vehicles preparing to crawl along the streets
    with goods;
These, ah these, how valued and toil'd for these!
How envied by all the earth!

### Poet

Fresh and rosy red the sun is mounting high,
On floats the sea in distant blue careering through its
    channels,
On floats the wind over the breast of the sea setting in toward
    land,
The great steady wind from west or west-by-south,
Floating so buoyant with milk-white foam on the waters.

But I am not the sea nor the red sun,
I am not the wind with girlish laughter,
Not the immense wind which strengthens, not the wind
    which lashes,
Not the spirit that ever lashes its own body to terror and
    death,
But I am that which unseen comes and sings, sings, sings,
Which babbles in brooks and scoots in showers on the land,
Which the birds know in the woods mornings and evenings,
And the shore-sands know and the hissing wave, and that
    banner and pennant,
Aloft there flapping and flapping.

### Child

O father it is alive—it is full of people—it has children,
O now it seems to me it is talking to its children,
I hear it—it talks to me—O it is wonderful!
O it stretches—it spreads and runs so fast—O my father,
It is so broad it covers the whole sky.

### Father

Cease, cease, my foolish babe,
What you are saying is sorrowful to me, much it displeases
me;
Behold with the rest again I say, behold not banners and
pennants aloft,
But the well-prepared pavements behold, and mark the solid-
wall'd houses.

### Banner and Pennant

Speak to the child O bard out of Manhattan,
To our children all, or north or south of Manhattan,
Point this day, leaving all the rest, to us over all—and yet we
know not why,
For what are we, mere strips of cloth profiting nothing,
Only flapping in the wind?

### Poet

I hear and see not strips of cloth alone,
I hear the tramp of armies, I hear the challenging sentry,
I hear the jubilant shouts of millions of men, I hear Liberty!
I hear the drums beat and the trumpets blowing,
I myself move abroad swift-rising flying then,
I use the wings of the land-bird and use the wings of the sea-
bird, and look down as from a height,
I do not deny the precious results of peace, I see populous
cities with wealth incalculable,
I see numberless farms, I see the farmers working in their
fields or barns,
I see mechanics working, I see buildings everywhere founded,
going up, or finish'd,
I see trains of cars swiftly speeding along railroad tracks
drawn by the locomotives,
I see the stores, depots, of Boston, Baltimore, Charleston,
New Orleans,
I see far in the West the immense area of grain, I dwell awhile
hovering,

I pass to the lumber forests of the North, and again to the
  Southern plantation, and again to California;
Sweeping the whole I see the countless profit, the busy
  gatherings, earn'd wages,
See the Identity formed out of thirty-eight spacious and
  haughty States, (and many more to come,)
See forts on the shores of harbors, see ships sailing in and
  out;
Then over all, (aye! aye!) my little and lengthen'd pennant
  shaped like a sword,
Runs swiftly up indicating war and defiance—and now the
  halyards have rais'd it,
Side of my banner broad and blue, side of my starry ban-
  ner,
Discarding peace over all the sea and land.


### Banner and Pennant

Yet louder, higher, stronger, bard! yet farther, wider cleave!
No longer let our children deem us riches and peace alone,
We may be terror and carnage, and are so now,
Not now are we any one of these spacious and haughty
  States, (nor any five, nor ten,)
Nor market nor depot we, nor money-bank in the city,
But these and all, and the brown and spreading land, and the
  mines below, are ours,
And the shores of the sea are ours, and the rivers great and
  small,
And the fields they moisten, and the crops and the fruits are
  ours,
Bays and channels and ships sailing in and out are ours—
  while we over all,
Over the area spread below, the three or four millions of
  square miles, the capitals,
The forty millions of people,—O bard! in life and death
  supreme,
We, even we, henceforth flaunt out masterful, high up above,
Not for the present alone, for a thousand years chanting
  through you,
This song to the soul of one poor little child.

### Child

O my father I like not the houses,
They will never to me be anything, nor do I like money,
But to mount up there I would like, O father dear, that banner I like,
That pennant I would be and must be.

### Father

Child of mine you fill me with anguish,
To be that pennant would be too fearful,
Little you know what it is this day, and after this day, forever,
It is to gain nothing, but risk and defy everything,
Forward to stand in front of wars—and O, such wars!—what have you to do with them?
With passions of demons, slaughter, premature death?

### Banner

Demons and death then I sing,
Put in all, aye all will I, sword-shaped pennant for war,
And a pleasure new and ecstatic, and the prattled yearning of children,
Blent with the sounds of the peaceful land and the liquid wash of the sea,
And the black ships fighting on the sea envelop'd in smoke,
And the icy cool of the far, far north, with rustling cedars and pines,
And the whirr of drums and the sound of soldiers marching, and the hot sun shining south,
And the beach-waves combing over the beach on my Eastern shore, and my Western shore the same,
And all between those shores, and my ever running Mississippi with bends and chutes,
And my Illinois fields, and my Kansas fields, and my fields of Missouri,
The Continent, devoting the whole identity without reserving an atom,
Pour in! whelm that which asks, which sings, with all and the yield of all,

Fusing and holding, claiming, devouring the whole,
No more with tender lip, nor musical labial sound,
But out of the night emerging for good, our voice persuasive
    no more,
Croaking like crows here in the wind.

### Poet

My limbs, my veins dilate, my theme is clear at last,
Banner so broad advancing out of the night, I sing you
    haughty and resolute,
I burst through where I waited long, too long, deafen'd and
    blinded,
My hearing and tongue are come to me, (a little child taught
    me,)
I hear from above O pennant of war your ironical call and
    demand,
Insensate! insensate (yet I at any rate chant you,) O banner!
Not houses of peace indeed are you, nor any nor all their
    prosperity, (if need be, you shall again have every one of
    those houses to destroy them,
You thought not to destroy those valuable houses, standing
    fast, full of comfort, built with money,
May they stand fast, then? not an hour except you above
    them and all stand fast;)
O banner, not money so precious are you, not farm produce
    you, nor the material good nutriment,
Nor excellent stores, nor landed on wharves from the
    ships,
Not the superb ships with sail-power or steam-power, fetch-
    ing and carrying cargoes,
Nor machinery, vehicles, trade, nor revenues—but you as
    henceforth I see you,
Running up out of the night, bringing your cluster of stars,
    (ever-enlarging stars,)
Divider of daybreak you, cutting the air, touch'd by the sun,
    measuring the sky,
(Passionately seen and yearn'd for by one poor little child,
While others remain busy or smartly talking, forever teach-
    ing thrift, thrift;)

O you up there! O pennant! where you undulate like a snake
    hissing so curious,
Out of reach, an idea only, yet furiously fought for, risking
    bloody death, loved by me,
So loved—O you banner leading the day with stars brought
    from the night!
Valueless, object of eyes, over all and demanding all—(ab-
    solute owner of all)—O banner and pennant!
I too leave the rest—great as it is, it is nothing—houses,
    machines are nothing—I see them not,
I see but you, O warlike pennant! O banner so broad, with
    stripes, I sing you only,
Flapping up there in the wind.
(1861–2?)                                                       1881


# RISE O DAYS FROM YOUR FATHOMLESS DEEPS

## 1

RISE O days from your fathomless deeps, till you loftier,
    fiercer sweep,
Long for my soul hungering gymnastic I devour'd what the
    earth gave me,
Long I roam'd the woods of the north, long I watch'd Nia-
    gara pouring,
I travel'd the prairies over and slept on their breast, I cross'd
    the Nevadas, I cross'd the plateaus,
I ascended the towering rocks along the Pacific, I sail'd out
    to sea,
I sail'd through the storm, I was refresh'd by the storm,
I watch'd with joy the threatening maws of the waves,
I mark'd the white combs where they career'd so high, curling
    over,
I heard the wind piping, I saw the black clouds,
Saw from below what arose and mounted, (O superb! O
    wild as my heart, and powerful!)
Heard the continuous thunder as it bellow'd after the light-
    ning,
Noted the slender and jagged threads of lightning as sudden
    and fast amid the din they chased each other across the
    sky;

These, and such as these, I, elate, saw—saw with wonder, yet
　　pensive and masterful,
All the menacing might of the globe uprisen around me,
Yet there with my soul I fed, I fed content, supercilious.

### 2

'Twas well, O soul—'twas a good preparation you gave me,
Now we advance our latent and ampler hunger to fill,
Now we go forth to receive what the earth and the sea never
　　gave us,
Not through the mighty woods we go, but through the
　　mightier cities,
Something for us is pouring now more than Niagara pouring,
Torrents of men, (sources and rills of the Northwest are you
　　indeed inexhaustible?)
What, to pavements and homesteads here, what were those
　　storms of the mountains and sea?
What, to passions I witness around me to-day? was the sea
　　risen?
Was the wind piping the pipe of death under the black clouds?
Lo! from deeps more unfathomable, something more deadly
　　and savage,
Manhattan rising, advancing with menacing front—Cincin-
　　nati, Chicago, unchain'd;
What was that swell I saw on the ocean? behold what comes
　　here,
How it climbs with daring feet and hands—how it dashes!
How the true thunder bellows after the lightning—how
　　bright the flashes of lightning!
How Democracy with desperate vengeful port strides on,
　　shown through the dark by those flashes of lightning!
(Yet a mournful wail and low sob I fancied I heard through
　　the dark,
In a lull of the deafening confusion.)

### 3

Thunder on! stride on, Democracy! strike with vengeful
　　stroke!
And do you rise higher than ever yet O days, O cities!

Crash heavier, heavier yet O storms! you have done me
    good,
My soul prepared in the mountains absorbs your immortal
    strong nutriment,
Long had I walk'd my cities, my country roads through
    farms, only half satisfied,
One doubt nauseous undulating like a snake, crawl'd on the
    ground before me,
Continually preceding my steps, turning upon me oft, ironi-
    cally hissing low;
The cities I love so well I abandon'd and left, I sped to the
    certainties suitable to me,
Hungering, hungering, hungering, for primal energies and
    Nature's dauntlessness,
I refresh'd myself with it only, I could relish it only,
I waited the bursting forth of the pent fire—on the water and
    air I waited long;
But now I no longer wait, I am fully satisfied, I am glutted,
I have witness'd the true lightning, I have witness'd my cities
    electric,
I have lived to behold man burst forth and warlike America
    rise,
Hence I will seek no more the food of the northern solitary
    wilds,
No more the mountains roam or sail the stormy sea.
1865                                           1867

## VIRGINIA—THE WEST

THE noble sire fallen on evil days,
I saw with hand uplifted, menacing, brandishing,
(Memories of old in abeyance, love and faith in abeyance,)
The insane knife toward the Mother of All.

The noble son on sinewy feet advancing,
I saw, out of the land of prairies, land of Ohio's waters and of
    Indiana,
To the rescue the stalwart giant hurry his plenteous off-
    spring,
Drest in blue, bearing their trusty rifles on their shoulders.

Then the Mother of All with calm voice speaking,
As to you Rebellious, (I seemed to hear her say,) why strive
against me, and why seek my life?
When you yourself forever provide to defend me?
For you provided me Washington—and now these also.
1872                                                                    1881

## CITY OF SHIPS

CITY of Ships!
(O the black ships! O the fierce ships!
O the beautiful sharp-bow'd steam-ships and sail-ships!)
City of the world! (for all races are here,
All the lands of the earth make contributions here;)
City of the sea! city of hurried and glittering tides!
City whose gleeful tides continually rush or recede, whirling
in and out with eddies and foam!
City of wharves and stores—city of tall façades of marble and
iron!
Proud and passionate city—mettlesome, mad, extravagant
city!
Spring up O city—not for peace alone, but be indeed your-
self, warlike!
Fear not—submit to no models but your own O city!
Behold me—incarnate me as I have incarnated you!
I have rejected nothing you offer'd me—whom you adopted
I have adopted,
Good or bad I never question you—I love all—I do not con-
demn anything,
I chant and celebrate all that is yours—yet peace no more,
In peace I chanted peace, but now the drum of war is mine,
War, red war is my song through your streets, O city!
1865                                                                    1867

## THE CENTENARIAN'S STORY

*Volunteer of* 1861-2, (*at Washington Park, Brooklyn, assisting
the Centenarian*)

GIVE me your hand old Revolutionary,
The hill-top is nigh, but a few steps, (make room gentlemen,)

Up the path you have follow'd me well, spite of your hundred
    and extra years,
You can walk old man, though your eyes are almost done,
Your faculties serve you, and presently I must have them
    serve me.

Rest, while I tell what the crowd around us means,
On the plain below recruits are drilling and exercising,
There is the camp, one regiment departs to-morrow,
Do you hear the officers giving their orders?
Do you hear the clank of the muskets?

Why what comes over you now old man?
Why do you tremble and clutch my hand so convulsively?
The troops are but drilling, they are yet surrounded with
    smiles,
Around them at hand the well-drest friends and the women,
While splendid and warm the afternoon sun shines down,
Green the midsummer verdure and fresh blows the dallying
    breeze,
O'er proud and peaceful cities and arm of the sea between.

But drill and parade are over, they march back to quarters,
Only hear that approval of hands! hear what a clapping!

As wending the crowds now part and disperse—but we old
    man,
Not for nothing have I brought you hither—we must remain,
You to speak in your turn, and I to listen and tell.

### The Centenarian

When I clutch'd your hand it was not with terror,
But suddenly pouring about me here on every side,
And below there where the boys were drilling, and up the
    slopes they ran,
And where tents are pitch'd, and wherever you see south and
    south-east and south-west,
Over hills, across lowlands and in the skirts of woods,
And along the shores in mire (now fill'd over) came again
    and suddenly raged,

As eighty-five years a-gone no mere parade receiv'd with
    applause of friends,
But a battle which I took part in myself—aye, long ago as it
    is, I took part in it,
Walking then this hilltop, this same ground.

Aye, this is the ground,
My blind eyes even as I speak behold it re-peopled from
    graves,
The years recede, pavements and stately houses disappear,
Rude forts appear again, the old hoop'd guns are mounted,
I see the lines of rais'd earth stretching from river to bay,
I mark the vista of waters, I mark the uplands and slopes;
Here we lay encamp'd, it was this time in summer also.

As I talk I remember all, I remember the Declaration,
It was read here, the whole army paraded, it was read to us
    here,
By his staff surrounded the General stood in the middle, he
    held up his unsheath'd sword,
It glitter'd in the sun in full sight of the army.

'Twas a bold act then—the English war-ships had just arrived,
We could watch down the lower bay where they lay at
    anchor,
And the transports swarming with soldiers.

A few days more and they landed and then the battle.

Twenty thousand were brought against us,
A veteran force furnish'd with good artillery.

I tell not now the whole of the battle,
But one brigade early in the forenoon order'd forward to
    engage the red-coats,
Of that brigade I tell, and how steadily it march'd,
And how long and well it stood confronting death.

Who do you think that was marching steadily sternly con-
    fronting death?

It was the brigade of the youngest men, two thousand strong,
Rais'd in Virginia and Maryland, and most of them known
    personally to the General.

Jauntily forward they went with quick step toward Gowanus'
    waters,
Till of a sudden unlook'd for by defiles through the woods,
    gain'd at night,
The British advancing, rounding in from the east, fiercely
    playing their guns,
That brigade of the youngest was cut off and at the enemy's
    mercy.

The General watch'd them from this hill,
They made repeated desperate attempts to burst their en-
    vironment,
Then drew close together, very compact, their flag flying in
    the middle,
But O from the hills how the cannon were thinning and thin-
    ning them!

It sickens me yet, that slaughter!
I saw the moisture gather in drops on the face of the
    General.
I saw how he wrung his hands in anguish.

Meanwhile the British manœuvr'd to draw us out for a
    pitch'd battle,
But we dared not trust the chances of a pitch'd battle.

We fought the fight in detachments,
Sallying forth we fought at several points, but in each the
    luck was against us,
Our foe advancing, steadily getting the best of it, push'd us
    back to the works on this hill,
Till we turn'd menacing here, and then he left us.

That was the going out of the brigade of the youngest men,
    two thousand strong,
Few return'd, nearly all remain in Brooklyn.

That and here my General's first battle,
No women looking on nor sunshine to bask in, it did not
conclude with applause,
Nobody clapp'd hands here then.

But in darkness in mist on the ground under a chill rain,
Wearied that night we lay foil'd and sullen,
While scornfully laugh'd many an arrogant lord off against
us encamp'd,
Quite within hearing, feasting, clinking wineglasses together
over their victory.

So dull and damp and another day,
But the night of that, mist lifting, rain ceasing,
Silent as a ghost while they thought they were sure of him,
my General retreated.

I saw him at the river-side,
Down by the ferry lit by torches, hastening the embarcation;
My General waited till the soldiers and wounded were all
pass'd over,
And then, (it was just ere sunrise,) these eyes rested on him
for the last time.

Every one else seem'd fill'd with gloom,
Many no doubt thought of capitulation.

But when my General pass'd me,
As he stood in his boat and look'd toward the coming sun,
I saw something different from capitulation.

### Terminus

Enough, the Centenarian's story ends,
The two, the past and present, have interchanged,
I myself as connecter, a chansonnier of a great future, am
now speaking.

And is this the ground Washington trod?
And these waters I listlessly daily cross, are these the waters
he cross'd,

As resolute in defeat as other generals in their proudest
    triumphs?

I must copy the story, and send it eastward and westward,
I must preserve that look as it beam'd on you rivers of
    Brooklyn.

See—as the annual round returns the phantoms return,
It is the 27th of August and the British have landed,
The battle begins and goes against us, behold through the
    smoke Washington's face,
The brigade of Virginia and Maryland have march'd forth to
    intercept the enemy,
They are cut off, murderous artillery from the hills plays
    upon them,
Rank after rank falls, while over them silently droops the
    flag,
Baptized that day in many a young man's bloody wounds,
In death, defeat, and sisters', mothers' tears.

Ah, hills and slopes of Brooklyn! I perceive you are more
    valuable than your owners supposed;
In the midst of you stands an encampment very old,
Stands forever the camp of that dead brigade.
(1861–2?)                                                              1881


## CAVALRY CROSSING A FORD

A LINE in long array where they wind betwixt green islands,
They take a serpentine course, their arms flash in the sun—
    hark to the musical clank,
Behold the silvery river, in it the splashing horses loitering
    stop to drink,
Behold the brown-faced men, each group, each person a
    picture, the negligent rest on the saddles,
Some emerge on the opposite bank, others are just entering
    the ford—while,
Scarlet and blue and snowy white,
The guidon flags flutter gayly in the wind.
1865                                                                    1871

## BIVOUAC ON A MOUNTAIN SIDE

I SEE before me now a traveling army halting,
Below a fertile valley spread, with barns and the orchards of
summer,
Behind, the terraced sides of a mountain, abrupt, in places
rising high,
Broken, with rocks, with clinging cedars, with tall shapes
dingily seen,
The numerous camp-fires scatter'd near and far, some away
up on the mountain,
The shadowy forms of men and horses, looming, large-sized,
flickering,
And over all the sky—the sky! far, far out of reach, studded,
breaking out, the eternal stars.
1865                                                    1871

## AN ARMY CORPS ON THE MARCH

WITH its cloud of skirmishers in advance,
With now the sound of a single shot snapping like a whip,
and now an irregular volley,
The swarming ranks press on and on, the dense brigades
press on,
Glittering dimly, toiling under the sun—the dust-cover'd
men,
In columns rise and fall to the undulations of the ground,
With artillery interspers'd—the wheels rumble, the horses
sweat,
As the army corps advances.
1865-6                                                  1871

## BY THE BIVOUAC'S FITFUL FLAME

BY the bivouac's fitful flame,
A procession winding around me, solemn and sweet and slow
—but first I note,
The tents of the sleeping army, the fields' and woods' dim
outline,
The darkness lit by spots of kindled fire, the silence,
Like a phantom far or near an occasional figure moving,

The shrubs and trees, (as I lift my eyes they seem to be
  stealthily watching me,)
While wind in procession thoughts, O tender and wondrous
  thoughts,
Of life and death, of home and the past and loved, and of
  those that are far away;
A solemn and slow procession there as I sit on the ground,
By the bivouac's fitful flame.
1865                                                    1867

## COME UP FROM THE FIELDS FATHER

COME up from the fields father, here's a letter from our Pete,
And come to the front door mother, here's a letter from thy
  dear son.

Lo, 'tis autumn,
Lo, where the trees, deeper green, yellower and redder,
Cool and sweeten Ohio's villages with leaves fluttering in the
  moderate wind,
Where apples ripe in the orchards hang and grapes on the
  trellis'd vines,
(Smell you the smell of the grapes on the vines?
Smell you the buckwheat where the bees were lately buzzing?)

Above all, lo, the sky so calm, so transparent after the rain,
  and with wondrous clouds,
Below too, all calm, all vital and beautiful, and the farm
  prospers well.

Down in the fields all prospers well,
But now from the fields come father, come at the daughter's
  call,
And come to the entry mother, to the front door come right
  away.

Fast as she can she hurries, something ominous, her steps
  trembling,
She does not tarry to smooth her hair nor adjust her cap.

Open the envelope quickly,
O this is not our son's writing, yet his name is sign'd,

O a strange hand writes for our dear son, O stricken mother's
soul!
All swims before her eyes, flashes with black, she catches the
main words only,
Sentences broken, *gunshot wound in the breast, cavalry skirmish, taken to hospital,*
*At present low, but will soon be better.*

Ah now the single figure to me,
Amid all teeming and wealthy Ohio with all its cities and
farms,
Sickly white in the face and dull in the head, very faint,
By the jamb of a door leans.

*Grieve not so, dear mother,* (the just-grown daughter speaks
through her sobs,
The little sisters huddle around speechless and dismay'd,)
*See, dearest mother, the letter says Pete will soon be better.*

Alas poor boy, he will never be better, (nor may-be needs to
be better, that brave and simple soul,)
While they stand at home at the door he is dead already,
The only son is dead.

But the mother needs to be better,
She with thin form presently drest in black,
By day her meals untouch'd, then at night fitfully sleeping,
often waking,
In the midnight waking, weeping, longing with one deep
longing,
O that she might withdraw unnoticed, silent from life escape
and withdraw,
To follow, to seek, to be with her dear dead son.
1865                                                    1867


## VIGIL STRANGE I KEPT ON THE FIELD ONE NIGHT

VIGIL strange I kept on the field one night;
When you my son and my comrade dropt at my side that
day,

One look I but gave which your dear eyes return'd with a
look I shall never forget,

One touch of your hand to mine O boy, reach'd up as you
lay on the ground,

Then onward I sped in the battle, the even-contested battle,

Till late in the night reliev'd to the place at last again I made
my way,

Found you in death so cold dear comrade, found your body
son of responding kisses, (never again on earth responding,)

Bared your face in the starlight, curious the scene, cool blew
the moderate night-wind,

Long there and then in vigil I stood, dimly around me the
battlefield spreading,

Vigil wondrous and vigil sweet there in the fragrant silent
night,

But not a tear fell, not even a long-drawn sigh, long, long I
gazed,

Then on the earth partially reclining sat by your side leaning
my chin in my hands,

Passing sweet hours, immortal and mystic hours with you
dearest comrade—not a tear, not a word,

Vigil of silence, love and death, vigil for you my son and my
soldier,

As onward silently stars aloft, eastward new ones upward
stole,

Vigil final for you brave boy, (I could not save you, swift was
your death,

I faithfully loved you and cared for you living, I think we
shall surely meet again,)

Till at latest lingering of the night, indeed just as the dawn
appear'd,

My comrade I wrapt in his blanket, envelop'd well his
form,

Folded the blanket well, tucking it carefully over head and
carefully under feet,

And there and then and bathed by the rising sun, my son in
his grave, in his rude-dug grave I deposited,

Ending my vigil strange with that, vigil of night and battle-
field dim,

Vigil for boy of responding kisses, (never again on earth
    responding,)
Vigil for comrade swiftly slain, vigil I never forget, how as
    day brighten'd,
I rose from the chill ground and folded my soldier well in his
    blanket,
And buried him where he fell.

1865                                        1867


## A MARCH IN THE RANKS HARD-PREST, AND
## THE ROAD UNKNOWN

A MARCH in the ranks hard-prest, and the road unknown,
A route through a heavy wood with muffled steps in the
    darkness,
Our army foil'd with loss severe, and the sullen remnant
    retreating,
Till after midnight glimmer upon us the lights of a dim-
    lighted building,
We come to an open space in the woods, and halt by the
    dim-lighted building,
'Tis a large old church at the crossing roads, now an im-
    promptu hospital,
Entering but for a minute I see a sight beyond all the pictures
    and poems ever made,
Shadows of deepest, deepest black, just lit by moving candles
    and lamps,
And by one great pitchy torch stationary with wild red flame
    and clouds of smoke,
By these, crowds, groups of forms vaguely I see on the floor,
    some in the pews laid down,
At my feet more distinctly a soldier, a mere lad, in danger of
    bleeding to death, (he is shot in the abdomen,)
I stanch the blood temporarily, (the youngster's face is white
    as a lily,)
Then before I depart I sweep my eyes o'er the scene fain to
    absorb it all,
Faces, varieties, postures beyond description, most in ob-
    scurity, some of them dead,

Surgeons operating, attendants holding lights, the smell of
ether, the odor of blood,
The crowd, O the crowd of the bloody forms, the yard out-
side also fill'd,
Some on the bare ground, some on planks or stretchers,
some in the death-spasm sweating,
An occasional scream or cry, the doctor's shouted orders or
calls,
The glisten of the little steel instruments catching the glint of
the torches,
These I resume as I chant, I see again the forms, I smell the
odor,
Then hear outside the orders given, *Fall in, my men, fall in;*
But first I bend to the dying lad, his eyes open, a half-smile
gives he me,
Then the eyes close, calmly close, and I speed forth to the
darkness,
Resuming, marching, ever in darkness marching, on in the
ranks,
The unknown road still marching.
1865                                                    1867


## A SIGHT IN CAMP IN THE DAYBREAK GRAY
## AND DIM

A SIGHT in camp in the daybreak gray and dim,
As from my tent I emerge so early sleepless,
As slow I walk in the cool fresh air the path near by the
hospital tent,
Three forms I see on stretchers lying, brought out there un-
tended lying,
Over each the blanket spread, ample brownish woolen blanket,
Gray and heavy blanket, folding, covering all.

Curious I halt and silent stand,
Then with light fingers I from the face of the nearest the first
just lift the blanket;
Who are you elderly man so gaunt and grim, with well-
gray'd hair, and flesh all sunken about the eyes?
Who are you my dear comrade?

Then to the second I step—and who are you my child and
 darling?
Who are you sweet boy with cheeks yet blooming?

Then to the third—a face nor child nor old, very calm, as of
 beautiful yellow-white ivory;
Young man I think I know you—I think this face is the face
 of the Christ himself,
Dead and divine and brother of all, and here again he lies.
1865                                                      1867


## AS TOILSOME I WANDER'D VIRGINIA'S WOODS

As toilsome I wander'd Virginia's woods,
To the music of rustling leaves kick'd by my feet, (for 'twas
 autumn,)
I mark'd at the foot of a tree the grave of a soldier;
Mortally wounded he and buried on the retreat, (easily all
 could I understand,)
The halt of a mid-day hour, when up! no time to lose—yet
 this sign left,
On a tablet scrawl'd and nail'd on the tree by the grave,
*Bold, cautious, true, and my loving comrade.*

Long, long I muse, then on my way go wandering,
Many a changeful season to follow, and many a scene of life,
Yet at times through changeful season and scene, abrupt,
 alone, or in the crowded street,
Comes before me the unknown soldier's grave, comes the
 inscription rude in Virginia's woods,
*Bold, cautious, true, and my loving comrade.*
1865                                                      1867


## NOT THE PILOT

Not the pilot has charged himself to bring his ship into port,
 though beaten back and many times baffled;
Not the pathfinder penetrating inland weary and long,
By deserts parch'd, snows chill'd, rivers wet, perseveres till he
 reaches his destination,

More than I have charged myself, heeded or unheeded, to
　　compose a march for these States,
For a battle-call, rousing to arms if need be, years, centuries
　　hence.
1860                                                               1881


## YEAR THAT TREMBLED AND REEL'D
## BENEATH ME

YEAR that trembled and reel'd beneath me!
Your summer wind was warm enough, yet the air I breathed
　　froze me,
A thick gloom fell through the sunshine and darken'd me,
Must I change my triumphant songs? said I to myself,
Must I indeed learn to chant the cold dirges of the baffled?
And sullen hymns of defeat?
1865                                                               1867


## THE WOUND-DRESSER

### 1

AN old man bending I come among new faces,
Years looking backward resuming in answer to children,
Come tell us old man, as from young men and maidens that
　　love me,
(Arous'd and angry, I'd thought to beat the alarum, and urge
　　relentless war,
But soon my fingers fail'd me, my face droop'd and I re-
　　sign'd myself,
To sit by the wounded and soothe them, or silently watch the
　　dead;)
Years hence of these scenes, of these furious passions, these
　　chances,
Of unsurpass'd heroes, (was one side so brave? the other was
　　equally brave;)
Now be witness again, paint the mightiest armies of earth,
Of those armies so rapid so wondrous what saw you to tell us?
What stays with you latest and deepest? of curious panics,
Of hard-fought engagements or sieges tremendous what
　　deepest remains?

2

O maidens and young men I love and that love me,
What you ask of my days those the strangest and sudden
    your talking recalls,
Soldier alert I arrive after a long march cover'd with sweat
    and dust,
In the nick of time I come, plunge in the fight, loudly shout
    in the rush of successful charge,
Enter the captur'd works—yet lo, like a swift running river
    they fade,
Pass and are gone they fade—I dwell not on soldiers' perils
    or soldiers' joys,
(Both I remember well—many of the hardships, few the joys,
    yet I was content.)

But in silence, in dreams' projections,
While the world of gain and appearance and mirth goes on,
So soon what is over forgotten, and waves wash the imprints
    off the sand,
With hinged knees returning I enter the doors, (while for you
    up there,
Whoever you are, follow without noise and be of strong
    heart.)

Bearing the bandages, water and sponge,
Straight and swift to my wounded I go,
Where they lie on the ground after the battle brought in,
Where their priceless blood reddens the grass the ground,
Or to the rows of the hospital tent, or under the roof'd
    hospital,
To the long rows of cots up and down each side I return,
To each and all one after another I draw near, not one do I
    miss,
An attendant follows holding a tray, he carries a refuse pail,
Soon to be fill'd with clotted rags and blood, emptied, and
    fill'd again.

I onward go, I stop,
With hinged knees and steady hand to dress wounds,
I am firm with each, the pangs are sharp yet unavoidable,

One turns to me his appealing eyes—poor boy! I never knew
you,
Yet I think I could not refuse this moment to die for you, if
that would save you.

### 3

On, on I go, (open doors of time! open hospital doors!)
The crush'd head I dress, (poor crazed hand tear not the
bandage away,)
The neck of the cavalry-man with the bullet through and
through I examine,
Hard the breathing rattles, quite glazed already the eye, yet
life struggles hard,
(Come sweet death! be persuaded O beautiful death!
In mercy come quickly.)

From the stump of the arm, the amputated hand,
I undo the clotted lint, remove the slough, wash off the mat-
ter and blood,
Back on his pillow the soldier bends with curv'd neck and
side falling head,
His eyes are closed, his face is pale, he dares not look on the
bloody stump,
And has not yet look'd on it.

I dress a wound in the side, deep, deep,
But a day or two more, for see the frame all wasted and
sinking,
And the yellow-blue countenance see.

I dress the perforated shoulder, the foot with the bullet-
wound,
Cleanse the one with a gnawing and putrid gangrene, so
sickening, so offensive,
While the attendant stands behind aside me holding the tray
and pail.

I am faithful, I do not give out,
The fractur'd thigh, the knee, the wound in the abdomen,
These and more I dress with impassive hand, (yet deep in **my**
breast a fire, a burning flame.)

### 4

Thus in silence in dreams' projections,
Returning, resuming, I thread my way through the hospitals,
The hurt and wounded I pacify with soothing hand,
I sit by the restless all the dark night, some are so young,
Some suffer so much, I recall the experience sweet and sad,
(Many a soldier's loving arms about this neck have cross'd
        and rested,
Many a soldier's kiss dwells on these bearded lips.)
1865                                                        1881

## LONG, TOO LONG AMERICA

Long, too long America,
Traveling roads all even and peaceful you learn'd from joys
        and prosperity only,
But now, ah now, to learn from crises of anguish, advancing,
        grappling with direst fate and recoiling not,
And now to conceive and show to the world what your chil-
        dren en-masse really are,
(For who except myself has yet conceiv'd what your children
        en-masse really are?)
1865                                                        1881

## GIVE ME THE SPLENDID SILENT SUN

### 1

Give me the splendid silent sun with all his beams full-
        dazzling,
Give me juicy autumnal fruit ripe and red from the orchard,
Give me a field where the unmow'd grass grows,
Give me an arbor, give me the trellis'd grape,
Give me fresh corn and wheat, give me serene-moving
        animals teaching content,
Give me nights perfectly quiet as on high plateaus west of the
        Mississippi, and I looking up at the stars,
Give me odorous at sunrise a garden of beautiful flowers
        where I can walk undisturb'd,
Give me for marriage a sweet-breath'd woman of whom I
        should never tire,

Give me a perfect child, give me away aside from the noise of
the world a rural domestic life,

Give me to warble spontaneous songs recluse by myself, for
my own ears only,

Give me solitude, give me Nature, give me again O Nature
your primal sanities!

These demanding to have them, (tired with ceaseless excitement, and rack'd by the war-strife,)

These to procure incessantly asking, rising in cries from my
heart,

While yet incessantly asking still I adhere to my city,

Day upon day and year upon year O city, walking your
streets,

Where you hold me enchain'd a certain time refusing to give
me up,

Yet giving to make me glutted, enrich'd of soul, you give me
forever faces;

(O I see what I sought to escape, confronting, reversing my
cries,

I see my own soul trampling down what it ask'd for.)


### 2

Keep your splendid silent sun,

Keep your woods O Nature, and the quiet places by the
woods,

Keep your fields of clover and timothy, and your corn-fields
and orchards,

Keep the blossoming buckwheat fields where the Ninth-
month bees hum;

Give me faces and streets—give me these phantoms incessant
and endless along the trottoirs!

Give me interminable eyes—give me women—give me comrades and lovers by the thousand!

Let me see new ones every day—let me hold new ones by the
hand every day!

Give me such shows—give me the streets of Manhattan!

Give me Broadway, with the soldiers marching—give me the
sound of the trumpets and drums!

(The soldiers in companies or regiments—some starting
    away, flush'd and reckless,
Some, their time up, returning with thinn'd ranks, young,
    yet very old, worn, marching, noticing nothing;)
Give me the shores and wharves heavy-fringed with black
    ships!
O such for me! O an intense life, full to repletion and varied!
The life of the theatre, bar-room, huge hotel, for me!
The saloon of the steamer! the crowded excursion for me!
    the torchlight procession!
The dense brigade bound for the war, with high piled military
    wagons following;
People, endless, streaming, with strong voices, passions,
    pageants,
Manhattan streets with their powerful throbs, with beating
    drums as now,
The endless and noisy chorus, the rustle and clank of mus-
    kets, (even the sight of the wounded,)
Manhattan crowds, with their turbulent musical chorus!
Manhattan faces and eyes forever for me.

1865                                          1867

## DIRGE FOR TWO VETERANS

THE last sunbeam
Lightly falls from the finish'd Sabbath,
On the pavement here, and there beyond it is looking,
    Down a new-made double grave.

Lo, the moon ascending,
Up from the east the silvery round moon,
Beautiful over the house-tops, ghastly, phantom moon,
    Immense and silent moon.

I see a sad procession,
And I hear the sound of coming full-key'd bugles,
All the channels of the city streets they're flooding,
    As with voices and with tears.

I hear the great drums pounding,
And the small drums steady whirring,

And every blow of the great convulsive drums,
  Strikes me through and through.

For the son is brought with the father,
(In the foremost ranks of the fierce assault they fell,
Two veterans son and father dropt together,
  And the double grave awaits them.)

Now nearer blow the bugles,
And the drums strike more convulsive,
And the daylight o'er the pavement quite has faded,
  And the strong dead-march enwraps me.

In the eastern sky up-buoying,
The sorrowful vast phantom moves illumin'd,
('Tis some mother's large transparent face,
  In heaven brighter growing.)

O strong dead-march you please me!
O moon immense with your silvery face you soothe me!
O my soldiers twain! O my veterans passing to burial!
  What I have I also give you.

The moon gives you light,
And the bugles and the drums give you music,
And my heart, O my soldiers, my veterans,
  My heart gives you love.

1865–6                                        1881


## OVER THE CARNAGE ROSE PROPHETIC A VOICE

OVER the carnage rose prophetic a voice,
Be not disthearten'd, affection shall solve the problems of
    freedom yet,
Those who love each other shall become invincible,
They shall yet make Columbia victorious.

Sons of the Mother of All, you shall yet be victorious,
You shall yet laugh to scorn the attacks of all the remainder
    of the earth.

K                                        W.

No danger shall balk Columbia's lovers,
If need be a thousand shall sternly immolate themselves for
one.

One from Massachusetts shall be a Missourian's comrade,
From Maine and from hot Carolina, and another an Ore-
gonese, shall be friends triune,
More precious to each other than all the riches of the earth.

To Michigan, Florida perfumes shall tenderly come,
Not the perfumes of flowers, but sweeter, and wafted beyond
death.

It shall be customary in the houses and streets to see manly
affection,
The most dauntless and rude shall touch face to face lightly,
The dependence of Liberty shall be lovers,
The continuance of Equality shall be comrades.

These shall tie you and band you stronger than hoops of iron,
I, ecstatic, O partners! O lands, with the love of lovers tie
you.

(Were you looking to be held together by lawyers?
Or by an agreement on a paper? or by arms?
Nay, nor the world, nor any living thing, will so cohere.)
1860                                                         1867


## I SAW OLD GENERAL AT BAY

I saw old General at bay,
(Old as he was, his gray eyes yet shone out in battle like stars,)
His small force was now completely hemm'd in, in his works,
He call'd for volunteers to run the enemy's lines, a desperate
emergency,
I saw a hundred and more step forth from the ranks, but two
or three were selected,
I saw them receive their orders aside, they listen'd with care,
the adjutant was very grave,
I saw them depart with cheerfulness, freely risking their lives.
1865                                                         1867

## THE ARTILLERYMAN'S VISION

WHILE my wife at my side lies slumbering, and the wars are
over long,

And my head on the pillow rests at home, and the vacant
midnight passes,

And through the stillness, through the dark, I hear, just hear,
the breath of my infant,

There in the room as I wake from sleep this vision presses
upon me;

The engagement opens there and then in fantasy unreal,

The skirmishers begin, they crawl cautiously ahead, I hear
the irregular snap! snap!

I hear the sounds of the different missiles, the short *t-h-t!*
*t-h-t!* of the rifle-balls,

I see the shells exploding leaving small white clouds, I hear
the great shells shrieking as they pass,

The grape like the hum and whirr of wind through the trees,
(tumultuous now the contest rages,)

All the scenes at the batteries rise in detail before me
again,

The crashing and smoking, the pride of the men in their
pieces,

The chief-gunner ranges and sights his piece and selects a fuse
of the right time,

After firing I see him lean aside and look eagerly off to note
the effect;

Elsewhere I hear the cry of a regiment charging, (the young
colonel leads himself this time with brandish'd sword,)

I see the gaps cut by the enemy's volleys, (quickly fill'd up, no
delay,)

I breathe the suffocating smoke, then the flat clouds hover
low concealing all;

Now a strange lull for a few seconds, not a shot fired on
either side,

Then resumed the chaos louder than ever, with eager calls
and orders of officers,

While from some distant part of the field the wind wafts
to my ears a shout of applause, (some special success,)

And ever the sound of the cannon far or near, (rousing even
　　　in dreams a devilish exultation and all the old mad joy in
　　　the depths of my soul,)
And ever the hastening of infantry shifting positions, bat-
　　　teries, cavalry, moving hither and thither,
(The falling, dying, I heed not, the wounded dripping and
　　　red I heed not, some to the rear are hobbling,)
Grime, heat, rush, aides-de-camp galloping by or on a full
　　　run,
With the patter of small arms, the warning *s-s-t* of the rifles,
　　　(these in my vision I hear or see,)
And bombs bursting in air, and at night the vari-color'd
　　　rockets.

1865　　　　　　　　　　　　　　　　　　　　　　　1881

## ETHIOPIA SALUTING THE COLORS

WHO are you dusky woman, so ancient hardly human,
With your woolly-white and turban'd head, and bare bony
　　　feet?
Why rising by the roadside here, do you the colors greet?

('Tis while our army lines Carolina's sands and pines,
Forth from thy hovel door thou Ethiopia com'st to me,
As under doughty Sherman I march toward the sea.)

*Me master years a hundred since from my parents sunder'd,*
*A little child, they caught me as the savage beast is caught,*
*Then hither me across the sea the cruel slaver brought.*

No further does she say, but lingering all the day,
Her high-borne turban'd head she wags, and rolls her dark-
　　　ling eye,
And courtesies to the regiments, the guidons moving by.

What is it fateful woman, so blear, hardly human?
Why wag your head with turban bound, yellow, red and
　　　green?
Are the things so strange and marvelous you see or have
　　　seen?

1871　　　　　　　　　　　　　　　　　　　　　　　1871

## NOT YOUTH PERTAINS TO ME

NOT youth pertains to me,
Nor delicatesse, I cannot beguile the time with talk,
Awkward in the parlor, neither a dancer nor elegant,
In the learn'd coterie sitting constrain'd and still, for learning
    inures not to me,
Beauty, knowledge, inure not to me—yet there are two or
    three things inure to me,
I have nourish'd the wounded and sooth'd many a dying
    soldier,
And at intervals waiting or in the midst of camp,
Composed these songs.

1865                                   1871

## RACE OF VETERANS

RACE of veterans—race of victors!
Race of the soil, ready for conflict—race of the conquering
    march!
(No more credulity's race, abiding-temper'd race,)
Race henceforth owning no law but the law of itself,
Race of passion and the storm.

1865–6                                 1871

## WORLD TAKE GOOD NOTICE

WORLD take good notice, silver stars fading,
Milky hue ript, weft of white detaching,
Coals thirty-eight, baleful and burning,
Scarlet, significant, hands off warning,
Now and henceforth flaunt from these shores.

1865                                   1867

## O TAN-FACED PRAIRIE-BOY

O TAN-FACED prairie-boy,
Before you came to camp came many a welcome gift,
Praises and presents came and nourishing food, till at last
    among the recruits,

You came, taciturn, with nothing to give—we but look'd on
    each other,
When lo! more than all the gifts of the world you gave me.
1865                                           1867

## LOOK DOWN FAIR MOON

LOOK down fair moon and bathe this scene,
Pour softly down night's nimbus floods on faces ghastly,
    swollen, purple,
On the dead on their backs with arms toss'd wide,
Pour down your unstinted nimbus sacred moon.
1865                                           1867

## RECONCILIATION

WORD over all, beautiful as the sky,
Beautiful that war and all its deeds of carnage must in time
    be utterly lost,
That the hands of the sisters Death and Night incessantly
    softly wash again, and ever again, this soil'd world;
For my enemy is dead, a man divine as myself is dead,
I look where he lies white-faced and still in the coffin—I
    draw near,
Bend down and touch lightly with my lips the white face in
    the coffin.
1865-6                                        1881

## HOW SOLEMN AS ONE BY ONE

### (*Washington City, 1865*)

How solemn as one by one,
As the ranks returning worn and sweaty, as the men file by
    where I stand,
As the faces the masks appear, as I glance at the faces study-
    ing the masks,
(As I glance upward out of this page studying you, dear
    friend, whoever you are,)
How solemn the thought of my whispering soul to each in
    the ranks, and to you!

I see behind each mask that wonder a kindred soul,
O the bullet could never kill what you really are, dear friend,
Nor the bayonet stab what you really are;
The soul! yourself I see, great as any, good as the best,
Waiting secure and content, which the bullet could never
    kill,
Nor the bayonet stab O friend.
(1865?)                                             1871


## AS I LAY WITH MY HEAD IN YOUR LAP
## CAMERADO

As I lay with my head in your lap camerado,
The confession I made I resume, what I said to you and the
    open air I resume,
I know I am restless and make others so,
I know my words are weapons full of danger, full of death,
For I confront peace, security, and all the settled laws, to
    unsettle them,
I am more resolute because all have denied me than I could
    ever have been had all accepted me,
I heed not and have never heeded either experience, cautions,
    majorities, nor ridicule,
And the threat of what is call'd hell is little or nothing to me,
And the lure of what is call'd heaven is little or nothing to me;
Dear camerado! I confess I have urged you onward with me,
        and still urge you, without the least idea what is our
        destination,
Or whether we shall be victorious, or utterly quell'd and
    defeated.
1865-6                                              1881


## DELICATE CLUSTER

DELICATE cluster! flag of teeming life!
Covering all my lands—all my seashores lining!
Flag of death! (how I watch'd you through the smoke of
    battle pressing!
How I heard you flap and rustle, cloth defiant!)
Flag cerulean—sunny flag, with the orbs of night dappled!

Ah my silvery beauty—ah my woolly white and crimson!
Ah to sing the song of you, my matron mighty!
My sacred one, my mother!
1871                                                      1871


## TO A CERTAIN CIVILIAN

DID you ask dulcet rhymes from me?
Did you seek the civilian's peaceful and languishing rhymes?
Did you find what I sang erewhile so hard to follow?
Why I was not singing erewhile for you to follow, to under-
        stand—nor am I now;
(I have been born of the same as the war was born,
The drum-corps' rattle is ever to me sweet music, I love well
        the martial dirge,
With slow wail and convulsive throb leading the officer's
        funeral;)
What to such as you anyhow such a poet as I? therefore leave
        my works,
And go lull yourself with what you can understand, and with
        piano-tunes,
For I lull nobody, and you will never understand me.
1865                                                     1871


## LO, VICTRESS ON THE PEAKS

Lo, Victress on the peaks,
Where thou with mighty brow regarding the world,
(The world O Libertad, that vainly conspired against thee,)
Out of its countless beleaguering toils, after thwarting them
        all,
Dominant, with the dazzling sun around thee,
Flauntest now unharm'd in immortal soundness and bloom
        —lo, in these hours supreme,
No poem proud, I chanting bring to thee, nor mastery's rap-
        turous verse,
But a cluster containing night's darkness and blood-dripping
        wounds,
And psalms of the dead.
1865–6                                                    1881

## SPIRIT WHOSE WORK IS DONE

(*Washington City*, 1865)

SPIRIT whose work is done—spirit of dreadful hours!
Ere departing fade from my eyes your forests of bayonets;
Spirit of gloomiest fears and doubts, (yet onward ever un-
     faltering pressing,)
Spirit of many a solemn day and many a savage scene—
     electric spirit,
That with muttering voice through the war now closed, like a
     tireless phantom flitted,
Rousing the land with breath of flame, while you beat and
     beat the drum,
Now as the sound of the drum, hollow and harsh to the last,
     reverberates round me,
As your ranks, your immortal ranks, return, return from the
     battles,
As the muskets of the young men yet lean over their shoulders,
As I look on the bayonets bristling over their shoulders,
As those slanted bayonets, whole forests of them appearing
     in the distance, approach and pass on, returning home-
     ward,
Moving with steady motion, swaying to and fro to the right
     and left,
Evenly, lightly rising and falling while the steps keep time;
Spirit of hours I knew, all hectic red one day, but pale as
     death next day,
Touch my mouth ere you depart, press my lips close,
Leave me your pulses of rage—bequeath them to me—fill me
     with currents convulsive,
Let them scorch and blister out of my chants when you are
     gone,
Let them identify you to the future in these songs.
1865–6                                                    1881

## ADIEU TO A SOLDIER

ADIEU O soldier,
You of the rude campaigning, (which we shared,)
The rapid march, the life of the camp,

The hot contention of opposing fronts, the long manœuvre,
Red battles with their slaughter, the stimulus, the strong
      terrific game,
Spell of all brave and manly hearts, the trains of time through
      you and like of you all fill'd,
With war and war's expression.

Adieu dear comrade,
Your mission is fulfill'd—but I, more warlike,
Myself and this contentious soul of mine,
Still on our own campaigning bound,
Through untried roads with ambushes opponents lined,
Through many a sharp defeat and many a crisis, often
      baffled,
Here marching, ever marching on, a war fight out—aye
      here,
To fiercer, weightier battles give expression.
1871                                                    1871


## TURN O LIBERTAD

Turn O Libertad, for the war is over,
From it and all henceforth expanding, doubting no more,
      resolute, sweeping the world,
Turn from lands retrospective recording proofs of the past,
From the singers that sing the trailing glories of the past,
From the chants of the feudal world, the triumphs of kings,
      slavery, caste,
Turn to the world, the triumphs reserv'd and to come—give
      up that backward world,
Leave to the singers of hitherto, give them the trailing past,
But what remains remains for singers for you—wars to come
      are for you,
(Lo, how the wars of the past have duly inured to you, and
      the wars of the present also inure;)
Then turn, and be not alarm'd O Libertad—turn your un-
      dying face,
To where the future, greater than all the past,
Is swiftly, surely preparing for you.
1865                                                    1871

## TO THE LEAVEN'D SOIL THEY TROD

To the leaven'd soil they trod calling I sing for the last,
(Forth from my tent emerging for good, loosing, untying the
tent-ropes,)
In the freshness the forenoon air, in the far-stretching circuits
and vistas again to peace restored,
To the fiery fields emanative and the endless vistas beyond,
to the South and the North,
To the leaven'd soil of the general Western world to attest
my songs,
To the Alleghanian hills and the tireless Mississippi,
To the rocks I calling sing, and all the trees in the woods,
To the plains of the poems of heroes, to the prairies spread-
ing wide,
To the far-off sea and the unseen winds, and the sane im-
palpable air;
And responding they answer all, (but not in words,)
The average earth, the witness of war and peace, acknow-
ledges mutely,
The prairie draws me close, as the father to bosom broad the
son,
The Northern ice and rain that began me nourish me to the
end,
But the hot sun of the South is to fully ripen my songs.
1865–6                                                    1881

# *Memories of President Lincoln*

## WHEN LILACS LAST IN THE DOORYARD BLOOM'D

### 1

WHEN lilacs last in the dooryard bloom'd,
And the great star early droop'd in the western sky in the night,
I mourn'd, and yet shall mourn with ever-returning spring.

Ever-returning spring, trinity sure to me you bring,
Lilac blooming perennial and drooping star in the west,
And thought of him I love.

### 2

O powerful western fallen star!
O shades of night—O moody, tearful night!
O great star disappear'd—O the black murk that hides the star!
O cruel hands that hold me powerless—O helpless soul of me!
O harsh surrounding cloud that will not free my soul.

### 3

In the dooryard fronting an old farm-house near the white-wash'd palings,
Stands the lilac-bush tall-growing with heart-shaped leaves of rich green,
With many a pointed blossom rising delicate, with the perfume strong I love,
With every leaf a miracle—and from this bush in the dooryard,
With delicate-color'd blossoms and heart-shaped leaves of rich green,
A sprig with its flower I break.

### 4

In the swamp in secluded recesses,
A shy and hidden bird is warbling a song.

Solitary the thrush,
The hermit withdrawn to himself, avoiding the settlements,
Sings by himself a song.

Song of the bleeding throat,
Death's outlet song of life, (for well dear brother I know,
If thou wast not granted to sing thou would'st surely die.)

### 5

Over the breast of the spring, the land, amid cities,
Amid lanes and through old woods, where lately the violets
    peep'd from the ground, spotting the gray debris,
Amid the grass in the fields each side of the lanes, passing the
    endless grass,
Passing the yellow-spear'd wheat, every grain from its shroud
    in the dark-brown fields uprisen,
Passing the apple-tree blows of white and pink in the or-
    chards,
Carrying a corpse to where it shall rest in the grave,
Night and day journeys a coffin.

### 6

Coffin that passes through lanes and streets,
Through day and night with the great cloud darkening the
    land,
With the pomp of the inloop'd flags with the cities draped in
    black,
With the show of the States themselves as of crape-veil'd
    women standing,
With processions long and winding and the flambeaus of the
    night,
With the countless torches lit, with the silent sea of faces and
    the unbared heads,
With the waiting depot, the arriving coffin, and the sombre
    faces,

With dirges through the night, with the thousand voices
    rising strong and solemn,
With all the mournful voices of the dirges pour'd around the
    coffin,
The dim-lit churches and the shuddering organs—where
    amid these you journey,
With the tolling tolling bells' perpetual clang,
Here, coffin that slowly passes,
I give you my sprig of lilac.

### 7

(Nor for you, for one alone,
Blossoms and branches green to coffins all I bring,
For fresh as the morning, thus would I chant a song for you
    O sane and sacred death.

All over bouquets of roses,
O death, I cover you over with roses and early lilies,
But mostly and now the lilac that blooms the first,
Copious I break, I break the sprigs from the bushes,
With loaded arms I come, pouring for you,
For you and the coffins all of you O death.)

### 8

O western orb sailing the heaven,
Now I know what you must have meant as a month since I
    walk'd,
As I walk'd in silence the transparent shadowy night,
As I saw you had something to tell as you bent to me night
    after night,
As you droop'd from the sky low down as if to my side,
    (while the other stars all look'd on,)
As we wander'd together the solemn night, (for something I
    know not what kept me from sleep,)
As the night advanced, and I saw on the rim of the west how
    full you were of woe,
As I stood on the rising ground in the breeze in the cool
    transparent night,
As I watch'd where you pass'd and was lost in the nether-
    ward black of the night,

As my soul in its trouble dissatisfied sank, as where you sad
  orb,
Concluded, dropt in the night, and was gone.

## 9

Sing on there in the swamp,
O singer bashful and tender, I hear your notes, I hear your
  call,
I hear, I come presently, I understand you,
But a moment I linger, for the lustrous star has detain'd me,
The star my departing comrade holds and detains me.

## 10

O how shall I warble myself for the dead one there I loved?
And how shall I deck my song for the large sweet soul that
  has gone?
And what shall my perfume be for the grave of him I love?

Sea-winds blown from east and west,
Blown from the Eastern sea and blown from the Western
  sea, till there on the prairies meeting,
These and with these and the breath of my chant,
I'll perfume the grave of him I love.

## 11

O what shall I hang on the chamber walls?
And what shall the pictures be that I hang on the walls,
To adorn the burial-house of him I love?

Pictures of growing spring and farms and homes,
With the Fourth-month eve at sundown, and the gray smoke
  lucid and bright,
With floods of the yellow gold of the gorgeous, indolent,
  sinking sun, burning, expanding the air,
With the fresh sweet herbage under foot, and the pale green
  leaves of the trees prolific,
In the distance the flowing glaze, the breast of the river, with
  a wind-dapple here and there,
With ranging hills on the banks, with many a line against the
  sky, and shadows,

And the city at hand with dwellings so dense, and stacks of
    chimneys,
And all the scenes of life and the workshops, and the work-
    men homeward returning.

### 12

Lo, body and soul—this land,
My own Manhattan with spires, and the sparkling and
    hurrying tides, and the ships,
The varied and ample land, the South and the North in the
    light, Ohio's shores and flashing Missouri,
And ever the far-spreading prairies cover'd with grass and
    corn.

Lo, the most excellent sun so calm and haughty,
The violet and purple morn with just-felt breezes,
The gentle soft-born measureless light,
The miracle spreading bathing all, the fulfill'd noon,
The coming eve delicious, the welcome night and the stars,
Over my cities shining all, enveloping man and land.

### 13

Sing on, sing on you gray-brown bird,
Sing from the swamps, the recesses, pour your chant from
    the bushes,
Limitless out of the dusk, out of the cedars and pines.

Sing on dearest brother, warble your reedy song,
Loud human song, with voice of uttermost woe.

O liquid and free and tender!
O wild and loose to my soul—O wondrous singer!
You only I hear—yet the star holds me, (but will soon
    depart,)
Yet the lilac with mastering odor holds me.

### 14

Now while I sat in the day and look'd forth,
In the close of the day with its light and the fields of spring,
    and the farmers preparing their crops,
In the large unconscious scenery of my land with its lakes
    and forests,

In the heavenly aerial beauty, (after the perturb'd winds and
the storms,)
Under the arching heavens of the afternoon swift passing,
and the voices of children and women,
The many-moving sea-tides, and I saw the ships how they sail'd,
And the summer approaching with richness, and the fields all
busy with labor,
And the infinite separate houses, how they all went on, each
with its meals and minutia of daily usages,
And the streets how their throbbings throbb'd, and the cities
pent—lo, then and there,
Falling upon them all and among them all, enveloping me
with the rest,
Appear'd the cloud, appear'd the long black trail,
And I knew death, its thought, and the sacred knowledge of
death.

Then with the knowledge of death as walking one side of me,
And the thought of death close-walking the other side of me,
And I in the middle as with companions, and as holding the
hands of companions,
I fled forth to the hiding receiving night that talks not,
Down to the shores of the water, the path by the swamp in
the dimness,
To the solemn shadowy cedars and ghostly pines so still.

And the singer so shy to the rest receiv'd me,
The gray-brown bird I know receiv'd us comrades three,
And he sang the carol of death, and a verse for him I love.

From deep secluded recesses,
From the fragrant cedars and the ghostly pines so still,
Came the carol of the bird.

And the charm of the carol rapt me,
As I held as if by their hands my comrades in the night,
And the voice of my spirit tallied the song of the bird.

*Come lovely and soothing death,*
*Undulate round the world, serenely arriving, arriving,*
*In the day, in the night, to all, to each,*
*Sooner or later delicate death*

*Prais'd be the fathomless universe,*
*For life and joy, and for objects and knowledge curious,*
*And for love, sweet love—but praise! praise! praise!*
*For the sure-enwinding arms of cool-enfolding death.*

*Dark mother always gliding near with soft feet,*
*Have none chanted for thee a chant of fullest welcome?*
*Then I chant it for thee, I glorify thee above all,*
*I bring thee a song that when thou must indeed come, come un-*
*falteringly.*

*Approach strong deliveress,*
*When it is so, when thou hast taken them I joyously sing the*
*dead,*
*Lost in the loving floating ocean of thee,*
*Laved in the flood of thy bliss O death.*

*From me to thee glad serenades,*
*Dances for thee I propose saluting thee, adornments and feast-*
*ings for thee,*
*And the sights of the open landscape and the high-spread sky*
*are fitting,*
*And life and the fields, and the huge and thoughtful night.*

*The night in silence under many a star,*
*The ocean shore and the husky whispering wave whose voice I*
*know,*
*And the soul turning to thee O vast and well-veil'd death,*
*And the body gratefully nestling close to thee.*

*Over the tree-tops I float thee a song,*
*Over the rising and sinking waves, over the myriad fields and*
*the prairies wide,*
*Over the dense-pack'd cities all and the teeming wharves and*
*ways,*
*I float this carol with joy, with joy to thee O death.*

## 15

To the tally of my soul,
Loud and strong kept up the gray-brown bird,
With pure deliberate notes spreading filling the night.

Loud in the pines and cedars dim,
Clear in the freshness moist and the swamp-perfume,
And I with my comrades there in the night.

While my sight that was bound in my eyes unclosed,
As to long panoramas of visions.

And I saw askant the armies,
I saw as in noiseless dreams hundreds of battle-flags,
Borne through the smoke of the battles and pierc'd with
    missiles I saw them,
And carried hither and yon through the smoke, and torn and
    bloody,
And at last but a few shreds left on the staffs, (and all in
    silence,)
And the staffs all splinter'd and broken.

I saw battle-corpses, myriads of them,
And the white skeletons of young men, I saw them,
I saw the debris and debris of all the slain soldiers of the war,
But I saw they were not as was thought,
They themselves were fully at rest, they suffer'd not,
The living remain'd and suffer'd, the mother suffer'd,
And the wife and the child and the musing comrade suffer'd,
And the armies that remain'd suffer'd.


## 16

Passing the visions, passing the night,
Passing, unloosing the hold of my comrades' hands,
Passing the song of the hermit bird and the tallying song of
    my soul,
Victorious song, death's outlet song, yet varying ever-altering
    song,
As low and wailing, yet clear the notes, rising and falling,
    flooding the night,
Sadly sinking and fainting, as warning and warning, and yet
    again bursting with joy,
Covering the earth and filling the spread of the heaven,
As that powerful psalm in the night I heard from recesses,

Passing, I leave thee lilac with heart-shaped leaves,
I leave thee there in the door-yard, blooming, returning with
spring.

I cease from my song for thee,
From my gaze on thee in the west, fronting the west, com-
muning with thee,
O comrade lustrous with silver face in the night.

Yet each to keep and all, retrievements out of the night,
The song, the wondrous chant of the gray-brown bird,
And the tallying chant, the echo arous'd in my soul,
With the lustrous and drooping star with the countenance
full of woe,
With the holders holding my hand nearing the call of the bird,
Comrades mine and I in the midst, and their memory ever to
keep, for the dead I loved so well,
For the sweetest, wisest soul of all my days and lands—and
this for his dear sake,
Lilac and star and bird twined with the chant of my soul,
There in the fragrant pines and the cedars dusk and dim.
1865–6                                                    1881

## O CAPTAIN! MY CAPTAIN!

O Captain! my Captain! our fearful trip is done,
The ship has weather'd every rack, the prize we sought is won,
The port is near, the bells I hear, the people all exulting,
While follow eyes the steady keel, the vessel grim and daring;
        But O heart! heart! heart!
            O the bleeding drops of red,
                Where on the deck my Captain lies,
                Fallen cold and dead.

O Captain! my Captain! rise up and hear the bells;
Rise up—for you the flag is flung—for you the bugle trills,
For you bouquets and ribbon'd wreaths—for you the shores
a-crowding,
For you they call, the swaying mass, their eager faces
turning;
        Here Captain! dear father!
            The arm beneath your head!

It is some dream that on the deck,
    You've fallen cold and dead.

My Captain does not answer, his lips are pale and still,
My father does not feel my arm, he has no pulse nor will,
The ship is anchor'd safe and sound, its voyage closed and
    done.
From fearful trip the victor ship comes in with object won:
        Exult O shores, and ring O bells!
            But I with mournful tread,
                Walk the deck my Captain lies,
                    Fallen cold and dead.

1865                                                    1871

## HUSH'D BE THE CAMPS TO-DAY

### (*May* 4, 1865)

HUSH'D be the camps to-day,
And soldiers let us drape our war-worn weapons,
And each with musing soul retire to celebrate,
Our dear commander's death.

No more for him life's stormy conflicts,
Nor victory, nor defeat—no more time's dark events,
Charging like ceaseless clouds across the sky.

But sing poet in our name,
Sing of the love we bore him—because you—dweller in
    camps, know it truly.

As they invault the coffin there,
Sing—as they close the doors of earth upon him—one verse,
For the heavy hearts of soldiers.
1865                                                    1871

## THIS DUST WAS ONCE THE MAN

THIS dust was once the man,
Gentle, plain, just and resolute, under whose cautious hand,
Against the foulest crime in history known in any land or age,
Was saved the Union of these States.
1871                                                    1871

# *By Blue Ontario's Shore*

### 1

By blue Ontario's shore,
As I mused of these warlike days and of peace return'd, and
    the dead that return no more,
A Phantom gigantic superb, with stern visage accosted me,
*Chant me the poem*, it said, *that comes from the soul of*
    *America, chant me the carol of victory,*
*And strike up the marches of Libertad, marches more powerful*
    *yet,*
*And sing me before you go the song of the throes of Demo-*
    *cracy.*

(Democracy, the destin'd conqueror, yet treacherous lip-
    smiles everywhere,
And death and infidelity at every step.)

### 2

A Nation announcing itself,
I myself make the only growth by which I can be appreciated,
I reject none, accept all, then reproduce all in my own forms.

A breed whose proof is in time and deeds,
What we are we are, nativity is answer enough to objections,
We wield ourselves as a weapon is wielded,
We are powerful and tremendous in ourselves,
We are executive in ourselves, we are sufficient in the variety
    of ourselves,
We are the most beautiful to ourselves and in ourselves,
We stand self-pois'd in the middle, branching thence over the
    world,
From Missouri, Nebraska, or Kansas, laughing attacks to
    scorn.

Nothing is sinful to us outside of ourselves,
Whatever appears, whatever does not appear, we are beautiful or sinful in ourselves only.

(O Mother—O Sisters dear!
If we are lost, no victor else has destroy'd us,
It is by ourselves we go down to eternal night.)

### 3

Have you thought there could be but a single supreme?
There can be any number of supremes—one does not countervail another any more than one eyesight countervails
another, or one life countervails another.

All is eligible to all,
All is for individuals, all is for you,
No condition is prohibited, not God's or any.

All comes by the body, only health puts you rapport with the
universe.

Produce great Persons, the rest follows.

### 4

Piety and conformity to them that like,
Peace, obesity, allegiance, to them that like,
I am he who tauntingly compels men, women, nations,
Crying, Leap from your seats and contend for your lives!

I am he who walks the States with a barb'd tongue, questioning every one I meet,
Who are you that wanted only to be told what you knew
before?
Who are you that wanted only a book to join you in your
nonsense?

(With pangs and cries as thine own O bearer of many children,
These clamors wild to a race of pride I give.)

O lands, would you be freer than all that has ever been
    before?
If you would be freer than all that has been before, come
    listen to me.

Fear grace, elegance, civilization, delicatesse,
Fear the mellow sweet, the sucking of honey-juice,
Beware the advancing mortal ripening of Nature,
Beware what precedes the decay of the ruggedness of states
    and men.

### 5

Ages, precedents, have long been accumulating undirected
    materials,
America brings builders, and brings its own styles.

The immortal poets of Asia and Europe have done their
    work and pass'd to other spheres,
A work remains, the work of surpassing all they have done.

America, curious toward foreign characters, stands by its
    own at all hazards,
Stands removed, spacious, composite, sound, initiates the
    true use of precedents,
Does not repel them or the past or what they have produced
    under their forms,
Takes the lesson with calmness, perceives the corpse slowly
    borne from the house,
Perceives that it waits a little while in the door, that it was
    fittest for its days,
That its life has descended to the stalwart and well-shaped
    heir who approaches,
And that he shall be fittest for his days.

Any period one nation must lead,
One land must be the promise and reliance of the future.

These States are the amplest poem,
Here is not merely a nation but a teeming Nation of nations,
Here the doings of men correspond with the broadcast do-
    ings of the day and night,

Here is what moves in magnificent masses careless of par-
    ticulars,
Here are the roughs, beards, friendliness, combativeness, the
    soul loves,
Here the flowing trains, here the crowds, equality, diversity,
    the soul loves.


### 6

Land of lands and bards to corroborate!
Of them standing among them, one lifts to the light a west-
    bred face,
To him the hereditary countenance bequeath'd both mother's
    and father's,
His first parts substances, earth, water, animals, trees,
Built of the common stock, having room for far and near,
Used to dispense with other lands, incarnating this land,
Attracting it body and soul to himself, hanging on its neck
    with incomparable love,
Plunging his seminal muscle into its merits and demerits,
Making its cities, beginnings, events, diversities, wars, vocal
    in him,
Making its rivers, lakes, bays, embouchure in him,
Mississippi with yearly freshets and changing chutes, Colum-
    bia, Niagara, Hudson, spending themselves lovingly in
    him,
If the Atlantic coast stretch or the Pacific coast stretch, he
    stretching with them North or South,
Spanning between them East and West, and touching what-
    ever is between them,
Growths growing from him to offset the growths of pine,
    cedar, hemlock, live-oak, locust, chestnut, hickory,
    cottonwood, orange, magnolia,
Tangles as tangled in him as any cranebake or swamp,
He likening sides and peaks of mountains, forests coated
    with northern transparent ice,
Off him pasturage sweet and natural as savanna, upland,
    prairie,
Through him flights, whirls, screams, answering those of the
    fish-hawk, mocking-bird, night-heron, and eagle,

His spirit surrounding his country's spirit, unclosed to good and evil,

Surrounding the essences of real things, old times and present times,

Surrounding just found shores, islands, tribes of red aborigines,

Weather-beaten vessels, landings, settlements, embryo stature and muscle,

The haughty defiance of the Year One, war, peace, the formation of the Constitution,

The separate States, the simple elastic scheme, the immigrants,

The Union always swarming with blatherers and always sure and impregnable,

The unsurvey'd interior, log-houses, clearings, wild animals, hunters, trappers,

Surrounding the multiform agriculture, mines, temperature, the gestation of new States,

Congress convening every Twelfth-month, the members duly coming up from the uttermost parts,

Surrounding the noble character of mechanics and farmers, especially the young men,

Responding their manners, speech, dress, friendships, the gait they have of persons who never knew how it felt to stand in the presence of superiors,

The freshness and candor of their physiognomy, the copiousness and decision of their phrenology,

The picturesque looseness of their carriage, their fierceness when wrong'd,

The fluency of their speech, their delight in music, their curiosity, good temper and open-handedness, the whole composite make,

The prevailing ardor and enterprise, the large amativeness,

The perfect equality of the female with the male, the fluid movement of the population,

The superior marine, free commerce, fisheries, whaling, gold-digging,

Wharf-hemm'd cities, railroad and steamboat lines intersecting all points,

Factories, mercantile life, labor-saving machinery, the Northeast, Northwest, Southwest,

Manhattan firemen, the Yankee swap, southern plantation
life,

Slavery—the murderous, treacherous conspiracy to raise it
upon the ruins of all the rest,

On and on to the grapple with it—Assassin! then your life or
ours be the stake, and respite no more.

### 7

(Lo, high toward heaven, this day,

Libertad, from the conqueress' field return'd,

I mark the new aureola around your head,

No more of soft astral, but dazzling and fierce,

With war's flames and the lambent lightnings playing,

And your port immovable where you stand,

With still the inextinguishable glance and the clinch'd and
lifted fist,

And your foot on the neck of the menacing one, the scorner
utterly crush'd beneath you,

The menacing arrogant one that strode and advanced with
his senseless scorn, bearing the murderous knife,

The wide-swelling one, the braggart that would yesterday do
so much,

To-day a carrion dead and damn'd, the despised of all the
earth,

An offal rank, to the dunghill maggots spurn'd.)

### 8

Others take finish, but the Republic is ever constructive and
ever keeps vista,

Others adorn the past, but you O days of the present, I adorn
you,

O days of the future I believe in you—I isolate myself for
your sake,

O America because you build for mankind I build for you,

O well-beloved stone-cutters, I lead them who plan with decision and science,

Lead the present with friendly hand toward the future.

(Bravas to all impulses sending sane children to the next age!
But damn that which spends itself with no thought of the stain, pains, dismay, feebleness, it is bequeathing.)

9

I listened to the Phantom by Ontario's shore,
I heard the voice arising demanding bards,
By them all native and grand, by them alone can these States be fused into the compact organism of a Nation.

To hold men together by paper and seal or by compulsion is no account,
That only holds men together which aggregates all in a living principle, as the hold of the limbs of the body or the fibres of plants.

Of all races and eras these States with veins full of poetical stuff most need poets, and are to have the greatest, and use them the greatest,
Their Presidents shall not be their common referee so much as their poets shall.

(Soul of love and tongue of fire!
Eye to pierce the deepest deeps and sweep the world!
Ah Mother, prolific and full in all besides, yet how long barren, barren?)

10

Of these States the poet is the equable man,
Not in him but off from him things are grotesque, eccentric, fail of their full returns,
Nothing out of its place is good, nothing in its place is bad,
He bestows on every object or quality its fit proportion, neither more nor less,
He is the arbiter of the diverse, he is the key,
He is the equalizer of his age and land,
He supplies what wants supplying, he checks what wants checking,

In peace out of him speaks the spirit of peace, large, rich,
  thrifty, building populous towns, encouraging agriculture, arts, commerce, lighting the study of man, the soul,
  health, immortality, government,
In war he is the best backer of the war, he fetches artillery as
  good as the engineer's, he can make every word he
  speaks draw blood,
The years straying toward infidelity he withholds by his
  steady faith,
He is no arguer, he is judgment, (Nature accepts him absolutely,)
He judges not as the judge judges but as the sun falling round
  a helpless thing,
As he sees the farthest he has the most faith,
His thoughts are the hymns of the praise of things,
In the dispute on God and eternity he is silent,
He sees eternity less like a play with a prologue and denoue-
  ment,
He sees eternity in men and women, he does not see men and
  women as dreams or dots.

For the great Idea, the idea of perfect and free individuals,
For that, the bard walks in advance, leader of leaders,
The attitude of him cheers up slaves and horrifies foreign
  despots.

Without extinction is Liberty, without retrograde is Equality,
They live in the feelings of young men and the best women,
(Not for nothing have the indomitable heads of the earth
  been always ready to fall for Liberty.)


### 11

For the great Idea,
That, O my brethren, that is the mission of poets.

Songs of stern defiance ever ready,
Songs of the rapid arming and the march,
The flag of peace quick-folded, and instead the flag we know,
Warlike flag of the great Idea.

(Angry cloth I saw there leaping!
I stand again in leaden rain your flapping folds saluting,
I sing you over all, flying beckoning through the fight—O the
    hard-contested fight!
The cannons ope their rosy-flashing muzzles—the hurtled
    balls scream,
The battle-front forms amid the smoke—the volleys pour
    incessant from the line,
Hark, the ringing word *Charge!*—now the tussle and the
    furious maddening yells,
Now the corpses tumble curl'd upon the ground,
Cold, cold in death, for precious life of you,
Angry cloth I saw there leaping.)


## 12

Are you he who would assume a place to teach or be a poet
    here in the States?
The place is august, the terms obdurate.

Who would assume to teach here may well prepare himself
    body and mind,
He may well survey, ponder, arm, fortify, harden, make lithe
    himself,
He shall surely be question'd beforehand by me with many
    and stern questions.

Who are you indeed who would talk or sing to America?
Have you studied out the land, its idioms and men?
Have you learn'd the physiology, phrenology, politics, geo-
    graphy, pride, freedom, friendship of the land? its sub-
    stratums and objects?
Have you consider'd the organic compact of the first day of
    the first year of Independence, sign'd by the Commis-
    sioners, ratified by the States, and read by Washington
    at the head of the army?
Have you possess'd yourself of the Federal Constitution?
Do you see who have left all feudal processes and poems
    behind them, and assumed the poems and processes of
    Democracy?

Are you faithful to things? do you teach what the land and
sea, the bodies of men, womanhood, amativeness,
heroic angers, teach?

Have you sped through fleeting customs, popularities?

Can you hold your hand against all seductions, follies, whirls,
fierce contentions? are you very strong? are you really of
the whole People?

Are you not of some coterie? some school or mere religion?

Are you done with reviews and criticisms of life? animating
now to life itself?

Have you vivified yourself from the maternity of these States?

Have you too the old ever-fresh forbearance and impartiality?

Do you hold the like love for those hardening to maturity?
for the last-born? little and big? and for the errant?


What is this you bring my America?

Is it uniform with my country?

Is it not something that has been better told or done before?

Have you not imported this or the spirit of it in some ship?

Is it not a mere tale? a rhyme? a prettiness?—is the good old
cause in it?

Has it not dangled long at the heels of the poets, politicians,
literats, of enemies' lands?

Does it not assume that what is notoriously gone is still here?

Does it answer universal needs? will it improve manners?

Does it sound with trumpet-voice the proud victory of the
Union in that secession war?

Can your performance face the open fields and the seaside?

Will it absorb into me as I absorb food, air, to appear again
in my strength, gait, face?

Have real employments contributed to it? original makers,
not mere amanuenses?

Does it meet modern discoveries, calibres, facts, face to face?

What does it mean to American persons, progresses, cities?
Chicago, Kanada, Arkansas?

Does it see behind the apparent custodians the real custodians
standing, menacing, silent, the mechanics, Manhattanese, Western men, Southerners, significant alike in their
apathy, and in the promptness of their love?

Does it see what finally befalls, and has always finally be-
  fallen, each temporizer, patcher, outsider, partialist,
  alarmist, infidel, who has ever ask'd any thing of
  America?
What mocking and scornful negligence?
The track strew'd with the dust of skeletons,
By the roadside others disdainfully toss'd.

## 13

Rhymes and rhymers pass away, poems distill'd from poems
  pass away,
The swarms of reflectors and the polite pass, and leave ashes,
Admirers, importers, obedient persons, make but the soil of
  literature,
America justifies itself, give it time, no disguise can deceive it
  or conceal from it, it is impassive enough,
Only toward the likes of itself will it advance to meet them,
If its poets appear it will in due time advance to meet them,
  there is no fear of mistake,
(The proof of a poet shall be sternly deferr'd till his country
  absorbs him as affectionately as he has absorb'd it.)

He masters whose spirit masters, he tastes sweetest who
  results sweetest in the long run,
The blood of the brawn beloved of time is unconstraint;
In the need of songs, philosophy, an appropriate native
  grand-opera, shipcraft, any craft,
He or she is greatest who contributes the greatest original
  practical example.

Already a nonchalant breed, silently emerging, appears on
  the streets,
People's lips salute only doers, lovers, satisfiers, positive
  knowers,
There will shortly be no more priests, I say their work is
  done,
Death is without emergencies here, but life is perpetual
  emergencies here,
Are your body, days, manners, superb? after death you shall
  be superb,

Justice, health, self-esteem, clear the way with irresistible
  power;
How dare you place any thing before a man?


14

Fall behind me States!
A man before all—myself, typical, before all.


Give me the pay I have served for,
Give to sing the songs of the great Idea, take all the rest,
I have loved the earth, sun, animals, I have despised riches,
I have given alms to every one that ask'd, stood up for the
  stupid and crazy, devoted my income and labor to
  others,
Hated tyrants, argued not concerning God, had patience and
  indulgence toward the people, taken off my hat to nothing known or unknown,
Gone freely with powerful uneducated persons and with the
  young, and with the mothers of families,
Read these leaves to myself in the open air, tried them by
  trees, stars, rivers,
Dismiss'd whatever insulted my own soul or defiled my
  body,
Claim'd nothing to myself which I have not carefully claim'd
  for others on the same terms,
Sped to the camps, and comrades found and accepted from
  every State,
(Upon this breast has many a dying soldier lean'd to breathe
  his last,
This arm, this hand, this voice, have nourish'd, rais'd,
  restored,
To life recalling many a prostrate form;)
I am willing to wait to be understood by the growth of the
  taste of myself,
Rejecting none, permitting all.


(Say O Mother, have I not to your thought been faithful?
Have I not through life kept you and yours before me?)

15

I swear I begin to see the meaning of these things,
It is not the earth, it is not America who is so great,
It is I who am great or to be great, it is You up there, or any
    one,
It is to walk rapidly through civilizations, governments,
    theories,
Through poems, pageants, shows, to form individuals.

Underneath all, individuals,
I swear nothing is good to me now that ignores individuals,
The American compact is altogether with individuals,
The only government is that which makes minute of indi-
    viduals,
The whole theory of the universe is directed unerringly to one
    single individual—namely to You.

(Mother! with subtle sense severe, with the naked sword in
    your hand,
I saw you at last refuse to treat but directly with individuals.)

16

Underneath all, Nativity,
I swear I will stand by my own nativity, pious or impious so
    be it;
I swear I am charm'd with nothing except nativity,
Men, women, cities, nations, are only beautiful from nativity.

Underneath all is the Expression of love for men and women,
(I swear I have seen enough of mean and impotent modes of
    expressing love for men and women,
After this day I take my own modes of expressing love for
    men and women.)

I swear I will have each quality of my race in myself,
(Talk as you like, he only suits these States whose manners
    favor the audacity and sublime turbulence of the States.)

Underneath the lessons of things, spirits, Nature, govern-
    ments, ownerships, I swear I perceive other lessons,

Underneath all to me is myself, to you yourself, (the same
    monotonous old song.)

### 17

O I see flashing that this America is only you and me,
Its power, weapons, testimony, are you and me,
Its crimes, lies, thefts, defections, are you and me,
Its Congress is you and me, the officers, capitols, armies,
    ships, are you and me,
Its endless gestations of new States are you and me,
The war, (that war so bloody and grim, the war I will hence-
    forth forget), was you and me,
Natural and artificial are you and me,
Freedom, language, poems, employments, are you and me,
Past, present, future, are you and me.

I dare not shirk any part of myself,
Not any part of America good or bad,
Not to build for that which builds for mankind,
Not to balance ranks, complexions, creeds, and the sexes,
Not to justify science nor the march of equality,
Nor to feed the arrogant blood of the brawn belov'd of time.

I am for those that have never been master'd,
For men and women whose tempers have never been mas-
    ter'd,
For those whom laws, theories, conventions, can never
    master.

I am for those who walk abreast with the whole earth,
Who inaugurate one to inaugurate all.

I will not be outfaced by irrational things,
I will penetrate what it is in them that is sarcastic upon me,
I will make cities and civilizations defer to me,
This is what I have learnt from America—it is the amount,
    and it I teach again.

(Democracy, while weapons were everywhere aim'd at your
    breast,

I saw you serenely give birth to immortal children, saw in
    dreams your dilating form,
Saw you with spreading mantle covering the world.)


### 18

I will confront these shows of the day and night,
I will know if I am to be less than they,
I will see if I am not as majestic as they,
I will see if I am not as subtle and real as they,
I will see if I am to be less generous than they,
I will see if I have no meaning, while the houses and ships
    have meaning,
I will see if the fishes and birds are to be enough for them-
    selves, and I am not to be enough for myself.

I match my spirit against yours you orbs, growths, moun-
    tains, brutes,
Copious as you are I absorb you all in myself, and become
    the master myself,
America isolated yet embodying all, what is it finally except
    myself?
These States, what are they except myself?

I know now why the earth is gross, tantalizing, wicked, it is
    for my sake,
I take you specially to be mine, you terrible, rude forms.

(Mother, bend down, bend close to me your face,
I know not what these plots and wars and deferments are for,
I know not fruition's success, but I know that through war
    and crime your work goes on, and must yet go on.)


### 19

Thus by blue Ontario's shore,
While the winds fann'd me and the waves came trooping to-
    ward me,
I thrill'd with the power's pulsations, and the charm of my
    theme was upon me,
Till the tissues that held me parted their ties upon me.

And I saw the free souls of poets,
The loftiest bards of past ages strode before me,
Strange large men, long unwaked, undisclosed, were disclosed to me.

### 20

O my rapt verse, my call, mock me not!
Not for the bards of the past, not to invoke them have I launch'd you forth,
Not to call even those lofty bards here by Ontario's shores,
Have I sung so capricious and loud my savage song.

Bards for my own land only I invoke,
(For the war, the war is over, the field is clear'd,)
Till they strike up marches henceforth triumphant and onward,
To cheer O Mother your boundless expectant soul.

Bards of the great Idea! bards of the peaceful inventions! (for the war, the war is over!)
Yet bards of latent armies, a million soldiers waiting everready,
Bards with songs as from burning coals or the lightning's fork'd stripes!
Ample Ohio's, Kanada's bards—bards of California! inland bards—bards of the war!
You by my charm I invoke.
1856                                         1881

### REVERSALS

LET that which stood in front go behind,
Let that which was behind advance to the front,
Let bigots, fools, unclean persons, offer new propositions,
Let the old propositions be postponed,
Let a man seek pleasure everywhere except in himself,
Let a woman seek happiness everywhere except in herself.
1856                                         1881

# *Autumn Rivulets*

## AS CONSEQUENT, Etc.

As consequent from store of summer rains,
Or wayward rivulets in autumn flowing,
Or many a herb-lined brook's reticulations,
Or subterranean sea-rills making for the sea,
Songs of continued years I sing.

Life's ever-modern rapids first, (soon, soon to blend,
With the old streams of death.)

Some threading Ohio's farm-fields or the woods,
Some down Colorado's cañons from sources of perpetual
    snow,
Some half-hid in Oregon, or away southward in Texas,
Some in the north finding their way to Erie, Niagara, Ottawa,
Some to Atlantica's bays, and so to the great salt brine.

In you whoe'er you are my book perusing,
In I myself, in all the world, these currents flowing,
All, all toward the mystic ocean tending.

Currents for starting a continent new,
Overtures sent to the solid out of the liquid,
Fusion of ocean and land, tender and pensive waves,
(Not safe and peaceful only, waves rous'd and ominous too,
Out of the depths the storm's abysmic waves, who knows
    whence?
Raging over the vast, with many a broken spar and tatter'd
    sail.)

Or from the sea of Time, collecting vasting all, I bring,
A windrow-drift of weeds and shells.

O little shells, so curious-convolute, so limpid-cold and
    voiceless,
Will you not little shells to the tympans of temples held,
Murmurs and echoes still call up, eternity's music faint and
    far,
Wafted inland, sent from Atlantica's rim, strains for the soul
    of the prairies,
Whisper'd reverberations, chords for the ear of the West
    joyously sounding,
Your tidings old, yet ever new and untranslatable,
Infinitesimals out of my life, and many a life,
(For not my life and yours alone I give—all, all I give,)
These waifs from the deep, cast high and dry,
Wash'd on America's shores?
1881                                                                                    1881


## THE RETURN OF THE HEROES

### 1

For the lands and for these passionate days and for myself,
Now I awhile retire to thee O soil of autumn fields,
Reclining on thy breast, giving myself to thee,
Answering the pulses of thy sane and equable heart,
Tuning a verse for thee.

O earth that hast no voice, confide to me a voice,
O harvest of my lands—O boundless summer growths,
O lavish brown parturient earth—O infinite teeming womb,
A song to narrate thee.

### 2

Ever upon this stage,
Is acted God's calm annual drama,
Gorgeous procession, songs of birds,
Sunrise that fullest feeds and freshens most the soul,
The heaving sea, the waves upon the shore, the musical,
    strong waves,
The woods, the stalwart trees, the slender, tapering trees,
The liliput countless armies of the grass,

The heat, the showers, the measureless pasturages,
The scenery of the snows, the winds' free orchestra,
The stretching light-hung roof of clouds, the clear cerulean
    and the silvery fringes,
The high dilating stars, the placid beckoning stars,
The moving flocks and herds, the plains and emerald mea-
    dows,
The shows of all the varied lands and all the growths and
    products.

### 3

Fecund America—to-day,
Thou art all over set in births and joys!
Thou groan'st with riches, thy wealth clothes thee as a
    swathing-garment,
Thou laughest loud with ache of great possessions,
A myriad-twining life like interlacing vines binds all thy vast
    demesne,
As some huge ship freighted to water's edge thou ridest into
    port,
As rain falls from the heaven and vapors rise from earth, so
    have the precious values fallen upon thee and risen out
    of thee;
Thou envy of the globe! thou miracle!
Thou, bathed, choked, swimming in plenty,
Thou lucky Mistress of the tranquil barns,
Thou Prairie Dame that sittest in the middle and lookest out
    upon thy world, and lookest East and lookest West,
Dispensatress, that by a word givest a thousand miles, a
    million farms, and missest nothing,
Thou all-acceptress—thou hospitable, (thou only art hospit-
    able as God is hospitable.)

### 4

When late I sang sad was my voice,
Sad were the shows around me with deafening noises of
    hatred and smoke of war;
In the midst of the conflict, the heroes, I stood,
Or pass'd with slow step through the wounded and dying.

But now I sing not war,
Nor the measur'd march of soldiers, nor the tents of camps,
Nor the regiments hastily coming up deploying in line of
    battle;
No more the sad, unnatural shows of war.

Ask'd room those flush'd immortal ranks, the first forth-
    stepping armies?
Ask room alas the ghastly ranks, the armies dread that
    follow'd.

(Pass, pass, ye proud brigades, with your tramping sinewy
    legs,
With your shoulders young and strong, with your knapsacks
    and your muskets;
How elate I stood and watch'd you, where starting off you
    march'd.

Pass—then rattle drums again,
For an army heaves in sight, O another gathering army,
Swarming, trailing on the rear, O you dread accruing army,
O you regiments so piteous, with your mortal diarrhœa, with
    your fever,
O my land's maim'd darlings, with the plenteous bloody
    bandage and the crutch,
Lo, your pallid army follows.)

5

But on these days of brightness,
On the far-stretching beauteous landscape, the roads and
    lanes, the high-piled farm-wagons, and the fruits and
    barns,
Should the dead intrude?

Ah the dead to me mar not, they fit well in Nature,
They fit very well in the landscape under the trees and grass,
And along the edge of the sky in the horizon's far margin.

Nor do I forget you Departed,
Nor in winter or summer my lost ones,

But most in the open air as now when my soul is rapt and at
    peace, like pleasing phantoms,
Your memories rising glide silently by me.

### 6

I saw the day the return of the heroes,
(Yet the heroes never surpass'd shall never return,
Them that day I saw not.)

I saw the interminable corps, I saw the processions of armies,
I saw them approaching, defiling by with divisions,
Streaming northward, their work done, camping awhile in
    clusters of mighty camps.

No holiday soldiers—youthful, yet veterans,
Worn, swart, handsome, strong, of the stock of homestead
    and workshop,
Harden'd of many a long campaign and sweaty march,
Inured on many a hard-fought bloody field.

A pause—the armies wait,
A million flush'd embattled conquerors wait,
The world too waits, then soft as breaking night and sure as
    dawn,
They melt, they disappear.

Exult O lands! victorious lands!
Not there your victory on those red shuddering fields,
But here and hence your victory.

Melt, melt away ye armies—disperse ye blue-clad soldiers,
Resolve ye back again, give up for good your deadly arms,
Other the arms the fields henceforth for you, or South or
    North,
With saner wars, sweet wars, life-giving wars.

### 7

Loud O my throat, and clear O soul!
The season of thanks and the voice of full-yielding,
The chant of joy and power for boundless fertility.

All till'd and untill'd fields expand before me,
I see the true arenas of my race, or first or last,
Man's innocent and strong arenas.

I see the heroes at other toils,
I see well-wielded in their hands the better weapons.

I see where the Mother of All,
With full-spanning eye gazes forth, dwells long,
And counts the varied gathering of the products.

Busy the far, the sunlit panorama,
Prairie, orchard, and yellow grain of the North,
Cotton and rice of the South and Louisianian cane,
Open unseeded fallows, rich fields of clover and timothy,
Kine and horses feeding, and droves of sheep and swine,
And many a stately river flowing and many a jocund brook,
And healthy uplands with herby-perfumed breezes,
And the good green grass, that delicate miracle the ever-
        recurring grass.

8

Toil on heroes! harvest the products!
Not alone on those warlike fields the Mother of All,
With dilated form and lambent eyes watch'd you.

Toil on heroes! toil well! handle the weapons well!
The Mother of All, yet here as ever she watches you.

Well-pleased America thou beholdest,
Over the fields of the West those crawling monsters,
The human-divine inventions, the labor-saving implements;
Beholdest moving in every direction imbued as with life the
        revolving hay-rakes,
The steam-power reaping-machines and the horse-power
        machines,
The engines, thrashers of grain and cleaners of grain, well
        separating the straw, the nimble work of the patent
        pitchfork,
Beholdest the newer saw-mill, the southern cotton-gin, and
        the rice-cleanser.

Beneath thy look O Maternal,
With these and else and with their own strong hands the
    heroes harvest.

All gather and all harvest,
Yet but for thee O Powerful, not a scythe might swing as now
    in security,
Not a maize-stalk dangle as now its silken tassels in peace.

Under thee only they harvest, even but a wisp of hay under
    thy great face only,
Harvest the wheat of Ohio, Illinois, Wisconsin, every barbed
    spear under thee,
Harvest the maize of Missouri, Kentucky, Tennessee, each
    ear in its light-green sheath,
Gather the hay to its myriad mows in the odorous tranquil
    barns,
Oats to their bins, the white potato, the buckwheat of Michi-
    gan, to theirs;
Gather the cotton in Mississippi or Alabama, dig and hoard
    the golden the sweet potato of Georgia and the Carolinas,
Clip the wool of California or Pennsylvania,
Cut the flax in the Middle States, or hemp or tobacco in the
    Borders,
Pick the pea and the bean, or pull apples from the trees or
    bunches of grapes from the vines,
Or aught that ripens in all these States or North or South,
Under the beaming sun and under thee.
1867                                                  1881


## THERE WAS A CHILD WENT FORTH

THERE was a child went forth every day,
And the first object he look'd upon, that object he became,
And that object became part of him for the day or a certain
    part of the day,
Or for many years or stretching cycles of years.

The early lilacs became part of this child,
And grass and white and red morning-glories, and white and
    red clover, and the song of the phœbe-bird,

And the Third-month lambs and the sow's pink-faint litter,
and the mare's foal and the cow's calf,
And the noisy brood of the barnyard or by the mire of the
pond-side,
And the fish suspending themselves so curiously below there,
and the beautiful curious liquid,
And the water-plants with their graceful flat heads, all became part of him.

The field-sprouts of Fourth-month and Fifth-month became
part of him,
Winter-grain sprouts and those of the light-yellow corn, and
the esculent roots of the garden,
And the apple-trees cover'd with blossoms and the fruit
afterward, and wood-berries, and the commonest weeds
by the road,
And the old drunkard staggering home from the outhouse of
the tavern whence he had lately risen,
And the schoolmistress that pass'd on her way to the school,
And the friendly boys that pass'd, and the quarrelsome boys,
And the tidy and fresh-cheek'd girls, and the barefoot negro
boy and girl,
And all the changes of city and country wherever he went.

His own parents, he that had father'd him and she that had
conceiv'd him in her womb and birth'd him,
They gave this child more of themselves than that,
They gave him afterward every day, they became part of him,

The mother at home quietly placing the dishes on the supper-
table,
The mother with mild words, clean her cap and gown, a
wholesome odor falling off her person and clothes as she
walks by,
The father, strong, self-sufficient, manly, mean, anger'd,
unjust,
The blow, the quick loud word, the tight bargain, the crafty
lure,
The family usages, the language, the company, the furniture,
the yearning and swelling heart,

Affection that will not be gainsay'd, the sense of what is real,
the thought if after all it should prove unreal,

The doubts of day-time and the doubts of night-time, the
curious whether and how,

Whether that which appears so is so, or is it all flashes and
specks?

Men and women crowding fast in the streets, if they are not
flashes and specks what are they?

The streets themselves and the façades of houses, and goods
in the windows,

Vehicles, teams, the heavy-plank'd wharves, the huge crossing at the ferries,

The village on the highland seen from afar at sunset, the
river between,

Shadows, aureola and mist, the light falling on roofs and
gables of white or brown two miles off,

The schooner near by sleepily dropping down the tide, the
little boat slack-tow'd astern,

The hurrying tumbling waves, quick-broken crests, slapping,

The strata of color'd clouds, the long bar of maroon-tint
away solitary by itself, the spread of purity it lies
motionless in,

The horizon's edge, the flying sea-crow, the fragrance of salt
marsh and shore mud,

These became part of that child who went forth every day,
and who now goes, and will always go forth every
day.

1855                                                        1871

## OLD IRELAND

FAR hence amid an isle of wondrous beauty,

Crouching over a grave an ancient sorrowful mother,

Once a queen, now lean and tatter'd seated on the ground,

Her old white hair drooping dishevel'd round her shoulders,

At her feet fallen an unused royal harp,

Long silent, she too long silent, mourning her shrouded hope
and heir,

Of all the earth her heart most full of sorrow because most
full of love.

Yet a word ancient mother,
You need crouch there no longer on the cold ground with
    forehead between your knees,
O you need not sit there veil'd in your old white hair so dis-
    hevel'd,
For know you the one you mourn is not in that grave,
It was an illusion, the son you love was not really dead,
The Lord is not dead, he is risen again young and strong in
    another country,
Even while you wept there by your fallen harp by the grave,
What you wept for was translated, pass'd from the grave,
The winds favor'd and the sea sail'd it,
And now with rosy and new blood,
Moves to-day in a new country.
1861                                                 1867

## THE CITY DEAD-HOUSE

By the city dead-house by the gate,
As idly sauntering wending my way from the clangor,
I curious pause, for lo, an outcast form, a poor dead prosti-
    tute brought,
Her corpse they deposit unclaim'd, it lies on the damp brick
    pavement,
The divine woman, her body, I see the body, I look on it
    alone,
That house once full of passion and beauty, all else I notice
    not,
Nor stillness so cold, nor running water from faucet, nor
    odors morbific impress me,
But the house alone—that wondrous house—that delicate
    fair house—that ruin!
That immortal house more than all the rows of dwellings
    ever built!
Or white-domed capitol with majestic figure surmounted, or
    all the old high-spired cathedrals,
That little house alone more than them all—poor, desperate
    house!
Fair, fearful wreck—tenement of a soul—itself a soul,
Unclaim'd, avoided house—take one breath from my tremu-
    lous lips,

Take one tear dropt aside as I go for thought of you,
Dead house of love—house of madness and sin, crumbled, crush'd,
House of life, erewhile talking and laughing—but ah, poor house, dead even then,
Months, years, an echoing, garnish'd house—but dead, dead, dead.

1867                                                1867

## THIS COMPOST

### 1

SOMETHING startles me where I thought I was safest,
I withdraw from the still woods I loved,
I will not go now on the pastures to walk,
I will not strip the clothes from my body to meet my lover the sea,
I will not touch my flesh to the earth as to other flesh to renew me.

O how can it be that the ground itself does not sicken?
How can you be alive you growths of spring?
How can you furnish health you blood of herbs, roots, orchards, grain?
Are they not continually putting distemper'd corpses within you?
Is not every continent work'd over and over with sour dead?

Where have you disposed of their carcasses?
Those drunkards and gluttons of so many generations?
Where have you drawn off all the foul liquid and meat?
I do not see any of it upon you to-day, or perhaps I am de-ceiv'd,
I will run a furrow with my plough, I will press my spade through the sod and turn it up underneath,
I am sure I shall expose some of the foul meat.

### 2

Behold this compost! behold it well!
Perhaps every mite has once form'd part of a sick person— yet behold!
The grass of spring covers the prairies,

The bean bursts noiselessly through the mould in the garden,
The delicate spear of the onion pierces upward,
The apple-buds cluster together on the apple-branches,
The resurrection of the wheat appears with pale visage out of
    its graves,
The tinge awakes over the willow-tree and the mulberry-tree,
The he-birds carol mornings and evenings while the she-birds
    sit on their nests,
The young of poultry break through the hatch'd eggs,
The new-born of animals appear, the calf is dropt from the
    cow, the colt from the mare,
Out of its little hill faithfully rise the potato's dark green
    leaves,
Out of its hill rises the yellow maize-stalk, the lilacs bloom in
    the door-yards,
The summer growth is innocent and disdainful above all
    those strata of sour dead.

What chemistry!
That the winds are really not infectious,
That this is no cheat, this transparent green-wash of the sea
    which is so amorous after me,
That it is safe to allow it to lick my naked body all over with
    its tongues,
That it will not endanger me with the fevers that have de-
    posited themselves in it,
That all is clean forever and forever,
That the cool drink from the well tastes so good,
That blackberries are so flavorous and juicy,
That the fruits of the apple-orchard and the orange-orchard,
    that melons, grapes, peaches, plums, will none of them
    poison me,
That when I recline on the grass I do not catch any disease,
Though probably every spear of grass rises out of what was
    once a catching disease.

Now I am terrified at the Earth, it is that calm and patient,
It grows such sweet things out of such corruptions,
It turns harmless and stainless on its axis, with such endless
    successions of diseas'd corpses,

It distills such exquisite winds out of such infused fetor,
It renews with such unwitting looks its prodigal, annual,
    sumptuous crops,
It gives such divine materials to men, and accepts such leav-
    ings from them at last.

1856                                                    1881


## TO A FOIL'D EUROPEAN REVOLUTIONAIRE

COURAGE yet, my brother or my sister!
Keep on—Liberty is to be subserv'd whatever occurs;
That is nothing that is quell'd by one or two failures, or any
    number of failures,
Or by the indifference or ingratitude of the people, or by any
    unfaithfulness,
Or the show of the tushes of power, soldiers, cannon, penal
    statutes.

What we believe in waits latent forever through all the con-
    tinents,
Invites no one, promises nothing, sits in calmness and light,
    is positive and composed, knows no discouragement,
Waiting patiently, waiting its time.

(Not songs of loyalty alone are these,
But songs of insurrection also,
For I am the sworn poet of every dauntless rebel the world
    over,
And he going with me leaves peace and routine behind him,
And stakes his life to be lost at any moment.)

The battle rages with many a loud alarm and frequent ad-
    vance and retreat,
The infidel triumphs, or supposes he triumphs,
The prison, scaffold, garrote, handcuffs, iron necklace and
    lead-balls do their work,
The named and unnamed heroes pass to other spheres,
The great speakers and writers are exiled, they lie sick in dis-
    tant lands,
The cause is asleep, the strongest throats are choked with
    their own blood,

The young men droop their eyelashes toward the ground
    when they meet;
But for all this Liberty has not gone out of the place, nor the
    infidel enter'd into full possession.

When Liberty goes out of a place it is not the first to go, nor
    the second or third to go,
It waits for all the rest to go, it is the last.

When there are no more memories of heroes and martyrs,
And when all life and all the souls of men and women are
    discharged from any part of the earth,
Then only shall liberty or the idea of liberty be discharged
    from that part of the earth,
And the infidel come into full possession.

Then courage European revolter, revoltress!
For till all ceases neither must you cease.

I do not know what you are for, (I do not know what I am
    for myself, nor what any thing is for,)
But I will search carefully for it even in being foil'd,
In defeat, poverty, misconception, imprisonment—for they
    too are great.

Did we think victory great?
So it is—but now it seems to me, when it cannot be help'd,
    that defeat is great,
And that death and dismay are great.
1856                              1881

## UNNAMED LANDS

NATIONS ten thousand years before these States, and many
    times ten thousand years before these States,
Garner'd clusters of ages that men and women like us grew
    up and travel'd their course and pass'd on,
What vast-built cities, what orderly republics, what pastoral
    tribes and nomads,
What histories, rulers, heroes, perhaps transcending all
    others,

What laws, customs, wealth, arts, traditions,
What sort of marriage, what costumes, what physiology and
　　phrenology,
What of liberty and slavery among them, what they thought
　　of death and the soul,
Who were witty and wise, who beautiful and poetic, who
　　brutish and undevelop'd,
Not a mark, not a record remains—and yet all remains.

O I know that those men and women were not for nothing,
　　any more than we are for nothing,
I know that they belong to the scheme of the world every bit
　　as much as we now belong to it.

Afar they stand, yet near to me they stand,
Some with oval countenances learn'd and calm,
Some naked and savage, some like huge collections of in-
　　sects,
Some in tents, herdsmen, patriarchs, tribes, horsemen,
Some prowling through woods, some living peaceably on
　　farms, laboring, reaping, filling barns,
Some traversing paved avenues, amid temples, palaces, fac-
　　tories, libraries, shows, courts, theatres, wonderful
　　monuments.

Are those billions of men really gone?
Are those women of the old experience of the earth gone?
Do their lives, cities, arts, rest only with us?
Did they achieve nothing for good for themselves?

I believe of all those men and women that fill'd the unnamed
　　lands, every one exists this hour here or elsewhere, in-
　　visible to us,
In exact proportion to what he or she grew from in life, and
　　out of what he or she did, felt, became, loved, sinn'd, in
　　life.

I believe that was not the end of those nations or any person
　　of them, any more than this shall be the end of my
　　nation, or of me;

Of their languages, governments, marriage, literature, pro-
    ducts, games, wars, manners, crimes, prisons, slaves,
    heroes, poets,
I suspect their results curiously await in the yet unseen world,
    counterparts of what accrued to them in the seen world,
I suspect I shall meet them there,
I suspect I shall there find each old particular of those un-
    named lands.

1860                                                              1881


## SONG OF PRUDENCE

MANHATTAN'S streets I saunter'd, pondering
On Time, Space, Reality—on such as these, and abreast with
    them Prudence.


The last explanation always remains to be made about prud-
    ence,
Little and large alike drop quietly aside from the prudence
    that suits immortality.


The soul is of itself,
All verges to it, all has reference to what ensues,
All that a person does, says, thinks, is of consequence,
Not a move can a man or woman make, that affects him or
    her in a day, month, any part of the direct lifetime, or
    the hour of death,
But the same affects him or her onward afterward through
    the indirect lifetime.


The indirect is just as much as the direct,
The spirit receives from the body just as much as it gives to
    the body, if not more.


Not one word or deed, not venereal sore, discoloration,
    privacy of the onanist,
Putridity of gluttons or rum-drinkers, peculation, cunning,
    betrayal, murder, seduction, prostitution,
But has results beyond death as really as before death.

Charity and personal force are the only investments worth
    any thing.

No specification is necessary, all that a male or female does,
        that is vigorous, benevolent, clean, is so much profit to
        him or her,
In the unshakable order of the universe and through the
        whole scope of it forever.

Who has been wise receives interest,
Savage, felon, President, judge, farmer, sailor, mechanic,
        literat, young, old, it is the same,
The interest will come round—all will come round.

Singly, wholly, to affect now, affected their time, will forever
        affect, all of the past and all of the present and all of the
        future,
All the brave actions of war and peace,
All help given to relatives, strangers, the poor, old, sorrow-
        ful, young children, widows, the sick, and to shunn'd
        persons,
All self-denial that stood steady and aloof on wrecks, and saw
        others fill the seats of the boats,
All offering of substance or life for the good old cause, or for
        a friend's sake, or opinion's sake,
All pains of enthusiasts scoff'd at by their neighbors,
All the limitless sweet love and precious suffering of mothers,
All honest men baffled in strifes recorded or unrecorded,
All the grandeur and good of ancient nations whose frag-
        ments we inherit,
All the good of the dozens of ancient nations unknown to us
        by name, date, location,
All that was ever manfully begun, whether it succeeded or no,
All suggestions of the divine mind of man or the divinity of
        his mouth, or the shaping of his great hands,
All that is well thought or said this day on any part of the
        globe, or on any of the wandering stars, or on any of the
        fix'd stars, by those there as we are here,
All that is henceforth to be thought or done by you whoever
        you are, or by any one,

These inure, have inured, shall inure, to the identities from
  which they sprang, or shall spring.

Did you guess any thing lived only its moment?
The world does not so exist, no parts palpable or impalpable
  so exist,
No consummation exists without being from some long previous consummation, and that from some other,
Without the farthest conceivable one coming a bit nearer the
  beginning than any.

Whatever satisfies souls is true;
Prudence entirely satisfies the craving and glut of souls,
Itself only finally satisfies the soul,
The soul has that measureless pride which revolts from every
  lesson but its own.

Now I breathe the word of the prudence that walks abreast
  with time, space, reality,
That answers the pride which refuses every lesson but its
  own.

What is prudence is indivisible,
Declines to separate one part of life from every part,
Divides not the righteous from the unrighteous or the living
  from the dead,
Matches every thought or act by its correlative,
Knows no possible forgiveness or deputed atonement,
Knows that the young man who composedly peril'd his life
  and lost it has done exceedingly well for himself without
  doubt,
That he who never peril'd his life, but retains it to old age in
  riches and ease, has probably achiev'd nothing for him-
  self worth mentioning,
Knows that only that person has really learn'd who has
  learn'd to prefer results,
Who favors body and soul the same,
Who perceives the indirect assuredly following the direct,
Who in his spirit in any emergency whatever neither hurries
  nor avoids death.
1856                                                     1881

## THE SINGER IN THE PRISON

### 1

*O sight of pity, shame and dole!*
*O fearful thought—a convict soul.*

RANG the refrain along the hall, the prison,
Rose to the roof, the vaults of heaven above,
Pouring in floods of melody in tones so pensive sweet and
    strong the like whereof was never heard,
Reaching the far-off sentry and the armed guards, who
    ceas'd their pacing,
Making the hearer's pulses stop for ecstasy and awe.

### 2

The sun was low in the west one winter day,
When down a narrow aisle amid the thieves and outlaws of
    the land,
(There by the hundreds seated, sear-faced murderers, wily
    counterfeiters,
Gather'd to Sunday church in prison walls, the keepers
    round,
Plenteous, well-armed, watching with vigilant eyes,)
Calmly a lady walk'd holding a little innocent child by either
    hand,
Whom seating on their stools beside her on the platform,
She, first preluding with the instrument a low and musical
    prelude,
In voice surpassing all, sang forth a quaint old hymn.

    A soul confined by bars and bands,
    Cries, help! O help! and wrings her hands,
    Blinded her eyes, bleeding her breast,
    Nor pardon finds, nor balm of rest.

    Ceaseless she paces to and fro,
    O heart-sick days! O nights of woe!
    Nor hand of friend, nor loving face,
    Nor favor comes, nor word of grace.

It was not I that sinn'd the sin,
The ruthless body dragg'd me in;
Though long I strove courageously,
The body was too much for me.

Dear prison'd soul bear up a space,
For soon or late the certain grace;
To set thee free and bear thee home,
The heavenly pardoner death shall come.

*Convict no more, nor shame, nor dole !*
*Depart—a God-enfranchis'd soul !*

### 3

The singer ceas'd,
One glance swept from her clear calm eyes o'er all those up-
turn'd faces,
Strange sea of prison faces, a thousand varied, crafty, brutal,
seam'd and beauteous faces,
Then rising, passing back along the narrow aisle between
them,
While her gown touch'd them rustling in the silence,
She vanish'd with her children in the dusk.

While upon all, convicts and armed keepers ere they
stirr'd,
(Convict forgetting prison, keeper his loaded pistol,)
A hush and pause fell down a wondrous minute,
With deep half-stifled sobs and sound of bad men bow'd and
moved to weeping,
And youth's convulsive breathings, memories of home,
The mother's voice in lullaby, the sister's care, the happy
childhood,
The long-pent spirit rous'd to reminiscence;
A wondrous minute then—but after in the solitary night, to
many, many there,
Years after, even in the hour of death, the sad refrain, the
tune, the voice, the words,

Resumed, the large calm lady walks the narrow aisle,
The wailing melody again, the singer in the prison sings,

> *O sight of pity, shame and dole!*
> *O fearful thought—a convict soul.*

1869                                                                   1881


## WARBLE FOR LILAC-TIME

WARBLE me now for joy of lilac-time, (returning in reminis-
    cence,)
Sort me O tongue and lips for Nature's sake, souvenirs of
    earliest summer,
Gather the welcome signs, (as children with pebbles or
    stringing shells,)
Put in April and May, the hylas croaking in the ponds, the
    elastic air,
Bees, butterflies, the sparrow with its simple notes,
Blue-bird and darting swallow, nor forget the high-hole
    flashing his golden wings,
The tranquil sunny haze, the clinging smoke, the vapor,
Shimmer of waters with fish in them, the cerulean above,
All that is jocund and sparkling, the brooks running,
The maple woods, the crisp February days and the sugar-
    making,
The robin where he hops, bright-eyed, brown-breasted,
With musical clear call at sunrise, and again at sunset,
Or flitting among the trees of the apple-orchard, building the
    nest of his mate,
The melted snow of March, the willow sending forth its
    yellow-green sprouts,
For spring-time is here! the summer is here! and what is this
    in it and from it?
Thou, soul, unloosen'd—the restlessness after I know not
    what;
Come, let us lag here no longer, let us be up and away!
O if one could but fly like a bird!
O to escape, to sail forth as in a ship!
To glide with thee O soul, o'er all, in all, as a ship o'er the
    waters;

Gathering these hints, the preludes, the blue sky, the grass,
  the morning drops of dew,
The lilac-scent, the bushes with dark green heart-shaped
  leaves,
Wood-violets, the little delicate pale blossoms called innocence,
Samples and sorts not for themselves alone, but for their
  atmosphere,
To grace the bush I love—to sing with the birds,
A warble for joy of lilac-time, returning in reminiscence.
1870                                                    1881


## OUTLINES FOR A TOMB

### (*G. P., Buried 1870*)

#### 1

WHAT may we chant, O thou within this tomb?
What tablets, outlines, hang for thee, O millionaire?
The life thou lived'st we know not,
But that thou walk'dst thy years in barter, 'mid the haunts of
  brokers,
Nor heroism thine, nor war, nor glory.


#### 2

Silent, my soul,
With drooping lids, as waiting, ponder'd,
Turning from all the samples, monuments of heroes.

While through the interior vistas,
Noiseless uprose, phantasmic, (as by night Auroras of the
  north,)
Lambent tableaus, prophetic, bodiless scenes,
Spiritual projections.

In one, among the city streets a laborer's home appear'd,
After his day's work done, cleanly, sweet-air'd, the gaslight
  burning,
The carpet swept and a fire in the cheerful stove.

In one, the sacred parturition scene,
A happy painless mother birth'd a perfect child.

In one, at a bounteous morning meal,
Sat peaceful parents with contented sons.

In one, by twos and threes, young people,
Hundreds concentring, walk'd the paths and streets and roads,
Toward a tall-domed school.

In one a trio beautiful,
Grandmother, loving daughter, loving daughter's daughter, sat,
Chatting and sewing.

In one, along a suite of noble rooms,
'Mid plenteous books and journals, paintings on the walls, fine statuettes,
Were groups of friendly journeymen, mechanics young and old,
Reading, conversing.

All, all the shows of laboring life,
City and country, women's, men's and children's,
Their wants provided for, hued in the sun and tinged for once with joy,
Marriage, the street, the factory, farm, the house-room, lodging-room,
Labor and toil, the bath, gymnasium, playground, library, college,
The student, boy or girl, led forward to be taught,
The sick cared for, the shoeless shod, the orphan father'd and mother'd,
The hungry fed, the houseless housed;
(The intentions perfect and divine,
The workings, details, haply human.)

### 3

O thou within this tomb,
From thee such scenes, thou stintless, lavish giver,

Tallying the gifts of earth, large as the earth,
Thy name an earth, with mountains, fields and tides.

Nor by your streams alone, you rivers,
By you, your banks Connecticut,
By you and all your teeming life old Thames,
By you Potomac laving the ground Washington trod, by you
     Patapsco,
You Hudson, you endless Mississippi—nor you alone,
But to the high seas launch, my thought, his memory.
1870                                                          1881


## OUT FROM BEHIND THIS MASK

### (*To Confront a Portrait*)

#### 1

OUT from behind this bending rough-cut mask,
These lights and shades, this drama of the whole,
This common curtain of the face contain'd in me for me, in
     you for you, in each for each,
(Tragedies, sorrows, laughter, tears—O heaven!
The passionate teeming plays this curtain hid!)
This glaze of God's serenest purest sky,
This film of Satan's seething pit,
This heart's geography's map, this limitless small continent,
     this soundless sea;
Out from the convolutions of this globe,
This subtler astronomic orb than sun or moon, than Jupiter,
     Venus, Mars,
This condensation of the universe, (nay here the only universe,
Here the idea, all in this mystic handful wrapt;)
These burin'd eyes, flashing to you to pass to future time,
To launch and spin through space revolving sideling, from
     these to emanate,
To you whoe'er you are—a look.


#### 2

A traveler of thoughts and years, of peace and war,
Of youth long sped and middle age declining,

(As the first volume of a tale perused and laid away, and this
　　the second,
Songs, ventures, speculations, presently to close,)
Lingering a moment here and now, to you I opposite turn,
As on the road or at some crevice door by chance, or open'd
　　window,
Pausing, inclining, baring my head, you specially I greet,
To draw and clinch your soul for once inseparably with mine,
Then travel travel on.
1876　　　　　　　　　　　　　　　　　　　　　　　　1881

## VOCALISM

### 1

VOCALISM, measure, concentration, determination, and the
　　divine power to speak words;
Are you full-lung'd and limber-lipp'd from long trial? from
　　vigorous practice? from physique?
Do you move in these broad lands as broad as they?
Come duly to the divine power to speak words?
For only at last after many years, after chastity, friendship,
　　procreation, prudence, and nakedness,
After treading ground and breasting river and lake,
After a loosen'd throat, after absorbing eras, temperaments,
　　races, after knowledge, freedom, crimes,
After complete faith, after clarifyings, elevations, and re-
　　moving obstructions,
After these and more, it is just possible there comes to a man,
　　a woman, the divine power to speak words;
Then toward that man or that woman swiftly hasten all—
　　none refuse, all attend,
Armies, ships, antiquities, libraries, paintings, machines,
　　cities, hate, despair, amity, pain, theft, murder, aspira-
　　tion, form in close ranks,
They debouch as they are wanted to march obediently
　　through the mouth of that man or that woman.

### 2

O what is it in me that makes me tremble so at voices?
Surely whoever speaks to me in the right voice, him or her I
　　shall follow,

As the water follows the moon, silently, with fluid steps, anywhere around the globe.

All waits for the right voices;
Where is the practis'd and perfect organ? where is the develop'd soul?
For I see every word utter'd thence has deeper, sweeter, new
 sounds, impossible on less terms.

I see brains and lips closed, tympans and temples unstruck,
Until that comes which has the quality to strike and to un-
 close,
Until that comes which has the quality to bring forth what
 lies slumbering forever ready in all words.
1860                                                    1881


## TO HIM THAT WAS CRUCIFIED

MY spirit to yours dear brother,
Do not mind because many sounding your name do not
 understand you,
I do not sound your name, but I understand you,
I specify you with joy O my comrade to salute you, and to
 salute those who are with you, before and since, and
 those to come also,
That we all labor together transmitting the same charge and
 succession,
We few equals indifferent of lands, indifferent of times,
We, enclosers of all continents, all castes, allowers of all
 theologies,
Compassionaters, perceivers, rapport of men,
We walk silent among disputes and assertions, but reject
 not the disputers nor any thing that is asserted,
We hear the bawling and din, we are reach'd at by divisions,
 jealousies, recriminations on every side,
They close peremptorily upon us to surround us, my comrade,
Yet we walk unheld, free, the whole earth over, journeying
 up and down till we make our ineffaceable mark upon
 time and the diverse eras,

Till we saturate time and eras, that the men and women of
    races, ages to come, may prove brethren and lovers as
    we are.
1860                                                    1881


## YOU FELONS ON TRIAL IN COURTS

You felons on trial in courts,
You convicts in prison-cells, you sentenced assassins chain'd
    and hand-cuff'd with iron,
Who am I too that I am not on trial or in prison?
Me ruthless and devilish as any, that my wrists are not
    chain'd with iron, or my ankles with iron?

You prostitutes flaunting over the trottoirs or obscene in
    your rooms,
Who am I that I should call you more obscene than myself?

O culpable! I acknowledge—I exposé!
(O admirers, praise not me—compliment not me—you make
    me wince,
I see what you do not—I know what you do not.)

Inside these breast-bones I lie smutch'd and choked,
Beneath this face that appears so impassive hell's tides con-
    tinually run,
Lusts and wickedness are acceptable to me,
I walk with delinquents with passionate love,
I feel I am of them—I belong to those convicts and prosti-
    tutes myself,
And henceforth I will not deny them—for how can I deny
    myself?
1860                                                    1867


## LAWS FOR CREATIONS

Laws for creations,
For strong artists and leaders, for fresh broods of teachers
    and perfect literats for America,
For noble savans and coming musicians.

All must have reference to the ensemble of the world, and the
 compact truth of the world,
There shall be no subject too pronounced—all works shall
 illustrate the divine law of indirections.

What do you suppose creation is?
What do you suppose will satisfy the soul, except to walk
 free and own no superior?
What do you suppose I would intimate to you in a hundred
 ways, but that man or woman is as good as God?
And that there is no God any more divine than Yourself?
And that that is what the oldest and newest myths finally
 mean?
And that you or any one must approach creations through
 such laws?
1860                                                        1871

## TO A COMMON PROSTITUTE

BE composed—be at ease with me—I am Walt Whitman,
 liberal and lusty as Nature,
Not till the sun excludes you do I exclude you,
Not till the waters refuse to glisten for you and the leaves to
 rustle for you, do my words refuse to glisten and rustle
 for you.

My girl I appoint with you an appointment, and I charge you
 that you make preparation to be worthy to meet me,
And I charge you that you be patient and perfect till I come.

Till then I salute you with a significant look that you do not
 forget me.
1860                                                        1860

## I WAS LOOKING A LONG WHILE

I WAS looking a long while for Intentions,
For a clew to the history of the past for myself, and for these
 chants—and now I have found it,
It is not in those paged fables in the libraries, (them I neither
 accept nor reject,)
M                                                           **W.**

It is no more in the legends than in all else,
It is in the present—it is this earth to-day,
It is in Democracy—(the purport and aim of all the past,)
It is the life of one man or one woman to-day—the average
　　man of to-day,
It is in languages, social customs, literatures, arts,
It is in the broad show of artificial things, ships, machinery,
　　politics, creeds, modern improvements, and the inter-
　　change of nations,
All for the modern—all for the average man of to-day.
1860　　　　　　　　　　　　　　　　　　　　　　　　1881


## THOUGHT

Of persons arrived at high positions, ceremonies, wealth,
　　scholarships, and the like;
(To me all that those persons have arrived at sinks away
　　from them, except as it results to their bodies and souls,
So that often to me they appear gaunt and naked,
And often to me each one mocks the others, and mocks him-
　　self or herself,
And of each one the core of life, namely happiness, is full of
　　the rotten excrement of maggots,
And often to me those men and women pass unwittingly the
　　true realities of life, and go toward false realities,
And often to me they are alive after what custom has served
　　them, but nothing more,
And often to me they are sad, hasty, unwaked sonnambules
　　walking the dusk.)
1860　　　　　　　　　　　　　　　　　　　　　　　　1871


## MIRACLES

Why, who makes much of a miracle?
As to me I know of nothing else but miracles,
Whether I walk the streets of Manhattan,
Or dart my sight over the roofs of houses toward the sky,
Or wade with naked feet along the beach just in the edge of
　　the water,
Or stand under trees in the woods,

Or talk by day with any one I love, or sleep in the bed at night
    with any one I love,
Or sit at table at dinner with the rest,
Or look at strangers opposite me riding in the car,
Or watch honey-bees busy around the hive of a summer fore-
    noon,
Or animals feeding in the fields,
Or birds, or the wonderfulness of insects in the air,
Or the wonderfulness of the sundown, or of stars shining so
    quiet and bright,
Or the exquisite delicate thin curve of the new moon in
    spring;
These with the rest, one and all, are to me miracles,
The whole referring, yet each distinct and in its place.

To me every hour of the light and dark is a miracle,
Every cubic inch of space is a miracle,
Every square yard of the surface of the earth is spread with
    the same,
Every foot of the interior swarms with the same.

To me the sea is a continual miracle,
The fishes that swim—the rocks—the motion of the waves—
    the ships with men in them,
What stranger miracles are there?
1856                                       1881

## SPARKLES FROM THE WHEEL

WHERE the city's ceaseless crowd moves on the livelong day,
Withdrawn I join a group of children watching, I pause
    aside with them.

By the curb toward the edge of the flagging,
A knife-grinder works at his wheel sharpening a great knife,
Bending over he carefully holds it to the stone, by foot and
    knee,
With measur'd tread he turns rapidly, as he presses with light
    but firm hand,
Forth issue then in copious golden jets,
Sparkles from the wheel.

The scene and all its belongings, how they seize and affect me,
The sad sharp-chinn'd old man with worn clothes and broad
　　shoulder-band of leather,
Myself effusing and fluid, a phantom curiously floating, now
　　here absorb'd and arrested,
The group, (an unminded point set in a vast surrounding,)
The attentive, quiet children, the loud, proud, restive base of
　　the streets,
The low hoarse purr of the whirling stone, the light-press'd
　　blade,
Diffusing, dropping, sideways-darting, in tiny showers of
　　gold,
Sparkles from the wheel.

1871　　　　　　　　　　　　　　　　　　　　　　　　　1871

## TO A PUPIL

Is reform needed? is it through you?
The greater the reform needed, the greater the Personality
　　you need to accomplish it.

You! do you not see how it would serve to have eyes, blood,
　　complexion, clean and sweet?
Do you not see how it would serve to have such a body and
　　soul that when you enter the crowd an atmosphere of
　　desire and command enters with you, and every one is
　　impress'd with your Personality?

O the magnet! the flesh over and over!
Go, dear friend, if need be give up all else, and commence
　　to-day to inure yourself to pluck, reality, self-esteem,
　　definiteness, elevatedness,
Rest not till you rivet and publish yourself of your own Per-
　　sonality.

1860　　　　　　　　　　　　　　　　　　　　　　　　　1860

## UNFOLDED OUT OF THE FOLDS

UNFOLDED out of the folds of the woman man comes un-
　　folded, and is always to come unfolded,
Unfolded only out of the superbest woman of the earth is to
　　come the superbest man of the earth,

Unfolded out of the friendliest woman is to come the friendliest man,
Unfolded only out of the perfect body of a woman can a man
be form'd of perfect body,
Unfolded only out of the inimitable poems of woman can
come the poems of man, (only thence have my poems
come;)
Unfolded out of the strong and arrogant woman I love, only
thence can appear the strong and arrogant man I love,
Unfolded by brawny embraces from the well-muscled woman
I love, only thence come the brawny embraces of the
man,
Unfolded out of the folds of the woman's brain come all the
folds of the man's brain, duly obedient,
Unfolded out of the justice of the woman all justice is unfolded,
Unfolded out of the sympathy of the woman is all sympathy;
A man is a great thing upon the earth and through eternity,
but every jot of the greatness of man is unfolded out of
woman;
First the man is shaped in the woman, he can then be shaped
in himself.

1856                                         1871

## WHAT AM I AFTER ALL

WHAT am I after all but a child, pleas'd with the sound of my
own name? repeating it over and over;
I stand apart to hear—it never tires me.

To you your name also;
Did you think there was nothing but two or three pronun-
ciations in the sound of your name?

1860                                         1867

## KOSMOS

WHO includes diversity and is Nature,
Who is the amplitude of the earth, and the coarseness and
sexuality of the earth, and the great charity of the earth,
and the equilibrium also,

Who has not look'd forth from the windows the eyes for
    nothing, or whose brain held audience with messengers
    for nothing,
Who contains believers and disbelievers, who is the most
    majestic lover,
Who holds duly his or her triune proportion of realism,
    spiritualism, and of the æsthetic or intellectual,
Who having consider'd the body finds all its organs and parts
    good,
Who, out of the theory of the earth and of his or her body
    understands by subtle analogies all other theories,
The theory of a city, a poem, and of the large politics of these
    States;
Who believes not only in our globe with its sun and moon,
    but in other globes with their suns and moons,
Who, constructing the house of himself or herself, not for a
    day but for all time, sees races, eras, dates, generations,
The past, the future, dwelling there, like space, inseparable
    together.

1860                       1867

## OTHERS MAY PRAISE WHAT THEY LIKE

OTHERS may praise what they like;
But I, from the banks of the running Missouri, praise nothing
    in art or aught else,
Till it has well inhaled the atmosphere of this river, also the
    western prairie-scent,
And exudes it all again.

1865                       1881

## WHO LEARNS MY LESSON COMPLETE?

WHO learns my lesson complete?
Boss, journeyman, apprentice, churchman and atheist,
The stupid and the wise thinker, parents and offspring, mer-
    chant, clerk, porter and customer,
Editor, author, artist, and schoolboy—draw nigh and com-
    mence;
It is no lesson—it lets down the bars to a good lesson,
And that to another, and every one to another still.

The great laws take and effuse without argument,
I am of the same style, for I am their friend,
I love them quits and quits, I do not halt and make salaams.

I lie abstracted and hear beautiful tales of things and the
    reasons of things,
They are so beautiful I nudge myself to listen.

I cannot say to any person what I hear—I cannot say it to
    myself—it is very wonderful.

It is no small matter, this round and delicious globe moving
    so exactly in its orbit for ever and ever, without one jolt
    or the untruth of a single second,
I do not think it was made in six days, nor in ten thousand
    years, nor ten billions of years,
Nor plann'd and built one thing after another as an architect
    plans and builds a house.

I do not think seventy years is the time of a man or woman,
Nor that seventy millions of years is the time of a man or
    woman,
Nor that years will ever stop the existence of me, or any one
    else.

Is it wonderful that I should be immortal? as every one is
    immortal;
I know it is wonderful, but my eyesight is equally wonderful,
    and how I was conceived in my mother's womb is
    equally wonderful,
And pass'd from a babe in the creeping trance of a couple of
    summers and winters to articulate and walk—all this is
    equally wonderful.

And that my soul embraces you this hour, and we affect each
    other without ever seeing each other, and never perhaps
    to see each other, is every bit as wonderful.

And that I can think such thoughts as these is just as wonder-
    ful,
And that I can remind you, and you think them and know
    them to be true, is just as wonderful.

And that the moon spins round the earth and on with the
    earth, is equally wonderful,
And that they balance themselves with the sun and stars is
    equally wonderful.

1855                                              1867

## TESTS

ALL submit to them where they sit, inner, secure, unap-
    proachable to analysis in the soul,
Not traditions, not the outer authorities are the judges,
They are the judges of outer authorities and of all traditions,
They corroborate as they go only whatever corroborates
    themselves, and touches themselves;
For all that, they have it forever in themselves to corroborate
    far and near without one exception.

1860                                              1860

## THE TORCH

ON my Northwest coast in the midst of the night a fisher-
    men's group stands watching,
Out on the lake that expands before them, others are spear-
    ing salmon,
The canoe, a dim shadowy thing, moves across the black water,
Bearing a torch ablaze at the prow.

1865                                            1867

## O STAR OF FRANCE

### 1870–71

O STAR of France,
The brightness of thy hope and strength and fame,
Like some proud ship that led the fleet so long,
Beseems to-day a wreck driven by the gale, a mastless hulk,
And 'mid its teeming madden'd half-drown'd crowds,
Nor helm nor helmsman.

Dim smitten star,
Orb not of France alone, pale symbol of my soul, its dearest
    hopes,
The struggle and the daring, rage divine for liberty,

Of aspirations toward the far ideal, enthusiast's dreams of
    brotherhood,
Of terror to the tyrant and the priest.

Star crucified—by traitors sold,
Star panting o'er a land of death, heroic land,
Strange, passionate, mocking, frivolous land.

Miserable! yet for thy errors, vanities, sins, I will not now
    rebuke thee,
Thy unexampled woes and pangs have quell'd them all,
And left thee sacred.

In that amid thy many faults thou ever aimedst highly,
In that thou wouldst not really sell thyself however great the
    price,
In that thou surely wakedst weeping from thy drugg'd sleep,
In that alone among thy sisters thou, giantess, didst rend the
    ones that shamed thee,
In that thou couldst not, wouldst not, wear the usual chains,
This cross, thy livid face, thy pierced hands and feet,
The spear thrust in thy side.

O star! O ship of France, beat back and baffled long!
Bear up O smitten orb!    O ship continue on!

Sure as the ship of all, the Earth itself,
Product of deathly fire and turbulent chaos,
Forth from its spasms of fury and its poisons,
Issuing at last in perfect power and beauty,
Onward beneath the sun following its course,
So thee O ship of France!

Finish'd the days, the clouds dispel'd,
The travail o'er, the long-sought extrication,
When lo! reborn, high o'er the European world,
(In gladness answering thence, as face afar to face, reflecting
    ours Columbia,)
Again thy star O France, fair lustrous star,
In heavenly peace, clearer, more bright than ever,
Shall beam immortal.
1871                                          1881

## THE OX-TAMER

IN a far-away northern county in the placid pastoral region,
Lives my farmer friend, the theme of my recitative, a famous
    tamer of oxen,
There they bring him the three-year-olds and the four-year-
    olds to break them,
He will take the wildest steer in the world and break him and
    tame him,
He will go fearless without any whip where the young bullock
    chafes up and down the yard,
The bullock's head tosses restless high in the air with raging
    eyes,
Yet see you! how soon his rage subsides—how soon this
    tamer tames him;
See you! on the farms hereabouts a hundred oxen young and
    old, and he is the man who has tamed them,
They all know him, all are affectionate to him;
See you! some are such beautiful animals, so lofty look-
    ing;
Some are buff-color'd, some mottled, one has a white line
    running along his back, some are brindled,
Some have wide flaring horns (a good sign)—see you! the
    bright hides,
See, the two with stars on their foreheads—see, the round
    bodies and broad backs,
How straight and square they stand on their legs—what fine
    sagacious eyes!
How they watch their tamer—they wish him near them—
    how they turn to look after him!
What yearning expression! how uneasy they are when he
    moves away from them;
Now I marvel what it can be he appears to them, (books,
    politics, poems, depart—all else departs,)
I confess I envy only his fascination—my silent, illiterate
    friend,
Whom a hundred oxen love there in his life on farms,
In the northern country far, in the placid pastoral region.
1874                                                    1881

## AN OLD MAN'S THOUGHT OF SCHOOL

*For the Inauguration of a Public School, Camden, New Jersey, 1874*

An old man's thought of school,
An old man gathering youthful memories and blooms that
    youth itself cannot.

Now only do I know you,
O fair auroral skies—O morning dew upon the grass!

And these I see, these sparkling eyes,
These stores of mystic meaning, these young lives,
Building, equipping like a fleet of ships, immortal ships,
Soon to sail out over the measureless seas,
On the soul's voyage.

Only a lot of boys and girls?
Only the tiresome spelling, writing, ciphering classes?
Only a public school?

Ah more, infinitely more;
(As George Fox rais'd his warning cry, "Is it this pile of
    brick and mortar, these dead floors, windows, rails, you
    call the church?
Why this is not the church at all—the church is living, ever
    living souls.")

And you America,
Cast you the real reckoning for your present?
The lights and shadows of your future, good or evil?
To girlhood, boyhood look, the teacher and the school.
1874                                                1881

## WANDERING AT MORN

Wandering at morn,
Emerging from the night from gloomy thoughts, thee in my
    thoughts,
Yearning for thee harmonious Union! thee, singing bird
    divine!

Thee coil'd in evil times my country, with craft and black
    dismay, with every meanness, treason thrust upon thee,
This common marvel I beheld—the parent thrush I watch'd
    feeding its young,
The singing thrush whose tones of joy and faith ecstatic,
Fail not to certify and cheer my soul.

There ponder'd, felt I,
If worms, snakes, loathsome grubs, may to sweet spiritual
    songs be turn'd,
If vermin so transposed, so used and bless'd may be,
Then may I trust in you, your fortunes, days, my country;
Who knows but these may be the lessons fit for you?
From these your future song may rise with joyous trills,
Destin'd to fill the world.
1873                          1881


## ITALIAN MUSIC IN DAKOTA

("*The Seventeenth—the finest Regimental Band I ever
heard.*")

THROUGH the soft evening air enwinding all,
Rocks, woods, fort, cannon, pacing sentries, endless wilds,
In dulcet streams, in flutes' and cornets' notes,
Electric, pensive, turbulent, artificial,
(Yet strangely fitting even here, meanings unknown before,
Subtler than ever, more harmony, as if born here, related
    here,
Not to the city's fresco'd rooms, not to the audience of the
    opera house,
Sounds, echoes, wandering strains, as really here at home,
*Sonnambula's* innocent love, trios with *Norma's* anguish,
And thy ecstatic chorus *Poliuto;*)
Ray'd in the limpid yellow slanting sundown,
Music, Italian music in Dakota.

While Nature, sovereign of this gnarl'd realm,
Lurking in hidden barbaric grim recesses,
Acknowledging rapport however far remov'd,

(As some old root or soil of earth its last-born flower or fruit,)
Listens well pleas'd.
1881                                                             1881

## WITH ALL THY GIFTS

WITH all thy gifts America,
Standing secure, rapidly tending, overlooking the world,
Power, wealth, extent, vouchsafed to thee—with these and
    like of these vouchsafed to thee,
What if one gift thou lackest? (the ultimate human problem
    never solving,)
The gift of perfect women fit for thee—what if that gift of
    gifts thou lackest?
The towering feminine of thee? the beauty, health, comple-
    tion, fit for thee?
The mothers fit for thee?
1876                                                             1881

## MY PICTURE-GALLERY

IN a little house keep I pictures suspended, it is not a fix'd
    house,
It is round, it is only a few inches from one side to the other;
Yet behold, it has room for all the shows of the world, all
    memories!
Here the tableaus of life, and here the groupings of death;
Here, do you know this? this is cicerone himself,
With finger rais'd he points to the prodigal pictures.
1880                                                             1881

## THE PRAIRIE STATES

A NEWER garden of creation, no primal solitude,
Dense, joyous, modern, populous millions, cities and farms,
With iron interlaced, composite, tied, many in one,
By all the world contributed—freedom's and law's and
    thrift's society,
The crown and teeming paradise, so far, of time's accumula-
    tions,
To justify the past.
1880                                                             1881

# *Proud Music of the Storm*

## 1

PROUD music of the storm,
Blast that careers so free, whistling across the prairies,
Strong hum of forest tree-tops—wind of the mountains,
Personified dim shapes—you hidden orchestras,
You serenades of phantoms with instruments alert,
Bending with Nature's rhythmus all the tongues of nations;
You chords left as by vast composers—you choruses,
You formless, free, religious dances—you from the Orient,
You undertone of rivers, roar of pouring cataracts,
You sounds from distant guns with galloping cavalry,
Echoes of camps with all the different bugle-calls,
Trooping tumultuous, filling the midnight late, bending me
    powerless,
Entering my lonesome slumber-chamber, why have you
    seiz'd me?

## 2

Come forward O my soul, and let the rest retire,
Listen, lose not, it is toward thee they tend,
Parting the midnight, entering my slumber-chamber,
For thee they sing and dance O soul.

A festival song,
The duet of the bridegroom and the bride, a marriage-
    march,
With lips of love, and hearts of lovers fill'd to the brim with
    love,
The red-flush'd cheeks and perfumes, the cortege swarming
    full of friendly faces young and old,
To flutes' clear notes and sounding harps' cantabile.

Now loud approaching drums,
Victoria! see'st thou in powder-smoke the banners torn but
    flying? the rout of the baffled?
Hearest those shouts of a conquering army?

(Ah soul, the sobs of women, the wounded groaning in
    agony,
The hiss and crackle of flames, the blacken'd ruins, the em-
    bers of cities,
The dirge and desolation of mankind.)

Now airs antique and mediæval fill me,
I see and hear old harpers with their harps at Welsh festivals,
I hear the minnesingers singing their lays of love,
I hear the minstrels, gleemen, troubadours, of the middle
    ages.

Now the great organ sounds,
Tremulous, while underneath, (as the hid footholds of the
    earth,
On which arising rest, and leaping forth depend,
All shapes of beauty, grace and strength, all hues we know,
Green blades of grass and warbling birds, children that gam-
    bol and play, the clouds of heaven above,)
The strong base stands, and its pulsations intermits not,
Bathing, supporting, merging all the rest, maternity of all the
    rest,
And with it every instrument in multitudes,
The players playing, all the world's musicians,
The solemn hymns and masses rousing adoration,
All passionate heart-chants, sorrowful appeals,
The measureless sweet vocalists of ages,
And for their solvent setting earth's own diapason,
Of winds and woods and mighty ocean waves,
A new composite orchestra, binder of years and climes, ten-
    fold renewer,
As of the far-back days the poets tell, the Paradiso,
The straying thence, the separation long, but now the wan-
    dering done,
The journey done, the journeyman come home,
And man and art with Nature fused again.

Tutti! for earth and heaven;
(The Almighty leader now for once has signal'd with his
    wand.)

The manly strophe of the husbands of the world,
And all the wives responding.

The tongues of violins,
(I think O tongues ye tell this heart, that cannot tell itself,
This brooding yearning heart, that cannot tell itself.)

### 3

Ah from a little child,
Thou knowest soul how to me all sounds became music,
My mother's voice in lullaby or hymn,
(The voice, O tender voices, memory's loving voices,
Last miracle of all, O dearest mother's, sister's, voices;)
The rain, the growing corn, the breeze among the long-
    leav'd corn,
The measur'd sea-surf beating on the sand,
The twittering bird, the hawk's sharp scream,
The wild-fowl's notes at night as flying low migrating north
    or south,
The psalm in the country church or mid the clustering trees,
    the open air camp-meeting,
The fiddler in the tavern, the glee, the long-strung sailor-
    song,
The lowing cattle, bleating sheep, the crowing cock at dawn.

All songs of current lands come sounding round me,
The German airs of friendship, wine and love,
Irish ballads, merry jigs and dances, English warbles,
Chansons of France, Scotch tunes, and o'er the rest,
Italia's peerless compositions.

Across the stage with pallor on her face, yet lurid passion,
Stalks Norma brandishing the dagger in her hand.

I see poor crazed Lucia's eyes' unnatural gleam,
Her hair down her back falls loose and dishevel'd.

I see where Ernani walking the bridal garden,
Amid the scent of night-roses, radiant, holding his bride by
    the hand,
Hears the infernal call, the death-pledge of the horn.

To crossing swords and gray hairs bared to heaven,
The clear electric base and baritone of the world,
The trombone duo, Libertad forever!

From Spanish chestnut trees' dense shade,
By old and heavy convent walls a wailing song,
Song of lost love, the torch of youth and life quench'd in
    despair,
Song of the dying swan, Fernando's heart is breaking.

Awaking from her woes at last retriev'd Amina sings,
Copious as stars and glad as morning light the torrents of her
    joy.

(The teeming lady comes,
The lustrous orb, Venus contralto, the blooming mother,
Sister of loftiest gods, Alboni's self I hear.)

#### 4

I hear those odes, symphonies, operas,
I hear in the *William Tell* the music of an arous'd and angry
    people,
I hear Meyerbeer's *Huguenots*, the *Prophet*, or *Robert*,
Gounod's *Faust*, or Mozart's *Don Juan*.

I hear the dance-music of all nations,
The waltz, some delicious measure, lapsing, bathing me in bliss,
The bolero to tinkling guitars and clattering castanets.

I see religious dances old and new,
I hear the sound of the Hebrew lyre,
I see the crusaders marching bearing the cross on high, to the
    martial clang of cymbals,
I hear dervishes monotonously chanting, interspers'd with
    frantic shouts, as they spin around turning always to-
    wards Mecca,

I see the rapt religious dances of the Persians and the Arabs,
Again, at Eleusis, home of Ceres, I see the modern Greeks
dancing,
I hear them clapping their hands as they bend their bodies,
I hear the metrical shuffling of their feet.

I see again the wild old Corybantian dance, the performers
wounding each other,
I see the Roman youth to the shrill sound of flageolets throwing and catching their weapons,
As they fall on their knees and rise again.

I hear from the Mussulman mosque the muezzin calling,
I see the worshippers within, nor form nor sermon, argument
nor word,
But silent, strange, devout, rais'd glowing heads, ecstatic
faces.

I hear the Egyptian harp of many strings,
The primitive chants of the Nile boatmen,
The sacred imperial hymns of China,
To the delicate sounds of the king, (the stricken wood and
stone,)
Or to Hindu flutes and the fretting twang of the vina,
A band of bayaderes.

5

Now Asia, Africa leave me, Europe seizing inflates me,
To organs huge and bands I hear as from vast concourses of
voices,
Luther's strong hymn *Eine feste Burg ist unser Gott*,
Rossini's *Stabat Mater dolorosa*,
Or floating in some high cathedral dim with gorgeous color'd
windows,
The passionate *Agnus Dei* or *Gloria in Excelsis*.

Composers! mighty maestros!
And you, sweet singers of old lands, soprani, tenori, bassi!
To you a new bard caroling in the West,
Obeisant sends his love.

(Such led to thee O soul,
All senses, shows and objects, lead to thee,
But now it seems to me sound leads o'er all the rest.)

I hear the annual singing of the children in St. Paul's cathedral,
Or, under the high roof of some colossal hall, the sym-
    phonies, oratorios of Beethoven, Handel, or Haydn,
The *Creation* in billows of godhood laves me.

Give me to hold all sounds, (I madly struggling cry,)
Fill me with all the voices of the universe,
Endow me with their throbbings, Nature's also,
The tempests, waters, winds, operas and chants, marches and
    dances,
Utter, pour in, for I would take them all!


6

Then I woke softly,
And pausing, questioning awhile the music of my dream,
And questioning all those reminiscences, the tempest in its
    fury,
And all the songs of sopranos and tenors,
And those rapt oriental dances of religious fervor,
And the sweet varied instruments, and the diapason of
    organs,
And all the artless plaints of love and grief and death,
I said to my silent curious soul out of the bed of the slumber-
    chamber,
Come, for I have found the clew I sought so long,
Let us go forth refresh'd amid the day,
Cheerfully tallying life, walking the world, the real,
Nourish'd henceforth by our celestial dream.

And I said, moreover,
Haply what thou hast heard O soul was not the sound of
    winds,
Nor dream of raging storm, nor sea-hawk's flapping wings
    nor harsh scream,
Nor vocalism of sun-bright Italy,

Nor German organ majestic, nor vast concourse of voices,
    nor layers of harmonies,
Nor strophes of husbands and wives, nor sound of marching
    soldiers,
Nor flutes, nor harps, nor the bugle-calls of camps,
But to a new rhythmus fitted for thee,
Poems bridging the way from Life to Death, vaguely wafted
    in night air, uncaught, unwritten,
Which let us go forth in the bold day and write.
(1868)                                1881

# *Passage to India*

## 1

SINGING my days,
Singing the great achievements of the present,
Singing the strong light works of engineers,
Our modern wonders, (the antique ponderous Seven out-
    vied,)
In the Old World the east the Suez canal,
The New by its mighty railroad spann'd,
The seas inlaid with eloquent gentle wires;
Yet first to sound, and ever sound, the cry with thee O soul,
The Past! the Past! the Past!

The Past—the dark unfathom'd retrospect!
The teeming gulf—the sleepers and the shadows!
The past—the infinite greatness of the past!
For what is the present after all but a growth out of the past?
(As a projectile form'd, impell'd, passing a certain line, still
    keeps on,
So the present, utterly form'd, impell'd by the past.)

## 2

Passage O soul to India!
Eclaircise the myths Asiatic, the primitive fables.

Not you alone proud truths of the world,
Nor you alone ye facts of modern science,
But myths and fables of eld, Asia's, Africa's fables,
The far-darting beams of the spirit, the unloos'd dreams,
The deep diving bibles and legends,
The daring plots of the poets, the elder religions;
O you temples fairer than lilies pour'd over by the rising
    sun!
O you fables spurning the known, eluding the hold of the
    known, mounting to heaven!
You lofty and dazzling towers, pinnacled, red as roses, bur-
    nish'd with gold!
Towers of fables immortal fashion'd from mortal dreams!
You too I welcome and fully the same as the rest!
You too with joy I sing.

Passage to India!
Lo, soul, seest thou not God's purpose from the first?
The earth to be spann'd, connected by network,
The races, neighbors, to marry and be given in marriage,
The oceans to be cross'd, the distant brought near,
The lands to be welded together.

A worship new I sing,
You captains, voyagers, explorers, yours,
You engineers, you architects, machinists, yours,
You, not for trade or transportation only,
But in God's name, and for thy sake O soul.


3

Passage to India!
Lo soul for thee of tableaus twain,
I see in one the Suez canal initiated, open'd,
I see the procession of steamships, the Empress Eugenie's
    leading the van,
I mark from on deck the strange landscape, the pure sky, the
    level sand in the distance,
I pass swiftly the picturesque groups, the workmen gather'd,
The gigantic dredging machines.

In one again, different, (yet thine, all thine, O soul, the same,)
I see over my own continent the Pacific railroad surmounting
    every barrier,
I see continual trains of cars winding along the Platte carry-
    ing freight and passengers,
I hear the locomotives rushing and roaring, and the shrill
    steam-whistle,
I hear the echoes reverberate through the grandest scenery in
    the world,
I cross the Laramie plains, I note the rocks in grotesque
    shapes, the buttes,
I see the plentiful larkspur and wild onions, the barren,
    colorless, sage-deserts,
I see in glimpses afar or towering immediately above me the
    great mountains, I see the Wind river and the Wahsatch
    mountains,
I see the Monument mountain and the Eagle's Nest, I pass
    the Promontory, I ascend the Nevadas,
I scan the noble Elk mountain and wind around its base,
I see the Humboldt range, I thread the valley and cross the
    river,
I see the clear waters of lake Tahoe, I see forests of majestic
    pines,
Or crossing the great desert, the alkaline plains, I behold en-
    chanting mirages of waters and meadows,
Marking through these and after all, in duplicate slender
    lines,
Bridging the three or four thousand miles of land travel,
Tying the Eastern to the Western sea,
The road between Europe and Asia.

(Ah Genoese thy dream! thy dream!
Centuries after thou art laid in thy grave,
The shore thou foundest verifies thy dream.)

#### 4

Passage to India!
Struggles of many a captain, tales of many a sailor dead,
Over my mood stealing and spreading they come,
Like clouds and cloudlets in the unreach'd sky.

Along all history, down the slopes,
As a rivulet running, sinking now, and now again to the sur-
        face rising,
A ceaseless thought, a varied train—lo, soul, to thee, thy
        sight, they rise,
The plans, the voyages again, the expeditions;
Again Vasco de Gama sails forth,
Again the knowledge gain'd, the mariner's compass,
Lands found and nations born, thou born America,
For purpose vast, man's long probation fill'd,
Thou rondure of the world at last accomplish'd.


5

O vast Rondure, swimming in space,
Cover'd all over with visible power and beauty,
Alternate light and day and the teeming spiritual darkness,
Unspeakable high processions of sun and moon and count-
        less stars above,
Below, the manifold grass and waters, animals, mountains,
        trees,
With inscrutable purpose, some hidden prophetic intention,
Now first it seems my thought begins to span thee.

Down from the gardens of Asia descending radiating,
Adam and Eve appear, then their myriad progeny after
        them,
Wandering, yearning, curious, with restless explorations,
With questionings, baffled, formless, feverish, with never-
        happy hearts,
With that sad incessant refrain, *Wherefore unsatisfied soul?*
        and *Whither O mocking life?*

Ah who shall soothe these feverish children?
Who justify these restless explorations?
Who speak the secret of impassive earth?
Who bind it to us? what is this separate Nature so unnatural?
What is this earth to our affections? (unloving earth, without
        a throb to answer ours,
Cold earth, the place of graves.)

Yet soul be sure the first intent remains, and shall be carried
out,
Perhaps even now the time has arrived.

After the seas are all cross'd, (as they seem already cross'd,)
After the great captains and engineers have accomplish'd
their work,
After the noble inventors, after the scientists, the chemist, the
geologist, ethnologist,
Finally shall come the poet worthy that name,
The true son of God shall come singing his songs.

Then not your deeds only O voyagers, O scientists and in-
ventors, shall be justified,
All these hearts as of fretted children shall be sooth'd,
All affection shall be fully responded to, the secret shall be
told,
All these separations and gaps shall be taken up and hook'd
and link'd together,
The whole earth, this cold, impassive, voiceless earth, shall
be completely justified,
Trinitas divine shall be gloriously accomplish'd and com-
pacted by the true son of God, the poet,
(He shall indeed pass the straits and conquer the mountains,
He shall double the cape of Good Hope to some purpose,)
Nature and Man shall be disjoin'd and diffused no more,
The true son of God shall absolutely fuse them.

6

Year at whose wide-flung door I sing!
Year of the purpose accomplish'd!
Year of the marriage of continents, climates and oceans!
(No mere doge of Venice now wedding the Adriatic,)
I see O year in you the vast terraqueous globe given and
giving all,
Europe to Asia, Africa join'd, and they to the New World,
The lands, geographies, dancing before you, holding a festi-
val garland,
As brides and bridegrooms hand in hand.

Passage to India!
Cooling airs from Caucasus, far, soothing cradle of man,
The river Euphrates flowing, the past lit up again.

Lo soul, the retrospect brought forward,
The old, most populous, wealthiest of earth's lands,
The streams of the Indus and the Ganges and their many
    affluents,
(I my shores of America walking to-day behold, resuming all,)
The tale of Alexander on his warlike marches suddenly dying,
On one side China and on the other side Persia and Arabia,
To the south the great seas and the bay of Bengal,
The flowing literatures, tremendous epics, religions, castes,
Old occult Brahma interminably far back, the tender and
    junior Buddha,
Central and southern empires and all their belongings, pos-
    sessors,
The wars of Tamerlane, the reign of Aurungzebe,
The traders, rulers, explorers, Moslems, Venetians, Byzan-
    tium, the Arabs, Portuguese,
The first travelers famous yet, Marco Polo, Batouta the Moor,
Doubts to be solv'd, the map incognita, blanks to be fill'd,
The foot of man unstay'd, the hands never at rest,
Thyself O soul that will not brook a challenge.

The mediæval navigators rise before me,
The world of 1492, with its awaken'd enterprise,
Something swelling in humanity now like the sap of the earth
    in spring,
The sunset splendor of chivalry declining.

And who art thou sad shade?
Gigantic, visionary, thyself a visionary,
With majestic limbs and pious beaming eyes,
Spreading around with every look of thine a golden world,
Enhuing it with gorgeous hues.

As the chief histrion,
Down to the footlights walks in some great scena,
Dominating the rest I see the Admiral himself,
(History's type of courage, action, faith,)

Behold him sail from Palos leading his little fleet,
His voyage behold, his return, his great fame,
His misfortunes, calumniators, behold him a prisoner,
    chain'd,
Behold his dejection, poverty, death.

(Curious in time I stand, noting the efforts of heroes,
Is the deferment long? bitter the slander, poverty, death?
Lies the seed unreck'd for centuries in the ground? lo, to
    God's due occasion,
Uprising in the night, it sprouts, blooms,
And fills the earth with use and beauty.)

### 7

Passage indeed O soul to primal thought,
Not lands and seas alone, thy own clear freshness,
The young maturity of brood and bloom,
To realms of budding bibles.

O soul, repressless, I with thee and thou with me,
Thy circumnavigation of the world begin,
Of man, the voyage of his mind's return,
To reason's early paradise,
Back, back to wisdom's birth, to innocent intuitions,
Again with fair creation.

### 8

O we can wait no longer,
We too take ship O soul,
Joyous we too launch out on trackless seas,
Fearless for unknown shores on waves of ecstasy to sail,
Amid the wafting winds, (thou pressing me to thee, I thee to
    me, O soul,)
Caroling free, singing our song of God,
Chanting our chant of pleasant exploration.

With laugh and many a kiss,
(Let others deprecate, let others weep for sin, remorse,
    humiliation,)
O soul thou pleasest me, I thee.

Ah more than any priest O soul we too believe in God,
But with the mystery of God we dare not dally.

O soul thou pleasest me, I thee,
Sailing these seas or on the hills, or waking in the night,
Thoughts, silent thoughts, of Time and Space and Death, like
    waters flowing,
Bear me indeed as through the regions infinite,
Whose air I breathe, whose ripples hear, lave me all over,
Bathe me O God in thee, mounting to thee,
I and my soul to range in range of thee.

O Thou transcendent,
Nameless, the fibre and the breath,
Light of the light, shedding forth universes, thou centre of
    them,
Thou mightier centre of the true, the good, the loving,
Thou moral, spiritual fountain—affection's source—thou
    reservoir,
(O pensive soul of me—O thirst unsatisfied—waitest not
    there?
Waitest not haply for us somewhere there the Comrade per-
    fect?)
Thou pulse—thou motive of the stars, suns, systems,
That, circling, move in order, safe, harmonious,
Athwart the shapeless vastnesses of space,
How should I think, how breathe a single breath, how speak,
    if, out of myself,
I could not launch, to those, superior universes?

Swiftly I shrivel at the thought of God,
At Nature and its wonders, Time and Space and Death,
But that I, turning, call to thee O soul, thou actual Me,
And lo, thou gently masterest the orbs,
Thou matest Time, smilest content at Death,
And fillest, swellest full the vastnesses of Space.

Greater than stars or suns,
Bounding O soul thou journeyest forth;
What love than thine and ours could wider amplify?
What aspirations, wishes, outvie thine and ours O soul?

What dreams of the ideal? what plans of purity, perfection,
    strength,
What cheerful willingness for others' sake to give up all?
For others' sake to suffer all?

Reckoning ahead O soul, when thou, the time achiev'd,
The seas all cross'd, weather'd the capes, the voyage done,
Surrounded, copest, frontest God, yieldest, the aim attain'd,
As fill'd with friendship, love complete, the Elder Brother
    found,
The Younger melts in fondness in his arms.


## 9

Passage to more than India!
Are thy wings plumed indeed for such far flights?
O soul, voyagest thou indeed on voyages like those?
Disportest thou on waters such as those?
Soundest below the Sanscrit and the Vedas?
Then have thy bent unleash'd.

Passage to you, your shores, ye aged fierce enigmas!
Passage to you, to mastership of you, ye strangling problems!
You, strew'd with the wrecks of skeletons, that, living, never
    reach'd you.

Passage to more than India!
O secret of the earth and sky!
Of you O waters of the sea! O winding creeks and rivers!
Of you O woods and fields! of you strong mountains of my
    land!
Of you O prairies! of you gray rocks!
O morning red! O clouds! O rain and snows!
O day and night, passage to you!
O sun and moon and all you stars! Sirius and Jupiter!
Passage to you!

Passage, immediate passage! the blood burns in my veins!
Away O soul! hoist instantly the anchor!
Cut the hawsers—haul out—shake out every sail!
Have we not stood here like trees in the ground long enough?

Have we not grovel'd here long enough, eating and drinking
    like mere brutes?
Have we not darken'd and dazed ourselves with books long
    enough?

Sail forth—steer for the deep waters only,
Reckless O soul, exploring, I with thee, and thou with me,
For we are bound where mariner has not yet dared to go,
And we will risk the ship, ourselves and all.

O my brave soul!
O farther farther sail!
O daring joy, but safe! are they not all the seas of God?
O farther, farther, farther sail!
(1868)                                          1871

# *Prayer of Columbus*

A BATTER'D, wreck'd old man,
Thrown on this savage shore, far, far from home,
Pent by the sea and dark rebellious brows, twelve dreary
    months,
Sore, stiff with many toils, sicken'd and nigh to death,
I take my way along the island's edge,
Venting a heavy heart.

I am too full of woe!
Haply I may not live another day;
I cannot rest O God, I cannot eat or drink or sleep,
Till I put forth myself, my prayer, once more to Thee,
Breathe, bathe myself once more in Thee, commune with
    Thee,
Report myself once more to Thee.

Thou knowest my years entire, my life,
My long and crowded life of active work, not adoration
    merely;
Thou knowest the prayers and vigils of my youth,

Thou knowest my manhood's solemn and visionary meditations,

Thou knowest how before I commenced I devoted all to come to Thee,

Thou knowest I have in age ratified all those vows and strictly kept them,

Thou knowest I have not once lost nor faith nor ecstasy in Thee,

In shackles, prison'd, in disgrace, repining not,

Accepting all from Thee, as duly come from Thee.

All my emprises have been fill'd with Thee,

My speculations, plans, begun and carried on in thought of Thee,

Sailing the deep or journeying the land for Thee;

Intentions, purports, aspirations mine, leaving results to Thee.

O I am sure they really came from Thee,

The urge, the ardor, the unconquerable will,

The potent, felt, interior command, stronger than words,

A message from the Heavens whispering to me even in sleep,

These sped me on.

By me and these the work so far accomplish'd,

By me earth's elder cloy'd and stifled lands uncloy'd, unloos'd,

By me the hemispheres rounded and tied, the unknown to the known.

The end I know not, it is all in Thee,

Or small or great I know not—haply what broad fields, what lands,

Haply the brutish measureless human undergrowth I know,

Transplanted there may rise to stature, knowledge worthy Thee,

Haply the swords I know may there indeed be turn'd to reaping-tools,

Haply the lifeless cross I know, Europe's dead cross, may bud and blossom there.

One effort more, my altar this bleak sand;
That Thou O God my life hast lighted,
With ray of light, steady, ineffable, vouchsafed of Thee,
Light rare untellable, lighting the very light,
Beyond all signs, descriptions, languages;
For that O God, be it my latest word, here on my knees,
Old, poor, and paralyzed, I thank Thee.

My terminus near,
The clouds already closing in upon me,
The voyage balk'd, the course disputed, lost,
I yield my ships to Thee.

My hands, my limbs grow nerveless,
My brain feels rack'd, bewilder'd,
Let the old timbers part, I will not part,
I will cling fast to Thee, O God, though the waves buffet me,
Thee, Thee at least I know.

Is it the prophet's thought I speak, or am I raving?
What do I know of life? what of myself?
I know not even my own work past or present,
Dim ever-shifting guesses of it spread before me,
Of newer better worlds, their mighty parturition,
Mocking, perplexing me.

And these things I see suddenly, what mean they?
As if some miracle, some hand divine unseal'd my eyes,
Shadowy vast shapes smile through the air and sky,
And on the distant waves sail countless ships,
And anthems in new tongues I hear saluting me.
1874                                          1881

# The Sleepers

## 1

I **WANDER** all night in my vision,
Stepping with light feet, swiftly and noiselessly stepping and
    stopping,

Bending with open eyes over the shut eyes of sleepers,
Wandering and confused, lost to myself, ill-assorted, contradictory,
Pausing, gazing, bending, and stopping.

How solemn they look there, stretch'd and still,
How quiet they breathe, the little children in their cradles.

The wretched features of ennuyés, the white features of corpses, the livid faces of drunkards, the sick-gray faces of onanists,
The gash'd bodies on battle-fields, the insane in their strong-door'd rooms, the sacred idiots, the new-born emerging from gates, and the dying emerging from gates,
The night pervades them and infolds them.

The married couple sleep calmly in their bed, he with his palm on the hip of the wife, and she with her palm on the hip of the husband,
The sisters sleep lovingly side by side in their bed,
The men sleep lovingly side by side in theirs,
And the mother sleeps with her little child carefully wrapt.

The blind sleep, and the deaf and dumb sleep,
The prisoner sleeps well in the prison, the runaway son sleeps,
The murderer that is to be hung next day, how does he sleep?
And the murder'd person, how does he sleep?

The female that loves unrequited sleeps,
And the male that loves unrequited sleeps,
The head of the money-maker that plotted all day sleeps,
And the enraged and treacherous dispositions, all, all sleep.

I stand in the dark with drooping eyes by the worst-suffering and the most restless,
I pass my hands soothingly to and fro a few inches from them,
The restless sink in their beds, they fitfully sleep.

Now I pierce the darkness, new beings appear,
The earth recedes from me into the night,

I saw that it was beautiful, and I see that what is not the
earth is beautiful.

I go from bedside to bedside, I sleep close with the other
sleepers each in turn,
I dream in my dream all the dreams of the other dreamers,
And I become the other dreamers.

I am a dance—play up there! the fit is whirling me fast!

I am the ever-laughing—it is new moon and twilight,
I see the hiding of douceurs, I see nimble ghosts whichever
way I look,
Cache and cache again deep in the ground and sea, and where
it is neither ground nor sea.

Well do they do their jobs those journeymen divine,
Only from me can they hide nothing, and would not if they
could,
I reckon I am their boss and they make me a pet besides,
And surround me and lead me and run ahead when I walk,
To lift their cunning covers to signify me with stretch'd arms,
and resume the way;
Onward we move, a gay gang of blackguards! with mirth-
shouting music and wild-flapping pennants of joy!

I am the actor, the actress, the voter, the politician,
The emigrant and the exile, the criminal that stood in the box,
He who has been famous and he who shall be famous after
to-day,
The stammerer, the well-formed person, the wasted or feeble
person.

I am she who adorn'd herself and folded her hair expectantly,
My truant lover has come, and it is dark.

Double yourself and receive me darkness,
Receive me and my lover too, he will not let me go without
him.

I roll myself upon you as upon a bed, I resign myself to the
dusk.

N                                                    W.

He whom I call answers me and takes the place of my lover,
He rises with me silently from the bed.

Darkness, you are gentler than my lover, his flesh was sweaty
    and panting,
I feel the hot moisture yet that he left me.

My hands are spread forth, I pass them in all directions,
I would sound up the shadowy shore to which you are jour-
    neying.

Be careful darkness! already what was it touch'd me?
I thought my lover had gone, else darkness and he are one,
I hear the heart-beat, I follow, I fade away.


2

I descend my western course, my sinews are flaccid,
Perfume and youth course through me and I am their wake.

It is my face yellow and wrinkled instead of the old woman's,
I sit low in a straw-bottom chair and carefully darn my
    grandson's stockings.

It is I too, the sleepless widow looking out on the winter
    midnight,
I see the sparkles of starshine on the icy and pallid earth.

A shroud I see and I am the shroud, I wrap a body and lie in
    the coffin,
It is dark here under ground, it is not evil or pain here, it is
    blank here, for reasons.

(It seems to me that every thing in the light and air ought to
    be happy,
Whoever is not in his coffin and the dark grave let him know
    he has enough.)

3

I see a beautiful gigantic swimmer swimming naked through
    the eddies of the sea,

His brown hair lies close and even to his head, he strikes out
    with courageous arms, he urges himself with his legs,
I see his white body, I see his undaunted eyes,
I hate the swift-running eddies that would dash him head-
    foremost on the rocks.

What are you doing you ruffianly red-trickled waves?
Will you kill the courageous giant? will you kill him in the
    prime of his middle age?

Steady and long he struggles,
He is baffled, bang'd, bruis'd, he holds out while his strength
    holds out,
The slapping eddies are spotted with his blood, they bear him
    away, they roll him, swing him, turn him,
His beautiful body is borne in the circling eddies, it is con-
    tinually bruis'd on rocks,
Swiftly and out of sight is borne the brave corpse.


4

I turn but do not extricate myself,
Confused, a past-reading, another, but with darkness yet.

The beach is cut by the razory ice-wind, the wreck-guns
    sound,
The tempest lulls, the moon comes floundering through the
    drifts.

I look where the ship helplessly heads end on, I hear the
    burst as she strikes, I hear the howls of dismay, they
    grow fainter and fainter.

I cannot aid with my wringing fingers,
I can but rush to the surf and let it drench me and freeze upon
    me.

I search with the crowd, not one of the company is wash'd to
    us alive,
In the morning I help pick up the dead and lay them in rows
    in a barn.

## 5

Now of the older war-days, the defeat at Brooklyn,
Washington stands inside the lines, he stands on the in-
trench'd hills amid a crowd of officers,
His face is cold and damp, he cannot repress the weeping
drops,
He lifts the glass perpetually to his eyes, the color is blanch'd
from his cheeks,
He sees the slaughter of the southern braves confided to him
by their parents.

The same at last and at last when peace is declared,
He stands in the room of the old tavern, the well-belov'd
soldiers all pass through,
The officers speechless and slow draw near in their turns,
The chief encircles their necks with his arm and kisses them
on the cheek,
He kisses lightly the wet cheeks one after another, he shakes
hands and bids good-by to the army.

## 6

Now what my mother told me one day as we sat at dinner
together,
Of when she was a nearly grown girl living home with her
parents on the old homestead.

A red squaw came one breakfast-time to the old homestead,
On her back she carried a bundle of rushes for rush-bottom-
ing chairs,
Her hair, straight, shiny, coarse, black, profuse, half-en-
velop'd her face,
Her step was free and elastic, and her voice sounded exquisitely as she spoke.

My mother looked in delight and amazement at the stranger,
She look'd at the freshness of her tall-borne face and full and
pliant limbs,
The more she look'd upon her she loved her,
Never before had she seen such wonderful beauty and purity,

She made her sit on a bench by the jamb of the fireplace, she
    cook'd food for her,
She had no work to give her, but she gave her remembrance
    and fondness.

The red squaw staid all the forenoon, and toward the middle
    of the afternoon she went away,
O my mother was loth to have her go away,
All the week she thought of her, she watch'd for her many a
    month,
She remember'd her many a winter and many a summer,
But the red squaw never came nor was heard of there again.

7

A show of the summer softness—a contact of something un-
    seen—an amour of the light and air,
I am jealous and overwhelm'd with friendliness,
And will go gallivant with the light and air myself.

O love and summer, you are in the dreams and in me,
Autumn and winter are in the dreams, the farmer goes with
    his thrift,
The droves and crops increase, the barns are well-fill'd.

Elements merge in the night, ships make tacks in the dreams,
The sailor sails, the exile returns home,
The fugitive returns unharm'd, the immigrant is back beyond
    months and years,
The poor Irishman lives in the simple house of his childhood
    with the well-known neighbors and faces,
They warmly welcome him, he is barefoot again, he forgets
    he is well off,
The Dutchman voyages home, and the Scotchman and
    Welshman voyage home, and the native of the Mediter-
    ranean voyages home,
To every port of England, France, Spain, enter well-fill'd
    ships,
The Swiss foots it toward his hills, the Prussian goes his way,
    the Hungarian his way, and the Pole his way,
The Swede returns, and the Dane and Norwegian return.

The homeward bound and the outward bound,
The beautiful lost swimmer, the ennuyé, the onanist, the
   female that loves unrequited, the money-maker,
The actor and actress, those through with their parts and
   those waiting to commence,
The affectionate boy, the husband and wife, the voter, the
   nominee that is chosen and the nominee that has fail'd,
The great already known and the great any time after to-day,
The stammerer, the sick, the perfect-form'd, the homely,
The criminal that stood in the box, the judge that sat and
   sentenced him, the fluent lawyers, the jury, the audience,
The laugher and weeper, the dancer, the midnight widow, the
   red squaw,
The consumptive, the erysipalite, the idiot, he that is wrong'd,
The antipodes, and every one between this and them in the
   dark,
I swear they are averaged now—one is no better than the other,
The night and sleep have liken'd them and restored them.

I swear they are all beautiful,
Every one that sleeps is beautiful, every thing in the dim light
   is beautiful,
The wildest and bloodiest is over, and all is peace.

Peace is always beautiful,
The myth of heaven indicates peace and night.

The myth of heaven indicates the soul,
The soul is always beautiful, it appears more or it appears
   less, it comes or it lags behind,
It comes from its embower'd garden and looks pleasantly on
   itself and encloses the world,
Perfect and clean the genitals previously jetting, and perfect
   and clean the womb cohering,
The head well-grown proportion'd and plumb, and the
   bowels and joints proportion'd and plumb.

The soul is always beautiful,
The universe is duly in order, every thing is in its place,
What has arrived is in its place and what waits shall be in its
   place,

The twisted skull waits, the watery or rotten blood waits,
The child of the glutton or venerealee waits long, and the
child of the drunkard waits long, and the drunkard himself waits long,
The sleepers that lived and died wait, the far advanced are to
go on in their turns, and the far behind are to come on in
their turns,
The diverse shall be no less diverse, but they shall flow and
unite—they unite now.

## 8

The sleepers are very beautiful as they lie unclothed,
They flow hand in hand over the whole earth from east to
west as they lie unclothed,
The Asiatic and African are hand in hand, the European and
American are hand in hand,
Learn'd and unlearn'd are hand in hand, and male and fe-
male are hand in hand,
The bare arm of the girl crosses the bare breast of her lover,
they press close without lust, his lips press her neck,
The father holds his grown or ungrown son in his arms
with measureless love, and the son holds the father in
his arms with measureless love,
The white hair of the mother shines on the white wrist of the
daughter,
The breath of the boy goes with the breath of the man, friend
is inarm'd by friend,
The scholar kisses the teacher and the teacher kisses the
scholar, the wrong'd is made right,
The call of the slave is one with the master's call, and the
master salutes the slave,
The felon steps forth from the prison, the insane becomes
sane, the suffering of sick persons is reliev'd,
The sweatings and fevers stop, the throat that was unsound is
sound, the lungs of the consumptive are resumed, the
poor distress'd head is free,
The joints of the rheumatic move as smoothly as ever, and
smoother than ever,
Stiflings and passages open, the paralyzed become supple,

They swell'd and convuls'd and congested awake to themselves in condition,
They pass the invigoration of the night and the chemistry of
 the night, and awake.

I too pass from the night,
I stay a while away O night, but I return to you again and
 love you.

Why should I be afraid to trust myself to you?
I am not afraid, I have been well brought forward by you,
I love the rich running day, but I do not desert her in whom I
 lay so long,
I know not how I came of you and I know not where I go
 with you, but I know I came well and shall go well.

I will stop only a time with the night, and rise betimes,
I will duly pass the day O my mother, and duly return to you.
1855                                                        1881

## TRANSPOSITIONS

Let the reformers descend from the stands where they are
 forever bawling—let an idiot or insane person appear on
 each of the stands;
Let judges and criminals be transposed—let the prison-
 keepers be put in prison—let those that were prisoners
 take the keys;
Let them that distrust birth and death lead the rest.
1856                                                        1881

# *To Think of Time*

### 1

To think of time—of all that retrospection,
To think of to-day, and the ages continued henceforward.

Have you guess'd you yourself would not continue?
Have you dreaded these earth-beetles?
Have you fear'd the future would be nothing to you?

Is to-day nothing? is the beginningless past nothing?
If the future is nothing they are just as surely nothing.

To think that the sun rose in the east—that men and women
were flexible, real, alive—that every thing was alive,
To think that you and I did not see, feel, think, nor bear our
part,
To think that we are now here and bear our part.


### 2

Not a day passes, not a minute or second without an ac-
couchement,
Not a day passes, not a minute or second without a corpse.

The dull nights go over and the dull days also,
The soreness of lying so much in bed goes over,
The physician after long putting off gives the silent and ter-
rible look for an answer,
The children come hurried and weeping, and the brothers
and sisters are sent for,
Medicines stand unused on the shelf, (the camphor-smell has
long pervaded the rooms,)
The faithful hand of the living does not desert the hand of the
dying,
The twitching lips press lightly on the forehead of the dying,
The breath ceases and the pulse of the heart ceases,
The corpse stretches on the bed and the living look upon it,
It is palpable as the living are palpable.

The living look upon the corpse with their eyesight,
But without eyesight lingers a different living and looks
curiously on the corpse.


### 3

To think the thought of death merged in the thought of
materials,
To think of all these wonders of city and country, and others
taking great interest in them, and we taking no interest
in them.

To think how eager we are in building our houses,
To think others shall be just as eager, and we quite indifferent.

(I see one building the house that serves him a few years, or
  seventy or eighty years at most,
I see one building the house that serves him longer than that.)

Slow-moving and black lines creep over the whole earth—
  they never cease—they are the burial lines,
He that was President was buried, and he that is now President shall surely be buried.

## 4

A reminiscence of the vulgar fate,
A frequent sample of the life and death of workmen,
Each after his kind.

Cold dash of waves at the ferry-wharf, posh and ice in the
  river, half-frozen mud in the streets,
A gray discouraged sky overhead, the short last daylight of
  December,
A hearse and stages, the funeral of an old Broadway stage-
  driver, the cortege mostly drivers.

Steady the trot to the cemetery, duly rattles the death-bell,
The gate is pass'd, the new-dug grave is halted at, the living
  alight, the hearse uncloses,
The coffin is pass'd out, lower'd and settled, the whip is laid
  on the coffin, the earth is swiftly shovel'd in,
The mound above is flatted with the spades—silence,
A minute—no one moves or speaks—it is done,
He is decently put away—is there any thing more?

He was a good fellow, free-mouth'd, quick-temper'd, not
  bad-looking,
Ready with life or death for a friend, fond of women, gam-
  bled, ate hearty, drank hearty,
Had known what it was to be flush, grew low-spirited toward
  the last, sicken'd, was help'd by a contribution,
Died, aged forty-one years—and that was his funeral.

Thumb extended, finger uplifted, apron, cape, gloves, strap,
    wet-weather clothes, whip carefully chosen,
Boss, spotter, starter, hostler, somebody loafing on you, you
    loafing on somebody, headway, man before and man
    behind,
Good day's work, bad day's work, pet stock, mean stock,
    first out, last out, turning-in at night,
To think that these are so much and so nigh to other drivers,
    and he there takes no interest in them.


### 5

The markets, the government, the working-man's wages, to
    think what account they are through our nights and
    days,
To think that other working-men will make just as great
    account of them, yet we make little or no account.

The vulgar and the refined, what you call sin and what you
    call goodness, to think how wide a difference,
To think the difference will still continue to others, yet we lie
    beyond the difference.

To think how much pleasure there is,
Do you enjoy yourself in the city? or engaged in business? or
    planning a nomination and election? or with your wife
    and family?
Or with your mother and sisters? or in womanly housework?
    or the beautiful maternal cares?
These also flow onward to others, you and I flow onward,
But in due time you and I shall take less interest in them.

Your farm, profits, crops—to think how engross'd you are,
To think there will still be farms, profits, crops, yet for you of
    what avail?


### 6

What will be will be well, for what is is well,
To take interest is well, and not to take interest shall be well.

The domestic joys, the daily housework or business, the
  building of houses, are not phantasms, they have weight,
  form, location,
Farms, profits, crops, markets, wages, government, are none
  of them phantasms,
The difference between sin and goodness is no delusion,
The earth is not an echo, man and his life and all the things of
  his life are well-consider'd.

You are not thrown to the winds, you gather certainly and
  safely around yourself,
Yourself! yourself! yourself, for ever and ever!

### 7

It is not to diffuse you that you were born of your mother
  and father, it is to identify you,
It is not that you should be undecided, but that you should
  be decided,
Something long preparing and formless is arrived and form'd
  in you,
You are henceforth secure, whatever comes or goes.

The threads that were spun are gather'd, the weft crosses the
  warp, the pattern is systematic.

The preparations have every one been justified,
The orchestra have sufficiently tuned their instruments, the
  baton has given the signal.

The guest that was coming, he waited long, he is now housed,
He is one of those who are beautiful and happy, he is one of
  those that to look upon and be with is enough.

The law of the past cannot be eluded,
The law of the present and future cannot be eluded,
The law of the living cannot be eluded, it is eternal,
The law of promotion and transformation cannot be eluded,
The law of heroes and good-doers cannot be eluded,
The law of drunkards, informers, mean persons, not one iota
  thereof can be eluded.

**8**

Slow moving and black lines go ceaselessly over the earth,
Northerner goes carried and Southerner goes carried, and
    they on the Atlantic side and they on the Pacific,
And they between, and all through the Mississippi country,
    and all over the earth.

The great masters and kosmos are well as they go, the heroes
    and good-doers are well,
The known leaders and inventors and the rich owners and
    pious and distinguish'd may be well,
But there is more account than that, there is strict account of
    all.

The interminable hordes of the ignorant and wicked are not
    nothing,
The barbarians of Africa and Asia are not nothing,
The perpetual successions of shallow people are not nothing
    as they go.

Of and in all these things,
I have dream'd that we are not to be changed so much, nor
    the law of us changed,
I have dream'd that heroes and good-doers shall be under the
    present and past law,
And that murderers, drunkards, liars, shall be under the
    present and past law,
For I have dream'd that the law they are under now is
    enough.

And I have dream'd that the purpose and essence of the
    known life, the transient,
Is to form and decide identity for the unknown life, the per-
    manent.

If all came but to ashes of dung,
If maggots and rats ended us, then Alarum! for we are be-
    tray'd,
Then indeed suspicion of death.

Do you suspect death? if I were to suspect death I should die
   now,
Do you think I could walk pleasantly and well-suited toward
   annihilation?

Pleasantly and well-suited I walk,
Whither I walk I cannot define, but I know it is good,
The whole universe indicates that it is good,
The past and the present indicate that it is good.

How beautiful and perfect are the animals!
How perfect the earth, and the minutest thing upon it!
What is called good is perfect, and what is called bad is just
   as perfect,
The vegetables and minerals are all perfect, and the impon-
   derable fluids perfect;
Slowly and surely they have pass'd on to this, and slowly and
   surely they yet pass on.

### 9

I swear I think now that every thing without exception has an
   eternal soul!
The trees have, rooted in the ground! the weeds of the sea
   have! the animals!

I swear I think there is nothing but immortality!
That the exquisite scheme is for it, and the nebulous float is
   for it, and the cohering is for it!
And all preparation is for it—and identity is for it—and life
   and materials are altogether for it!

1855                                             1881

# *Whispers of Heavenly Death*

## DAREST THOU NOW O SOUL

Darest thou now O soul,
Walk out with me toward the unknown region,
Where neither ground is for the feet nor any path to follow?

No map there, nor guide,
Nor voice sounding, nor touch of human hand,
Nor face with blooming flesh, nor lips, nor eyes, are in that
    land.

I know it not O soul,
Nor dost thou, all is a blank before us,
All waits undream'd of in that region, that inaccessible land.

Till when the ties loosen,
All but the ties eternal, Time and Space,
Nor darkness, gravitation, sense, nor any bounds bounding
    us.

Then we burst forth, we float,
In Time and Space O soul, prepared for them,
Equal, equipt at last, (O joy! O fruit of all!) them to fulfil O
    soul.
1868                                                    1881

## WHISPERS OF HEAVENLY DEATH

Whispers of heavenly death murmur'd I hear,
Labial gossip of night, sibilant chorals,
Footsteps gently ascending, mystical breezes wafted soft and
    low,

399

Ripples of unseen rivers, tides of a current flowing, forever
    flowing,
(Or is it the plashing of tears? the measureless waters of
    human tears?)

I see, just see skyward, great cloud-masses,
Mournfully slowly they roll, silently swelling and mixing,
With at times a half-dimm'd sadden'd far-off star,
Appearing and disappearing.

(Some parturition rather, some solemn immortal birth;
On the frontiers to eyes impenetrable,
Some soul is passing over.)
1868                            1871

## CHANTING THE SQUARE DEIFIC

### 1

CHANTING the square deific, out of the One advancing, out of
    the sides,
Out of the old and new, out of the square entirely divine,
Solid, four-sided, (all the sides needed,) from this side Jeho-
    vah am I,
Old Brahm I, and I Saturnius am;
Not Time affects me—I am Time, old, modern as any,
Unpersuadable, relentless, executing righteous judgments,
As the Earth, the Father, the brown old Kronos, with laws,
Aged beyond computation, yet ever new, ever with those
    mighty laws rolling,
Relentless I forgive no man—whoever sins dies—I will have
    that man's life;
Therefore let none expect mercy—have the seasons, gravita-
    tion, the appointed days, mercy? no more have I,
But as the seasons and gravitation, and as all the appointed
    days that forgive not,
I dispense from this side judgments inexorable without the
    least remorse.

### 2

Consolator most mild, the promis'd one advancing,
With gentle hand extended, the mightier God am I,

Foretold by prophets and poets in their most rapt prophecies
and poems,
From this side, lo! the Lord Christ gazes—lo! Hermes I—
lo! mine is Hercules' face,
All sorrow, labor, suffering, I, tallying it, absorb in myself,
Many times have I been rejected, taunted, put in prison, and
crucified, and many times shall be again,
All the world have I given up for my dear brothers' and sisters' sake, for the soul's sake,
Wending my way through the homes of men, rich or poor,
with the kiss of affection,
For I am affection, I am the cheer-bringing God, with hope
and all-enclosing charity,
With indulgent words as to children, with fresh and sane
words, mine only,
Young and strong I pass knowing well I am destin'd myself
to an early death;
But my charity has no death—my wisdom dies not, neither
early nor late,
And my sweet love bequeath'd here and elsewhere never
dies.

### 3

Aloof, dissatisfied, plotting revolt,
Comrade of criminals, brother of slaves,
Crafty, despised, a drudge, ignorant,
With sudra face and worn brow, black, but in the depths of
my heart, proud as any,
Lifted now and always against whoever scorning assumes to
rule me,
Morose, full of guile, full of reminiscences, brooding, with
many wiles,
(Though it was thought I was baffled and dispel'd, and my
wiles done, but that will never be,)
Defiant, I, Satan, still live, still utter words, in new lands duly
appearing, (and old ones also,)
Permanent here from my side, warlike, equal with any, real
as any,
Nor time nor change shall ever change me or my words.

4

Santa Spirita, breather, life.
Beyond the light, lighter than light,
Beyond the flames of hell, joyous, leaping easily above hell,
Beyond Paradise, perfumed solely with mine own perfume,
Including all life on earth, touching, including God, includ-
      ing Saviour and Satan,
Ethereal, pervading all, (for without me what were all? what
      were God?)
Essence of forms, life of the real identities, permanent, posi-
      tive, (namely the unseen,)
Life of the great round world, the sun and stars, and of man,
      I, the general soul,
Here the square finishing, the solid, I the most solid,
Breathe my breath also through these songs.
1865-6

## OF HIM I LOVE DAY AND NIGHT

Of him I love day and night I dream'd I heard he was dead,
And I dream'd I went where they had buried him I love, but
      he was not in that place,
And I dream'd I wander'd searching among burial-places to
      find him,
And I found that every place was a burial-place;
The houses full of life were equally full of death, (this house
      is now,)
The streets, the shipping, the places of amusement, the Chi-
      cago, Boston, Philadelphia, the Mannahatta, were as
      full of the dead as of the living,
And fuller, O vastly fuller of the dead than of the living;
And what I dream'd I will henceforth tell to every person and
      age,
And I stand henceforth bound to what I dream'd,
And now I am willing to disregard burial-places and dis-
      pense with them,
And if the memorials of the dead were put up indifferently
      everywhere, even in the room where I eat or sleep, I
      should be satisfied,

And if the corpse of any one I love, or if my own corpse, be
    duly render'd to powder and pour'd in the sea, I shall be
    satisfied,
Or if it be distributed to the winds I shall be satisfied.
1871                                              1871

## YET, YET, YE DOWNCAST HOURS

YET, yet, ye downcast hours, I know ye also,
Weights of lead, how ye clog and cling at my ankles,
Earth to a chamber of mourning turns—I hear the o'er-
    weening, mocking voice,
*Matter is conqueror—matter, triumphant only, continues on-
    ward.*

Despairing cries float ceaselessly toward me,
The call of my nearest lover, putting forth, alarm'd, un-
    certain,
*The sea I am quickly to sail, come tell me,*
*Come tell me where I am speeding, tell me my destination.*

I understand your anguish, but I cannot help you,
I approach, hear, behold, the sad mouth, the look out of the
    eyes, your mute inquiry,
*Whither I go from the bed I recline on, come tell me;*
Old age, alarm'd, uncertain—a young woman's voice, ap-
    pealing to me for comfort;
A young man's voice, *Shall I not escape?*
1860                                              1871

## AS IF A PHANTOM CARESS'D ME

As if a phantom caress'd me,
I thought I was not alone walking here by the shore;
But the one I thought was with me as now I walk by the
    shore, the one I loved that caress'd me,
As I lean and look through the glimmering light, that one has
    utterly disappear'd,
And those appear that are hateful to me and mock me.
1860                                              1867

## ASSURANCES

I NEED no assurances, I am a man who is pre-occupied of his
own soul;
I do not doubt that from under the feet and beside the hands
and face I am cognizant of, are now looking faces I am
not cognizant of, calm and actual faces,
I do not doubt but the majesty and beauty of the world are
latent in any iota of the world,
I do not doubt I am limitless, and that the universes are
limitless, in vain I try to think how limitless,
I do not doubt that the orbs and the systems of orbs play
their swift sports through the air on purpose, and that I
shall one day be eligible to do as much as they, and more
than they,
I do not doubt that temporary affairs keep on and on millions of years,
I do not doubt interiors have their interiors, and exteriors
have their exteriors, and that the eyesight has another
eyesight, and the hearing another hearing, and the voice
another voice,
I do not doubt that the passionately-wept deaths of young
men are provided for, and that the deaths of young
women and the deaths of little children are provided for,
(Did you think Life was so well provided for, and Death, the
purport of all Life, is not well provided for?)
I do not doubt that wrecks at sea, no matter what the horrors
of them, no matter whose wife, child, husband, father,
lover, has gone down, are provided for, to the minutest
points,
I do not doubt that whatever can possibly happen anywhere
at any time, is provided for in the inherences of things,
I do not think Life provides for all and for Time and Space,
but I believe Heavenly Death provides for all.

1856                                              1871

## QUICKSAND YEARS

QUICKSAND years that whirl me I know not whither,
Your schemes, politics, fail, lines give way, substances mock
and elude me,

Only the theme I sing, the great and strong-possess'd soul,
    eludes not,
One's-self must never give way—that is the final substance—
    that out of all is sure,
Out of politics, triumphs, battles, life, what at last finally
    remains?
When shows break up what but One's-Self is sure?
(1861-2)                                    1867


## THAT MUSIC ALWAYS ROUND ME

THAT music always round me, unceasing, unbeginning, yet
    long untaught I did not hear,
But now the chorus I hear and am elated,
A tenor, strong, ascending with power and health, with glad
    notes of daybreak I hear,
A soprano at intervals sailing buoyantly over the tops of im-
    mense waves,
A transparent base shuddering lusciously under and through
    the universe,
The triumphant tutti, the funeral wailings with sweet flutes
    and violins, all these I fill myself with,
I hear not the volumes of sound merely, I am moved by the
    exquisite meanings,
I listen to the different voices winding in and out, striving,
    contending with fiery vehemence to excel each other in
    emotion;
I do not think the performers know themselves—but now I
    think I begin to know them.
1860                                      1867


## WHAT SHIP PUZZLED AT SEA

WHAT ship puzzled at sea, cons for the true reckoning?
Or coming in, to avoid the bars and follow the channel a
    perfect pilot needs?
Here, sailor! here, ship! take aboard the most perfect pilot,
Whom, in a little boat, putting off and rowing, I hailing you
    offer.
1860                                      1881

## A NOISELESS PATIENT SPIDER

A NOISELESS patient spider,
I mark'd where on a little promontory it stood isolated,
Mark'd how to explore the vacant vast surrounding,
It launched forth filament, filament, filament, out of itself,
Ever unreeling them, ever tirelessly speeding them.

And you O my soul where you stand,
Surrounded, detached, in measureless oceans of space,
Ceaselessly musing, venturing, throwing, seeking the spheres
    to connect them,
Till the bridge you will need be form'd, till the ductile anchor
    hold,
Till the gossamer thread you fling catch somewhere, O my
    soul.
(1862-3)                                                    1881


## O LIVING ALWAYS, ALWAYS DYING

O LIVING always, always dying!
O the burials of me past and present,
O me while I stride ahead, material, visible, imperious as
    ever;
O me, what I was for years, now dead, (I lament not, I am
    content;)
O to disengage myself from those corpses of me, which I turn
    and look at where I cast them,
To pass on, (O living! always living!) and leave the corpses
    behind.
1860                                                        1867


## TO ONE SHORTLY TO DIE

FROM all the rest I single out you, having a message for you,
You are to die—let others tell you what they please, I cannot
    prevaricate,
I am exact and merciless, but I love you—there is no escape
    for you.

Softly I lay my right hand upon you, you just feel it,
I do not argue, I bend my head close and half envelop it,
I sit quietly by, I remain faithful,
I am more than nurse, more than parent or neighbor,
I absolve you from all except yourself spiritual bodily, that is
    eternal, you yourself will surely escape,
The corpse you will leave will be but excrementitious.

The sun bursts through in unlooked-for directions,
Strong thoughts fill you and confidence, you smile,
You forget you are sick, as I forget you are sick,
You do not see the medicines, you do not mind the weeping
    friends, I am with you,
I exclude others from you, there is nothing to be commiserated,
I do not commiserate, I congratulate you.
1860                              1871

## NIGHT ON THE PRAIRIES

NIGHT on the prairies,
The supper is over, the fire on the ground burns low,
The wearied emigrants sleep, wrapt in their blankets;
I walk by myself—I stand and look at the stars, which I think
    now I never realized before.

Now I absorb immortality and peace,
I admire death and test propositions.

How plenteous! how spiritual! how résumé!
The same old man and soul—the same old aspirations, and
    the same content.

I was thinking the day most splendid till I saw what the not-
    day exhibited,
I was thinking this globe enough till there sprang out so
    noiseless around me myriads of other globes.

Now while the great thoughts of space and eternity fill me I
    will measure myself by them,
And now touch'd with the lives of other globes arrived as far
    along as those of the earth,

Or waiting to arrive, or pass'd on farther than those of the
earth,
I henceforth no more ignore them than I ignore my own life,
Or the lives of the earth arrived as far as mine, or waiting to
arrive.

O I see now that life cannot exhibit all to me, as the day cannot,
I see that I am to wait for what will be exhibited by death.
1860                                                    1871

## THOUGHT

As I sit with others at a great feast, suddenly while the music
is playing,
To my mind, (whence it comes I know not,) spectral in mist
of a wreck at sea,
Of certain ships, how they sail from port with flying streamers
and wafted kisses, and that is the last of them,
Of the solemn and murky mystery about the fate of the
President,
Of the flower of the marine science of fifty generations founder'd off the Northeast coast and going down—of the
steamship Arctic going down,
Of the veil'd tableau—women gather'd together on deck,
pale, heroic, waiting the moment that draws so close—O
the moment!
A huge sob—a few bubbles—the white foam spirting up—
and then the women gone,
Sinking there while the passionless wet flows on—and I now
pondering, Are those women indeed gone?
Are souls drown'd and destroy'd so?
Is only matter triumphant?
1860                                                    1871

## THE LAST INVOCATION

At the last, tenderly,
From the walls of the powerful fortress'd house,
From the clasp of the knitted locks, from the keep of the
well-closed doors,
Let me be wafted.

Let me glide noiselessly forth;
With the key of softness unlock the locks—with a whisper,
Set ope the doors O soul.

Tenderly—be not impatient,
(Strong is your hold O mortal flesh,
Strong is your hold O love.)
1868                                                    1871


## AS I WATCH'D THE PLOUGHMAN PLOUGHING

As I watch'd the ploughman ploughing,
Or the sower sowing in the fields, or the harvester harvesting,
I saw there too, O life and death, your analogies;
(Life, life is the tillage, and Death is the harvest according.)
1871                                                    1871


## PENSIVE AND FALTERING

PENSIVE and faltering,
The words *the Dead* I write,
For living are the Dead,
(Haply the only living, only real,
And I the apparition, I the spectre.)

1868                                                    1871

# *Thou Mother with Thy Equal Brood*

## 1

THOU Mother with thy equal brood,
Thou varied chain of different States, yet one identity only,
A special song before I go I'd sing o'er all the rest,
For thee, the future.

I'd sow a seed for thee of endless Nationality,
I'd fashion thy ensemble including body and soul,
I'd show away ahead thy real Union, and how it may be
    accomplish'd.

The paths to the house I seek to make,
But leave to those to come the house itself.

Belief I sing, and preparation;
As Life and Nature are not great with reference to the pre-
    sent only,
But greater still from what is yet to come,
Out of that formula for thee I sing.

## 2

As a strong bird on pinions free,
Joyous, the amplest spaces heavenward cleaving,
Such be the thought I'd think of thee America,
Such be the recitative I'd bring for thee.

The conceits of the poets of other lands I'd bring thee not,
Nor the compliments that have served their turn so long,
Nor rhyme, nor the classics, nor perfume of foreign court or
    indoor library;

But an odor I'd bring as from forests of pine in Maine, or
    breath of an Illinois prairie,
With open airs of Virginia or Georgia or Tennessee, or from
    Texas uplands, or Florida's glades,
Or the Saguenay's black stream, or the wide blue spread of
    Huron,
With presentment of Yellowstone's scenes, or Yosemite,
And murmuring under, pervading all, I'd bring the rustling
    sea-sound,
That endlessly sounds from the two Great Seas of the world.

And for thy subtler sense subtler refrains dread Mother,
Preludes of intellect tallying these and thee, mind-formulas
    fitted for thee, real and sane and large as these and thee,
Thou! mounting higher, diving deeper than we knew, thou
    transcendental Union!
By thee fact to be justified, blended with thought,
Thought of man justified, blended with God,
Through thy idea, lo, the immortal reality!
Through thy reality, lo, the immortal ideal!

### 3

Brain of the New World, what a task is thine,
To formulate the Modern—out of the peerless grandeur of
    the modern,
Out of thyself, comprising science, to recast poems, churches,
    art,
(Recast, maybe discard them, end them—maybe their work
    is done, who knows?)
By vision, hand, conception, on the background of the
    mighty past, the dead,
To limn with absolute faith the mighty living present.

And yet thou living present brain, heir of the dead, the Old
    World brain,
Thou that lay folded like an unborn babe within its fold so
    long,
Thou carefully prepared by it so long—haply thou but un-
    foldest it, only maturest it,

It to eventuate in thee—the essence of the by-gone time con-
    tain'd in thee,
Its poems, churches, arts, unwitting to themselves, destined
    with reference to thee;
Thou but the apples, long, long, long a-growing,
The fruit of all the Old ripening to-day in thee.

#### 4

Sail, sail thy best, ship of Democracy,
Of value is thy freight, 'tis not the Present only,
The Past is also stored in thee,
Thou holdest not the venture of thyself alone, not of the
    Western continent alone,
Earth's *résumé* entire floats on thy keel O ship, is steadied by
    thy spars,
With thee Time voyages in trust, the antecedent nations sink
    or swim with thee,
With all their ancient struggles, martyrs, heroes, epics, wars,
    thou bear'st the other continents,
Theirs, theirs as much as thine, the destination-port trium-
    phant;
Steer then with good strong hand and wary eye O helmsman,
    thou carriest great companions,
Venerable priestly Asia sails this day with thee,
And royal feudal Europe sails with thee.

#### 5

Beautiful world of new superber birth that rises to my eyes,
Like a limitless golden cloud filling the western sky,
Emblem of general maternity lifted above all,
Sacred shape of the bearer of daughters and sons,
Out of thy teeming womb thy giant babes in ceaseless pro-
    cession issuing,
Acceding from such gestation, taking and giving continual
    strength and life,
World of the real—world of the twain in one,
World of the soul, born by the world of the real alone, led to
    identity, body, by it alone,

Yet in beginning only, incalculable masses of composite precious materials,

By history's cycles forwarded, by every nation, language, hither sent,

Ready, collected here, a freer, vast, electric world, to be constructed here,

(The true New World, the world of orbic science, morals, literatures to come,)

Thou wonder world yet undefined, unform'd, neither do I define thee,

How can I pierce the impenetrable blank of the future?

I feel thy ominous greatness evil as well as good,

I watch thee advancing, absorbing the present, transcending the past,

I see thy light lighting, and thy shadow shadowing, as if the entire globe,

But I do not undertake to define thee, hardly to comprehend thee,

I but thee name, thee prophesy, as now,

I merely thee ejaculate!

Thee in thy future,

Thee in thy only permanent life, career, thy own unloosen'd mind, thy soaring spirit,

Thee as another equally needed sun, radiant, ablaze, swift-moving, fructifying all,

Thee risen in potent cheerfulness and joy, in endless great hilarity,

Scattering for good the cloud that hung so long, that weigh'd so long upon the mind of man,

The doubt, suspicion, dread, of gradual, certain decadence of man;

Thee in thy larger, saner brood of female, male—thee in thy athletes, moral, spiritual, South, North, West, East,

(To thy immortal breasts, Mother of All, thy every daughter, son, endear'd alike, forever equal,)

Thee in thy own musicians, singers, artists, unborn yet, but certain,

Thee in thy moral wealth and civilization, (until which thy proudest material civilization must remain in vain,)

Thee in thy all-supplying, all-enclosing worship—thee in no
    single bible, saviour, merely,
Thy saviours countless, latent within thyself, thy bibles in-
    cessant within thyself, equal to any, divine as any,
(Thy soaring course thee formulating, not in thy two great
    wars, nor in thy century's visible growth,
But far more in these leaves and chants, thy chants, great
    Mother!)
Thee in an education grown of thee, in teachers, studies,
    students, born of thee,
Thee in thy democratic fêtes en-masse, thy high original fes-
    tivals, operas, lecturers, preachers,
Thee in thy ultimata, (the preparations only now completed,
    the edifice on sure foundations tied,)
Thee in thy pinnacles, intellect, thought, thy topmost rational
    joys, thy love and godlike aspiration,
In thy resplendent coming literati, thy full-lung'd orators,
    thy sacerdotal bards, kosmic savans,
These! these in thee, (certain to come,) to-day I prophesy.

### 6

Land tolerating all, accepting all, not for the good alone, all
    good for thee,
Land in the realms of God to be a realm unto thyself,
Under the rule of God to be a rule unto thyself.

(Lo, where arise three peerless stars,
To be thy natal stars my country, Ensemble, Evolution,
    Freedom,
Set in the sky of Law.)

Land of unprecedented faith, God's faith,
Thy soil, thy very subsoil, all upheav'd,
The general inner earth so long so sedulously draped over,
    now hence for what it is boldly laid bare,
Open'd by thee to heaven's light for benefit or bale.

Not for success alone,
Not to fair-sail unintermitted always,
The storm shall dash thy face, the murk of war and worse
    than war shall cover thee all over,

(Wert capable of war, its tug and trials? be capable of peace,
 its trials,
For the tug and mortal strain of nations come at last in prosperous peace, not war;)
In many a smiling mask death shall approach beguiling thee,
 thou in disease shalt swelter,
The livid cancer spread its hideous claws, clinging upon thy
 breasts, seeking to strike thee deep within,
Consumption of the worst, moral consumption, shall rouge
 thy face with hectic,
But thou shalt face thy fortunes, thy diseases, and surmount
 them all,
Whatever they are to-day and whatever through time they
 may be,
They each and all shall lift and pass away and cease from thee,
While thou, Time's spirals rounding, out of thyself, thyself
 still extricating, fusing,
Equable, natural, mystical Union thou, (the mortal with im-
 mortal blent,)
Shalt soar toward the fulfilment of the future, the spirit of
 the body and the mind,
The soul, its destinies.

The soul, its destinies, the real real,
(Purport of all these apparitions of the real;)
In thee America, the soul, its destinies,
Thou globe of globes! thou wonder nebulous!
By many a throe of heat and cold convuls'd, (by these thyself
 solidifying,)
Thou mental, moral orb—thou New, indeed new, Spiritual
 World!
The Present holds thee not—for such vast growth as thine,
For such unparallel'd flight as thine, such brood as thine,
The FUTURE only holds thee and can hold thee.
1872                 1881

## A PAUMANOK PICTURE

Two boats with nets lying off the sea-beach, quite still,
Ten fishermen waiting—they discover a thick school of moss-
 bonkers—they drop the join'd seine-ends in the water,

The boats separate and row off, each on its rounding course
    to the beach, enclosing the mossbonkers,
The net is drawn in by a windlass by those who stop ashore,
Some of the fishermen lounge in their boats, others stand
    ankle-deep in the water, pois'd on strong legs,
The boats partly drawn up, the water slapping against them,
Strew'd on the sand in heaps and windrows, well out from
    the water, the green-back'd spotted mossbonkers.

1881                                                      1881

# From Noon to Starry Night

## THOU ORB ALOFT FULL-DAZZLING

THOU orb aloft full-dazzling! thou hot October noon!
Flooding with sheeny light the gray beach sand,
The sibilant near sea with vistas far and foam,
And tawny streaks and shades and spreading blue;
O sun of noon refulgent! my special word to thee.

Hear me illustrious!
Thy lover me, for always I have loved thee,
Even as basking babe, then happy boy alone by some wood
  edge, thy touching-distant beams enough,
Or man matured, or young or old, as now to thee I launch
  my invocation.

(Thou canst not with thy dumbness me deceive,
I know before the fitting man all Nature yields,
Though answering not in words, the skies, trees, hear his
  voice—and thou O sun,
As for thy throes, thy perturbations, sudden breaks and
  shafts of flame gigantic,
I understand them, I know those flames, those perturbations
  well.)

Thou that with fructifying heat and light,
O'er myriad farms, o'er lands and waters North and South,
O'er Mississippi's endless course, o'er Texas' grassy plains,
  Kanada's woods,
O'er all the globe that turns its face to thee shining in space,
Thou that impartially infoldest all, not only continents, seas,
Thou that to grapes and weeds and little wild flowers givest
  so liberally,

o           **417**           w.

Shed, shed thyself on mine and me, with but a fleeting ray out
    of thy million millions,
Strike though these chants.

Nor only launch thy subtle dazzle and thy strength for these,
Prepare the later afternoon of me myself—prepare my
    lengthening shadows,
Prepare my starry nights.
1881                                                              1881

## FACES

### 1

SAUNTERING the pavement or riding the country by-road, lo,
    such faces!
Faces of friendship, precision, caution, sauvity, ideality,
The spiritual-prescient face, the always welcome common
    benevolent face,
The face of the singing of music, the grand faces of natural
    lawyers and judges broad at the back-top,
The faces of hunters and fishers bulged at the brows, the
    shaved blanch'd faces of orthodox citizens,
The pure, extravagant, yearning, questioning artist's face,
The ugly face of some beautiful soul, the handsome detested
    or despised face,
The sacred faces of infants, the illuminated face of the mother
    of many children,
The face of an amour, the face of veneration,
The face as of a dream, the face of an immobile rock,
The face withdrawn of its good and bad, a castrated face,
A wild hawk, his wings clipp'd by the clipper,
A stallion that yielded at last to the thongs and knife of the
    gelder.

Sauntering the pavement thus, or crossing the ceaseless ferry,
    faces and faces and faces,
I see them and complain not, and am content with all.

### 2

Do you suppose I could be content with all if I thought them
    their own finalè?

This now is too lamentable a face for a man,
Some abject louse asking leave to be, cringing for it,
Some milk-nosed maggot blessing what lets it wrig to its hole.

This face is a dog's snout sniffing for garbage,
Snakes nest in that mouth, I hear the sibilant threat.

This face is a haze more chill than the arctic sea,
Its sleepy and wabbling icebergs crunch as they go.

This is a face of bitter herbs, this an emetic, they need no
    label,
And more of the drug-shelf, laudanum, caoutchouc, or hog's-
    lard.

This face is an epilepsy, its wordless tongue gives out the
    earthly cry,
Its veins down the neck distend, its eyes roll till they show
    nothing but their whites,
Its teeth grit, the palms of the hands are cut by the turn'd-in
    nails,
The man falls struggling and foaming to the ground, while he
    speculates well.

This face is bitten by vermin and worms,
And this is some murderer's knife with a half-pull'd scabbard.

This face owes to the sexton his dismalest fee,
An unceasing death-bell tolls there.

3

Features of my equals would you trick me with your creas'd
    and cadaverous march?
Well, you cannot trick me.

I see your rounded never-erased flow,
I see 'neath the rims of your haggard and mean disguises.

Splay and twist as you like, poke with the tangling fores of
    fishes or rats,
You'll be unmuzzled, you certainly will.

I saw the face of the most smear'd and slobbering idiot they
    had at the asylum,
And I knew for my consolation what they knew not,
I knew of the agents that emptied and broke my brother,
The same wait to clear the rubbish from the fallen tenement,
And I shall look again in a score or two of ages,
And I shall meet the real landlord perfect and unharm'd,
    every inch as good as myself.

### 4

The Lord advances, and yet advances,
Always the shadow in front, always the reach'd hand bring-
    ing up the laggards.

Out of this face emerge banners and horses—O superb! I see
    what is coming,
I see the high pioneer-caps, see staves of runners clearing the
    way,
I hear victorious drums.

This face is a life-boat,
This is the face commanding and bearded, it asks no odds of
    the rest,
This face is flavor'd fruit ready for eating,
This face of a healthy honest boy is the programme of all good.

These faces bear testimony slumbering or awake,
They show their descent from the Master himself.

Off the word I have spoken I except not one—red, white,
    black, are all deific,
In each house is the ovum, it comes forth after a thousand
    years.

Spots or cracks at the windows do not disturb me,
Tall and sufficient stand behind and make signs to me,
I read the promise and patiently wait.

This is a full-grown lily's face,
She speaks to the limber-hipp'd man near the garden pickets,
*Come here* she blushingly cries, *Come nigh to me limber-
    hipp'd man,*

*Stand at my side till I lean as high as I can upon you,*
*Fill me with albescent honey, bend down to me,*
*Rub to me with your chafing beard, rub to my breast and*
*shoulders.*

### 5

The old face of the mother of many children,
Whist! I am fully content.

Lull'd and late is the smoke of the First-day morning,
It hangs low over the rows of trees by the fences,
It hangs thin by the sassafras and wild-cherry and cat-brier
under them.

I saw the rich ladies in full dress at the soiree,
I heard what the singers were singing so long,
Heard who sprang in crimson youth from the white froth and
the water-blue.

Behold a woman!
She looks out from her quaker cap, her face is clearer and
more beautiful than the sky.

She sits in an armchair under the shaded porch of the farm-
house,
The sun just shines on her old white head.

Her ample gown is of cream-hued linen,
Her grandsons raised the flax, and her grand-daughters spin
it with the distaff and the wheel.

The melodious character of the earth,
The finish beyond which philosophy cannot go and does not
wish to go,
The justified mother of men.
1855                                                                    1881

## THE MYSTIC TRUMPETER

### 1

HARK, some wild trumpeter, some strange musician,
Hovering unseen in air, vibrates capricious tunes to-night.

I hear thee trumpeter, listening alert I catch thy notes,
Now pouring, whirling like a tempest round me,
Now low, subdued, now in the distance lost.


## 2

Come nearer bodiless one, haply in thee resounds
Some dead composer, haply thy pensive life
Was fill'd with aspirations high, unform'd ideals,
Waves, oceans musical, chaotically surging,
That now ecstatic ghost, close to me bending, thy cornet
    echoing, pealing,
Gives out to no one's ears but mine, but freely gives to mine,
That I may thee translate.


## 3

Blow trumpeter free and clear, I follow thee,
While at thy liquid prelude, glad, serene,
The fretting world, the streets, the noisy hours of day with-
    draw,
A holy calm descends like dew upon me,
I walk in cool refreshing night the walks of Paradise,
I scent the grass, the moist air and the roses;
Thy song expands my numb'd imbonded spirit, thou freest,
    launchest me,
Floating and basking upon heaven's lake.


## 4

Blow again trumpeter! and for my sensuous eyes,
Bring the old pageants, show the feudal world.

What charm thy music works! thou makest pass before me,
Ladies and cavaliers long dead, barons are in their castle halls,
    the troubadours are singing,
Arm'd knights go forth to redress wrongs, some in quest of
    the holy Graal;
I see the tournament, I see the contestants incased in heavy
    armor seated on stately champing horses,
I hear the shouts, the sounds of blows and smiting steel;

I see the Crusaders' tumultuous armies—hark, how the cymbals clang,

Lo, where the monks walk in advance, bearing the cross on high.

### 5

Blow again trumpeter! and for thy theme,

Take now the enclosing theme of all, the solvent and the setting,

Love, that is pulse of all, the sustenance and the pang,

The heart of man and woman all for love,

No other theme but love—knitting, enclosing, all-diffusing love.

O how the immortal phantoms crowd around me!

I see the vast alembic ever working, I see and know the flames that heat the world,

The glow, the blush, the beating hearts of lovers,

So blissful happy some, and some so silent, dark, and nigh to death;

Love, that is all the earth to lovers—love, that mocks time and space,

Love, that is day and night—love, that is sun and moon and stars,

Love, that is crimson, sumptuous, sick with perfume,

No other words but words of love, no other thought but love.

### 6

Blow again trumpeter—conjure war's alarums.

Swift to thy spell a shuddering hum like distant thunder rolls,

Lo, where the arm'd men hasten—lo, mid the clouds of dust the glint of bayonets,

I see the grime-faced cannoneers, I mark the rosy flash amid the smoke, I hear the cracking of the guns;

Nor war alone—thy fearful music-song, wild prayer, brings every sight of fear,

The deeds of ruthless brigands, rapine, murder—I hear the cries for help!

I see ships foundering at sea, I behold on deck and below deck the terrible tableaus.

### 7

O trumpeter, methinks I am myself the instrument thou
　　playest,
Thou melt'st my heart, my brain—thou movest, drawest,
　　changest them at will;
And now thy sullen notes send darkness through me,
Thou takest away all cheering light, all hope,
I see the enslaved, the overthrown, the hurt, the opprest of
　　the whole earth,
I feel the measureless shame and humiliation of my race, it
　　becomes all mine,
Mine too the revenges of humanity, the wrongs of ages,
　　baffled feuds and hatreds,
Utter defeat upon me weighs—all lost—the foe victorious,
(Yet 'mid the ruins Pride colossal stands unshaken to the
　　last,
Endurance, resolution to the last.)

### 8

Now trumpeter for thy close,
Vouchsafe a higher strain than any yet,
Sing to my soul, renew its languishing faith and hope,
Rouse up my slow belief, give me some vision of the future,
Give me for once its prophecy and joy.

O glad, exulting, culminating song!
A vigor more than earth's is in thy notes,
Marches of victory—man disenthral'd—the conqueror at
　　last,
Hymns to the universal God from universal man—all joy!
A reborn race appears—a perfect world, all joy!
Women and men in wisdom innocence and health—all joy!
Riotous laughing bacchanals fill'd with joy!
War, sorrow, suffering gone—the rank earth purged—no-
　　thing but joy left!
The ocean fill'd with joy—the atmosphere all joy!　·
Joy! joy! in freedom, worship, love! joy in the ecstasy of life!
Enough to merely be! enough to breathe!
Joy! joy! all over joy!
1872　　　　　　　　　　　　　　　　　　　　　　1881

## TO A LOCOMOTIVE IN WINTER

THEE for my recitative,

Thee in the driving storm even as now, the snow, the winter-
day declining,

Thee in thy panoply, thy measur'd dual throbbing and thy
beat convulsive,

Thy black cylindric body, golden brass and silvery steel,

Thy ponderous side-bars, parallel and connecting rods,
gyrating, shuttling at thy sides,

Thy metrical, now swelling pant and roar, now tapering in
the distance,

Thy great protruding head-light fix'd in front,

Thy long, pale, floating vapor-pennants, tinged with delicate
purple,

The dense and murky clouds out-belching from thy smoke-
stack,

Thy knitted frame, thy springs and valves, the tremulous
twinkle of thy wheels,

Thy train of cars behind, obedient, merrily following,

Through gale or calm, now swift, now slack, yet steadily
careering;

Type of the modern—emblem of motion and power—pulse
of the continent,

For once come serve the Muse and merge in verse, even as
here I see thee,

With storm and buffeting gusts of wind and falling snow,

By day thy warning ringing bell to sound its notes,

By night thy silent signal lamps to swing.

Fierce-throated beauty!

Roll through my chant with all thy lawless music, thy swinging lamps at night,

Thy madly-whistled laughter, echoing, rumbling like an
earthquake, rousing all,

Law of thyself complete, thine own track firmly holding,

(No sweetness debonair of tearful harp or glib piano thine,)

Thy trills of shrieks by rocks and hills return'd,

Launch'd o'er the prairies wide, across the lakes,

To the free skies unpent and glad and strong.

1876                                                      1881

## O MAGNET-SOUTH

O MAGNET-SOUTH! O glistening perfumed South! my South!
O quick mettle, rich blood, impulse and love! good and evil!
  O all dear to me!
O dear to me my birth-things—all moving things and the
  trees where I was born—the grains, plants, rivers,
Dear to me my own slow sluggish rivers where they flow,
  distant, over flats of silvery sands or through swamps,
Dear to me the Roanoke, the Savannah, the Altamahaw, the
  Pedee, the Tombigbee, the Santee, the Coosa, and the
  Sabine,
O pensive, far away wandering, I return with my soul to
  haunt their banks again,
Again in Florida I float on transparent lakes, I float on the
  Okeechobee, I cross the hummock-land or through
  pleasant openings or dense forests,
I see the parrots in the woods, I see the papaw-tree and the
  blossoming titi;
Again, sailing in my coaster on deck, I coast off Georgia, I
  coast up the Carolinas,
I see where the live-oak is growing, I see where the yellow-
  pine, the scented bay-tree, the lemon and orange, the
  cypress, the graceful palmetto,
I pass rude sea-headlands and enter Pamlico sound through
  an inlet, and dart my vision inland;
O the cotton plant! the growing fields of rice, sugar, hemp!
The cactus guarded with thorns, the laurel-tree with large
  white flowers,
The range afar, the richness and barrenness, the old woods
  charged with mistletoe and trailing moss,
The piney odor and the gloom, the awful natural stillness,
  (here in these dense swamps the freebooter carries his
  gun, and the fugitive has his conceal'd hut;)
O the strange fascination of these half-known half-impass-
  able swamps, infested by reptiles, resounding with the
  bellow of the alligator, the sad noises of the night-owl
  and the wild-cat, and the whirr of the rattlesnake,
The mocking-bird, the American mimic, singing all the forenoon, singing through the moon-lit night,

The humming-bird, the wild turkey, the raccoon, the opossum;
A Kentucky corn-field, the tall, graceful, long-leav'd corn,
    slender, flapping, bright green, with tassels, with beauti-
    ful ears each well-sheath'd in its husk;
O my heart! O tender and fierce pangs, I can stand them not,
    I will depart;
O to be a Virginian where I grew up! O to be a Carolinian!
O longings irrepressible! O I will go back to old Tennessee
    and never wander more.

1860                                   1881

## MANNAHATTA

I WAS asking for something specific and perfect for my city,
Whereupon lo! upsprang the aboriginal name.

Now I see what there is in a name, a word, liquid, sane,
    unruly, musical, self-sufficient,
I see that the word of my city is that word from of old,
Because I see that word nested in nests of water-bays, superb,
Rich, hemm'd thick all around with sailships and steamships,
    an island sixteen miles long, solid-founded,
Numberless crowded streets, high growths of iron, slender,
    strong, light, splendidly uprising toward clear skies,
Tides swift and ample, well-loved by me, toward sundown,
The flowing sea-currents, the little islands, larger adjoining
    islands, the heights, the villas,
The countless masts, the white shore-steamers, the lighters,
    the ferry-boats, the black sea-steamers well-model'd,
The down-town streets, the jobbers' houses of business, the
    houses of business of the ship-merchants and money-
    brokers, the river-streets,
Immigrants arriving, fifteen or twenty thousand in a week,
The carts hauling goods, the manly race of drivers of horses,
    the brown-faced sailors,
The summer air, the bright sun shining, and the sailing clouds
    aloft,
The winter snows, the sleigh-bells, the broken ice in the river,
    passing along up or down with the flood-tide or ebb-tide,
The mechanics of the city, the masters, well-form'd, beauti-
    ful-faced, looking you straight in the eyes,

Trottoirs throng'd, vehicles, Broadway, the women, the shops
   and shows,
A million people—manners free and superb—open voices—
   hospitality—the most courageous and friendly young
   men,
City of hurried and sparkling waters! city of spires and masts!
City nested in bays! my city!
1860                                                                          1881

## ALL IS TRUTH

O ME, man of slack faith so long,
Standing aloof, denying portions so long,
Only aware to-day of compact all-diffused truth,
Discovering to-day there is no lie or form of lie, and can be
   none, but grows as inevitably upon itself as the truth
   does upon itself,
Or as any law of the earth or any natural production of the
   earth does.

(This is curious and may not be realized immediately, but it
   must be realized,
I feel in myself that I represent falsehoods equally with the rest,
And that the universe does.)

Where has fail'd a perfect return indifferent of lies or the truth?
Is it upon the ground, or in water or fire? or in the spirit of
   man? or in the meat and blood?

Meditating among liars and retreating sternly into myself, I
   see that there are really no liars or lies after all,
And that nothing fails its perfect return, and that what are
   called lies are perfect returns,
And that each thing exactly represents itself and what has
   preceded it,
And that the truth includes all, and is compact just as much
   as space is compact,
And that there is no flaw or vacuum in the amount of the
   truth—but that all is truth without exception;
And henceforth I will go celebrate any thing I see or am,
And sing and laugh and deny nothing.
1860                                                                          1871

## A RIDDLE SONG

THAT which eludes this verse and any verse,
Unheard by sharpest ear, unform'd in clearest eye or cun-
    ningest mind,
Nor lore nor fame, nor happiness nor wealth,
And yet the pulse of every heart and life throughout the
    world incessantly,
Which you and I and all pursuing ever ever miss,
Open but still a secret, the real of the real, an illusion,
Costless, vouchsafed to each, yet never man the owner,
Which poets vainly seek to put in rhyme, historians in prose,
Which sculptor never chisel'd yet, not painter painted,
Which vocalist never sung, nor orator nor actor ever utter'd,
Invoking here and how I challenge for my song.

Indifferently, 'mid public, private haunts, in solitude,
Behind the mountain and the wood,
Companion of the city's busiest streets, through the assem-
    blage,
It and its radiations constantly glide.

In looks of fair unconscious babes,
Or strangely in the coffin'd dead,
Or show of breaking dawn or stars by night,
As some dissolving delicate film of dreams,
Hiding yet lingering.

Two little breaths of words comprising it,
Two words, yet all from first to last comprised in it.

How ardently for it!
How many ships have sail'd and sunk for it!
How many travelers started from their homes and ne'er
    return'd!
How much of genius boldly staked and lost for it!
What countless stores of beauty, love, ventur'd for it!
How all superbest deeds since Time began are traceable to it
    —and shall be to the end!
How all heroic martyrdoms to it!

How, justified by it, the horrors, evils, battles of the earth!
How the bright fascinating lambent flames of it, in every age
    and land, have drawn men's eyes,
Rich as a sunset on the Norway coast, the sky, the islands,
    and the cliffs,
Or midnight's silent glowing northern lights unreachable.

Haply God's riddle it, so vague and yet so certain,
The soul for it, and all the visible universe for it,
And heaven at last for it.

1881                                                 1881


## EXCELSIOR

WHO has gone farthest? for I would go farther,
And who has been just? for I would be the most just person
    of the earth,
And who most cautious? for I would be more cautious,
And who has been happiest? O I think it is I—I think no one
    was ever happier than I,
And who has lavish'd all? for I lavish constantly the best I
    have,
And who proudest? for I think I have reason to be the
    proudest son alive—for I am the son of the brawny and
    tall-topt city,
And who has been bold and true? for I would be the boldest
    and truest being of the universe,
And who benevolent? for I would show more benevolence
    than all the rest,
And who has receiv'd the love of the most friends? for I
    know what it is to receive the passionate love of many
    friends,
And who possesses a perfect and enamour'd body? for I do
    not believe any one possesses a more perfect or en-
    amour'd body than mine,
And who thinks the amplest thoughts? for I would surround
    those thoughts,
And who has made hymns fit for the earth? for I am mad
    with devouring ecstasy to make joyous hymns for the
    whole earth.

1856                                                 1881

## AH POVERTIES, WINCINGS, AND SULKY RETREATS

AH poverties, wincings, and sulky retreats,

Ah you foes that in conflict have overcome me,

(For what is my life or any man's life but a conflict with foes, the old, the incessant war?)

You degradations, you tussle with passions and appetites,

You smarts from dissatisfied friendships, (ah wounds the sharpest of all!)

You toil of painful and choked articulations, you mean-nesses,

You shallow tongue-talks at tables, (my tongue the shallowest of any;)

You broken resolutions, you racking angers, you smother'd ennuis!

Ah think not you finally triumph, my real self has yet to come forth,

It shall yet march forth o'ermastering, till all lies beneath me,

It shall yet stand up the soldier of ultimate victory.

1865–6                                                          1881

## THOUGHTS

OF public opinion,

Of a calm and cool fiat sooner or later, (how impassive! how certain and final!)

Of the President with pale face asking secretly to himself, *What will the people say at last?*

Of the frivolous Judge—of the corrupt Congressman, Governor, Mayor—of such as these standing helpless and exposed,

Of the mumbling and screaming priest, (soon, soon deserted,)

Of the lessening year by year of venerableness, and of the dicta of officers, statutes, pulpits, schools,

Of the rising forever taller and stronger and broader of the intuitions of men and women, and of Self-esteem and Personality;

Of the true New World—of the Democracies resplendent en-masse,

Of the conformity of politics, armies, navies, to them,

Of the shining sun by them—of the inherent light, greater
  than the rest,
Of the envelopment of all by them, and the effusion of all
  from them.
1860                                                    1881

## MEDIUMS

THEY shall arise in the States,
They shall report Nature, laws, physiology, and happiness,
They shall illustrate Democracy and the kosmos,
They shall be alimentive, amative, perceptive,
They shall be complete women and men, their pose brawny
  and supple, their drink water, their blood clean and clear,
They shall fully enjoy materialism and the sight of products,
  they shall enjoy the sight of the beef, lumber, bread-
  stuffs, of Chicago the great city,
They shall train themselves to go in public to become orators
  and oratresses,
Strong and sweet shall their tongues be, poems and materials
  of poems shall come from their lives, they shall be
  makers and finders,
Of them and of their works shall emerge divine conveyers, to
  convey gospels,
Characters, events, retrospections, shall be convey'd in gospels, trees, animals, waters, shall be convey'd,
Death, the future, the invisible faith, shall all be convey'd.
1860                                                    1871

## WEAVE IN, MY HARDY LIFE

WEAVE in, weave in, my hardy life,
Weave yet a soldier strong and full for great campaigns to
  come,
Weave in red blood, weave sinews in like ropes, the senses,
  sight weave in,
Weave lasting sure, weave day and night the weft, the warp,
  incessant weave, tire not,
(We know not what the use O life, nor know the aim, the end,
  nor really aught we know,
But know the work, the need goes on and shall go on, the
  death-envelop'd march of peace as well as war goes on,)

For great campaigns of peace the same the wiry threads to
    weave,
We know not why or what, yet weave, forever weave.
1865                                            1881

## SPAIN, 1873–74

Out of the murk of heaviest clouds,
Out of the feudal wrecks and heap'd-up skeletons of kings,
Out of that old entire European debris, the shatter'd mum-
    meries,
Ruin'd cathedrals, crumble of palaces, tombs of priests,
Lo, Freedom's features fresh undimm'd look forth—the same
    immortal face looks forth;
(A glimpse as of thy Mother's face Columbia,
A flash significant as of a sword,
Beaming towards thee.)

Nor think we forget thee maternal;
Lag'd'st thou so long? shall the clouds close again upon thee?
Ah, but thou hast thyself now appear'd to us—we know thee,
Thou hast given us a sure proof, the glimpse of thyself,
Thou waitest there as everywhere thy time.
1873                                           1881

## BY BROAD POTOMAC'S SHORE

By broad Potomac's shore, again old tongue,
(Still uttering, still ejaculating, canst never cease this babble?)
Again old heart so gay, again to you, your sense, the full
    flush spring returning,
Again the freshness and the odors, again Virginia's summer
    sky, pellucid blue and silver,
Again the forenoon purple of the hills,
Again the deathless grass, so noiseless soft and green,
Again the blood-red roses blooming.

Perfume this book of mine O blood-red roses!
Lave subtly with your waters every line Potomac!
Give me of you O spring, before I close, to put between its
    pages!
O forenoon purple of the hills, before I close, of you!
O deathless grass, of you!
1876                                           1881

## FROM FAR DAKOTA'S CAÑONS

*June* 25, 1876

FROM far Dakota's cañons,
Lands of the wild ravine, the dusky Sioux, the lonesome
stretch, the silence,
Haply to-day a mournful wail, haply a trumpet-note for
heroes.

The battle-bulletin,
The Indian ambuscade, the craft, the fatal environment,
The cavalry companies fighting to the last in sternest hero-
ism,
In the midst of their little circle, with their slaughter'd horses
for breastworks,
The fall of Custer and all his officers and men.

Continues yet the old, old legend of our race,
The loftiest of life upheld by death,
The ancient banner perfectly maintain'd,
O lesson opportune, O how I welcome thee!

As sitting in dark days,
Lone, sulky, through the time's thick murk looking in vain
for light, for hope,
From unsuspected parts a fierce and momentary proof,
(The sun there at the centre though conceal'd,
Electric life forever at the centre,)
Breaks forth a lightning flash.

Thou of the tawny flowing hair in battle,
I erewhile saw, with erect head, pressing ever in front, bear-
ing a bright sword in thy hand,
Now ending well in death the splendid fever of thy deeds,
(I bring no dirge for it or thee, I bring a glad triumphal
sonnet,)
Desperate and glorious, aye in defeat most desperate, most
glorious,
After thy many battles in which never yielding up a gun or a
color,

Leaving behind thee a memory sweet to soldiers,
Thou yieldest up thyself.
1876                                                          1881

## OLD WAR-DREAMS

IN midnight sleep of many a face of anguish,
Of the look at first of the mortally wounded, (of that inde-
      scribable look,)
Of the dead on their backs with arms extended wide,
            I dream, I dream, I dream.

Of scenes of Nature, fields and mountains,
Of skies so beauteous after a storm, and at night the moon so
      unearthly bright,
Shining sweetly, shining down, where we dig the trenches and
      gather the heaps,
            I dream, I dream, I dream.

Long have they pass'd, faces and trenches and fields,
Where through the carnage I moved with a callous com-
      posure, or away from the fallen,
Onward I sped at the time—but now of their forms at night,
            I dream, I dream, I dream.
1865-6                                                       1881

## THICK-SPRINKLED BUNTING

THICK-SPRINKLED bunting! flag of stars!
Long yet your road, fateful flag—long yet your road, and
      lined with bloody death,
For the prize I see at issue at last is the world,
All its ships and shores I see interwoven with your threads
      greedy banner;
Dream'd again the flags of kings, highest borne, to flaunt
      unrival'd?
O hasten flag of man— O with sure and steady step, passing
      highest flags of kings,
Walk supreme to the heavens mighty symbol—run up above
      them all,
Flag of stars! thick-sprinkled bunting!
1865                                                         1871

## WHAT BEST I SEE IN THEE

### *To U. S. G. return'd from his World's Tour*

WHAT best I see in thee,
Is not that where thou mov'st down history's great highways,
Ever undimm'd by time shoots warlike victory's dazzle,
Or that thou sat'st where Washington sat, ruling the land in
　　peace,
Or thou the man whom feudal Europe fêted, venerable Asia
　　swarm'd upon,
Who walk'd with kings with even pace the round world's
　　promenade;
But that in foreign lands, in all thy walks with kings,
Those prairie sovereigns of the West, Kansas, Missouri,
　　Illinois,
Ohio's, Indiana's millions, comrades, farmers, soldiers, all to
　　the front,
Invisibly with thee walking with kings with even pace the
　　round world's promenade,
Were all so justified.
(1879?)　　　　　　　　　　　　　　　　　　　　　　1881


## SPIRIT THAT FORM'D THIS SCENE

### *Written in Platte Cañon, Colorado*

SPIRIT that form'd this scene,
These tumbled rock-piles grim and red,
These reckless heaven-ambitious peaks,
These gorges, turbulent-clear streams, this naked freshness,
These formless wild arrays, for reasons of their own,
I know thee, savage spirit—we have communed together,
Mine too such wild arrays, for reasons of their own;
Was't charged against my chants they had forgotten art?
To fuse within themselves its rules precise and delicatesse?
The lyrist's measur'd beat, the wrought-out temple's grace—
　　column and polish'd arch forgot?
But thou that revelest here—spirit that form'd this scene,
They have remember'd thee.
1881　　　　　　　　　　　　　　　　　　　　　　1881

## AS  I  WALK  THESE  BROAD  MAJESTIC  DAYS

As I walk these broad majestic days of peace,
(For the war, the struggle of blood finish'd, wherein, O
      terrific Ideal,
Against vast odds erewhile having gloriously won,
Now thou stridest on, yet perhaps in time toward denser wars,
Perhaps to engage in time in still more dreadful contests,
      dangers,
Longer campaigns and crises, labors beyond all others,)
Around me I hear that eclat of the world, politics, produce,
The announcements of recognized things, science,
The approved growth of cities and the spread of inventions.

I see the ships, (they will last a few years,)
The vast factories with their foremen and workmen,
And hear the indorsement of all, and do not object to it.

But I too announce solid things,
Science, ships, politics, cities, factories, are not nothing,
Like a grand procession to music of distant bugles pouring,
      triumphantly moving, and grander heaving in sight,
They stand for realities—all is as it should be.

Then my realities;
What else is so real as mine?
Libertad and the divine average, freedom to every slave on
      the face of the earth,
The rapt promises and luminè of seers, the spiritual world,
      these centuries-lasting songs,
And our visions, the visions of poets, the most solid an-
      nouncements of any.
1860                                                    1881

## A CLEAR MIDNIGHT

THIS is thy hour O soul, thy free flight into the wordless,
Away from books, away from art, the day erased, the lesson
      done,
Thee fully forth emerging, silent, gazing, pondering the
      themes thou lovest best,
Night, sleep, death and the stars.
1881                                                    1881

# Songs of Parting

## AS THE TIME DRAWS NIGH

As the time draws nigh glooming a cloud,
A dread beyond of I know not what darkens me.

I shall go forth,
I shall traverse the States awhile, but I cannot tell whither or
    how long,
Perhaps soon some day or night while I am singing my voice
    will suddenly cease.

O book, O chants! must all then amount to but this?
Must we barely arrive at this beginning of us?—and yet it is
    enough, O soul;
O soul, we have positively appear'd—that is enough.
1860                                  1871

## YEARS OF THE MODERN

YEARS of the modern! years of the unperform'd!
Your horizon rises, I see it parting away for more august
    dramas,
I see not America only, not only Liberty's nation but other
    nations preparing,
I see tremendous entrances and exits, new combinations, the
    solidarity of races,
I see that force advancing with irresistible power on the
    world's stage,
(Have the old forces, the old wars, played their parts? are the
    acts suitable to them closed?)
I see Freedom, completely arm'd and victorious and very
    haughty, with Law on one side and Peace on the other,
A stupendous trio all issuing forth against the idea of caste;

What historic denouements are these we so rapidly approach?

I see men marching and countermarching by swift millions,

I see the frontiers and boundaries of the old aristocracies broken,

I see the landmarks of European kings removed,

I see this day the People beginning their landmarks, (all others give way;)

Never were such sharp questions ask'd as this day,

Never was average man, his soul, more energetic, more like a God,

Lo, how he urges and urges, leaving the masses no rest!

His daring foot is on land and sea everywhere, he colonizes the Pacific, the archipelagoes,

With the steamship, the electric telegraph, the newspaper, the wholesale engines of war,

With these and the world-spreading factories he interlinks all geography, all lands;

What whispers are these O lands, running ahead of you, passing under the seas?

Are all nations communing? is there going to be but one heart to the globe?

Is humanity forming en-masse? for lo, tyrants tremble, crowns grow dim,

The earth, restive, confronts a new era, perhaps a general divine war,

No one knows what will happen next, such portents fill the days and nights;

Years prophetical! the space ahead as I walk, as I vainly try to pierce it, is full of phantoms,

Unborn deeds, things soon to be, project their shapes around me,

This incredible rush and heat, this strange ecstatic fever of dreams O years!

Your dreams O years, how they penetrate through me! (I know not whether I sleep or wake;)

The perform'd America and Europe grow dim, retiring in shadow behind me,

The unperform'd, more gigantic than ever, advance, advance upon me.

1865                                        1881

## ASHES OF SOLDIERS

Ashes of soldiers South or North,
As I muse retrospective murmuring a chant in thought,
The war resumes, again to my sense your shapes,
And again the advance of the armies.

Noiseless as mists and vapors,
From their graves in the trenches ascending,
From cemeteries all through Virginia and Tennessee,
From every point of the compass out of the countless graves,
In wafted clouds, in myriads large, or squads of twos or
     threes or single ones they come,
And silently gather round me.

Now sound no note O trumpeters,
Not at the head of my cavalry parading on spirited horses,
With sabres drawn and glistening, and carbines by their
     thighs, (ah my brave horsemen!
My handsome tan-faced horsemen! what life, what joy and
     pride,
With all the perils were yours.)

Nor you drummers, neither at reveillé at dawn,
Nor the long roll alarming the camp, nor even the muffled
     beat for a burial,
Nothing from you this time O drummers bearing my warlike
     drums.

But aside from these and the marts of wealth and the crowded
     promenade,
Admitting around me comrades close unseen by the rest and
     voiceless,
The slain elate and alive again, the dust and debris alive,
I chant this chant of my silent soul in the name of all dead
     soldiers.

Faces so pale with wondrous eyes, very dear, gather closer
     yet,
Draw close, but speak not.

Phantoms of countless lost,
Invisible to the rest henceforth become my companions,
Follow me ever—desert me not while I live.

Sweet are the blooming cheeks of the living—sweet are the
    musical voices sounding,
But sweet, ah sweet, are the dead with their silent eyes.

Dearest comrades, all is over and long gone,
But love is not over—and what love, O comrades
Perfume from battle-fields rising, up from the fœtor arising.

Perfume therefore my chant, O love, immortal love,
Give me to bathe the memories of all dead soldiers,
Shroud them, embalm them, cover them all over with tender
    pride.

Perfume all—make all wholesome,
Make these ashes to nourish and blossom,
O love, solve all, fructify all with the last chemistry.

Give me exhaustless, make me a fountain,
That I exhale love from me wherever I go like a moist
    perennial dew,
For the ashes of all dead soldiers South or North.
1865                            1881

## THOUGHTS

### 1

Of these years I sing,
How they pass and have pass'd through convuls'd pains, as
    through parturitions,
How America illustrates birth, muscular youth, the promise,
    the sure fulfilment, the absolute success, despite of
    people—illustrates evil as well as good,
The vehement struggle so fierce for unity in one's -self;
How many hold despairingly yet to the models departed,
    caste, myths, obedience, compulsion, and to infidelity,
How few see the arrived models, the athletes, the Western
    States, or see freedom or spirituality, or hold any faith
    in results,

(But I see the athletes, and I see the results of the war glorious
    and inevitable, and they again leading to other results.)

How the great cities appear—how the Democratic masses,
    turbulent, wilful, as I love them,
How the whirl, the contest, the wrestle of evil with good, the
    sounding and resounding, keep on and on,
How society waits unform'd, and is for a while between
    things ended and things begun,
How America is the continent of glories, and of the triumph
    of freedom and of the Democracies, and of the fruits of
    society, and of all that is begun,
And how the States are complete in themselves—and how all
    triumphs and glories are complete in themselves, to lead
    onward,
And how these of mine and of the States will in their turn be
    convuls'd, and serve other parturitions and transitions,
And how all people, sights, combinations, the democratic
    masses too, serve—and how every fact, and war itself,
    with all its horrors, serves,
And how now or at any time each serves the exquisite transi-
    tion of death.


2

Of seeds dropping into the ground, of births,
Of the steady concentration of America, inland, upward, to
    impregnable and swarming places,
Of what Indiana, Kentucky, Arkansas, and the rest, are to be,
Of what a few years will show there in Nebraska, Colorado,
    Nevada, and the rest,
(Or afar, mounting the Northern Pacific to Sitka or Aliaska,)
Of what the feuillage of America is the preparation for—and
    of what all sights, North, South, East and West, are,
Of this Union welded in blood, of the solemn price paid, of
    the unnamed lost ever present in my mind;
Of the temporary use of materials for identity's sake,
Of the present, passing, departing—of the growth of com-
    pleter men than any yet,
Of all sloping down there where the fresh free giver the
    mother, the Mississippi flows,

Of mighty inland cities yet unsurvey'd and unsuspected,
Of the new and good names, of the modern developments, of
    inalienable homesteads,
Of a free and original life there, of simple diet and clean and
    sweet blood,
Of litheness, majestic faces, clear eyes, and perfect physique
    there,
Of immense spiritual results future years far West, each side
    of the Anahuacs,
Of these songs, well understood there, (being made for that
    area,)
Of the native scorn of grossness and gain there,
(O it lurks in me night and day—what is gain after all to
    savageness and freedom?)

1860                                  1881

## SONG AT SUNSET

SPLENDOR of ended day floating and filling me,
Hour prophetic, hour resuming the past,
Inflating my throat, you divine average,
You earth and life till the last ray gleams I sing.

Open mouth of my soul uttering gladness,
Eyes of my soul seeing perfection,
Natural life of me faithfully praising things,
Corroborating forever the triumph of things.

Illustrious every one!
Illustrious what we name space, sphere of unnumber'd
    spirits,
Illustrious the mystery of motion in all beings, even the
    tiniest insect,
Illustrious the attribute of speech, the senses, the body,
Illustrious the passing light—illustrious the pale reflection
    on the new moon in the western sky,
Illustrious whatever I see or hear or touch, to the last.

Good in all,
In the satisfaction and aplomb of animals,
In the annual return of the seasons,

In the hilarity of youth,
In the strength and flush of manhood,
In the grandeur and exquisiteness of old age,
In the superb vistas of death.


Wonderful to depart!
Wonderful to be here!
The heart, to jet the all-alike and innocent blood!
To breathe the air, how delicious!
To speak—to walk—to seize something by the hand!
To prepare for sleep, for bed, to look on my rose-color'd
    flesh!
To be conscious of my body, so satisfied, so large!
To be this incredible God I am!
To have gone forth among other Gods, these men and
    women I love.


Wonderful how I celebrate you and myself!
How my thoughts play subtly at the spectacles around!
How the clouds pass silently overhead!
How the earth darts on and on! and how the sun, moon,
    stars, dart on and on!
How the water sports and sings! (surely it is alive!)
How the trees rise and stand up, with strong trunks, with
    branches and leaves!
(Surely there is something more in each of the trees, some
    living soul.)


O amazement of things—even the least particle!
O spirituality of things!
O strain musical flowing through ages and continents, now
    reaching me and America!
I take your strong chords, intersperse them, and cheerfully
    pass them forward.


I too carol the sun, usher'd or at noon, or as now, set-
    ting,
I too throb to the brain and beauty of the earth and of all the
    growths of the earth,
I too have felt the resistless call of myself.

As I steam'd down the Mississippi,
As I wander'd over the prairies,
As I have lived, as I have look'd through my windows my eyes,
As I went forth in the morning, as I beheld the light breaking
in the east,
As I bathed on the beach of the Eastern Sea, and again on the
beach of Western Sea,
As I roam'd the streets of inland Chicago, whatever streets I
have roam'd,
Or cities or silent woods, or even amid the sights of war,
Wherever I have been I have charged myself with content-
ment and triumph.

I sing to the last the equalities modern or old,
I sing the endless finalés of things,
I say Nature continues, glory continues,
I praise with electric voice,
For I do not see one imperfection in the universe,
And I do not see one cause or result lamentable at last in the
universe.

O setting sun! though the time has come,
I still warble under you, if none else does, unmitigated adoration.
1860                                                      1881

## AS AT THY PORTALS ALSO DEATH

As at thy portals also death,
Entering thy sovereign, dim, illimitable grounds,
To memories of my mother, to the divine blending, maternity,
To her, buried and gone, yet buried not, gone not from me,
(I see again the calm benignant face fresh and beautiful still,
I sit by the form in the coffin,
I kiss and kiss convulsively again the sweet old lips, the
cheeks, the closed eyes in the coffin;)
To her, the ideal woman, practical, spiritual, of all of earth,
life, love, to me the best,
I grave a monumental line, before I go, amid these songs,
And set a tombstone here.
1881                                                      1881

## MY LEGACY

THE business man the acquirer vast,
After assiduous years surveying results, preparing for de-
    parture,
Devises houses and lands to his children, bequeaths stocks,
    goods, funds for a school or hospital,
Leaves money to certain companions to buy tokens, sou-
    venirs of gems and gold.

But I, my life surveying, closing,
With nothing to show to devise from its idle years,
Nor houses nor lands, nor tokens of gems or gold for my
    friends,
Yet certain remembrances of the war for you, and after you,
And little souvenirs of camps and soldiers, with my love,
I bind together and bequeath in this bundle of songs.
1872                                            1881

## PENSIVE ON HER DEAD GAZING

PENSIVE on her dead gazing I heard the Mother of All,
Desperate on the torn bodies, on the forms covering the
    battle-fields gazing,
(As the last gun ceased, but the scent of the powder-smoke
    linger'd,)
As she call'd to her earth with mournful voice while she
    stalk'd,
Absorb them well O my earth, she cried, I charge you lose
    not my sons, lose not an atom,
And you streams absorb them well, taking their dear blood,
And you local spots, and you airs that swim above lightly
    impalpable,
And all you essences of soil and growth, and you my rivers'
    depths,
And you mountain sides, and the woods where my dear chil-
    dren's blood trickling redden'd,
And you trees down in your roots to bequeath to all future
    trees,
My dead absorb or South or North—my young men's bodies
    absorb, and their precious precious blood,

Which holding in trust for me faithfully back again give me
    many a year hence,
In unseen essence and odor of surface and grass, centuries
    hence,
In blowing airs from the fields back again give me my dar-
    lings, give my immortal heroes,
Exhale me them centuries hence, breathe me their breath, let
    not an atom be lost,
O years and graves! O air and soil! O my dead, an aroma
    sweet!
Exhale them perennial sweet death, years, centuries hence.
1865                                1881

## CAMPS OF GREEN

Not alone those camps of white, old comrades of the wars,
When as order'd forward, after a long march,
Footsore and weary, soon as the light lessens we halt for the
    night,
Some of us so fatigued carrying the gun and knapsack, drop-
    ping asleep in our tracks,
Others pitching the little tents, and the fires lit up begin to
    sparkle,
Outposts of pickets posted surrounding alert through the dark,
And a word provided for countersign, careful for safety,
Till to the call of the drummers at daybreak loudly beating
    the drums,
We rise up refresh'd, the night and sleep pass'd over, and
    resume our journey,
Or proceed to battle.

Lo, the camps of the tents of green,
Which the days of peace keep filling, and the days of war
    keep filling,
With a mystic army, (is it too order'd forward? is it too only
    halting awhile,
Till night and sleep pass over?)

Now in those camps of green, in their tents dotting the world,
In the parents, children, husbands, wives, in them, in the old
    and young,

Sleeping under the sunlight, sleeping under the moonlight,
    content and silent there at last,
Behold the mighty bivouac-field and waiting-camp of all,
Of the corps and generals all, and the President over the
    corps and generals all,
And of each of us O soldiers, and of each and all in the ranks
    we fought,
(There without hatred we all, all meet.)

For presently O soldiers, we too camp in our place in the
    bivouac-camps of green,
But we need not provide for outposts, nor word for the
    counter-sign,
Nor drummer to beat the morning drum.
1865                                         1881

## THE SOBBING OF THE BELLS

### (*Midnight, Sept.* 19–20, 1881)

THE sobbing of the bells, the sudden death-news everywhere,
The slumberers rouse, the rapport of the People,
(Full well they know that message in the darkness,
Full well return, respond within their breasts, their brains,
    the sad reverberations,)
The passionate toll and clang—city to city, joining, sounding,
    passing,
Those heart-beats of a Nation in the night.
1881                                           1881

## AS THEY DRAW TO A CLOSE

As they draw to a close,
Of what underlies the precedent songs—of my aims in them,
Of the seed I have sought to plant in them,
Of joy, sweet joy, through many a year, in them,
(For them, for them have I lived, in them my work is done,)
Of many an aspiration fond, of many a dream and plan;
Through Space and Time fused in a chant, and the flowing
    eternal identity,
To Nature encompassing these, encompassing God—to the
    joyous, electric all,

To the sense of Death, and accepting exulting in Death in its
    turn the same as life,
The entrance of man to sing;
To compact you, ye parted, diverse lives,
To put rapport the mountains and rocks and streams,
And the winds of the north, and the forests of oak and pine,
With you O soul.
1871                                                                                         1881

## JOY, SHIPMATE, JOY!

JOY, shipmate, joy!
(Pleas'd to my soul at death I cry,)
Our life is closed, our life begins,
The long, long anchorage we leave,
The ship is clear at last, she leaps!
She swiftly courses from the shore,
Joy, shipmate, joy!

1871                                                                                         1871

## THE UNTOLD WANT

THE untold want by life and land ne'er granted,
Now voyager sail thou forth to seek and find.

1871                                                                                         1871

## PORTALS

WHAT are those of the known but to ascend and enter the
    Unknown?
And what are those of life but for Death?

1871                                                                                         1871

## THESE CAROLS

THESE carols sung to cheer my passage through the world I
    see,
For completion I dedicate to the Invisible World.

1871                                                                                         1871

## NOW FINALÈ TO THE SHORE

Now finalè to the shore,
Now land and life finalè and farewell,
Now Voyager depart, (much, much for thee is yet in store,)

P                                                                                         W.

Often enough hast thou adventur'd o'er the seas,
Cautiously cruising, studying the charts,
Duly again to port and hawser's tie returning;
But now obey thy cherish'd secret wish,
Embrace thy friends, leave all in order,
To port and hawser's tie no more returning,
Depart upon thy endless cruise old Sailor.
1871                                                      1871

## SO LONG!

To conclude, I announce what comes after me.

I remember I said before my leaves sprang at all,
I would raise my voice jocund and strong with reference to
  consummations.

When America does what was promis'd,
When through these States walk a hundred millions of superb
  persons,
When the rest part away for superb persons and contribute
  to them,
When breeds of the most perfect mothers denote America,
Then to me and mine our due fruition.

I have press'd through in my own right,
I have sung the body and the soul, war and peace have I sung,
  and the songs of life and death,
And the songs of birth, and shown that there are many
  births.

I have offer'd my style to every one, I have journey'd with
  confident step;
While my pleasure is yet at the full I whisper *So long !*
And take the young woman's hand and the young man's
  hand for the last time.

I announce natural persons to arise,
I announce justice triumphant,
I announce uncompromising liberty and equality,
I announce the justification of candor and the justification of
  pride.

I announce that the identity of these States is a single identity
only,
I announce the Union more and more compact, indissoluble,
I announce splendors and majesties to make all the previous
politics of the earth insignificant.

I announce adhesiveness, I say it shall be limitless, unloosen'd,
I say you shall yet find the friend you were looking for.

I announce a man or woman coming, perhaps you are the
one, (*So long!*)
I announce the great individual, fluid as Nature, chaste,
affectionate, compassionate, fully arm'd.

I announce a life that shall be copious, vehement, spiritual,
bold,
I announce an end that shall lightly and joyfully meet its
translation.

I announce myriads of youths, beautiful, gigantic, sweet-
blooded,
I announce a race of splendid and savage old men.

O thicker and faster—(*So long!*)
O crowding too close upon me,
I foresee too much, it means more than I thought,
It appears to me I am dying.

Hasten throat and sound your last,
Salute me—salute the days once more. Peal the old cry once
more.

Screaming electric, the atmosphere using,
At random glancing, each as I notice absorbing,
Swiftly on, but a little while alighting,
Curious envelop'd messages delivering,
Sparkles hot, seed ethereal down in the dirt dropping,
Myself unknowing, my commission obeying, to question it
never daring,
To ages and ages yet the growth of the seed leaving,

To troops out of the war arising, they the tasks I have set
    promulging,
To women certain whispers of myself bequeathing, their
    affection me more clearly explaining,
To young men my problems offering—no dallier I—I the
    muscle of their brains trying,
So I pass, a little time vocal, visible, contrary,
Afterward a melodious echo, passionately bent for, (death
    making me really undying,)
The best of me then when no longer visible, for toward that
    I have been incessantly preparing.

What is there more, that I lag and pause and crouch extended
    with unshut mouth?
Is there a single final farewell?

My songs cease, I abandon them,
From behind the screen where I hid I advance personally
    solely to you.

Camerado, this is no book,
Who touches this touches a man,
(Is it night? are we here together alone?)
It is I you hold and who holds you,
I spring from the pages into your arms—decease calls me
    forth.

O how your fingers drowse me,
Your breath falls around me like dew, your pulse lulls the
    tympans of my ears,
I feel immerged from head to foot,
Delicious, enough.

Enough O deed impromptu and secret,
Enough O gliding present—enough O summ'd-up past.

Dear friend whoever you are take this kiss,
I give it especially to you, do not forget me,
I feel like one who has done work for the day to retire awhile,
I receive now again of my many translations, from my ava-
    taras ascending, while others doubtless await me,

An unknown sphere more real than I dream'd, more direct,
    darts awakening rays about me, *So long!*
Remember my words, I may again return,
I love you, I depart from materials,
I am as one disembodied, triumphant, dead.
1860                                                     1881

# Sands at Seventy

## [First Annex]

### MANNAHATTA

My city's fit and noble name resumed,
Choice aboriginal name, with marvellous beauty, meaning,
*A rocky founded island—shores where ever gayly dash the
    coming, going, hurrying sea waves.*
1888                                                1888–9

### PAUMANOK

Sea-beauty! stretch'd and basking!
One side thy inland ocean laving, broad, with copious com-
    merce, steamers, sails,
And one the Atlantic's wind caressing, fierce or gentle—
    mighty hulls dark-gliding in the distance.
Isle of sweet brooks of drinking-water—healthy air and soil!
Isle of the salty shore and breeze and brine!
1888                                                1888–9

### FROM MONTAUK POINT

I stand as on some mighty eagle's beak,
Eastward the sea absorbing, viewing, (nothing but sea and
    sky,)
The tossing waves, the foam, the ships in the distance.
The wild unrest, the snowy, curling caps—that inbound urge
    and urge of waves,
Seeking the shores forever.
1888                                                1888–9

### TO THOSE WHO'VE FAIL'D

To those who've fail'd, in aspiration vast,
To unnam'd soldiers fallen in front on the lead,

454

To calm, devoted engineers—to over-ardent travelers—to
    pilots on their ships,
To many a lofty song and picture without recognition—I'd
    rear a laurel-cover'd monument,
High, high above the rest—To all cut off before their time,
Possess'd by some strange spirit of fire,
Quench'd by an early death.
1888                                    1888–9

## A CAROL CLOSING SIXTY-NINE

A CAROL closing sixty-nine—a *résumé*—a repetition,
My lines in joy and hope continuing on the same,
Of ye, O God, Life, Nature, Freedom, Poetry;
Of you, my Land—your rivers, prairies, States—you, mottled
    Flag I love,
Your aggregate retain'd entire—Of north, south, east and
    west, your items all;
Of me myself—the jocund heart yet beating in my breast,
The body wreck'd, old, poor and paralyzed—the strange
    inertia falling pall-like round me,
The burning fires down in my sluggish blood not yet extinct,
The undiminish'd faith—the groups of loving friends.
1888                                      1888–9

## THE BRAVEST SOLDIERS

BRAVE, brave were the soldiers (high named to-day) who
    lived through the fight;
But the bravest press'd to the front and fell, unnamed, un-
    known.
1888                                      1888–9

## A FONT OF TYPE

THIS latent mine—these unlaunch'd voices—passionate
    powers,
Wrath, argument, or praise, or comic leer, or prayer devout,
(Not nonpareil, brevier, bourgeois, long primer merely,)
These ocean waves arousable to fury and to death,
Or sooth'd to ease and sheeny sun and sleep,
Within the pallid slivers slumbering.
1888                                      1888–9

## AS I SIT WRITING HERE

As I sit writing here, sick and grown old,
Not my least burden is that dulness of the years, querilities,
Ungracious glooms, aches, lethargy, constipation, whimper-
 ing *ennui*,
May filter in my daily songs.
1888             1888–9

## MY CANARY BIRD

Dɪᴅ we count great, O soul, to penetrate the themes of
 mighty books,
Absorbing deep and full from thoughts, plays, speculations?
But now from thee to me, caged bird, to feel thy joyous
 warble,
Filling the air, the lonesome room, the long forenoon,
Is it not just as great, O soul?
1888             1888–9

## QUERIES TO MY SEVENTIETH YEAR

Aᴘᴘʀᴏᴀᴄʜɪɴɢ, nearing, curious,
Thou dim, uncertain spectre—bringest thou life or death?
Strength, weakness, blindness, more paralysis and heavier?
Or placid skies and sun? Wilt stir the waters yet?
Or haply cut me short for good? Or leave me here as now,
Dull, parrot-like and old, with crack'd voice harping,
 screeching?
1888             1888–9

## THE WALLABOUT MARTYRS

*(In Brooklyn, in an old vault, mark'd by no special recogni-
tion, lie huddled at this moment the undoubtedly authentic remains of the stanchest and earliest Revolutionary patriots from
the British prison ships and prisons of the times of 1776–83, in
and around New York, and from all over Long Island; originally buried—many thousands of them—in trenches in the
Wallabout sands.)*

Gʀᴇᴀᴛᴇʀ than memory of Achilles or Ulysses,
More, more by far to thee than tomb of Alexander,

Those cart loads of old charnel ashes, scales and splints of
    mouldy bones,
Once living men—once resolute courage, aspiration, strength,
The stepping stones to thee to-day and here, America.
1888                                   1888–9

## THE FIRST DANDELION

SIMPLE and fresh and fair from winter's close emerging,
As if no artifice of fashion, business, politics, had ever been,
Forth from its sunny nook of shelter'd grass—innocent,
    golden, calm as the dawn,
The spring's first dandelion shows its trustful face.
1888                                   1888–9

## AMERICA

CENTRE of equal daughters, equal sons,
All, all alike endear'd, grown, ungrown, young or old,
Strong, ample, fair, enduring, capable, rich,
Perennial with the Earth, with Freedom, Law and Love,
A grand, sane, towering, seated Mother,
Chair'd in the adamant of Time.
1888                                   1888–9

## MEMORIES

How sweet the silent backward tracings!
The wanderings as in dreams—the meditation of old times
    resumed—their loves, joys, persons, voyages.
1888                                   1888–9

## TO-DAY AND THEE

THE appointed winners in a long-stretch'd game;
The course of Time and nations—Egypt, India, Greece and
    Rome;
The past entire, with all its heroes, histories, arts, experi-
    ments,
Its store of songs, inventions, voyages, teachers, books,
Garner'd for now and thee—To think of it!
The heirdom all converged in thee!
1888                                   1888–9

## AFTER THE DAZZLE OF DAY

AFTER the dazzle of day is gone,
Only the dark, dark night shows to my eyes the stars;
After the clangor of organ majestic, or chorus, or perfect
    band,
Silent, athwart my soul, moves the symphony true.
1888                                  1888–9

## ABRAHAM LINCOLN, BORN FEB. 12, 1809

### (*Publish'd Feb.* 12, 1888)

TO-DAY, from each and all, a breath of prayer—a pulse of
    thought,
To memory of Him—to birth of Him.
1888                                  1888–9

## OUT OF MAY'S SHOWS SELECTED

APPLE orchards, the trees all cover'd with blossoms;
Wheat fields carpeted far and near in vital emerald green;
The eternal, exhaustless freshness of each early morning;
The yellow, golden, transparent haze of the warm afternoon
    sun;
The aspiring lilac bushes with profuse purple or white
    flowers.
1888                                  1888–9

## HALCYON DAYS

NOT from successful love alone,
Nor wealth, nor honor'd middle age, nor victories of politics
    or war;
But as life wanes, and all the turbulent passions calm,
As gorgeous, vapory, silent hues cover the evening sky,
As softness, fulness, rest, suffuse the frame, like fresher,
    balmier air,
As the days take on a mellower light, and the apple at last
    hangs really finish'd and indolent-ripe on the tree,
Then for the teeming quietest, happiest days of all!
The brooding and blissful halcyon days!
1888                                  1888–9

## FANCIES AT NAVESINK

### THE PILOT IN THE MIST

Steaming the northern rapids—(an old St. Lawrence re-
    miniscence,
A sudden memory-flash comes back, I know not why,
Here waiting for the sunrise, gazing from this hill;)*
Again 'tis just at morning—a heavy haze contends with day-
    break,
Again the trembling, laboring vessel veers me—I press
    through foam-dash'd rocks that almost touch me,
Again I mark where aft the small thin Indian helmsman
Looms in the mist, with brow elate and governing hand.

### HAD I THE CHOICE

Had I the choice to tally greatest bards,
To limn their portraits, stately, beautiful, and emulate at
    will,
Homer with all his wars and warriors—Hector, Achilles,
    Ajax,
Or Shakspere's woe-entangled Hamlet, Lear, Othello—
    Tennyson's fair ladies,
Metre or wit the best, or choice conceit to wield in perfect
    rhyme, delight of singers;
These, these, O sea, all these I'd gladly barter,
Would you the undulation of one wave, its trick to me trans-
    fer,
Or breathe one breath of yours upon my verse,
And leave its odor there,

### YOU TIDES WITH CEASELESS SWELL

You tides with ceaseless swell! you power that does this
    work!
You unseen force, centripetal, centrifugal, through space's
    spread,
Rapport of sun, moon, earth, and all the constellations,

* Navesink—a sea-side mountain, lower entrance of New York Bay.

What are the messages by you from distant stars to us? what
  Sirius'? what Capella's?
What central heart—and you the pulse—vivifies all? what
  boundless aggregate of all?
What subtle indirection and significance in you? what clue to
  all in you? what fluid, vast identity,
Holding the universe with all its parts as one—as sailing in a
  ship?

## LAST OF EBB, AND DAYLIGHT WANING

LAST of ebb, and daylight waning,
Scented sea-cool landward making, smells of sedge and salt
  incoming,
With many a half-caught voice sent up from the eddies,
Many a muffled confession—many a sob and whisper'd
  word,
As of speakers far or hid.

How they sweep down and out! how they mutter!
Poets unnamed—artists greatest of any, with cherish'd lost
  designs,
Love's unresponse—a chorus of age's complaints—hope's
  last words,
Some suicide's despairing cry, *Away to the boundless waste,
  and never again return.*

On to oblivion then!
On, on, and do your part, ye burying, ebbing tide!
On for your time, ye furious debouché!

## AND YET NOT YOU ALONE

AND yet not you alone, twilight and burying ebb,
Nor you, ye lost designs alone—nor failures, aspirations;
I know, divine deceitful ones, your glamour's seeming;
Duly by you, from you, the tide and light again—duly the
  hinges turning,
Duly the needed discord-parts offsetting, blending,
Weaving from you, from Sleep, Night, Death itself,
The rhythmus of Birth eternal.

### PROUDLY THE FLOOD COMES IN

PROUDLY the flood comes in, shouting, foaming, advancing,
Long it holds at the high, with bosom broad outswelling,
All throbs, dilates—the farms, woods, streets of cities—
    workmen at work,
Mainsails, topsails, jibs, appear in the offing—steamers'
    pennants of smoke—and under the forenoon sun,
Freighted with human lives, gaily the outward bound, gaily
    the inward bound,
Flaunting from many a spar the flag I love.


### BY THAT LONG SCAN OF WAVES

BY that long scan of waves, myself call'd back, resumed upon
    myself,
In every crest some undulating light or shade—some retro-
    spect,
Joys, travels, studies, silent panoramas—scenes, ephemeral,
The long past war, the battles, hospital sights, the wounded
    and the dead,
Myself through every by-gone phase—my idle youth—old
    age at hand,
My three-score years of life summ'd up, and more, and
    past,
By any grand ideal tried, intentionless, the whole a nothing,
And haply yet some drop within God's scheme's ensemble—
    some wave, or part of wave,
Like one of yours, ye multitudinous ocean.


### THEN LAST OF ALL

THEN last of all, caught from these shores, this hill,
Of you O tides, the mystic human meaning:
Only by law of you, your swell and ebb, enclosing me the
    same,
The brain that shapes, the voice that chants this song.
1885                                                    1888–9

## ELECTION DAY, NOVEMBER, 1884

I<small>F</small> I should need to name, O Western World, your powerfulest
scene and show,

'Twould not be you, Niagara—nor you, ye limitless prairies
—nor your huge rifts of canyons, Colorado,

Nor you, Yosemite—nor Yellowstone, with all its spasmic
geyser loops ascending to the skies, appearing and disappearing,

Nor Oregon's white cones—nor Huron's belt of mighty lakes
—nor Mississippi's stream:

—This seething hemisphere's humanity, as now, I'd name—
*the still small voice* vibrating—America's choosing day,

(The heart of it not in the chosen—the act itself the main, the
quadrennial choosing,)

The stretch of North and South arous'd—sea-board and inland—Texas to Maine—the Prairie States—Vermont,
Virginia, California,

The final ballot-shower from East to West—the paradox and
conflict,

The countless snow-flakes falling—(a swordless conflict,

Yet more than all Rome's wars of old, or modern Napoleon's:) the peaceful choice of all,

Or good or ill humanity—welcoming the darker odds, the
dross:

—Foams and ferments the wine? it serves to purify—while
the heart pants, life glows:

These stormy gusts and winds waft precious ships,

Swell'd Washington's, Jefferson's, Lincoln's sails.

1884                                                    1888–9

## WITH HUSKY-HAUGHTY LIPS, O SEA!

W<small>ITH</small> husky-haughty lips, O sea!

Where day and night I wend thy surf-beat shore,

Imaging to my sense thy varied strange suggestions,

(I see and plainly list thy talk and conference here,)

Thy troops of white-maned racers racing to the goal,

Thy ample, smiling face, dash'd with the sparkling dimples of
the sun,

Thy brooding scowl and murk—thy unloos'd hurricanes,

Thy unsubduedness, caprices, wilfulness;

Great as thou art above the rest, thy many tears—a lack from
    all eternity in thy content,

(Naught but the greatest struggles, wrongs, defeats, could
    make thee greatest—no less could make thee,)

Thy lonely state—something thou ever seek'st and seek'st,
    yet never gain'st,

Surely some right withheld—some voice, in huge monoton-
    ous rage, of freedom-lover pent,

Some vast heart, like a planet's, chain'd and chafing in those
    breakers,

By lengthen'd swell, and spasm, and panting breath,

And rhythmic rasping of thy sands and waves,

And serpent hiss, and savage peals of laughter,

And undertones of distant lion roar,

(Sounding, appealing to the sky's deaf ear—but now, rapport
    for once,

A phantom in the night thy confidant for once,)

The first and last confession of the globe,

Outsurging, muttering from thy soul's abysms,

The tale of cosmic elemental passion,

Thou tellest to a kindred soul.

(1883)                                 1888–9


## DEATH OF GENERAL GRANT

As one by one withdraw the lofty actors,

From that great play on history's stage eterne,

That lurid, partial act of war and peace—of old and new
    contending,

Fought out through wrath, fears, dark dismays, and many a
    long suspense;

All past—and since, in countless graves receding, mellowing,

Victor's and vanquish'd—Lincoln's and Lee's—now thou
    with them,

Man of the mighty days—and equal to the days!

Thou from the prairies!—tangled and many-vein'd and hard
    has been thy part,

To admiration has it been enacted!

1885                                   1888–9

## RED JACKET (FROM ALOFT)

*(Impromptu on Buffalo City's monument to, and re-burial of
the old Iroquois orator, October 9, 1884)*

UPON this scene, this show,
Yielded to-day by fashion, learning, wealth,
(Nor in caprice alone—some grains of deepest meaning,)
Haply, aloft, (who knows?) from distant sky-clouds' blended
    shapes,
As some old tree, or rock or cliff, thrill'd with its soul,
Product of Nature's sun, stars, earth direct—a towering
    human form,
In hunting-shirt of film, arm'd with the rifle, a half-ironical
    smile curving its phantom lips,
Like one of Ossian's ghosts looks down.
(1884)                                1888–9

## WASHINGTON'S MONUMENT, FEBRUARY, 1885

AH, not this marble, dead and cold:
Far from its base and shaft expanding—the round zones
    circling, comprehending,
Thou, Washington, art all the world's, the continents' entire
    —not yours alone, America,
Europe's as well, in every part, castle of lord or laborer's
    cot,
Or frozen North, or sultry South—the African's—the Arab's
    in his tent,
Old Asia's there with venerable smile, seated amid her
    ruins;
(Greets the antique the hero new? 'tis but the same—the heir
    legitimate, continued ever,
The indomitable heart and arm—proofs of the never-broken
    line,
Courage, alertness, patience, faith, the same—e'en in defeat
    defeated not, the same:)
Wherever sails a ship, or house is built on land, or day or
    night,
Through teeming cities' streets, indoors or out, factories or
    farms,

Now, or to come, or past—where patriot wills existed or
    exist,
Wherever Freedom, pois'd by Toleration, sway'd by Law,
Stands or is rising thy true monument.
(1885?)                           1888-9

## OF THAT BLITHE THROAT OF THINE

*(More than eighty-three degrees north—about a good day's
steaming distance to the Pole by one of our fast oceaners in
clear water—Greely the explorer heard the song of a single
snow-bird merrily sounding over the desolation.)*

OF that blithe throat of thine from arctic bleak and blank,
I'll mind the lesson, solitary bird—let me too welcome chill-
    ing drifts,
E'en the profoundest chill, as now—a torpid pulse, a brain
    unnerv'd,
Old age land-lock'd within its winter bay—(cold, cold, O
    cold!)
These snowy hairs, my feeble arm, my frozen feet,
For them thy faith, thy rule I take, and grave it to the last;
Not summer's zones alone—not chants of youth, or south's
    warm tides alone,
But held by sluggish floes, pack'd in the northern ice, the
    cumulus of years,
These with gay heart I also sing.
(1884)                           1888-9

## BROADWAY

WHAT hurrying human tides, or day or night!
What passions, winnings, losses, ardors, swim thy waters!
What whirls of evil, bliss and sorrow, stem thee!
What curious questioning glances—glints of love!
Leer, envy, scorn, contempt, hope, aspiration!
Thou portal—thou arena—thou of the myriad long-drawn
    lines and groups!
(Could but thy flagstones, curbs, façades, tell their inimitable
    tales;
Thy windows rich, and huge hotels—thy side-walks wide;)

Thou of the endless sliding, mincing, shuffling feet!
Thou, like the parti-colored world itself—like infinite, teeming, mocking life!
Thou visor'd, vast, unspeakable show and lesson!
1888                                                    1888-9


## TO GET THE FINAL LILT OF SONGS

To get the final lilt of songs,
To penetrate the inmost lore of poets—to know the mighty ones,
Job, Homer, Eschylus, Dante, Shakspere, Tennyson, Emerson;
To diagnose the shifting-delicate tints of love and pride and doubt—to truly understand,
To encompass these, the last keen faculty and entrance-price,
Old age, and what it brings from all its past experiences.
1888                                                    1888-9


## OLD SALT KOSSABONE

FAR back, related on my mother's side,
Old Salt Kossabone, I'll tell you how he died:
(Had been a sailor all his life—was nearly 90—lived with his married grandchild, Jenny;
House on a hill, with view of bay at hand, and distant cape, and stretch to open sea;
The last of afternoons, the evening hours, for many a year his regular custom,
In his great arm chair by the window seated,
(Sometimes, indeed, through half the day,)
Watching the coming, going of the vessels, he mutters to himself—And now the close of all:
One struggling outbound brig, one day, baffled for long—cross-tides and much wrong going,
At last at nightfall strikes the breeze aright, her whole luck veering,
And swiftly bending round the cape, the darkness proudly entering, cleaving, as he watches,

"She's free—she's on her destination"—these the last words
    —when Jenny came, he sat there dead,
Dutch Kossabone, Old Salt, related on my mother's side, far
    back.
1888                                      1888-9

## THE DEAD TENOR

As down the stage again,
With Spanish hat and plumes, and gait inimitable,
Back from the fading lessons of the past, I'd call, I'd tell and
    own,
How much from thee! the revelation of the singing voice
    from thee!
(So firm—so liquid soft—again that tremulous, manly timbre!
The perfect singing voice—deepest of all to me the lesson—
    trial and test of all:)
How through those strains distill'd—how the rapt ears, the
    soul of me, absorbing
*Fernando's* heart, *Manrico's* passionate call, *Ernani's*, sweet
    *Gennaro's*,
I fold thenceforth, or seek to fold, within my chants trans-
    muting,
Freedom's and Love's and Faith's unloos'd cantabile,
(As perfume's, color's, sunlight's correlation:)
From these, for these, with these, a hurried line, dead tenor,
A wafted autumn leaf, dropt in the closing grave, the
    shovel'd earth,
To memory of thee.
1884                                        1888-9

## CONTINUITIES

*(From a talk I had lately with a German spiritualist)*

NOTHING is ever really lost, or can be lost,
No birth, identity, form—no object of the world,
Nor life, nor force, nor any visible thing;
Appearance must not foil, nor shifted sphere confuse thy
    brain.
Ample are time and space—ample the fields of Nature.
The body, sluggish, aged, cold—the embers left from earlier
    fires,

The light in the eye grown dim, shall duly flame again;
The sun now low in the west rises for mornings and for noons
　　continual;
To frozen clods ever the spring's invisible law returns,
With grass and flowers and summer fruits and corn.
1888　　　　　　　　　　　　　　　　　　　　1888-9

## YONNONDIO

(*The sense of the word is* lament for the aborigines. *It is an
Iroquois term; and has been used for a personal name.*)

A SONG, a poem of itself—the word itself a dirge,
Amid the wilds, the rocks, the storm and wintry night,
To me such misty, strange tableaux the syllables calling up;
Yonnondio—I see, far in the west or north, a limitless ravine,
　　with plains and mountains dark,
I see swarms of stalwart chieftains, medicine-men, and war-
　　riors,
As flitting by like clouds of ghosts, they pass and are gone in
　　the twilight,
(Race of the woods, the landscapes free, and the falls!
No picture, poem, statement, passing them to the future:)
Yonnondio! Yonnondio!—unlimn'd they disappear;
To-day gives place, and fades—the cities, farms, factories
　　fade;
A muffled sonorous sound, a wailing word is borne through
　　the air for a moment,
Then blank and gone and still, and utterly lost.
1887　　　　　　　　　　　　　　　　　　　　1888-9

## LIFE

EVER the undiscouraged, resolute, struggling soul of man;
(Have former armies fail'd? then we send fresh armies—and
　　fresh again;)
Ever the grappled mystery of all earth's ages old or new;
Ever the eager eyes, hurrahs, the welcome-clapping hands,
　　the loud applause;
Ever the soul dissatisfied, curious, unconvinced at last;
Struggling to-day the same—battling the same.
1888　　　　　　　　　　　　　　　　　　　　1888-9

## "GOING SOMEWHERE"

MY science-friend, my noblest woman-friend,
(Now buried in an English grave—and this a memory-leaf
    for her dear sake,)
Ended our talk—"The sum, concluding all we know of old
    or modern learning, intuitions deep,
"Of all Geologies—Histories—of all Astronomy—of Evolu-
    tion, Metaphysics all,
"Is, that we all are onward, onward, speeding slowly, surely
    bettering,
"Life, life an endless march, an endless army, (no halt, but it
    is duly over,)
"The world, the race, the soul—in space and time the uni-
    verses,
"All bound as is befitting each—all surely going some-
    where."

1887                                       1888–9


## SMALL THE THEME OF MY CHANT

### (*From the* 1867 *edition* "*L. of G.*")

SMALL the theme of my Chant, yet the greatest—namely,
    One's-Self—a simple, separate person. That, for the use
    of the New World, I sing,
Man's physiology complete, from top to toe, I sing. Not
    physiognomy alone, nor brain alone, is worthy for the
    Muse;—I say the Form complete is worthier far. The
    Female equally with the Male, I sing.
Nor cease at the theme of One's-Self. I speak the word of the
    modern, the word En-Masse.
My Days I sing, and the Lands—with interstice I knew of
    hapless War.
(O friend, whoe'er you are, at last arriving hither to com-
    mence, I feel through every leaf the pressure of your
    hand, which I return.
And thus upon our journey, footing the road, and more than
    once, and link'd together let us go.)

1867                                           1888–9

## TRUE CONQUERORS

Old farmers, travelers, workmen (no matter how crippled or
  bent,)
Old sailors, out of many a perilous voyage, storm and wreck,
Old soldiers from campaigns, with all their wounds, defeats
  and scars;
Enough that they've survived at all—long life's unflinching
  ones!
Forth from their struggles, trials, fights, to have emerged at
  all—in that alone,
True conquerors o'er all the rest.
1888                                                  1888–9


## THE UNITED STATES TO OLD WORLD CRITICS

Here first the duties of to-day, the lessons of the concrete,
Wealth, order, travel, shelter, products, plenty;
As of the building of some varied, vast, perpetual edifice,
Whence to arise inevitable in time, the towering roofs, the
  lamps,
The solid-planted spires tall shooting to the stars.
1888                                                  1888–9


## THE CALMING THOUGHT OF ALL

That coursing on, whate'er men's speculations,
Amid the changing schools, theologies, philosophies,
Amid the bawling presentations new and old,
The round earth's silent vital laws, facts, modes continue.
1888                                                  1888–9


## THANKS IN OLD AGE

Thanks in old age—thanks ere I go,
For health, the midday sun, the impalpable air—for life,
  mere life,
For precious ever-lingering memories, (of you my mother
  dear—you father—you, brothers, sisters, friends,)
For all my days—not those of peace alone—the days of war
  the same,

For gentle words, caresses, gifts from foreign lands,
For shelter, wine and meat—for sweet appreciation,
(You distant, dim unknown—or young or old—countless,
    unspecified, readers belov'd,
We never met, and ne'er shall meet—and yet our souls em-
    brace, long, close and long;)
For beings, groups, love, deeds, words, books—for colors,
    forms,
For all the brave strong men—devoted, hardy men—who've
    forward sprung in freedom's help, all years, all lands,
For braver, stronger, more devoted men—(a special laurel
    ere I go, to life's war's chosen ones,
The cannoneers of song and thought—the great artillerists—
    the foremost leaders, captains of the soul:)
As soldier from an ended war return'd—As traveler out of
    myriads, to the long procession retrospective,
Thanks—joyful thanks!—a soldier's, traveler's thanks.
1888                                  1888–9

## LIFE AND DEATH

THE two old, simple problems ever intertwined,
Close home, elusive, present, baffled, grappled.
By each successive age insoluble, pass'd on,
To ours to-day—and we pass on the same.
1888                                  1888–9

## THE VOICE OF THE RAIN

AND who art thou? said I to the soft-falling shower,
Which, strange to tell, gave me an answer, as here translated:
I am the Poem of Earth, said the voice of the rain,
Eternal I rise impalpable out of the land and the bottomless
    sea,
Upward to heaven, whence, vaguely form'd, altogether
    changed, and yet the same,
I descend to lave the drouths, atomies, dust-layers of the
    globe,
And all that in them without me were seeds only, latent, un-
    born;

And forever, by day and night, I give back life to my own
    origin and make pure and beautify it;
(For song, issuing from its birth-place, after fulfilment, wan-
    dering,
Reck'd or unreck'd, duly with love returns.)
(1885)                         1888-9

## SOON SHALL THE WINTER'S FOIL BE HERE

Soon shall the winter's foil be here;
Soon shall these icy ligatures unbind and melt—A little
    while,
And air, soil, wave, suffused shall be in softness, bloom and
    growth—a thousand forms shall rise
From these dead clods and chills as from low burial graves.
Thine eyes, ears—all thy best attributes—all that takes cog-
    nizance of natural beauty,
Shall wake and fill. Thou shalt perceive the simple shows,
    the delicate miracles of earth,
Dandelions, clover, the emerald grass, the early scents and
    flowers,
The arbutus under foot, the willow's yellow-green, the blos-
    soming plum and cherry;
With these the robin, lark and thrush, singing their songs—
    the flitting bluebird;
For such the scenes the annual play brings on.
1888                         1888-9

## WHILE NOT THE PAST FORGETTING

### (*Publish'd May* 30, 1888)

While not the past forgetting,
To-day, at least, contention sunk entire—peace, brotherhood
    uprisen;
For sign reciprocal our Northern, Southern hands,
Lay on the graves of all dead soldiers, North or South,
(Nor for the past alone—for meanings to the future,)
Wreaths of roses and branches of palm.
1888                         1888-9

## THE DYING VETERAN

*(A Long Island incident—early part of the nineteenth century)*

Amid these days of order, ease, prosperity,
Amid the current songs of beauty, peace, decorum,
I cast a reminiscence—(likely 'twill offend you,
I heard it in my boyhood;)—More than a generation since,
A queer old savage man, a fighter under Washington himself,
(Large, brave, cleanly, hot-blooded, no talker, rather spiritualistic,
Had fought in the ranks—fought well—had been all through the Revolutionary war,)
Lay dying—sons, daughters, church-deacons, lovingly tending him,
Sharping their sense, their ears, towards his murmuring, half-caught words:
"Let me return again to my war-days,
To the sights and scenes—to forming the line of battle,
To the scouts ahead reconnoitering,
To the cannons, the grim artillery,
To the galloping aids, carrying orders,
To the wounded, the fallen, the heat, the suspense,
The perfume strong, the smoke, the deafening noise;
Away with your life of peace!—your joys of peace!
Give me my old wild battle-life again!"
(1887)                                           1888–9

## STRONGER LESSONS

Have you learn'd lessons only of those who admired you, and were tender with you, and stood aside for you?
Have you not learn'd great lessons from those who reject you, and brace themselves against you? or who treat you with contempt, or dispute the passage with you?
1888                                              1888–9

## A PRAIRIE SUNSET

Shot gold, maroon and violet, dazzling silver, emerald, fawn,
The earth's whole amplitude and Nature's multiform power consign'd for once to colors;

The light, the general air possess'd by them—colors till now
    unknown,
No limit, confine—not the Western sky alone—the high
    meridian—North, South, all,
Pure luminous color fighting the silent shadows to the last.
1888                                         1888-9

## TWENTY YEARS

DOWN on the ancient wharf, the sand, I sit, with a new-
    comer chatting:
He shipp'd as green-hand boy, and sail'd away, (took some
    sudden, vehement notion;)
Since, twenty years and more have circled round and round,
While he the globe was circling round and round,—and now
    returns:
How changed the place—all the old land-marks gone—the
    parents dead;
(Yes, he comes back *to lay in port for good—to settle*—has a
    well-fill'd purse—no spot will do but this;)
The little boat that scull'd him from the sloop, now held in
    leash I see,
I hear the slapping waves, the restless keel, the rocking in the
    sand,
I see the sailor kit, the canvas bag, the great box bound with
    brass,
I scan the face all berry-brown and bearded—the stout-
    strong frame,
Dress'd in its russet suit of good Scotch cloth:
(Then what the told-out story of those twenty years? What
    of the future?)
(1887)                                       1888-9

## ORANGE BUDS BY MAIL FROM FLORIDA

(*Voltaire closed a famous argument by claiming that a ship
of war and the grand opera were proofs enough of civilization's
and France's progress, in his day.*)

A LESSER proof than old Voltaire's, yet greater,
Proof of this present time, and thee, thy broad expanse,
    America,

To my plain Northern hut, in outside clouds and snow,
Brought safely for a thousand miles o'er land and tide,
Some three days since on their own soil live-sprouting,
Now here their sweetness through my room unfolding,
A bunch of orange buds by mail from Florida.
1888                                        1888–9


## TWILIGHT

THE soft voluptuous opiate shades,
The sun just gone, the eager light dispell'd—(I too will soon
    be gone, dispell'd,)
A haze—nirwana—rest and night—oblivion.
(1887)                                      1888–9


## YOU LINGERING SPARSE LEAVES OF ME

YOU lingering sparse leaves of me on winter-nearing
    boughs,
And I some well-shorn tree of field or orchard-row;
You tokens diminute and lorn—(not now the flush of May,
    or July clover-bloom—no grain of August now;)
You pallid banner-staves—you pennants valueless—you
    overstay'd of time,
Yet my soul-dearest leaves confirming all the rest,
The faithfulest—hardiest—last.
1887                                        1888–9


## NOT MEAGRE, LATENT BOUGHS ALONE

NOT meagre, latent boughs alone, O songs! (scaly and bare,
    like eagles' talons,)
But haply for some sunny day (who knows?) some future
    spring, some summer—bursting forth,
To verdant leaves, or sheltering shade—to nourishing
    fruit,
Apples and grapes—the stalwart limbs of trees emerging—
    the fresh, free, open air,
And love and faith, like scented roses blooming.
1887                                        1888–9

## THE DEAD EMPEROR

(*Publish'd March* 10, 1888)

To-DAY, with bending head and eyes, thou, too, Columbia,
Less for the mighty crown laid low in sorrow—less for the
    Emperor,
Thy true condolence breathest, sendest out o'er many a salt
    sea mile,
Mourning a good old man—a faithful shepherd, patriot.
1888                                       1888–9

## AS THE GREEK'S SIGNAL FLAME

(*For Whittier's eightieth birthday, December* 17, 1887)

As the Greek's signal flame, by antique records told,
Rose from the hill-top, like applause and glory,
Welcoming in fame some special veteran, hero,
With rosy tinge reddening the land he'd served,
So I aloft from Mannahatta's ship-fringed shore,
Lift high a kindled brand for thee, Old Poet.
1887                                      1888–9

## THE DISMANTLED SHIP

IN some unused lagoon, some nameless bay,
On sluggish, lonesome waters, anchor'd near the shore,
An old, dismasted, gray and batter'd ship, disabled, done,
After free voyages to all the seas of earth, haul'd up at last
    and hawser'd tight,
Lies rusting, mouldering.
1888                                       1888–9

## NOW PRECEDENT SONGS, FAREWELL

Now precedent songs, farewell—by every name farewell,
(Trains of a staggering line in many a strange procession,
    waggons,
From ups and downs—with intervals—from elder years,
    mid-age, or youth,)
"In Cabin'd Ships", or "Thee Old Cause" or "Poets to
    Come"

Or "Paumanok", "Song of Myself", "Calamus", or "Adam",
Or "Beat! Beat! Drums!" or "To the Leaven'd Soil they
    Trod,"
Or "Captain! My Captain!" "Kosmos", "Quicksand Years",
    or "Thoughts",
"Thou Mother with thy Equal Brood", and many, many
    more unspecified,
From fibre heart of mine—from throat and tongue—(My
    life's hot pulsing blood,
The personal urge and form for me—not merely paper, auto-
    matic type and ink,)
Each song of mine—each utterance in the past—having its
    long, long history,
Of life or death, or soldier's wound, of country's loss or
    safety,
(O heaven! what flash and started endless train of all! com-
    pared indeed to that!
What wretched shred e'en at the best of all!)
1888                                      1888–9

## AN EVENING LULL

AFTER a week of physical anguish,
Unrest and pain, and feverish heat,
Toward the ending day a calm and lull comes on,
Three hours of peace and soothing rest of brain. *
1888                                      1888–9

## OLD AGE'S LAMBENT PEAKS

THE touch of flame—the illuminating fire—the loftiest look
    at last,
O'er city, passion, sea—o'er prairie, mountain, wood—the
    earth itself;
The airy, different, changing hues of all, in falling twilight,
Objects and groups, bearings, faces, reminiscences;

* The two songs on pages 476-477 ["Now Precedent Songs, Farewell"
and "an Evening Lull"] are eked out during an afternoon, June, 1888,
in my seventieth year, at a critical spell of illness. Of course no reader
and probably no human being at any time will ever have such phases of
emotional and solemn action as these involve to me. I feel in them an
end and close of all.

The calmer sight—the golden setting, clear and broad:
So much i' the atmosphere, the points of view, the situations
whence we scan,
Bro't out by them alone—so much (perhaps the best) unreck'd before;
The lights indeed from them—old age's lambent peaks.
1888                                                      1889


## AFTER THE SUPPER AND TALK

AFTER the supper and talk—after the day is done,
As a friend from friends his final withdrawal prolonging,
Good-bye and Good-bye with emotional lips repeating,
(So hard for his hand to release those hands—no more will
they meet,
No more for communion of sorrow and joy, of old and
young,
A far-stretching journey awaits him, to return no more,)
Shunning, postponing severance—seeking to ward off the
last word ever so little,
E'en at the exit-door turning—charges superfluous calling
back—e'en as he descends the steps,
Something to eke out a minute additional—shadows of
nightfall deepening,
Farewells, messages lessening—dimmer the forthgoer's vis-
age and form,
Soon to be lost for aye in the darkness—loth, O so loth to
depart!
Garrulous to the very last.
1887                                                    1888-9

# Good-bye My Fancy

(*Second Annex*)

## SAIL OUT FOR GOOD, EIDÓLON YACHT!

HEAVE the anchor short!
Raise main-sail and jib—steer forth,
O little white-hull'd sloop, now speed on really deep
    waters,
(I will not call it our concluding voyage,
But outset and sure entrance to the truest, best, maturest;)
Depart, depart from solid earth—no more returning to these
    shores,
Now on for aye our infinite free venture wending,
Spurning all yet tried ports, seas, hawsers, densities, gravi-
    tation,
Sail out for good, eidólon yacht of me!
1891                                    1891–2

## LINGERING LAST DROPS

AND whence and why come you?

We know not whence, (was the answer,)
We only know that we drift here with the rest,
That we linger'd and lagg'd—but were wafted at last, and are
    now here,
To make the passing shower's concluding drops,
1891                                    1891–2

## GOOD-BYE MY FANCY

GOOD-BYE* my fancy—(I had a word to say,
But 'tis not quite the time—The best of any man's word or say,
Is when its proper place arrives—and for its meaning,
I keep mine till the last.)
1891                                        1891-2


## ON, ON THE SAME, YE JOCUND TWAIN!

ON, on the same, ye jocund twain!
My life and recitative, containing birth, youth, mid-age years,
Fitful as motley-tongues of flame, inseparably twined and
    merged in one—combining all,
My single soul—aims, confirmations, failures, joys—Nor
    single soul alone,
I chant my nation's crucial stage, (America's, haply human-
    ity's)—the trial great, the victory great,
A strange *eclaircissement* of all the masses past, the eastern
    world, the ancient, medieval,
Here, here from wanderings, strayings, lessons, wars, defeats
    —here at the west a voice triumphant—justifying all,
A gladsome pealing cry—a song for once of utmost pride and
    satisfaction;
I chant from it the common bulk, the general average horde,
    (the best no sooner than the worst)—And now I chant
    old age,
(My verses, written first for forenoon life, and for the sum-
    mer's, autumn's spread,
I pass to snow-white hairs the same, and give to pulses win-
    ter-cool'd the same;)
As here in careless trill, I and my recitatives, with faith and
    love,

   * Behind a Good-bye there lurks much of the salutation of another
beginning—to me, Development, Continuity, Immortality, Transformation, are the chiefest life-meanings of Nature and Humanity, and
are the *sine qua non* of all facts, and each fact.
   Why do folks dwell so fondly on the last words, advice. appearance,
of the departing? Those last words are not samples of the best, which
involve vitality at its full, and balance, and perfect control and scope.
But they are valuable beyond measure to confirm and endorse the
varied train, facts, theories and faith of the whole preceding life.

Wafting to other work, to unknown songs, conditions,
On, on, ye jocund twain! continue on the same!
1891                                    1891–2


## MY 71st YEAR

AFTER surmounting three-score and ten,
With all their chances, changes, losses, sorrows,
My parents' deaths, the vagaries of my life, the many tearing
    passions of me, the war of '63 and '4,
As some old broken soldier, after a long, hot, wearying
    march, or haply after battle,
To-day at twilight, hobbling, answering company roll-call,
    *Here*, with vital voice,
Reporting yet, saluting yet the Officer over all.
1889                                    1891–2


## APPARITIONS

A VAGUE mist hanging 'round half the pages:
(Sometimes how strange and clear to the soul,
That all these solid things are indeed but apparitions, con-
    cepts, non-realities.)
1891                                    1891–2


## THE PALLID WREATH

SOMEHOW I cannot let it go yet, funeral though it is,
Let it remain back there on its nail suspended,
With pink, blue, yellow, all blanch'd, and the white now gray
    and ashy,
One wither'd rose put years ago for thee, dear friend;
But I do not forget thee. Hast thou then faded?
Is the odor exhaled? Are the colors, vitalities, dead?
No, while memories subtly play—the past vivid as ever;
For but last night I woke, and in that spectral ring saw
    thee,
Thy smile, eyes, face, calm, silent, loving as ever;
So let the wreath hang still awhile within my eye-reach,
It is not yet dead to me, nor even pallid.
1891                                    1891–2
    Q                                    W

## AN ENDED DAY

THE soothing sanity and blitheness of completion,
The pomp and hurried contest-glare and rush are done;
Now triumph! transformation! jubilate!*

1891                            1891-2

## OLD AGE'S SHIP & CRAFTY DEATH'S

FROM east and west across the horizon's edge,
Two mighty masterful vessels sailers steal upon us:
But we'll make race a-time upon the seas—a battle-contest
    yet! bear lively there!
(Our joys of strife and derring-do to the last!)
Put on the old ship all her power to-day!
Crowd top-sail, top-gallant and royal studding-sails,
Out challenge and defiance—flags and flaunting pennants
    added,
As we take to the open! take to the deepest, freest waters.

1890                            1891-2

* NOTE.—*Summer country life.—Several years.*—In my rambles and explorations I found a woody place near the creek, where for some reason the birds in happy mood seem'd to resort in unusual numbers. Especially at the beginning of the day, and again at the ending, I was sure to get there the most copious bird-concerts. I repair'd there frequently at sunrise——and also at sunset, or just before. . . . Once the question arose in me: Which is the best singing, the first or the latter-most? The first always exhilarated, and perhaps seem'd more joyous and stronger; but I always felt the sunset or late afternoon sounds more penetrating and sweeter—seem'd to touch the soul—often the evening thrushes, two or three of them, responding and perhaps blending. Though I miss'd some of the mornings, I found myself getting to be quite strictly punctual at the evening utterances.

ANOTHER NOTE.—"He went out with the tide and the sunset," was a phrase I heard from a surgeon describing an old sailor's death under peculiarly gentle conditions.

During the Secession War, 1863 and '4, visiting the Army Hospitals around Washington, I form'd the habit, and continued it to the end, whenever the ebb or flood tide began the latter part of the day, of punctually visiting those at that time populous wards of suffering men. Somehow (or I thought so) the effect of the hour was palpable. The badly wounded would get some ease, and would like to talk a little, or be talk'd to. Intellectual and emotional natures would be at their best: Deaths were always easier; medicines seem'd to have better effect when given then, and a lulling atmosphere would pervade the wards.

Similar influences, similar circumstances and hours, day-close, after great battles, even with all their horrors. I had more than once the same experience on the fields cover'd with fallen or dead.

## TO THE PENDING YEAR

HAVE I no weapon-word for thee—some message brief and
 fierce?
(Have I fought out and done indeed the battle?) Is there no
 shot left,
For all thy affectations, lisps, scorns, manifold silliness?
Nor for myself—my own rebellious self in thee?

Down, down, proud gorge!—though choking thee;
Thy bearded throat and high-borne forehead to the gutter;
Crouch low thy neck to eleemosynary gifts.
(1889)                                                    1891–2

### SHAKSPERE-BACON'S CIPHER

I DOUBT it not—then more, far more;
In each old song bequeath'd—in every noble page or text,
(Different—something unreck'd before—some unsuspected
 author,)
In every object, mountain, tree, and star—in every birth and
 life,
As part of each—evolv'd from each—meaning, behind the
 ostent,
A mystic cipher waits infolded.
1891                                                      1891–2

### LONG, LONG HENCE

AFTER a long, long course, hundreds of years, denials,
Accumulations, rous'd love and joy and thought,
Hopes, wishes, aspirations, ponderings, victories, myriads of
 readers,
Coating, compassing, covering—after ages' and ages' en-
 crustations,
Then only may these songs reach fruition.
1891                                                      1891–2

### BRAVO, PARIS EXPOSITION!

ADD to your show, before you close it, France,
With all the rest, visible, concrete, temples, towers, goods,
 machines and ores,
Our sentiment wafted from many million heart-throbs,
 ethereal but solid,

(We grand-sons and great-grand-sons do not forget your
  grand-sires,)
From fifty Nations and nebulous Nations, compacted, sent
  oversea to-day,
America's applause, love, memories and good-will.
1889                                                    1891–2

## INTERPOLATION SOUNDS

(*General Philip Sheridan was buried at the Cathedral,
Washington, D.C., August,* 1888, *with all the pomp, music, and
ceremonies of the Roman Catholic service.*)

OVER and through the burial chant,
Organ and solemn service, sermon, bending priests,
To me come interpolation sounds not in the show—plainly
  to me, crowding up the aisle and from the window,
Of sudden battle's hurry and harsh noises—war's grim game
  to sight and ear in earnest;
The scout call'd up and forward—the general mounted and
  his aids around him—the new-brought word—the in-
  stantaneous order issued;
The rifle crack—the cannon thud—the rushing forth of men
  from their tents;
The clank of cavalry—the strange celerity of forming ranks
  —the slender bugle note;
The sound of horses' hoofs departing—saddles, arms, accoutrements. *
1888                                                    1891–2

* NOTE.—CAMDEN, N.J., August 7, 1888.—Walt Whitman asks the
*New York Herald* "to add his tribute to Sheridan":
  "In the grand constellation of five or six names, under Lincoln's
Presidency, that history will bear for ages in her firmament as marking
the last life-throbs of secession, and beaming on its dying gasps,
Sheridan's will be bright. One consideration rising out of the now dead
soldier's example as it passes my mind, is worth taking notice of. If the
war had continued any long time these States, in my opinion, would
have shown and proved the most conclusive military talents ever
evinced by any nation on earth. That they possess'd a rank and file
ahead of all other known in points of quality and limitlessness of number are easily admitted. But we have, too, the eligibility of organizing,
handling and officering equal to the other. These two, with modern
arms, transportation and inventive American genius, would make the
United States, with earnestness, not only able to stand the whole
world, but conquer that world united against us."

## TO THE SUNSET BREEZE

AH, whispering, something again, unseen,
Where late this heated day thou enterest at my window, door,
Thou, laving, tempering all, cool-freshing, gently vitalizing
Me, old, alone, sick, weak-down, melted-worn with sweat;
Thou, nestling, folding close and firm yet soft, companion
    better than talk, book, art,
(Thou hast, O Nature! elements! utterance to my heart be-
    yond the rest—and this is of them,)
So sweet thy primitive taste to breathe within—thy soothing
    fingers on my face and hands,
Thou, messenger-magical strange bringer to body and spirit
    of me,
(Distances balk'd—occult medicines penetrating me from
    head to foot,)
I feel the sky, the prairies vast—I feel the mighty northern
    lakes,
I feel the ocean and the forest—somehow I feel the globe
    itself swift-swimming in space;
Thou blown from lips so loved, now gone—haply from end-
    less store, God-sent,
(For thou art spiritual, Godly, most of all known to my
    sense,)
Minister to speak to me, here and now, what word has never
    told, and cannot tell,
Art thou not universal concrete's distillation? Law's, all
    Astronomy's last refinement?
Hast thou no soul? Can I not know, identify thee?
1890                                          1891-2

## OLD CHANTS

AN ancient song, reciting, ending,
Once gazing toward thee, Mother of All,
Musing, seeking themes fitted for thee,
*Accept for me*, thou saidst, *the elder ballads*,
*And name for me before thou goest each ancient poet.*

(Of many debts incalculable,
Haply our New World's chiefest debt is to old poems.)

Ever so far back, preluding thee, America,
Old chants, Egyptian priests, and those of Ethiopia,
The Hindu epics, the Grecian, Chinese, Persian,
The Biblic books and prophets, and deep idyls of the Nazarene,
The Iliad, Odyssey, plots, doings, wanderings of Eneas,
Hesiod, Eschylus, Sophocles, Merlin, Arthur,
The Cid, Roland at Roncesvalles, the Nibelungen,
The troubadours, minstrels, minnesingers, skalds,
Chaucer, Dante, flocks of singing birds,
The Border Minstrelsy, the bye-gone ballads, feudal tales,
    essays, plays,
Shakspere, Schiller, Walter Scott, Tennyson,
As some vast wondrous weird dream-presences,
The great shadowy groups gathering around,
Darting their mighty masterful eyes forward at thee,
Thou! with as now thy bending neck and head, with cour-
    teous hand and word, ascending,
Thou! pausing a moment, drooping thine eyes upon them,
    blent with their music,
Well pleased, accepting all, curiously prepared for by them,
Thou enterest at thy entrance porch.
1891                                              1891-2


# A CHRISTMAS GREETING

*(From a Northern Star-Group to a Southern, 1889-90)*

WELCOME, Brazilian brother—thy ample place is ready;
A loving hand—a smile from the north—a sunny instant hail!
(Let the future care for itself, where it reveals its troubles,
    impedimentas,
Ours, ours the present throe, the democratic aim, the accept-
    ance and the faith;)
To thee to-day our reaching arm, our turning neck—to thee
    from us the expectant eye,
Thou cluster free! thou brilliant lustrous one! thou, learning
    well,
The true lesson of a nation's light in the sky,
(More shining than the Cross, more than the Crown,)
The height to be superb humanity.
(1889)                                            1891-2

## SOUNDS OF THE WINTER

SOUNDS of the winter too,
Sunshine upon the mountains—many a distant strain
From cheery railroad train—from nearer field, barn, house,
The whispering air—even the mute crops, garner'd apples,
    corn,
Children's and women's tones—rhythm of many a farmer
    and of flail,
An old man's garrulous lips among the rest, *Think not we
    give out yet,*
*Forth from these snowy hairs we keep up yet the lilt.*
1891                                          1891–2

## A TWILIGHT SONG

As I sit in twilight late alone by the flickering oak-flame,
Musing on long-pass'd war-scenes—of the countless buried
    unknown soldiers,
Of the vacant names, as unindented air's and sea's—the un-
    return'd,
The brief truce after battle, with grim burial-squads, and the
    deep-fill'd trenches
Of gather'd dead from all America, North, South, East,
    West, whence they came up,
From wooded Maine, New-England's farms, from fertile
    Pennsylvania, Illinois, Ohio,
From the measureless West, Virginia, the South, the Caro-
    linas, Texas,
(Even here in my room-shadows and half-lights in the noise-
    less flickering flames,
Again I see the stalwart ranks on-filing, rising—I hear the
    rhythmic tramp of the armies;)
You million unwrit names all, all—you dark bequest from all
    the war,
A special verse for you—a flash of duty long neglected—your
    mystic roll strangely gather'd here,
Each name recall'd by me from out the darkness and death's
    ashes,
Henceforth to be, deep, deep within my heart recording, for
    many a future year,

Your mystic roll entire of unknown names, or North or
     South,
Embalm'd with love in this twilight song.
1890                                                    1891–2


## WHEN THE FULL-GROWN POET CAME

WHEN the full-grown poet came,
Out spake pleased Nature (the round impassive globe, with
     all its shows of day and night,) saying, *He is mine;*
But out spake too the Soul of man, proud, jealous and unre-
     conciled, *Nay, he is mine alone;*
—Then the full-grown poet stood between the two, and took
     each by the hand;
And to-day and ever so stands, as blender, uniter, tightly
     holding hands,
Which he will never release until he reconciles the two,
And wholly and joyously blends them.
1891                                                    1891–2


## OSCEOLA

*(When I was nearly grown to manhood in Brooklyn, New
York (middle of 1838), I met one of the return'd U.S. Marines
from Fort Moultrie, S. C., and had long talks with him—
learn'd the occurrence below described—death of Osceola. The
latter was a young, brave, leading Seminole, in the Florida war
of that time—was surrender'd to our troops, imprison'd, and
literally died of "a broken heart", at Fort Moultrie. He
sicken'd of his confinement—the doctor and officers made
every allowance and kindness possible for him; then the close.)*

WHEN his hour for death had come,
He slowly rais'd himself from the bed on the floor,
Drew on his war-dress, shirt, leggings, and girdled the belt
     around his waist,
Call'd for vermilion paint (his looking-glass was held before
     him,)
Painted half his face and neck, his wrists, and back-hands,
Put the scalp-knife carefully in his belt—then lying down,
     resting a moment,

Rose again, half sitting, smiled, gave in silence his extended
hand to each and all,
Sank faintly low to the floor (tightly grasping the tomahawk
handle,)
Fix'd his look on wife and little children—the last:
(And here a line in memory of his name and death.)
1890                                                           1891-2

## A VOICE FROM DEATH

(*The Johnstown, Penn., cataclysm, May* 31, 1889)

A VOICE from Death, solemn and strange, in all his sweep and
power,
With sudden, indescribable blow—towns drown'd—human-
ity by thousands slain,
The vaunted work of thrift, goods, dwellings, forge, street,
iron bridge,
Dash'd pell-mell by the blow—yet usher'd life continuing on,
(Amid the rest, amid the rushing, whirling, wild debris,
A suffering woman saved—a baby safely born!)
Although I come and unannounc'd, in horror and in pang,
In pouring flood and fire, and wholesale elemental crash,
(this voice so solemn, strange,)
I too a minister of Deity.

Yea, Death, we bow our faces, veil our eyes to thee,
We mourn the old, the young untimely drawn to thee,
The fair, the strong, the good, the capable,
The household wreck'd, the husband and the wife, the en-
gulf'd forger in his forge,
The corpses in the whelming waters and the mud,
The gather'd thousands to their funeral mounds, and thou-
sands never found or gather'd.

Then after burying, mourning the dead,
(Faithful to them found or unfound, forgetting not, bearing
the past, here new musing,)
A day—a passing moment or an hour—America itself bends
low,
Silent, resign'd, submissive.

War, death, cataclysm like this, America,
Take deep to thy proud prosperous heart.

E'en as I chant, lo! out of death, and out of ooze and slime,
The blossoms rapidly blooming, sympathy, help, love,
From West and East, from South and North and over sea,
Its hot-spurr'd hearts and hands humanity to human aid
    moves on;
And from within a thought and lesson yet.

Thou ever-darting Globe! through Space and Air!
Thou waters that encompass us!
Thou that in all the life and death of us, in action or in sleep!
Thou laws invisible that permeate them and all,
Thou that in all, and over all, and through and under all,
    incessant!
Thou! thou! the vital, universal, giant force resistless, sleep-
    less, calm,
Holding Humanity as in thy open hand, as some ephemeral
    toy,
How ill to e'er forget thee!

For I too have forgotten,
(Wrapt in these little potencies of progress, politics, culture,
    wealth, inventions, civilization,)
Have lost my recognition of your silent ever-swaying power,
    ye mighty, elemental throes,
In which and upon which we float, and every one of us is
    buoy'd.

1889                                              1891-2

## A PERSIAN LESSON

FOR his o'erarching and last lesson the greybeard sufi,
In the fresh scent of the morning in the open air,
On the slope of a teeming Persian rose-garden,
Under the ancient chestnut-tree wide spreading its branches,
Spoke to the young priests and students.

Finally my children, to envelop each word, each part of the
    rest,
Allah is all, all, all—is immanent in every life and object,

May-be at many and many-a-more removes—yet Allah,
  Allah, Allah is there.

"Has the estray wander'd far?  Is the reason-why strangely
  hidden?
Would you sound below the restless ocean of the entire world?
Would you know the dissatisfaction? the urge and spur of
  every life;
The something never still'd—never entirely gone? the invisible need of every seed?

"It is the central urge in every atom,
(Often unconscious, often evil, downfallen,)
To return to its divine source and origin, however distant,
Latent the same in subject and in object, without one excep-
  tion."
1891                                                    1891-2

## THE COMMONPLACE

THE commonplace I sing;
How cheap is health! how cheap nobility!
Abstinence, no falsehood, no gluttony, lust;
The open air I sing, freedom, toleration,
(Take here the mainest lesson—less from books—less from
  the schools,)
The common day and night—the common earth and waters,
Your farm—your work, trade, occupation,
The democratic wisdom underneath, like solid ground for all.
1891                                                    1891-2

## "THE ROUNDED CATALOGUE DIVINE
## COMPLETE"

*(Sunday —— — ——. —Went this forenoon to church. A
college professor, Rev. Dr. ——, gave us a fine sermon, during
which I caught the above words; but the minister included in his
"rounded catalogue" letter and spirit, only the esthetic things,
and entirely ignored what I name in the following:)*

THE devilish and the dark, the dying and diseas'd,
The countless (nineteen-twentieths) low and evil, crude and
  savage,

The crazed, prisoners in jail, the horrible, rank, malig-
nant,
Venom and filth, serpents, the ravenous sharks, liars, the
dissolute;
(What is the part the wicked and the loathsome bear within
earth's orbic scheme?)
Newts, crawling things in slime and mud, poisons,
The barren soil, the evil men, the slag and hideous rot.

1891                                                      1891–2


## MIRAGES

*(Noted verbatim after a supper-talk out doors in Nevada with
two old miners)*

MORE experiences and sights, stranger, than you'd think
for;
Times again, now mostly just after sunrise or before sunset,
Sometimes in spring, oftener in autumn, perfectly clear
weather, in plain sight,
Camps far or near, the crowded streets of cities and the shop-
fronts,
(Account for it or not—credit or not—it is all true,
And my mate there could tell you the like—we have often
confab'd about it,)
People and scenes, animals, trees, colors and lines, plain as
could be,
Farms and dooryards of home, paths border'd with box,
lilacs in corners,
Weddings in churches, thanksgiving dinners, returns of long-
absent sons,
Glum funerals, the crape-veil'd mother and the daughters,
Trials in courts, jury and judge, the accused in the box,
Contestants, battles, crowds, bridges, wharves,
Now and then mark'd faces of sorrow or joy,
(I could pick them out this moment if I saw them again,)
Show'd to me just aloft to the right in the sky-edge,
Or plainly there to the left on the hill-tops.

1891                                                      1891–2

## L. OF G.'S PURPORT

NOT to exclude or demarcate, or pick out evils from their
formidable masses (even to expose them,)
But add, fuse, complete, extend—and celebrate the immortal
and the good.

Haughty this song, its words and scope,
To span vast realms of space and time,
Evolution—the cumulative—growths and generations.

Begun in ripen'd youth and steadily pursued,
Wandering, peering, dallying with all—war, peace, day and
night absorbing,
Never even for one brief hour abandoning my task,
I end it here in sickness, poverty, and old age.

I sing of life, yet mind me well of death:
To-day shadowy Death dogs my steps, my seated shape, and
has for years—
Draws sometimes close to me, as face to face.
1891                                                      1891-2


## THE UNEXPRESS'D

How dare one say it?
After the cycles, poems, singers, plays,
Vaunted Ionia's, India's—Homer, Shakspere—the long, long
times, thick dotted roads, areas,
The shining clusters and the Milky Ways of stars—Nature's
pulses reap'd,
All retrospective passions, heroes, war, love, adoration,
All ages' plummets dropt to their utmost depths,
All human lives, throats, wishes, brains—all experiences'
utterance;
After the countless songs, or long or short, all tongues, all
lands,
Still something not yet told in poesy's voice or print— some-
thing lacking,
(Who knows? the best yet unexpress'd and lacking.)
1891                                                      1891-2

## GRAND IS THE SEEN

GRAND is the seen, the light, to me—grand are the sky and
    stars,
Grand is the earth, and grand are lasting time and space,
And grand their laws, so multiform, puzzling, evolutionary;
But grander far the unseen soul of me, comprehending, en-
    dowing all those,
Lighting the light, the sky and stars, delving the earth, sailing
    the sea,
(What were all those, indeed, without thee, unseen soul? of
    what amount without thee?)
More evolutionary, vast, puzzling, O my soul!
More multiform far—more lasting thou than they.
1891                                        1891–2

## UNSEEN BUDS

UNSEEN buds, infinite, hidden well,
Under the snow and ice, under the darkness, in every square
    or cubic inch,
Germinal, exquisite, in delicate lace, microscopic, unborn,
Like babes in wombs, latent, folded, compact, sleeping;
Billions of billions, and trillions of trillions of them waiting,
(On earth and in the sea—the universe—the stars there in the
    heavens,)
Urging slowly, surely forward, forming endless,
And waiting ever more, forever more behind.
1891                                        1891–2

## GOOD-BYE MY FANCY!

GOOD-BYE my Fancy!
Farewell dear mate, dear love!
I'm going away, I know not where,
Or to what fortune, or whether I may ever see you again,
So Good-bye my Fancy.

Now for my last—let me look back a moment;
The slower fainter ticking of the clock is in me,
Exit, nightfall, and soon the heart-thud stopping.

Long have we lived, joy'd, caress'd together;
Delightful!—now separation—Good-bye my Fancy.

Yet let me not be too hasty,
Long indeed have we lived, slept, filter'd, become really
    blended into one;
Then if we die we die together, (yes, we'll remain one,)
If we go anywhere we'll go together to meet what happens,
May-be we'll be better off and blither, and learn something,
May-be it is yourself now really ushering me to the true songs,
    (who knows?)
May-be it is you the mortal knob really undoing, turning—
    so now finally,
Good-bye—and hail! my Fancy.
1891                                                    1891-2

# Old Age Echoes

*(Posthumous Additions)*

### TO SOAR IN FREEDOM AND IN FULLNESS OF POWER

I HAVE not so much emulated the birds that musically sing,
I have abandon'd myself to flights, broad circles.
The hawk, the seagull, have far more possess'd me than the
    canary or mocking-bird,
I have not felt to warble and trill, however sweetly,
I have felt to soar in freedom and in the fullness of power,
    joy, volition.
1897                                                    1897


### THEN SHALL PERCEIVE

IN softness, languor, bloom, and growth,
Thine eyes, ears, all thy sense—thy loftiest attribute—all that
    takes cognizance of beauty,
Shall rouse and fill—then shall perceive!
1897                                                    1897


### THE FEW DROPS KNOWN

OF heroes, history, grand events, premises, myths, poems,
The few drops known must stand for oceans of the un-
    known,
On this beautiful and thick peopl'd earth, here and there a
    little specimen put on record,
A little of Greeks and Romans, a few Hebrew canticles, a few
    death odors as from graves, from Egypt—
What are they to the long and copious retrospect of anti-
    quity?
1897                                                    1897

## ONE THOUGHT EVER AT THE FORE

ONE thought ever at the fore—
That in the Divine Ship, the World, breasting Time and
    Space,
All Peoples of the globe together sail, sail the same voyage,
    are bound to the same destination.
1897                                                      1897

## WHILE BEHIND ALL FIRM AND ERECT

WHILE behind all, firm and erect as ever,
Undismay'd amid the rapids—amid the irresistible and
    deadly urge,
Stands a helmsman, with brow elate and strong hand.
1897                                                      1897

## A KISS TO THE BRIDE

### *Marriage of Nelly Grant, May* 21, 1874

SACRED, blithesome, undenied,
With benisons from East and West,
And salutations North and South,
Through me indeed to-day a million hearts and hands,
Wafting a million loves, a million soulfelt prayers;
—Tender and true remain the arm that shields thee!
Fair winds always fill the ship's sails that sail thee!
Clear sun by day, and light stars at night, beam on thee!
Dear girl—through me the ancient privilege too,
For the New World, through me, the old, old wedding greeting,
O youth and health! O sweet Missouri rose! O bonny bride!
Yield thy red cheeks, thy lips, to-day,
Unto a Nation's loving kiss.
1874                                                      1897

## NAY, TELL ME NOT TO-DAY THE PUBLISH'D SHAME

### *Winter of* 1873, *Congress in Session*

NAY, tell me not to-day the publish'd shame,
Read not to-day the journal's crowded page,
The merciless reports still branding forehead after forehead,
The guilty column following guilty column.

To-day to me the tale refusing,
Turning from it—from the white capitol turning,
Far from these swelling domes, topt with statues,
More endless, jubilant, vital visions rise
Unpublish'd, unreported.

Through all your quiet ways, or North or South, you Equal
    States, you honest farms,
Your million untold manly healthy lives, or East or West,
    city or country,
Your noiseless mothers, sisters, wives, unconscious of their
    good,
Your mass of homes nor poor nor rich, in visions rise—(even
    your excellent poverties,)
Your self-distilling, never-ceasing virtues, self-denials, graces,
Your endless base of deep integrities within, timid but cer-
    tain,
Your blessings steadily bestow'd, sure as the light, and still,
(Plunging to these as a determin'd diver down the deep
    hidden waters,)
These, these to-day I brood upon—all else refusing, these
    will I con,
To-day to these give audience.
1873                                            1897

## SUPPLEMENT HOURS

SANE, random, negligent hours,
Sane, easy, culminating hours,
After the flush, the Indian summer, of my life,
Away from Books—away from Art—the lesson learn'd,
    pass'd o'er,
Soothing, bathing, merging all—the sane, magnetic,
Now for the day and night themselves—the open air,
Now for the fields, the seasons, insects, trees—the rain and
    snow,
Where wild bees flitting hum,
Or August mulleins grow, or winter's snowflakes fall,
Or stars in the skies roll round—
The silent sun and stars.
1897                                            1897

## OF MANY A SMUTCH'D DEED REMINISCENT

FULL of wickedness, I—of many a smutch'd deed reminiscent—of worse deeds capable,
Yet I look composedly upon nature, drink day and night the
joys of life, and await death with perfect equanimity.
Because of my tender and boundless love for him I love and
because of his boundless love for me.

1897                                                                    1897


## TO BE AT ALL

*(Cf. Stanza 27, "Song of Myself," p. 53)*

To be at all—what is better than that?
I think if there were nothing more developed, the clam in its
callous shell in the sand were august enough.
I am not in any callous shell;
I am cased with supple conductors, all over,
They take every object by the hand, and lead it within me;
They are thousands, each one with his entry to himself;
They are always watching with their little eyes, from my head
to my feet;
One no more than a point lets in and out of me such bliss and
magnitude,
I think I could lift the girder of the house away if it lay be-
tween me and whatever I wanted.

1855                                                                    1897


## DEATH'S VALLEY

*To accompany a picture; by request. "The Valley of the
Shadow of Death," from the painting by George Inness*

NAY, do not dream, designer dark,
Thou hast portray'd or hit thy theme entire;
I, hoverer of late by this dark valley, by its confines, having
glimpses of it,
Here enter lists with thee, claiming my right to make a sym-
bol too.

For I have seen many wounded soldiers die,
After dread suffering—have seen their lives pass off with smiles;
And I have watch'd the death-hours of the old; and seen the infant die;
The rich with all his nurses and his doctors;
And then the poor, in meagreness and poverty;
And I myself for long, O Death, have breath'd my every breath
Amid the nearness and the silent thought of thee.
And out of these and thee,
I make a scene, a song (not fear of thee,
Nor gloom's ravines, nor bleak, nor dark—for I do not fear thee,
Nor celebrate the struggle, or contortion, or hard-tied knot),
Of the broad blessed light and perfect air, with meadows, rippling tides, and trees and flowers and grass,
And the low hum of living breeze—and in the midst God's beautiful eternal right hand,
Thee, holiest minister of Heaven—thee, envoy, usherer, guide at last of all,
Rich, florid, loosener of the stricture-knot call'd life,
Sweet, peaceful, welcome Death.
1892                                                                 1897


## ON THE SAME PICTURE

*Intended for first stanza of "Death's Valley"*

AYE, well I know 'tis ghastly to descend that valley:
Preachers, musicians, poets, painters, always render it,
Philosophs exploit—the battlefield, the ship at sea, the myriad beds, all lands,
All, all the past have enter'd, the ancientest humanity we know,
Syria's, India's, Egypt's, Greece's, Rome's;
Till now for us under our very eyes spreading the same to-day,
Grim, ready, the same to-day, for entrance, yours and mine,
Here, here 'tis limn'd.
1892                                                                 1897

## A THOUGHT OF COLUMBUS

THE mystery of mysteries, the crude and hurried ceaseless
    flame, spontaneous, bearing on itself.
The bubble and the huge, round, concrete orb!
A breath of Deity, as thence the bulging universe unfolding!
The many issuing cycles from their precedent minute!
The eras of the soul incepting in an hour,
Haply the widest, farthest evolutions of the world and
    man.

Thousands and thousands of miles hence, and now four
    centuries back,
A mortal impulse thrilling its brain cell,
Reck'd or unreck'd, the birth can no longer be postpon'd:
A phantom of the moment, mystic, stalking, sudden,
Only a silent thought, yet toppling down of more than walls
    of brass or stone.
(A flutter at the darkness' edge as if old Time's and Space's
    secret near revealing.)
A thought! a definite thought works out in shape.
Four hundred years roll on.
The rapid cumulus—trade, navigation, war, peace, demo-
    cracy, roll on;
The restless armies and the fleets of time following their
    leader—the old camps of ages pitch'd in newer, larger
    areas,
The tangl'd, long-deferr'd, éclaircissement of human life and
    hopes boldly begins untying,
As here to-day up-grows the Western World.

(An added word yet to my song, far Discoverer, as ne'er
    before sent back to son of earth—
If still thou hearest, hear me,
Voicing as now—lands, races, arts, bravas to thee,
O'er the long backward path to thee—one vast consensus
    north, south, east, west,
Soul plaudits! acclamation! reverent echoes!
One manifold, huge memory to thee! oceans and lands!
The modern world to thee and thought of thee!)
(1891)                                 1897

# Uncollected and Rejected Poems

## AMBITION

ONE day an obscure youth, a wanderer,
Known but to few, lay musing with himself
About the chances of his future life.
In that youth's heart, there dwelt the coal Ambition,
Burning and glowing; and he asked himself,
"Shall I, in time to come, be great and famed?"
Now soon an answer wild and mystical
Seemed to sound forth from out the depths of air;
And to the gazer's eye appeared a shape
Like one as of a cloud—and thus it spoke:

"O, many a panting, noble heart
    Cherishes in its deep recess
The hope to win renown o'er earth
    From Glory's prized caress.

"And some will win that envied goal,
    And have their deeds known far and wide;
And some—by far the most—will sink
    Down in oblivion's tide.

"But *thou*, who visions bright dost cull
    From the imagination's store,
With dreams, such as the youthful dream
    Of grandeur, love, and power,

"Fanciest that thou shalt build a name
    And come to have the nations know
What conscious might dwells in the brain
    That throbs beneath that brow?

"And see thick countless ranks of men
    Fix upon *thee* their reverent gaze—

And listen to the plaudits loud
   To *thee* that thousands raise?

"Weak, childish soul! the very place
   That pride has made for folly's rest;
What thoughts, with vanity all rife,
   Fill up thy heaving breast!

"At night, go view the solemn stars
   Those wheeling worlds through time the same—
How puny seem the widest power,
   The proudest mortal name!

"Think too, that all, lowly and rich,
   Dull idiot mind and teeming sense,
Alike must sleep the endless sleep,
   A hundred seasons hence.

"So, frail one, never more repine,
   Though thou livest on obscure, unknown;
Though after death unsought may be
   Thy markless resting stone."

And as these accents dropped in the youth's ears,
He felt him sick at heart; for many a month
His fancy had amused and charmed itself
With lofty aspirations, visions fair
Of what he *might be*. And it pierced him sore
To have his airy castles thus dashed down.

1842

## BLOOD-MONEY

*"Guilty of the body and tne blood of Christ"*

### 1

OF olden time, when it came to pass
That the beautiful god, Jesus, should finish his work on earth,
Then went Judas, and sold the divine youth,
And took pay for his body.

Curs'd was the deed, even before the sweat of the clutching
　　hand grew dry;
And darkness frown'd upon the seller of the like of God,
Where, as though earth lifted her breast to throw him from
　　her, and heaven refused him,
He hung in the air, self-slaughter'd.

The cycles, with their long shadows, have stalk'd silently
　　forward,
Since those ancient days—many a pouch enwrapping mean-
　　while
Its fee, like that paid for the son of Mary.

And still goes one, saying,
"What will ye give me, and I will deliver this man unto
　　you?"
And they make the covenant, and pay the pieces of silver.


2

Look forth, deliverer,
Look forth, first-born of the dead,
Over the tree-tops of Paradise;
See thyself in yet continued bonds,
Toilsome and poor, thou bear'st man's form again,
Thou art reviled, scourged, put into prison,
Hunted from the arrogant equality of the rest;
With staves and swords throng the willing servants of
　　authority,
Again they surround thee, mad with devilish spite;
Toward thee stretch the hands of a multitude, like vultures'
　　talons,
The meanest spit in thy face, they smite thee with their
　　palms;
Bruised, bloody, and pinion'd is thy body,
More sorrowful than death is thy soul.

Witness of anguish, brother of slaves,
Not with thy price closed the price of thine image:
And still Iscariot plies his trade.
1850

## RESURGEMUS

SUDDENLY, out of its stale and drowsy air, the air of slaves,
Like lightning Europe le'pt forth,
Sombre, superb and terrible,
As Ahimoth, brother of Death.
God, 'twas delicious!
That brief, tight, glorious grip
Upon the throats of kings.
You liars paid to defile the People,

Mark you now:
Not for numberless agonies, murders, lusts,
For court thieving in its manifold mean forms,
Worming from his simplicity the poor man's wages;
For many a promise sworn by royal lips
And broken, and laughed at in the breaking;
Then, in their power, not for all these,
Did a blow fall in personal revenge,
Or a hair draggle in blood:
The People scorned the ferocity of kings.

But the sweetness of mercy brewed bitter destruction,
And frightened rulers come back:
Each comes in state, with his train,
Hangman, priest, and tax-gatherer,
Soldier, lawyer, and sycophant;
As appalling procession of locusts,
And the king struts grandly again.

Yet behind all, lo, a Shape
Vague as the night, draped interminably,
Head, front and form, in scarlet folds,
Whose face and eyes none may see,
Out of its robes only this,
The red robes, lifted by the arm,
One finger pointed high over the top,
Like the head of a snake appears.

Meanwhile, corpses lie in new-made graves,
Bloody corpses of young men;
The rope of the gibbet hangs heavily,

The bullets of tyrants are flying,
The creatures of power laugh aloud:
And all these things bear fruits, and they are good.

Those corpses of young men,
Those martyrs that hang from the gibbets,
Those hearts pierced by the grey lead,
Cold and motionless as they seem,
Live elsewhere with undying vitality;
They live in other young men, O, kings,
They live in brothers, again ready to defy you;
They were purified by death,
They were taught and exalted.
Not a grave of those slaughtered ones,
But is growing its seed of freedom,
In its turn to bear seed,
Which the winds shall carry afar and resow,
And the rain nourish.
Not a disembodied spirit
Can the weapon of tyrants let loose,
But it shall stalk invisibly over the earth,
Whispering, counselling, cautioning.

Liberty, let others despair of thee,
But I will never despair of thee:
Is the house shut? Is the master away?
Nevertheless, be ready, be not weary of watching,
He will surely return; his messengers come anon.
1850

## GREAT ARE THE MYTHS

### 1

GREAT are the myths—I too delight in them;
Great are Adam and Eve—I too look back and accept them;
Great the risen and fallen nations, and their poets, women,
    sages, inventors, rulers, warriors, and priests.

Great is Liberty! great is Equality! I am their follower;
Helmsmen of nations, choose your craft! where you sail, I sail,
I weather it out with you, or sink with you.

Great is Youth—equally great is Old Age—great are the Day
and Night;
Great is Wealth—great is Poverty—great is Expression—
great is Silence.

Youth, large, lusty, loving—Youth, full of grace, force, fascination!
Do you know that Old Age may come after you, with equal
grace, force, fascination?

Day, full-blown and splendid—Day of the immense sun,
action, ambition, laughter,
The Night follows close, with millions of suns, and sleep, and
restoring darkness.

Wealth, with the flush hand, fine clothes, hospitality;
But then the Soul's wealth, which is candor, knowledge,
pride, enfolding love;
(Who goes for men and women showing Poverty richer than
wealth?)

Expression of speech! in what is written or said, forget not
that Silence is also expressive,
That anguish as hot as the hottest, and contempt as cold as
the coldest, may be without words.

2

Great is the Earth, and the way it became what it is;
Do you imagine it has stopt at this? the increase abandon'd?
Understand then that it goes as far onward from this, as this
is from the times when it lay in covering waters and
gases, before man had appear'd.

Great is the quality of Truth in man;
The quality of truth in man supports itself through all
changes,
It is inevitably in the man—he and it are in love, and never
leave each other.

The truth in man is no dictum, it is vital as eyesight;
If there be any Soul, there is truth—if there be man or woman
     there is truth—if there be physical or moral, there is
     truth;
If there be equilibrium or volition, there is truth—if there be
     things at all upon the earth, there is truth.

O truth of the earth! I am determin'd to press my way to-
     ward you;
Sound your voice! I scale mountains, or dive in the sea after
     you.

### 3

Great is Language—it is the mightiest of the sciences,
It is the fulness, color, form, diversity of the earth, and of
     men and women, and of all qualities and processes;
It is greater than wealth—it is greater than buildings, ships,
     religions, paintings, music.

Great is the English speech—what speech is so great as the
     English?
Great is the English brood—what brood has so vast a des-
     tiny as the English?
It is the mother of the brood that must rule the earth with the
     new rule;
The new rule shall rule as the Soul rules, and as the love,
     justice, equality in the Soul rule.

Great is Law—great are the few old land-marks of the law,
They are the same in all times, and shall not be disturb'd.

### 4

Great is Justice!
Justice is not settled by legislators and laws—it is in the Soul;
It cannot be varied by statutes, any more than love, pride,
     the attraction of gravity, can;
It is immutable—it does not depend on majorities—majori-
     ties or what not, come at last before the same passion-
     less and exact tribunal.

For justice are the grand natural lawyers, and perfect judges
   —it is in their Souls;
It is well assorted—they have not studied for nothing—the
   great includes the less;
They rule on the highest grounds—they oversee all eras,
   states, administrations.

The perfect judge fears nothing—he could go front to front
   before God;
Before the perfect judge all shall stand back—life and death
   shall stand back—heaven and hell shall stand back.

5

Great is Life, real and mystical, wherever and whoever;
Great is Death—sure as life holds all parts together, Death
   holds all parts together.

Has Life much purport?—Ah, Death has the greatest purport.
1855

## POEM OF REMEMBRANCE FOR A GIRL OR A BOY OF THESE STATES

You just maturing youth! You male or female!
Remember the organic compact of These States,
Remember the pledge of the Old Thirteen thenceforward to
   the rights, life, liberty, equality of man,
Remember what was promulged by the founders, ratified by
   The States, signed in black and white by the Commis-
   sioners, and read by Washington at the head of the
   army,
Remember the purposes of the founders,—Remember Wash-
   ington;
Remember the copious humanity streaming from every
   direction toward America;
Remember the hospitality that belongs to nations and men;
   (Cursed be nation, woman, man, without hospitality!)
Remember, government is to subserve individuals,

Not any, not the President, is to have one jot more than you
or me,
Not any habitan of America is to have one jot less than you
or me.

Anticipate when the thirty or fifty millions, are to become the
hundred or two hundred millions, of equal freemen and
freewomen, amicably joined.

Recall ages—One age is but a part—ages are but a part;
Recall the angers, bickerings, delusions, superstitions, of the
idea of caste,
Recall the bloody cruelties and crimes.

Anticipate the best women;
I say an unnumbered new race of hardy and well-defined
women are to spread through all These States,
I say a girl fit for These States must be free, capable, dauntless, just the same as a boy.

Anticipate your own life—retract with merciless power,
Shirk nothing—retract in time—Do you see those errors,
diseases, weaknesses, lies, thefts?
Do you see that lost character?—Do you see decay, consumption, rum-drinking, dropsy, fever, mortal cancer or
inflammation?
Do you see death, and the approach of death?
1856

## THINK OF THE SOUL

Think of the Soul;
I swear to you that body of yours gives proportions to your
Soul somehow to live in other spheres;
I do not know how, but I know it is so.

Think of loving and being loved;
I swear to you, whoever you are, you can interfuse yourself
with such things that everybody that sees you shall look
longingly upon you.

Think of the past;
I warn you that in a little while others will find their past in
    you and your times.

The race is never separated—nor man nor woman escapes;
All is inextricable—things, spirits, Nature, nations, you too
    —from precedents you come.

Recall the ever-welcome defiers, (The mothers precede them;)
Recall the sages, poets, saviors, inventors, lawgivers, of the
    earth;
Recall Christ, brother of rejected persons—brother of slaves,
    felons, idiots, and of insane and diseas'd persons.

Think of the time when you were not yet born;
Think of times you stood at the side of the dying;
Think of the time when your own body will be dying.

Think of spiritual results,
Sure as the earth swims through the heavens, does every one
    of its objects pass into spiritual results.

Think of manhood, and you to be a man;
Do you count manhood, and the sweet of manhood, no-
    thing?

Think of womanhood, and you to be a woman;
The creation is womanhood;
Have I not said that womanhood involves all?
Have I not told how the universe has nothing better than the
    best womanhood?
1856

## RESPONDEZ!

RESPONDEZ! Respondez!
(The war is completed—the price is paid—the title is settled
    beyond recall;)
Let every one answer! let those who sleep be waked! let none
    evade!
Must we still go on with our affections and sneaking?

Let me bring this to a close—I pronounce openly for a new distribution of roles;

Let that which stood in front go behind! and let that which was behind advance to the front and speak;

Let murderers, bigots, fools, unclean persons, offer new propositions!

Let the old propositions be postponed!

Let faces and theories be turn'd inside out! let meanings be freely criminal, as well as results!

Let there be no suggestion above the suggestion of drudgery!

Let none be pointed toward his destination! (Say! do you know your destination?)

Let men and women be mock'd with bodies and mock'd with Souls!

Let the love that waits in them, wait! let it die, or pass stillborn to other spheres!

Let the sympathy that waits in every man, wait! or let it also pass, a dwarf, to other spheres!

Let contradictions prevail! let one thing contradict another! and let one line of my poems contradict another!

Let the people sprawl with yearning, aimless hands! let their tongues be broken! let their eyes be discouraged! let none descend into their hearts with the fresh lusciousness of love!

(Stifled, O days! O lands! in every public and private corruption!

Smother'd in thievery, impotence, shamelessness, mountain-high;

Brazen effrontery, scheming, rolling like ocean's waves around and upon you, O my days! my lands!

For not even those thunderstorms, nor fiercest lightnings of the war, have purified the atmosphere;)

—Let the theory of America still be management, caste, comparison! (Say! what other theory would you?)

Let them that distrust birth and death still lead the rest! (Say! why shall they not lead you?)

Let the crust of hell be neared and trod on! let the days be darker than the nights! let slumber bring less slumber than waking time brings!

Let the world never appear to him or her for whom it was all made!

Let the heart of the young man still exile itself from the heart of the old man! and let the heart of the old man be exiled from that of the young man!

Let the sun and moon go! let scenery take the applause of the audience! let there be apathy under the stars!

Let freedom prove no man's inalienable right! every one who can tyrannize, let him tyrannize to his satisfaction!

Let none but infidels be countenanced!

Let the eminence of meanness, treachery, sarcasm, hate, greed, indecency, impotence, lust, be taken for granted above all! let writers, judges, governments, households, religions, philosophies, take such for granted above all!

Let the worst men beget children out of the worst women!

Let the priest still play at immortality!

Let death be inaugurated!

Let nothing remain but the ashes of teachers, artists, moralists, lawyers, and learn'd and polite persons!

Let him who is without my poems be assassinated!

Let the cow, the horse, the camel, the garden-bee—let the mud-fish, the lobster, the mussel, eel, the sting-ray, and the grunting pig-fish—let these, and the like of these, be put on a perfect equality with man and woman!

Let churches accommodate serpents, vermin, and the corpses of those who have died of the most filthy of diseases!

Let marriage slip down among fools, and be for none but fools!

Let men among themselves talk and think forever obscenely of women! and let women among themselves talk and think obscenely of men!

Let us all, without missing one, be exposed in public, naked, monthly, at the peril of our lives! let our bodies be freely handled and examined by whoever chooses!

Let nothing but copies at second hand be permitted to exist upon the earth!

Let the earth desert God, nor let there ever henceforth be mention'd the name of God!

Let there be no God!

R                                                                    W.

Let there be money, business, imports, exports, custom, authority, precedents, pallor, dyspepsia, smut, ignorance, unbelief!

Let judges and criminals be transposed! let the prison-keepers be put in prison! let those that were prisoners take the keys! (Say! why might they not just as well be transposed?)

Let the slaves be masters! let the masters become slaves!

Let the reformers descend from the stands where they are forever bawling! let an idiot or insane person appear on each of the stands!

Let the Asiatic, the African, the European, the American, and the Australian, go armed against the murderous stealthiness of each other! let them sleep armed! let none believe in good will!

Let there be no unfashionable wisdom! let such be scorn'd and derided off from the earth!

Let a floating cloud in the sky—let a wave of the sea—let growing mint, spinach, onions, tomatoes—let these be exhibited as shows, at a great price for admission!

Let all the men of These States stand aside for a few smouchers! let the few seize on what they choose! let the rest gawk, giggle, starve, obey!

Let shadows be furnish'd with genitals! let substances be deprived of their genitals!

Let there be wealthy and immense cities—but still through any of them, not a single poet, savior, knower, lover!

Let the infidels of These States laugh all faith away!

If one man be found who has faith, let the rest set upon him!

Let them affright faith! let them destroy the power of breeding faith!

Let the she-harlots and the he-harlots be prudent! let them dance on, while seeming lasts! (O seeming! seeming! seeming!)

Let the preachers recite creeds! let them still teach only what they have been taught!

Let insanity still have charge of sanity!

Let books take the place of trees, animals, rivers, clouds!

Let the daub'd portraits of heroes supersede heroes!

Let the manhood of man never take steps after itself!

Let it take steps after eunuchs, and after consumptive and
    genteel persons!
Let the white person again tread the black person under his
    heel! (Say! which is trodden under heel, after all?)
Let the reflections of the things of the world be studied in
    mirrors! let the things themselves still continue un-
    studied!
Let a man seek pleasure everywhere except in himself!
Let a woman seek happiness everywhere except in herself!
(What real happiness have you had one single hour through
    your whole life?)
Let the limited years of life do nothing for the limitless years
    of death! (What do you suppose death will do, then?)
1856

## APOSTROPH

O MATER! O fils!
O brood continental!
O flowers of the prairies!
O space boundless! O hum of mighty products!
O you teeming cities! O so invincible, turbulent, proud!
O race of the future! O women!
O fathers! O you men of passion and the storm!
O native power only! O beauty!
O yourself! O God! O divine average!
O you bearded roughs! O bards! O all those slumberers!
O arouse! the dawn-bird's throat sounds shrill! Do you not
    hear the cock crowing?
O, as I walk'd the beach, I heard the mournful notes fore-
    boding a tempest—the low, oft-repeated shriek of the
    diver, the long-lived loon;
O I heard, and yet hear, angry thunder;—O you sailors! O
    ships! make quick preparation!
O from his masterful sweep, the warning cry of the eagle!
(Give way there, all! It is useless! Give up your spoils;)
O sarcasms! Propositions! (O if the whole world should
    prove indeed a sham, a sell!)
O I believe there is nothing real but America and freedom!
O to sternly reject all except Democracy!
O imperator! O who dare confront you and me?

O to promulgate our own! O to build for that which build
for mankind!

O feuillage! O North! O the slope drained by the Mexican
sea!

O all, all inseparable—ages, ages, ages!

O a curse on him that would dissever this Union for any
reason whatever!

O climate, labors! O good and evil! O death!

O you strong with iron and wood! O Personality!

O the village or place which has the greatest man or woman!
even if it be only a few ragged huts;

O the city where women walk in public processions in the
streets, the same as the men;

O a wan and terrible emblem, by me adopted!

O shapes arising! shapes of the future centuries!

O muscle and pluck forever for me!

O workmen and workwomen forever for me!

O farmers and sailors! O drivers of horses forever for me!

O I will make the new bardic list of trades and tools!

O you coarse and wilful! I love you!

O South! O longings for my dear home! O soft and sunny
airs!

O pensive! O I must return where the palm grows and the
mocking bird sings, or else I die!

O equality! O organic compacts! I am come to be your born
poet!

O whirl, contest, sounding and resounding! I am your poet,
because I am part of you;

O days by-gone! Enthusiasts! Antecedents!

O vast preparations for These States! O years!

O what is now being sent forward thousands of years to
come!

O mediums! O to teach! to convey the invisible faith!

To promulge real things! to journey through all The States!

O creation! O to-day! O laws! O unmitigated adoration!

O for mightier broods of orators, artists, and singers!

O for native songs! carpenter's, boatman's, ploughman's
songs! shoemaker's songs!

O haughtiest growth of time! O free and extatic!

O what I, here, preparing, warble for!

O you hastening light! O the sun of the world will ascend,
    dazzling, and take his height—and you too will ascend;
O so amazing and so broad! up there resplendent, darting
    and burning;
O prophetic! O vision staggered with weight of light! with
    pouring glories!
O copious! O hitherto unequalled!
O Libertad! O compact! O union impossible to dissever!
O my Soul! O lips becoming tremulous, powerless!
O centuries, centuries yet ahead!
O voices of greater orators! I pause—I listen for you!
O you States! Cities! defiant of all outside authority! I
    spring at once into your arms! you I most love!
O you grand Presidentiads! I wait for you!
New history! New heroes! I project you!
Visions of poets! only you really last! O sweep on! sweep on!
O Death! O you striding there! O I cannot yet!
O heights! O infinitely too swift and dizzy yet!
O purged lumine! you threaten me more than I can stand!
O present! I return while yet I may to you!
O poets to come, I depend upon you!
1860

## O SUN OF REAL PEACE

O SUN of real peace! O hastening light!
O free and extatic! O what I here, preparing, warble for!
O the sun of the world will ascend, dazzling, and take his
    height—and you too, O my Ideal will surely ascend!
O so amazing and broad—up there resplendent, darting and
    burning!
O vision prophetic, stagger'd with weight of light! with pour-
    ing glories!
O lips of my soul, already becoming powerless!
O ample and grand Presidentiads! Now the war, the war is
    over!
New history! new heroes! I project you!
Visions of poets! only you really last! sweep on! sweep on!
O heights too swift and dizzy yet!
O purged and luminous! you threaten me more than I can
    stand!

(I must not venture—the ground under my feet menaces me
  —it will not support me:
O future too immense,)—O present, I return, while yet I may,
  to you.
1860


## [SO FAR AND SO FAR, AND ON TOWARD
THE END]

So far, and so far, and on toward the end,
Singing what is sung in this book, from the irresistible im-
  pulses of me;
But whether I continue beyond this book, to maturity,
Whether I shall dart forth the true rays, the ones that wait
  unfired,
(Did you think the sun was shining its brightest?
No—it has not yet fully risen;)
Whether I shall complete what is here started,
Whether I shall attain my own height, to justify these, yet
  unfinished,
Whether I shall make THE POEM OF THE NEW WORLD, trans-
  cending all others—depends, rich persons, upon you,
Depends, whoever you are now filling the current Presiden-
  tiad, upon you,
Upon you, Governor, Mayor, Congressman,
And you, contemporary America.
1860


## IN THE NEW GARDEN, IN ALL THE PARTS

IN the new garden, in all the parts,
In cities now, modern, I wander,
Though the second or third result, or still further, primitive
  yet,
Days, places, indifferent—though various, the same,
Time, Paradise, the Mannahatta, the prairies, finding me un-
  changed,
Death indifferent—Is it that I lived long since? Was I buried
  very long ago?
For all that, I may now be watching you here, this moment;

For the future, with determined will, I seek—the woman of
    the future,
You, born years, centuries after me, I seek.
1860


### [STATES!]

STATES!
Were you looking to be held together by the lawyers?
By an agreement on a paper? Or by arms?

Away!
I arrive, bringing these, beyond all the forces of courts and
    arms,
These! to hold you together as firmly as the earth itself is
    held together.

The old breath of life, ever new,
Here! I pass it by contact to you, America.

O mother! have you done much for me?
Behold, there shall from me be much done for you.

There shall from me be a new friendship—It shall be called
    after my name,
It shall circulate through The States, indifferent of place,
It shall twist and intertwist them through and around each
    other—Compact shall they be, showing new signs,
Affection shall solve every one of the problems of freedom,
Those who love each other shall be invincible,
They shall finally make America completely victorious, in
    my name.

One from Massachusetts shall be a comrade to a Missourian,
One from Maine or Vermont, and a Carolinian and an Ore-
    gonese, shall be friends triune, more precious to each
    other than all the riches of the earth.

To Michigan shall be wafted perfume from Florida,
To the Mannahatta from Cuba or Mexico,
Not the perfume of flowers, but sweeter, and wafted beyond
    death.

No danger shall balk Columbia's lovers,
If need be, a thousand shall sternly immolate themselves for one,
The Kanuck shall be willing to lay down his life for the Kansian, and the Kansian for the Kanuck, on due need.

It shall be customary in all directions, in the houses and streets, to see manly affection,
The departing brother or friend shall salute the remaining brother or friend with a kiss.

There shall be innovations,
There shall be countless linked hands—namely, the Northeasterner's, and the Northwesterner's, and the Southwesterner's, and those of the interior, and all their brood,
These shall be masters of the world under a new power,
They shall laugh to scorn the attacks of all the remainder of the world.

The most dauntless and rude shall touch face to face lightly,
The dependence of Liberty shall be lovers,
The continuance of Equality shall be comrades.

These shall tie and band stronger than hoops of iron,
I, extatic, O partners! O lands! henceforth with the love of lovers tie you.
1860

### [LONG I THOUGHT THAT KNOWLEDGE]

LONG I thought that knowledge alone would suffice me—O if I could but obtain knowledge!
Then my lands engrossed me—Lands of the prairies, Ohio's land, the southern savannas, engrossed me—For them I would live—I would be their orator;
Then I met the examples of old and new heroes—I heard of warriors, sailors, and all dauntless persons—And it seemed to me that I too had it in me to be as dauntless as any—and would be so;

And then, to enclose all, it came to me to strike up the songs
  of the New World—And then I believed my life must be
  spent in singing;
But now take notice, land of the prairies, land of the south
  savannas, Ohio's land,
Take notice, you Kanuck woods—and you Lake Huron—
  and all that with you roll toward Niagara—and you
  Niagara also,
And you, Californian mountains—That you each and all find
  somebody else to be your singer of songs,
For I can be your singer of songs no longer—One who loves
  me is jealous of me, and withdraws me from all but love,
With the rest I dispense—I sever from what I thought would
  suffice me, for it does not—it is now empty and tasteless
  to me,
I heed knowledge, and the grandeur of The States, and the
  example of heroes, no more,
I am indifferent to my own songs—I will go with him I love,
It is to be enough for us that we are together—We never
  separate again.

1860

## [HOURS CONTINUING LONG, SORE AND HEAVY-HEARTED]

HOURS continuing long, sore and heavy-hearted,
Hours of the dusk, when I withdraw to a lonesome and unfrequented spot, seating myself, leaning my face in my
  hands;
Hours sleepless, deep in the night, when I go forth, speeding
  swiftly the country roads, or through the city streets, or
  pacing miles and miles, stifling plaintive cries;
Hours discouraged, distracted—for the one I cannot content
  myself without, soon I saw him content himself without
  me;
Hours when I am forgotten, (O weeks and months are passing, but I believe I am never to forget!)
Sullen and suffering hours! (I am ashamed—but it is useless
  —I am what I am;)
Hours of my torment—I wonder if other men ever have the
  like, out of the like feelings?

Is there even one other like me—distracted—his friend, his
  lover, lost to him?
Is he too as I am now? Does he still rise in the morning, de-
  jected, thinking who is lost to him? and at night, awaking, think who is lost?
Does he too harbor his friendship silent and endless? harbor
  his anguish and passion?
Does some stray reminder, or the casual mention of a name,
  bring the fit back upon him, taciturn and deprest?
Does he see himself reflected in me? In these hours, does he
  see the face of his hours reflected?
1860

## [WHO IS NOW READING THIS?]

WHO is now reading this?

May-be one is now reading this who knows some wrong-
  doing of my past life,
Or may-be a stranger is reading this who has secretly loved me,
Or may-be one who meets all my grand assumptions and
  egotisms with derision,
Or may-be one who is puzzled at me.

As if I were not puzzled at myself!
Or as if I never deride myself! (O conscience-struck! O self-
  convicted!)
Or as if I do not secretly love strangers! (O tenderly, a long
  time, and never avow it;)
Or as if I did not see, perfectly well, interior in myself, the
  stuff of wrong-doing,
Or as if it could cease transpiring from me until it must cease.
1860

## TO YOU

LET us twain walk aside from the rest;
Now we are together privately, do you discard ceremony,
Come! vouchsafe to me what has yet been vouchsafed to
  none—Tell me the whole story,
Tell me what you would not tell your brother, wife, husband,
  or physician.
1860

## [OF THE VISAGES OF THINGS]

OF the visages of things—And of piercing through to the accepted hells beneath;

Of ugliness—To me there is just as much in it as there is in beauty—And now the ugliness of human beings is acceptable to me;

Of detected persons—To me, detected persons are not, in any respect, worse than undetected persons—and are not in any respect worse than I am myself;

Of criminals—To me, any judge, or any juror, is equally criminal—and any reputable person is also—and the President is also.

1860

## SAYS

### 1

I SAY whatever tastes sweet to the most perfect person, that is finally right.

### 2

I SAY nourish a great intellect, a great brain;
If I have said anything to the contrary, I hereby retract it.

### 3

I SAY man shall not hold property in man;
I say the least developed person on earth is just as important and sacred to himself or herself, as the most developed person is to himself or herself.

### 4

I SAY where liberty draws not the blood out of slavery, there slavery draws the blood out of liberty,
I say the word of the good old cause in These States, and resound it hence over the world.

### 5

I SAY the human shape or face is so great, it must never be made ridiculous;
I say for ornaments nothing outre can be allowed,

And that anything is most beautiful without ornament,
And that exaggerations will be sternly revenged in your own
    physiology, and in other persons' physiology also;
And I say that clean-shaped children can be jetted and con-
    ceived only where natural forms prevail in public, and
    the human face and form are never caricatured;
And I say that genius need never more be turned to romances,
(For facts properly told, how mean appear all romances.)

## 6

I SAY the word of lands fearing nothing—I will have no other
    land;
I say discuss all and expose all—I am for every topic openly;
I say there can be no salvation for These States without inno-
    vators—without free tongues, and ears willing to hear
    the tongues;
And I announce as a glory of These States, that they respect-
    fully listen to propositions, reforms, fresh views and
    doctrines, from successions of men and women,
Each age with its own growth.

## 7

I HAVE said many times that materials and the Soul are great,
    and that all depends on physique;
Now I reverse what I said, and affirm that all depends on the
    æsthetic or intellectual,
And that criticism is great—and that refinement is greatest of
    all;
And I affirm now that the mind governs—and that all de-
    pends on the mind.

## 8

WITH one man or woman—(no matter which one—I even
    pick out the lowest,)
With him or her I now illustrate the whole law;
I say that every right, in politics or what-not, shall be elig-
    ible to that one man or woman, on the same terms as
    any.
1860

## DEBRIS

HE is wisest who has the most caution,
He only wins who goes far enough.

ANY thing is as good as established, when that is established
that will produce and continue it.

WHAT General has a good army in himself, has a good army;
He happy in himself, or she happy in herself, is happy,
But I tell you you cannot be happy by others, any more than
you can beget or conceive a child by others.

ONE sweeps by, attended by an immense train,
All emblematic of peace—not a soldier or menial among
them.

ONE sweeps by, old, with black eyes, and profuse white hair,
He has the simple magnificence of health and strength,
His face strikes as with flashes of lightning whoever it turns
toward.

THREE old men slowly pass, followed by three others, and
they by three others,
They are beautiful—the one in the middle of each group
holds his companions by the hand,
As they walk, they give out perfume wherever they walk.

WHAT weeping face is that looking from the window?
Why does it stream those sorrowful tears?
Is it for some burial place, vast and dry?
Is it to wet the soil of graves?

I WILL take an egg out of the robin's nest in the orchard,
I will take a branch of gooseberries from the old bush in the
garden, and go and preach to the world;
You shall see I will not meet a single heretic or scorner,
You shall see how I stump clergymen, and confound them,
You shall see me showing a scarlet tomato, and a white
pebble from the beach.

BEHAVIOR—fresh, native, copious, each one for himself or
    herself,
Nature and the Soul expressed—America and freedom ex-
    pressed—in it the finest art,
In it pride, cleanliness, sympathy, to have their chance,
In it physique, intellect, faith—in it just as much as to man-
    age an army or a city, or to write a book—perhaps more,
The youth, the laboring person, the poor person, rivalling all
    the rest—perhaps outdoing the rest,
The effects of the universe no greater than its;
For there is nothing in the whole universe that can be more
    effective than a man's or a woman's daily behavior can
    be,
In any position, in any one of These States.

I THOUGHT I was not alone, walking here by the shore,
But the one I thought was with me, as now I walk by the
    shore,
As I lean and look through the glimmering light—that one
    has utterly disappeared,
And those appear that perplex me.
1860

## THOUGHT

OF what I write from myself—As if that were not the resumé;
Of Histories—As if such, however complete, were not less
    complete than the preceding poems;
As if those shreds, the records of nations, could possibly be
    as lasting as the preceding poems;
As if here were not the amount of all nations, and of all the
    lives of heroes.
1860

## SOLID, IRONICAL, ROLLING ORB

SOLID, ironical, rolling orb!
Master of all, and matter of fact!—at last I accept your
    terms;
Bringing to practical, vulgar tests, of all my ideal dreams,
And of me, as lover and hero.
1865

## BATHED IN WAR'S PERFUME

BATHED in war's perfume—delicate flag!
(Should the days needing armies, needing fleets, come again,)
O to hear you call the sailors and the soldiers! flag like a
    beautiful woman!
O to hear the tramp, tramp, of a million answering men! O
    the ships they arm with joy!
O to see you leap and beckon from the tall masts of ships!
O to see you peering down on the sailors on the decks!
Flag like the eyes of women.
1865

## NOT MY ENEMIES EVER INVADE ME

NOT my enemies ever invade me—no harm to my pride from
    them I fear;
But the lovers I recklessly love—lo! how they master me!
Lo! me, ever open and helpless, bereft of my strength!
Utterly abject, grovelling on the ground before them.
1865–6

## THIS DAY, O SOUL

THIS day, O Soul, I give you a wondrous mirror;
Long in the dark, in tarnish and cloud it lay—But the cloud
    has pass'd, and the tarnish gone;
. . . Behold, O Soul! it is now a clean and bright mirror,
Faithfully showing you all the things of the world.
1865–6

## LESSONS

THERE are who teach only the sweet lessons of peace and safety;
But I teach lessons of war and death to those I love,
That they readily meet invasions, when they come.
1871

## ONE SONG, AMERICA, BEFORE I GO

ONE song, America, before I go,
I'd sing, o'er all the rest, with trumpet sound,
For thee—the Future.

I'd sow a seed for thee of endless Nationality;
I'd fashion thy Ensemble, including Body, and Soul;
I'd show, away ahead, the real Union, and how it may be
accomplish'd.

(The paths to the House I seek to make,
But leave to those to come, the House itself.)

Belief I sing—and Preparation;
As Life and Nature are not great with reference to the Pre-
sent only,
But greater still from what is to come,
Out of that formula for Thee I sing.
1872

## AFTER AN INTERVAL

### (*Nov.* 22, 1875, *midnight—Saturn and Mars in conjunction*)

AFTER an interval, reading, here in the midnight,
With the great stars looking on—all the stars of Orion looking,
And the silent Pleiades—and the duo looking of Saturn and
ruddy Mars;
Pondering, reading my own songs, after a long interval,
(sorrow and death familiar now,)
Ere closing the book, what pride! what joy! to find them,
Standing so well the test of death and night!
And the duo of Saturn and Mars!
1875

## THE BEAUTY OF THE SHIP

WHEN, staunchly entering port,
After long ventures, hauling up, worn and old,
Battered by sea and wind, torn by many a fight,
With the original sails all gone, replaced, or mended,
I only saw, at last, the beauty of the Ship.
1876

## TWO RIVULETS

Two Rivulets side by side,
Two blended, parallel, strolling tides,
Companions, travelers, gossiping as they journey.

For the Eternal Ocean bound,
These ripples, passing surges, streams of Death and Life,
Object and Subject hurrying, whirling by,
The Real and Ideal,

Alternate ebb and flow the Days and Nights,
(Strands of a Trio twining, Present, Future, Past.)

In You, whoe'er you are, my book perusing,
In I myself—in all the World—these ripples flow,
All, all, toward the mystic Ocean tending.

(O yearnful waves! the kisses of your lips!
Your breast so broad, with open arms, O firm, expanded
     shore!)
1876

## OR FROM THAT SEA OF TIME

### 1

OR, from that Sea of Time,
Spray, blown by the wind—a double winrow-drift of weeds
     and shells;
(O little shells, so curious-convolute! so limpid-cold and
     voiceless!
Yet will you not, to the tympans of temples held,
Murmurs and echoes still bring up—Eternity's music, faint
     and far,
Wafted inland, sent from Atlantica's rim—strains for the
     Soul of the Prairies,
Whisper'd reverberations—chords for the ear of the West,
     joyously sounding
Your tidings old, yet ever new and untranslatable;)
Infinitesimals out of my life, and many a life,
(For not my life and years alone I give—all, all I give;)
These thoughts and Songs—waifs from the deep—here, cast
     high and dry,
Wash'd on America's shores.

### 2

Currents of starting a Continent new,
Overtures sent to the solid out of the liquid,

Fusion of ocean and land—tender and pensive waves,
(Not safe and peaceful only—waves rous'd and ominous too.

Out of the depths, the storm's abysms—who knows whence?
    Death's waves,
Raging over the vast, with many a broken spar and tatter'd
    sail.)
1876

## FROM MY LAST YEARS

FROM my last years, last thoughts I here bequeath,
Scatter'd and dropt, in seeds, and wafted to the West,
Through moisture of Ohio, prairie soil of Illinois—through
    Colorado, California air,
For Time to germinate fully.
1876

## IN FORMER SONGS

IN former songs Pride have I sung, and Love, and passionate,
    joyful Life,
But here I twine the strands of Patriotism and Death.

And now, Life, Pride, Love, Patriotism and Death,
To you, O FREEDOM, purport of all!
(You that elude me most—refusing to be caught in songs of
    mine,)
I offer all to you.

### 2

'Tis not for nothing, Death,
I sound out you, and words of you, with daring tone—em·
    bodying you,
In my new Democratic chants—keeping you for a close,
For last impregnable retreat—a citadel and tower,
For my last stand—my pealing, final cry.
1876

# II. Prose

# Prose

## GENEALOGY—VAN VELSOR AND WHITMAN

THE later years of the last century found the Van Velsor family, my mother's side, living on their own farm at Cold Spring, Long Island, New York State, near the eastern edge of Queen's county, about a mile from the harbor.* My father's side—probably the fifth generation from the first English arrivals in New England—were at the same time farmers on their own land—(and a fine domain it was, 500 acres, all good soil, gently sloping east and south, about one-tenth woods, plenty of grand old trees,) two or three miles off, at West Hills, Suffolk county. The Whitman name in the Eastern States, and so branching West and South, starts undoubtedly from one John Whitman, born 1602, in Old England, where he grew up, married, and his eldest son was born in 1629. He came over in the *True Love* in 1640 to America, and lived in Weymouth, Mass., which place became the mother-hive of the New-Englanders of the name; he died in 1692. His brother, Rev. Zechariah Whitman, also came over in the *True Love*, either at that time or soon after, and lived at Milford, Conn. A son of this Zechariah, named Joseph, migrated to Huntington, Long Island, and permanently settled there. Savage's *Genealogical Dictionary* (vol. iv, p. 524) gets the Whitman family establish'd at Huntington, per this Joseph, before 1664. It is quite certain that from that beginning, and from Joseph, the West Hill Whitmans, and all others in Suffolk county, have since radiated, myself among the number. John and Zechariah both went to England and back again divers times; they had large families, and several of their children were born in the old country. We hear of the father of John and Zechariah, Abijah Whitman, who goes over into the 1500's, but we know little about him, except that he also was for some time in America.

* Long Island was settled first on the west end by the Dutch from Holland, then on the east end by the English—the dividing line of the two nationalities being a little west of Huntington, where my father's folks lived, and where I was born.

These old pedigree-reminiscences come up to me vividly from a visit I made not long since (in my 63d year) to West Hills, and to the burial grounds of my ancestry, both sides. I extract from notes of that visit, written there and then:

## THE OLD WHITMAN AND VAN VELSOR CEMETERIES

*July* 29, 1881.—After more than forty years' absence, (except a brief visit, to take my father there once more, two years before he died,) went down Long Island on a week's jaunt to the place where I was born, thirty miles from New York city. Rode around the old familiar spots, viewing and pondering and dwelling long upon them, everything coming back to me. Went to the old Whitman homestead on the upland and took a view eastward, inclining south, over the broad and beautiful farm lands of my grandfather (1780,) and my father. There was the new house (1810,) the big oak a hundred and fifty or two hundred years old; there the well, the sloping kitchen-garden, and a little way off even the well-kept remains of the dwelling of my great-grandfather (1750-'60) still standing, with its mighty timbers and low ceilings. Near by, a stately grove of tall, vigorous black-walnuts, beautiful, Apollo-like, the sons or grandsons, no doubt, of black-walnuts during or before 1776. On the other side of the road spread the famous apple orchard, over twenty acres, the trees planted by hands long mouldering in the grave (my uncle Jesse's,) but quite many of them evidently capable of throwing out their annual blossoms and fruit yet.

I now write these lines seated on an old grave (doubtless of a century since at least) on the burial hill of the Whitmans of many generations. Fifty or more graves are quite plainly traceable, and as many more decay'd out of all form—depress'd mounds, crumbled and broken stones, cover'd with moss—the gray and sterile hill, the clumps of chestnuts outside, the silence, just varied by the soughing wind. There is always the deepest eloquence of sermon or poem in any of these ancient graveyards of which Long Island has so many;

so what must this one have been to me? My whole family history, with its succession of links, from the first settlement down to date, told here—three centuries concentrate on this sterile acre.

The next day, July 30, I devoted to the maternal locality, and if possible was still more penetrated and impress'd. I write this paragraph on the burial hill of the Van Velsors, near Cold Spring, the most significant depository of the dead that could be imagin'd, without the slightest help from art, but far ahead of it, soil sterile, a mostly bare plateau-flat of half an acre, the top of a hill, brush and well grown trees and dense woods bordering all around, very primitive, secluded, no visitors, no road (you cannot drive here, you have to bring the dead on foot, and follow on foot.) Two or three-score graves quite plain; as many more almost rubb'd out. My grandfather Cornelius and my grandmother Amy (Naomi) and numerous relatives nearer or remoter, on my mother's side, lie buried here. The scene as I stood or sat, the delicate and wild odor of the woods, a slightly drizzling rain, the emotional atmosphere of the place, and the inferr'd reminiscences, were fitting accompaniments.

## THE MATERNAL HOMESTEAD

I WENT down from this ancient grave place eighty or ninety rods to the site of the Van Velsor homestead, where my mother was born (1795,) and where every spot had been familiar to me as a child and youth (1825-'40.) Then stood there a long rambling, dark-gray, shingle-sided house, with sheds, pens, a great barn, and much open road-space. Now of all those not a vestige left; all had been pull'd down, erased, and the plough and harrow pass'd over foundations, road-spaces and everything, for many summers; fenced in at present, and grain and clover growing like any other fine fields. Only a big hole from the cellar, with some little heaps of broken stone, green with grass and weeds, identified the place. Even the copious old brook and spring seem'd to have mostly dwindled away. The whole scene, with what it arous'd, memories of my young days there half a century ago, the vast kitchen and ample fireplace and the sitting-room adjoining, the plain furniture, the meals, the house full of merry people, my grandmother Amy's sweet old face in its Quaker cap, my grandfather "the Major", jovial, red, stout, with sonorous voice and characteristic physiognomy, with the actual sights themselves, made the most pronounc'd half-day's experience of my whole jaunt.

For there with all those wooded, hilly, healthy surroundings, my dearest mother, Louisa Van Velsor, grew up—(her mother, Amy Williams, of the Friends' or Quakers' denomination—the Williams family, seven sisters and one brother—the father and brother sailors, both of whom met their deaths at sea.) The Van Velsor people were noted for fine horses, which the men bred and train'd from blooded stock. My mother, as a young woman, was a daily and daring rider. As to the head of the family himself, the old race of the Netherlands, so deeply grafted on Manhattan island and in Kings and Queens counties, never yielded a more mark'd and full Americanized specimen than Major Cornelius Van Velsor.

## TWO OLD FAMILY INTERIORS

OF the domestic and inside life of the middle of Long Island, at and just before that time, here are two samples:

"The Whitmans, at the beginning of the present century, lived in a long story-and-a-half farm-house, hugely timber'd, which is still standing. A great smoke-canopied kitchen, with vast hearth and chimney, form'd one end of the house. The existence of slavery in New York at that time, and the possession by the family of some twelve or fifteen slaves, house and field servants, gave things quite a patriarchial look. The very young darkies could be seen, a swarm of them, toward sundown, in this kitchen, squatted in a circle on the floor, eating their supper of Indian pudding and milk. In the house, and in food and furniture, all was rude, but substantial. No carpets or stoves were known, and no coffee, and tea or sugar only for the women. Rousing wood fires gave both warmth and light on winter nights. Pork, poultry, beef, and all the ordinary vegetables and grains were plentiful. Cider was the men's common drink, and used at meals. The clothes were mainly homespun. Journeys were made by both men and women on horseback. Both sexes labor'd with their own hands—the men on the farm—the women in the house and around it. Books were scarce. The annual copy of the almanac was a treat, and was pored over through the long winter evenings. I must not forget to mention that both these families were near enough to the sea to behold it from the high places, and to hear in still hours the roar of the surf; the latter, after a storm, giving a peculiar sound at night. Then all hands, male and female, went down frequently on beach and bathing parties, and the men on practical expeditions for cutting salt hay, and for clamming and fishing."—*John Burroughs's* NOTES.

"The ancestors of Walt Whitman, on both the paternal and maternal sides, kept a good table, sustained the hospitalities, decorums, and an excellent social reputation in the county, and they were often of mark'd individuality. If space permitted, I should consider some of the men worthy special description; and still more some of the women. His great-grandmother on the paternal side, for instance, was a large swarthy woman, who lived to a very old age. She smoked tobacco, rode on horseback like a man, managed the most vicious horse, and, becoming a widow in later life, went forth every day over her farm-lands, frequently in the saddle, directing the labor of her slaves, in language in which, on exciting occasions, oaths were not spared. The two immediate grandmothers were, in the best sense, superior women. The maternal one (Amy Williams before marriage) was a Friend, or Quakeress, of sweet, sensible character, housewifely proclivities, and deeply intuitive and spiritual. The other (Hannah Brush,) was an equally noble, perhaps stronger character, lived to be very old, had quite a family of sons, was a natural lady, was in early life a school-mistress, and had great solidity of mind. W. W. himself makes much of the women of his ancestry."—*The Same.*

Out from these arrieres of persons and scenes, I was born May 31, 1819. And now to dwell awhile on the locality itself —as the successive growth-stages of my infancy, childhood, youth and manhood were all pass'd on Long Island, which I sometimes feel as if I had incorporated. I roam'd, as boy and man, and have lived in nearly all parts, from Brooklyn to Montauk point.

## PAUMANOK, AND MY LIFE ON IT AS CHILD AND YOUNG MAN

WORTH fully and particularly investigating indeed this Paumanok, (to give the spot its aboriginal name,*) stretching east through Kings, Queens and Suffolk counties, 120 miles altogether—on the north Long Island sound, a beautiful, varied and picturesque series of inlets, "necks" and sea-like expansions, for a hundred miles to Orient point. On the ocean side the great south bay dotted with countless hummocks, mostly small, some quite large, occasionally long bars of sand out two hundred rods to a mile-and-a-half from the shore. While now and then, as at Rockaway and far east along the Hamptons, the beach makes right on the island, the sea dashing up without intervention. Several light-houses on the shores east; a long history of wrecks tragedies, some even of late years. As a youngster, I was in the atmosphere and traditions of many of these wrecks—of one or two almost an observer. Off Hempstead beach for example, was the loss of the ship *Mexico* in 1840, (alluded to in "the Sleepers" in L. of G.) And at Hampton, some years later, the destruction of the brig *Elizabeth*, a fearful affair, in one of the worst winter gales, where Margaret Fuller went down, with her husband and child.

Inside the outer bars or beach this south bay is everywhere comparatively shallow; of cold winters all thick ice on the surface. As a boy I often went forth with a chum or two, on those frozen fields, with hand-sled, axe and eel-spear, after messes of eels. We would cut holes in the ice, sometimes striking quite an eel-bonanza, and filling our baskets with great, fat, sweet, white-meated fellows. The scenes, the ice, drawing the hand-sled, cutting holes, spearing the eels, &c., were of course just such fun as is dearest to boyhood. The

* "Paumanok, (or Paumanake, or Paumanack, the Indian name of Long Island,) over a hundred miles long; shaped like a fish—plenty of sea shore, sandy, stormy, uninviting, the horizon boundless, the air too strong for invalids, the bays a wonderful resort for aquatic birds, the south-side meadows cover'd with salt hay, the soil of the island generally tough, but good for the locust-tree, the apple orchard, and the blackberry, and with numberless springs of the sweetest water in the world. Years ago, among the bay-men—a strong, wild race, now extinct, or rather entirely changed—a native of Long Island was called a *Paumanacker*, or *Creole-Paumanacker*."—*John Burroughs.*

shores of this bay, winter and summer, and my doings there in early life, are woven all through L. of G. One sport I was very fond of was to go on a bay-party in summer to gather sea-gull's eggs. (The gulls lay two or three eggs, more than half the size of hen's eggs, right on the sand, and leave the sun's heat to hatch them.)

The eastern end of Long Island, the Peconic bay region, I knew quite well too—sail'd more than once round Shelter island, and down to Montauk—spent many an hour on Turtle hill by the old light-house, on the extreme point, looking out over the ceaseless roll of the Atlantic. I used to like to go down there and fraternize with the blue-fishers, or the annual squads of sea-bass takers. Sometimes, along Montauk peninsula, (it is some 15 miles long, and good grazing,) met the strange, unkempt, half-barbarous herdsmen, at that time living there entirely aloof from society or civilization, in charge, on those rich pasturages, of vast droves of horses, kine or sheep, own'd by farmers of the eastern towns. Sometimes, too, the few remaining Indians, or half-breeds, at that period left on Montauk peninsula, but now I believe altogether extinct.

More in the middle of the island were the spreading Hempstead plains, then (1830-'40) quite prairie-like, open, uninhabited, rather sterile, cover'd with kill-calf and huckleberry bushes, yet plenty of fair pasture for the cattle, mostly milch-cows, who fed there by hundreds, even thousands, and at evening, (the plains too were own'd by the towns, and this was the use of them in common,) might be seen taking their way home, branching off regularly in the right places. I have often been out on the edges of these plains toward sundown, and can yet recall in fancy the interminable cow-processions, and hear the music of the tin or copper bells clanking far or near, and breathe the cool of the sweet and slightly aromatic evening air, and note the sunset.

Through the same region of the island, but further east, extended wide central tracts of pine and scrub-oak, (charcoal was largely made here,) monotonous and sterile. But many a good day or half-day did I have, wandering through those solitary cross-roads, inhaling the peculiar and wild aroma. Here, and all along the island and its shores, I spent intervals many years, all seasons, sometimes riding, sometimes boating, but generally afoot, (was always then a good walker,) absorbing fields, shores, marine incidents, characters, the bay-men, farmers, pilots—always had a plentiful acquaintance with the latter, and with fishermen—went every summer on sailing trips—always liked the bare sea-beach, south side, and have some of my happiest hours on it to this day.

As I write, the whole experience comes back to me after the lapse of forty and more years—the soothing rustle of the waves, and the saline smell—boyhood's times, the clam-digging, bare-foot, and with trowsers roll'd up—hauling down the creek—the perfume of the sedge-meadows—the hay-boat, and the chowder and fishing excursions;—or, of later years, little voyages down and out New York bay, in the pilot boats. Those same later years, also, while living in Brooklyn, (1836-'50) I went regularly every week in the mild seasons down to Coney Island, at that time a long, bare unfrequented shore, which I had all to myself, and where I loved, after bathing, to race up and down the hard sand, and declaim Homer or Shakspere to the surf and sea gulls by the hour. But I am getting ahead too rapidly, and must keep more in my traces.

## MY FIRST READING—LAFAYETTE

From 1824 to '28 our family lived in Brooklyn in Front, Cranberry and Johnson streets. In the latter my father built a nice house for a home, and afterwards another in Tillary street. We occupied them, one after the other, but they were mortgaged, and we lost them. I yet remember Lafayette's visit.* Most of these years I went to the public schools. It

* "On the visit of General Lafayette to this country, in 1824, he came over to Brooklyn in state, and rode through the city. The children of the schools turn'd out to join in the welcome. An edifice for a free public library for youths was just then commencing, and Lafayette consented to stop on his way and lay the corner-stone. Numerous children arriving on the ground, where a huge irregular excavation for the building was already dug, surrounded with heaps of rough stone, several gentlemen assisted in lifting the children to safe or convenient spots to see the ceremony. Among the rest, Lafayette, also helping the children, took up the five-year-old Walt Whitman, and pressing the child a moment to his breast, and giving him a kiss, handed him down to a safe spot in the excavation."—*John Burroughs.*

must have been about 1829 or '30 that I went with my father and mother to hear Elias Hicks preach in a ball-room on Brooklyn heights. At about the same time employ'd as a boy in an office, lawyers', father and two sons, Clarke's, Fulton street, near Orange. I had a nice desk and window-nook to myself; Edward C. kindly help'd me at my handwriting and composition, and, (the signal event of my life up to that time,) subscribed for me to a big circulating library. For a time I now revel'd in romance-reading of all kinds; first, the *Arabian Nights*, all the volumes, an amazing treat. Then, with sorties in very many other directions, took in Walter Scott's novels, one after another, and his poetry, (and continue to enjoy novels and poetry to this day.)

## PRINTING OFFICE—OLD BROOKLYN

AFTER about two years went to work in a weekly newspaper and printing office, to learn the trade. The paper was the *Long Island Patriot*, owned by S. E. Clements, who was also postmaster. An old printer in the office, William Hartshorne, a revolutionary character, who had seen Washington, was a special friend of mine, and I had many a talk with him about long past times. The apprentices, including myself, boarded with his grand-daughter. I used occasionally to go out riding with the boss, who was very kind to us boys; Sundays he took us all to a great old rough, fortress-looking stone church, on Joralemon street, near where the Brooklyn city hall now is—(at that time broad fields and country roads everywhere around.) Afterward I work'd on the *Long Island Star*, Alden Spooner's paper. My father all these years pursuing his trade as carpenter and builder, with varying fortune. There was a growing family of children—eight of us—my brother Jesse the oldest, myself the second, my dear sisters Mary and Hannah Louisa, my brothers Andrew, George, Thomas Jefferson, and then my youngest brother, Edward, born 1835, and always badly crippled, as I am myself of late years.

# GROWTH—HEALTH—WORK

I DEVELOP'D (1833-4-5) into a healthy, strong youth (grew too fast, though, was nearly as big as a man at 15 or 16.) Our family at this period moved back to the country, my dear mother very ill for a long time, but recover'd. All these years I was down Long Island more or less every summer, now east, now west, sometimes months at a stretch. At 16, 17, and so on, was fond of debating societies, and had an active membership with them, off and on, in Brooklyn and one or two country towns on the island. A most omnivorous novel-reader, these and later years, devour'd everything I could get. Fond of the theatre, also, in New York, went whenever I could—sometimes witnessing fine performances.

1836-7, work'd as compositor in printing offices in New York city. Then, when little more than 18, and for a while afterwards, went to teaching country schools down in Queens and Suffolk counties, Long Island, and "boarded round". (This latter I consider one of my best experiences and deepest lessons in human nature behind the scenes and in the masses.) In '39, '40, I started and publish'd a weekly paper in my native town, Huntington. Then returning to New York city and Brooklyn, work'd on as printer and writer, mostly prose, but an occasional shy at "poetry".

## SUN-DOWN PAPERS [No. 8]

### *From the Desk of a Schoolmaster*

ON a pleasant, still, summer evening, I once took a walk down a lane that borders our village. The moon was shining with a luscious brightness; I gazed on the glorious evidences of divinity hanging above me, and as I gazed strange and fit-ful thoughts occupied my brain. I reflected on the folly and vanity of those objects with which most men occupy their lives; and the awe and dread with which they approach its close. I remembered the strife for temporary and puerile distinctions—the seeking after useless and cumbersome wealth —the yielding up the diseased mind to be a prey to constant melancholy and discontent; all which may be daily seen by those who have intercourse with the sons of men. But, most of all, I thought on the troubles caused under the name of Truth and Religion—the dissentions which have arisen between those of opposing creeds—and the quarrels and bickerings that even now prevail among men upon the slightest and most trivial points of opinion in these things. While such imaginings possessed my mind, I unconsciously seated myself upon a grassy bank; weariness, induced by the fatigues of the day, overpowered me; I sank into a tranquil sleep, and the spirit of dreams threw his misty veil about my soul.

I was wandering over the earth in search of TRUTH. Cities were explored by my enterprise; and the mouldy volumes which for years had lain undisturbed, were eagerly scanned to discover the object of my labours. Among the pale and attenuated votaries of science, I mixed as with kindred spirits; and the proudest of the learned were my familiars. My piercing gaze penetrated far down into the mines of knowledge, endeavouring to reach that jewel fairer, and brighter, and more precious than earthly jewels; but in vain, for it eluded my sight. Through the crowded ranks of men who swarm in thickly peopled places, I took my way, silent and unobserved, but ever on the alert for a clew to guide me toward the attainment of that which was the hope of my soul. I entered the gorgeous temples where pride, dressed in rich robes, preaches the doctrine of the holy and just Nazarene: I waited at the courts of powerful princes, where pomp, and grandeur, and adoration combined to make a frail mortal think himself mighty: I stood in the presence of the youthful and the gay—beauty, flashing in its bloom—strength, rearing itself in pride—revellers, and dancers, and feasters. But my heart turned comfortless from them all, for it had not attained its desire, and disappointment was heavy upon it. I then travelled to distant and uncivilized regions. Far in the north, among mountains of snow and rivers of ice, I sought what alone could gratify me. I lived, too, with the rude Tartar in his tent, and installed myself in all the mysteries which are known to the Lamas of Thibet. I wandered to a more southern clime, and disputed with the Brahmins, who profess to believe in a religion that has existed for more centuries than any other one has years. The swarthy wor·

shipper of fire made known to me his belief; and the devotee of the camel-driver of Mecca strived for my conversion to his faith. But useless was all my toil, and valueless were all the immense stores of learning I had acquired. I was baffled in all my attempts, and only began new projects to find them meet with as little success as the former.

Sick and disheartened, I retired far from the inhabited portions of the earth, and lived in solitude amid a wild and mountainous country. I there spent my time in reflection, and the pursuit of the various branches of learning, and lived upon the frugal produce of the neighbouring fields. I had one day travelled to some distance from my usual retreat, and kept insensibly wandering onward and onward, till I found myself suddenly brought to a stand by an immense ledge of rocks which rose almost perpendicularly in front of me, and, reaching far away on each side, effectually closed up my advance. The top of this stupendous pile was hidden in the clouds, and so steep was it that it seemed impossible to ascend. I stood perplexed and wondering, incited by curiosity to explore its heights and warned by prudence to return to my cell, when I heard a low but clear and silvery voice pronounce these words, as if from the cloud over my head:

"Mortal, thou hast now an opportunity of seeing what has been the search of thy life. From the top of the mountain which rises before thee, thou mayest behold on the opposite side the holy altar of Truth. Ascend, and refresh thine eyes with the picture of its loveliness."

Amazed and transported with this assurance, I immediately began to climb the precipice. The ascent was rugged and difficult, but perseverance and incessant vigour enabled me to surmount every bar. I succeeded in reaching the top, and threw myself, panting and covered with sweat, on the stony sand. When weariness had at length given way before the power of repose, I walked onwards over the mountain, which was composed of sterile black rocks and sand, with not a spot of verdure to relieve its gloomy appearance, and at length arrived at the brow of the precipice. On this side, the mountain appeared still more steep, and to advance to the edge was evidently attended with great danger. I did so, however, and my dazzled eyes fell on a sight more beautiful than was ever before revealed to mortals. Far below stretched a country exceeding the imagination of the seeker after pleasure, and more lovely than the dreams which benignant spirits sometimes weave around the couch of youth and innocence. The surface of the land was covered with soft grass, and with fragrant trees, and shrubs, and flowers, far fresher and fairer than those of our world. Here and there it was decked with sparkling streams of water, sweet as the tear which falls in behalf of sorrow from the eye of virtue, and fair as snow-drops in the tresses of beauty. These brooks broke occasionally into little cascades, which gushed forth joyously, and seemed to murmur their happiness in sounds of thankful gratitude to heaven.

But it was not the flowers, or the rich verdure, or the bubbling waters that attracted my attention. The scene was delightfully variegated with rolls and slight elevations of land: on the highest of these I beheld a white marble base, on which were raised several columns, and over the whole was thrown a roof of the same material, presenting an edifice of singular appearance, but of the most exquisite finish. I could not at once make out its proportions, for there appeared around it something like a mist, which was the more singular, as in every other place the light was of a radiant clearness. In fact, when I first viewed the spot, though I was on the alert, this temple, if so it may be called, did not strike my eye at all; but now, by dint of the most intent gazing, I could perceive its various parts with tolerable accuracy. While I was communing with myself in what manner I should endeavor to reach the ground below, and explore the very recesses of the marble temple, the silence around me was suddenly broken, and I heard the voice which had once before addressed me at the foot of the mountain, speaking in tones which sounded like the notes of a flute breathed through groves of spicy flowers:

"Seek not, O child of clay," it said, "to discover that which is hidden by an allseeing God, from the knowledge of mortals! Wert thou to attain thy desire, thou wouldst still be impotent, for thine eyes, covered as they are with the dark web of mortality, would be unable to comprehend the awful mysteries which Nature veils from thy mind. But turn thy

s                                                    w

gaze to the left, below the hill on which the temple stands, and learn a lesson of instruction which will repay all thy fatigue."

The voice ceased, and, struck with awe, I looked in the direction it had pointed out to me. I beheld a country different entirely from the one I have just described, and in almost every respect like that earth on which we live. It was not far from the temple of Truth, which could be perceived from it, but the two were divided by an impassable vacuum. Upon the small spot of ground which resembled our native planet, I beheld many people, of all classes, and nations, and tongues and dresses, constantly passing, with their attention directed toward the temple. Each one seemed to view it with the utmost care, and to wish to penetrate the veil of surrounding mist that dimmed its clearness. There was one thing, however, which astonished and at first somewhat bewildered me. I observed that each one of these inquirers after Truth held in his hand an optical glass and never gazed at the temple but through its medium. Upon observing closely, I saw that these glasses were of the most incongruous shapes and forms, and exercised singular and amazing power over the appearance of whatever was beheld through them. With some they were narrow and contracted, making the temple appear insignificant and mean. Some had them of one colour, and others of a different. Many of the glasses were of so gross a texture, that the temple was completely hid from view. Some of them distorted it into the most grotesque shapes and forms: others again would make it appear an ordinary edifice; and few were so true as to give a view of the temple nigh to its correct representation. But of whatever correctness were these glasses, each individual persisted in looking at the object of his attention through their aid. No one, or at least very few, was seen to examine the temple with the clear and undistorted organs which nature had given him: and that few, I found, were scoffed at and persecuted by all the others, who, though they differed to the utmost in their manner of viewing Truth among themselves, yet united to a man in condemning those who endeavoured to see what little could be perceived of the temple without the false assistance of some glass or other.

1 stood gazing on these things, perplexed, and hardly knowing what to think of them, when I once more heard the voice which had twice addressed me. It had lost none of its sweetness, but there was now in it an admonishing tone which sank into my soul as the rich stores of learning penetrate the open ears of attention:

"Behold!" thus it spoke, "and learn wisdom from the spectacles which have been this day unfolded to thine eyes. Thou hast gazed upon the altar of Nature; but hast seen how impossible it is to penetrate the knowledge which is stored within it. Let pride therefore depart from thy soul, and let a sense of the littleness of all earthly acquirements bow down thy head in awe before the mighty Creator of a million worlds. Thou hast seen that whatever of the great light of Truth it has been deemed expedient to show to mortals can be most truly and usefully contemplated by the plain eye of simplicity, unaccompanied by the clogs and notions which dim the gaze of most men—and hast with wonder seen how all will still continue to view the noblest objects of desire through the distorted medium of their own prejudices and bigotry. The altar of Truth is immutable, unchangeable and firm, ever the same bright emanation from God, and ever consistent with its founder. Though worlds shoot out of existence—though stars grow dim, and whole systems are blotted out of being by the hand of the mighty conqueror, Change—yet will Nature and Truth, for they two in [are] one, stand up in everlasting youth and bloom and power. Thou seest, then, how miserable are all the creeds and doctrines prevailing among men, which profess to bring down these awful mysteries, [as] things which they can fathom and search out. Kneel, then, oh! insect of an hour, whose every formation is subject enough for an eternity of wonder—and whose fate is wrapped in a black shroud of uncertainty—kneel on that earth which thou makest the scene of thy wretched strife after corruptible honors—of thy own little schemes for happiness—and of thy crimes and guilt—kneel, bend thy face to the sand, spread out the puny arms with which thy pride would win so much glory—and adore with a voiceless awe, that Unknown Power, the very minutest idea of whose abode and strength, and formation, and intentions, it would be more difficult for thee to comprehend than for a stroke of thy hand to push out of their orbits the suns and systems which make the slightest evidence of his strength."

Speechless and trembling, I listened to the sounds of this awful voice. I had sunk to the earth in fear, for a strange and pervading terror had filled my frame, while the unseen spirit had given utterance to his words. But at length I arose, and endeavored to return the gratitude of my soul for the priceless treasures which had been showered upon my mind.

The agitations of my thoughts, however, broke my slumbers. I awoke and found that the moon had long raised her radiant face, and was throwing down floods of light to illuminate the earth. The cold mists of night had stiffened my limbs, and were falling heavy around on the wet grass. I slowly wended my way homeward, my soul improved in knowledge, and determined to treasure during life the instruction I had gained from the vision that night.


## BOZ AND DEMOCRACY

Is it not your fortune, reader, occasionally, in your path through life, to meet with one whose custom it is to look alway upon the dark points of a picture—to seek out faults, and where they do not really exist, to fancy them—whose disposition is sour and whose soul seems anxious to condemn all that other people praise? A man of this description is to cheerfulness and soul-confidence what a cloud is to the sun. Malignant and envious, he would rob a patriot of his countrymen's love—a saint of his reverence—a glorious writer of his well-deserved fame.

The Washington *Globe* discourseth after the following manner:

"If to delineate the human character in its lowest stage of ignorance, vice and degradation, and give it the most unbounded scope in every species of wickedness and crime, is to be a Democratic writer, then most assuredly Mr. Dickens is emphatically one. He has exhibited human nature in its naked, ragged deformity, reeking with vice and pollution; as ignorant as wicked, and absolutely below the standard of the very beasts of the field. He has made his exhibitions of human character more disgusting and abhorrent, by a degree of brutal ignorance and stupendous depravity, which constitute, in their combination, a spectacle so absolutely and exclusively hateful, as to absorb all consideration of the means by which this miserable desecration of humanity was produced, and all sympathy for the brutes who to us, as it were, misrepresent their fellow creatures. Incidentally, these spectacles may connect themselves in our minds, with the means by which this extremity of vice and ignorance was produced, but the overwhelming feeling is that of disgust and abhorrence. There are physical diseases so revolting to the senses as to convert pity into sickening disgust, and there is a degree of moral corruption and wickedness which annihilates all sympathy.

"To call this the literature of Democracy is to make Democracy as brutal as this gentleman has been pleased to represent it in his native country. It may suit there, where it has perhaps its prototypes, so numerous as to constitute a class, but it does not actually belong to the United States, nor is it applicable to the state of society in this country. Such a school of literature can only aid the course and progress of vice among us, by placing before the already degraded, examples of new modes of wickedness, with which they were hitherto unacquainted, and degrees of degradation of which they never had any perception, until they became so conspicuous in the polite and fashionable literature of the day. The extraordinary cheapness with which these works have been got up among us, and the allurements they present in a series of embellishments with the grossness of the scenes they are intended to illustrate, have given them a general circulation among those classes most likely to overlook the latent imperceptible moral, if any such exists, and to concentrate their attention on those broad caricatures of wickedness, which are too often represented by the author in combination with ludicrous circumstances, admirably calculated to make those who have no very distinct notions of right and wrong, consider the whole an excellent joke, worthy of all imitation.

"I cannot, for my part, comprehend how a writer can be fairly entitled to the credit of being the champion of that class of mankind which he pictures in colors so revolting to our feelings and sympathies; nor by what process of induction this intimate association with this perpetual contemplation with all the varieties of extreme degradation coupled with a boundless latitude of crime, can be converted into a school of morals. If this is indeed the tendency of such contemplations and associations, let us send our children to bridewells and penitentiaries for their education, and to the quarter sessions for lessons of morality. Indeed it seems to me that Mr. Dickens' moral writings are very much on a par with Le Bœuf's great moral picture of Adam and Eve, in the moment of being tempted by the serpent. They were represented as large as life, perfectly naked, the female in the attitude of a lascivious courtesan, tempting a bashful youth; and if the artist had not fortunately bethought himself of calling it a great moral picture, no decent female would have dared to visit its exhibition. At this rate, I should not be at all surprised at seeing some strenuous amateur writing a criticism to prove the displays of Fanny Elssler a great moral spectacle."

The above is evidently the offering of no unpractised hand. I wish I could speak as favorably of the author's appreciation of merit, and of his candor and judgment.

A "democratic writer", I take it, is one the tendency of whose pages is to destroy those old land-marks which pride and fashion have set up, making impassable distinctions between the brethren of the Great Family—to render in their deformity before us the tyranny of partial laws—to show us the practical workings of the thousand distortions engrafted by custom upon our notions of what justice is—to make us love our fellow-creatures, and own that although social distinctions place others far higher or far lower than we, yet are human beings alike, as links of the same chain; one whose lines are imbued, from preface to finis, with that philosophy which teaches to pull down the high and bring up the low. I consider Mr. Dickens to be a democratic writer.

The mere fact of a man's delineating human character in its lowest stages of degradation, and giving it unbounded scope in every species of wickedness, proves neither his "democracy" nor its opposite. If it be done in such a way as that a kind of charm is thrown all the time around the guilty personage described—in such a way that excuses and palliations for his vice are covertly conveyed, every now and then—such writings, most assuredly, would have no fair claim to rank among "the literature of democracy". But when these specimens of naked, ragged deformity, as ignorant as wicked, are drawn out before us, and surrounded with their fit accompaniments, filth and darkness, and the deepest discomfort—when crime is portrayed, never so that by any possibility the reader can find the slightest temptation to go and do likewise—when we see how evil doing is followed by its sure and long and weary punishment—when our minds are led to the irresistible conclusion that iniquity is loathsome, and by the magic of the pen-painter have its pictures so stamped upon them that we ever after associate depraved actions with lowness and the very vulgarity of pollution—in such case, I say, the delineations of life in its lowest aspect, and even characterized by grossest ignorance and brutality, do not militate against their author's claim for admiration from all true democrats. And, then, the effect of the contrast which Mr. Dickens seems fond of forcing us to make between these wicked ones and the beings of purity and truth whom he also draws with a master hand! How he brings these characters together, and places them side by side, and makes them play into each other's hands, as it were, for the purpose of bringing out their distinctive traits! He not only teaches his readers to abhor vice, but he exhibits before them, for imitation, examples of the beauty of honesty—not as in the abstract style of the essayist, or the lofty dreams of the poet—but by examples that everyone can copy, examples in familiar life, that come home to us all. Who is not in love with truth when he follows, through trouble, poverty, and temptation, a little child that never swerves, but in its simplicity conducts itself as though there were no such thing as falsehood? What impropriety is there in the process of induction which calls that a school of morals where the pupil sees mapped out before him the parish boy's progress through sin and ignorance—resisting the tempter when yielding would have procured ease—steadily holding to the truth at all risks—living like an angel of light amid spirits of darkness—never giving up, though often his prospects seemed desperate—and being rewarded, at last, with prosperity?

The writer in the *Globe* thinks that the spectacles of misery pictured in the Boz novels constitute a combination so exclusively hateful as to absorb all consideration of the means which produce them, and all sympathy for the performers themselves. Did not the writer in the *Globe*, when he read the graphically drawn and deeply colored picture of the life led by Oliver Twist and his mates in the poor house, and of all the transactions there, and of the conduct of those who had to do with the institution—did he not have some reflections upon the evils of such a state of society as led to the existence of these things? When he read of Squeers and Do-the-boys hall, did he not entertain the most distant idea of how such a boarding-school system, if prevalent, might be rooted out, by thus showing it up?

The critic in the *Globe* compares Mr. Dickens' portraitures to the exhibition of those physical diseases so revolting to the senses as to create nothing but horror and sickening disgust. I suppose that in order to please our critic, a writer must speak mincingly, and with much delicacy lest he should introduce a vigorous turn or idea, which would offend him for its grossness. I fear me he is too dainty. Such exquisite sensitiveness—such affectation of being overcome by the strength of description in the novelist—such refined horror at some fancied overstepping of the limits wherein an author should confine himself, if he aspires to please the polite taste —bespeak the literary fop much more than they mark a man really fit to measure the length and breadth of that genius he so maligns. Besides, Mr. Dickens makes a sparing use of these strong features. The criticism in the *Globe* seems imbued throughout with the notion that the Boz works tell of nothing but the horrible and the awful—of desperate crime, and sensual vice. Surely it is not so. Boz is not altogether a feeder upon Newgate Calendars, and Police Reports, and whatever else reflects from the mind of him who looks thereon a sombre and a sorrowful hue. Pickwick, and the Wellers, and the Fat Boy, forbid! Dick Swiveller and the Marchioness—Kit, and pony—Miggs and Joe Willett, condemn the imputation. And thy sweet face, Kate Nickleby, and thy Christian nature, Cheeryble brothers—and thou, poor Nell —and thou, G. Varden—repel the slander!

The familiarity with low life wherein Mr. Dickens places his readers is a wholesome familiarity. For those moving in a kindred sphere it is wholesome, because it holds out to them continually the spectacle of beings of their own grade, engaged either in worthy actions which are held up to emulation, and shown to be rewarded both in themselves and in their results—or engaged in avocations of guilt which in themselves and their results are fearful, and only to be thought of with shuddering. For the richer classes this familiarity is wholesome because they are taught to feel, in fancy, what poverty is, and what thousands of fellow-creatures, as good as they, toil on year after year, amid discouragements and evils, whose bare relation is enough to make the hearer heart-sick. The rich cannot taste the distresses of want from their own experience; it is something if they are made to do so through the power of the pen.

He cannot comprehend, this critic tells us, how a writer can be called the champion of that class of mankind which he pictures in colors so revolting. A good parent or teacher sometimes has to lay before those whom he would reform the strong, naked, hideous truth. But Mr. Dickens never maligns the poor. He puts the searing iron to wickedness, whether among poor or rich; and yet when he describes the guilty, poor and oppressed man, we are always in some way reminded how much need there is that certain systems of law and habit which lead to this poverty and consequent crime should be remedied.

I would say more, but my limits prevent me. I cannot, however, close this paper without alluding once more, as in the beginning of the article, to those men who are always prone to carping and detraction. Mr. Dickens' charming manners, his modesty, his freedom from haughtiness, his *lovable* nature, his pleasant tenor of mind, as displayed in his personal conduct—might, it would seem, have saved him from those snappish and sour flings which some of the third-rate editorial fry are indulging in toward him. There are men among us with that unfortunate disposition—unfortunate as well for themselves as for those who have any intercourse with them—which picks out by preference every chance to snarl, and bite, and find fault. Honor paid to a fellow-creature is hateful to them: they turn pale with envy and malignance.

As I think that my humble lance, wielded in defense of Mr. Dickens, may meet the sight of that gentleman himself, I cannot lose the opportunity of saying how much I love and esteem him for what he has taught me through his writings—and for the genial influence that these writings spread around them wherever they go. Never having seen Boz in the body, we have yet had many a tête-à-tête. And I cannot tamely hear one whom I have long considered as a personal friend, and as a friend to his species, thus falsely and uncharitably and groundlessly attacked.

## "HOME" LITERATURE

HE WHO desires to see this noble Republic independent, not only in name but in fact, of all unwholesome foreign sway must ever bear in mind the influence of European literature over us—its tolerable amount of good, and its, we hope, "not to be endured" much longer, immense amount of evil. That there is often some clap-trap in denunciations of English books, we have no disposition to deny,—but the evil generally leans on the other side: we receive with a blind homage whatever comes to us stamped with the approbation of foreign critics—merely because it *is* so stamped. We have not enough confidence in our own judgment; we forget that God has given the American mind powers of analysis and acuteness superior to those possessed by any other nation on earth.

For the beautiful creations of the great intellects of Europe —for the sweetness of majesty of Shakespeare, Goethe, and some of the Italian poets—the fiery breath of Byron, the fascinating melancholy of Rousseau, the elegance and candor of Hume and Gibbon—and much more beside—we of the western world bring our tribute of admiration and respect. Presumptuous and vain would it be for us to decry their glorious merits. But it must not be forgotten, that many of the most literary men of England are the advocates of doctrines that in such a land as ours are the rankest and foulest poison.—Cowper teaches blind loyalty to the "divine right of kings",—Johnson was a burly aristocrat—and many more of that age were the scorners of the common people, and pour adulation on the shrine of "toryism". Walter Scott, Croly, Alison, Southey, and many others well known in America, exercise an evil influence through their books, in more than one respect; for they laugh to scorn the idea of republican freedom and virtue.

And what perfect cataracts of trash come to us at the present day from abroad! The tinsel sentimentality of Bulwer is but a relief from the inflated, unnatural, high-life-below-stairs, "historical" romances of Harrison Ainsworth. As to the vulgar coarseness of Marryatt, the dish-water senility of Lady Blessington, and the stuff (there is no better word,) of a long string of literary quacks, tapering down to the nastiness of the French Paul de Kock (who in reality has perhaps more talent than all the others put together—malgre his awfully murderous translations into English,)—who can say they have any qualities which recommend them to that wide circulation they enjoy on this side of the Atlantic? Let us be more just to ourselves and our own good taste. Why, "Professor" Ingraham, and those—their name is legion—Misters and Madams who write tales (does any body ever really read them through?) for the monthly magazines, have quite as much genuine ability as these coiners of unwholesome reading from abroad!

But where is the remedy? says the inquisitive reader. *In ourselves* we must look for it. Let those who read (and in this country who does not read?) no more condescend to patronize an inferior foreign author, when they have so many respectable writers at home. Shall Hawthorne get a paltry *seventy-five dollars* for a two-volume work—shall real American genius shiver with neglect—while the public run after this foreign trash? We hope, and we confidently expect, that the people of this land will come to their "sober second thought" upon the subject, and that soon.

## NEW STATES: SHALL THEY BE SLAVE OR FREE?

It is of not so much importance, the difference in the idea of a proper time to discuss, if we are only united in the *principle* that whatever new territory may be annexed to the United States, shall be free territory, and not for slaves. With the present slave states, of course, no human being any where

out from themselves has the least shadow of a right to interfere; but in new land, added to our surface by the national
arms, and by the action of our government, and where
slavery does not exist, it is certainly of momentous importance one way or the other, whether that land shall be slave
land or not. All ordinarily "weighty issues" are insignificant
before this: it swallows them up as Aaron's rod swallowed
the other rods. It involves the question whether the mighty
power of this republic, put forth in its greatest strength, shall
be used to root deeper and spread wider an institution which
Washington, Jefferson, Madison, and all the old fathers of
our freedom, anxiously, and avowedly from the bottom of
their hearts, sought the extinction of, and considered inconsistent with the other institutions of the land. And if those
true and brave old men were now among us, can any candid
person doubt which "side" they would espouse in this argument? Would the great apostle of democracy—in his clear
views of right and wrong, and their linked profit and loss—
would he *now*, seeing the stalwart giants of the free young
west, contrasted with the meagre leanness of the south—
meagre with all her noble traits—would *he* hesitate in bending his divine energies to the side of freedom?

The man who accustoms himself to *think*, when such matters are put before him, and does not whiff his opinion rapidly
out, from mere heedlessness, or from a more degrading
motive, will see the wide and radical difference between the
unquestionable folly, and wicked wrong, of "abolitionist"
interference with slavery in the southern states—and this
point of establishing slavery in fresh land. With the former
we have nothing to do; but with the latter, we should all be
derelict to our highest duties as christians, as men, and as
democrats, if we did not throw ourselves into the field of discussion, using the utmost display of every energy wherewith
God has endowed us, in behalf of the side which reason and
religion proclaim as the right one. Is *this* the country, and
*this* the age, where and when we are to be told that slavery
must be propped up and extended? And shall any respectable portion of our citizens be deluded either by the sophisms
of Mr. Calhoun, or those far, very far, lower influences of the
darkest and meanest phases of demagoguism, which are rife

more at the north than at the south, to act in a matter which asks consideration purely on points of high justice, human rights, national advantage, and the safety of the union in the future?

## CROSSING THE ALLEGHANIES

WE left Baltimore on Saturday morning at seven o'clock, on the railroad for Cumberland, which is about a hundred and seventy miles distant, at the eastern edge of the Alleghanies. Of course, at this season of the year the country is not re- markably fascinating anywhere; and here a very large por- tion of the road is bounded on one side or the other by cliffs and steeps of an Alp-like loftiness. We seemed, for at least a hundred miles, to follow the course of an interminable brook, winding with its windings, and twisting with its twists, in a, to me, singular fashion. But even with so many circuits, the road had to be cut through very many bad places; and was probably one of the most expensive railroads ever built. It pays enormous profits, however; and they seriously "talk" about having it continued to some place on the Ohio, perhaps Wheeling. After "talking about it" awhile, it will very likely be done; it only wants money enough—and an enormous lot of that it *will* want, too!

At Harper's Ferry, where they gave us twenty minutes to dine, the scenery is strikingly abrupt and varied. Houses were perched up over our heads—backs in the ground—and others perched up over *their* heads, and so on. The finest scenery, though, even here, (if it be not a bull to say so,) is about half a mile off. As soon as the cars stopped, a frightful sound of bells and discordant screams surrounded us, and we were all but torn in pieces by the assault, as it were! Re- covering from the first shock of such an unexpected salute, we found that there were several "hotels", each moved by a bitter rivalry for getting the passengers to eat their dinner. One "opposition house", in particular, seemed bent upon proceeding to extremities—and most of the passengers were fain to go quietly in. For a good dinner here, the price was only twenty-five cents.

Cumberland, at which we arrived about sunset, is a thriving town, with several public edifices, a newspaper or two, and those [institutions] invariably to be found in every western and southern community, some big "hotels". The town has a peculiar character, from its being the great rendezvous and landing place of the immense Pennsylvania wagons, and the drovers from hundreds of miles west. You may see Tartar-looking groups of these wagons, and their drivers, in the open grounds about,—the horses being loosed—and the whole having not a little the appearance of a caravan of the Steppes. Hundreds and hundreds of these enormous vehicles, with their arched roofs of white canvas, wend their way into Cumberland from all quarters, during a busy season, with goods to send on eastward, and to take goods brought by the railroad. They are in shape not a little like the "Chinese junk", whilom exhibited at New York—being built high at each end, and scooping down in the waist. With their teams of four and six horses, they carry an almost incalculable quantity of "freight"; and if one should accidentally get in the road-ruts before their formidable wheels, they would perform the work of a *Juggernaut* upon him in most effectual order. The drivers of these vehicles and the drovers of cattle, hogs, horses, etc., in this section of the land, form a large slice of "society".

Night now falling down around us like a very large cloak of black broadcloth, (I fancy *that* figure, at least, hasn't been used up by the poets) and the Alleghanies rearing themselves up "some pumpkins" (as they say here,) right before our nasal members, we got into one of the several four-horse stage coaches of the "National Road and Good Intent Stage Company", whereby we were to be transported over those big hills. They did the thing systematically, whatever may be said elsewise. All the passengers' names were inscribed on a roll, (we purchased tickets in Philadelphia, at $13 a head, to go to Wheeling,) and a clerk stands by and two or three negroes with a patent weighing machine. The clerk calls your name—your baggage is whipped on the machine, and if it weighs over fifty pounds, you have to pay extra. You are then put in the stage, (literally put in, like a package, unless you move quickly,) your baggage packed on behind—and the next name called off—baggage weighed—and so on to the end of the chapter. If six passengers desire it, or any smaller number who will pay for six, they can wait and have a coach sent with them the next morning, or at any hour they choose. One cunning trick of the company is, that they give you no check or receipt for your baggage, for which they pretend not to be responsible. It is best, therefore, if possible, for each passenger to have some witness to his baggage and its amount, in which case, if it be lost, the company will have to pay up—whatever they publish to the contrary.

So they boxed us up in our coach, nine precious souls, and we dashed through the town and up the mountains, with an apparent prospect of as comfortable a night as could be expected, considering all things. One or two of the passengers tried to get up a conversational entertainment; one old gentleman, in particular, *did* talk. He resided on a farm in the interior of Ohio. He had been on to Washington, (I heard the fact at least twenty-five times in the course of that night and the next day,) to claim a certain $5,000 from the Government for capturing a British merchant brig off the coast of Maine, in the last war. She got becalmed, or something of that sort, and he being thereabout, in command of a fishing smack, sailed or rowed up, captured her and brought her into port, where the Government functionaries took possession of her and sold her cargo for some $30,000. Our old gentleman, however, (not *then* old, of course,) had no privateering papers, and [was] consequently not a dollar the gainer. He had now been on to Washington to see about it, and was in hopes of getting at least his share of the sale. (Poor old man! if he lives till he gets Congress to pay him, he will be immortal.) This famous old gentleman moreover informed us that his wife had had thirteen children, one in every month of the year, and one over besides—all being alive and kicking! He did not know exactly what to think about the Mexican war; but he thought that Congress might at least grant decent pensions to those who were severely maimed in it, and to the widows of both officers and privates who were killed. Sage and sound conclusions, thought the rest of us too. And here I may say, once for all, that, though expecting to find a shrewd population as I journeyed to the interior, and down through the great rivers, I was by no means prepared for the sterling vein of common sense that seemed to pervade them —even the roughest shod and roughest clad of all. A satirical person could no doubt find an ample field for his powers in many of the manners and the ways of the West; and so can he, indeed, in the highest circles of fashion. But I fully believe that in a comparison of actual manliness and what the Yankees call "gumption", the well-to-do *citizens* (for I am not speaking so much of the country,) particularly the young men, of New York, Philadelphia, Boston, Brooklyn and so on, with all the advantages of compact neighborhood, schools, etc., are not up to the men of the West. Among the latter, probably, attention is more turned to the *realities* of life, and a habit formed of thinking for one's self; in the cities, frippery and artificial fashion are too much the ruling powers.

Up we toiled, and down we clattered, (for the first fifty miles it was nearly *all* up,) over these mighty warts on the great breast of nature. It was excessively cold; the moon shone at intervals; and whenever we stopped, I found the ground thickly covered with snow. The places at which we changed horses, (which was done every ten miles,) were generally long, old, one-story houses, with stupendous fires of soft coal that is so plentiful and cheap here. In the night, with the mountains on all sides, the precipitous and turning road, the large, bare-armed trees looming up around us, the room half filled with men curiously enwrapped in garments of a fashion till then never seen—and the flickering light from the mighty fire putting a red glow upon most objects, and casting others into a strong shadow—I can tell you these stoppages were not without interest. They might, it seems to me, afford first rate scenes for an *American* painter—one who, not continually straining to be merely second or third best, in *imitation*, seizes original and really picturesque occasions of this sort for his pieces. There was one of the Alleghany inns, in particular, that we stopped at about an hour after midnight. (All the staging across these mountains, both to and fro, is done in the night, which engrafts a somewhat weird character upon the public houses—their busy time being from sunset to sunrise.) There were some ten or twelve great strapping drovers, reclining about the room on benches, and as many more before the huge fire. The beams overhead were low and smoke-dried. I stepped to the farther end of the long porch; the view from the door was grand, though vague, even in the moonlight. We had just descended a large and very steep hill, and just off on one side of us was a precipice of apparently hundreds of feet. The silence of the grave spread over this solemn scene; the mountains were covered in their white shrouds of snow—and the towering trees looked black and threatening; only the largest stars were visible, and they glittered with a tenfold brightness. One's heart, at such times, is irresistibly lifted to Him of whom these august appearances are but the least emanation. Faith! if I had an infidel to convert, I would take him on the mountains, of a clear and beautiful night, when the stars are shining.

Journeying in this manner, the time and the distance slipped away, until we welcomed the gray dawn of the morning. Half an hour more brought us to Uniontown, at the western side of the Alleghanies—and glad enough were "all hands" to arrive there.

## MY PASSION FOR FERRIES

LIVING in Brooklyn or New York city from this time forward, my life, then, and still more the following years, was curiously identified with Fulton ferry, already becoming the greatest of its sort in the world for general importance, volume, variety, rapidity, and picturesqueness. Almost daily, later, ('50 to '60,) I cross'd on the boats, often up in the pilot-houses where I could get a full sweep, absorbing shows, accompaniments, surroundings. What oceanic currents, eddies, underneath—the great tides of humanity also, with ever-shifting movements. Indeed, I have always had a passion for ferries; to me they afford inimitable, streaming, never-failing, living poems. The river and bay scenery, all about New York island, any time of a fine day—the hurrying, splashing sea-tides—the changing panorama of steamers, all sizes, often a string of big ones outward bound to distant ports—the myriads of white-sail'd schooners, sloops, skiffs, and the marvellously beautiful yachts—the majestic sound boats as they rounded the Battery and came along towards 5, afternoon, eastward bound—the prospect off towards Staten Island, or down the Narrows, or the other way up the Hudson—what refreshment of spirit such sights and experiences gave me years ago (and many a time since). My old pilot friends, the Balsirs, Johnny Cole, Ira Smith, William White, and my young ferry friend, Tom Gere—how well I remember them all.

## BROADWAY SIGHTS

BESIDES Fulton ferry, off and on for years, I knew and frequented Broadway—that noted avenue of New York's crowded and mixed humanity, and of so many notables. Here I saw, during those times, Andrew Jackson, Webster, Clay, Seward, Martin Van Buren, filibuster Walker, Kossuth, Fitz Greene Halleck, Bryant, the Prince of Wales, Charles Dickens, the first Japanese ambassadors, and lots of other celebrities of the time. Always something novel or inspiriting; yet mostly to me the hurrying and vast amplitude of those never-ending human currents. I remember seeing James Fenimore Cooper in a court-room in Chambers street, back of the city hall, where he was carrying on a law case—(I think it was a charge of libel he had brought against some one). I also remember seeing Edgar A. Poe, and having a short interview with him, (it must have been in 1845 or '6,) in his office, second story of a corner building, (Duane or Pearl street). He was editor and owner or part owner of *the Broadway Journal.* The visit was about a piece of mine he had publish'd. Poe was very cordial, in a quiet way, appear'd well in person, dress, etc. I have a distinct and pleasing remembrance of his looks, voice, manner and matter; very kindly and human, but subdued, perhaps a little jaded. For another of my reminiscences, here on the west side, just below Houston street, I once saw (it must have been about 1832, of a sharp, bright January day) a bent, feeble but stout-built very old man, bearded, swathed in rich furs, with a great ermine cap on his head, led and assisted, almost carried, down the steps of his high front stoop (a dozen friends and servants, emulous, carefully holding, guiding him) and then lifted and tuck'd in a gorgeous sleigh, envelop'd in other furs, for a ride. The sleigh was drawn by as fine a team of horses as I ever saw. (You needn't think all the best animals are brought up nowadays; never was such horseflesh as fifty years ago on Long Island, or south, or in New York city; folks look'd for spirit and mettle in a nag, not tame speed merely.) Well, I, a boy of perhaps 13 or 14, stopp'd and gazed long at the spectacle of that fur-swathed old man, surrounded by friends and servants, and the careful seating of him in the sleigh. I remember the spirited, champing horses, the driver with his whip, and a fellow-driver by his side, for extra prudence. The old man, the subject of so much attention, I can almost see now. It was John Jacob Astor.

The years 1846, '47, and there along, see me still in New York city, working as writer and printer, having my usual good health, and a good time generally.

## OMNIBUS JAUNTS AND DRIVERS

ONE phase of those days must by no means go unrecorded—namely, the Broadway omnibuses, with their drivers. The vehicles still (I write this paragraph in 1881) give a portion of the character of Broadway—the Fifth avenue, Madison avenue, and Twenty-third street lines yet running. But the flush days of the old Broadway stages, characteristic and copious, are over. The Yellow-birds, the Red-birds, the original Broadway, the Fourth avenue, the Knickerbocker, and a dozen others of twenty or thirty years ago, are all gone. And the men specially identified with them, and giving vitality and meaning to them—the drivers—a strange, natural, quick-eyed and wondrous race—(not only Rabelais and Cervantes would have gloated upon them, but Homer and Shakspere would)—how well I remember them, and must here give a word about them. How many hours, forenoons and afternoons—how many exhilarating night-times I have had —perhaps June or July, in cooler air—riding the whole length of Broadway, listening to some yarn, (and the most vivid yarns ever spun, and the rarest mimicry)—or perhaps I declaiming some stormy passage from Julius Caesar or Richard, (you could roar as loudly as you chose in that heavy, dense, uninterrupted street-bass.) Yes, I knew all the drivers then, Broadway Jack, Dressmaker, Balky Bill, George Storms, Old Elephant, his brother Young Elephant (who came afterward,) Tippy, Pop Rice, Big Frank, Yellow Joe, Pete Callahan, Patsey Dee, and dozens more; for there were hundreds. They had immense qualities, largely animal—eating, drinking; women—great personal pride, in their way—perhaps a few slouches here and there, but I should have trusted the general run of them, in their simple good-will and honor, under all circumstances. Not only for comradeship, and sometimes affection—great studies I found them also. (I suppose the critics will laugh heartily, but the influence of those Broadway omnibus jaunts and drivers and declamations and escapades undoubtedly enter'd into the gestation of *Leaves of Grass*.)

## PLAYS AND OPERAS TOO

AND certain actors and singers, had a good deal to do with the business. All through these years, off and on, I frequented the old Park, the Bowery, Broadway and Chatham-square theatres, and the Italian operas at Chambers-street, Astor-place or the Battery—many seasons was on the free list, writing for papers even as quite a youth. The old Park theatre—what names, reminiscences, the words bring back! Placide, Clarke, Mrs. Vernon, Fisher, Clara F., Mrs. Wood, Mrs. Seguin, Ellen Tree, Hackett, the younger Kean, Macready, Mrs. Richardson, Rice—singers, tragedians, comedians. What perfect acting! Henry Placide in *Napoleon's Old Guard* or *Grandfather Whitehead*,—or *the Provoked Husband* of Cibber, with Fanny Kemble as Lady Townley—or Sheridan Knowles in his own *Virginius*—or inimitable Power in *Born to Good Luck*. These, and many more, the years of youth and onward. Fanny Kemble—name to conjure up great mimic scenes withal—perhaps the greatest. I remember well her rendering of Bianca in *Fazio*, and Marianna in *the Wife*. Nothing finer did ever stage exhibit—the veterans of all nations said so, and my boyish heart and head felt it in every minute cell. The lady was just matured, strong, better than merely beautiful, born from the footlights, had had three years' practice in London and through the British towns, and then she came to give America that young maturity and roseate power in all their noon, or rather fore-noon, flush. It was my good luck to see her nearly every night she play'd at the old Park—certainly in all her princi-pal characters.

I heard, these years, well render'd, all the Italian and other operas in vogue, *Sonnambula, the Puritans, Der Freischutz, Huguenots, Fille d'Regiment, Faust, Etoile du Nord, Poliuto* and others. Verdi's *Ernani, Rigoletto,* and *Trovatore,* with Donizetti's *Lucia* or *Favorita* or *Lucrezia,* and Auber's *Massaniello,* or Rossini's *William Tell* and *Gazza Ladra,* were among my special enjoyments. I heard Alboni every time she sang in New York and vicinity—also Grisi, the tenor Mario, and the baritone Badiali, the finest in the world.

This musical passion follow'd my theatrical one. As a boy or young man I had seen, (reading them carefully the day beforehand,) quite all Shakspere's acting dramas, play'd wonderfully well. Even yet I cannot conceive anything finer than old Booth in *Richard Third,* or *Lear,* (I don't know which was best,) or Iago, (or Pescara, or Sir Giles Overreach, to go outside of Shakspere)—or Tom Hamblin in *Macbeth*—or old Clarke, either as the ghost in *Hamlet,* or as Prospero in *the Tempest,* with Mrs. Austin as Ariel, and Peter Richings as Caliban. Then other dramas, and fine players in them, For-rest as Metamora or Damon or Brutus—John R. Scott as Tom Cringle or Rolla—or Charlotte Cushman's Lady Gay Spanker in *London Assurance.* Then of some years later, at Castle Garden, Battery, I yet recall the splendid seasons cf the Havana musical troupe under Maretzek—the fine band, the cool sea-breezes, the unsurpass'd vocalism—Steffanone, Bosio, Truffi, Marini in *Marino Faliero, Don Pasquale,* or *Favorita.* No better playing or singing ever in New York. It was here too I afterward heard Jenny Lind. (The Battery—its past associations—what tales those old trees and walks and sea-walls could tell!)

## THROUGH EIGHT YEARS

In 1848, '49, I was occupied as editor of the *Daily Eagle* news-paper, in Brooklyn. The latter year went off on a leisurely journey and working expedition (my brother Jeff with me) through all the middle States, and down the Ohio and Mississippi rivers. Lived awhile in New Orleans, and work'd there on the editorial staff of *Daily Crescent* newspaper. After a time plodded back northward, up the Mississippi, and around to, and by way of the great lakes, Michigan, Huron, and Erie, to Niagara falls and lower Canada, finally returning through central New York and down the Hudson; traveling altogether probably 8,000 miles this trip, to and fro. '51, '53, occupied in house-building in Brooklyn. (For a little of the first part of that time in printing a daily and weekly paper, *the Freeman*.) '55 lost my dear father this year by death. Commenced putting *Leaves of Grass* to press for good, at the job printing office of my friends, the brothers Rome, in Brooklyn, after many MS. doings and undoings—(I had great trouble in leaving out the stock "poetical" touches, but succeeded at last.) I am now (1856-'7) passing through my 37th year.

## THE OLD CATHEDRAL

THIS venerable building was, on Thursday last, resorted to by hundreds of those who wished to show their penitence and humility. The old monastic church stood, as it were, aloof from the wings on either side. The temples dedicated to the law—the higher Courts on the one side, and the Municipal Court on the other—have been renovated, and now look like modern structures by the side of some monument of old. The tall, gray Cathedral reared its ancient spire to Heaven; but the towers wherein [were] the bells that have tolled the death knell, and rung the merry marriage music of thousands, were silent. It was a day dedicated to the "King of Kings"—it was the Holy Thursday of Passion week. It commemorated the occasion of the "Last Supper" of our Saviour, who, when surrounded by his disciples, gave them his last earthly blessing. There were over two thousand communicants kneeling at the altars, at various periods of the day, and all seemed fully sensible of the solemnity of the occasion. Grand Mass was celebrated—after which, many persons came in to adore or communicate in spirit with the

"Son of Man". In the niche upon the right-hand side, stood a *basse relievo* of the Virgin and her Child. Upon a table near by, was a bronze figure of the Crucifixion, and underneath a higher portion of the altar, a cross, covered with purple silk —the color emblematical of the blood that gushed from the wound inflicted by the spearman, upon the person of the Divine Nazarene. On the other side was a niche dedicated to St. Francis; this was half covered with a parti-colored drapery, which entirely concealed the face of the Saint, but beneath, there was an altar composed of the most gorgeous flowers—whose radiant beauties were lighted up by innumerable candles in silver candlesticks. The church was crowded by those devoted to the Catholic religion, and presented a scene that was solemn and interesting in the highest degree. Our dark-eyed Creole beauties, with their gilt-edged prayer-books in their hands, would walk in with an air that seemed to say that beauty was a part of religion. Dipping their taper fingers into the holy water and crossing their foreheads, they would then walk up the aisle and kneel down to prayer. We saw many women there whose garments betokened that some dear friend had not long been laid in the grave. They knelt before the picture of Christ carrying his cross, and prayed, no doubt, that they might have strength to carry theirs. Persons of all classes went down before the shrine of Religion. There was the broken-hearted man of the world— the gray-haired man, whose feet were on the brink of the grave—the blooming girl whose charms were budding into womanhood—and the wrinkled, care-worn widow, to whom love was but a memory. Then again, were the old servants of ancient families; and then ragged, pale-faced creatures, who looked as though they did not dare to approach too near the altar. The whole scene was beautiful and solemn, and calculated to impress the heart with the purity of virtue, and endow the soul with full reliance in the power of Him who rules above. Yesterday was Good-Friday—the anniversary of the Crucifixion. The ceremonies on this occasion were of the most imposing nature, and showed reverence and respect for the tortures endured by the God-like Hero of Calvary, for the benefit of a sinful world.

# LETTERS FROM PAUMANOK

BROOKLYN, *August* 11, [1851.]

THE hot day was over at last; though the opera at Castle Garden did not commence till eight; and even had it not been leisure enough and to spare, was there any escape from those imperial commands in the west? So with wool-hat crushed in my hand behind me, for the sundown breezes felt good, there on old "Clover Hill", (modernized Brooklyn Heights,) I took my time, and expanded to the glory spread over heaven and earth.

Sails of sloops bellied gracefully upon the river, with mellower light and deepened shadows. And the dark and glistening water formed an undertone to the play of vehement color above.

Rapidly, an insatiable greediness grew within me for brighter and stronger hues; oh, brighter and stronger still. It seemed as if all that the eye could bear, were unequal to the fierce voracity of my soul for intense, glowing color.

And yet there were the most choice and fervid fires of the sunset, in their brilliancy and richness almost terrible.

Have not you, too, at such a time, known this thirst of the eye? Have not you, in like manner, while listening to the well-played music of some band like Maretzek's, felt an overwhelming desire for measureless sound—a sublime orchestra of a myriad orchestras—a colossal volume of harmony, in which the thunder might roll in its proper place; and above it, the vast, pure Tenor,—identity of the Creative Power itself—rising through the universe, until the boundless and unspeakable capacities of that mystery, the human soul, should be filled to the uttermost, and the problem of human cravingness be satisfied and destroyed?

Of this sort are the promptings of good music upon me. How is it possible, that among the performers there, with their instruments, are some who can jest, and giggle, and look flippantly over the house meanwhile? And even good singers upon the stage beyond them, you may see presently, who will mar their parts with quizzing and ill-timed smiles, and looks of curiosity at the amount of their audience.

Come, I will not talk to you as to one of the superficial crowd who saunter here because it is a fashion; who take opera glasses with them, and make you sick with shallow words, upon the sublimest and most spiritual of the arts. I will trust you with confidence; I will divulge secrets.

The delicious music of *the Favorite*, is upon us. Gradually, we see not this huge amphitheatre, nor the cropped heads and shaved faces of the men; nor coal-skuttle bonnets; nor hear the rattle of fans, nor even the ill-bred chatter. We see the groves of a Spanish convent, and the procession of monks; we hear the chant, now dim and faint, then swelling loudly, and then again dying away among the trees. The aged Superior and the young Fernando, we see. In answer to the old man's rebukes and questions, we hear the story of love.

Those fresh vigorous tones of Bettini!—I have often wished to know this man, for a minute, that I might tell him how much of the highest order of pleasure he has conferred upon me. His voice has often affected me to tears. Its clear, firm, wonderfully exalting notes, filling and expanding away; dwelling like a poised lark up in heaven; have made my very soul tremble.—Critics talk of others who are more perfectly artistical—yes, as the well-shaped marble is artistical. But the singing of this man has breathing blood within it; the living soul, of which the lower stage they call art, is but the shell and sham.

Yes, let me dwell a moment here. After travelling through the fifteen years' display in this city, of musical celebrities, from Mrs. Austin up to Jenny Lind, from Old Bull on to conductor Benedict, with much fair enjoyment of the talent of all; none have thoroughly satisfied, overwhelmed me, but this man. Never before did I realize what an indescribable volume of delight the recesses of the soul can bear from the sound of the honied perfection of the human voice. The *manly* voice it must be, too. The female organ, however curious and high, is but as the pleasant moonlight.

The Swedish Swan, with all her blandishments, never touched my heart in the least. I wondered at so much vocal dexterity; and indeed they were all very pretty, those leaps and double somersets. But even in the grandest religious airs, genuine masterpieces as they are, of the German composers, executed by this strangely overpraised woman in perfect scientific style, let critics say what they like, it was a failure, for there was a vacuum in the head of the performance. Beauty pervaded it no doubt, and that of a high order. It was the beauty of Adam before God breathed into his nostrils.

Let us return to Balthazar, and his prophetic announcements. "Ah, Fernando," we hear him say, "this magnificent world, which allures you, is deceptive and false. The angel you now love may prove treacherous. Yes, tossed by tempests, you will gladly seek again this haven of peace."

I always thought the plot of the *Favorite* a peculiarly well-proportioned and charming story. It is a type of the experience of the human kind, and, like Shakspeare's dramas, its moral is world-wide.

Fernando, young, enthusiastic, full of manly vigor, and at the same time of tenderness, trusted and loved a beautiful unknown woman. She, Leonara [Leonora], though the favorite and mistress of the king, returned the young man's love. Thus, he would not complete the burial of himself among the priesthood. He left the convent, and having received from Leonara a commission of rank in the army, joined the camp, and rendered such important services, that the king, in person, thanked him before the court. He, however, abruptly discovered the amour between his favorite and the young officer.

The king's own love was faithful, but the Papal court interfered, and Leonara confessing her genuine attachment to Fernando, the royal consent sealed their marriage. Previously to this, the disgraced woman had sent her lover a true account of herself; but it was intercepted, and Fernando immediately afterwards found that his idol was the cast-off mistress of the king.

All the indignant passions of his soul then broke forth. He upbraided the king with such perfidy, tore the golden order from his neck, broke his sword, and cast it at the monarch's feet, and retired in a fury of sorrow and disappointment, back into the shadows from which he had sallied forth into the world.

Now we approach the close of the legend. We see again the dark groves of the convent. Up through the venerable trees peal the strains of the chanting voices. Oh, sweet music of Donizetti, how can men hesitate what rank to give you!

With his pale face at the foot of the cross kneels the returned novice, his breast filled with a devouring anguish, his eyes showing the death that has fallen upon his soul. The strains of death, too, come plaintively from his lips. Never before did you hear such wonderful gushing sorrow, poured forth like ebbing blood, from a murdered heart. Is it for peace he prays with that appealing passion? Is it the story of his own sad wreck he utters?

Listen. Pure and vast, that voice now rises, as on clouds, to the heaven where it claims audience. Now, firm and unbroken, it spreads like an ocean around us. Ah, welcome that I know not the mere language of the earthly words in which the melody is embodied; as all words are mean before the language of true music.

Thanks, great artist. For one, at least, it is no extravagance to say, you have justified his ideal of the loftiest of the arts. Thanks, limner of the spirit of life, and hope and peace; of the red fire of passion, the cavernous vacancy of despair, and the black pall of the grave.

I write as I feel; and I feel that there are not a few who will pronounce a Yes to my own confession.

## PREFACE, 1855

### *To first issue of* Leaves of Grass. *Brooklyn, N.Y.*

AMERICA does not repel the past, or what the past has produced under its forms, or amid other politics, or the idea of castes, or the old religions—accepts the lesson with calmness —is not impatient because the slough still sticks to opinions and manners in literature, while the life which served its requirements has passed into the new life of the new forms— perceives that the corpse is slowly borne from the eating and sleeping rooms of the house—perceives that it waits a little while in the door—that it was fittest for its days—that its action has descended to the stalwart and well-shaped heir who approaches—and that he shall be fittest for his days.

The Americans of all nations at any time upon the earth,

have probably the fullest poetical nature. The United States themselves are essentially the greatest poem. In the history of the earth hitherto, the largest and most stirring appear tame and orderly to their ampler largeness and stir. Here at last is something in the doings of man that corresponds with the broadcast doings of the day and night. Here is action untied from strings, necessarily blind to particulars and details, magnificently moving in masses. Here is the hospitality which for ever indicates heroes. Here the performance, disdaining the trivial, unapproach'd in the tremendous audacity of its crowds and groupings, and the push of its perspective, spreads with crampless and flowing breadth, and showers its prolific and splendid extravagance. One sees it must indeed own the riches of the summer and winter, and need never be bankrupt while corn grows from the ground, or the orchards drop apples, or the bays contain fish, or men beget children upon women.

Other states indicate themselves in their deputies—but the genius of the United States is not best or most in its executives or legislatures, nor in its ambassadors or authors, or colleges or churches or parlors, nor even in its newspapers or inventors—but always most in the common people, south, north, west, east, in all its States, through all its mighty amplitude. The largeness of the nation, however, were monstrous without a corresponding largeness and generosity of the spirit of the citizen. Not swarming states, nor streets and steamships, nor prosperous business, nor farms, nor capital, nor learning, may suffice for the ideal of man—nor suffice the poet. No reminiscences may suffice either. A live nation can always cut a deep mark, and can have the best authority the cheapest—namely, from its own soul. This is the sum of the profitable uses of individuals or states, and of present action and grandeur, and of the subjects of poets. (As if it were necessary to trot back generation after generation to the eastern records! As if the beauty and sacredness of the demonstrable must fall behind that of the mythical! As if men do not make their mark out of any times! As if the opening of the western continent by discovery, and what has transpired in North and South America, were less than the small theatre of the antique, or the aimless sleep-walking of the middle ages!) The pride of the United States leaves the wealth and finesse of the cities, and all returns of commerce and agriculture, and all the magnitude of geography or shows of exterior victory, to enjoy the sight and realization of full-sized men, or one full-sized man unconquerable and simple.

The American poets are to enclose old and new, for America is the race of races. The expression of the American poet is to be transcendent and new. It is to be indirect, and not direct or descriptive or epic. Its quality goes through these to much more. Let the age and wars of other nations be chanted, and their eras and characters be illustrated, and that finish the verse. Not so the great psalm of the republic. Here the theme is creative, and has vista. Whatever stagnates in the flat of custom or obedience or legislation, the great poet never stagnates. Obedience does not master him, he masters it. High up out of reach he stands, turning a concentrated light—he turns the pivot with his finger—he baffles the swiftest runners as he stands, and easily overtakes and envelopes them. The time straying toward infidelity and confections and persiflage he withholds by steady faith. Faith is the antiseptic of the soul—it pervades the common people and preserves them—they never give up believing and expecting and trusting. There is that indescribable freshness and unconsciousness about an illiterate person, that humbles and mocks the power of the noblest expressive genius. The poet sees for a certainty how one not a great artist may be just as sacred and perfect as the greatest artist.

The power to destroy or remould is freely used by the greatest poet, but seldom the power of attack. What is past is past. If he does not expose superior models, and prove himself by every step he takes, he is not what is wanted. The presence of the great poet conquers—not parleying, or struggling, or any prepared attempts. Now he has passed that way, see after him! There is not left any vestige of despair, or misanthropy, or cunning, or exclusiveness, or the ignominy of a nativity or color, or delusion of hell or the necessity of hell—and no man thenceforward shall be degraded for ignorance or weakness or sin. The greatest poet hardly knows pettiness or triviality. If he breathes into anything that was before thought small, it dilates with the grandeur and life of the universe. He is a seer—he is individual—he is complete in himself—the others are as good as he, only he sees it, and they do not. He is not one of the chorus—he does not stop for any regulation—he is the president of regulation. What the eyesight does to the rest, he does to the rest. Who knows the curious mystery of the eyesight? The other senses corroborate themselves, but this is removed from any proof but its own, and foreruns the identities of the spiritual world. A single glance of it mocks all the investigations of man, and all the instruments and books of the earth, and all reasoning. What is marvellous? what is unlikely? what is impossible or baseless or vague—after you have once just open'd the space of a peach-pit, and given audience to far and near, and to the sunset, and had all things enter with electric swiftness, softly and duly, without confusion or jostling or jam?

The land and sea, the animals, fishes and birds, the sky of heaven and the orbs, the forests, mountains and rivers, are not small themes—but folks expect of the poet to indicate more than the beauty and dignity which always attach to dumb real objects—they expect him to indicate the path between reality and their souls. Men and women perceive the beauty well enough—probably as well as he. The passionate tenacity of hunters, woodmen, early risers, cultivators of gardens and orchards and fields, the love of healthy women for the manly form, seafaring persons, drivers of horses, the passion for light and the open air, all is an old varied sign of the unfailing perception of beauty, and of a residence of the poetic in out-door people. They can never be assisted by poets to perceive—some may, but they never can. The poetic quality is not marshal'd in rhyme or uniformity, or abstract addresses to things, nor in melancholy complaints or good precepts, but is the life of these and much else, and is in the soul. The profit of rhyme is that it drops seeds of a sweeter and more luxuriant rhyme, and of uniformity that it conveys itself into its own roots in the ground out of sight. The rhyme and uniformity of perfect poems show the free growth of metrical laws, and bud from them as unerringly and loosely as lilacs and roses on a bush, and take shapes as compact as the shapes of chestnuts and oranges, and melons and pears, and shed the perfume impalpable to form. The fluency and ornaments of the finest poems or music or orations or recitations, are not independent but dependent. All beauty comes from beautiful blood and a beautiful brain. If the greatnesses are in conjunction in a man or woman, it is enough—the fact will prevail through the universe; but the gaggery and gilt of a million years will not prevail. Who troubles himself about his ornaments or fluency is lost. This is what you shall do: Love the earth and sun and the animals, despise riches, give alms to every one that asks, stand up for the stupid and crazy, devote your income and labor to others, hate tyrants, argue not concerning God, have patience and indulgence toward the people, take off your hat to nothing known or unknown, or to any man or number of men—go freely with powerful uneducated persons, and with the young, and with the mothers of families—re-examine all you have been told in school or church or in any book, and dismiss whatever insults your own soul; and your very flesh shall be a great poem, and have the richest fluency, not only in its words, but in the silent lines of its lips and face, and between the lashes of your eyes, and in every motion and joint of your body. The poet shall not spend his time in unneeded work. He shall know that the ground is already plough'd and manured; others may not know it, but he shall. He shall go directly to the creation. His trust shall master the trust of everything he touches—and shall master all attachment.

The known universe has one complete lover, and that is the greatest poet. He consumes an eternal passion, and is indifferent which chance happens, and which possible contingency of fortune or misfortune, and persuades daily and hourly his delicious pay. What balks or breaks others is fuel for his burning progress to contact and amorous joy. Other proportions of the reception of pleasure dwindle to nothing to his proportions. All expected from heaven or from the highest, he is rapport with in the sight of the daybreak, or the scenes of the winter woods, or the presence of children playing, or with his arm round the neck of a man or woman. His love above all love has leisure and expanse—he leaves room ahead of himself. He is no irresolute or suspicious lover—he is sure—he scorns intervals. His experience and the showers and thrills are not for nothing. Nothing can jar him—suffering and darkness cannot—death and fear cannot. To him complaint and jealousy and envy are corpses buried and rotten in the earth—he saw them buried. The sea is not surer of the shore, or the shore of the sea, than he is the fruition of his love, and of all perfection and beauty.

The fruition of beauty is no chance of miss or hit—it is as inevitable as life—it is exact and plumb as gravitation. From the eyesight proceeds another eyesight, and from the hearing proceeds another hearing, and from the voice proceeds another voice, eternally curious of the harmony of things with man. These understand the law of perfection in masses and floods—that it is profuse and impartial—that there is not a minute of the light or dark, nor an acre of the earth and sea, without it—nor any direction of the sky, nor any trade or employment, nor any turn of events. This is the reason that about the proper expression of beauty there is precision and balance. One part does not need to be thrust above another. The best singer is not the one who has the most lithe and powerful organ. The pleasure of poems is not in them that take the handsomest measure and sound.

Without effort, and without exposing in the least how it is done, the greatest poet brings the spirit of any or all events and passions and scenes and persons, some more and some less, to bear on your individual character as you hear or read. To do this well is to compete with the laws that pursue and follow Time. What is the purpose must surely be there, and the clue of it must be there—and the faintest indication is the indication of the best, and then becomes the clearest indication. Past and present and future are not disjoin'd but join'd. The greatest poet forms the consistence of what is to be, from what has been and is. He drags the dead out of their coffins and stands them again on their feet. He says to the past, Rise and walk before me that I may realize you. He learns the lesson—he places himself where the future becomes present. The greatest poet does not only dazzle his rays over character and scenes and passions—he finally ascends, and finishes all —he exhibits the pinnacles that no man can tell what they are for, or what is beyond—he glows a moment on the extremest verge. He is most wonderful in his last half-hidden smile or frown; by that flash of the moment of parting the one that sees it shall be encouraged or terrified afterward for many years. The greatest poet does not moralize or make applications of morals—he knows the soul. The soul has that measureless pride which consists in never acknowledging any lessons or deductions but its own. But it has sympathy as measureless as its pride, and the one balances the other, and neither can stretch too far while it stretches in company with the other. The inmost secrets of art sleep with the twain. The greatest poet has lain close betwixt both, and they are vital in his style and thoughts.

The art of art, the glory of expression and the sunshine of the light of letters, is simplicity. Nothing is better than simplicity—nothing can make up for excess, or for the lack of definiteness. To carry on the heave of impulse and pierce intellectual depths and give all subjects their articulations are powers neither common nor very uncommon. But to speak in literature with the perfect rectitude and insouciance of the movements of animals, and the unimpeachableness of the sentiment of trees in the woods and grass by the roadside, is the flawless triumph of art. If you have look'd on him who has achiev'd it you have look'd on one of the masters of the artists of all nations and times. You shall not contemplate the flight of the gray gull over the bay, or the mettlesome action of the blood horse, or the tall leaning of sunflowers on their stalk, or the appearance of the sun journeying through heaven, or the appearance of the moon afterward, with any more satisfaction than you shall contemplate him. The great poet has less a mark'd style, and is more the channel of thoughts and things without increase or diminution, and is the free channel of himself. He swears to his art, I will not be meddlesome, I will not have in my writing any elegance, or effect, or originality, to hang in the way between me and the rest like curtains. I will have nothing hang in the way, not the richest curtains. What I tell I tell for precisely what it is. Let who may exalt or startle or fascinate or soothe, I will have purposes as health or heat or snow has, and be as regardless of observation. What I experience or portray shall go from my composition without a shred of my composition. You shall stand by my side and look in the mirror with me.

T                                                                                                W.

The old red blood and stainless gentility of great poets will be proved by their unconstraint. A heroic person walks at his ease through and out of that custom or precedent or authority that suits him not. Of the traits of the brotherhood of first-class writers, savans, musicians, inventors and artists, nothing is finer than silent defiance advancing from new free forms. In the need of poems, philosophy, politics, mechanism, science, behavior, the craft of art, an appropriate native grand opera, shipcraft, or any craft, he is greatest for ever and ever who contributes the greatest original practical example. The cleanest expression is that which finds no sphere worthy of itself, and makes one.

The messages of great poems to each man and woman are, Come to us on equal terms, only then can you understand us. We are no better than you, what we inclose you inclose, what we enjoy you may enjoy. Did you suppose there could be only one Supreme? We affirm there can be unnumber'd Supremes, and that one does not countervail another any more than one eyesight countervails another—and that men can be good or grand only of the consciousness of their supremacy within them. What do you think is the grandeur of storms and dismemberments, and the deadliest battles and wrecks, and the wildest fury of the elements, and the power of the sea, and the motion of Nature, and the throes of human desires, and dignity and hate and love? It is that something in the soul which says, Rage on, whirl on, I tread master here and everywhere—Master of the spasms of the sky and of the shatter of the sea, Master of nature and passion and death, and of all terror and all pain.

The American bards shall be mark'd for generosity and affection, and for encouraging competitors. They shall be Kosmos, without monopoly or secrecy, glad to pass anything to any one—hungry for equals night and day. They shall not be careful of riches and privilege—they shall be riches and privilege—they shall perceive who the most affluent man is. The most affluent man is he that confronts all the shows he sees by equivalents out of the stronger wealth of himself. The American bard shall delineate no class of persons, nor one or two out of the strata of interests, nor love most nor truth most, nor the soul most, nor the body most—and not be for the Eastern States more than the Western, or the Northern States more than the Southern.

Exact science and its practical movements are no checks on the greatest poet, but always his encouragement and support. The outset and remembrance are there—there the arms that lifted him first, and braced him best—there he returns after all his goings and comings. The sailor and traveler—the anatomist, chemist, astronomer, geologist, phrenologist, spiritualist, mathematician, historian, and lexicographer, are not poets, but they are the lawgivers of poets, and their construction underlies the structure of every perfect poem. No matter what rises or is utter'd, they sent the seed of the conception of it—of them and by them stand the visible proofs of souls. If there shall be love and content between the father and the son, and if the greatness of the son is the exuding of the greatness of the father, there shall be love between the poet and the man of demonstrable science. In the beauty of poems are henceforth the tuft and final applause of science.

Great is the faith of the flush of knowledge, and of the investigation of the depths of qualities and things. Cleaving and circling here swells the soul of the poet, yet is president of itself always. The depths are fathomless, and therefore calm. The innocence and nakedness are resumed—they are neither modest nor immodest. The whole theory of the supernatural, and all that was twined with it or educed out of it, departs as a dream. What has ever happen'd—what happens, and whatever may or shall happen, the vital laws inclose all. They are sufficient for any case and for all cases— none to be hurried or retarded—any special miracle of affairs or persons inadmissible in the vast clear scheme where every motion and every spear of grass, and the frames and spirits of men and women and all that concerns them, are unspeakably perfect miracles, all referring to all, and each distinct and in its place. It is also not consistent with the reality of the soul to admit that there is anything in the known universe more divine than men and women.

Men and women, and the earth and all upon it, are to be taken as they are, and the investigation of their past and present and future shall be unintermitted, and shall be done with perfect candor. Upon this basis philosophy speculates, ever looking towards the poet, ever regarding the eternal tendencies of all toward happiness, never inconsistent with what is clear to the senses and to the soul. For the eternal tendencies of all toward happiness make the only point of sane philosophy. Whatever comprehends less than that—whatever is less than the laws of light and of astronomical motion —or less than the laws that follow the thief, the liar, the glutton and the drunkard, through this life and doubtless afterward—or less than vast stretches of time, or the slow formation of density, or the patient upheaving of strata—is of no account. Whatever would put God in a poem or system of philosophy as contending against some being or influence, is also of no account. Sanity and ensemble characterize the great master—spoilt in one principle, all is spoilt. The great master has nothing to do with miracles. He sees health for himself in being one of the mass—he sees the hiatus in singular eminence. To the perfect shape comes common ground. To be under the general law is great, for that is to correspond with it. The master knows that he is unspeakably great, and that all are unspeakably great—that nothing, for instance, is greater than to conceive children, and bring them up well—that to *be* is just as great as to perceive or tell.

In the make of the great masters the idea of political liberty is indispensable. Liberty takes the adherence of heroes wherever man and woman exist—but never takes any adherence or welcome from the rest more than from poets. They are the voice and exposition of liberty. They out of ages are worthy the grand idea—to them it is confided, and they must sustain it. Nothing has precedence of it, and nothing can warp or degrade it.

As the attributes of the poets of the kosmos concentre in the real body, and in the pleasure of things, they possess the superiority of genuineness over all fiction and romance. As they emit themselves, facts are shower'd over with light—the daylight is lit with more volatile light—the deep between the setting and rising sun goes deeper many fold. Each precise object or condition or combination or process exhibits a beauty—the multiplication table its—old age its—the carpenter's trade its—the grand opera its—the huge-hull'd clean-shap'd New York clipper at sea under steam or full sail gleams with unmatch'd beauty—the American circles and large harmonies of government gleam with theirs—and the commonest definite intentions and actions with theirs. The poets of the kosmos advance through all interpositions and coverings and turmoils and stratagems to first principles. They are of use—they dissolve poverty from its need, and riches from its conceit. You large proprietor, they say, shall not realize or perceive more than any one else. The owner of the library is not he who holds a legal title to it, having bought and paid for it. Any one and every one is owner of the library, (indeed he or she alone is owner,) who can read the same through all the varieties of tongues and subjects and styles, and in whom they enter with ease, and make supple and powerful and rich and large.

These American States, strong and healthy and accomplish'd, shall receive no pleasure from violations of natural models, and must not permit them. In paintings or mouldings or carvings in mineral or wood, or in the illustrations of books or newspapers, or in the patterns of woven stuffs, or anything to beautify rooms or furniture or costumes, or to put upon cornices or monuments, or on the prows or sterns of ships, or to put anywhere before the human eye indoors or out, that which distorts honest shapes, or which creates unearthly beings or places or contingencies, is a nuisance and revolt. Of the human form especially, it is so great it must never be made ridiculous. Of ornaments to a work nothing outre can be allow'd—but those ornaments can be allow'd that conform to the perfect facts of the open air, and that flow out of the nature of the work, and come irrepressibly from it, and are necessary to the completion of the work. Most works are most beautiful without ornament. Exaggerations will be revenged in human physiology. Clean and vigorous children are jetted and conceiv'd only in those communities where the models of natural forms are public every day. Great genius and the people of these States must never be demean'd to romances. As soon as histories are properly told, no more need of romances.

The great poets are to be known by the absence in them of tricks, and by the justification of perfect personal candor. All faults may be forgiven of him who has perfect candor.

Henceforth let no man of us lie, for we have seen that openness wins the inner and outer world, and that there is no single exception, and that never since our earth gather'd itself in a mass have deceit or subterfuge or prevarication attracted its smallest particle or the faintest tinge of a shade—and that through the enveloping wealth and rank of a state, or the whole republic of states, a sneak or sly person shall be discover'd and despised—and that the soul has never once been fool'd and never can be fool'd—and thrift without the loving nod of the soul is only a fœtid puff—and there never grew up in any of the continents of the globe, nor upon any planet or satellite, nor in that condition which precedes the birth of babes, nor at any time during the changes of life, nor in any stretch of abeyance or action of vitality, nor in any process of formation or reformation anywhere, a being whose instinct hated the truth.

Extreme caution or prudence, the soundest organic health, large hope and comparison and fondness for women and children, large alimentiveness and destructiveness and causality, with a perfect sense of the oneness of nature, and the propriety of the same spirit applied to human affairs, are called up of the float of the brain of the world to be parts of the greatest poet from his birth out of his mother's womb, and from her birth out of her mother's. Caution seldom goes far enough. It has been thought that the prudent citizen was the citizen who applied himself to solid gains, and did well for himself and for his family, and completed a lawful life without debt or crime. The greatest poet sees and admits these economies as he sees the economies of food and sleep, but has higher notions of prudence than to think he gives much when he gives a few slight attentions at the latch of the gate. The premises of the prudence of life are not the hospitality of it, or the ripeness and harvest of it. Beyond the independence of a little sum laid aside for burial-money, and of a few clap-boards around and shingles overhead on a lot of American soil own'd, and the easy dollars that supply the year's plain clothing and meals, the melancholy prudence of the abandonment of such a great being as a man is, to the toss and pallor of years of money-making, with all their scorching days and icy nights, and all their stifling deceits and underhand dodgings, or infinitesimals of parlors, or shameless stuffing while others starve, and all the loss of the bloom and odor of the earth, and of the flowers and atmosphere, and of the sea, and of the true taste of the women and men you pass or have to do with in youth or middle age, and the issuing sickness and desperate revolt at the close of a life without elevation or naïvete, (even if you have achiev'd a secure 10,000 a year, or election to Congress or the Governorship,) and the ghastly chatter of a death without serenity or majesty, is the great fraud upon modern civilization and forethought, blotching the surface and system which civilization undeniably drafts, and moistening with tears the immense features it spreads and spreads with such velocity before the reach'd kisses of the soul.

Ever the right explanation remains to be made about prudence. The prudence of the mere wealth and respectability of the most esteem'd life appears too faint for the eye to observe at all, when little and large alike drop quietly aside at the thought of the prudence suitable for immortality. What is the wisdom that fills the thinness of a year, or seventy or eighty years—to the wisdom spaced out by ages, and coming back at a certain time with strong reinforcements and rich presents, and the clear faces of wedding-guests as far as you can look, in every direction, running gaily toward you? Only the soul is of itself—all else has reference to what ensues. All that a person does or thinks is of consequence. Nor can the push of charity or personal force ever be anything else than the profoundest reason, whether it brings argument to hand or no. No specification is necessary—to add or subtract or divide is in vain. Little or big, learn'd or unlearn'd, white or black, legal or illegal, sick or well, from the first inspiration down the windpipe to the last expiration out of it, all that a male or female does that is vigorous and benevolent and clean is so much sure profit to him or her in the unshakable order of the universe, and through the whole scope of it forever. The prudence of the greatest poet answers at last the craving and glut of the soul, puts off nothing, permits no let-up for its own case or any case, has no particular sabbath or judgment day, divides not the living from the dead, or the righteous from the unrighteous, is satisfied with the present, matches every thought or act by its correlative, and knows no possible forgiveness or deputed atonement.

The direct trial of him who would be the greatest poet is to-day. If he does not flood himself with the immediate age as with vast oceanic tides—if he be not himself the age transfigur'd, and if to him is not open'd the eternity which gives similitude to all periods and locations and processes, and animate and inanimate forms, and which is the bond of time, and rises up from its inconceivable vagueness and infiniteness in the swimming shapes of to-day, and is held by the ductile anchors of life, and makes the present spot the passage from what was to what shall be, and commits itself to the representation of this wave of an hour, and this one of the sixty beautiful children of the wave—let him merge in the general run, and wait his development.

Still the final test of poems, or any character or work, remains. The prescient poet projects himself centuries ahead, and judges performer or performance after the changes of time. Does it live through them? Does it still hold on untired? Will the same style, and the direction of genius to similar points, be satisfactory now? Have the marches of tens and hundreds and thousands of years made willing detours to the right hand and the left hand for his sake? Is he beloved long and long after he is buried? Does the young man think often of him? and the young woman think often of him? and do the middle-aged and the old think of him?

A great poem is for ages and ages in common, and for all degrees and complexions, and all departments and sects, and for a woman as much as a man, and a man as much as a woman. A great poem is no finish to a man or woman, but rather a beginning. Has any one fancied he could sit at last under some due authority, and rest satisfied with explanations, and realize, and be content and full? To no such terminus does the greatest poet bring—he brings neither cessation nor shelter'd fatness and ease. The touch of him, like Nature, tells in action. Whom he takes he takes with firm sure grasp into live regions previously unattain'd—thenceforward is no rest—they see the space and ineffable sheen that turn the old spots and lights into dead vacuums. Now there shall be a man cohered out of tumult and chaos—the elder encourages the younger and shows him how—they two shall launch off fearlessly together till the new world fits an orbit for itself, and looks unabash'd on the lesser orbits of the stars, and sweeps through the ceaseless rings, and shall never be quiet again.

There will soon be no more priests. Their work is done. A new order shall arise, and they shall be the priests of man, and every man shall be his own priest. They shall find their inspiration in real objects to-day, symptoms of the past and future. They shall not deign to defend immortality or God, or the perfection of things, or liberty, or the exquisite beauty and reality of the soul. They shall arise in America, and be responded to from the remainder of the earth.

The English language befriends the grand American expression—it is brawny enough, and limber and full enough. On the tough stock of a race who through all change of circumstance was never without the idea of political liberty, which is the animus of all liberty, it has attracted the terms of daintier and gayer and subtler and more elegant tongues. It is the powerful language of resistance—it is the dialect of common sense. It is the speech of the proud and melancholy races, and of all who aspire. It is the chosen tongue to express growth, faith, self-esteem, freedom, justice, equality, friendliness, amplitude, prudence, decision, and courage. It is the medium that shall wellnigh express the inexpressible.

No great literature, nor any like style of behavior or oratory, or social intercourse or household arrangements, or public institutions, or the treatment by bosses of employ'd people, nor executive detail, or detail of the army and navy, nor spirit of legislation or courts, or police or tuition or architecture, or songs or amusements, can long elude the jealous and passionate instinct of American standards. Whether or no the sign appears from the mouths of the people, it throbs a live interrogation in every freeman's and freewoman's heart, after that which passes by, or this built to remain. Is it uniform with my country? Are its disposals without ignominious distinctions? Is it for the ever-growing communes of brothers and lovers, large, well united, proud, beyond the old models, generous beyond all models? Is it something grown fresh out of the fields, or drawn from the sea for use to me to-day here? I know that what answers for me, an American, in Texas, Ohio, Canada, must answer for any individual or nation that serves for a part of my materials. Does this answer? Is it for the nursing of the young of the republic? Does it solve readily with the sweet milk of the nipples of the breasts of the Mother of Many Children?

America prepares with composure and good-will for the visitors that have sent word. It is not intellect that is to be their warrant and welcome. The talented, the artist, the ingenious, the editor, the statesman, the erudite, are not unappreciated—they fall in their place and do their work. The soul of the nation also does its work. It rejects none, it permits all. Only toward the like of itself will it advance halfway. An individual is as superb as a nation when he has the qualities which make a superb nation. The soul of the largest and wealthiest and proudest nation may well go half-way to meet that of its poets.

## THE EIGHTEENTH PRESIDENCY!

*Voice of Walt Whitman to each Young Man in the Nation, North, South, East, and West*

BEFORE the American era, the programme of the classes of a nation read thus, first the king, second the noblemen and gentry, third the great mass of mechanics, farmers, men following the water, and all laboring persons. The first and second classes are unknown to the theory of the government of These States; the likes of the class rated third on the old programme were intended to be, and are in fact, and to all intents and purposes, the American nation, the people.

Mechanics, farmers, sailors, etc., constitute some six millions of the inhabitants of These States; merchants, lawyers, doctors, teachers, and priests, count up as high as five hundred thousand; the owners of slaves number three hundred and fifty thousand; the population of The States being altogether about thirty millions, seven tenths of whom are women and children. At present, the personnel of the government of these thirty millions, in executives and elsewhere, is drawn from limber-tongued lawyers, very fluent but empty, feeble old men, professional politicians, dandies, dyspeptics, and so forth, and rarely drawn from the solid body of the people; the effects now seen, and more to come. Of course the fault, if it be a fault, is for reasons, and is of the people themselves, and will mend when it should mend.

Has much been done in the theory of These States? Very good; more remains. Who is satisfied with the theory, or a parade of the theory? I say, delay not, come quickly to its most courageous facts and illustrations. I say no body of men are fit to make Presidents, Judges, and Generals, unless they themselves supply the best specimens of the same, and that supplying one or two such specimens illuminates the whole body for a thousand years.

I expect to see the day when the like of the present personnel of the governments, federal, state, municipal, military and naval, will be looked upon with derision, and when qualified mechanics and young men will reach Congress and other official stations, sent in their working costumes, fresh from their benches and tools, and returning to them again with dignity. The young fellows must prepare to do credit to this destiny, for the stuff is in them. Nothing gives place, recollect, and never ought to give place except to its clean superiors. There is more rude and undeveloped bravery, friendship, conscientiousness, clear-sightedness, and practical genius for any scope of action, even the broadest and highest, now among the American mechanics and young men, than in all the official persons in These States, legislative, executive, judicial, military and naval, and more than among all the literary persons. I would be much pleased to see some heroic, shrewd, fully-informed, healthy-bodied, middle-aged, beard-faced American blacksmith or boatman come down from the West across the Alleghanies, and walk into the Presidency, dressed in a clean suit of working attire, and with the tan all over his face, breast, and arms; I would certainly vote for that sort of man, possessing the due requirements, before any other candidate. Such is the thought that must become familiar to you, whoever you are, and to the people of These States; and must eventually take shape in action.

At present, we are environed with nonsense under the name of respectability. Everywhere lowers that stifling atmosphere that makes all the millions of farmers and mechanics of These States the helpless supple-jacks of a comparatively few politicians. Somebody must make a bold push. The people, credulous, generous, deferential, allow the American government to be managed in many respects as is only proper under the personnel of a king and hereditary lords; or, more truly, not proper under any decent men anywhere. If this were to go on, we ought to change the title of the President, and issue patents of nobility. Of course it is not to go on; the Americans are no fools. I perceive meanwhile that nothing less than marked inconsistencies and usurpations will arouse a nation, and make ready for better things afterwards.

But what ails the present way of filling the offices of The States? Is it not good enough? I should say it was not. To-day, of all the persons in public office in These States, not one in a thousand has been chosen by any spontaneous movement of the people, nor is attending to the interests of the people; all have been nominated and put through by great or small caucuses of the politicians, or appointed as rewards for electioneering; and all consign themselves to personal and party interests. Neither in the Presidency, nor in Congress, nor in the foreign ambassadorships, nor in the governorships of the States, nor in legislatures, nor in the mayoralties of cities, nor the aldermanships, nor among the police, nor on the benches of judges, do I observe a single bold, muscular, young, well-informed, well-beloved, resolute American man, bound to do a man's duty, aloof from all parties, and with a manly scorn of all parties. Instead of that, every trustee of the people is a traitor, looking only to his own gain, and to boost up his party. The berths, the Presidency included, are bought, sold, electioneered for, prostituted, and filled with prostitutes. In the North and East, swarms of dough-faces, office-vermin, kept-editors, clerks, attaches of ten thousand officers and their parties, aware of nothing further than the drip and spoil of politics—ignorant of principles, the true glory of a man. In the South, no end of blusterers, braggarts, windy, melodramatic, continually screaming in falsetto, a nuisance to These States, their own just as much as any; altogether the most impudent persons that have yet appeared in the history of lands, and with the most incredible successes, having pistol'd, bludgeoned, yelled and threatened America, the past twenty years into one long train of cowardly concessions, and still not through but rather at the commencement. Their cherished secret scheme is to dissolve the union of These States.

Well, what more? Is nothing but breed upon breed like these to be represented in the Presidency? Are parties to forever usurp the government? Are lawyers, dough-faces, and the three hundred and fifty thousand owners of slaves, to sponge the mastership of thirty millions? Where is the real America? Where are the laboring persons, ploughmen, men with axes, spades, scythes, flails? Where are the carpenters, masons, machinists, drivers of horses, workmen in factories? Where is the spirit of the manliness and common sense of These States? It does not appear in the government. It does not appear at all in the Presidency.

The sixteenth and seventeenth terms of the American Presidency have shown that the villainy and shallowness of great rulers are just as eligible to These States as to any foreign despotism, kingdom, or empire—there is not a bit of difference. History is to record these two Presidencies as so far our topmost warning and shame. Never were publicly displayed more deformed, mediocre, snivelling, unreliable, false-hearted men! Never were These States so insulted, and attempted to be betrayed! All the main purposes for which the government was established are openly denied. The perfect equality of slavery with freedom is flauntingly preached in the North, nay, the superiority of slavery. The slave trade is proposed to be renewed. Everywhere frowns and misunderstandings—everywhere exasperations and humiliations. The President eats dirt and excrement for his daily meals, likes it, and tries to force it on The States. The cushions of the Presidency are nothing but filth and blood. The pavements of Congress are also bloody. The land that flushed amazed at the basest outrage of our times, grows pale with a far different feeling to see the outrage unanimously commended back again to those who only half rejected it. The national tendency toward populating territories full of free work-people, established by the organic compacts of These

States, promulged by the fathers, the Presidents, the old warriors, and the earlier Congresses, a tendency vital to the life and thrift of the masses of the citizens, is violently put back under the feet of slavery, and against the free people the masters of slaves are everywhere held up by the President by the red hand. In fifteen of The States the three hundred and fifty thousand masters keep down the true people, the millions of white citizens, mechanics, farmers, boatmen, manufacturers, and the like, excluding them from politics and from office, and punishing by the lash, by tar and feathers, binding fast to rafts on the river or trees in the woods, and sometimes by death, all attempts to discuss the evils of slavery in its relations to the whites. The people of the territories are denied the power to form State governments unless they consent to fasten upon them the slave-hopple, the iron wristlet, and the neck-spike. For refusing such consent, the governor and part of the legislature of the State of Kansas are chased, seized, chained, by the creatures of the President, and are to-day in chains. Over the vast continental tracts of unorganized American territory, equal in extent to all the present organized States, and in future to give the law to all, the whole executive, judicial, military and naval power of These States is forsworn to the people, the rightful owners, and sworn to the help of the three hundred and fifty thousand masters of slaves, to put them through this continent, with their successors, at their pleasure, and to maintain by force their mastership over their slave men and women, slave-farmers, slave-miners, slave-cartmen, slave-sailors, and the like. Slavery is adopted as an American institution, superior, national, constitutional, right in itself, and under no circumstances to take any less than freedom takes. Nor is that all; to-day, to-night, the constables and commissioners of the President can by law step into any part of These States and pick out whom they please, deciding which man or woman they will allow to be free, and which shall be a slave, no jury to intervene, but the commissioner's mandate to be enforced by the federal troops and cannon, and has been actually so enforced.

Are the states retarded then? No; while all is drowned and desperate that the government has had to do with, all the outside influence of government, (forever the largest part,) thrives and smiles. The sun shines, corn grows, men go merrily about their affairs, houses are built, ships arrive and depart. Through evil and through good, the republic stands, and is for centuries yet to stand, immovable from its foundations. No, no; out at dastards and disgraces, fortunate are the wrongs that call forth stout and angry men; then is shown what stuff there is in a nation.

The young genius of America is not going to be emasculated and strangled just as it arrives toward manly age. It shall live, and yet baffle the politicians and the three hundred and fifty thousand masters of slaves.

Now the term of the seventeenth Presidency passing hooted and spurned to its close, the delegates of the politicians have nominated for the eighteenth term, Buchanan of Pennsylvania, and Fillmore of New York, separate tickets, but men both patterned to follow and match the seventeenth term, both disunionists, both old politicians, both sworn down to the theories of special parties, and of all others the theories that balk and reverse the main purposes of the founders of These States. Such are the nominees that have arisen out of the power of the politicians, but another power has also arisen. A new race copiously appears, with resolute tread, soon to confront Presidents, congresses and parties, to look them sternly in the face, to stand no nonsense, American young men, the offspring and proof of These States, the West the same as the East, and the South alike with the North.

America sends these young men in good time, for they were needed. Much waits to be done. First, people need to realize who are poisoning the politics of These States.

Whence the delegates of the politicians? Whence the Buchanan and Fillmore Conventions? Not from sturdy American freemen; not from industrious homes; not from thrifty farms; not from the ranks of fresh-bodied young men; not from among teachers, poets, savans, learned persons, beloved persons, temperate persons; not from among shipbuilders, engineers, agriculturists, scythe-swingers, cornhoers; not from the race of mechanics; not from that great strong stock of Southerners that supplied the land in old times; not from the real West, the log-hut, the clearing, the woods, the prairie, the hill-side; not from the sensible, generous, rude Californian miners; not from the best specimens of Massachusetts, Maine, New Jersey, Pennsylvania, Ohio, Illinois, Wisconsin, Indiana, nor from the untainted unpolitical citizens of the cities.

Whence then do these nominating dictators of America year after year start out? From lawyers' offices, secret lodges, back-yards, bed-houses, and bar-rooms; from out of the custom-houses, marshals' offices, post-offices, and gambling hells; from the President's house, the jail, the venereal hospital, the station-house; from unnamed by-places where devilish disunion is hatched at midnight; from political hearses, and from the coffins inside, and from the shrouds inside the coffins; from the tumors and abscesses of the land; from the skeletons and skulls in the vaults of the federal almshouses; from the running sores of the great cities; thence to the national, state, city, and district nominating conventions of These States, come the most numerous and controlling delegates.

Who are they personally? Office-holders, office-seekers, robbers, pimps, exclusives, malignants, conspirators, murderers, fancy-men, port-masters, custom-house clerks, contractors, kept-editors, Spaniels well-trained to carry and fetch, jobbers, infidels, disunionists, terrorists, mail-riflers, slave-catchers, pushers of Slavery, creatures of the President, creatures of would-be Presidents, spies, blowers, electioneers, body-snatchers, bawlers, bribers, compromisers, runaways, lobbyers, sponges, ruined sports, expelled gamblers, policy backers, monte-dealers, duelists, carriers of concealed weapons, blind men, deaf men, pimpled men, scarred inside with the vile disorder, gaudy outside with gold chains made from the people's money and harlot's money twisted together; crawling, serpentine men, the lousy combings and born freedom sellers of the earth.

Stript of padding and paint, who are Buchanan and Fillmore? What has this age to do with them? Two galvanized old men, close on the summons to depart this life, their early contemporaries long since gone, only they two left, relics and proofs of the little political bargains, chances, combinations, resentments of a past age, having nothing in common with this age, standing for the first crop of political graves and

grave-stones planted in These States, but in no sort standing
for the lusty young growth of the modern times of The
States. It is clear from all these two men say and do, that
their hearts have not been touched in the least by the flowing
fire of the humanitarianism of the new world, its best glory
yet, and a moral control stronger than all its governments.
It is clear that neither of these nominees of the politicians has
thus far reached an inkling of the real scope and character of
the contest of the day, probably now only well begun, to
stretch through years, with varied temporary successes and
reverses. Still the two old men live in respectable little spots,
with respectable little wants. Still their eyes stop at the edges
of the tables of committees and cabinets, beholding not the
great round world beyond. What has this age to do with them?

You Americans who travel with such men, or who are
nominated on tickets any where with them, or who support
them at popular meetings, or write for them in the newspapers, or who believe that any good can come out of them,
you also understand not the present age, the fibre of it, the
countless currents it brings of American young men, a different superior race. All this effervescence is not for nothing;
the friendlier, vaster, more vital modern spirit, hardly yet
arrived at definite proportions, or to the knowledge of itself,
will have the mastery. The like turmoil prevails in the expressions of literature, manners, trade, and other departments.

To butchers, sailors, stevedores, and drivers of horses—
to ploughmen, wood-cutters, marketmen, carpenters,
masons, and laborers—to workmen in factories—and
to all in These States who live by their daily toil.
Mechanics! A parcel of windy northern liars are bawling
in your ears the easily-spoken words Democracy and the
democratic party. Others are making a great ado with the
word Americanism, a solemn and great word. What the so-
called democracy are now sworn to perform would eat the
faces off the succeeding generations of common people worse
than the most horrible disease. The others are contributing
to the like performance, and are using the great word Americanism without yet feeling the first aspiration of it, as the
great word Religion has been used, probably loudest and
oftenest used, by men that made indiscriminate massacres at

night, and filled the world so full with hatreds, horrors, par-
tialities, exclusions, bloody revenges, penal conscience laws
and test oaths. To the virtue of Americanism is happening
to-day, what happens many days to many virtues, namely,
the masses who possess them but do not understand them
are sought to be sold by that very means to those who neither
possess them nor understand them. What are the young mer
suspicious of? I will tell them what it stands them in hand to
be suspicious of, and that is American craft; it is subtler than
Italian craft; I guess it is about the subtlest craft upon the earth.

What is there in prospect for free farmers and work
people? A few generations ago, the general run of farmers
and work-people like us were slaves, serfs, deprived of their
liberty by law; they are still so deprived on some parts of the
continent of Europe. To-day, those who are free here, and
free in the British islands and elsewhere, are free through
deeds that were done, and men that lived, some of them an
age or so ago, and some of them many ages ago. The men
and deeds of these days also decide for generations ahead, as
past men and deeds decided for us.

As the broad fat States of the West, the largest and best
parts of the inheritance of the American farmers and mechanics, were ordained to common people and workmen long in
advance by Jefferson, Washington, and the earlier Congresses,
now a far ampler west is to be ordained. Is it to be ordained
to workmen, or the masters of workmen? Shall the future
mechanics of America be serfs? Shall labor be degraded, and
women be whipt in the fields for not performing their tasks?
If slaves are not prohibited from all national territory
by law, as prohibited in the beginning, as the organic
compacts authorize and require, and if, on the contrary, the
entrance and establishment of slave labor through the continent is secured, there will steadily wheel into this Union, for
centuries to come, slave state after slave state, the entire
surface of the land owned by great proprietors, in plantations of thousands of acres, showing no more sight for free
races of farmers and work-people than there is now in any
European despotism or aristocracy; and the existence of our
present Free States put in jeopardy, because out of that vast
territory are to come states enough to overbalance all.

Workmen! Workwomen! Those immense national American tracts belong to you; they are in trust with you; they are latent with the populous cities, numberless farms, herds, granaries, groves, golden gardens, and inalienable homesteads, of your successors. The political blowers and kept-editors of the North are raising a fog of prevarications around you. But the manlier Southern disunionists, the chieftains among the three hundred and fifty thousand masters, clearly distinguish the issue, and the principle it rests upon. McDuffie, disunionist governor, lays it down with candid boldness that the workingmen of a state are unsafe depositaries of political powers and rights, and that a republic can not permanently exist unless those who ply the mechanical trades and attend to the farm-work are slaves, subordinated by strict laws to their masters. Calhoun, disunionist senator, denounces and denies, in the presence of the world, the main article of the organic compact of These States, that all men are born free and equal, and bequeaths to his followers, at present leaders of the three hundred and fifty thousand masters, guides of the so-called democracy, counsellors of Presidents, and getters-up of the nominations of Buchanan and Fillmore, his deliberate charge, to be carried out against that main article, that it is the most false and dangerous of all political errors; such being the words of that charge, spoken in the summer of the 73d year of These States, and, indeed, carried out since in the spirit of congressional legislation, executive action, and the candidates offered by the political parties to the people.

Are not political parties about played out? I say they are, all round. America has outgrown parties; henceforth it is too large, and they too small. They habitually make common cause just as soon in advocacy of the worst deeds and men as the best, or probably a little sooner for the worst. I place no reliance upon any old party, nor upon any new party. Suppose one to be formed under the noblest auspices, and getting into power with the noblest intentions, how long would it remain so? How many years? Would it remain so one year? As soon as it becomes successful, and there are offices to be bestowed, the politicians leave the unsuccessful parties, and rush toward it, and it ripens and rots with the rest.

What right has one political party, no matter which, to wield the American government? No right at all. Not the so-called democratic, not abolition, opposition to foreigners, nor any other party, should be permitted the exclusive use of the Presidency; and every American young man must have sense enough to comprehend this. I have said the old parties are defunct; but there remains of them empty flesh, putrid mouths, mumbling and squeaking the tones of these conventions, the politicians standing back in shadow, telling lies, trying to delude and frighten the people; and nominating such candidates as Fillmore and Buchanan.

What impudence! for any one platform, section, creed, no matter which, to expect to subordinate all the rest, and rule the immense diversity of These free and equal States! Platforms are of no account. The right man is every thing. With the downfall of parties go the platforms they are forever putting up, lowering, turning, repainting, and changing.

The platforms for the Presidency of These States are simply the organic compacts of The States, the Declaration of Independence, the Federal Constitution, the action of the earlier Congresses, the spirit of the fathers and warriors, the official lives of Washington, Jefferson, Madison, and the now well-understood and morally established rights of man, wherever the sun shines, the rain falls, and the grass grows.

Much babble will always be heard in the land about the Federal Constitution, this, that, and the other concerning it. The Federal Constitution is a perfect and entire thing, an edifice put together, not for the accommodation of a few persons, but for the whole human race; not for a day or a year, but for many years, perhaps a thousand, perhaps many thousand. Its architecture is not a single brick, a beam, an apartment, but only the whole. It is the grandest piece of moral building ever constructed; I believe its architects were some mighty prophets and gods. Few appreciate it, Americans just as few as any. Like all perfect works or persons, time only is great enough to give it area. Five or six centuries hence, it will be better understood from results, growths.

The Federal Constitution is the second of the American organic compacts. The premises, outworks, guard, defense, entrance of the Federal Constitution, is the primary compact of These States, sometimes called the Declaration of Independence; and the groundwork, feet, understratum of that again, is its deliberate engagement, in behalf of the States, thenceforward to consider all men to be born free and equal into the world, each one possessed of inalienable rights to his life and liberty, (namely, that no laws passed by any government could be considered to alienate or take away those born rights, the penalties upon criminals being, of course, for the very purpose of preserving those rights). This is the covenant of the Republic from the beginning, now and forever. It is not a mere opinion; its is the most venerable pledge, with all the forms observed, signed by the commissioners, ratified by The States, and sworn to by Washington at the head of his army, with his hand upon the Bible. It is supreme over all American law, and greater than Presidents, Congresses, elections and what not, for they hurry out of the way, but it remains. Above all, it is carefully to be observed in all that relates to the continental territories. When they are organized into States, it is to be passed over to the good faith of those States.

One or 2 radical parts of the American theory of government. Man can not hold property in man. As soon as there are clear-brained original American judges, this saying will be simplified by their judgments, and no State out of the whole confederacy but will confirm and approve those judgments.

Any one of These States is perfect mistress of itself; and each additional State the same. When States organize themselves, the Federal government withdraws, absolved from its duties, except certain specific ones under the Constitution, and only in behalf of them can it interfere in The States.

The true government is much simpler than is supposed, and abstains from much more. Nine tenths of the laws passed every winter at the Federal Capitol, and all the State Capitols, are not only unneeded laws, but positive nuisances, job got up for the service of special classes or persons.

Every rational uncriminal person, twenty-one years old, should be eligible to vote, on actual residence, no other requirement needed. The day will come when this will prevail.

The whole American government is itself simply a compact with each individual of the thirty millions of persons now inhabitants of These States, and prospectively with each individual of the hundred millions and five hundred millions that are in time to become inhabitants, to protect each one's life, liberty, industry, acquisitions, without excepting one single individual out of the whole number, and without making ignominious distinctions. Thus is government sublime; thus is it equal; otherwise it is government of castes on exactly the same principles with the kingdoms of Europe.

I said the national obligation is passed over to The States. Then if they are false to it, and impose upon certain persons, can the national government interfere? It can not, under any circumstances whatever. We must wait, no matter how long. There is no remedy, except in The State itself. A cornerstone of the organic compacts of America is that a State is perfect mistress of itself. If that is taken away, all the rest may just as well be taken away. When that is taken away, this Union is dissolved.

Must runaway slaves be delivered back? They must. Many things may have the go-by, but good faith shall never have the go-by.

By a section of the fourth article of the Federal Constitution, These States compact each with the other, that any person held to service or labor in one State under its law, and escaping into another State, shall not be absolved from service by any law of that other State, but shall be delivered up to the persons to whom such service or labor is due. This part of the second organic compact between the original States should be carried out by themselves in their usual forms, but in spirit and in letter. Congress has no business to pass any law upon the subject, any more than upon the hundred other of the compacts between the States, left to be carried out by their good faith. Why should Congress pick out this particular one? I had quite as lief depend on the good faith of any of These States, as on the laws of Congress and the President. Good faith is irresistible among men, and friendship is; which lawyers can not understand, thinking nothing but compulsion will do.

But cannot that requirement of the fourth article of the Second Compact be evaded, on any plea whatever, even the plea of its unrighteousness? Nay, I perceive it is not to be evaded on any plea whatever, not even the plea of its un-righteousness. It should be observed by The States, in spirit and in letter, whether it is pleasant to them or unpleasant, beholding in it one item among many items, each of the rest as important as it, and each to be so carried out as not to contravene the rest. As to what is called the Fugitive Slave Law, insolently put over the people by their Congress and President, it contravenes the whole of the organic compacts, and is all times to be defied in all parts of These States, South or North, by speech, by pen, and, if need be, by the bullet and the sword.

Shall we determine upon such things, then, and not leave them to the great judges and the scholars? Yes, it is best that we determine upon such things.

Whenever the day comes for him to appear, the man who shall be the Redeemer President of These States, is to be the one that fullest realizes the rights of individuals, signified by the impregnable rights of The States, the substratum of this Union. The Redeemer President of These States is not to be exclusive, but inclusive. In both physical and political America there is plenty of room for the whole human race; if not, more room can be provided.

To the American young men, mechanics, farmers, etc. How much longer do you intend to submit to the espionage and terrorism of the three hundred and fifty thousand owners of slaves? Are you too their slaves, and their most obedient slaves? Shall no one among you dare open his mouth to say he is opposed to slavery, as a man should be, on account of the whites, and wants it abolished for their sake? Is not a writer, speaker, teacher to be left alive, but those who lick up the spit that drops from the mouths of the three hundred and fifty thousand masters? Is there hardly one free, courageous soul left in fifteen large and populous States? Do the ranks of the owners of slaves themselves contain no men desperate and tired of that service and sweat of the mind, worse than any service in sugar-fields or corn-fields, under the eyes of over-seers? Do the three hundred and fifty thousand expect to bar off forever all preachers, poets, philosophers—all that makes the brain of These States, free literature, free thought, the good old cause of liberty? Are they blind? Do they not see those unrelaxed circles of death narrowing and narrowing every hour around them?

You young men of the Southern States! is the word **Abolitionist** so hateful to you, then? Do you know that Washington, Jefferson, Madison, and all the great Presidents and primal warriors and sages were declared abolitionists?

You young men! American mechanics, farmers, boatmen, manufacturers, and all work-people of the South, the same as the North! you are either to abolish slavery, or it will abolish you.

To the three hundred and fifty thousand owners of slaves: Suppose you get Kansas, do you think it would be ended? Suppose you and the politicians put Buchanan into the Eighteenth Presidency, or Fillmore into the Presidency, do you think it would be ended? I know nothing more desirable for those who contend against you than that you should get Kansas. Then would the melt begin in These States that would not cool till Kansas should be redeemed, as of course it would be.

O gentlemen, you do not know whom Liberty has nursed in These States, and depends on in time of need. You have not received any report of the Free States, but have received only the reports of the trustees who have betrayed the Free States. Do you suppose they will betray many thousand men, and stick at betraying a few men like you? Raised on plantations or in towns full of menial workmen and workwomen, you do not know, as I know, these fierce and turbulent races that fill the Northeast, the East, the West, the Northwest, the Pacific shores, the great cities, Manhattan Island, Brooklyn, Newark, Boston, Worcester, Hartford, New Haven, Providence, Portland, Bangor, Augusta, Albany, Buffalo, Rochester, Syracuse, Lockport, Cleaveland, Detroit, Milwaukee, Racine, Sheboygan, Madison, Galena, Burlington, Iowa City, Chicago, St. Louis, Cincinnati, Columbus, Pittsburgh, Philadelphia, San Francisco, Sacramento, and many more. From my mouth hear the will of These States taking form in the great cities. Where slavery is, there it is. The American compacts, common sense, all things unite to make it the affair of the States diseased with it, to cherish the same as long as they see fit, and to apply the remedy when they see fit.

But not one square mile of continental territory shall hence-forward be given to slavery, to slaves, or to the masters of slaves—not one square foot. If any laws are passed giving up such territory, those laws will be repealed. In organizing the territories, what laws are good enough for the American freeman must be good enough for you; if you come in under the said laws, well and good; if not stay away. What is done, is done; henceforth there is no further compromise. All this is now being cast in the stuff that makes the tough national resolves of These States, that every hour only anneals tougher. It is not that putty you see in Congress and in the Presidency; it is iron—it the undissuadable swift metal of death.

To editors of the independent press, and to rich persons. Circulate and reprint this Voice of mine for the working-men's sake. I hereby permit and invite any rich person, any-where, to stereotype it, or re-produce it in any form, to de-luge the cities of The States with it, North, South, East and West. It is those millions of mechanics you want; the writers, thinkers, learned and benevolent persons, merchants, are already secured almost to a man. But the great masses of the mechanics, and a large portion of the farmers, are unsettled, hardly know whom to vote for, or whom to believe. I am not afraid to say that among them I seek to initiate my name, Walt Whitman, and that I shall in future have much to say to them. I perceive that the best thoughts they have wait un-spoken, impatient to be put in shape; also that the character, power, pride, friendship, conscience of America have yet to be proved to the remainder of the world.

The times are full of great portents in These States and in the whole world. Freedom against slavery is not issuing here alone, but is issuing everywhere. The horizon rises, it divides I perceive, for a more august drama than any of the past. Old men have played their parts, the act suitable to them is closed, and if they will not withdraw voluntarily, must be bid to do so with unmistakable voice. Landmarks of masters, slaves, kings, aristocracies, are moth-eaten, and the peoples of the earth are planting new vast landmarks for themselves. Frontiers and boundaries are less and less able to divide men. The modern inventions, the wholesale engines of war, the world-spreading instruments of peace, the steamship, the locomotive, the electric telegraph, the common newspaper, the cheap book, the ocean mail, are interlinking the inhabitants of the earth together as groups of one family —America standing, and for ages to stand, as the host and champion of the same, the most welcome spectacle ever presented among nations. Every thing indicates unparalleled reforms. Races are marching and countermarching by swift millions and tens of millions. Never was justice so mighty amid injustice; never did the idea of equality erect itself so haughty and uncompromising amid inequality, as to-day. Never were such sharp questions asked as to-day. Never was there more eagerness to know. Never was the representative man more energetic, more like a god, than to-day. He urges on the myriads before him, he crowds them aside, his daring step approaches the arctic and antarctic poles, he colonizes the islands of the Pacific, the Asiatic Indias, the birthplace of languages and of races, the archipelagoes, Australia; he explores Africa, he unearths Assyria and Egypt, he restates history, he enlarges morality, he speculates anew upon the soul, upon original premises; nothing is left quiet, nothing but he will settle by demonstrations for himself. What whispers are these running through the eastern continents, and crossing the Atlantic and Pacific? What historic denouements are these we are approaching? On all sides tyrants tremble, crowns are unsteady, the human race restive, on the watch for some better era, some divine war. No man knows what will happen next, but all know that some such things are to happen as mark the greatest moral convulsions of the earth. Who shall play the hand for America in these tremendous games? A pretty time for two dead corpses to go walking up and down the earth, to guide by feebleness and ashes a proud, young, friendly, fresh, heroic nation of thirty millions of live and electric men!

## STREET YARN

SOLDIERS and militiamen are not the only people who wear uniforms. A uniform serves two purposes; first, to distinguish the wearers from others, and secondly, to assimilate them to each other. The universal uniform is more for the former of these than the latter; and is not only the style and substance of garments, but appearance and carriage. Come and walk in New York streets, or sit in a restaurant; we will detect some people for you by their uniforms.

Mild, foolish, dough-colored, simpering face; black cloth suit—shad-bellied, single-breasted coat, with low standing collar all round, vest buttoned close to throat, knees a little bent, toes turned out, and chin down. Episcopalian deacon.

Wild cataract of hair; absurd, bunged-up felt hat, with peaked crown; velvet coat, all friggled over with gimp, but worn; eyes rather staring, look upward. Third-rate artist.

Dress strictly respectable; hat well down on forehead; face thin, dry, close-shaven; mouth with a gripe like a vice; eye sharp and quick; brows bent; forehead scowling; step jerky and bustling. Wall Street broker.

Hands crossed behind him; step slow; dress well enough, but careless all over; face bent downward, and full of thought. Leading lawyer.

Rusty black costume; white choker; look oddly compounded of severity, superiority, curiosity, apprehension, and suspicion; shoulders stooping, chest flat. Country clergyman.

Half-a-dozen ill-dressed fellows together (this in the evening); dirty, unshorn faces; debauched expression; the half-shut eyes, and loose, hanging lips of the tribe; hoarse voices, incredibly tuneless; oaths and curses; laughs made up of a yell and a cackle; a peculiar quick, eager step, as they flock along close together. Short-boys; damnable dangerous villains.

Dirty finery, excessively plentiful; paint, both red and white; draggle-tailed dress, ill-fitting; coarse features, unintelligent; bold glance, questioning, shameless, perceptibly anxious; hideous croak or dry, brazen ring in voice; affected, but awkward, mincing, waggling gait. Harlot.

Heavy moustache; obtrusively expensive dress; big breast pin; heavy gold chain; rings; hat down over brows; loafing attitude on corner; eye furtive, glassy, expressionless; oaths; tobacco-spit. Gambler.

There, somewhat in that manner, you may learn even to

distinguish the trades from each other. But now let us sketch individuals. We are sitting, we will suppose, in the St. Nicholas front windows, or standing in front of Delmonico's, or anywhere in a thoroughfare. The crowd flows by; among it goes, now and then, one of these following:

A tall, slender man, round-shouldered, chin stuck out, deep-set eyes, sack-coat. His step is quick, and his arms swing awkwardly, as if he were trying to knock his elbows together behind him. Albert Brisbane the Socialist; the capitalist, too—an odd circumstance for a radical in New York! Somehow or other he always looks as if he were attempting to think out some problem a little too hard for him.

Old gentleman in carriage. A well-built, portly old man, full, ruddy face, abundant wavy—almost frizzly—white hair, good forehead, kindly, intelligent look. Dr. Francis, the encyclopædia of historical information, especially in local history and genealogy.

Tall, large, rough-looking man, in a journeyman carpenter's uniform. Coarse, sanguine complexion; strong, bristly, grizzled beard; singular eyes, of a semi-transparent, indistinct light blue, and with that sleepy look that comes when the lid rests half way down over the pupil; careless, lounging gait. Walt Whitman, the sturdy, self-conscious microcosmic, prose-poetical author of that incongruous hash of mud and gold—*Leaves of Grass*.

Middle-sized person, upright and alert; dark, sallow, Spanish-looking phiz; jet black hair and beard, a wild and glittering eye, and a certain air of satisfaction, as if well content to be of importance. That is Stephen H. Branch, the Alligator; the burr in the skirts of Mr. Matsell; the "indefatigable" searcher after Brandon records; the great worm-doctor, and the only writer of the Branch school known to exist.

Oldish, tall, large-framed, slouching man, in negligent costume of blue cloth; drags his feet along like "flat irons hung on a string"; seems much interested in the sidewalk; if he looks up, shows a face as blank as a brick wall, yet with a benign and pleasant look. The benign and pleasant look Professor Robinson can't get rid of; and if his learning and intelligence don't always appear on the outside of his capacious head, it is because they are "urgently engaged" within.

For that careless, lumbering old gentleman is Professor Edward Robinson, of Union Theological Seminary; the first scholar of the country, if not of his time, in Biblical Learning, and whose discoveries in Palestine, and other labors, have made him a name all over Protestant Christendom, and proved him fully equal to the greatest of the great Germans who have done so much in that department, and in whose own language and literature he is himself so thorough a scholar.

A short, "chunked", light-haired, fair-faced, big-headed, jolly roly-poly man, with a ready smile and a prompt step, like a bold little game-cock. Robert Bonner, the hero of unheard-of and tremendous advertising, who fires cannon, fills page upon page of newspapers, and—if he could—would placard the very walls of Paradise with hifalutin hand-bills, to sell that gorgeous and unprecedented sheet, the New York *Ledger*.

Somebody in an open barouche, driving daintily. He looks like a doll; is it alive? We'll cross the street and so get close to him. Did you see? Fantastic hat, turned clear over in the rim above the ears; blue coat and shiny brass buttons; patent leathers; shirt-frill; gold specs; bright red cheeks, and singularly definite jetty black eyebrows, moustache, and imperial. You could see that from the sidewalk; but you saw, when you stood at his wheel, not only the twinkling diamond ring and breast-pin, but the heavy, slabby red paint; and even the substratum of grizzly gray under that jetty dye; and upon our word there's a hair of the same straggling out under the jaunty oiled wig! How straight he sits, and how he simpers, and how he fingers the reins with a delicate white little finger stuck out, as if a mere touch were all—as if his whole hand might govern a team of elephants! The Baron Spolasco, with no end of medical diplomas from all sorts of universities across the ocean, who cures everything immediately; you may consult him confidentially, or by letter, if you choose. It would be worth money to see that old gentleman —they say he is nearly eighty—undress himself! Clothes, wig, calves, stays, moustache, teeth, complexion—what a bald, bare, wizened, shriveled old granny he would be!

A lady—slender and elegant—in black from head to foot; pure white complexion, pale, striking chiseled features, perfect profile, abundant fair hair; abstracted look, and rather rapid, purposeful step. That is Miss Ada Clare, called by many a perfect beauty; questionless, of decided talent; one about whom many interesting stories might be told, and a persevering and energetic votary of the mimetic art. Possessed of some wealth, great personal attractions, no inconsiderable share of intellect and cultivation, she has already often appeared upon the stage, which she may possibly adopt as a profession.

A straight, trim-built, prompt, vigorous man, well dressed with strong brown hair, beard, and moustache, and a quick and watchful eye. He steps alertly by, watching everybody. Charles A. Dana, chief editor of the New York *Tribune*, a man of rough, strong intellect, tremendous prejudices firmly relied on, and excellent intentions.

Down the other side goes one with a dry, spare, hard visage, black eyes, and a huge white beard of somewhat ragged appearance. He strides along regardlessly and rapidly, a book in his hand, a thought—and more too—inside of his head, a most rustical straw hat outside of it, turned sharp up behind and down before, like a country boy's, and a summer coat streaming flag-like from his shoulders. He is senior partner of a book and job printing firm, down town. "Pshaw! what is he worth describing for?" Wait a minute. That firm is also a firm of newspaper editors and publishers. It is the firm of William C. Bryant & Co.; and the senior partner, the white-bearded, scrawny, striding old gentleman, is, if not our foremost and noblest poet, abreast with the foremost; and, moreover, a strong, valiant, and uncompromising—and more yet, and rarer—an absolutely fair and courteous political newspaper editor, on what side it is unnecessary to say.

A big, heavy, overgrown man, with a face like a raw beefsteak, little piggy eyes, queer, dry, straight, harsh, coarse hair, "of a speckled color", made up of brownish red and gray, rather dirty clothes, and quite dirty, yellow dogskin gloves. He goes rolling along in an elephantine style, and for fear of being trod on, probably, people get out of the way. That is George Law, who never will be President. Those people, and many more, go about the streets of New York.

# WICKED ARCHITECTURE

NOT wicked in carelessness of material construction, like the crumbly structures sometimes run up in our city by mercenary builders, that prove death-traps to the inmates; nor in purpose, like an Inquisition or a panel-thief's haunt; but in the unrighteous spirit of ostentation that unconsciously directs it, and in the manifold and frightful social evils flowing from it.

It may not at first appear that the architecture of New York has any very distinct connection with any thing good or evil. But there *is* a connection, and one startlingly close and efficient. The domestic architecture—the dwelling-house architecture—of the city (for our Architectural Wickedness exists mainly there), even though perhaps not absolutely in itself the efficient cause of evil, is the most striking type of that condition of social morals which is the fertile hot-bed for evils the most enormous.

A house to live in is the third great necessity; food and clothing only being before it. And furthermore, it is in some sense true that a man is not a whole and complete man unless he *owns* a house and the ground it stands on. Men are created owners of the earth. Each was intended to possess his piece of it; and however the modifications of civilized life have covered this truth, or changed the present phase of it, it is still indicated by the universal instinctive desire for landed property, and by the fuller sense of independent manhood which comes from the possession of it.

In New York, closed in by rivers, pressing desperately toward the business center at its southern end, and characterized by an unparalleled fierceness in money-chasing, land is dear. This of course makes the possession of it a basis for an increased ostentation of it; for the dearer a thing is, the more pride in showing it, and wonder in staring at it.

Next; ways of thinking, throughout society, are more or less formed on the patterns set by the rich. And accordingly it may be stated, as a general principle, that in New York city, among all ranks, except the poorest, there is a habit of occupying houses outrageously and absurdly too expensive, whether in prime cost or in rent, for the resources of the occupant. The wealthy began by building such houses for themselves. Then they, as land-owners, or builders as speculators, went on to build blocks and ranges of similar edifices, to lease to people of less wealth; and these again were not slow to hire them on the great American principle, that I am as good as anybody; which, however, is unfortunately taken to include this: that I may therefore have whatever anybody else has, *whether I can afford it or not.*

This ambitious folly, however, is operative only among the better classes. The great mass of the poor live in insufficient tenements, because the competition on the narrow island for dwelling-places is so keen that dwellings both "cheap and nasty", to use an expressive late English Saxonism, pay large rents; and if the landlords get their rent, what matter whether the house be a house or a sty? And the poor tenants, knowing that landlords can always find occupants, and consequently not being able to coerce improvement by threatening to remove, must live in such dens as they may. What too many of those dens are, the reports of the Legislative Tenement Committee, now engaged in examining the leased dwelling-houses occupied by our city poor, most impressively show; but with this branch of the subject we have not now to deal.

*In no other city in the whole world does rent occupy so large a proportion of expenses as in New York;* in no other city in the world would so many years' income be required from the man of whatsoever pecuniary and social standing to purchase for himself a piece of ground and a house, whereon and wherein to live.

London is the most expensive capital in Europe. From it economical Englishmen flee to the continental cities, large and small, to live in equal comfort at less expense. Rents in London are from one half to one fourth of New York rates. A house corresponding with our "first-class brown-stone front English basement" tenements, on a twenty-five foot lot, renting for $2,000, may be had in London for about £200; roughly, $1,000. A "second-class" house may here rent for $800 to $1,200. The corresponding house in London costs but about $500. A very large number of houses are rented in New York for from $600 to $800; say at an average of $700. In London such houses would be rented at about $200.

"Twenty years' purchase", that is, the total of rent for twenty years, is in London considered a fair rate for valuing the house and lot; so that one twentieth of the value, or five *per cent.* on it, is paid for rent. In New York, twelve and ten years' rent would buy many houses; that is, eight or ten *per cent.* on the value is paid for rent.

Such is a succinct statement, illustrated by statistics and comparison, of our domestic architectural habits in New York city. Next comes the development of those consequences of them which make us call it Wicked Architecture.

They may be stated in brief and in mass as, *Difficulty of Marriage and Settlement in Life.* Mr. Brown, we will suppose, is a substantial, well-to-do old gentleman. His house is a four-story one, if you please, brown-stone front, and all that sort of thing.

Mrs. Brown tells her daughters, "Now, girls, it's all very well to have a loving husband, and to love him; but it's a great deal better to have substantial comfort and a sufficient pecuniary income. Have a good husband, and love him, if possible; but marry well, at any rate. That's sound, common sense; I've lived longer than you have; and I know better what's flummery and what isn't."

The girls are well prepared by their city training for such advice as that, and they take it.

A worthy young clerk or just-established junior partner, perhaps a thriving mechanic, even—if it be not a profane presumption!—asks leave of old Brown to seek one of his daughters in marriage.

*Mr. Brown.* "Mr. Driver, you are doubtless a very excellent young man. But can you maintain Melinda Ann in the style to which she has been accustomed?"

Driver rather confusedly begins to talk about present narrow circumstances, good prospects, future wealth, earnest devotion, etc.

*Mr. Brown.* "Yes, yes. I know. But it appears to me, young man, that you'd a little better wait awhile until you are certain of this position. As a friend, Mr. Driver," etc.

Driver leaves. This specimen (from actual life, by the way) abundantly expresses the state of expectation on the one

U                                                           W.

hand, and the necessary hesitation on the part of all but the already rich on the other, to which we refer. Illogical old Brown! Did you begin at the large end of the horn? You would have been wiser to remember the pride with which you and Mrs. B. stood within the first little two-story whole house that you rented; the cheap struggling year through which you crawled like a caterpillar up to the riches that now gild you so grandly!

Well. Very large numbers of young men, some of no principle and some of a little, well-intentioned enough, but not fortified very strongly against fierce temptations, stand in this relation to the maidens from among whom they should select their wives.

Either they marry, or they do not. If not, they at best live single and imperfect lives, losing the healthy beautifying power which God intended them to find in the family relations, isolated units in a world whose essence is association. But if they are not strong enough for that, facts show that in great numbers they lose the very nucleus and essence of all usefulness and power—purity of soul—and, degrading themselves by submission under the tyranny of ignoble lusts, fall into one or the other of two states—or into both of them—of which we can here say but very little; in brief, into the practice of haunting those abodes which are the gates of hell, or into an illegitimate and unblest association with some one woman, necessarily of coarse and impure mind, or low character and social standing, and of downward tendency in every channel of Life. The mothers who send beloved sons into the city to live, would feel little hope and much and painful fear, could they know how large a proportion of the business men and active male population of the city generally, under the age of twenty-five years, are either in the constant practice of visiting houses of ill-fame or are living in a quasi household with a kept mistress. Upon this point we can not enlarge. Suffice it to say that there is no man of *general* and *thorough* acquaintance in New York who can not point out, if he chooses, five, or ten, or twenty young men, almost—and perhaps quite—to his personal knowledge so circumstanced!

But suppose that, in spite of all, our young friends marry.

They can not afford a house. And consequently, as the little girl aptly said when asked where her parents lived, "They don't *live;* they BOARD."

Few are aware of the extent of boarding-house life in New York. Whole neighborhoods of boarding-houses now stand, for instance, around St. John's Park; in Houston and Bleecker streets; in many other localities formerly as aristocratic as "Fifth Avenoodledom". Thousands of young or "moderately well off " people, absolutely unable to find the right residence for them, hire a house quite too large, and eke out the rent by sub-letting one, two, three, or more rooms, or entire floors, to such lodgers as they can find. This custom prevails everywhere. Fifth Avenue, Fourteenth Street, from river to river, Twenty-second and Twenty-third Streets and indeed nearly every other respectable portion of the city, are dotted with houses thus portioned off. Judicious and extensively informed observers estimate the proportion of dwelling-houses which are either professedly boarding-houses, or in which one or more rooms are thus sub-let to "one or two respectable young gentlemen", "a married couple without incumbrance", etc., as seven out of every ten. Counting in this class of residences those hotels which are occupied mostly by permanent boarders, it is probable that nearer three quarters than two thirds of all the adult inhabitants of New York city, of the middle and wealthy classes, live in boarding houses.

What is this boarding-house life? Simply a place to keep a man's trunk and his wife while he is at work, and where he has breakfast, tea, and sleeping-room. All day long, these thousands and thousands of wives, many of them with their children, are left alone, without responsibility, with little or no employment; they may read or study; probably with a master; and, if so, under the inevitable risks of such avocations; they spin street yarns in Broadway; shop; dine at Taylor's or Thompson's; make calls; talk scandal; sleep. There is no chance for the gathering of the wretched husband's family. There is no chance for the development of the unhappy wife into a mature and noble woman—the

"Perfect being, nobly planned,
To warn, to comfort, to command."

of the poet. Listlessness; emptiness; sloth; nerves; dyspepsia; flirtations; prodigality; vain show; perhaps—often, might we not say?—immorality, nay, infamy. These are the accomplishments which the boarding-house life most tends to develop.

We must hasten. Of whatever remedies are applicable to this state of things, many are too profound and remote even to be stated in a newspaper article. That which we shall mention—we can do little more—is one which combines the recommendation of practicability and profit. It is simply the erection of tenement-houses, so arranged that each floor is a complete isolated habitation by itself. There are already a few such buildings, and they are eagerly sought for. In London they have been introduced within the last few years, and meet with great favor. By the arrangement of two tenements on each floor, space is given for a well, which will afford light and ventilation to the midmost of the tier of rooms; and the two end apartments may be used for the social daylight uses of the family. Such tenements as these, judiciously located and handsomely finished, could be rented at reasonable rates; would restore to many of these wretched "married bachelors" a place for their household goods, a home and a hearth of their own, if not forever, at least in independent separation for the time being; would furnish the unoccupied mind and listless bodies of their wives with the stimulus and responsibilities which they need, and which God meant for them: and last—and least—yet most necessary of all, could, as may be demonstrated, yield a remunerative per-centage on the investment of the capitalist.

Perhaps we may add, that if any persons desire further information in this matter of tenement homes, it shall be given as far as practicable upon application at the office of this paper.

## CHARLES DICKENS

*Blackwood's Magazine* for April contains several very interesting articles. Among them is a "Remonstrance with Dickens", in which Magu takes the great novelist to task for the degeneracy so evident in his later works from the high standard of his earlier novels.

This is not the first time that a similar complaint has been made against Dickens' later works, and for our own part we admit its justice, and hope that that once most humorous of authors will take the rebuke in good part, and follow the advice of his reviewer, who recommends him to "lay aside his pen for awhile, collecting fitting materials in his own fields, without wandering into regions strange to him, and when fully ripe, expressing the results of his marvelous faculty of observation in his old natural, humorous, graphic pathetic way". The impression which we have felt in reading Dickens' later works has been that made by John Wesley's sermon on Dr. Johnson. Being asked what he thought of the sermon the lexicographer replied, "It was not a good sermon, Sir, but it was one which none but a good preacher could have made." So say we of *Dombey & Son*, *Bleak House* and especially the 1st volume of *Little Dorrit*. Taken as a whole, neither of them is a good novel, but there is enough of excellence in each, and especially in the two former works, to show that none but a good novelist could have written it.

## [EMERSON'S "BRAHMA"]

SOME of the papers are poking fun at Emerson on account of the unintelligibility of his little Mystic Song entitled "Brahma" in the new *Atlantic Monthly*. The name of the poem is a facile key to it; Brahma, the Indian Deity, is the absolute and omnipresent god, besides whom all is illusion and fancy, and to whom everything apparent reverts in the end. This pantheistic thought Emerson expresses, not only clearly, but with remarkable grace and melody.

## PROFESSIONAL MEN

AMONG the silly paragraphs which frequently go the rounds of the press none are more absurd than those which represent the editorial existence as one of ceaseless labor and annoyance, coupled with ungrateful returns and ill-pay. We can only account for the appearance of such items in the papers by supposing them to be the productions of the individuals who have entered upon the profession destitute of the most ordinary qualifications for it, who have established journals in such locations, or under such circumstances, as inevitably preclude success. For our own part we are convinced that neither do the labors of journalism exceed, nor are its returns unworthy of comparison with, those of any other profession. A journalist will not succeed at once in an illiterate neighborhood any more than a physician will flourish in a healthy, a clergyman in a wicked, or a lawyer in a peace-loving community. But as a whole the rewards of journalism bear comparison fairly [well] with those of any of the other professional callings. The leading editors of the Union reap as large income as any men earn in the pulpit, the bar, or the consulting room; and the proportion of starving country editors is no greater than that of briefless attorneys, doctors without practice, and under-paid ministers. The generality of the editorial profession throughout the country earn as good livings as the great body of members of the other professions. Yet even were it otherwise, allowance would have to be made for the fact that while comparatively few men dare to attempt prescribing for diseases of the soul or body, or to venture into the legal arena, on the other hand at least every sixth man flatters himself that he is capable of instructing the community through the press. Hence there are more quacks and pretenders in the newspaper profession than in any other, though goodness knows there are too many in all!

Then again, journalism possesses indirect advantages which no other except the legal profession can present the like of. It furnishes the readiest road to political preferment if a change from the editorial stool to the legislative desk is a preferment, which we doubt. Still, in estimating the material advantages attending the pursuit of the different professions, it is fair to take this into account. Thus it will be seen that the editor can afford to laugh in his sleeve at the pitying comparisons which are so often drawn between his own and the rival professional modes of getting a living.

But we had wellnigh forgotten the collateral advantages accruing from the profession of journalism. There is the consciousness of possessing power and influence, in a greater or less degree—the feeling of self-complacency which is kept alive in the editorial breast by the deferential respect paid him by all who have an office to solicit, a nostrum to vend or an axe to grind, and who are anxious to secure the potent aid of his "truly valuable and widely circulated organ of public opinion", to advertise their projects. There is also the silent veneration of the public who regard the terrible "We" as a semi-omniscient and omnipotent being; there is the possibility of dead headism on a large scale if he chooses to stoop to it, and the numberless compliments and contributions which the grateful public bestows upon its benefactor; and last, though not least, there are fragrant offerings occasionally in the shape of notes of thanks from meetings, especially if the paper has "come out strong" on behalf of the object promoted by the individuals constituting said meetings.

Nor are the thorns spread over this bed of roses so thickly as the uninitiated are taught to believe. The editorial responsibilities are not half so consequential as those of a ferry boat pilot. The intellectual labors do not begin to equal those of a lawyer in a civil suit of any importance, nor does the hardest-worked news-hunter undergo physical toil at all comparable with that of a physician in active practice. It would be vain to deny that the literary labor of a newspaper is accompanied by a great deal of annoyance, worry, and exhaustion; but it does not compare in these respects with the monotonous drudgery of preparation for the pulpit, or the weary plodding through the devious labyrinths of the law-books.

You light-hearted and good natured individuals, who have been hitherto disposed to commiserate the perplexed editor in his dusty sanctum, spare your pity, we entreat you, for those who need it more. Bestow it if you will on office-seekers, cringing for the favors of a superior; on politicians, doomed to listen daily to the wearisome platitudes of their colleagues; on doctors, wearing out their own lives in vain attempts to prolong those of others; on lawyers, inextricably entangled in an ever-shifting ocean of contradictory enactments;—at any rate, waste not your commiseration on journalists, who need it not and who can be, if they know how, at once the most self-reliant, the most contented and the most useful of mortals.

## [REFORMERS]

THE cant of the reformers is quite as barefaced and disgusting in its way as that of other descriptions of trade. Sleek Mawworms cry out from the lecturing-desk against the vice and brutality of the masses. These are the moral reformers. Another school—the bouncing, bumptious Bounderby school— inveigh against the filth and disease and neglect of Hygiene among the masses. These are the physical reformers. They preach long discourses and write long-winded articles against ignorance and rum and debauchery. They safely assume that the time is out of joint, and tack to it the bold assumption that it is they who are born to set it right. One imagines the millennium would be at hand if a Bible were in every household, or a church or a school house at every corner, another finds his universal panacea for the ills that flesh is heir to in turning humans into amphibious animals, in deluging their insides and outsides with the liquid element, and in forswearing of beef-steak for bran-bread and turnips. Cure yourselves, O physicians, and search not for motes in the eyes of people, when you cannot see straightly for the beams that blind your own. Think not so brainsickly of things. There is no mental or moral or philosophical philosopher's stone that can transmute by its specific virtue the base metal of the diseased into the refined gold of the Normal. There is no magic hey-presto-change! which can snatch the round men from the square holes and the square men from the round holes, and make all right and tight in an instant in this great old terrestrial ball of ours. If there be balm in Gilead for the correction of abuses and the healing of moral and physical evil, it can be found in no such little doses as you make specialities and hobbies withal. The origin of evil is a question that has puzzled all developed thoughtful minds through all the ages, and it is so deep and dark and mystic a problem that not the wisest of them has ever been able to peer behind one fold of the thick veil. And you approach this mighty mystery, and hold forth in your puny hands your potent "specific" for its cure. With your farthing rush-light you seek to illumine the illimitable caverns of the infinite. With your favorite (pint) measure, you would ladle out the ocean.

It is pitiful. These problems lie so deep, and you approach them so superficially—these qualities are so momentous, and you talk of them so childishly! Heaven is so high, and yet you play before it such fantastic tricks! Nature is so calm, so serene, so certain in her workings, and yet you cannot perceive the beauty and the grandeur of the lesson she inculcates. You can accept nothing unquestioned. You place the blatant enthusiast before the reverent philosopher. Fanaticism with you stands in the stead of Faith.

## DOWN BELOW

WHO of the thousands of the gay upper circles who are flitting to the watering places on their usual summer round of fashions and folly thinks of the elements of woe and crime that are festering beneath their feet! Who of the pseudo-philanthropists whose eyes are intent on Africa and who solicit with smooth tongued sweetness alms for the South Sea Island Mission, or a donation for the founding of an asylum for superannuated lap dogs, even think of or care for the gaunt physical want and heathenish spiritual ignorance that make the city's stews and purlieus hideous? Who among the loud mouthed lady-reformers ever suggested any practical plan of relief for those of their own sister-hood who are toiling out life and blood and brain for the miserable pittance which the cupidity of men grants the poor seamstress? Whoever cares to reflect upon the fact that while the Tract Society counts its contributions by millions, the Magdalen Asylum is left with half-a-dozen inmates for lack of means, the News Boy's Home in pretty much the same condition, and every enterprise that has some real, substantial, practical good for its basis may be placed in the same category?

Nobody knows and nobody cares about these things. The impudent, the pretending, the tinselled and the superficial—these claim the great world's attention and admiration. Nobody wishes to look deeper—it is unpleasant and inconvenient. It is not pleasant to grope among the muck and the slime. Cover it up! Do you say that pestilence will arise? Never mind—cover it up—never look "Down below".

## SOURCES OF CHARACTER—RESULTS—1860

To sum up the foregoing from the outset (and, of course, far, far more unrecorded,) I estimate three leading sources and formative stamps to my own character, now solidified for good or bad, and its subsequent literary and other outgrowth —the maternal nativity-stock brought hither from far-away Netherlands, for one, (doubtless the best)—the subterranean tenacity and central bony structure (obstinacy, wilfulness) which I get from my paternal English elements, for another —and the combination of my Long Island birth-spot, sea-shores, childhood's scenes, absorptions, with teeming Brooklyn and New York—with, I suppose, my experiences afterward in the secession outbreak, for the third.

For, in 1862, startled by news that my brother George, an officer in the 51st New York volunteers, had been seriously wounded (first Fredericksburg battle, December 13th,) I hurriedly went down to the field of war in Virginia. But I must go back a little.

## OPENING OF THE SECESSION WAR

NEWS of the attack on fort Sumter and *the flag* at Charleston harbor, S. C., was receiv'd in New York city late at night (13th April, 1861,) and was immediately sent out in extras of the newspapers. I had been to the opera in Fourteenth street that night, and after the performance was walking down Broadway toward twelve o'clock, on my way to Brooklyn, when I heard in the distance the loud cries of the newsboys, who came presently tearing and yelling up the street, rushing from side to side even more furiously than usual. I bought an extra and cross'd to the Metropolitan hotel (Niblo's) where the great lamps were still brightly blazing, and, with a crowd of others, who gather'd impromptu, read the news, which was evidently authentic. For the benefit of some who had no papers, one of us read the telegram aloud, while all listen'd silently and attentively. No remark was made by any of the crowd, which had increas'd to thirty or forty, but all stood a minute or two, I remember, before they dispers'd. I can almost see them there now, under the lamps at midnight again.

# NATIONAL UPRISING AND VOLUNTEERING

I HAVE said somewhere that the three Presidentiads preceding 1861 show'd how the weakness and wickedness of rulers are just as eligible here in America under republican, as in Europe under dynastic influences. But what can I say of that prompt and splendid wrestling with secession slavery, the arch-enemy personified, the instant he unmistakably show'd his face? The volcanic upheaval of the nation, after that firing on the flag at Charleston, proved for certain something which had been previously in great doubt, and at once substantially settled the question of disunion. In my judgment it will remain as the grandest and most encouraging spectacle yet vouchsafed in any age, old or new, to political progress and democracy. It was not for what came to the surface merely—though that was important—but what it indicated below, which was of eternal importance. Down in the abysms of New World humanity there had form'd and harden'd a primal hardpan of national Union will, determin'd and in the majority, refusing to be tamper'd with or argued against, confronting all emergencies, and capable at any time of bursting all surface bonds, and breaking out like an earthquake. It is, indeed, the best lesson of the century, or of America, and it is a mighty privilege to have been part of it. (Two great spectacles, immortal proofs of democracy, unequall'd in all the history of the past, are furnish'd by the secession war—one at the beginning, the other at its close. Those are, the general, voluntary, arm'd upheaval, and the peaceful and harmonious disbanding of the armies in the summer of 1865.)

# CONTEMPTUOUS FEELING

EVEN after the bombardment of Sumter, however, the gravity of the revolt, and the power and will of the slave States for a strong and continued military resistance to national authority, were not at all realized at the North, except by a few. Nine-tenths of the people of the free States look'd upon the rebellion, as started in South Carolina, from a feeling one-half of contempt, and the other half composed of anger and incredulity. It was not thought it would be join'd in by Virginia, North Carolina, or Georgia. A great and cautious national official predicted that it would blow over "in sixty days", and folks generally believ'd the prediction. I remember talking about it on a Fulton ferry-boat with the Brooklyn mayor, who said he only "hoped the Southern fire-eaters would commit some overt act of resistance, as they would then be at once so effectually squelch'd, we would never hear of secession again—but he was afraid they never would have the pluck to really do anything". I remember, too, that a couple of companies of the Thirteenth Brooklyn, who rendezvou'd at the city armory, and started thence as thirty days' men, were all provided with pieces of rope, conspicuously tied to their musket barrels, with which to bring back each man a prisoner from the audacious South, to be led in a noose, on our men's early and triumphant return!

## BATTLE OF BULL RUN, JULY, 1861

ALL this sort of feeling was destin'd to be arrested and revers'd by a terrible shock—the battle of first Bull Run—certainly, as we now know it, one of the most singular fights on record. (All battles, and their results, are far more matters of accident than is generally thought; but this was throughout a casualty, a chance. Each side supposed it had won, till the last moment. One had, in point of fact, just the same right to be routed as the other. By a fiction, or series of fictions, the national forces at the last moment exploded in a panic and fled from the field.) The defeated troops commenced pouring into Washington over the Long Bridge at daylight on Monday, 22d—day drizzling all through with rain. The Saturday and Sunday of the battle (20th, 21st,) had been parch'd and hot to an extreme—the dust, the grime and smoke, in layers, sweated in, follow'd by other layers again sweated in, absorb'd by those excited souls—their clothes all saturated with the clay-powder filling the air—stirr'd up everywhere on the dry roads and trodden fields by the regiments, swarming wagons, artillery, etc.—all the men with this coating of murk and sweat and rain, now recoiling back, pouring over the Long Bridge—a horrible march of twenty miles, returning to Washington baffled, humiliated, panic-struck. Where are the vaunts, and the proud boasts with which you went forth? Where are your banners, and your bands of music, and your ropes to bring back your prisoners? Well, there isn't a band playing—and there isn't a flag but clings ashamed and lank to its staff.

The sun rises, but shines not. The men appear, at first sparsely and shame-faced enough, then thicker, in the streets of Washington—appear in Pennsylvania avenue, and on the steps and basement entrances. They come along in disorderly mobs, some in squads, stragglers, companies. Occasionally, a rare regiment, in perfect order, with its officers (some gaps, dead, the true braves,) marching in silence, with lowering faces, stern, weary to sinking, all black and dirty, but every man with his musket, and stepping alive; but these are the exceptions. Sidewalks of Pennsylvania avenue, Four-teenth street, etc., crowded, jamm'd with citizens, darkies, clerks, everybody, lookers-on; women in the windows, curious expressions from faces, as those swarms of dirt-cover'd return'd soldiers there (will they never end?) move by; but nothing said, no comments; (half our lookers-on secesh of the most venomous kind—they say nothing; but the devil snickers in their faces.) During the forenoon Wash-ington gets all over motley with these defeated soldiers—queer-looking objects, strange eyes and faces, drench'd (the steady rain drizzles on all day) and fearfully worn, hungry, haggard, blister'd in the feet. Good people (but not over-many of them either,) hurry up something for their grub. They put wash-kettles on the fire, for soup, for coffee. They set tables on the sidewalks—wagon-loads of bread are pur-chas'd, swiftly cut in stout chunks. Here are two aged ladies, beautiful, the first in the city for culture and charm, they stand with store of eating and drink at an improvis'd table of rough plank, and give food, and have the store replenish'd from their house every half-hour all that day; and there in the rain they stand, active, silent, white-hair'd, and give food, though the tears stream down their cheeks, almost without intermission, the whole time. Amid the deep excitement, crowds and motion, and desperate eagerness, it seems strange to see many, very many, of the soldiers sleeping—in the midst of all, sleeping sound. They drop down anywhere, on the steps of houses, up close by the basements or fences, on the sidewalk, aside on some vacant lot, and deeply sleep. A poor 17 or 18 year old boy lies there, on the stoop of a grand house; he sleeps so calmly, so profoundly. Some clutch their muskets firmly even in sleep. Some in squads; comrades, brothers, close together—and on them, as they lay, sulkily drips the rain.

As afternoon pass'd, and evening came, the streets, the bar-rooms, knots everywhere, listeners, questioners, terrible yarns, bugaboo, mask'd batteries, our regiment all cut up, etc.—stories and story-tellers, windy, bragging, vain centres of street-crowds. Resolution, manliness, seem to have abandon'd Washington. The principal hotel, Willard's, is full of shoulder-straps—thick, crush'd, creeping with shoulder-straps. (I see them, and must have a word with them. There you are, shoulder-straps!—but where are your companies? where are your men? Incompetents! never tell me of chances of battle, of getting stray'd, and the like. I think this is your work, this retreat, after all. Sneak, blow, put on airs there in Willard's sumptuous parlors and bar-rooms, or anywhere—no explanation shall save you. Bull Run is your work; had you been half or one-tenth worthy your men, this would never have happen'd.)

Meantime, in Washington, among the great persons and their entourage, a mixture of awful consternation, uncertainty, rage, shame, helplessness, and stupefying disappointment. The worst is not only imminent, but already here. In a few hours—perhaps before the next meal—the secesh generals, with their victorious hordes, will be upon us. The dream of humanity, the vaunted Union we thought so strong, so impregnable—lo! it seems already smash'd like a china plate. One bitter, bitter hour—perhaps proud America will never again know such an hour. She must pack and fly—no time to spare. Those white palaces—the dome-crown'd capitol there on the hill, so stately over the trees—shall they be left —or destroy'd first? For it is certain that the talk among certain of the magnates and officers and clerks and officials everywhere, for twenty-four hours in and around Washington after Bull Run, was loud and undisguised for yielding out and out, and substituting the southern rule, and Lincoln promptly abdicating and departing. If the secesh officers and forces had immediately follow'd, and by a bold Napoleonic movement had enter'd Washington the first day, (or even the second,) they could have had things their own way, and a powerful faction north to back them. One of our returning colonels express'd in public that night, amid a swarm of officers and gentlemen in a crowded room, the opinion that it was useless to fight, that the southerners had made their title clear, and that the best course for the national government to pursue was to desist from any further attempt at stopping them, and admit them again to the lead, on the best terms they were willing to grant. Not a voice was rais'd against this judgment, amid that large crowd of officers and gentlemen. (The fact is, the hour was one of the three or four of those crises we had then and afterward, during the fluctuations of four years, when human eyes appear'd at least just as likely to see the last breath of the Union as to see it continue.)

## THE STUPOR PASSES—SOMETHING ELSE BEGINS

But the hour, the day, the night pass'd, and whatever returns, an hour, a day, a night like that can never again return. The President, recovering himself, begins that very night—sternly, rapidly sets about the task of reorganizing his forces, and placing himself in positions for future and surer work. If there were nothing else of Abraham Lincoln for history to stamp him with, it is enough to send him with his wreath to the memory of all future time, that he endured that hour, that day, bitterer than gall—indeed a crucifixion day—that it did not conquer him—that he unflinchingly stemm'd it, and resolv'd to lift himself and the Union out of it.

Then the great New York papers at once appear'd, (commencing that evening, and following it up the next morning, and incessantly through many days afterwards,) with leaders that rang out over the land with the loudest, most reverberating ring of clearest bugles, full of encouragement, hope, inspiration, unfaltering defiance. Those magnificent editorials! they never flagg'd for a fortnight. The *Herald* commenced them—I remember the articles well. The *Tribune* was equally cogent and inspiriting—and the *Times, Evening Post,* and other principal papers, were not a whit behind. They came in good time, for they were needed. For in the humiliation of Bull Run, the popular feeling north, from its extreme of superciliousness, recoil'd to the depth of gloom and apprehension.

(Of all the days of the war, there are two especially I can never forget. Those were the day following the news, in New York and Brooklyn, of that first Bull Run defeat, and the day of Abraham Lincoln's death. I was home in Brooklyn on both occasions. The day of the murder we heard the news very early in the morning. Mother prepared breakfast—and other meals afterward—as usual; but not a mouthful was eaten all day by either of us. We each drank half a cup of coffee; that was all. Little was said. We got every newspaper morning and evening, and the frequent extras of that period, and pass'd them silently to each other.)

## THE BOWERY

### *Lager Beer, The Germans, etc.*

THE Bowery, and the demesnes east of it, represent the real democratic lager element of New York. There is lager enough on Broadway, but it is not imbibed, as it is here, with the genuine working-man's thirst; nor associated, as here, with so many memories of friendship, and with the ideas of relief from toil, and with the social relaxations and pleasures of life.

All the east side is full of German operatives. To go off for a couple of hours of an evening, or six or seven hours of a Sunday, is their main hold upon life outside of their daily work. And these hours are identified with lager.

### *A Popular Lager-Beer Hall in the Bowery*

Through a somewhat lengthy passage, you reach a great round open place, formerly a circus, or something of that kind. Here is plenty of room, and the roof of canvas, red, white and blue, makes it all cool and nice for summer. The crowd is dense; they surround the little and big tables, and fill up the interstices.

Waiters clutching in their hands astonishing quantities of glasses, glide to and fro, working their way through impossible places, with snake-like agility. (This feat of carrying a couple of dozen glasses in each hand is worth noticing.)

There is a stage, with theatrical and lyric performances; also a brass band, in another part of the house, up in a gallery that runs all round the house; the brass is very loud and vehement.

Among the audience are numerous descendants of the race that escaped from Egypt and crossed a certain sea dry-shod. Here they are in the Bowery, many of them with hats of the Mose-style. Some of them have brought their wives and babies—the latter they frequently toddle and dance to the sound of the music. Of course Germany predominates, although the European continent is all more or less represented. There are, here and there, young couples, apparently not long married—some of them very loving. But their loving is unnoticed; there is great freedom of the individual permitted here. There are some good-looking women. The best of the matter is a general show of health and hilarity, and those make up for other deficiencies.

There is a restaurant on one side of the large room. On another side, cigar and confectionery stands, etc. Somewhere around is a shooting-gallery attached, for amid all the din of the band, the click of glasses, the unrestrained laughter and talk of six or eight hundred people, and the raps on the tables to call the waiters, you hear the crack, crack! of the bogus rifles, firing wooden missiles at a target against the wall (at two cents a shot).

Boys run round with trays of pretzels; others with cheap cigars. At a bar off one side, you see three men drinking each a large cylindrical glass of wheat beer—that aristocratic cousin of the popular russet lager. With the rest, you hear the merry pop of the innocent soda water, in bottles, the corks being abruptly liberated from their bonds of twine. In the midst of all the bell rings and the curtain rises for a performance, in German on the stage.

Now there is some trouble. There is an "officer", with big black whiskers, a fearful looking man, deputed to keep the peace in this reckless assemblage. Everything has gone on well enough till this moment, but now he becomes frantic in his futile endeavors to make the standees become seated, so that all can see the magnificent achievements on the stage. But all the evening each one of the mass has been doing what seemed best in his own sight, and now the tide is resistless. There is much hubbub. The officer with the ferocious whiskers has a special squabble with a weak, pale-faced young man (evidently a journeyman shoemaker), who has come there to do the handsome with a chosen one of the other sex.

The pale-faced young man retorts upon the officer with indignation, in a foreign tongue. Whiskers attempts to bully him, but the frau takes a hand in. Then whiskers suddenly beholds (although positively invisible to me and the rest) a mortal row over in a distant part of the hall, which requires his attention and personal presence.

Meantime the actors and actresses on the stage proceed with admirable nonchalance, not disturbed in the least by the rumpus, which at one time made more noise by far than the play (or whatever it was).

But lo! a balloon is suddenly let down, as from the high meridian, covered with an inscription in large, strange characters. I ask for their decipherment from a learned person in my neighborhood. He courteously informs me that it is an advertisement of a ball, of some guild or society, to come off the ensuing week, with the place, price of tickets, etc. I look with horror at this method of abstracting money from the daily and weekly papers; also with some curiosity at the ingenious utensil. After about five minutes it ascends, and is lost to sight.

The mixture of sounds now affords one who hath ears to hear that sort of thing, something very novel and varied. The band up in the gallery plays ambitious pieces from the great composers, etc.; but it does not disturb you so much in connection with all the rest. In every direction are men's voices, animated with lager. There is much friendship—occasionally an embrace. I hear the orders sung out from the waiters in the restaurant to the carver very plainly. A disturbed infant, a rod off, is squalling at the top of its strength. Then there is the continual clicking of glasses, the calling of friends to each other from outside to inside; a boy crying as he passes with a tray, "Cakes, pretzel, ice cream;" and the pounding of a beefsteak to make it tender back in the restaurant. These are only samples, for there are plenty more to make up the combination.

Such are the sights and sounds at a lager establishment, pure and simple. Then there is the larger hall, with dancing accompaniments for the crowd.

### *Lindmuller's*

Have you never spent an hour of an evening at Lindmuller's dance hall? Then you shall go thither with us this instant, only promising that you may consider yourself transported, without expense or trouble, to the east side of the Bowery, opposite Spring street.

Lindmuller's might be taken for a large hot-house, with the usual glass roof. It, too, like the spot previously described, is roomy and democratic and devoted to lager; but the further speciality here, is in letting joy be unconfined, and everybody going in for a good buxom dance.

Up around the one story, toward the roof, along the pillars and gas-fixing, etc., are trained slender threads of vines; but their pale green leaves have a suspicion of the artificial. All the ample center of the "halle", a space of sixty or seventy feet by forty, is kept clear for the waltzers. Around this are motley groups, seated or standing, with their glasses of lager, and looking at the dance. It is about 10 o'clock, Thursday evening, May 9th, '62.

Now a waiter dashes out and sprinkles the floor with a watering-pot. Then the waltzing band strikes up—very good music—the young fellows seize their partners, and off they whirl.

Now a trivial episode occurs. The "officer" (here shaved very clean) rushes through the crowd of dancers, and taps a young man on the shoulder; the mild young man having violated the etiquette of the hour by engaging in the merry dance with his hat on. The young man removes the offending article, and proceeds.

The crowd of dancers thickens, and becomes thick and agitated. Some grow very red in the face. One fleshy young lady shines conspicuously, like the full moon among the stars. If there is any accidental jostling, it is received with great good nature, altogether the people seeming to have a first rate time.

Here, too, on one side, is a shooting gallery. A placard annexed informs patriots who wish to join the army, and desire first to perfect themselves in the art and mystery of hitting the mark, that they will here be taught free by an accomplished professor.

Another placard, a little distance off, nominates John C. Fremont for the Presidency in 1864.

Meanwhile, the young fellows (good-looking and healthy) waltz, waltz, waltz away. Of course there are the inevitable cakes and pretzel.

VELSOR BRUSH.

## DOWN AT THE FRONT

FALMOUTH, Va., *opposite Fredericksburgh, December* 21, 1862.—Begin my visits among the camp hospitals in the army of the Potomac. Spend a good part of the day in a large brick mansion on the banks of the Rappahannock, used as a hospital since the battle—seems to have receiv'd only the worst cases. Out doors, at the foot of a tree, within ten yards of the front of the house, I notice a heap of amputated feet, legs, arms, hands, etc., a full load for a one-horse cart. Several dead bodies lie near, each covered with its brown woolen blanket. In the door-yard, towards the river, are fresh graves, mostly of officers, their names on pieces of barrel-staves or broken boards, stuck in the dirt. (Most of these bodies were subsequently taken up and transported north to their friends.) The large mansion is quite crowded upstairs and down, everything impromptu, no system, all bad enough, but I have no doubt the best that can be done; all the wounds pretty bad, some frightful, the men in their old clothes, unclean and bloody. Some of the wounded are rebel soldiers and officers, prisoners. One, a Mississippian, a captain, hit badly in leg, I talk'd with some time; he ask'd me for papers, which I gave him. (I saw him three months afterward in Washington, with his leg amputated, doing well.) I went through the rooms, downstairs and up. Some of the men were dying. I had nothing to give at that visit, but wrote a few letters to folks home, mothers, etc. Also talk'd to three or four, who seem'd most susceptible to it, and needing it.

## AFTER FIRST FREDERICKSBURG

*December* 23 *to* 31.—The results of the late battle are exhibited everywhere about here in thousands of cases, (hundreds die every day,) in the camp, brigade, and division hospitals. These are merely tents, and sometimes very poor ones, the wounded lying on the ground, lucky if their blankets are spread on layers of pine or hemlock twigs, or small leaves. No cots; seldom even a mattress. It is pretty cold. The ground is frozen hard, and there is occasional snow. I go around from one case to another. I do not see that I do much good to those wounded and dying; but I cannot leave them. Once in a while some youngster holds on to me convulsively, and I do what I can for him; at any rate, stop with him and sit near him for hours, if he wishes it.

Besides the hospitals, I also go occasionally on long tours through the camps, talking with the men, etc. Sometimes at night among the groups around the fires, in their shebang enclosures of bushes. These are curious shows, full of characters and groups. I soon get acquainted anywhere in camp, with officers or men, and am always well used. Sometimes I go down on picket with the regiments I know best. As to rations, the army here at present seems to be tolerably well supplied, and the men have enough, such as it is, mainly salt pork and hard tack. Most of the regiments lodge in the flimsy little shelter-tents. A few have built themselves huts of logs and mud, with fire-places.

## BACK TO WASHINGTON

*January,* '63.—Left camp at Falmouth, with some wounded, a few days since, and came here by Aquia creek railroad, and so on government steamer up the Potomac. Many wounded were with us on the cars and boat. The cars were just common platform ones. The railroad journey of ten or twelve miles was made mostly before sunrise. The soldiers guarding the road came out from their tents or shebangs of bushes with rumpled hair and half-awake look. Those on duty were walking their posts, some on banks over us, others down far below the level of the track. I saw large cavalry camps off the road. At Aquia creek landing were numbers of wounded going north. While I waited some three hours, I went around among them. Several wanted word sent home to parents, brothers, wives, etc., which I did for them, (by mail the next day from Washington.) On the boat I had my hands full. One poor fellow died going up.

I am now remaining in and around Washington, daily visiting the hospitals. Am much in Patent-office, Eighth street, H street, Armory-square, and others. Am now able to do a little good, having money, (as almoner of others home,) and getting experience. To-day, Sunday afternoon and till nine in the evening, visited Campbell hospital; attended specially to one case in ward I, very sick with pleurisy and typhoid fever, young man, farmer's son, D. F. Russell, company E, 60th New York, downhearted and feeble; a long time before he would take any interest; wrote a letter home to his mother, in Malone, Franklin county, N. Y., at his request; gave him some fruit and one or two other gifts; envelop'd and directed his letter, etc. Then went thoroughly through ward 6, observ'd every case in the ward, without, I think, missing one; gave perhaps from twenty to thirty persons, each one some little gift, such as oranges, apples, sweet crackers, figs, etc.

## THE WHITE HOUSE BY MOONLIGHT

*February 24th.*—A spell of fine soft weather. I wander about a good deal, sometimes at night under the moon. To-night took a long look at the President's house. The white portico —the palace-like, tall, round columns, spotless as snow—the walls also—the tender and soft moonlight, flooding the pale marble, and making peculiar faint languishing shades, not shadows—everywhere a soft transparent hazy, thin, blue moon-lace, hanging in the air—the brilliant and extra-plentiful clusters of gas, on and around the façade, columns, por-

tico, etc.—everything so white, so marbly pure and dazzling,
yet soft—the White House of future poems, and of dreams
and dramas, there in the soft and copious moon—the gorgeous front, in the trees, under the lustrous flooding moon,
full of reality, full of illusion—the forms of the trees, leafless,
silent, in trunk and myriad-angles of branches, under the
stars and sky—the White House of the land, and of beauty
and night—sentries at the gates, and by the portico, silent,
pacing there in blue overcoats—stopping you not at all, but
eyeing you with sharp eyes, whichever way you move.

## AN ARMY HOSPITAL WARD

LET me specialize a visit I made to the collection of barrack-
like one-story edifices, Campbell hospital, out on the flats, at
the end of the then horse railway route, on Seventh street.
There is a long building appropriated to each ward. Let us
go into ward 6. It contains, to-day, I should judge, eighty or
a hundred patients, half sick, half wounded. The edifice is
nothing but boards, well white-wash'd inside, and the usual
slender-framed iron bedsteads, narrow and plain. You walk
down the central passage, with a row on either side, their feet
towards you, and their heads to the wall. There are fires in
large stoves, and the prevailing white of the walls is reliev'd
by some ornaments, stars, circles, etc., made of evergreens.
The view of the whole edifice and occupants can be taken at
once, for there is no partition. You may hear groans or other
sounds of unendurable suffering from two or three of the
cots, but in the main there is quite—almost a painful absence
of demonstration; but the pallid face, the dull'd eye, and the
moisture of the lip, are demonstration enough. Most of
these sick or hurt are evidently young fellows from the country, farmers' sons, and such like. Look at the fine large
frames, the bright and broad countenances, and the many
yet lingering proofs of strong constitution and physique.
Look at the patient and mute manner of our American
wounded as they lie in such a sad collection; representatives
from all New England, and from New York, and New Jersey,
and Pennsylvania—indeed from all the States and all the
cities—largely from the west. Most of them are entirely

without friends or acquaintances here—no familiar face, and hardly a word of judicious sympathy or cheer, through their sometimes long and tedious sickness, or the pangs of aggravated wounds.

## THE GREAT ARMY OF THE WOUNDED

The military hospitals, convalescent camps, etc., in Washington and its neighborhood, sometimes contain over fifty thousand sick and wounded men. Every form of wound (the mere sight of some of them having been known to make a tolerably hardy visitor faint away), every kind of malady, like a long procession, with typhoid fever and diarrhœa at the head as leaders, are here in steady motion. The soldier's hospital! how many sleepless nights, how many women's tears, how many long and waking hours and days of suspense, from every one of the Middle, Eastern, and Western States, have concentrated here! Our own New York, in the form of hundreds and thousands of her young men, may consider herself here —Pennsylvania, Ohio, Indiana, and all the West and Northwest the same—and all the New England States the same.

Upon a few of these hospitals I have been almost daily calling as a missionary, on my own account, for the sustenance and consolation of some of the most needy cases of sick and dying men, for the last two months. One has much to learn to do good in these places. Great tact is required. These are not like other hospitals. By far the greatest proportion (I should say five sixths) of the patients are American young men, intelligent, of independent spirit, tender feelings, used to a hardy and healthy life; largely the farmers are represented by their sons—largely the mechanics and workingmen of the cities. Then they are soldiers. All these points must be borne in mind.

People through our Northern cities have little or no idea of the great and prominent feature which these military hospitals and convalescent camps make in and around Washington. There are not merely two or three or a dozen, but some fifty of them, of different degrees of capacity. Some have a thousand and more patients. The newspapers here find it necessary to print every day a directory of the hospitals—a long list, something like what a directory of the churches would be in New York, Philadelphia, or Boston.

The Government (which really tries, I think, to do the best and quickest it can for these sad necessities) is gradually settling down to adopt the plan of placing the hospitals in clusters of one-story wooden barracks, with their accompanying tents and sheds for cooking and all needed purposes. Taking all things into consideration, no doubt these are best adapted to the purpose; better than using churches and large public buildings like the Patent office. These sheds now adopted are long, one-story edifices, sometimes ranged along in a row, with their heads to the street, and numbered either alphabetically, Wards A or B, C, D, and so on; or Wards 1, 2, 3, etc. The middle one will be marked by a flagstaff, and is the office of the establishment, with rooms for the ward surgeons, etc. One of these sheds, or wards, will contain sixty cots; sometimes, on an emergency, they move them close together, and crowd in more. Some of the barracks are larger, with, of course, more inmates. Frequently there are tents, more comfortable here than one might think, whatever they may be down in the army.

Each ward has a ward-master, and generally a nurse for every ten or twelve men. A ward surgeon has, generally, two wards—although this varies. Some of the wards have a woman nurse; the Armory-square wards have some very good ones. The one in Ward E is one of the best.

A few weeks ago the vast area of the second story of that noblest of Washington buildings, the Patent office, was crowded close with rows of sick, badly wounded, and dying soldiers. They were placed in three very large apartments. I went there several times. It was a strange, solemn, and, with all its features of suffering and death, a sort of fascinating sight. I went sometimes at night to soothe and relieve particular cases; some, I found, needed a little cheering up and friendly consolation at that time, for they went to sleep better afterwards. Two of the immense apartments are filled with high and ponderous glass cases crowded with models in miniature of every kind of utensil, machine, or invention it ever entered into the mind of man to conceive, and with curiosities and foreign presents. Between these cases were lateral openings, perhaps eight feet wide, and quite deep, and in these were placed many of the sick; besides a great long double row of them up and down through the middle of the hall. Many of them were very bad cases, wounds and amputations. Then there was a gallery running above the hall, in which there were beds also. It was, indeed, a curious scene at night when lit up. The glass cases, the beds, the sick, the gallery above and the marble pavement under foot; the suffering, and the fortitude to bear it in the various degrees; occasionally, from some, the groan that could not be repressed; sometimes a poor fellow dying, with emaciated face and glassy eyes, the nurse by his side, the doctor also there, but no friend, no relative—such were the sights but lately in the Patent office. The wounded have since been removed from there, and it is now vacant again.

Of course there are among these thousands of prostrated soldiers in hospital here all sorts of individual cases. On recurring to my note-book, I am puzzled which cases to select to illustrate the average of these young men and their experiences. I may here say, too, in general terms, that I could not wish for more candor and manliness, among all their sufferings, than I find among them.

Take this case in Ward 6, Campbell hospital: a young man from Plymouth county, Massachusetts; a farmer's son, aged about twenty or twenty-one; a soldierly, American young fellow, but with sensitive and tender feelings. Most of December and January last he lay very low, and for quite a while I never expected he would recover. He had become prostrated with an obstinate diarrhœa: his stomach would hardly keep the least thing down; he was vomiting half the time. But that was hardly the worst of it. Let me tell his story—it is but one of thousands.

He had been some time sick with his regiment in the field, in front, but did his duty as long as he could; was in the battle of Fredericksburg; soon after was put in the regimental hospital. He kept getting worse—could not eat anything they had there; the doctor told him nothing could be done for him there. The poor fellow had fever also; received (perhaps it could not be helped) little or no attention; lay on the ground, getting worse. Toward the latter part of

December, very much enfeebled, he was sent up from the front, from Falmouth station, in an open platform car (such as hogs are transported upon North), and dumped with a crowd of others on the boat at Aquia creek, falling down like a rag where they deposited him, too weak and sick to sit up or help himself at all. No one spoke to him or assisted him; he had nothing to eat or drink; was used (amid the great crowds of sick) either with perfect indifference, or, as in two or three instances, with heartless brutality.

On the boat, when night came and when the air grew chilly, he tried a long time to undo the blankets he had in his knapsack, but was too feeble. He asked one of the employees, who was moving around deck, for a moment's assistance to get the blankets. The man asked him back if he could not get them himself. He answered, no, he had been trying for more than half an hour, and found himself too weak. The man rejoined, he might then go without them, and walked off. So H. lay chilled and damp on deck all night, without anything under or over him, while two good blankets were within reach. It caused him a great injury—nearly cost him his life.

Arrived at Washington, he was brought ashore and again left on the wharf, or above it, amid the great crowds, as before, without any nourishment—not a drink for his parched mouth; no kind hand had offered to cover his face from the forenoon sun. Conveyed at last some two miles by the ambulance to the hospital, and assigned a bed (Bed 49, Ward 6, Campbell hospital, January and February, 1863), he fell down exhausted upon the bed. But the ward-master (he has since been changed) came to him with a growling order to get up: the rules, he said, permitted no man to lie down in that way with his own clothes on; he must sit up—must first go to the bath-room, be washed, and have his clothes completely changed. (A very good rule, properly applied.) He was taken to the bath-room and scrubbed well with cold water. The attendants, callous for a while, were soon alarmed, for suddenly the half-frozen and lifeless body fell limpsy in their hands, and they hurried it back to the cot, plainly insensible, perhaps dying.

Poor boy! the long train of exhaustion, deprivation, rudeness, no food, no friendly word or deed, but all kinds of upstart airs and impudent, unfeeling speeches and deeds, from all kinds of small officials (and some big ones), cutting like razors into that sensitive heart, had at last done the job. He now lay, at times out of his head but quite silent, asking nothing of any one, for some days, with death getting a closer and a surer grip upon him; he cared not, or rather he welcomed death. His heart was broken. He felt the struggle to keep up any longer to be useless. God, the world, humanity —all had abandoned him. It would feel so good to shut his eyes forever on the cruel things around him and toward him.

As luck would have it, at this time I found him. I was passing down Ward No. 6 one day about dusk (4th January, I think), and noticed his glassy eyes, with a look of despair and hopelessness, sunk low in his thin, pallid-brown young face. One learns to divine quickly in the hospital, and as I stopped by him and spoke some commonplace remark (to which he made no reply), I saw as I looked that it was a case for ministering to the affection first, and other nourishment and medicines afterward. I sat down by him without any fuss; talked a little; soon saw that it did him good; led him to talk a little himself; got him somewhat interested; wrote a letter for him to his folks in Massachusetts (to L. H. Campbell, Plymouth county); soothed him down as I saw he was getting a little too much agitated, and tears in his eyes; gave him some small gifts, and told him I should come again soon. (He has told me since that this little visit, at that hour, just saved him; a day more, and it would have been perhaps too late.)

Of course I did not forget him, for he was a young fellow to interest any one. He remained very sick—vomiting much every day, frequent diarrhœa, and also something like bronchitis, the doctor said. For a while I visited him almost every day, cheered him up, took him some little gifts, and gave him small sums of money (he relished a drink of new milk, when it was brought through the ward for sale). For a couple of weeks his condition was uncertain—sometimes I thought there was no chance for him at all; but of late he is doing better—is up and dressed, and goes around more and more (February 21) every day. He will not die, but will recover.

The other evening, passing through the ward, he called me

—he wanted to say a few words, particular. I sat down by his side on the cot in the dimness of the long ward, with the wounded soldiers there in their beds, ranging up and down. H. told me I had saved his life. He was in the deepest earnest about it. It was one of those things that repay a soldiers' hospital missionary a thousandfold—one of the hours he never forgets.

A benevolent person, with the right qualities and tact, cannot, perhaps, make a better investment of himself, at present, anywhere upon the varied surface of the whole of this big world, than in these military hospitals, among such thousands of most interesting young men. The army is very young—and so much more American than I supposed. Reader, how can I describe to you the mute appealing look that rolls and moves from many a manly eye, from many a sick cot, following you as you walk slowly down one of these wards? To see these, and to be incapable of responding to them, except in a few cases (so very few compared to the whole of the suffering men), is enough to make one's heart crack. I go through in some cases, cheering up the men, distributing now and then little sums of money—and, regularly, letter-paper and envelopes, oranges, tobacco, jellies, etc., etc.

Many things invite comment, and some of them sharp criticism, in these hospitals. The Government, as I said, is anxious and liberal in its practice toward its sick; but the work has to be left, in its personal application to the men, to hundreds of officials of one grade or another about the hospitals, who are sometimes entirely lacking in the right qualities. There are tyrants and shysters in all positions, and especially those dressed in subordinate authority. Some of the ward doctors are careless, rude, capricious, needlessly strict. One I found who prohibited the men from all enlivening amusements; I found him sending men to the guardhouse for the most trifling offence. In general, perhaps, the officials—especially the new ones, with their straps or badges —put on too many airs. Of all places in the world, the hospitals of American young men and soldiers, wounded in the volunteer service of their country, ought to be exempt from mere conventional military airs and etiquette of shoulder-straps. But they are not exempt. **W. W.**

## A NIGHT BATTLE, OVER A WEEK SINCE

*May* 12 [1863].—There was part of the late battle at Chancellorsville, (second Fredericksburgh,) a little over a week ago, Saturday, Saturday night and Sunday, under Gen. Joe Hooker, I would like to give just a glimpse of—(a moment's look in a terrible storm at sea—of which a few suggestions are enough, and full details impossible). The fighting had been very hot during the day, and after an intermission the latter part, was resumed at night, and kept up with furious energy till 3 o'clock in the morning. That afternoon (Saturday) an attack sudden and strong by Stonewall Jackson had gain'd a great advantage to the southern army, and broken our lines, entering us like a wedge, and leaving things in that position at dark. But Hooker at 11 at night made a desperate push, drove the secesh forces back, restored his original lines, and resumed his plans. This night scrimmage was very exciting, and afforded countless strange and fearful pictures. The fighting had been general both at Chancellorsville and northeast at Fredericksburgh. (We hear of some poor fighting, episodes, skedaddling on our part. I think not of it. I think of the fierce bravery, the general rule.) One corps, the 6th, Sedgewick's, fights four dashing and bloody battles in thirty-six hours, retreating in great jeopardy, losing largely but maintaining itself, fighting with the sternest desperation under all circumstances, getting over the Rappahannock only by the skin of its teeth, yet getting over. It lost many, many brave men, yet it took vengeance, ample vengeance.

But it was the tug of Saturday evening, and through the night and Sunday morning, I wanted to make a special note of. It was largely in the woods, and quite a general engagement. The night was very pleasant, at times the moon shining out full and clear, all Nature so calm in itself, the early summer grass so rich, and foliage of the trees—yet there the battle raging, and many good fellows lying helpless, with new accessions to them, and every minute amid the rattle of muskets and crash of cannon, (for there was an artillery contest too,) the red life-blood oozing out from heads or trunks or limbs upon that green and dew-cool grass. Patches of the woods take fire, and several of the wounded, unable to move, are consumed—quite large spaces are swept over, burning the dead also—some of the men have their hair and beards singed—some, burns on their faces and hands—others holes burnt in their clothing. The flashes of fire from the cannon, the quick flaring flames and smoke, and the immense roar— the musketry so general, the light nearly bright enough for each side to see the other—the crashing, tramping of men— the yelling—close quarters—we hear the secesh yells—our men cheer loudly back, especially if Hooker is in sight—hand to hand conflicts, each side stands up to it, brave, determin'd as demons, they often charge upon us—a thousand deeds are done worth to write newer greater poems on—and still the woods on fire—still many are not only scorch'd—too many, unable to move, are burned to death.

Then the camps of the wounded—O heavens, what scene is this?—is this indeed *humanity*—these butchers' shambles? There are several of them. There they lie, in the largest, in an open space in the woods, from 200 to 300 poor fellows—the groans and screams—the odor of blood, mixed with the fresh scent of the night, the grass, the trees—that slaughter-house! O well is it their mothers, their sisters cannot see them—cannot conceive, and never conceiv'd, these things. One man is shot by a shell, both in the arm and leg—both are amputated —there lie the rejected members. Some have their legs blown off—some bullets through the breast—some indescribably horrid wounds in the face or head, all mutilated, sickening, torn, gouged out—some in the abdomen—some mere boys— many rebels, badly hurt—they take their regular turns with the rest, just the same as any—the surgeons use them just the same. Such is the camp of the wounded—such a fragment, a reflection afar off of the bloody scene—while all over the clear, large moon comes out at times softly, quietly shining. Amid the woods, that scene of flitting souls—amid the crack and crash and yelling sounds—the impalpable perfume of the woods—and yet the pungent, stifling smoke—the radiance of the moon, looking from heaven at intervals so placid—the sky so heavenly—the clear-obscure up there, those buoyant upper oceans—a few large placid stars beyond, coming silently and languidly out, and then disappearing—the melancholy, draperied night above, around. And there, upon the roads, the fields, and in those woods, that contest, never one more desperate in any age or land—both parties now in force—masses—no fancy battle, no semi-play, but fierce and savage demons fighting there—courage and scorn of death the rule, exceptions almost none.

What history, I say, can ever give—for who can know—the mad, determin'd tussle of the armies, in all their separate large and little squads—as this—each steep'd from crown to toe in desperate, mortal purports? Who know the conflict, hand-to-hand—the many conflicts in the dark, those shadowy-tangled, flashing moonbeam'd woods—the writhing groups and squads—the cries, the din, the cracking guns and pistols—the distant cannon—the cheers and calls and threats and awful music of the oaths—the indescribable mix—the officers' orders, persuasions, encouragements—the devils fully rous'd in human hearts—the strong shout, *Charge, men, charge*—the flash of the naked sword, and rolling flame and smoke? And still the broken, clear and clouded heaven—and still again the moonlight pouring silvery soft its radiant patches over all. Who paint the scene, the sudden partial panic of the afternoon, at dusk? Who paint the irrepressible advance of the second division of the Third corps, under Hooker himself, suddenly order'd up—those rapid-filing phantoms through the woods? Who show what moves there in the shadows, fluid and firm—to save, (and it did save,) the army's name, perhaps the nation? as there the veterans hold the field. (Brave Berry falls not yet—but death has mark'd him—soon he falls.)

## THE MOST INSPIRITING OF ALL WAR'S SHOWS

*June* 29 [1863].—Just before sundown this evening a very large cavalry force went by—a fine sight. The men evidently had seen service. First came a mounted band of sixteen bugles, drums and cymbals, playing wild martial tunes—made my heart jump. Then the principal officers, then company after company, with their officers at their heads, making of course the main part of the cavalcade; then a long train of men with led horses, lots of mounted negroes with special horses—and a long string of baggage-wagons, each drawn by four horses—and then a motley rear guard.

It was a pronouncedly warlike and gay show; the sabres clank'd, the men look'd young and healthy and strong; the electric tramping of so many horses on the hard road, and the gallant bearing, fine seat, and bright faced appearance of a thousand and more handsome young American men, were so good to see. An hour later another troop went by, smaller in numbers, perhaps three hundred men. They too look'd like serviceable men, campaigners used to field and fight.

*July* 3.—This forenoon, for more than an hour, again long strings of cavalry, several regiments, very fine men and horses, four or five abreast. I saw them in Fourteenth street, coming in town from north. Several hundred extra horses, some of the mares with colts, trotting along. (Appear'd to be a number of prisoners too.) How inspiriting always the cavalry regiments. Our men are generally well mounted, feel good, are young, gay on the saddle, their blankets in a roll behind them, their sabres clanking at their sides. This noise and movement and the tramp of many horses' hoofs has a curious effect upon one. The bugles play—presently you hear them afar off, deaden'd, mix'd with other noises. Then just as they had all pass'd, a string of ambulances commenc'd from the other way, moving up Fourteenth street north, slowly wending along, bearing a large lot of wounded to the hospitals.

### BATTLE OF GETTYSBURG

*July* 4*th* [1863].—The weather to-day, upon the whole, is very fine, warm, but from a smart rain last night, fresh enough, and no dust, which is a great relief for this city. I saw the parade about noon, Pennsylvania avenue, from Fifteenth street down toward the capitol. There were three regiments of infantry, (I suppose the ones doing patrol duty here,) two or three societies of Odd Fellows, a lot of children in barouches, and a squad of policemen. (A useless imposition upon the soldiers—they have work enough on their backs without piling the like of this.)

x                                                    w.

As I went down the Avenue, saw a big flaring placard on the bulletin board of a newspaper office, announcing "Glorious Victory for the Union Army!" Meade had fought Lee at Gettysburg, Pennsylvania, yesterday and day before, and repuls'd him most signally, taken 3,000 prisoners, etc. (I afterwards saw Meade's despatch, very modest, and a sort of order of the day from the President himself, quite religious, giving thanks to the Supreme, and calling on the people to do the same.)

I walk'd on to Armory hospital—took along with me several bottles of blackberry and cherry syrup, good and strong, but innocent. Went through several of the wards, announc'd to the soldiers the news from Meade, and gave them all a good drink of the syrups with ice water, quite refreshing—prepar'd it all myself, and serv'd it around. Meanwhile the Washington bells are ringing their sundown peals for Fourth of July, and the usual fusilades of boys' pistols, crackers, and guns.

## A CAVALRY CAMP

I AM writing this, nearly sundown, watching a cavalry company (acting Signal service,) just come in through a shower, making their night's camp ready on some broad, vacant ground, a sort of hill, in full view opposite my window. There are the men in their yellow-striped jackets. All are dismounted; the freed horses stand with drooping heads and wet sides; they are to be led off presently in groups, to water. The little wall-tents and shelter tents spring up quickly. I see the fires already blazing, and pots and kettles over them. Some among the men are driving in tent-poles, wielding their axes with strong, slow blows. I see great huddles of horses, bundles of hay, groups of men (some with unbuckled sabres yet on their sides,) a few officers, piles of wood, the flames of the fires, saddles, harness, etc. The smoke streams upward, additional men arrive and dismount—some drive in stakes, and tie their horses to them; some go with buckets for water, some are chopping wood, and so on.

*July 6th.*—A steady rain, dark and thick and warm. A train of six-mule wagons has just pass'd bearing pontoons, great square-end flat-boats, and the heavy planking for over-laying them. We hear that the Potomac above here is flooded and are wondering whether Lee will be able to get back across again, or whether Meade will indeed break him to pieces. The cavalry camp on the hill is a ceaseless field of observation for me. This forenoon there stand the horses, tether'd together, dripping, steaming, chewing their hay. The men emerge from their tents, dripping also. The fires are half quench'd.

*July* 10*th*.—Still the camp opposite—perhaps fifty or sixty tents. Some of the men are cleaning their sabres (pleasant to-day,) some brushing boots, some laying off, reading, writing—some cooking, some sleeping. On long temporary cross-sticks back of the tents are cavalry accoutrements—blankets and overcoats are hung out to air—there are the squads of horses tether'd, feeding, continually stamping and whisking their tails to keep off flies. I sit long in my third story window and look at the scene—a hundred little things going on—peculiar objects connected with the camp that could not be described, any one of them justly, without much minute drawing and coloring in words.

## A NEW YORK SOLDIER

THIS afternoon, July 22d, I have spent a long time with Oscar F. Wilber, company G, 154th New York, low with chronic diarrhœa, and a bad wound also. He asked me to read him a chapter in the New Testament. I complied, and ask'd him what I should read. He said, "Make your own choice." I open'd at the close on one of the first books of the evangelists, and read the chapters describing the latter hours of Christ, and the scenes at the crucifixion. The poor, wasted young man ask'd me to read the following chapter also, how Christ rose again. I read very slowly, for Oscar was feeble. It pleased him very much, yet the tears were in his eyes. He ask'd me if I enjoy'd religion. I said, "Perhaps not, my dear, in the way you mean, and yet, may-be, it is the same thing." He said, "It is my chief reliance." He talk'd of death, and said he did not fear it. I said, "Why, Oscar, don't you think you will get well?" He said, "I may, but it is not probable."

He spoke calmly of his condition. The wound was very bad, it discharg'd much. Then the diarrhœa had prostrated him, and I felt that he was even then the same as dying. He behaved very manly and affectionate. The kiss I gave him as I was about leaving he return'd fourfold. He gave me his mother's address, Mrs. Sally D. Wilber, Alleghany post-office, Cattaraugus county, N. Y. I had several such interviews with him. He died a few days after the one just described.

## ABRAHAM LINCOLN

*August* 12*th*, [1863].—I see the President almost every day, as I happen to live where he passes to or from his lodgings out of town. He never sleeps at the White House during the hot season, but has quarters at a healthy location some three miles north of the city, the Soldiers' home, a United States military establishment. I saw him this morning about $8\frac{1}{2}$ coming in to business, riding on Vermont avenue, near L street. He always has a company of twenty-five or thirty cavalry, with sabres drawn and held upright over their shoulders. They say this guard was against his personal wish, but he let his counselors have their way. The party makes no great show in uniform or horses. Mr. Lincoln on the saddle generally rides a good-sized, easy-going gray horse, is dress'd in plain black, somewhat rusty and dusty, wears a black stiff hat, and looks about as ordinary in attire, etc., as the commonest man. A lieutenant, with yellow straps, rides at his left, and following behind, two by two, come the cavalry men, in their yellow-striped jackets. They are generally going at a slow trot, as that is the pace set them by the one they wait upon. The sabres and accoutrements clank, and the entirely unornamental *cortège* as it trots towards Lafayette square arouses no sensation, only some curious stranger stops and gazes. I see very plainly ABRAHAM LINCOLN's dark brown face, with the deep-cut lines, the eyes, always to me with a deep latent sadness in the expression. We have got so that we exchange bows, and very cordial ones. Sometimes the President goes and comes in an open barouche. The cavalry always accompany him, with drawn sabres. Often I notice as he goes out evenings—and sometimes in the morning, when he returns early—he turns off and halts at the large and handsome residence of the Secretary of War, on K street, and holds conference there. If in his barouche, I can see from my window he does not alight, but sits in his vehicle, and Mr. Stanton comes out to attend him. Sometimes one of his sons, a boy of ten or twelve, accompanies him, riding at his right on a pony. Earlier in the summer I occasionally saw the President and his wife, toward the latter part of the afternoon, out in a barouche, on a pleasure ride through the city. Mrs. Lincoln was dress'd in complete black, with a long crape veil. The equipage is of the plainest kind, only two horses, and they nothing extra. They pass'd me once very close, and I saw the President in the face fully, as they were moving slowly, and his look, though abstracted, happen'd to be directed steadily in my eye. He bow'd and smiled, but far beneath his smile I noticed well the expression I have alluded to. None of the artists or pictures has caught the deep, though subtle and indirect expression of this man's face. There is something else there. One of the great portrait painters of two or three centuries ago is needed.

## DOWN AT THE FRONT

CULPEPPER, VA., *Feb.* '64.—Here I am pretty well down toward the extreme front. Three or four days ago General S., who is now in chief command, (I believe Meade is absent, sick,) moved a strong force southward from camp as if intending business. They went to the Rapidan; there has since been some manœuvering and a little fighting, but nothing of consequence. The telegraphic accounts given Monday morning last, make entirely too much of it, I should say. What General S. intended we here know not, but we trust in that competent commander. We were somewhat excited, (but not so very much either,) on Sunday, during the day and night, as orders were sent out to pack up and harness, and be ready to evacuate, to fall back towards Washington. But I was very sleepy and went to bed. Some tremendous shouts arousing me during the night, I went forth and found it was from the men above mention'd, who were returning. I talk'd with some of the men; as usual I found them full of gayety, endurance, and many fine little outshows, the signs of the most excellent good manliness of the world. It was a curious sight to see those shadowy columns moving through the night. I stood unobserv'd in the darkness and watch'd them long. The mud was very deep. The men had their usual burdens, overcoats, knapsacks, guns and blankets. Along and along they filed by me, with often a laugh, a song, a cheerful word, but never once a murmur. It may have been odd, but I never before so realized the majesty and reality of the American people *en masse*. It fell upon me like a great awe. The strong ranks moved neither fast nor slow. They had march'd seven or eight miles already through the slipping unctuous mud. The brave First corps stopt here. The equally brave Third corps moved on to Brandy station. The famous Brooklyn 14th are here, guarding the town. You see their red legs actively moving everywhere. Then they have a theatre of their own here. They give musical performances, nearly everything done capitally. Of course the audience is a jam. It is good sport to attend one of these entertainments of the 14th. I like to look around at the soldiers, and the general collection in front of the curtain, more than the scene on the stage.

## A NEW ARMY ORGANIZATION FIT FOR AMERICA

It is plain to me out of the events of the war, north and south, and out of all considerations, that the current military theory, practice, rules and organization, (adopted from Europe from the feudal institutes, with, of course, the "modern improvements", largely from the French,) though tacitly follow'd, and believ'd in by the officers generally, are not at all consonant with the United States, nor our people, nor our days. What it will be I know not—but I know that as entire an abnegation of the present military system, and the naval too, and a building up from radically different root-bases and centres appropriate to us, must eventually result, as that our political system has resulted and become establish'd, different from feudal Europe, and built up on itself from original, perennial, democratic premises. We have undoubtedly in the United States the greatest military power—an exhaustless, intelligent, brave and reliable rank and file—in the world, any land, perhaps all lands. The problem is to organize this in the manner fully appropriate to it, to the principles of the republic, and to get the best service out of it. In the present struggle, as already seen and review'd, probably three-fourths of the losses, men, lives, etc., have been sheer superfluity, extravagance, waste.

## A GLIMPSE OF WAR'S HELL-SCENES

In one of the late movements of our troops in the valley, (near Upperville, I think,) a strong force of Moseby's mounted guerillas attack'd a train of wounded, and the guard of cavalry convoying them. The ambulances contain'd about 60 wounded, quite a number of them officers of rank. The rebels were in strength, and the capture of the train and its partial guard after a short snap was effectually accomplish'd. No sooner had our men surrender'd, the rebels instantly commenced robbing the train and murdering their prisoners, even the wounded. Here is the scene, or a sample of it, ten minutes after. Among the wounded officers in the ambulances were one, a lieutenant of regulars, and another of higher rank. These two were dragg'd out on the ground on their backs, and were now surrounded by the guerillas, a demoniac crowd, each member of which was stabbing them in different parts of their bodies. One of the officers had his feet pinn'd firmly to the ground by bayonets stuck through them and thrust into the ground. These two officers, as afterwards found on examination, had receiv'd about twenty such thrusts, some of them through the mouth, face, etc. The wounded had all been dragg'd (to give a better chance also for plunder,) out of their wagons; some had been effectually dispatch'd, and their bodies were lying there lifeless and bloody. Others, not yet dead, but horribly mutilated, were moaning or groaning. Of our men who surrender'd, most had been thus maim'd or slaughter'd.

At this instant a force of our cavalry, who had been following the train at some interval, charged suddenly upon the secesh captors, who proceeded at once to make the best escape they could. Most of them got away, but we gobbled two officers and seventeen men, in the very acts just described. The sight was one which admitted of little discussion, as may be imagined. The seventeen captur'd men and two officers were put under guard for the night, but it was decided there and then that they should die. The next morning the two officers were taken in the town, separate places, put in the centre of the street, and shot. The seventeen men were taken to an open ground, a little one side. They were placed in a hollow square, half-encompass'd by two of our cavalry regiments, one of which regiments had three days before found the bloody corpses of three of their men hamstrung and hung up by the heels to limbs of trees by Moseby's guerillas, and the other had not long before had twelve men, after surrendering, shot and then hung by the neck to limbs of trees, and jeering inscriptions pinn'd to the breast of one of the corpses, who had been a sergeant. Those three, and those twelve, had been found, I say, by these environing regiments. Now, with revolvers, they form'd the grim cordon of the seventeen prisoners. The latter were placed in the midst of the hollow square, unfasten'd, and the ironical remark made to them that they were now to be given "a chance for themselves". A few ran for it. But what use? From every side the deadly pills came. In a few minutes the seventeen corpses strew'd the hollow square. I was curious to know whether some of the Union soldiers, some few, (some one or two at least of the youngsters,) did not abstain from shooting on the helpless men. Not one. There was no exultation, very little said, almost nothing, yet every man there contributed his shot.

Multiply the above by scores, aye hundreds—verify it in all the forms that different circumstances, individuals, places, could afford—light it with every lurid passion, the wolf's, the lion's lapping thirst for blood—the passionate, boiling volcanoes of human revenge for comrades, brothers slain—with the light of burning farms, and heaps of smutting, smouldering black embers—and in the human heart everywhere black, worse embers—and you have an inkling of this war.

## [EXCHANGE OF PRISONERS]

*December* 27, 1864.

To the Editor of the *Brooklyn Eagle:*

The public mind is deeply excited, and most righteously so, at the starvation of the United States prisoners of war in the hands of the Secessionists. The dogged sullenness and scoundrelism prevailing everywhere among the prison guards and officials, (with, I think, the general exception of the surgeons,) the measureless torments of the forty or fifty thousand helpless young men, with all their humiliations, hunger, cold, filth, despair, hope utterly given out, and the more and more frequent imbecility, I have myself seen the proofs of in so many instances, that I know the facts well, and know that the half has not been told, nor the tithe either. But there is another and full as important side to the story. Whose fault is it at bottom that our men have not been exchanged? To my knowledge it is understood by Col. Mulford, our capital Executive Officer of Exchange, and also by those among us who have had longest and nearest contact with the secession exchange officers, that the Government of the latter have been and are ready to exchange man for man as far as prisoners go, (certainly all the whites, and, as I understand it, a large proportion of the blacks also).

Under the President (whose humane, conscientious and fatherly heart, I have abiding faith in,) the control of exchange has remained with the Secretary of War, and also with such personages as Major General Butler and Major General Hitchcock. In my opinion the Secretary has taken and obstinately held a position of cold-blooded policy, (that is he thinks it policy,) more cruel than anything done by the Secessionists. Ostensibly and officially saying he will not exchange at all, unless the Secession leaders will give us, on average terms, all the blacks they capture in military action, the Secretary has also said (and this is the basis of his course and policy,) that it is not for the benefit of the Government of the United States that the power of the Secessionists should be repleted by some 50,000 men in good condition now in our hands, besides getting relieved of the support of nearly the same number of human wrecks and ruins, of no advantage to us, now in theirs.

Major General Butler, in my opinion, has also incorporated in the question of exchange a needless amount of personal pique, and an unbecoming obstinacy. He, too, has taken his stand on the exchange of all black soldiers, has persisted in it without regard to consequences, and has made the whole of the large and complicated question of general exchange turn upon that one item alone, while it is but a drop in the bucket. Then he makes it too much a personal contest who shall conquer, and an occasion to revenge the bad temper and insults of the South towards himself.

Of Major General Hitchcock, the public may judge what a valuable contribution he brings to this matter of exchange, from a remark he has made not long since, that "none but cowards are ever taken prisoners in war".

This is the spirit in which the faith of the Government of the United States toward fifty thousand of its bravest young men—soldiers faithful to it in its hours of extremest peril—has been, for the past year, and is now handled. Meantime, while the thing has been held in abeyance in this manner, considerably more than one-fourth of those helpless and most wretched men, (their last hours passed in the thought that they were abandoned by their Government, and left to their fate,) have been exchanged by deaths of starvation, (Mr. Editor, or you, reader, do you know what a death by starvation actually is?) leaving half the remainder closely prepared to follow, from mental and physical atrophy; and even the remnant cannot long tarry behind. So that the Secretary and the Major Generals mentioned, may find their policy work out even more than they calculated.

In my opinion, the anguish and death of these ten to fifteen thousand American young men, with all the added and incalculable sorrow, long drawn out, amid families at home, rests mainly upon the heads of members of our own government; and if they persist, the death of the remainder of the Union prisoners and often worse than death, will be added.

WALT WHITMAN.

## BOYS IN THE ARMY

As I walk'd home about sunset, I saw in Fourteenth street a very young soldier, thinly clad, standing near the house I was about to enter. I stopt a moment in front of the door and call'd him to me. I knew that an old Tennessee regiment, and also an Indiana regiment, were temporarily stopping in new barracks, near Fourteenth street. This boy I found belonged to the Tennessee regiment. But I could hardly believe he carried a musket. He was but 15 years old, yet had been twelve months a soldier, and had borne his part in several battles, even historic ones. I ask'd him if he did not suffer from the cold, and if he had no overcoat. No, he did not suffer from cold, and had no overcoat, but could draw one whenever he wish'd. His father was dead, and his mother living in some part of East Tennessee; all the men were from that part of the country. The next forenoon I saw the Tennessee and Indiana regiments marching down the Avenue. My boy was with the former, stepping along with the rest. There were many other boys no older. I stood and watch'd them as they tramp'd along with slow, strong, heavy, regular steps. There did not appear to be a man over 30 years of age, and a large proportion were from 15 to perhaps 22 or 23. They had all the look of veterans, worn, stain'd, impassive, and a certain unbent, lounging gait, carrying in addition to their regular arms and knapsacks, frequently a frying-pan, broom, etc. They were all of pleasant physiognomy; no refinement, nor blanch'd with intellect, but as my eye pick'd them, moving along, rank by rank, there did not seem to be a single repulsive, brutal or markedly stupid face among them.

## DEATH OF PRESIDENT LINCOLN

*April* 16, '65.—I find in my notes of the time, this passage on the death of Abraham Lincoln: He leaves for America's history and biography, so far, not only its most dramatic reminiscence—he leaves, in my opinion, the greatest, best, most characteristic, artistic, moral personality. Not but that he had faults, and show'd them in the Presidency; but honesty, goodness, shrewdness, conscience, and (a new virtue, unknown to other lands, and hardly yet really known here, but the foundation and tie of all, as the future will grandly develop,) UNIONISM, in its truest and amplest sense, form'd the hard-pan of his character. These he seal'd with his life. The tragic splendor of his death, purging, illuminating all, throws round his form, his head, an aureole that will remain and will grow brighter through time, while history lives, and love of country lasts. By many has this Union been help'd; but if one name, one man, must be pick'd out, he, most of all, is the conservator of it, to the future. He was assassinated—but the Union is not assassinated—*ça ira!* One falls and another falls. The soldier drops, sinks like a wave—but the ranks of the ocean eternally press on. Death does its work, obliterates a hundred, a thousand—President, general, captain, private, —but the Nation is immortal.

## WESTERN SOLDIERS

*May* 26–7 [1865].—The streets, the public buildings and grounds of Washington, still swarm with soldiers from Illinois, Indiana, Ohio, Missouri, Iowa, and all the Western States. I am continually meeting and talking with them. They often speak to me first, and always show great sociability, and glad to have a good interchange of chat. These Western soldiers are more slow in their movements, and in their intellectual quality also; have no extreme alertness. They are larger in size, have a more serious physiognomy, are continually looking at you as they pass in the street. They are largely animal, and handsomely so. During the war I have been at times with the Fourteenth, Fifteenth, Seventeenth, and Twentieth Corps. I always feel drawn toward the men, and like their personal contact when we are crowded close together, as frequently these days in the street-cars. They all think the world of General Sherman; call him "old Bill", or sometimes "uncle Billy".

## THREE YEARS SUMM'D UP

DURING those three years in hospital, camp or field, I made over six hundred visits or tours, and went, as I estimate, counting all, among from eighty thousand to a hundred thousand of the wounded and sick, as sustainer of spirit and body in some degree, in time of need. These visits varied from an hour or two, to all day or night; for with dear or critical cases I generally watch'd all night. Sometimes I took up my quarters in the hospital, and slept or watch'd there several nights in succession. Those three years I consider the greatest privilege and satisfaction, (with all their feverish excitements and physical deprivations and lamentable sights,) and, of course, the most profound lesson of my life. I can say that in my ministerings I comprehended all, whoever came in my way, northern or southern, and slighted none. It arous'd and brought out and decided undream'd-of depths of emotion. It has given me my most fervent views of the true *ensemble* and extent of the States. While I was with wounded and sick in thousands of cases from the New England States, and from New York, New Jersey, and Pennsylvania, and from Michigan, Wisconsin, Ohio, Indiana, Illinois, and all the Western States, I was with more or less from all the States, North and South, without exception. I was with many from the border States, especially from Maryland and Virginia, and found, during those lurid years 1862-63, far more Union southerners, especially Tennesseans, than is supposed. I was with many rebel officers and men among our wounded, and gave them always what I had, and tried to cheer them the same as any. I was among the army teamsters considerably, and, indeed, always found myself drawn to them. Among the black soldiers, wounded or sick, and in the contraband camps, I also took my way whenever in their neighborhood, and did what I could for them.

## THE MILLION DEAD, TOO, SUMM'D UP

THE dead in this war—there they lie, strewing the fields and woods and valleys and battle-fields of the south—Virginia, the Peninsula—Malvern hill and Fair Oaks—the banks of the Chickahominy—the terraces of Fredericksburgh—Antietam bridge—the grisly ravines of Manassas—the bloody promenade of the Wilderness—the varieties of the *strayed* dead, (the estimate of the War department is 25,000 national soldiers kill'd in battle and never buried at all, 5,000 drown'd —15,000 inhumed by strangers, or on the march in haste, in hitherto unfound localities—2,000 graves cover'd by sand and mud by Mississippi freshets, 3,000 carried away by caving-in of banks, etc.,)—Gettysburgh, the West, South-west—Vicksburgh—Chattanooga—the trenches of Peters-burg—the numberless battles, camps, hospitals everywhere —the crop reap'd by the mighty reapers, typhoid, dysentery, inflammations—and blackest and loathesomest of all, the dead and living burial-pits, the prison-pens of Andersonville, Salisbury, Belle-Isle, etc., (not Dante's pictured hell and all its woes, its degradations, filthy torments, excell'd those prisons)—the dead, the dead, the dead—*our* dead—or South or North, ours all, (all, all, all, finally dear to me)—or East or West—Atlantic coast or Mississippi valley—somewhere they crawl'd to die, alone, in bushes, low gullies, or on the sides of hills—(there, in secluded spots, their skeletons, bleach'd bones, tufts of hair, buttons, fragments of clothing, are occa-sionally found yet)—our young men once so handsome and so joyous, taken from us—the son from the mother, the hus-band from the wife, the dear friend from the dear friend—the clusters of camp graves, in Georgia, the Carolinas, and in Tennessee—the single graves left in the woods or by the road-side, (hundreds, thousands, obliterated)—the corpses floated down the rivers, and caught and lodged, (dozens, scores, floated down the upper Potomac, after the cavalry engage-ments, the pursuit of Lee, following Gettysburgh)—some lie at the bottom of the sea—the general million, and the special cemeteries in almost all the States—the infinite dead—(the land entire saturated, perfumed with their impalpable ashes' exhalation in Nature's chemistry distill'd, and shall be so for-ever, in every future grain of wheat and ear of corn, and every flower that grows, and every breath we draw)—not only Northern dead leavening Southern soil—thousands, aye tens of thousands, of Southerners, crumble to-day in Northern earth.

And everywhere among these countless graves—every-where in the many soldier Cemeteries of the Nation, (there are now, I believe, over seventy of them)—as at the time in the vast trenches, the depositories of slain, Northern and

Southern, after the great battles—not only where the scathing
trail passed those years, but radiating since in all the peaceful
quarters of the land—we see, and ages yet may see, on monuments and gravestones, singly or in masses, to thousands or
tens of thousands, the significant word UNKNOWN.

(In some of the cemeteries nearly *all* the dead are unknown.
At Salisbury, N. C., for instance, the known are only 85, while
the unknown are 12,027, and 11,700 of these are buried in
trenches. A national monument has been put up here, by
order of Congress, to mark the spot—but what visible,
material monument can ever fittingly commemorate that
spot?)

## THE REAL WAR WILL NEVER GET IN THE BOOKS

AND so good-bye to the war. I know not how it may have
been, or may be, to others—to me the main interest I found,
(and still, on recollection, find,) in the rank and file of the
armies, both sides, and in those specimens amid the hospitals, and even the dead on the field. To me the points illustrating the latent personal character and eligibilities of these
States, in the two or three millions of American young and
middle-aged men, North and South, embodied in those
armies—and especially the one-third or one-fourth of their
number, stricken by wounds or disease at some time in the
course of the contest—were of more significance even than
the political interests involved. (As so much of a race depends
on how it faces death, and how it stands personal anguish
and sickness. As, in the glints of emotions under emergencies,
and the indirect traits and asides in Plutarch, we get far profounder clues to the antique world than all its more formal
history.)

Future years will never know the seething hell and the
black infernal background of countless minor scenes and
interiors, (not the official surface-courteousness of the Generals, not the few great battles) of the Secession war; and it is
best they should not—the real war will never get in the books.
In the mushy influences of current times, too, the fervid atmosphere and typical events of those years are in danger of

being totally forgotten. I have at night watch'd by the side of a sick man in the hospital, one who could not live many hours. I have seen his eyes flash and burn as he raised himself and recurr'd to the cruelties on his surrender'd brother, and mutilations of the corpse afterward. (See in the preceding pages, the incident at Upperville—the seventeen kill'd as in the description, were left there on the ground. After they dropt dead, no one touch'd them—all were made sure of, however. The carcasses were left for the citizens to bury or not, as they chose.)

Such was the war. It was not a quadrille in a ball-room. Its interior history will not only never be written—its practicality, minutiæ of deeds and passions, will never be even suggested. The actual soldier of 1862-'65, North and South, with all his ways, his incredible dauntlessness, habits, practices, tastes, language, his fierce friendship, his appetite, rankness, his superb strength and animality, lawless gait, and a hundred unnamed lights and shades of camp, I say, will never be written—perhaps must not and should not be.

The preceding notes may furnish a few stray glimpses into that life, and into those lurid interiors, never to be fully convey'd to the future. The hospital part of the drama from '61 to '65, deserves indeed to be recorded. Of that many-threaded drama, with its sudden and strange surprises, its confounding of prophecies, its moments of despair, the dread of foreign interference, the interminable campaigns, the bloody battles, the mighty and cumbrous and green armies, the drafts and bounties—the immense money expenditure, like a heavy-pouring constant rain—with, over the whole land, the last three years of the struggle, an unending, universal mourning-wail of women, parents, orphans—the marrow of the tragedy concentrated in those Army Hospitals —(it seem'd sometimes as if the whole interest of the land, North and South, was one vast central hospital, and all the rest of the affair but flanges)—those forming the untold and unwritten history of the war—infinitely greater (like life's) than the few scraps and distortions that are ever told or written. Think how much, and of importance, will be—how much, civic and military, has already been—buried in the grave, in eternal darkness.

## [TROWBRIDGE ANECDOTE CONCERNING EMERSON AND WHITMAN]

WASHINGTON,

*Sept.* 6, 1865.

J. T. TROWBRIDGE has called on me to-day, stopt an hour. Told me, on authority of Mr. Emerson, the following. An English gentleman who came to America, and among the Boston literati, not long since, was the bearer of a letter to me from Lord Houghton (Richard Moncton Milnes, the poet)—a friendly and generous letter about *Leaves of Grass* and also intended as a letter of introduction for the gentleman bearing it. But the Boston literati talked severely and warmly about the author of *Leaves*, dwelt on the manner in which he treated Mr. Emerson, and, in short, made such a story that the gentleman changed his plan of visiting W. W. and never delivered the letter sent him.

J. T. T. told me of Mr. Emerson's lectures—one in which he said, speaking of the very few who wrote English greatly— "there is also Walt Whitman, but he belongs yet to the fire clubs, and has not got into the parlors."

By J. T. T.'s account it is plain that Mr. E. has quite thoroughly shifted his position from that taken in the letter of 1855, and makes the largest qualifications.


## DEMOCRATIC VISTAS

As the greatest lessons of Nature through the universe are perhaps the lessons of variety and freedom, the same present the greatest lessons also in New World politics and progress. If a man were ask'd, for instance, the distinctive points contrasting modern European and American political and other life with the old Asiatic cultus, as lingering-bequeath'd yet in China and Turkey, he might find the amount of them in John Stuart Mill's profound essay on Liberty in the future, where he demands two main constituents, or sub-strata, for a truly grand nationality—1st, a large variety of character—and 2d, full play for human nature to expand itself in numberless and even conflicting directions—(seems to be for general humanity much like the influences that make up, in their limitless field, that perennial health-action of the air we call the weather—an infinite number of currents and forces, and contributions, and temperatures, and cross-purposes, whose ceaseless play of counterpart upon counterpart brings constant restoration and vitality). With this thought—and not for itself alone, but all it necessitates, and draws after it—let me begin my speculations.

America, filling the present with greatest deeds and problems, cheerfully accepting the past, including feudalism, (as, indeed, the present is but the legitimate birth of the past, including feudalism,) counts, as I reckon, for her justification and success, (for who, as yet, dare claim success?) almost entirely on the future. Nor is that hope unwarranted. To-day, ahead, though dimly yet, we see, in vistas, a copious, sane, gigantic offspring. For our New World I consider far less important for what it has done, or what it is, than for results to come. Sole among nationalities, these States have assumed the task to put in forms of lasting power and practicality, on areas of amplitude rivaling the operations of the physical kosmos, the moral political speculations of ages, long, long deferr'd, the democratic republican principle, and the theory of development and perfection by voluntary standards, and self-reliance. Who else, indeed, except the United States, in history, so far, have accepted in unwitting faith, and, as we now see, stand, act upon, and go security for, these things?

But preluding no longer, let me strike the key-note of the following strain. First premising that, though the passages of it have been written at widely different times, (it is, in fact, a collection of memoranda, perhaps for future designers, comprehenders,) and though it may be open to the charge of one part contradicting another—for there are opposite sides to the great question of democracy, as to every great question —I feel the parts harmoniously blended in my own realization and convictions, and present them to be read only in such oneness, each page and each claim and assertion modified and temper'd by the others. Bear in mind, too, that they are not the result of studying up in political economy, but of the ordinary sense, observing, wandering among men, these States, these stirring years of war and peace. I will not gloss over the appaling dangers of universal suffrage in the United States. In fact, it is to admit and face these dangers I am writing. To him or her within whose thought rages the battle, advancing, retreating, between democracy's convictions, aspirations, and the people's crudeness, vice, caprices, I mainly write this essay. I shall use the words America and democracy as convertible terms. Not an ordinary one is the issue. The United States are destined either to surmount the gorgeous history of feudalism, or else prove the most tremendous failure of time. Not the least doubtful am I on any prospects of their material success. The triumphant future of their business, geographic and productive departments, on larger scales and in more varieties than ever, is certain. In those respects the republic must soon (if she does not already) outstrip all examples hitherto afforded, and dominate the world.*

Admitting all this, with the priceless value of our political institutions, general suffrage, (and fully acknowledging the latest, widest opening of the doors,) I say that, far deeper than these, what finally and only is to make of our western world a nationality superior to any hither known, and out-

---

* "From a territorial area of less than nine hundred thousand square miles, the Union has expanded into over four millions and a half—fifteen times larger than that of Great Britain and France combined—with a shore-line, including Alaska, equal to the entire circumference of the earth, and with a domain within these lines far wider than that of the Romans in their proudest days of conquest and renown. With a river, lake, and coastwise commerce estimated at over two thousand millions of dollars per year; with a railway traffic of four to six thousand millions per year, and the annual domestic exchanges of the country running up to nearly ten thousand millions per year; with over two thousand millions of dollars invested in manufacturing, mechanical, and mining industry; with over five hundred millions of acres of land in actual occupancy, valued, with their appurtenances, at over seven thousand millions of dollars, and producing annually crops valued at over three thousand millions of dollars; with a realm which, if the density of Belgium's population were possible, would be vast enough to include all the present inhabitants of the world; and with equal rights guaranteed to even the poorest and humblest of our forty millions of people—we can, with a manly pride akin to that which distinguish'd the palmiest days of Rome, claim," etc., etc., etc.—*Vice-President Colfax's Speech, July 4*, 1870.

LATER—*London "Times"*, (*Weekly,*) *June 23*, '82.

"The wonderful wealth-producing power of the United States defies and sets at naught the grave drawbacks of a mischievous protective tariff, and has already obliterated, almost wholly, the traces of the

topping the past, must be vigorous, yet unsuspected Literatures, perfect personalities and sociologies, original, trans-
cendental, and expressing (what, in highest sense, are not yet
express'd at all,) democracy and the modern. With these,
and out of these, I promulge new races of Teachers, and of
perfect Women, indispensable to endow the birth-stock of a
New World. For feudalism, caste, the ecclesiastic traditions,
though palpably retreating from political institutions, still
hold essentially, by their spirit, even in this country, entire
possession of the more important fields, indeed the very subsoil, of education, and of social standards and literature.

I say that democracy can never prove itself beyond cavil,
until it founds and luxuriantly grows its own forms of art,
poems, schools, theology, displacing all that exists, or that
has been produced anywhere in the past, under opposite influences. It is curious to me that while so many voices, pens,
minds, in the press, lecture-rooms, in our Congress, etc., are
discussing intellectual topics, pecuniary dangers, legislative
problems, the suffrage, tariff and labor questions, and the
various business and benevolent needs of America, with propositions, remedies, often worth deep attention, there is one
need, a hiatus the profoundest, that no eye seems to perceive,
no voice to state. Our fundamental want to-day in the
United States, with closest, amplest reference to present conditions, and to the future, is of a class, and the clear idea of a
class, of native authors, literatuses, far different, far higher in
grade than any yet known, sacerdotal, modern, fit to cope
with our occasions, lands, permeating the whole mass of
American mentality, taste, belief, breathing into it a new

greatest of modern civil wars. What is especially remarkable in the
present development of American energy and success is its wide and
equable distribution. North and south, east and west, on the shores
of the Atlantic and the Pacific, along the chain of the great lakes, in
the valley of the Mississippi, and on the coasts of the gulf of Mexico,
the creation of wealth and the increase of population are signally exhibited. It is quite true, as has been shown by the recent apportion-
ment of population in the House of Representatives, that some sections
of the Union have advanced, relatively to the rest, in an extraordinary
and unexpected degree. But this does not imply that the States which
have gain'd no additional representatives or have actually lost some
have been stationary or have receded. The fact is that the present tide
of prosperity has risen so high that it has overflow'd all barriers, and
has fill'd up the back-waters, and establish'd something like an approach to uniform success."

breath of life, giving it decision, affecting politics far more than the popular superficial suffrage, with results inside and underneath the elections of Presidents or Congresses—radiating, begetting appropriate teachers, schools, manners, and, as its grandest result, accomplishing, (what neither the schools nor the churches and their clergy have hitherto accomplish'd, and without which this nation will no more stand, permanently, soundly, than a house will stand without a substratum,) a religious and moral character beneath the political and productive and intellectual bases of the States. For know you not, dear, earnest reader, that the people of our land may all read and write, and may all possess the right to vote—and yet the main things may be entirely lacking?—(and this to suggest them.)

View'd, to-day, from a point of view sufficiently overarching, the problem of humanity all over the civilized world is social and religious, and is to be finally met and treated by literature. The priest departs, the divine literatus comes. Never was anything more wanted than, to-day, and here in the States, the poet of the modern is wanted, or the great literatus of the modern. At all times, perhaps, the central point in any nation, and that whence it is itself really sway'd the most, and whence it sways others, is its national literature, especially its archetypal poems. Above all previous lands, a great original literature is surely to become the justification and reliance, (in some respects the sole reliance,) of American democracy.

Few are aware how the great literature penetrates all, gives hue to all, shapes aggregates and individuals, and, after subtle ways, with irresistible power, constructs, sustains, demolishes at will. Why tower, in reminiscence, above all the nations of the earth, two special lands, petty in themselves, yet inexpressibly gigantic, beautiful, columnar? Immortal Judah lives, and Greece immortal lives, in a couple of poems.

Nearer than this. It is not generally realized, but it is true, as the genius of Greece, and all the sociology, personality, politics and religion of those wonderful states, resided in their literature or esthetics, that what was afterwards the main support of European chivalry, the feudal, ecclesiastical, dynastic world over there—forming its osseous structure, holding it together for hundreds, thousands of years, preserving its flesh and bloom, giving it form, decision, rounding it out, and so saturating it in the conscious and unconscious blood, breed, belief, and intuitions of men, that it still prevails powerful to this day, in defiance of the mighty changes of time—was its literature, permeating to the very marrow, especially that major part, its enchanting songs, ballads, and poems.*

To the ostent of the senses and eyes, I know, the influences which stamp the world's history are wars, uprisings or downfalls of dynasties, changeful movements of trade, important inventions, navigation, military or civil governments, advent of powerful personalities, conquerors, etc. These of course play their part; yet, it may be, a single new thought, imagination, abstract principle, even literary style, fit for the time, put in shape by some great literatus, and projected among mankind, may duly cause changes, growths, removals, greater than the longest and bloodiest war, or the most stupendous merely political, dynastic, or commercial overturn.

In short, as, though it may not be realized, it is strictly true, that a few first-class poets, philosophs, and authors, have substantially settled and given status to the entire religion, education, law, sociology, etc., of the hitherto civilized world, by tinging and often creating the atmospheres out of which they have arisen, such also must stamp, and more than ever stamp, the interior and real democratic construction of this American continent, to-day, and days to come. Remember also this fact of difference, that, while through the antique and through the mediæval ages, highest thoughts and ideals realized themselves, and their expression made its way by

* See, for hereditaments, specimens, Walter Scott's Border Minstrelsy, Percy's collection, Ellis's early English Metrical Romances, the European continental poems of Walter of Aquitania, and the Nibelungen, of pagan stock, but monkish-feudal redaction; the history of the Troubadours, by Fauriel; even the far-back cumbrous old Hindu epics, as indicating the Asian eggs out of which European chivalry was hatch'd; Ticknor's chapters on the Cid, and on the Spanish poems and poets of Calderon's time. Then always, and, of course, as the superbest poetic culmination-expression of feudalism, the Shaksperean dramas, in the attitudes, dialogue, characters, etc., of the princes, lords and gentlemen, the pervading atmosphere, the implied and express'd standard of manners, the high port and proud stomach, the regal embroidery of style, etc.

other arts, as much as, or even more than by, technical literature, (not open to the mass of persons, or even to the majority of eminent persons,) such literature in our day and for
current purposes, is not only more eligible than all the other
arts put together, but has become the only general means of
morally influencing the world. Painting, sculpture, and the
dramatic theatre, it would seem, no longer play an indispensable or even important part in the workings and medium-
ship of intellect, utility, or even high esthetics. Architecture
remains, doubtless with capacities, and a real future. Then
music, the combiner, nothing more spiritual, nothing more
sensuous, a god, yet completely human, advances, prevails,
holds highest place; supplying in certain wants and quarters
what nothing else could supply. Yet in the civilization of to-
day it is undeniable that, over all the arts, literature dominates, serves beyond all—shapes the character of church and
school—or, at any rate, is capable of doing so. Including the
literature of science, its scope is indeed unparallel'd.

Before proceeding further, it were perhaps well to dis-
criminate on certain points. Literature tills its crops in many
fields, and some may flourish, while others lag. What I say in
these Vistas has its main bearing on imaginative literature,
especially poetry, the stock of all. In the department of
science, and the specialty of journalism, there appear, in these
States, promises, perhaps fulfilments, of highest earnestness,
reality, and life. These, of course, are modern. But in the
region of imaginative, spinal and essential attributes, something equivalent to creation is, for our age and lands, imperatively demanded. For not only is it not enough that the new
blood, new frame of democracy shall be vivified and held together merely by political means, superficial suffrage, legislation, etc., but it is clear to me that, unless it goes deeper,
gets at least as firm and as warm a hold in men's hearts,
emotions and belief, as, in their days, feudalism or ecclesiasticism, and inaugurates its own perennial sources, welling
from the centre forever, its strength will be defective, its
growth doubtful, and its main charm wanting. I suggest,
therefore, the possibility, should some two or three really
original American poets, (perhaps artists or lecturers,) arise,
mounting the horizon like planets, stars of the first magni-

tude, that, from their eminence, fusing contributions, races, far localities, etc., together, they would give more compaction and more moral identity, (the quality to-day most needed,) to these States, than all its Constitutions, legislative and judicial ties, and all its hitherto political, warlike, or materialistic experiences. As, for instance, there could hardly happen anything that would more serve the States, with all their variety of origins, their diverse climes, cities, standards, etc., than possessing an aggregate of heroes, characters, exploits, sufferings, prosperity or misfortune, glory or disgrace, common to all, typical of all—no less, but even greater would it be to possess the aggregation of a cluster of mighty poets, artists, teachers, fit for us, national expressers, comprehending and effusing for the men and women of the States, what is universal, native, common to all, inland and seaboard, northern and southern. The historians say of ancient Greece, with her ever-jealous autonomies, cities, and states, that the only positive unity she ever own'd or receiv'd, was the sad unity of a common subjection, at the last, to foreign conquerors. Subjection, aggregation of that sort, is impossible to America; but the fear of conflicting and irreconcilable interiors, and the lack of a common skeleton, knitting all close, continually haunts me. Or, if it does not, nothing is plainer than the need, a long period to come, of a fusion of the States into the only reliable identity, the moral and artistic one. For, I say, the true nationality of the States, the genuine union, when we come to a moral crisis, is, and is to be, after all, neither the written law, nor, (as is generally supposed,) either self-interest, or common pecuniary or material objects —but the fervid and tremendous IDEA, melting everything else with resistless heat, and solving all lesser and definite distinctions in vast, indefinite, spiritual, emotional power.

It may be claim'd, (and I admit the weight of the claim,) that common and general worldly prosperity, and a populace well-to-do, and with all life's material comforts, is the main thing, and is enough. It may be argued that our republic is, in performance, really enacting to-day the grandest arts, poems, etc., by beating up the wilderness into fertile farms, and in her railroads, ships, machinery, etc. And it may be ask'd, Are these not better, indeed, for America, than any utterances even of greatest rhapsode, artist, or literatus?

I too hail those achievements with pride and joy: then answer that the soul of man will not with such only—nay, not with such at all—be finally satisfied; but needs what, (standing on these and on all things, as the feet stand on the ground,) is address'd to the loftiest, to itself alone.

Out of such considerations, such truths, arises for treatment in these Vistas the important question of character, of an American stock-personality, with literatures and arts for outlets and return-expressions, and, of course, to correspond, within outlines common to all. To these, the main affair, the thinkers of the United States, in general so acute, have either given feeblest attention, or have remain'd, and remain, in a state of somnolence.

For my part, I would alarm and caution even the political and business reader, and to the utmost extent, against the prevailing delusion that the establishment of free political institutions, and plentiful intellectual smartness, with general good order, physical plenty, industry, etc., (desirable and precious advantages as they all are,) do, of themselves, determine and yield to our experiment of democracy the fruitage of success. With such advantages at present fully, or almost fully, possess'd—the Union just issued, victorious, from the struggle with the only foes it need ever fear, (namely, those within itself, the interior ones,) and with unprecedented materialistic advancement—society, in these States, is canker'd, crude, superstitious, and rotten. Political, or law-made society is, and private, or voluntary society, is also. In any vigor, the element of the moral conscience, the most important, the verteber to State or man, seems to me either entirely lacking, or seriously enfeebled or ungrown.

I say we had best look our times and lands searchingly in the face, like a physician diagnosing some deep disease. Never was there, perhaps, more hollowness at heart than at present, and here in the United States. Genuine belief seems to have left us. The underlying principles of the States are not honestly believ'd in, (for all this hectic glow, and these melo-dramatic screamings,) nor is humanity itself believ'd in. What penetrating eye does not everywhere see through the mask? The spectacle is appaling. We live in an atmosphere of hypocrisy throughout. The men believe not in the women, nor the women in the men. A scornful superciliousness rules in literature. The aim of all the *littérateurs* is to find something to make fun of. A lot of churches, sects, etc., the most dismal phantasms I know, usurp the name of religion. Conversation is a mass of badinage. From deceit in the spirit, the mother of all false deeds, the offspring is already incalculable. An acute and candid person, in the revenue department in Washington, who is led by the course of his employment to regularly visit the cities, north, south and west, to investigate frauds, has talk'd much with me about his discoveries. The depravity of the business classes of our country is not less than has been supposed, but infinitely greater. The official services of America, national, state, and municipal, in all their branches and departments, except the judiciary, are saturated in corruption, bribery, falsehood, maladministration; and the judiciary is tainted. The great cities reek with respectable as much as non-respectable robbery and scoundrelism. In fashionable life, flippancy, tepid amours, weak infidelism, small aims, or no aims at all, only to kill time. In business, (this all-devouring modern word, business,) the one sole object is, by any means, pecuniary gain. The magician's serpent in the fable ate up all the other serpents; and money-making is our magician's serpent, remaining to-day sole master of the field. The best class we show, is but a mob of fashionably dress'd speculators and vulgarians. True, indeed, behind this fantastic farce, enacted on the visible stage of society, solid things and stupendous labors are to be discover'd, existing crudely and going on in the background, to advance and tell themselves in time. Yet the truths are none the less terrible. I say that our New World democracy, however great a success in uplifting the masses out of their sloughs, in materialistic development, products, and in a certain highly-deceptive superficial popular intellectuality, is, so far, an almost complete failure in its social aspects, and in really grand religious, moral, literary, and esthetic results. In vain do we march with unprecedented strides to empire so colossal, outvying the antique, beyond Alexander's, beyond the proudest sway of Rome. In vain have we annex'd Texas, California, Alaska, and reach north for Canada and south for Cuba. It is as if we were somehow being endow'd with a vast and more and more thoroughly-appointed body, and then left with little or no soul.

Let me illustrate further, as I write, with current observations, localities, etc. The subject is important, and will bear repetition. After an absence, I am now again (September, 1870) in New York city and Brooklyn, on a few weeks' vacation. The splendor, picturesqueness, and oceanic amplitude and rush of these great cities, the unsurpass'd situation, rivers and bay, sparkling sea-tides, costly and lofty new buildings, façades of marble and iron, of original grandeur and elegance of design, with the masses of gay color, the preponderance of white and blue, the flags flying, the endless ships, the tumultuous streets, Broadway, the heavy, low, musical roar, hardly ever intermitted, even at night; the jobbers' houses, the rich shops, the wharves, the great Central Park, and the Brooklyn Park of hills, (as I wander among them this beautiful fall weather, musing, watching, absorbing)—the assemblages of the citizens in their groups, conversations, trades, evening amusements, or along the by-quarters—these I say, and the like of these, completely satisfy my senses of power, fulness, motion, etc., and give me, through such senses and appetites, and through my esthetic conscience, a continued exaltation and absolute fulfilment. Always and more and more, as I cross the East and North rivers, the ferries, or with the pilots in their pilot-houses, or pass an hour in Wall street, or the gold exchange, I realize, (if we must admit such partialisms,) that not Nature alone is great in her fields of freedom and the open air, in her storms, the shows of night and day, the mountains, forests, seas—but in the artificial, the work of man too is equally great—in this profusion of teeming humanity—in these ingenuities, streets, goods, houses, ships—these hurrying, feverish, electric crowds of men, their complicated business genius, (not least among the geniuses,) and all this mighty, many-threaded wealth and industry concentrated here.

But sternly discarding, shutting our eyes to the glow and grandeur of the general superficial effect, coming down to what is of the only real importance, Personalities, and examining minutely, we question, we ask, Are there, indeed, *men* here worthy the name? Are there athletes? Are there perfect women, to match the generous material luxuriance? Is there a pervading atmosphere of beautiful manners? Are there crops of fine youths, and majestic old persons? Are there arts worthy freedom and a rich people? Is there a great moral and religious civilization—the only justification of a great material one? Confess that to severe eyes, using the moral microscope upon humanity, a sort of dry and flat Sahara appears, these cities, crowded with petty grotesques, malformations, phantoms, playing meaningless antics. Confess that everywhere, in shop, street, church, theatre, barroom, official chair, are pervading flippancy and vulgarity, low cunning, infidelity—everywhere the youth puny, impudent, foppish, prematurely ripe—everywhere an abnormal libidinousness, unhealthy forms, male, female, painted, padded, dyed, chignon'd, muddy complexions, bad blood, the capacity for good motherhood deceasing or deceas'd, shallow notions of beauty, with a range of manners, or rather lack of manners, (considering the advantages enjoy'd,) probably the meanest to be seen in the world.*

Of all this, and these lamentable conditions, to breathe into them the breath recuperative of sane and heroic life, I say a new founded literature, not merely to copy and reflect existing surfaces, or pander to what is called taste—not only to amuse, pass away time, celebrate the beautiful, the refined, the past, or exhibit technical, rhythmic, or grammatical dexterity—but a literature underlying life, religious, consistent

* Of these rapidly-sketch'd hiatuses, the two which seem to me most serious are, for one, the condition, absence, or perhaps the singular abeyance, of moral conscientious fibre all through American society; and, for another, the appaling depletion of women in their powers of sane athletic maternity, their crowning attribute, and ever making the woman, in loftiest spheres, superior to the man.

I have sometimes thought, indeed, that the sole avenue and means of a reconstructed sociology depended, primarily, on a new birth, elevation, expansion, invigoration of woman, affording, for races to come, (as the conditions that antedate birth are indispensable,) a perfect motherhood. Great, great, indeed, far greater than they know, is the sphere of women. But doubtless the question of such new sociology all goes together, includes many varied and complex influences and premises, and the man as well as the woman, and the woman as well as the man.

with science, handling the elements and forces with competent power, teaching and training men—and, as perhaps the most precious of its results, achieving the entire redemption of woman out of these incredible holds and webs of silliness, millinery, and every kind of dyspeptic depletion—and thus insuring to the States a strong and sweet Female Race, a race of perfect Mothers—is what is needed.

And now, in the full conception of these facts and points, and all that they infer, pro and con—with yet unshaken faith in the elements of the American masses, the composites, of both sexes, and even consider'd as individuals—and ever recognizing in them the broadest bases of the best literary and esthetic appreciation—I proceed with my speculations, Vistas.

First, let us see what we can make out of a brief, general, sentimental consideration of political democracy, and whence it has arisen, with regard to some of its current features, as an aggregate, and as the basic structure of our future literature and authorship. We shall, it is true, quickly and continually find the origin-idea of the singleness of man, individualism, asserting itself, and cropping forth, even from the opposite ideas. But the mass, or lump character, for imperative reasons, is to be ever carefully weigh'd, borne in mind, and provided for. Only from it, and from its proper regulation and potency, comes the other, comes the chance of individualism. The two are contradictory, but our task is to reconcile them.*

The political history of the past may be summ'd up as having grown out of what underlies the words, order, safety, caste, and especially out of the need of some prompt deciding authority, and of cohesion at all cost. Leaping time, we come to the period within the memory of people now living, when, as from some lair where they had slumber'd long, accumulating wrath, sprang up and are yet active, (1790, and

---

* The question hinted here is one which time only can answer. Must not the virtue of modern Individualism, continually enlarging, usurping all, seriously affect, perhaps keep down entirely, in America, the like of the ancient virtue of Patriotism, the fervid and absorbing love of general country? I have no doubt myself that the two will merge, and will mutually profit and brace each other, and that from them a greater product, a third, will arise. But I feel that at present they and their oppositions form a serious problem and paradox in the United States.

on even to the present, 1870,) those noisy eructations, destructive iconoclasms, a fierce sense of wrongs, amid which
moves the form, well known in modern history, in the old
world, stain'd with much blood, and mark'd by savage reactionary clamors and demands. These bear, mostly, as on one
inclosing point of need.

For after the rest is said—after the many time-honor'd and
really true things for subordination, experience, rights of
property, etc., have been listen'd to and acquiesced in—after
the valuable and well-settled statement of our duties and relations in society is thoroughly conn'd over and exhausted—
it remains to bring forward and modify everything else with
the idea of that Something a man is, (last precious consolation of the drudging poor,) standing apart from all else,
divine in his own right, and a woman in hers, sole and un-
touchable by any canons of authority, or any rule derived
from precedent, state-safety, the acts of legislatures, or even
from what is called religion, modesty, or art. The radiation
of this truth is the key of the most significant doings of our
immediately preceding three centuries, and has been the political genesis and life of America. Advancing visibly, it still
more advances invisibly. Underneath the fluctuations of the
expressions of society, as well as the movements of the politics
of the leading nations of the world, we see steadily pressing
ahead and strengthening itself, even in the midst of immense
tendencies toward aggregation, this image of completeness in
separatism, of individual personal dignity, of a single person,
either male or female, characterized in the main, not from
extrinsic acquirements or position, but in the pride of himself
or herself alone; and, as an eventual conclusion and summing up, (or else the entire scheme of things is aimless, a
cheat, a crash,) the simple idea that the last, best dependence
is to be upon humanity itself, and its own inherent, normal,
full-grown qualities, without any superstitious support whatever. This idea of perfect individualism it is indeed that deepest tinges and gives character to the idea of the aggregate.
For it is mainly or altogether to serve independent separatism
that we favor a strong generalization, consolidation. As it is
to give the best vitality and freedom to the rights of the
States, (every bit as important as the right of nationality, the

union,) that we insist on the identity of the Union at all hazards.

The purpose of democracy—supplanting old belief in the necessary absoluteness of establish'd dynastic rulership, temporal, ecclesiastical, and scholastic, as furnishing the only security against chaos, crime, and ignorance—is, through many transmigrations, and amid endless ridicules, arguments, and ostensible failures, to illustrate, at all hazards, this doctrine or theory that man, properly train'd in sanest, highest freedom, may and must become a law, and series of laws, unto himself, surrounding and providing for, not only his own personal control, but all his relations to other individuals, and to the State; and that, while other theories, as in the past histories of nations, have proved wise enough, and indispensable perhaps for their conditions, *this*, as matters now stand in our civilized world, is the only scheme worth working from, as warranting results like those of Nature's laws, reliable, when once establish'd, to carry on themselves.

The argument of the matter is extensive, and, we admit, by no means all on one side. What we shall offer will be far, far from sufficient. But while leaving unsaid much that should properly even prepare the way for the treatment of this many-sided question of political liberty, equality, or republicanism —leaving the whole history and consideration of the feudal plan and its products, embodying humanity, its politics and civilization, through the retrospect of past time, (which plan and products, indeed, make up all of the past, and a large part of the present)—leaving unanswer'd, at least by any specific and local answer, many a well-wrought argument and instance, and many a conscientious declamatory cry and warning—as, very lately, from an eminent and venerable person abroad*—things, problems, full of doubt, dread, sus-

* "SHOOTING NIAGARA."—I was at first roused to much anger and abuse by this essay from Mr. Carlyle, so insulting to the theory of America—but happening to think afterwards how I had more than once been in the like mood, during which his essay was evidently cast, and seen persons and things in the same light, (indeed some might say there are signs of the same feeling in these Vistas)—I have since read it again. not only as a study, expressing as it does certain judgments from the highest feudal point of view, but have read it with respect as coming from an earnest soul, and as contributing certain sharp-cutting metallic grains, which, if not gold or silver, may be good, hard, honest iron.

pense, (not new to me, but old occupiers of many an anxious hour in city's din, or night's silence,) we still may give a page or so, whose drift is opportune. Time alone can finally answer these things. But as a substitute in passing, let us, even if fragmentarily, throw forth a short direct or indirect suggestion of the premises of that other plan, in the new spirit, under the new forms, started here in our America.

As to the political section of Democracy, which introduces and breaks ground for further and vaster sections, few probably are the minds, even in these republican States, that fully comprehend the aptness of that phrase, "THE GOVERNMENT OF THE PEOPLE, BY THE PEOPLE, FOR THE PEOPLE," which we inherit from the lips of Abraham Lincoln; a formula whose verbal shape is homely wit, but whose scope includes both the totality and all minutiæ of the lesson.

The People! Like our huge earth itself, which, to ordinary scansion, is full of vulgar contradictions and offence, man, viewed in the lump, displeases, and is a constant puzzle and affront to the merely educated classes. The rare, cosmical, artist-mind, lit with the Infinite, alone confronts his manifold and oceanic qualities—but taste, intelligence and culture, (so-called,) have been against the masses, and remain so. There is plenty of glamour about the most damnable crimes and hoggish meannesses, special and general, of the feudal and dynastic world over there, with its *personnel* of lords and queens and courts, so well-dress'd and so handsome. But the People are ungrammatical, untidy, and their sins gaunt and ill-bred.

Literature, strictly consider'd, has never recognized the People, and, whatever may be said, does not to-day. Speaking generally, the tendencies of literature, as hitherto pursued, have been to make mostly critical and querulous men. It seems as if, so far, there were some natural repugnance between a literary and professional life, and the rude rank spirit of the democracies. There is, in later literature, a treatment of benevolence, a charity business, rife enough it is true; but I know nothing more rare, even in this country, than a fit scientific estimate and reverent appreciation of the People— of their measureless wealth of latent power and capacity, their vast, artistic contrasts of lights and shades—with, in

America, their entire reliability in emergencies, and a certain breadth of historic grandeur, of peace or war, far surpassing all the vaunted samples of book-heroes, or any *haut ton* coteries, in all the records of the world.

The movements of the late secession war, and their results, to any sense that studies well and comprehends them, show that popular democracy, whatever its faults and dangers, practically justifies itself beyond the proudest claims and wildest hopes of its enthusiasts. Probably no future age can know, but I well know, how the gist of this fiercest and most resolute of the world's war-like contentions resided exclusively in the unnamed, unknown rank and file; and how the brunt of its labor of death was, to all essential purposes, volunteer'd. The People, of their own choice, fighting, dying for their own idea, insolently attack'd by the secession-slave-power, and its very existence imperil'd. Descending to detail, entering any of the armies, and mixing with the private soldiers, we see and have seen august spectacles. We have seen the alacrity with which the American-born populace, the peaceablest and most good-natured race in the world, and the most personally independent and intelligent, and the least fitted to submit to the irksomeness and exasperation of regimental discipline, sprang, at the first tap of the drum, to arms —not for gain, nor even glory, nor to repel invasion—but for an emblem, a mere abstraction—for the life, *the safety of the flag*. We have seen the unequal'd docility and obedience of these soldiers. We have seen them tried long and long by hopelessness, mismanagement, and by defeat; have seen the incredible slaughter toward or through which the armies (as at first Fredericksburg, and afterward at the Wilderness,) still unhesitatingly obey'd orders to advance. We have seen them in trench, or crouching behind breastwork, or tramping in deep mud, or amid pouring rain or thick-falling snow, or under forced marches in hottest summer (as on the road to get to Gettysburg)—vast suffocating swarms, divisions, corps, with every single man so grimed and black with sweat and dust, his own mother would not have known him—his clothes all dirty, stain'd and torn, with sour, accumulated sweat for perfume—many a comrade, perhaps a brother, sun-struck, staggering out, dying, by the roadside, of exhaustion—yet the

Y                                                          W.

great bulk bearing steadily on, cheery enough, hollow-bellied from hunger, but sinewy with unconquerable resolution.

We have seen this race proved by wholesale, by drearier, yet more fearful tests—the wound, the amputation, the shatter'd face or limb, the slow hot fever, long impatient anchorage in bed, and all the forms of maiming, operation and disease. Alas! America have we seen, though only in her early youth, already to hospital brought. There have we watch'd these soldiers, many of them only boys in years—mark'd their decorum, their religious nature and fortitude, and their sweet affection. Wholesale, truly. For at the front, and through the camps, in countless tents, stood the regimental, brigade and division hospitals; while everywhere amid the land, in or near cities, rose clusters of huge, white-wash'd, crowded, one-story wooden barracks; and there ruled agony with bitter scourge, yet seldom brought a cry; and there stalk'd death by day and night along the narrow aisles between the rows of cots, or by the blankets on the ground, and touch'd lightly many a poor sufferer, often with blessed, welcome touch.

I know not whether I shall be understood, but I realize that it is finally from what I learn'd personally mixing in such scenes that I am now penning these pages. One night in the gloomiest period of the war, in the Patent-office hospital in Washington city, as I stood by the bedside of a Pennsylvania soldier, who lay, conscious of quick approaching death, yet perfectly calm, and with noble, spiritual manner, the veteran surgeon, turning aside, said to me, that though he had witness'd many, many deaths of soldiers, and had been a worker at Bull Run, Antietam, Fredericksburg, etc., he had not seen yet the first case of man or boy that met the approach of dissolution with cowardly qualms or terror. My own observation fully bears out the remark.

What have we here, if not, towering above all talk and argument, the plentifully-supplied, last-needed proof of democracy, in its personalities? Curiously enough, too, the proof of this point comes, I should say, every bit as much from the south, as from the north. Although I have spoken only of the latter, yet I deliberately include all. Grand, common stock! to me the accomplish'd and convincing growth, prophetic of the future; proof undeniable to sharpest sense, of perfect beauty, tenderness and pluck, that never feudal lord, nor Greek, nor Roman breed, yet rival'd. Let no tongue ever speak in disparagement of the American races, north or south, to one who has been through the war in the great army hospitals.

Meantime, general humanity, (for to that we return, as, for our purposes, what it really is, to bear in mind,) has always, in every department, been full of perverse maleficence, and is so yet. In downcast hours the soul thinks it always will be— but soon recovers from such sickly moods. I myself see clearly enough the crude, defective streaks in all the strata of the common people; the specimens and vast collections of the ignorant, the credulous, the unfit and uncouth, the incapable, and the very low and poor. The eminent person just mention'd sneeringly asks whether we expect to elevate and improve a nation's politics by absorbing such morbid collections and qualities therein. The point is a formidable one, and there will doubtless always be numbers of solid and reflective citizens who will never get over it. Our answer is general, and is involved in the scope and letter of this essay. We believe the ulterior object of political and all other government, (having, of course, provided for the police, the safety of life, property, and for the basic statute and common law, and their administration, always first in order,) to be among the rest, not merely to rule, to repress disorder, etc., but to develop, to open up to cultivation, to encourage the possibilities of all beneficent and manly outcroppage, and of that aspiration for independence, and the pride and self-respect latent in all characters. (Or, if there be exceptions, we cannot, fixing our eyes on them alone, make theirs the rule for all.)

I say the mission of government, henceforth, in civilized lands, is not repression alone, and not authority alone, not even of law, nor by that favorite standard of the eminent writer, the rule of the best men, the born heroes and captains of the race, (as if such ever, or one time out of a hundred, get into the big places, elective or dynastic)—but higher than the highest arbitrary rule, to train communities through all their grades, beginning with individuals and ending there again, to rule themselves. What Christ appear'd for in the moral-spiritual field for human-kind, namely, that in respect to the absolute soul, there is in the possession of such by each single individual, something so transcendent, so incapable of gradations, (like life,) that, to that extent, it places all beings on a common level, utterly regardless of the distinctions of intellect, virtue, station, or any height or lowliness whatever—is tallied in like manner, in this other field, by democracy's rule that men, the nation, as a common aggregate of living identities, affording in each a separate and complete subject for freedom, worldly thrift and happiness, and for a fair chance for growth, and for protection in citizenship, etc., must, to the political extent of the suffrage or vote, if no further, be placed, in each and in the whole, on one broad, primary, universal, common platform.

The purpose is not altogether direct; perhaps it is more indirect. For it is not that democracy is of exhaustive account, in itself. Perhaps, indeed, it is, (like Nature,) of no account in itself. It is that, as we see, it is the best, perhaps only, fit and full means, formulater, general caller-forth, trainer, for the million, not for grand material personalities only, but for immortal souls. To be a voter with the rest is not so much; and this, like every institute, will have its imperfections. But to become an enfranchised man, and now, impediments removed, to stand and start without humiliation, and equal with the rest; to commence, or have the road clear'd to commence, the grand experiment of development, whose end, (perhaps requiring several generations,) may be the forming of a full-grown man or woman—that *is* something. To ballast the State is also secured, and in our times is to be secured, in no other way.

We do not, (at any rate I do not,) put it either on the ground that the People, the masses, even the best of them, are, in their latent or exhibited qualities, essentially sensible and good—nor on the ground of their rights; but that good or bad, rights or no rights, the democratic formula is the only safe and preservative one for coming times. We endow the masses with the suffrage for their own sake, no doubt; then, perhaps still more, from another point of view, for community's sake. Leaving the rest to the sentimentalists, we present freedom as sufficient in its scientific aspect, cold as ice, reasoning, deductive, clear and passionless as crystal.

Democracy too is law, and of the strictest, amplest kind. Many suppose, (and often in its own ranks the error,) that it means a throwing aside of law, and running riot. But, briefly, it is the superior law, not alone that of physical force, the body, which, adding to, it supersedes with that of the spirit. Law is the unshakable order of the universe forever; and the law over all, and law of laws, is the law of successions; that of the superior law, in time, gradually supplanting and overwhelming the inferior one. (While, for myself, I would cheerfully agree—first covenanting that the formative tendencies shall be administer'd in favor, or at least not against it, and that this reservation be closely construed—that until the individual or community show due signs, or be so minor and fractional as not to endanger the State, the condition of authoritative tutelage may continue, and self-government must abide its time.) Nor is the esthetic point, always an important one, without fascination for highest aiming souls. The common ambition strains for elevations, to become some privileged exclusive. The master sees greatness and health in being part of the mass; nothing will do as well as common ground. Would you have in yourself the divine, vast, general law? Then merge yourself in it.

And, topping democracy, this most alluring record, that it alone can bind, and ever seeks to bind, all nations, all men, of however various and distant lands, into a brotherhood, a family. It is the old, yet ever-modern dream of earth, out of her eldest and her youngest, her fond philosophers and poets. Not that half only, individualism, which isolates. There is another half, which is adhesiveness or love, that fuses, ties and aggregates, making the races comrades, and fraternizing all. Both are to be vitalized by religion, (sole worthiest elevator of man or State,) breathing into the proud, material tissues, the breath of life. For I say at the core of democracy, finally, is the religious element. All the religions, old and new, are there. Nor may the scheme step forth, clothed in resplendent beauty and command, till these, bearing the best, the latest fruit, the spiritual, shall fully appear.

A portion of our pages we might indite with reference toward

Europe, especially the British part of it, more than our own land, perhaps not absolutely needed for the home reader. But the whole question hangs together, and fastens and links all peoples. The liberalist of to-day has this advantage over antique or mediæval times, that his doctrine seeks not only to individualize but to universalize. The great word Solidarity has arisen. Of all dangers to a nation, as things exist in our day, there can be no greater one than having certain portions of the people set off from the rest by a line drawn—they not privileged as others, but degraded, humiliated, made of no account. Much quackery teems, of course, even on democracy's side, yet does not really affect the orbic quality of the matter. To work in, if we may so term it, and justify God, his divine aggregate, the People, (or, the veritable horn'd and sharp-tail'd Devil, *his* aggregate, if there be who convulsively insist upon it)—this, I say, is what democracy is for; and this is what our America means, and is doing—may I not say, has done? If not, she means nothing more, and does nothing more, than any other land. And as, by virtue of its kosmical, antiseptic power, Nature's stomach is fully strong enough not only to digest the morbific matter always presented, not to be turn'd aside, and perhaps, indeed, intuitively gravitating thither—but even to change such contributions into nutriment for highest use and life—so American democracy's. That is the lesson we, these days, send over to European lands by every western breeze.

And, truly, whatever may be said in the way of abstract argument, for or against the theory of a wider democratizing of institutions in any civilized country, much trouble might well be saved to all European lands by recognizing this palpable fact, (for a palpable fact it is,) that some form of such democratizing is about the only resource now left. *That*, or chronic dissatisfaction continued, mutterings which grow annually louder and louder, till, in due course, and pretty swiftly in most cases, the inevitable crisis, crash, dynastic ruin. Anything worthy to be call'd statesmanship in the Old World, I should say, among the advanced students, adepts, or men of any brains, does not debate to-day whether to hold on, attempting to lean back and monarchize, or to look forward and democratize—but *how*, and in what degree and part, most prudently to democratize.

The eager and often inconsiderate appeals of reformers and revolutionists are indispensable, to counterbalance the inertness and fossilism making so large a part of human institutions. The latter will always take care of themselves—the danger being that they rapidly tend to ossify us. The former is to be treated with indulgence, and even with respect. As circulation to air, so is agitation and a plentiful degree of speculative license to political and moral sanity. Indirectly, but surely, goodness, virtue, law, (of the very best,) follow freedom. These, to democracy, are what the keel is to the ship, or saltness to the ocean.

The true gravitation-hold of liberalism in the United States will be a more universal ownership of property, general homesteads, general comfort—a vast, intertwining reticulation of wealth. As the human frame, or, indeed, any object in this manifold universe, is best kept together by the simple miracle of its own cohesion, and the necessity, exercise and profit thereof, so a great and varied nationality, occupying millions of square miles, were firmest held and knit by the principle of the safety and endurance of the aggregate of its middling property owners. So that, from another point of view, ungracious as it may sound, and a paradox after what we have been saying, democracy looks with suspicious, ill-satisfied eye upon the very poor, the ignorant, and on those out of business. She asks for men and women with occupations, well-off, owners of houses and acres, and with cash in the bank—and with some cravings for literature, too; and must have them, and hastens to make them. Luckily, the seed is already well-sown, and has taken ineradicable root.*

* For fear of mistake, I may as well distinctly specify, as cheerfully included in the model and standard of these Vistas, a practical, stirring, worldly, money-making, even materialistic character. It is undeniable that our farms, stores, offices, dry-goods, coal and groceries, enginery, cash-accounts, trades, earnings, markets, etc., should be attended to in earnest, and actively pursued, just as if they had a real and permanent existence. I perceive clearly that the extreme business energy, and this almost maniacal appetite for wealth prevalent in the United States, are parts of amelioration and progress, indispensably needed to prepare the very results I demand  My theory includes riches, and the getting of riches, and the amplest products, power, activity, inventions, movements, etc. Upon them, as upon substrata, I raise the edifice design'd in these Vistas.

Huge and mighty are our days, our republican lands—and most in their rapid shiftings, their changes, all in the interest of the cause. As I write this particular passage, (November, 1868,) the din of disputation rages around me. Acrid the temper of the parties, vital the pending questions. Congress convenes; the President sends his message; reconstruction is still in abeyance; the nomination and the contest for the twenty-first Presidentiad draw close, with loudest threat and bustle. Of these, and all the like of these, the eventuations I know not; but well I know that behind them, and whatever their eventuations, the vital things remain safe and certain, and all the needed work goes on. Time, with soon or later superciliousness, disposes of Presidents, Congressmen, party platforms, and such. Anon, it clears the stage of each and any mortal shred that thinks itself so potent to its day; and at and after which, (with precious, golden exceptions once or twice in a century,) all that relates to sir potency is flung to moulder in a burial-vault, and no one bothers himself the least bit about it afterward. But the People ever remain, tendencies continue, and all the idiocratic transfers in unbroken chain go on.

In a few years the dominion-heart of America will be far inland, toward the west. Our future national capital may not be where the present one is. It is possible, nay likely, that in less than fifty years, it will migrate a thousand or two miles, will be re-founded, and every thing belonging to it made on a different plan, original, far more superb. The main social, political, spine-character of the States will probably run along the Ohio, Missouri and Mississippi rivers, and west and north of them, including Canada. Those regions, with the group of powerful brothers toward the Pacific, (destined to the mastership of that sea and its countless paradises of islands,) will compact and settle the traits of America, with all the old retain'd, but more expanded, grafted on newer, hardier, purely native stock. A giant growth, composite from the rest, getting their contribution, absorbing it, to make it more illustrious. From the north, intellect, the sun of things, also the idea of unswayable justice, anchor amid the last, the wildest tempests. From the south the living soul, the animus of good and bad, haughtily admitting no demonstration but its own. While from the west itself comes solid personality, with blood and brawn, and the deep quality of all-accepting fusion.

Political democracy, as it exists and practically works in America, with all its threatening evils, supplies a training-school for making first-class men. It is life's gymnasium, not of good only, but of all. We try often, though we fall back often. A brave delight, fit for freedom's athletes, fills these arenas, and fully satisfies, out of the action in them, irrespective of success. Whatever we do not attain, we at any rate attain the experiences of the fight, the hardening of the strong campaign, and throb with currents of attempt at least. Time is ample. Let the victors come after us. Not for nothing does evil play its part among us. Judging from the main portions of the history of the world, so far, justice is always in jeopardy, peace walks amid hourly pitfalls, and of slavery, misery, meanness, the craft of tyrants and the credulity of the populace, in some of their protean forms, no voice can at any time say, They are not. The clouds break a little, and the sun shines out—but soon and certain the lowering darkness falls again, as if to last forever. Yet is there an immortal courage and prophecy in every sane soul that cannot, must not, under any circumstances, capitulate. *Vive*, the attack—the perennial assault! *Vive*, the unpopular cause—the spirit that audaciously aims—the never-abandon'd efforts, pursued the same amid opposing proofs and precedents.

Once, before the war, (alas! I dare not say how many times the mood has come!) I, too, was fill'd with doubt and gloom. A foreigner, an acute and good man, had impressively said to me, that day—putting in form, indeed, my own observations: "I have travel'd much in the United States, and watch'd their politicians, and listen'd to the speeches of the candidates, and read the journals, and gone into the public houses, and heard the unguarded talk of men. And I have found your vaunted America honeycomb'd from top to toe with infidelism, even to itself and its own programme. I have mark'd the brazen hell-faces of secession and slavery gazing defiantly from all the windows and doorways. I have everywhere found, primarily, thieves and scalliwags arranging the nominations to offices, and sometimes filling the offices themselves. I have found the north just as full of bad stuff as the south. Of the holders of public office in the Nation or the States or their municipalities, I have found that not one in a hundred has been chosen by any spontaneous selection of the outsiders, the people, but all have been nominated and put through by little or large caucuses of the politicians, and have got in by corrupt rings and electioneering, not capacity or desert. I have noticed how the millions of sturdy farmers and mechanics are thus the helpless supple-jacks of comparatively few politicians. And I have noticed more and more, the alarming spectacle of parties usurping the government, and openly and shamelessly wielding it for party purposes."

Sad, serious, deep truths. Yet are there other, still deeper, amply confronting, dominating truths. Over those politicians and great and little rings, and over all their insolence and wiles, and over the powerfulest parties, looms a power, too sluggish maybe, but ever holding decisions and decrees in hand, ready, with stern process, to execute them as soon as plainly needed—and at times, indeed, summarily crushing to atoms the mightiest parties, even in the hour of their pride.

In saner hours far different are the amounts of these things from what, at first sight, they appear. Though it is no doubt important who is elected governor, mayor, or legislator, (and full of dismay when incompetent or vile ones get elected, as they sometimes do,) there are other, quieter contingencies, infinitely more important. Shams, etc., will always be the show, like ocean's scum; enough, if waters deep and clear make up the rest. Enough, that while the piled embroider'd shoddy gaud and fraud spreads to the superficial eye, the hidden warp and weft are genuine, and will wear forever. Enough, in short, that the race, the land which could raise such as the late rebellion, could also put it down.

The average man of a land at last only is important. He, in these States, remains immortal owner and boss, deriving good uses, somehow, out of any sort of servant in office, even the basest; (certain universal requisites, and their settled regularity and protection, being first secured,) a nation like ours, in a sort of geological formation state, trying continually new experiments, choosing new delegations, is not served

by the best men only, but sometimes more by those that provoke it—by the combats they arouse. Thus national rage,
fury, discussions, etc., better than content. Thus, also, the
warning signals, invaluable for after times.

What is more dramatic than the spectacle we have seen
repeated, and doubtless long shall see—the popular judgment taking the successful candidates on trial in the offices—
standing off, as it were, and observing them and their doings
for a while, and always giving, finally, the fit, exactly due
reward? I think, after all, the sublimest part of political history, and its culmination, is currently issuing from the
American people. I know nothing grander, better exercise,
better digestion, more positive proof of the past, the triumphant result of faith in human-kind, than a well-contested
American national election.

Then still the thought returns, (like the thread-passage in
overtures,) giving the key and echo to these pages. When I
pass to and fro, different latitudes, different seasons, beholding the crowds of the great cities, New York, Boston, Philadelphia, Cincinnati, Chicago, St. Louis, San Francisco, New
Orleans, Baltimore—when I mix with these interminable
swarms of alert, turbulent, good-natured, independent citizens, mechanics, clerks, young persons—at the idea of this
mass of men, so fresh and free, so loving and so proud, a
singular awe falls upon me. I feel, with dejection and amazement, that among our geniuses and talented writers or speakers, few or none have yet really spoken to this people, created
a single image-making work for them, or absorb'd the central spirit and the idiosyncrasies which are theirs—and which,
thus, in highest ranges, so far remain entirely uncelebrated,
unexpress'd.

Dominion strong is the body's; dominion stronger is the
mind's. What has fill'd, and fills to-day our intellect, our
fancy, furnishing the standards therein, is yet foreign. The
great poems, Shakspere included, are poisonous to the idea
of the pride and dignity of the common people, the life-blood
of democracy. The models of our literature, as we get it from
other lands, ultra-marine, have had their birth in courts, and
bask'd and grown in castle sunshine; all smells of princes'
favors. Of workers of a certain sort, we have, indeed, plenty,

contributing after their kind; many elegant, many learn'd, all complacent. But touch'd by the national test, or tried by the standards of democratic personality, they wither to ashes. I say I have not seen a single writer, artist, lecturer, or what-not, that has confronted the voiceless but ever erect and active, pervading, underlying will and typic aspiration of the land, in a spirit kindred to itself. Do you call those genteel little creatures American poets? Do you term that perpetual, pistareen, paste-pot work, American art, American drama, taste, verse? I think I hear, echoed as from some mountain-top afar in the west, the scornful laugh of the Genius of these States.

Democracy, in silence, biding its time, ponders its own ideals, not of literature and art only—not of men only, but of women. The idea of the women of America, (extricated from this daze, this fossil and unhealthy air which hangs about the word *lady*,) develop'd, raised to become the robust equals, workers, and, it may be, even practical and political deciders with the men—greater than man, we may admit, through their divine maternity, always their towering, emblematical attribute—but great, at any rate, as man, in all departments; or, rather, capable of being so, soon as they realize it, and can bring themselves to give up toys and fictions, and launch forth, as men do, amid real, independent, stormy life.

Then, as towards our thought's finalé, (and, in that, over-arching the true scholar's lesson,) we have to say there can be no complete or epical presentation of democracy in the ag-gregate, or anything like it, at this day, because its doctrines will only be effectually incarnated in any one branch, when, in all, their spirit is at the root and centre. Far, far, indeed, stretch, in distance, our Vistas! How much is still to be disentangled, freed! How long it takes to make this Ameri-can world see that it is, in itself, the final authority and reliance!

Did you, too, O friend, suppose democracy was only for elections, for politics, and for a party name? I say democracy is only of use there that it may pass on and come to its flower and fruits in manners, in the highest forms of interaction be-tween men, and their beliefs—in religion, literature, colleges, and schools—democracy in all public and private life, and in the army and navy.* I have intimated that, as a paramount scheme, it has yet few or no full realizers and believers. I do not see, either, that it owes any serious thanks to noted propagandists or champions, or has been essentially help'd, though often harm'd, by them. It has been and is carried on by all the moral forces, and by trade, finance, machinery, intercommunications, and, in fact, by all the developments of history, and can no more be stopp'd than the tides, or the earth in its orbit. Doubtless, also, it resides, crude and latent, well down in the hearts of the fair average of the American-born people, mainly in the agricultural regions. But it is not yet, there or anywhere, the fully-receiv'd, the fervid, the absolute faith.

I submit, therefore, that the fruition of democracy, on aught like a grand scale, resides altogether in the future. As, under any profound and comprehensive view of the gorgeous-composite feudal world, we see in it, through the long ages and cycles of ages, the results of a deep, integral, human and divine principle, or fountain, from which issued laws, ecclesia, manners, institutes, costumes, personalities, poems, (hitherto unequall'd,) faithfully partaking of their source, and indeed only arising either to betoken it, or to furnish parts of that varied-flowing display, whose centre was one and absolute—so, long ages hence, shall the due historian or critic make at least an equal retrospect, an equal history for the democratic principle. It too must be adorn'd, credited with its results—then, when it, with imperial power, through amplest time, has dominated mankind—has been the source and test of all the moral, esthetic, social, political, and religious expressions and institutes of the civilized world—has begotten them in spirit and in form, and has carried them to its own unprecedented heights—has had, (it is possible,) monastics and ascetics, more numerous, more devout than the monks and priests of all previous creeds—has sway'd the ages with a breadth and rectitude tallying Nature's own—has

* The whole present system of the officering and personnel of the army and navy of these States, and the spirit and letter of their trebly-aristocratic rules and regulations, is a monstrous exotic, a nuisance and revolt, and belong here just as much as orders of nobility, or the Pope's council of cardinals. I say if the present theory of our army and navy is sensible and true, then the rest of America is an unmitigated fraud.

fashion'd, systematized, and triumphantly finish'd and carried out, in its own interest, and with unparallel'd success, a new earth and a new man.

Thus we presume to write, as it were, upon things that exist not, and travel by maps yet unmade, and a blank. But the throes of birth are upon us; and we have something of this advantage in seasons of strong formations, doubts, suspense—for then the afflatus of such themes haply may fall upon us, more or less; and then, hot from surrounding war and revolution, our speech, though without polish'd coherence, and a failure by the standard called criticism, comes forth, real at least as the lightnings.

And may-be we, these days, have, too, our own reward—(for there are yet some, in all lands, worthy to be so encouraged). Though not for us the joy of entering at the last the conquer'd city—not ours the chance ever to see with our own eyes the peerless power and splendid *éclat* of the democratic principle, arriv'd at meridian, filling the world with effulgence and majesty far beyond those of past history's kings, or all dynastic sway—there is yet, to whoever is eligible among us, the prophetic vision, the joy of being toss'd in the brave turmoil of these times—the promulgation and the path, obedient, lowly reverent to the voice, the gesture of the god, or holy ghost, which others see not, hear not—with the proud consciousness that amid whatever clouds, seductions, or heart-wearying postponements, we have never deserted, never despair'd, never abandon'd the faith.

So much contributed, to be conn'd well, to help prepare and brace our edifice, our plann'd Idea—we still proceed to give it in another of its aspects—perhaps the main, the high façade of all. For to democracy, the leveler, the unyielding principle of the average, is surely join'd another principle, equally unyielding, closely tracking the first, indispensable to it, opposite, (as the sexes are opposite,) and whose existence, confronting and ever modifying the other, often clashing, paradoxical, yet neither of highest avail without the other, plainly supplies to these grand cosmic politics of ours, and to the launch'd-forth mortal dangers of republicanism, to-day or any day, the counterpart and offset whereby Nature restrains the deadly original relentlessness of all her first-class laws. This second principle is individuality, the pride and centripetal isolation of a human being in himself—identity—personalism. Whatever the name, its acceptance and thorough infusion through the organizations of political commonalty now shooting Aurora-like about the world, are of utmost importance, as the principle itself is needed for very life's sake. It forms, in a sort, or is to form, the compensating balance-wheel of the successful working machinery of aggregate America.

And, if we think of it, what does civilization itself rest upon —and what object has it, with its religions, arts, schools, etc., but rich, luxuriant, varied personalism? To that, all bends; and it is because toward such result democracy alone, on anything like Nature's scale, breaks up the limitless fallows of humankind, and plants the seed, and gives fair play, that its claims now precede the rest. The literature, songs, esthetics, etc., of a country are of importance principally because they furnish the materials and suggestions of personality for the women and men of that country, and enforce them in a thousand effective ways.* As the topmost claim of a strong

* After the rest is satiated, all interest culminates in the field of persons, and never flags there. Accordingly in this field have the great poets and literatuses signally toil'd. They too, in all ages, all lands, have been creators, fashioning, making types of men and women, as Adam and Eve are made in the divine fable. Behold, shaped, bred by orientalism, feudalism, through their long growth and culmination, and breeding back in return—(when shall we have an equal series, typical of democracy?)—behold, commencing in primal Asia, (apparently formulated, in what beginning we know, in the gods of the mythologies, and coming down thence,) a few samples out of the countless product, bequeath'd to the moderns, bequeath'd to America as studies. For the men, Yudishtura, Rama, Arjuna, Solomon, most of the Old and New Testament characters; Achilles, Ulysses, Theseus, Prometheus, Hercules, Æneas, Plutarch's heroes; the Merlin of Celtic bards; the Cid, Arthur and his knights, Siegfried and Hagen in the Nibelungen; Roland and Oliver; Roustam in the Shah-Nemah; and so on to Milton's Satan, Cervantes' Don Quixote, Shakspere's Hamlet, Richard II, Lear, Marc Antony, etc., and the modern Faust. These, I say, are models, combined, adjusted to other standards than America's, but of priceless value to her and hers.

Among women, the goddesses of the Egyptian, Indian and Greek mythologies, certain Bible characters, especially the Holy Mother; Cleopatra, Penelope; the portraits of Brunhelde and Chriemhilde in the Nibelungen; Oriana, Una, etc.; the modern Consuelo, Walter Scott's Jeanie and Effie Deans, etc., etc. (Yet woman portray'd or outlin'd at her best, or as perfect human mother, does not hitherto, it seems to me, fully appear in literature.)

consolidating of the nationality of these States, is, that only by such powerful compaction can the separate States secure that full and free swing within their spheres, which is becoming to them, each after its kind, so will individuality, with unimpeded branchings, flourish best under imperial republican forms.

Assuming Democracy to be at present in its embryo condition, and that the only large and satisfactory justification of it resides in the future, mainly through the copious production of perfect characters among the people, and through the advent of a sane and pervading religiousness, it is with regard to the atmosphere and spaciousness fit for such characters, and of certain nutriment and cartoon-draftings proper for them, and indicating them for New-World purposes, that I continue the present statement—an exploration, as of new ground, wherein, like other primitive surveyors, I must do the best I can, leaving it to those who come after me to do much better. (The service, in fact, if any, must be to break a sort of first path or track, no matter how rude and ungeometrical.)

We have frequently printed the word Democracy. Yet I cannot too often repeat that it is a word the real gist of which still sleeps, quite unawaken'd, notwithstanding the resonance and the many angry tempests out of which its syllables have come, from pen or tongue. It is a great word, whose history, I suppose, remains unwritten, because that history has yet to be enacted. It is, in some sort, younger brother of another great and often-used word, Nature, whose history also waits unwritten. As I perceive, the tendencies of our day, in the States, (and I entirely respect them,) are toward those vast and sweeping movements, influences, moral and physical, of humanity, now and always current over the planet, on the scale of the impulses of the elements. Then it is also good to reduce the whole matter to the consideration of a single self, a man, a woman, on permanent grounds. Even for the treatment of the universal, in politics, metaphysics, or anything, sooner or later we come down to one single, solitary soul.

There is, in sanest hours, a consciousness, a thought that rises, independent, lifted out from all else, calm, like the stars, shining eternal. This is the thought of identity—yours for you, whoever you are, as mine for me. Miracle of miracles, beyond statement, most spiritual and vaguest of earth's dreams, yet hardest basic fact, and only entrance to all facts. In such devout hours, in the midst of the significant wonders of heaven and earth, (significant only because of the Me in the centre,) creeds, conventions, fall away and become of no account before this simple idea. Under the luminousness of real vision, it alone takes possession, takes value. Like the shadowy dwarf in the fable, once liberated and look'd upon, it expands over the whole earth, and spreads to the roof of heaven.

The quality of BEING, in the object's self, according to its own central idea and purpose, and of growing therefrom and thereto—not criticism by other standards, and adjustments thereto—is the lesson of Nature. True, the full man wisely gathers, culls, absorbs; but if, engaged disproportionately in that, he slights or overlays the precious idiocrasy and special nativity and intention that he is, the man's self, the main thing, is a failure, however wide his general cultivation. Thus, in our times, refinement and delicatesse are not only attended to sufficiently, but threaten to eat us up, like a cancer. Already, the democratic genius watches, ill-pleased, these tendencies. Provision for a little healthy rudeness, savage virtue, justification of what one has in one's self, whatever it is, is demanded. Negative qualities, even deficiencies, would be a relief. Singleness and normal simplicity and separation, amid this more and more complex, more and more artificialized state of society—how pensively we yearn for them! how we would welcome their return!

In some such direction, then—at any rate enough to preserve the balance—we feel called upon to throw what weight we can, not for absolute reasons, but current ones. To prune, gather, trim, conform, and ever cram and stuff, and be genteel and proper, is the pressure of our days. While aware that much can be said even in behalf of all this, we perceive that we have not now to consider the question of what is demanded to serve a half-starved and barbarous nation, or set of nations, but what is most applicable, most pertinent, for numerous congeries of conventional, over-corpulent societies, already becoming stifled and rotten with flatulent, infidelistic literature, and polite conformity and art. In addition to establish'd sciences, we suggest a science as it were of healthy average personalism, on original-universal grounds, the object of which should be to raise up and supply through the States a copious race of superb American men and women, cheerful, religious, ahead of any yet known.

America has yet morally and artistically originated nothing. She seems singularly unaware that the models of persons, books, manners, etc., appropriate for former conditions and for European lands, are but exiles and exotics here. No current of her life, as shown on the surfaces of what is authoritatively called her society, accepts or runs into social or esthetic democracy; but all the currents set squarely against it. Never, in the Old World, was thoroughly upholster'd exterior appearance and show, mental and other, built entirely on the idea of caste, and on the sufficiency of mere outside acquisition—never were glibness, verbal intellect, more the test, the emulation—more loftily elevated as head and sample —than they are on the surface of our republican States this day. The writers of a time hint the mottoes of its gods. The word of the modern, say these voices, is the word Culture.

We find ourselves abruptly in close quarters with the enemy. This word Culture, or what it has come to represent, involves, by contrast, our whole theme, and has been, indeed, the spur, urging us to engagement. Certain questions arise. As now taught, accepted and carried out, are not the processes of culture rapidly creating a class of supercilious infidels, who believe in nothing? Shall a man lose himself in countless masses of adjustments, and be so shaped with reference to this, that, and the other, that the simply good and healthy and brave parts of him are reduced and clipp'd away, like the bordering of box in a garden? You can cultivate corn and roses and orchards—but who shall cultivate the mountain peaks, the ocean, and the tumbling gorgeousness of the clouds? Lastly—is the readily-given reply that culture only seeks to help, systematize, and put in attitude, the elements of fertility and power, a conclusive reply?

I do not so much object to the name, or word, but I should certainly insist, for the purposes of these States, on a radical change of category, in the distribution of precedence. I should demand a programme of culture, drawn out, not for a single class alone, or for the parlors or lecture-rooms, but with an eye to practical life, the west, the working-men, the facts of farms and jack-planes and engineers, and of the broad range of the women also of the middle and working strata, and with reference to the perfect equality of women, and of a grand and powerful motherhood. I should demand of this programme or theory a scope generous enough to include the widest human area. It must have for its spinal meaning the formation of a typical personality of character, eligible to the uses of the high average of men—and *not* restricted by conditions ineligible to the masses. The best culture will always be that of the manly and courageous instincts, and loving perceptions, and of self-respect—aiming to form, over this continent, an idiocrasy of universalism, which, true child of America, will bring joy to its mother, returning to her in her own spirit, recruiting myriads of offspring, able, natural, perceptive, tolerant, devout believers in her, America, and with some definite instinct why and for what she has arisen, most vast, most formidable of historic births, and is, now and here, with wonderful step, journeying through Time.

The problem, as it seems to me, presented to the New World is, under permanent law and order, and after preserving cohesion, (ensemble-Individuality,) at all hazards, to vitalize man's free play of special Personalism, recognizing in it something that calls ever more to be consider'd, fed, and adopted as the substratum for the best that belongs to us, (government indeed is for it,) including the new esthetics of our future.

To formulate beyond this present vagueness—to help line and put before us the species, or a specimen of the species, of the democratic ethnology of the future, is a work toward which the genius of our land, with peculiar encouragement, invites her well-wishers. Already certain limnings, more or less grotesque, more or less fading and watery, have appear'd. We too, (repressing doubts and qualms,) will try our hand.

Attempting, then, however crudely, a basic model or portrait of personality for general use for the manliness of the States, (and doubtless that is most useful which is most simple and comprehensive for all, and toned low enough,) we should prepare the canvas well beforehand. Parentage must consider itself in advance. (Will the time hasten when father-hood and motherhood shall become a science—and the noblest science?) To our model, a clear-blooded, strong-fibred physique, is indispensable; the questions of food, drink, air, exercise, assimilation, digestion, can never be in-termitted. Out of these we descry a well-begotten self hood—in youth, fresh, ardent, emotional, aspiring, full of adven-ture; at maturity, brave, perceptive, under control, neither too talkative nor too reticent, neither flippant nor sombre; of the bodily figure, the movements easy, the complexion show-ing the best blood, somewhat flush'd, breast expanded, an erect attitude, a voice whose sound outvies music, eyes of calm and steady gaze, yet capable also of flashing—and a general presence that holds its own in the company of the highest. (For it is native personality, and that alone, that endows a man to stand before presidents or generals, or in any distinguish'd collection, with *aplomb*—and *not* culture, or any knowledge or intellect whatever.)

With regard to the mental-educational part of our model, enlargement of intellect, stores of cephalic knowledge, etc., the concentration thitherward of all the customs of our age, especially in America, is so overweening, and provides so fully for that part, that, important and necessary as it is, it really needs nothing from us here—except, indeed, a phrase of warning and restraint. Manners, costumes, too, though important, we need not dwell upon here. Like beauty, grace of motion, etc., they are results. Causes, original things, being attended to, the right manners unerringly follow. Much is said, among artists, of "the grand style", as if it were a thing by itself. When a man, artist or whoever, has health, pride, acuteness, noble aspirations, he has the motive-ele-ments of the grandest style. The rest is but manipulation, (yet that is no small matter).

Leaving still unspecified several sterling parts of any model fit for the future personality of America, I must not fail, again and ever, to pronounce myself on one, probably the least attended to in modern times—a hiatus, indeed, threatening its gloomiest consequences after us. I mean the simple, unsophisticated Conscience, the primary moral element. If I were asked to specify in what quarter lie the grounds of darkest dread, respecting the America of our hopes, I should have to point to this particular. I should demand the invariable application to individuality, this day and any day, of that old, ever-true plumb-rule of persons, eras, nations. Our triumphant modern civilizee, with his all-schooling and his wondrous appliances, will still show himself but an amputation while this deficiency remains. Beyond, (assuming a more hopeful tone,) the vertebration of the manly and womanly personalism of our western world, can only be, and is, indeed, to be, (I hope,) its all-penetrating Religiousness.

The ripeness of Religion is doubtless to be looked for in this field of individuality, and is a result that no organization or church can ever achieve. As history is poorly retain'd by what the technists call history, and is not given out from their pages, except the learner has in himself the sense of the well-wrapt, never yet written, perhaps impossible to be written, history—so Religion, although casually arrested, and, after a fashion, preserv'd in the churches and creeds, does not depend at all upon them, but is a part of the identified soul, which, when greatest, knows not bibles in the old way, but in new ways—the identified soul, which can really confront Religion when it extricates itself entirely from the churches, and not before.

Personalism fuses this, and favors it. I should say, indeed, that only in the perfect uncontamination and solitariness of individuality may the spirituality of religion positively come forth at all. Only here, and on such terms, the meditation, the devout ecstasy, the soaring flight. Only here, communion with the mysteries, the eternal problems, whence? whither? Alone, and identity, and the mood—and the soul emerges, and all statements, churches, sermons, melt away like vapors. Alone, and silent thought and awe, and aspiration—and then the interior consciousness, like a hitherto unseen inscription, in magic ink, beams out its wondrous lines to the sense. Bibles may convey, and priests expound, but it is exclusively for the noiseless operation of one's isolated Self, to enter the pure ether of veneration, reach the divine levels, and commune with the unutterable.

**To** practically enter into politics is an important part of American personalism. To every young man, north and south, earnestly studying these things, I should here, as an offset to what I have said in former pages, now also say, that may-be to views of very largest scope, after all, perhaps the political, (perhaps the literary and sociological,) America goes best about its development its own way—sometimes, to temporary sight, appaling enough. It is the fashion among dillettants and fops (perhaps I myself am not guiltless,) to decry the whole formulation of the active politics of America, as beyond redemption, and to be carefully kept away from. See you that you do not fall into this error. America, it may be, is doing very well upon the whole, notwithstanding these antics of the parties and their leaders, these half-brain'd nominees, the many ignorant ballots, and many elected failures and blatherers. It is the dillettants, and all who shirk their duty, who are not doing well. As for you, I advise you to enter more strongly yet into politics. I advise every young man to do so. Always inform yourself; always do the best you can; always vote. Disengage yourself from parties. They have been useful, and to some extent remain so; but the floating, uncommitted electors, farmers, clerks, mechanics, the masters of parties—watching aloof, inclining victory this side or that side—such are the ones most needed, present and future. For America, if eligible at all to downfall and ruin, is eligible within herself, not without; for I see clearly that the combined foreign world could not beat her down. But these savage, wolfish parties alarm me. Owning no law but their own will, more and more combative, less and less tolerant of the idea of ensemble and of equal brotherhood, the perfect equality of the States, the ever-overarching American ideas, it behooves you to convey yourself implicitly to no party, nor submit blindly to their dictators, but steadily hold yourself judge and master over all of them.

So much, (hastily toss'd together, and leaving far more unsaid,) for an ideal, or intimations of an ideal, toward American manhood. But the other sex, in our land, requires at least a basis of suggestion.

I have seen a young American woman, one of a large family of daughters, who, some years since, migrated from her meagre country home to one of the northern cities, to gain her own support. She soon became an expert seamstress, but finding the employment too confining for health and comfort, she went boldly to work for others, to house-keep, cook, clean, etc. After trying several places, she fell upon one where she was suited. She has told me that she finds nothing degrading in her position; it is not inconsistent with personal dignity, self-respect, and the respect of others. She confers benefits and receives them. She has good health; her presence itself is healthy and bracing; her character is un-stain'd; she has made herself understood, and preserves her independence, and has been able to help her parents, and educate and get places for her sisters; and her course of life is not without opportunities for mental improvement, and of much quiet uncosting happiness and love.

I have seen another woman who, from taste and necessity conjoin'd, has gone into practical affairs, carries on a mechanical business, partly works at it herself, dashes out more and more into real hardy life, is not abash'd by the coarseness of the contact, knows how to be firm and silent at the same time, holds her own with unvarying coolness and decorum, and will compare, any day, with superior carpenters, farmers, and even boatmen and drivers. For all that, she has not lost the charm of the womanly nature, but preserves and bears it fully, though through such rugged presentation.

Then there is the wife of a mechanic, mother of two children, a woman of merely passable English education, but of fine wit, with all her sex's grace and intuitions, who exhibits, indeed, such a noble female personality, that I am fain to record it here. Never abnegating her own proper independence, but always genially preserving it, and what belongs to it—cooking, washing, child-nursing, house-tending—she beams sunshine out of all these duties, and makes them illustrious. Physiologically sweet and sound, loving work, practical, she yet knows that there are intervals, however few, devoted to recreation, music, leisure, hospitality—and affords such intervals. Whatever she does, and wherever she is, that charm, that indescribable perfume of genuine womanhood attends her, goes with her, exhales from her, which belongs of right to all the sex, and is, or ought to be, the invariable atmosphere and common aureola of old as well as young.

My dear mother once described to me a resplendent person, down on Long Island, whom she knew in early days. She was known by the name of the Peacemaker. She was well toward eighty years old, of happy and sunny temperament, had always lived on a farm, and was very neighborly, sensible and discreet, an invariable and welcom'd favorite, especially with young married women. She had numerous children and grandchildren. She was uneducated, but possess'd a native dignity. She had come to be a tacitly agreed upon domestic regulator, judge, settler of difficulties, shepherdess, and reconciler in the land. She was a sight to draw near and look upon, with her large figure, her profuse snow-white hair, (uncoil'd by any head-dress or cap,) dark eyes, clear complexion, sweet breath, and peculiar personal magnetism.

The foregoing portraits, I admit, are frightfully out of line from these imported models of womanly personality—the stock feminine characters of the current novelists, or of the foreign court poems, (Ophelias, Enids, princesses, or ladies of one thing or another,) which fill the envying dreams of so many poor girls, and are accepted by our men, too, as supreme ideals of feminine excellence to be sought after. But I present mine just for a change.

Then there are mutterings, (we will not now stop to heed them here, but they must be heeded,) of something more revolutionary. The day is coming when the deep questions of woman's entrance amid the arenas of practical life, politics, the suffrage, etc., will not only be argued all around us, but may be put to decision, and real experiment.

Of course, in these States, for both man and woman, we must entirely recast the types of highest personality from what the oriental, feudal, ecclesiastical worlds bequeath us, and which yet possess the imaginative and esthetic fields of the United States, pictorial and melodramatic, not without use as studies, but making sad work, and forming a strange anachronism upon the scenes and exigencies around us. Of course, the old undying elements remain. The task is, to successfully adjust them to new combinations, our own days.

Nor is this so incredible. I can conceive a community, to-day and here, in which, on a sufficient scale, the perfect personalities, without noise meet; say in some pleasant western settlement or town, where a couple of hundred best men and women, of ordinary worldly status, have by luck been drawn together, with nothing extra of genius or wealth, but virtuous, chaste, industrious, cheerful, resolute, friendly and devout. I can conceive such a community organized in running order, powers judiciously delegated—farming, building, trade, courts, mails, schools, elections, all attended to; and then the rest of life, the main thing, freely branching and blossoming in each individual, and bearing golden fruit. I can see there, in every young and old man, after his kind, and in every woman after hers, a true personality, develop'd, exercised proportionately in body, mind, and spirit. I can imagine this case as one not necessarily rare or difficult, but in buoyant accordance with the municipal and general requirements of our times. And I can realize in it the culmination of something better than any stereotyped *éclat* of history or poems. Perhaps, unsung, undramatized, unput in essays or biographies—perhaps even some such community already exists, in Ohio, Illinois, Missouri, or somewhere, practically fulfilling itself, and thus outvying, in cheapest vulgar life, all that has been hitherto shown in best ideal pictures.

In short, and to sum up, America, betaking herself to formative action, (as it is about time for more solid achievement, and less windy promise,) must, for her purposes, cease to recognize a theory of character grown of feudal aristocracies, or form'd by merely literary standards, or from any ultramarine, full-dress formulas of culture, polish, caste, etc., and must sternly promulgate her own new standard, yet old enough, and accepting the old, the perennial elements, and combining them into groups, unities, appropriate to the modern, the democratic, the west, and to the practical occasions and needs of our own cities, and of the agricultural regions. Ever the most precious in the common. Ever the fresh breeze of field, or hill, or lake, is more than any palpitation of fans, though of ivory, and redolent with perfume; and the air is more than the costliest perfumes.

And now, for fear of mistake, we may not intermit to beg

our absolution from all that genuinely is, or goes along with, even Culture. Pardon us, venerable shade! if we have seem'd to speak lightly of your office. The whole civilization of the earth, we know, is yours, with all the glory and the light thereof. It is, indeed, in your own spirit, and seeking to tally the loftiest teachings of it, that we aim these poor utterances. For you, too, mighty minister! know that there is something greater than you, namely, the fresh, eternal qualities of Being. From them, and by them, as you, at your best, we too evoke the last, the needed help, to vitalize our country and our days. Thus we pronounce not so much against the principle of culture; we only supervise it, and promulge along with it, as deep, perhaps a deeper, principle. As we have shown the New World including in itself the all-leveling aggregate of democracy, we show it also including the all-varied, all-permitting, all-free theorem of individuality, and erecting therefor a lofty and hitherto unoccupied framework or platform, broad enough for all, eligible to every farmer and mechanic—to the female equally with the male—a towering selfhood, not physically perfect only—not satisfied with the mere mind's and learning's stores, but religious, possessing the idea of the infinite, (rudder and compass sure amid this troublous voyage, o'er darkest, wildest wave, through stormiest wind, of man's or nation's progress)— realizing, above the rest, that known humanity, in deepest sense, is fair adhesion to itself, for purposes beyond—and that, finally, the personality of mortal life is most important with reference to the immortal, the unknown, the spiritual, the only permanently real, which as the ocean waits for and receives the rivers, waits for us each and all.

Much is there, yet, demanding line and outline in our Vistas, not only on these topics, but others quite unwritten. Indeed, we could talk the matter, and expand it, through lifetime. But it is necessary to return to our original premises. In view of them, we have again pointedly to confess that all the objective grandeurs of the world, for highest purposes, yield themselves up, and depend on mentality alone. Here, and here only, all balances, all rests. For the mind, which alone builds the permanent edifice, haughtily builds it to itself. By it, with what follows it, are convey'd to mortal sense the culminations of the materialistic, the known, and a prophecy of the unknown. To take expression, to incarnate, to endow a literature with grand and archetypal models—to fill with pride and love the utmost capacity, and to achieve spiritual meanings, and suggest the future—these, and these only, satisfy the soul. We must not say one word against real materials; but the wise know that they do not become real till touched by emotions, the mind. Did we call the latter imponderable? Ah, let us rather proclaim that the slightest song-tune, the countless ephemera of passions arous'd by orators and tale-tellers, are more dense, more weighty than the engines there in the great factories, or the granite blocks in their foundations.

Approaching thus the momentous spaces, and considering with reference to a new and greater personalism, the needs and possibilities of American imaginative literature, through the medium-light of what we have already broach'd, it will at once be appreciated that a vast gulf of difference separates the present accepted condition of these spaces, inclusive of what is floating in them, from any condition adjusted to, or fit for, the world, the America, there sought to be indicated, and the copious races of complete men and women, along these Vistas crudely outlined. It is, in some sort, no less a difference than lies between that long-continued nebular state and vagueness of the astronomical worlds, compared with the subsequent state, the definitely-form'd worlds themselves, duly compacted, clustering in systems, hung up there, chandeliers of the universe, beholding and mutually lit by each other's lights, serving for ground of all substantial foot-hold, all vulgar uses—yet serving still more as an undying chain and echelon of spiritual proofs and shows. A bound-less field to fill! A new creation, with needed orbic works launch'd forth, to revolve in free and lawful circuits—to move, self-poised, through the ether, and shine like heaven's own suns! With such, and nothing less, we suggest that New World literature, fit to rise upon, cohere, and signalize in time, these States.

What, however, do we more definitely mean by New World literature? Are we not doing well enough here already? Are not the United States this day busily using, working, more printer's type, more presses, than any other country? uttering and absorbing more publications than any other? Do not our publishers fatten quicker and deeper? (helping themselves, under shelter of a delusive and sneaking law, or rather absence of law, to most of their forage, poetical, pictorial, historical, romantic, even comic, without money and without price—and fiercely resisting the timidest proposal to pay for it.) Many will come under this delusion—but my purpose is to dispel it. I say that a nation may hold and circulate rivers and oceans of very readable print, journals, magazines, novels, library-books, "poetry", etc.—such as the States to-day possess and circulate—of unquestionable aid and value —hundreds of new volumes annually composed and brought out here, respectable enough, indeed unsurpass'd in smartness and erudition—with further hundreds, or rather millions, (as by free forage or theft aforemention'd,) also thrown into the market—and yet, all the while, the said nation, land, strictly speaking, may possess no literature at all.

Repeating our inquiry, what, then, do we mean by real literature? especially the democratic literature of the future? Hard questions to meet. The clues are inferential, and turn us to the past. At best, we can only offer suggestions, comparisons, circuits.

It must still be reiterated, as, for the purpose of these memoranda, the deep lesson of history and time, that all else in the contributions of a nation or age, through its politics, materials, heroic personalities, military éclat, etc., remains crude, and defers, in any close and thorough-going estimate, until vitalized by national, original archetypes in literature. They only put the nation in form, finally tell anything— prove, complete anything—perpetuate anything. Without doubt, some of the richest and most powerful and populous communities of the antique world, and some of the grandest personalities and events, have, to after and present times, left themselves entirely unbequeath'd. Doubtless, greater than any that have come down to us, were among those lands, heroisms, persons, that have not come down to us at all, even by name, date, or location. Others have arrived safely, as from voyages over wide, century-stretching seas. The little ships, the miracles that have buoy'd them, and by incredible chances safely convey'd them, (or the best of them, their meaning and essence,) over long wastes, darkness, lethargy, ignorance, etc., have been a few inscriptions—a few immortal compositions, small in size, yet compassing what measureless values of reminiscence, contemporary portraitures, manners, idioms and beliefs, with deepest inference, hint and thought, to tie and touch forever the old, new body, and the old, new soul! These! and still these! bearing the freight so dear—dearer than pride—dearer than love. All the best experience of humanity, folded, saved, freighted to us here. Some of these tiny ships we call Old and New Testament, Homer, Eschylus, Plato, Juvenal, etc. Precious minims! I think, if we were forced to choose, rather than have you, and the likes of you, and what belongs to, and has grown of you, blotted out and gone, we could better afford, appaling as that would be, to lose all actual ships, this day fasten'd by wharf, or floating on wave, and see them, with all their cargoes, scuttled and sent to the bottom.

Gather'd by geniuses of city, race or age, and put by them in highest of art's forms, namely, the literary form, the peculiar combinations and the outshows of that city, age, or race, its particular modes of the universal attributes and passions, its faiths, heroes, lovers and gods, wars, traditions, struggles, crimes, emotions, joys, (or the subtle spirit of these,) having been pass'd on to us to illumine our own selfhood, and its experiences—what they supply, indispensable and highest, if taken away, nothing else in all the world's boundless storehouses could make up to us, or ever again return.

For us, along the great highways of time, those monuments stand—those forms of majesty and beauty. For us those beacons burn through all the nights. Unknown Egyptians, graving hieroglyphs; Hindus, with hymn and apothegm and endless epic; Hebrew prophet, with spirituality, as in flashes of lightning, conscience like red-hot iron, plaintive songs and screams of vengeance for tyrannies and enslavement; Christ, with bent head, brooding love and peace, like a dove; Greek, creating external shapes of physical and esthetic proportion; Roman, lord of satire, the sword, and the codex;—of the figures, some far off and veil'd, others nearer and visible; Dante, stalking with lean form, nothing but fibre, not a grain of superfluous flesh; Angelo, and the great painters, architects, musicians; rich Shakspere, luxuriant as the sun, artist and singer of feudalism in its sunset, with all the gorgeous colors, owner thereof, and using them at will; and so to such as German Kant and Hegel, where they, though near us, leaping over the ages, sit again, impassive, imperturbable, like the Egyptian gods. Of these, and the like of these, is it too much, indeed, to return to our favorite figure, and view them as orbs and systems of orbs, moving in free paths in the spaces of that other heaven, the kosmic intellect, the soul?

Ye powerful and resplendent ones! ye were, in your atmospheres, grown not for America, but rather for her foes, the feudal and the old—while our genius is democratic and modern. Yet could ye, indeed, but breathe your breath of life into our New World's nostrils—not to enslave us, as now, but, for our needs, to breed a spirit like your own—perhaps, (dare we to say it?) to dominate, even destroy, what you yourselves have left! On your plane, and no less, but even higher and wider, must we mete and measure for to-day and here. I demand races of orbic bards, with unconditional uncompromising sway. Come forth, sweet democratic despots of the west!

By points like these we, in reflection, token what we mean by any land's or people's genuine literature. And thus compared and tested, judging amid the influence of loftiest products only, what do our current copious fields of print, covering in manifold forms, the United States, better, for an analogy, present, than, as in certain regions of the sea, those spreading, undulating masses of squid, through which the whale swimming, with head half out, feeds?

Not but that doubtless our current so-called literature, (like an endless supply of small coin,) performs a certain service, and may-be, too, the service needed for the time, (the preparation-service, as children learn to spell.) Everybody reads, and truly nearly everybody writes, either books, or for the magazines or journals. The matter has magnitude, too, after a sort. But is it really advancing? or, has it advanced for a long while? There is something impressive about the huge editions of the dailies and weeklies, the mountain-stacks of white paper piled in the press-vaults, and the proud, crashing, ten-cylinder presses, which I can stand and watch any time by the half hour. Then, (though the States in the field of imagination present not a single first-class work, not a single great literatus,) the main objects, to amuse, to titillate, to pass away time, to circulate the news, and rumors of news, to rhyme and read rhyme, are yet attain'd, and on a scale of infinity. To-day, in books, in the rivalry of writers, especially novelists, success, (so-call'd,) is for him or her who strikes the mean flat average, the sensational appetite for stimulus, incident, persiflage, etc., and depicts, to the common calibre, sensual, exterior life. To such, or the luckiest of them, as we see, the audiences are limitless and profitable; but they cease presently. While this day, or any day, to workmen portraying interior or spiritual life, the audiences were limited, and often laggard—but they last forever.

Compared with the past, our modern science soars, and our journals serve—but ideal and even ordinary romantic literature, does not, I think, substantially advance. Behold the prolific brood of the contemporary novel, magazine-tale, theatre-play, etc. The same endless thread of tangled and superlative love-story, inherited, apparently from the Amadises and Palmerins of the 13th, 14th, and 15th centuries over there in Europe. The costumes and associations brought down to date, the seasoning hotter and more varied, the dragons and ogres left out—but the *thing*, I should say, has not advanced—is just as sensational, just as strain'd—remains about the same, nor more, nor less.

What is the reason our time, our lands, that we see no fresh local courage, sanity, of our own—the Mississippi, stalwart Western men, real mental and physical facts, Southerners, etc., in the body of our literature? especially the poetic part of it. But always, instead, a parcel of dandies and ennuyees, dapper little gentlemen from abroad, who flood us with their thin sentiment of parlors, parasols, piano-songs, tinkling rhymes, the five-hundredth importation—or whimpering and crying about something, chasing one aborted conceit after another, and forever occupied in dyspeptic amours with dyspeptic women. While, current and novel, the grandest events and revolutions, and stormiest passions of history, are crossing to-day with unparallel'd rapidity and magnificence over the stages of our own and all the continents, offering new materials, opening new vistas, with largest needs, inviting the daring launching forth of conceptions in literature, inspired by them, soaring in highest regions, serving art in its highest, (which is only the other name for serving God, and serving humanity,) where is the man of letters, where is the book, with any nobler aim than to follow in the old track, repeat what has been said before—and, as its utmost triumph, sell well, and be erudite or elegant?

Mark the roads, the processes, through which these States have arrived, standing easy, henceforth ever-equal, ever-compact, in their range to-day. European adventures? the most antique? Asiatic or African? old history—miracles—romances? Rather, our own unquestion'd facts. They hasten, incredible, blazing bright as fire. From the deeds and days of Columbus down to the present, and including the present—and especially the late secession war—when I con them, I feel, every leaf, like stopping to see if I have not made a mistake, and fall'n on the splendid figments of some dream. But it is no dream. We stand, live, move, in the huge flow of our age's materialism—in its spirituality. We have had founded for us the most positive of lands. The founders have pass'd to other spheres—but what are these terrible duties they have left us?

Their politics the United States have, in my opinion, with all their faults, already substantially establish'd, for good, on their own native, sound, long-vista'd principles, never to be overturn'd, offering a sure basis for all the rest. With that, their future religious forms, sociology, literature, teachers, schools, costumes, etc., are of course to make a compact whole, uniform, on tallying principles. For how can we remain, divided, contradicting ourselves, this way?* I say we can only attain harmony and stability by consulting ensemble

---

* Note, to-day, an instructive, curious spectacle and conflict. Science, (twin, in its fields, of Democracy in its)—Science, testing absolutely all thoughts, all works, has already burst well upon the world—a sun, mounting, most illuminating, most glorious—surely never again to set. But against it, deeply entrench'd, holding possession, yet remains, (not only through the churches and schools, but by imaginative literature, and unregenerate poetry,) the fossil theology of the mythic-materialistic, superstitious, untaught and credulous, fable-loving, primitive ages of humanity.

and the ethic purports, and faithfully building upon them. For the New World, indeed, after two grand stages of preparation-strata, I perceive that now a third stage, being ready for, (and without which the other two were useless,) with unmistakable signs appears. The First stage was the planning and putting on record the political foundation rights of immense masses of people—indeed all people—in the organization of republican National, State, and municipal governments, all constructed with reference to each, and each to all. This is the American programme, not for classes, but for universal man, and is embodied in the compacts of the Declaration of Independence, and, as it began and has now grown, with its amendments, the Federal Constitution—and in the State governments, with all their interiors, and with general suffrage; those having the sense not only of what is in themselves, but that their certain several things started, planted, hundreds of others in the same direction duly arise and follow. The Second stage relates to material prosperity, wealth, produce, labor-saving machines, iron, cotton, local, State and continental railways, intercommunication and trade with all lands, steamships, mining, general employment, organization of great cities, cheap appliances for comfort, numberless technical schools, books, newspapers, a currency for money circulation, etc. The Third stage, rising out of the previous ones, to make them and all illustrious, I, now, for one, promulge, announcing a native expression-spirit, getting into form, adult, and through mentality, for these States, self-contain'd, different from others, more expansive, more rich and free, to be evidenced by original authors and poets to come, by American personalities, plenty of them, male and female, traversing the States, none excepted—and by native superber tableaux and growths of language, songs, operas, orations, lectures, architecture—and by a sublime and serious Religious Democracy sternly taking command, dissolving the old, sloughing off surfaces, and from its own interior and vital principles, reconstructing, democratizing society.

For America, type of progress, and of essential faith in man, above all his errors and wickedness—few suspect how deep, how deep it really strikes. The world evidently sup-

z                                                        w.

poses, and we have evidently supposed so too, that the States are merely to achieve the equal franchise, an elective government—to inaugurate the respectability of labor, and become a nation of practical operatives, law-abiding, orderly and well off. Yes, those are indeed parts of the task of America; but they not only do not exhaust the progressive conception, but rather arise, teeming with it, as the mediums of deeper, higher progress. Daughter of a physical revolution—mother of the true revolutions, which are of the interior life, and of the arts. For so long as the spirit is not changed, any change of appearance is of no avail.

The old men, I remember as a boy, were always talking of American independence. What is independence? Freedom from all laws or bonds except those of one's own being, control'd by the universal ones. To lands, to man, to woman, what is there at last to each, but the inherent soul, nativity, idiocrasy, free, highest-poised, soaring its own flight, following out itself?

At present, these States, in their theology and social standards, (of greater importance than their political institutions,) are entirely held possession of by foreign lands. We see the sons and daughters of the New World, ignorant of its genius, not yet inaugurating the native, the universal, and the near, still importing the distant, the partial, and the dead. We see London, Paris, Italy—not original, superb, as where they belong—but second-hand here, where they do not belong. We see the shreds of Hebrews, Romans, Greeks; but where, on her own soil, do we see, in any faithful, highest, proud expression, America herself? I sometimes question whether she has a corner in her own house.

Not but that in one sense, and a very grand one, good theology, good art, or good literature, has certain features shared in common. The combination fraternizes, ties the races—is, in many particulars, under laws applicable indifferently to all, irrespective of climate or date, and, from whatever source, appeals to emotions, pride, love, spirituality common to human kind. Nevertheless, they touch a man closest, (perhaps only actually touch him,) even in these, in their expression through autochthonic lights and shades, flavors, fondnesses, aversions, specific incidents, illustrations,

out of his own nationality, geography, surroundings, antecedents, etc. The spirit and the form are one, and depend far
more on association, identity and place, than is supposed.
Subtly interwoven with the materiality and personality of a
land, a race—Teuton, Turk, Californian, or what-not—there
is always something—I can hardly tell what it is—history but
describes the results of it—it is the same as the untellable
look of some human faces. Nature, too, in her stolid forms,
is full of it—but to most it is there a secret. This something is
rooted in the invisible roots, the profoundest meanings of
that place, race, or nationality; and to absorb and again
effuse it, uttering words and products as from its midst, and
carrying it into highest regions, is the work, or a main part of
the work, of any country's true author, poet, historian, lecturer, and perhaps even priest and philosoph. Here, and
here only, are the foundations for our really valuable and
permanent verse, drama, etc.

But at present, (judged by any higher scale than that which
finds the chief ends of existence to be to feverishly make
money during one-half of it, and by some "amusement", or
perhaps foreign travel, flippantly kill time, the other half,)
and consider'd with reference to purposes of patriotism,
health, a noble personality, religion, and the democratic adjustments, all these swarms of poems, literary magazines,
dramatic plays, resultant so far from American intellect, and
the formation of our best ideas, are useless and a mockery.
They strengthen and nourish no one, express nothing characteristic, give decision and purpose to no one, and suffice only
the lowest level of vacant minds.

Of what is called the drama, or dramatic presentation in
the United States, as now put forth at the theatres, I should
say it deserves to be treated with the same gravity, and on a
par with the questions of ornamental confectionery at public
dinners, or the arrangement of curtains and hangings in a
ball-room—nor more, nor less. Of the other, I will not insult
the reader's intelligence, (once really entering into the atmosphere of these Vistas,) by supposing it necessary to show, in
detail, why the copious dribble, either of our little or well-
known rhymesters, does not fulfil, in any respect, the needs
and august occasions of this land. America demands a

poetry that is bold, modern, and all-surrounding and kos-mical, as she is herself. It must in no respect ignore science or the modern, but inspire itself with science and the modern. It must bend its vision toward the future, more than the past. Like America, it must extricate itself from even the greatest models of the past, and, while courteous to them, must have entire faith in itself, and the products of its own democratic spirit only. Like her, it must place in the van, and hold up at all hazards, the banner of the divine pride of man in himself, (the radical foundation of the new religion). Long enough have the People been listening to poems in which common humanity, deferential, bends low, humiliated, acknowledging superiors. But America listens to no such poems. Erect, in-flated, and fully self-esteeming be the chant; and then America will listen with pleased ears.

Nor may the genuine gold, the gems, when brought to light at last, be probably usher'd forth from any of the quar-ters currently counted on. To-day, doubtless, the infant genius of American poetic expression, (eluding those highly-refined imported and gilt-edged themes, and sentimental and butterfly flights, pleasant to orthodox publishers—causing tender spasms in the coteries, and warranted not to chafe the sensitive cuticle of the most exquisitely artificial gossamer delicacy,) lies sleeping far away, happily unrecognized and uninjur'd by the coteries, the art-writers, the talkers and critics of the saloons, or the lecturers in the colleges—lies sleeping, aside, unrecking itself, in some western idiom, or native Michigan or Tennessee repartee, or stump-speech—or in Kentucky or Georgia, or the Carolinas—or in some slang or local song or allusion of the Manhattan, Boston, Phila-delphia or Baltimore mechanic—or up in the Maine woods— or off in the hut of the California miner, or crossing the Rocky mountains, or along the Pacific railroad—or on the breasts of the young farmers of the northwest, or Canada, or boatmen of the lakes. Rude and coarse nursing-beds, these; but only from such beginnings and stocks, indigenous here, may haply arrive, be grafted, and sprout, in time, flowers of genuine American aroma, and fruits truly and fully our own.

I say it were a standing disgrace to these States—I say it

were a disgrace to any nation, distinguish'd above others by
the variety and vastness of its territories, its materials, its inventive activity, and the splendid practicality of its people,
not to rise and soar above others also in its original styles in
literature and art, and its own supply of intellectual and esthetic masterpieces, archetypal, and consistent with itself. I
know not a land except ours that has not, to some extent,
however small, made its title clear. The Scotch have their
born ballads, subtly expressing their past and present, and
expressing character. The Irish have theirs. England, Italy,
France, Spain, theirs. What has America? With exhaustless
mines of the richest ore of epic, lyric, tale, tune, picture, etc.,
in the Four Years' War; with, indeed, I sometimes think, the
richest masses of material ever afforded a nation, more variegated, and on a larger scale—the first sign of proportionate,
native, imaginative Soul, and first-class works to match, is,
(I cannot too often repeat,) so far wanting.

Long ere the second centennial arrives, there will be some
forty to fifty great States, among them Canada and Cuba.
When the present century closes, our population will be sixty
or seventy millions. The Pacific will be ours, and the Atlantic
mainly ours. There will be daily electric communication
with every part of the globe. What an age! What a land!
Where, elsewhere, one so great? The individuality of one
nation must then, as always, lead the world. Can there be
any doubt who the leader ought to be? Bear in mind, though,
that nothing less than the mightiest original non-subordin-
ated Soul has ever really, gloriously led, or ever can lead.
(This Soul—its other name, in these Vistas, is Literature.)

In fond fancy leaping those hundred years ahead, let us
survey America's works, poems, philosophies, fulfilling prophecies, and giving form and decision to best ideals. Much
that is now undream'd of, we might then perhaps see establish'd, luxuriantly cropping forth, richness, vigor of letters
and of artistic expression, in whose products character will
be a main requirement, and not merely erudition or elegance.

Intense and loving comradeship, the personal and passionate attachment of man to man—which, hard to define, underlies the lessons and ideals of the profound saviours of every

land and age, and which seems to promise, when thoroughly develop'd, cultivated and recognized in manners and literature, the most substantial hope and safety of the future of these States, will then be fully express'd. *

A strong fibred joyousness and faith, and the sense of health *al fresco*, may well enter into the preparation of future noble American authorship. Part of the test of a great literatus shall be the absence in him of the idea of the covert, the lurid, the maleficent, the devil, the grim estimates inherited from the Puritans, hell, natural depravity, and the like. The great literatus will be known, among the rest, by his cheerful simplicity, his adherence to natural standards, his limitless faith in God, his reverence, and by the absence in him of doubt, ennui, burlesque, persiflage, or any strain'd and temporary fashion.

Nor must I fail, again and yet again, to clinch, reiterate more plainly still, (O that indeed such survey as we fancy, may show in time this part completed also!) the lofty aim, surely the proudest and the purest, in whose service the future literatus, of whatever field, may gladly labor. As we have intimated, offsetting the material civilization of our race, our nationality, its wealth, territories, factories, population, products, trade, and military and naval strength, and breathing breath of life into all these, and more, must be its moral civilization—the formulation, expression, and aidancy whereof, is the very highest height of literature. The climax of this loftiest range of civilization, rising above all the gorgeous shows and results of wealth, intellect, power, and art, as such —above even theology and religious fervor—is to be its de-

---

* It is to the development, identification, and general prevalence of that fervid comradeship, (the adhesive love, at least rivaling the amative love hitherto possessing imaginative literature, if not going beyond it,) that I look for the counterbalance and offset of our materialistic and vulgar American democracy, and for the spiritualization thereof. Many will say it is a dream, and will not follow my inferences : but I confidently expect a time when there will be seen, running like a half-hid warp through all the myriad audible and visible worldly interests of America, threads of manly friendship, fond and loving, pure and sweet, strong and life-long, carried to degrees hitherto unknown—not only giving tone to individual character, and making it unprecedently emotional, muscular, heroic, and refined, but having the deepest relations to general politics. I say democracy infers such loving comradeship, as its most inevitable twin or counterpart, without which it will be incomplete, in vain, and incapable of perpetuating itself.

velopment, from the eternal bases, and the fit expression, of absolute Conscience, moral soundness, Justice. Even in religious fervor there is a touch of animal heat. But moral conscientiousness, crystalline, without flaw, not Godlike only, entirely human, awes and enchants forever. Great is emotional love, even in the order of the rational universe. But, if we must make gradations, I am clear there is something greater. Power, love, veneration, products, genius, esthetics, tried by subtlest comparisons, analyses, and in serenest moods, somewhere fail, somehow become vain. Then noiseless, with flowing steps, the lord, the sun, the last ideal comes. By the names right, justice, truth, we suggest, but do not describe it. To the world of men it remains a dream, an idea as they call it. But no dream is it to the wise—but the proudest, almost only solid, lasting thing of all. Its analogy in the material universe is what holds together this world, and every object upon it, and carries its dynamics on forever sure and safe. Its lack, and the persistent shirking of it, as in life, sociology, literature, politics, business, and even sermonizing, these times, or any times, still leaves the abysm, the mortal flaw and smutch, mocking civilization to-day, with all its unquestion'd triumphs, and all the civilization so far known.*

Present literature, while magnificently fulfilling certain popular demands, with plenteous knowledge and verbal smartness, is profoundly sophisticated, insane, and its very

* I am reminded as I write that out of this very conscience, or idea of conscience, of intense moral right, and in its name and strain'd construction, the worst fanaticisms, wars, persecutions, murders, etc., have yet, in all lands, in the past, been broach'd, and have come to their devilish fruition. Much is to be said—but I may say here, and in response, that side by side with the unflagging stimulation of the elements of religion and conscience must henceforth move with equal sway, science, absolute reason, and the general proportionate development of the whole man. These scientific facts, deductions, are divine too—precious counted parts of moral civilization, and, with physical health, indispensable to it, to prevent fanaticism. For abstract religion, I perceive, is easily led astray, ever credulous, and is capable of devouring, remorseless, like fire and flame. Conscience, too, isolated from all else, and from the emotional nature, may but attain the beauty and purity of glacial, snowy ice. We want, for these States, for the general character, a cheerful, religious fervor, endued with the ever-present modifications of the human emotions, friendship, benevolence, with a fair field for scientific inquiry, the right of individual judgment, and always the cooling influences of material Nature.

joy is morbid. It needs tally and express Nature, and the spirit of Nature, and to know and obey the standards. I say the question of Nature, largely consider'd, involves the questions of the esthetic, the emotional, and the religious—and involves happiness. A fitly born and bred race, growing up in right conditions of out-door as much as in-door harmony, activity and development, would probably, from and in those conditions, find it enough merely *to live*—and would, in their relations to the sky, air, water, trees, etc., and to the countless common shows, and in the fact of life itself, discover and achieve happiness—with Being suffused night and day by wholesome extasy, surpassing all the pleasures that wealth, amusement, and even gratified intellect, erudition, or the sense of art, can give.

In the prophetic literature of these States, (the reader of my speculations will miss their principal stress unless he allows well for the point that a new Literature, perhaps a new Metaphysics, certainly a new Poetry, are to be, in my opinion, the only sure and worthy supports and expressions of the American Democracy,) Nature, true Nature, and the true idea of Nature, long absent, must, above all, become fully restored, enlarged, and must furnish the pervading atmosphere to poems, and the test of all high literary and esthetic compositions. I do not mean the smooth walks, trimm'd hedges, poseys and nightingales of the English poets, but the whole orb, with its geologic history, the kosmos, carrying fire and snow, that rolls through the illimitable areas, light as a feather, though weighing billions of tons. Furthermore, as by what we now partially call Nature is intended, at most, only what is entertainable by the physical conscience, the sense of matter, and of good animal health—on these it must be distinctly accumulated, incorporated, that man, comprehending these, has, in towering superaddition, the moral and spiritual consciences, indicating his destination beyond the ostensible, the mortal.

To the heights of such estimate of Nature indeed ascending, we proceed to make observations for our Vistas, breathing rarest air. What is I believe called Idealism seems to me to suggest, (guarding against extravagance, and ever modified even by its opposite,) the course of inquiry and desert of favor for our New World metaphysics, their foundation of and in literature, giving hue to all.*

The elevating and etherealizing ideas of the unknown and of unreality must be brought forward with authority, as they are the legitimate heirs of the known, and of reality, and at least as great as their parents. Fearless of scoffing, and of the ostent, let us take our stand, our ground, and never desert it, to confront the growing excess and arrogance of realism. To the cry, now victorious—the cry of sense, science, flesh, incomes, farms, merchandise, logic, intellect, demonstrations, solid perpetuities, buildings of brick and iron, or even the facts of the shows of trees, earth, rocks, etc., fear not, my brethren, my sisters, to sound out with equally determin'd voice, that conviction brooding within the recesses of every envision'd soul—illusions! apparitions! figments all! True, we must not condemn the show, neither absolutely deny it, for the indispensability of its meanings; but how clearly we see that, migrate in soul to what we can already conceive of superior and spiritual points of view, and, palpable as it seems under present relations, it all and several might, nay certainly would, fall apart and vanish.

* The culmination and fruit of literary artistic expression, and its final fields of pleasure for the human soul, are in metaphysics, including the mysteries of the spiritual world, the soul itself, and the question of the immortal continuation of our identity. In all ages, the mind of man has brought up here—and always will. Here, at least, of whatever race or era, we stand on common ground. Applause, too, is unanimous, antique or modern. Those authors who work well in this field—though their reward, instead of a handsome percentage, or royalty, may be but simply the laurel-crown of the victors in the great Olympic games—will be dearest to humanity, and their works, however esthetically defective, will be treasur'd forever. The altitude of literature and poetry has always been religion—and always will be. The Indian Vedas, the Naçkas of Zoroaster, the Talmud of the Jews, the Old Testament, the Gospel of Christ and his disciples, Plato's works, the Koran of Mohammed, the Edda of Snorro, and so on toward our own day, to Swedenborg, and to the invaluable contributions of Leibnitz, Kant and Hegel—these, with such poems only in which, (while singing well of persons and events, of the passions of man, and the shows of the material universe,) the religious tone, the consciousness of mystery, the recognition of the future, of the unknown, of Deity over and under all, and of the divine purpose, are never absent, but indirectly give tone to all—exhibit literature's real heights and elevations, towering up like the great mountains of the earth.

Standing on this ground—the last, the highest, only permanent ground—and sternly criticizing, from it, all works, either of the literary, or any art, we have peremptorily to dismiss every pretensive produc-

I hail with joy the oceanic, variegated, intense practical energy, the demand for facts, even the business materialism of the current age, our States. But wo to the age or land in which these things, movements, stopping at themselves, do not tend to ideas. As fuel to flame, and flame to the heavens, so must wealth, science, materialism—even this democracy of which we make so much—unerringly feed the highest mind, the soul. Infinitude the flight: fathomless the mystery. Man, so diminutive, dilates beyond the sensible universe, competes with, outcopes space and time, meditating even one great idea. Thus, and thus only, does a human being, his spirit, ascend above, and justify, objective Nature, which, probably nothing in itself, is incredibly and divinely serviceable, indispensable, real, here. And as the purport of objective Nature is doubtless folded, hidden, somewhere here—as somewhere here is what this globe and its manifold forms, and the light of day, and night's darkness, and life itself, with all its experiences, are for—it is here the great literature, especially verse, must get its inspiration and throbbing blood. Then may we attain to a poetry worthy the immortal soul of man, and which, while absorbing materials, and, in their own sense, the shows of Nature, will, above all, have, both directly and indirectly, a freeing, fluidizing, expanding, religious character,

---

tion, however fine its esthetic or intellectual points, which violates or ignores, or even does not celebrate, the central divine idea of All, suffusing universe, of eternal trains of purpose, in the development, by however slow degrees, of the physical, moral, and spiritual kosmos. I say he has studied, meditated to no profit, whatever may be his mere erudition, who has not absorb'd this simple consciousness and faith. It is not entirely new—but it is for Democracy to elaborate it, and look to build upon and expand from it, with uncompromising reliance. Above the doors of teaching the inscription is to appear, Though little or nothing can be absolutely known, perceiv'd, except from a point of view which is evanescent yet we know at least one permanency, that Time and Space, in the will of God, furnish successive chains, completions of material births and beginnings, solve all discrepancies, fears and doubts, and eventually fulfil happiness—and that the prophecy of those births, namely spiritual results, throws the true arch over all teaching, all science. The local considerations of sin, disease, deformity, ignorance, death, etc., and their measurement by the superficial mind, and ordinary legislation and theology, are to be met by science, boldly accepting, promulging this faith, and planting the seeds of superber laws—of the explication of the physical universe through the spiritual—and clearing the way for a religion, sweet and unimpugnable alike to little child or great savan.

exulting with science, fructifying the moral elements, and stimulating aspirations, and meditations on the unknown.

The process, so far, is indirect and peculiar, and though it may be suggested, cannot be defined. Observing, rapport, and with intuition, the shows and forms presented by Nature, the sensuous luxuriance, the beautiful in living men and women, the actual play of passions, in history and life—and, above all, from those developments either in Nature or human personality in which power, (dearest of all to the sense of the artist,) transacts itself—out of these, and seizing what is in them, the poet, the esthetic worker in any field, by the divine magic of his genius, projects them, their analogies, by curious removes, indirections, in literature and art, (No useless attempt to repeat the material creation, by daguerreotyping the exact likeness by mortal mental means). This is the image-making faculty, coping with material creation, and rivaling, almost triumphing over it. This alone, when all the other parts of a specimen of literature or art are ready and waiting, can breathe into it the breath of life, and endow it with identity.

"The true question to ask," says the librarian of Congress in a paper read before the Social Science Convention at New York, October, 1869, "The true question to ask respecting a book, is, *has it help'd any human soul?*" This is the hint, statement, not only of the great literatus, his book, but of every great artist. It may be that all works of art are to be first tried by their art qua lities, their image-forming talent, and their dramatic, pictor al, plot-constructing, euphonious and other talents. Then, whenever claiming to be first-class works, they are to be strictly and sternly tried by their foundation in, and radiation, in the highest sense, and always indirectly, of the ethic principles, and eligibility to free, arouse, dilate.

As, within the purposes of the Kosmos, and vivifying all meteorology, and all the congeries of the mineral, vegetable and animal worlds—all the physical growth and development of man, and all the history of the race in politics, religions, wars, etc., there is a moral purpose, a visible or invisible intention, certainly underlying all—its results and proof needing to be patiently waited for—needing intuition, faith, idiosyncrasy, to its realization, which many, and especially the intellectual, do not have—so in the product, or congeries of the product, of the greatest literatus. This is the last, profoundest measure and test of a first-class literary or esthetic achievement, and when understood and put in force must fain, I say, lead to works, books, nobler than any hitherto known. Lo! Nature, (the only complete, actual poem,) existing calmly in the divine scheme, containing all, content, careless of the criticisms of a day, or these endless and wordy chatterers. And lo! to the consciousness of the soul, the permanent identity, the thought, the something, before which the magnitude even of democracy, art, literature, etc., dwindles, becomes partial, measurable—something that fully satisfies, (which those do not). That something is the All, and the idea of All, with the accompanying idea of eternity, and of itself, the soul, buoyant, indestructible, sailing space forever, visiting every region, as a ship the sea. And again lo! the pulsations in all matter, all spirit, throbbing forever—the eternal beats, eternal systole and diastole of life in things— wherefrom I feel and know that death is not the ending, as was thought, but rather the real beginning—and that nothing ever is or can be lost, nor ever die, nor soul, nor matter.

In the future of these States must arise poets immenser far, and make great poems of death. The poems of life are great, but there must be the poems of the purports of life, not only in itself, but beyond itself. I have eulogized Homer, the sacred bards of Jewry, Eschylus, Juvenal, Shakspere, etc., and acknowledged their inestimable value. But, (with perhaps the exception, in some, not all respects, of the second-mention'd,) I say there must, for future and democratic purposes, appear poets, (dare I to say so?) of higher class even than any of those—poets not only possess'd of the religious fire and abandon of Isaiah, luxuriant in the epic talent of Homer, or for proud characters as in Shakspere, but consistent with the Hegelian formulas, and consistent with modern science. America needs, and the world needs, a class of bards who will, now and ever, so link and tally the rational physical being of man, with the ensembles of time and space, and with this vast and multiform show, Nature, surrounding him, ever tantalizing him, equally a part, and yet not a part of him, as to essentially harmonize, satisfy, and put at rest. Faith, very old, now scared away by science, must be restored, brought back by the same power that caused her departure—restored with new sway, deeper, wider, higher than ever. Surely, this universal ennui, this coward fear, this shuddering at death, these low, degrading views, are not always to rule the spirit pervading future society, as it has the past, and does the present. What the Roman Lucretius sought most nobly, yet all too blindly, negatively to do for his age and its successors, must be done positively by some great coming literatus, especially poet, who, while remaining fully poet, will absorb whatever science indicates, with spiritualism, and out of them, and out of his own genius, will compose the great poem of death. Then will man indeed confront Nature, and confront time and space, both with science, and *con amore*, and take his right place, prepared for life, master of fortune and misfortune. And then that which was long wanted will be supplied, and the ship that had it not before in all her voyages, will have an anchor.

There are still other standards, suggestions, for products of high literatuses. That which really balances and conserves the social and political world is not so much legislation, police, treaties, and dread of punishment, as the latent eternal intuitional sense, in humanity, of fairness, manliness, decorum, etc. Indeed, this perennial regulation, control, and oversight, by self-suppliance, is *sine qua non* to democracy; and a highest widest aim of democratic literature may well be to bring forth, cultivate, brace, and strengthen this sense, in individuals and society. A strong mastership of the general inferior self by the superior self, is to be aided, secured, indirectly, but surely, by the literatus, in his works, shaping, for individual or aggregate democracy, a great passionate body, in and along with which goes a great masterful spirit.

And still, providing for contingencies, I fain confront the fact, the need of powerful native philosophs and orators and bards, these States, as rallying points to come, in times of danger, and to fend off ruin and defection. For history is long, long, long. Shift and turn the combinations of the statement as we may, the problem of the future of America is in certain respects as dark as it is vast. Pride, competition, segregation, vicious wilfulness, and license beyond example, brood already upon us. Unwieldy and immense, who shall hold in behemoth? who bridle leviathan? Flaunt it as we choose, athwart and over the roads of our progress loom huge uncertainty, and dreadful, threatening gloom. It is useless to deny it: Democracy grows rankly up the thickest, noxious, deadliest plants and fruits of all—brings worse and worse invaders—needs newer, larger, stronger, keener compensations and compellers.

Our lands, embracing so much, (embracing indeed the whole, rejecting none,) hold in their breast that flame also, capable of consuming themselves, consuming us all. Short as the span of our national life has been, already have death and downfall crowded close upon us—and will again crowd close, no doubt, even if warded off. Ages to come may never know, but I know, how narrowly during the late secession war—and more than once, and more than twice or thrice— our Nationality, (wherein bound up, as in a ship in a storm, depended, and yet depend, all our best life, all hope, all value,) just grazed, just by a hair escaped destruction. Alas! to think of them! the agony and bloody sweat of certain of those hours! those cruel, sharp, suspended crises!

Even to-day, amid these whirls, incredible flippancy, and blind fury of parties, infidelity, entire lack of first-class captains and leaders, added to the plentiful meanness and vulgarity of the ostensible masses—that problem, the labor question, beginning to open like a yawning gulf, rapidly widening every year—what prospect have we? We sail a dangerous sea of seething currents, cross and under-currents, vortices—all so dark, untried—and whither shall we turn? It seems as if the Almighty had spread before this nation charts of imperial destinies, dazzling as the sun, yet with many a deep intestine difficulty, and human aggregate of cankerous imperfection—saying, lo! the roads, the only plans of development, long and varied with all terrible balks and ebullitions. You said in your soul, I will be empire of empires, overshadowing all else, past and present, putting the history of Old-World dynasties, conquests behind me, as of no account—making a new history, a history of democracy, making old history a dwarf—I alone inaugurating largeness, culminating time. If these, O lands of America, are indeed the prizes, the determinations of your soul, be it so. But behold the cost, and already specimens of the cost. Thought you greatness was to ripen for you like a pear? If you would have greatness, know that you must conquer it through ages, centuries—must pay for it with a proportionate price. For you too, as for all lands, the struggle, the traitor, the wily person in office, scrofulous wealth, the surfeit of prosperity, the demonism of greed, the hell of passion, the decay of faith, the long postponement, the fossil-like lethargy, the ceaseless need of revolutions, prophets, thunder-storms, deaths, births, new projections and invigorations of ideas and men.

Yet I have dream'd, merged in that hidden-tangled problem of our fate, whose long unraveling stretches mysteriously through time—dream'd out, portray'd, hinted already—a little or a larger band—a band of brave and true, unprecedented yet—arm'd and equipt at every point—the members separated, it may be, by different dates and States, or south, or north, or east, or west—Pacific, Atlantic, Southern, Canadian—a year, a century here, and other centuries there—but always one, compact in soul, conscience-conserving, God-inculcating, inspired achievers, not only in literature, the greatest art, but achievers in all art—a new, undying order, dynasty, from age to age transmitted—a band, a class, at least as fit to cope with current years, our dangers, needs, as those who, for their times, so long, so well, in armor or in cowl, upheld and made illustrious, that far-back feudal, priestly world. To offset chivalry, indeed, those vanish's countless knights, old altars, abbeys, priests, ages and stringd of ages, a knightlier and more sacred cause to-day demands, and shall supply, in a New World, to larger, grander work, more than the counterpart and tally of them.

Arrived now, definitely, at an apex for these Vistas, I confess that the promulgation and belief in such a class or institution—a new and greater literatus order—its possibility, (nay certainty,) underlies these entire speculations—and that the rest, the other parts, as superstructures, are all founded upon it. It really seems to me the condition, not only of our future national and democratic development, but of our perpetuation. In the highly artificial and materialistic bases of modern civilization, with the corresponding arrangements and methods of living, the force-infusion of intellect alone, the depraving influences of riches just as much as poverty, the absence of all high ideals in character—with the long series of tendencies, shapings, which few are strong enough to resist, and which now seem, with steam-engine speed, to be everywhere turning out the generations of humanity like uniform iron castings—all of which, as compared with the feudal ages, we can yet do nothing better than accept, make the best of, and even welcome, upon the whole, for their oceanic practical grandeur, and their restless wholesale kneading of the masses—I say of all this tremendous and dominant play of solely materialistic bearings upon current life in the United States, with the results as already seen, accumulating, and reaching far into the future, that they must either be confronted and met by at least an equally subtle and tremendous force-infusion for purposes of spiritualization, for the pure conscience, for genuine esthetics, and for absolute and primal manliness and womanliness—or else our modern civilization, with all its improvements, is in vain, and we are on the road to a destiny, a status, equivalent, in its real world, to that of the fabled damned.

Prospecting thus the coming unsped days, and that new order in them—marking the endless train of exercise, development, unwind, in nation as in man, which life is for—we see, fore-indicated, amid these prospects and hopes, new law-forces of spoken and written language—not merely the peda-gogue-forms, correct, regular, familiar with precedents, made for matters of outside propriety, fine words, thoughts definitely told out—but a language fann'd by the breath of Nature, which leaps overhead, cares mostly for impetus and effects, and for what it plants and invigorates to grow—tallies life and character, and seldomer tells a thing than suggests or necessitates it. In fact, a new theory of literary composition for imaginative works of the very first class, and especially for highest poems, is the sole course open to these States. Books are to be call'd for, and supplied, on the assumption that the process of reading is not a half-sleep, but, in highest sense, an exercise, a gymnast's struggle; that the reader is to do something for himself, must be on the alert, must himself or herself construct indeed the poem, argument, history, metaphysical essay—the text furnishing the hints, the clue, the start or frame-work. Not the book needs so much to be the complete thing, but the reader of the book does. That were to make a nation of supple and athletic minds, well-train'd, intuitive, used to depend on themselves, and not on a few coteries of writers.

Investigating here, we see, not that it is a little thing we have, in having the bequeath'd libraries, countless shelves of volumes, records, etc.; yet how serious the danger, depending entirely on them, of the bloodless vein, the nerveless arm, the false application, at second or third hand. We see that the real interest of this people of ours in the theology, history, poetry, politics, and personal models of the past, (the British islands, for instance, and indeed all the past,) is not necessarily to mould ourselves or our literature upon them, but to attain fuller, more definite comparisons, warnings, and the insight to ourselves, our own present, and our own far grander, different, future history, religion, social customs, etc. We see that almost everything that has been written, sung, or stated, of old, with reference to humanity under the feudal and oriental institutes, religions, and for other lands, needs to be re-written, re-sung, re-stated, in terms consistent with the institution of these States, and to come in range and obedient uniformity with them.

We see, as in the universes of the material kosmos, after meteorological, vegetable, and animal cycles, man at last arises, born through them, to prove them, concentrate them, to turn upon them with wonder and love—to command them, adorn them, and carry them upward into superioli realms—so, out of the series of the preceding social and political universes, now arise these States. We see that wher many were supposing things establish'd and completed, really the grandest things always remain; and discover that the work of the New World is not ended, but only fairly begun.

We see our land, America, her literature, esthetics, etc., as, substantially, the getting in form, or effusement and statement, of deepest basic elements and loftiest final meanings, of history and man—and the portrayal, (under the eternal laws and conditions of beauty,) of our own physiognomy, the subjective tie and expression of the objective, as from our own combination, continuation, and points of view—and the deposit and record of the national mentality, character, appeals, heroism, wars, and even liberties—where these, and all, culminate in native literary and artistic formulation, to be perpetuated; and not having which native, first-class formulation, she will flounder about, and her other, however imposing, eminent greatness, prove merely a passing gleam; but truly having which, she will understand herself, live nobly, nobly contribute, emanate, and, swinging, poised safely on herself, illumin'd and illuming, become a full-form'd world, and divine Mother not only of material but spiritual worlds, in ceaseless succession through time—the main thing being the average, the bodily, the concrete, the democratic, the popular, on which all the superstructures of the future are to permanently rest.

## [PREFACE TO "AS A STRONG BIRD ON PINIONS FREE"]

THE impetus and ideas urging me, for some years past, to an utterance, or attempt at utterance, of New World songs, and an epic of Democracy, having already had their publish'd expression, as well as I can expect to give it, in *Leaves of Grass*, the present and any future pieces from me are really but the surplusage forming after that volume, or the wake eddying behind it. I fulfill'd in that an imperious conviction, and the commands of my nature as total and irresistible as those which make the sea flow, or the globe revolve. But of this supplementary volume, I confess I am not so certain. Having from early manhood abandon'd the business pursuits and applications usual in my time and country, and obediently yielded myself up ever since to the impetus mention'd, and to the work of expressing those ideas, it may be that mere habit has got dominion of me, when there is no real need of saying anything further. But what is life but an experiment? and mortality but an exercise? with reference to results beyond. And so shall my poems be. If incomplete here, and superfluous there, *n'importe*—the earnest trial and persistent exploration shall at least be mine, and other success failing shall be success enough. I have been more anxious, anyhow, to suggest the songs of vital endeavor and manly evolution, and furnish something for races of outdoor athletes, than to make perfect rhymes, or reign in the parlors. I ventur'd from the beginning my own way, taking chances— and would keep on venturing.

I will therefore not conceal from any persons, known or unknown to me, who take an interest in the matter, that I have the ambition of devoting yet a few more years to poetic composition. The mighty present age! To absorb and express in poetry, anything of it—of its wor!d,—America— cities and States—the years, the events of our Nineteenth century—the rapidity of movement—the violent contrasts, fluctuations of light and shade, of hope and fear—the entire revolution made by science in the poetic method—these great new underlying facts and new ideas rushing and spreading everywhere;—truly a mighty age! As if in some colossal drama, acted again like those of old under the open sun, the Nations of our time, and all the characteristics of Civilization, seem hurrying, stalking across, flitting from wing to wing, gathering, closing up, toward some long-prepared, most tremendous denouement. Not to conclude the infinite scenas of the race's life and toil and happiness and sorrow, but haply that the boards be clear'd from oldest, worst incumbrances, accumulations, and Man resume the eternal play anew, and under happier, freer auspices. To me, the United States are important because in this colossal drama they are unquestionably designated for the leading parts, for many a century to come. In them history and humanity seem to seek to culminate. Our broad areas are even now the busy theatre of plots, passions, interests, and suspended problems, compared to which the intrigues of the past of Europe, the wars of dynasties, the scope of kings and kingdoms, and even the development of peoples, as hitherto, exhibit scales of measurement comparatively narrow and trivial. And on these areas of ours, as on a stage, sooner or later, something like an *éclaircissement* of all the past civilization of Europe and Asia is probably to be evolved.

The leading parts. Not to be acted, emulated here, by us again, that role till now foremost in history—not to become a conqueror nation, or to achieve the glory of mere military, or diplomatic, or commercial superiority—but to become the grand producing land of nobler men and women—of copious races, cheerful, healthy, tolerant, free—to become the most friendly nation, (the United States indeed)—the modern composite nation, form'd from all, with room for all, welcoming all immigrants—accepting the work of our own interior development, as the work fitly filling ages and ages to come;—the leading nation of peace, but neither ignorant nor incapable of being the leading nation of war;—not the man's nation only, but the woman's nation—a land of splendid mothers, daughters, sisters, wives.

Our America to-day I consider in many respects as but indeed a vast seething mass of *materials*, ampler, better, (worse also,) than previously known—eligible to be used to carry towards its crowning stage, and build for good, the great ideal nationality of the future, the nation of the body and the soul,*—no limit here to land, help, opportunities, mines, products, demands, supplies, etc.;—with (I think) our political organization, National, State, and Municipal, permanently establish'd, as far ahead as we can calculate—but, so far, no social, literary, religious, or esthetic organizations, consistent with our politics, or becoming to us—which organizations can only come, in time, through great democratic ideas, religion—through science, which now, like a new sunrise, ascending, begins to illuminate all—and through our own begotten poets and literatuses. (The moral of a late well-written book on civilization seems to be that the only real foundation-walls and bases—and also *sine qua non* afterward—of true and full civilization, is the eligibility and certainty of boundless products for feeding, clothing, sheltering everybody—perennial fountains of physical and domestic

* The problems of the achievements of this crowning stage through future first-class National Singers, Orators, Artists, and others—of creating in literature an *imaginative* New World, the correspondent and counterpart of the current Scientific and Political New Worlds,—and the perhaps distant, but still delightful prospect, (for our children, if not in our own day,) of delivering America, and, indeed, all Christian lands everywhere, from the thin moribund and watery, but appallingly extensive nuisance of conventional poetry—by putting something really alive and substantial in its place—I have undertaken to grapple with, and argue, in the preceding "Democratic Vistas" [p. 657].

comfort, with intercommunication, and with civil and ecclesiastical freedom—and that then the esthetic and mental
business will take care of itself. Well, the United States have
establish'd this basis, and upon scales of extent, variety,
vitality, and continuity, rivaling those of Nature; and have
now to proceed to build an edifice upon it. I say this edifice
is only to be fitly built by new literatures, especially the
poetic. I say a modern image-making creation is indispensable to fuse and express the modern political and scientific
creations—and then the trinity will be complete.)

When I commenced, years ago, elaborating the plan of my
poems, and continued turning over that plan, and shifting it
in my mind through many years, (from the age of twenty-
eight to thirty-five,) experimenting much, and writing and
abandoning much, one deep purpose underlay the others, and
has underlain it and its execution ever since—and that has
been the religious purpose. Amid many changes, and a formulation taking far different shape from what I at first supposed, this basic purpose has never been departed from in the
composition of my verses. Not of course to exhibit itself in
the old ways, as in writing hymns or psalms with an eye to
the church-pew, or to express conventional pietism, or the
sickly yearnings of devotees, but in new ways, and aiming at
the widest sub-bases and inclusions of humanity, and tallying
the fresh air of sea and land. I will see, (said I to myself,)
whether there is not, for my purposes as poet, a religion, and
a sound religious germenancy in the average human race, at
least in their modern development in the United States, and
in the hardy common fiber and native yearnings and elements, deeper and larger, and affording more profitable returns, than all mere sects or churches—as boundless, joyous,
and vital as Nature itself—a germenancy that has too long
been unencouraged, unsung, almost unknown. With science,
the old theology of the East, long in its dotage, begins evidently to die and disappear. But (to my mind) science—and
may-be such will prove its principal service—as evidently
prepares the way for One indescribably grander—Time's
young but perfect offspring—the new theology—heir of the
West—lusty and loving, and wondrous beautiful. For
America, and for to-day, just the same as any day, the

supreme and final science is the science of God—what we call science being only its minister—as Democracy is, or shall be also. And a poet of America (I said) must fill himself with such thoughts, and chant his best out of them. And as those were the convictions and aims, for good or bad, of *Leaves of Grass*, they are no less the intention of this volume. As there can be, in my opinion, no sane and complete personality, nor any grand and electric nationality, without the stock element of religion imbuing all the other elements, (like heat in chemistry, invisible itself, but the life of all visible life,) so there can be no poetry worthy the name without that element behind all. The time has certainly come to begin to discharge the idea of religion, in the United States, from mere ecclesiasticism, and from Sundays and churches and church-going, and assign it to that general position, chiefest, most indispensable, most exhilarating, to which the others are to be adjusted, inside of all human character, and education, and affairs. The people, especially the young men and women of America, must begin to learn that religion, (like poetry,) is something far, far different from what they supposed. It is, indeed, too important to the power and perpetuity of the New World to be consign'd any longer to the churches, old or new, Catholic or Protestant—Saint this, or Saint that. It must be consign'd henceforth to democracy *en masse*, and to literature. It must enter into the poems of the nation. It must make the nation.

The Four Years' War is over—and in the peaceful, strong, exciting, fresh occasions of to-day, and of the future, that strange, sad war is hurrying even now to be forgotten. The camp, the drill, the lines of sentries, the prisons, the hospitals —(ah! the hospitals!)—all have passed away—all seem now like a dream. A new race, a young and lusty generation, already sweeps in with oceanic currents, obliterating the war, and all its scars, its mounded graves, and all its reminiscences of hatred, conflict, death. So let it be obliterated. I say the life of the present and the future makes undeniable demands upon us each and all, south, north, east, west. To help put the United States (even if only in imagination) hand in hand, in one unbroken circle in a chant—to rouse them to the unprecedented grandeur of the part they are to play, and are even now playing—to the thought of their great future, and the attitude conform'd to it—especially their great esthetic, moral, scientific future, (of which their vulgar material and political present is but as the preparatory tuning of instruments by an orchestra,) these, as hitherto, are still, for me, among my hopes, ambitions.

*Leaves of Grass*, already publish'd, is, in its intentions, the song of a great composite *democratic individual*, male or female. And following on and amplifying the same purpose, I suppose I have in my mind to run through the chants of this volume, (if ever completed,) the thread-voice, more or less audible, of an aggregated, inseparable, unprecedented, vast, composite, electric *democratic nationality*.

Purposing, then, to still fill out, from time to time through years to come, the following volume, (unless prevented,) I conclude this preface to the first instalment of it, pencil'd in the open air, on my fifty-third birth-day, by wafting to you, dear reader, whoever you are, (from amid the fresh scent of the grass, the pleasant coolness of the forenoon breeze, the lights and shades of tree-boughs silently dappling and playing around me, and the notes of the cat-bird for undertone and accompaniment,) my true good-will and love.

WASHINGTON, D. C., *May* 31, 1872.　　　　W. W.


## AN INTERREGNUM PARAGRAPH

SEVERAL years now elapse before I resume my diary. I continued at Washington working in the Attorney-General's department through '66 and '67, and some time afterward. In February '73 I was stricken down by paralysis, gave up my desk, and migrated to Camden, New Jersey, where I lived during '74 and '75, quite unwell—but after that began to grow better; commenc'd going for weeks at a time, even for months, down in the country, to a charmingly recluse and rural spot along Timber creek, twelve or thirteen miles from where it enters the Delaware river. Domicil'd at the farm-house of my friends, the Staffords, near by, I lived half the time along this creek and its adjacent fields and lanes. And it is to my life here that I, perhaps, owe partial recovery (a sort of second wind, or semi-renewal of the lease of life) from the prostration of 1874-'75. If the notes of that outdoor life could only prove as glowing to you, reader dear, as the experience itself was to me. Doubtless in the course of the following, the fact of invalidism will crop out, (I call myself *a half-Paralytic* these days, and reverently bless the Lord it is no worse,) between some of the lines—but I get my share of fun and healthy hours, and shall try to indicate them. (The trick is, I find, to tone your wants and tastes low down enough, and make much of negatives, and of mere daylight and the skies.)

## [PREFACE TO THE CENTENNIAL EDITION]

AT the eleventh hour, under grave illness, I gather up the pieces of prose and poetry left over since publishing, a while since, my first and main volume, *Leaves of Grass*—pieces, here, some new, some old—nearly all of them (sombre as many are, making this almost death's book) composed in by-gone atmospheres of perfect health—and preceded by the freshest collection, the little "Two Rivulets", now send them out, embodied in the present melange, partly as my contribution and outpouring to celebrate, in some sort, the feature of the time, the first centennial of our New World nationality—and then as chyle and nutriment to that moral, indissoluble union, equally representing all, and the mother of many coming centennials.

And e'en for flush and proof of our America—for reminder, just as much, or more, in moods of towering pride and joy, I keep my special chants of death and immortality* to stamp the coloring-finish of all, present and past. For terminus and temperer to all, they were originally written; and that shall be their office at the last.

---

* PASSAGE TO INDIA.—As in some ancient legend-play, to close the plot and the hero's career, there is a farewell gathering on ship's deck and on shore, a loosing of hawsers and ties, a spreading of sails to the wind—a starting out on unknown seas, to fetch up no one knows whither—to return no more—and the curtain falls, and there is the end of it—so I have reserv'd that poem, with its cluster, to finish and explain much that, without them, would not be explain'd, and to take leave, and escape for good, from all that has preceded them. (Then probably "Passage to India", and its cluster, are but freer vent and

For some reason—not explainable or definite to my own mind, yet secretly pleasing and satisfactory to it—I have not hesitated to embody in, and run through the volume, two altogether distinct veins, or strata—politics for one, and for the other, the pensive thought of immortality. Thus, too, the prose and poetic, the dual forms of the present book. The volume, therefore, after its minor episodes, probably divides into these two, at first sight far diverse, veins of topic and treatment. Three points, in especial, have become very dear to me, and all through I seek to make them again and again, in many forms and repetitions, as will be seen: 1. That the

---

fuller expression to what, from the first, and so on throughout, more or less lurks in my writings, underneath every page, every line, everywhere.)

I am not sure but the last inclosing sublimation of race or poem is, what it thinks of death. After the rest has been comprehended and said, even the grandest—after those contributions to mightiest nationality, or to sweetest song, or to the best personalism, male or female, have been glean'd from the rich and varied themes of tangible life, and have been fully accepted and sung, and the pervading fact of visible existence, with the duty it devolves, is rounded and apparently completed, it still remains to be really completed by suffusing through the whole and several, that other pervading invisible fact, so large a part, (is it not the largest part?) of life here, combining the rest and furnishing, for person or State, the only permanent and unitary meaning to all, even the meanest life, consistently with the dignity of the universe, in Time. As from the eligibility to this thought, and the cheerful conquest of this fact, flash forth the first distinctive proofs of the soul, so to me, (extending it only a little further,) the ultimate Democratic purports, the ethereal and spiritual ones, are to concentrate here, and as fixed stars, radiate hence. For, in my opinion, it is no less than this idea of immortality, above all other ideas, that is to enter into, and vivify, and give crowning religious stamp, to democracy in the New World.

It was originally my intention, after chanting in *Leaves of Grass* the songs of the body and existence, to then compose a further, equally needed volume, based on those convictions of perpetuity and conservation which, enveloping all precedents, make the unseen soul govern absolutely at last. I meant, while in a sort continuing the theme of my first chants, to shift the slides, and exhibit the problem and paradox of the same ardent and fully appointed personality entering the sphere of the resistless gravitation of spiritual law, and with cheerful face estimating death, not at all as the cessation, but as somehow what I feel it must be, the entrance upon by far the greatest part of existence, and something that life is at least as much for, as it is for itself. But the full construction of such a work is beyond my powers, and must remain for some bard in the future. The physical and the sensuous, in themselves or in their immediate continuations, retain holds upon me which I think are never entirely releas'd; and those holds I have not only not denied, but hardly wish'd to weaken.

Meanwhile, not entirely to give the go-by to my original plan, and

true growth-characteristics of the democracy of the New World are henceforth to radiate in superior literary, artistic and religious expressions, far more than in its republican forms, universal suffrage, and frequent elections, (though these are unspeakably important). 2. That the vital political mission of the United States is, to practically solve and settle the problem of two sets of rights—the fusion, thorough compatibility and junction of individual State prerogatives, with the indispensable necessity of centrality and Oneness—the national identity power—the sovereign Union, relentless, permanently comprising all, and over all, and in that never yielding an inch: then 3d. Do we not, amid a general malaria

---

far more to avoid a mark'd hiatus in it, than to entirely fulfil it, I end my books with thoughts, or radiations from thoughts, on death, immortality, and a free entrance into the spiritual world. In those thoughts, in a sort, I make the first steps or studies toward the mighty theme, from the point of view necessitated by my foregoing poems, and by modern science. In them I also seek to set the key-stone to my democracy's enduring arch. I recollate them now, for the press, in order to partially occupy and offset days of strange sickness, and the heaviest affliction and bereavement of my life; and I fondly please myself with the notion of leaving that cluster to you, O unknown reader of the future, as "something to remember me by", more especially than all else. Written in former days of perfect health, little did I think the pieces had the purport that now, under present circumstances, opens to me.

[As I write these lines, May 31, 1875, it is again early summer,— again my birth-day—now my fifty-sixth. Amid the outside beauty and freshness, the sunlight and verdure of the delightful season, O how different the moral atmosphere amid which I now revise this Volume, from the jocund influence surrounding the growth and advent of *Leaves of Grass.* I occupy myself, arranging these pages for publication, still envelopt in thoughts of the death two years since of my dear Mother, the most perfect and magnetic character, the rarest combination of practical, moral and spiritual, and the least selfish, of all and any I have ever known—and by me O so much the most deeply loved— and also under the physical affliction of a tedious attack of paralysis, obstinately lingering and keeping its hold upon me, and quite suspending all bodily activity and comfort.]

Under these influences, therefore, I still feel to keep "Passage to India" for last words even to this centennial dithyramb. Not as, in antiquity, at highest festival of Egypt, the noisome skeleton of death was sent on exhibition to the revelers, for zest and shadow to the occasion's joy and light—but as the marble statue of the normal Greeks at Elis, suggesting death in the form of a beautiful and perfect young man, with closed eyes, leaning on an inverted torch—emblem of rest and aspiration after action—of crown and point which all lives and poems should steadily have reference to, namely, the justified and noble termination of our identity, this grade of it, and outlet-preparation to another grade.

of fogs and vapors, our day, unmistakably see two pillars of promise, with grandest, indestructible indications—one, that the morbid facts of American politics and society everywhere are but passing incidents and flanges of our unbounded impetus of growth? weeds, annuals, of the rank, rich soil—not central, enduring, perennial things? The other, that all the hitherto experience of the States, their first century, has been but preparation, adolescence—and that this Union is only now and henceforth, (*i.e.* since the secession war,) to enter on its full democratic career?

Of the whole, poems and prose, (not attending at all to chronological order, and with original dates and passing allusions in the heat and impression of the hour, left shuffled in, and undisturb'd,) the chants of *Leaves of Grass*, my former volume, yet serve as the indispensable deep soil, or basis, out of which, and out of which only, could come the roots and stems more definitely indicated by these later pages. (While that volume radiates physiology alone, the present one, though of the like origin in the main, more palpably doubtless shows the pathology which was pretty sure to come in time from the other.)

In that former and main volume, composed in the flush of my health and strength, from the age of 30 to 50 years, I dwelt on birth and life, clothing my ideas in pictures, days, transactions of my time, to give them positive place, identity —saturating them with that vehemence of pride and audacity of freedom necessary to loosen the mind of still-to-be-form'd America from the accumulated folds, the superstitions, and all the long, tenacious and stifling anti-democratic authorities of the Asiatic and European past—my enclosing purport being to express, above all artificial regulation and aid, the eternal bodily composite, cumulative, natural character of one's self. *

* Namely, a character, making most of common and normal elements, to the superstructure of which not only the precious accumulations of the learning and experiences of the Old World, and the settled social and municipal necessities and current requirements, so long a-building, shall still faithfully contribute, but which at its foundations and carried up thence, and receiving its impetus from the democratic spirit, and accepting its gauge in all departments from the democratic formulas, shall again directly be vitalized by the perennial influences of Nature at first hand, and the old heroic stamina of Nature, the strong air of prairie and mountain, the dash of the briny sea, the primary antiseptics—of the passions, in all their fullest heat and potency, of

Estimating the American Union as so far, and for some time to come, in its yet formative condition, I bequeath poems and essays as nutriment and influences to help truly assimilate and harden, and especially to furnish something toward what the States most need of all, and which seems to me yet quite unsupplied in literature, namely, to show them, or begin to show them, themselves distinctively, and what they are for. For though perhaps the main points of all ages and nations are points of resemblance, and, even while granting evolution, are substantially the same, there are some vital things in which this Republic, as to its individualities, and as a compacted Nation, is to specially stand forth, and culminate modern humanity. And these are the very things it least morally and mentally knows—(though, curiously enough, it is at the same time faithfully acting upon them).

I count with such absolute certainty on the great future of

---

courage, rankness, amativeness, and of immense pride. Not to lose at all, therefore, the benefits of artificial progress and civilization, but to re-occupy for Western tenancy the oldest though ever-fresh fields, and reap from them the savage and sane nourishment indispensable to a hardy nation, and the absence of which, threatening to become worse and worse, is the most serious lack and defect to-day of our New World literature.

Not but what the brawn of *Leaves of Grass* is, I hope, thoroughly spiritualized everywhere, for final estimate, but, from the very subjects, the direct effect is a sense of the life, as it should be, of flesh and blood, and physical urge, and animalism. While there are other themes, and plenty of abstract thoughts and poems in the volume—while I have put in it passing and rapid but actual glimpses of the great struggle between the nation and the slave-power, (1861–'65,) as the fierce and bloody panorama of that contest unroll'd itself: while the whole book, indeed, revolves around that four years' war, which, as I was in the midst of it, becomes, in "Drum-Taps", pivotal to the rest entire—and here and there, before and afterward, not a few episodes and speculations—*that*—namely, to make a type-portrait for living, active, worldly, healthy personality, objective as well as subjective, joyful and potent, and modern and free, distinctively for the use of the United States, male and female, through the long future—has been, I say, my general object. (Probably, indeed, the whole of these varied songs, and all my writings, both volumes, only ring changes in some sort, on the ejaculation, How vast, how eligible, how joyful, how real, is a human being, himself or herself.)

Though from no definite plan at the time, I see now that I have unconsciously sought, by indirections at least as much as directions, to express the whirls and rapid growth and intensity of the United States, the prevailing tendency and events of the Nineteenth century, and largely the spirit of the whole current world, my time; for I feel that I have partaken of that spirit, as I have been deeply interested in all those events, the closing of long-stretch'd eras and ages, and, illus-

the United States—different from, though founded on, the past—that I have always invoked that future, and surrounded myself with it, before or while singing my songs. (As ever, all tends to followings—America, too, is a prophecy. What, even of the best and most successful, would be justified by itself alone? by the present, or the material ostent alone? Of men or States, few realize how much they live in the future. That, rising like pinnacles, gives its main significance to all You and I are doing to-day. Without it, there were little meaning in lands or poems—little purport in human lives. All ages, all Nations and States, have been such prophecies. But where any former ones with prophecy so broad, so clear, as our times, our lands—as those of the West?)

Without being a scientist, I have thoroughly adopted the conclusions of the great savans and experimentalists of our time, and of the last hundred years, and they have interiorly

---

trated in the history of the United States, the opening of larger ones. (The death of President Lincoln, for instance, fitly, historically closes, in the civilization of feudalism, many old influences—drops on them, suddenly, a vast, gloomy, as it were, separating curtain.)

Since I have been ill, (1873-'74-'75,) mostly without serious pain, and with plenty of time and frequent inclination to judge my poems, (never composed with eye on the book-market, nor for fame, nor for any pecuniary profit,) I have felt temporary depression more than once, for fear that in *Leaves of Grass* the *moral* parts were not sufficiently pronounc'd. But in my clearest and calmest moods I have realized that as those *Leaves*, all and several, surely prepare the way for, and necessitate morals, and are adjusted to them, just the same as Nature does and is, they are what, consistently with my plan, they must and probably should be. (In a certain sense, while the Moral is the purport and last intelligence of all Nature, there is absolutely nothing of the moral in the works, or laws, or shows of Nature. Those only lead inevitably to it—begin and necessitate it.)

Then I meant *Leaves of Grass*, as publish'd, to be the Poem of average Identity, (of *yours*, whoever you are, now reading these lines.) A man is not greatest as victor in war, nor inventor or explorer, nor even in science, or in his intellectual or artistic capacity, or exemplar in some vast benevolence. To the highest democratic view, man is most acceptable in living well the practical life and lot which happens to him as ordinary farmer, sea-farer, mechanic, clerk, laborer, or driver—upon and from which position as a central basis or pedestal, while performing its labors, and his duties as citizen, son, husband, father and employ'd person, he preserves his physique, ascends, developing, radiating himself in other regions—and especially where and when, (greatest of all, and nobler than the proudest mere genius or magnate in any field,) he fully realizes the conscience, the spiritual, the divine faculty, cultivated well, exemplified in all his deeds and words, through life, uncompromising to the end—a flight loftier than any of Homer's or Shakspere's—broader than all poems and bibles—namely, Nature's

tinged the chyle of all my verse, for purposes beyond. Following the modern spirit, the real poems of the present, ever solidifying and expanding into the future, must vocalize the vastness and splendor and reality with which scientism has invested man and the universe, (all that is called creation,) and must henceforth launch humanity into new orbits, consonant with that vastness, splendor, and reality, (unknown to the old poems,) like new systems of orbs, balanced upon themselves, revolving in limitless space, more subtle than the stars. Poetry, so largely hitherto and even at present wedded to children's tales, and to mere amorousness, upholstery and superficial rhyme, will have to accept, and, while not denying the past, nor the themes of the past, will be revivified by this tremendous innovation, the kosmic spirit, which must henceforth, in my opinion, be the background and underlying impetus, more or less visible, of all first-class songs.

---

own, and in the midst of it, Yourself, your own Identity, body and soul. (All serves, helps—but in the centre of all, absorbing all, giving, for your purpose, the only meaning and vitality to all, master or mistress of all, under the law, stands Yourself.) To sing the Song of that law of average Identity, and of Yourself, consistently with the divine law of the universal, is a main intention of those *Leaves*.

Something more may be added—for, while I am about it, I would make a full confession. I also sent out *Leaves of Grass* to arouse and set flowing in men's and women's hearts, young and old, endless streams of living, pulsating love and friendship, directly from them to myself, now and ever. To this terrible, irrepressible yearning, (surely more or less down underneath in most human souls)—this never-satisfied appetite for sympathy, and this boundless offering of sympathy—this universal democratic comradeship—this old, eternal, yet ever-new interchange of adhesiveness, so fitly emblematic of America—I have given in that book, undisguisedly, declaredly, the openest expression. Besides, important as they are in my purpose as emotional expressions for humanity, the special meaning of the "Calamus" cluster of *Leaves of Grass*, (and more or less running through the book, and cropping out in "Drum-Taps",) mainly resides in its political significance. In my opinion, it is by a fervent, accepted development of comradeship, the beautiful and sane affection of man for man, latent in all the young fellows, north and south, east and west—it is by this, I say, and by what goes directly and indirectly along with it, that the United States of the future, (I cannot too often repeat,) are to be most effectually welded together, intercalated, anneal'd into a living union.

Then, for enclosing clue of all, it is imperatively and ever to be borne in mind that *Leaves of Grass* entire is not to be construed as an intellectual or scholastic effort or poem mainly, but more as a radical utterance out of the Emotions and the Physique—an utterance adjusted to, perhaps born of, Democracy and the Modern—in its very nature regardless of the old conventions, and, under the great laws, following only its own impulses.

Only, (for me, at any rate, in all my prose and poetry,) joyfully accepting modern science, and loyally following it without the slightest hesitation, there remains ever recognized still a higher flight, a higher fact, the eternal soul of man, (of all else too,) the spiritual, the religious—which it is to be the greatest office of scientism, in my opinion, and of future poetry also, to free from fables, crudities and superstitions, and launch forth in renew'd faith and scope a hundred fold. To me, the worlds of religiousness, of the conception of the divine, and of the ideal, though mainly latent, are just as absolute in humanity and the universe as the world of chemistry, or anything in the objective worlds. To me

The prophet and the bard,
Shall yet maintain themselves—in higher circles yet,
Shall mediate to the modern, to democracy—interpret yet
to them,
God and eidólons.

To me, the crown of savantism is to be, that it surely opens the way for a more splendid theology, and for ampler and diviner songs. No year, nor even century, will settle this. There is a phase of the real, lurking behind the real, which it is all for. There is also in the intellect of man, in time, far in prospective recesses, a judgment, a last appellate court, which will settle it.

In certain parts in these flights, or attempting to depict or suggest them, I have not been afraid of the charge of obscurity, in either of my two volumes—because human thought, poetry or melody, must leave dim escapes and outlets—must possess a certain fluid, aerial character, akin to space itself, obscure to those of little or no imagination, but indispensable to the highest purposes. Poetic style, when address'd to the soul, is less definite form, outline, sculpture, and becomes vista, music, half-tints, and even less than half-tints. True, it may be architecture; but again it may be the forest wildwood, or the best effect thereof, at twilight, the waving oaks and cedars in the wind, and the impalpable odor.

Finally, as I have lived in fresh lands, inchoate, and in a revolutionary age, future-founding, I have felt to identify the points of that age, these lands, in my recitatives, altogether in my own way. Thus my form has strictly grown from my purports and facts, and is the analogy of them. Within my time the United States have emerged from nebulous vagueness and suspense, to full orbic, (though varied,) decision—have done the deeds and achiev'd the triumphs of half a score of centuries—and are henceforth to enter upon their real history —the way being now, (*i.e.* since the result of the secession war,) clear'd of death-threatening impedimenta, and the free areas around and ahead of us assured and certain, which were not so before—(the past century being but preparations, trial voyages and experiments of the ship, before her starting out upon deep water).

In estimating my volumes, the world's current times and deeds, and their spirit, must be first profoundly estimated. Out of the hundred years just ending, (1776-1876,) with their genesis of inevitable wilful events, and new experiments and introductions, and many unprecedented things of war and peace, (to be realized better, perhaps only realized, at the remove of a century hence;) out of that stretch of time, and especially out of the immediately preceding twenty-five years, (1850-'75,) with all their rapid changes, innovations, and audacious movements—and bearing their own inevitable wilful birth-marks—the experiments of my poems too have found genesis.                                    W. W.


## A WINTER DAY ON THE SEA-BEACH

ONE bright December mid-day lately I spent down on the New Jersey sea-shore, reaching it by a little more than an hour's railroad trip over the old Camden and Atlantic. I had started betimes, fortified by nice strong coffee and a good breakfast (cook'd by the hands I love, my dear sister Lou's— how much better it makes the victuals taste, and then assimilate, strengthen you, perhaps make the whole day comfortable afterwards.) Five or six miles at the last, our track enter'd a broad region of salt grass meadows, intersected by lagoons, and cut up everywhere by watery runs. The sedgy perfume, delightful to my nostrils, reminded me of "the mash" and south bay of my native island. I could have journey'd contentedly till night through these flat and odorous sea-prairies. From half-past 11 till 2 I was nearly all the time along the beach, or in sight of the ocean, listening to its hoarse murmur, and inhaling the bracing and welcome breezes. First, a rapid five-mile drive over the hard sand—our carriage wheels hardly made dents in it. Then after dinner (as there were nearly two hours to spare) I walk'd off in another direction, (hardly met or saw a person,) and taking possession of what appear'd to have been the reception-room of an old bath-house range, had a broad expanse of view all to myself—quaint, refreshing, unimpeded—a dry area of sedge and Indian grass immediately before and around me—space, simple, unornamented space. Distant vessels, and the far-off, just visible trailing smoke of an inward bound steamer; more plainly, ships, brigs, schooners, in sight, most of them with every sail set to the firm and steady wind.

The attractions, fascinations there are in sea and shore! How one dwells on their simplicity, even vacuity! What is it in us, arous'd by those indirections and directions? That spread of waves and gray-white beach, salt, monotonous, senseless—such an entire absence of art, books, talk, elegance—so indescribably comforting, even this winter day—grim, yet so delicate-looking, so spiritual— striking emotional, impalpable depths, subtler than all the poems, paintings, music, I have ever read, seen, heard. (Yet let me be fair, perhaps it is because I have read those poems and heard that music.)

## SEA-SHORE FANCIES

EVEN as a boy, I had the fancy, the wish, to write a piece, perhaps a poem, about the sea-shore—that suggesting, dividing line, contact, junction, the solid marrying the liquid—that curious, lurking something, (as doubtless every objective form finally becomes to the subjective spirit,) which means far more than its mere first sight, grand as that is—blending the real and ideal, and each made portion of the other. Hours, days, in my Long Island youth and early manhood, I haunted the shores of Rockaway or Coney island, or away east to the Hamptons or Montauk. Once, at the latter place, (by the old lighthouse, nothing but sea-tossings in sight in every direction as far as the eye could reach,) I remember well, I felt that I must one day write a book express-ing this liquid, mystic theme. Afterward, I recollect, how it came to me that instead of any special lyrical or epical or literary attempt, the sea-shore should be an invisible *influence*, a pervading gauge and tally for me, in my composition. (Let me give a hint here to young writers. I am not sure but I have unwittingly follow'd out the same rule with other powers besides sea and shores—avoiding them, in the way of any dead set at poetizing them, as too big for formal handling—quite satisfied if I could indirectly show that we have met and fused, even if only once, but enough—that we have really absorb'd each other and understand each other.)

There is a dream, a picture, that for years at intervals, (sometimes quite long ones, but surely again, in time,) has come noiselessly up before me, and I really believe, fiction as it is, has enter'd largely into my practical life—certainly into my writings, and shaped and color'd them. It is nothing more or less than a stretch of interminable white-brown sand, hard and smooth and broad, with the ocean perpetually, grandly, rolling in upon it, with slow-measured sweep, with rustle and hiss and foam, and many a thump as of low bass drums. This scene, this picture, I say, has risen before me at times for years. Sometimes I wake at night and can hear and see it plainly.

## SPRING OVERTURES—RECREATIONS

*February* 10.—The first chirping, almost singing, of a bird to-day. Then I noticed a couple of honey-bees spirting and humming about the open window in the sun.

*February* 11.—In the soft rose and pale gold of the declin-ing light, this beautiful evening, I heard the first hum and preparation of awakening spring—very faint—whether in the earth or roots, or starting of insects, I know not—but it was audible, as I lean'd on a rail (I am down in my country quarters awhile,) and look'd long at the western horizon. Turning to the east, Sirius, as the shadows deepen'd, came forth in dazzling splendor. And great Orion; and a little to the north-east the big Dipper, standing on end.

*February* 20.—A solitary and pleasant sundown hour at

the pond, exercising arms, chest, my whole body, by a tough
oak sapling thick as my wrist, twelve feet high—pulling and
pushing, inspiring the good air. After I wrestle with the tree
awhile, I can feel its young sap and virtue welling up out of
the ground and tingling through me from crown to toe, like
health's wine. Then for addition and variety I launch forth
in my vocalism; shout declamatory pieces, sentiments, sorrow, anger, etc., from the stock poets or plays—or inflate my
lungs and sing the wild tunes and refrains I heard of the
blacks down south, or patriotic songs I learn'd in the army.
I make the echoes ring, I tell you! As the twilight fell, in a
pause of these ebullitions, an owl somewhere the other side
of the creek sounded *too-oo-oo-oo-oo*, soft and pensive (and
I fancied a little sarcastic) repeated four or five times. Either
to applaud the negro songs—or perhaps an ironical comment
on the sorrow, anger, or style of the stock poets.

## ONE OF THE HUMAN KINKS

How is it that in all the serenity and lonesomeness of solitude, away off here amid the hush of the forest, alone, or as I
have found in prairie wilds, or mountain stillness, one is
never entirely without the instinct of looking around, (I never
am, and others tell me the same of themselves, confidentially,)
for somebody to appear, or start up out of the earth, or from
behind some tree or rock? Is it a lingering, inherited remains
of man's primitive wariness, from the wild animals? or from
his savage ancestry far back? It is not at all nervousness or
fear. Seems as if something unknown were possibly lurking
in those bushes, or solitary places. Nay, it is quite certain
there is—some vital unseen presence.

## AN AFTERNOON SCENE

*February* 22.—Last night and to-day rainy and thick, till
mid-afternoon, when the wind chopp'd round, the clouds
swiftly drew off like curtains, the clear appear'd, and with it
the fairest, grandest, most wondrous rainbow I ever saw, all
complete, very vivid at its earth-ends, spreading vast effusions of illuminated haze, violet, yellow, drab-green, in all

directions overhead, through which the sun beam'd an indescribable utterance of color and light, so gorgeous yet so soft,
such as I had never witness'd before. Then its continuance:
a full hour pass'd before the last of those earth-ends disappear'd. The sky behind was all spread in translucent blue,
with many little white clouds and edges. To these a sunset,
filling, dominating the esthetic and soul senses, sumptuously,
tenderly, full. I end this note by the pond, just light enough
to see, through the evening shadows, the western reflections
in its water-mirror surface, with inverted figures of trees. I
hear now and then the *flup* of a pike leaping out, and rippling
the water.

## DISTANT SOUNDS

THE axe of the wood-cutter, the measured thud of a single
threshing-flail, the crowing of chanticleer in the barn-yard,
(with invariable responses from other barn-yards,) and the
lowing of cattle—but most of all, or far or near, the wind—
through the high tree-tops, or through low bushes, laving
one's face and hands so gently, this balmy-bright noon, the
coolest for a long time, (September 2)—I will not call it *sigh-
ing*, for to me it is always a firm, sane, cheery expression,
through a monotone, giving many varieties, or swift or slow,
or dense or delicate. The wind in the patch of pine woods off
there—how sibilant. Or at sea, I can imagine it this moment,
tossing the waves, with spirits of foam flying far, and the free
whistle, and the scent of the salt—and that vast paradox
somehow with all its action and restlessness conveying a
sense of eternal rest.

## A SUN-BATH—NAKEDNESS

*Sunday, August* 27, [1878].—Another day quite free from
mark'd prostration and pain. It seems indeed as if peace and
nutriment from heaven subtly filter into me as I slowly hobble
down these country lanes and across fields, in the good air—
as I sit here in solitude with Nature—open, voiceless, mystic,
far removed, yet palpable, eloquent Nature. I merge myself
in the scene, in the perfect day. Hovering over the clear
brook-water, I am sooth'd by its soft gurgle in one place, and

the hoarser murmurs of its three-foot fall in another. Come, ye disconsolate, in whom any latent eligibility is left—come get the sure virtues of creek-shore, and wood and field. Two months (July and August, '77,) have I absorb'd them, and they begin to make a new man of me. Every day, seclusion— every day at least two or three hours of freedom, bathing, no talk, no bonds, no dress, no books, no *manners*.

Shall I tell you, reader, to what I attribute my already much-restored health? That I have been almost two years, off and on, without drugs and medicines, and daily in the open air. Last summer I found a particularly secluded little dell off one side by my creek, originally a large dug-out marl-pit, now abandon'd, fill'd, with bushes, trees, grass, a group of willows, a straggling bank, and a spring of delicious water running right through the middle of it, with two or three little cascades. Here I retreated every hot day, and follow it up this summer. Here I realize the meaning of that old fellow who said he was seldom less alone than when alone. Never before did I get so close to Nature; never before did she come so close to me. By old habit, I pencill'd down from time to time, almost automatically, moods, sights, hours, tints and outlines, on the spot. Let me specially record the satisfaction of this current forenoon, so serene and primitive, so conventionally exceptional, natural.

An hour or so after breakfast I wended my way down to the recesses of the aforesaid dell, which I and certain thrushes, cat-birds, etc., had all to ourselves. A light south-west wind was blowing through the tree-tops. It was just the place and time for my Adamic air-bath and flesh-brushing from head to foot. So hanging clothes on a rail near by, keeping old broadbrim straw on head and easy shoes on feet, havn't I had a good time the last two hours! First with the stiff-elastic bristles rasping arms, breast, sides, till they turn'd scarlet— then partially bathing in the clear waters of the running brook—taking everything very leisurely, with many rests and pauses—stepping about barefooted every few minutes now and then in some neighboring black ooze, for unctuous mud-bath to my feet—a brief second and third rinsing in the crystal running waters—rubbing with the fragrant towel—slow negligent promenades on the turf up and down in the sun, varied with occasional rests, and further frictions of the bristle-brush—sometimes carrying my portable chair with me from place to place, as my range is quite extensive here, nearly a hundred rods, feeling quite secure from intrusion, (and that indeed I am not at all nervous about, if it accidentally happens).

As I walk'd slowly over the grass, the sun shone out enough to show the shadow moving with me. Somehow I seem'd to get identity with each and every thing around me, in its condition. Nature was naked, and I was also. It was too lazy, soothing, and joyous-equable to speculate about. Yet I might have thought somehow in this vein: Perhaps the inner never-lost rapport we hold with earth, light, air, trees, etc., is not to be realized through eyes and mind only, but through the whole corporeal body, which I will not have blinded or bandaged any more than the eyes. Sweet, sane, still Nakedness in Nature!—ah if poor, sick, prurient humanity in cities might really know you once more! Is not nakedness then indecent? No, not inherently. It is your thought, your sophistication, your fear, your respectability, that is indecent. There come moods when these clothes of ours are not only too irksome to wear, but are themselves indecent. Perhaps indeed he or she to whom the free exhilarating extasy of nakedness in Nature has never been eligible (and how many thousands there are!) has not really known what purity is—nor what faith or art or health really is. (Probably the whole curriculum of first-class philosophy, beauty, heroism, form, illustrated by the old Hellenic race—the highest height and deepest depth known to civilization in those departments—came from their natural and religious idea of Nakedness.)

Many such hours, from time to time, the last two summers —I attribute my partial rehabilitation largely to them. Some good people may think it a feeble or half-crack'd way of spending one's time and thinking. May-be it is.


## THOUGHTS UNDER AN OAK—A DREAM

*June* 2, [1878].—This is the fourth day of a dark northeast storm, wind and rain. Day before yesterday was my birthday. I have now enter'd on my 60th year. Every day of the storm, protected by overshoes and a waterproof blanket, I regularly come down to the pond, and ensconce myself under the lee of the great oak; I am here now writing these lines. The dark smoke-color'd clouds roll in furious silence athwart the sky; the soft green leaves dangle all around me; the wind steadily keeps up its hoarse, soothing music over my head—Nature's mighty whisper. Seated here in solitude I have been musing over my life—connecting events, dates, as links of a chain, neither sadly nor cheerily, but somehow, to-day here under the oak, in the rain, in an unusually matter-of-fact spirit.

But my great oak—sturdy, vital, green—five feet thick at the butt. I sit a great deal near or under him. Then the tulip tree near by—the Apollo of the woods—tall and graceful, yet robust and sinewy, inimitable in hang of foliage and throwing-out of limb; as if the beauteous, vital, leafy creature could walk, if it only would. (I had a sort of dream-trance the other day, in which I saw my favorite trees step out and promenade up, down and around, very curiously—with a whisper from one, leaning down as he pass'd me, *We do all this on the present occasion, exceptionally, just for you.*)

## THREE OF US

*July* 14, [1878].—My two kingfishers still haunt the pond. In the bright sun and breeze and perfect temperature of to-day, noon, I am sitting here by one of the gurgling brooks, dipping a French water-pen in the limpid crystal, and using it to write these lines, again watching the feather'd twain, as they fly and sport athwart the water, so close, almost touching into its surface. Indeed there seem to be three of us. For nearly an hour I indolently look and join them while they dart and turn and take their airy gambols, sometimes far up the creek disappearing for a few moments, and then surely returning again, and performing most of their flight within sight of me, as if they knew I appreciated and absorb'd their vitality, spirituality, faithfulness, and the rapid, vanishing, delicate lines of moving yet quiet electricity they draw for me across the spread of the grass, the trees, and the blue sky.

While the brook babbles, babbles, and the shadows of the boughs dapple in the sunshine around me, and the cool west-by-nor'-west wind faintly soughs in the thick bushes and tree tops.

Among the objects of beauty and interest now beginning to appear quite plentifully in this secluded spot, I notice the humming-bird, the dragon-fly with its wings of slate-color'd gauze, and many varieties of beautiful and plain butterflies, idly flapping among the plants and wild posies. The mullein has shot up out of its nest of broad leaves, to a tall stalk towering sometimes five or six feet high, now studded with knobs of golden blossoms. The milk-weed, (I see a great gorgeous creature of gamboge and black lighting on one as I write,) is in flower, with its delicate red fringe; and there are profuse clusters of a feathery blossom waving in the wind on taper stems. I see lots of these and much else in every direction, as I saunter or sit. For the last half hour a bird has persistently kept up a simple, sweet, melodious song, from the bushes. (I have a positive conviction that some of these birds sing, and others fly and flirt about here for my special benefit.)

## DEATH OF WILLIAM CULLEN BRYANT

*New York City.*—Came on from West Philadelphia, June 13, in the 2 p.m. train to Jersey City, and so across and to my friends, Mr. and Mrs. J. H. J., and their large house, large family (and large hearts,) amid which I feel at home, at peace —away up on Fifth avenue, near Eighty-sixth street, quiet breezy, overlooking the dense woody fringe of the park— plenty of space and sky, birds chirping, and air comparatively fresh and odorless. Two hours before starting, saw the announcement of William Cullen Bryant's funeral, and felt a strong desire to attend. I had known Mr. Bryant over thirty years ago, and he had been markedly kind to me. Off and on, along that time for years as they pass'd, we met and chatted together. I thought him very sociable in his way, and a man to become attach'd to. We were both walkers, and when I work'd in Brooklyn he several times came over, middle of afternoons, and we took rambles miles long, till dark, out towards Bedford or Flatbush, in company. On these occasions he gave me clear accounts of scenes in Europe—the cities, looks, architecture, art, especially Italy—where he had travel'd a good deal.

*June* 14, [1878].—*The Funeral.*—And so the good, stainless, noble old citizen and poet lies in the closed coffin there —and this is his funeral. A solemn, impressive, simple scene, to spirit and senses. The remarkable gathering of gray heads, celebrities—the finely render'd anthem, and other music— the church, dim even now at approaching noon, in its light from the mellow-stain'd windows—the pronounc'd eulogy on the bard who loved Nature so fondly, and sung so well her shows and seasons—ending with these appropriate well-known lines:

> I gazed upon the glorious sky,
>     And the green mountains round,
> And thought that when I came to lie
>     At rest within the ground,
> 'Twere pleasant that in flowery June,
> When brooks send up a joyous tune,
>     And groves a cheerful sound,
> The sexton's hand, my grave to make,
> The rich green mountain turf should break.

## MANHATTAN FROM THE BAY

*June* 25, [1878].— Returned to New York last night. Out to-day on the waters for a sail in the wide bay, southeast of Staten island—a rough, tossing ride, and a free sight—the long stretch of Sandy Hook, the highlands of Navesink, and the many vessels outward and inward bound. We came up through the midst of all, in the full sun. I especially enjoy'd the last hour or two. A moderate sea-breeze had set in; yet over the city, and the waters adjacent, was a thin haze, concealing nothing, only adding to the beauty. From my point of view, as I write amid the soft breeze, with a sea-temperature, surely nothing on earth of its kind can go beyond this show. To the left the North river with its far vista—nearer, three or four war-ships, anchor'd peacefully—the Jersey side, the banks of Weehawken, the Palisades, and the gradually receding blue, lost in the distance—to the right the East river—the

mast-hemm'd shores—the grand obelisk-like towers of the
bridge, one on either side, in haze, yet plainly defin'd, giant
brothers twain, throwing free graceful interlinking loops high
across the tumbled tumultuous current below—(the tide is
just changing to its ebb)—the broad water-spread everywhere
crowded—no, not crowded, but thick as stars in the sky—
with all sorts and sizes of sail and steam vessels, plying ferry-
boats, arriving and departing coasters, great ocean Dons,
iron-black, modern, magnificent in size and power, fill'd with
their incalculable value of human life and precious merchandise—with here and there, above all, those daring, careening
things of grace and wonder, those white and shaded swift-
darting fish-birds, (I wonder if shore or sea elsewhere can
outvie them,) ever with their slanting spars, and fierce, pure,
hawk-like beauty and motion—first-class New York sloop or
schooner yachts, sailing, this fine day, the free sea in a good
wind. And rising out of the midst, tall-topt, ship-hemm'd,
modern, American, yet strangely oriental, V-shaped Manhattan, with its compact mass, its spires, its cloud-touching
edifices group'd at the centre—the green of the trees, and all
the white, brown and gray of the architecture well blended,
as I see it, under a miracle of limpid sky, delicious light of
heaven above, and June haze on the surface below.

## HUMAN AND HEROIC NEW YORK

The general subjective view of New York and Brooklyn—
(will not the time hasten when the two shall be municipally
united in one, and named Manhattan?)—what I may call the
human interior and exterior of these great seething oceanic
populations, as I get it in this visit, is to me best of all. After
an absence of many years, (I went away at the outbreak of
the secession war, and have never been back to stay since,)
again I resume with curiosity the crowds, the streets, I knew
so well, Broadway, the ferries, the west side of the city, democratic Bowery—human appearances and manners as seen in
all these, and along the wharves, and in the perpetual travel
of the horse-cars, or the crowded excursion steamers, or in
Wall and Nassau streets by day—in the places of amusement
at night—bubbling and whirling and moving like its own en-

vironment of waters—endless humanity in all phases—
Brooklyn also—taken in for the last three weeks. No need to
specify minutely—enough to say that (making all allowances
for the shadows and side-streaks of a million-headed-city)
the brief total of the impressions, the human qualities, of
these vast cities, is to me comforting, even heroic, beyond
statement. Alertness, generally fine physique, clear eyes that
look straight at you, a singular combination of reticence and
self-possession, with good nature and friendliness—a prevailing range of according manners, taste and intellect, surely
beyond any elsewhere upon earth—and a palpable outcropping of that personal comradeship I look forward to as the
subtlest, strongest future hold of this many-item'd Union—
are not only constantly visible here in these mighty channels
of men, but they form the rule and average. To-day, I should
say—defiant of cynics and pessimists, and with a full knowledge of all their exceptions—an appreciative and perceptive
study of the current humanity of New York gives the direct-
est proof yet of successful Democracy, and of the solution of
that paradox, the eligibility of the free and fully developed
individual with the paramount aggregate. In old age, lame
and sick, pondering for years on many a doubt and danger
for this republic of ours—fully aware of all that can be said
on the other side—I find in this visit to New York, and the
daily contact and rapport with its myriad people, on the scale
of the oceans and tides, the best, most effective medicine my
soul has yet partaken—the grandest physical habitat and
surroundings of land and water the globe affords—namely,
Manhattan island and Brooklyn, which the future shall join
in one city—city of superb democracy, amid superb surroundings.

## HOURS FOR THE SOUL

*July* 22*d*, 1878.—Living down in the country again. A wonderful conjunction of all that goes to make those sometime
miracle-hours after sunset—so near and yet so far. Perfect,
or nearly perfect days, I notice, are not so very uncommon;
but the combinations that make perfect nights are few, even
in a life time. We have one of those perfections to-night.

Sunset left things pretty clear; the larger stars were visible soon as the shades allow'd. A while after 8, three or four great black clouds suddenly rose, seemingly from different points, and sweeping with broad swirls of wind but no thunder, underspread the orbs from view everywhere, and indicated a violent heat-storm. But without storm, clouds, blackness and all, sped and vanish'd as suddenly as they had risen; and from a little after 9 till 11 the atmosphere and the whole show above were in that state of exceptional clearness and glory just alluded to. In the northwest turned the Great Dipper with its pointers round the Cynosure. A little south of east the constellation of the Scorpion was fully up, with red Antares glowing in its neck; while dominating, majestic Jupiter swam, an hour and a half risen, in the east—(no moon till after 11.) A large part of the sky seem'd just laid in great splashes of phosphorus. You could look deeper in, farther through, than usual; the orbs thick as heads of wheat in a field. Not that there was any special brilliancy either— nothing near as sharp as I have seen of keen winter nights, but a curious general luminousness throughout to sight, sense, and soul. The latter had much to do with it. (I am convinced there are hours of Nature, especially of the atmosphere, mornings and evenings, address'd to the soul. Night transcends, for that purpose, what the proudest day can do.) Now, indeed, if never before, the heavens declared the glory of God. It was to the full sky of the Bible, of Arabia, of the prophets, and of the oldest poems. There, in abstraction and stillness, (I had gone off by myself to absorb the scene, to have the spell unbroken,) the copiousness, the removedness, vitality, loose-clear-crowdedness, of that stellar concave spreading overhead, softly absorb'd into me, rising so free, interminably high, stretching east, west, north, south—and I, though but a point in the centre below, embodying all.

As if for the first time, indeed, creation noiselessly sank into and through me its placid and untellable lesson, beyond —O, so infinitely beyond!—anything from art, books, sermons, or from science, old or new. The spirit's hour—religion's hour—the visible suggestion of God in space and time —now once definitely indicated, if never again. The untold pointed at—the heavens all paved with it. The Milky Way, as if some superhuman symphony, some ode of universal vagueness, disdaining syllable and sound—a flashing glance of Deity, address'd to the soul. All silently—the indescribable night and stars—far off and silently.

THE DAWN.—*July* 23.—This morning, between one and two hours before sunrise, a spectacle wrought on the same background, yet of quite different beauty and meaning. The moon well up in the heavens, and past her half, is shining brightly—the air and sky of that cynical-clear, Minerva-like quality, virgin cool—not the weight of sentiment or mystery, or passion's ecstasy indefinable—not the religious sense, the varied All, distill'd and sublimated into one, of the night just described. Every star now clear-cut, showing for just what it is, there in the colorless ether. The character of the heralded morning, ineffably sweet and fresh and limpid, but for the esthetic sense alone, and for purity without sentiment. I have itemized the night—but dare I attempt the cloudless dawn? (What subtle tie is this between one's soul and the break of day? Alike, and yet no two nights or morning shows ever exactly alike.) Preceded by an immense star, almost unearthly in its effusion of white splendor, with two or three long unequal spoke-rays of diamond radiance, shedding down through the fresh morning air below—an hour of this, and then the sunrise.

THE EAST.—What a subject for a poem! Indeed, where else a more pregnant, more splendid one? Where one more idealistic-real, more subtle, more sensuous-delicate? The East, answering all lands, all ages, peoples; touching all senses, here, immediate, now—and yet so indescribably far off—such retrospect! The East—long-stretching—so losing itself—the orient, the gardens of Asia, the womb of history and song—forth-issuing all those strange, dim cavalcades—

Florid with blood, pensive, rapt with musings, hot with passion,
Sultry with perfume, with ample and flowing garments,
With sunburnt visage, intense soul and glittering eyes.

Always the East—old, how incalculably old! And yet here the same—ours yet, fresh as a rose, to every morning, every life, to-day—and always will be.

*September* 17.—Another presentation—same theme—just before sunrise again, (a favorite hour with me.) The clear gray sky, a faint glow in the dull liver-color of the east, the cool fresh odor and the moisture—the cattle and horses off there grazing in the fields—the star Venus again, two hours high. For sounds, the chirping of crickets in the grass, the clarion of chanticleer, and the distant cawing of an early crow. Quietly over the dense fringe of cedars and pines rises that dazzling, red, transparent disk of flame, and the low sheets of white vapor roll and roll into dissolution.

THE MOON.—*May* 18.—I went to bed early last night, but found myself waked shortly after 12, and, turning awhile, sleepless and mentally feverish, I rose, dress'd myself, sallied forth and walk'd down the lane. The full moon, some three or four hours up—a sprinkle of light and less-light clouds just lazily moving—Jupiter an hour high in the east, and here and there throughout the heavens a random star appearing and disappearing. So beautifully veiled and varied—the air, with that early-summer perfume, not at all damp or raw—at times Luna languidly emerging in richest brightness for minutes, and then partially envelop'd again. Far off a poor whip-poor-will plied his notes incessantly. It was that silent time between 1 and 3.

The rare nocturnal scene, how soon it sooth'd and pacified me! Is there not something about the moon, some relation or reminder, which no poem or literature has yet caught? (In very old and primitive ballads I have come across lines or asides that suggest it.) After a while the clouds mostly clear'd, and as the moon swam on, she carried, shimmering and shifting, delicate color-effects of pellucid green and tawny vapor. Let me conclude this part with an extract, (some writer in the *Tribune*, May 16, 1878:)

"No one ever gets tired of the moon. Goddess that she is by dower of her eternal beauty, she is a true woman by her tact—knows the charm of being seldom seen, of coming by surprise and staying but a little while; never wears the same dress two nights running, nor all night the same way; commends herself to the matter-of-fact people by her usefulness, and makes her uselessness adored by poets, artists, and all lovers in all lands; lends herself to every symbolism and to every emblem; is Diana's bow and Venus's mirror and Mary's throne; is a sickle, a scarf, an eyebrow, his face or her face, and look'd at by her or by him; is the madman's hell, the poet's heaven, the baby's toy, the philosopher's study; and while her admirers follow her footsteps, and hang on her lovely looks, she knows how to keep her woman's secret—her other side —unguess'd and unguessable."

*Furthermore. February* 19, 1880.—Just before 10 p.m. cold and entirely clear again, the show overhead, bearing southwest, of wonderful and crowded magnificence. The moon in her third quarter—the clusters of the Hyades and Pleiades, with the planet Mars between—in full crossing sprawl in the sky the great Egyptian X, (Sirius, Procyon, and the main stars in the constellations of the Ship, the Dove, and of Orion;) just north of east Boötes, and in his knee Arcturus, an hour high, mounting the heaven, ambitiously large and sparkling, as if he meant to challenge with Sirius the stellar supremacy.

With the sentiment of the stars and moon such nights I get all the free margins and indefiniteness of music or poetry, fused in geometry's utmost exactness.

## STRAW-COLOR'D AND OTHER PSYCHES

*August* 4, [1878].—A pretty sight! Where I sit in the shade— a warm day, the sun shining from cloudless skies, the forenoon well advanc'd—I look over a ten-acre field of luxuriant clover-hay, (the second crop)—the livid-ripe red blossoms and dabs of August brown thickly spotting the prevailing dark-green. Over all flutter myriads of light-yellow butterflies, mostly skimming along the surface, dipping and oscillating, giving a curious animation to the scene. The beautiful, spiritual insects! straw-color'd Psyches! Occasionally one of them leaves his mates, and mounts, perhaps spirally, perhaps in a straight line in the air, fluttering up, up, till literally out of sight. In the lane as I came along just now I noticed one spot, ten feet square or so, where more than a hundred had collected, holding a revel, a gyration-dance, or butterfly good-time, winding and circling, down and across, but always keeping within the limits. The little creatures have come out all of a sudden the last few days, and are now very plentiful. As I sit outdoors, or walk, I hardly look around without somewhere seeing two (always two) fluttering through the air in amorous dalliance. Then their inimitable color, their fragility, peculiar motion—and that strange, frequent way of one leaving the crowd and mounting up, up in the free ether, and apparently never returning. As I look over the field, these yellow-wings everywhere mildly sparkling, many snowy blossoms of the wild carrot gracefully bending on their tall and taper stems—while for sounds, the distant guttural screech of a flock of guinea-hens comes shrilly yet somehow musically to my ears. And now a faint growl of heat-thunder in the north—and ever the low rising and falling wind-purr from the tops of the maples and willows.

## DEATH OF ABRAHAM LINCOLN

LECTURE *deliver'd in New York, April* 14, 1879—*in Philadelphia,* '80—*in Boston,* '81

How often since that dark and dripping Saturday—that chilly April day, now fifteen years bygone—my heart has entertain'd the dream, the wish, to give of Abraham Lincoln's death, its own special thought and memorial. Yet now the sought-for opportunity offers, I find my notes incompetent, (why, for truly profound themes, is statement so idle? why does the right phrase never offer?) and the fit tribute I dream'd of, waits unprepared as ever. My talk here indeed is less because of itself or anything in it, and nearly altogether because I feel a desire, apart from any talk, to specify the day, the martyrdom. It is for this, my friends, I have call'd you together. Oft as the rolling years bring back this hour, let it again, however briefly, be dwelt upon. For my own part, I hope and desire, till my own dying day, whenever the 14th or 15th of April comes, to annually gather a few friends, and hold its tragic reminiscence. No narrow or sectional reminiscence. It belongs to these States in their entirety—not the North only, but the South—perhaps belongs most tenderly and devoutly to the South, of all; for there, really, this man's birth-stock. There and thence his antecedent stamp. Why should I not say that thence his manliest traits—his universality—his canny, easy ways and words upon the surface—his inflexible determination and courage at heart?

Have you never realized it, my friends, that Lincoln, though grafted on the West, is essentially, in personnel and character, a Southern contribution?

And though by no means proposing to resume the secession war to-night, I would briefly remind you of the public conditions preceding that contest. For twenty years, and especially during the four or five before the war actually began, the aspect of affairs in the United States, though without the flash of military excitement, presents more than the survey of a battle, or any extended campaign, or series, even of Nature's convulsions. The hot passions of the South—the strange mixture at the North of inertia, incredulity, and conscious power—the incendiarism of the abolitionists—the rascality and *grip* of the politicians, unparallel'd in any land, any age. To these I must not omit adding the honesty of the essential bulk of the people everywhere—yet with all the seething fury and contradiction of their natures more arous'd than the Atlantic's waves in wildest equinox. In politics, what can be more ominous, (though generally unappreciated then)—what more significant than the Presidentiads of Fillmore and Buchanan? proving conclusively that the weakness and wickedness of elected rulers are just as likely to afflict us here, as in the countries of the Old World, under their monarchies, emperors, and aristocracies. In that Old World were everywhere heard underground rumblings, that died out, only to again surely return. While in America the volcano, though civic yet, continued to grow more and more convulsive—more and more stormy and threatening.

In the height of all this excitement and chaos, hovering on the edge at first, and then merged in its very midst, and destined to play a leading part, appears a strange and awkward figure. I shall not easily forget the first time I ever saw Abraham Lincoln. It must have been about the 18th or 19th of February, 1861. It was rather a pleasant afternoon, in New York city, as he arrived there from the West, to remain a few hours, and then pass on to Washington, to prepare for his inauguration. I saw him in Broadway, near the site of the present Post-office. He came down, I think from Canal street, to stop at the Astor House. The broad spaces, sidewalks, and street in the neighborhood, and for some distance, were crowded with solid masses of people, many thousands. The omnibuses and other vehicles had all been turn'd off, leaving an unusual hush in that busy part of the city. Presently two or three shabby hack barouches made their way with some difficulty through the crowd, and drew up at the Astor House entrance. A tall figure stepp'd out of the centre of these barouches, paus'd leisurely on the sidewalk, look'd up at the granite walls and looming architecture of the grand old hotel —then, after a relieving stretch of arms and legs, turn'd round for over a minute to slowly and good-humoredly scan the appearance of the vast and silent crowds. There were no speeches—no compliments—no welcome—as far as I could hear, not a word said. Still much anxiety was conceal'd in that quiet. Cautious persons had fear'd some mark'd insult or indignity to the President-elect—for he possess'd no personal popularity at all in New York city, and very little political. But it was evidently tacitly agreed that if the few political supporters of Mr. Lincoln present would entirely abstain from any demonstration on their side, the immense majority, who were anything but supporters, would abstain on their side also. The result was a sulky, unbroken silence, such as certainly never before characterized so great a New York crowd.

Almost in the same neighborhood I distinctly remember'd seeing Lafayette on his visit to America in 1825. I had also personally seen and heard, various years afterward, how Andrew Jackson, Clay, Webster, Hungarian Kossuth, Filibuster Walker, the Prince of Wales on his visit, and other celebres, native and foreign, had been welcom'd there—all that indescribable human roar and magnetism, unlike any other sound in the universe—the glad exulting thunder-shouts of countless unloos'd throats of men! But on this occasion, not a voice—not a sound. From the top of an omnibus, (driven up one side, close by, and block'd by the curbstone and the crowds,) I had, I say, a capital view of it all, and especially of Mr. Lincoln, his look and gait—his perfect composure and coolness—his unusual and uncouth height, his dress of complete black, stovepipe hat push'd back on the head, dark-brown complexion, seam'd and wrinkled yet canny-looking face, black, bushy head of hair, disproportionately long neck, and his hands held behind as he stood observing the people. He look'd with curiosity upon that immense sea of faces, and the sea of faces return'd the look with similar curiosity. In both there was a dash of comedy, almost farce, such as Shakspere puts in his blackest tragedies. The crowd that hemm'd around consisted I should think of thirty to forty thousand men, not a single one his personal friend—while I have no doubt, (so frenzied were the ferments of the time,) many an assassin's knife and pistol lurk'd in hip or breast-pocket there, ready, soon as break and riot came.

But no break or riot came. The tall figure gave another relieving stretch or two of arms and legs; then with moderate pace, and accompanied by a few unknown-looking persons, ascended the portico-steps of the Astor House, disappear'd through its broad entrance—and the dumb-show ended.

I saw Abraham Lincoln often the four years following that date. He changed rapidly and much during his Presidency— but this scene, and him in it, are indelibly stamp'd upon my recollection. As I sat on the top of my omnibus, and had a good view of him, the thought, dim and inchoate then, has since come out clear enough, that four sorts of genius, four mighty and primal hands, will be needed to the complete limning of this man's future portrait—the eyes and brains and finger-touch of Plutarch and Eschylus and Michel Angelo, assisted by Rabelais.

And now—(Mr. Lincoln passing on from this scene to Washington, where he was inaugurated, amid armed cavalry, and sharpshooters at every point—the first instance of the kind in our history—and I hope it will be the last)—now the rapid succession of well-known events, (too well known—I believe, these days, we almost hate to hear them mention'd) —the national flag fired on at Sumter—the uprising of the North, in paroxysms of astonishment and rage—the chaos of divided councils—the call for troops—the first Bull Run— the stunning cast-down, shock, and dismay of the North— and so in full flood the secession war. Four years of lurid, bleeding, murky, murderous war. Who paint those years, with all their scenes?—the hard-fought engagements—the defeats, plans, failures—the gloomy hours, days, when our Nationality seem'd hung in pall of doubt, perhaps death—

the Mephistophelean sneers of foreign lands and attachés—the dreaded Scylla of European interference, and the Charybdis of the tremendously dangerous latent strata of secession sympathizers throughout the free States, (far more numerous than is supposed)—the long marches in summer—the hot sweat, and many a sunstroke, as on the rush to Gettysburg in '63—the night battles in the woods, as under Hooker at Chancellorsville—the camps in winter—the military prisons —the hospitals—(alas! alas! the hospitals.)

The secession war? Nay, let me call it the Union war. Though whatever call'd, it is even yet too near us—too vast and too closely overshadowing—its branches unform'd yet, (but certain,) shooting too far into the future—and the most indicative and mightiest of them yet ungrown. A great literature will yet arise out of the era of those four years, those scenes—era compressing centuries of native passion, first-class pictures, tempests of life and death—an inexhaustible mine for the histories, drama, romance, and even philosophy, of peoples to come—indeed the verteber of poetry and art, (of personal character too,) for all future America—far more grand, in my opinion, to the hands capable of it, than Homer's siege of Troy, or the French wars to Shakspere.

But I must leave these speculations, and come to the theme I have assign'd and limited myself to. Of the actual murder of President Lincoln, though so much has been written, probably the facts are yet very indefinite in most persons' minds. I read from my memoranda, written at the time, and revised frequently and finally since.

The day, April 14, 1865, seems to have been a pleasant one throughout the whole land—the moral atmosphere pleasant too—the long storm, so dark, so fratricidal, full of blood and doubt and gloom, over and ended at last by the sun-rise of such an absolute National victory, and utter break-down of Secessionism—we almost doubted our own senses! Lee had capitulated beneath the apple-tree of Appomattox. The other armies, the flanges of the revolt, swiftly follow'd. And could it really be, then? Out of all the affairs of this world of woe and failure and disorder, was there really come the confirm'd, unerring sign of plan, like a shaft of pure light—of rightful rule—of God? So the day, as I say, was propitious.

Early herbage, early flowers, were out. (I remember where I was stopping at the time, the season being advanced, there were many lilacs in full bloom. By one of those caprices that enter and give tinge to events without being at all a part of them, I find myself always reminded of the great tragedy of that day by the sight and odor of these blossoms. It never fails.)

But I must not dwell on accessories. The deed hastens. The popular afternoon paper of Washington, the little *Evening Star*, had spatter'd all over its third page, divided among the advertisements in a sensational manner, in a hundred different places, *The President and his Lady will be at the Theatre this evening.* . . . (Lincoln was fond of the theatre. I have myself seen him there several times. I remember thinking how funny it was that he, in some respects the leading actor in the stormiest drama known to real history's stage through centuries, should sit there and be so completely interested and absorb'd in those human jack-straws, moving about with their silly little gestures, foreign spirit, and flatulent text.)

On this occasion the theatre was crowded, many ladies in rich and gay costumes, officers in their uniforms, many well-known citizens, young folks, the usual clusters of gas-lights, the usual magnetism of so many people, cheerful, with perfumes, music of violins and flutes—(and over all, and saturating all, that vast, vague wonder, *Victory*, the nation's victory, the triumph of the Union, filling the air, the thought, the sense, with exhilaration more than all music and perfumes.)

The President came betimes, and, with his wife, witness'd the play from the large stage-boxes of the second tier, two thrown into one, and profusely drap'd with the national flag. The acts and scenes of the piece—one of those singularly written compositions which have at least the merit of giving entire relief to an audience engaged in mental action or business excitements and cares during the day, as it makes not the slightest call on either the moral, emotional, esthetic, or spiritual nature—a piece, (*Our American Cousin,*) in which, among other characters, so call'd, a Yankee, certainly such a one as was never seen, or the least like it ever seen, in North America, is introduced in England, with a varied fol-de-rol of talk, plot, scenery, and such phantasmagoria as goes to make up a modern popular drama—had progress'd through perhaps a couple of its acts, when in the midst of this comedy, or non-such, or whatever it is to be call'd, and to offset it, or finish it out, as if in Nature's and the great Muse's mockery of those poor mimes, came interpolated that scene, not really or exactly to be described at all, (for on the many hundreds who were there it seems to this hour to have left a passing blur, a dream, a blotch)—and yet partially to be described as I now proceed to give it. There is a scene in the play representing a modern parlor, in which two unprecedented English ladies are inform'd by the impossible Yankee that he is not a man of fortune, and therefore undesirable for marriage-catching purposes; after which, the comments being finish'd, the dramatic trio make exit, leaving the stage clear for a moment. At this period came the murder of Abraham Lincoln. Great as all its manifold train, circling round it, and stretching into the future for many a century, in the politics, history, art, etc., of the New World, in point of fact the main thing, the actual murder, transpired with the quiet and simplicity of any commonest occurrence—the bursting of a bud or pod in the growth of vegetation, for instance. Through the general hum following the stage pause, with the change of positions, came the muffled sound of a pistol-shot, which not one-hundredth part of the audience heard at the time—and yet a moment's hush—somehow, surely, a vague startled thrill—and then, through the ornamented, draperied, starr'd and striped space-way of the President's box, a sudden figure, a man, raises himself with hands and feet, stands a moment on the railing, leaps below to the stage, (a distance of perhaps fourteen or fifteen feet,) falls out of position, catching his boot-heel in the copious drapery, (the American flag,) falls on one knee, quickly recovers himself, rises as if nothing had happen'd, (he really sprains his ankle, but unfelt then)—and so the figure, Booth, the murderer, dress'd in plain black broadcloth, bare-headed, with full, glossy, raven hair, and his eyes like some mad animal's flashing with light and resolution, yet with a certain strange calmness, holds aloft in one hand a large knife—walks along not much back from the footlights—turns fully toward the audience his face of sta-

tuesque beauty, lit by those basilisk eyes, flashing with desperation, perhaps insanity—launches out in a firm and steady
voice the words *Sic semper tyrannis*—and then walks with
neither slow nor very rapid pace diagonally across to the
back of the stage, and disappears. (Had not all this terrible
scene—making the mimic ones preposterous—had it not all
been rehears'd, in blank, by Booth, beforehand?)

A moment's hush—a scream—the cry of *murder*—Mrs.
Lincoln leaning out of the box, with ashy cheeks and lips,
with involuntary cry, pointing to the retreating figure, *He has
kill'd the President.* And still a moment's strange, incredul-
ous suspense—and then the deluge!—then that mixture of
horror, noises, uncertainty—(the sound, somewhere back, of
a horse's hoofs clattering with speed)—the people burst
through chairs and railings, and break them up—there is inextricable confusion and terror—women faint—quite feeble
persons fall, and are trampl'd on—many cries of agony are
heard—the broad stage suddenly fills to suffocation with a
dense and motley crowd, like some horrible carnival—the
audience rush generally upon it, at least the strong men do—
the actors and actresses are all there in their play-costumes
and painted faces, with mortal fright showing through the
rouge—the screams and calls, confused talk—redoubled,
trebled—two or three manage to pass up water from the stage
to the President's box—others try to clamber up—etc., etc.

In the midst of all this, the soldiers of the President's guard,
with others, suddenly drawn to the scene, burst in—(some
two hundred altogether)—they storm the house, through all
the tiers, especially the upper ones, inflam'd with fury, literally charging the audience with fix'd bayonets, muskets and
pistols, shouting *Clear out! clear out! you sons of* ——. . . .
Such the wild scene, or a suggestion of it rather, inside the
play-house that night.

Outside, too, in the atmosphere of shock and craze,
crowds of people, fill'd with frenzy, ready to seize any outlet
for it, come near committing murder several times on innocent individuals. One such case was especially exciting. The
infuriated crowd, through some chance, got started against
one man, either for words he utter'd, or perhaps without any
cause at all, and were proceeding at once to actually hang

him on a neighboring lamp-post, when he was rescued by a few heroic policemen, who placed him in their midst, and fought their way slowly and amid great peril toward the station house. It was a fitting episode of the whole affair. The crowd rushing and eddying to and fro—the night, the yells, the pale faces, many frighten'd people trying in vain to extricate themselves—the attack'd man, not yet freed from the jaws of death, looking like a corpse—the silent, resolute, half-dozen policemen, with no weapons but their little clubs, yet stern and steady through all those eddying swarms— made a fitting side-scene to the grand tragedy of the murder. They gain'd the station house with the protected man, whom they placed in security for the night, and discharged him in the morning.

And in the midst of that pandemonium, infuriated soldiers, the audience and the crowd, the stage, and all its actors and actresses, its paint-pots, spangles, and gas-lights—the life blood from those veins, the best and sweetest of the land, drips slowly down, and death's ooze already begins its little bubbles on the lips.

Thus the visible incidents and surroundings of Abraham Lincoln's murder, as they really occur'd. Thus ended the attempted secession of these States; thus the four years' war. But the main things come subtly and invisibly afterward, perhaps long afterward—neither military, political, nor (great as those are,) historical. I say, certain secondary and indirect results, out of the tragedy of this death, are, in my opinion, greatest. Not the event of the murder itself. Not that Mr. Lincoln strings the principal points and personages of the period, like beads, upon the single string of his career. Not that his idiosyncrasy, in its sudden appearance and disappearance, stamps this Republic with a stamp more mark'd and enduring than any yet given by any one man—(more even than Washington's;)—but, join'd with these, the immeasurable value and meaning of that whole tragedy lies, to me, in senses finally dearest to a nation, (and here all our own)—the imaginative and artistic senses—the literary and dramatic ones. Not in any common or low meaning of those terms, but a meaning precious to the race, and to every age. A long and varied series of contradictory events arrives at

last at its highest poetic, single, central, pictorial denouement. The whole involved, baffling, multiform whirl of the
secession period comes to a head, and is gather'd in one brief
flash of lightning-illumination—one simple, fierce deed. Its
sharp culmination, and as it were solution, of so many bloody
and angry problems, illustrates those climax-moments on the
stage of universal Time, where the historic Muse at one entrance, and the tragic Muse at the other, suddenly ringing
down the curtain, close an immense act in the long drama of
creative thought, and give it radiation, tableau, stranger than
fiction. Fit radiation—fit close! How the imagination—how
the student loves these things! America, too, is to have them.
For not in all great deaths, nor far or near—not Cæsar in the
Roman senate-house, or Napoleon passing away in the wild
night-storm at St. Helena—not Paleologus, falling, desperately fighting, piled over dozens deep with Grecian corpses—
not calm old Socrates, drinking the hemlock—outvies that
terminus of the secession war, in one man's life, here in our
midst, in our own time—that seal of the emancipation of
three million slaves—that parturition and delivery of our at
last really free Republic, born again, henceforth to commence its career of genuine homogeneous Union, compact,
consistent with itself.

Nor will ever future American Patriots and Unionists, indifferently over the whole land, or North or South, find a
better moral to their lesson. The final use of the greatest men
of a Nation is, after all, not with reference to their deeds in
themselves, or their direct bearing on their times or lands.
The final use of a heroic-eminent life—especially of a heroic-
eminent death—is its indirect filtering into the nation and the
race, and to give, often at many removes, but unerringly, age
after age, color and fibre to the personalism of the youth and
maturity of that age, and of mankind. Then there is a cement
to the whole people, subtler, more underlying, than any thing
in written constitution, or courts or armies—namely, the
cement of a death identified thoroughly with that people, at
its head, and for its sake. Strange, (is it not?) that battles,
martyrs, agonies, blood, even assassination, should so condense—perhaps only really, lastingly condense—a Nationality.

I repeat it—the grand deaths of the race—the dramatic

deaths of every nationality—are its most important inherit-
ance-value—in some respects beyond its literature and art—
(as the hero is beyond his finest portrait, and the battle itself
beyond its choicest song or epic.) Is not here indeed the
point underlying all tragedy? the famous pieces of the
Grecian masters—and all masters? Why, if the old Greeks
had had this man, what trilogies of plays—what epics—
would have been made out of him! How the rhapsodes
would have recited him! How quickly that quaint tall form
would have enter'd into the region where men vitalize gods,
and gods divinify men! But Lincoln, his times, his death—
great as any, any age—belong altogether to our own, and
our autochthonic. (Sometimes indeed I think our American
days, our own stage—the actors we know and have shaken
hands, or talk'd with—more fateful than any thing in Eschylus—more heroic than the fighters around Troy—afford
kings of men for our Democracy prouder than Agamemnon
—models of character cute and hardy as Ulysses—deaths
more pitiful than Priam's.)

When, centuries hence, (as it must, in my opinion, be centuries hence before the life of these States, or of Democracy,
can be really written and illustrated,) the leading historians
and dramatists seek for some personage, some special event,
incisive enough to mark with deepest cut, and mnemonize,
this turbulent Nineteenth century of ours, (not only these
States, but all over the political and social world)—something, perhaps, to close that gorgeous procession of European feudalism, with all its pomp and caste-prejudices, (of
whose long train we in America are yet so inextricably the
heirs)—something to identify with terrible identification, by
far the greatest revolutionary step in the history of the
United States, (perhaps the greatest of the world, our century)—the absolute extirpation and erasure of slavery from
the States—those historians will seek in vain for any point to
serve more thoroughly their purpose, than Abraham Lincoln's death.

Dear to the Muse—thrice dear to Nationality—to the
whole human race—precious to this Union—precious to
Democracy—unspeakably and forever precious—their first
great Martyr Chief.

## AN EGOTISTICAL "FIND"

"I HAVE found the law of my own poems," was the unspoken but more-and-more decided feeling that came to me as I pass'd, hour after hour, amid all this grim yet joyous elemental abandon—this plenitude of material, entire absence of art, untrammel'd play of primitive Nature—the chasm, the gorge, the crystal mountain stream, repeated scores, hundreds of miles—the broad handling and absolute uncramped-ness—the fantastic forms, bathed in transparent browns, faint reds and grays, towering sometimes a thousand, sometimes two or three thousand feet high—at their tops now and then huge masses pois'd, and mixing with the clouds, with only their outlines, hazed in misty lilac, visible. ("In Nature's grandest shows," said an old Dutch writer, an ecclesiastic, "amid the ocean's depth, if so might be, or countless worlds rolling above at night, a man thinks of them, weighs all, not for themselves or the abstract, but with reference to his own personality, and how they may affect him or color his destinies.")

## THE PRAIRIES AND GREAT PLAINS IN POETRY

### (*After traveling Illinois, Missouri, Kansas and Colorado*)

GRAND as is the thought that doubtless the child is already born who will see a hundred millions of people, the most prosperous and advanc'd of the world, inhabiting these Prairies, the great Plains, and the valley of the Mississippi, I could not help thinking it would be grander still to see all those inimitable American areas fused in the alembic of a perfect poem, or other esthetic work, entirely western, fresh and limitless—altogether our own, without a trace or taste of Europe's soil, reminiscence, technical letter or spirit. My days and nights, as I travel here—what an exhilaration!—not the air alone, and the sense of vastness, but every local sight and feature. Everywhere something characteristic—the cactuses, pinks, buffalo grass, wild sage—the receding perspective, and the far circle-line of the horizon all times of day, especially forenoon—the clear, pure, cool, rarefied nutriment for the lungs, previously quite unknown—the black patches and streaks left by surface-conflagrations—the deep-plough'd furrow of the "fire-guard"—the slanting snow-racks built all along to shield the railroad from winter drifts—the prairie-dogs and the herds of antelope—the curious "dry rivers"—occasionally a "dug-out" or corral—Fort Riley and Fort Wallace—those towns of the northern plains, (like ships on the sea,) Eagle-Tail, Coyotè, Cheyenne, Agate, Monotony, Kit Carson—with ever the ant-hill and the buffalo-wallow—ever the herds of cattle and the cow-boys ("cow-punchers") to me a strangely interesting class, bright-eyed as hawks, with their swarthy complexions and their broad-brimm'd hats—apparently always on horseback, with loose arms slightly raised and swinging as they ride.

## AMERICA'S CHARACTERISTIC LANDSCAPE

SPEAKING generally as to the capacity and sure future destiny of that plain and prairie area (larger than any European kingdom) it is the inexhaustible land of wheat, maize, wool, flax, coal, iron, beef and pork, butter and cheese, apples and grapes—land of ten million virgin farms—to the eye at present wild and unproductive—yet experts say that upon it when irrigated may easily be grown enough wheat to feed the world. Then as to scenery (giving my own thought and feeling,) while I know the standard claim is that Yosemite, Niagara falls, the upper Yellowstone and the like, afford the greatest natural shows, I am not so sure but the Prairies and the Plains, while less stunning at first sight, last longer, fill the esthetic sense fuller, precede all the rest, and make North America's characteristic landscape.

Indeed through the whole of this journey, with all its shows and varieties, what most impress'd me, and will longest remain with me, are these same prairies. Day after day, and night after night, to my eyes, to all my senses—the esthetic one most of all—they silently and broadly unfolded. Even their simplest statistics are sublime.

## EARTH'S MOST IMPORTANT STREAM

THE valley of the Mississippi river and its tributaries, (this stream and its adjuncts involve a big part of the question,) comprehends more than twelve hundred thousand square miles, the greater part prairies. It is by far the most important stream on the globe, and would seem to have been marked out by design, slow-flowing from north to south, through a dozen climates, all fitted for man's healthy occupancy, its outlet unfrozen all the year, and its line forming a safe, cheap continental avenue for commerce and passage from the north temperate to the torrid zone. Not even the mighty Amazon (though larger in volume) on its line of east and west—not the Nile in Africa, nor the Danube in Europe, nor the three great rivers of China, compare with it. Only the Mediterranean sea has play'd some such part in history, and all through the past, as the Mississippi is destined to play in the future. By its demesnes, water'd and welded by its branches, the Missouri, the Ohio, the Arkansas, the Red, the Yazzo, the St. Francis and others, it already compacts twenty-five millions of people, not merely the most peaceful and money-making, but the most restless and warlike on earth. Its valley, or reach, is rapidly concentrating the political power of the American Union. One almost thinks it *is* the Union—or soon will be. Take it out, with its radiations, and what would be left? From the car windows through Indiana, Illinois, Missouri, or stopping some days along the Topeka and Santa Fe road, in southern Kansas, and indeed wherever I went, hundreds and thousands of miles through this region, my eyes feasted on primitive and rich meadows, some of them partially inhabited, but far, immensely far more untouch'd, unbroken—and much of it more lovely and fertile in its unplough'd innocence than the fair and valuable fields of New York's, Pennsylvania's, Maryland's or Virginia's richest farms.

## MISSISSIPPI VALLEY LITERATURE

LYING by one rainy day in Missouri to rest after quite a long exploration—first trying a big volume I found there of "Milton, Young, Gray, Beattie and Collins", but giving it up for a bad job—enjoying however for awhile, as often before, the reading of Walter Scott's poems, *Lay of the Last Minstrel*, *Marmion*, and so on—I stopp'd and laid down the book, and ponder'd the thought of a poetry that should in due time express and supply the teeming region I was in the midst of, and have briefly touch'd upon. One's mind needs but a moment's deliberation anywhere in the United States to see clearly enough that all the prevalent book and library poets, either as imported from Great Britain, or follow'd and *doppel-gang'd* here, are foreign to our States, copiously as they are read by us all. But to fully understand not only how absolutely in opposition to our times and lands, and how little and cramp'd, and what anachronisms and absurdities many of their pages are, for American purposes, one must dwell or travel awhile in Missouri, Kansas and Colorado. and get rapport with their people and country.

Will the day ever come—no matter how long deferr'd— when those models and lay-figures from the British islands— and even the precious traditions of the classics—will be reminiscences, studies only? The pure breath, primitiveness, boundless prodigality and amplitude, strange mixture of delicacy and power, of continence, of real and ideal, and of all original and first-class elements, of these prairies, the Rocky mountains, and of the Mississippi and Missouri rivers —will they ever appear in, and in some sort form a standard for our poetry and art? (I sometimes think that even the ambition of my friend Joaquin Miller to put them in, and illustrate them, places him ahead of the whole crowd.)

Not long ago I was down New York bay, on a steamer, watching the sunset over the dark green heights of Navesink, and viewing all that inimitable spread of shore, shipping and sea, around Sandy Hook. But an intervening week or two, and my eyes catch the shadowy outlines of the Spanish peaks. In the more than two thousand miles between, though of infinite and paradoxical variety, a curious and absolute fusion is doubtless steadily annealing, compacting, identifying all. But subtler and wider and more solid, (to produce such compaction,) than the laws of the States, or the common ground of Congress, or the Supreme Court, or the grim welding of our national wars, or the steel ties of railroads, or all the kneading and fusing processes of our material and business history, past or present, would in my opinion be a great throbbing, vital, imaginative work, or series of works, or literature, in constructing which the Plains, the Prairies, and the Mississippi river, with the demesnes of its varied and ample valley, should be the concrete background, and America's humanity, passions, struggles, hopes, there and now—an *éclaircissement* as it is and is to be, on the stage of the New World, of all Time's hitherto drama of war, romance and evolution—should furnish the lambent fire, the ideal.

## THE SILENT GENERAL

*September* 28, '79.—So General Grant, after circumambiating the world, has arrived home again, landed in San Francisco yesterday, from the ship *City of Tokio* from Japan. What a man he is! what a history! what an illustration—his life—of the capacities of that American individuality common to us all. Cynical critics are wondering "what the people can see in Grant" to make such a hubbub about. They aver (and it is no doubt true) that he has hardly the average of our day's literary and scholastic culture, and absolutely no pronounc'd genius or conventional eminence of any sort. Correct: but he proves how an average western farmer, mechanic, boatman, carried by tides of circumstances, perhaps, caprices, into a position of incredible military or civic responsibilities, (history has presented none more trying, no born monarch's, no mark more shining for attack or envy,) may steer his way fitly and steadily through them all, carrying the country and himself with credit year after year—command over a million armed men—fight more than fifty pitch'd battles—rule for eight years a land larger than all the kingdoms of Europe combined—and then, retiring, quietly (with a cigar in his mouth) make the promenade of the whole world, through its courts and coteries, and kings and czars and mikados, and splendidest glitters and etiquettes, as phlegmatically as he ever walk'd the portico of a Missouri hotel after dinner. I say all this is what people like—and I am sure I like it. Seems to me it transcends Plutarch. How those old Greeks, indeed, would have seized on him! A mere plain man—no art, no poetry—only practical sense, ability to do, or try his best to do, what devolv'd upon him.

A common trader, money-maker, tanner, farmer of Illinois —general for the republic, in its terrific struggle with itself, in the war of attempted secession—President following, (a task of peace, more difficult than the war itself)—nothing heroic, as the authorities put it—and yet the greatest hero. The gods, the destinies, seem to have concentrated upon him.

## PRESIDENT HAYES'S SPEECHES

*September* 30, [1879].—I see President Hayes has come out West, passing quite informally from point to point, with his wife and a small cortege of big officers, receiving ovations, and making daily and sometimes double-daily addresses to the people. To these addresses—all impromptu, and some would call them ephemeral—I feel to devote a memorandum. They are shrewd, good-natur'd, face-to-face speeches, on easy topics not too deep; but they give me some revised ideas of oratory—of a new, opportune theory and practice of that art, quite changed from the classic rules, and adapted to our days, our occasions, to American democracy, and to the swarming populations of the West. I hear them criticized as wanting in dignity, but to me they are just what they should be, considering all the circumstances, who they come from, and who they are address'd to. Underneath, his objects are to compact and fraternize the States, encourage their materialistic and industrial development, soothe and expand their self-poise, and tie all and each with resistless double ties not only of inter-trade barter, but human comradeship.

From Kansas City I went on to St. Louis, where I remain'd nearly three months, with my brother T. J. W., and my dear nieces.

## EDGAR POE'S SIGNIFICANCE

*January* 1, '80.—In diagnosing this disease called humanity —to assume for the nonce what seems a chief mood of the personality and writings of my subject—I have thought that poets, somewhere or other on the list, present the most mark'd indications. Comprehending artists in a mass, musicians, painters, actors, and so on, and considering each and all of them as radiations or flanges of that furious whirling wheel, poetry, the centre and axis of the whole, where else indeed may we so well investigate the causes, growths, tally-marks of the time—the age's matter and malady?

By common consent there is nothing better for man or woman than a perfect and noble life, morally without flaw, happily balanced in activity, physically sound and pure, giving its due proportion, and no more, to the sympathetic, the human emotional element—a life, in all these, unhasting, unresting, untiring to the end. And yet there is another shape of personality dearer far to the artist-sense, (which likes the play of strongest lights and shades,) where the perfect character, the good, the heroic, although never attain'd, is never lost sight of, but through failures, sorrows, temporary downfalls, is return'd to again and again, and while often violated, is passionately adhered to as long as mind, muscles, voice, obey the power we call volition. This sort of personality we see more or less in Burns, Byron, Schiller, and George Sand. But we do not see it in Edgar Poe. (All this is the result of reading at intervals the last three days a new volume of his poems—I took it on my rambles down by the pond, and by degrees read it all through there.) While to the character first outlined the service Poe renders is certainly that entire contrast and contradiction which is next best to fully exemplifying it.

Almost without the first sign of moral principle, or of the concrete or its heroisms, or the simpler affections of the heart, Poe's verses illustrate an intense faculty for technical and abstract beauty, with the rhyming art to excess, an incorrigible propensity toward nocturnal themes, a demoniac undertone behind every page—and, by final judgment, probably belong among the electric lights of imaginative literature, brilliant and dazzling, but with no heat. There is an indescribable magnetism about the poet's life and reminiscences, as well as the poems. To one who could work out their subtle retracing and retrospect, the latter would make a close tally no doubt between the author's birth and antecedents, his childhood and youth, his physique, his so-call'd education, his studies and associates, the literary and social Baltimore, Richmond, Philadelphia and New York, of those

2B                                                W.

times—not only the places and circumstances in themselves, but often, very often, in a strange spurning of, and reaction from them all.

The following from a report in the Washington *Star* of November 16, 1875, may afford those who care for it something further of my point of view toward this interesting figure and influence of our era. There occurr'd about that date in Baltimore a public reburial of Poe's remains, and dedication of a monument over the grave:

"Being in Washington on a visit at the time, 'the old gray' went over to Baltimore, and though ill from paralysis, consented to hobble up and silently take a seat on the platform, but refused to make any speech, saying, 'I have felt a strong impulse to come over and be here to-day myself in memory of Poe, which I have obey'd, but not the slightest impulse to make a speech, which, my dear friends, must also be obeyed.' In an informal circle, however, in conversation after the ceremonies, Whitman said: 'For a long while, and until lately, I had a distaste for Poe's writings. I wanted, and still want for poetry, the clear sun shining, and fresh air blowing—the strength and power of health, not of delirium, even amid the stormiest passions—with always the background of the eternal moralities. Non-complying with these requirements, Poe's genius has yet conquer'd a special recognition for itself, and I too have come to fully admit it, and appreciate it and him.

" 'In a dream I once had, I saw a vessel on the sea, at midnight, in a storm. It was no great full-rigg'd ship, nor majestic steamer, steering firmly through the gale, but seem'd one of those superb little schooner yachts I had often seen lying anchor'd, rocking so jauntily, in the waters around New York, or up Long Island sound —now flying uncontroll'd with torn sails and broken spars through the wild sleet and winds and waves of the night. On the deck was a slender, slight, beautiful figure, a dim man, apparently enjoying all the terror, the murk, and the dislocation of which he was the centre and the victim. That figure of my lurid dream might stand for Edgar Poe, his spirit, his fortunes, and his poems—themselves all lurid dreams.' "

Much more may be said, but I most desired to exploit the idea put at the beginning. By its popular poets the calibres of an age, the weak spots of its embankments, its sub-currents, (often more significant than the biggest surface ones,) are unerringly indicated. The lush and the weird that have taken such extraordinary possession of Nineteenth century verse-lovers—what mean they? The inevitable tendency of poetic culture to morbidity, abnormal beauty—the sickliness of all technical thought or refinement in itself—the abnegation of the perennial and democratic concretes at first hand, the body, the earth and sea, sex and the like—and the substitution of something for them at second or third hand—what bearings have they on current pathological study?

## BEETHOVEN'S SEPTETTE

*February* 11, '80.—At a good concert to-night in the foyer of the opera house, Philadelphia—the band a small but first-rate one. Never did music more sink into and soothe and fill me—never so prove its soul-rousing power, its impossibility of statement. Especially in the rendering of one of Bee-thoven's master septettes by the well-chosen and perfectly-combined instruments (violins, viola, clarionet, horn, 'cello and contrabass,) was I carried away, seeing, absorbing many wonders. Dainty abandon, sometimes as if Nature laughing on a hillside in the sunshine; serious and firm monotonies, as of winds; a horn sounding through the tangle of the forest, and the dying echoes; soothing floating of waves, but pre-sently rising in surges, angrily lashing, muttering, heavy; piercing peals of laughter, for interstices; now and then weird, as Nature herself is in certain moods—but mainly spontaneous, easy, careless—often the sentiment of the pos-tures of naked children playing or sleeping. It did me good even to watch the violinists drawing their bows so masterly—every motion a study. I allow'd myself, as I sometimes do, to wander out of myself. The conceit came to me of a copious grove of singing birds, and in their midst a simple harmonic duo, two human souls, steadily asserting their own pensive-ness, joyousness.

## A CONTRALTO VOICE

*May* 9, [1880 ?] *Sunday*.—Visit this evening to my friends the J.'s—good supper, to which I did justice—lively chat with Mrs. J. and I. and J. As I sat out front on the walk afterward, in the evening air, the church-choir and organ on the corner opposite gave Luther's hymn, *Ein feste berg*, very finely. The air was borne by a rich contralto. For nearly half an hour there in the dark (there was a good string of English stanzas,) came the music, firm and unhurried, with long pauses. The full silver star-beams of Lyra rose silently over the church's dim roof-ridge. Vari-color'd lights from the stain'd glass windows broke through the tree-shadows. And under all—under the Northern Crown up there, and in the fresh breeze below, and the *chiaroscuro* of the night, that liquid-full contralto.

## SEEING NIAGARA TO ADVANTAGE

*June* 4, '80.—For really seizing a great picture or book, or piece of music, or architecture, or grand scenery—or perhaps for the first time even the common sunshine, or landscape, or may-be even the mystery of identity, most curious mystery of all—there comes some lucky five minutes of a man's life, set amid a fortuitous concurrence of circumstances, and bringing in a brief flash the culmination of years of reading and travel and thought. The present case about two o'clock this afternoon, gave me Niagara, its superb severity of action and color and majestic grouping, in one short, indescribable show. We were very slowly crossing the Suspension bridge —not a full stop anywhere, but next to it—the day clear, sunny, still—and I out on the platform. The falls were in plain view about a mile off, but very distinct, and no roar— hardly a murmur. The river tumbling green and white, far below me; the dark high banks, the plentiful umbrage, many bronze cedars, in shadow; and tempering and arching all the immense materiality, a clear sky overhead, with a few white clouds, limpid, spiritual, silent. Brief, and as quiet as brief, that picture—a remembrance always afterwards. Such are the things, indeed, I lay away with my life's rare and blessed bits of hours, reminiscent, past—the wild sea-storm I once saw one winter day, off Fire island—the elder Booth in *Richard*, that famous night forty years ago in the old Bowery —or Alboni in the children's scene in *Norma*—or night-views, I remember, on the field, after battles in Virginia—or the peculiar sentiment of moonlight and stars over the great

Plains, western Kansas—or scooting up New York bay, with a stiff breeze and a good yacht, off Navesink. With these, I say, I henceforth place that view, that afternoon, that combination complete, that five minutes' perfect absorption of Niagara—not the great majestic gem alone by itself, but set complete in all its varied, full, indispensable surroundings.

## TENNYSON'S "DE PROFUNDIS"

*[London, Ontario], June* 24, [1880]

To-day I spent half an hour (in a recluse summer-house embowered) leisurely reading Tennyson's new poem "De Profundis". I should call the piece (to coin a term) a specimen of the mystical-recherché—and a mighty choice specimen. It has several exquisite little verses, not simple like rosebuds, but gem-like like garnets or sapphires, cut by a lapidary artist. These, for instance (some one has had a baby):

> "O young life
> Breaking with laughter from the dark!"

> "O dear Spirit half-lost
> In thine own shadow and this fleshly sign
> That thou art thou—who wailest being born."

Then from "The Human Cry Attached":

> "We feel we are nothing—for all is
> Thou and in Thee;
> We feel we are something—
> That also has come from thee."

Some cute friends afterwards said it was altogether vague and could not be grasped. Very likely: It sounded to me like organ-playing, *capriccio*, which also cannot be grasped.

## THE SAVAGE SAGUENAY

Up these black waters, over a hundred miles—always strong, deep, (hundreds of feet, sometimes thousands,) ever with high, rocky hills for banks, green and gray—at times a little like some parts of the Hudson, but much more pronounc'd and defiant. The hills rise higher—keep their ranks more unbroken. The river is straighter and of more resolute flow, and its hue, though dark as ink, exquisitely polish'd and sheeny under the August sun. Different, indeed, this Saguenay from all other rivers—different effects—a bolder, more vehement play of lights and shades. Of a rare charm of singleness and simplicity. (Like the organ-chant at midnight from the old Spanish convent, in *Favorita*—one strain only, simple and monotonous and unornamented—but indescribably penetrating and grand and masterful.) Great place for echoes: while our steamer was tied at the wharf at Tadousac (taj-oo-sac) waiting, the escape-pipe letting off steam, I was sure I heard a band at the hotel up in the rocks—could even make out some of the tunes. Only when our pipe stopp'd, I knew what caused it. Then at cape Eternity and Trinity rock, the pilot with his whistle producing similar marvellous results, echoes indescribably weird, as we lay off in the still bay under their shadows.

## CAPES ETERNITY AND TRINITY

But the great, haughty, silent capes themselves; I doubt if any crack points, or hills, or historic places of note, or anything of the kind elsewhere in the world, outvies these objects —(I write while I am before them face to face). They are very simple, they do not startle—at least they did not me— but they linger in one's memory forever. They are placed very near each other, side by side, each a mountain rising flush out of the Saguenay. A good thrower could throw a stone on each in passing—at least it seems so. Then they are as distinct in form as a perfect physical man or a perfect physical woman. Cape Eternity is bare, rising, as just said, sheer out of the water, rugged and grim (yet with an indescribable beauty) nearly two thousand feet high. Trinity rock, even a little higher, also rising flush, top-rounded like a great head with close-cut verdure of hair. I consider myself well repaid for coming my thousand miles to get the sight and memory of the unrivall'd duo. They have stirr'd me more profoundly than anything of the kind I have yet seen. If Europe or Asia had them, we should certainly hear of them in all sorts of sent-back poems, rhapsodies, etc., a dozen times a year through our papers and magazines.

## CEDAR-PLUMS LIKE—NAMES

*(Back again in Camden and down in Jersey)*

ONE time I thought of naming this collection "Cedar-Plums
Like" (which I still fancy wouldn't have been a bad name,
nor inappropriate.) A melange of loafing, looking, hobbling,
sitting, traveling—a little thinking thrown in for salt, but
very little—not only summer but all seasons—not only days
but nights—some literary meditations—books, authors examined, Carlyle, Poe, Emerson tried, (always under my
cedar-tree, in the open air, and never in the library)—mostly
the scenes everybody sees, but some of my own caprices,
meditations, egotism—truly an open air and mainly summer
formation—singly, or in clusters—wild and free and somewhat acrid—indeed more like cedar-plums than you might
guess at first glance.

But do you know what they are? (To city man, or some
sweet parlor lady I now talk.) As you go along roads, or
barrens, or across country, anywhere through these States,
middle, eastern, western, or southern, you will see, certain
seasons of the year, the thick woolly tufts of the cedar mottled with bunches of china-blue berries, about as big as fox-
grapes. But first a special word for the tree itself: everybody
knows that the cedar is a healthy, cheap, democratic wood,
streak'd red and white—an evergreen—that it is not a *cultivated* tree—that it keeps away moths—that it grows inland or
seaboard, all climates, hot or cold, any soil—in fact rather
prefers sand and bleak side spots—content if the plough, the
fertilizer and the trimming-axe, will but keep away and let it
alone. After a long rain, when everything looks bright, often
have I stopt in my wood-saunters, south or north, or far west,
to take in its dusky green, wash'd clean and sweet, and
speck'd copiously with its fruit of clear, hardy blue. The
wood of the cedar is of use—but what profit on earth are
those sprigs of acrid plums? A question impossible to answer satisfactorily. True, some of the herb doctors give them
for stomachic affections, but the remedy is as bad as the disease. Then in my rambles down in Camden county I once
found an old crazy woman gathering the clusters with zeal
and joy. She show'd, as I was told afterward, a sort of in-

fatuation for them, and every year placed and kept profuse bunches high and low about her room. They had a strange charm on her uneasy head, and effected docility and peace. (She was harmless, and lived near by with her well-off married daughter.) Whether there is any connection between those bunches, and being out of one's wits, I cannot say, but I myself entertain a weakness for them. Indeed, I love the cedar, anyhow—its naked ruggedness, its just palpable odor, (so different from the perfumer's best,) its silence, its equable acceptance of winter's cold and summer's heat, of rain or drouth—its shelter to me from those, at times—its associations—(well, I never could explain *why* I love anybody, or anything.) The service I now specially owe to the cedar is, while I cast around for a name for my proposed collection, hesitating, puzzled—after rejecting a long, long string, I lift my eyes, and lo! the very term I want. At any rate, I go no further—I tire in the search. I take what some invisible kind spirit has put before me. Besides, who shall say there is not affinity enough between (at least the bundle of sticks that produced) many of these pieces, or granulations, and those blue berries? their uselessness growing wild—a certain aroma of Nature I would so like to have in my pages—the thin soil whence they come—their content in being let alone—their stolid and deaf repugnance to answering questions, (this latter the nearest, dearest trait affinity of all).

Then reader dear, in conclusion, as to the point of the name for the present collection, let us be satisfied to *have* a name—something to identify and bind it together, to concrete all its vegetable, mineral, personal memoranda, abrupt raids of criticism, crude gossip of philosophy, varied sands and clumps—without bothering ourselves because certain pages do not present themselves to you or me as coming under their own name with entire fitness or amiability. (It is a profound, vexatious never-explicable matter—this of names. I have been exercised deeply about it my whole life.*)

* In the pocket of my receptacle-book I find a list of suggested and rejected names for this volume, or parts of it—such as the following:

> As the wild bee hums in May,
> & August mulleins grow,
> & Winter snow-flakes fall,
> & stars in the sky roll round.

After all of which the name "Cedar-Plums Like" got its nose put out of joint; but I cannot afford to throw away what I pencill'd down the lane there, under the shelter of my old friend, one warm October noon. Besides, it wouldn't be civil to the cedar tree.


## DEATH OF THOMAS CARLYLE

*February* 10, '81.—And so the flame of the lamp, after long wasting and flickering, has gone out entirely.

As a representative author, a literary figure, no man else will bequeath to the future more significant hints of our stormy era, its fierce paradoxes, its din, and its struggling parturition periods, than Carlyle. He belongs to our own branch of the stock too; neither Latin nor Greek, but altogether Gothic. Rugged, mountainous, volcanic, he was himself more a French revolution than any of his volumes. In some respects, so far in the Nineteenth century, the best equipt, keenest mind, even from the college point of view, of all Britain; only he had an ailing body. Dyspepsia is to be traced in every page, and now and then fills the page. One may include among the lessons of his life—even though that life stretch'd to amazing length—how behind the tally of genius and morals stands the stomach, and gives a sort of casting vote.

Two conflicting agonistic elements seem to have contended

---

*Away from Books—away from Art,*
*Now for the Day and Night—the lesson done,*
*Now for the Sun and Stars,*

| | |
|---|---|
| *Notes of a Half-Paralytic,* | *As Voices in the Dusk, from Speakers* |
| *Week in and Week out,* | *far or hid,* |
| *Embers of Ending Days,* | *Autochthons . . . Embryons,* |
| *Ducks and Drakes,* | *Wing-and-Wing,* |
| *Flood Tide and Ebb,* | *Notes and Recallés,* |
| *Gossip at Early Candle-light,* | *Only Mulleins and Bumble-Bees,* |
| *Echoes and Escapades,* | *Pond-Babble . . . Tête-à-Têtes,* |
| *Such as I . . . Evening Dews,* | *Echoes of a Life in the 19th Century in* |
| *Notes after Writing a Book,* | *the New World,* |
| *Far and Near at 63,* | *Flanges of Fifty Years,* |
| *Drifts and Cumulus,* | *Abandons . . . Hurry Notes,* |
| *Maize-Tassels . . . Kindlings,* | *A Life-Mosaic . . . Native Moments,* |
| *Fore and Aft . . . Vestibules,* | *Types and Semi-Tones,* |
| *Scintilla at 60 and after,* | *Oddments . . . Sand-Drifts,* |
| *Sands on the Shores of 64,* | *Again and Again.* |

in the man, sometimes pulling him different ways like wild horses. He was a cautious, conservative Scotchman, fully aware what a fœtid gas-bag much of modern radicalism is; but then his great heart demanded reform, demanded change —often terribly at odds with his scornful brain. No author ever put so much wailing and despair into his books, sometimes palpable, oftener latent. He reminds me of that passage in Young's poems where as death presses closer and closer for his prey, the soul rushes hither and thither, appealing, shrieking, berating, to escape the general doom.

Of short-comings, even positive blur-spots, from an American point of view, he had serious share.

Not for his merely literary merit, (though that was great)— not as "maker of books", but as launching into the self-complacent atmosphere of our days a rasping, questioning, dislocating agitation and shock, is Carlyle's final value. It is time the English-speaking peoples had some true idea about the verteber of genius, namely power. As if they must always have it cut and bias'd to the fashion, like a lady's cloak! What a needed service he performs! How he shakes our comfortable reading circles with a touch of the old Hebraic anger and prophecy—and indeed it is just the same.    Not Isaiah himself more scornful, more threatening: "The crown of pride, the drunkards of Ephraim, shall be trodden under feet: And the glorious beauty which is on the head of the fat valley shall be a fading flower." (The word prophecy is much misused; it seems narrow'd to prediction merely. That is not the main sense of the Hebrew word translated "prophet"; it means one whose mind bubbles up and pours forth as a fountain, from inner, divine spontaneities revealing God. Prediction is a very minor part of prophecy. The great matter is to reveal and outpour the God-like suggestions pressing for birth in the soul. This is briefly the doctrine of the Friends or Quakers.)

Then the simplicity and amid ostensible frailty the towering strength of this man—a hardy oak knot, you could never wear out—an old farmer dress'd in brown clothes, and not handsome—his very foibles fascinating. Who cares that he wrote about Dr. Francia, and "Shooting Niagara"—and "the Nigger Question",—and didn't at all admire our United

States? (I doubt if he ever thought or said half as bad words about us as we deserve.) How he splashes like leviathan in the seas of modern literature and politics! Doubtless, respecting the latter, one needs first to realize, from actual observation, the squalor, vice and doggedness ingrain'd in the bulk-population of the British islands, with the red tape, the fatuity, the flunkeyism everywhere, to understand the last meaning in his pages. Accordingly, though he was no chartist or radical, I consider Carlyle's by far the most indignant comment or protest anent the fruits of feudalism to-day in Great Britain—the increasing poverty and degradation of the homeless, landless twenty millions, while a few thousands, or rather a few hundreds, possess the entire soil, the money, and the fat berths. Trade and shipping, and clubs and culture, and prestige, and guns, and a fine select class of gentry and aristocracy, with every modern improvement, cannot begin to salve or defend such stupendous hoggishness.

The way to test how much he has left his country were to consider, or try to consider, for a moment, the array of British thought, the resultant *ensemble* of the last fifty years, as existing to-day, *but with Carlyle left out*. It would be like an army with no artillery. The show were still a gay and rich one—Byron, Scott, Tennyson, and many more—horsemen and rapid infantry, and banners flying—but the last heavy roar so dear to the ear of the train'd soldier, and that settles fate and victory, would be lacking.

For the last three years we in America have had transmitted glimpses of a thin-bodied, lonesome, wifeless, childless, very old man, lying on a sofa, kept out of bed by indomitable will, but, of late, never well enough to take the open air. I have noted this news from time to time in brief descriptions in the papers. A week ago I read such an item just before I started out for my customary evening stroll between eight and nine. In the fine cold night, unusually clear, (Feb. 5, '81,) as I walk'd some open grounds adjacent, the condition of Carlyle, and his approaching—perhaps even then actual—death, filled me with thoughts eluding statement, and curiously blending with the scene. The planet Venus, an hour high in the west, with all her volume and lustre recover'd, (she has been shorn and languid for nearly a year,) including an additional sentiment I never noticed before—not merely voluptuous, Paphian, steeping, fascinating—now with calm commanding seriousness and hauteur—the Milo Venus now. Upward to the zenith, Jupiter, Saturn, and the moon past her quarter, trailing in procession, with the Pleiades following, and the constellation Taurus, and red Aldebaran. Not a cloud in heaven. Orion strode through the southeast, with his glittering belt—and a trifle below hung the sun of the night, Sirius. Every star dilated, more vitreous, nearer than usual. Not as in some clear nights when the larger stars entirely outshine the rest. Every little star or cluster just as distinctly visible, and just as nigh. Berenice's hair showing every gem, and new ones. To the northeast and north the Sickle, the Goat and kids, Cassiopeia, Castor and Pollux, and the two Dippers. While through the whole of this silent indescribable show, inclosing and bathing my whole receptivity, ran the thought of Carlyle dying. (To soothe and spiritualize, and, as far as may be, solve the mysteries of death and genius, consider them under the stars at midnight.)

And now that he has gone hence, can it be that Thomas Carlyle, soon to chemically dissolve in ashes and by winds, remains an identity still? In ways perhaps eluding all the statements, lore and speculations of ten thousand years—eluding all possible statements to mortal sense—does he yet exist, a definite, vital being, a spirit, an individual—perhaps now wafted in space among those stellar systems, which, suggestive and limitless as they are, merely edge more limitless, far more suggestive systems? I have no doubt of it. In silence of a fine night, such questions are answer'd to the soul, the best answers that can be given. With me, too, when depress'd by some specially sad event, or tearing problem, I wait till I go out under the stars for the last voiceless satisfaction.

# CARLYLE FROM AMERICAN POINTS OF VIEW

## *Later Thoughts and Jottings*

THERE is surely at present an inexplicable *rapport* (all the more piquant from its contradictoriness) between that deceas'd author and our United States of America—no matter whether it lasts or not.* As we Westerners assume definite shape, and result in formations and fruitage unknown before, it is curious with what a new sense our eyes turn to representative outgrowths of crises and personages in the Old World. Beyond question, since Carlyle's death, and the publication of Froude's memoirs, not only the interest in his books, but every personal bit regarding the famous Scotchman—his dyspepsia, his buffetings, his parentage, his paragon of a wife, his career in Edinburgh, in the lonesome nest on Craigenputtock moor, and then so many years in London—is probably wider and livelier to-day in this country than in his own land. Whether I succeed or no, I, too, reaching across the Atlantic and taking the man's dark fortune-telling of humanity and politics, would offset it all, (such is the fancy that comes to me,) by a far more profound horoscope-casting of those themes—G. F. Hegel's.†

First, about a chance, a never-fulfill'd vacuity of this pale cast of thought—this British Hamlet from Cheyne row, more puzzling than the Danish one, with his contrivances for settling the broken and spavin'd joints of the world's government, especially its democratic dislocation. Carlyle's grim fate was cast to live and dwell in, and largely embody, the parturition agony and qualms of the old order, amid crowded

---

* It will be difficult for the future—judging by his books, personal dis-sympathies, etc.,—to account for the deep hold this author has taken on the present age, and the way he has color'd its method and thought. I am certainly at a loss to account for it all as affecting myself. But there could be no view, or even partial picture, of the middle and latter part of our Nineteenth century, that did not markedly include Thomas Carlyle. In his case (as so many others, literary productions, works of art, personal identities, events,) there has been an impalpable something more effective than the palpable. Then I find no better text, (it is always important to have a definite, special, even oppositional, living man to start from,) for sending out certain speculations and comparisons for home use. Let us see what they amount to —those reactionary doctrines, fears, scornful analyses of democracy— even from the most erudite and sincere mind of Europe.

† Not the least mentionable part of the case, (a streak, it may be, of that humor with which history and fate love to contrast their gravity,) is that although neither of my great authorities during their lives consider'd the United States worthy of serious mention, all the principal works of both might not inappropriately be this day collected and bound up under the conspicuous title: *Speculations for the use of North America, and Democracy there with the relations of the same to Metaphysics, including Lessons and Warnings (encouragements too, and of the vastest,) from the Old World to the New.*

accumulations of ghastly morbidity, giving birth to the new. But conceive of him (or his parents before him) coming to America, recuperated by the cheering realities and activity of our people and country—growing up and delving face-to-face resolutely among us here, especially at the West—inhaling and exhaling our limitless air and eligibilities—devoting his mind to the theories and developments of this Republic amid its practical facts as exemplified in Kansas, Missouri, Illinois, Tennessee, or Louisiana. I say *facts*, and face-to-face confrontings—so different from books, and all those quiddities and mere reports in the libraries, upon which the man (it was wittily said of him at the age of thirty, that there was no one in Scotland who had glean'd so much and seen so little,) almost wholly fed, and which even his sturdy and vital mind but reflected at best.

Something of the sort narrowly escaped happening. In 1835, after more than a dozen years of trial and non-success, the author of *Sartor Resartus* removing to London, very poor, a confirmed hypochondriac, *Sartor* universally scoffed at, no literary prospects ahead, deliberately settled on one last casting throw of the literary dice—resolv'd to compose and launch forth a book on the subject of *the French Revolution*—and if that won no higher guerdon or prize than hitherto, to sternly abandon the trade of author forever, and emigrate for good to America. But the venture turn'd out a lucky one, and there was no emigration.

Carlyle's work in the sphere of literature as he commenced and carried it out, is the same in one or two leading respects that Immanuel Kant's was in speculative philosophy. But the Scotchman had none of the stomachic phlegm and never-perturb'd placidity of the Konigsberg sage, and did not, like the latter, understand his own limits, and stop when he got to the end of them. He clears away jungle and poison-vines and underbrush—at any rate hacks valiantly at them, smiting hip and thigh. Kant did the like in his sphere, and it was all he profess'd to do; his labors have left the ground fully prepared ever since—and greater service was probably never perform'd by mortal man. But the pang and hiatus of Carlyle seem to me to consist in the evidence everywhere that amid a whirl of fog and fury and cross-purposes, he firmly believ'd he had a clue to the medication of the world's ills, and that his bounden mission was to exploit it.*

There were two anchors, or sheet-anchors, for steadying, as a last resort, the Carlylean ship. One will be specified presently. The other, perhaps the main, was only to be found in some mark'd form of personal force, an extreme degree of competent urge and will, a man or men "born to command". Probably there ran through every vein and current of the Scotchman's blood something that warm'd up to this kind of trait and character above aught else in the world, and which makes him in my opinion the chief celebrater and promulger of it in literature—more than Plutarch, more than Shakspere. The great masses of humanity stand for nothing—at least nothing but nebulous raw material; only the big planets and shining suns for him. To ideas almost invariably languid or cold, a number-one forceful personality was sure to rouse his eulogistic passion and savage joy. In such case, even the standard of duty hereinafter rais'd, was to be instantly lower'd and vail'd. All that is comprehended under the terms republicanism and democracy were distasteful to him from the first, and as he grew older they became hateful and contemptible. For an undoubtedly candid and penetrating faculty such as his, the bearings he persistently ignored were marvellous. For instance, the promise, nay certainty, of the democratic principle, to each and every State of the current world, not so much of helping it to perfect legislators and executives, but as the only effectual method for surely, however slowly, training people on a large scale toward voluntarily ruling and managing themselves (the ultimate aim of political and all other development)—to gradually reduce the fact of *governing* to its minimum, and to subject all its staffs and their doings to the telescopes and microscopes of committees and parties—and greatest of all, to afford (not stagnation and obedient content, which went well enough with

---

* I hope I shall not myself fall into the error I charge upon him, of prescribing a specific for indispensable evils. My utmost pretension is probably but to offset that old claim of the exclusively curative power of first-class individual men, as leaders and rulers, by the claims, and general movement and result, of ideas. Something of the latter kind seems to me the distinctive theory of America, of democracy, and of the modern—or rather, I should say, it *is* democracy, and *is* the modern.

the feudalism and ecclesiasticism of the antique and medieval world, but) a vast and sane and recurrent ebb and tide action for those floods of the great deep that have henceforth palpably burst forever their old bounds—seem never to have enter'd Carlyle's thought. It was splendid how he refus'd any compromise to the last. He was curiously antique. In that harsh, picturesque, most potent voice and figure, one seems to be carried back from the present of the British islands more than two thousand years, to the range between Jerusalem and Tarsus. His fullest best biographer justly says of him:

"He was a teacher and a prophet, in the Jewish sense of the word. The prophecies of Isaiah and Jeremiah have become a part of the permanent spiritual inheritance of mankind, because events proved that they had interpreted correctly the sign of their own times, and their prophecies were fulfill'd. Carlyle, like them, believ'd that he had a special message to deliver to the present age. Whether he was correct in that belief, and whether his message was a true message, remains to be seen. He has told us that our most cherish'd ideas of political liberty, with their kindred corollaries, are mere illusions, and that the progress which has seem'd to go along with them is a progress towards anarchy and social dissolution. If he was wrong, he has misused his powers. The principles of his teachings are false. He has offer'd himself as a guide upon a road of which he had no knowledge; and his own desire for himself would be the speediest oblivion both of his person and his works. If, on the other hand, he has been right; if, like his great predecessors, he has read truly the tendencies of this modern age of ours, and his teaching is authenticated by facts, then Carlyle, too, will take his place among the inspired seers."

To which I add an amendment that under no circumstances, and no matter how completely time and events disprove his lurid vaticinations, should the English-speaking world forget this man, nor fail to hold in honor his unsurpass'd conscience, his unique method, and his honest fame. Never were convictions more earnest and genuine. Never was there less of a flunkey or temporizer. Never had political progressivism a foe it could more heartily respect.

The second main point of Carlyle's utterance was the idea of *duty being done*. (It is simply a new codicil—if it be particularly new, which is by no means certain—on the time-honor'd bequest of dynasticism, the mould-eaten rules of legitimacy and kings.) He seems to have been impatient sometimes to madness when reminded by persons who thought at least as deeply as himself, that this formula, though precious, is rather a vague one, and that there are many other considerations to a philosophical estimate of each and every department either in general history or individual affairs.

Altogether, I don't know anything more amazing than these persistent strides and throbbings so far through our Nineteenth century of perhaps its biggest, sharpest, and most erudite brain, in defiance and discontent with everything; contemptuously ignoring, (either from constitutional inaptitude, ignorance itself, or more likely because he demanded a definite cure-all here and now,) the only solace and solvent to be had.

There is, apart from mere intellect, in the make-up of every superior human identity, (in its moral completeness, considered as *ensemble*, not for that moral alone, but for the whole being, including physique,) a wondrous something that realizes without argument, frequently without what is called education, (though I think it the goal and apex of all education deserving the name)—an intuition of the absolute balance, in time and space, of the whole of this multifarious, mad chaos of fraud, frivolity, hoggishness—this revel of fools, and incredible make-believe and general unsettledness, we call *the world;* a soul-sight of that divine clue and unseen thread which holds the whole congeries of things, all history and time, and all events, however trivial, however momentous, like a leash'd dog in the hand of the hunter. Such soul-sight and root-centre for the mind—mere optimism explains only the surface or fringe of it—Carlyle was mostly, perhaps entirely without. He seems instead to have been haunted in the play of his mental action by a spectre, never entirely laid from first to last, (Greek scholars, I believe, find the same mocking and fantastic apparition attending Aristophanes, his comedies,)—the spectre of world-destruction.

How largest triumph or failure in human life, in war or peace, may depend on some little hidden centrality, hardly more than a drop of blood, a pulse-beat, or a breath of air! It is certain that all these weighty matters, democracy in

America, Carlyleism, and the temperament for deepest political or literary exploration, turn on a simple point in speculative philosophy.

The most profound theme that can occupy the mind of man—the problem on whose solution science, art, the bases and pursuits of nations, and everything else, including intelligent human happiness, (here to-day, 1882, New York, Texas, California, the same as all times, all lands,) subtly and finally resting, depends for competent outset and argument, is doubtless involved in the query: What is the fusing explanation and tie—what the relation between the (radical, democratic) Me, the human identity of understanding, emotions, spirit, etc., on the one side, of and with the (conservative) Not Me, the whole of the material objective universe and laws, with what is behind them in time and space, on the other side? Immanuel Kant, though he explain'd or partially explain'd, as may be said, the laws of the human understanding, left this question an open one. Schelling's answer, or suggestion of answer, is (and very valuable and important, as far as it goes,) that the same general and particular intelligence, passion, even the standards of right and wrong, which exist in a conscious and formulated state in man, exist in an unconscious state, or in perceptible analogies, throughout the entire universe of external Nature, in all its objects large or small, and all its movements and processes—thus making the impalpable human mind, and concrete nature, notwithstanding their duality and separation, convertible, and in centrality and essence one. But G. F. Hegel's fuller statement of the matter probably remains the last best word that has been said upon it, up to date. Substantially adopting the scheme just epitomized, he so carries it out and fortifies it and merges everything in it, with certain serious gaps now for the first time fill'd, that it becomes a coherent metaphysical system, and substantial answer (as far as there can be any answer) to the foregoing question—a system which, while I distinctly admit that the brain of the future may add to, revise, and even entirely reconstruct, at any rate beams forth to-day, in its entirety, illuminating the thought of the universe, and satisfying the mystery thereof to the human mind, with a more consoling scientific assurance than any yet.

According to Hegel the whole earth, (an old nucleus-thought, as in the Vedas, and no doubt before, but never hitherto brought so absolutely to the front, fully surcharged with modern scientism and facts, and made the sole entrance to each and all,) with its infinite variety, the past, the sur-roundings of to-day, or what may happen in the future, the contrarieties of material with spiritual, and of natural with artificial, are all, to the eye of the *ensemblist*, but necessary sides and unfoldings, different steps or links, in the endless process of Creative thought, which, amid numberless appar-ent failures and contradictions, is held together by central and never-broken unity—not contradictions or failures at all, but radiations of one consistent and eternal purpose; the whole mass of everything steadily, unerringly tending and flowing toward the permanent *utile* and *morale*, as rivers to oceans. As life is the whole law and incessant effort of the visible universe, and death only the other or invisible side of the same, so the *utile*, so truth, so health are the continuous-immutable laws of the moral universe, and vice and disease, with all their perturbations, are but transient, even if ever so prevalent expressions.

To politics throughout, Hegel applies the like catholic standard and faith. Not any one party, or any one form of government, is absolutely and exclusively true. Truth con-sists in the just relations of objects to each other. A majority or democracy may rule as outrageously and do as great harm as an oligarchy or despotism—though far less likely to do so. But the great evil is either a violation of the relations just referr'd to, or of the moral law. The specious, the unjust, the cruel, and what is called the unnatural, though not only per-mitted but in a certain sense, (like shade to light,) inevitable in the divine scheme, are by the whole constitution of that scheme, partial, inconsistent, temporary, and though having ever so great an ostensible majority, are certainly destin'd to failures, after causing great suffering.

Theology, Hegel translates into science.* All apparent contradictions in the statement of the Deific nature by differ-ent ages, nations, churches, points of view, are but fractional and imperfect expressions of one essential unity, from which

* I am much indebted to J. Gostick's abstract.

they all proceed—crude endeavors or distorted parts, to be regarded both as distinct and united. In short (to put it in our own form, or summing up,) that thinker or analyzer or overlooker who by an inscrutable combination of train'd wisdom and natural intuition most fully accepts in perfect faith the moral unity and sanity of the creative scheme, in history, science, and all life and time, present and future, is both the truest cosmical devotee or religioso, and the profoundest philosopher. While he who, by the spell of himself and his circumstance, sees darkness and despair in the sum of the workings of God's providence, and who, in that, denies or prevaricates, is, no matter how much piety plays on his lips, the most radical sinner and infidel.

I am the more assured in recounting Hegel a little freely here,* not only for offsetting the Carlylean letter and spirit—cutting it out all and several from the very roots, and below the roots—but to counterpoise, since the late death and deserv'd apotheosis of Darwin, the tenets of the evolutionists. Unspeakably precious as those are to biology, and henceforth indispensable to a right aim and estimate in study, they neither comprise or explain everything—and the last word or whisper still remains to be breathed, after the utmost of those claims, floating high and forever above them all, and above technical metaphysics. While the contributions which German Kant and Fichte and Schelling and Hegel have bequeath'd to humanity—and which English Darwin has also in his field—are indispensable to the erudition of America's future, I should say that in all of them, and the best of them, when compared with the lightning flashes and flights of the old prophets and *exaltés*, the spiritual poets and poetry of all lands, (as in the Hebrew Bible,) there seems to be, nay certainly is, something lacking—something cold, a failure to

* I have deliberately repeated it all, not only in offset to Carlyle's ever-lurking pessimism and world-decadence, but as presenting the most thoroughly *American points of view* I know. In my opinion the above formulas of Hegel are an essential and crowning justification of New World democracy in the creative realms of time and space. There is that about them which only the vastness, the multiplicity and the vitality of America would seem able to comprehend, to give scope and illustration to, or to be fit for, or even originate. It is strange to me that they were born in Germany, or in the old world at all. While a Carlyle, I should say, is quite the legitimate European product to be expected.

satisfy the deepest emotions of the soul—a want of living glow, fondness, warmth, which the old *exaltés* and poets supply, and which the keenest modern philosophers so far do not.

Upon the whole, and for our purposes, this man's name certainly belongs on the list with the just-specified, first-class moral physicians of our current era—and with Emerson and two or three others—though his prescription is drastic, and perhaps destructive, while theirs is assimilating, normal and tonic. Feudal at the core, and mental offspring and radiation of feudalism as are his books, they afford ever-valuable lessons and affinities to democratic America. Nations or individuals, we surely learn deepest from unlikeness, from a sincere opponent, from the light thrown even scornfully on dangerous spots and liabilities. (Michel Angelo invoked heaven's special protection against his friends and affectionate flatterers; palpable foes he could manage for himself.) In many particulars Carlyle was indeed, as Froude terms him, one of those far-off Hebraic utterers, a new Micah or Habbakuk. His words at times bubble forth with abysmic inspiration. Always precious, such men; as precious now as any time. His rude, rasping, taunting, contradictory tones—what ones are more wanted amid the supple, polish'd, money-worshipping, Jesus-and-Judas-equalizing, suffrage-sovereignty echoes of current America? He has lit up our Nineteenth century with the light of a powerful, penetrating, and perfectly honest intellect of the first class, turn'd on British and European politics, social life, literature, and representative personages—thoroughly dissatisfied with all, and mercilessly exposing the illness of all. But while he announces the malady, and scolds and raves about it, he himself, born and bred in the same atmosphere, is a mark'd illustration of it.

## A WEEK'S VISIT TO BOSTON

*May* 1, '81.—Seems as if all the ways and means of American travel to-day had been settled, not only with reference to speed and directness, but for the comfort of women, children, invalids, and old fellows like me. I went on by a through train that runs daily from Washington to the Yankee metropolis without change. You get in a sleeping-car soon after dark in Philadelphia, and after ruminating an hour or two, have your bed made up if you like, draw the curtains, and go to sleep in it—fly on through Jersey to New York—hear in your half-slumbers a dull jolting and bumping sound or two —are unconsciously toted from Jersey City by a midnight steamer around the Battery and under the big bridge to the track of the New Haven road—resume your flight eastward, and early the next morning you wake up in Boston. All of which was my experience. I wanted to go to the Revere house. A tall unknown gentleman, (a fellow-passenger on his way to New-port he told me, I had just chatted a few moments before with him,) assisted me out through the depot crowd, procured a hack, put me in it with my traveling bag, saying smilingly and quietly, "Now I want you to let this be *my* ride," paid the driver, and before I could remonstrate bow'd himself off.

The occasion of my jaunt, I suppose I had better say here, was for a public reading of "the death of Abraham Lincoln" essay, on the sixteenth anniversary of that tragedy; which reading duly came off, night of April 15. Then I linger'd a week in Boston—felt pretty well (the mood propitious, my paralysis lull'd)—went around everywhere, and saw all that was to be seen, especially human beings. Boston's immense material growth—commerce, finance, commission stores, the plethora of goods, the crowded streets and sidewalks—made of course the first surprising show. In my trip out West, last year, I thought the wand of future prosperity, future empire, must soon surely be wielded by St. Louis, Chicago, beautiful Denver, perhaps San Francisco; but I see the said wand stretch'd out just as decidedly in Boston, with just as much certainty of staying; evidences of copious capital—indeed no centre of the New World ahead of it, (half the big railroads in the West are built with Yankees' money, and they take the dividends.) Old Boston with its zigzag streets and multi-tudinous angles, (crush up a sheet of letter-paper in your hand, throw it down, stamp it flat, and that is a map of old Boston)—new Boston with its miles upon miles of large and costly houses—Beacon street, Commonwealth avenue, and a hundred others. But the best new departures and expan-sions of Boston, and of all the cities of New England, are in another direction.

## MY TRIBUTE TO FOUR POETS

*April* 16, [1885].—A short but pleasant visit to Longfellow. I
am not one of the calling kind, but as the author of "Evan-
geline" kindly took the trouble to come and see me three
years ago in Camden, where I was ill, I felt not only the impulse of my own pleasure on that occasion, but a duty. He
was the only particular eminence I called on in Boston, and I
shall not soon forget his lit-up face and glowing warmth and
courtesy, in the modes of what is called the old school.

And now just here I feel the impulse to interpolate something about the mighty four who stamp this first American
century with its birth-marks of poetic literature. In a late
magazine one of my reviewers, who ought to know better,
speaks of my "attitude of contempt and scorn and intoler-
ance" toward the leading poets—of my "deriding" them, and
preaching their "uselessness". If anybody cares to know
what I think—and have long thought and avow'd—about
them, I am entirely willing to propound. I can't imagine any
better luck befalling these States for a poetical beginning and
initiation than has come from Emerson, Longfellow, Bryant,
and Whittier. Emerson, to me, stands unmistakably at the
head, but for the others I am at a loss where to give any precedence. Each illustrious, each rounded, each distinctive.
Emerson for his sweet, vital-tasting melody, rhym'd philosophy, and poems as amber-clear as the honey of the wild bee
he loves to sing. Longfellow for rich color, graceful forms
and incidents—all that makes life beautiful and love refined
—competing with the singers of Europe on their own ground,
and, with one exception, better and finer work than that of
any of them. Bryant pulsing the first interior verse-throbs of
a mighty world—bard of the river and the wood, ever conveying a taste of open air, with scents as from hayfields,
grapes, birch-borders—always lurkingly fond of threnodies
—beginning and ending his long career with chants of death,
with here and there through all, poems, or passages of poems,
touching the highest universal truths, enthusiasms, duties—
morals as grim and eternal, if not as stormy and fateful, as
anything in Eschylus. While in Whittier, with his special
themes—(his outcropping love of heroism and war, for all

his Quakerdom, his verses at times like the measur'd step of Cromwell's old veterans)—in Whittier lives the zeal, the moral energy, that founded New England—the splendid rectitude and ardor of Luther, Milton, George Fox—I must not, dare not, say the wilfulness and narrowness—though doubtless the world needs now, and always will need, almost above all, just such narrowness and wilfulness.

## MILLET'S PICTURES—LAST ITEMS

*April* 18, [1881].—Went out three or four miles to the house of Quincy Shaw, to see a collection of J. F. Millet's pictures. Two rapt hours. Never before have I been so penetrated by this kind of expression. I stood long and long before "the Sower". I believe what the picture-men designate "the first Sower", as the artist executed a second copy, and a third, and, some think, improved in each. But I doubt it. There is something in this that could hardly be caught again—a sublime murkiness and original pent fury. Besides this masterpiece, there were many others, (I shall never forget the simple evening scene, "Watering the Cow,") all inimitable, all perfect as pictures, works of mere art; and then it seem'd to me, with that last impalpable ethic purpose from the artist (most likely unconscious to himself) which I am always looking for. To me all of them told the full story of what went before and necessitated the great French revolution—the long precedent crushing of the masses of a heroic people into the earth, in abject poverty, hunger—every right denied, humanity attempted to be put back for generations—yet Nature's force, titanic here, the stronger and hardier for that repression—waiting terribly to break forth, revengeful—the pressure on the dykes, and the bursting at last—the storming of the Bastile—the execution of the king and queen—the tempest of massacres and blood. Yet who can wonder?

> Could we wish humanity different?
> Could we wish the people made of wood or stone?
> Or that there be no justice in destiny or time?

The true France, base of all the rest, is certainly in these pictures. I comprehend "Field-People Reposing", "the Diggers", and "the Angelus" in this opinion. Some folks always think of the French as a small race, five or five and a half feet high, and ever frivolous and smirking. Nothing of the sort. The bulk of the personnel of France, before the Revolution, was large-sized, serious, industrious as now, and simple. The revolution and Napoleon's wars dwarf'd the standard of human size, but it will come up again. If for nothing else, I should dwell on my brief Boston visit for opening to me the new world of Millet's pictures. Will America ever have such an artist out of her own gestation, body, soul?

## "CUSTER'S LAST RALLY"

WENT to-day to see this just-finish'd painting by John Mulvany, who has been out in far Dakota, on the spot, at the forts, and among the frontiersmen, soldiers and Indians, for the last two years, on purpose to sketch it in from reality, or the best that could be got of it. Sat for over an hour before the picture, completely absorb'd in the first view. A vast canvas, I should say twenty or twenty-two feet by twelve, all crowded, and yet not crowded, conveying such a vivid play of color, it takes a little time to get used to it. There are no tricks; there is no throwing of shades in masses; it is all at first painfully real, overwhelming, needs good nerves to look at it. Forty or fifty figures, perhaps more, in full finish and detail in the mid-ground, with three times that number, or more, through the rest—swarms upon swarms of savage Sioux, in their war-bonnets, frantic, mostly on ponies, driving through the background, through the smoke, like a hurricane of demons. A dozen of the figures are wonderful. Altogether a western, autochthonic phase of America, the frontiers, culminating, typical, deadly, heroic to the uttermost—nothing in the books like it, nothing in Homer, nothing in Shakspere; more grim and sublime than either, all native, all our own, and all a fact. A great lot of muscular, tan-faced men, brought to bay under terrible circumstances—death ahold of them, yet every man undaunted, not one losing his head, wringing out every cent of the pay before they sell their lives. Custer (his hair cut short) stands in the middle, with dilated eye and extended arm, aiming a huge cavalry pistol. Captain Cook is there, partially wounded, blood on the white handkerchief around his head, aiming his carbine coolly, half kneeling—(his body was afterwards found close by Custer's). The slaughter'd or half-slaughter'd horses, for breastworks, make a peculiar feature. Two dead Indians, herculean, lie in the foreground, clutching their Winchester rifles, very characteristic. The many soldiers, their faces and attitudes, the carbines, the broad-brimm'd western hats, the powder-smoke in puffs, the dying horses with their rolling eyes almost human in their agony, the clouds of war-bon-neted Sioux in the background, the figures of Custer and Cook—with indeed the whole scene, dreadful, yet with an attraction and beauty that will remain in my memory. With all its color and fierce action, a certain Greek continence pervades it. A sunny sky and clear light envelop all. There is an almost entire absence of the stock traits of European war pictures. The physiognomy of the work is realistic and Western. I only saw it for an hour or so; but it needs to be seen many times—needs to be studied over and over again. I could look on such a work at brief intervals all my life without tiring; it is very tonic to me; then it has an ethic purpose below all, as all great art must have. The artist said the sending of the picture abroad, probably to London, had been talk'd of. I advised him if it went abroad to take it to Paris. I think they might appreciate it there—nay, they certainly would. Then I would like to show Messieur Crapeau that some things can be done in America as well as others.

## A VISIT, AT THE LAST, TO R. W. EMERSON

CONCORD, MASS.—Out here on a visit—elastic, mellow, Indian-summery weather. Came to-day from Boston, (a pleasant ride of 40 minutes by steam, through Somerville, Belmont, Waltham, Stony Brook, and other lively towns,) convoy'd by my friend F. B. Sanborn, and to his ample house, and the kindness and hospitality of Mrs. S. and their fine family. Am writing this under the shade of some old hickories and elms, just after 4 P.M., on the porch, within a stone's throw of the Concord river. Off against me, across stream, on a meadow and side-hill, haymakers are gathering and wagoning-in probably their second or third crop. The

spread of emerald-green and brown, the knolls, the score or
two of little haycocks dotting the meadow, the loaded-up
wagons, the patient horses, the slow-strong action of the men
and pitchforks—all in the just-waning afternoon, with
patches of yellow sun-sheen, mottled by long shadows—a
cricket shrilly chirping, herald of the dusk—a boat with two
figures noiselessly gliding along the little river, passing under
the stone bridge-arch—the slight settling haze of aerial moisture, the sky and the peacefulness expanding in all directions
and overhead—fill and soothe me.

*Same Evening.*—Never had I a better piece of luck befall
me: a long and blessed evening with Emerson, in a way I
couldn't have wish'd better or different. For nearly two
hours he has been placidly sitting where I could see his face in
the best light, near me. Mrs. S.'s back-parlor well fill'd with
people, neighbors, many fresh and charming faces, women,
mostly young, but some old. My friend A. B. Alcott and his
daughter Louisa were there early. A good deal of talk, the
subject Henry Thoreau—some new glints of his life and fortunes, with letters to and from him—one of the best by Margaret Fuller, others by Horace Greeley, Channing, etc.—one
from Thoreau himself, most quaint and interesting. (No
doubt I seem'd very stupid to the roomful of company, taking hardly any part in the conversation; but I had "my own
pail to milk in", as the Swiss proverb puts it.) My seat and
the relative arrangement were such that, without being rude,
or anything of the kind, I could just look squarely at E.,
which I did a good part of the two hours. On entering, he
had spoken very briefly and politely to several of the company, then settled himself in his chair, a trifle push'd back,
and, though a listener and apparently an alert one, remain'd
silent through the whole talk and discussion. A lady friend
quietly took a seat next him, to give special attention. A
good color in his face, eyes clear, with the well-known expression of sweetness, and the old clear-peering aspect quite the
same.

*Next Day.*—Several hours at E.'s house, and dinner there.
An old familiar house, (he has been in it thirty-five years,)
with surroundings, furnishment, roominess, and plain elegance and fullness, signifying democratic ease, sufficient

opulence, and an admirable old-fashioned simplicity—modern luxury, with its mere sumptuousness and affectation, either touch'd lightly upon or ignored altogether. Dinner the same. Of course the best of the occasion (Sunday, September 18, '81) was the sight of E. himself. As just said, a healthy color in the cheeks, and good light in the eyes, cheery expression, and just the amount of talking that best suited, namely, a word or short phrase only where needed, and almost always with a smile. Besides Emerson himself, Mrs. E., with their daughter Ellen, the son Edward and his wife, with my friend F. S. and Mrs. S., and others, relatives and intimates. Mrs. Emerson, resuming the subject of the evening before, (I sat next to her,) gave me further and fuller information about Thoreau, who, years ago, during Mr. E.'s absence in Europe, had lived for some time in the family, by invitation.

## OTHER CONCORD NOTATIONS

THOUGH the evening at Mr. and Mrs. Sanborn's, and the memorable family dinner at Mr. and Mrs. Emerson's, have most pleasantly and permanently fill'd my memory, I must not slight other notations of Concord. I went to the old Manse, walk'd through the ancient garden, enter'd the rooms, noted the quaintness, the unkempt grass and bushes, the little panes in the windows, the low ceilings, the spicy smell, the creepers embowering the light. Went to the Concord battle ground, which is close by, scann'd French's statue, "the Minute Man," read Emerson's poetic inscription on the base, linger'd a long while on the bridge, and stopp'd by the grave of the unnamed British soldiers buried there the day after the fight in April, '75. Then riding on, (thanks to my friend Miss M. and her spirited white ponies, she driving them,) a half hour at Hawthorne's and Thoreau's graves. I got out and went up of course on foot, and stood a long while and ponder'd. They lie close together in a pleasant wooded spot well up the cemetery hill, "Sleepy Hollow." The flat surface of the first was densely cover'd by myrtle, with a border of arbor-vitæ, and the other had a brown headstone, moderately elaborate, with inscriptions. By Henry's side lies his brother John, of whom much was expected, but he died young. Then to Walden pond, that beautiful embower'd sheet of water, and spent over an hour there. On the spot in the woods where Thoreau had his solitary house is now quite a cairn of stones, to mark the place; I too carried one and deposited on the heap. As we drove back, saw the "School of Philosophy", but it was shut up, and I would not have it open'd for me. Near by stopp'd at the house of W. T. Harris, the Hegelian, who came out, and we had a pleasant chat while I sat in the wagon. I shall not soon forget those Concord drives, and especially that charming Sunday forenoon one with my friend Miss M., and the white ponies.

## BOSTON COMMON—MORE OF EMERSON

*October* 10-13, [1881].—I spend a good deal of time on the Common, these delicious days and nights—every mid-day from 11.30 to about 1—and almost every sunset another hour. I know all the big trees, especially the old elms along Tremont and Beacon streets, and have come to a sociable-silent understanding with most of them, in the sunlit air, (yet crispy-cool enough,) as I saunter along the wide unpaved walks. Up and down this breadth by Beacon street, between these same old elms, I walk'd for two hours, of a bright sharp February mid-day twenty-one years ago, with Emerson, then in his prime, keen, physically and morally magnetic, arm'd at every point, and when he chose, wielding the emotional just as well as the intellectual. During those two hours he was the talker and I the listener. It was an argument-statement, reconnoitring, review, attack, and pressing home, (like an army corps in order, artillery, cavalry, infantry,) of all that could be said against that part (and a main part) in the construction of my poems, "Children of Adam." More precious than gold to me that dissertation—it afforded me, ever after, this strange and paradoxical lesson; each point of E.'s statement was unanswerable, no judge's charge ever more complete or convincing, I could never hear the points better put—and then I felt down in my soul the clear and unmistakable conviction to disobey all, and pursue my own way. "What have you to say then to such things?" said E., pausing in conclusion. "Only that while I can't answer them at all, I feel more settled than ever to adhere to my own theory, and ex-emplify it," was my candid response. Whereupon we went and had a good dinner at the American House. And thence-forward I never waver'd or was touch'd with qualms, (as I confess I had been two or three times before.)

## DEATH OF LONGFELLOW

CAMDEN, *April* 3, '82.—I have just return'd from an old forest haunt, where I love to go occasionally away from par-lors, pavements, and the newspapers and magazines—and where, of a clear forenoon, deep in the shade of pines and cedars and a tangle of old laurel-trees and vines, the news of Longfellow's death first reach'd me. For want of anything better, let me lightly twine a sprig of the sweet ground-ivy trailing so plentifully through the dead leaves at my feet, with reflections of that half hour alone, there in the silence, and lay it as my contribution on the dead bard's grave.

Longfellow in his voluminous works seems to me not only to be eminent in the style and forms of poetical expression that mark the present age, (an idiosyncrasy, almost a sick-ness, of verbal melody,) but to bring what is always dearest as poetry to the general human heart and taste, and probably must be so in the nature of things. He is certainly the sort of bard and counteractant most needed for our materialistic, self-assertive, money-worshipping, Anglo-Saxon races, and especially for the present age in America—an age tyrannically regulated with reference to the manufacturer, the merchant, the financier, the politician and the day workman—for whom and among whom he comes as the poet of melody, courtesy, deference—poet of the mellow twilight of the past in Italy, Germany, Spain, and in Northern Europe—poet of all sym-pathetic gentleness—and universal poet of women and young people. I should have to think long if I were ask'd to name the man who has done more, and in more valuable directions, for America.

I doubt if there ever was before such a fine intuitive judge and selecter of poems. His translations of many German and Scandinavian pieces are said to be better than the verna-culars. He does not urge or lash. His influence is like good drink or air. He is not tepid either, but always vital, with flavor, motion, grace. He strikes a splendid average, and does not sing exceptional passions, or humanity's jagged escapades. He is not revolutionary, brings nothing offensive or new, does not deal hard blows. On the contrary, his songs soothe and heal, or if they excite, it is a healthy and agreeable excitement. His very anger is gentle, is at second hand, (as in the "Quadroon Girl" and the "Witnesses").

There is no undue element of pensiveness in Longfellow's strains. Even in the early translation, the Manrique, the movement is as of strong and steady wind or tide, holding up and buoying. Death is not avoided through his many themes, but there is something almost winning in his original verses and renderings on that dread subject—as, closing "the Happiest Land" dispute,

> And then the landlord's daughter
> Up to heaven rais'd her hand,
> And said, "Ye may no more contend,
> There lies the happiest land."

To the ungracious complaint-charge of his want of racy nativity and special originality, I shall only say that America and the world may well be reverently thankful—can never be thankful enough—for any such singing-bird vouchsafed out of the centuries, without asking that the notes be different from those of other songsters; adding what I have heard Longfellow himself say, that ere the New World can be worthily original, and announce herself and her own heroes, she must be well saturated with the originality of others, and respectfully consider the heroes that lived before Agamemnon.

## STARTING NEWSPAPERS

### *Reminiscences (From the "Camden Courier")*

As I sat taking my evening sail across the Delaware in the staunch ferry-boat *Beverly*, a night or two ago, I was join'd by two young reporter friends. "I have a message for you," said one of them; "the C. folks told me to say they would like a piece sign'd by your name, to go in their first number. Can you do it for them?" "I guess so," said I; "what might it be about?" "Well, anything on newspapers, or perhaps what you've done yourself, starting them." And off the boys went, for we had reach'd the Philadelphia side. The hour was fine and mild, the bright half-moon shining; Venus, with excess of splendor, just setting in the west, and the great Scorpion rearing its length more than half up in the southeast. As I cross'd leisurely for an hour in the pleasant night-scene, my young friend's words brought up quite a string of reminiscences.

I commenced when I was but a boy of eleven or twelve writing sentimental bits for the old *Long Island Patriot*, in Brooklyn; this was about 1832. Soon after, I had a piece or two in George P. Morris's then celebrated and fashionable *Mirror*, of New York city. I remember with what half-suppress'd excitement I used to watch for the big, fat, red-faced, slow-moving, very old English carrier who distributed the *Mirror* in Brooklyn; and when I got one, opening and cutting the leaves with trembling fingers. How it made my heart double-beat to see *my piece* on the pretty white paper, in nice type.

My first real venture was the *Long Islander*, in my own beautiful town of Huntington, in 1839. I was about twenty years old. I had been teaching country school for two or three years in various parts of Suffolk and Queens counties, but liked printing; had been at it while a lad, learn'd the trade of compositor, and was encouraged to start a paper in the region where I was born. I went to New York, bought a press and types, hired some little help, but did most of the work myself, including the press-work. Everything seem'd turning out well; (only my own restlessness prevented me gradually establishing a permanent property there). I bought a good horse, and every week went all round the country serving my papers, devoting one day and night to it. I never had happier jaunts—going over to south side, to Babylon, down the south road, across to Smithtown and Comac, and back home. The experiences of those jaunts, the dear old-fashion'd farmers and their wives, the stops by the hay-fields, the hospitality, nice dinners, occasional evenings, the girls, the rides through the brush, come up in my memory to this day.

I next went to the *Aurora* daily in New York city—a sort of free lance. Also wrote regularly for the *Tattler*, an evening paper. With these and a little outside work I was occupied off and on, until I went to edit the *Brooklyn Eagle*, where for two years I had one of the pleasantest sits of my life—a good owner, good pay, and easy work and hours. The troubles in the Democratic party broke forth about those times (1848-'49) and I split off with the radicals, which led to rows with the boss and "the party", and I lost my place.

Being now out of a job, I was offer'd impromptu, (it happen'd between the acts one night in the lobby of the old Broadway theatre near Pearl street, New York city,) a good chance to go down to New Orleans on the staff of the *Crescent*, a daily to be started there with plenty of capital behind it. One of the owners, who was north buying material, met me walking in the lobby, and though that was our first acquaintance, after fifteen minutes' talk (and a drink) we made a formal bargain, and he paid me two hundred dollars down to bind the contract and bear my expenses to New Orleans. I started two days afterwards; had a good leisurely time, as the paper wasn't to be out in three weeks. I enjoy'd my journey and Louisiana life much. Returning to Brooklyn a year or two afterward I started the *Freeman*, first as a weekly, then daily. Pretty soon the secession war broke out, and I, too, got drawn in the current southward, and spent the following three years there, (as memorandized preceding).

Besides starting them as aforementioned, I have had to do, one time or another, during my life, with a long list of papers, at divers places, sometimes under queer circumstances. During the war, the hospitals at Washington, among other means of amusement, printed a little sheet among themselves, surrounded by wounds and death, the *Armory Square Gazette*, to which I contributed. The same long afterward, casually, to a paper—I think it was call'd the *Jimplecute*—out in Colorado where I stopp'd at the time. When I was in Quebec province, in Canada, in 1880, I went into the queerest little old French printing-office near Tadousac. It was far more primitive and ancient than my Camden friend William Kurtz's place up on Federal street. I remember, as a youngster, several characteristic old printers of a kind hard to be seen these days.

2C                                             W.

## BY EMERSON'S GRAVE

*May* 6, '82.—We stand by Emerson's new-made grave without sadness—indeed a solemn joy and faith, almost hauteur
—our soul-benison no mere

"Warrior, rest, thy task is done,"

for one beyond the warriors of the world lies surely symboll'd
here. A just man, poised on himself, all-loving, all-inclosing,
and sane and clear as the sun. Nor does it seem so much
Emerson himself we are here to honor—it is conscience, simplicity, culture, humanity's attributes at their best, yet applicable if need be to average affairs, and eligible to all. So used
are we to suppose a heroic death can only come from out of
battle or storm, or mighty personal contest, or amid dramatic incidents or danger, (have we not been taught so for ages
by all the plays and poems?) that few even of those who most
sympathizingly mourn Emerson's late departure will fully
appreciate the ripen'd grandeur of that event, with its play of
calm and fitness, like evening light on the sea.

How I shall henceforth dwell on the blessed hours when,
not long since, I saw that benignant face, the clear eyes, the
silently smiling mouth, the form yet upright in its great age—
to the very last, with so much spring and cheeriness, and such
an absence of decrepitude, that even the term *venerable* hardly
seem'd fitting.

Perhaps the life now rounded and completed in its mortal
development, and which nothing can change or harm more,
has its most illustrious halo, not in its splendid intellectual or
esthetic products, but as forming in its entirety one of the few
(alas! how few!) perfect and flawless excuses for being, of the
entire literary class.

We can say, as Abraham Lincoln at Gettysburg, It is not
we who come to consecrate the dead—we reverently come to
receive, if so it may be, some consecration to ourselves and
daily work from him.

## FINAL CONFESSIONS—LITERARY TESTS

So draw near their end these garrulous notes. There have
doubtless occurr'd some repetitions, technical errors in the

consecutiveness of dates, in the minutiæ of botanical, astronomical, etc., exactness, and perhaps elsewhere;—for in
gathering up, writing, peremptorily dispatching copy, this
hot weather, (last of July and through August, '82,) and delaying not the printers, I have had to hurry along, no time to
spare. But in the deepest veracity of all—in reflections of
objects, scenes, Nature's outpourings, to my senses and receptivity, as they seem'd to me—in the work of giving those
who care for it, some authentic glints, specimen-days of my
life—and in the *bona fide* spirit and relations, from author to
reader, on all the subjects design'd, and as far as they go, I
feel to make unmitigated claims.

The synopsis of my early life, Long Island, New York city,
and so forth, and the diary-jottings in the Secession war, tell
their own story. My plan in starting what constitutes most of
the middle of the book, was originally for hints and data of a
Nature-poem that should carry one's experiences a few hours,
commencing at noon-flush, and so through the after-part of
the day—I suppose led to such idea by my own life-afternoon
now arrived. But I soon found I could move at more ease, by
giving the narrative at first hand. (Then there is a humiliating
lesson one learns, in serene hours, of a fine day or night.
Nature seems to look on all fixed-up poetry and art as something almost impertinent.)

Thus I went on, years following, various seasons and areas,
spinning forth my thought beneath the night and stars, (or as
I was confined to my room by half-sickness,) or at midday
looking out upon the sea, or far north steaming over the
Saguenay's black breast, jotting all down in the loosest sort
of chronological order, and here printing from my impromptu
notes, hardly even the seasons group'd together, or anything corrected—so afraid of dropping what smack of out-
doors or sun or starlight might cling to the lines, I dared not
try to meddle with or smooth them. Every now and then,
(not often, but for a foil,) I carried a book in my pocket—or
perhaps tore out from some broken or cheap edition a bunch
of loose leaves; most always had something of the sort ready,
but only took it out when the mood demanded. In that way,
utterly out of reach of literary conventions, I re-read many
authors.

I cannot divest my appetite of literature, yet I find myself eventually trying it all by Nature—*first premises* many call it, but really the crowning results of all, laws, tallies and proofs. (Has it never occur'd to any one how the last deciding tests applicable to a book are entirely outside of technical and grammatical ones, and that any truly first-class production has little or nothing to do with the rules and calibres of ordinary critics? or the bloodless chalk of Allibone's Dictionary? I have fancied the ocean and the daylight, the mountain and the forest, putting their spirit in a judgment on our books. I have fancied some disembodied human soul giving its verdict.)

## A MEMORANDUM AT A VENTURE

"All is proper to be express'd, provided our aim is only high enough."—*J. F. Millet.*

"The candor of science is the glory of the modern. It does not hide and repress; it confronts, turns on the light. It alone has perfect faith—faith not in a part only, but all. Does it not undermine the old religious standards? Yes, in God's truth, by excluding the devil from the theory of the universe—by showing that evil is not a law in itself, but a sickness, a perversion of the good, and the other side of the good—that in fact all of humanity, and of everything, is divine in its bases, its eligibilities."

SHALL the mention of such topics as I have briefly but plainly and resolutely broach'd in the "Children of Adam" section of *Leaves of Grass* be admitted in poetry and literature? Ought not the innovation to be put down by opinion and criticism? and, if those fail, by the District Attorney? True, I could not construct a poem which declaredly took, as never before, the complete human identity, physical, moral, emotional, and intellectual, (giving precedence and compass in a certain sense to the first,) nor fulfil that *bona fide* candor and entirety of treatment which was a part of my purpose, without comprehending this section also. But I would entrench myself more deeply and widely than that. And while I do not ask any man to indorse my theory, I confess myself anxious that what I sought to write and express, and the ground I built on, shall be at least partially understood, from its own platform. The best way seems to me to confront the question with entire frankness.

There are, generally speaking, two points of view, two conditions of the world's attitude toward these matters; the first, the conventional one of good folks and good print everywhere, repressing any direct statement of them, and making allusions only at second or third hand—(as the Greeks did of death, which, in Hellenic social culture, was not mention'd point-blank, but by euphemisms). In the civilization of to-day, this condition—without stopping to elaborate the arguments and facts, which are many and varied and perplexing —has led to states of ignorance, repressal, and cover'd over disease and depletion, forming certainly a main factor in the world's woe. A non-scientific, non-esthetic, and eminently non-religious condition, bequeath'd to us from the past, (its origins diverse, one of them the far-back lessons of benevolent and wise men to restrain the prevalent coarseness and animality of the tribal ages—with Puritanism, or perhaps Protestantism itself for another, and still another specified in the latter part of this memorandum)—to it is probably due most of the ill births, inefficient maturity, snickering pruriency, and of that human pathologic evil and morbidity which is, in my opinion, the keel and reason-why of every evil and morbidity. Its scent, as of something sneaking, furtive, mephitic, seems to lingeringly pervade all modern literature, conversation, and manners.

The second point of view, and by far the largest—as the world in working-day dress vastly exceeds the world in parlor toilette—is the one of common life, from the oldest times down, and especially in England, (see the earlier chapters of Taine's *English Literature*, and see Shakspere almost anywhere,) and which our age to-day inherits from riant stock, in the wit, or what passes for wit, of masculine circles, and in erotic stories and talk, to excite, express, and dwell on, that merely sensual voluptuousness which, according to Victor Hugo, is the most universal trait of all ages, all lands. This second condition, however bad, is at any rate like a disease which comes to the surface, and therefore less dangerous than a conceal'd one.

The time seems to me to have arrived, and America to be

the place, for a new departure—a third point of view. The same freedom and faith and earnestness which, after centuries of denial, struggle, repression, and martyrdɔm, the present day brings to the treatment of politics and religion, must work out a plan and standard ɔn this subject, not so much for what is call'd society, as for thoughtfulest men and women, and thoughtfulest literature. The same spirit that marks the physiological author and demonstrator on these topics in his important field, I have thought necessary to be exemplified, for once, in another certainly not less important field.

In the present memorandum I only venture to indicate that plan and view—decided upon more than twenty years ago, for my own literary action, and formulated tangibly in my printed poems—(as Bacon says an abstract thought or theory is of no moment unless it leads to a deed or work done, exemplifying it in the concrete)—that the sexual passion in itself, while normal and unperverted, is inherently legitimate, creditable, not necessarily an improper theme for poet, as confessedly not for scientist—that, with reference to the whole construction, organism, and intentions of *Leaves of Grass*, anything short of confronting that theme, and making myself clear upon it, as the enclosing basis of everything, (as the sanity of everything was to be the atmosphere of the poems,) I should beg the question in its most momentous aspect, and the superstructure that follow'd, pretensive as it might assume to be, would all rest on a poor foundation, or no foundation at all. In short, as the assumption of the sanity of birth, Nature and humanity, is the key to any true theory of life and the universe—at any rate, the only theory ɔut of which I wrote—it is, and must inevitably be, the only key to *Leaves of Grass*, and every part of it. *That*, (and not a vain consistency or weak pride, as a late "Springfield Republican" charges,) is the reason that I have stood out for these particular verses uncompromisingly for over twenty years, and maintain them to this day. *That* is what I felt in my inmost brain and heart, when I only answer'd Emerson's vehement arguments with silence, under the old elms of Boston Common.

Indeed, might not every physiologist and every good

physician pray for the redeeming of this subject from its hitherto relegation to the tongues and pens of blackguards, and boldly putting it for once at least, if no more, in the demesne of poetry and sanity—as something not in itself gross or impure, but entirely consistent with highest manhood and womanhood, and indispensable to both? Might not only every wife and every mother—not only every babe that comes into the world, if that were possible—not only all marriage, the foundation and *sine qua non* of the civilized state—bless and thank the showing, or taking for granted, that motherhood, fatherhood, sexuality, and all that belongs to them, can be asserted, where it comes to question, openly, joyously, proudly, "without shame or the need of shame", from the highest artistic and human considerations—but, with reverence be it written, on such attempt to justify the base and start of the whole divine scheme in humanity, might not the Creative Power itself deign a smile of approval?

To the movement for the eligibility and entrance of women amid new spheres of business, politics, and the suffrage, the current prurient, conventional treatment of sex is the main formidable obstacle. The rising tide of "woman's rights", swelling and every year advancing farther and farther, recoils from it with dismay. There will in my opinion be no general progress in such eligibility till a sensible, philosophic, democratic method is substituted.

The whole question—which strikes far, very far deeper than most people have supposed, (and doubtless, too, something is to be said on all sides,) is peculiarly an important one in art—is first an ethic, and then still more an esthetic one. I condense from a paper read not long since at Cheltenham, England, before the "Social Science Congress", to the Art Department, by P. H. Rathbone of Liverpool, on the "Undraped Figure in Art", and the discussion that follow'd:

"When coward Europe suffer'd the unclean Turk to soil the sacred shores of Greece by his polluting presence, civilization and morality receiv'd a blow from which they have never entirely recover'd, and the trail of the serpent has been over European art and European society ever since. The Turk regarded and regards women as animals without soul, toys to be play'd with or broken at pleasure, and to be hidden, partly from shame, but chiefly for the purpose of stimulating exhausted passion. Such is the unholy origin of the objection to the nude as a fit subject for art; it is purely Asiatic, and though not introduced for the first time in the fifteenth century, is yet to be traced to the source of all impurity— the East. Although the source of the prejudice is thoroughly un- healthy and impure, yet it is now shared by many pure-minded and honest, if somewhat uneducated, people. But I am prepared to maintain that it is necessary for the future of English art and of English morality that the right of the nude to a place in our gal- leries should be boldly asserted; it must, however, be the nude as represented by thoroughly trained artists, and with a pure and noble ethic purpose. The human form, male and female, is the type and standard of all beauty of form and proportion, and it is necessary to be thoroughly familiar with it in order safely to judge of all beauty which consists of form and proportion. To women it is most necessary that they should become thoroughly imbued with the knowledge of the ideal female form, in order that they should recognize the perfection of it at once, and without effort, and so far as possible avoid deviations from the ideal. Had this been the case in times past, we should not have had to deplore the distortions effected by tight-lacing, which destroy'd the figure and ruin'd the health of so many of the last generation. Nor should we have had the scandalous dresses alike of society and the stage. The extreme development of the low dresses which obtain'd some years ago, when the stays crush'd up the breasts into suggestive promin- ence, would surely have been check'd, had the eye of the public been properly educated by familiarity with the exquisite beauty of line of a well-shaped bust. I might show how thorough acquaint- ance with the ideal nude foot would probably have much modified the foot-torturing boots and high heels, which wring the foot out of all beauty of line, and throw the body forward into an awkward and ungainly attitude.

"It is argued that the effect of nude representation of women upon young men is unwholesome, but it would not be so if such works were admitted without question into our galleries, and be- came thoroughly familiar to them. On the contrary, it would do much to clear away from healthy-hearted lads one of their sorest trials—that prurient curiosity which is bred of prudish concealment. Where there is mystery there is the suggestion of evil, and to go to a theatre, where you have only to look at the stalls to see one, half of the female form, and to the stage to see the other half un-draped, is far more pregnant with evil imaginings than the most objectionable of totally undraped figures. In French art there have been questionable nude figures exhibited; but the fault was not that they were nude, but that they were the portraits of ugly im-modest women."

Some discussion follow'd. There was a general concurrence in the principle contended for by the reader of the paper. Sir Walter Stirling maintain'd that the perfect male figure, rather than the female, was the model of beauty. After a few remarks from Rev. Mr. Roberts and Colonel Oldfield, the Chairman regretted that no opponent of nude figures had taken part in the discussion. He agreed with Sir Walter Stirling as to the male figure being the most perfect model of proportion. He join'd in defending the exhibition of nude figures, but thought considerable supervision should be exercis'd over such exhibitions.

No, it is not the picture or nude statue or text, with clear aim, that is indecent; it is the beholder's own thought, infer-ence, distorted construction. True modesty is one of the most precious of attributes, even virtues, but in nothing is there more pretense, more falsity, than the needless assump-tion of it. Through precept and consciousness, man has long enough realized how bad he is. I would not so much disturb or demolish that conviction, only to resume and keep unerr-ingly with it the spinal meaning of the Scriptural text, *God overlook'd all that he had made*, (including the apex of the whole—humanity—with its elements, passions, appetites,) *and behold, it was very good.*

Does not anything short of that third point of view, when you come to think of it profoundly and with amplitude, im-pugn Creation from the outset? In fact, however overlaid, or unaware of itself, does not the conviction involv'd in it per-ennially exist at the centre of all society, and of the sexes, and of marriage? Is it not really an intuition of the human race? For, old as the world is, and beyond statement as are the countless and splendid results of its culture and evolution, perhaps the best and earliest and purest intuitions of the human race have yet to be develop'd.

## EMERSON'S BOOKS, (THE SHADOWS OF THEM)

In the regions we call Nature, towering beyond all measurement, with infinite spread, infinite depth and height—in those regions, including Man, socially and historically, with his moral-emotional influences—how small a part, (it came in my mind to-day,) has literature really depicted— even summing up all of it, all ages. Seems at its best some little fleet of boats, hugging the shores of a boundless sea, and never venturing, exploring the unmapp'd—never, Columbus-like, sailing out for New Worlds, and to complete the orb's rondure. Emerson writes frequently in the atmosphere of this thought, and his books report one or two things from that very ocean and air, and more legibly address'd to our age and American polity than by any man yet. But I will begin by scarifying him—thus proving that I am not insensible to his deepest lessons. I will consider his books from a democratic and western point of view. I will specify the shadows on these sunny expanses. Somebody has said of heroic character that "wherever the tallest peaks are present, must inevitably be deep chasms and valleys". Mine be the ungracious task (for reasons) of leaving unmention'd both sunny expanses and sky-reaching heights, to dwell on the bare spots and darknesses. I have a theory that no artist or work of the very first class may be or can be without them.

First, then, these pages are perhaps too perfect, too concentrated. (How good, for instance, is good butter, good sugar. But to be eating nothing but sugar and butter all the time! even if ever so good.) And though the author has much to say of freedom and wildness and simplicity and spontaneity, no performance was ever more based on artificial scholarships and decorums at third or fourth removes, (he calls it culture,) and built up from them. It is always a *make*, never an unconscious *growth*. It is the porcelain figure or statuette of lion, or stag, or Indian hunter—and a very choice statuette too—appropriate for the rosewood or marble bracket of parlor or library; never the animal itself, or the hunter himself. Indeed, who wants the real animal or hunter? What would that do amid astral and bric-a-brac and tapestry, and ladies and gentlemen talking in subdued tones of Browning and

Longfellow and art? The least suspicion of such actual bull, or Indian, or of Nature carrying out itself, would put all those good people to instant terror and flight.

Emerson, in my opinion, is not most eminent as poet or artist or teacher, though valuable in all those. He is best as critic, or diagnoser. Not passion or imagination or warp or weakness, or any pronounced cause or specialty, dominates him. Cold and bloodless intellectuality dominates him. (I know the fires, emotions, love, egotisms, glow deep, perennial, as in all New Englanders—but the façade, hides them well—they give no sign.) He does not see or take one side, one presentation only or mainly, (as all the poets, or most of the fine writers anyhow)—he sees all sides. His final influence is to make his students cease to worship anything—almost cease to believe in anything, outside of themselves. These books will fill, and well fill, certain stretches of life, certain stages of development—are, (like the tenets or theology the author of them preach'd when a young man,) unspeakably serviceable and precious as a stage. But in old or nervous or solemnest or dying hours, when one needs the impalpably soothing and vitalizing influences of abysmic Nature, or its affinities in literature or human society, and the soul resents the keenest mere intellection, they will not be sought for.

For a philosopher, Emerson possesses a singularly dandified theory of manners. He seems to have no notion at all that manners are simply the signs by which the chemist or metallurgist knows his metals. To the profound scientist, all metals are profound, as they really are. The little one, like the conventional world, will make much of gold and silver only. Then to the real artist in humanity, what are called bad manners are often the most picturesque and significant of all. Suppose these books becoming absorb'd, the permanent chyle of American general and particular character—what a well-wash'd and grammatical, but bloodless and helpless, race we should turn out! No, no, dear friend; though the States want scholars, undoubtedly, and perhaps want ladies and gentlemen who use the bath frequently, and never laugh loud, or talk wrong, they don't want scholars, or ladies and gentlemen, at the expense of all the rest. They want good farmers, sailors, mechanics, clerks, citizens—perfect business and social relations—perfect fathers and mothers. If we could only have these, or their approximations, plenty of them, fine and large and sane and generous and patriotic, they might make their verbs disagree from their nominatives, and laugh like volleys of musketeers, if they should please. Of course these are not all America wants, but they are first of all to be provided on a large scale. And, with tremendous errors and escapades, this, substantially, is what the States seem to have an intuition of, and to be mainly aiming at. The plan of a select class, superfined, (demarcated from the rest,) the plan of Old World lands and literatures, is not so objectionable in itself, but because it chokes the true plan for us, and indeed is death to it. As to such special class, the United States can never produce any equal to the splendid show, (far, far beyond comparison or competition here,) of the principal European nations, both in the past and at the present day. But an immense and distinctive commonalty over our vast and varied area, west and east, south and north —in fact, for the first time in history, a great, aggregated, real PEOPLE, worthy the name, and made of develop'd heroic individuals, both sexes—is America's principal, perhaps only, reason for being. If ever accomplish'd, it will be at least as much, (I lately think, doubly as much,) the result of fitting and democratic sociologies, literatures and arts—if we ever get them—as of our democratic politics.

At times it has been doubtful to me if Emerson really knows or feels what Poetry is at its highest, as in the Bible, for instance, or Homer or Shakspere. I see he covertly or plainly likes best superb verbal polish, or something old or odd—Waller's "Go, lovely rose", or Lovelace's lines "to Lucusta"—the quaint conceits of the old French bards, and the like. Of *power* he seems to have a gentleman's admiration—but in his inmost heart the grandest attribute of God and Poets is always subordinate to the octaves, conceits, polite kinks, and verbs.

The reminiscence that years ago I began like most youngsters to have a touch (though it came late, and was only on the surface) of Emerson-on-the-brain—that I read his writings reverently, and address'd him in print as "Master", and for a month or so thought of him as such—I retain not only with composure, but positive satisfaction. I have noticed that most young people of eager minds pass through this stage of exercise.

The best part of Emersonianism is, it breeds the giant that destroys itself. Who wants to be any man's mere follower? lurks behind every page. No teacher ever taught, that has so provided for his pupil's setting up independently—no truer evolutionist.

## VENTURES, ON AN OLD THEME

A DIALOGUE—*One party says*—We arrange our lives—even the best and boldest men and women that exist, just as much as the most limited—with reference to what society conventionally rules and makes right. We retire to our rooms for freedom; to undress, bathe, unloose everything in freedom. These, and much else, would not be proper in society.

*Other party answers*—Such is the rule of society. Not always so, and considerable exceptions still exist. However, it must be called the general rule, sanction'd by immemorial usage, and will probably always remain so.

*First party*—Why not, then, respect it in your poems?

*Answer*—One reason, and to me a profound one, is that the soul of a man or woman demands, enjoys compensation in the highest directions for this very restraint of himself or herself, level'd to the average, or rather mean, low, however eternally practical, requirements of society's intercourse. To balance this indispensable abnegation, the free minds of poets relieve themselves, and strengthen and enrich mankind with free flights in all the directions not tolerated by ordinary society.

*First party*—But must not outrage or give offence to it.

*Answer*—No, not in the deepest sense—and do not, and cannot. The vast averages of time and the race *en masse* settle these things. Only understand that the conventional standards and laws proper enough for ordinary society apply neither to the action of the soul, nor its poets. In fact the latter know no laws but the laws of themselves, planted in them by God, and are themselves the last standards of the law, and its final exponents—responsible to Him directly, and not at all to mere etiquette. Often the best service that can be done to the race, is to lift the veil, at least for a time, from these rules and fossil-etiquettes.

NEW POETRY—*California, Canada, Texas*—In my opinion the time has arrived to essentially break down the barriers of form between prose and poetry. I say the latter is henceforth to win and maintain its character regardless of rhyme, and the measurement-rules of iambic, spondee, dactyl, etc., and that even if rhyme and those measurements continue to furnish the medium for inferior writers and themes, (especially for persiflage and the comic, as there seems henceforward, to the perfect taste, something inevitably comic in rhyme, merely in itself, and anyhow,) the truest and greatest *Poetry*, (while subtly and necessarily always rhythmic, and distinguishable easily enough,) can never again, in the English language, be express'd in arbitrary and rhyming metre, any more than the greatest eloquence, or the truest power and passion. While admitting that the venerable and heavenly forms of chiming versification have in their time play'd great and fitting parts—that the pensive complaint, the ballads, wars, amours, legends of Europe, etc., have, many of them, been inimitably render'd in rhyming verse—that there have been very illustrious poets whose shapes the mantle of such verse has beautifully and appropriately envelopt—and though the mantle has fallen, with perhaps added beauty, on some of our own age—it is, notwithstanding, certain to me, that the day of such conventional rhyme is ended. In America, at any rate, and as a medium of highest esthetic practical or spiritual expression, present or future, it palpably fails, and must fail, to serve. The Muse of the Prairies, of California, Canada, Texas, and of the peaks of Colorado, dismissing the literary, as well as social etiquette of over-sea feudalism and caste, joyfully enlarging, adapting itself to comprehend the size of the whole people, with the free play, emotions, pride, passions, experiences, that belong to them, body and soul—to the general globe, and all its relations in astronomy, as the savans portray them to us—to the modern, the busy Nineteenth century, (as grandly poetic as any, only different,) with steamships, railroads, factories, electric telegraphs, cylinder presses—to the thought of the solidarity of nations, the brotherhood and sisterhood of the entire earth— to the dignity and heroism of the practical labor of farms, factories, foundries, workshops, mines, or on shipboard, or on lakes and rivers—resumes that other medium of expression, more flexible, more eligible—soars to the freer, vast, diviner heaven of prose.

Of poems of the third or fourth class, (perhaps even some of the second,) it makes little or no difference who writes them—they are good enough for what they are; nor is it necessary that they should be actual emanations from the personality and life of the writers. The very reverse sometimes gives piquancy. But poems of the first class, (poems of the depth, as distinguished from those of the surface,) are to be sternly tallied with the poets themselves, and tried by them and their lives. Who wants a glorification of courage and manly defiance from a coward or a sneak?—a ballad of benevolence or chastity from some rhyming hunks, or lascivious, glib *roue*?

In these States, beyond all precedent, poetry will have to do with actual facts, with the concrete States, and—for we have not much more than begun—with the definitive getting into shape of the Union. Indeed I sometimes think *it* alone is to define the Union, (namely, to give it artistic character, spirituality, dignity.) What American humanity is most in danger of is an overwhelming prosperity, "business" worldliness, materialism: what is most lacking, east, west, north, south, is a fervid and glowing Nationality and patriotism, cohering all the parts into one. Who may fend that danger, and fill that lack in the future, but a class of loftiest poets?

If the United States haven't grown poets, on any scale of grandeur, it is certain they import, print, and read more poetry than any equal number of people elsewhere—probably more than all the rest of the world combined.

Poetry (like a grand personality) is a growth of many generations—many rare combinations.

To have great poets, there must be great audiences, too.

# DARWINISM—(THEN FURTHERMORE)

RUNNING through prehistoric ages—coming down fro.
them into the daybreak of our records, founding theology,
suffusing literature, and so brought onward—(a sort of verteber and marrow to all the antique races and lands, Egypt,
India, Greece, Rome, the Chinese, the Jews, etc., and giving
cast and complexion to their art, poems, and their politics as
well as ecclesiasticism, all of which we more or less inherit,)
appear those venerable claims to origin from God himself, or
from gods and goddesses—ancestry from divine beings of
vaster beauty, size, and power than ours. But in current and
latest times, the theory of human origin that seems to have
most made its mark, (curiously reversing the antique,) is that
we have come on, originated, develop, from monkeys,
baboons—a theory more significant perhaps in its indirections, or what it necessitates, than it is even in itself. (Of the
twain, far apart as they seem, and angrily as their conflicting
advocates to-day oppose each other, are not both theories to
be possibly reconcil'd, and even blended? Can we, indeed,
spare either of them? Better still, out of them is not a third
theory, the real one, or suggesting the real one, to arise?)

Of this old theory, evolution, as broach'd anew, trebled,
with indeed all-devouring claims, by Darwin, it has so much
in it, and is so needed as a counterpoise to yet widely prevailing and unspeakably tenacious, enfeebling superstitions—is
fused, by the new man, into such grand, modest, truly scientific accompaniments—that the world of erudition, both
moral and physical, cannot but be eventually better'd and
broaden'd in its speculations, from the advent of Darwinism.
Nevertheless, the problem of origins, human and other, is not
the least whit nearer its solution. In due time the Evolution
theory will have to abate its vehemence, cannot be allow'd to
dominate every thing else, and will have to take its place as
a segment of the circle, the cluster—as but one of many
theories, many thoughts, of profoundest value—and re-
adjusting and differentiating much, yet leaving the divine
secrets just as inexplicable and unreachable as before—may-
be more so.

*Then furthermore*—What is finally to be done by priest or

poet—and by priest or poet only—amid all the stupendous and dazzling novelties of our century, with the advent of America, and of science and democracy—remains just as indispensable, after all the work of the grand astronomers, chemists, linguists, historians, and explorers of the last hundred years—and the wondrous German and other metaphysicians of that time—and will continue to remain, needed, America and here, just the same as in the world of Europe, or Asia, of a hundred, or a thousand, or several thousand years ago. I think indeed *more* needed, to furnish statements from the present points, the added arriere, and the unspeakably immenser vistas of to-day. Only the priests and poets of the modern, at least as exalted as any in the past, fully absorbing and appreciating the results of the past, in the commonalty of all humanity, all time, (the main results already, for there is perhaps nothing more, or at any rate not much, strictly new, only more important modern combinations, and new relative adjustments,) must indeed recast the old metal, the already achiev'd material, into and through new moulds, current forms.

Meantime, the highest and subtlest and broadest truths of modern science wait for their true assignment and last vivid flashes of light—as Democracy waits for its—through first-class metaphysicians and speculative philosophs—laying the basements and foundations for those new, more expanded, more harmonious, more melodious, freer American poems.

## THE TRAMP AND STRIKE QUESTIONS

*Part of a Lecture proposed, (never deliver'd)*

Two grim and spectral dangers—dangerous to peace, to health, to social security, to progress—long known in concrete to the governments of the Old World, and there eventuating, more than once or twice, in dynastic overturns, bloodshed, days, months, of terror—seem of late years to be nearing the New World, nay, to be gradually establishing themselves among us. What mean these phantoms here? (I personify them in fictitious shapes, but they are very real.) Is the fresh and broad demesne of America destined also to give them foothold and lodgment, permanent domicile?

Beneath the whole political world, what most presses and perplexes to-day, sending vastest results affecting the future, is not the abstract question of democracy, but of social and economic organization, the treatment of working-people by employers, and all that goes along with it—not only the wages-payment part, but a certain spirit and principle, to vivify anew these relations; all the questions of progress, strength, tariffs, finance, etc., really evolving themselves more or less directly out of the Poverty Question, ("the Science of Wealth," and a dozen other names are given it, but I prefer the severe one just used.) I will begin by calling the reader's attention to a thought upon the matter which may not have struck you before—the wealth of the civilized world, as contrasted with its poverty—what does it derivatively stand for, and represent? A rich person ought to have a strong stomach. As in Europe the wealth of to-day mainly results from, and represents, the rapine, murder, outrages, treachery, hoggishness, of hundreds of years ago, and onward, later, so in America, after the same token—(not yet so bad, perhaps, or at any rate not so palpable—we have not existed long enough—but we seem to be doing our best to make it up.)

Curious as it may seem, it is in what are call'd the poorest, lowest characters you will sometimes, nay generally, find glints of the most sublime virtues, eligibilities, heroisms. Then it is doubtful whether the State is to be saved, either in the monotonous long run, or in tremendous special crises, by its good people only. When the storm is deadliest, and the disease most imminent, help often comes from strange quarters—(the homœopathic motto, you remember, *cure the bite with a hair of the same dog*.)

The American Revolution of 1776 was simply a great strike, successful for its immediate object—but whether a real success judged by the scale of the centuries, and the long-striking balance of Time, yet remains to be settled. The French Revolution was absolutely a strike, and a very terrible and relentless one, against ages of bad pay, unjust division of wealth-products, and the hoggish monopoly of a few, rolling in superfluity, against the vast bulk of the work-people, living in squalor.

If the United States, like the countries of the Old World, are also to grow vast crops of poor, desperate, dissatisfied, nomadic, miserably-waged populations, such as we see looming upon us of late years—steadily, even if slowly, eating into them like a cancer of lungs or stomach—then our republican experiment, notwithstanding all its surface-successes, is at heart an unhealthy failure.

*February '79.*—I saw to-day a sight I had never seen before —and it amazed, and made me serious; three quite good-looking American men, of respectable personal presence, two of them young, carrying chiffonier-bags on their shoulders, and the usual long iron hooks in their hands, plodding along, their eyes cast down, spying for scraps, rags, bones, etc.

## THE BIBLE AS POETRY

I SUPPOSE one cannot at this day say anything new, from a literary point of view, about those autochthonic bequests of Asia—the Hebrew Bible, the mighty Hindu epics, and a hundred lesser but typical works; (not now definitely including the Iliad—though that work was certainly of Asiatic genesis, as Homer himself was—considerations which seem curiously ignored.) But will there ever be a time or place—ever a student, however modern, of the grand art, to whom those compositions will not afford profounder lessons than all else of their kind in the garnerage of the past? Could there be any more opportune suggestion, to the current popular writer and reader of verse, what the office of poet was in primeval times—and is yet capable of being, anew, adjusted entirely to the modern?

All the poems of Orientalism, with the Old and New Testaments at the centre, tend to deep and wide, (I don't know but the deepest and widest,) psychological development—with little, or nothing at all, of the mere esthetic, the principal verse-requirement of our day. Very late, but unerringly, comes to every capable student the perception that it is not in beauty, it is not in art, it is not even in science, that the profoundest laws of the case have their eternal sway and out-cropping.

In his discourse on "Hebrew Poets" De Sola Mendes said: "The fundamental feature of Judaism, of the Hebrew nationality, was religion; its poetry was naturally religious. Its subjects, God and Providence, the covenants with Israel, God in Nature, and as reveal'd, God the Creator and Governor, Nature in her majesty and beauty, inspired hymns and odes to Nature's God. And then the checker'd history of the nation furnish'd allusions, illustrations, and subjects for epic display—the glory of the sanctuary, the offerings, the splendid ritual, the Holy City, and lov'd Palestine with its pleasant valleys and wild tracts." Dr. Mendes said "that rhyming was not a characteristic of Hebrew poetry at all. Metre was not a necessary mark of poetry. Great poets discarded it; the early Jewish poets knew it not."

Compared with the famed epics of Greece, and lesser ones since, the spinal supports of the Bible are simple and meagre. All its history, biography, narratives, etc., are as beads, strung on and indicating the eternal thread of the Deific purpose and power. Yet with only deepest faith for impetus, and such Deific purpose for palpable or impalpable theme, it often transcends the masterpieces of Hellas, and all masterpieces. The metaphors daring beyond account, the lawless soul, extravagant by our standards, the glow of love and friendship, the fervent kiss—nothing in argument or logic, but unsurpass'd in proverbs, in religious ecstasy, in suggestions of common mortality and death, man's great equalizers —the spirit everything, the ceremonies and forms of the churches nothing, faith limitless, its immense sensuousness immensely spiritual—an incredible, all-inclusive non-worldliness and dew-scented illiteracy (the antipodes of our Nineteenth Century business absorption and morbid refinement) —no hair-splitting doubts, no sickly sulking and sniffling, no *Hamlet*, no "Adonais", no "Thanatopsis", no "In Memoriam".

The culminated proof of the poetry of a country is the quality of its personnel, which, in any race, can never be really superior without superior poems. The finest blending of individuality with universality (in my opinion nothing out of the galaxies of the *Iliad* or Shakspere's heroes, or from the Tennysonian *Idylls*, so lofty, devoted and starlike,) typified in the songs of those old Asiatic lands. Men and Women as great columnar trees. Nowhere else the abnegation of self towering in such quaint sublimity; nowhere else the simplest human emotions conquering the gods of heaven, and fate itself. (The episode, for instance, toward the close of the *Mahabharata*—the journey of the wife Savitri with the god of death, Yama,

> "One terrible to see—blood-red his garb,
>  His body huge and dark, bloodshot his eyes,
>  Which flamed like suns beneath his turban cloth,
>  Arm'd was he with a noose,"

who carries off the soul of the dead husband, the wife tenaciously following, and—by the resistless charm of perfect poetic recitation!—eventually redeeming her captive mate.)

I remember how enthusiastically William H. Seward, in his last days, once expatiated on these themes, from his travels in Turkey, Egypt, and Asia Minor, finding the oldest Biblical narratives exactly illustrated there to-day with apparently no break or change along three thousand years—the veil'd women, the costumes, the gravity and simplicity, all the manners just the same. The veteran Trelawney said he found the only real *nobleman* in the world in a good average specimen of the mid-aged or elderly Oriental. In the East the grand figure, always leading, is the *old man*, majestic, with flowing beard, paternal, etc. In Europe and America, it is, as we know, the young fellow—in novels, a handsome and interesting hero, more or less juvenile—in operas, a tenor with blooming cheeks, black mustache, superficial animation, and perhaps good lungs, but no more depth than skim-milk. But reading folks probably get their information of those Bible areas and current peoples, as depicted in print by English and French cads, the most shallow, impudent, supercilious brood on earth.

I have said nothing yet of the cumulus of associations (perfectly legitimate parts of its influence, and finally in many respects the dominant parts,) of the Bible as a poetic entity, and of every portion of it. Not the old edifice only—the congeries also of events and struggles and surroundings, of which it has been the scene and motive—even the horrors, dreads, deaths. How many ages and generations have brooded and wept and agonized over this book! What un-tellable joys and ecstasies—what support to martyrs at the stake—from it. (No really great song can ever attain full purport till long after the death of its singer—till it has accrued and incorporated the many passions, many joys and sorrows, it has itself arous'd.) To what myriads has it been the shore and rock of safety—the refuge from driving tem-pest and wreck! Translated in all languages, how it has united this diverse world! Of civilized lands to-day, whose of our retrospects has it not interwoven and link'd and per-meated? Not only does it bring us what is clasp'd within its covers; nay, that is the least of what it brings. Of its thou-sands, there is not a verse, not a word, but is thick-studded with human emotions, successions of fathers and sons, mothers and daughters, of our own antecedents, inseparable from that background of us, on which, phantasmal as it is, all that we are to-day inevitably depends—our ancestry, our past.

Strange, but true, that the principal factor in cohering the nations, eras and paradoxes of the globe, by giving them a common platform of two or three great ideas, a commonalty of origin, and projecting kosmic brotherhood, the dream of all hope, all time—that the long trains, gestations, attempts and failures, resulting in the New World, and in modern solidarity and politics—are to be identified and resolv'd back into a collection of old poetic lore, which, more than any one thing else, has been the axis of civilization and history through thousands of years—and except for which this America of ours, with its polity and essentials, could not now be existing.

No true bard will ever contravene the Bible. If the time ever comes when iconoclasm does its extremest in one direc-tion against the Books of the Bible in its present form, the collection must still survive in another, and dominate just as much as hitherto, or more than hitherto, through its divine and primal poetic structure. To me, that is the living and definite element-principle of the work, evolving everything else. Then the continuity; the oldest and newest Asiatic utterance and character, and all between, holding together, like the appari-tion of the sky, and coming to us the same. Even to our Nineteenth Century here are the fountain heads of song.

# A THOUGHT ON SHAKSPERE

THE most distinctive poems—the most permanently rooted and with heartiest reason for being—the copious cycle of Arthurian legends, or the almost equally copious Charlemagne cycle, or the poems of the Cid, or Scandinavian Eddas, or Nibelungen, or Chaucer, or Spenser, or *bona fide* Ossian, or *Inferno*—probably had their rise in the great historic perturbations, which they came in to sum up and confirm, indirectly embodying results to date. Then however precious to "culture", the grandest of those poems, it may be said, preserve and typify results offensive to the modern spirit, and long past away. To state it briefly, and taking the strongest examples, in Homer lives the ruthless military prowess of Greece, and of its special god-descended dynastic houses; in Shakspere the dragon-rancors and stormy feudal splendor of mediæval caste.

Poetry, largely consider'd, is an evolution, sending out improved and ever-expanded types—in one sense, the past, even the best of it, necessarily giving place, and dying out. For our existing world, the bases on which all the grand old poems were built have become vacuums—and even those of many comparatively modern ones are broken and half-gone. For us to-day, not their own intrinsic value, vast as that is, backs and maintains those poems—but a mountain-high growth of associations, the layers of successive ages. Everywhere—their own lands included—(is there not something terrible in the tenacity with which the one book out of millions holds its grip?)—the Homeric and Virgilian works, the interminable ballad-romances of the middle ages, the utterances of Dante, Spenser, and others, are upheld by their cumulus-entrenchment in scholarship, and as precious, always welcome, unspeakably valuable reminiscences.

Even the one who at present reigns unquestion'd—of Shakspere—for all he stands for so much in modern literature, he stands entirely for the mighty esthetic sceptres of the past, not for the spiritual and democratic, the sceptres of the future. The inward and outward characteristics of Shakspere are his vast and rich variety of persons and themes, with his wondrous delineation of each and all—not only limitless funds of verbal and pictorial resource, but great excess, superfœtation—mannerism, like a fine, aristocratic perfume, holding a touch of musk (Euphues, his mark)—with boundless sumptuousness and adornment, real velvet and gems, not shoddy nor paste—but a good deal of bombast and fustian—(certainly some terrific mouthing in Shakspere!)

Superb and inimitable as all is, it is mostly an objective and physiological kind of power and beauty the soul finds in Shakspere—a style supremely grand of the sort, but in my opinion stopping short of the grandest sort, at any rate for fulfilling and satisfying modern and scientific and democratic American purposes. Think, not of growths as forests primeval, or Yellowstone geysers, or Colorado ravines, but of costly marble palaces, and palace rooms, and the noblest fixings and furniture, and noble owners and occupants to correspond—think of carefully built gardens from the beautiful but sophisticated gardening art at its best, with walks and bowers and artificial lakes, and appropriate statue-groups and the finest cultivated roses and lilies and japonicas in plenty—and you have the tally of Shakspere. The low characters, mechanics, even the loyal henchmen—all in themselves nothing—serve as capital foils to the aristocracy. The comedies (exquisite as they certainly are) bringing in admirably portray'd common characters, have the unmistakable hue of plays, portraits, made for the divertisement only of the élite of the castle, and from its point of view. The comedies are altogether non-acceptable to America and Democracy.

But to the deepest soul, it seems a shame to pick and choose from the riches Shakspere has left us—to criticize his infinitely royal, multiform quality—to gauge, with optic glasses, the dazzle of his sun-like beams.

The best poetic utterance, after all, can merely hint, or remind, often very indirectly, or at distant removes. Aught of real perfection, or the solution of any deep problem, or any completed statement of the moral, the true, the beautiful, eludes the greatest, deftest poet—flies away like an always uncaught bird.

## ROBERT BURNS AS POET AND PERSON

WHAT the future will decide about Robert Burns and his works—what place will be assign'd them on that great roster of geniuses and genius which can only be finish'd by the slow but sure balancing of the centuries with their ample average —I of course cannot tell. But as we know him, from his recorded utterances, and after nearly one century, and its diligence of collections, songs, letters, anecdotes, presenting the figure of the canny Scotchman in a fullness and detail wonderfully complete, and the lines mainly by his own hand, he forms to-day, in some respects, the most interesting personality among singers. Then there are many things in Burns's poems and character that specially endear him to America. He was essentially a Republican—would have been at home in the Western United States, and probably become eminent there. He was an average sample of the good-natured, warm-blooded, proud-spirited, amative, alimentive, convivial, young and early-middle-aged man of the decent-born middle classes everywhere and any how. Without the race of which he is a distinct specimen, (and perhaps his poems) America and her powerful Democracy could not exist to-day—could not project with unparallel'd historic sway into the future.

Perhaps the peculiar coloring of the era of Burns needs always first to be consider'd. It included the times of the '76-'83 Revolution in America, of the French Revolution, and an unparallel'd chaos development in Europe and elsewhere. In every department, shining and strange names, like stars, some rising, some in meridian, some declining—Voltaire, Franklin, Washington, Kant, Goethe, Fulton, Napoleon, mark the era. And while so much, and of grandest moment, fit for the trumpet of the world's fame, was being transacted—that little tragi-comedy of R. B.'s life and death was going on in a country by-place in Scotland!

Burns's correspondence, generally collected and publish'd since his death, gives wonderful glints into both the amiable and weak (and worse than weak) parts of his portraiture, habits, good and bad luck, ambition and associations. His letters to Mrs. Dunlop, Mrs. McLehose, (Clarinda), Mr. Thompson, Dr. Moore, Robert Muir, Mr. Cunningham,

Miss Margaret Chalmers, Peter Hill, Richard Brown, Mrs.
Riddel, Robert Ainslie, and Robert Graham, afford valuable
lights and shades to the outline, and with numerous others,
help to a touch here, and fill-in there, of poet and poems.
There are suspicions, it is true, of "the Genteel Letter-
Writer", with scraps and words from "the Manual of French
Quotations", and, in the love-letters, some hollow mouth-
ings. Yet we wouldn't on any account lack the letters. A full
and true portrait is always what is wanted; veracity at every
hazard. Besides, do we not all see by this time that the story
of Burns, even for its own sake, requires the record of the
whole and several, with nothing left out? Completely and
every point minutely told out its fullest, explains and justifies
itself—(as perhaps almost any life does). He is very close to
the earth. He pick'd up his best words and tunes directly
from the Scotch home-singers, but tells Thompson they
would not please his, T.'s, "learn'd lugs", adding, "I call
them simple—you would pronounce them silly." Yes, indeed; the idiom was undoubtedly his happiest hit. Yet Dr.
Moore, in 1789, writes to Burns, "If I were to offer an opinion, it would be that in your future productions you should
abandon the Scotch stanza and dialect, and adopt the measure and language of modern English poetry"!

As the 128th birth-anniversary of the poet draws on,
(January, 1887,) with its increasing club-suppers, vehement
celebrations, letters, speeches, and so on—(mostly, as William O'Connor says, from people who would not have
noticed R. B. at all during his actual life, nor kept his company, or read his verses, on any account)—it may be opportune to print some leisurely-jotted notes I find in my budget.
I take my observation of the Scottish bard by considering him
as an individual amid the crowded clusters, galaxies, of the
old world—and fairly inquiring and suggesting what out of
these myriads he too may be to the Western Republic. In the
first place no poet on record so fully bequeaths his own personal magnetism,* nor illustrates more pointedly how one's

---

* Probably no man that ever lived—a friend has made the statement
—was so fondly loved, both by men and women, as Robert Burns. The
reason is not hard to find: he had a real heart of flesh and blood beating in his bosom; you could almost hear it throb. "Some one said,
that if you had shaken hands with him his hand would have burnt

verses, by time and reading, can so curiously fuse with the versifier's own life and death, and give final light and shade to all.

I would say a large part of the fascination of Burns's homely, simple dialect-melodies is due, for all current and future readers, to the poet's personal "errors", the general bleakness of his lot, his ingrain'd pensiveness, his brief dash into dazzling, tantalizing, evanescent sunshine—finally culminating in those last years of his life, his being taboo'd and in debt, sick and sore, yaw'd as by contending gales, deeply dissatisfied with everything, most of all with himself—high-spirited too—(no man ever really higher-spirited than Robert Burns.) I think it a perfectly legitimate part too. At any rate it has come to be an impalpable aroma through which only both the songs and their singer must henceforth be read and absorb'd. Through that view-medium of misfortune—of a noble spirit in low environments, and of a squalid and premature death—we view the undoubted facts, (giving, as we read them now, a sad kind of pungency,) that Burns's were, before all else, the lyrics of illicit loves and carousing intoxication. Perhaps even it is this strange, impalpable *post-mortem* comment and influence referr'd to, that gives them their contrast, attraction, making the zest of their author's after fame. If he had lived steady, fat, moral, comfortable, well-to-do years, on his own grade, (let alone, what of course was out of the question, the ease and velvet and rosewood and copious royalties of Tennyson or Victor Hugo or Longfellow,) and died well-ripen'd and respectable, where could have come in that burst of passionate sobbing and remorse which well'd forth instantly and generally in Scotland, and soon follow'd everywhere among English-speaking races, on

---

yours. The gods, indeed, made him poetical, but Nature had a hand in him first. His heart was in the right place; he did not pile up cantos of poetic diction; he pluck'd the mountain daisy under his feet; he wrote of field-mouse hurrying from its ruin'd dwelling. He held the plough or the pen with the same firm, manly grasp. And he was loved. The simple roll of the women who gave him their affection and their sympathy would make a long manuscript; and most of these were of such noble worth that, as Robert Chambers says, 'their character may stand as a testimony in favor of that of Burns.' " [As I understand, the foregoing is from an extremely rare book publish'd by M'Kie, in Kilmarnock. I find the whole beautiful paragraph in a capital paper on Burns, by Amelia Barr.]

♠

the announcement of his death? and which, with no sign of stopping, only regulated and vein'd with fitting appreciation, flows deeply, widely yet?

Dear Rob! manly, witty, fond, friendly, full of weak spots as well as strong ones—essential type of so many thousands —perhaps the average, as just said, of the decent-born young men and the early mid-aged, not only of the British Isles, but America, too, North and South, just the same. I think, indeed, one best part of Burns is the unquestionable proof he presents of the perennial existence among the laboring classes, especially farmers, of the finest latent poetic elements in their blood. (How clear it is to me that the common soil has always been, and is now, thickly strewn with just such gems.) He is well-called the *Ploughman*. "Holding the plough", said his brother Gilbert, "was the favorite situation with Robert for poetic compositions; and some of his best verses were produced while he was at that exercise." "I must return to my humble station, and woo my rustic muse in my wonted way, at the plough-tail." 1787, to the Earl of Buchan. He has no high ideal of the poet or the poet's office; indeed quite a low and contracted notion of both:

> "Fortune! if thou'll but gie me still
> Hale breeks, a scone, and whiskey gill,
> An' rowth o' rhyme to rave at will,
> Tak' a' the rest."

See also his rhym'd letters to Robert Graham invoking patronage; "one stronghold", Lord Glencairn, being dead, now these appeals to "Fintra, my other stay", (with in one letter a copious shower of vituperation generally.) In his collected poems there is no particular unity, nothing that can be called a leading theory, no unmistakable spine or skeleton. Perhaps, indeed, their very desultoriness is the charm of his songs: "I take up one or another", he says in a letter to Thompson, "just as the bee of the moment buzzes in my bonnet-lug."

Consonantly with the customs of the time—yet markedly inconsistent in spirit with Burns's own case, (and not a little painful as it remains on record, as depicting some features of the bard himself,) the relation called *patronage* existed between the nobility and gentry on one side, and literary people on the other, and gives one of the strongest side-lights to the general coloring of poems and poets. It crops out a good deal in Burns's Letters, and even necessitated a certain flunkeyism on occasions, through life. It probably, with its requirements, (while it help'd in money and countenance) did as much as any one cause in making that life a chafed and unhappy one, ended by a premature and miserable death.

Yes, there is something about Burns peculiarly acceptable to the concrete, human points of view. He poetizes work-a-day agricultural labor and life, (whose spirit and sympathies, as well as practicalities, are much the same everywhere,) and treats fresh, often coarse, natural occurrences, loves, persons, not like many new and some old poets in a genteel style of gilt and china, or at second or third removes, but in their own born atmosphere, laughter, sweat, unction. Perhaps no one ever sang "lads and lasses"—that universal race, mainly the same, too, all ages, all lands—down on their own plane, as he has. He exhibits no philosophy worth mentioning; his morality is hardly more than parrot-talk—not bad or deficient, but cheap, shopworn, the platitudes of old aunts and uncles to the youngsters (be good boys and keep your noses clean.) Only when he gets at Poosie Nansie's, celebrating the "barley bree", or among tramps, or democratic bouts and drinking generally,

("Freedom and whiskey gang thegither,")

we have, in his own unmistakable color and warmth, those interiors of rake-helly life and tavern fun—the cantabile of jolly beggars in highest jinks—lights and groupings of rank glee and brawny amorousness, outvying the best painted pictures of the Dutch school, or any school.

By America and her democracy such a poet, I cannot too often repeat, must be kept in loving remembrance; but it is best that discriminations be made. His admirers (as at those anniversary suppers, over the "hot Scotch") will not accept for their favorite anything less than the highest rank, alongside of Homer, Shakspere, etc. Such, in candor, are not the true friends of the Ayrshire bard, who really needs a different place quite by himself. The Iliad and the Odyssey express courage, craft, full-grown heroism in situations of danger, the sense of command and leadership, emulation, the last and fullest evolution of self-poise as in kings, and god-like even while animal appetites. The Shaksperean compositions, on vertebers and framework of the primary passions, portray (essentially the same as Homer's,) the spirit and letter of the feudal world, the Norman lord, ambitious and arrogant, taller and nobler than common men—with much underplay and gusts of heat and cold, volcanoes and stormy seas. Burns (and some will say to his credit) attempts none of these themes. He poetizes the humor, riotous blood, sulks, amorous torments, fondness for the tavern and for cheap objective nature, with disgust at the grim and narrow ecclesiasticism of his time and land, of a young farmer on a bleak and hired farm in Scotland, through the years and under the circumstances of the British politics of that time, and of his short personal career as author, from 1783 to 1796. He is intuitive and affectionate, and just emerged or emerging from the shackles of the kirk, from poverty, ignorance, and from his own rank appetites—(out of which latter, however, he never extricated himself.) It is to be said that amid not a little smoke and gas in his poems, there is in almost every piece a spark of fire, and now and then the real afflatus. He has been applauded as democratic, and with some warrant; while Shakspere, and with the greatest warrant, has been called monarchical or aristocratic (which he certainly is). But the splendid personalizations of Shakspere, formulated on the largest, freest, most heroic, most artistic mould, are to me far dearer as lessons, and more precious even as models for Democracy, than the humdrum samples Burns presents. The motives of some of his effusions are certainly discreditable personally—one or two of them markedly so. He has, moreover, little or no spirituality. This last is his mortal flaw and defect, tried by highest standards. The ideal he never reach'd (and yet I think he leads the way to it). He gives melodies, and now and then the simplest and sweetest ones; but harmonies, complications, oratorios in words, never. (I do not speak this in any deprecatory sense. Blessed be the memory of the warm-hearted Scotchman for what he has left us, just as it is!) He likewise did not know himself, in more ways

than one.  Though so really free and independent, he prided
himself in his songs on being a reactionist and a Jacobite—on
persistent sentimental adherency to the cause of the Stuarts
—the weakest, thinnest, most faithless, brainless dynasty that
ever held a throne.

Thus, while Burns is not at all great for New World study,
in the sense that Isaiah and Eschylus and the book of Job are
unquestionably great—is not to be mention'd with Shakspere
—hardly even with current Tennyson or our Emerson—he
has a nestling niche of his own, all fragrant, fond, and quaint
and homely—a lodge built near but outside the mighty
temple of the gods of song and art—those universal strivers,
through their works of harmony and melody and power, to
ever show or intimate man's crowning, last, victorious fusion
in himself of Real and Ideal.  Precious, too—fit and precious
beyond all singers, high or low—will Burns ever be to the
native Scotch, especially to the working-classes of North
Britain; so intensely one of them, and so racy of the soil,
sights, and local customs.  He often apostrophizes Scotland,
and is, or would be, enthusiastically patriotic.  His country
has lately commemorated him in a statue.*  His aim is declaredly to be "a Rustic Bard".  His poems were all written in
youth or young manhood, (he was little more than a young
man when he died).  His collected works in giving everything,
are nearly one half first drafts.  His brightest hit is his use of
the Scotch patois, so full of terms flavor'd like wild fruits or
berries.  Then I should make an allowance to Burns which
cannot be made for any other poet.  Curiously even the frequent crudeness, haste, deficiencies, (flatness and puerilities
by no means absent) prove upon the whole not out of keep-

* The Dumfries statue of Robert Burns was successfully unveil'd
April 1881 by Lord Rosebery, the occasion having been made national
in its character.  Before the ceremony, a large procession paraded the
streets of the town, all the trades and societies of that part of Scotland
being represented, at the head of which went dairymen and ploughmen,
the former driving their carts and being accompanied by their maids.
The statue is of Sicilian marble.  It rests on a pedestal of gray stone five
feet high.  The poet is represented as sitting easily on an old tree root,
holding in his left hand a cluster of daisies.  His face is turn'd toward
the right shoulder, and the eyes gaze into the distance.  Near by lie a
collie dog, a broad bonnet half covering a well-thumb'd song-book,
and a rustic flageolet.  The costume is taken from the Nasmyth portrait, which has been follow'd for the features of the face.

ing in any comprehensive collection of his works, heroically printed, "following copy", every piece, every line according to originals. Other poets might tremble for such boldness, such rawness. In "this odd-kind chiel" such points hardly mar the rest. Not only are they in consonance with the underlying spirit of the pieces, but complete the full abandon and veracity of the farm-fields and the home-brew'd flavor of the Scotch vernacular. (Is there not often something in the very neglect, unfinish, careless nudity, slovenly hiatus, coming from intrinsic genius, and not "put on", that secretly pleases the soul more than the wrought and re-wrought polish of the most perfect verse?) Mark the native spice and untranslatable twang in the very names of his songs—"O for ane and twenty, Tam," "John Barleycorn," "Last May a braw Wooer," "Rattlin roarin' Willie," "O wert thou in the cauld, cauld blast," "Gude e'en to you, Kimmer," "Merry hae I been teething a Heckle," "O lay thy loof in mine, lass," and others.

The longer and more elaborated poems of Burns are just such as would please a natural but homely taste, and cute but average intellect, and are inimitable in their way. The "Twa Dogs", (one of the best) with the conversation between Cesar and Luath, the "Brigs of Ayr", "the Cotter's Saturday Night", "Tam O' Shanter"—all will be long read and re-read and admired, and ever deserve to be. With nothing profound in any of them, what there is of moral and plot has an inimitably fresh and racy flavor. If it came to question, Literature could well afford to send adrift many a pretensive poem, and even book of poems, before it could spare these compositions.

Never indeed was there truer utterance in a certain range of idiosyncrasy than by this poet. Hardly a piece of his, large or small, but has "snap" and raciness. He puts in cantering rhyme (often doggerel) much cutting irony and idiomatic ear-cuffing of the kirk-deacons—drily good-natured addresses to his cronies, (he certainly would not stop us if he were here this moment, from classing that "to the De'il" among them)—"to Mailie and her Lambs", "to auld Mare Maggie", "to a Mouse",

> "Wee, sleekit, cowrin, tim'rous beastie:"

"to a Mountain Daisy", "to a Haggis", "to a Louse", "to the Toothache", etc.—and occasionally to his brother bards and lady or gentleman patrons, often with strokes of tenderest sensibility, idiopathic humor, and genuine poetic imagination —still oftener with shrewd, original, sheeny, steel-flashes of wit, home-spun sense, or lance-blade puncturing. Then, strangely, the basis of Burns's character, with all its fun and manliness, was hypochondria, the blues, palpable enough in "Despondency", "Man was made to Mourn", "Address to Ruin", a "Bard's Epitaph", etc. From such deep-down elements sprout up, in very contrast and paradox, those riant utterances of which a superficial reading will not detect the hidden foundation. Yet nothing is clearer to me than the black and desperate background behind those pieces—as I shall now specify them. I find his most characteristic, Nature's masterly touch and luxuriant life-blood, color and heat, not in "Tam O' Shanter", "the Cotter's Saturday Night", "Scots wha hae", "Highland Mary", "the Twa Dogs", and the like, but in "the Jolly Beggars", "Rigs of Barley", "Scotch Drink", "the Epistle to John Rankine", "Holy Willie's Prayer", and in "Halloween", (to say nothing of a certain cluster, known still to a small inner circle in Scotland, but, for good reasons, not published anywhere.) In these compositions, especially the first, there is much indelicacy (some editions flatly leave it out,) but the composer reigns alone, with handling free and broad and true, and is an artist. You may see and feel the man indirectly in his other verses, all of them, with more or less life-likeness—but these I have named last call out pronouncedly in his own voice,

"I, Rob, am here."

Finally, in any summing-up of Burns, though so much is to be said in the way of fault-finding, drawing black marks, and doubtless severe literary criticism—(in the present outpouring I have "kept myself in", rather than allow'd any free flow)— after full retrospect of his works and life, the aforesaid "odd-kind chiel" remains to my heart and brain as almost the tenderest, manliest, and (even if contradictory) dearest flesh-and-blood figure in all the streams and clusters of by-gone poets.

# WALT WHITMAN IN CAMDEN

## By George Selwyn

It is not a little difficult to write an article about Walt Whitman's *home*, for it was humorously said by himself, not long ago, that he had all his life possessed a home only in the sense that a ship possesses one. Hardly, indeed, till the year 1884 could he be called the occupant of such a definite place, even the kind of one I shall presently describe. To illustrate his own half-jocular remark as just given, and to jot down a few facts about the poet in Camden during the last sixteen years, and about his present home, is my only purpose in this article. I have decided to steer clear of any criticism of *Leaves of Grass*, and confine myself to his condition and a brief outline of his personal history. I should also like to dwell a moment on what may be called the peculiar outfit or schooling he has chosen, to fulfil his mission as poet, according to his own ideal.

In the observation of the drama of human nature—if, indeed, "all the world's a stage"—Walt Whitman has had rare advantages as auditor, from the beginning. Several of his earlier years, embracing the age of fifteen to twenty-one, were spent in teaching country schools in Queens and Suffolk counties, New York, following the quaint old fashion of "boarding around", that is, moving from house to house and farm to farm, among high and low, living a few days alternately at each, until the quarter was up, and then commencing over again. His occupation, for a long period, as printer, with frequent traveling, is to be remembered; also as carpenter. Quite a good deal of his life has been passed in boarding-houses and hotels. The three years in the Secession War of course play a marked part. He never made any long sea-voyages, but for years at one period (1846-60) went out in their boats, sometimes for a week at a time, with the New York Bay pilots, among whom he was a great favorite. In 1848-49 his location was in New Orleans, with occasional sojourns in the other Gulf States besides Louisiana. From 1865 to '73 he lived in Washington. Born in 1819, his life through childhood and as a young and middle-aged man— that is, up to 1862—was mainly spent, with a few intervals of

Western and Southern jaunts, on his native Long Island, mostly in Brooklyn. At that date, aged forty-two, he went down to the field of war in Virginia, and for the three subsequent years he was actively engaged as volunteer attendant and nurse on the battlefields, to the Southern soldiers equally with the Northern, and among the wounded in the army hospitals. He was prostrated by hospital malaria and "inflammation of the veins" in 1864, but recovered. He worked "on his own hook", had indomitable strength, health, and activity, was on the move night and day, not only till the official close of the Secession struggle, but for a long time afterward, for there was a vast legacy of suffering soldiers left when the contest was over. He was permanently appointed under President Lincoln, in 1865, to a respectable office in the Attorney-General's department. (This followed his removal from a temporary clerkship in the Indian Bureau of the Interior Department. Secretary Harlan dismissed him from that post specifically for being the author of *Leaves of Grass*.) He worked on for some time in the Attorney-General's office, and was promoted, but the seeds of the hospital malaria seemed never to have been fully eradicated. He was at last struck down, quite suddenly, by a severe paralytic shock (left hemiplegia), from which—after some weeks—he was slowly recovering, when he lost by death his mother and his sister. Soon followed two additional shocks of paralysis, though slighter than the first. Summer had now commenced at Washington, and his doctor imperatively ordered the sick man an entire change of scene—the mountains or the seashore. Whitman accordingly left Washington, destined for the New Jersey or Long Island coast, but at Philadelphia found himself too ill to proceed any further. He was brought over to Camden, and has been living there ever since. . . .

I must forbear expanding on the poet's career these fifteen years, only noting that during them (1880) occurs the final completion of *Leaves of Grass*, the object of his life. His present domicile is a little old-fashioned frame house, situated about gunshot from the Delaware River on a clean, quiet, democratic street. This "shanty", as he calls it, was purchased by the poet five years ago for $2,000—two-thirds being paid in cash. In it he occupies the second floor. I commenced by likening his home to that of a ship, and the comparison might go farther. Though larger than any vessel's cabin, Walt Whitman's room, at 328 Mickle Street, Camden, has all the rudeness, simplicity, and free-and-easy character of the quarters of some old sailor. In the good-sized, three-windowed apartment, 20 by 20 feet or over, there are a wood stove, a bare board floor of narrow planks, a comfortable bed, divers big and little boxes, a good gas lamp, two big tables, a few old uncushioned seats, and lots of pegs and hooks and shelves. Hung or tacked on the walls are pictures, those of his father, mother and sisters holding the places of honor, a portrait of a sweetheart of long ago, a large print of Osceola the Seminole chief (given to Whitman many years since by Catlin the artist), some rare old engravings by Strange, and "Banditti Regaling", by Mortimer. Heaps of books, manuscripts, memoranda, scissorings, proof-sheets, pamphlets, newspapers, old and new magazines, mysterious-looking literary bundles tied up with stout strings, lie about the floor here and there. Off against a back wall looms a mighty trunk having double locks and bands of iron—such a receptacle as comes over sea with the foreign emigrants, and you in New York may have seen hoisted by powerful tackle from the hold of some Hamburg ship.

On the main table more books, some of them evidently old-timers, a Bible, several Shakespeares—a nook devoted to translations of Homer and Aeschylus and the other Greek poets and tragedians, with Felton's and Symond's books on Greece—a collection of the works of Fauriel and Ellis on mediaeval poetry—a well-thumbed volume (his companion, off and on, for fifty years) of Walter Scott's *Border Minstrelsy*, —Tennyson, Ossian, Burns, Omar Khayyám, all miscellaneously together. Whitman's stalwart form itself luxuriates in a curious, great cane-seat chair, with posts and rungs like ship's spars; altogether the most imposing, heavy-timbered, broad-armed and broad-bottomed edifice of the kind possible. It was the Christmas gift of the young son and daughter of Thomas Donaldson, of Philadelphia, and was specially made for the poet. . . .

(If I slightly infringe the rule laid down at the beginning, to attempt no literary criticism, I hope the reader will excuse it.)

Both Walt Whitman's book and personal character need to be studied a long time and in the mass, and are not to be gauged by custom. I never knew a man who—for all he takes an absorbing interest in politics, literature, and what is called "the world"—seems to be so poised on himself alone. Dr. Drinkard, the Washington physician who attended him in his paralysis, wrote to the Philadelphia doctor into whose hands the case passed, saying among other things: "In his bodily organism, and in his constitution, tastes and habits, Whitman is the most *natural* man I have ever met." The primary foundation of the poet's character, at the same time, is certainly spiritual. Helen Price, who knew him for fifteen years, pronounces him (in Dr. Bucke's book) the most essentially religious person she ever knew. On this foundation has been built up, layer by layer, the rich, diversified, concrete experience of his life, from its earliest years. Then his aim and ideal have not been the technical literary ones. His strong individuality, willfulness, audacity, with his scorn of convention and rote, have unquestionably carried him far outside the regular metes and bounds. No wonder there are some who refuse to consider his *Leaves* as "literature". It is perhaps only because he was brought up a printer, and worked during his early years as newspaper and magazine writer, that he has put his expression in typographical form, and made a regular book of it, with lines, leaves and binding.

Of late years the poet, who will be sixty-six years old on the last day of May ensuing, has been in a state of half-paralysis. He gets out of doors regularly in fair weather, much enjoys the Delaware River, is a great frequenter of the Camden and Philadelphia Ferry, and may occasionally be seen sauntering along Chestnut or Market Street in the latter city. He has a curious sort of public sociability, talking with black and white, high and low, male and female, old and young, of all grades. He gives a word or two of friendly recognition, or a nod or smile, to each. Yet he is by no means a marked talker or logician anywhere. I know an old book-stand man who always speaks of him as Socrates. But in one respect the likeness is entirely deficient. Whitman never argues, disputes, or holds or invites a cross-questioning bout with any human being.

Through his paralysis, poverty, the embezzlement of book-agents (1874-1876), the incredible slanders and misconstructions that have followed him through life, and the quite complete failure of his book from a worldly and financial point of view, his splendid fund of personal equanimity and good spirits has remained inexhaustible, and is to-day, amid bodily helplessness and a most meagre income, more vigorous and radiant than ever.

## THE OLD BOWERY

### *A Reminiscence of New York Plays and Acting Fifty Years Ago*

In an article not long since, "Mrs. Siddons as Lady Macbeth," in *The Nineteenth Century*, after describing the bitter regretfulness to mankind from the loss of those first-class poems, temples, pictures, gone and vanish'd from any record of men, the writer (Fleeming Jenkin) continues:

"If this be our feeling as to the more durable works of art, what shall we say of those triumphs which, by their very nature, last no longer than the action which creates them—the triumphs of the orator, the singer, or the actor? There is an anodyne in the words, 'must be so,' 'inevitable,' and there is even some absurdity in longing for the impossible. This anodyne and our sense of humor temper the unhappiness we feel when, after hearing some great performance, we leave the theatre and think, 'Well, this great thing has been, and all that is now left of it is the feeble print upon my brain, the little thrill which memory will send along my nerves, mine and my neighbors; as we live longer the print and thrill must be feebler, and when we pass away the impress of the great artist will vanish from the world.' The regret that a great art should in its nature be transitory, explains the lively interest which many feel in reading anecdotes or descriptions of a great actor."

All this is emphatically my own feeling and reminiscence about the best dramatic and lyric artists I have seen in by-gone days—for instance, Marietta Alboni, the elder Booth, Forrest, the tenor Bettini, the baritone Badiali, "old man Clarke"—(I could write a whole paper on the latter's peerless rendering of the Ghost in *Hamlet* at the Park, when I was a young fellow)—an actor named Ranger, who appear'd in America forty years ago in *genre* characters; Henry Placide, and many others. But I will make a few memoranda at least of the best one I knew.

For the elderly New Yorker of to-day, perhaps, nothing were more likely to start up memories of his early manhood than the mention of the Bowery and the elder Booth. At the date given, the more stylish and select theatre (prices, 50 cents pit, $1 boxes) was "The Park", a large and well-appointed house on Park Row, opposite the present Post-office. English opera and the old comedies were often given in capital style; the principal foreign stars appear'd here, with Italian opera at wide intervals. The Park held a large part in my boyhood's and young manhood's life. Here I heard the English actor, Anderson, in *Charles de Moor*, and in the fine part of "Gisippus". Here I heard Fanny Kemble, Charlotte Cushman, the Seguins, Daddy Rice, Hackett as Falstaff, Nimrod Wildfire, Rip Van Winkle, and in his Yankee-characters. (See pages 19, 20, *Specimen Days* [*supra*, pp. 564-565]. It was here (some years later than the date in the headline) I also heard Mario many times, and at his best. In such parts as Gennaro, in *Lucrezia Borgia*, he was inimitable—the sweetest of voices, a pure tenor, of considerable compass and respectable power. His wife, Grisi, was with him, no longer first-class or young—a fine Norma, though, to the last.

Perhaps my dearest amusement reminiscences are those musical ones. I doubt if ever the senses and emotions of the future will be thrill'd as were the auditors of a generation ago by the deep passion of Alboni's contralto (at the Broadway Theatre, south side, near Pearl street)—or by the trumpet notes of Badiali's baritone, or Bettini's pensive and incomparable tenor in Fernando in *Favorita*, or Marini's bass in *Faliero*, among the Havana troupe, Castle Garden.

But getting back more specifically to the date and theme I started from—the heavy tragedy business prevail'd more decidedly at the Bowery Theatre, where Booth and Forrest were frequently to be heard. Though Booth *père*, then in his prime, ranging in age from 40 to 44 years (he was born in 1796,) was the loyal child and continuer of the traditions of orthodox English play-acting, he stood out "himself alone" in many respects beyond any of his kind on record, and with effects and ways that broke through all rules and all traditions. He has been well describ'd as an actor "whose instant and tremendous concentration of passion in his delineations overwhelm'd his audience, and wrought into it such enthusiasm that it partook of the fever of inspiration surging through his own veins." He seems to have been of beautiful private character, very honorable, affectionate, good-natured, no arrogance, glad to give the other actors the best chances. He knew all stage points thoroughly, and curiously ignored the mere dignities. I once talk'd with a man who had seen him do the Second Actor in the mock play to Charles Kean's Hamlet in Baltimore. He was a marvellous linguist. He play'd Shylock once in London, giving the dialogue in Hebrew, and in New Orleans Oreste (Racine's *Andromaque*) in French. One trait of his habits, I have heard, was strict vegetarianism. He was exceptionally kind to the brute creation. Every once in a while he would make a break for solitude or wild freedom, sometimes for a few hours, sometimes for days. (He illustrated Plato's rule that to the forming an artist of the very highest rank a dash of insanity or what the world calls insanity is indispensable.) He was a small-sized man—yet sharp observers noticed that however crowded the stage might be in certain scenes, Booth never seem'd overtopt or hidden. He was singularly spontaneous and fluctuating; in the same part each rendering differ'd from any and all others. He had no stereotyped positions and made no arbitrary requirements on his fellow-performers.

As is well known to old play-goers, Booth's most effective part was Richard III. Either that, or Iago, or Shylock, or Pescara in *The Apostate*, was sure to draw a crowded house. (Remember heavy pieces were much more in demand those days than now.) He was also unapproachably grand in Sir Giles Overreach, in *A New Way to Pay Old Debts*, and the principal character in *The Iron Chest*.

In any portraiture of Booth, those years, the Bowery Theatre, with its leading lights, and the lessee and manager, Thomas Hamblin, cannot be left out. It was at the Bowery I first saw Edwin Forrest (the play was John Howard Payne's

*Brutus, or the Fall of Tarquin*, and it affected me for weeks;
or rather I might say permanently filter'd into my whole
nature,) then in the zenith of his fame and ability. Sometimes (perhaps a veteran's benefit night,) the Bowery would
group together five or six of the first-class actors of those
days—Booth, Forrest, Cooper, Hamblin, and John R. Scott,
for instance. At that time and here George Jones ("Count
Joannes") was a young, handsome actor, and quite a favorite. I remember seeing him in the title role in *Julius Cæsar*,
and a capital performance it was.

To return specially to the manager. Thomas Hamblin
made a first-rate foil to Booth, and was frequently cast with
him. He had a large, shapely, imposing presence, and dark
and flashing eyes. I remember well his rendering of the main
role in Maturin's *Bertram, or the Castle of St. Aldobrand*.
But I thought Tom Hamblin's best acting was in the comparatively minor part of Faulconbridge in *King John*—he
himself evidently revell'd in the part, and took away the
house's applause from young Kean (the King) and Ellen
Tree (Constance,) and everybody else on the stage—some
time afterward at the Park. Some of the Bowery actresses
were remarkably good. I remember Mrs. Pritchard in *Tour
de Nesle*, and Mrs. McClure in *Fatal Curiosity*, and as Mill-
wood in *George Barnwell*. (I wonder what old fellow reading
these lines will recall the fine comedietta of *The Youth That
Never Saw a Woman*, and the jolly acting in it of Mrs. Her-
ring and old Gates.)

The Bowery, now and then, was the place, too, for spec-
tacular pieces, such as *The Last Days of Pompeii, The Lion-
Doom'd* and the yet undying *Mazeppa*. At one time *Jonathan
Bradford, or the Murder at the Roadside Inn*, had a long and
crowded run; John Sefton and his brother William acted in
it. I remember well the Frenchwoman Celeste, a splendid
pantomimist, and her emotional *Wept of the Wishton-Wish*.
But certainly the main "reason for being" of the Bowery
Theatre those years was to furnish the public with Forrest's
and Booth's performances—the latter having a popularity
and circles of enthusiastic admirers and critics fully equal to
the former—though people were divided as always. For
some reason or other, neither Forrest nor Booth would

accept engagements at the more fashionable theatre, the Park. And it is a curious reminiscence, but a true one, that both these great actors and their performances were taboo'd by "polite society" in New York and Boston at the time— probably as being too robustuous. But no such scruples affected the Bowery.

Recalling from that period the occasion of either Forrest or Booth, any good night at the old Bowery, pack'd from ceiling to pit with its audience mainly of alert, well-dress'd, full-blooded young and middle-aged men, the best average of American-born mechanics—the emotional nature of the whole mass arous'd by the power and magnetism of as mighty mimes as ever trod the stage—the whole crowded auditorium, and what seeth'd in it, and flush'd from its faces and eyes, to me as much a part of the show as any—bursting forth in one of those long-kept-up tempests of hand-clapping peculiar to the Bowery—no dainty kid-glove business, but electric force and muscle from perhaps 2,000 full-sinew'd men—(the inimitable and chromatic tempest of one of those ovations to Edwin Forrest, welcoming him back after an absence, comes up to me this moment)—Such sounds and scenes as here resumed will surely afford to many old New Yorkers some fruitful recollections.

I can yet remember (for I always scann'd an audience as rigidly as a play) the faces of the leading authors, poets, editors, of those times—Fenimore Cooper, Bryant, Paulding, Irving, Charles King, Watson Webb, N. P. Willis, Hoffman, Halleck, Mumford, Morris, Leggett, L. G. Clarke, R. A. Locke and others, occasionally peering from the first tier boxes; and even the great National Eminences, Presidents Adams, Jackson, Van Buren and Tyler, all made short visits there on their Eastern tours.

Awhile after 1840 the character of the Bowery as hitherto described completely changed. Cheap prices and vulgar pro- grammes came in. People who of after years saw the pande- monium of the pit and the doings on the boards must not gauge by them the times and characters I am describing. Not but what there was more or less rankness in the crowd even then. For types of sectional New York those days—the streets East of the Bowery, that intersect Division, Grand,

and up to Third avenue—types that never found their Dickens, or Hogarth, or Balzac, and have pass'd away unportraitured—the young ship-builders, cartmen, butchers, firemen (the old time "soap-lock" or exaggerated "Mose" or "Sikesey", of Chanfrau's plays,) they, too, were always to be seen in these audiences, racy of the East river and the Dry Dock. Slang, wit, occasional shirt sleeves, and a picturesque freedom of looks and manners, with a rude good-nature and restless movement, were generally noticeable. Yet there never were audiences that paid a good actor or an interesting play the compliment of more sustain'd attention or quicker rapport. Then at times came the exceptionally decorous and intellectual congregations I have hinted it; for the Bowery really furnish'd plays and players you could get nowhere else. Notably, Booth always drew the best hearers; and to a specimen of his acting I will now attend in some detail.

I happen'd to see what has been reckon'd by experts one of the most marvellous pieces of histrionism ever known. It must have been about 1834 or '35. A favorite comedian and actress at the Bowery, Thomas Flynn and his wife, were to have a joint benefit, and, securing Booth for Richard, advertised the fact many days beforehand. The house fill'd early from top to bottom. There was some uneasiness behind the scenes, for the afternoon arrived, and Booth had not come from down in Maryland, where he lived. However, a few minutes before ringing-up time he made his appearance in lively condition.

After a one-act farce over, as contrast and prelude, the curtain rising for the tragedy, I can, from my good seat in the pit, pretty well front, see again Booth's quiet entrance from the side, as, with head bent, he slowly and in silence, (amid the tempest of boisterous hand-clapping,) walks down the stage to the footlights with that peculiar and abstracted gesture, musingly kicking his sword, which he holds off from him by its sash. Though fifty years have pass'd since then, I can hear the clank, and feel the perfect following hush of perhaps three thousand people waiting. (I never saw an actor who could make more of the said hush or wait, and hold the audience in an indescribable, half-delicious, half-irritating suspense.) And so throughout the entire play, all parts, voice, atmosphere, magnetism, from

"Now is the winter of our discontent,"

to the closing death fight with Richmond, were of the finest and grandest. The latter character was play'd by a stalwart young fellow named Ingersoll. Indeed, all the renderings were wonderfully good. But the great spell cast upon the mass of hearers came from Booth. Especially was the dream scene very impressive. A shudder went through every nervous system in the audience; it certainly did through mine.

Without question Booth was royal heir and legitimate representative of the Garrick-Kemble-Siddons dramatic traditions; but he vitalized and gave an unnamable *race* to those traditions with his own electric personal idiosyncrasy. (As in all art-utterance it was the subtle and powerful something *special to the individual* that really conquer'd.)

To me, too, Booth stands for much else besides theatricals. I consider that my seeing the man those years glimps'd for me, beyond all else, that inner spirit and form—the unquestionable charm and vivacity, but intrinsic sophistication and artificiality—crystallizing rapidly upon the English stage and literature at and after Shakspere's time, and coming on accumulatively through the seventeenth and eighteenth centuries to the beginning, fifty or forty years ago, of those disintegrating, decomposing processes now authoritatively going on. Yes; although Booth must be class'd in that antique, almost extinct school, inflated, stagy, rendering Shakspere (perhaps inevitably, appropriately) from the growth of arbitrary and often cockney conventions, his genius was to me one of the grandest revelations of my life, a lesson of artistic expression. The words fire, energy, *abandon*, found in him unprecedented meanings. I never heard a speaker or actor who could give such a sting to hauteur or the taunt. I never heard from any other the charm of unswervingly perfect vocalization without trenching at all on mere melody, the province of music.

So much for a Thespian temple of New York fifty years since, where "sceptred tragedy went trailing by" under the gaze of the Dry Dock youth, and both players and auditors were of a character and like we shall never see again. And so much for the grandest histrion of modern times, as near as I can deliberately judge (and the phrenologists put my "caution" at 7)—grander, I believe, than Kean in the expression of electric passion, the prime eligibility of the tragic artist. For though those brilliant years had many fine and even magnificent actors, undoubtedly at Booth's death (in 1852) went the last and by far the noblest Roman of them all.

## SLANG IN AMERICA

View'd freely, the English language is the accretion and growth of every dialect, race, and range of time, and is both the free and compacted composition of all. From this point of view, it stands for Language in the largest sense, and is really the greatest of studies. It involves so much; is indeed a sort of universal absorber, combiner, and conqueror. The scope of its etymologies is the scope not only of man and civilization, but the history of Nature in all departments, and of the organic Universe, brought up to date; for all are comprehended in words, and their backgrounds. This is when words become vitaliz'd, and stand for things, as they unerringly and soon come to do, in the mind that enters on their study with fitting spirit, grasp, and appreciation.

Slang, profoundly consider'd, is the lawless germinal element, below all words and sentences, and behind all poetry, and proves a certain perennial rankness and protestantism in speech. As the United States inherit by far their most precious possession—the language they talk and write—from the Old World, under and out of its feudal institutes, I will allow myself to borrow a simile even of those forms farthest removed from American Democracy. Considering Language then as some mighty potentate, into the majestic audience-hall of the monarch ever enters a personage like one of Shakspere's clowns, and takes position there, and plays a part even in the stateliest ceremonies. Such is Slang, or indirection, an attempt of common humanity to escape from bald literalism, and express itself illimitably, which in highest walks produces poets and poems, and doubtless in pre-historic times gave the start to, and perfected, the whole immense tangle of the old mythologies. For, curious as it may appear, it is strictly the same impulse-source, the same thing. Slang, too, is the wholesome fermentation or eructation of those processes eternally active in language, by which froth and specks are thrown up, mostly to pass away; though occasionally to settle and permanently crystallize.

To make it plainer, it is certain that many of the oldest and solidest words we use, were originally generated from the daring and license of slang. In the processes of word-formation, myriads die, but here and there the attempt attracts superior meanings, becomes valuable and indispensable, and lives forever. Thus the term *right* means literally only straight. *Wrong* primarily meant twisted, distorted. *Integrity* meant oneness. *Spirit* meant breath, or flame. A *supercilious* person was one who rais'd his eyebrows. To *insult* was to leap against. If you *influenc'd* a man, you but flow'd into him. The Hebrew word which is translated *prophesy* meant to bubble up and pour forth as a fountain. The enthusiast bubbles up with the Spirit of God within him, and it pours forth from him like a fountain. The word prophecy is misunderstood. Many suppose that it is limited to mere prediction; that is but the lesser portion of prophecy. The greater work is to reveal God. Every true religious enthusiast is a prophet.

Language, be it remember'd, is not an abstract construction of the learn'd, or of dictionary-makers, but is something arising out of the work, needs, ties, joys, affections, tastes, of long generations of humanity, and has its bases broad and low, close to the ground. Its final decisions are made by the masses, people nearest the concrete, having most to do with actual land and sea. It impermeates all, the Past as well as the Present, and is the grandest triumph of the human intellect. "Those mighty works of art", says Addington Symonds, "which we call languages, in the construction of which whole peoples unconsciously co-operated, the forms of which were determin'd not by individual genius, but by the instincts of successive generations, acting to one end, inherent in the nature of the race—Those poems of pure thought and fancy, cadenced not in words, but in living imagery, fountain-heads of inspiration, mirrors of the mind of nascent nations, which we call Mythologies—these surely are more marvellous in

their infantine spontaneity than any more mature production
of the races which evolv'd them. Yet we are utterly ignorant
of their embryology; the true science of Origins is yet in its
cradle."

Daring as it is to say so, in the growth of Language it is
certain that the retrospect of slang from the start would be
the recalling from their nebulous conditions of all that is
poetical in the stores of human utterance. Moreover, the
honest delving, as of late years, by the German and British
workers in comparative philology, has pierc'd and dispers'd
many of the falsest bubbles of centuries; and will disperse
many more. It was long recorded that in Scandinavian myth-
ology the heroes in the Norse Paradise drank out of the
skulls of their slain enemies. Later investigation proves the
word taken for skulls to mean *horns* of beasts slain in the
hunt. And what reader had not been exercis'd over the traces
of that feudal custom, by which *seigneurs* warm'd their feet in
the bowels of serfs, the abdomen being open'd for the purpose? It now is made to appear that the serf was only required to submit his unharm'd abdomen as a foot cushion
while his lord supp'd, and was required to chafe the legs of
the seigneur with his hands.

It is curiously in embryons and childhood, and among the
illiterate, we always find the groundwork and start, of this
great science, and its noblest products. What a relief most
people have in speaking of a man not by his true and formal
name, with a "Mister" to it, but by some odd or homely ap-
pellative. The propensity to approach a meaning not directly
and squarely, but by circuitous styles of expression, seems
indeed a born quality of the common people everywhere,
evidenced by nick-names, and the inveterate determination
of the masses to bestow sub-titles, sometimes ridiculous,
sometimes very apt. Always among the soldiers during the
secession war, one heard of "Little Mac" (Gen. McClellan),
or of "Uncle Billy" (Gen. Sherman.) "The old man" was, of
course, very common. Among the rank and file, both armies, it was very general to speak of the different States they
came from by their slang names. Those from Maine were
call'd Foxes; New Hampshire, Granite Boys; Massachusetts,
Bay Staters; Vermont, Green Mountain Boys; Rhode

Island, Gun Flints; Connecticut, Wooden Nutmegs; New York, Knickerbockers; New Jersey, Clam Catchers; Pennsylvania, Logher Heads; Delaware, Muskrats; Maryland, Claw Thumpers; Virginia, Beagles; North Carolina, Tar Boilers; South Carolina, Weasels; Georgia, Buzzards; Louisiana, Creoles; Alabama, Lizards; Kentucky, Corn Crackers; Ohio, Buckeyes; Michigan, Wolverines; Indiana, Hoosiers; Illinois, Suckers; Missouri, Pukes; Mississippi, Tadpoles; Florida, Fly up the Creeks; Wisconsin, Badgers; Iowa, Hawkeyes; Oregon, Hard Cases. Indeed I am not sure but slang names have more than once made Presidents. "Old Hickory," (Gen. Jackson) is one case in point. "Tippecanoe, and Tyler too," another.

I find the same rule in the people's conversations everywhere. I heard this among the men of the city horse-cars, where the conductor is often call'd a "snatcher" (*i.e.* because his characteristic duty is to constantly pull or snatch the bell-strap, to stop or go on). Two young fellows are having a friendly talk, amid which, says 1st conductor, "What did you do before you was a snatcher?" Answer of 2d conductor, "Nail'd." (Translation of answer: "I work'd as carpenter.") What is a "boom"? says one editor to another. " Esteem'd contemporary," says the other, "a boom is a bulge." "Barefoot whiskey" is the Tennessee name for the undiluted stimulant. In the slang of the New York common restaurant waiters a plate of ham and beans is known as "stars and stripes", codfish balls as "sleeve-buttons", and hash as "mystery".

The Western States of the Union are, however, as may be supposed, the special areas of slang, not only in conversation, but in names of localities, towns, rivers, etc. A late Oregon traveller says:

"On your way to Olympia by rail, you cross a river called the Shookum-Chuck; your train stops at places named Newaukum, Tumwater, and Toutle; and if you seek further you will hear of whole counties labell'd Wahkiakum, or Snohomish, or Kitsar, or Klikatat; and Cowlitz, Hookium, and Nenolelops greet and offend you. They complain in Olympia that Washington Territory gets but little immigration; but what wonder? What man, having the whole American continent to choose from, would willingly date his letters from the county of Snohomish or bring up his children

in the city of Nenolelops? The village of Tumwater is, as I am
ready to bear witness, very pretty indeed; but surely an emigrant
would think twice before he establish'd himself either there or at
Toutle. Seattle is sufficiently barbarous; Stelicoom is no better;
and I suspect that the Northern Pacific Railroad terminus has been
fixed at Tacoma because it is one of the few places on Puget Sound
whose name does not inspire horror."

Then a Nevada paper chronicles the departure of a mining
party from Reno: "The toughest set of roosters that ever
shook the dust off any town left Reno yesterday for the new
mining district of Cornucopia. They came here from Virginia. Among the crowd were four New York cock-fighters,
two Chicago murderers, three Baltimore bruisers, one Philadelphia prize-fighter, four San Francisco hoodlums, three
Virginia beats, two Union Pacific roughs, and two check
guerillas." Among the far-west newspapers, have been, or
are, *The Fairplay* (Colorado) *Flume*, *The Solid Muldoon*, of
Ouray, *The Tombstone Epitaph*, of Nevada, *The Jimplecute*,
of Texas, and *The Bazoo*, of Missouri. Shirttail Bend, Whiskey Flat, Puppytown, Wild Yankee Ranch, Squaw Flat,
Rawhide Ranch, Loafer's Ravine, Squitch Gulch, Toenail
Lake, are a few of the names of places in Butte county, Cal.

Perhaps indeed no place or term gives more luxuriant
illustrations of the fermentation processes I have mention'd,
and their froth and specks, than those Mississippi and Pacific
coast regions, at the present day. Hasty and grotesque as are
some of the names, others are of an appropriateness and
originality unsurpassable. This applies to the Indian words,
which are often perfect. Oklahoma is proposed in Congress
for the name of one of our new Territories. Hog-eye, Lick-
skillet, Rake-pocket and Steal-easy are the names of some
Texan towns. Miss Bremer found among the aborigines the
following names: *Men's*, Horn-point; Round-Wind; Stand-
and-look-out; The-Cloud-that-goes-aside; Iron-toe; Seek-
the-sun; Iron-flash; Red-bottle; White-spindle; Black-dog;
Two-feathers-of-honor; Gray-grass; Bushy-tail; Thunder-
face; Go-on-the-burning-sod; Spirits-of-the-dead. *Women's*,
Keep-the-fire; Spiritual-woman; Second-daughter-of-the-
house; Blue-bird.

Certainly philologists have not given enough attention to

this element and its results, which, I repeat, can probably be found working every where to-day, amid modern conditions, with as much life and activity as in far-back Greece or India, under prehistoric ones. Then the wit—the rich flashes of humor and genius and poetry—darting out often from a gang of laborers, railroad-men, miners, drivers or boatmen! How often have I hover'd at the edge of a crowd of them, to hear their repartee and impromptus! You get more real fun from half an hour with them than from the books of all "the American humorists".

The science of language has large and close analogies in geological science, with its ceaseless evolution, its fossils, and its numberless submerged layers and hidden strata, the in-finite go-before of the present. Or, perhaps Language is more like some vast living body, or perennial body of bodies. And slang not only brings the first feeders of it, but is after-ward the start of fancy, imagination and humor, breathing into its nostrils the breath of life.

## A WORD ABOUT TENNYSON

BEAUTIFUL as the song was, the original "Locksley Hall" of half a century ago was essentially morbid, heart-broken, finding fault with everything, especially the fact of money's being made (as it ever must be, and perhaps should be) the paramount matter in worldly affairs;

Every door is barr'd with gold, and opens but to golden keys.
First, a father, having fallen in battle, his child (the singer)
        Was left a trampled orphan, and a selfish uncle's ward.
Of course love ensues. The woman in the chant or mono-logue proves a false one; and as far as appears the ideal of woman, in the poet's reflections, is a false one—at any rate for America. Woman is *not* "the lesser man". (The heart is not the brain.) The best of the piece of fifty years since is its concluding line:

        For the mighty wind arises roaring seaward and I go.
Then for this current 1886-7, a just-out sequel, which (as an apparently authentic summary says) "reviews the life of mankind during the past sixty years, and comes to the con-

clusion that its boasted progress is of doubtful credit to the world in general and to England in particular. A cynical vein of denunciation of democratic opinions and aspirations runs throughout the poem in mark'd contrast with the spirit of the poet's youth." Among the most striking lines of this sequel are the following:

> Envy wears the mask of love, and, laughing sober fact to scorn,
> Cries to weakest as to strongest, "Ye are equals, equal born,"
> Equal-born! Oh yes, if yonder hill be level with the flat.
> Charm us, orator, till the lion look no larger than the cat:
> Till the cat, through that mirage of overheated language, loom
> Larger than the lion Demo—end in working its own doom.
> Tumble Nature heel o'er head, and, yelling with the yelling street,
> Set the feet above the brain, and swear the brain is in the feet,
> Bring the old dark ages back, without the faith, without the hope
> Beneath the State, the Church, the Throne, and roll their ruins down the slope.

I should say that all this is a legitimate consequence of the tone and convictions of the earlier standards and points of view. Then some reflections, down to the hard-pan of this sort of thing.

The course of progressive politics (democracy) is so certain and resistless, not only in America but in Europe, that we can well afford the warning calls, threats, checks, neutralizings, in imaginative literature, or any department, of such deep-sounding, and high-soaring voices as Carlyle's and Tennyson's. Nay, the blindness, excesses, of the prevalent tendency —the dangers of the urgent trends of our times—in my opinion, need such voices almost more than any. I should, too, call it a signal instance of democratic humanity's luck that it has such enemies to contend with—so candid, so fervid, so heroic. But why do I say enemies? Upon the whole is not Tennyson—and was not Carlyle (like an honest and stern physician)—the true friend of our age?

Let me assume to pass verdict, or perhaps momentary judgment, for the United States on this poet—a remov'd and distant position giving some advantages over a nigh one. What is Tennyson's service to his race, times, and especially to America? First, I should say—or at least not forget—his personal character. He is not to be mention'd as a rugged, evolutionary, aboriginal force—but (and a great lesson is in it) he has been consistent throughout with the native, healthy, patriotic spinal element and promptings of himself. His moral line is local and conventional, but it is vital and genuine. He reflects the uppercrust of his time, its pale cast of thought—even its *ennui*. Then the simile of my friend John Burroughs is entirely true, "his glove is a glove of silk, but the hand is a hand of iron." He shows how one can be a royal laureate, quite elegant and "aristocratic", and a little queer and affected, and at the same time perfectly manly and natural. As to his non-democracy, it fits him well, and I like him the better for it. I guess we all like to have (I am sure I do) some one who presents those sides of a thought, or possibility, different from our own—different and yet with a sort of home-likeness—a tartness and contradiction offsetting the theory as we view it, and construed from tastes and proclivities not at all his own.

To me, Tennyson shows more than any poet I know (perhaps has been a warning to me) how much there is in finest verbalism. There is such a latent charm in mere words, cunning collocations, and in the voice ringing them, which he has caught and brought out, beyond all others—as in the line,

> And hollow, hollow, hollow, all delight,

in "The Passing of Arthur", and evidenced in "The Lady of Shalott", "The Deserted House", and many other pieces. Among the best (I often linger over them again and again) are "Lucretius", "The Lotus Eaters", and "The Northern Farmer". His mannerism is great, but it is a noble and welcome mannerism. His very best work, to me, is contain'd in the books of *The Idylls of the King*, and all that has grown out of them. Though indeed we could spare nothing of Tennyson, however small or however peculiar—not "Break, Break", nor "Flower in the Crannied Wall", nor the old, eternally-told passion of "Edward Gray":

> Love may come and love may go,
>   And fly like a bird from tree to tree.
> But I will love no more, no more
>   Till Ellen Adair come back to me.

Yes, Alfred Tennyson's is a superb character, and will help give illustriousness, through the long roll of time, to our Nineteenth Century. In its bunch of orbic names, shining like a constellation of stars, his will be one of the brightest. His very faults, doubts, swervings, doublings upon himself, have been typical of our age. We are like the voyagers of a ship, casting off for new seas, distant shores. We would still dwell in the old suffocating and dead haunts, remembering and magnifying their pleasant experiences only, and more than once impell'd to jump ashore before it is too late, and stay where our fathers stay'd, and live as they lived.

May-be I am non-literary and non-decorous (let me at least be human, and pay part of my debt) in this word about Tennyson. I want him to realize that here is a great and ardent Nation that absorbs his songs, and has a respect and affection for him personally, as almost for no other foreigner. I want this word to go to the old man at Farringford as conveying no more than the simple truth; and that truth (a little Christmas gift) no slight one either. I have written impromptu, and shall let it all go at that. The readers of more than fifty millions of people in the New World not only owe to him some of their most agreeable and harmless and healthy hours, but he has enter'd into the formative influences of character here, not only in the Atlantic cities, but inland and far West, out in Missouri, in Kansas, and away in Oregon, in farmer's house and miner's cabin.

Best thanks, anyhow, to Alfred Tennyson—thanks and appreciation in America's name.


## GEORGE FOX (AND SHAKSPERE)

WHILE we are about it, we must almost inevitably go back to the origin of the Society of which Elias Hicks has so far prov'd to be the most mark'd individual result. We must revert to the latter part of the 16th, and all, or nearly all of that 17th century, crowded with so many important historical events, changes, and personages. Throughout Europe, and especially in what we call our Mother Country, men were unusually arous'd—(some would say demented). It was a special age of the insanity of witch-trials and witch-hangings.

In one year 60 were hung for witchcraft in one English county alone. It was peculiarly an age of military-religious conflict. Protestantism and Catholicism were wrestling like giants for the mastery, straining every nerve. Only to think of it—that age! its events, persons—Shakspere just dead, (his folios publish'd, complete)—Charles 1st, the shadowy spirit and the solid block! To sum up all, it was *the age of Cromwell*!

As indispensable foreground, indeed, for Elias Hicks, and perhaps *sine qua non* to an estimate of the kind of man, we must briefly transport ourselves back to the England of that period. As I say, it is the time of tremendous moral and political agitation; ideas of conflicting forms, governments, theologies, seethe and dash like ocean storms, and ebb and flow like mighty tides. It was, or had been, the time of the long feud between the Parliament and the Crown. In the midst of the sprouts, began George Fox—born eight years after the death of Shakspere. He was the son of a weaver, himself a shoemaker, and was "converted" before the age of 20. But O the sufferings, mental and physical, through which those years of the strange youth pass'd! He claim'd to be sent by God to fulfil a mission. "I come", he said, "to direct people to the spirit that gave forth the Scriptures." The range of his thought, even then, cover'd almost every important subject of after times, anti-slavery, women's rights, etc. Though in a low sphere, and among the masses, he forms a mark'd feature in the age.

And how, indeed, beyond all any, that stormy and perturb'd age! The foundations of the old, the superstitious, the conventionally poetic, the credulous, all breaking—the light of the new, and of science and democracy, definitely beginning—a mad, fierce, almost crazy age! The political struggles of the reigns of the Charleses, and of the Protectorate of Cromwell, heated to frenzy by theological struggles. Those were the years following the advent and practical working of the Reformation—but Catholicism is yet strong, and yet seeks supremacy. We think our age full of the flush of men and doings, and culminations of war and peace; and so it is. But there could hardly be a grander and more picturesque and varied age than that.

Born out of and in this age, when Milton, Bunyan, Dryden

and John Locke were still living—amid the memories of Queen Elizabeth and James First, and the events of their reigns—when the radiance of that galaxy of poets, warriors, statesmen, captains, lords, explorers, wits and gentlemen, that crowded the courts and times of those sovereigns still fill'd the atmosphere—when America commencing to be explor'd and settled commenc'd also to be suspected as destin'd to overthrow the old standards and calculations—when Feudalism, like a sunset, seem'd to gather all its glories, reminiscences, personalisms, in one last gorgeous effort, before the advance of a new day, a new incipient genius—amid the social and domestic circles of that period—indifferent to reverberations that seem'd enough to wake the dead, and in a sphere far from the pageants of the court, the awe of any personal rank or charm of intellect, or literature, or the varying excitement of Parliamentarian or Royalist fortunes—this curious young rustic goes wandering up and down England.

George Fox, born 1624, was of decent stock, in ordinary lower life—as he grew along toward manhood, work'd at shoemaking, also at farm labors—loved to be much by himself, half-hidden in the woods, reading the Bible—went about from town to town, dress'd in leather clothes—walk'd much at night, solitary, deeply troubled ("the inward divine teaching of the Lord")—sometimes goes among the ecclesiastical gatherings of the great professors, and though a mere youth bears bold testimony—goes to and fro disputing—(must have had great personality)—heard the voice of the Lord speaking articulately to him, as he walk'd in the fields—feels resistless commands not to be explain'd, but follow'd, to abstain from taking off his hat, to say *Thee* and *Thou,* and not bid others Good morning or Good evening—was illiterate, could just read and write—testifies against shows, games, and frivolous pleasures—enters the court, and warns the judges that they see to doing justice—goes into public houses and market-places, with denunciations of drunkenness and money-making—rises in the midst of the church-services, and gives his own explanation of the ministers' explanations, and of Bible passages and texts—sometimes for such things put in prison, sometimes struck fiercely on the mouth on the spot, or knock'd down, and lying there beaten and bloody—was of keen wit, ready to any question with the most apropos of answers—was sometimes press'd for a soldier, (*him* for a soldier!)—was indeed terribly buffeted; but goes, goes, goes —often sleeping out-doors, under hedges, or hay stacks— forever taken before justices—improving such, and all occasions, to *bear testimony*, and give good advice—still enters the "steeple-houses", (as he calls churches,) and though often dragg'd out and whipt till he faints away, and lies like one dead, when he comes-to—stands up again, and offering himself all bruis'd and bloody, cries out to his tormentors, "Strike—strike again, here where you have not yet touch'd! my arms, my head, my cheeks,"—Is at length arrested and sent up to London, confers with the Protector, Cromwell,— is set at liberty, and holds great meetings in London.

Thus going on, there is something in him that fascinates one or two here, and three or four there, until gradually there were others who went about in the same spirit, and by degrees the Society of Friends took shape, and stood among the thousand religious sects of the world. Women also catch the contagion, and go round, often shamefully misused. By such contagion those ministerings, by scores, almost hundreds of poor travelling men and women, keep on year after year, through ridicule, whipping, imprisonment, etc.—some of the Friend-ministers emigrate to New England—where their treatment makes the blackest part of the early annals of the New World. Some were executed, others maim'd, par-burnt, and scourg'd—two hundred die in prison—some on the gallows, or at the stake.

George Fox himself visited America, and found a refuge and hearers, and preach'd many times on Long Island, New York State. In the village of Oysterbay they will show you the rock on which he stood, (1672,) addressing the multitude, in the open air—thus rigidly following the fashion of apostolic times.—(I have heard myself many reminiscences of him.) Flushing also contains (or contain'd—I have seen them) memorials of Fox, and his son, in two aged white-oak trees, that shaded him while he bore his testimony to people gather'd in the highway.—Yes, the American Quakers were much persecuted—almost as much, by a sort of consent of all the other sects, as the Jews were in Europe in the middle ages.

In New England, the cruelest laws were pass'd, and put in execution against them. As said, some were whipt—women the same as men. Some had their ears cut off—others their tongues pierc'd with hot irons—others their faces branded. Worse still, a woman and three men had been hang'd, (1660). —Public opinion, and the statutes, join'd together, in an odious union, Quakers, Baptists, Roman Catholics and Witches.—Such a fragmentary sketch of George Fox and his time—and the advent of "the Society of Friends" in America.

Strange as it may sound, Shakspere and George Fox, (think of them! compare them!) were born and bred of similar stock, in much the same surroundings and station in life—from the same England—and at a similar period. One to radiate all of art's, all literature's splendor—a splendor so dazzling that he himself is almost lost in it, and his contemporaries the same—his fictitious Othello, Romeo, Hamlet, Lear, as real as any lords of England or Europe then and there—more real to us, the mind sometimes thinks, than the man Shakspere himself. Then the other—may we indeed name him the same day? What is poor plain George Fox compared to William Shakspere—to fancy's lord, imagination's heir? Yet George Fox stands for something too—a thought—the thought that wakes in silent hours—perhaps the deepest, most eternal thought latent in the human soul. This is the thought of God, merged in the thoughts of moral right and the immortality of identity. Great, great is this thought—aye, greater than all else. When the gorgeous pageant of Art, refulgent in the sunshine, color'd with roses and gold—with all the richest mere poetry, old or new, (even Shakspere's) with all that statue, play, painting, music, architecture, oratory, can effect, ceases to satisfy and please— When the eager chase after wealth flags, and beauty itself becomes a loathing—and when all worldly or carnal or esthetic, or even scientific values, having done their office to the human character, and minister'd their part to its development —then, if not before, comes forward this over-arching thought, and brings its eligibilities, germinations. Most neglected in life of all humanity's attributes, easily cover'd with crust, deluded and abused, rejected, yet the only certain source of what all are seeking, but few or none find—in it I for myself clearly see the first, the last, the deepest depths and highest heights of art, of literature, and of the purposes of life. I say whoever labors here, makes contributions here, or best of all sets an incarnated example here, of life or death, is dearest to humanity—remains after the rest are gone. And here, for these purposes, and up to the light that was in him, the man Elias Hicks—as the man George Fox had done years before him—lived long, and died, faithful in life, and faithful in death.

# A BACKWARD GLANCE O'ER TRAVEL'D ROADS

[*Preface to* November Boughs, 1888]

PERHAPS the best of songs heard, or of any and all true love, or life's fairest episodes, or sailors', soldiers' trying scenes on land or sea, is the *résumé* of them, or any of them, long after-wards, looking at the actualities away back past, with all their practical excitations gone. How the soul loves to float amid such reminiscences!

So here I sit gossiping in the early candle-light of old age—I and my book—casting backward glances over our travel'd road. After completing, as it were, the journey—(a varied jaunt of years, with many halts and gaps of intervals—or some lengthen'd ship-voyage, wherein more than once the last hour had apparently arrived, and we seem'd certainly going down—yet reaching port in a sufficient way through all discomfitures at last)—After completing my poems, I am curious to review them in the light of their own (at the time unconscious, or mostly unconscious) intentions, with certain unfoldings of the thirty years they seek to embody. These lines, therefore, will probably blend the weft of first purposes and speculations, with the warp of that experience afterwards, always bringing strange developments.

Result of seven or eight stages and struggles extending through nearly thirty years, (as I nigh my three-score-and-ten I live largely on memory,) I look upon *Leaves of Grass*, now finish'd to the end of its opportunities and powers, as my definitive *carte visite* to the coming generations of the New World,* if I may assume to say so. That I have not gain'd the acceptance of my own time, but have fallen back on fond dreams of the future—anticipations—("still lives the song, though Regnar dies")—That from a worldly and business point of view *Leaves of Grass* has been worse than a failure— that public criticism on the book and myself as author of it yet shows mark'd anger and contempt more than anything else—("I find a solid line of enemies to you everywhere,"— letter from W. S. K., Boston, May 28, 1884)—And that solely for publishing it I have been the object of two or three pretty serious special official buffetings—is all probably no more than I ought to have expected. I had my choice when I commenc'd. I bid neither for soft eulogies, big money returns, nor the approbation of existing schools and conventions. As fulfill'd or partially fulfill'd, the best comfort of the whole business (after a small band of the dearest friends and up-holders ever vouchsafed to man or cause—doubtless all the more faithful and uncompromising—this little phalanx!—for being so few) is that, unstopp'd and unwarp'd by any influ-ence outside the soul within me, I have had my say entirely my own way, and put it unerringly on record—the value thereof to be decided by time.

In calculating that decision, William O'Connor and Dr. Bucke are far more peremptory than I am. Behind all else that can be said, I consider *Leaves of Grass* and its theory ex-perimental—as, in the deepest sense, I consider our American republic itself to be, with its theory. (I think I have at least enough philosophy not to be too absolutely certain of any-thing, or any results.) In the second place, the volume is a *sortie*—whether to prove triumphant, and conquer its field of aim and escape and construction, nothing less than a hun-dred years from now can fully answer. I consider the point that I have positively gain'd a hearing, to far more than make up for any and all ot her lacks and withholdings. Essentially, *that* was from the first, and has remain'd throughout, the main object. Now it seems to be achiev'd, I am certainly

---

* When Champollion, on his death-bed, handed to the printer the revised proof of his *Egyptian Grammar*, he said gayly, "Be careful of this—it is my *carte de visite* to posterity."

contented to waive any otherwise momentous drawbacks, as of little account. Candidly and dispassionately reviewing all my intentions, I feel that they were creditable—and I accept the result, whatever it may be.

After continued personal ambition and effort, as a young fellow, to enter with the rest into competition for the usual rewards, business, political, literary, etc.—to take part in the great *mêlée*, both for victory's prize itself and to do some good—After years of those aims and pursuits, I found myself remaining possess'd, at the age of thirty-one to thirty-three, with a special desire and conviction. Or rather, to be quite exact, a desire that had been flitting through my previous life, or hovering on the flanks, mostly indefinite hitherto, had steadily advanced to the front, defined itself, and finally dominated everything else. This was a feeling or ambition to articulate and faithfully express in literary or poetic form, and uncompromisingly, my own physical, emotional, moral, intellectual, and æsthetic Personality, in the midst of, and tallying, the momentous spirit and facts of its immediate days, and of current America—and to exploit that Personality, identified with place and date, in a far more candid and comprehensive sense than any hitherto poem or book.

Perhaps this is in brief, or suggests, all I have sought to do. Given the Nineteenth Century, with the United States, and what they furnish as area and points of view, *Leaves of Grass* is, or seeks to be, simply a faithful and doubtless self-will'd record. In the midst of all, it gives one man's— the author's—identity, ardors, observations, faiths, and thoughts, color'd hardly at all with any decided coloring from other faiths or other identities. Plenty of songs had been sung—beautiful, matchless songs—adjusted to other lands than these—another spirit and stage of evolution; but I would sing, and leave out or put in, quite solely with reference to America and to-day. Modern science and democracy seem'd to be throwing out their challenge to poetry to put them in its statements in contradistinction to the songs and myths of the past. As I see it now (perhaps too late,) I have unwittingly taken up that challenge and made an attempt at such statements—which I certainly would not assume to do now, knowing more clearly what it means.

For grounds for *Leaves of Grass*, as a poem, I abandon'd the conventional themes, which do not appear in it: none of the stock ornamentation, or choice plots of love or war, or high, exceptional personages of Old-World song; nothing, as I may say, for beauty's sake—no legend, or myth, or romance, nor euphemism, nor rhyme. But the broadest average of humanity and its identities in the now ripening Nineteenth Century, and especially in each of their countless examples and practical occupations in the United States to-day.

One main contrast of the ideas behind every page of my verses, compared with establish'd poems, is their different relative attitude towards God, towards the objective universe, and still more (by reflection, confession, assumption, etc.) the quite changed attitude of the ego, the one chanting or talking, towards himself and towards his fellow-humanity. It is certainly time for America, above all, to begin this readjustment in the scope and basic point of view of verse; for everything else has changed. As I write, I see in an article on Wordsworth, in one of the current English magazines, the lines, "A few weeks ago an eminent French critic said that, owing to the special tendency to science and to its all-devouring force, poetry would cease to be read in fifty years." But I anticipate the very contrary. Only a firmer, vastly broader, new area begins to exist—nay, is already form'd—to which the poetic genius must emigrate. Whatever may have been the case in years gone by, the true use for the imaginative faculty of modern times is to give ultimate vivification to facts, to science, and to common lives, endowing them with glows and glories and final illustriousness which belong to every real thing, and to real things only. Without that ultimate vivification—which the poet or other artist alone can give—reality would seem incomplete, and science, democracy, and life itself, finally in vain.

Few appreciate the moral revolutions, our age, which have been profounder far than the material or inventive or war-produced ones. The Nineteenth Century, now well towards its close (and ripening into fruit the seeds of the two preced-

ing centuries*)—the uprisings of national masses and shiftings of boundary-lines—the historical and other prominent
facts of the United States—the war of attempted Secession—
the stormy rush and haste of nebulous forces—never can
future years witness more excitement and din of action—
never completer change of army front along the whole line,
the whole civilized world. For all these new and evolutionary
facts, meanings, purposes, new poetic messages, new forms
and expressions, are inevitable.

My Book and I—what a period we have presumed to span!
those thirty years from 1850 to '80—and America in them!
Proud, proud indeed may we be, if we have cull'd enough of
that period in its own spirit to worthily waft a few live breaths
of it to the future!

Let me not dare, here or anywhere, for my own purposes,
or any purposes, to attempt the definition of Poetry, nor
answer the question what it is. Like Religion, Love, Nature,
while those terms are indispensable, and we all give a sufficiently accurate meaning to them, in my opinion no definition that has ever been made sufficiently encloses the name
Poetry; nor can any rule or convention ever so absolutely
obtain but some great exception may arise and disregard and
overturn it.

Also it must be carefully remember'd that first-class literature does not shine by any luminosity of its own; nor do its
poems. They grow of circumstances, and are evolutionary.
The actual living light is always curiously from elsewhere—
follows unaccountable sources, and is lunar and relative at
the best. There are, I know, certain controlling themes that
seem endlessly appropriated to the poets—as war, in the past
—in the Bible, religious rapture and adoration—always love,
beauty, some fine plot, or pensive or other emotion. But,
strange as it may sound at first, I will say there is something
striking far deeper and towering far higher than those themes
for the best elements of modern song.

* The ferment and germination even of the United States to-day,
dating back to, and in my opinion mainly founded on, the Elizabethan
age in English history, the age of Francis Bacon and Shakspere. Indeed, when we pursue it, what growth or advent is there that does not
date back, back, until lost—perhaps its most tantalizing clues lost—in
the receded horizons of the past?

Just as all the old imaginative works rest, after their kind, on long trains of presuppositions, often entirely unmention'd by themselves, yet supplying the most important bases of them, and without which they could have had no reason for being, so *Leaves of Grass*, before a line was written, presupposed something different from any other, and, as it stands, is the result of such presupposition. I should say, indeed, it were useless to attempt reading the book without first carefully tallying that preparatory background and quality in the mind. Think of the United States to-day—the facts of these thirty-eight or forty empires solder'd in one—sixty or seventy millions of equals, with their lives, their passions, their future —these incalculable, modern, American, seething multitudes around us, of which we are inseparable parts! Think, in comparison, of the petty environage and limited area of the poets of past or present Europe, no matter how great their genius. Think of the absence and ignorance in all cases hitherto, of the multitudinousness, vitality, and the unprecedented stimulants of to-day and here. It almost seems as if a poetry with cosmic and dynamic features of magnitude and limitlessness suitable to the human soul, were never possible before. It is certain that a poetry of absolute faith and equality for the use of the democratic masses never was.

In estimating first-class song, a sufficient Nationality, or, on the other hand, what may be call'd the negative and lack of it, (as in Goethe's case, it sometimes seems to me,) is often, if not always, the first element. One needs only a little penetration to see, at more or less removes, the material facts of their country and radius, with the coloring of the moods of humanity at the time, and its gloomy or hopeful prospects, behind all poets and each poet, and forming their birthmarks. I know very well that my *Leaves* could not possibly have emerged or been fashion'd or completed, from any other era than the latter half of the Nineteenth Century, nor any other land than democratic America, and from the absolute triumph of the National Union arms.

And whether my friends claim it for me or not, I know well enough, too, that in respect to pictorial talent, dramatic situations, and especially in verbal melody and all the conventional technique of poetry, not only the divine works that to-day stand ahead in the world's reading, but dozens more, transcend (some of them immeasurably transcend) all I have done, or could do. But it seem'd to me, as the objects in Nature, the themes of æstheticism, and all special exploitations of the mind and soul, involve not only their own inherent quality, but the quality, just as inherent and important, of *their point of view,*\* the time had come to reflect all themes and things, old and new, in the lights thrown on them by the advent of America and democracy—to chant those themes through the utterance of one, not only the grateful and reverent legatee of the past, but the born child of the New World—to illustrate all through the genesis and ensemble of to-day; and that such illustration and ensemble are the chief demands of America's prospective imaginative literature. Not to carry out, in the approved style, some choice plot of fortune or misfortune, or fancy, or fine thoughts, or incidents, or courtesies— all of which has been done overwhelmingly and well, probably never to be excell'd—but that while in such æsthetic presentation of objects, passions, plots, thoughts, etc., our lands and days do not want, and probably will never have, anything better than they already possess from the bequests of the past, it still remains to be said that there is even towards all those a subjective and contemporary point of view appropriate to ourselves alone, and to our new genius and environments, different from anything hitherto; and that such conception of current or gone-by life and art is for us the only means of their assimilation consistent with the Western world.

Indeed, and anyhow, to put it specifically, has not the time arrived when, (if it must be plainly said, for democratic America's sake, if for no other) there must imperatively come a readjustment of the whole theory and nature of Poetry? The question is important, and I may turn the argument over and repeat it: Does not the best thought of our day and Republic conceive of a birth and spirit of song superior to anything past or present? To the effectual and moral consolidation of our lands (already, as materially establish'd, the great-

---

\* According to Immanuel Kant, the last essential reality, giving shape and significance to all the rest.

est factors in known history, and far, far greater through what they prelude and necessitate, and are to be in future)— to conform with and build on the concrete realities and theories of the universe furnish'd by science, and henceforth the only irrefragable basis for anything, verse included—to root both influences in the emotional and imaginative action of the modern time, and dominate all that precedes or opposes them—is not either a radical advance and step forward, or a new verteber of the best song indispensable?

The New World receives with joy the poems of the antique, with European feudalism's rich fund of epics, plays, ballads —seeks not in the least to deaden or displace those voices from our ear and area—holds them indeed as indispensable studies, influences, records, comparisons. But though the dawn-dazzle of the sun of literature is in those poems for us of to-day—though perhaps the best parts of current character in nations, social groups, or any man's or woman's individuality, Old World or New, are from them—and though if I were ask'd to name the most precious bequest to current American civilization from all the hitherto ages, I am not sure but I would name those old and less old songs ferried hither from east and west—some serious words and debits remain ; some acrid considerations demand a hearing. Of the great poems receiv'd from abroad and from the ages, and to-day enveloping and penetrating America, is there one that is consistent with these United States, or essentially applicable to them as they are and are to be? Is there one whose underlying basis is not a denial and insult to democracy? What a comment it forms, anyhow, on this era of literary fulfilment, with the splendid day-rise of science and resuscitation of history, that our chief religious and poetical works are not our own, nor adapted to our light, but have been furnish'd by far-back ages out of their arriere and darkness, or, at most, twilight dimness! What is there in those works that so imperiously and scornfully dominates all our advanced civilization, and culture?

Even Shakspere, who so suffuses current letters and art (which indeed have in most degrees grown out of him,) belongs essentially to the buried past. Only he holds the proud distinction for certain important phases of that past, of being the loftiest of the singers life has yet given voice to. All, however, relate to and rest upon conditions, standards, politics, sociologies, ranges of belief, that have been quite eliminated from the Eastern hemisphere, and never existed at all in the Western. As authoritative types of song they belong in America just about as much as the persons and institutes they depict. True, it may be said, the emotional, moral, and æsthetic natures of humanity have not radically changed—that in these the old poems apply to our times and all times, irrespective of date; and that they are of incalculable value as pictures of the past. I willingly make those admissions and to their fullest extent; then advance the points herewith as of serious, even paramount importance.

I have indeed put on record elsewhere my reverence and eulogy for those never-to-be-excell'd poetic bequests, and their indescribable preciousness as heirlooms for America. Another and separate point must now be candidly stated. If I had not stood before those poems with uncover'd head, fully aware of their colossal grandeur and beauty of form and spirit, I could not have written *Leaves of Grass*. My verdict and conclusions as illustrated in its pages are arrived at through the temper and inculcation of the old works as much as through anything else—perhaps more than through anything else. As America fully and fairly construed is the legitimate result and evolutionary outcome of the past, so I would dare to claim for my verse. Without stopping to qualify the averment, the Old World has had the poems of myths, fictions, feudalism, conquest, caste, dynastic wars, and splendid exceptional characters and affairs, which have been great; but the New World needs the poems of realities and science and of the democratic average and basic equality, which shall be greater. In the centre of all, and object of all, stands the Human Being, towards whose heroic and spiritual evolution poems and everything directly or indirectly tend, Old World or New.

Continuing the subject, my friends have more than once suggested—or may be the garrulity of advancing age is possessing me—some further embryonic facts of *Leaves of Grass*, and especially how I enter'd upon them. Dr. Bucke has, in his volume, already fully and fairly described the preparation of my poetic field, with the particular and general plowing, planting, seeding, and occupation of the ground, till everything was fertilized, rooted, and ready to start its own way for good or bad. Not till after this, did I attempt any serious acquaintance with poetic literature. Along in my sixteenth year I had become the possessor of a stout, well-cramm'd one thousand page octavo volume (I have it yet,) containing Walter Scott's poetry entire—an inexhaustible mine and treasury of poetic forage (especially the endless forests and jungles of notes)—has been so to me for fifty years, and remains so to this day.*

Later, at intervals, summers and falls, I used to go off, sometimes for a week at a stretch, down in the country, or to Long Island's sea-shores—there, in the presence of outdoor influences, I went over thoroughly the Old and New Testaments, and absorb'd (probably to better advantage for me than in any library or indoor room—it makes such difference *where* you read,) Shakspere, Ossian, the best translated versions I could get of Homer, Eschylus, Sophocles, the old German Nibelungen, the ancient Hindoo poems, and one or two other masterpieces, Dante's among them. As it happen'd, I read the latter mostly in an old wood. The *Iliad* (Buckley's prose version) I read first thoroughly on the peninsula of Orient, northeast end of Long Island, in a shelter'd hollow of rocks and sand, with the sea on each side. (I have wonder'd since why I was not overwhelm'd by those mighty masters. Likely because I read them, as described, in the full presence of Nature, under the sun, with the far-spreading landscape and vistas, or the sea rolling in.)

Toward the last I had among much else look'd over Edgar Poe's poems—of which I was not an admirer, tho' I always saw that beyond their limited range of melody (like perpetual

---

* Sir Walter Scott's *Complete Poems;* especially including BORDER MINSTRELSY; then Sir Tristrem; Lay of the Last Minstrel; Ballads from the German; Marmion; Lady of the Lake; Vision of Don Roderick; Lord of the Isles; Rokeby; Bridal of Triermain; Field of Waterloo; Harold the Dauntless; all the Dramas; various Introductions, endless interesting Notes, and Essays on Poetry, Romance, etc.

Lockhart's 1833 (or '34) edition with Scott's latest and copious revisions and annotations. (All the poems were thoroughly read by me, but the ballads of the Border Minstrelsy over and over again.)

chimes of music bells, ringing from lower *b* flat up to *g*) they were melodious expressions, and perhaps never excell'd ones, of certain pronounc'd phases of human morbidity. (The Poetic area is very spacious—has room for all—has so many mansions!) But I was repaid in Poe's prose by the idea that (at any rate for our occasions, our day) there can be no such thing as a long poem. The same thought had been haunting my mind before, but Poe's argument, though short, work'd the sum and proved it to me.

Another point had an early settlement, clearing the ground greatly. I saw, from the time my enterprise and questionings positively shaped themselves (how best can I express my own distinctive era and surroundings, America, Democracy?) that the trunk and centre whence the answer was to radiate, and to which all should return from straying however far a distance, must be an identical body and soul, a personality—which personality, after many considerations and ponderings I deliberately settled should be myself—indeed could not be any other. I also felt strongly (whether I have shown it or not) that to the true and full estimate of the Present both the Past and the Future are main considerations.

These, however, and much more might have gone on and come to naught (almost positively would have come to naught,) if a sudden, vast, terrible, direct and indirect stimulus for new and national declamatory expression had not been given to me. It is certain, I say, that, although I had made a start before, only from the occurrence of the Secession War, and what it show'd me as by flashes of lightning, with the emotional depths it sounded and arous'd (of course, I don't mean in my own heart only, I saw it just as plainly in others, in millions)—that only from the strong flare and provocation of that war's sights and scenes the final reasons-for-being of an autochthonic and passionate song definitely came forth.

I went down to the war fields in Virginia (end of 1862), lived thenceforward in camp—saw great battles and the days and nights afterward—partook of all the fluctuations, gloom, despair, hopes again arous'd, courage evoked—death readily risk'd—*the cause*, too—along and filling those agonistic and lurid following years, 1863-'64-'65—the real parturition years (more than 1776-'83) of this henceforth homogeneous Union. Without those three or four years and the experiences they gave, *Leaves of Grass* would not now be existing.

But I set out with the intention also of indicating or hinting some point-characteristics which I since see (though I did not then, at least not definitely) were bases and object-urgings toward those *Leaves* from the first. The word I myself put primarily for the description of them as they stand at last, is the word Suggestiveness. I round and finish little, if anything; and could not, consistently with my scheme. The reader will always have his or her part to do, just as much as I have had mine. I seek less to state or display any theme or thought, and more to bring you, reader, into the atmosphere of the theme or thought—there to pursue your own flight. Another impetus-word is Comradeship as for all lands, and in a more commanding and acknowledg'd sense than hitherto. Other word signs would be Good Cheer, Content, and Hope.

The chief trait of any given poet is always the spirit he brings to the observation of Humanity and Nature—the mood out of which he contemplates his subjects. What kind of temper and what amount of faith report these things? Up to how recent a date is the song carried? What the equipment, and special raciness of the singer—what his tinge of coloring? The last value of artistic expressers, past and present—Greek æsthetes, Shakspere—or in our own day Tennyson, Victor Hugo, Carlyle, Emerson—is certainly involv'd in such questions. I say the profoundest service that poems or any other writings can do for their reader is not merely to satisfy the intellect, or supply something polish'd and interesting, not even to depict great passions, or persons or events, but to fill him with vigorous and clean manliness, religiousness, and give him *good heart* as a radical possession and habit. The educated world seems to have been growing more and more ennuyed for ages, leaving to our time the inheritance of it all. Fortunately there is the original inexhaustible fund of buoyancy, normally resident in the race, forever eligible to be appeal'd to and relied on.

As for native American individuality, though certain to come, and on a large scale, the distinctive and ideal type of

Western character (as consistent with the operative political and even money-making features of United States' humanity in the Nineteenth Century as chosen knights, gentlemen and warriors were the ideals of the centuries of European feudalism) it has not yet appear'd. I have allow'd the stress of my poems from beginning to end to bear upon American individuality and assist it—not only because that is a great lesson in Nature, amid all her generalizing laws, but as counterpoise to the leveling tendencies of Democracy—and for other reasons. Defiant of ostensible literary and other conventions, I avowedly chant "the great pride of man in himself", and permit it to be more or less a *motif* of nearly all my verse. I think this pride indispensable to an American. I think it not inconsistent with obedience, humility, deference, and self-questioning.

Democracy has been so retarded and jeopardized by powerful personalities, that its first instincts are fain to clip, conform, bring in stragglers, and reduce everything to a dead level. While the ambitious thought of my song is to help the forming of a great aggregate Nation, it is, perhaps, altogether through the forming of myriads of fully develop'd and enclosing individuals. Welcome as are equality's and fraternity's doctrines and popular education, a certain liability accompanies them all, as we see. That primal and interior something in man, in his soul's abysms, coloring all, and, by exceptional fruitions, giving the last majesty to him—something continually touch'd upon and attain'd by the old poems and ballads of feudalism, and often the principal foundation of them—modern science and democracy appear to be endangering, perhaps eliminating. But that forms an appearance only; the reality is quite different. The new influences, upon the whole, are surely preparing the way for grander individualities than ever. To-day and here personal force is behind everything, just the same. The times and depictions from the *Iliad* to Shakspere inclusive can happily never again be realized—but the elements of courageous and lofty manhood are unchanged.

Without yielding an inch the working-man and working-woman were to be in my pages from first to last. The ranges of heroism and loftiness with which Greek and feudal poets endow'd their god-like or lordly born characters—indeed prouder and better based and with fuller ranges than those— I was to endow the democratic averages of America. I was to show that we, here and to-day, are eligible to the grandest and the best—more eligible now than any times of old were. I will also want my utterances (I said to myself before beginning) to be in spirit the poems of the morning. (They have been founded and mainly written in the sunny forenoon and early midday of my life.) I will want them to be the poems of women entirely as much as men. I have wish'd to put the complete Union of the States in my songs without any preference or partiality whatever. Henceforth, if they live and are read, it must be just as much South as North—just as much along the Pacific as Atlantic—in the valley of the Mississippi, in Canada, up in Maine, down in Texas, and on the shores of Puget Sound.

From another point of view *Leaves of Grass* is avowedly the song of Sex and Amativeness, and even Animality— though meanings that do not usually go along with those words are behind all, and will duly emerge; and all are sought to be lifted into a different light and atmosphere. Of this feature, intentionally palpable in a few lines, I shall only say the espousing principle of those lines so gives breath of life to my whole scheme that the bulk of the pieces might as well have been left unwritten were those lines omitted. Difficult as it will be, it has become, in my opinion, imperative to achieve a shifted attitude from superior men and women towards the thought and fact of sexuality, as an element in character, personality, the emotions, and a theme in literature. I am not going to argue the question by itself; it does not stand by itself. The vitality of it is altogether in its relations, bearings, significance—like the clef of a symphony. At last analogy the lines I allude to, and the spirit in which they are spoken, permeate all *Leaves of Grass*, and the work must stand or fall with them, as the human body and soul must remain as an entirety.

Universal as are certain facts and symptoms of communities or individuals all times, there is nothing so rare in modern conventions and poetry as their normal recognizance. Literature is always calling in the doctor for consultation and confession, and always giving evasions and swathing suppressions in place of that "heroic nudity"* on which only a genuine diagnosis of serious cases can be built. And in respect to editions of *Leaves of Grass* in time to come (if there should be such) I take occasion now to confirm those lines with the settled convictions and deliberate renewals of thirty years, and to hereby prohibit, as far as word of mine can do so, any elision of them.

Then still a purpose enclosing all, and over and beneath all. Ever since what might be call'd thought, or the budding of thought, fairly began in my youthful mind, I had had a desire to attempt some worthy record of that entire faith and acceptance ("to justify the ways of God to man" is Milton's well-known and ambitious phrase) which is the foundation of moral America. I felt it all as positively then in my young days as I do now in my old ones; to formulate a poem whose every thought or fact should directly or indirectly be or connive at an implicit belief in the wisdom, health, mystery, beauty of every process, every concrete object, every human or other existence, not only consider'd from the point of view of all, but of each.

While I cannot understand it or argue it out, I fully believe in a clue and purpose in Nature, entire and several; and that invisible spiritual results, just as real and definite as the visible, eventuate all concrete life and all materialism, through Time. My book ought to emanate buoyancy and gladness legitimately enough, for it was grown out of those elements, and has been the comfort of my life since it was originally commenced.

One main genesis-motive of the *Leaves* was my conviction (just as strong to-day as ever) that the crowning growth of the United States is to be spiritual and heroic. To help start and favor that growth—or even to call attention to it, or the need of it—is the beginning, middle and final purpose of the poems. (In fact, when really cipher'd out and summ'd to the last, plowing up in earnest the interminable average fallows of humanity—not "good government" merely, in the common sense—is the justification and main purpose of these United States.)

* *Nineteenth Century*, July, 1883.

Isolated advantages in any rank or grace or fortune—the direct or indirect threads of all the poetry of the past—are in my opinion distasteful to the republican genius, and offer no foundation for its fitting verse. Establish'd poems, I know, have the very great advantage of chanting the already perform'd, so full of glories, reminiscences dear to the minds of men. But my volume is a candidate for the future. "All original art", says Taine, anyhow, "is self-regulated, and no original art can be regulated from without; it carries its own counterpoise, and does not receive it from elsewhere—lives on its own blood"—a solace to my frequent bruises and sulky vanity.

As the present is perhaps mainly an attempt at personal statement or illustration, I will allow myself as further help to extract the following anecdote from a book, *Annals of Old Painters*, conn'd by me in youth. Rubens, the Flemish painter, in one of his wanderings through the galleries of old convents, came across a singular work. After looking at it thoughtfully for a good while, and listening to the criticisms of his suite of students, he said to the latter, in answer to their questions, (as to what school the work implied or belong'd,) "I do not believe the artist, unknown and perhaps no longer living, who has given the world this legacy, ever belong'd to any school, or ever painted anything but this one picture, which is a personal affair—a piece out of a man's life."

*Leaves of Grass* indeed (I cannot too often reiterate) has mainly been the outcropping of my own emotional and other personal nature—an attempt, from first to last, to put *a Person*, a human being (myself, in the latter half of the Nineteenth Century, in America,) freely, fully and truly on record. I could not find any similar personal record in current literature that satisfied me. But it is not on *Leaves of Grass* distinctively as *literature*, or a specimen thereof, that I feel to dwell, or advance claims. No one will get at my verses who insists upon viewing them as a literary performance, or attempt at such performance, or as aiming mainly toward art or æstheticism.

I say no land or people or circumstances ever existed so needing a race of singers and poems differing from all others, and rigidly their own, as the land and people and circum-

stances of the United States need such singers and poems to-
day, and for the future. Still further, as long as the States
continue to absorb and be dominated by the poetry of the
Old World, and remain unsupplied with autochthonous song,
to express, vitalize and give color to and define their material
and political success, and minister to them distinctively, so
long will they stop short of first-class Nationality and remain
defective.

In the free evening of my day I give to you, reader, the
foregoing garrulous talk, thoughts, reminiscences,

> As idly drifting down the ebb,
>
> Such ripples, half-caught voices, echo from the shore.

Concluding with two items for the imaginative genius of
the West, when it worthily rises—First, what Herder taught
to the young Goethe, that really great poetry is always (like
the Homeric or Biblical canticles) the result of a national
spirit, and not the privilege of a polish'd and select few;
Second, that the strongest and sweetest songs yet remain to
be sung.

## THE PERFECT HUMAN VOICE

STATING it briefly and pointedly I should suggest that the
human voice is a cultivation or form'd growth on a fair native foundation. This foundation probably exists in nine
cases out of ten. Sometimes nature affords the vocal organ in
perfection, or rather I would say near enough to whet one's
appreciation and appetite for a voice that might be truly
call'd perfection. To me the grand voice is mainly physiological—(by which I by no means ignore the mental help, but
wish to keep the emphasis where it belongs.) Emerson says
*manners* form the representative apex and final charm and
captivation of humanity: but he might as well have changed
the typicality to voice.

Of course there is much taught and written about elocu-
tion, the best reading, speaking, etc., but it finally settles
down to *best* human vocalization. Beyond all other power
and beauty, there is something in the quality and power of
the right voice (*timbre* the schools call it) that touches the
soul, the abysms. It was not for nothing that the Greeks de-

pended, at their highest, on poetry's and wisdom's vocal utterance by *tête-à-tête* lectures—(indeed all the ancients did).

Of celebrated people possessing this wonderful vocal power, patent to me, in former days, I should specify the contralto Alboni, Elias Hicks, Father Taylor, the tenor Bettini, Fanny Kemble, and the old actor Booth, and in private life many cases, often women. I sometimes wonder whether the best philosophy and poetry, or something like the best, after all these centuries, perhaps waits to be rous'd out yet, or suggested, by the perfect physiological human voice.


## OLD ACTORS, SINGERS, SHOWS, Etc., IN NEW YORK

### *Flitting mention—(with much left out)*

SEEMS to me I ought acknowledge my debt to actors, singers, public speakers, conventions, and the Stage in New York, my youthful days, from 1835 onward—say to '60 or '61—-and to plays and operas generally. (Which nudges a pretty big disquisition: of course it should be all elaborated and penetrated more deeply—but I will here give only some flitting mentionings of my youth.) Seems to me now when I look back, the Italian contralto Marieta Alboni (she is living yet, in Paris, 1891, in good condition, good voice yet, considering) with the then prominent histrions Booth, Edwin Forrest and Fanny Kemble and the Italian singer Bettini, have had the deepest and most lasting effect upon me. I should like well if Madame Alboni and the old composer Verdi, (and Bettini the tenor, if he is living) could know how much noble pleasure and happiness they gave me, and how deeply I always remember them and thank them to this day. For theatricals in literature and doubtless upon me personally, including opera, have been of course serious factors. (The experts and musicians of my present friends claim that the new Wagner and his pieces belong far more truly to me, and I to them, likely. But I was fed and bred under the Italian dispensation, and absorb'd it, and doubtless show it.)

As a young fellow, when possible I always studied a play or libretto quite carefully over, by myself, (sometimes twice through) before seeing it on the stage; read it the day or two days before. Tried both ways—not reading some beforehand; but I found I gain'd most by getting that sort of mastery first, if the piece had depth. (Surface effects and glitter were much less thought of, I am sure, those times). There were many fine old plays, neither tragedies nor comedies— the names of them quite unknown to to-day's current audiences. *All is not Gold that Glitters*, in which Charlotte Cushman had a superbly enacted part, was of that kind. C. C., who revel'd in them, was great in such pieces; I think better than in the heavy popular roles.

We had some fine music those days. We had the English opera of *Cinderella* (with Henry Placide as the pompous old father, an unsurpassable bit of comedy and music). We had *Bombastes Furioso*. Must have been in 1844 (or '5) I saw Charles Kean and Mrs. Kean (Ellen Tree)—saw them in the Park in Shakspere's *King John*. He, of course, was the chief character. She play'd "Queen Constance". Tom Hamblin was "Faulconbridge", and probably the best ever on the stage. It was an immense show-piece, too; lots of grand set scenes and fine armor-suits and all kinds of appointments imported from London (where it had been first render'd.) The large brass bands—the three or four hundred "supes"—the interviews between the French and English armies—the talk with "Hubert" (and the hot irons) the delicious acting of "Prince Arthur" (Mrs. Richardson, I think)—and all the fine *blare* and court pomp—I remember to this hour. The death-scene of the King in the orchard of Swinstead Abbey, was very effective. Kean rush'd in, gray-pale and yellow, and threw himself on a lounge in the open. His pangs were horribly realistic. (He must have taken lessons in some hospital.)

Fanny Kemble play'd to wonderful effect in such pieces as *Fazio, or the Italian wife*. The turning-point was jealousy. It was a rapid-running, yet heavy-timber'd, tremendous wrenching, passionate play. Such old pieces always seem'd to me built like an ancient ship of the line, solid and lock'd from keel up—oak and metal and knots. One of the finest characters was a great court lady, "Aldabella," enacted by Mrs. Sharpe. O how it all entranced us, and knock'd us about, as the scenes swept on like a cyclone!

Saw Hackett at the old Park many times, and remember him well. His renderings were first-rate in everything. He inaugurated the true "Rip Van Winkle", and look'd and acted and dialogued it to perfection (he was of Dutch breed, and brought up among old Holland descendants in Kings and Queens counties, Long Island). The play and the acting of it have been adjusted to please popular audiences since; but there was in that original performance certainly something of a far higher order, more art, more reality, more resemblance, a bit of fine pathos, a lofty *brogue*, beyond anything afterward.

One of my big treats was the rendering at the old Park of Shakspere's *Tempest* in musical version. There was a very fine instrumental band, not numerous, but with a capital leader. Mrs. Austin was the "Ariel", and Peter Richings the "Caliban"; both excellent. The drunken song of the latter has probably been never equal'd. The perfect actor Clarke (old Clarke) was "Prospero".

Yes; there were in New York and Brooklyn some fine non-technical singing performances, concerts, such as the Hutchinson band, three brothers, and the sister, the red-cheek'd New England carnation, sweet Abby; sometimes plaintive and balladic—sometimes anti-slavery, anti-calomel, and comic. There were concerts by Templeton, Russell, Dempster, the old Alleghanian band, and many others. Then we had lots of "negro minstrels", with capital character songs and voices. I often saw Rice the original "Jim Crow" at the old Park Theatre filling up the gap in some short bill—and the wild chants and dances were admirable—probably ahead of anything since. Every theatre had some superior voice, and it was common to give a favorite song between the acts. "The Sea" at the bijou Olympic, (Broadway near Grand,) was always welcome from a little Englishman named Edwin, a good balladist. At the Bowery the loves of "Sweet William",

"When on the Downs the fleet was moor'd,"

always bro't an encore, and sometimes a treble.

I remember Jenny Lind and heard her (1850 I think) several times. She had the most brilliant, captivating, popular musical style and expression of any one known; (the canary, and several other sweet birds are wondrous fine—but there is something in song that goes deeper—isn't there?)

The great "Egyptian Collection" was well up in Broadway, and I got quite acquainted with Dr. Abbott, the proprietor— paid many visits there, and had long talks with him, in connection with my readings of many books and reports on Egypt—its antiquities, history, and how things and the scenes really look, and what the old relics stand for, as near as we can now get. (Dr. A. was an Englishman of say 54—had been settled in Cairo as physician for 25 years, and all that time was collecting these relics, and sparing no time or money seeking and getting them. By advice and for a change of base for himself, he brought the collection to America. But the whole enterprise was a fearful disappointment, in the pay and commercial part.) As said, I went to the Egyptian Museum many many times; sometimes had it all to myself— delved at the formidable catalogue—and on several occasions had the invaluable personal talk, correction, illustration and guidance of Dr. A. himself. He was very kind and helpful to me in those studies and examinations; once, by appointment, he appear'd in full and exact Turkish (Cairo) costume, which long usage there had made habitual to him.

One of the choice places of New York to me then was the "Phrenological Cabinet" of Fowler & Wells, Nassau street near Beekman. Here were all the busts, examples, curios and books of that study obtainable. I went there often, and once for myself had a very elaborate and leisurely examination and "chart of bumps" written out (I have it yet,) by Nelson Fowler (or was it Sizer?) there.

And who remembers the renown'd New York "Tabernacle" of those days "before the war"? It was on the east side of Broadway, near Pearl street—was a great turtle-shaped hall, and you had to walk back from the street entrance thro' a long wide corridor to get to it—was very strong—had an immense gallery—altogether held three or four thousand people. Here the huge annual conventions of the windy and cyclonic "reformatory societies" of those times were held—especially the tumultuous Anti-Slavery ones. I remember hearing Wendell Phillips, Emerson, Cassius Clay, John P. Hale, Beecher, Fred Douglas, the Burleighs, Garrison, and others. Sometimes the Hutchinsons would sing—very fine. Sometimes there were angry rows. A chap named Isaiah Rhynders, a fierce politician of those days, with a band of robust supporters, would attempt to contradict the speakers and break up the meetings. But the Anti-Slavery, and Quaker, and Temperance, and Missionary and other conventicles and speakers were tough, tough, and always maintained their ground, and carried out their programs fully. I went frequently to these meetings, May after May—learn'd much from them—was sure to be on hand when J. P. Hale or Cash Clay made speeches.

There were also the smaller and handsome halls of the Historical and Athenæum Societies up on Broadway. I very well remember W. C. Bryant lecturing on Homœopathy in one of them, and attending two or three addresses by R. W. Emerson in the other.

There was a series of plays and dramatic *genre* characters by a gentleman bill'd as Ranger—very fine, better than merely technical, full of exquisite shades, like the light touches of the violin in the hands of a master. There was the actor Anderson, who brought us Gerald Griffin's *Gysippus*, and play'd it to admiration. Among the actors of those times I recall: Cooper, Wallack, Tom Hamblin, Adams (several), Old Gates, Scott, Wm. Sefton, John Sefton, Geo. Jones, Mitchell, Seguin, Old Clarke, Richings, Fisher, H. Placide, T. Placide, Thorne, Ingersoll, Gale (Mazeppa) Edwin, Horncastle. Some of the women hastily remember'd were: Mrs. Vernon, Mrs. Pritchard, Mrs. McClure, Mary Taylor, Clara Fisher, Mrs. Richardson, Mrs. Flynn. Then the singers, English, Italian and other: Mrs. Wood, Mrs. Seguin, Mrs. Austin, Grisi, La Grange, Steffanone, Bosio, Truffi, Parodi, Vestvali, Bertucca, Jenny Lind, Gazzaniga, Laborde. And the opera men: Bettini, Badiali, Marini, Mario, Brignoli, Amodio, Beneventano, and many, many others whose names I do not at this moment recall.

In another paper I have described the elder Booth, and the Bowery Theatre of those times. Afterward there was the Chatham. The elder Thorne, Mrs. Thorne, William and John Sefton, Kirby, Brougham, and sometimes Edwin Forrest himself play'd there. I remember them all, and many more, and especially the fine theatre on Broadway near Pearl, in 1855 and '6.

There were very good circus performances, or horseman-ship, in New York and Brooklyn. Every winter in the first-named city, a regular place in the Bowery, nearly opposite the old theatre; fine animals and fine riding, which I often witness'd. (Remember seeing near here, a young, fierce, splendid lion, presented by an African Barbary Sultan to President Andrew Jackson. The gift comprised also a lot of jewels, a fine steel sword, and an Arab stallion; and the lion was made over to a show-man.)

If it is worth while I might add that there was a small but well-appointed amateur-theatre up Broadway, with the usual stage, orchestra, pit, boxes, etc., and that I was myself a member for some time, and acted parts in it several times— "second parts" as they were call'd. Perhaps it too was a lesson, or help'd that way; at any rate it was full of fun and enjoyment.

And so let us turn off the gas. Out in the brilliancy of the footlights—filling the attention of perhaps a crowded audi-ence, and making many a breath and pulse swell and rise—O so much passion and imparted life!—over and over again, the season through—walking, gesticulating, singing, reciting his or her part—But then sooner or later inevitably wending to the flies or exit door—vanishing to sight and ear—and never materializing on this earth's stage again!

# III. Letters

# Letters

## I

### N. HALE Sr., Boston, Mass.

[Brooklyn, New York]
Tuesday June 14th [1842]

I took the liberty, two or three weeks since, of forwarding you a MS. tale "The Angel of Tears", intended for the *Boston Miscellany*.—

Be so kind, if you accept it, to forward a note, informing me thereof, to this place (your agency in New York), and if you decline, please return the MS.

My stories, I believe, have been pretty popular, and extracted liberally. Several of them in the *Democratic Review* have received public favor, instance "Death in the School-Room", &c. &c.

Walter Whitman.

## II

### T. G. BERGEN

Brooklyn, Jan. 15, '49.

T. G. Bergen, Esq.

Dear Sir: It would be a great obligation to me if you would present the enclosed bill and start it on its passage, so that I could get my pay as quickly as possible,—For, like most printers, I am horribly in need of cash.—

Do, my dear sir, oblige me, in this matter, if possible.

Yours truly

Walter Whitman

## III

### TO AN UNKNOWN CORRESPONDENT

Brooklyn, Saturday Afternoon,
July 20, 1857

Dear Friend,

Do not suppose, because I have delayed writing to you, that I have forgotten you.—No, that will never be.—I often recall your visits to me and your goodness.—I think profoundly of my friends—though I cannot write to them by the post office.—I write to them more to my satisfaction, through my poems.—

Tell Hector I thank him heartily for his invitation and letter—O it is not from any mind to slight him that I have not answered it, or accepted the friendly call.—I am so non-polite—so habitually wanting in my responses and cere-monies.—That is *me*—much that is bad, harsh, an undutiful person, a thriftless debtor, is me.—

I spent an evening with Mr. Arnold and Mrs. Price lately. —Mrs. Price and Helen had been out all day with the sewing machine, at Mr. Beecher's—either Henry Ward's, or his father's. They had done a great day's work—as much, one of the Beecher ladies said, as a sempstress could have got through with in six months.—Mrs. P. and Helen had engage-ments for a fortnight ahead, to go out among families and take the sewing machine.—What a revolution this little piece of furniture is producing.—Isn't it quite an *encouragement*.—

I got into quite a talk with Mr. Arnold about Mrs. Hatch. —He says the pervading thought of her speeches is that *first* exists the spirituality of any thing, and *that* gives existence to things, the earth, plants, animals, men, women. But that Andrew Jackson Davis puts *matter* as the subject of his homilies, and the primary source of all results—I suppose the soul among the rest. Both are quite determined in their theories.—Perhaps when they know more, both of them will be much less determined.—

A minister, Rev. Mr. Porter, was introduced to me this morning,—a Dutch Reformed minister, and editor of the *Christian Intelligencer*, N.Y.—Would you believe it,—he had been reading *Leaves of Grass*, and wanted *more*? He said he hoped I retained the true Reformed faith which I must have inherited from my mother's Dutch ancestry.—I not only assured him of my retaining faith in that sect, but that I had perfect faith in all sects, and was not inclined to reject one single one—but believed each to be about as far advanced as it could be, considering what had preceded it—and moreover that every one was the needed representative of *its* truth—or of something needed as much as truth.—I had quite a good hour with Mr. Porter—we grew friends—and I am to go dine with the head man of the head congregation of Dutch Presbyterians in Brooklyn, Eastern District!

I have seen Mrs. Walton once since you left Brooklyn,—I dined there.—I feel great sympathy with her, on some accounts.—Certainly, she is not happy.—

Fowler & Wells are bad persons for me.—They retard my book very much.—It is worse than ever.—I wish now to bring out a third edition—I have now *a hundred* poems ready (the last edition had thirty-two.)—and shall endeavor to make an arrangement with some publisher here to take the plates from F. & W. and make the additions needed, and so bring out the third edition.—F. & W. are very willing to give up the plates—they want the thing off their hands.—In the forthcoming Vol. I shall have, as I said, a hundred poems, and no other matter but poems—(no letters to or from Emerson—no Notices or any thing of that sort.)—It is, I know Well enough, that *that* must be the *true Leaves of Grass* —and I think it has an aspect of completeness, and makes its case clearer.—The old poems are all retained.—The difference is in the new character given to the mass, by the additions.—

Dear friend, I do not feel like fixing a day on which I will come and make my promised visit.—How it is I know not, but I hang back more and more from making visits, even to those I have much happiness in being with.—

Mother is well—all are well.—Mother often speaks about you.—We shall all of us remember you always with more affection than you perhaps suppose.—Before I come to Philadelphia, I shall send you or Hector a line.—

—Wishing Peace & Friendship

Walt Whitman.

# IV

## JAMES RUSSELL LOWELL, Boston

Portland av. near Myrtle
Brooklyn, N.Y.
Jan. 20, '60

Dear Sir:

Mr. House informed me that you accepted, and would publish, my " Bardic Symbols". If so, would you, as soon as convenient, have it put in type and send me the proof?

About the two lines:

(See from my dead lips the ooze exuding at last!
See the prismatic colors glistening and rolling!)

I have in view, from them an effect in the piece which I clearly feel, but cannot as clearly define—Though I should prefer them in still, as I told Mr. House, I agree that you may omit them, if you decidedly wish to.

Yours &c.

Walt Whitman

# V

## MRS. ABBY H. PRICE, Brooklyn

Boston, Thursday night, March 29 [1860].

As I know you would like to hear from me, my dear friend, I will not yet go to bed—but sit down to write to you, that I have been here in Boston, to-day is a fortnight, and that my book is well under way. About a hundred and twenty pages are set up—it will probably make from six to seven hundred pages—and of a larger size than the last edition. It is to be very finely printed, good paper, and new, rather large-sized type. Thayer & Eldridge, the publishers, are a couple of young Yankees—so far very good specimens, to me of this Eastern race of yours. They have treated me first rate—have not asked me at all what I was going to put into the book—just took me to the stereotype foundry and gave orders to follow my directions. It will be out in a month—a great relief to have the thing off my mind.

I am more pleased with Boston than I anticipated. It is full of life, and criss-cross streets. I am very glad I came, if only to rub out of me the deficient notions I had of New England character. I am getting to like it, every way—even the Yankee twang.

Emerson called upon me immediately, treated me with the greatest courtesy—kept possession of me all day—gave me a bully dinner, &c.

I go on the Common—walk considerable in Washington street—and occupy about three hours a day at work in the printing office. All I have to do is to read proofs. I wish you lived here—I should visit you regularly every day—probably twice a day. I create an immense sensation in Washington Street. Everybody here is so like everybody else—and I am Walt Whitman!—Yankee curiosity and cuteness—for once is thoroughly stumped, confounded petrified, made desperate.

Let me see—have I anything else to say to you? Indeed, what does it all amount to,—this saying business? Of course I had better tear up this note—only I want to let you see how I cannot have forgotten you—sitting up here after half past 12, to write this precious document. I send my love to Helen and Emmy.

Walt.

## VI

### J. R. LOWELL, Boston

Brooklyn, Tuesday morning,<br>October 1st 1861.

Mr Lowell,

Dear Sir:—The price of "1861", if you print it, is $20. You are at liberty to make any verbal alterations. The envelope is of course to return it in, if you cannot use it.

Yours truly<br>W. Whitman

## VII

### MRS. LOUISA WHITMAN, Brooklyn

Washington,
*Monday forenoon*, Dec. 29, 1862.

Dear, Dear Mother—Friday the 19th inst. I succeeded in reaching the camp of the 51st New York, and found George alive and well. In order to make sure that you would get the good news, I sent back by messenger to Washington a telegraphic dispatch (I dare say you did not get it for some time) as well as a letter—and the same to Hannah at Burlington. I have staid in camp with George ever since, till yesterday, when I came back to Washington, about the 24th. George got Jeff's letter of the 20th. Mother, how much you must have suffered, all that week, till George's letter came—and all the rest must too. As to me, I know I put in about three days of the greatest suffering I ever experienced in my life. I wrote to Jeff how I had my pocket picked in a jam and hurry, changing cars, at Philadelphia—so that I landed here without a dime. The next two days I spent hunting through the hospitals, walking day and night, unable to ride, trying to get information—trying to get access to big people, etc.—I could not get the least clue to anything. Odell would not see me at all. But Thursday afternoon, I lit on a way to get down on the Government boat that runs to Aquia creek, and so by railroad to the neighborhood of Falmouth, opposite Fredericksburg—so by degrees I worked my way to Ferrero's brigade, which I found Friday afternoon without much trouble after I got in camp. When I found dear brother George, and found that he was alive and well, O you may imagine how trifling all my little cares and difficulties seemed —they vanished into nothing. And now that I have lived for eight or nine days amid such scenes as the camps furnish, and had a practical part in it all, and realize the way that hundreds of thousands of good men are now living, and have had to live for a year or more, not only without any of the comforts, but with death and sickness and hard marching and hard fighting (and no success at that) for their continual experience—really nothing we call trouble seems worth talking about. One of the first things that met my eyes in camp was a heap of feet, arms, legs, etc., under a tree in front of a hospital, the Lacy house.

George is very well in health, has a good appetite—I think he is at times more wearied out and homesick than he shows, but stands it upon the whole very well. Every one of the soldiers, to a man, wants to get home.

I suppose Jeff got quite a long letter I wrote, from camp, about a week ago. I told you that George had been promoted to captain—his commission arrived while I was there. When you write, address, Capt. George W. Whitman, Co. K., 51st New York Volunteers, Ferrero's brigade, near Falmouth, Va. Jeff must write oftener, and put in a few lines from mother, even if it is only two lines—then in the next letter a few lines from Mat, and so on. You have no idea how letters from home cheer one up in camp, and dissipate homesickness.

While I was there George still lived in Capt. Francis's tent —there were five of us altogether, to eat, sleep, write, etc., in a space twelve feet square, but we got along very well—the weather all along was very fine—and would have got along to perfection, but Capt. Francis is not a man I could like much —I had very little to say to him. George is about building a place, half hut and half tent, for himself, (he is probably about it this very day,) and then he will be better off, I think. Every captain has a tent, in which he lives, transacts company business, etc., has a cook, (or a man of all work,) and in the same tent mess and sleep his lieutenants, and perhaps the first sergeant. They have a kind of fire-place—and the cook's fire is outside on the open ground. George had very good times while Francis was away—the cook, a young disabled soldier, Tom, is an excellent fellow and a first-rate cook, and the second lieutenant, Pooley, is a tip-top young Pennsylvanian. Tom thinks all the world of George; when he heard he was wounded, on the day of the battle, he left everything, got across the river, and went hunting for George through the field, through thick and thin. I wrote to Jeff that George was wounded by a shell, a gash in the cheek—you could stick a splint through into the mouth, but it has healed up without difficulty already. Everything is uncertain about the army, whether it moves or stays where it is. There are no furloughs granted at present. I will stay here for the present, at any rate long enough to see if I can get any employment at anything, and shall write what luck I have. Of course I am unsettled at present. Dear mother, my love.

Walt.

If Jeff or any writes, address me, care of Major Hapgood, paymaster, U.S.A. Army, Washington, D.C. I send my love to dear sister Mat, and little Sis—and to Andrew and all my brothers. O Mat, how lucky it was you did not come—together, we could never have got down to see George.

# VIII

## MRS. MARTHA WHITMAN, Brooklyn

Washington, Friday morning,
Jan. 2, 1863.

Dear Sister—You have heard of my fortunes and misfortunes of course, (through my letters to mother and Jeff,) since I left home that Tuesday afternoon. But I thought I would write a few lines to you, as it is a comfort to write home, even if I have nothing particular to say. Well, dear sister, I hope you are well and hearty, and that little Sis keeps as well as she always had, when I left home so far. Dear little plague, how I would like to have her with me, for one day; I can fancy I see her, and hear her talk. Jeff must have got a note from me about a letter I have written to the *Eagle*—you may be sure you will get letters enough from me, for I have little else to do at present. Since I laid my eyes on dear brother George, and saw him alive and well—and since I have spent a week in camp, down there opposite Fredericksburg, and seen what well men, and sick men, and mangled men endure—it seems to me I can be satisfied and happy henceforward if I can get one meal a day, and know that mother and all are in good health, and especially be with you again, and have some little steady paying occupation in N.Y. or Brooklyn.

I am writing this in the office of Major Hapgood, way up in the top of a big high house, corner of 15th and F street; there is a splendid view, away down south of the Potomac river, and across to the Georgetown side, and the grounds and houses of Washington spread out beneath my high point of view. The weather is perfect—I have had that in my favor ever since leaving home—yesterday and to-day it is bright, and plenty warm enough. The poor soldiers are continually coming in from the hospitals, etc., to get their pay—some of them waiting for it to go home. They climb up here, quite exhausted, and then find it is no good, for there is no money to pay them; there are two or three paymasters' desks in this room, and the scenes of disappointment are quite affecting. Here they wait in Washington, perhaps week after week, wretched and heart-sick—this is the greatest place of delays and puttings off, and no finding the clue to anything. This building is the Paymaster-general's quarters, and the crowds on the walk and corner of poor, sick, pale, tattered soldiers are awful—many of them day after day disappointed and tired out. Well, Mat, I will suspend my letter for the present, and go through the city—I have a couple of poor fellows in the hospital to visit also.

Walt.

Saturday evening, Jan. 3. I write this in the place where I have my lodging-room, 394 L street, 4th door above 14th street. A friend of mine, William D. O'Connor, has two apartments on the 3rd floor, very ordinarily furnished, for which he pays the *extra*ordinary price of $25 a month. I have a werry little bedroom on the 2nd floor. Mr. and Mrs. O'Connor and their little girl have all gone out "down town" for an hour or two, to make some Saturday evening purchases, and I am left in possession of the premises—so I sit by the fire, and scribble more of my letter. I have not heard anything from dear brother George since I left the camp last Sunday morning, 28th Dec. I wrote to him on Tuesday last. I wish to get to him the two blue woolen shirts Jeff sent, as they would come very acceptable to him—and will try to do it yet. I think of sending them by mail, if the postage is not more than $1.

Yesterday I went out to the Campbell hospital to see a couple of Brooklyn boys, of the 51st. They knew I was in Washington, and sent me a note, to come and see them. O my dear sister, how your heart would ache to go through the rows of wounded young men, as I did—and stopt to speak a comforting word to them. There were about 100 in one long room, just a long shed neatly whitewashed inside. One young man was very much prostrated, and groaning with pain. I stopt and tried to comfort him. He was very sick. I found he had not had any medical attention since he was brought there; among so many he had been overlooked; so I sent for the doctor, and he made an examination of him. The doctor behaved very well—seemed to be anxious to do right—said that the young man would recover; he had been brought pretty low with diarrhœa, and now had bronchitis, but not so serious as to be dangerous. I talked to him some time—he seemed to have entirely given up, and lost heart—he had not a cent of money—not a friend or acquaintance. I wrote a letter from him to his sister—his name is John A. Holmes, Campello, Plymouth county, Mass. I gave him a little change I had—he said he would like to buy a drink of milk when the woman came through with milk. Trifling as this was, he was overcome and began to cry. Then there were many, many others. I mention the one, as a specimen. My Brooklyn boys were John Lowery, shot at Fredericksburg, and lost his left forearm, and Amos H. Vliet—Jeff knows the latter—he has his feet frozen, and is doing well. The 100 are in a ward, (6), and there are, I should think, eight or ten or twelve such wards in the Campbell hospital—indeed a real village. Then there are 38 more hospitals here in Washingtin, some of them much larger.

Sunday forenoon, Jan. 4, 1863. Mat, I hope and trust dear mother and all are well, and everything goes on good [at] home. The envelope I send, Jeff or any of you can keep for direction, or use it when wanted to write to me. As near as I can tell, the army at Falmouth remains the same. Dear sister, good-bye.

Walt.

I send my love to Andrew and Jesse and Eddy and all. What distressing news this is of the loss of the Monitor.

## IX

## MR. WOOD

Washington,
Saturday morning Jan 17 '63.

Dear Mr. Wood,

So your generous heart moved you to send the sick and dying young men in the hospitals a handsome little contribution of money (toward $4) I thank you, dear sir, in their name,—and in my own, as the organ of your charity. I have distributed part of it in Ward 6, (Dr. Leman, ward surgeon) Campbell Hospital—and shall to-day bestow the rest in the Patent Office Hosp. My friend, I must meet you soon again.

Truly yours,

Walt Whitman.

## X

### JEFFERSON WHITMAN, Brooklyn

Office Major Hapgood, cor. 15th & F sts,
Washington, Feb. 13, 1863.

Dear Brother—Nothing new; still I thought I would write you a line this morning. The $4, namely $2 from Theo A. Drake and $2 from John D. Martin, enclosed in your letter of the 10th, came safe. They too will please accept the grateful thanks of several poor fellows, in hospital here.

The letter of introduction to Mr. Webster, chief clerk, State department, will be very acceptable. If convenient, I should like Mr. Lane to send it immediately. I do not so much look for an appointment from Mr. Seward as his backing me from the State of New York. I have seen Preston King this morning for the second time (it is very amusing to hunt for an office—so the thing seems to me just now, even if one don't get it). I have seen Charles Sumner three times— he says ev'ry thing here moves as part of a great machine, and that I must consign myself to the fate of the rest—still [in] an interview I had with him yesterday he talked and acted as though he had life in him, and would exert himself to any reasonable extent for me to get something. Meantime I make about enough to pay my expenses by hacking on the press here, and copying in the paymasters' offices, a couple of hours a day. One thing is favorable here, namely, pay for whatever one does is at a high rate. I have not yet presented my letters to either Seward or Chase—I thought I would get my forces all in a body, and make one concentrated dash, if possible with the personal introduction and presence of some big bug. I like fat old Preston King very much—he is fat as a hogshead, with great hanging chops. The first thing he said to me the other day in the parlor chambers of the Senate, when I sent in for him and he came out, was, "Why, how can I do this thing, or any thing for you—how do I know but you are a Secessionist? You look for all the world like an old Southern planter—a regular Carolina or Virginia planter." I treated him with just as much hauteur as he did me with bluntness—this was the first time—it afterward proved that Charles Sumner had not prepared the way for me, as I supposed, or rather not so strongly as I supposed, and Mr. King had even forgotten it—so I was an entire stranger. But the same day C. S. talked further with Mr. King in the Senate, and the second interview I had with the latter (this forenoon) he has given me a sort of general letter, endorsing me from New York—one envelope is addressed to Secretary Chase, and another to Gen. Meigs, head Quartermaster's dept. Meantime, I am getting better and better acquainted with office-hunting wisdom and Washington peculiarities generally. I spent several hours in the Capitol the other day. The incredible gorgeousness of some of the rooms, (interior decorations, etc.)—rooms used perhaps but for merely three or four committee meetings in the course of the whole year—is beyond one's flightiest dreams. Costly frescoes of the style of Taylor's saloon in Broadway, only really the best and choicest of their sort, done by imported French and Italian artists, are the prevailing sorts. (Imagine the work you see on the fine china vases in Tiffany's, the paintings of Cupids and goddesses, etc., spread recklessly over the arched ceiling and broad panels of a big room—the whole floor underneath paved with tesselated pavement, which is a sort of cross between marble

and china, with little figures, drab, blue, cream color, etc.)
These things, with heavy elaborately wrought balustrades,
columns, and steps—all of the most beautiful marbles I ever
saw, some white as milk, other of all colors, green, spotted,
lined, or of our old chocolate color—all these marbles used
as freely as if they were common blue flags—with rich door-
frames and window-casings of bronze and gold—heavy chandeliers and mantles, and clocks in every room—and indeed
by far the richest and gayest, and most un-American and
inappropriate ornamenting and finest interior workmanship
I ever conceived possible, spread in profusion through scores,
hundreds, (and almost thousands) of rooms—such are what
I find, or rather would find to interest me, if I devoted time to
it. But a few of the rooms are enough for me—the style is
without grandeur, and without simplicity. These days, the
state our country is in, and especially filled as I am from top
to toe of late with scenes and thoughts of the hospitals,
(America seems to me now, though only in her youth, but
brought already here, feeble, bandaged, and bloody in hospital)—these days I say, Jeff, all the poppy-show goddesses,
and all the pretty blue and gold in which the interior Capitol
is got up, seems to me out of place beyond anything I could
tell—and I get away from it as quick as I can when that kind
of thought comes over me. I suppose it is to be described
throughout—those interiors—as all of them got up in the
French style—well, enough for a New York.

## XI

NAT GRAY AND FRED GRAY, New York

Washington, March 19, 1863.

Dear Nat and Fred Gray:

Since I left New York I was down in the Army of the
Potomac in front with my brother a good part of the winter,
commencing time of the battle of Fredericksburgh—have
seen *war-life*, the real article—folded myself in a blanket,
lying down in the mud with composure—relished salt pork
and hard tack—have been on the battlefield among the

wounded, the faint and the bleeding, to give them nourishment—have gone over with a flag of truce the next day to help direct the burial of the dead—have struck up a tremendous friendship with a young Mississippi captain (about 19) that we took prisoner badly wounded at Fredericksburgh (he has followed me here, is in the Emory hospital here minus a leg—he wears his confederate uniform, proud as the devil—I met him first at Falmouth, in the Lacy house middle of December last, his leg just cut off, and cheered him up—poor boy, he has suffered a great deal, and still suffers—has eyes bright as a hawk, but face pale—our affection is an affair quite romantic—sometimes when I lean over to say I am going, he puts his arms around my neck, draws my face down, etc., quite a scene for the New Bowery). I spent the Christmas holidays on the Rappahannock.—During January came up hither, took a lodging room here. Did the 37th Congress, especially the night sessions the last three weeks, explored the Capitol, meandering the gorgeous painted interminable Senate corridors, getting lost in them (a new sensation, rich and strong, that endless painted interior at night)—got very much interested in some particular cases in Hospitals here—go now steadily to more or less of said Hospitals by day or night—find always the sick and dying soldiers forthwith begin to cling to me in a way that makes a fellow feel funny enough. These Hospitals, so different from all others—these thousands, and tens and twenties of thousands of American young men, badly wounded, all sorts of wounds, operated on, pallid with diarrhœa, languishing, dying with fever, pneumonia, etc., open a new world somehow to me, giving closer insights, new things, exploring deeper mines, than any yet, showing our humanity (I sometimes put myself in fancy in the cot, with typhoid, or under the knife) tried by terrible, fearfullest tests, probed deepest, the living soul's, the body's tragedies, bursting the petty bonds of art. To these, what are your dramas and poems, even the oldest and the fearfullest? Not old Greek mighty ones; where man contends with fate (and always yields)—not Virgil showing Dante on and on among the agonized and damned, approach what here I see and take part in. For here I see, not at intervals, but quite always, how certain man, our American man—how he holds himself cool and unquestioned master above all pains and bloody mutilations. It is immense, the best thing of all—nourishes me of all men. This then, what frightened us all so long. Why, it is put to flight with ignominy—a mere stuffed scarecrow of the fields. Oh death, where is thy sting? Oh grave, where is thy victory?

In the Patent Office, as I stood there one night, just off the cot-side of a dying soldier, in a large ward that had received the worst cases of Second Bull Run, Antietam, and Fredericksburgh, the surgeon, Dr. Stone (Horatio Stone the Sculptor) told me, of all who had died in that crowded ward the past six months, he had still to find the *first man* or *boy* who had met the approach of death with a single tremor or unmanly fear. But let me change the subject—I have given you screed enough about Death and the Hospitals—and too much—since I got started. Only I have some curious yarns I promise you my darlings and gossips, by word of mouth whene'er we meet.

Washington and its points I find bear a second and a third perusal, and doubtless many. My first impressions, architectural, etc., were not favorable; but upon the whole, the city, the spaces, buildings, etc., make no unfit emblem of our country, so far, so broadly planned, everything in plenty, money and materials staggering with plenty, but the fruit of the plans, the knit, the combination yet wanting—Determined to express ourselves greatly in a Capitol but no fit Capitol yet here (time, associations, wanting I suppose) many a hiatus yet—many a thing to be taken down and done over again yet—perhaps an entire change of base—maybe a succession of changes.

Congress does not seize very hard upon me; I studied it and its members with curiosity, and long—much gab, great fear of public opinion, plenty of low business talent, but no masterful man in Congress (probably best so). I think well of the President. He has a face like a Hoosier Michael Angelo, so awful ugly it becomes beautiful, with its strange mouth, its deep cut, criss-cross lines, and its doughnut complexion.—My notion is too, that underneath his outside smutched mannerism, and stories from third-class county barrooms (it is his humor), Mr. Lincoln keeps a fountain of first-class practical telling wisdom. I do not dwell on the supposed failures of his government; he has shown, I sometimes think an almost supernatural tact in keeping the ship afloat at all, with head steady, not only not going down, and now certain not to, but with proud and resolute spirit, and flag flying in sight of the world, menacing and high as ever. I say never yet captain, never ruler, had such a perplexing dangerous task as his, the past two years. I more and more rely upon his idiomatic western genius, careless of court dress or court decorum.

I am living here without much definite aim (except going to the hospitals)—yet I have quite a good time—I make some money by scribbling for the papers, and as copyist. I have had (and have) thoughts of trying to get a clerkship or something, but I only try in a listless sort of way, and of course do not succeed. I have strong letters of introduction from Mr. Emerson to Mr. Seward and Mr. Chase, but I have not presented them. I have seen Mr. Sumner several times anent my office hunting—he promised fair once—but he does not seem to be finally fascinated. I hire a bright little 3rd story front room, with service, etc., for $7 a month, dine in the same house (394 L St. a private house)—and remain yet much of the old vagabond that so gracefully becomes me. I miss you all, my darlings and gossips, Fred Gray, and Bloom and Russell and everybody. I wish you would all come here in a body—that would be divine (we would drink ale, which is here the best). My health, strength, personal beauty, etc., are, I am happy to inform you, without diminution, but on the contrary quite the reverse. I weigh full 220 pounds avoirdupois, yet still retain my usual perfect shape—a regular model. My beard, neck, etc., are woolier, fleecier, whiteyer than ever. I wear army boots, with magnificent black morocco tops, the trousers put in, wherein shod and legged, confront I Virginia's deepest mud with supercilious eyes. The scenery around Washington is really fine, the Potomac a lordly river, the hills, woods, etc., all attractive. I poke about quite a good deal. Much of the weather here is from heaven —of late though, a stretch decidedly from the other point. To-night (for it is night about 10) I sit alone writing this epistle (which will doubtless devour you all with envy and admiration) in a room adjoining my own particular. A gentleman and his wife who occupy the two other apartments on this floor have gone to see Heron in *Medea*—have put their little child in bed and left me in charge. The little one is sleeping soundly there in the back room, and I (plagued with a cold in the head) sit here in the front by a good fire writing as aforesaid to my gossips and darlings. The evening is lonesome and still, I am entirely alone "Oh, Solitude where are the charms, etc."

Now you write to me good long letters, my own boys. You, Bloom, give me your address particular, dear friend. Tell me Charles Russell's address, particular—also write me about Charles Chauncey. Tell me about everybody. For, dearest gossips, as the heart panteth, etc., so my soul after any and all sorts of items about you all. My darling, dearest boys, if I could be with you this hour, long enough to take only just three mild hot rums, before cool weather closes.

Friday Morning, 20th—I finish my letter in the office of Major Hapgood, a paymaster, and a friend of mine. This is a large building filled with paymaster's offices, some thirty or forty or more. This room is up on the fifth floor (a most noble and broad view from my window) curious scenes around here—a continual stream of soldiers, officers, cripples, etc., some climbing wearily up the stairs. They seek their pay—and every hour, almost every minute, has its incident, its hitch, its romance, farce or tragedy. There are two paymasters in this room. A sentry at the street door, another halfway up the stairs, another at the chief clerk's door, all with muskets and bayonets—sometimes a great swarm, hundreds around the side walk in front waiting (everybody is waiting for something here). I take a pause, look up a couple of minutes from my pen and paper—see spread, off there the Potomac, very fine, nothing petty about it—the Washington monument, not half finished—the public grounds around it filled with ten thousand beeves on the hoof—to the left the Smithsonian with its brown turrets—to the right far across, Arlington Heights, the forts, eight or ten of them—then the long bridge, and down a ways but quite plain, the shipping of Alexandria. Opposite me, and in a stone throw is the Treasury Building, and below the bustle and life of Pennsylvania Avenue. I shall hasten with my letter, and then go forth and take a stroll down "the avenue" as they call it here.

Now you boys, don't you think I have done the handsome thing by writing this astoundingly magnificent letter—certainly the longest I ever wrote in my life. Fred, I wish you to present my best respects to your father, Bloom and all; one of these days we will meet, and make up for lost time, my dearest boys.

Walt.

Address me, care Major Hapgood, paymaster U.S. Army, Cor. 15th & F St., Washington. How is Mullen? Give him my respects—How is Ben Knower? How the twinkling and temperate Towle? Remember me to them.

XII

MRS. LOUISA WHITMAN, Brooklyn

Washington, March 31, 1863.

Dearest Mother—I have not heard from George, except a note he wrote me a couple of days after he got back from his furlough. I think it likely the regiment has gone with its corps to the West, the Kentucky or Tennessee region—Burnside at last accounts was in Cincinnati. Well, it will be a change for George, if he is out there. I sent a long letter to Han last Saturday—enclosed George's note to me. Mother, when you or Jeff writes again, tell me if my papers and MSS. are all right; I should be very sorry indeed if they got scattered, or used up or anything—especially the copy of *Leaves of Grass* covered in blue paper, and the little MS. book *Drum-Taps*, and the MS. tied up in the square, spotted (stone-paper) loose covers—I want them all carefully kept.

Mother, it is quite a snow-storm here this morning—the ground is an inch and a half deep with snow—and it is snowing and drizzling—but I feel very independent in my stout army-boots; I go anywhere. I *have* felt quite well of my deafness and cold in my head for four days or so, but it is back again bad as ever this morning.

Dear mother, I wrote the above in my room—I have now come down to Major Hapgood's office. I do not find anything from home, and no particular news in the paper this morning—no news about the Ninth Army Corps, or where they are. I find a good letter from one of my New York boys, (Fifth avenue) a young fellow named Hugo Fritsch, son of the Austrian Consul-General—he writes me a long, first-rate letter this morning. He too speaks about the Opera—like Jeff he goes there a good deal—says that Medori, the soprano, as Norma made the greatest success ever seén—says that the whole company there now, the singers, are very fine. All this I write for Jeff and Mat—I hope they will go once in a while when it is convenient.

It is a most disagreeable day here, mother, walking poshy and a rain and drizzle.

There is nothing new with me, no particular sight for an office that I can count on. But I can make enough with the papers, for the present necessities. I hear that the paymaster, Major Yard, that pays the 51st, has gone on West, I suppose to Cincinnati, or wherever the brigade has gone—of course to pay up—he pays up to 1st of March—all the Army is going to be paid up to 1st March everywhere.

Mother, I hope you are well and hearty as usual. I am so glad you are none of you going to move. I would like to have the pleasure of Miss Mannahatta Whitman's company, the first fine forenoon, if it were possible; I think we might have first-rate times, for one day at any rate. I hope she will not forget her Uncle Walt. I received a note from Probasco, requesting me not to put his name in my next letter. I appreciate his motive, and wish to please him always—but in this matter I shall do what I think appropriate. Mother, I see some very interesting persons here—a young master's mate, who was on the *Hatteras*, when surprised and broadsided by the *Alabama*, Capt Semmes—he gave me a very good acc't of it all—then Capt. Mullen, U.S. Army, (engineer) who has been six years out in the Rocky mts. making a Gov't road 650 miles from Ft. Benton to Walla Walla—very, very interesting to know such men intimately, and talk freely with them. Dearest mother, I shall have great yarns to spin, when I come home. I am not a bit homesick, yet I should like to see you and Mat very, very much—one thinks of the women when he is away. Walt.

Shall send the shirts in a day or two.

## XIII

### MRS. LOUISA WHITMAN, Brooklyn

Washington, Tuesday, May 5, 1863.

Dearest Mother—Your letter came safe, and was very welcome, and always will be. Mother, I am sorry about your rheumatism—if it still continues I think it would be well for me to write a line to Mrs. Piercy, and get Jeff to stop with it, so that you could take the baths again, as I am sure they are very beneficial. Dear mother, you write me, or Jeff must in the next letter, how you are getting along, whether it is any better or worse—I want to know. Mother, about George's fund in the bank; I hope by all means you can scratch along so as to leave $250 there—I am so anxious that our family should have a little ranch, even if it is the meanest kind, off somewhere that you can call your own, and that would do for Ed etc.—it might be a real dependence, and comfort—and may-be for George as much as any one. I mean to come home one of these days, and get the acre or half acre somewhere out in some by-place on Long Island, and build it—you see if I don't. About Hannah, dear mother, I hardly know what advice to give you—from what I know at present I can't tell what course to pursue. I want Han to come home, from the bottom of my heart. Then there are other thoughts and considerations that come up. Dear mother, I cannot advise, but shall acquiesce in anything that is settled upon, and try to help.

The condition of things here in the hospitals is getting pretty bad—the wounded from the battles around Fredericksburg are coming up in large numbers. It is very sad to see them. I have written to Mr. Lane, asking him to get his friends to forward me what they think proper—but somehow I feel delicate about sending such requests, after all.

I have almost made up my mind to do what I can personally, and not seek assistance from others.

Dear mother, I have not received any letter from George. I write to him and send papers to Winchester. Mother, while I have been writing this a very large number of Southern prisoners, I should think 1,000 at least, has past up Pennsylvania avenue, under a strong guard. I went out in the street, close to them. Poor fellows, many of them mere lads—it brought the tears; they seemed our flesh and blood too, some wounded, all miserable in clothing, all in dirt and tatters—many of them fine young men. Mother, I cannot tell you how I feel to see those prisoners marched.

XIV

MRS. LOUISA WHITMAN, Brooklyn

Washington, Tuesday forenoon, May 19, 1863.

Dearest Mother—. . . I sent George a letter yesterday—have not got any letter myself from Georgy, but have sent him quite a good many and papers. Mother, what a tramp the 51st has had—they only need now to go to California, and they will finish the job complete. O mother, how welcome the shirts were—I was putting off, and putting off, to get some new ones. I could not find any one to do them as I want them, and it would have cost such a price—and so my old ones had got to be. When they came back from the wash I had to laugh; they were a lot of rags, held together with starch. I have a very nice old black aunty for a washwoman, but she bears down pretty hard, I guess, when she irons them, and they showed something like the poor old city of Fredericksburg does, since Burnside bombarded it. Well, mother, when the bundle came, I was so glad—and the coats too, worn as they are, they come in very handy—and the cake, dear mother, I am almost like the boy that put it under his pillow and woke up in the night and eat some. I carried a good chunk to a young man wounded I think a good deal of, and it did him so much good—it is dry, but all the better, as he eat it with tea and it relished. I eat a piece with him, and drinked some tea out of his cup, as I sat by the side of his cot. Mother, I have neglected, I think, what I ought to have told you two or three weeks ago, that is that I have discarded my old clothes—somewhat because they were too thick, and more still because they were worse gone in than any I have ever yet wore, I think, in my life, especially the trowsers. Wearing my big boots had caused the inside of the legs just above the knee to wear two beautiful round holes right through cloth and partly through the lining, producing a novel effect, which was not necessary, as I produce a sufficient sensation without—then they were desperately faded. I have a nice plain suit of a dark wine color; looks very well, and feels good—single breasted sack coat with breast pockets, etc., and vest and pants same as what I always wear (pants pretty full), so upon the whole all looks unusually good for me. My hat is very good yet, boots ditto; have a new necktie, nice shirts—you can imagine I cut quite a swell. I have not trimmed my beard since I left home, but it is not grown much longer, only perhaps a little bushier. I keep about as stout as ever, and the past five or six days I have felt wonderful well, indeed never did I feel better. About ten or twelve days ago, we had a short spell of very warm weather here, but for about six days now it has been delightful, just warm enough. I generally go to the hospitals from 12 to 4— and then again from 6 to 9; some days I only go in the middle of the day or evening, not both—and then when I feel somewhat opprest, I skip over a day, or make perhaps a light call only, as I have several cautions from the doctors, who tell me that one must beware of continuing too steady and long in the air and influences of the hospitals. I find the caution a wise one.

Mother, you or Jeff must write me what Andrew does about going to North Carolina. I should think it might have a beneficial effect upon his throat. I wrote Jeff quite a long letter Sunday. Jeff must write to me whenever he can, I like dearly to have them—and whenever you feel like it you too, dear mother. Tell Sis her uncle Walt will come back one of these days from the sick soldiers and take her out on Fort Greene again. Mother, I received a letter yesterday from John Elliot's father, in Bedford co., Pennsylvania (the young man I told you about, who died under the operation). It was very sad; it was the first he knew about it. I don't know whether I told you of Dennis Barrett, pneumonia three weeks since, had got well enough to be sent home. Dearest mother, I hope you will take things as easy as possible and try to keep a good heart. Matty, my dear sister, I have to inform you that I was treated to a splendid dish of ice cream Sunday night; I wished you was with me to have another. I send you my love, dear sister. Mother, I hope by all means it will be possible to keep the money whole to get some ranch next spring, if not before; I mean to come home and build it. Good-bye for the present, dear mother.

Walt.

## XV

### MRS. LOUISA WHITMAN, Brooklyn

Washington, Tuesday morning, June 9, 1863.

Dearest Mother—Jeff's letter came yesterday and was very welcome, as I wanted to hear about you all. I wrote to George yesterday and sent Jeff's letter enclosed. It looks from some accounts as though the 9th Army Corps might be going down into East Tennessee (Cumberland Gap, or perhaps bound for Knoxville). It is an important region, and has many Southern Unionists. The staunchest Union man I have ever met is a young Southerner in the 2nd Tennessee (Union reg't)—he was ten months in Southern prisons; came up from Richmond paroled about ten weeks ago, and has been in hospital here sick until lately. He suffered everything but death—he is [the] one they hung up by the heels, head downwards—and indeed worse than death, but stuck to his convictions like a hero—John Barker, a real manly fellow; I saw much of him and heard much of that country that can be relied on. He is now gone home to his reg't.

Mother, I am feeling very well these days—my head that was stopt up so and hard of hearing seems to be all right; I only hope you have had similar good fortune with your rheumatism, and that it will continue so. I wish I could come in for a couple of days and see you; if I should succeed in getting a transportation ticket that would take me to New York and back I should be tempted to come home for two or three days, as I want some MSS. and books, and the trunk, etc.—but I will see. Mother, your letter week before last was very good—whenever you feel like it you write me, dear mother, and tell me everything about the neighborhood and all the items of our family.

And sister Mat, how is she getting along—I believe I will have to write a letter especially to her and Sis one of these times.

It is awful dry weather here, no rain of any consequence for five or six weeks. We have strawberries good and plenty, 15 cents a quart, with the hulls on—I go down to market sometimes of a morning and buy two or three quarts, for the folks I take my meals with. Mother, do you know I have not paid, as you may say, a cent of board since I have been in Washington, that is for meals—four or five times I have made a rush to leave the folks and find a moderate-priced boarding-house, but every time they have made such a time about it that I have kept on. It is Mr. and Mrs. O'Connor (he is the author of *Harrington*); he has a $1600 office in the Treasury, and she is a first-rate woman, a Massachusetts girl. They keep house in a moderate way; they have one little girl (lost a fine boy about a year ago); they have two rooms in the same house where I hire my rooms, and I take breakfast (half-past 8) and dinner (half-past 4) with them, as they will have it so. That's the way it has gone on now over five months, and as I say, they won't listen to my leaving—but I shall do so, I think. I can never forget the kindness and real friendship, and it appears as though they would continue just the same, if it were for all our lives. But I have insisted on going to market (it is pleasant in the cool of the morning) and getting the things at my own expense, two or three times a week lately. I pay for the room I occupy now $7 a month—the landlord is a mixture of booby, miser, and hog; his name is G——; the landlady is a good woman, Washington raised —they are quite rich; he is Irish of the worst kind—has had a good office for ten years until Lincoln came in. They have bought another house, smaller, to live in, and are going to move (were to have moved 1st of June). They had an auction of the house we live in yesterday, but nobody came to buy, so it was ridiculous—we had a red flag out, and a nigger walked up and down ringing a big bell, which is the fashion here for auctions.

Well, mother, the war still goes on, and everything as much in a fog as ever—and the battles as bloody, and the wounded and sick getting worse and plentier all the time. I see a letter

in the *Tribune* from Lexington, Ky., June 5th, headed "The
9th Army Corps departing for Vicksburg"—but I cannot
exactly make it out on reading the letter carefully—I don't
see anything in the letter about the 9th Corps moving from
Vicksburg; at any rate I think the 2nd division is more likely
to be needed in Kentucky (or as I said, in Eastern Tennessee), as the Secesh are expected to make trouble there. But
one can hardly tell—the only thing is to resign oneself to
events as they occur; it is a sad and dreary time, for so many
thousands of parents and relatives, not knowing what will
occur next. Mother, I told you, I think last week, that I had
wrote to Han, and enclosed George's last letter to me—I
wrote a week ago last Sunday—I wonder if she got the letter.
About the pictures, I should like Jeff to send them, as soon as
convenient—might send 20 of the big head, 10 or 12 of the
standing figure, and 3 of the carte visite.

I am writing this in Major Hapgood's office—it is bright
and pleasant, only the dust here in Washington is a great
nuisance. Mother, your shirts do first rate—I am wearing
them; the one I have on to-day suits me better than any I
have ever yet had. I have not worn the thin coat the last
week or so, as it has not been very hot lately. Mother, I
think something of commencing a series of lectures and reading, etc., through different cities of the North, to supply myself with funds for my hospital and soldiers' visits, as I do not
like to be beholden to the medium of others. I need a pretty
large supply of money, etc., to do the good I would like to,
and the work grows upon me, and fascinates me—it is the
most affecting thing you ever see, the lots of poor sick and
wounded young men that depend so much, in one word or
another, upon my petting or soothing or feeding, sitting by
them and feeding them their dinner or supper—some are
quite helpless, some wounded in both arms—or giving some
trifle (for a novelty or a change, it isn't for the value of it), or
stopping a little while with them. Nobody will do but me—
so, mother, I feel as though I would like to inaugurate a plan
by which I could raise means on my own hook, and perhaps
quite plenty too. Best love to you, dearest mother, and to
sister Mat, and Jeff.

Walt.

## XVI

### MRS. LOUISA WHITMAN, Brooklyn

Washington, June 30th, 1863.

Dearest Mother—Your letter, with Han's, I have sent to George, though whether it will find him or not I cannot tell, as I think the 51st must be away down at Vicksburg. I have not had a word from George yet. Mother, I have had quite an attack of sore throat and distress in my head for some days past, up to last night, but to-day I feel nearly all right again. I have been about the city same as usual nearly—to the hospitals, etc., I mean. I am told that I hover too much over the beds of the hospitals, with fever and putrid wounds, etc. One soldier brought here about fifteen days ago, very low with typhoid fever, Livingston Brooks, Co. B., 17th Penn. Cavalry, I have particularly stuck to, as I found him to be in what appeared to be a dying condition, from negligence and a horrible journey of about forty miles, bad roads and fast driving; and then after he got here, as he is a simple country boy, very shy and silent, and made no complaint, they neglected him. I found him something like I found John Holmes last winter. I called the doctor's attention to him, shook up the nurses, had him bathed in spirits, gave him lumps of ice, and ice to his head; he had a fearful bursting pain in his head, and his body was like fire. He was very quiet, a very sensible boy, old fashioned; he did not want to die, and I had to lie to him without stint, for he thought I knew everything, and I always put in of course that what I told him was exactly the truth, and that if he got really dangerous I would tell him and not conceal it. The rule is to remove bad fever patients out from the main wards to a tent by themselves, and the doctor told me he would have to be removed. I broke it gently to him, but the poor boy got it immediately in his head that he was marked with death, and was to be removed on that account. It had a great effect upon him, and although I told the truth this time it did not have as good a result as my former fibs. I persuaded the doctor to let him remain. For three days he lay just about an even chance, go or stay, with a little leaning toward the first. But, mother, to make a long story short, he is now out of any immediate danger. He has been perfectly rational throughout—begins to taste a little food (for a week he ate nothing; I had to compel him to take a quarter of an orange now and then), and I will say, whether anyone calls it pride or not, that if he *does* get up and around again it's me that saved his life. Mother, as I have said in former letters, you can have no idea how these sick and dying youngsters cling to a fellow, and how fascinating it is, with all its hospital surroundings of sadness and scenes of repulsion and death. In this same hospital, Armory-square, where this cavalry boy is, I have about fifteen or twenty particular cases I see much to—some of them as much as him. There are two from East Brooklyn: George Monk, Co. A, 78th N.Y., and Stephen Redgate (his mother is a widow in East Brooklyn—I have written to her). Both are pretty badly wounded—both are youngsters under 19. O mother, it seems to me as I go through these rows of cots as if it was too bad to accept these *children*, to subject them to such premature experiences. I devote myself much to Armory-square hospital because it contains by far the worst cases, most repulsive wounds, has the most suffering and most need of consolation. I go every day without fail, and often at night—sometimes stay very late. No one interferes with me, guards, nurses, doctors, nor anyone. I am let to take my own course.

Well, mother, I suppose you folks think we are in a somewhat dubious position here in Washington, with Lee in strong force almost between us and you Northerners. Well, it does look ticklish; if the Rebs cut the connection then there will be fun. The Reb cavalry come quite near us, dash in and steal wagon trains, etc.; it would be funny if they should come some night to the President's country house (Soldier's home), where he goes out to sleep every night; it is in the same direction as their saucy raid last Sunday. Mr. Lincoln passes here (14th st.) every evening on his way out. I noticed him last evening about half-past 6—he was in his barouche, two horses, guarded by about thirty cavalry. The barouche comes first under a slow trot, driven by one man in the box, no servant or footmen beside; the cavalry all follow closely after with a lieutenant at their head. I had a good view of the President last evening. He looks more careworn

even than usual, his face with deep cut lines, seams, and his
*complexion gray* through very dark skin—a curious looking
man, very sad. I said to a lady who was looking with me,
"Who can see that man without losing all wish to be sharp
upon him personally?" The lady assented, although she is
almost vindictive on the course of the administration (thinks
it wants nerve, etc.—the usual complaint). The equipage is
rather shabby, horses indeed almost what my friends the
Broadway drivers would call *old plugs*. The President
dresses in plain black clothes, cylinder hat—he was alone
yesterday. As he came up, he first drove over to the house of
the Sec. of War, on K st., about 300 feet from here; sat in his
carriage while Stanton came out and had a 15 minutes interview with him (I can see from my window), and then wheeled
around the corner and up Fourteenth st., the cavalry after him.
I really think it would be safer for him just now to stop at the
White House, but I expect he is too proud to abandon the
former custom. Then about an hour after we had a large cavalry regiment pass, with blankets, arms, etc., on the war march
over the same track. The regt. was very full, over a thousand
—indeed thirteen or fourteen hundred. It was an old regt.,
veterans, *old fighters*, young as they were. They were pre-
ceeded by a fine mounted band of sixteen (about ten bugles,
the rest cymbals and drums). I tell you, mother, it made
everything ring—made my heart leap. They played with a
will. Then the accompaniment: the sabers rattled on a
thousand men's sides—they had pistols, their heels were
spurred—handsome American young men (I make no acc't
of any other); rude uniforms, well worn, but good cattle,
prancing—all good riders, full of the devil; nobody shaved,
very sunburnt. The regimental officers (splendidly mounted,
but just as roughly dressed as the men) came immediately
after the band, then company after company, with each its
officers at its head—the tramps of so many horses (there is
a good hard turnpike)—then a long train of men with led
horses, mounted negroes, and a long, long string of baggage
wagons, each with four horses, and then a strong rear guard.
I tell you it had the look of *real war*—noble looking fellows;
a man feels so proud on a good horse, and armed. They are
off toward the region of Lee's (supposed) rendezvous, **to-**

ward Susquehannah, for the great anticipated battle. Alas! how many of these healthy, handsome, rollicking young men will lie cold in death before the apples ripen in the orchard. Mother, it is curious and stirring here in some respects. Smaller or larger bodies of troops are moving continually— many just-well men are turned out of the hospitals. I am where I see a good deal of them. There are getting to be *many black troops*. There is one very good regt. here black as tar; they go around, have the regular uniform—they submit to no nonsense. Others are constantly forming. It is getting to be a common sight. [The rest of the letter is lost.—ED. of *Wound Dresser*.]

## XVII

### MRS. LOUISA WHITMAN, Brooklyn

Washington, Wednesday forenoon,
July 15, 1863.

Dear Mother—So the mob has risen at last in New York—I have been expecting it, but as the day for the draft had arrived and everything was so quiet, I supposed all might go on smoothly; but it seems the passions of the people were only sleeping, and have burst forth with terrible fury, and they have destroyed life and property, the enrolment build- ings, etc., as we hear. The accounts we get are a good deal in a muddle, but it seems bad enough. The feeling here is savage and hot as fire against New York (the mob—"Cop- perhead mob" the papers here call it), and I hear nothing in all directions but threats of ordering up the gunboats, can- nonading the city, shooting down the mob, hanging them in a body, etc., etc. Meantime I remain silent, partly amused, partly scornful, or occasionally put a dry remark, which only adds fuel to the flame. I do not feel it in my heart to abuse the poor people, or call for a rope or bullets for them, but that is all the talk here, even in the hospitals. The acc'ts from N.Y. this morning are that the Gov't has ordered the draft to be suspended there—I hope it is true, for I find that the deeper they go in with the draft, the more trouble it is likely to make. I have changed my opinion and feelings on the

subject—we are in the midst of strange and terrible times—
one is pulled a dozen different ways in his mind, and hardly
knows what to think or do. Mother, I have not much fear
that the troubles in New York will affect any of our family,
still I feel somewhat uneasy about Jeff, if any one, as he is
more around. I have had it much on my mind what could be
done, if it should so happen that Jeff should be drafted—of
course he could not go without its being the downfall almost
of our whole family, as you may say, Mat and his young ones,
and sad blow to you too, mother, and to all. I didn't see any
other way than to try to raise the $300, mostly by borrowing
if possible of Mr. Lane. Mother, I have no doubt I shall
make a few hundred dollars by the lectures I shall certainly
commence soon (for my hospital missionary purposes and
my own, for that purpose), and I could lend that am't to Jeff
to pay it back. May-be the draft will not come off after all; I
should say it was very doubtful if they can carry it out in
N.Y. and Brooklyn—and besides, it is only one chance out of
several, to be drawn if it does. I don't wonder dear brother
Jeff feels the effect it would have on domestic affairs; I think
it is right to feel so, full as strongly as a man can. I do hope
all will go well and without such an additional trouble falling
upon us, but as it can be met with money, I hope Jeff and
Mat and all of you, dear mother, will not worry any more
about it. I wrote to Jeff a few lines last Sunday, I suppose he
got. Mother, I don't know whether you have had a kind of
gloomy week the past week, but somehow I feel as if you all
had; but I hope it has passed over. How is dear sister Mat,
and how is Miss Mannahatta, and little Black Head? I sometimes feel as if I *must* come home and see you all—I want to
very much.

My hospital life still continues the same—I was in Armory
all day yesterday—and day and night before. They have the
men wounded in the railroad accident at Laurel station (bet.
here and Baltimore), about 30 soldiers, some of them horribly
injured at 3 o'clock a.m. last Saturday by collision—poor,
poor, poor men. I go again this afternoon and night—I see
so much of butcher sights, so much sickness and suffering, I
must get away a while, I believe, for self-preservation. I have
felt quite well though the past week—we have had rain con

tinually. Mother, I have not heard from George since, have you? I shall write Han to-day and send George's letter—if you or Jeff has not written this week, I hope Jeff will write on receiving this. Good-bye for [the] present, dearest mother, and Jeff, and Mat.

Walt.

Mother, the army is to be paid off two months more, right away. Of course George will get two months more pay. Dear mother, I hope you will keep untouched and put in bank every cent you can. I want us to have a ranch somewhere by or before next spring.

## XVIII

### LEWIS KIRK BROWN

Washington, August 1, 1863.

Both your letters have been received Lewy—the second one came this morning, & was welcome, as any thing from you will always be, & the sight of your face welcomer than all, my darling—I see you write in good spirits, & appear to have first rate times—Lew you must not go around too much, nor eat & drink too promiscuous, but be careful & moderate, & not let the kindness of friends carry you away, lest you break down again, dear son—I was at the hospital yesterday four or five hours, was in Ward K—Taber has been down sick, so he had to lay abed, but he is better now, & goes around as usual—Curly is the same as usual—most of the others are the same—there have been quite a good many deaths—the young man who lay in bed 2 with a very bad leg is dead—I saw Johnny Mahay in ward E,—poor fellow, he is very poorly, he is very thin, & his face is like wax—Lew I must tell you what a curious thing happened in the Chaplain's house night before last—there has been a man in Ward I, named Lane, with two fingers amputated, very bad with gangrene, so they removed him to a tent by himself—last Thursday his wife came to see him. She seemed a nice woman but very poor. She stopt at the Chaplain's—about 3 o'clock in the morning she got up & went to the sink, & there she gave birth to a child, which fell down the sink into the sewer runs beneath,

fortunately the water was not turned on—the Chaplain got
up, carried Mrs. Lane out, & then roused up a lot of men
from the hospital, with spades &c. dug a trench outside, &
got into the sink, & took out the poor little child, it lay there
on its back, in about two inches of water—well, strange as it
may seem, the child was alive, (it fell about five feet through
the sink)—& is now living & likely to live, is quite bright, has
a head of thick black hair—the Chaplain took me in yesterday, showed me the child, & Mrs. Jackson, his wife, told me
the whole story, with a good deal I haven't told you—& then
she treated me to a good plate of ice cream—so I staid there
nearly an hour & had quite a pleasant visit. Mrs. Lane lay in
an adjoining room. Lew, as to me & my affairs there is nothing very new or important—I have not succeeded in getting any employment here yet, except that I write a little,
(newspaper correspondence &c) barely enough to pay my
expenses—but it is my fault, for I have not tried hard enough
for anything—the last three weeks I have not felt very well—
for two or three days I was down sick, for the first time in my
life, (as I have never before been sick)—I feel pretty fair to-
day—I go round most every day, the same as usual—I have
some idea of giving myself a furlough of three or four weeks,
& going home to Brooklyn, N Y but I should return again to
Washington, probably. Lew, it is pretty hot weather here, &
the sun affects me—(I had a sort of sun stroke about five
years ago.)—You speak of being here in Washington again
about the last of August—O Lewy how glad I should be to
see you, to have you with me—I have thought if it could
be so that you & one other person & myself could be where
we could work & live together, & have each other's society,
we three, I should like it so much—but it is probably a
dream—Well, Lew they had the great battle of Gettysburgh,
but it does not seem to have settled anything, except to have
killed & wounded a great many thousand men—It seems as
though the two armies were falling back again to near their
old positions on the Rappahannock—it is hard to tell what
will be the next move—Yet Lewy I think we shall conquer
yet—I don't believe it is destined that this glorious Union is
to be broken up by all the Secesh South, or Copheads north
either—Well my darling I have scribbled you off something

to show you where I am & that I have rec'd your welcome letters—but my letter is not of much interest, for I don't feel very bright to-day—Dear son you must write me whenever you can—take opportunity—when you have nothing to do, & write me a good long letter—Your letters & your love for me are very precious to me, for I appreciate it all Lew, & give you the like in return. It is now about 3 o'clock & I will go out & mail this letter, & then go & get my dinner—So good bye Lewy—good bye my dear son & comrade & I hope it will prove God's will that you get well & sound yet, & have many good years yet——.

Walt

Address my letters care Major Hapgood paymaster U S A at cor. 15th & F st Washington D C

XIX

HUGO FRITSCH, New York

Aug. 7 '63.

Dear Hugo, I received a letter from Bloom yesterday—but before responding to it (which I will do soon) I must write to you my friend. Your good letter of June 27th was duly rec'd.—I have read it many times—indeed Hugo, you know not how much comfort you give, by writing me your letters—posting me up.

Well Hugo, I am still as much as ever, indeed more, in the great military hospitals here. Every day or night I spend four five or six hours among my sick, wounded, prostrate, boys. It is fascinating, sad, and with varied fortune, of course. Some of my boys get well, some die. After I finish this letter (and then dining at a restaurant) I shall give the latter part of the afternoon and some hours of the night to Armory Square Hospital, a large establishment and one I find most calling on my sympathies and ministrations. I am welcomed by the surgeons as by the soldiers—very grateful to me. You must remember that these government hospitals are not filled as with human débris like the old established city hospitals, New York, &c., but mostly with these good-born American young men appealing to me most profoundly, good stock, often mere boys, full of sweetness and heroism—often they seem very near to me, even as my own children or younger brothers. I make no bones of petting them just as if they were—have long given up formalities and reserves in my treatment of them.

Let me see, Hugo. I will not write anything about the topics of the horrible riots of last week, nor Gen. Meade nor Vicksburgh, nor Charleston—I leave them to the newspapers. Nor will I write you this time so much about hospitals as I did last. Tell Fred his letter was received. I appreciate it, received real pleasure from it—'twas a true friend's letter, characteristic, full of vivacity, off-hand, and below all a thorough base of genuine remembrance and good will—was not wanting in the *sentimental* either (so I take back all about the *apostate*, do you understand, Freddy, my dear?)—and only write this for you till I reply to that said letter a good long and special measure to yourself.

Tell Nat Bloom that if he expects to provoke me into a dignified not mentioning him, nor writing anything about him, by his studious course of heartbreaking neglect (which has already reduced me to a skeleton of but little over 200 lbs and a countenance of raging hectic, indicating an early grave), I was determined not to do anything of the sort, but shall speak of him every time, and send him love, just as if he were adorned with faithful troth instead of (as I understand) beautiful whiskers—Does he think that beautiful whiskers can fend off the pangs of remorse? In conclusion I have to say, Nathaniel, you just keep on if you think there's no hell.

Hugo, I suppose you were at Charles Channing's funeral—tell me all you hear about the particulars of his death—Tell me of course about the boys, what you do, say, anything, everything—

Hugo, write oftener—you express your thoughts perfectly —do you not know how much more agreeable to me is the conversation or writing that does not take hard paved tracks, the usual and stereotyped, but has little peculiarities and even kinks of its own, making its genuineness—its vitality? Dear friend, your letters are precious to me—none I have ever received from anyone are more so.

Ah I see in your letter, Hugo, you speak of my being reformed—no, I am not so frightfully reformed either, only the hot weather here does not permit of drinking heavy drinks, and there is no good lager here—then besides I have no society—I expect to prove to you and all yet that I am no backslider—But here I go nowhere for mere amusement, only occasionally a walk.

And Charles Russell—how I should like to see him—how like to have one of our old times again—Ah Fred, and you dear Hugo, and you repentant one with the dark shining whiskers—must there not be an hour, an evening in the future when we four returning concentrating New York-ward or elsewhere, shall meet, allowing no interloper, and have our drinks and things, and resume the chain and con-solidate and achieve a night better and mellower than ever,—we four?

Hugo, I wish you to give my love to all the boys—I re-ceived a letter from Ben Knower, very good—I shall answer it soon. Give my love to Ben—If Charles Kingsley is in town same to him—ditto Mullen—ditto Park. (I hope to hear that sweet sweet fiddler one of these days, that strain again)

I wish to have Fred Gray say something for me, giving my love to his mother and father—I bear them both in mind—I count on having good interviews with them when I see New York.

## XX

### MISS GREGG

Sept. 7, '63.

Dear friend. You spoke the other day, partly in fun, about the men being so undemonstrative. I thought I would write you a line as I hear you leave the hospital tomorrow for a few weeks. Your labor of love and disinterestedness here in Hospital is appreciated. I have heard the ward A patients speak of you with gratitude, sometimes with enthusiasm. They have their own invariable ways (not outside éclat, but in manly American hearts however rude however undemon-strative to you). I thought it would be sweet to your tender and womanly heart to know what I have so often heard from the soldiers about you as I sat by their sick cots. I too have learnt to love you, seeing your tender heart, and your goodness to these wounded and dying young men—for they have grown to seem to me as my sons or dear young brothers.

As I am poor I cannot make you a present, but I write you this note dear girl, knowing you will receive it in the same candor and good faith it is written.

## XXI

### W. S. DAVIS, Worcester, Massachusetts

Oct. 1, 1863

The noble gift of your brother Joseph P. Davis of $20 for the aid of the wounded, sick, dying soldiers here came safe to hand—it is being sacredly distributed to them—part of it has been so already—I may another time give you special cases— I go every day or night in the hospitals a few hours—As to physical comforts, I attempt to have some—generally a lot of —something harmless and not too expensive to go round to each man, even if it is nothing but a good home-made biscuit to each man—or a couple of spoonfuls of blackberry preserve —I take a ward or two of an evening and two more next evening &c—as an addition to his supper—sometimes one thing, sometimes another, (judgment of course has to be carefully used)—then after such general round I fall back upon the main thing, after all, the special cases, alas too common—those that need some special attention, some little delicacy, some trifle—very often far above all else, soothing kindness wanted—personal magnetism—poor boys, their sick hearts and wearied and exhausted bodies hunger for the sustenance of love or their deprest spirits must be cheered up —I find often young men, some hardly more than children in age yet—so good, so sweet, so brave, so decorous, I could not feel them nearer to me if my own sons or your brothers— Some cases even I could not tell anyone, how near to me, from their yearning ways and their sufferings—it is comfort and delight to me to minister to them, to sit by them—some wind themselves around one's heart and will be kissed at parting at night just like children—though veterans of two

years of battles and camp life—I always carry a haversack
with some articles most wanted—physical comforts are a
sort of basis—I distribute nice large biscuit, sweet crackers,
sometimes cut up a lot of peaches with sugar, give preserves
of all kinds, jellies, &c. tea, oysters, butter, condensed milk,
plugs of tobacco (I am the only one that doles out this last,
and the men have grown to look to me)—wine, brandy,
sugar, pickles, letter-stamps, envelopes and note paper, the
morning papers, common handkerchiefs and napkins, un-
dershirts, socks, dressing gowns, and fifty other things—I
have lots of special little requests. Frequently I give small
sums of money,—shall do so with your brother's contribution—the wounded are very frequently brought and lay here
a long while without a cent. I have been here and in front
nine months doing this thing and have learned much—the
soldiers are from fifteen to twenty-five or six years of age—
lads of fifteen or sixteen more frequent than you have any
idea—seven-eighths of the army are Americans, our own
stock—the foreign element in the army is much overrated
and is of not much account anyhow. There are no hospitals
(there are dozens of them in and around Washington) you
must understand like the diseased half-foreign collections
under that name common at all times in cities—in these here,
the noblest cleanest stock I think of the world, and the most
precious.

## XXII

### To ———

Dear Friend. I am going to write to you to ask any friends
you may be in communication with for aid for my soldiers. I
remain here in Washington still occupied among the hospitals—I have now been engaged in this over seven months. As
time passes on it seems as if sad cases of old and lingering
wounded accumulate, regularly recruited with new ones
every week—I have been most of this day in Armory Square
Hospital Seventh st. I seldom miss a day or evening. Out of
the six or seven hundred in this Hospital I try to give a word
or a trifle to every one without exception, making regular
rounds among them all. I give all kinds of sustenance,

blackberries, peaches, lemons and sugar, wines, all kinds of preserves, pickles, brandy, milk, shirts and all articles of underclothing, tobacco, tea, handkerchiefs, &c &c &c. I always give paper, envelopes, stamps, &c. I want a supply for this purpose. To many I give (when I have it) small sums of money—half of the soldiers in hospital have not a cent. There are many returned prisoners sick, lost all—and every day squads of men from the front, cavalry or infantry-- brought in wounded or sick, generally without a cent of money. I select the most needy cases and devote my time and services much to them. I find it tells best—some are mere lads, 17, 18, 19, or 20—some are silent, sick, heavy-hearted, (things, attentions, &c. are very rude in the army and hospitals, nothing but the mere hard routine, no time for tenderness or extras)—so I go round,—some of my boys die, some get well.

O what a sweet unwonted love (those good American boys of good stock, decent, clean, well-raised boys, so near to me) —what an attachment grows up between us, started from hospital cots, where pale young faces lie and wounded or sick bodies. My brave young American soldiers—now for so many months I have gone around among them, where they lie. I have long discarded all stiff conventions (they and I are too near to each other, there is no time to lose, and death and anguish dissipate ceremony here between my lads and me)— I pet them, some of them it does so much good, they are so faint and lonesome—at parting at night sometimes I kiss them right and left—The doctors tell me I supply the patients with a medicine which all their drugs and bottles and powders are helpless to yield.

I wish you would ask anybody you know who is likely to contribute—It is a good holy cause, surely nothing nobler—I desire you if possible could raise for me, forthwith, for application to these wounded and sick here, (they are from Massachusetts and all the New England states, there is not a day but I am with some Yankee boys, and doing some trifle for them)—a sum—if possible fifty dollars—if not then less— thirty dollars—or indeed any amount——.

I am at present curiously almost alone here, as visitor and consolator to Hospitals—the work of the different Reliefs and Commissions is nearly all off in the field—and as to private visitors, there are few or none—I wish you or some of your friends could just make a round with me, for an hour or so, at some of my hospitals or camps—I go among all our own dear soldiers, hospital camps and any, our teamsters' hospitals, among sick and dying, the rebels, the contrabands, &c &c. What I reach is necessarily but a drop in the bucket but it is done in good faith, and with now some experience and I hope with good heart.

## XXIII

### MRS. MARGARET S. CURTIS, Boston

Washington, Armory Sq Hospital,
Sunday Evening Oct 4 [1863]

Dear Madam, Your letter reached me this forenoon with the $30 for my dear boys, for very dear they have become to me, wounded and sick here in the government hospitals.—As it happens I find myself rapidly making acknowledgment of your welcome letter and contribution from the midst of those it was sent to aid—and best by a sample of actual hospital life on the spot, and of my own goings around the last two or three hours—As I write I sit in a large pretty well-filled ward by the cot of a lad of 18 belonging to Company M 2d N Y cavalry, wounded three weeks ago to-day at Culpeper—hit by fragment of a shell in the leg below the knee—a large part of the calf of the leg is torn away, (it killed his horse)—still no bones broken, but a pretty large ugly wound—I have been writing to his mother at Comac, Suffolk co. N.Y—. She must have a letter just as if from him, about every three days—it pleases the boy very much—he has four married sisters—them also I have to write to occasionally—Although so young he has been in many fights and tells me shrewdly about them, but only when I ask him. He is a cheerful good-natured child— has to lie in bed constantly his leg in a box—I bring him things—he says little or nothing in the way of thanks—is a country boy—always smiles and brightens much when I appear—looks straight in my face and never at what I may have in my hand for him—I mention him for a specimen as he is within reach of my hand and I can see that his eyes have been steadily fixed on me from his cot ever since I began to write this letter. This youngster is no special favorite—only a needful case—it will not do at all to show partiality here—there are some 25 or 30 wards, barracks, tents, &c in this hospital—This is ward C, has beds for 60 patients—they are mostly full—most of the other principal wards about the same—so you see a U S general hospital here is quite an establishment—this has a regular police, armed sentries at the gates and in the passages &c,—and a great staff of surgeons, cadets, women and men nurses &c &c. I come here pretty regularly because this hospital receives I think the worst cases and is one of the least visited—there is not much hospital visiting here now—it has become an old story—the principal here, Dr. Bliss, is a very fine operating surgeon—sometimes he performs several amputations or other operations of importance in a day—amputations, blood, death are nothing to him—you will see a group absorbed in playing cards up at the other end of the room.

I visit the sick every day or evening—sometimes I stay far in the night, on special occasions. I believe I have not missed more than two days in past six months. It is quite an art to visit the hospitals to advantage. The amount of sickness, and the number of poor, wounded, dying young men is appalling. One often feels lost, despondent, his labors not even a drop in the bucket—the wretched little he can do in proportion.

I believe I mentioned in my letter to Dr. Russell that I try to distribute something, even if but the merest trifle, all round, without missing any, when I visit a ward, going round rather rapidly—and then devoting myself more at leisure to the cases that need special attention. One who is experienced may find in almost any ward at any time one or two patients or more who are at that time trembling in the balance, the crisis of the wound, recovery uncertain, yet death also uncertain. I will confess to you madam that I think I have an instinct and faculty for these cases. Poor young men, how many have I seen and know—how pitiful it is to see them,—one must be calm and cheerful, and not let on how their case really is, must stop much with them, find out their idiosyncrasies—do anything for them—nourish them—judiciously give them the right things to drink,—bringing in the affections, soothe them, brace them up, kiss them, discard all ceremony, and fight for them, as it were, with all weapons. I need not tell your womanly soul that such work blesses him that works as much as the object of it. I have never been happier than in some of these hospital ministering hours.

It is now between 8 and 9 evening—the atmosphere is rather solemn here to-night—there are some very sick men here—the scene is a curious one—the ward is perhaps 120 or 30 feet long—the cots each have their white mosquito curtains—all is quite still—an occasional sigh or groan—up in the middle of the ward the lady nurse sits at a little table with a shaded lamp, reading—the walls, roof, &c are all whitewashed—the light up and down the ward from a few gasburners about half turned down—It is Sunday evening—today I have been in the hospital, one part or another, since three o'clock—to a few of the men, pretty sick, or just convalescing and with delicate stomachs or perhaps badly wounded arms, I have fed their suppers—partly peaches pealed, and cut up with powdered sugar, very cool and refreshing,— they like to have me sit by them and peel them, cut them in a glass, and sprinkle on the sugar—(all these little items maybe may interest you).

I have given three of the men this afternoon, small sums of money—I provide myself with a lot of bright new 10 ct and 5 ct bills, and when I give little sums of change I give the bright new bills. Every little thing even must be taken advantage of—to give bright fresh 10 ct bills instead of any other helps break the dullness of hospital life——

## XXIV

### HUGO FRITSCH, New York

[Oct. 8. '63.]

Dear Hugo. I don't know why I have delayed so long as a month to write to you, for your affectionate and lively letter of September 5th gave me as much pleasure as I ever received from correspondence. I read it even yet & have taken the liberty to show it to one or two persons I knew would be interested. Dear comrade, you must be assured that my

heart is much with you in New York, & with my other dear
friends, your associates—& my dear I wish you to excuse me
to Fred Gray & to Perk, & Ben Knower, for not yet writing
to them, also to Charles Kingsley, should you see him—I am
contemplating a tremendous letter to my dear comrade
Frederickus, which will make up for deficiencies,—my own
comrade Fred, how I should like to see him and have a good
heart's time with him, & a mild orgie, just for a basis, you
know, for talk & interchange of reminiscences & the play of
the quiet lambent electricity of real friendship—O Hugo, as
my pen glides along writing these thoughts, I feel as if I
could not delay coming right off to New York & seeing you
all, you & Fred & Bloom, & everybody—I want to see you,
to be within hand's reach of you, and hear your voices, even
if only for one evening for only three hours—I want to hear
Perk's fiddle—I want to hear Perk himself, (& I will humbly
submit to drink to the Church of England)—I want to be
with Bloom (that wretched young man who I hear continually adorns himself outwardly, but I hear nothing of the interior) and I want to see Charley Russell, & if he is in N.Y.
you see him I wish you to say that I sent him my love, particular, & that he & Fred & Charles Chauncey remain a group
of itself in the portrait-gallery of my heart and mind yet &
forever—for so it happened for our dear times, when we first
got acquainted, (we recked not of them as they passed,) were
so good, so hearty, those friendship times, our talk, our
knitting together, it may be a whim, but I think nothing
could be better or quieter & more happy of the kind—& is
there any better kind in life's experiences?—

Dear comrade, I still live here as a hospital missionary
after my own style, & on my own hook—I go every day or
night without fail to some of the great government hospitals
—O the sad scenes I witness—scenes of death, anguish, the
fevers, amputations, friendlessness, hungering & thirsting
young hearts, for some loving presence—such noble young
men as some of these wounded are—such endurance, such
native decorum, such candor—I will confess to you dear
Hugo that in some respects I find myself in my element amid
these scenes—shall I not say to you that I find I supply often
to some of these dear suffering boys in my presence & mag-

netism that which nor doctors, nor medicines, nor skill, nor any routine assistance can give? Dear Hugo, you must write to me often as you can, & not delay it, your letters are very dear to me. Did you see my newspaper letter in N Y *Times* of Sunday Oct 4? About my dear comrade Bloom, is he still out in Pleasant Valley? Does he meet you often? Do you & the fellows meet at Gray's or anywhere? O Hugo I wish I could hear with you the current opera—I saw Devereux in the N Y papers of Monday announced for that night, & I knew in all probability you would be there—tell me how it goes, & about the principal singers—only don't run away with that theme, & occupy too much of your letter with it— but tell me mainly about all my dear friends, & every little personal item, & what you all do, & say &c.

I am excellent well. I have cut my beard short & hair ditto: (all my acquaintances are in anger & despair & go about wringing their hands) my face is all tanned & red. If the weather is moist or has been lately, or looks as if it thought of going to be, I perambulate this land in big army boots outside & up to my knees. Then around my majestic brow around my well-brimmed felt hat—a black & gold cord with acorns. Altogether the effect is satisfactory. The guards as I enter or pass places often salute me. All of which I tell, as you will of course take pride in your friend's special & expanding glory.

Fritschy, I am writing this in Major Hapgood's office, fifth story, by a window that overlooks all down the city, & over & down the beautiful Potomac, & far across the hills & shores for many a mile. We have had superb weather lately, yes for a month—it has just rained, so the dust is provided for, (that is the only thing I dread in Washington, the dust, I don't mind the mud). It is now between one and two o'clock Thursday afternoon. I am much alone in this pleasant far-up room, as Major is absent sick, & the clerk lays off a good deal. From three to five hours a day or night I go regularly among the sick, wounded, dying young men. I am enabled to give them things, food. There are very few visitors, amateurs, now. It has become an old story. The suffering ones cling to me poor children very close. I think of coming to New York quite soon to stay perhaps three weeks, then sure return here.

## XXV

### MRS. ABBY H. PRICE, Brooklyn

Washington, October 11th, 1863.

Dear Friend: Your letters were both received, and were indeed welcome. Don't mind my not answering them promptly, for you know what a wretch I am about such things. But you must write just as often as you conveniently can. Tell me all about your folks, especially the girls, and about Mr. A. Of course you won't forget Arthur, and always when you write to him send my love. Tell me about Mrs. U. and the dear little rogues. Tell Mrs. B. she ought to be here, hospital matron, only it is a harder pull than folks anticipate. You wrote about Emma, her thinking she might and ought to come as nurse for the soldiers. Dear girl, I know it would be a blessed thing for the men to have her loving spirit and hand. But, my darling, it is a dreadful thing—you don't know these wounds, sickness, etc., the sad condition in which many of the men are brought here, and remain for days; sometimes the wounds full of crawling corruption, etc. Down in the field-hospitals in front they have no proper care (can't have), and after a battle go for many days unattended to.

Abby, I think often about you and the pleasant days, the visits I used to pay you, and how good it was always to be made so welcome. Oh, I wish I could come in this afternoon and have a good tea with you, and have three or four hours of mutual comfort, and rest and talk, and be all of us together again. Is Helen home and well? and what is she doing now? And you, my dear friend, how sorry I am to hear that your health is not rugged—but, dear Abby, you must not dwell on anticipations of the worst (but I know that is not your nature, or did not use to be). I hope this will find you feeling quite well and in good spirits—I feel so tremendously well myself—I will have to come and show myself to you, I think—I am so fat, good appetite, out considerably in the open air, and all red and tanned worse than ever. You see, therefore, that my life amid these sad and death-stricken hospitals has not told at all badly upon me, for I am this fall so running over with health I feel as if I ought to go on, on that account, working among all who are deprived of it—and O how gladly I would bestow upon them a liberal share of mine, dear Abby, if such a thing were possible.

I am continually moving around among the hospitals. One I go to oftenest these last three months is "Armory Square", as it is large, generally full of the worst wounds and sickness, and is among the least visited. To this or some other I never miss a day or evening. Above all, the poor boys welcome simple kindness, loving affection (some are so fervent, so hungering for this)—poor fellows, how young they are, lying there with their pale faces, and that mute look in the eyes. Oh, how one gets to love them, often, particular cases, so suffering, so good, so manly and yet simple. Abby, you would all smile to see me among them—many of them like children. Ceremony is quite discarded—they suffer and get exhausted and so weary—not a few are on their dying beds—lots of them have grown to expect, as I leave at night, that we should kiss each other, sometimes quite a number; I have to go round. There is little petting in a soldier's life in the field, but, Abby, I know what is in their hearts, always waiting, though they may be unconscious of it themselves.

I have a place where I buy very nice home-made biscuits, sweet crackers, etc. Among others, one of my ways is to get a good lot of these, and for supper, go through a couple of wards and give a portion to each man—next day two wards more, and so on. Then each marked case needs something to itself. I spend my evenings altogether at the hospitals—my days often. I give little gifts of money in small sums, which I am enabled to do—all sorts of things, indeed, food, clothing, letter-stamps (I write lots of letters), now and then a good pair of crutches or a cane, etc. Then I read to them—the whole ward that can walk gathers around me and listens.

All this I tell you, my dear, because I know it will interest you. There is much else—many exceptions—those I leave out. I like Washington very well; I have three or four hours my own work every day copying, and in writing letters for the press, etc.; make enough to pay my way—live in an inexpensive manner anyhow. I like the mission I am at here, and as it is deeply holding me I shall continue.

[*On a second sheet*] October 15.

Well, Abby, I will send you enough to make up lost time.
I ought to have finished and sent off the letter last Sunday,
when it was written. I have been unusually busy. We are
having new arrivals of wounded and sick now all the time—
some very bad cases. I have found some good friends here, a
few, but true as steel—W. D. O'C. and wife above all the rest.
He is a clerk in the Treasury—she is a Yankee girl. Then
C. W. E. in Paymaster's Department. He is a Boston boy,
too—their friendship and assistance have been unswerving.

In the hospitals among these American soldiers from East
and West, North and South, I could not describe to you what
mutual attachments, passing deep and tender. Some have
died, but the love for them lives as long as I draw breath.
These soldiers know how to love too, when once they have
the right person. It is wonderful. You see I am running off
into the clouds (perhaps my element). Abby, I am writing
this last note this afternoon in Major H.'s office—he is away
sick—I am here a good deal of the time alone—it is a dark,
rainy afternoon—we don't know what is going on down in
front, whether Meade is getting the worst of it, or not—(but
the result of the big elections permanently cheers us)—I
believe fully in Lincoln—few know the rocks and quicksands
he has to steer through and over. I inclose you a note
Mrs. O'C. handed me to send you, written, I suppose, upon
impulse. She is a noble Massachusetts woman, is not very
rugged in health—I am there very much—her husband and I
are great friends. Well, I must close—the rain is pouring, the
sky leaden, it is between 2 and 3—I am going to get some
dinner and then to the hospital. Good-by, dear friends; I
send my love to all.                                W. W.


## XXVI

### JULIA ELIZABETH STILWELL
South Norwalk, Connecticut

[Oct. 21, '63.]

*Dear friend,* Jimmy is getting along favorably but of course
slowly. I was with him night before last and am going again
this afternoon. It requires a good deal of patience in him to

lay so steadily confined in bed, but he has the good luck to continue remarkably free from any acute suffering so far. Night before last he had some pain and swelling in the foot below the wound, but nothing of serious account. They bandaged it pretty tightly and that relieved it. He wished me to write to *you* this time, and I promised him to do so night before last. I wrote at that time from the hospital to your parents at Comac, and sent the letter yesterday. Jim is not satisfied unless I write pretty often, whether there is anything to tell or not.

My friend I received your note about your folks getting your dear brother's body from down in Virginia. Lately, as you doubtless know, the Rebels have advanced upon us, and have held Culpepper and around there for many days past; and of course nothing could be done. The rumor just now is that they are falling back, and may soon yield us our old ground. At present still I should think nothing could be done. The authorities here don't grant passes yet. But I suppose you inferred all this from what you read in the papers.

Dear friends all I say to you as I have to Jimmy's parents, that I shall try to keep watch of the boy, as according to all I know at present I shall probably continue in Washington for some time, and if any thing should occur I will write you. Dear friends, as it may be some reliance to you and make you feel less uneasy to know Jim can have nothing happen to him without you being informed. Though as far as now appears he will go on favorably, and his wound will heal up, so that he can sit up, and then gradually move about, and then in due time be able to travel.

So farewell for [the] present, and I pray that God may be with you, and though we are strangers I send my love to you and Jimmy's sisters and brothers in law, for in times of trouble and death, I see we draw near in spirit, regardless of being separated by distance, or of being unknown.

### XXVII

#### MRS. MARGARET S. CURTIS, Boston

Oct. 28 '63

Dear Madam. Since I last wrote you I have continued my hospital visitations daily or nightly without intermission and shall continue them this fall and winter. Your contributions, and those of your friends, sent me for the soldiers wounded and sick, have been used among them in manifold ways, little sums of money given, (the wounded very generally come up here without a cent and in lamentable plight,) and in purchases of various kinds, often impromptu as I see things wanted on the moment... train is standing tediously waiting, &c. as they often are here. But what I write this note for particularly is to see if your sister, Hannah Stevenson, or yourself, might find it eligible to see a young man whom I love very much, who has fallen into deepest affliction, and is now in your city. He is a young Massachusetts soldier from Barre. He was sun-struck here in Washington last July, was taken to hospital here, I was with him a good deal for many weeks—he then went home to Barre,—became worse,—has now been sent from his home to your city—is at times (as I infer) so troubled . . . I received a letter from Boston this morning from a stranger about him telling me (he appears too ill to write himself) that he is in Mason General Hospital, Boston. His name is Caleb H. Babbitt of Co E 34th Mass Vol. He must have been brought there lately. My dear friend, if you should be able to go, or if not able yourself give this to your sister or some friend who will go,—it may be that my dear boy and comrade is not so very bad, but I fear he is. Tell him you come from me like, and if he is in a situation to talk, his loving heart will open to you at once. He is a manly, affectionate boy. I beg whoever goes would write a few lines to me how the young man is. I send my thanks and love to yourself, your sister, husband, and the sisters Wigglesworth. Or else give this to Dr. Russell. The letter from the stranger above referred to is dated also Pemberton square hospital.

## XXVIII

### LEWIS KIRK BROWN AND HOSPITAL COMRADES, Washington

Brooklyn, November 8, 1863.

Dear son and comrade, and all my dear comrades in the hospital I sit down this pleasant Sunday forenoon intending to write you all a good stout letter to try to amuse you as I am not able at present to visit you like I did—yet what I shall write about I hardly know until I get started—but my dear comrades I wish to help you pass away the time for a few minutes anyhow—I am now home at my mother's in Brooklyn N. Y.—I am in good health as ever and eat my rations without missing one time—Lew I wish you was here with me, and I wish my dear comrade Elijah Fox in ward G was here with me—but perhaps he is on his way to Wisconsin—Lewy I came through from Washington to New York by day train, 2nd Nov. had a very pleasant trip, everything went lovely, and I got home in the evening between 8 and 9—Next morning I went up to the polls bright and early—I suppose it is not necessary to tell you how I voted—we have gained a great victory in this city—it went union this time, though it went democratic strong only a year ago, and for many years past—and all through the State the election was a very big thing for the union—I tell you the copperheads got flaxed out handsomely—indeed these late elections are about as great a victory for us as if we had flaxed General Lee himself, and all his men—and so for personal good will I feel as if I could have more for Lee or any of his fighting men, than I have for the northern copperheads—Lewy I was very glad to get your letter of the 5th—I want you to tell Oscar Cunningham in your ward that I sent him my love and he must try to keep up good courage while he is confined there with his wound. Lewy I want you to give my love to Charley Cate and all the boys in ward K, and to Benton if he is there still—I wish you would go in ward C and see James O. Stilwell, and also Thomas Carson in same ward, and Chambers that lays next to him, and tell them I sent them my love. Give Carson this letter to read if he wishes it. Tell James Stilwell I have writ from here to his folks in Comac L I, and it may be I shall go down there next week on the L I railroad; and let him have this letter to read if he wishes it. Tell Manvill Winterstein that lays next to him in ward C that I send him my love, and I hope his wound is healing good. Lew I wish you to go in ward B and tell a young cavalry man, his first name is Edwin, he is wounded in the right arm, that I send him my love, and on the opposite side a young man wounded in the right knee, and also a young man named Charley wounded in left hand,

and Jennings and also a young man I love that lays now up by the door just above Jennings, that I sent them all my love. So Lew you see I am giving you a good round job, with so many messages—but I want you to do them all dear son, and leave my letter with each of the boys that wish it, to read for themselves—tell Miss Gregg in ward A that I send my love to Pleasant Barley, if he is still there, and if so I hope it will be God's will that he will live and get strong to go home yet—I send my love to little Billy the Ohio boy in ward A, and to Miss Gregg herself—and if Miss Doolittle is in ward B, please ask her to tell the boys in the ward I sent them my love, and to her too, and give her this letter some evening to read to the boys, and one of these days I will come back and read to them myself—and the same to Mrs. Southwick in ward H, if she wishes to read it to the boys for my sake. Lew I wish you would go in ward G and find a very dear friend of mine in bed 11, Elijah D. Fox if he is still there. Tell him I sent him my best love and that I made reckoning of meeting him again, and that he must not forget me, though that I know he never will—I want to hear how he is, and whether he has got his papers through yet—Lewy I wish you would go to him first and let him have this letter to read if he is there—Lewy I would like you to give my love to a young man named Burns in ward I, and to all the boys in ward I.—and indeed in every ward, from A to K inclusive, and all through the hospital, as I find I cannot particularize without being tedious—so I send my love sincerely to each and all, for every sick and wounded soldier is dear to me as a son or brother, and furthermore every man that wears the union uniform and sticks to it like a man, is to me a dear comrade, and I will do what I can for him though it may not be much—and I will add that my mother and all my folks feel just the same about it, and would show it by their words too when they can——

Well, dear comrades, what shall I tell you to pass away the time? I am going around quite a good deal, more than I really desire to. Two or three nights ago I went to the N Y Academy of Music, to the Italian opera. I suppose you know that is a performance, a play, all in music and singing, in the Italian language, very sweet and beautiful. There is a large company of singers and a large band, altogether two or three hundred. It is a splendid great house, four or five tiers high, and a broad parquette on the main floor. The opera here now has some of the greatest singers in the world—the principal lady singer (her name is Medori) has a voice that would make you hold your breath with wonder and delight—it is like a miracle—no mocking bird or clearest flute can begin with it —and besides she is a tall and handsome lady, and her actions are so graceful as she moves about the stage, playing her part. Boys, I must tell you just one scene in the opera I saw—things have worked so in the piece that this lady is compelled, although she tries very hard to avoid it, to give the cup of poisoned wine to her lover—the king her husband forces her to do it—she pleads hard, but her husband threatens to take both their lives (all this is in the singing and music, very fine)—so the lover is brought in as a prisoner, and the king pretends to pardon him and make up, and asks the young man to drink a cup of wine, and orders the lady to pour it out. The lover drinks it, then the king gives her and him a look, and walks off the stage. And now came as good a piece of performance as I ever saw in my life. The lady as soon as she saw that her husband was really gone, she sprang to her lover, clutched him by the arm, and poured out the greatest singing you ever heard—it poured like a raging river more than anything else I could compare it to—she tells him he is poisoned—he tries to inquire &c and hardly knows what to make of it—she breaks in trying to pacify him, and explain &c—all this goes on very rapid indeed, and the band accompanying—she quickly draws out from her bosom a little vial, to neutralize the poison, then the young man in his desperation abuses her and tells her perhaps it is to poison him still more as she has already poisoned him once—this puts her in such agony, she begs and pleads with him to take the antidote at once before it is too late—her voice is so wild and high it goes through one like a knife, yet it is delicious— she holds the little vial to his mouth with one hand and with the other springs open a secret door in the wall for him to escape from the palace—he swallows the antidote, and as she pushes him through the door, the husband returns with some armed guards, but she slams the door to, and stands back up against the door, and her arms spread wide open across it, one fist clenched, and her eyes glaring like a wildcat, so they dare not touch her—and that ends the scene. Comrades, recollect all this is in singing and music, and lots of it too, on a big scale, in the band, every instrument you can think of, and the best players in the world, and sometimes the whole band and the whole men's chorus and the women's chorus all putting on the steam together—and all in a vast house, light as day, and with a crowded audience of ladies and men. Such singing and strong rich music always give me the greatest pleasure—and so the opera is the only amusement I have gone to, for my own satisfaction, for last ten years.

But my dear comrades I will now tell you something about my own folks—home here there is quite a lot of us—my father is not living—my dear mother is very well indeed for her age, which is 67—she is cheerful and hearty and still does all her light housework and cooking—She never tires of hearing about the soldiers, and I sometimes think she is the greatest patriot I ever met, one of the old stock—I believe she would cheerfully give her life for the union, if it would avail anything—and the last mouthful in the house to any union soldier that needed it—then I have a very excellent sister-in-law,—she has two fine young ones—so I am very happy in the women and family arrangements. Lewy, the brother I mentioned as sick, lives near here, he is very poorly indeed, and I fear will never be much better—he too was a soldier, has for several months had throat disease—he is married and has a family—I believe I have told you of still another brother in the army, down in the 9th Army Corps, has been in the service over two years, he is very rugged and healthy—has been in many battles, but only once wounded, at first Fredericksburg.

## XXIX

### ELIJAH FOX

Brooklyn Saturday night Nov 21, '63.

Dear son and comrade. I wrote a few lines about five days ago and sent on to Armory Square, but as I have not heard from it I suppose you have gone on to Michigan. I got your letter of Nov. 10th and it gave me much comfort. Douglass I shall return to Washington about the 24th so when you write direct to care of Major Hapgood, paymaster U S A, Washington D C—Dearest comrade I only write this lest the one I wrote five days ago may not reach you from the hospital. I am still here at my mother's and feel as if I have had enough of going around New York—enough of amusements, suppers, drinking, and what is called *pleasure*.—Dearest son: it would be more pleasure if we could be together just in quiet, in some plain way of living, with some good employment and reasonable income, where I could have you often with me, than all the dissipations and amusements of this great city— O I hope things may work so that we can yet have each other's society—for I cannot bear the thought of being separated from you—I know I am a great fool about such things but I tell you the truth dear son. I do not think one night has passed in New York or Brooklyn when I have been at the theatre or opera or afterward to some supper party or carousal made by the young fellows for me, but what amid the play or the singing I would perhaps think of you,—and the same at the gayest supper party of men where all was fun and noise and laughing and drinking, of a dozen young men and I among them I would see your face before me in my thought as I have seen it so often there in Ward G, and my amusement or drink would be all turned to nothing, and I would realize how happy it would be if I could leave all the fun and noise and the crowd and be with you—I don't wish to disparage my dear friends and acquaintances here, there are so many of them and all so good, many so educated, traveled, &c. some so handsome and witty, some rich &c. some among the literary class—many young men—all good —many of them educated and polished and brilliant in conversation, &c—and I thought I valued their society and friendship—and I do, for it is worth valuing—But Douglass I will tell you the truth. You are so much closer to me than any of them that there is no comparison—there has never passed so much between them and me as we have—besides there is something that takes down all artificial accomplishments, and that is a manly and loving soul—My dearest comrade, I am sitting here writing to you very late at night—

I have been reading—it is indeed after 12, and my mother
and all the rest have gone to bed two hours ago, and I am
here above writing to you, and I enjoy it too. Although it is
not much yet I know it will please you dear boy. If you get
this you must write and tell me where and how you are. I
hope you are quite well and with your dear wife, for I know
you have long wished to be with her, and I wish you to give
her my best respects and love too.

Douglass I haven't written any news for there is nothing
particular I have to write. Well, it is now past midnight,
pretty well on to one o'clock, and my sheet is mostly written
out—so my dear darling boy, I must bid you good night, or
rather good morning, and I hope it may be God's will we
shall yet be with each other—but I must indeed bid you good
night my dear loving comrade, and the blessing of God on
you by night and day my darling boy.

## XXX

### MRS. LOUISA WHITMAN, Brooklyn

Culpepper, Virginia, Friday night,
Feb. 12, 1864.

Dearest Mother—I am still stopping down in this region. I
am a good deal of the time down within half a mile of our
picket lines, so that you see I can indeed call myself in the
front. I stopped yesterday with an artillery camp in the 1st
Corps at the invitation of Capt. Crawford, who said that he
knew me in Brooklyn. It is close to the lines—I asked him if
he did not think it dangerous. He said, No, he could have a
large force of infantry to help him there, in very short metre,
if there was any sudden emergency. The troops here are
scattered all around, much more apart than they seemed to
me to be opposite Fredericksburg last winter. They mostly
have good huts and fireplaces, etc. I have been to a great
many of the camps, and I must say I am astonished [how]
good the houses are almost everywhere. I have not seen
one regiment, nor any part of one, in the poor uncomfortable little shelter tents that I saw so common last winter
after Fredericksburg—but all the men have built huts of logs

and mud. A good many of them would be comfortable enough to live in under any circumstances. I have been in the division hospitals around here. There are not many men sick here, and no wounded—they now send them on to Washington. I shall return there in a few days, as I am very clear that the real need of one's services is there after all— there the worst cases concentrate, and probably will, while the war lasts. I suppose you know that what we call hospital here in the field is nothing but a collection of tents on the bare ground for a floor—rather hard accomodation for a sick man. They heat them there by digging a long trough in the ground under them, covering it over with old railroad iron and earth, and then building a fire at one end and letting it draw through and go out at the other, as both ends are open. This heats the ground through the middle of the hospital quite hot. I find some poor creatures crawling about pretty weak with diarrhœa; there is a great deal of that; they keep them until they get very bad indeed, and then send them to Washington. This aggravates the complaint, and they come into Washington in a terrible condition. O mother, how often and how many I have seen come into Washington from this awful complaint after such an experience as I have described—with the look of death on their poor young faces; they keep them so long in the field hospitals with poor accomodations the disease gets too deeply seated.

To-day I have been out among some of the camps of the 2nd division of the 1st Corps. I have been wandering around all day, and have had a very good time, over woods, hills, and gullies—indeed, a real soldier's march. The weather is good and the travelling quite tolerable. I have been in the camps of some Massachusetts, Pennsylvania, and New York regiments. I have friends in them, and went out to see them, and see soldiering generally, as I can never cease to crave more and more knowledge of actual soldier's life, and to be among them as much as possible. This evening I have also been in a large wagoner's camp. They had good fires and were very cheerful. I went to see a friend there, too, but did not find him in. It is curious how many I find that I know and that know me. Mother, I have no difficulty at all in making myself at home among the soldiers, teamsters, or any—I most always find they like to have me very much; it seems to do them good. No doubt they soon feel that my heart and sympathies are truly with them, and it is both a novelty and pleases them and touches their feelings, and so doubtless does them good—and I am sure it does that to me. There is more fun around here than you would think for. I told you about the theatre the 14th Brooklyn has got up—they have songs and burlesques, etc.; some of the performers are real good. As I write this I have heard in one direction or another two or three good bands playing—and hear one tooting away some gay tunes now, though it is quite late at night. Mother, I don't know whether I mentioned in my last letter that I took dinner with Col. Fowler one day early part of the week. His wife is stopping here. I was down at the 14th as I came along this evening, too—one of the officers told me about a presentation to George of a sword, etc.—he said he see it in the papers. The 14th invited me to come and be their guest while I staid here, but I have not been able to accept. Col. Fowler uses me tip-top—he is provost marshal of this region; makes a good officer. Mother, I could get no pen and ink to-night. Well, dear mother, I send you my love, and to George and Jeff and Mat and little girls and all.

Walt.

Direct to care of Major Hapgood as before, and write soon. Mother, I suppose you got a letter I wrote from down here last Monday.

## XXXI

### MRS. LOUISA WHITMAN, Brooklyn

Washington, March 29, 1864.

Dearest Mother—I have written to George again to Knoxville. Things seem to be quiet down there so far. We think here that our forces are going to be made strongest here in Virginia this spring, and every thing bent to take Richmond. Grant is here; he is now down at headquarters in the field, Brandy station. We expect fighting before long; there are many indications. I believe I told you they had sent up all the sick from front. [*The letter is here mutilated so as to be illegible; from the few remaining words, however, it is possible to gather that the writer is describing the arrival of a train* of wounded, over 600, *in Washington during* a terribly rainy afternoon. *The letter continues:*] I could not keep the tears out of my eyes. Many of the poor young men had to be moved on stretchers, with blankets over them, which soon soaked as wet as water in the rain. Most were sick cases, but some badly wounded. I came up to the nearest hospital and helped. Mother, it was a dreadful night (last Friday night)— pretty dark, the wind gusty, and the rain fell in torrents. One poor boy—this is a sample of one case out of the 600—he seemed to be quite young, he was quite small (I looked at his body afterwards), he groaned some as the stretcher bearers were carrying him along, and again as they carried him through the hospital gate. They set down the stretcher and examined him, and the poor boy was dead. They took him into the ward, and the doctor came immediately, but it was all of no use. The worst of it is, too, that he is entirely un-known—there was nothing on his clothes, or anyone with him to identify him, and he is altogether unknown. Mother, it is enough to rack one's heart—such things. Very likely his folks will never know in the world what has become of him. Poor, poor child, for he appeared as though he could be but 18. I feel lately as though I must have some intermission. I feel well and hearty enough, and was never better, but my feelings are kept in a painful condition a great part of the time. Things get worse and worse, as to the amount and suf-ferings of the sick, and as I have said before, those who have to do with them are getting more and more callous and in-different. Mother, when I see the common soldiers, what they go through, and how everybody seems to try to pick upon them, and what humbug there is over them every how, even the dying soldier's money stolen from his body by some scoundrel attendant, or from [the] sick one, even from under his head, which is a common thing, and then the agony I see every day, I get almost frightened at the world. Mother, I will try to write more cheerfully next time—but I see so much. Well, good-bye for present, dear mother.

Walt.

## XXXII

### MRS. LOUISA WHITMAN, Brooklyn

Washington, April 10, 1864.

Dearest Mother—I rec'd your letter and sent the one you sent for George immediately—he must have got it the next day. I had got one from him before yours arrived. I mean to go to Annapolis and see him.

Mother, we expect a commencement of the fighting below very soon; there is every indication of it. We have had about as severe rain storms here lately as I ever see. It is middling pleasant now. There are exciting times in Congress—the Copperheads are getting furious and want to recognize the Southern Confederacy. This is a pretty time to talk of recognizing such villains after what they have done, and after what has transpired the last three years. After first Fredericksburg I felt discouraged myself, and doubted whether our rulers could carry on the war—but that has passed away. The war must be carried on, and I could willingly go myself in the ranks if I thought it would profit more than at present, and I don't know sometimes but I shall as it is. Mother, you don't know what a feeling a man gets after being in the active sights and influences of the camp, the army, the wounded, etc. He gets to have a deep feeling he never experienced before—the flag, the tune of Yankee Doodle and similar things, produce an effect on a fellow never such before. I have seen some bring tears on the men's cheeks, and others turn pale, under such circumstances. I have a little flag; it belonged to one of our cavalry reg'ts; presented to me by one of the wounded. It was taken by the Secesh in a cavalry fight, and rescued by our men in a bloody little skirmish. It cost three men's lives, just to get one little flag, four by three. Our men rescued it, and tore it from the breast of a dead Rebel—all that just for the name of getting their little banner back again. The man that got it was very badly wounded, and they let him keep it. I was with him a good deal; he wanted to give me something, he said, he didn't expect to live, so he gave me the little banner as a keepsake. I mention this, mother, to show you a specimen of the feeling. There is n't a reg't, cavalry or infantry, that would n't do the same on occasion.

Tuesday morning, April 12. Mother, I will finish my letter this morning. It is a beautiful day to-day. I was up in Congress very late last night. The house had a very excited night session about expelling the men that want to recognize the Southern Confederacy. You ought to hear the soldiers talk. They are excited to madness. We shall probably have hot times here, not in the army alone. The soldiers are true as the North Star. I send you a couple of envelopes, and one to George. Write how you are, dear mother, and all the rest. I want to see you all. Jeff, my dear brother, I wish you was here, and Mat too. Write how Sis is. I am well, as usual; indeed first rate every way. I want to come on in a month and try to print my *Drum-Taps*. I think it may be a success pecuniarily, too. Dearest mother, I hope this will find you entirely well, and dear sister Mat and all.

Walt.

## XXXIII

### MRS. LOUISA WHITMAN, Brooklyn

Washington, April 26, 1864.

Dearest Mother—Burnside's army passed through here yesterday. I saw George and walked with him in the regiment for some distance and had quite a talk. He is very well; he is very much tanned and looks hardy. I told him all the latest news from home. George stands it very well, and looks and behaves the same noble and good fellow he always was and always will be. It was on 14th st. I watched three hours before the 51st came along. I joined him just before they came to where the President and Gen. Burnside were standing with others on a balcony, and the interest of seeing me, etc., made George forget to notice the President and salute him. He was a little annoyed at forgetting it. I called his attention to it, but we had passed a little too far on, and George wouldn't turn round even ever so little. However, there was a great many more than half the army passed without noticing Mr. Lincoln and the others, for there was a great crowd all through the streets, especially here, and the place where the

President stood was not conspicuous from the rest. The 9th Corps made a very fine show indeed. There were, I should think, five very full regiments of new black troops, under Gen. Ferrero. They looked and marched very well. It looked funny to see the President standing with his hat off to them just the same as the rest as they passed by. Then there [were the] Michigan regiments; one of them was a regiment of sharpshooters, partly composed of Indians. Then there was a pretty strong force of artillery and a middling force of cavalry—many New York, Pennsylvania, Massachusetts, R. I., etc., reg'ts. All except the blacks were veterans [that had] seen plenty of fighting. Mother, it is very different to see a real army of fighting men, from one of those shows in Brooklyn, or New York, or on Fort Greene. Mother, it was a curious sight to see these ranks after rank of our own dearest blood of men, mostly young, march by, worn and sunburnt and sweaty, with well-worn clothes and thin bundles, and knapsacks, tin cups, and some with frying pans strapt over their backs, all dirty and sweaty, nothing real neat about them except their muskets; but they were all as clean and bright as silver. They were four or five hours passing along, marching with wide ranks pretty quickly, too. It is a great sight to see an army 25 or 30,000 on the march. They are all so gay, too. Poor fellows, nothing dampens their spirits. They all got soaked with rain the night before. I saw Fred McReady and Capt. Sims, and Col. Le Gendre, etc. I don't know exactly where Burnside's army is going. Among other rumors it is said they [are] to go [with] the Army of the Potomac to act as a reserve force, etc. Another is that they are to make a flank march, to go round and get Lee on the side, etc. I have n't been out this morning and don't know what news—we know nothing, only that there is without doubt to be a terrible campaign here in Virginia this summer, and that all who know deepest about it are very serious about it. Mother, it is serious times. I do not feel to fret or whimper, but in my heart and soul about our country, the forthcoming campaign with all its vicissitudes and the wounded and slain —I dare say, mother, I feel the reality more than some because I am in the midst of its saddest results so much. Others may say what they like, I believe in Grant and in

Lincoln, too. I think Grant deserves to be trusted. He is working continually. No one knows his plans; we will only know them when he puts them in operation. Our army is very large here in Virginia this spring, and they are still pouring in from east and west. You don't see about it in the papers, but we have a very large army here.

Mother, I am first rate in health, thank God; I never was better. Dear mother, have you got over all that distress and sickness in your head? You must write particular about it. Dear brother Jeff, how are you, and how is Matty, and how the dear little girls? Jeff, I believe the devil is in it about my writing you; I have laid out so many weeks to write you a good long letter, and something has shoved it off each time. Never mind, mother's letters keep you posted. You must write, and don't forget to tell me all about Sis. Is she as good and interesting as she was six months ago? Mother, have you heard anything from Han? Mother, I have just had my breakfast. I had it in my room—some hard biscuit warmed on the stove, and a bowl of strong tea with good milk and sugar. I have given a Michigan soldier his breakfast with me. He relished it, too; he has just gone. Mother, I have just heard again that Burnside's troops are to be a reserve to protect Washington, so there may be something in it.

Walt.

It is very fine weather here yesterday and today. The hospitals are very full; they are putting up hundreds of hospital tents.

## XXXIV

### MRS. LOUISA WHITMAN, Brooklyn

Washington, June 3, 1864.

Dearest Mother—Your letter came yesterday. I have not heard the least thing from the 51st since—no doubt they are down there with the army near Richmond. I have not written to George lately. I think the news from the Army is very good. Mother, you know of course that it is now very near Richmond indeed, from five to ten miles. Mother, if this campaign was not in progress I should not stop here, as it is now beginning to tell a little upon me, so many bad wounds, many putrefied, and all kinds of dreadful ones, I have been rather too much with—but as it is, I certainly remain here while the thing remains undecided. It is impossible for me to abstain from going to see and minister to certain cases, and that draws me into others, and so on. I have just left Oscar Cunningham, the Ohio boy—he is in a dying condition—there is no hope for him—it would draw tears from the hardest heart to look at him—he is all wasted away to a skeleton, and looks like some one fifty years old. You remember I told you a year ago, when he was first brought in, I thought him the noblest specimen of a young Western man I had seen, a real giant in size, and always with a smile on his face. O what a change. He has long been very irritable to every one but me, and his frame is all wasted away. The young Massachusetts 1st artillery boy, Cutter, I wrote about is dead. He is the one that was brought in a week a go last Sunday badly wounded in the breast. The deaths in the principal hospital I visit, Armory-square, average one an hour.

I saw Capt. Baldwin of the 14th this morning; he has lost his left arm—is going home soon. Mr. Kalbfleisch and Anson Herrick, (M. C. from New York) came in one of the wards where I was sitting writing a letter this morning, in the midst of the wounded. Kalbfleisch was so much affected by the sight that he burst into tears. O, I must tell you, I [gave] in Carver hospital a great treat of ice cream, a couple of days ago—went round myself through about 15 large wards—(I bought some ten gallons, very nice). You would have cried and been amused too. Many of the men had to be fed; several of them I saw cannot probably live, yet they quite enjoyed it. I gave everybody some—quite a number [of] Western country boys had never tasted ice cream before. They relish such things [as] oranges, lemons, etc. Mother, I feel a little blue this morning, as two young men I knew very well have just died. One died last night, and the other about half an hour before I went to the hospital. I did not anticipate the death of either of them. Each was a very, very sad case, so young. Well mother, I see I have written you another gloomy sort of letter. I do not feel as first rate as usual.

Walt.

You don't know how I want to come home and see you all; you, dear mother, and Jeff and Mat and all. I believe I am homesick—something new for me—then I have seen all the horrors of soldiers' life and not been kept up by its excitement. It is awful to see so much, and not be able to relieve it.

## XXXV

### MRS. LOUISA WHITMAN, Brooklyn

Washington, June 7, 1864.

Dearest Mother—I cannot write you anything about the 51st, as I have not heard a word. I felt very much disturbed yesterday afternoon, as Major Hapgood came up from the paymaster general's office, and said that news had arrived that Burnside was killed, and that the 9th Corps had had a terrible slaughter. He said it was believed at the paymaster general's office. Well, I went out to see what reliance there was on it. The rumor soon spread over the town, and was believed by many—but as near as I can make it out, it proves to be one of those unaccountable stories that get started these times. Saturday night we heard that Grant was routed completely, etc. etc.—so that's the way stories fly. I suppose you hear the same big lies there in Brooklyn. Well, the truth is sad enough, without adding anything to it—but Grant is not destroyed yet, but I think is going into Richmond yet, but the cost is terrible. Mother, I have not felt well at all the last week. I had spells of deathly faintness and bad trouble in my head too, and sore throat (quite a little budget, ain't they?) My head was the worst, though I don't know, the faint spells were not very pleasant—but I feel so much better this forenoon I believe it has passed over. There is a very horrible collection in Armory building, (in Armory-square hospital)—about 200 of the worst cases you ever see, and I had been probably too much with them. It is enough to melt the heart of a stone; over one third of them are amputation cases. Well, mother, poor Oscar Cunningham is gone at last. He is the 82d Ohio boy (wounded May 3d, '63). I have written so much of him I suppose you feel as if you almost knew him. I was with him Saturday forenoon and also evening. He was more composed than usual, could not articulate very well. He died about 2 o'clock Sunday morning—very easy they told me. I was not there. It was a blessed relief; his life has been misery for months. The cause of death at last was the system absorbing the pus, the bad matter, instead of discharging it from [the] wound. I believe I told you I was quite blue from the deaths of several of the poor young men I knew well, especially two I had strong hopes of their getting up. Things are going pretty badly with the wounded. They are crowded here in Washington in immense numbers, and all those that come up from the Wilderness and that region, arrived here so neglected, and in such plight, it was awful—(those that were at Fredericksburg and also from Ball Plain). The papers are full of puffs, etc., but the truth is, the largest proportion of worst cases got little or no attention. We receive them here with their wounds full of worms —some all swelled and inflamed. Many of the amputations have to be done over again. One new feature is that many of the poor afflicted young men are crazy. Every ward has some in it that are wandering. They have suffered too much, and it is perhaps a privilege that they are out of their senses. Mother, it is most too much for a fellow, and I sometimes wish I was out of it—but I suppose it is because I have not felt first rate myself. I am going to write to George to-day, as I see there is a daily mail to White House. O, I must tell you that we get the wounded from our present field near Richmond much better than we did from the Wilderness and Fredericksburg. We get them now from White House. They are put on boats there, and come all the way here, about 160 or 170 miles. White House is only twelve or fifteen miles from the field, and is our present depot and base of supplies. It is very pleasant here to-day, a little cooler than it has been—a good rain shower last evening. The Western reg'ts continue to pour in here, the 100 days men;—may go down to front to guard posts, trains, etc.

Well, mother, how do things go on with you all? It seems to me if I could only be home two or three days, and have some good teas with you and Mat, and set in the old basement a while, and have a good time and talk with Jeff, and see the little girls, etc., I should be willing to keep on afterward among these sad scenes for the rest of the summer—but I shall remain here until this Richmond campaign is settled, anyhow, unless I get sick, and I don't anticipate that. Mother dear, I hope you are well and in fair spirits—you must try to. Have you heard from sister Han?

Walt.

You know I am living at 502 Pennsylvania av. (near 3d st.) —it is not a very good place. I don't like it so well as I did cooking my own grub—and the air is not good. Jeff, you must write.

## XXXVI

### MRS. LOUISA WHITMAN, Brooklyn

Washington, June 14, 1864.

Dearest Mother. I am not feeling very well these days—the doctors have told me not to come inside the hospitals for the present. I send there by a friend every day; I send things and aid to some cases I know, and hear from there also, but I do not go myself at present. It is probable that the hospital poison has affected my system, and I find it worse than I calculated. I have spells of faintness and very bad feeling in my head, fullness and pain—and besides sore throat. My boarding place, 502 Pennsylvania av., is a miserable place, very bad air. But I shall feel better soon, I know—the doctors say it will pass over—they have long told me I was going in too strong. Some days I think it has all gone and I feel well again, but in a few hours I have a spell again. Mother, I have not heard anything of the 51st. I sent George's letter to Han. I have written to George since. I shall write again to him in a day or two. If Mary comes home, tell her I sent her my love. If I don't feel better before the end of this week or beginning of next, I may come home for a week or fortnight for a change. The rumor is very strong here that Grant is over the James river on south side—but it is not in the papers. We are having quite cool weather here. Mother, I want to see you and Jeff so much. I have been working a little at copying, but have stopt it lately.

Walt.

## XXXVII

### MRS. LOUISA WHITMAN, Brooklyn

Washington, June 17, 1864.

Dearest Mother. I got your letter this morning. This place and the hospitals seem to have got the better of me. I do not feel so badly this forenoon—but I have bad nights and bad days too. Some of the spells are pretty bad—still I am up some and around every day. The doctors have told me for a fortnight I must leave; that I need an entire change of air, etc.

I think I shall come home for a short time, and pretty soon. (I will try it two or three days yet though, and if I find my illness goes over I will stay here yet awhile. All I think about is to be here if any thing should happen to George).

We don't hear anything more of the army than you do there in the papers.

Walt.

Mother, if I should come I will write a day or so before.

## XXXVIII

### CHARLES W. ELDRIDGE

Brooklyn, N. Y.,
October 8, 1864.

... I am perhaps not so unconscionably hearty as before my sickness. We are deprest in spirits here about my brother George—if not killed, he is a prisoner—he was in the engagement of Sept. 30—on the extreme left——

My book is not yet being printed. I still wish to stereotype it myself. I could easily still put it in the hands of a proper publisher then and make better terms with him.

If you write to William I wish you to enclose him this letter—I wish him to receive again my faithful friendship—while health and sense remain I cannot forget what he has been to me. I love him dearly——

... The political meetings in New York and Brooklyn immense. I go to them as to shows—fireworks, cannon, clusters of gas lights, countless torches, banners and mottoes. 15, 20, 50,000 people—Per contra I occasionally go riding off in the country, in quiet lanes, or a sail on the water, and many times to . . . Coney Island.

All the signs are that Grant is going to strike farther, perhaps risk all. One feels solemn when one sees what depends. The military success though first class of war, is the least that depends.

Good by, dearest comrade. . . .

Walt.

## XXXIX

WILLIAM D. O'CONNOR [Washington, **D. C.**]

Brooklyn, January 6, 1865.

Dear friend

Your welcome letter of December 30 came safe. I have written & sent my application to Mr. Otto, & also a few lines to Mr. Ashton, with a copy of it. I am most desirous to get the appointment, as enclosing with the rest of the points, my attentions to the soldiers & to my poems, as you intimate.

—It may be *Drum-Taps* may come out this winter yet, (in the way I have mentioned in times past). It is in a state to put right through, a perfect copy being ready for the printers. I feel at last, & for the first time without any demur, that I am satisfied with it—content to have it go to the world verbatim & punctuatim. It is in my opinion superior to *Leaves of Grass*—certainly more perfect as a work of art, being adjusted in all its proportions, & its passion having the indispensable merit that though to the ordinary reader let loose with wildest abandon, the true artist can see it is yet under control. But I am perhaps mainly satisfied with *Drum-Taps* because it delivers my ambition of the task that has haunted me, namely, to express in a poem (& in the way I like, which is not at all by directly stating it) the pending action of this *Time & Land we swim in*, with all their large conflicting fluctuations of despair & hope, the shiftings, masses, & the whirl & deafening din, (yet over all, as by invisible hand, a definite purport & idea)—with the unprecedented anguish of wounded & suffering, the beautiful young men, in wholesale death & agony, everything sometimes as if blood color, & dripping blood. The book is therefore unprecedently sad, (as these days are, are they not?)—but it also has the blast of the trumpet, & the drum pounds & whirrs in it, & then an undertone of sweetest comradeship & human love, threading its steady thread inside the chaos, & heard at every lull & interstice thereof—truly, also it has clear notes of faith & triumph.

—— *Drum-Taps* has none of the perturbations of *Leaves of Grass.* I am satisfied with *Leaves of Grass*, (by far the most of it) as expressing what was intended, namely, to express by sharp-cut self assertion, One's Self & also, or may be still more, to map out, to throw together for American use, a gigantic embryo or skeleton of Personality,—fit for the West, for native models—but there are a few things I shall carefully eliminate in the next issue, & a few more I shall considerably change.

I see I have said I consider *Drum-Taps* superior to *Leaves of Grass.* I probably mean as a piece of art, & from the more simple & winning nature of the subject, & also because I have in it only succeeded to my satisfaction in removing all superfluity from it, verbal superfluity I mean, I delight to make a poem where I feel clear that not a word but is indispensable part thereof & of my meaning.

Still *Leaves of Grass* is dear to me, always dearest to me, as my first born, as daughter of my life's first hopes, doubts, & the putting in form of those days' efforts & aspirations— true, I see now, with some things in it I should not put in if I were to write now, but yet I shall certainly let them stand, even if but for proofs of phases passed away.

Mother and all home are well as usual. Not a word for over three months from my brother George—the probabilities are most gloomy.—I see the Howells now & then. I am well, but need to leave here—need a change. If you see Miss Howard tell her Jesse Mullery has been to see me—came yesterday & has just left this forenoon. He talked of nothing but her. His life is saved, & he will have tolerably good strength & health, at least for present. His address is ward 7

Centre St Hospital Newark New Jersey. I was up at Mrs. Price's the other night. She is better this winter. Mrs. Paulina Wright Davis is stopping with her this winter. I have sent a paper with sketch of Hospital Visits, to Dr. Wm. F. Channing. I cannot forgive myself for not acknowledging his assistance for the Hospitals, by letter at the time. I send you another paper also, as you might like it. I take it by a line in your letter that Charles Eldridge has not gone to Boston. I have been reading the strange articles from the Richmond press. A thousand Satans baffled with terror, hatred, malignant squirming, appear in every paragraph. Little California is playing around me as I finish, & has been for half an hour. Love to dear Nelly & Jeannie & all.

Walt Whitman

## XL

### JEFFERSON WHITMAN, Brooklyn

Washington, Jan 30. 1865.

My dear brother: Your letter has only just reached me though I see the Brooklyn post office is January 27th—I was gratified with Babcock's and Smith's letters, though I am very sorry they neither of them mentioned the date of Lt. Caldwell's letter from Danville. If it should be much later than George's, which was November 27th, it would be a relief to know it—but I presume it was one of the same batch. Jeff, I have this morning written to Capt Mason, telling him where George is, and asking him, as that would be ten times more likely to get through, if he will have (or direct some proper person) to put up a box of things to eat, and given him George's address to send it through the lines, and said that I or you would pay the bill of course, and be most deeply obliged to him and that I would have enclosed the money in the letter I sent him, but thought it safer to wait and see whether it reached him. I have written to George since I have been here in Washington. Also a few lines to Han. We have had very cold mean weather here ever since I arrived till to-day,—it is now moderated and very pleasant overhead. I am quite comfortable, have a comfortable room enough, with a wood stove, and a pile of wood in the room, a first rate and good big bed, and a very friendly old Secesh landlady, whose husband and son are off in the Southern army—she is different from any I have found yet here, is very obliging, starts my fire for me at 5 o'clock every afternoon and lights the gas even and then turns it down to be ready for me when I come home.—I get my meals where I can—they are poor and expensive—You speak of the Indian Office—It is a Bureau in the Department of the Interior, which has charge of quite a large mass of business relating to the numerous Indian tribes in West and Northwest, large numbers of whom are under annuities, supplies, &c. from the government. All I have hitherto employed myself about has been making copies of reports and bids &c. for the office to send up to the Congressional Committee on Indian Affairs.—It is easy enough—I take things very easy—the rule is to come at 9, and go at 4—but I don't come at 9, and only stay till 4 when I want, as at present to finish a letter for the mail—I am treated with great courtesy, as an evidence of which I have to inform you that since I began this letter, I have been sent for by the Cashier to receive my *pay* for the arduous and invaluable services I have already rendered to the government—I feel quite well, perhaps not as completely so as I used to was, but I think I shall get so this spring—as I did indeed feel yesterday better than I have since I was taken sick last summer. I spent yesterday afternoon in Armory Square Hospital, and had a real good time, and the boys had too. Jeff you need not be afraid about my overdoing the matter. I shall go regularly enough, but I shall be on my guard against trouble. I am also going to some of the camps about here; there is a great chance among them to do good, and they are interesting places every way, for one who goes among the men. I have thought every day of Mother—dear Mother I hope she gets along well this bitter weather—(about the hoop iron, I think it was the right thing to do—the least they can do is to take it off )—My dear brother you must by all means come and see me—Martha my dear sister, I send you and the dear little torments my best love. Jeff give my respects to Mrs. Lane and Dr. Ruggles.

Walt.

## XLI

### J. T. TROWBRIDGE [Boston?]

Washington, Monday February 6, 1865.

My dear Friend:

As you see by the date of this, I am back again in Washington, moving around regularly, but not to excess, among the hospitals. . . . My health is pretty good, but since I was prostrated last July, I have not had that unconscious and perfect health I formerly had. The physicians says my system has been penetrated by the malaria,—it is tenacious, peculiar and somewhat baffling—but tells it will go over in due time. It is my first appearance in the character of a man not entirely well.

The talk here is about the late Peace Conference—the general statement accepted is that it has been a failure and a bubble—even the war is to go on worse than ever—but I find a few shrewd persons whose theory is that it is not at all sure of its being a failure—they say that the President and Mr. Seward are willing to avoid at present the tempest of rage which would beat about their heads, if it were known among the Radicals that Peace, Amnesty, *every thing*, were given up to the Rebels on the single price of re-assuming their place in the Union—so the said shrewd ones say the thing is an open question yet. For *my* part I see no light or knowledge in any direction on the matter of the conference, or what it amounted to, or where it left off. I say nothing, and have no decided opinion about it—not even a guess (but rather leaning to the generally accepted statement above).

My dear friend, I haven't your last letter at hand to see whether there is anything that needs special answer—I hope to hear from you often. For the present Farewell.

Walt Whitman

Direct to me simply Washington, D. C., as I call for my letters daily at the post office. Should you have an opportunity to see Dr. Le Baron Russel, 3 Mt. Vernon St., tell him I wished you to thank him for many favors and contributions to the men in times past, and that I am now back in Washington. If perfectly eligible, it might help me in the cause of the men, if you were to prepare a paragraph for Mr. Shillaber's paper, if he were willing to publish it, stating that I am now as a volunteer nurse among the Hospitals at Washington & in the field as formerly. Write soon as convenient.

W. W.

## XLII

### CAPTAIN WILLIAM COOK, New York

Washington, Feb. 27, 1865.

Captain: Could you give me a little further information about my brother Capt. George W. Whitman 51st New York, who gave you the slip you sent from Annapolis Feb 19 with his and mother's address, Feb 14th?—Why did not he, and the other officers, 51st N. Y. come up with the main body, for exchange?—were the other officers 51st there at Danville, time you left?—Please tell me all you know, or think probable, on this subject of why they did not come. Have they been sent further south, to avoid exchanging them, or are they still at Danville?—*Was* my brother *really well* & hearty —was Lieut. Sam'l Pooley, 51st N. Y. there, & how was he?— Do you know whether my brother got letters & boxes we sent him?—Was he in the attempt to escape, Dec. 10, last?—My dear Sir, if you could take a leisure half hour and write me, *soon as possible*, what you know on these or other points relating to my brother, it would deeply oblige me—Address—

Walt Whitman

Washington, D. C.

## XLIII

### WILLIAM D. O'CONNOR

Dear friend,                    Brooklyn, April 7, 1865

I am stopping longer than I first intended, as I have decided to print the book, and am now under way with it. Probably I will not be back till 16th or 17th.

I have been to Christern's the great importer of foreign & special London books—he said he had no Hugo's Shakespeare & had heard of none—English I mean: if any Scribner would know about it—I have been to Scribner's today—He thinks he has seen one announced in English literary announcements—but thinks it is not yet printed—has not had or seen any such book.

The grand culminations of last week impress me profoundly of course. I feel more than ever how America has been entirely re-stated by them—and they will shape the destinies of the future of the whole of mankind.

My dear mother is well. My brother George has been unwell, again, and has sulkily permitted me to get an extension of his leave of absence, 20 days longer.

Please go to the Post Office & get all letters & send me. Please inquire for last week's advertised letters, & the present weeks also. I will not trouble to send any after next Wednesday night. My book will be small & not thick at all—but will be well printed. (The commissioner has granted me the two weeks longer.)

## XLIV

### MRS. IRWIN, ———, Pennsylvania

[May, 1865]

Dear madam: No doubt you and Frank's friends have heard the sad fact of his death in hospital here, through his uncle, or the lady from Baltimore, who took his things. (I have not seen them, only heard of them visiting Frank.) I will write you a few lines—as a casual friend that sat by his death-bed. Your son, corporal Frank H. Irwin, was wounded near fort Fisher, Virginia, March 25th, 1865—the wound was in the left knee, pretty bad. He was sent up to Washington, was receiv'd in Ward C, Armory-square hospital, March 28th—the wound became worse, and on the 4th of April the leg was amputated a little above the knee—the operation was perform'd by Dr. Bliss, one of the best surgeons in the army—he did the whole operation himself—there was a good deal of bad matter gather'd—the bullet was found in the knee. For a couple of weeks afterwards he was doing pretty well. I visited and sat by him frequently, as he was fond of having me. The last ten or twelve days of April I saw that his case was critical. He previously had some fever, with cold spells.

The last week in April he was much of the time flighty—but always mild and gentle. He died first of May. The actual cause of death was pyaemia, (the absorption of the matter in the system instead of its discharge.) Frank, as far as I saw, had everything requisite in surgical treatment, nursing, &c. He had watches much of the time. He was so good and well-behaved and affectionate, I myself liked him very much. I was in the habit of coming in afternoons and sitting by him, and soothing him, and he liked to have me—liked to put his arm out and lay his hand on my knee—would keep it so a long while. Toward the last he was more restless and flighty at night—often fancied himself with his regiment—by his talk sometimes seem'd as if his feelings were hurt by being blamed by his officers for something he was entirely innocent of—said, "I never in my life was thought capable of such a thing, and never was." At other times he would fancy himself talking as it seem'd to children or such like, his relatives I suppose, and giving them good advice; would talk to them a long while. All the time he was out of his head not one single bad word or idea escaped him. It was remark'd that many a man's conversation in his senses was not half as good as Frank's delirium. He seem'd quite willing to die—he had become very weak and had suffer'd a good deal, and was perfectly resign'd, poor boy. I do not know his past life, but I feel as if it must have been good. At any rate what I saw of him here, under the most trying circumstances, with a painful wound, and among strangers, I can say that he behaved so brave, so composed, and so sweet and affectionate, it could not be surpass'd. And now like many other noble and good men, after serving his country as a soldier, he has yielded up his young life at the very outset in her service. Such things are gloomy—yet there is a text, "God doeth all things well" —the meaning of which, after due time, appears to the soul.

I thought perhaps a few words, though from a stranger, about your son, from one who was with him at the last, might be worth while—for I loved the young man, though I but saw him immediately to lose him. I am merely a friend visiting the hospitals occasionally to cheer the wounded and sick.

W. W.

## XLV

JEFFERSON WHITMAN, Brooklyn

Attorney General's Office,
Washington, May 7, 1866.

Dear Brother Jeff, By Mother's letter I have heard about the moving & the new quarters—Mother says that she is glad they are no worse, under all the circumstances. I enclose an envelope to mother, with a little money in it.—As you see, I am still in the same place, with easy times enough, & a good place as I could expect.—The Attorney General is absent now in Kentucky. There is not much work. I can't tell whether I shall keep on here, or not. There is nothing at present that looks like a change—I feel quite well this spring—but a clerk's life here is not very interesting—I went down last Thursday to Mt. Vernon 16 miles down the Potomac—I think it is the pleasantest spot & farm I ever saw—went through the house & grounds &c—I was very glad I went—Yesterday we had the funeral here of a man you must have seen mentioned in the papers, old Count Gurowski,—I have been very well acquainted with him since I have lived here—he was a strange old man, a great lord in his own country, Poland, owner of 30,000 serfs & great estates—an exile for conspiracy against the government—he knew everything & growled & found fault with everybody—but was always very courteous to me, & spoke very highly of me in his book, his *Diary* printed last winter—his funeral was simple but very impressive—all the big radicals were there—The fight between Congress & the President is still going on—I think the President is rather afraid of going too far against Congress, for Stevens & the rest of 'em are very determined.

My hospitals are dwindled down to a small force—but there are plenty of cases to occupy me a couple of visits a week—I always go Sunday, sometimes in the middle of the week—Julius Mason is here in barracks yet—Jeff, I wish I could now & then be home and see you all, even if it was only a couple of hours—

Give my best respects to Mr. Lane and the Doctor—I send my love to Mat & the little girls. Write & tell me all about

home affairs, & how George is getting along—dear old
Mother, as she gets older & older, I think about her every
day & night.

                                                              Walt.

## XLVI

### MRS. LOUISA WHITMAN, Brooklyn

Washington, Thursday, May 25, '65

Dear Mother, I received your letter of the 22d—I feel uneasy
about you all the time, & hope I shall get a letter to-day, &
find you have recovered.

Well, the Review is over, & it was very grand—it was too
much & too impressive, to be described—but you will see a
good deal about it in the papers. If you can imagine a great
wide avenue like Flatbush avenue, quite flat, & stretching as
far as you can see with a great white building half as big as
Fort Greene on a hill at the commencement of the avenue,
and then through this avenue marching solid ranks of soldiers, 20 or 25 abreast, just marching steady all day long for
two days without intermission, one regiment after another,
real war-worn soldiers, that have been marching & fighting
for years—sometimes for an hour nothing but cavalry, just
solid ranks, on good horses, with sabres glistening & carbines hanging by their saddles, & their clothes showing hard
service, but they mostly all good-looking hardy young men—
then great masses of guns, batteries of cannon, four or six
abreast, each drawn by six horses, with the gunners seated on
the ammunition wagons—& these perhaps a long while in
passing, nothing but batteries,—(it seemed as if all the cannon
in the world were here)—then great battalions of blacks,
with axes & shovels & pick axes, (real Southern darkies,
black as tar)—then again hour after hour the old infantry
regiments, the men all sunburnt—nearly every one with
some old tatter all in shreds, (that *had been* a costly and
beautiful *flag*)—the great drum corps of sixty or eighty
drummers massed at the heads of the brigades, playing away
—now & then a fine brass band,—but oftener nothing but
the drums & whistling fifes,—but they sounded very lively—
(perhaps a band of sixty drums & fifteen or twenty fifes play-

ing "Lannigan's ball")—the different corps banners, the generals with their staffs &c—the Western Army, led by Gen. Sherman, (old Bill, the soldiers all call him)—well, dear mother, that is a brief sketch, give you some idea of the great panorama of the Armies that have been passing through here the last two days.

—I saw the President several times, stood close by him, & took a good look at him—& like his expression much—he is very plain & substantial—it seemed wonderful that just that plain middling-sized ordinary man, dressed in black, without the least badge or ornament, should be the master of all these myriads of soldiers, the best that ever trod the earth, with forty or fifty Major-Generals, around him or riding by with their broad yellow-satin belts around their waists,—and of all the artillery & cavalry,—to say nothing of all the Forts & ships, &c. &c.—I saw Gen. Grant too several times—He is the noblest Roman of them all—none of the pictures do justice to him—about sundown I saw him again riding on a large fine horse, with his hat off in answer to the hurrahs—he rode by where I stood, & I saw him well, as he rode by on a slow canter, with nothing but a single orderly after him—He looks like a good man—(& I believe there is much in looks) —I saw Gen. Meade, Gen. Thomas, Secretary Stanton, & lots of other celebrated government officers & generals—but the *rank* and *file* was the greatest sight of all.

The 51st was in the line Tuesday with the 9th Corps. I saw George but did not get a chance to speak to him. He is well. George is now *Major* George W. Whitman,—has been commissioned & mustered in. (Col. Wright & Col. Shephard have done it, I think.) The 51st is over to the Old Convalescent camp, between here and Alexandria, doing provost duty. It, the old camp is now called Amgur General Hospital. If you should write direct,

> Major G. W. Whitman
> 51st New York V. V.
> on provost duty at
> Amgur Gen'l Hospital
> near Alexandria Va

It is thought that the 51st will not be mustered out for the present—It is thought the Government will retain the re-enlisted veteran regiments, such as the 51st—If that is so George will remain as he is for the summer, or most of it—The reason I haven't seen him is, I knew they had left provost duty in the Prince st. prison, but didn't know where they had gone till Tuesday—I saw Capt. Caldwell Tuesday, also Col. Wright Tuesday night—they said they all have pleasant quarters over there.

Dear brother Jeff, I was very sorry you wasnt able to come on to see the Review—we had perfect weather & everything just as it should be—the streets now are full of soldiers scattered around loose, as the armies are in camp near here getting ready to be mustered out.—I am quite well & visit the Hospitals the same.—Mother you didn't write whether you got the package of 5 *Drum-Taps*—I keep thinking about you every few minutes all day—I wish I was home a couple of days—Jeff, you will take this acc't of the Review, same as if it were written to you.

Walt

## XLVII

### MRS. LOUISA WHITMAN, Brooklyn

Attorney General's Office, Washington,
Nov. 16, 1866. Friday afternoon.

Dearest Mother, I only write again this week—(I wrote last Tuesday) to inform you that the Attorney General has promoted me.—I have now a real good berth, what they call a third class clerk with the pay of $1600 a year.—I shall have about $127 a month (they take a little off, every time they pay, on acc't of gov't tax).—Besides I have now a regular appointment, instead of being a temporary clerk, as before. I was appointed last Wednesday, my new grade & pay commence on Nov. 1st—I have n't got a letter from home for ten or twelve days. The Attorney General has gone to New York—he is badly afflicted with sore eyes, & has gone there to see the best oculists——

My cold, or whatever it is, is better to-day—I hope you are all well—Good bye dear mother—*Write soon.*

Walt.

Mother, I send some envelopes—You must have paper—you know I left you a great lot, when I was home. I hope you are not sick, dear mother.

## XLVIII

### MRS. LOUISA WHITMAN, Brooklyn

Attorney General's Office, Washington,
Nov. 23, 1866.

Dearest Mother,—I feel middling well to-day. I got to the office just the same as usual—If I had a good home where I could have a decent time, & keep in for three or four days, I should get all right—the principal trouble with me, I think, is neuralgia—it gives me great distress in the head at times—but the spells do not last long at a time—I eat pretty nearly the same as usual—but do not sleep well——

But I think I am making too much of it—I thought I would write you just a few lines, you would get Saturday.

You must tell Jeff or George to get the *Galaxy* of Dec. 1, it is a magazine—it is for sale at most of the book-stands—30 cts—it has a piece in about me—I think it is very good—John Burroughs is a young man from Delaware County, New York—he lives here, now, is married—I am well acquainted with him, & he & his wife have been very hospitable & friendly to me.

Mr. Conway's article was about as impudent as it was friendly—quite a mixture of good & bad.

I am glad you like Emily Price,—she is a good girl. She seems to me one that you need n't make any fuss or change—but let domestic things go on just as they may be, when she comes to visit you.

It is pleasant this afternoon—the sun is shining out—the river & hills on the other side look beautiful.

I sent Han a book *Lady Audley's Secret*—& shall send her a letter to-day.

Don't forget, George or Jeff, to get the *Galaxy* of Dec. 1.

2H                                                                          W.

Mother if any of you want another copy of the new *Leaves of Grass*, I can send you an order for one on the binder in New York, & you can get it.

Well mother dear, I believe that is all—except that I am getting a new pair of trouserloons—Shall not get any other new clothes this winter——

Love to George & all.                                   Walt.

### XLIX

### MRS. LOUISA WHITMAN

Attorney General's Office, Washington,
Dec. 24, 1866.

Dearest Mother, I got Jeff's letter sending the money toward the soldiers' dinner—it was more than I asked for, & was very good of them all—I have not had any trouble myself worth mentioning—the dinner has been got up at my instigation—I have contributed handsomely—but they (the Hospital steward &c.) have done the work.

Mother I sent Han a handsome little volume of *Florence Percy's Poems*, & $5 for a Christmas present. Sent it to-day —Poor Han—I suppose every such thing does her so much good——

Don't you believe that fool Heyde lately wrote a long letter to Mr. Raymond, editor of the N. Y. *Times*—in it he said "Walt was a good fellow *enough*—*but*"—& then he went on to run down *Leaves of Grass*, like the rest of 'em—The way I know is Wm. O'Connor was invited by Raymond to come & see him—& he told O'Connor he had received a number of letters about that piece in the *Times* of Dec. 2, which I sent you. He said they all praised the piece, & thanked him (Raymond) for printing it, except one he got from a fellow in Vermont who called himself Walt Whitman's relation—a brother-in-law, he believed—quite a good deal of stuff. Raymond seemed to think the man was either crazy or a fool, & he treated the letter with contempt.—I don't want you to write any thing about it to Han, of course—only if she was here we would tell her. The puppy thought I suppose that he could get his letter printed, & injure me & my book——

We are likely to have a pleasant day for Christmas—when

I next write I will tell you about the dinner—I must inform you that I have had a present of a beautiful knife, a real Rogers steel, to-day from the Attorney General—Mother $2 is for Nance—you can give it to her in money, or in any way you like.

Well, dear mother, this is Christmas eve, & I am writing it in the office by gas light, so as it will be ready to go to-morrow—I have not heard since from Mrs. Grayson.—Good night mother dear.

Walt.

## L

## M. D. CONWAY

July 24, 1867.

Dear friend. I avail myself of an opportunity to send you, by the hands of Mr. Philp, just starting for London, a copy of my Poems prepared with care for the printers, with reference to republication in England. The Introduction is written by William O'Connor. All is sent you, so that in case there comes any opening you may have a proper copy of latest date, prepared by me, to publish from. Of course I do not expect you, and would not permit you, to make yourself the job of running around and seeking after a publisher; only, please take charge of the copy—I hereby clothe you with power over it, and should any good chance befall, it is what I should wish a London edition set up from.

Mr. O'Connor has shown me your note of April 30th last to him. I wish to send you, as also to those other friends and well-wishers whom it seems I have in England, my true thanks and love.

Many serious and wonderful things have occurred in our dear country since you and I last met, my friend. But of these I will not now talk. I too have had many deep experiences since.

Mr. Philp starts from Washington this evening so I must cut short my letter. I will add that I remain well and hearty. For occupation I hold a pleasant clerkship in the Attorney General's office—of pay sufficient and duties agreeable and consistent with my tastes. I may write you, by mail, further about the book, and other matters. Write me on receipt of the copy. Farewell.

## LI

### M. D. CONWAY

Washington, Nov. 1st '67.

My feeling and attitude about a volume of selections from my *Leaves* by Mr. Rossetti, for London publication, are simply passive ones, yet with decided satisfaction that if the job is to be done, it is to be by such hands. Perhaps, too, "good-natured" as you advise—certainly not ill-natured. I wish Mr. Rossetti to know that I appreciate *his* appreciation, realize his delicacy and honor, and warmly thank him for his literary friendliness.

I have no objection to his substituting other words—leaving it all to his own tact—for "onanist", "father-stuff", &c. &c. Briefly, I hereby empower him (since that is the pivotal affair and since he has the kindness to shape his action so much by my wishes—and since, indeed, the sovereignty of the responsibility is not mine in the case) to make verbal changes of that sort wherever, for reasons sufficient for him, he decides that they are indispensible.

I would add that it is a question with me whether the introductory essay, or prose preface of the first edition, is worth printing.

"Calamus" is a common word here; it is the very large and aromatic grass, or root, spears three feet high—often called "sweet flag"—grows all over the Northern and Middle States—(see Webster's Large Dictionary—Calamus—definition 2).—The récherché or ethereal sense, as used in my book, arises probably from it, Calamus presenting the biggest and hardiest kind of spears of grass, and from its fresh, aromatic, pungent bouquet.

I write this to catch to-morrow's steamer from New York. It is every way likely I shall think of other points, and write you again in a week or so.

## LII

### WILLIAM MICHAEL ROSSETTI

Nov. 22, '67.

I suppose Mr. Conway has received and you have read, the letter I sent over about three weeks since, assenting to the substitution of other words, &c. as prepared by you, in your reprint of my book, or selections therefrom.

I suppose the reprint intends to avoid any expressed or implied character of being an expurgated edition—and hope it will simply assume the form and name of a selection from the various editions of my pieces, printed here. I suggest, in the interest of that view, whether the following might not be a good form of Title-page: "Walt Whitman's Poems Selected from the American Editions By William M. Rossetti."

When I have my next edition brought out here, I shall change the title of the piece, "When lilacs in the Dooryard bloom'd," to "President Lincoln's Funeral Hymn". You are at liberty to take the latter name, or the old one, at your option, (if you include the piece in your reprint).

I wish particularly not [only] that the little figures numbering the stanzas, but also that the larger figures dividing the pieces into separate passages or sections, be carefully preserved as in copy.

It is quite certain that I shall add to my next edition (according to my plan from the start) a brief cluster of pieces, born of thoughts on the deep themes—Death and Immortality.

You will allow me to send you an article I have printed on "Democracy"—a hasty charcoal-sketch of a piece, but indicative, to any one interested in *Leaves of Grass*, as of the audience the book supposes and in whose interest it is made.

Allow me also to send you (as the ocean postage law is now so easy,) a copy of Mr. Burroughs' Notes and some papers.

And now, my dear sir, and with uninterested candor, you must just make what use, or no use at all, of anything I suggest or send as your own occasions call for. Very likely some of my suggestions may have been anticipated.


## LIII

### W. M. ROSSETTI

Washington, Dec. 3, 1867.

My dear Mr. Rossetti: I have just received, and have considered, your letter of Nov. 17. In order that there may be the frankest understanding with respect to my position, I

hasten to write you that the authorization in my letter of
Nov. 1st to Mr. Conway, for you, to make verbal alterations,
substitute words, &c. was meant to be construed as an answer to the case presented in Mr. Conway's letter of Oct. 12.
Mr. Conway stated the case of a volume of selections, in
which it had been decided that the poems reprinted in London should appear verbatim, and asking my authority to
change certain words in the preface to first edition of poems,
&c. I will be candid with you, and say I had not the slightest
idea of applying my authorization to a reprint of the full
volume of my poems. As such a volume was not proposed,
and as your courteous and honorable course and attitude
called and call for no niggardly or hesitating response from
me, I penned that authorization, and did not feel to set
limits to it. But abstractly, and standing alone, and not read
in connection with Mr. C.'s letter of Oct. 12, I see now it is
far too loose, and needs distinct guarding. I cannot and will
not consent, of my own volition, to countenance an expurgated edition of my pieces. I have steadily refused to do so
here in my own country, even under seductive offers, and
must not do so in another country.

I feel it due to myself to write you explicitly thus, my dear
Mr. Rossetti, though it may seem harsh, and perhaps un-
generous. Yet I rely upon you to absolve me, sooner or
later. Could you see Mr. Conway's letter of Oct. 12, you
would, I think, more fully comprehend the integrity of my
explanation.

I have to add that the points made in that letter, in relation
to the proposed reprint, as originally designed, exactly correspond with those, on the same subject, in your late letter,—
that the kind and appreciative tone of both letters is in the
highest degree gratifying, and is most cordially and affectionately responded to by me—and that the fault of sending
the loose authorization has surely been, to a large degree, my
own.

And now, my friend, having set myself right in that matter,
I proceed to say, on the other hand, for you and for Mr.
Hotten, that if, before the arrival of this letter, you have practically invested in and accomplished, or partially accomplished, any plan, even contrary to this letter, I do not expect

you to abandon it, at loss of outlay, but shall *bona fide* consider you blameless if you let it go on and be carried out as you may have arranged. It is the question of the authorization of an expurgated edition proceeding from me that deepest engages me. The facts of the different ways, one way or another, in which the book may appear in England, out of influences not under the shelter of my umbrage, are of much less importance to me.

After making the foregoing explanation, I shall, I think, accept kindly whatever happens. For I feel, indeed know, that I am in the hands of a friend, and that my pieces will receive that truest, brightest, of light and perception coming from love. In that, all other and lesser requisites become pale.

It would be better, in any introduction, to make no allusion to me as authorizing, or not prohibiting, &c.

The whole affair is somewhat mixed, and I write off-hand to catch to-morrow's New York steamer—but I guess you will pick out my meaning. Probably, indeed, Mr. Hotten has preferred to go on after the original plan—which, if so, saves all trouble.

I have to add that I only wish you could know how deeply the beautiful personal tone and passages of your letter of Nov. 17 have penetrated and touched me. It is such things that go to our hearts, and reward us, and make up for all else, for years. Permit me to offer you my friendship.

I sent you hence, Nov. 23, a letter through Mr. Conway. Also a copy of Mr. Burroughs's Notes, Mr. O'Connor's pamphlet, and some papers containing criticisms on *Leaves of Grass*. Also, later, a prose article of mine, named Democracy, in a magazine.

Let me know how the work goes on, what shape it takes, &c. Finally, I charge you to construe all I have written through my declared and fervent realization of your goodness to me, nobleness of intention, and, I am fain to hope, personal, as, surely, literary and moral sympathy and attachment. And so, for the present, farewell.

Walt Whitman.

## LIV

## EDMUND ROUTLEDGE

Edmund Routledge:                    Washington, Jan. 17, '68.

Dear Sir: In compliance with request in your name in letter from George Routledge and Sons, New York, of December 28th and my own reply thereto of December 30th, I send you herewith a poem for the Magazine, if found acceptable. For my own convenience and to insure correctness I have had the manuscript put in type and transmit it to you in the shape of a printed proof. The price is one hundred and twenty dollars in gold, payable here, and I should like thirty copies of the magazine sent me here. It is to be distinctly understood that I reserve the right to print it in any future editions of my book. Hoping success to the Magazine, and that my piece may be found acceptable for it, I remain

Respectfully &c yours

Walt Whitman.

## LV

## M. D. CONWAY, London

Feb. 17th, 1868.

Dear Conway: Your letter of Feb 1st has just come to hand. I am willing that Mr. Hotten should sell his English publication of my Poems in the United States, on condition of paying me one shilling for every copy disposed of here, and hereby give consent to that arrangement. Furthermore, to save trouble, I hereby fully empower you to decide or act for me, in any matters or propositions relating to the book, in England, should any such arise—and what you agree to, is agreed to by me. If convenient I should like Mr. Hotten to send me two copies of the book, by mail, immediately. I should also consider it a special favor if you would forward me from time to time any of the English magazines or journals that might contain *noteworthy* criticisms of my poems. But you must allow me to repay you the favor.

William O'Connor is well and remains employed as before. Ellen O'Connor is absent, in Providence, but returns here soon—their little girl has been very ill, is now convalescent.

Our American politics, as you notice, are in an unusually effervescent condition, with, perhaps (to the mere eye observation, from a distance)—divers alarming and deadly portending stars and signals:—Yet we old stagers take things very easily, and count on coming out all right in due time. The Republicans have exploited the negro too intensely, and there comes a reaction. But that is going to be provided for. According to present appearances the good, worthy, non-demonstrative courage-representing Grant will be elected President. What about him, then? As at present advised I shall vote for him, non-demonstrative as he is— but admit I can tell much better about him some five years hence.

I remain well in health—occupy the same agreeable quiet place in the Attorney General's office—and am writing a prose piece or two (which I will send you when printed). I wish to send my sincerest thanks and personal regards to Mr. Rossetti. To have had my book and my cause fall into his hands, in London, in the way they have, I consider one of the greatest pieces of good fortune.

Mr. Morley called upon me. Did you get my piece I sent— Democracy?—I have just received a letter from A. B. Alcott —he was with Emerson the previous evening, talking.

Remember my request to Mr. Hotten for a couple of copies by mail—also, by your own kindness, any English criticisms of value, should such appear.

I have not yet seen the February Fortnightly, nor the book William Blake, but shall procure and read both. I feel prepared in advance to render my cordial and admirant respect to Mr. Swinburne—and would be glad to have him know that I thank him heartily for the mention which I understand he has made of me, in the Blake.

Indeed, my dear friend, I may here confess to you that to be accepted by these young men of England, and treated with highest courtesy and even honor, touches me deeply. In my own country, so far,—from the press, and from authoritative quarters, I have received but one long tirade of impudence, mockery, and scurrilous jeers. Only since the English recognition have the skies here lighted up a little.

With remembrance and love, to you, Rossetti, and all my good friends—I write for the present Farewell.

## LVI

### JOHN CAMDEN HOTTEN, London

Feb. 18, 1868.

Dear Sir: In response to your letter of the 5th instant, which has just reached me, I have to say that I accept the proposal in it respecting your English publication of my poems—and hereby agree that you have the privilege of selling that publication in the United States, on payment to me, or my agent, of a royalty of one shilling, (or 25 cents gold) upon every copy sold in the U.S. Of course it is distinctly understood that this grant from me does not affect my copyright here but that said copyright in each of its particulars and in the whole, is absolutely and fully and exclusively retained by me.

It is not improbable that a very handsome and steady sale of the English volume may be effected here, by the right business manipulation, a moderate, judicious advertising &c.

My book has never been really published here at all and the market is in a sort vacant of supply. I will suggest something to you on these points in a future letter.

I received yesterday a letter from Mr. Conway conveying your proposition, to which I mailed an immediate answer, to the same effect as herewith.

Accept my thanks for the William Blake. It has not yet come from the post office, but I know it will prove to me a profoundly interesting study and a handsome gift. It is, in fact, a book I was wanting.,

After the reception of the copy you speak of—my own volume—(now probably on its way)—I shall doubtless have occasion to express genuine pleasure—with gratitude both to its editor and publisher.

And now, my dear sir, please accept with my trust in the success of the enterprise my kindest respects to yourself personally.

## LVII

### JOHN CAMDEN HOTTEN, London

March 9, '68.

*Mr. Hotten.* I thank you for the copy of my poems sent by you. It has just reached me. I consider it a beautiful volume. The portrait as given in it is, however, a marked blemish. I was thinking, if you wish to have a portrait, you might like to own the original plate of 1855 which I believe I can procure in good order—and from which you can print something much better—as per impression enclosed. If so, send me word immediately. The price of the plate would probably be forty dollars gold—or eight pounds. It would suit just such a volume, and would perfectly coincide with the text as it now stands in note and preface. If I receive your favorable response, I will, if possible, procure the plate and send it you by express—on receipt of which, and not till then, you can send me the money.

I will thank you to convey to Mr. Swinburne my heartiest thanks for the copy of William Blake sent me, and also for his kind and generous mention of me in it.

## LVIII

### M. D. CONWAY, London

Washington, March 18, '68.

My dear Conway. I send the accompanying article in hopes you can do me the favor to dispose of it to an English magazine. The one I first think of is the *Fortnightly Review.* If not that some other. I place the whole business, price, &c. in your absolute control. Only understand that the piece is to be published here in the *Galaxy* for May. Some English magazine for May is what would suit best. In haste.

## LIX

### MRS. ABBY H. PRICE, Brooklyn

Attorney General's Office,
Washington, April 10, 1868

My Dear Friend,

I received your first letter of about a month ago, (March 9,)—I enquired of a friend in the revenue office, about the tax under the new law,—& whether ruffles would be exempted, &c.—& on or about the 11th March, I wrote you what I had learned—viz: that they were to be exempted—& also all the gossip and news,—about the O'Connors, & about myself, literary matters with me, and how I was situated here, and about things in general—*of course* a mighty interesting letter it must have been—and a dreadful loss not to get!—for I infer by your second letter April 7, just rec'd, that you did *not* get it—which I deeply regret, for I don't like to be supposed capable of not responding to those that are almost the same as *my own* folks. (I put both the old & new No's on the address—perhaps that made it miscarry.)—but let them go.

The changes in the Attorney Gen's office have made no difference in my situation—I have had the good luck to be treated with "distinguished consideration" by all the Attorney Gen's.—Mr. Speed, Mr. Stanberry & the present one Mr. Browning. I couldn't wish to have better bosses—& as to the pleasantness and permanency of my situation here, it is not likely to be affected, as far as present appears, unless Wade coming in power, should appoint Harlan, or some pious & modest Radical of similar stripe, to the Attorney Generalship—in which case, doubtless, I should have to tumble out.

My dear friends, I often think about you all—Helen & Emily in particular, & wish I could look in upon you—Sunday afternoons—I warmly thank you for your hospitable offers.

Give my best respects to Mr. Arnold & Mr. Price—I shall have a piece in the *Galaxy* for May—it will be called "Personalism"—is a continuation of the piece on Democracy—shall have a poem soon, (perhaps in May No.) in the *Broad-*

*way magazine*—I am well as usual—the Impeachment is growing shaky—it is a doubtful business—I am writing this at my table in office—as I look out it is dark & cloudy with a chill rain, but the grass is green & I see the river flowing beyond.

With love.

Walt Whitman.

## LX

### JOHN CAMDEN HOTTEN, London

April 24 '68

*To Mr. Hotten.* I am glad to hear you are having Mr Conway's photograph engraved in place of the bad print now in the book. If a faithful presentation of that photograph can be given it will satisfy me well—of course it should be reproduced with all its shaggy, dappled, rough-skinned character, and not attempted to be smoothed or prettyfied—(if in time I send the following hints)—let the costume be kept very simple and broad, and rather kept down too, little as there is of it—preserve the effect of the sweeping lines making all that fine free angle below the chin—I would suggest not to bring in so fully the shoulders and bust as the photograph does—make only the neck, the collar with the immediately neighboring part of the shirt delineated. You will see that the spot at the left side of the hair, near the temple, is a white blur, and does not belong to the picture. The eyes part and all around the eyes try to re-produce fully and faithfully, exactly as in the photograph. I hope you have a good artist at the work. It is perhaps worth your taking special pains about, both to achieve a successful picture and likeness, something characteristic, and as certain to be a marked help to your edition of the book. Send me an early proof of the engraving.

Thank you for the papers with notices in them—and for your *Academia* criticism. Please continue to send any special notices. I receive them safely and promptly. The *London Review* article is reprinted in Littell's *Living Age*. I should like to know who wrote the piece in the *Morning Star*

—it flushed my friends and myself too, like a sun dash, brief, hot, and dazzling.

I have several things more to say and will write again soon —Also to Mr. Rossetti to whom meantime, please offer my friendliest, truest regards.

## LXI

### A. BRONSON ALCOTT, Concord, Massachusetts

To Mr. Alcott. April 26, '68.

Your kind and welcome letter came to hand. Pardon me for not responding sooner. I esteem your friendly appreciation of Democracy. I have just sent you Personalism— which is to be followed, in perhaps a couple of months or so, by another article addressing itself mainly to the question of what kind of Literature we must seek for our coming America, &c. In the three articles (to be gathered probably in a book) I put forth, to germinate if they may, what I would fain hope might prove little seeds and roots.

I am still living here in Washington, employed in a post in the Attorney General's office, very pleasantly, with sufficient leisure, and almost entirely without those peculiar belongings that make the Treasury Interior Dep't &c. clerkships disagreeable. I am, as ever, working on *Leaves of Grass*— hoping to bring it yet into fitter and fuller proportions. I am well as usual. My dear mother is living and well; we speak of you. I wish you to give my best respects and love to Mr. Emerson.

## LXII

### MRS. LOUISA WHITMAN, Brooklyn

Attorney General's Office, Tuesday afternoon, Washington, April 28, 1868.

Dearest Mother, I have received your letter of Saturday 25th this morning,—& glad to hear from you indeed—I suppose by this time you have rec'd the letter I sent yesterday 27th—I sent you the *Galaxy*, but I see by your letter that George had already bought one. I have seen the piece in Thursday's *Times*,—John Swinton sent me one—so you can enclose it to Jeff—I have just received a letter from England, enclosing other notices—&c.—Mr. Conway is very friendly—but my friend Col. Hinton, (in his letter some weeks ago in the *Rochester Express*,) has given him, Conway, some pretty sharp cuts about his ridiculous anecdotes of me & of you too —Still Conway seems to mean all the good he can.—But such descriptions of me as, "he was never known to smile or laugh" is altogether too jolly—Don't you think so?——

*Thursday evening* 8 *o'clock*. Well mother I will again write a few lines—I have been out most all the afternoon—went up first to the Impeachment Trial, & heard Mr. Evarts speak a while, & then left, for it seemed too pleasant outdoors to stay in there—I took a long walk, & ride in the cars away out in the suburbs, & so back to dinner, & now this evening another walk—& have fetched in here at the office to sit awhile, read the papers &c.—I received to-day another letter from old Mr. Alcott—I sent him the *Galaxy* with "Personalism"— and he compliments me highly & speaks of Mr. Emerson too and his friendliness to me—We have had a warm but very pleasant day—I am feeling very well—I only hope, dear mother, you are feeling well & in good spirits.

*Friday evening, May* 1.

Mother your letter of Wednesday, 29th, came this fore-noon—it was too bad you did n't get mine Tuesday, as I put it in the P. O. myself Monday—So you are not going to move at present—I too remain in the same place, but have been going to move all winter & the spring too—I have been in the office all day to-day—all the rest of the clerks wanted to go up to the Impeachment trial, but I didn't care to go.

I have received another paper from England to-day, with a tremendous big favorable notice of my book, between three and four columns—one of the friendliest notices yet written. The English publisher of my book, Mr. Hotten, sends them to me——

*Saturday, noon*—I am going off for the afternoon—Mr. Stanbery is to speak on the trial, & I may go in & hear him a few minutes, but I guess I shall spend my half-holiday mostly in jaunting around in the open air. Every thing begins to look like summer here—the trees are all green—we are having it pretty warm to-day, but a little hazy—it is now 12 o'clock, the noon bell has just rung & I am off for the rest of the day—Take good care of yourself, dear mother——

*Sunday afternoon* Mother you see I am determined to make you out a letter—I have been sitting here in the office all alone, fixing up my new piece for the *Galaxy*—for I have still another piece besides those that have already appeared— Two have appeared, & now this is the third one, addressed to the literary classes—I want the *Galaxy* folks to print it in the July number—but they havn't sent me word yet whether they will or no.—It is a pleasant day—we have had quite a rain storm yesterday afternoon & last night—I am going out at 6 o'clock to O'Connor's to tea—Mother I hope you are having a pleasant Sunday.

*Monday forenoon, May* 4. Well, I had a quiet, agreeable sort of Sunday,—wrote & read most of the forenoon, & rambled out in the afternoon—& went up to O'Connor's in the evening—he had two or three others there, visitors— O'Connors & Burroughs are very hospitable to me, the same as they always have been—they are almost the only places I go—I send you a couple of papers same mail with this—I am going to send the MS of my piece to the *Galaxy* to-day, as I have just rec'd a note from them by mail this morning—I suppose George is well, & busy—I should like to see you all. Love to you dearest mother—I will write again next Monday.

Walt.

## LXIII

### W. C. AND F. P. CHURCH, New York

April 30, 1868.

To W. C. & F. P. Church.

I have now just ready an article intended as the third and concluding one to the two already published by you on Democracy and Personalism. This is upon the general subject of a needed American literature in the highest sense, and of our imaginative mental &c growths, home-born, appropriate to and towering high enough for The States, and in the interests of their democratic institutions. I have, of course, treated the subject in my own way,—certain parts strong and earnest,—but there is nothing in it to make the piece at all improper for the magazine—probably indeed may be found more appropriate and serviceable, and more to rouse editorial and critical attention, &c., than the already published articles. I propose to you to print it in The *Galaxy* for July. It will make from eleven to twelve pages in the new form and type. The name is "Orbic Literature". The price will be the same as for each of the previous articles, $100. I reserve the right of printing it in [a] future book. I can send it on immediately. I think it will be best to not delay too long as the interest in the thing is now up, something like a serial story. This is the conclusion and I should like to have it in the July number.

## LXIV

### CHARLES HINE

Washington, May 9, '68.

My dear Charles Hine: I received with gladness the authentic sign and proof that you are on hand and doing,—viz. Watson's *Art Journal* with notice &c—I am anxious to see the picture. I am sure it must be a thing of beauty, glowing, human and true. Believe me, my friend, I have not forgotten you nor your old kindness and friendliness. Also Mrs. Hine and the daughter—to whom I send best remembrances.

As soon as I come to New York again I will visit you at the studio. In the meantime, I send you by same mail as this a copy of my last edition, also a little book, written by Mr. Burroughs, (a second Thoreau,)—and a newspaper, with letter—the book and letter all about my precious self,—and I dare say may interest you. If the books are not brought by the carrier, you must send to p.o. for them. I have seen Faris here, but now he has gone back to N.Y. I am working in the Attorney General's office—have a pleasant berth, moderate pay, but sufficient. I am well, weigh nearly 200, and eat my rations every time. You must write and let me know whether the books come safe.

## LXV

## MRS. ABBY H. PRICE, Brooklyn

Attorney General's Office
Washington, Monday, Sept. 14, 1868

Dear Abby,

I shall come on in the train that leaves here in the middle of the day, to-morrow Tuesday, 15th, & gets in New York at 10 at night—so I shall be up there by or before 11 to-morrow night—(*to-night* for you reading this).

I am really pleased that you can accomodate me & make great reckoning of being with you, & of my room, &c—but wish to have it distinctly understood, in all friendship, that I *pay* for *my room*, &, just the same as anybody else—*positively* I will not come on any other terms—& you must let it be as I say this time—I have lots of money—in fact *untold wealth*—& I shall not feel right if you undertake to alter this part of my programme—I am feeling well & hearty—I wish you to read my piece in the *Broadway London Magazine*, just out—it was written for you among the rest—In a few hours I shall be with you.

Walt

## LXVI

## PETER DOYLE, Washington

Oct. 6, 1868.

Dear Pete. There is nothing special with me to write to you about. The time slips away mighty quick. It seems but a day or two since I left Washington yet am now on the fourth week of my furlough. Last night was about the greatest political show I ever saw even in New York—a grand Democratic meeting and torch light processions. I was out in the midst of them, to see the sights. I always enjoy seeing the City let loose and on the rampage as it was last night to the fullest extent. I cannot begin to tell you how the Democrats showed themselves by thousands and tens of thousands. The whole City was lit up with torches. Cannons were fired all night in various parts of the City. As I was on my way home in a 2nd Avenue car between 12 and 1 o'clock we got blocked in by a great part of the returning procession. Of course we had to just stand and take it. I enjoyed it hugely from the front platform. They were nearly an hour passing us, streaming both sides. In the procession were all sorts of objects, models of ships forty or fifty feet long, full manned, cars of liberty with women, etc., etc. The ranks spread across the street, and everybody carried a blazing torch. Fireworks were going off in every direction. The sky was full of big balloons letting off rockets and Roman candles 'way up among the stars. The excitement, the rush, and the endless torches gave me great pleasure. Ever and anon the cannon, some near some distant. I heard them long after I got to bed. It sounded like a distant engagement. I send you the *Herald* with a sort of account of the show, but it doesn't do half justice to it—The speeches were of no account at all.

I suppose you got a letter and paper from me Saturday, Oct. 3rd. I received your welcome letter of Oct. 1st, also the *Star*. I read Mr. Noyes' western letters with pleasure. So you have something new in R. R.—new offices and rules. The R. R. business here is very different. They go through these long routes on the rush—no mercy to the cattle. The 3rd Avenue R. R. lost 36 horses in one day last summer, one of those hot days. We are having pleasant weather just now, seems like Indian summer. So long, dear Pete. From your loving comrade,

Walt.

## LXVII

### PETER DOYLE, Washington

Providence, R. I.,
Oct. 17, 1868.

Dear Pete. According to announcement in my last I have made a movement and change of base from tumultuous, close-packed, world-like New York to this half-rural, brisk, handsome, New England, third-class town. I came on here last Thursday. I came as guest of Thomas Davis, formerly M.C. from this City—Arrived between 8 and 9 o'clock at night—found his carriage at the depot waiting for me. At the house—a sort of castle built of stone, on fine grounds, a mile and a half from the town—a hearty welcome from his hospitable wife and a family of young ladies and children—a hot supper—a tip top room, etc., etc.,—so you see, Pete, your old man is in clover. I have since been round the City and suburbs considerably. I am going down to Newport before I return—Invitations, etc., are numerous—I am, in fact, already dividing myself between two hospitalities, part of the time with Mr. and Mrs. Davis and part with Dr. and Mrs. Channing, old acquaintances of mine in another part of the City. I stopt last night at the house of the latter. It is on a high and pleasant hill at the side of the City which it entirely overlooks. From the window of my room I can look down across the city, the river, and off miles upon miles in the distance. The woods are a real spectacle, colored with all the rich colors of autumn. Yesterday it was beautiful and balmy beyond description, like the finest Indian summer. I wandered around, partly walking, partly in a carriage, a good part of the day. To-day there is an entire change of scene. As I am writing this, what do you think, Pete? great flakes of snow are falling—quite a thick flurry—sometimes the wind blows in gusts—in fact a real snow storm has been going on all the forenoon, though without the look or feeling of winter as the grass and foliage are autumnal and the cold is not severe yet. Still it [is] disagreeable and wet and dark and prevents me from going out. So I will make up by writing a couple of letters, one to mother and one to you, telling you about things. Providence is a handsome city of about 70,000 inhabitants, has numerous manufactories in full operation—everything looks lively. From the house up here I can hear almost any time, night or day, the sound of factory bells and the steam whistles of locomotives half a mile distant. Then the lights at night seen from here make a curious exhibition. At both places I stop we have plenty of ripe fresh fruit and lots of flowers. Pete, I could now send you a boquet every morning far better than I used to—of much choicer flowers. And how are you getting along, dearest comrade? I hope you are well and that everything is going on right with you. I have not heard from you for a good while, it seems. I suppose you got my last letter of 14th, from N.Y. I expect to return to N.Y. about the 22nd. Should you feel to write after receiving this you might direct to 331 East 55th Street as before. I am well as usual. I am luxuriating on excellent grapes. I wish I could send you a basket. At both places I stop they have vineyards and the grapes are very good and plenty this year. Last night when I went up at 11 o'clock to my room I took up three great bunches each as big as my fist and sat down and eat them before I turned in. I like to eat them in this way and it agrees with me. It is quite a change here from my associations and surroundings either in Washington or New York. Evenings and meal times I find myself thrown amidst a mild, pleasant society, really intellectual, composed largely of educated women, some young, some not so young, everything refined and polite, *not* disposed to small talk, conversing in earnest on profound subjects, but with a moderate rather slow tone and in a kind of conciliatory manner—delighting in this sort of conversation and spending their evenings till late, in it. I take a hand in, for a change. I find it entertaining, as I say, for novelty's sake, for a week or two—but I know very well that would be enough for me. It is all first rate, good and smart but too constrained and bookish for a free old hawk like me. I send you my love, dear Pete. *So long*. Will write from N.Y. soon as I return there. *P.S.* Just after 12 o'clock noon. As I am just finishing the storm lightens up—I am sure I see a bit of blue sky in the clouds—yes, the sun is certainly breaking out.

## LXVIII

### RALPH WALDO EMERSON, Concord, Massachusetts

Washington, Nov. 30, '68
sent Dec. 2.

Dear Mr. Emerson: On the eve of sending the enclosed piece abroad I have taken a notion to first offer it to the *Atlantic* and, if not too great a liberty, to solicit your services for that purpose. I would be obliged if you would take it in to Mr. Fields the first time you go to Boston. If available at all, I propose it for the February number of the magazine. The price is one hundred dollars; and thirty copies of the number in which it may be printed. Of course Mr. F. may read this letter.

I shall require an answer from Mr. Fields within a week from the time of the reception of the piece.

I scrupulously reserve the right to print the piece in the future in my book.

## LXIX

### DR. THAYER, Burlington, Vermont

December 8, 1868.

Dr. Thayer,

Dear Sir: Won't you do me the very great favor to write me a few lines regarding the condition of my sister, Mrs. H. L. Heyde. I am sure, from what I hear, that it is mainly to your medical skill, and your kindness as a good man, that she got through her late illness. She seems by her letters to be left in an extremely nervous state. Doctor, please write me as fully as you think proper. Though we have never met personally, I have heard of you from my mother and sister. I must ask you to keep this letter, and the whole matter, strictly confidential, and mention it to no person. My sister in a late letter wished me to write you and thank you for your great kindness to her.

## LXX

### JOHN MORLEY, London

[Washington, D. C.]
Dec. 17, '68.

John Morley.

Dear Sir: I send you an original piece of mine, in hopes it will be found available for say the March Number of your Magazine. The price is four pounds—twenty dollars—in gold—and four copies of the number in which it is printed, sent me by mail.

Please send me an answer, with decision, by next or succeeding mail.

My address is to Attorney General's Office, this city.

## LXXI

## JAMES T. FIELDS

Washington,
Jan. 20, 1869

James T. Fields,

Dear Sir: The package of February Magazines sent on the 16th arrived safely yesterday. Accept my thanks. I am pleased with the typographical appearance and correctness of my piece.

I enclose a piece, Thou vast Rondure swimming in Space, of which I have to say to you as follows. It is to appear in the April number of the *London Fortnightly Review*. Having just received a note from the editor of that *Review*, Mr. Morley, in which he intimates that he has no objection to its appearing simultaneously in America, I thought I would show it to you. Very possibly you will not care to print a piece any how which is to appear elsewhere. Should that, however, be no objection, and should you consider the piece available for your purposes, the price is $20. Of course it would have to go in your number of April. I reserve the right of printing in future book.

## LXXII

## MRS. LOUISA WHITMAN

Saturday forenoon.
Feb. 6th [1869]

Mother, your letter has just come this forenoon—you must not worry about Han—one can't tell any thing about it—but it is probable things go on with them just as they always did —I believe I shall write to Han again—shall not say any thing about Heyde, of course——

—We have had a cold snap here—but this forenoon it is very pleasant, bright, & comfortable enough—I did not have any bad spells in the head yesterday—nor, so far, to-day— My cold in the head has been extremely bad & is not well yet——. Went up to Ashton's Thursday even'g to spend the even'g with some company—had supper about 9 o'clock.

*Wednesday afternoon.—*

It commenced snowing yesterday noon, & stormed all day, & a rain at night—I have been out to-day—not any work hardly in the office—still I have to be around—it is a dark & muddy day here—a young man has just been in with a photograph of me,—his mother had bought it at a place here, & sent it to me for me to write my name—I gratified him— They have taken a very good little photo of me here lately— I will send you one before long—It is now three o'clock, & the colored man has commenced to clean up—so I will vamose——

—Great excitement here among the politicians—Cant tell who will be the new Attorney General under Grant— but don't think Mr. Evart will continue on—still I don't know——

## LXXIII

### PETER DOYLE, Washington

Brooklyn, N.Y.,
Saturday evening, Aug. 21 [1869].

Dear Pete. I have been very sick the last three days—I don't know what to call it—it makes me prostrated and deadly weak, and little use of my limbs. I have thought of you, my darling boy, very much of the time. I have not been out of the house since the first day after my arrival. I had a pleasant journey through on the cars Wednesday afternoon and night —felt quite well then. My mother and folks are all well. We are in our new house—we occupy part and rent out part. I have a nice room, where I now sit writing this. It is the latter part of the afternoon. I feel better the last hour or so. It has been extremely hot here the last two days—I see it has been so in Washington too. I hope I shall get out soon—I hanker to get out doors, and down the bay. And now dear Pete for yourself. How is it with you, dearest boy—and is there any- thing different with the face? Dear Pete, you must forgive me for being so cold the last day and evening. I was unspeakably shocked and repelled from you by that talk and proposition of yours—you know what—there by the fountain. It seemed indeed to me, (for I will talk out plain to you, dearest comrade) that the one I loved, and who had always been so manly and sensible, was gone, and a fool and intentional suicide stood in his place. I spoke so sternly and cutting. (Though I see now that my words might have appeared to have a certain other meaning, which I didn't dream of—insulting to you, never for one moment in my thoughts.) But will say no more of this—for I know such thoughts must have come when you was not yourself but in a moment of derangement,—and have passed away like a bad dream. Dearest boy I have not a doubt but you will get well and entirely well—and we will one day look back on these drawbacks and sufferings as things long past. The extreme cases of that malady, (as I told you before) are persons that have very deeply diseased blood so they have no foundation to build on—you are of healthy stock, with a sound constitution and good blood—and I know it is impossible for it to continue long. My darling, if you are not well when I come back I will get a good room or two in some quiet place, and we will live together and devote ourselves altogether to the job of curing you, and making you stronger and healthier than ever. I have had this in my mind before but never broached it to you. I could go on with my work in the Attorney General's office just the same—and we should see that your mother should have a small sum every week to keep the pot a-boiling at home. Dear comrade, I think of you very often. My love for you is indestructible, and since that night and morning has returned more than before. Dear Pete, dear son, my darling boy, my young and loving brother, don't let the devil put such thoughts in your mind again—wickedness unspeakable—death and disgrace here, and hell's agonies hereafter—Then what would it be afterward to the mother? What to *me*?—Pete, I send you some money by Adams' Express—you use it, dearest son, and when it is gone you shall have some more, for I have plenty. I will write again before long—give my love to Johnny Lee, my dear darling boy. I love him truly—(let him read these three last lines)—Dear Pete, *remember*——

                                        Walt.

## LXXIV

### WILLIAM O'CONNOR, Washington

Washington, Sept. 28, 1869.

Dear William O'Connor: As you were interested in Mr. Parton's money-borrowing item about me, I enclose you the receipts signed and given me by his attorney at the time, (June 1857)—The sum borrowed by me of Mr. Parton was Two hundred dollars. He had, just before, kindly volunteered the loan himself, without the least request or hint from me. I then declined, but afterward borrowed the money, and gave a short-time Note. I felt soon and feel now, that it was a great impropriety on my part, and it has caused me much compunction and real unhappiness since. Anyhow when the time for paying the note came, I had no money. Mr. Parton then put the matter in the hands of his Attorney, Mr. Oliver Dyer, who sued. My recollection is that I confessed judgment, and proposed to Mr. Dyer that he should receive payment in goods. He came by appointment to my room in Classen avenue, Brooklyn, June 17, 1857, talked over the matter, behaved very kindly,—positively accepted there and then, and conveyed away, goods to the amount of One hundred and eighty one dollars, and receipted for them, on account. He also, for the balance, conditionally accepted other goods, (which he also conveyed away with him,) on the agreement between us that if they, when more deliberately examined, proved acceptable, they would requite the balance, and the debt would be considered paid;—otherwise they would be returned, and the balance would still stand against me. These goods he retained, and subsequently told me that they had proved acceptable, and consented to give me a receipt in full, and satisfaction paper—but, (I think), said the latter would require the signature of Mr. Parton. This was a meeting either in the street, or on the Brooklyn ferry. On meeting him afterwards in a similar way, once or twice, I mentioned the matter of a receipt in full, but never pressed it —never procured such receipt, nor the original note either.

I consider the debt *paid*—(though if I had wealth, to-day, I should certainly pay it over again, in cash.) Among the goods rendered I remember an oil painting, an original of marked beauty and value, by Jesse Talbot, illustrating a scene from *Pilgrim's Progress*, worth from four to five hundred dollars. This I put, if I remember right, at one hundred dollars. I presume Mr. Dyer or Mr. Parton has it yet.

The enclosed receipt marked 1, was, on turning over the goods, written by me and signed by Mr. Dyer, who then re-marked that he would also give me one in more technical form, and wrote, signed, and handed me the receipt marked 2. I presume (but do not know for certain) that Mr. Dyer considers the debt fully paid.

(The balance of thirty-five dollars mentioned, besides the one hundred and eighty one, includes sixteen dollars as Mr. Dyer's fee, or more probably costs of suit, over and above the original two hundred.)
                                                    Walt Whitman.

## LXXV

## WILLIAM MICHAEL ROSSETTI

Washington December 9, 1869.

Dear Mr. Rossetti. Your letter of last summer to William O'Connor with the passages transcribed from a lady's cor-respondence, has been shown me by him, and copy lately furnished me, which I have just been rereading. I am deeply touched by these sympathies and convictions, coming from a woman and from England, and am sure that if the lady knew how much comfort it has been to me to get them, she would not only pardon you for transmitting them to Mr. O'Connor but approve that action. I realize indeed of this emphatic and smiling *well done* from the heart and conscience of a true wife and mother, and one too whose sense of the poetic, as I glean from your letter, after flowing through the heart and conscience, must also move through and satisfy science as much as the esthetic, that I had hitherto received no eulo-gium so magnificent.

I send by same mail with this, same address as this letter, two photographs, taken within a few months. One is inten-ded for the lady (if I may be permitted to send it her)—and will you please accept the other, with my respects and love?

The picture is by some criticised very severely indeed, but I hope you will not dislike it, for I confess to myself a perhaps capricious fondness for it, as my own portrait, over some scores that have been made or taken at one time or another.

I am still employed in the Attorney General's office. My p.o. address remains the same. I am quite well and hearty. My new editions, considerably expanded, with what suggestions &c I have to offer, presented I hope in more definite form, will probably get printed the coming spring. I shall forward you early copies. I send my love to Moncure Conway, if you see him. I wish he would write to me. If the pictures don't come, or get injured on the way, I will try again by express. I want you to loan this letter to the lady, or, if she wishes it, give it to her to keep.

## LXXVI

### BENTON WILSON

April 15, 1870.

Dear Benton Wilson.

Dear loving comrade, As I have just been again reading your last letter to me of December 19, last. I think I wrote to you on receiving it, but cannot now remember for certain. Sometimes, after an interval, the thought of one I much love comes upon me strong and full all of a sudden—and now as I sit here by a big open window, this beautiful afternoon, every thing quiet and sunny—I have been and am now, thinking so of you, dear young man, and of your love, or more rightly speaking, our love for each other—so curious, so sweet, I say so *religious*—We met there in the Hospital—how little we have been together—seems to me we ought to be some together every day of our lives—I don't care about talking, or amusement—but just to be together, and work together, or go off in the open air together—Now it is a long while since we have been together—and it seems a long while since I have had a letter. Don't blame me for not writing oftener. I know you would feel satisfied if you could only realize how and how much I am thinking of you, and with what great love, this afternoon. I can hardly express it in a letter—but I thought I would just write a letter this time off-hand to you, dearest soldier, only for love to you—I thought it might please you.

Nothing very new or different in my affairs. I am still working here in Atty Gens office—same posish—have good health—expect to bring out new editions of my books before long—how is the little boy—I send my love to him and to your wife and parents.

## LXXVII

### THOMAS DIXON, Sunderland

June 30, '70.

I must render you thanks for the box of books, as they have at last reached me in good condition. The delay in their arrival is unaccountable. But they are welcome, and will all be read in due time, with sincere gratitude to the donor.

Both your letters also reached me, and were cordially welcomed. I should have acknowledged them at date, only that for many weeks I have been disabled from writing and from my clerical work by reason of a wound in the right hand, which is now better.

There is nothing new or noteworthy in my own affairs. I still remain in the Attorney General's office here—still enjoying good health. I keep freshening and shaping my books at my leisure, and hope to put them in type the coming year.

You speak of my prose preface to first *Leaves of Grass*. I am unable to send it you having not a copy left. It was written hastily while the first edition was being printed in 1855—I do not consider it of permanent value. I shall send you (probably in the mail that follows this—certainly very soon,) a piece written some while since by me on Democracy—in which Mr. Carlyle's "shooting Niagara" is alluded to. I shall also send an article by an English lady, put in print here, that may interest you.

I am writing this at my desk in the Treasury building here, an immense pile, in which our office occupies rooms. From my large open window I have an extensive view of sky, Potomac river, hills and fields of Virginia many many miles. We are having a spell of that oppressive heat which so much falls upon us here.

## LXXVIII

### PETER DOYLE, Washington

Brooklyn, Wednesday night, Aug. 3, [1870].

Dear Pete. Dear son, I received your second letter to-day—also the *Star*. I sent you a letter Tuesday evening, which I suppose you have received. As I am now sitting in my room and have no desire to go to bed yet, I will commence another. Give my best respects to George Smith—also to Pensey Bell and his brother George—also to Mr. Shedd—and in fact to all my railroad friends whenever they enquire after me— Dear son, I can almost see you drowsing and nodding since last Sunday, going home late—especially as we wait there at 7th St. and I am telling you something deep about the heavenly bodies—and in the midst of it I look around and find you fast asleep, and your head on my shoulder like a chunk of wood—an awful compliment to my lecturing powers. All the talk here now is either the war on the Rhine, or the murder of old Mr. Nathan, or some other murder—for there are plenty of them—I send you a couple of papers with pieces about them. Say whether they come safe. I believe that is all for to-night, as it is getting late. Good night, Pete—Good night, my darling son—here is a kiss for you, dear boy—on the paper here—a good long one. *Thursday—4th*—I have been out all the forenoon and until about 2 o'clock—had some business in New York, which I attended, then came back and spent an hour and a half on the river, with one of the pilots, a particular friend of mine—saw the yachts, several of them, including the *America*, out practising for the great race that comes off Monday—the *Dauntless* was out yesterday—and the *Cambria* went down three days ago—the *America* is the handsomest little craft I ever laid eyes on—I also saw Henry Ward Beecher and had some talk with him—I find myself going with the pilots muchly—there are several that were little boys, now grown up, and remember me well—fine hearty fellows—always around the water—sons of old pilots —they make much of me, and of course I am willing. 10 *o'clock at night*—As this is lying here on my table to be sent off to-morrow, I will imagine you with your arm around my

neck saying Good night, Walt—and me—Good night, Pete.
—*Friday morning*, *Aug*. 5.—All well—fine weather and I feel
in good spirits. I am just going out and across to New York.
We had a heavy shower here yesterday afternoon 4th, the
weather is not too hot here.                    Walt.


## LXXIX

### PETER DOYLE, Washington

Brooklyn, August 12, [1870].

Dear Son. Yours of yesterday 11th, has just this minute
come, and I wish to write a few lines so that you may get
them before Sunday. I have not time to write much, as it is
now about 5 P.M. Dear son, I hope you will not feel discouraged at the situation, even if it comes to the worst. It is
now thought that business generally throughout the country
is ready to revive as soon as the hot season is done, and that
everything will be brisker this fall than any time since the
war. Dear Pete, whatever happens, in such ups and downs,
you must try to meet it with a stout heart. As long as the
Almighty vouchsafes you health, strength, and a clear conscience, let other things do their worst,—and let Riker go
to hell. You are better off to-day to be what you are than to
be him with his $10,000 a year—poor thin-livered cuss that
he is.—My darling son, I will send you $5 every Saturday,
should you be idle—as I can easily spare that, and you can
depend upon it—it won't go far, but it may take the edge off.
Many, many loving kisses to you, dear son—for I must close,
or I shall lose to-night's mail.                    Walt.


## LXXX

### PETER DOYLE, Washington

Brooklyn, September 2, 1870

Dear Pete.

I received your welcome letter of Aug. 27th and also 31st,
enclosing Ned Stewart's—when you write tell Ned I am here

in Brooklyn, loafing around—and that I send my love. Pete, there is nothing particular to write about this time—pretty much the same story—every day out on the bay awhile, or going down to Coney Island beach—and every day from two to four or five hours in the printing office—I still keep well and hearty, and the weather is fine—warm through the middle of the day, and cool morning and nights—I fall in with a good many of my acquaintances of years ago—the young fellows, (now not so young)—that I knew intimately here before the war—some are dead—and some have got married—and some have grown rich—one of the latter I was up with yesterday and last night—he has a big house on Fifth Avenue I was there to—dinner (dinner at 8 P.M.!)—everything in the loudest sort of style, with wines, silver, nigger waiters, etc. etc. etc. But my friend is just one of the manliest, jovialest, best sort of fellows—no airs, and just the one to suit you and me,—no women in the house—he is single—he wants me to make my home there—I shall not do that, but shall go there very frequently—the dinners and good wines are attractive—then there is a fine library. Well Pete, I am on the second month of my furlough—to think it is almost six weeks since we parted there that night—my dear loving boy, how much I want to see you—it seems a long while. I have received a good letter from Mr. O'Connor, and also one from John Rowland who is in the office for me. Nothing new in office—Well, Pete, about half of our separation is over—the next six weeks will soon pass away—indeed it may be only four, as John Rowland told me he might wish to go away—Good-bye for the present, my loving son, and give my respects to any of the boys that ask about me.

Walt.

## LXXXI

PETER DOYLE, Washington

Brooklyn, September 6th, 1870.

Dear Son.

I see by your letter of the 4th, that you are working as usual. I sometimes fancy I see you—and 14—and Mr. Shedd

going up or down the avenue—or at the end at Georgetown
—or Navy Yard—the old familiar route and scenes—the
circle, the President's House—Willards'—7th Street—Capitol Gate—the Hill, etc. etc. etc. I keep pretty busy, writing,
proof-reading, etc. I am at the printing office several hours
every day—I feel in capital health and spirits—weigh several
pounds heavier—but, as a small drawback, and something
new for me, find myself needing glasses every time I read or
write—this has grown upon me very rapidly since and during
the hot weather, and especially since I left Washington—so I
read and write as little as possible, beyond my printing matters, etc.—as that occupies several hours and tires my eyes
sometimes. We are having splendid fall weather, both days
and nights. Last night I was out late—the scene on the river
was heavenly—the sky clear, and the moon shining her
brightest—I felt almost chilly at last with the cold—and so
put for home. One of the prettiest sights now is to see the
great German steamers, and other ships, as they lay tied up
along the shore, all covered with gay flags and streamers—
"dress ship" as they call it—flaunting out in the breeze,
under a brilliant sky and sun—all in honor, of course, of the
victory of the German Armies—all the spars and rigging are
hid with hundreds and hundreds of flags—a big red, white
and black flag capping all. Of course you may know that the
way the war turns out suits me to death—Louis Napoleon
fully deserves his fate—I consider him by far the meanest
scoundrel (with all his smartness) that ever sat on a throne. I
make a distinction, however, I admire and love the French,
and France as a nation—of all foreign nations, she has my
sympathy first of all. Pete, I was just reading over your last
letter again. Dear son, you must try to keep up a good heart.
You say you do—but I am afraid you are feeling, (or have
felt,) somewhat unhappy. One soon falls into the habit of
getting low spirited or deprest and moody—if a man allows
himself, he will always find plenty to make him so—Everyone
has [his] trouble, disappointments, rebuffs, etc. especially
every young and proud-spirited man who has to work for his
living. But I want you to try and put a brave face against
everything that happens—for it is not so much the little misfortunes of life themselves, as the way we take them and

brood over them, that causes the trouble. About the "tiresome" all I have to say is—to say nothing—only a good smacking kiss and many of them—and taking in return many, many, many, from my dear son—good loving ones too— which will do more credit to his lips than growling and complaining at his father.

Walt.

## LXXXII

## JOHN BURROUGHS

107 north Portland av.
Brooklyn, N.Y. March 15, '71.

Dear John Burroughs:

We have had cold & spiteful weather all the time of my visit here—over a month—& I have not had my usual outdoor enjoyment, loafing about &c—have been indoors most of the time—I also caught cold just on coming here, & it has bothered ever since. How are you dear friend? & how is 'Sula—dear friend, too—— —Write me a few lines, John— let me know how Chauncey is getting along—if he finds any difficulty—but I guess not---I guess he is getting along well— Is there any thing new among my friends in Wash'n there?—I have got out my new edition, from same plates as the last, only all bound in One Vol.—neatly done in green cloth, vellum—looks the best & most ship-shape of any edition yet —have not added any of my later pieces in this,—leaving them to some future issue——

—Rec'd a letter from Mrs. Gilchrist in England—she has been read'g "Wake Robin" & takes to it greatly—says Rossetti dined at her house not long since—(you know she is the authoress of the "Woman's Estimate", in the *Radical*)——

John, I think it likely I shall return about the 1st of April— Mother has had a bad spell for three days, but is about as usual again, yesterday & to-day—Direct to me here—love to all.

Walt.

## LXXXIII

## WILLIAM D. O'CONNOR

Brooklyn,
107 North Portland Av.
July 14, 1871

Dear friend,

There is nothing special to write about, yet I will send you a line. I wrote to Nelly between two & three weeks ago—with a line to you and Charles Eldridge—which I suppose came all right at the time. I have been having a comfortable time, absolutely doing nothing, sleeping a good deal, eating & drinking what suits me, and going out a few hours a day, a good part of the time on the water. Mother has had an attack of illness, somewhat severe the last few days—& I have been sort of nurse and doctor—(as none of my sisters are home at present)—result is that Mother is very much better this morning——

John Burroughs has called on me—looking well. I must tell you that the *Westminster* for July has for the 2d article of the number a long article of 33 or 4 pages, headed "*The Poetry of Democracy: Walt Whitman*" and capped with the names of the three last issued books—rather quiet in tone, but essentially very favorable & appreciative—undertakes to define the character of Democratic art & poetic literature, as discriminated from Aristocratic—quotes freely from all my books—will please you, I think.

Wednesday's brush in N.Y. you have seen in the papers—in five sixths of the city, it was curiously almost unfelt, every thing went on the same—30 or 40 killed and a hundred wounded—yet it falls very languidly on our people—we have supped full of horrors of late years—the *policemen* looked & behaved splendidly. I have been looking on them & been with them much, & am refreshed by their presence—it is something new—in some respects they afford the most encouraging sign I have got—brown, bearded, worn, resolute, American-looking men, dusty & sweaty—looked like veterans—the stock here even in these cities is in the main magnificent—the heads either shysters, villains or impotents

—Love to Nelly, Charles Eldridge & Jeannie.

**Walt.**

## LXXXIV

### PETER DOYLE

[Sunday, 16 July, 1871.]
By the sea-shore, Coney Island,
Sunday 3 p.m.

Dear Pete.

I will write you a few lines as I sit here, on a clump of sand by the sea shore—having some paper in my haversack, and an hour or two yet before I start back. Pete, I wish you were with me the few hours past—I have just had a splendid swim and souse in the surf—the waves are slowly rolling in, with hoarse roar that is music to my ears—the breeze blows pretty brisk from southwest, and the sun is partially clouded—from where I sit I look out on the bay and down the Narrows, vessels sailing in every direction in the distance—a great big black long ocean steamship streaking it up toward New York —and the lines of hills and mountains, far, far away on the Jersey coast, a little veiled with blue vapor—here around me, as I sit is nothing but barren sand—but I don't know how long I could sit here, to that soothing, rumbling murmuring of the waves—and then the salt breeze. Friday, July [21]. Dear Son. I wrote the preceding nearly a week ago, intending to finish and send it then—Nothing very new or special with me—Mother has been quite unwell, gets better, then worse again—I have applied for a few days' further leave— The weather here remains nearly perfect—we have had but three or four uncomfortably hot days the past five weeks— every day a fine breeze smelling of the sea. Pete, if you are still working, and all is going on smooth, you can send me that $50.—you might get Mr. Milburn to send it to me by Post Office Order—give it to him with this envelope, and ask him to go to P.O. and send a P.O. Order to me—it will save you the trouble—But Pete, dear boy, if anything has turned up in meantime, you needn't send it, as I can get along otherwise—I am doing well, both in health and *business prospects* here—my book is doing first rate—so everything is lovely and the goose hangs high—Your loving comrade and father.

Walt.

## LXXXV

## GEORGE PEYTON, CHAS. E. BURD AND JAMES B. YOUNG, New York

Department of Justice,
Washington, Aug. 5, 1871.

Messrs. George Peyton, Chas. E. Burd and James B. Young, *Committee on Invitations*. [American Institute]

Dear Sirs: I have received your letter of 1st instant containing your invitation to deliver an appropriate original poem at the opening of the 40th Annual Exhibition of the American Institute, Sept. 7, and stating terms, &c. I accept with pleasure, and shall be ready without fail to deliver the poem at the time specified.

Address me here if anything further.

## LXXXVI

## F. S. ELLIS, 33 King st, Covent Garden, London

Sent By Steamer, Aug. 12 '71.

I take the liberty of writing at a venture to propose to you the publication, in a moderate-priced volume, of a full edition of my poems, *Leaves of Grass*, in England under my sanction. I send by same mail as this, a revised copy of *L. of G*. I should like a fair remuneration or percentage.

I make this proposition not only to get my poems before the British public, but more because I am annoyed at the horrible dismemberment of my book there already and possibility of something worse.

Should my proposal suit you, go right on with the book. Style of setting it up, price, rate of remuneration to me, &c, I leave it entirely to you. Only the text must be sacredly preserved, verbatim.

Please direct to me here as soon as convenient.

## LXXXVII

### EDWARD DOWDEN, Dublin

Washington, Aug. 22, '71.

Dear Mr. Dowden. I have received your kind letter and your review in the *Westminster*, and thank you heartily. I wish to write to you at more length, and may do so before long. I take real comfort in the thought that I have such friends in Ireland including yourself. I wish to hear more of Mr. Tyrrell, whom you speak of.

## LXXXVIII

### ANNE GILCHRIST, Earl's Colne, Halstead, Essex

Washington City, U.S.
November 3, 1871.

Dear friend,

I have been waiting quite a long while for time & the right mood to answer your letter in a spirit as serious as its own, & in the same unmitigated trust & affection. But more daily work than ever has fallen upon me to do the current season, & though I am well & contented, my best moods seem to shun me. I wished to give to it a day, a sort of Sabbath, or holy day apart to itself, under serene & propitious influences —confident that I could then write you a letter which would do you good, & me too. But I must at least show, without further delay, that I am not insensible to your love. I too send you my love. And do you feel no disappointment because I now write but briefly. My book is my best letter, my response, my truest explanation of all. In it I have put my body & spirit. You understand this better & fuller & clearer than any one else. And I too fully & clearly understand the loving & womanly letter it has evoked. Enough that there surely exists between us so beautiful & delicate a relation, accepted by both of us with joy.

Walt Whitman

## LXXXIX

RUDOLF SCHMIDT, Kopenhagen, Denmark

Dec. 7, 1871.

Dear Sir: I have received (through Mr. Clausen) your letter of 19th October from Kopenhagen, and I cheerfully forward you my poems *Leaves of Grass* and a small prose work *Democratic Vistas.* I also enclose several articles and criticisms, written about my book in England and America, within the last ten years. May I say there is something about your letter and application that has deeply pleased me. How I should like to know your country and people—and especially you yourself, and your poet Björnson and Hans Andersen. How proud I should be to become known to you all. Pray let me hear from you, and if the books and papers reach you.

My address is Washington, D.C. United States of America.

## XC

MRS. LOUISA WHITMAN, Brooklyn

Department of Justice
Washington [December] 187[1]

Friday evening—after 6. Mama dear, I believe I must send you a line for Saturday though I have little or nothing to write about—I am sitting here alone in the office, writing by my lamp—I went over to Baltimore last evening for a little trip—saw Mr. Emerson—he lectured there—John Burroughs wanted to go over and hear him—it was not interesting to me at all—but we had a pleasant little jaunt—got back about ½ past 11.

Nothing different in the office—I expect to go over in the Treasury Building, in the office of the Solicitor of the Treasury, as I told you. The new Attorney Gen'l., Mr. Williams, has assigned me there but several important bits of work have had to be done just now, & today & yesterday I have had to do them—(as the old ladies say "I guess they'll miss me a good deal more than they 'spected"—) so I have been held on to here so far.—Mama Dear I met a man who saw Jeff about nine days ago in St. Louis. Good bye for the time. Dear Mother——

Walt

## XCI

### MRS. LOUISA WHITMAN

Department of Justice, *Monday noon*—Jan. 1, 1872.

Well mother dear, New Year has begun—it is the funniest one yet—there is a fog as dark as Egypt, sometimes you cant see a rod before you—it has been so for two days steady—very muddy, & spells of drizzling rain—I am well & hearty—I am just informed that I am to be transferred over to the Treasury Building, into the Solicitor of the Treasurer's office (it is in the Department of Justice—is a branch of it.)—Mr. Williams, the new boss, wishes to bring some friend of his here—I do not know that I shall dislike the change—I can tell better all about it in a week or two—I have applied for a good long leave of absence, to commence about Feb. 1st—I shall probably get it, but without pay, (or with only a small part pay)—I am willing to take a leave without pay—I want to come home for a while, both to be home, & to see about the new edition of my books—I am real well & fat & hearty this winter—but I believe I have got a little set against one thing & another here, (especially the grub,) & I want a change for a couple of months very much——

—Mama dear, I want to hear about your last week—& George & Lou—I sent three letters to you last week, & papers—I knew that policeman Doyle that was shot dead here—he was Pete Doyle's brother—I was at the funeral yesterday—it was in the papers I sent you—Love to you dear mama.

Walt.

I forgot to say Arthur Price is here, on the iron-clad *Mahopac*—the vessel is at the navy-yard—expects to sail soon—I am going down this afternoon to go on board the ship & see him—he is well & hearty.

## XCII

### RUDOLF SCHMIDT, Copenhagen

[Jan. 16 and 20th, 1872.]

Supposing that the books and papers I sent you in response to your letter have safely arrived, I thought I would now write you a few lines. What I have to submit and say I will just say without ceremony—confident you will receive it in the same spirit in which it is written. I sent you (By Mr. Clausen) my poems *Leaves of Grass*, and little prose work *Democratic Vistas*. Also a piece I recited at the opening of the American Institute in New York; and then several criticisms, sketches &c. about the books and about myself by different persons, from different points of view. These will furnish you with sufficient material for your examination, digest and proposed review.

When you are composing your review, I would like to have you bring in, in the proper place, the following mentioned facts—that neither my book of poems or *Democratic Vistas* is cordially accepted in the United States—nor do any of the chief Literary persons or organs of that country admit *Leaves of Grass* as having (possessing) any value or recognize the author as a poet at all—that he has indeed been ignominiously dismissed from a moderate government employment by special order of a cabinet officer at Washington, for the sole and avowed reason that he was the writer of the book—that, up to this time, no American publisher will publish it (the author having had to print its various editions himself)—that many of the bookstores refuse to keep it for sale—and that the position of the author both as to literary rank and worldly prosperity, in his own country, has been and remains to day under a heavy and depressing cloud.

Of course at the same time you will hardly need to be told that my book is written in the sun, and with a gay heart—for these surely fully belong to me. But I think a good foreign criticism of my works would be more complete by giving these facts above, for they are substantial facts, notwithstanding a very few exceptions, and in truth they are a necessary part of any complete criticism.

Abroad, my book and myself have had a welcome quite dazzling. Tennyson writes me friendly letters. Freiligrath translates and commends me. Robert Buchanan, Swinburne, the great English and Dublin colleges, affectionately receive me and doughtily champion me. And while I, the author, am without any recompense at all in America, the English pirate-publisher, Hotten, draws a handsome annual income from a bad London reprint of my poems.

I wish you to speak of the purpose of *Democratic Vistas*— (It is at present in danger of falling still-born here.)

I should be glad to hear more from you, your magazine, your country too. For all, accept my friendliest good wishes.

Direct, W. W. Solicitor's office, Treasury, Washington, D.C. United States America.

*Later.* Upon reading over my letter, previous to mailing it, I had almost decided not to send it as a part of it may be open to the suspicion of querulousness—yet as nothing can be further from my real state of mind (which is more than satisfied with my literary fortune upon the whole) I will let it go.

## XCIII

### EDWARD DOWDEN

Jan. 20, 1872.

Dear Sir—I must no longer delay writing and to acknowledge your letters of Sept 5 and Oct. 15. I had previously (Aug 22) written you very briefly in response to your friendly letter of July 23d—the first you wrote accompanying copy of the review. All—letters and review—have been read and re-read. I am sure I appreciate them and you in them. May I say you do not seem to be afar off, but stand very near to me. What John Burroughs brings adds confirmation. I was deeply interested in the accounts given me by you of your friends—I do not hesitate to call them mine also—Tyrrell, Cross, your brother, Miss West, Todhunter, O'Grady,—Yeats, Ellis, Nettleship. Affectionate remembrance to all of them. You especially and Mrs. Dowden—and indeed all of you— already I say stand near to me. I wish each to be told what I write—or to see this letter when convenient.

There is one point touched by you in the *Westminster* criticism that if occasion arise should be dwelt on with more stress—and that is defended—stating the attitude of general denial and sneering which magazines, editors, authors, publishers, "critics", &c. in the United States hold towards

*Leaves of Grass* and myself as author of it. As to *Democratic Vistas*, it remains quite unread, uncalled for, here in America.

If you write again for publication about my books, or have opportunity to influence any forthcoming article on them, I think it would be a proper and an even essential part of such article to distinctly include the important facts, (for facts they are,) that *Leaves of Grass* and their author are contemptuously ignored by the recognized literary organs here in the United States, rejected by the publishing houses here, the author turned out of a government clerkship and deprived of his means of support by a Head of Department at Washington solely on account of having written the book.

I say I think the statement of these things proper and even indispensible to any complete foreign criticism of my poems. True, I take the whole matter very coolly. I know that my book has been composed in a cheerful and happy spirit—and that the same still substantially remains with me. (And I would like my friends, indeed, when writing for publication about my poetry, to present its gay-heartedness, as one of its chief points.)

I am in excellent health and still employed as a clerk here in Washington. I saw John Burroughs very lately: he is well, and showed me a letter he had just received from you. I wish more and more (and especially now that I feel I know you, and should be no stranger)—to journey over sea, and visit England and your country.

Tennyson has written to me twice—and very cordial and hearty letters. He invites me to become his guest.

I have received a letter from Joaquin Miller. He was at last accounts in Oregon, recuperating, studying, enjoying free nature, and writing new poems.

Emerson has just been this way (Baltimore and Washington) lecturing. He maintains about the same attitude as twenty-five or thirty years ago. It seems to me pretty thin. Immense upheavals have occurred since then, putting the world in new relations. I send you a newspaper report of his lectures here a night or two ago. It seems to be a fine average specimen of his current lectures.

And now my friend, I must close my letter. I have long

wished to write you a letter to show that I heartily realize your kindness and sympathy, and would draw the communion closer between us. I shall probably send you any thing I publish, and any thing about me from time to time. You must write freely to me, and I hope frequently.

## XCIV

### RUDOLF SCHMIDT

Feb. 2, 1872

Dear Mr. Rudolf Schmidt, Your note of Jan. 5, acknowledging receipt of "papers", and enclosing to me your photograph, is just received. I like your photograph and thank you for it—I like indeed the good frank way of sending such pictures when interested and curious. I wish to know whether you have safely received the particular copy of the last edition of my poems, in one volume with loose sheet photos enclosed, which I sent you by Mr. Clausen. Mr. Clausen tells me that he put up the various matter I furnished in three parcels—if you have got the three it is all right. I mailed you a letter of some length, Jan. 16. I shall send you, probably by next mail, my latest piece, in a Western Magazine for February. Also a second copy of my pamphlet *Democratic Vistas* —If the first copy reached you, send the second to Mr. Björnson—if not, not. Yes, I am sure I should like your friend Björnson much.

I am going next week to New York to stay there until April 10—my address there will be 107 *North* Portland av. Brooklyn, New York, U.S. Amer—about April 10, I shall return here again and my address will be——

I am writing this at my desk—as above, Treasury Building, middle of afternoon. From my great south window I can see a far-stretching and noble view, many, many miles of open ground, the Potomac river, the hilly banks, the mountains of Virginia, &c. We are having a severe cold spell. Everything is white with snow but the sun has been clear and dazzling all day. The hour of office-closing is nigh and I too must close. I have much pleasure in writing to you and expecting yours. Adieu.

## XCV

### ANNE GILCHRIST [Camden Square, London]

Washington, D.C.
February 8, 1872

Dear friend,

I send by same mail with this, my latest piece, copied in a newspaper—& write you just a line or two. I suppose you duly received my former letters (two)—I ought to have written something about your children (described to me in your letter of last summer, July 23d, which I have just been reading again) Dear boys & girls—how my heart goes out to them——

Did I tell you that I had received letters from Tennyson, & that he cordially invites me to visit him? Sometimes I dream of coming to Old England, on such a visit—& then of seeing you & your children—but it is a dream only.

I am still living here in employment in a Government office—My health is good—Life is rather sluggish here—though not without the sunshine—(Your letters too were warm, bright rays of it.)

I am going on to New York soon, to remain there a few weeks—but my address will still be here—I wrote lately to Mr. Rossetti quite a long letter——

Best love & remembrance to you, dear friend, & to the young folk—My exact address is *Solicitor's Office, Treasury, Washington, D.C.—U.S. America.*

Walt Whitman.

## XCVI

### ANNE GILCHRIST

Brooklyn, N.Y.
March 20, 1872

My dear friend,

Your letter is rec'd, having been sent on to me from Washington. My address still remains Solicitor's office, Treasury there. I am moving about a good deal the past year, & shall be for the ensuing year—I am to start for northern New England, & remain awhile—am also arranging for a trip afterward to California—a journey I have had in contemplation for several years, & which has been two or three times fixed, but postponed, during that time.

I have been stopping for two months, (Feb. & March,) home with my Mother, & am writing this home. Mother is towards eighty—has had an active domestic & maternal life —has had eight children—has brought them all up—has been healthy & strong, always worked hard—now shows the infirmities of age (indeed rapidly advancing) but looks finely, & is cheerful hearted—will probably soon give up her own housekeeping & go to live with one of my brothers, who is married.—My father died seventeen years since.

Dear friend, I am quite sure that *every one* of your letters has safely reached me—sometimes after delays & circuits, (as you will now understand better) on account of my more & more frequent wanderings—The letter with the photographs gave me great pleasure—& was acknowledged by a letter I sent you—Have you not received it?

Walt Whitman

Dear friend, let me warn you somewhat about myself—& yourself also.—You must not construct such an unauthorized & imaginary ideal Figure & call it W. W. and so devotedly invest your loving nature in it. The actual W. W. is a very plain personage & entirely unworthy such devotion.

## XCVII

### ALFRED TENNYSON

My Dear Mr. Tennyson:                    April 27, 1872.

This morning's paper has a vague sort of an item about your coming to America, or wanting to come, to view the working of our institutions, etc. Is there anything in it? I hope so, for I want more and more to meet you and be with you. Then I should like to give my explanations and comments of America and her shows, affairs, persons, doings, offhand, as you witness them, and become puzzled, perhaps, dismayed by them. America is at present a vast seething mass of varied material human and other, of the richest, best, worst, and plentiest kind. Wealthy inventive, no limit to food, land, money, work, opportunity, smart and industrious citizens, but (though real and permanently politically organized by birth and acceptance) without fusion or definite heroic identity in form and purpose or organization, which can only come by native schools of great ideas,—religion, poets, literature,—and will surely come, even through the measureless crudity of the States in those fields so far, and to-day.

The lesson of Buckle's books on civilization always seemed to me to be that the preceding main basis and continual *sine qua non* of civilization is the eligibility to, and certainty of boundless products for feeding, clothing, and sheltering everybody, infinite comfort, personal and inter-communication and plenty with mental and ecclesiastical freedom, and that then all the rest, moral and esthetic, will take care of itself. Well, the United States have secured the requisite bases, and must now proceed to build upon them.

I send you by same mail with this, a more neatly printed copy of my *Leaves;* also *Dem. Vistas.*

Your letter of last fall reached me at the time. [Not found] Have you forgotten that you put a promise in it, to send me your picture when "you could lay hands on a good one"?— [In letter of September 22, 1871.]

I have been in Brooklyn and New York most of the past winter and current spring, visiting my aged dear mother, near eighty. Am now back here at work. Am well and hearty. I have received two letters from you, July 12 and September 22, of last year 1872. This is the second letter I have written to you. My address is: Solicitor's Office, Treasury, Washington, D.C., United States. Write soon, my friend. Don't forget the picture.

Walt Whitman.

## XCVIII

### PETER DOYLE, Washington

Hanover, N.H.,<br>Thursday, June 27 [1872].

Dear Son.

I will write you just a line to show you I am here away north, and alive and kicking. I delivered my poem here be-

fore the College yesterday. All went off very well.—(It is
rather provoking—after feeling unusually well this whole
summer,—since Sunday last I have been about half sick and
am so yet, by spells.) I am to go to Vermont for a couple of
days, and then back to Brooklyn.—Pete I received your
letter, that you had been taken off—write to me Saturday
30th, or Sunday—direct to usual address 107 Portland Ave.,
Brooklyn. I will send you the little book with my poem, (and
others) when I get back to Brooklyn. Pete, did my poem
appear in the Washington papers—I suppose Thursday or
Friday—*Chronicle* or *Patriot?* If so send me one—(or one of
each).—It is a curious scene here, as I write, a beautiful old
New England village, 150 years old, large houses and gardens,
great elms, plenty of hills—every thing comfortable, but very
Yankee—*not an African to be seen all day*—not a grain of
dust—not a car to be seen or heard—green grass everywhere
—no smell of coal tar.—As I write a party are playing base
ball on a large green in front of the house—the weather suits
me first rate—cloudy but no rain. Your loving

Walt.

## XCIX

### CHARLES W. ELDRIDGE, Washington (?)

[New York]
July 19, [1872]

... Charley, I went leisurely up the Connecticut valley, by
way of Springfield, through the best part (agriculturally and
other) of Massachusetts, Connecticut, and New Hampshire,
June 24th and 25th by daylight—26th and 27th at Hanover,
N.H.—28th and 29th slowly up the White River valley, a
captivating wild region, by Vermont Central RR, and so to
Burlington, and about Lake Champlain, where I spent a
week, filling myself every day (especially mornings and sunsets) with the grandest ensembles of the Adirondacks always
on one side, and the Green Mountains on the other; sailed
after that down Champlain by day, stopt at Albany over
night, and down the Hudson by boat, 4th of July, through a
succession of splendid and magnificent thunderstorms (10 or

12 of them), alternated by spells of clearest sunlight. Then home—some five or six days immediately following I was ill, real ill—I suppose the excessive heat, etc. etc.—but am now feeling all right.

Upon the whole, I have stood the unprecedented heat pretty well. Mother is not very well—has spells of weakness —has rheumatism, then good days again—will break up from Brooklyn in September and go with George at Camden —as they are vehement for it.

My sister Martha at St. Louis is better far than one would expect after the alarm of two months ago—she has since no trouble with the cancer (or supposed cancer)— Jeff and the children well—My sister Hannah in Burlington I found better than I had anticipated—*everything much better*——

Charley, who do you think I have been spending some three hours with today, from 12 to 3—(it is now 4½)—Joaquin Miller. He saw me yesterday toward dusk in 5th Av., on a stage, and rushed out of the house and mounting the stage gave me his address, and made an appointment. He lives here. . . . I am much pleased (upon the whole) with him— *really pleased and satisfied*—his presence, conversation, atmosphere, are infinitely more satisfying than his poetry. He is, however, mopish, ennuyéed, a *California Hamlet*, unhappy every way—but a natural prince, maybe an illiterate one—but tender, sweet, and magnetic.

Love to you, dear Charley, and to all—I will soon be with you again.

Walt

# C

## THOMAS CARLYLE

Sept 3 '72

Dear Sir: Following an impulse of the moment, I have just mailed to you two little books of mine—writing this to introduce them—and taking permission to personally offer, as it were, from America true respects and love.

## CI

### MRS. ABBY H. PRICE

Washington, Friday evening, Feb. 21, [1873]

Dear Friend Abby, and all my friends Helen & Emmy & Mr. Arnold

I will write a line only—My paralysis still leaves me extremely feeble—& with great distress in the head—*but I shall certainly recover*—mind just as clear as ever—I have lost my dear, dear sister Martha, in St. Louis— I appreciate your kind letter Abby dear, and it is possible when I get better it may be just the thing for me to come on a few days—but at present I can hardly move ten steps without feeling sick——

I am sitting here now in the rocking chair in my room writing this—most of the time alone which suits me best—it is paralysis of left side—Love to all

Walt

(My address is Solicitors Office Treasury)

## CII

### MANNAHATTA WHITMAN [St. Louis]

Washington Saturday afternoon
March 1, '73

Dear Hattie,

I have received your letter, & read it over & over again—it is very, very good—so much about your dear mother, it brought the tears to my eyes, & I had to stop many times—my dear, dear Sister Martha, she must have suffered so much, & to keep up such fortitude & patience & even cheerfulness, while life lasted——

Hattie, I got a letter from your grandmother written Thursday afternoon, & she had not got your letter then—did you send her one a week ago, as you spoke of having written to her? She was very uneasy at not hearing from Jeff or any cf you, since your mother's death.—I wish you to write *immediately* to your grandmother, direct to her

care of Geo. W. Whitman
at Starr's foundry
Camden,
N. Jersey

I have got just well enough to go out, in a carriage, but dear Hattie, I am in a miserable condition, as to my power of moving—The doctor says I shall get well, but it is very, very slow and irksome—my mind is clear, but I have to sit in my room alone, by the fire, most of the time—visitors generally have been prohibited—but only a few come in—but now I have ventured out for a few minutes every fair day—It is now afternoon, very pleasant, & I shall just get out on the side-walk & then back——

—O how often I have thought of my dear sister Martha, as I have been alone here, both night & day—I think of your father too, & of you & California—but here I am, unable to move—— I hope Jeff will feel like writing to mother, & she will send it to me—As soon as I can travel I think of going on to Camden——

Dearest Hattie, if we had a house to invite you and California to, how much comfort it would be to your grand-mother & me—But I have great thoughts—at any rate—a great desire—to get one, here, when I get well, & have grand-mother & Eddy here—& then you & California shall surely come——

Love to you dearest Hattie—& love to your dear father, & to California—If you can, dear neice, write me again, & dont wait very long dear Hattie— Hattie dear you must mind the address—(My letters from St. Louis are addressed wrong) My right address is

> Walt Whitman
> Solicitor's office Treasury,
> Washington, D.C.

## CIII

### PETER DOYLE

> Camden,
> Tuesday afternoon, July 15 [1873].

Dear Pete.

There is nothing new or different with me—I am no better in any respect, don't know what is going to come out of it all —We are having pretty hot weather here just now, but it does not affect me much—it is not near as oppressive here as the Washington heat—I received your letter, my dear son—with the paper—I will write more to-morrow. Wednesday afternoon. Pete, I have little to write to you about, as I remain anchored here in the house nearly all the time. As I write I am sitting in my mother's former room, in her old arm-chair. —Spend a great deal of my time here, as I haven't felt like going out lately—half a block tires me. Pete, my darling son, I still think I shall weather it but time only can show— Mother's death is on my mind yet, time does not lift the cloud from me at all—I want much to get to the sea-shore, either Long Island or the Jersey coast, and shall make a start if I get strong enough—It is not so hot here to-day. So long, my darling boy.

                                                          Walt.

## CIV

ANNE GILCHRIST, Earls Colne, Halsted, Essex

Camden, New Jersey,
August 17, 1873.

I must write you a few lines dear loving friend once more at any rate. Since I last wrote clouds have darkened over me, & still remain. On the night of 23d of January last I was paralyzed, left side, & have remained so since. February 19th I lost a dear sister, who died in St. Louis, leaving two young daughters. May 23d my inexpressibly beloved mother died in Camden. I was just able to get from Washington to her dying bed, & sit there. I thought I was bearing it all stoutly but I find it affecting the progress of my recovery since & now. The doctor says my disease is cerebral anaemia, resulting in paralysis. I am still feeble, palsied, & have spells of great distress in the head—But there are favorable points—I am up & dressed every day, sleep & eat middling well, & do not change much yet in flesh & face, only look very old. Though I move slowly very short distances, I walk with difficulty, & have to remain in or near the house. I think the probabilities are quite strong *yet that I shall get well,* (*though I may not.*) Many times during the past year, especially during the past six months, have I thought of you & your children—Many times indeed have I been going to write, but did not. I have just been reading over again several of this & last year's letters from you & looking at the pictures sent in the one of January 24, '72. The letters of Jan 24, June 3 & July 11, of '72, and of Jan 31 & May 20, this year—with certainly one other & may-be two—all came safe. Do not think hard of me for not writing oftener, especially the last seven months—if you could look into my spirit & emotions you would be entirely satisfied & at peace.

I am at present temporarily here at Camden, on the Delaware river, immediately opposite Philadelphia, at the house of my brother. I am occupying the rooms where my mother died—every object of furniture &c. is familiar & has an emotional history. You must not be unhappy about me, for I am comfortably situated as can be—and many things—indeed every thing,—in my case might be so much worse. Though my plans depend on yet uncertain results, my intention, as far as any thing, is, on getting stronger, & after the hot season passes, to get back to Washington for the fall & winter. My post office address continues there, (Solicitor's Office Treasury.) I send my love to Percy, & all your dear children. The enclosed ring I have just taken from my finger & send you with my love.

Walt Whitman

## CV

### PETER DOYLE

Camden,<br>Friday afternoon, Oct. 3 [1873].

Dear Pete, Dear Son.

I received your letter the first of the week, and was interested in your account of your week, of laying off, and of the playing of the band under Schneider and Petrola—also about City R.R. men—I send my love and best respects to all of them—I have had a bad spell again this week—for three days I have had a succession of those *blurs* again—only very much worse than ever before—last night I slept pretty well, and

haven't had any of them yet, to-day, but my head feels sore
and ready to have them, almost if I move across the room—I
am sitting here, feeling pretty bad, my head unsettled and
dizzy—I don't go out any more—but am up and dressed—
Still Pete, I do not get discouraged but think it will pass over,
and I shall feel better, and strong enough to come back to
Washington. Still I don't know, I think it best to face my
situation—it is pretty serious. I send you a card—and if I
should get bad, I will certainly send you word, or telegraph—
I will write Monday or Tuesday next—We have moved into
my brother's new house—I am up here in the 3rd story room,
fronting south—the sun is shining in bright—it is beautiful
October weather here—My brother had a large room, very
handsome, on second floor, with large bay window fronting west, built for me, but I moved up here instead, it is
much more retired, and has the sun—I am very comfortable
here indeed, but my *heart* is blank and lonesome utterly.
11 *o'clock a.m. sitting by the window* 1*st floor.* I have just
been talking with a young married R.R. man, Thomas Osler,
I fell in with—he has a bad bone-gathering on his left hand,
sort of felon, suffered greatly with it 5 days and nights—had
it lanced yesterday, and is better—he stood by the open
window 1st floor, and talked with me, while I sat in an arm-
chair inside—he is a regular R.R. man—you could tell by the
cut of his jib, low collar, cap, clean shirt (for holiday) dark
complexion, and hard dark hands, I took quite a fancy to
him and, *of course*, I suppose he did to me—I believe he
works on the locomotive—Pete, you must tell me how you
put in the past week—I like such a letter as your last one—
written two or three different times—It gave me a good idea
of what you are doing—and also of how things look in
Washington—I have written a line to Col. Hinton and shall
write a line to Eldridge.

3 *o'clock* P.M. My head is feeling very sore and touchy and
sensitive—I don't go out—I have re-written my will—What
little I have to leave I have left mainly to my lame brother
Ed., poor man—Pete, I have left you $200, and my gold
watch—(but it will be much better for us to spend the money
together, and I have no doubt we shall do so). This house is
quite pleasant—it is on the corner—fronts south—side to

west—plenty of light and air and view—This afternoon I am quite in hopes I am getting better of my spells to-day, as I have not had any actual spells though I have felt pretty sick all day. But I have been up all day, and eat quite a bite for dinner—Pete, I have written plainly, because I want you to be prepared if anything should happen to me—but I tell you *honest*, I still think I shall pull through—and that I shall be able to write better news early next week—don't you be alarmed yet.

Walt.

## CVI

### JOHN BURROUGHS

431 Stevens st, cor West,
Camden, N. Jersey,
Dec. 11—p.m. '73

Dear John Burroughs,

I have had another severe spell the last five weeks—head troubles, & stomach troubles, & *liver* troubles—the doctor thinks the latter the seat & basis this time of all, or nearly all —head-swimming, faintness, vomiting, &c—but for three or four days past have been easier—am up—didn't go out for three to four weeks, but am venturing out a little now—hope & quite expect to get at least as well as I was before this spell —Eldridge has made me a call of two or three hours, (on his return from Boston to Wash'n), seems to be nothing very new among our friends at Wash'n—Marvin has written me twice—he has been reading your *Notes*, & is quite possessed with them—also *Dem. Vistas*—I am writing very little—have a piece a *melange*, prose & verse, in the *Christmas Graphic* (comes out in a week or so.) in which I say a brief word about Emerson—To eke out my letter I send a scrap from paper about death of a young friend of mine—also another scrap— also another from London *Academy*, (which latter only please return when you write)—Best love to 'Sula—*Merry Christmas*—Do you get in the new house?—Write me a good long letter—I wish I was with you——

Walt.

## CVII

## JOHN BURROUGHS

431 Stevens st. cor West.
Camden, N. Jersey, Dec. 17. '73

Dear John Burroughs,

I have been back here two weeks & over—My Washington jaunt occupied some seventeen or eighteen days, & was a very pleasant one for me—(started out with the idea of a two days visit only)—Am perhaps now lately not so well, but not much different—the gravest trouble is the liver and stomachic business now—Still I keep up about the same, (& get mad at myself for grunting)—your letter of two days since rec'd. Best love to 'Sula, & to Jenny Grant if there—My new edition is nearly ready—Two Vols—will give you early advice of their appearance—only 100 copies issued—Is the *Winter Sunshine* out?—Eldridge call'd to see me on his return home two weeks since. Marvin has gone to England, with a Treas. squad. He has call'd on Mrs. Gilchrist. M. D. Conway called on me, Lord Houghton also. We have great times in *this house*—a baby has arrived, a fine lusty little fellow, now five weeks old —(he has been named Walt)—just now though he is quite sick, but I opine will get along—The rest all very well, except that my sister, the mother, is part of the time only middling. —I hear young Walt raising *his* song in the room overhead as I conclude my letter—Love to you as always, my friend——

Walt

## CVIII

## MRS. ABBY H. PRICE and HELEN PRICE

431 Stevens St., Cor. West.,
Camden N. Jersey.
Sunday afternoon—4½—[January, 1874]

Dear Abby & Dear H. [Helen],
Not forgetting E. & all.

As I am sitting here along in the parlor, the sun near setting pleasantly and brightly, (though cold to-day) I just think that I ought to write you, even if but a line,—that I am neglecting you—that perhaps you will be glad enough to hear from me. Well, I am still here—still alive, after quite a many pretty hard pulls and pressures—maintain pretty good spirits —which *would* be quite *first rate & good*—but every day and every night comes the thought of my mother,—I am not despondent or blue, nor disposed to be any more *ennuyed* than ever—but that thought remains to temper the rest of my life.

I am probably improving, though very slowly—go out a little most every day—go over to Philadelphia—get along pretty well in the cars & crossing the ferry, (and the car fellows and ferrymen are very kind & helpful—almost all know me, I suppose instinctively)—Appetite fair—rest at night tolerable—general strength better than at any time (it is now just a year since I was paralysed). Can't use my left leg yet with any freedom—bad spells in the head too frequent yet— then, with all these, I am certainly encouraged to believe I am on the gain. (But I am not out of the woods yet.) I write some—(must occupy my mind). I am writing some pieces in the *Weekly Graphic*—my reminiscences of war times—first number appears in *Weekly Graphic* of Jan. 24—three or four others to follow.

We are in the new house my brother has built—very nice. I find myself *very lonesome* here, for all social & emotional consolation—(Man cannot live on *bread* alone—can he?)—I want to come to see you—must do so before long—want to pay a moderate board (same as [I] do here), if convenient for you to have me.—*Shall not come on any other condition.*

Well, Abby, I have just scurried rapidly over the sheet, & will send it to you just as it is, with love,

Walt Whitman

## CIX

### RUDOLPH SCHMIDT, Copenhagen

[Camden, New Jersey]
Jan 25 '74.

My dear Rudolph Schmidt, Your letter of Jan. 2, has just reached me here. I am always glad to hear from you. Write oftener. I have been very ill, just a year, from paralysis and cerebral anaemia—I have been at death's door. I sent you a paper with acct four or five months since but as you do not allude to it I suppose you did not rec. it. I send another by this mail. I have sent you several papers and magazines. I am not in bed but go out a little every day, and shall probably get well again yet, but remain paralyzed yet—have bad spells in my head, and walk with great difficulty—ameliorate very, very slowly. Still I write and publish a little.

What about Björnson? Is he coming to America? If so give him my address and tell him to come and see me. It is almost a part of Philadelphia where I live on the opposite side of the Delaware river. When you write or send *Democratic Vistas*, direct here. Write me from Germany.

What did I hear a while since of some great German university putting up for discussion? I have no thought of visiting England. In a letter two years since Tennyson kindly invited me to come and accept his hospitality—which aroused some thought of it in my mind—but it has passed over.

## CX

JOHN BURROUGHS, Esopus, New York

[Camden, New Jersey?]
June 5, 1874

Dear Friend,

Your second letter, with sad news—following the sad, sad, inexpressibly sad news of the first—has just reached me.

I will not write any of the usual condolences—Channy's malady and death seem to be of those events sometimes mocking with unaccountable sudden tragedies and cross-purposes all of us & all our affairs. ...

Walt

## CXI

PETER DOYLE

431 Stevens St. cor. West,
Camden, N. Jersey, Friday noon, Feb. 6 [1874].

Dear Boy Pete.

Both your letters came this week—also one from my friend Eldridge, he too speaks of meeting and talking with you. It is real winter here, the ground all covered with snow, as I look out—not the least thaw to-day, as it is cloudy—I rise pretty late mornings—had my breakfast a little while ago, mutton-chop, coffee, nice brown bread and sweet butter, very nice—eat with very fair appetite—I enjoy my breakfast better than any other meal—(eat a light dinner pretty late, and no sup-per)—Feel generally about the same as before described—no worse no better, (nothing to brag of anyhow). I have men-tioned about my crossing the ferry—from our house the cars run by the next corner, (200 feet or less) a half mile or so to the ferry—the Delaware here is full three quarters of a mile wide—it is a noble river, not so wide as the Potomac nor with fine banks like Arlington, but grander, and with more style, and with powerful rushing tides, now great processions of broken ice, many little and some great big cakes—the boats are very fine and strong, go crashing right ahead, with a loud noise, breaking the cakes often a foot thick and more—I enjoy crossing these days—it does me good—the ferry men are all very kind and respectful—I have been reading a book *Merrie England in the Olden Time*, a London book, with pic-tures, full of fun and humor—I have enjoyed it much—There is an awful amount of want and suffering from no work, here about—a young man was here yesterday—Had seen me in Washington—wanted help—I gave him a little—I see the cars and locomotives skurrying by as I close.

Walt.

## CXII

## PETER DOYLE

431 Stevens St. cor. West,
Camden, N Jersey, July 10 [1874].

Dear, Dear Son

I am still here suffering pretty badly—have great distress in my head, and an almost steady pain in left side—but my worst troubles let up on me part of the time—the evenings are my best times—and somehow I still keep up in spirit, and, (the same old story) *expect* to get better. I have been dis-charged from my clerkship in the solicitor's office, Treasury, by the new Solicitor, Mr. Wilson. I think of laying up here in Camden, I have bought a cheap lot—and think of putting up a little two or three room house for myself, my darling son, you must not be unhappy about me—I hope and trust things may work so that we can yet be with each other, at least from time to time—and meanwhile we must adapt ourselves to circumstances. You keep on and try to do right, and live the same square life you always have, and maintain as cheerful a heart as possible, and as for the way things finally turn out, leave that to the Almighty—Pete, I shall want you or Mr. Eldridge to see to the sending on here of my boxes at Dr White's—I will write further about it—I have not heard anything from Eldridge, or Mrs. O'Connor, or any of the Washington folk for quite a long time. Have you been up to see Mrs. O'C.? Pete, didn't you get my last Saturday's postal card? I wrote you one, I got yours last Monday—Did you get the Camden paper with my College piece in? I sent one. Very hot here yesterday and to-day. I don't fret at all about being discharged—it is just as well—I wonder it didn't come before—How are your folks at home?—your dear mother and all—write about all and Mr and Mrs. Nash, Wash Milburn, and the R.R. boys.

Your old Walt

## CXIII

### JOHN BURROUGHS. Esopus, New York

[Camden, New Jersey]<br>April 1, 1875

Dear John,

I have looked over the Emerson notes—read them all over once—am precluded from anything more, or giving any very deep or elaborate analysis of them, in connection with the Emerson question (as my brain is in a state not allowing thought, argument or study)—but still I will give you my first impressions of your pages:

In their totality they produce a not agreeable notion of being written by one who has been largely grown and ripened and gristled by Emerson, but has at last become dissatisfied and finicky about him, and would pitch into him, but cannot

—perhaps dare not—and so keeps running around in a sort of circle of praises and half praises, like a horse tied by a tether.

Your *Notes* also seem to me (to be plain) a good deal too diffuse, and too Emersony in themselves—I should select about one third of the MS. as *first rate* (including the opening part). My opinion is that you had perhaps better work it all over, and leave out at least half.

About the allusions to me, my off-hand thought is that my name might be brought in, in one or two places, as foil or suggestive comparison—but *my name only*, without any praise or comments (only the silently inferred ones). To my friends and circle who know the relations and history between me and Emerson, the mere mention of the name itself, in that way, will be significant (and it might give pungency to the sentence.)

I have had a bad time the last two weeks—head and belly —and I almost wonder I stand it so well—for I *do* stand it— I go out most every day, a little. John Swinton from N.Y. has been to see me.

Love to you and 'Sula.

W. W.

## CXIV

### EDMUND CLARENCE STEDMAN

431 Stevens st. cor West,
Camden, N. Jersey,
June 17, '75.

My dear Stedman,

I have rec'd your kind note, & am pleased that you remember me. I shall select some scrap of my MS. & send you soon. The last fortnight I have had an extra spell of debility & head distress, but feel better to-day. Should you come to Philadelphia come over here, (by ferry from foot of Market st. Phil., very accessible) & see me, & have a chat. I am leisurely preparing a Volume, *Two Rivulets* (i.e. Real and Ideal) all sorts of things, prose & (my) poetry. Won't be out though for five or six months. Pleasant in some respects here, for me—but pretty lonesome.

Walt Whitman

## CXV

## ALFRED TENNYSON

My Dear Mr. Tennyson:                    [July 24, 1875]

Since I last wrote you, (your kind response was duly received) I have been laid up here nearly all the time, and still
continue so,—quite shattered, but, somehow with good
spirits; not well enough to go out in the world and go to
work, but not sick enough to give up either, or lose my interest in affairs, life, literature, etc. I keep up and dressed, and
go out a little nearly every day.

I have been reading your *Queen Mary*, and think you have
excelled yourself in it. I did not know until I read it, how
much eligibility to passion, character, and art arousings was
still left to me in my sickness and old age. Though I am democrat enough to realize the deep criticism of *Jefferson* (?)
[*sic*] on Walter Scott's writings (and many of the finest plays,
poems, and romances) that they fail to give at all the life of
the great mass of the people then and there.

I shall print a new volume before long and will send you a
copy. I send you a paper about same mail as this. Soon as
convenient write me a few lines. (Put in letter your exact
P.O. address.) If you have leisure, tell me about yourself. I
shall never see you and talk to you, so I hope you will write
to make it up.

                    Your friend
                              Walt Whitman

## CXVI

## —— EINSTEIN

                              Camden, Nov. 26, '75.

My dear Einstein: On coming back here I find your letter of
the 20th. It is so kind (bringing up old memories, and making prologue and ceremony unnecessary) that I will at once
answer it in its own spirit, and reveal the situation.

My paralysis has left me permanently disabled, unable to do
anything of any consequence, and yet with perhaps (though
old, not yet 60.) some lease of life yet. I had saved up a little
money, and when I came here, nearly three years ago, I

bought a nice cheap lot, intending to put on a small house to haul in, and live out the rest of my days. I had and yet have a sort of idea that my books (I am getting ready, or about have ready, my completed writings, in two Volumes—*Leaves of Grass*, and *Two Rivulets*) will yet henceforth reliably furnish me with sufficient for grub, pocket money, &c., if I have my own shanty to live in. But my means, meagre at the best, have gone, for my expenses since, and now, while not hitherto actually wanting (and not worrying much about the future, either) I have come to the end of my rope, and am in fact ridiculously poor. I have my lot yet clear, and it would be a great thing for me to be able to build forthwith a four or five room shanty on it and haul in snug and quiet, with the sense of security for the rest of my days—for I feel yet about as cheerful and *vimmy* as ever, and may live several years yet—indeed probably will—and may write some—though my days of active participation, and ganging about in the world, are over.

I get out a little nearly every day and enjoy it, but am very lame—keep stout and red as ever—grayer than ever—am feeling pretty comfortable as I write—have just returned from a three weeks' jaunt to Washington and Baltimore—which has much refreshed me, (the first time I have been away from my anchorage here for nearly three years.) I often recall the old times in New York, or on Broadway, or at Pfaff's—and the faces and voices of *the boys*.

## CXVII

### ANNE GILCHRIST, London

431 Stevens st.
cor West,
Camden, N. Jersey
U S America—March 17, '76.

Dearest friend:

To your good & comforting letter of Feb. 25th I at once answer, at least with a few lines. I have already to day written (answering one just rec'd from him) a pretty long letter to Mr. Rossetti, & requested him to loan it to you for perusal. In that I have described my situation fully & candidly.

My new edition is printed & ready. On receipt of your letter I have mailed you a set, two Vols. which you ought to have rec'd by this time. I wish you to send me word soon as they arrive.

My health, I am encouraged to think, is perhaps a shade better—certainly as well as any time of late. I even already vaguely contemplate plans, (they may never be fulfilled, but yet again they may,) of changes, journeys—even of coming to London, of seeing you, of visiting my friends, &c.

My dearest friend *I do not approve your American trans-settlement—I see so many things here, you have yet no idea of —the American social & almost every other kind of crudeness, meagreness, (at least in appearance)—Don't do any thing toward it, nor resolve on it, nor indeed make any move at all in it, without further advice from me. If I should get well enough to voyage, we will talk about it yet in London—*You must not be uneasy about me—dear friend, I get along much better than you suppose. As to the literary situation here, my rejection by the coteries & my poverty, (which is the least of my troubles)—am not sure but I enjoy them all.

Besides, as to the latter, I am not in want. Best love to you, & to your children.

Walt Whitman

## CXVIII

### W. M. ROSSETTI

[Camden, New Jersey]<br>March 17, 1876.

My books are out, the new edition; a set of which, immediately on receiving your letter of 28th, I have sent you, (by mail, March 15,) and I suppose you have before this receiv'd them. My dear friend, your offers of help, and those of my other British friends, I think I fully appreciate, in the right spirit, welcome and acceptive—leaving the matter altogether in your and their hands, and to your and their convenience, discretion, leisure, and nicety. Though poor now, even to penury, I have not so far been deprived of any physical thing I need or wish whatever, and I feel confident I shall not [be] in the future. During my employment of seven years or more in Washington after the war (1865-72) I regularly saved part of my wages: and, though the sum has now become about exhausted by my expenses of the last three years, there are already beginning at present welcome dribbles hitherward from the sales of my new edition, which I just job and sell, myself, (all through this illness, my book-agents for three years in New York successively, badly cheated me,) and shall continue to dispose of the books myself. And *that* is the way I should prefer to glean my support. In that way I cheerfully accept all the aid my friends find it convenient to proffer.

To repeat a little, and without undertaking details, understand, dear friend, for yourself and all, that I heartily and most affectionately thank my British friends, and that I accept their sympathetic generosity in the same spirit in which I believe (nay, know) it is offer'd—that though poor I am not in want—that I maintain good heart and cheer; and that by far the most satisfaction to me (and I think it can be done, and believe it will be) will be to live, as long as possible, on the sales, by myself, of my own works, and perhaps, if practicable, by further writings for the press.

W. W.

I am prohibited from writing too much, and I must make this candid statement of the situation serve for all my dear friends over there.

## CXIX

### ROBERT BUCHANAN, London

431 Stevens St Cor West
Camden N Jersey U S America
April 4 '76

Robert Buchanan—

My dear friend—I merely want to say that I have read your letter in the London *Daily News*—all your three letters —and that I deeply appreciate them, and do not hesitate to accept and respond to them in the same spirit in which they were surely impelled and written.

May God bless you and yours,

Walt Whitman

W.

## CXX

### ROBERT BUCHANAN, London

[Camden, New Jersey]
May 16, 1876.

**Your two** letters including the cheque for £25 reached me, for which accept deepest thanks. I have already written you my approval of your three communications in L. *D. News* and saying that in my opinion (and now with fullest deliberation reaffirming it) *all the points assumed as facts on which your letter of March* 13 *is grounded are substantially true and most of them are true to the minutest particular* as far as could be stated in a one column letter.

Then let me quite definitely explain myself about one or two things. I should not have instigated this English move, and if I had been consulted should have peremptorily stopped it —but now that it has started and grown, and under the circumstances, and by the person, and in the spirit, (and especially as I can and will give, to each generous donor, my book, portrait, autograph, myself as it were) I am determined to respond to it in the same spirit in which it has risen—to accept most thankfully, cordially and unhesitatingly all that my friends feel to convey to me, which determination I here deliberately express once for all. This you are at liberty to make known to all who feel any interest in the matter.

The situation at present may be briefly and candidly told. I am, and have for three years during my paralysis, been boarding here with a relative, comfortable and nice enough, but steadily paying just the same as at an inn,—and the whole affair in precisely the same business spirit. My means would by this time have entirely given out but that have been temporarily replenished from sales of my new edition and as now by this most welcome present and purchase—the £25 herein acknowledged.

Though without employment, means or income you augur truly that I am not in what may be called pinching want— nor do I anticipate it.

My object I may say farther has lately been and still is to build a cheap little three or four room house on a little lot in a rural skirt of this town—for a nook, where I can haul in and eke out in a sort of independent economy and comfort and as satisfactorily as may be the rest of my years—for I may live several of them yet.—To attain this would be quite a triumph, and I feel assured I could then live very nicely indeed on the income from my books.

I shall (as I see now) continue to be my own publisher and bookseller. Accept all subscriptions to the New Edition. All will be supplied upon remittance. There are Two Volumes. *Leaves of Grass*, 384 pages, $5, has two portraits. Then *Two Rivulets*, poems and prose, (including Memoranda of the War) with photos, 359 pages—also $5. Each book has my autograph. The Two Volumes are my complete works, $10 the set.

I wish the particular address of each generous friend given, so as he or she can be reach'd by mail or express—either with the autographic volume *Two Rivulets* or a complete set of my works in Two Volumes, with autograph and portraits, or some other of my books.

It may be some while before the books arrive but they *will* arrive in time.

### CXXI

JOHN BURROUGHS, Esopus, New York

Saturday afternoon,
[Camden, New Jersey]
June 17, [1876]

John, I have just been reading your *Galaxy* article, seated by the open window, front room, in my shirt sleeves & must write a word about it—Your late pieces show marked *vitality* —*vivacity*—(struggling, almost chafing, underneath a continent, respectable form or exterior) & *this is the best of them* —has those peculiarities, not without one or two foibles, but the *whole* of the piece is glorious—leaves the impression now upon me (after two readings) of the noblest piece of criticism on these things yet in America—as much nobler than the superb Emersonian pages on those subjects as lines & opinions with *the blood of life* & throb of hot conviction in them, are nobler than the superbest *marble statue lines*——

—It would be possible that I might be swayed into a warm feeling about the piece by the magnificent & very 'cute page about me, but as it happens by accident I had look'd over & read the piece in parts, *accidentally omitting at first the entire lines in the second column* of the page, about me (which finally please me best)—& had made up my mind very decidedly as aforesaid—then when I *did* read them, you can imagine *they* didn't hurt me much—nor my estimation of the piece— I have much to write—or tell you—about my own concerns—things in England—here too—&c. &c—have been waiting for the chance to write you fully ever since I got your kind generous note & present—but it dont seem to occur— Physically I am not much different—get along about as well as usual these times—am just now going down to our old farm house & big family down in Jersey at *White Horse*, to spend a couple of days—and it is now (4½ p m ) while I am waiting for the hack to come & take me to the depot that I write this—George and Lou are well—baby only pretty well —hot weather, & teething—(but behaves like a little hero)— expect my two neices nere next week from St Louis—Love to 'Sula—write soon——

                                                        Walt

<br>

## CXXII

### ROBERT BUCHANAN

                                    [Camden, New Jersey?]
                                    Sept. 4 '76.
R. Buchanan.

I forward you by Express today same address as this letter the package of Books (see list on other side)—I wish Tennyson to have a set and have enclosed one, and would ask you to do me the favor of seeing that it is safely transmitted to him. Notwithstanding the disclaimer in yours of April 23 I also send a set for Richard Bentley in response to his kindness and generosity : (if anything I know not of prevents its reaching him, I wish *you* to keep it for yourself.)

Please see that the photograph is given to the School of Art, with my affectionate respects.

Trusting to your kindness to see that they are carefully sent to the subscribers.

## CXXIII

### JOHN BURROUGHS, Esopus, New York

Kirkwood, New Jersey,
May 17, 1877

I am passing a good part of my time down here at the farm. . . . Still keep well for me, and jolly, am all tanned and sunburnt—eat my rations every time.

I was up yesterday to Camden to get my mail and found *the book*—read it all over with appreciative and I think critical eyes, my impression of liking it, as a curiously *homogeneous* work (just enough radiations to make it *piquant*) and, in connection *liking the name*, etc., all deepened and clinched. I especially much like, and more like, the chapter about me. There has certainly been nothing yet said that so makes the points (and eloquently makes them) I most want brought out and put on record.

Are you coming to the Gilchrists, and when?

W. W.

## CXXIV

### JOHN R. JOHNSTON, Philadelphia

1929 North 22d St.
Phila : June 20, 1877

Dear boy Jack,

I thought of coming round to see you all last Sunday, but it was so hot & I didn't get over to Camden—didn't feel like walking up from the ferry—Jack I am stopping up here in 22d Street for a week or two—they are very kind to me, & very jovial & we have real good times—the young man, about 21, he & I are very thick—then there are two grown daughters—the eldest one is a *first class trump*, she is my favorite every way—she is studying at the woman's medical university here—the mother Mrs. Gilchrist, is a very fine lady,—we have good meals, & take our time over them—I have the best room in the house, breezy & cool (& the water in it)—& a young English college Professor, Mr. Carpenter, is staying here for a few days—though a stranger he is a great friend of mine & indeed has come over from England to see me—(But I have written enough of all that——

Dear Jack, I wonder if I shall ever be with you, or rather have you with me, so that we can have some good times together on land and water—I used to think of having a shanty of my own there in Camden, & I thought I shouldn't be satisfied without having you & Ida up there to take supper with me two evenings in the week, at least—I wonder if it is ever coming to pass—meantime I shall come around *next Sunday*, if you are all at home—Tell Ida to put her hair in curl papers Saturday morning—*I hope there will be some spear mint ready to pull in the garden*—Johnny how does it go with you?— Love to mother & father & tell 'Em I'm coming round next Sunday—Here is a kiss for you, Jack, & take care of yourself, & don't forget

Your loving friend

old W W

## CXXV

### MR. AND MRS. GEORGE W. WHITMAN
[Camden, New Jersey]

1309 Fifth avenue
New York June 15 [1878]

Dear brother & sister

I will write you a line to let you know I am all right—I sent you a N Y paper the *Sun* of to-day with an acc't of the funeral —I am feeling pretty well for me—am stopping with Mr. Johnston and his wife & family—there is a big family & they have moved up here—a big four or five story house, near 86th St overlooking the Park, cool & fresh as can be—all are very kind, especially Mrs. J. (the new one)—the children all call me Uncle Walt—the baby is bright & interesting, but not rugged—(I hardly think its tenure of life secure)—I have many invitations, but don't accept them I have seen John Burroughs & he wants me to go up there to Esopus, but I don't think I shall go—I find my gray clothes very seasonable here, as it is cool enough all the time except at mid-day—I suppose Hattie and Jessie are there, all right—Dear girls I send you my best love, & I will soon be home & see you— I will finish to-night.

Sunday 3½ p m
West Point
50 miles above N Y on the Hudson

I finish my letter here—having had a very pleasant 3 hours trip up here on the *Plymouth Rock* to Mr. & Mrs John Bigelow's—I met her at Mr Bryant's funeral & she invited me up here—I came up for the sail as well as to see the good folks & this beautiful spot—I think it is the finest I have ever seen— Had dinner about an hour ago, and in about an hour more, shall return on the boat—Shall get to N Y before sundown.

—The weather is perfect—I am feeling all right—shall probably mail this to you when I get in to night—Hope you are all well &c—

Walt

Monday 17th
11 a m

I was so tired out & got in so late from the West Point trip that I did not go to mail this last night—At present I am sitting alone in the front parlor with the Park opposite like a dense wood—is pleasant, but cloudy & *almost cold* to-day— (if I had not my old grays wearing I should be uncomfortable) —Lou you would like the folks & everything here—especially Mrs Johnston—at meals there is a great big table & the little children sit up the same as any—toward the last the baby & the little 4 year old girl are generally down crawling around on the floor—— the whole squad are model children lively & free & *children*, but no bother & no whimpering or quarrelling at all under any circumstances they form a great part of my comfort—Yesterday was such a strain that to-day I am going to keep still—Best love to you all—I enclose a card— write me about the girls & all——

W W

CXXVI

ALFRED TENNYSON

My Dear Tennyson:　　　　　　　August 9, 1878.

The last letter I sent you was September 14, 1876, (nearly two years ago), to which I have received no response. I also sent you my two volumes; new edition, having received your subscription of five pounds (with an intimation from Robert Buchanan that no books were expected in return, but I preferred to send them).

I am still in the land of the living, much better and robuster the last two years, and especially the last six months, (though a partial paralytic yet). I find the experiences of invalidism and the losing of corporeal ties not without their advantages, at least, if one reserve enough physique to, as it were, confront the invalidism. But all this summer I have been, and am well enough to be out on the water or down in the fields or woods of the country more than half the time and am quite "hefty" (as we say here) and sunburnt.

Best regards and love to you, dear friend. Write me first leisure and opportunity. Haven't you a son—lately married —I have heard about? Pray, tell me something about him and the respected lady, your wife, whom you mentioned in your last as prostrated with illness, and yourself, most of all.

Walt Whitman.

## CXXVII

### GEORGE W. CHILDS, [Philadelphia]

431 Stevens Street

Dear Mr. Childs       Camden Friday noon Jan 31 [1879]

If nothing prevents, I shall do myself the pleasure of accepting your invitation for to-morrow night—'Twould be a kindness to me if you would have one of your young men (Mr Johan perhaps) come down & meet me at the foot of Market street (Camden Federal street Ferry—Philadelphia side) at ¼ to 8, and convoy me up to your house——

Walt Whitman

## CXXVIII

### ANNE GILCHRIST [Lower Shincliffe, Durham]

431 Stevens Street

Dear friend,       Camden August 18 [1879]

Yours of 2d just rec'd—(the one from Scotland came also) —I am pretty well—full as well as when I last saw you in New York—if any thing perhaps a little *plus*. I went down last month to spend a while with the Staffords at their new farm, but I miss'd my main attraction & comfort, *the Creek* & did not make a long visit—Mrs S and the rest are as usual, except Debbie, who was not at all hearty—Brother & Sister here well—sister seems to be engaged this morning with her new girl, (who seems to be doing marvellous! (sic) in early fall house-cleaning)—at any rate I noticed every thing tumbled & heaped just now as I have been down stairs to see what the postman left me.

I am sitting up in my room Stevens street writing this— copious rains all the morning and (sic) last night—(& indeed this is the third day of them)—Hattie and Jessie left for St. Louis last Thursday night—Lou and I went over to the West Phil: depot and saw them off—(dear girls, how we miss them)——

I am busy a little leisurely writing—think of printing soon a smallish 100 page book of my accumulated memoranda down at the Creek, & across the Ferry, days & nights, under the title of *Idle Days & Nights of a half-Paralytic* prose, free gossip mostly, (you saw some specimens in that Jersey letter, last winter in the Phila : *Times*)

—Isn't that sad about the sudden death of our young Mrs. Sartoris in your country?—Something strange too (I hope nothing uncanny will turn out)——

—Thank you dear friend for your letter (—came in just right) —how I should indeed like to see that *Cathedral*—I don't know which I should go for first, the Cathedral, or *that baby*——

Best love

to you—to Bee, Herb, Giddy and all—I write in haste but I am determined you shall have a word at least promptly in response.

## CXXIX

### JOHN BURROUGHS, Esopus, New York

[Camden, New Jersey]
August 29, 1879

Dear Jack,

As I sit here the weather is now perfect, day and night—I have jotted off the enclosed I send you (of course use it or not).

Your letter arrived with the enclosures. I keep well, go out most every day.... I sell a book now and then.

No, I have not been to any watering-place—they are no company for me—the cities, magnificent for their complex play and oceans of eager human faces—but the country or sea for me, in some sparse place, old barn and farm house, or bleak seashore, nobody round—meanwhile I get along very well here.

Walt

## CXXX

### PETER DOYLE

2316 Pine St.
St. Louis, Missouri, Nov. 5 [1879].

Dear Pete.

You will be surprised to get a letter from me away off here —I have been taking quite a journey the last two months— have been out to the Rocky Mountains and Colorado (2000 miles) (Seems to me I sent you a paper six weeks ago from Denver)—I got along very well until three weeks ago when I was taken sick and disabled, and hauled in here in St. Louis for repairs, have been here ever since—am fixed comfortable —still somewhat under the weather, (but have no doubt I shall be well as usual for me before long)—shall stay here probably two or three weeks longer, and then back east to Camden.—Pete, this is a wonderful country out here, and no one knows how big it is till he launches out in the midst of it —But there are plenty of hard-up fellows in this City and out in the mines, and all over here—you have no idea how many run ashore, get sick from exposure, poor grub, etc.—many young men, some old chaps, some boys of 15 or 16—I met them everywhere, especially at the R. R. stoppings, out of money and trying to get home—But the general run of all these Western places, City and country is very prosperous, on the rush, plenty of people, plenty to eat, and apparently plenty of money—Colorado you know is getting to be the great silver land of the world—in Denver I visited a big smelting establishment, purifying the ore, goes through many processes—takes a week—well they showed me silver by the cart load—Then in middle Colorado, in one place, as we stopt in a mining camp, I saw rough bullion bars piled up in stacks outdoors five or six feet high, like haycocks—so it is— a few make great strikes—like the prizes in the lottery—but most are blanks—I was at Pike's Peak—I liked Denver City very much—But the most interesting part of my travel has been *the Plains*, (the great American desert the old geographies call it, but it is no desert) largely through Colorado and Western Kansas, all flat, hundreds and even thousands of miles—some real good, nearly all pretty fair soil, all for stock raising, thousands of herds of cattle, some very large— the herdsmen, (the principal common employment) a wild hardy race, always on horse back, they call 'em cow-boys altogether—I used to like to get among them and talk to them —I stopt some days at a town right in the middle of those Plains, in Kansas, on the Santa Fe road—found a soldier there who had known me in the War 15 years ago—was married and running the hotel there—I had hard work to get away from him—he wanted me to stay all winter—The picture at the beginning of this letter is the St. Louis bridge over the Mississippi river—I often go down to the river, or across this bridge—it is one of my favorite sights—but the air of this City don't agree with me—I have not had a well day, (even for me) since I have been here—Well, Pete, dear boy, I guess I have written enough—How are you getting along? I often think of you and no doubt you often do of me—God bless you, my darling friend, and however it goes, you must keep up a good heart—for I do—So long—from your old Walt.

## CXXXI

## JOHN BURROUGHS

Camden [New Jersey,]
Dec 23 [1879]

Dear John Burroughs

Yours rec'd last week—Nothing new with me—I still keep well—The lecture is a *fixed fact* (to come)—but I shall wait till I get good & ready—I suppose as I am writing this you & 'Sula are now home—I 'most envy you—very cold here to day, but bright—& I am just going out for a couple of hours

*25th Christmas afternoon*

Went out—also yesterday—but not long or far, as we are having a sharp spell of cold & gusty winds here these days —Rec'd a letter from Herbert Gilchrist this morning—they are at 315 west 19 street, N.Y. now, in their own apartments, & I believe expect to be for the winter—Call on them, & 'Sula call too, when down—— Write me more fully about your proposed book of next spring—(it is in the gestation of a book— the melting of the fluid metal, before the casting—that it receives that something to make its idiosyncrasy, identity—its 'excuse for being' if it is to have any)—I have written to Jenny Gilder & sent her a small budget of printed slips &c. (I would like best to be *told about* in strings of continuous anecdotes, incidents, *mots*, thumb nail personal sketches, characteristic —& true—such for instance as are in the 2d edition of your old Wash'n *Notes*)—Yours of 17th Dec. rec'd—Tennyson & the criticism safely rec'd *back*—I suppose you rec'd the hat photo. you spoke of—(I sent it to you Oct 1st)—I mailed you also a pair of buck gloves—& Smith a pair too—four days since—I shall send this to Delaware County, as you say you are going home for a few days—Write me if you get it all right

W. W.

Happy New Year to you & all

## CXXXII

JOHN BURROUGHS, Esopus, New York

[Camden, New Jersey]
[March 29, 1881]

Dear Friend,

Yours rec'd with the good 10—God bless you—I half-moped along, all through February, but am coming round, same as before. I go down three or four days at a time to my friends, the Staffords and get out in the woods a great deal. . . . It is only half an hour's journey. Should have come up there with you a month ago but was hardly able. I got a bad chill six weeks ago, struck in (was quite well up to that time)

Your letter *don't contain* the slip about the Emerson busi-

ness you allude to—the just-published Carlyle Reminiscences, so well and strongly praised in the *Herald*, the
*Critic*, and everywhere, don't confirm or add to my estimation of C—*much the contrary*——

Kennedy comes here quite often and is disposed to be
friendly—I guess he is a pretty good man, but has *the fever
called literature*, and I shouldn't wonder if he was in for it for
life. Lathrop has visited me—very pleasant. Shall be glad to
supply you with a set of books of course. I have plenty yet

Walt Whitman

## CXXXIII

### HELEN PRICE, Woodside, New York

431 Stevens Street,<br>Camden, New Jersey,<br>April 21, '81.

Dear Helen Price,

Your good letter has come & I am glad indeed to hear
from you & sister & father, & have you located.—All sorrowful, solemn, yet soothing thoughts come up in my mind at
reminiscences of my dear friend, your dear mother—have
often thought of you all since '73 the last time I saw you so
briefly—so sadly—[At his mother's funeral].

About Dr. Bucke (he is a long-established medical doctor
& head of the Asylum for the Insane at London, Ontario,
Canada)—you can write to him freely & send him what you
feel to—he is a true & trusted friend of mine—I know him
well—I have just returned from Boston where I have been
the past week—went on to read my annual *Death of Abraham
Lincoln* on the anniversary of that tragedy—I am pretty well
for me—am still under the benumbing influence of paralysis,
but thankful to be as well as I am—still board here (make my
headquarters here) with my brother & his wife—Eddy my
brother is living & well, he is now boarding ab't 40 miles
from here—Yes, Helen dear, when I come to New York, I
will send you word sure—Best love to you, Emmy, father &
all—especially little Walter.

Walt Whitman

## CXXXIV

### JOHN BURROUGHS, Esopus, New York

Concord, Massachusetts,
September 19, 1881

Dear John,

I keep on fairly in health and strength—have been out here a few days the guest of Mr. and Mrs. F. B. Sanborn—& everything most affectionate and hospitable from them both—& from others—Have had a curiously full and satisfactory time with Emerson—he came to see me Saturday evening early, Mrs. E also, & staid two hours—Yesterday I went there (by pressing invitation) to dinner, & staid two hours—a wonderfully good two hours—the whole family were very cordial, including Mrs. E and the son, Edward, a doctor, a fine, handsome, 'cute, glowing young man, with a beautiful wife and child—I took to them all—I cannot tell you how sweet and good (and all as it should be) Emerson look'd and behaved —he did not talk in the way of joining in any animated conversation, but pleasantly and hesitatingly & sparsely—fully enough—to me it seemed just as it should be.

The book is about through—will appear last of October— every thing satisfactory. I go from here in about a week to Johnston's, Cor. Mott Avenue & 149th Street, N. Y.—then to Camden. Shall go to Canada this winter.

Walt Whitman

## CXXXV

### JOHN BURROUGHS, Esopus, New York

[Boston, Massachusetts,
September 24, 1881]

... I am now back here finishing up, only staid a few days in Concord, but they were marked days. . . . For my part I thought the old man in his smiling and alert quietude and withdrawnness (he has a good color in his face and ate just as much dinner as anybody) more eloquent, grand, appropriate and impressive than ever, more indeed than could be described. Isn't it comforting that I have had, in the sunset, as it were, so many significant, affectionate hours with him, under such quiet, beautiful, appropriate circumstances? . . .

Besides this general death-gloom of the nation, have you heard of the sudden and dreadful death of our young friend, Beatrice Gilchrist, in performing some chemical experiment with ether?

Joaquin Miller is here, is with me every day. Longfellow has been to see me. I have met O. W. Holmes, and old Mr. James.

With love

Walt Whitman

## CXXXVI

### ALMA CALDER JOHNSTON

Rand, Avery & Co., Printers<br>Boston, Monday noon Oct: 10 '81

My dear friend

Yours rec'd & thanks—I still linger along here—the printing of my book is finished—but one or two little things I want to see to—& then I am in no hurry. Shall probably finish up altogether this week—& then shall come on to your house—shall send you word a day before hand—I am well as usual—Have had a very pleasant time here & the book printed &c to my entire satisfaction—Best love to John, Ally, and the dear girls——

Walt Whitman

## CXXXVII

TO ——— ——— ——— Dresden, Saxony

Camden, New Jersey, U.S.A.,<br>Dec. 20, '81.

Dear Sir:—Your letter asking definite endorsement to your translation of my *Leaves of Grass* into Russian is just received, and I hasten to answer it. Most warmly and willingly I consent to the translation, and waft a prayerful *God speed* to the enterprise.

You Russians and we Americans! Our countries so distant, so unlike at first glance—such a difference in social and political conditions, and our respective methods of moral and practical development the last hundred years;—and yet in certain features, and vastest ones, so resembling each other. The variety of stock-elements and tongues, to be resolutely fused in a common identity and union at all hazards—the idea, perennial through the ages, that they both have their historic and divine mission—the fervent element of manly friendship throughout the whole people, surpass'd by no other races—the grand expanse of territorial limits and boundaries—the unform'd and nebulous state of many things, not yet permanently settled, but agreed on all hands to be the preparations of an infinitely greater future—the fact that both Peoples have their independent and leading positions to hold, keep, and if necessary, fight for, against the rest of the world—the deathless aspirations at the inmost centre of each great community, so vehement, so mysterious, so abysmic—are certainly features you Russians and we Americans possess in common.

As my dearest dream is for an internationality of poems and poets, binding the lands of the earth closer than all treaties and diplomacy—as the purpose beneath the rest in my book is such hearty comradeship, for individuals to begin with, and for all the nations of the earth as a result—how happy I should be to get the hearing and emotional contact of the great Russian peoples.

To whom, now and here, (addressing you for Russia and Russians, and empowering you, should you see fit, to print the present letter, in your book, as a preface,) I waft affectionate salutation from these shores, in America's name.

W. W.

## CXXXVIII

### JOHN BURROUGHS

April 28, 1882

. . . So Emerson is dead—the leading man in all Israel. If I feel able I shall go to his funeral—improbable though. A new deal in the fortunes of *Leaves of Grass*—the District Attorney at Boston has threatened Osgood with indictment "under the statues against obscene literature,—specifies a long list of pieces, lines, &c—Osgood is frightened, asks me to change and expurgate—I refuse peremptorily—*he throws up the book and will not publish it any more*—wants me to take the plates, wh. I shall try to do and publish it as before (in some respects shall like it just as well). Can you help me? Can you loan me $100?

The next *N. A. Review* (June number) will have a piece, "A Memorandum at a Venture," signed by my name, in which I ventilate my theory of sexual matter, treatment and allusion in *Children of Adam*—I shall have some slips and will send you some to England.

—Am writing this in great haste, angry with myself for not having responded before to your good letter of April 10. Love to 'Sula and the kid.

## CXXXIX

### JOHN BURROUGHS, Esopus, New York

[Camden, New Jersey?]
[Before June] 1882

I have run over the Carlyle proof and being in the mood have thought best to mark (of course for your consideration—you may have something behind which I do not see) *out* certain passages just as they summarily impresst me—clearly though rapidly feeling as I went along that the article would be bettered and more unitary without them.

What you set out mainly to say, and have to say, seems to me very well said indeed, and I *like the article*—What you have to offer as the Carlyle foil, in defence of America, I don't like so well—besides, it is unnecessary anyhow—unless one has got something outsmashing Carlyle himself—a battering-ram that batters *his* ram to the dust.

## CXL

## JOHN BURROUGHS, Esopus, New York

[New York?]
[August 13, 1882]

I commenced publishing *L of G* in June on my own hook, but
found it vexatious from the start, and having quite vehement
proposals from Rees Welsh (2d hand book dealer and law
book publisher, 23 South 9th St. Phila.) I passed the use of
the plates into his hands—he printed it (the plates are here in
Phila.) an exact copy of the Osgood edition—Welsh's first
edition (a cautious 1000) was ready about three weeks ago
and was exhausted in a day—the second came in ab't five
days ago, and is now nearly gone—a third is ordered—I am
very glad I let him have it——

I am throwing together a prose jumble, *Specimen Days*—
(see slips enclosed)—nearly 200 pages already cast——

... When you have a leisure hour reel me off a letter—put
in about Mrs. Gilchrist and Herbert. Dr. Bucke is keeping
back his book till *Specimen Days* comes out—will come out
by winter likely.

Walt Whitman

## CXLI

## WILLIAM D. O'CONNOR

431 Stevens Street Camden New Jersey
Nov. 12 '82—Sunday a.m.

......

I have rec'd a long letter from Ezra Heywood dated
Princeton, Mass:—Heywood has been arrested by Comstock
—part at least of the *cause* appears to be sending printed
slips by mail with "to a common prostitute" and "A woman
waits for me"—supplements to Heywood's paper *the Word*
—(I believe I will just enclose H's letter—slips & all)—My
impression is that *Comstock's chief object is to get (by snap
judgment probably) a judicial decision on which he can base a
show to go before the P.M. General* (as per the late decision of

P.M.G. in such questions)—the hearing is to come off before U.S. Commissioner Hallett in Boston, Nov. 16——

—(As to the vehement action of the Free religious and lover folk, in their conventions, papers &c. in my favor—and even proceedings like those of Heywood—I see nothing better for myself or friends to do than quietly stand aside & let it go on) what do you think?

As I write it is a cloudy moist warmish Sunday, 10-¼ a.m. pleasant—quiet here—I am up in my 3d story, south-front room, writing this——

There is a long & supercilious notice of S. D. in *N. Y. World*, Oct 30,—I wonder if written by Hurlbut himself?—an examination of that New York nest of little malignants, (Stoddard, little Winter, and half a dozen more)—the *Boston Herald* some weeks since (Oct 15) had a lengthy and very warm notice—very judicious extracts (Sylvester Baxter author)—the best I have seen from the book's own standpoint (which of course is everything)

—Are you then going to make a brochure of the *Tribune* letters? *Good,* if so—Shall I furnish you with more detailed and verbatim data of the Osgood transaction & correspondence—or have you them sufficiently?——

—Where is Ashton? Is he there in W. & do you see him?— If so tell him I have not forgotten him—& that I send him & Mrs. A my love——

—In a late note I asked you, if eligible, to send me Charley Eldridge's address—(Do you know what *ducks and drakes* are? Well S.D. is a rapid skimming over the pond-surface of my life, thoughts, *expressions* that way—the real are altogether untouched, but the flat pebble making a few dips as it flies & flits along—enough at least to give some living touches and contact points)—I was quite willing to make an immense *negative* book.

I am holding my own in the recovery of my *half state* of health—am contemplating some changes of base, (residence, domicile—sometimes I have thought of coming to Washington, settling there, getting a lot & small house in fee simple) —Have you sent Dowden's letter to Dr. Bucke?—I got a letter from Dr. Channing asking me to lecture in the Tilton sisters' course this winter in Boston—but I cannot lecture at present—besides I shall certainly not do anything to identify myself specially with free love.                                    W. W.

Write as often as you can—the days are quite stagnant with me—(a spell at any rate)

## CXLII

### PETER DOYLE, Washington

[June, 1883]

Pete do you remember—(of course you do—I do well)—those great long jovial walks we had at times for years, (1866-'72) out of Washington City—often moonlight nights, 'way to "Good Hope"; or, Sundays, up and down the Potomac shores, one side or the other, sometimes ten miles at a stretch? Or when you work'd on the horse-cars, and I waited for you, coming home late together—or resting and chatting at the Market, corner 7th street and the Avenue, and eating those nice musk or water-melons? Or during my tedious sickness and first paralysis ('73) how you used to come to my solitary garret room and make up my bed, and enliven me and chat for an hour or so—or perhaps go out and get the medicines Dr. Drinkard had order'd for me—before you went on duty? . . . Give my love to dear Mrs. and Mr. Nash, and tell them I have not forgotten them, and never will.

W. W.

## CXLIII

### JAMES REDPATH

August 12, 1885.

All right my dear J. R.—$60 for the Booth article will do, in full—(I reserve the right of printing it in future collections of my writings—this is indispensable) I have been and am lingering under the miserable inertia following my sunstroke —otherwise should have sent you one or two articles—have them on the stocks—Am very slowly gaining the tally of my strength—had none to spare before.

Thank you, dear friend, for your services and affectionate good will.

## CXLIV

## HERBERT GILCHRIST

15th December 1885.
Camden, United States, America.

Dear Herbert:

I have received your letter. Nothing now remains but a sweet and rich memory—none more beautiful all time, all life all the earth—I cannot write anything of a letter to-day. I must sit alone and think.

Walt Whitman.

## CXLV

## CENTURY MAGAZINE, New York City

328 Mickle street
Camden N J July 15 '86

—Thanks for the three slips. I shall keep them carefully in my own hands until I see "Father Taylor" printed in the magazine—if I am indebted, as I fancy, to the printing office, for the courtesy of the slips, please send this card there if convenient.

Walt Whitman

## CXLVI

## W. S. KENNEDY, Belmont, Massachusetts

Camden, Feb. 25, '87—*Noon*

Dear W. S. K.—It is of no importance whether I had read Emerson before starting *L. of G.* or not. The fact happens to be positively that I had *not*. The basis and body and genesis of the *L[eaves]* differing I suppose from Em[erson] and many grandest poets and artists was and is that I found and find everything in the *common concrete*, the broadest materials, the flesh, the common passions, the tangible and visible, etc., and in *the average*, and that I radiate, work from, these outward—or rather hardly wish to leave here but to remain and celebrate it all. Whatever the amount of this may be or not be, it is certainly *not Emersonian*, not Shakspere, not Tennyson—indeed, the antipodes of E. and the others in essential respects. But I have not suggested or exprest myself well in my book unless I have in a sort included them and their sides and expressions too—as this orb the world means and includes all climes, all sorts, *L. of G.'s* word is *the body, including all*, including the intellect and soul; E.'s word is mind (or intellect or soul).

If I were to unbosom to you in the matter I should say that I never cared so very much for E.'s writings, prose or poems, but from his first personal visit and two hours with me (in Brooklyn in 1866 or '65?) [the query mark his; he means '55 or '56] I had a strange attachment and love for *him* and his contact, talk, company, magnetism. I welcomed *him* deepest and always—yet it began and continued *on his part*, quite entirely; HE always sought ME. We probably had a dozen (possibly twenty) of these meetings, talks, walks, etc.—some five or six times (sometimes New York, sometimes Boston) had good long dinners together. I was very happy—I don't think I was at my best with him—he always did most of the talking—I am sure he was happy too. That visit to me at Sanborn's, by E. and family (see pp. 189-90 *Specimen Days*), and the splendid formal-informal family dinner *to me*, next day, Sunday, Sept. 18, '81, by E., Mrs. E., and all, I consider not only a victor-event in my life, but it is an after-explanation of so much and offered as an apology, peace-offering, justification, of much that the world knows not of. My dear friend, I think I know R. W. E. better than anybody else knows him—and loved him in proportion, but quietly. Much was revealed to me.

Walt Whitman.

## CXLVII

### KARL KNORTZ

Camden, N.J. March 24. '87.

I am still here in good heart (good spirits) mainly—but am almost entirely disabled and powerless to move about at all.

Dr. Bucke is well and active at his post in Canada. O'Connor is very ill and is now in Southern California. W. S. Kennedy (Belmont, Mass.) has a book about me that is to be published in England soon. I am quiescent, but think of publishing in collected and revised form my pieces of last four years in a little book *November Boughs*.

Walt Whitman

## CXLVIII

### EDWARD CARPENTER, Sheffield, England

328 Mickle st —Camden New Jersey
U S America May 3 '87

Yours of Ap: 20 just rec'd & welcomed. Write oftener—The Staffords & I remember you with greatest affection & esteem —I also with deepest gratitude.—I am still here in the same little old house—of course gradually sinking and dissolving —Harry S. had a surgical operation on his throat—it seems to have been properly done,—& the cut is healing—He is at Marlton, New Jersey, married, has a child—I send you some papers—always best love

Walt Whitman

## CXLIX

### KARL KNORTZ

Camden, N.J. May 3. '87.

Your letter received and welcomed as always. My visit to New York was a hasty flash only. I am more and more wretchedly physically disabled and feel better off here in my own den.

The "Anne Gilchrist" book is a wonderful well done vol. and interesting very to me, because I knew and loved Mrs. G—but I doubt whether it contains much (or any thing) for you. I can loan you my copy if you wish. I will certainly keep you posted about myself, or any literary movement or change or happening of my work.

Walt Whitman

## CL

### [TO THE EDITORS OF THE *CRITIC*]

328 Mickle Street
Camden New Jersey
May 30 '87

I wish to warmly thank Elizabeth Porter Gould and yourselves for the article ab't myself & the war hospitals—Nothing I have received has touch'd me deeper or been more
comforting & agreeable to me. If convenient I sh'd like to
have you send this note to E. P. G. with my thanks &
regards——

Walt Whitman

## CLI

### WILLIAM SLOANE KENNEDY, Belmont.
Massachusetts

Tues., p.m. [Oct. 4, '87].

Hear from Dr. Bucke frequently; he always writes me
cheerily and chipper, which I like, for it is pretty monotonous here. I return Symonds's letter herewith. The whole
matter—this letter and the *Fortnightly* note [by him]—seems
to me funny.

"Perhaps there may be bairns, kind sir,
Perhaps there may be *not*."

## CLII

### EDITOR PALL MALL GAZETTE

[1887]

First thank you again for the handsome money present of
some months ago, which did me more good than you perhaps
think for—it has helped me in meals, clothing, debts, &c ever
since. My best help however has come in my old age and
paralysis from the British Islands. The piece in your paper
(was it early in May last?) from "a distinguished American
man of letters" about me was a very large inflation into

fiction of a very little amount of fact—in spirit it is altogether, and in letter mainly untrue about my affairs, &c. My income from my books (royalties &c) does not realize $100 a year. I am now in my 69th year, living plainly, but very comfortably, in a little wooden cottage of my own, good spirits invariably, but physically a sad wreck, and failing more and more each successive season, unable even to get about the house without help—most of the time, though, without serious pain or suffering, except extreme weakness which I have a good deal—the paralysis that prostrated me after the Secession War (several shocks) never lifting entirely since, but leaving me mentally unimpaired absolutely (thank God!) I have a few, very few, staunch and loving friends and upholders here in America. I am gathering a lot of pieces— verse and prose—uttered within the last six years, and shall send them out under the name of *November Boughs* before long—a little book (200 pages or less), some new pieces—a sort of continuation or supplement. Then I think of printing a revised edition of complete writings ("Leaves of Grass," "Specimen Days and Collect," and "November Boughs" all in one volume) soon. Please accept personal thanks from me (never mind the literary) and I know you will accept this impromptu note in the same spirit in which it is written. Best thanks and love to all my British helpers, readers, and defenders.

## CLIII

### W. S. KENNEDY AND JOHN BURROUGHS

My dear friends W S K & J B     Camden Feb: 11 '88

I send you Dr. Bucke's letter from Florida just rec'd with the latest from our dear friend O'Connor (tho' I think Dr B's view is ab't as severe & dark as the case will stand)

—Nothing is very new or special with me—I am jogging along much the same—down hill no doubt even if slowly (this is the most nipping winter I have ever had)—at present am sitting here by the fire in my little front room—have had my late breakfast (I rise late these cold days) of chocolate & buckwheat cakes with quince jelly—feel so-so fair.—Ernest

Rhys is here (was here last ev'n'g)—his lecture, debate & advocacy of *L of G.* last Tuesday ev'n'g. in N Y. seems to have been quite an affair—a success—the leaning of the full dress audience (many ladies) was palpably certainly on our side—quite remarkable—Tho' little Fawcett & Rev. Lloyd had their say against *L of G.* Rhys delivers lecture again here in Phila. next Tuesday evn'g. I still have little bits in N Y *Herald*——

                                        Walt Whitman

## CLIV

### JOHN BURROUGHS, West Park, New York

                                    [December 21, 1888.]
My Dear Friend,

Real glad to hear from you once more. . . . The death of Mrs. Gilchrist is indeed a gloomy fact. She had cancer and suffered much the last three months of her life with asthma—for a long time "every breath was a struggle", Herbert expresses it. The actual cause of death was dilation of the heart. Seems to me mortality never enclosed a more beautiful spirit.

The trouble ab't my eyesight passed over, and I use both eyes now same as before.

I am living here, rather monotonously, but get along. As I write, feel ab't the same as of late years—only the walking power seems quite gone from me. I can hardly get from one room to another—sometimes quite force myself to get out a few yards, but difficult and risky——

O'Connor seems to be holding on at Washington. I think he is middling well, except the leg power—his "gelatine legs" he calls them—will pass over, I rather think.

I drove down yesterday (Sunday) to my friends, the Staffords, 10 miles from here, and staid three hours, had dinner, etc. I go there every Sunday. So I get stirred up some, but not half enough—three reasons, my natural sluggishness and the paralysis of late years, the weather and my old, stiff, slow horse, with a lurking propensity to stumble down——

The "free-will offering" of the English, through Rossetti, has amounted in the past year to over 400—I am still living on it—I get a miserable return of royalties from McKay, my

Philad. publisher—not $50 for both books, *L of G* and *S.D* for the past year.

John, I like *both the names* in your note—I cannot choose —if I lean at all it is in favor of "Spring Relish"—either would be first rate—Did you get W. S. Kennedy's pamphlet, *the Poet as a Craftsman*?

I hear from Dr. Bucke quite often, he was, the past season, somewhat broken in physical stamina and health but is better—he gives up for the present his European tour, but is coming here soon for a week.

As I close my bird is singing like a house afire, and the sun is shining out—I wish you were here to spend the day with me.

W. W.

## CLV

### EDMUND CLARENCE STEDMAN [New York City]

328 Mickle Street
Camden New Jersey March 31 '89

Thanks my dear E C S for the box of noble books with the endless mines in them—& double thanks for the loving cheering (I fear flattering,) long letter, wh' has done me good, & I have read twice—My friendly & liberal presentation 7th Vol. is thoroughly appreciated by me—& the picture is certainly printed at its best—The whole presentation indeed is by far the best of that sort I ever received. I wish to convey my best regards to the printers, proof-readers & print-plate presser &c—I have been laid up for nearly a year almost entirely disabled—imprison'd in sick room—last fall & during winter sometimes low, serious, but just now easier, comparatively free from pain,—getting along better than you might suppose. —Our dear friend O'Connor is very ill at Washington (lower legs paralyzed, & lately attacks of epilepsy)—Burroughs is pretty well—is at his place West Park Ulster Co: with his wife & boy (with a book in press, I believe)—Best regards & love to you & yours—Have put off this letter of thanks & good wishes waiting for a day I sh'd feel pretty well to write it in, but such day lagging I delay no longer.

Walt Whitman

## CLVI

### THOMAS B. HARNED, Philadelphia

Tom:                                    May 10th, 1889.

If you will, fill the brown bottle with sherry for me, and the small white bottle with Cognac. My dear friend O'Connor is dead.

                                        Walt Whitman

## CLVII

### JOHN ADDINGTON SYMONDS

                                Camden, New Jersey
                                August 19, 1890

. . . About the questions on *Calamus* etc., they quite daze me. *Leaves of Grass* is only rightly to be construed by and within its own atmosphere and essential character—all its pages and pieces so coming strictly under. That the *Calamus* part has ever allowed the possibility of such construction as mentioned is terrible. I am fain to hope that the pages themselves are not to be even mentioned for such gratuitous and quite at the time undreamed and unwished possibility of morbid inference—which are disavowed by me and seem damnable.

. . . My life, young manhood, mid-age, times South, etc., have been jolly bodily, and doubtless open to criticism. Though unmarried I have had six children—two are dead— one living Southern grandchild, fine boy, writes to me occasionally—circumstances (connected with their fortune and benefit) have separated me from intimate relations.

## CLVIII

### J. W. WALLACE, Bolton, Lancashire

                                        Sept: 8, '90.

Y'r kind letter rec'd & I have enc'd it in my letter to Dr. Bucke to-day. I continue well as usual of late—had melon & rye bread for my breakfast—fair appetite. Have just written a card to Dr. J.—his photos rec'd good. I am getting some sharp notices in print here lately. One I hear of (I have not seen it yet) in Sept. *Atlantic* Mag: by Dr. Holmes (the physician, you doubtless know, wants to achieve a good job more than to get the love of the patient).

## CLIX

### J. W. WALLACE, Bolton, Lancashire

Sept: 22, '90.

Yr's of 11th rec'd—P.O. order rec'd—& thank you. Sent the little *L. of G.* pocket-bk ed'n three or four days since—possibly I may have made the mistake of directing it to Dr. J. (hope I have not also made the mistake of writing y'r or his name in it—cannot now remember distinctly,)—but at any rate you must have rec'd it by this time.

The little "new volume" to be put out by me will be only a further annex (the 2d, one) to *L. of G.*—fixing the bits of the last year and a half in book shape. Will send you word of it and probably the sheets themselves. Tell Dr. J. the photos (of myself & Frank Warren Fritzinger, my friend & gillie) are rec'd & valued both by me & Warry. Cooler weather here, but I get out in wheel chair a little. Keep as well as usual. Enclose a printed slip (a 2d. one, give to Dr. J.). Respects to F. R. C. Hutton & all the friends.

## CLX

### J. JOHNSTON, Bolton, Lancashire

[Camden, New Jersey]
Dec: 2, '90.

The *Notes* & "Good Words" have come all right. Of the *Notes* I w'd like you to send a copy each to:

Mrs. O'Connor, 112, M. Street, N.W., Washington, D.C.

Mrs. Mary E. Van Nostrand, Greenport, Suffolk Co., New York.

Miss Whitman, 2436 2d. Carondelet Av. St. Louis, Missouri.

Mrs. H. L. Heyde, 21, Pearl Street, Burlington, Vermont.

R. G. Ingersoll, 45, Wall Street, New York City.

Sloane Kennedy, Belmont, Mass.

David McKay, Publisher, 23, South 9th St. Philadelphia.

Talcott Williams, Press Newspaper Office, Philadelphia.

Bernard O'Dowd, Supreme Court Library, Melbourne, Victoria.

R. Pearsall Smith, 44, Grosvenor Road, Westminster Embankm't, London.

Edw'd Carpenter, Millthorpe, near Chesterfield, England.

M. Gabriel Sarrazin, Magistrat, Nouméa, Nouvelle Calédonie (Colonies Françaises).

? to Tennyson.

W. M. Rossetti, Euston Square, London.

J. Addington Symonds, Davos Platz, Switzerland.

Have read the Notes all through & accept & like them— (am pleased & flatter'd always best in the human side). Hope you have had a good lot struck off by the printer, as they will surely be wanted—& (barring their fearfully eulogistic tinge) I endorse all. Nothing very new or different here—physically bad off these times. The pict: in *Good Words* has got a decidedly better turn to it than the big Ill: one. A gloomy blue week here—death of my brother Jeff six days ago at St. Louis, Missouri. Cold weather here—all white f'm snow out. Affectionate remembrances to all. I am sitting here in the big old chair with wolf skin spread—sun shining merrily out on the snow.

## CLXI

### J. JOHNSTON, Bolton, Lancashire

[Camden, New Jersey]
Feb: 17th, '91. Noon.

The item was right, am in a bad way: "may blow over—may not", but it will be all right either way.

Remembrance to you & J. W. W. & all the friends. Am sitting here as usual—& have had a cup of coffee. God bless you & all.

## CLXII

### J. JOHNSTON

March 30, '91.

Pleasant sunny day out & I am getting on fairly considering —have pretty good nights—must have five or six hours sleep—no vehement pain night or day that I make acc't of. Eat my two meals daily or something of them, farina, roast apple, rare fried egg, mutton & rice, &c. &c. Dr. Longaker, (652 North 8th Street, Philadelphia) comes every 2d day, and I like him & his doings. There has been some little correspondence bet'n him & Dr. Bucke. The latter is well—I got letter to-day. Wish you to pass this scrawl to J. W. W., as he may like to know particulars. The *Nat. Review* comes to-day & I have been looking at W. Sharp's piece. (All guessing ab't future American National Literature seems to me guessing on the weather of years f'm now.) The proofs of *Good Bye My Fancy* are slowly getting along. Have sent back 31 pp. to be corrected—(there may be ab't 45). Don't you look out for anything stirring—it is small anyhow & mostly to untune (let down) clinch what I have said before, pass the fingers again carelessly over the strings, & probably some parrot-like repetitions & *to close the book*, avoiding anything like trumpet blasts or attempts at them. Intend it to be bound in with *November Boughs* & make its supplementary part.

## CLXIII

### J. W. WALLACE, Bolton, Lancashire

[Camden, New Jersey]
May 9, '91. Even'g.

Thanks for y'r loving cable missive, rec'd to-day. Everything with me is at low ebb—perhaps the lowest—perhaps the waters may come in again—perhaps not—it will be all right either way. Dr. Longaker has come in to-day after ten days absence—is very welcome. Y'rs & Dr. J's good letters rec'd to-day & a good letter f'm Dr. Bucke. Have sent a Copy May *N.E. Magazine* to Dr. J. for his and y'r service. Seems a spell of warm sunny weather started here.

May 10, noon.—Fine sunny warm day. . . . Do you keep at all the American presidential trip Pacific-ward & South-westward, with the tip-top off-hand speeches of Prest. Harri-son? All curious & significant & satisfactory to me—a lunch trip of 10,000 miles, "& all on our own land".

## CLXIV

### DR. RICHARD MAURICE BUCKE
London, Ontario

Camden pm May 23 '91

Nothing very new or different—bad bad enough—*the fiend-ish indigestion block* continued—heavy torpor increasing—the burial house in Harleigh well toward finished—I paid the constructor $500 last week—(as far as I can see I am favored in having Ralph Moore as my *alter ego* in making it)—I wish to collect the remains of my parents & two or three other near relations & shall doubtless do so—I have two deceased children (young man & woman—illegitimate of course) that I much desired to bury here with me—but have ab't aban-doned the plan on account of angry litigation and fuss gener-ally, and disinterment from down South—Kennedy has printed a short criticism of *Good Bye*—finds it without the sign-marks of early *L. of G.*—praises it highly tho'—As I get toward estimate, but that is more in the forming than settled state, from my own point of view I accept without demur its spurty (old Lear's irascibility)—its off-handedness, even evid-ence of decrepitude & old fisherman's seine character as part of the *artism* (from my point of view) & as adherent as the determined cartoon of personality that dominates or rather stands behind all *L. of G.* like the unseen master & director of the show.

W. W.

## CLXV

### J. W. WALLACE, Bolton, Lancashire

May 29, '91.

Still badly prostrated—horrible torpidity, y'rs & Dr.'s letters rec'd & cheer me much. Am sitting here in big chair at this moment. I guess I have a good deal of the feeling of Epictetus & stoicism—or tried to have. They are specially needed in a rich & luxurious, & even scientific age. But I am clear that I include & allow & probably teach some things stoicism would frown upon & discard. One's pulses & marrow are not *democratic* & *natural* for nothing. Let Plato's steeds prance & curvet & drive at their utmost, but the master's grip & eyes & brain must retain the ultimate power for all or things are lost. Give my loving compliments to all the boys, & give this scrawl to Wentworth Dixon to keep if he cares for it.

### CLXVI

#### J. JOHNSTON, Bolton, Lancashire

[Camden, New Jersey]
June 1, '91.

Well, here I am launched on my 73rd year. We had our birth anniversary spree last evn'g. Ab't 40 people—choice friends mostly—twelve or so women. Tennyson sent a short and sweet letter over his own sign manual. Y'r cable was rec'd & read. Lots of bits of speeches with gems in them. We had a capital good supper, (or dinner,)—chicken soup. salmon, roast lamb, &c., &c., &c. I had been under a horrible spell f'm 5 to 6, but Warry got me dress'd & down—(like carrying down a great log)—& Traubel had all ready for me a big goblet of first-rate iced champagne—I suppose I swigged it off at once. I certainly welcom'd them all forthwith & at once felt if I was to go down I would not fail without a desperate struggle. Must have taken near two bottles champagne the even'g. So I added (I felt to) a few words of honor & reverence for our Emerson, Bryant, Longfellow dead—and then for Whittier & Tennyson, the boss of us all, (specifying all)—not four minutes altogether—then held out with them *for three hours*, talking lots, lots impromptu. Dr. B. is here. Horace T. is married. Fine sunny noon.

P.S. Doctor, if easy and cheap photo (fac-simile) this June 1 note, not the mask, & give one to each of the friends that desires, send Tennyson one, send Symonds one, send Whittier one (Amesbury, Mass.) & half a dozen to me. Just send them without explanation.

2L.                                                                W.

## CLXVII

### DR. R. M. BUCKE, London, Ontario

[Camden, New Jersey]
June 25, '91.

Hot wave set in again—quite mark'd depression with me to-day—fairish night last. The birthday report, &c., is all left out (*not* printed) in July Lippincott's for some reason, (probably excessive crowd of matter,) so don't look out for the Mag. Rec'd letters f'm the Bolton friends to-day & fac-similes of one I sent the next day after the birth-supper. (I believe one of the f.s. is sent to you—if not I will send you one.) What staunch tender fellows those Englishmen are! when they take a turn. I doubt if ever a fellow had such a splendid emotional send-back response as I have had f'm those Lancashire chaps under the lead of Dr. J. & J. W. W.—it cheers & nourishes my very heart. If you go down to Bolton & convenient, read publicly to them the last five or six lines as f'm my living pulse.—But I feel a bad spell coming on me & must lie down—hot oppressive to-day. (I fear a long continued spell of heat—piled on the rest—may tell badly on me.) Am again sitting here by open window—some breeze.

## CLXVIII

### J. JOHNSTON, Bolton, Lancashire

Nov: 3, '91.

Sunny cool day. Wallace went hence this mn'g well & in good spirits to take *City of Berlin* f'm N.Y. to-morrow mn'g. Sir Edwin Arnold & others here yesterday—all went well. A is being *recepted* here finely—he is evidently one of my warmest and solid friends. I continue ab't same as of late.

## CLXIX

### J. JOHNSTON, Bolton, Lancashire

Feb: 6, 1892.

Well I must send you all dear fellows a word from my own hand—propp'd up in bed, deadly weak yet, but the spark seems to glimmer yet—the doctors & nurses & N.Y. friends as faithful as ever. Here is the adv. of the '92 edn. Dr. Bucke is well & hard at work. Col. Ingersoll has been here, sent a basket of champagne. All are good—physical conditions &c. are not so bad as you might suppose, only my sufferings much of the time are fearful. Again I repeat my thanks to you & cheery British friends, may be last—my right arm giving out.

Walt Whitman.

*Feb:* 7.—Same cond'n cont'd—More & more it comes to the fore that the only theory worthy our modern times for g't literature politics and sociology must combine all the bulk-people of all lands, the women not forgetting. But the mustard plaster on my side is stinging & I must stop—Good-bye to all.

**W. W**

# Notes

# ABBREVIATIONS

*The following abbreviations have been used:*

Barrus for *Whitman and Burroughs Comrades*, 1931, Clara Barrus.

Bucke for *Walt Whitman*, 1883, Richard Maurice Bucke, M.D.

Comp. Prose for *Complete Prose*, 1907, Walt Whitman.

Donaldson for *Walt Whitman the Man*, 1896, Thomas Donaldson.

Furness for *Walt Whitman's Workshop*, 1928, Clifton Joseph Furness.

Glicksberg for *Walt Whitman and the Civil War*, 1933, Charles I. Glicksberg.

Harned for *The Letters of Anne Gilchrist and Walt Whitman*, 1918, ed. Thomas B. Harned.

Holloway for *Whitman; An Interpretation in Narrative*, 1926, Emory Holloway.

*In Re* for *In Re Walt Whitman*, 1893, eds. Horace L. Traubel, Richard Maurice Bucke, Thomas B. Harned.

Kennedy for *Reminiscences of Walt Whitman*, 1896, William Sloane Kennedy.

N. and F. for *Notes and Fragments Left by Walt Whitman*, 1899, ed. by Dr. Richard Maurice Bucke.

Perry for *Walt Whitman*, 1906, Bliss Perry.

Saunders for *Whitman Music List*, 1926, compiled and privately published by Henry S. Saunders.

S.D.C. for *Specimen Days—Collect*, 1907, Walt Whitman.

Traubel for *With Walt Whitman in Camden*, 1915, Horace Traubel.

U.P.P. for *Uncollected Poetry and Prose of Walt Whitman*, 1914, ed. Emory Holloway

# Notes

## *Poems*

"*Come, Said My Soul*" (motto). Various drafts of this poem, first published in "A Christmas Garland", Christmas *Graphic*, 1874, are to be found in *The Conservator*, June 1896, the Putnam edition of Whitman's *Complete Writings*, 1902, X, p. 131 ff., and in U.P.P., II, p. 56.

"*One's Self I Sing*" (p. 3). Cf. "Small the Theme of my Chant" (p. 469).

"*Eidólons*" (p. 6). For an explanation of Whitman's use of this word see Kennedy, pp. 140-141, and Carleton Noyes, *An Approach to Walt Whitman*, p. 166. Frank Harris quotes Whitman as saying that the poem was "returned by Scribner's with a 'very insulting and contemptuous letter'". (*Contemporary Portraits*, Third Series, p. 221.)

"*To the States*" (p. 10). Title in the 1860 Edition, "Walt Whitman's Caution".

"*To a Certain Cantatrice*" (p. 10). Addressed to Marietta Alboni, according to Isaac Hull Platt. (*Walt Whitman*, p. 15.)

"*Starting from Paumanok*" (p. 14). Whitman was fond of the old Indian name for Long Island and sometimes used it as a *nom de plume*, e.g. U.P.P., I, p. 247. In "Brooklyniana" he gives the meaning as "The island with its breast long drawn out, and laid against the sea". (U.P.P., II, p. 274.)

p. 18, ll. 9-10: "*It may be*", etc. Cf. "Ambition" (p. 502).

"*Song of Myself*" (p. 26). First printed with a title, "A Poem of Walt Whitman, An American", in 1860.

p. 29, l. 8: "*show me to a cent*" substituted for "show to me a cent" in 1888 edition. (See Traubel, II, p. 324.)

p. 30, ll. 9-12: These lines were on the list of passages Osgood asked to be expurgated if he should continue the publication of *Leaves of Grass* in 1880. (Bucke, p. 149.)

p. 31, l. 11: "*Tuckahoe*"—a native of Virginia, the inhabitants of the poor lands of which state were supposed to live on tuckahoe, an underground fungus-sclerotium (*Standard Dictionary*). "*Cuff*" —short for Cuffy, a local nickname for a negro.

p. 33, ll. 14 ff.: "*the heavy omnibus*", etc. Cf. pp. 563 ff.

p. 36, l. 15: "*shuffle and break-down*", a form of negro dance.

p. 39, l. 7: "*The jour printer with gray head*", etc. A line probably suggested by William Hartshorne, the old printer who taught Whitman to set type. (U.P.P., I, p. 234 n.: II, pp. 245-249, 294.)

p. 41, l. 4: "*the fourth of Seventh-month*", a form of expression appearing in Whitman's early editions which reflects the Quaker influences of his childhood.

p. 49, ll. 14-23: "*And of the threads*", etc. These lines were also on the Osgood list of expurgations demanded.

p. 50, ll. 9-18: "*You my rich blood . . . it shall be you*". These lines were also on the Osgood list. (Bucke, p. 149.)

p. 53, l. 18: "*To be in any form*", etc. Cf. "To Be At All" (p. 499).

p. 54, ll. 1-23: "*Is this then a touch? . . . too much for me*". This passage was also on the Osgood list of recommended expurgations. The original manuscript of this passage is to be seen in U.P.P., II, pp. 72-73.

p. 55, ll. 20 ff.: "*I believe a leaf of grass*", etc. The original manuscript version of this passage is to be found in U.P.P., I, p. 70.

p. 57, ll. 23 ff.: "*My ties and ballasts leave me*", etc. Cf. U.P.P., II, p. 66. "*I am afoot with my vision*". Cf. *The Sleepers* (p. 383) and Holloway, pp. 123 ff.

p. 59, l. 6: "*Swims with her calf*". Originally "her calves", but altered when Whitman discovered that the whale usually has but one calf. See J. Johnston and J. W. Wallace, *Visits to Walt Whitman in* 1890-1891, p. 46.

p. 62, ll. 15-16: "*I turn the bridegroom out of bed*", etc. These lines were on the Osgood list of expurgations demanded.

p. 62, ll. 19 ff.: "*I understand the large hearts of heroes*", etc. According to Dr. R. M. Bucke this passage describes an actual shipwreck. ("Notes on the Text of Leaves of Grass", *Conservator*, VIII, p. 40.)

p. 64, ll. 20 ff.: "*Now I tell what I knew in Texas*", etc. Though Whitman may have been in Texas on some unidentified journey, this anecdote came from his reading rather than his personal experience. As editor of the Brooklyn *Eagle*, he had published, on March 11, 1846, an excerpt entitled "Fanning's Men, or The Massacre at Goliad", which he had found in *Blackwood's*. The original article was based in part on *A Campaign in Texas*, by Von H. Ehrenberg, Leipzig, 1845.

p. 66, ll. 1 ff.: "*Would you hear of an old-time sea-fight?*" etc. According to Dr. Bucke this passage describes the engagement between the *Bon Homme Richard*, John Paul Jones, commander, and the *Serapis*, Richard Pearson, commander, in the North Sea, September 23, 1779. (*Conservator*, VII, p. 88.)

p. 69, l. 12: "*Eleves*". For Whitman's attitude toward the incorporation of foreign words into English speech, see his article "America's Mightiest Inheritance", *New York Dissected*, pp. 55-65.

p. 70, ll. 21-22: "*On women*", etc. Cf. "*To the Garden the World*" (p. 86). These lines were included in the Osgood list.

p. 70, ll. 23 ff.: "*To any one dying*", etc. The original manuscript version of this passage is to be seen in U.P.P., II, p. 69.

p. 74, ll. 16 ff.: "*I do not despise you priests*", etc. For a very early employment of the device used in this passage see *Sun-Down Papers—No.* 8, p. 542. Albert Mordell (*Erotic Motive in Literature*, p. 240) thinks this passage may have been suggested by George Sand's *Consuelo*, a book of which Whitman was very fond. A fictional use of the method is made by Jack London in *The Star Rover*.

p. 79, ll. 10 ff.: "*I have no chair*", etc. For the original prose version of this passage see U.P.P., II, p. 66.

"*Children of Adam*" (pp. 86-105). For Whitman's statements concerning his purpose in writing this group of poems see "A Memorandum at a Venture" (p. 804) and "Boston Common— More of Emerson" (p. 797). Whitman said to Traubel in March, 1888: " 'Children of Adam' stumps the worst and the best: I have even tried hard to see if it might not as I grow older or experience new moods stump me: I have even almost deliberately tried to retreat. But it would not do. When I tried to take these pieces out of the scheme the whole scheme came down about my ears." (Traubel, I, p. 3.) Cf. Letter XXXVIII (p. 948).

"*From Pent-up Aching Rivers*" (p. 86):

p. 86, ll. 15-16: "*From my own voice*", etc. and p. 87, l. 12; p. 88, l. 19: "*The female form approaching*", etc. These lines were on the Osgood list.

"*I Sing the Body Electric*" (p. 88).

p. 91, l. 15-p. 92, l. 3: "*Mad filaments*", etc. These lines were on the Osgood list.

p. 93, l. 13: During his visit to New Orleans in 1848 Whitman had an opportunity to observe the slave auctions in the basement of the old St. Louis Hotel. Advertisements of these auctions were carried in the daily *Crescent*, on which he worked.

p. 95, l. 17-p. 96, l. 10: "*Hips, lip-sockets . . . meat of the body*." Osgood included these lines in his list.

"*A Woman Waits for Me*" (p. 96). The entire poem was on the Osgood list.

"*Spontaneous Me*" (p. 98, l. 17-p. 100, l. 10). "This poem . . . where it may". This passage was on the Osgood list.

"*Out of the Rolling Ocean the Crowd*" (p. 101). All that is known of the romantic attachment celebrated in this poem is given in U.P.P., I, lviii, n. 15. This poem has been set to music by Weda Cook Addicks, but the song has not been published.

*"Once I Pass'd through a Populous City"* (p. 104). This poem, often cited in support of the theory that Whitman had a love-affair in New Orleans, is shown in the original manuscript (U.P.P., II, p. 102) to have been addressed to a man. Mr. H. B. Binns mentions Whitman's "express desire that the poem be regarded merely in its universal application" (*A Life of Walt Whitman*, p. 51); since it was not published until 1860, it is possible to argue that, in his desire to celebrate the permanence of human affection as contrasted with other experiences, Whitman chose from his own memories, first, his memory of a "Calamus" relationship, and substituted later a reminiscence of some "Children of Adam" experience, both being equally suitable as illustrations, but the latter more likely to prove poetically effective. As bearing upon this interpretation, compare "Fast-Anchor'd Eternal O Love", published in the same edition as this poem (1860); it contained, until they were dropped from the 1881 edition, two lines whose phraseology is so similar to that of "Once I Pass'd through a Populous City" as to suggest the possibility of a common origin in Whitman's experience:

> "Singing what, to the Soul, entirely redeemed her, the faithful one, the prostitute, who detained me when I went to the city;
> Singing the song of prostitutes."

*"I Heard You Solemn-Sweet Pipes of the Organ"* (p. 104). I am indebted to Mr. Ralph Adimari for information concerning the first publication of this poem. Apparently it does not refer, as did "Out of the Rolling Ocean the Crowd", to Whitman's Washington inamorata, for it was first published in the New York *Leader*, October 12, 1861, as follows:

## LITTLE BELLS LAST NIGHT

War-suggesting trumpets, I heard you;
And you I heard beating, you chorus of small and large drums;
You round-lipp'd cannons!—you I heard, thunder-cracking, saluting the frigate from France;
I heard you, solemn-sweet pipes of the organ, as last Sunday morn I pass'd the church;
Winds of Autumn!—as I walk'd the woods at dusk, I heard your long-stretch'd sighs, up above, so mournful;
I heard the perfect Italian tenor, singing at the opera; I heard the soprano in the midst of the quartet singing;
Lady! you, too, I heard, as with white arms in your parlor, you play'd for me delicious music on the harp;
Heart of my love!—you, too, I heard, murmuring low, through one of the wrists around my head—
Heard the pulse of you, when all was still, ringing little bells last night under my ear.

*"Calamus"* (pp. 106-125). Cf. Letter LI (p. 964), Letter CLVII (p. 1052), and Letter CLXI, n. (p. 1054). This group of poems has long been the subject of conflicting interpretation, which Whitman's own comments have not always helped to clarify. Some writers see in them plain evidence that Whitman was simply a Uranian. (See Eduard Bertz, *Walt Whitman Ein Charakterbild* and other writings; W. W. Rivers, *Walt Whitman's Anomaly*; Ludwig Lewisohn, *Expression in America*; and Edgar Lee Masters, *Whitman*.) Others, like George Rice Carpenter (*Walt Whitman*), and Leon Bazalgette (*Walt Whitman*) interpret these poems of comradeship purely in their spiritual sense. No evidence has ever been made public which would convict Whitman of homosexual practices, and to classify him psychologically as a simple Uranian raises difficulties in the interpretation of the "Children of Adam" poems, their counterpart, which are as outspoken on the subject of the attraction between man and woman. Havelock Ellis indicates his view, always worthy of respect, by including Whitman in his *Intermediate Sex.* Jean Catel (*Walt Whitman, La Naissance du Poète*) seeks to reconcile the two expressions given to the affectionate nature of Whitman by a theory of autoeroticism, a kind of narcissism which employed others, of either sex, as mirrors in whom he could admire himself. The poems which follow certainly contain some esoteric elements, but this is not the place to analyse them. Suffice it to say that it is difficult to believe that any very simple explanation can fit all the facts.

*"In Paths Untrodden"* (p. 106). A part of an early manuscript of this poem is to be found in the Camden Edition of Whitman's *Complete Writings*, III, p. 137.

*"These I Singing in Spring"* (p. 111, l. 11): "*a live-oak*". Cf. "I Saw in Louisiana a Live-Oak Growing" (p. 118).

*"I Saw in Louisiana a Live-Oak Growing"* (p. 118). An early draft of this poem is published in *Complete Writings*, III, p. 140.

*"Here the Frailest Leaves of Me"* (p. 121). This poem was set to music as a song (unpublished) by Nicolas Dority. (Henry S. Saunders in his privately published *Whitman Music List*, 1926. To this I am indebted for most of the notes on Whitman music.)

*"Sometimes with One I Love"* (p. 124). Set to music in an unpublished song by Nicolas Dority.

*"That Shadow My Likeness"* (p. 125). An early manuscript version of this poem is to be found in U.P.P., II, p. 91.

*"Salut au Monde!"* (p. 126). Cf. "Excelsior" (p. 430), also "Sun-Down Papers—No. 8" (p. 542), and *Pictures, An Unpublished Poem of Walt Whitman*, New York and London, 1927. For a description of this poem as presented in a musical festival at the Neighborhood Playhouse in New York in April, 1922, with pantomime and choral music by Charles T. Griffes and Edmund Rickett, see New York *Sun*, April 24, 1922. There was a revival

of this festival in 1936 under the direction of Blanche Yurka, as a Federal Theater Project.

p. 130, l. 12: "*the full limb'd Bacchus*". Moncure Conway reports seeing a picture of Bacchus in Whitman's room when he visited him in Brooklyn. (*Fortnightly Review*, October 1866.)

"*Song of the Open Road*" (p. 136). William Sloane Kennedy is probably right in suggesting (*Conservator*, February 1907) that a hint for this poem may have been found by Whitman in George Sand's *Consuelo*, Chapter III: "What is more beautiful than a road? It is the symbol and the image of an active and varied life," etc. Whitman's unbounded enthusiasm for George Sand, and for this novel in particular, is well known. John Burroughs suggested that the idea of the poem might have come from Thoreau's essay on "Walking". (*Life and Letters of John Burroughs*, vol. II, p. 102.)

p. 140, ll. 21 ff.: "*Why are there trees*", etc. Cf. "I Saw in Louisiana a Live-Oak Growing" (p. 118).

p. 144, ll. 11-14: "*To see no possession*", etc. Cf. Emerson's 'Monadnoc".

p. 146, ll. 13-16: "*Let the paper remain on the desk*", etc. Cf. "Beat! Beat! Drums!" (p. 259).

"*Crossing Brooklyn Ferry*" (p. 147). Cf. "To Think of Time" (p. 392).

p. 148, ll. 11 ff.: "*I too many and many a time*". For a contemporary description of one of the many experiences out of which this poem confessedly grew see "Letters from Paumanok—No. 3", U.P.P., I, pp. 255-256.

p. 150, ll. 11-26: "*I am he who knew*", etc. Cf. "Of Many a Smutch'd Deed Reminiscent" (p. 499).

"*Song of the Answerer*" (p. 153). Cf. Emerson's essay, "The Poet".

p. 156, l. 13: "*The singers do not beget*", etc. Cf. "To the Garden the World" (p. 86).

"*Our Old Feuillage*" (p. 158). This poem, though substituting thumbnail descriptions of "catalogues", is a sort of "Salut au Monde" limited to the national horizon.

"*A Song of Joys*" (p. 163). Edward Hungerford seeks to trace each of the joys celebrated in this poem to a phrenological attribute. ("Walt Whitman and His Chart of Bumps", *American Literature*, January 1931.)

p. 166, ll. 16 ff.: "*O the whaleman's joys*", etc. This passage may well have been suggested by *Moby Dick* (1851).

"*Song of the Exposition*" (p. 181). Cf. "After All, Not to Create Only". The poem was read at the opening of the annual exhibition of the American Institute in New York, September 7, 1881. It was widely published at the time in the New York and Boston news-papers. (Camden Edition of Whitman's *Complete Writings*, X, p. 180.) The manuscript of this poem is said to have been sold in London in 1921 for $1500 (New York *Times*, February 6, 1921). For a discussion of Whitman's methods of turning the occasion to account see "Whitman as His Own Press Agent" (Emory Holloway), *American Mercury*, December 1929.

The poem was published in a second edition by Roberts Bros., Boston, in 1871, which contained a description of the occasion, probably written by Whitman himself for the *Washington Chronicle*. (See Kennedy, *The Fight of a Book for the World*, p. 196.)

"*Song of the Redwood-Tree*" (p. 191). Published in *Harper's Magazine*, February 1874; price paid, $100 (Kennedy, p. 16).

"*Song of the Universal*" (p. 209). First published in the *New Republic*, Camden, New Jersey, June 20, 1874. Read as a commencement poem at Tuft's College, June 17, 1874. (See *Two Rivulets*, "Centennial Songs", p. 15.)

"*Pioneers! O Pioneers!*" (p. 211). The title of this poem was borrowed by Willa Cather for one of her novels.

"*France*" (p. 217). Cf. "To a Foil'd European Revolutionaire" (p. 338), "O Star of France" (p. 360), "Spain, 1873-74" (p. 433), and "Resurgemus" (p. 505).

"*Year of Meteors*" (p. 220).

p. 220, ll. 20 ff.: "*I would sing how an old man*", etc. The reference is to John Brown, executed in 1859 for inciting slaves to rebellion.

p. 221, l. 6: "*young prince of England*", the Prince of Wales (Edward VII).

"*A Broadway Pageant*" (p. 224). This poem was occasioned by the reception given to the Japanese Embassy in June 1860.

p. 227, l. 6: "*her eldest son*", the Prince of Wales. Cf. "Year of Meteors" (p. 221).

"*Out of the Cradle Endlessly Rocking*" (p. 228). Originally published as "A Child's Reminiscence" in the New York *Saturday Press*, December 24, 1859. The poem was perhaps written about 1858 (see Bucke, p. 29). For a full discussion of its first appearance and reception see Thomas Olive Mabott and Rollo G. Silver, *A Child's Reminiscence*.

p. 228, l. 2: "*The Mocking Bird's Throat*." As to whether Whitman was at fault in placing the mocking bird on Long Island, it may be noted that J. P. Giraud, Jr., says that the gray mocking bird sometimes was seen there in the mating season at the period to which Whitman's poem refers. (*The Birds of Long Island*, New York, 1843, p. 82.)

p. 229, ll. 7 ff.: "*Shine! shine! shine!*" etc. The exalted music of this poem has been highly commended, and many passages of it, especially these lines, have been set to music by Stanley Addicks, W. W. Gilchrist, Arthur Hartmann, Marshall Kernochan, A. H. Ryder and Frank O. Warner.

"*As I Ebb'd with the Ocean of Life*" (p. 234). First published in the *Atlantic Monthly*, April 1860, as "Bardic Symbols".

"*Tears*" (p. 237). Set to music, 1905, by C. V. Stanford, Opus 97, No. 5.

"*To the Man-of-War Bird*" (p. 237). Published in the *Athenæum*, April 1, 1876.

"*Aboard at the Ship's Helm*" (p. 238). Set to music in an unpublished song by Phillip Dalmas.

"*Song for All Seas, All Ships*" (p. 241). Published in the New York *Daily Graphic*, April 4, 1873, under the title, "Sea Captains, Young or Old".

"*Patroling Barnegat*" (p. 242). Published in the *American*, June 1880 (Vol. X, p. 179) and republished in *Harper's Monthly*, April 1881. Set to music by Eugene Bonner.
The Barnegat Shoals are off the shore of New Jersey at the Barnegat Inlet and Long Beach.

"*After the Sea-Ship*" (p. 243). First published under the title "In the Wake Following", New York *Daily Graphic*, Christmas Number, 1874.

"*A Boston Ballad*" (p. 244). The occasion of this poem was the arrest of Anthony Burns in Boston and his rendition to slavery, on May 24, 1854, despite an attempt to free him led by T. W. Higginson. According to William Sloane Kennedy, Whitman intended to drop this poem, but was persuaded to retain it by John T. Trowbridge. (*The Fight of a Book for the World*, p. 175.)

"*Europe, the 72d and 73d Years of These States*" (p. 246). Whitman's chronology dates from the Declaration of Independence (1776), so that he refers to the years 1848 and 1849. The poem, one of his earliest in free verse, was published as "Resurgemus" in the New York *Tribune*, June 21, 1850. For a collection of the poems in the two versions, and the growth of Whitman's characteristic verse form, see U.P.P., I, pp. 27-30. The occasion was, of course, the abortive popular movements in Italy, Hungary, France and Germany, in these years. Compare "To a Foil'd European Revolutionaire" (p. 338), "O Star of France" (p. 360), "Spain, 1873-74" (p. 433), and "Resurgemus" (p. 505).

"*To a President*" (p. 251). The poem is apparently addressed to President Buchanan. Cf. poem entitled, "To the States" (p. 255).

"*The Dalliance of the Eagles*" (p. 252). First published in *Cope's Tobacco Plant*, November 1880. This poem was included in the Osgood list of expurgations (Bucke, p. 149). This poem seems to have been based on a description given to the poet by John Burroughs. (Barrus, p. 170.)

"*Roaming in Thought*" (p. 252). Cf. "Carlyle from American Points of View" (p. 780).

"*To the States*" (p. 255). Cf. "To a President" (p. 251).

"*Drum-Taps*" (p. 256). Apparently this group of poems, or some of them, was in manuscript as early as March 1863. (*Wound Dresser*, p. 61 ; also see pp. 163, 164, 188.)

"*Eighteen Sixty-One*" (p. 258). Cf. Letter VI (p. 887). Although Whitman in 1861 and 1862 was supporting himself by doing hack work for the Brooklyn *Standard* and the New York *Leader*, much of which had no reference to the war, it is unfair to assume that he was not profoundly moved by it from the start. (See U.P.P., I, LVII, 2, 222 ff., Glicksberg, and the note following.)

"*Beat! Beat! Drums!*" (p. 259). A manuscript letter dated October 1, 1861, offered this poem for $20, to James Russell Lowell, then editor of the *Atlantic Monthly* (Bayard Wyman collection). But the poem was actually published in *Harper's Weekly*, September 28, 1861, and copied in the New York *Leader* on the same date, where the third line from the end concluded with the exhortation, "Recruit! Recruit!" It seems clear that the poem, like Bryant's "Our Country's Call", which appeared in the New York *Ledger* on November 2, and Whittier's "The Summons", in the *Leader*, July 27, was written in an effort to counteract the moral effect of the defeat at Bull Run on July 21. See "Battle of Bull Run", and "The Stupor Passes" (pp. 620-624). For information concerning the original version of this poem, the editor is indebted to Mr. Ralph Adimari.

This poem was set to music by Coleridge-Taylor, Opus 45, No. 6.

"*Song of the Banner at Daybreak*" (p. 260). This is the only poem of Whitman's cast in dramatic form.

"*The Centenarian's Story*" (p. 270). According to Whitman's literary executors, Traubel, Bucke and Harned (Camden Edition, I, p. xix) the poet had a great uncle, the son of Nehemiah Whitman, his great grandfather, who "was a lieutenant in Col. Josiah Smith's regiment of the American Army. He participated in the disastrous battle of Brooklyn and there lost his life. In the 'Centennarian' story will be found some informal account of this portentious event". As editor of the *Eagle*, Whitman urged the creation of Washington Park (Fort Greene), wrote a patriotic ode about the patriots buried there (U.P.P., I, pp. 22-23), and gave considerable space to it in his "Brooklyniana" (U.P.P., II, pp. 242-246). Cf. also "The Sleepers", § 5 (p. 388).

"*Cavalry Crossing a Ford*" (p. 275). This poem has been set to music by Tillie White.

"*By the Bivouac's Fitful Flame*" (p. 276). This poem was set to music by Harvey Gaul.

"*Come Up from the Fields Father*" (p. 277). Manuscripts in the Bayard Wyman collection seem to identify this poem with the case of Oscar Cunningham, mentioned in one of Whitman's letters to his mother (p. 944). Whitman wrote such a letter to Cunningham's sister when he died in June 1864.

"*A March in the Ranks, Hard Pres't, and the Road Unknown*" (p. 280). For an early manuscript version of this incident see Glicksberg, pp. 123-125.

"*Dirge for Two Veterans*" (p. 288). This poem was set to music by F. L. Ritter, Opus 13.

"*The Artilleryman's Vision*" (p. 291). Cf. "The Sleepers", § 5 (p. 388).

"*Ethiopia Saluting the Colors*" (p. 292). Set to music by Coleridge-Taylor, Opus 51, and by Charles Wood.

"*World Take Good Notice*" (p. 293). A longer manuscript version of this poem was printed in *facsimile* by J. H. Johnston, a friend of the poet, in the *Century Magazine*, February 1911, Vol. 59, p. 532, as follows:

"Rise, lurid stars, woolly white no more;
Change, angry cloth—weft of the silver stars no more;
Orbs blushing scarlet—thirty four stars, red as flame,
On the blue bunting this day we sew.

World take good notice, silver stars have vanished;
Orbs now of scarlet—now mortal coals all aglow
Dots of molten iron, wakeful and ominous,
On the blue bunting henceforth appear."

"*O Tan-Faced Prairie-Boy*" (p. 293). This poem was set to music by Weda Cook Addicks.

"*Look Down Fair Moon*" (p. 294). This poem was set to music by Phillip Dalmas.

"*Reconciliation*" (p. 294). This poem was set to music by Phillip Dalmas.

"*As I Lay with My Head in Your Lap Camerado*" (p. 295). In William Rossetti's selected edition of Whitman's poems the title of this poem was "Questionable".

"*Memories of President Lincoln*" (p. 300). The relationship of Whitman and Lincoln is the subject of an entire volume by William E. Barton, an unsympathetic study, the occasional inaccuracies of which are pointed out by Charles I. Glicksberg in his *Walt Whitman and the Civil War*. For Whitman's contemporary references to Lincoln, see pp. 644, 651, 959; his memorial lecture on Lincoln is given on pp. 752-762.

Abraham Lincoln was shot in Ford's theater in Washington, Good Friday night, April 14, 1865, and died the next morning, After the funeral in Washington, the funeral train passed through Maryland, Pennsylvania, New Jersey, New York, Ohio, Indiana, to Springfield, Illinois, where the body was buried in the Oak Ridge Cemetery. Whitman makes use of this fact in his poem. An article in the *Atlantic Monthly*, June 1865, declared: "Along the line of more than 1500 miles his remains were borne, as it were, through continued lines of the people; and the number of mourners and the sincerity and unanimity of grief was such as never before attended the obsequies of a human being. So that the terrible catastrophe of his end hardly struck more awe than the majestic sorrow of the people."

p. 305, l. 25–p. 306, l. 24 : "*Come Lovely and Soothing Death*", etc. In the 1876 Edition this passage was called "Death Carol". This poem was set to music by W. H. Neidlinge and by Nicolas Douty : the "Death Carol" passage by Stanley Addicks.

"*O Captain! My Captain!*" (p. 308). First published in New York *Saturday Press*, November 4, 1865. The poem has been set to music by Weda Cook Addicks, Frank Butcher, H. H. Huss, E. S. Kelley, Charles F. Manning, Cyril Scott, Donald Nicholas Tweedy and Charles Wood.

Although this is perhaps Whitman's best-known poem, it is so atypical that he at times resented the fact that its popularity tended to obscure his more individual work. Horace Traubel gives (II, pp. 332-333), with partial *facsimile* reproduction, an early manuscript version which varies considerably from the one printed :

## MY CAPTAIN

The mortal voyage over, the gales and tempests done,
The ship that bears me nears her home the prize I sought is won,
The port is close, the bells I hear, the people all exulting,
While (As) steady sails and enters straight my wondrous veteran
    vessel ;
But O heart! heart! heart! leave you not the little spot,
Where on the deck my Captain lies—sleeping pale and dead.

O Captain! dearest Captain! get up and hear the bells ;
Get up and see the flying flags, and see the splendid sun,
For you it is the citics shout—for you the shores are crowded ;
For you the red-rose garlands, and electric eyes of women ;
O Captain! O my father! My arm I push beneath you ;
It is some dream that on the deck you slumber pale and dead.

My captain does not answer, his lips are closed and still,
My father does not feel my arm—he has no pulse nor will ;
But his ship, his ship, is anchor'd safe, the fearful trip is done,
The wondrous ship, the ship divine, its mighty object won,
And our cities walk in triumph—but O heart, heart, you stay,
Where on the deck my captain lies sleeping cold   dead.

And cities shout and thunder—but my heart.

And all career in triumph wide—but I with gentle tread,
Walk the deck my captain lies, sleeping cold and dead.

My captain does not answer, his lips are closed and still,
My father does not feel my arm, he has no pulse nor will,
But his ship, his ship is anchor'd safe—the fearful trip is done,
The wondrous ship, the well-tried ship, its proudest object won;
And my lands career in triumph—but I with gentle tread
Walk the spot my captain lies sleeping pale and dead.

"*By Blue Ontario's Shore*" (p. 310). Parts of this poem have been taken from the prose Preface to the 1855 Edition, others were composed for the 1856 Edition, and several passages, including §§ 1, 7, and 20, and parts of 14, 17, and 18, were added in 1867. A few lines were added in 1871.

p. 313, ll. 10-11: "*Attracting it body and soul . . . merits and demerits*". Included in the Osgood list of expurgations.

p. 315, ll. 3-4: "*Slavery—the murderous, treacherous conspiracy*", etc. Cf. "The Eighteenth Presidency" (p. 586), also composed in 1856.

p. 317, l. 5: "*He judges not . . . a helpless thing*". Cf. "To a Common Prostitute" (p. 353).

pp. 318-320, § 12: Compare "Democratic Vistas" (pp. 657-722, *passim*), and "Poetry To-Day in America". (Comp. Prose, p. 281.)

"*Reversals*" (p. 325). This is only a fragment of a poem called "Poem of the Proposition of Nakedness" in the 1856 edition, and "Respondez!" in 1867 and 1871 editions. The original poem appears on p. 511.

"*The Return of the Heroes*" (p. 327). First published in *Galaxy*, in September 1867, under the title, "A Carol of Harvest".

"*There Was a Child Went Forth*" (p. 332). Though this poem with its description of Whitman's father and mother is obviously more or less autobiographical, yet Traubel records (II, p. 228): "People have often asked him the meaning of the poem There was a Child Went Forth and he has always made the same answer: 'What is the meaning? I wonder what? I wonder what?' Once he said to Bonsall: 'Harry, maybe it has no meaning.' "

p. 333, l. 16: "*The mother at home*", etc. Cf. "The Sleepers" (p. 383), and "Faces" (p. 418).

p. 334, l. 13: "*These became part of that child*", etc. Cf. Tennyson's "Ulysses": "I am a part of all that I have met."

"*Old Ireland*" (p. 334). First published in the New York *Leader* November 2, 1861. The editor is indebted to Mr. Ralph Adimari for information about its first publication. Originally the last two lines read:

"And now with rosy and new blood, again among the nations of
     the earth,
Moves to-day, an armed man, in a new country."

Like "Beat! Beat! Drums!" this was published not long after the defeat at Bull Run and may have been intended also to stimulate recruiting among the Irish.

"*The City Dead-House*" (p. 335). Cf. "To A Common Prostitute" (p. 353).

"*To a Foil'd European Revolutionaire*" (p. 338). Cf. "Europe" (p. 246), "O Star of France" (p. 360), and "Spain" (p. 433).

"*Song of Prudence*" (p. 341). Parts of this poem are taken from the Preface to the 1855 edition. It is apparently indebted somewhat to Emerson's essay on "Prudence". Cf. also "Song of the Rolling Earth" (p. 203).

"*The Singer in the Prison*" (p. 344). First published in the *Saturday Evening Visitor*, December 1869, with the subtitle, "A Christmas Incident". Sidney H. Morse, when sculpturing Whitman, was told that this poem was based on a personal observation. As Morse recalled it, the singer was Parepa Rosa singing to the convicts in a prison in New York. (*In Re.*, p. 370.)

"*Warble for Lilac-time*" (p. 346). Published in *Galaxy*, May 1870.

"*Outlines for a Tomb*" (p. 347). Originally published in *Galaxy*, 1870, with the title, "Brother of All, With Generous Hand". The poem was a tribute to George Peabody, who gave large sums for science, for the education of the negro, and for improving living conditions among the poor in London. Though he died in London, November 14, 1869, he was buried in Massachusetts, February 1870. In "Two Rivulets", above the title appeared the following inscription:

☞ "To any Hospital or School-Founder, or Public Beneficiary, anywhere."

"*Out from Behind this Mask*" (p. 349). In "Two Rivulets" appeared under the title this explanatory note: "To confront My Portrait, illustrating 'the Wound Dresser', in *Leaves of Grass*."

"*To A Common Prostitute*" (p. 353). This poem was on the Osgood list, notwithstanding the fact that Whitman said, "It is nothing but the beautiful little idyl of the New Testament concerning the woman taken in adultery." (See Kennedy, pp. 125-127.)

"*Unfolded Out of the Folds*" (p. 356). It is not clear why Whitman did not include this poem in the "Children of Adam" group, where it would seem to belong.

p. 357, ll. 6-7: "*Unfolded out of the strong . . . embraces of the man.*" These two lines were on the Osgood list of expurgations.

"*Kosmos*" (p. 357). Cf. "Walt Whitman, a kosmos", etc., p. 48, l. 21.

"*O Star of France*" (p. 360). First published in *Galaxy*, June

1871. The occasion of this poem was the defeat of France in the Franco-Prussian War.

"*The Ox-Tamer*" (p. 362). First published in the New York *Daily Graphic*, Christmas Number, 1874.

"*An Old Man's Thought of School*" (p. 363). Recited by the author at the Cooper Public School in Camden and published in the New York *Daily Graphic*, November 3, 1874.

"*Wandering at Morn*" (p. 363). First published as "The Singing Thrush" in the New York *Daily Graphic*, March 15, 1873.

"*Italian Music in Dakota*" (p. 364). Cf. "Proud Music of the Storm" (p. 366), "The Mystic Trumpeter" (p. 421), "Plays and Operas Too" (p. 564), "Old Actors, Singers, Shows, Etc., in New York" (p. 875), "The Opera" (*New York Dissected*, pp. 18-23), and Louise Pound "Walt Whitman and Italian Music" (*American Mercury*, September 1925).

"*My Picture-Gallery*" (p. 365). First published in the *American*, October 1880. For a long manuscript out of which this short poem grew, see *Pictures, An Unpublished Poem of Walt Whitman* (Emory Holloway, editor), New York and London, 1927. Cf. also N. and F., pp. 77, 177.

"*The Prairie States*" (p. 365). A *facsimile* manuscript of this poem was printed in the catalogue of the Saltus Sale at the Anderson Galleries (1922), and in the *Art Autograph*, March 16, 1880. It is said to have been published on behalf of the Irish Famine Fund.

"*Proud Music of the Storm*" (p. 366). First published in the *Atlantic Monthly*, February 1869, but written some months earlier. For this poem Whitman received $100. (See Traubel, II, 21-23.) The poem was offered to the *Atlantic* through Whitman's friend, Ralph Waldo Emerson (Letter LXVIII, p. 981). Cf. For other Whitman compositions on music, see note on "Italian Music in Dakota" (p. 364).

"*Passage to India*" (p. 372). This poem was rejected by Bret Harte when submitted to the *Overland Monthly* in April 1870. It was first printed as a thin booklet in 1871 (copyright 1870), but parts of it had been written earlier. Section 5 was printed from a manuscript by the Brooklyn *Eagle*, October 26, 1911, where the date of composition is said to be about 1848. This, however, seems to be a mistake, for Traubel gives a letter to James T. Fields, offering it to the *Atlantic* on January 20, 1869, and it appeared in the London *Fortnightly Review* in April of that year. Another passage apparently intended for a separate poem is that in §8, beginning, "O soul thou pleasest me", and ending with the section. Mr. Oscar Lion of New York owns this manuscript.

The occasion of the poem was the completion of the Suez Canal and the Pacific Railroad. Of the poem Whitman said, "There's more of me, the essential ultimate me, in that than in any of the poems ... the burden of it is evolution—the one thing escaping the other—the unfolding of cosmic purposes." (Traubel, I, pp. 156-157.)

"*Prayer of Columbus*" (p. 381). First published in *Harper's Magazine*, March 1874, where it was accompanied by the following explanatory note:

"It was near the close of his indomitable and pious life—on his last voyage when nearly 70 years of age—that Columbus, to save his two remaining ships from foundering in the Caribbean Sea in a terrible storm, had to run them ashore on the Island of Jamaica where, laid up for a long and miserable year—1503—he was taken very sick, had several relapses, his men revolted, and death seem'd daily imminent; though he was eventually rescued, and sent home to Spain to die, unrecognized, neglected and in want. . . . It is only ask'd, as preparation and atmosphere for the following lines, that the bare authentic facts be recall'd and realized, and nothing contributed by the fancy. See, the Antillean Island, with its florid skies and rich foliage and scenery, the waves beating the solitary sands, and the hulls of the ships in the distance. See, the figure of the great Admiral, walking the beach, as a stage, in this sublimest tragedy—for what tragedy, what poem, so piteous and majestic as the real scene?—and hear him uttering—as his mystical and religious soul surely utter'd, the ideas following—perhaps, in their equivalents, the very words." (Inclusive Edition, *Leaves*, p. 682.)

Whitman wrote to Pete Doyle concerning this poem: "I am told that I have colored it with thoughts of myself—very likely." (*Calamus*, p. 145.)

"*The Sleepers*" (p. 383). Though on the surface this poem is an attempt to picture the mind in sleep (see Bucke, p. 171), it serves also as a key to Whitman's poetic method (see Holloway, pp. 123 ff.).

p. 384, l. 9: "*he with his palm . . . of the husband*". These phrases were on the Osgood list of expurgations.

p. 387, § 4: The reference here is to the *Mexico*, wrecked off Hempstead, Long Island, in 1840. (See "Paumanok, and my Life on it as Child and Young Man" (p. 538).

p. 390, ll. 21-22: "*Perfect and clean . . . and plumb*". These lines were on the Osgood list of expurgations.

"*Transpositions*" (p. 392). Part of the much longer poem "Respondez!" from the 1856 edition (p. 511).

"*To think of Time*" (p. 392). Cf. "Crossing Brooklyn Ferry" (p. 147).

"*Darest Thou Now O Soul*" (p. 399). First published in the *Broadway Magazine* (London), October 1868. This poem has been set to music by Rutland Boughton, G. W. Chadwick, Harper Seed and Eva Ruth Spalding.

"*Whispers of Heavenly Death*" (p. 399). First published in *Broadway Magazine* (London), October 1868

"*Chanting the Square Deific*" (p. 400). To Daniel G. Brinton, Whitman commented on this poem as follows: "It would be hard to give the idea mathematical expression: the idea of spiritual equity—of spiritual substance: the four-square entity—the north, south, east, west of the constituted universe (even the soul universe)—the four sides as sustaining the universe (the supernatural something): this is not the poem, but the idea back of the poem or below the poem. I am lame enough trying to explain it in other words—the idea seems to fit its own words better than mine. You see, at the time the poem wrote itself: now I am trying to write it." (Traubel, I, p. 156.) See also Leon Howard, "A Critique of Whitman's Transcendentalism" (*Modern Language Notes*, January 1931).

"*That Music Always Round Me*" (p. 405). Cf. "The Mystic Trumpeter" (p. 421), and "Proud Music of the Storm" (p. 366).

"*Quicksand Years*" (p. 404). For manuscript versions of this poem differing from the text, see Glicksberg, pp. 125-126.

"*A Noiseless Patient Spider*" (p. 406). First published in *Broadway Magazine* (London), October 1868. For an early manuscript of this poem, see U.P.P., II, p. 93.

"*The Last Invocation*" (p. 408). First published in the *Broadway Magazine* (London), October 1868. Originally without title, this poem is sometimes called "The Imprisoned Soul" (*Oxford Book of English Verse*). This poem was set to music by Eugene Bonner, Frank Bridge, Ada Weigle Powers and Eva Ruth Spalding.

"*Pensive and Flattering*" (p. 409). First published in *Broadway Magazine* (London), October 1868.

"*Thou mother with Thy Equal Brood*" (p. 410). This poem was read by Whitman before the United Literary Societies of Dartmouth College at commencement on Wednesday, June 26, 1872 (*Calamus*, p. 96). For an account of the circumstances connected with this occasional poem, see Perry, pp. 203-210, and Harold W. Blodgett, "Walt Whitman's Dartmouth Visit". (*Dartmouth Alumni Magazine*, February 1933.)

"*A Paumanok Picture*" (p. 415). Cf. "Paumanok, and my Life on it as Child and Young Man" (p. 538).

"*Faces*" (p. 418). For a counterpart of this poem, see "Street Yarn". (*New York Dissected*, pp. 128-132.)

p. 420, ll. 1-6: "*I saw the face*", etc. This passage Whitman said, was suggested by his brother Eddie, who was mentally defective.

p. 421, § 5: This is commonly interpreted as a description of Whitman's Quaker grandmother, Amy Williams Van Velsor.

p. 420, l. 25-p. 421, l. 3: "*She speaks . . . my breast and shoulders*". This passage was on the Osgood list of expurgations.

"*The Mystic Trumpeter*" (p. 421). First published in the *Kansas Magazine*, February 1872. Cf. "Proud Music of the Storm" (p. 366), "Italian Music in Dakota", and "That Music Always Round Me" (p. 405). Many years ago the present editor examined a manuscript, then in the collection of Mr. W. R. Benjamin, which indicated that one Julius Bing supplied Whitman with notes on classical music when he was writing this poem.

"*Mannahatta*" (p. 427). Whitman was fond of referring to Manhattan in this way in his poetry, and in compliment to him his brother Jefferson named a daughter Mannahatta.

"*A Riddle Song*" (p. 429). Whitman never gave the key to this riddle, but Dr. Bucke suggested that it is "good cause" of "old cause" (Traubel, II, 228); Kennedy offers "the Ideal" (*The Fight of a Book for the World*, p. 188). In the Bayard Wyman collection is a printed proof of the poem which omits lines 2-10, 29, and makes many changes in punctuation. Apparently it was published in the first number of *Sunnyside Press* in the spring of 1880 (see Barrus, p. 191).

"*Excelsior*" (p. 430). Whitman was an admirer of Longfellow, and may have borrowed the title from him. Cf. "Ambition" (p. 502).

"*Ah Poverties, Wincings, and Sulky Retreats*" (p. 431). Cf. "Crossing Brooklyn Ferry", § 6 (p. 150).

"*Weave in, My Hearty Life*" (p. 432). To show the metrical regularity of this poem, William Sloane Kennedy has arranged it in conventional form. (Kennedy, p. 167.)

"*Spain, 1873-74*" (p. 433). First published without the date and the title in the New York *Daily Graphic*, March 24, 1873, with the signature, "Washington, March 23, 1873, Walt Whitman".

"*From Far Dakota's Cañons*" (p. 434). First published as "A Death-Sonnet for Custer", in the New York *Tribune*, July 10, 1876. Cf. "Custer's Last Rally" (p. 793).

"*What Best I See In Thee*" (p. 436). President Grant returned from his world tour in the fall of 1879. Cf. "Death of General Grant" (p. 463), and "The Silent General" (p. 767).

"*Spirit that Form'd This Scene*" (p. 436). First published in the *Critic*, September 10, 1881.

"*A Clear Midnight*" (p. 437). Set to music by Eugene Bonner, F. S. Converse, Phillip Dalmas, W. H. Pommer, Ada Weigle Powers, Lynnel Reed, and Eva Ruth Spalding.

"*Years of the Modern*" (p. 438). Though first published in 1865 (in *Drum-Taps*), parts of this poem were written in prose form in 1856. (Cf. "The Eighteenth Presidency", pp. 586-602.)

"*As at Thy Portals also Death*" (p. 445). Whitman's mother died, May 23, 1873.

"*The Artilleryman's Vision*" (p. 291). Cf. "The Dying Veteran" (p. 473), and "The Sleepers", § 5 (p. 388).

"*The Sobbing of the Bells*" (p. 448). This tribute to President Garfield, whom Whitman had known personally (Traubel, I, p. 324), written at the Hotel Bulfinch in Boston (Kennedy, p. 3), was first published in the Boston *Daily Globe*, September 27, 1881. A *facsimile* reproduction of the manuscript is to be found in Bucke, facing p. 54. Whitman once expressed a doubt about the propriety of retaining the poem because it borrows a line from Poe's "The Bells" for its title. (Traubel, III, p. 129.)

"*So Long*" (p. 450). First appearing in the 1860 edition, this poem was always kept at the end of *Leaves of Grass* (though the Annexes in late editions came after it).

"*Mannahatta*" (p. 454). First published in New York *Herald*, February 27, 1888. Whitman has another poem with the same title (p. 427).

"*Paumanok*" (p. 454). First published in New York *Herald*, February 29, 1888.

"*From Montauk Point*" (p. 454). First published in New York *Herald*, March 1, 1888.

"*A Carol Closing Sixty-nine*" (p. 455). First published in New York *Herald*, May 21, 1888. Whitman had offered this poem to *Lippincott's Magazine*, but when it did not appear in the June issue, he withdrew it and sent it to the *Herald* in order that it might appear near his birthday (Traubel, I, p. 179). A *Critic* paragraph taking note of his approaching birthday, declared that "the number of those who greatly admire his writings, though without thinking them the be-all and the end-all of American poetry, and who feel for his personality a heartfelt and growing affection has increased in proportion as his work and the story of his career have become better known". (*Critic*, May 25, 1889.)

"*The Bravest Soldiers*" (p. 455). First published in New York *Herald*, March 18, 1888.

"*A Font of Type*" (p. 455). In John Russell Young's *Men and Memories* (Vol. I, p. 107) the original version of this poem is given as follows:

> "O latent mine! O unlaunched voices!
>     passionate powers, all eligible.
> Wrath, argument, praise, or comic leer, or
>     prayer devout, or love's caress,
> (Not nonpareil, brevier, bourgeois, long primer, merely),
> Shores, oceans, roused to fury and to death,
> Or soothed to ease and sheeny sun, and sleep,
> With these pallid slivers, waiting.

"*As I Sit Writing Here*" (p. 456). First published in New York *Herald*, May 14, 1888.

"*My Canary Bird*" (p. 456). First published in New York *Herald*, March 2, 1888.

"*Queries to My Seventieth Year*" (p. 456). First published in New York *Herald*, May 2, 1888.

"*The Wallabout Martyrs*" (p. 456). First published in New York *Herald*, March 16, 1888. Cf. "The Centenarian's Story" (p. 270).

"*The First Dandelion*" (p. 457). First published in New York *Herald*, March 12, 1888. It appeared, ironically, on the morning of New York's greatest blizzard, and was parodied in the press.

"*America*" (p. 457). First published in New York *Herald*, February 11, 1888.

"*To-day and Thee*" (p. 457). First published in New York *Herald*, April 23, 1888.

"*After the Dazzle of Day*" (p. 458). First published in New York *Herald*, February 3, 1888.

"*Out of May's Shows Selected*" (p. 458). First published in New York *Herald*, May 10, 1888.

"*Halcyon Days*" (p. 458). First published in New York *Herald*, January 29, 1888.

"*Fancies at Navesink*" (p. 459). All these poems except the fifth were published in *Nineteenth Century Magazine*, August 1885, after having been declined by Mr. H. M. Alden for *Harper's Magazine*. (Traubel, I, p. 61.)

"*Election Day, November* 1884" (p. 462). This poem was first published in the *Philadelphia Press*, October 26, 1884, using a part of the first line for a title. *Diary in Canada* (p. 73) contains the following explanatory note:

PRESIDENTIAL ELECTION. *Oct.* 31, '84

The political parties are trying—but mostly in vain—to get up some fervor of excitement on the pending Presidential election. It comes off next Tuesday. There is no question at issue of any importance. I cannot "enthuse" at all. I think of the elections of '30 and '20. Then there was something to arouse a fellow. But I like well the *fact* of all these national elections—have written a little poem about it (to order)—published in a Philadelphia daily of 26th instant. [The candidates in '84 were Blaine and Cleveland; the issues, tariff and Chinese exclusion. Blaine was defeated, owing to Conkling's defection.]

"*With Husky-Haughty Lips, O Sea!*" (p. 462). First published in *Harper's Magazine*, March 1884. Fifty dollars was paid for the poem on November 30, 1883 (Traubel, II, p. 220). The poem was written at Ocean Grove, New Jersey, where Whitman was visiting with John Burroughs, September 26–October 1, 1883 (Traubel, I, p. 406).

"*Death of General Grant*" (p. 463). Cf. "What Best I See in Thee" (p. 436), and "The Silent General" (p. 767). First published in the *Critic*, August 15, 1885, as "Grant". In a printed proofsheet the first line was used as a title and a second section was added as follows:

> "And still shall be;—resume again, thou hero heart!
> Strengthen to firmest day, O rosy dawn of hope!
>
> Thou dirge I started first, to joyful shout reversed!—
>     and thou, O grave,
>
> Wait long and long."

"*Red Jacket (from Aloft)*" (p. 464). First published in the *Philadelphia Press*, October 10, 1884. (Rollo G. Silver, "Thirty-one Letters of Walt Whitman", *American Literature*, January 1937, p. 430.)

"*Washington's Monument, February, 1885*" (p. 464). Probably first printed in *Philadelphia Press*, February 22, 1885.

"*Of that Blythe Throat of Thine*" (p. 465). First published in *Harper's Monthly*, January 1885. The price paid was $30. (Traubel, II, p. 218-219.)

"*Broadway*" (p. 465). First published in New York *Herald*, April 10, 1888. Cf. "Broadway". (*New York Dissected*, pp. 119-124.)

"*To Get the Final Lilt of Songs*" (p. 466). First published in New York *Herald*, April 16, 1888, after having been rejected by the *Cosmopolitan*. (Traubel, I, p. 37.)

"*Old Salt Kossabone*" (p. 466). First published in New York *Herald*, February 25, 1888.

"*Continuities*" (p. 467). First published in New York *Herald*, March 20, 1888.

"*Yonnondio*" (p. 468): First published in the *Critic*, November 26, 1887. For a discussion of the meaning of the Indian word, see Traubel, II, p. 269. A *Critic* correspondent, who signed his letter "Etymologist", said Whitman had been misinformed—that the Hurons and Iroquois used it to mean "Beautiful Mountain", and applied it to the Canadian Governor, Montmagny, whose name had been incorrectly explained to them. (*Critic*, December 17, 1887.)

"*Life*" (p. 468): First published in New York *Herald*, April 5, 1888.

"*Going Somewhere*" (p. 469): First published in *Lippincott's Magazine*, November 1887. This elegiac poem was a tribute to Mrs. Anne Gilchrist. For the story of her friendship with the poet, see Harned; also Letters LXXV (p. 987), LXXXVIII (p. 998), XCVI (p. 1005), CIV (p. 1012), CVII (p. 1016), CXXIV (p. 1029), CXXVIII (p. 1032), CXXXI (p. 1035), CXL (p. 1042), and

CLXIV (p. 1045). The manuscript of this poem is reproduced in *facsimile* in Thomas Donaldson, *Walt Whitman, the Man,* facing p. 74.

"*Small the Theme of My Chant*" (p. 469): Cf. "One's Self I Sing" (p. 3).

"*True Conquerors*" (p. 470): First published in New York *Herald,* February 15, 1888.

"*The United States to Old World Critics*" (p. 470). First published in New York *Herald,* May 27, 1888.

"*The Calming Thought of All*" (p. 470). First published in New York *Herald,* May 27, 1888.

"*Life and Death*" (p. 471). First published in New York *Herald,* May 23, 1888.

"*Soon shall the Winter's Foil be Here*" (p. 472). First published in New York *Herald,* February 21, 1888.

"*The Dying Veteran*" (p. 473). Cf. "The Artilleryman's Vision" (p. 291). Whitman wrote to Kennedy, "A New York newspaper syndicate (S. S. McClure, Tribune Building) vehemently solicited and gave me $25 (far more than it is worth)." (Kennedy, p. 55.)

"*A Prairie Sunset*" (p. 473). First published in New York *Herald,* March 9, 1888.

"*Twenty Years*" (p. 474). First published in *Magazine of Art* (in England, July 1888; in America, August 1888), with a line drawing. The poem had been requested by M. H. Spielmann, editor of the magazine, on November 30, 1887. (Traubel, II, p. 232-233.)

"*Orange Buds by Mail from Florida*" (p. 474). First published in New York *Herald,* March 19, 1888.

"*Twilight*" (p. 475). First published in the *Century Magazine,* December 1887. The price paid was $10 (Kennedy, p. 55). The word "oblivion" in the poem called forth numerous protests from Whitman readers as being inconsistent with his philosophy. For his self defense, see Traubel, I, pp. 140-141.

"*You Lingering Sparse Leaves of Me*" (p. 475). First published in *Lippincott's Magazine,* November 1887.

"*Not Meager Latent Boughs Alone*" (p. 475). First published in *Lippincott's Magazine,* November 1887.

"*The Dead Emperor*" (p. 476). First published in New York *Herald,* March 10, 1888, where it is dated March 9. The poem was written at the request of the *Herald.* Concerning the criticism it aroused among Whitman's democratic and liberal friends, he said: "You know, I include Kings, Queens, Emperors, Nobles, Barons, and the aristocracy generally, in my net—excluding nobody and nothing human—and this does not seem to be relished by these narrow-minded folks." (J. Johnston and J. W. Wallace, *Visits to Walt Whitman in* 1890-1891, 1917, p. 50.)

"*As the Greek's Signal Flame*" (p. 476). First published in the New York *Herald*, December 15, 1887, with the heading, "Walt Whitman's Praise". In the *Herald* version, between lines 1 and 2, appears the line, "(Tally of many hard strain'd battle struggle, year—triumphant only at the last.)" Although Whittier is said to have thrown into the fire the complimentary copy of the first edition which Whitman sent him (Perry, 1908, p. 100), the poets admired each other personally, and Whitman at his seventy-second birthday dinner drank a toast to the Quaker poet, "a noble old man". (*In Re*, p. 297.)

"*The Dismantled Ship*" (p. 476). First published in New York *Herald*, February 23, 1888. Whitman said to Traubel: "Yes, it was suggested by the picture in Harned's parlor: that's me—that's my old hulk—was laid up at last: no good anymore—no good"—pausing—"a fellow might get melancholy seeing himself in such a mirror—but I guess we can see through as well as in the mirrors when the test comes!" (Traubel, I, p. 390.) Mr. Harned gave to the present editor a similar account of the origin of this poem.

"*An Evening Lull*" (p. 477). For a discussion concerning the poem, between Whitman, Traubel, and Bucke, see Traubel, I, pp. 354, 472-491.

"*Old Age's Lambent Peaks*" (p. 477). First published in the *Century*, September 1888.

"*After the Supper and Talk*" (p. 478). First published in *Lippincott's Magazine*, 1887. The manuscript of this poem is reproduced in *facsimile* in the *Complete Writings* (1902), Vol. II, facing p. 322.

"*Second Annex*" (*Good-Bye My Fancy*) (p. 479). In Whitman's final edition this group of poems had the following preface:

"Had I not better withhold (in this old age and paralysis of me) such little tags and fringe-dots (maybe specks, stains), as follow a long dusty journey, and witness it afterward? I have probably not been enough afraid of careless touches, from the first—and am not now—nor of parrot-like repetitions—nor platitudes and the commonplace. Perhaps I am too democratic for such avoidances. Besides, is not the verse-field, as originally plann'd by my theory, now sufficiently illustrated—and full time for me to silently retire? —(indeed amid no loud call or market for my sort of poetic utterance).

In answer, or rather defiance, to that kind of well-put interrogation, here comes this little cluster, and conclusion of my preceding clusters. Though not at all clear that, as here collated, it is worth printing (certainly I have nothing fresh to write)—I while away the hours of my 72d year—hours of forced confinement in my den—by putting in shape this small old age collation:

Last droplets of and after spontaneous rain,
From many limpid distillations and past showers;
(Will they germinate anything? mere exhalations as they all are
—the land's and sea's—America's;
Will they filter to any deep emotion? any heart and brain?

However that may be, I feel like improving to-day's opportunity and wind up. During the last two years I have sent out, in the lulls of illness and exhaustion, certain chirps—lingering-dying ones probably (undoubtedly)—which I may as well gather and put in fair type while able to see correctly—(for my eyes plainly warn me they are dimming, and my brain more and more palpably neglects or refuses, month after month, even slight tasks or revisions).

In fact, here I am these current years 1890 and '91, (each successive fortnight getting stiffer and stuck deeper) much like some hard-cased dilapidated grim ancient shell-fish or time-bang'd conch (no legs, utterly non-locomotive) cast up high and dry on the shore-sands, helpless to move anywhere—nothing left but behave myself quiet, and while away the days yet assign'd, and discover if there is anything for the said grim and time-bang'd conch to be got at last out of inherited good spirits and primal buoyant centre-pulses down there deep somewhere within his gray-blurr'd old shell. . . . (Reader, you must allow a little fun here—for one reason there are too many of the following poemets about death, &c., and for another the passing hours (July 5, 1890) are so sunny-fine. And old as I am I feel to-day almost a part of some frolicsome wave, or for sporting yet like a kid or kitten—probably a streak of physical adjustment and perfection here and now. I believe I have it in me perennially anyhow.)

Then behind all, the deep down consolation (it is a glum one, but I dare not be sorry for the fact of it in the past, nor refrain from dwelling, even vaunting here at the end) that this late-years palsied old shorn and shell-fish condition of me is the indubitable outcome and growth, now near for 20 years along, of too over-zealous, over-continued bodily and emotional excitement and action through the times of 1862, '3, '4, and '5, visiting and waiting on wounded and sick army volunteers, both sides, in campaigns or contests, or after them, or in hospitals or fields south of Washington City, or in that place and elsewhere—those hot, sad, wrenching times—the army volunteers, all States—or North or South—the wounded, suffering, dying—the exhausting, sweating summers, marches, battles, carnage—those trenches hurriedly heap'd by the corpse-thousands, mainly unknown—Will the America of the future—will this vast rich Union ever realize what itself cost, back theré after all?—those hecatombs of battle-deaths—Those times of which, O far-off reader, this whole book is indeed finally but a reminiscent memorial from thence by me to you?"

"*Sail Out for Good, Eidólon Yacht*" (p. 479). First published in *Lippincott's Magazine*, March 1881.

"*On, on the Same, Ye Jocund Twain!*" (p. 480). Whitman is

quoted as saying that this poem was rejected by the *Century Magazine* as being merely personal. (Frank Harris, *Contemporary Portraits*, Third Series, p. 221.)

"*My 71st Year*" (p. 481). First published in the *Century Magazine*, November 1889.

"*The Pallid Wreath*" (p. 481). First published in the *Critic*, January 10, 1891.

"*Old Age's Ship & Crafty Death's*" (p. 482). First published in the *Century Magazine*, February 1890.

"*To the Pending Year*" (p. 483). First published in the *Critic*, with the title, "To the Year 1889", January 5, 1889.

"*Bravo, Paris Exposition!*" (p. 483). First published in *Harper's Weekly*, September 28, 1889.

"*Interpolation Sounds*" (p. 484). First published in New York *Herald*, August 12, 1888, without title. Whitman was chagrined that this poem, written in "ten minutes or so", was displayed so prominently in the paper. (Traubel, II, p. 125.)

"*To the Sun-set Breeze*" (p. 485). First published in *Lippincott's Magazine*, December 1890; previously rejected by *Harper's*. (Frank Harris, *Contemporary Portraits*, Third Series, p. 221.)

"*Old Chants*" (p. 485). First published in *Truth*, New York, March 19, 1891. Cf. "With Antecedents" (p. 222); also "Preparatory Reading and Thought". (N. and F., pp. 75-149.)

"*Sounds of the Winter*" (p. 487). First published in *Lippincott's Magazine*, March 1891.

"*A Twilight Song*" (p. 487). First published in the *Century Magazine*, May 1890.

"*When the Full-Grown Poet Came*" (p. 488). Cf. "Passage to India", § 5 (p. 375).

"*Osceola*" (p. 488). First published in *Munson's Illustrated World*, April 1890.

"*A Voice from Death*" (p. 489). First published in New York *World*, June 7, 1889.

"*The Commonplace*" (p. 491). First published, in *facsimile*, in *Munson's Illustrated World*, March 1891. (Rollo G. Silver, *American Literature*, January 1937, p. 435.)

"*The Unexpressed*" (p. 493). First published in *Lippincott's Magazine*, March 1891. A Whitman manuscript, on display in the Whitman Exhibition at the New York Public Library in 1925, indicates that the poem had been offered to *Harper's*, October 18, 1890.

"*Grand is the Seen*" (p. 494). A manuscript showing several variations was published in the *Conservator*, January 1897:

"Grand is the seen, the light—grand are the sky & stars.
Grand is the earth, & grand are time & space,

And grand their laws so multiform, so evolutionary, puzzling,
    lasting;
Then grander is one's unseen soul, endowing comprehending
    those—
Lighting the light, the sky & stars, sailing the sea, delving the
    earth,
More multiform—more puzzling than they, more evolutionary
    vast & lasting."

"*A Kiss to the Bride*" (p. 497). Cf. Letter CXXVIII, n. (p. 1032).

"*Nay, Tell Me Not To-day the Published Shame*" (p. 497). First published in New York *Daily Graphic*, March 5, 1873.

"*Of Many a Smutch'd Deed Reminiscent*" (p. 499). Cf. "Ah Poverties, Wincings and Sulky Retreats" (p. 431), and "Crossing Brooklyn Ferry, § 6 (p. 150). The manuscript of this poem appears in N. and F., p. 39. Probably it was first published after the poet's death. Other "Old Age Echoes" may belong in the same category such as the first five poems in the group and "Supplement Hours".

"*Death's Valley*" (p. 499). First published in *Harper's Magazine*, April 1892.

"*A Thought of Columbus*" (p. 501). A *facsimile* of the manuscript of this, Whitman's last deliberate composition, was published in *Once a Week*, July 9, 1892. Cf. "Prayer of Columbus" (p. 381).


## EARLY POEMS

"*Ambition*" (p. 502). First published in *Brother Jonathan*, January 29, 1842. The poem is an elaboration of "Fame's Vanity", published in the *Long Island Democrat*, October 23, 1839. Both poems were reprinted in U.P.P. (I, pp. 4-5, 19-20). A comparison of them shows gradual improvement in verse composition. Cf. "A Backward Glance O'er Travel'd Roads" (p. 858).

"*Blood-Money*" (p. 503). This poem, almost the first that Whitman published in free verse, appeared in Horace Greeley's New York *Tribune*, Supplement, March 22, 1850. It was inspired, like Whittier's "Ichabod", by Webster's speech conciliating the slave states, on the 7th of March, and by the Fugitive Slave Law.

"*Resurgemus*" (p. 505). First published in the New York *Daily Tribune*, June 21, 1850. Cf. "Europe, The 72d and 73d Years of These States" (p. 246). A comparison of the two versions is made in U.P.P., I, pp. xci, 27-30.

# Prose

"*Two Old Family Interiors*". The quotations in this section of *Specimen Days* were doubtless written by Whitman himself. Cf. "End of a Literary Mystery", Frederick P. Hier, *American Mercury*, April 1924. Not only is the style Whitman's, but John Burroughs informed the present editor that he had got his biographical material for the *Notes* from Whitman.

"*Printing Office—Old Brooklyn*" (p. 541).

p. 541, l. 18: "*William Hartshorne*". Cf. "Song of Myself" (p. 39, l. 7).

"*Sun-Down Papers*" (p. 542). First published in the *Long Island Democrat*, October 20, 1840. (For a description of Whitman at the time he was employed by this country newspaper, see U.P.P., I, xxxiii, ff.) It is imitative of eighteenth century essay visions and reflects the Quaker influences which surrounded Whitman's youth.

"*Boz and Democracy*" (p. 548). First published in *Brother Jonathan*, February 26, 1842. Charles Dickens, whose influence appears in Whitman's *Franklin Evans*, published later in the year, was at this time being fêted in New York.

"*Home Literature*" (p. 554). First published in the Brooklyn *Daily Eagle*, July 11, 1846.

p. 554, l. 36: "*Croly*"—George Crowly (1780-1860), an Irish poet and clergyman and a writer of such romances as *Salthiel*; "*Alison*", probably Sir Archibald Allison (1792-1867) the Scotch historian.

p. 555, l. 8: "*Marryatt*". Captain Frederic Marryat (1792-1848), author of *Mr. Midshipman Easy* and other novels; "*Lady Blessington*", Marguerite Power, Countess of Blessington (1789-1849), author of *Conversations With Lord Byron*.

p. 555, ll. 16, 17: " '*Professor' Ingraham*": Joseph Holt Ingraham (1809-1860), a college professor and later a Protestant Episcopal rector, who wrote *Lafitte, or the Pirate of the Gulf*, and *The Prince of the House of David*.

"*New States: Shall they be Slave or Free*" (p. 555). First published in Brooklyn *Daily Eagle*, April 22, 1847. It was this editorial and others advocating free-soil in the territories of the United States, which caused Whitman to lose his position as editor of the *Eagle*. Cf. "The Eighteenth Presidency" (p. 586).

1088

"*Crossing the Alleghanies*" (p. 557). First published in the New Orleans *Daily Crescent*, March 5, 1848. This is one of three travel articles descriptive of Whitman's journey to New Orleans.

p. 560, ll. 2, 3: "*A satirical person*". Perhaps a reference to Dickens' *American Notes*, which, though distasteful to Whitman, the latter was willing to forgive. Cf. "Boz and Democracy" (p. 548).

"*The Old Cathedral*" (p. 566). First published in New Orleans *Daily Crescent*, April 22, 1848.

"*Letters from Paumanok*" (p. 568). First published in New York *Evening Post*, August 14, 1851. "Old Actors, Singers, Shows, Etc. in New York".

"*Preface* 1855" (p. 571). The original preface to the first edition of *Leaves of Grass*, of which this is Whitman's revision, is available in the Inclusive Edition of *Leaves of Grass* (1924). Various parts of the preface were later incorporated in some of the poems, e.g. "By Blue Ontario's Shore". The text given is that of Whitman's revision in Comp. Prose.

"*The Eighteenth Presidency*" (p. 586). The manuscript of this campaign address was not printed until 1928, when it was issued at Montpellier in pamphlet form by Professor Jean Catel and by Professor Furness in *Walt Whitman's Workshop*, *q.v.* for an excellent analysis.

p. 588, l. 33: "*swarms of dough-faces*". On March 2, 1850, Whitman published in the New York *Evening Post* a poem, "Song for Certain Congressmen", which was preserved in Comp. Prose (p. 334) as "Dough-Face Song".

p. 592, l. 7: "*these nominating dictators*". Though Whitman did not print the present political essay, so far as is known, he did employ parts of this virulent passage in "Origins of Attempted Secession". (Comp. Prose, p. 252.)

p. 599, l. 16: "*The Redeemer President*". Professor Furness calls attention to the accuracy of this prophecy. But in 1858, when Lincoln was making his first bid for the larger influence that was to be his, Whitman seems not to have been so much impressed by him as by Douglas. See *I Sit and Look Out*, pp. 95-99.

p. 601, l. 30: "*great portents*", etc. Cf. "Years of the Modern" (p. 438).

"*Street Yarn*" (p. 602). First published in *Life Illustrated*, August 16, 1856. For detailed annotation of the Whitman articles from this periodical, see *New York Dissected* (Emory Holloway and Ralph Adimari).

"*Wicked Architecture*" (p. 607). First published in *Life Illustrated*, July 19, 1856. The article illustrates Whitman's belief in the influence of environment on morals. Many of the evils he (and other journalists) dealt with were attacked in the first tenement house law, in 1867.

*"Charles Dickens"* (p. 612). First published in Brooklyn *Daily Times*, May 6, 1857. Cf. "Boz and Democracy", n. (p. 548).

*"Emerson's 'Brahma'"* (p. 613). From the Brooklyn *Daily Times*, November 16, 1857.

*"Professional Men"* (p. 613). First published in Brooklyn *Daily Times*, January 30, 1858.

*"Reformers"* (p. 616). First published in Brooklyn *Daily Times*, April 19, 1858.

*"Down Below"* (p. 617). From the Brooklyn *Daily Times*, July 12, 1858.

*"Opening of the Secession War"* (p. 618). First published in "'Tis But Ten Years Since", New York *Weekly Graphic*, January 24, 1874.

*"National Uprising and Volunteering"* (p. 619). This and most of the next three sections of *Specimen Days* were first published in "'Tis But Ten Years Since", New York *Weekly Graphic*, February 7, 1874.

*"The Bowery"* (p. 624). First published in the New York *Leader*, in 1862. The pseudonym "Velsor Brush" is a combination of the family names of two of Whitman's ancestors.

*"Down at the Front"* (p. 645). This and the next two sections were first published in "'Tis But Ten Years Since", New York *Weekly Graphic*, February 14, 1874.

p. 645, l. 24: *"General S."*. General John Sedgewick. (See Comp. Prose, p. 420.)

*"After First Fredericksburg"* (p. 629). First printed in "Our Wounded and Sick Soldiers—Visits Among the Hospitals", New York *Times*, December 11, 1864.

*"The White House by Moonlight"* (p. 630). A manuscript memorandum once in the possession of Mr. Walter R. Benjamin indicated that Whitman intended to make a poem of this material.

*"An Army Hospital Ward"* (p. 631). First published in "'Tis But Ten Years Since", New York *Weekly Graphic*, February 21, 1874.

*"The Great Army of the Wounded"* (p. 632). This is a specimen of the human interest war correspondence Whitman sent to various New York and Brooklyn papers from Washington. It appeared in the New York *Times*, February 26, 1863.

*"A Night Battle Over a Week Since"* (p. 638). Lee defeated Hooker at Chancellorsville, May 1-4, 1864. Published in S.D.C.

*"The Most Inspiriting of All War's Shows"* (p. 640). 1863. Published in S.D.C.

*"Battle of Gettysburg"* (p. 641). Meade defeated Lee at Gettysburg, July 1-3, 1863. Published in S.D.C.

"*A Cavalry Camp*" (p. 642). July 1863. Printed in **S.D.C.**

"*A New York Soldier*" (p. 643). 1863. Printed in "Hospital Visits", New York *Times*, December 11, 1864. Reprinted in "'Tis But Ten Years Since", February 28, 1874.

"*Abraham Lincoln*" (p. 644). From "Washington in the Hot Season", New York *Times*, August 16, 1863. Reprinted in revised form in "'Tis But Ten Years Since", New York *Weekly Graphic*, February 28, 1874; both newspaper versions vary considerably from the text, which is taken from *Specimen Days*. Cf. "Death of President Lincoln" (p. 651), and "Death of Abraham Lincoln" (p. 752).

"*A New Army Organization Fit for America*" (p. 646). From S.D.C.

"*A Glimpse of War's Hell-Scenes*" (p. 647). Apparently written in the fall of 1864. Printed in S.D.C.

"[*Exchange of Prisoners*]" (p. 649). This is one of the letters Whitman sent to the press urging a change in the government policy toward the exchange of prisoners, his brother being a prisoner at the time, though he was later exchanged.

"*Boys in the Army*" (p. 651). Apparently written in January-February 1865. Published in S.D.C.

"*Death of President Lincoln*" (p. 651). April 1865. Published in S.D.C. Cf. "Death of Abraham Lincoln" (p. 752), and "Memories of President Lincoln" (pp. 300-325).

"*Western Soldiers*" (p. 652). First published in "'Tis But Ten Years Since", New York *Weekly Graphic*, March 7, 1874, where it is dated, "May 26-9, 1865".

"*Three Years Summ'd Up*" (p. 652). First published in "'Tis But Ten Years Since", New York *Weekly Graphic*, March 7, 1874.

"*The Million Dead, Too, Summ'd Up*" (p. 653). Published in S.D.C.

"*The Real War Will Never Get in the Books*" (p. 655). Published in S.D.C.

"[*Trowbridge Anecdote*]" (p. 657). This is a memorandum which Whitman made after an interview with Trowbridge and twenty-three years later gave to Horace Traubel. (Traubel, I, p. 101.)

"*Democratic Vistas*" (p. 657). Published as a separate volume, 1871. This important statement of Whitman's faith in democracy and his conception of the relation of literature to democracy was composed by combining, somewhat inexpertly, earlier essays: "Democracy", *Galaxy*, December 1867, and "Personalism", *ibidem*, May 1868.

"*Preface to 'As a Strong Bird on Pinions Free*' " (p. 722). Published in 1872. Present title, "Thou Mother With thy Equal Brood". The text is that of Comp. Prose.

"*An Interregnum Paragraph*" (p. 727). Published in S.D.C. p. 728, ll. 5, 6; "*a half-Paralytic.*" Cf. letter CXXI.

"*Preface to the Centennial Edition*" (p. 728). This preface to the two-volume edition of *Leaves of Grass* and *Two Rivulets*, published to mark the Centennial of the Declaration of Independence, in 1876, employs the text of Comp. Prose.

"*A Winter-Day on the Sea Beach*" (p. 736). Originally captioned "A Fine Winter Day on the Beach" as a section of "How I Still Get Around at Sixty and Take Notes", No. 1, *Critic*, January 29, 1881. Republished in S.D.C.

"*Sea-Shore Fancies*" (p. 737). Originally published without this caption as a part of the preceding *Critic* article. The last paragraph was there captioned "A Sea Vision". In the S.D.C. reprint, Whitman omitted the following concluding sentence: "What country, or what else anyhow, I do not define; but the vast and lonesome beaches there—an unknown, unsailed, untrod sea and shore." Cf. "With Husky-Haughty Lips O Sea" (p. 462).

"*One of the Human Kinks*" (p. 739). Originally published in "How I Still Get Around at Sixty and Take Notes", No. 3, *Critic*, July 16, 1881.

"*An Afternoon Scene*" (p. 739). Dated February 22, 1878, this appeared as part of the same article as the preceding paragraph. The last two sentences there constituted a separate paragraph.

"*Distant Sounds*" (p. 740). Originally published as part of "How I Still Get Around at Sixty and Take Notes", No. 2, *Critic*, April 9, 1881.

"*A Sun-Bath—Nakedness*" (p. 740). Under the caption "Convalescent Hours", this was first published as part of the same article as the preceding paragraph. Cf. "A Memorandum at a Venture" (p. 804), and "Ventures on an Old Theme" (p. 813).

"*Thoughts Under an Oak—A Dream*" (p. 742). Published in S.D.C.

"*Three of Us*" (p. 743). Published in S.D.C.

"*Death of William Cullen Bryant*" (p. 744). Originally published in "The Poet's Recreation", New York *Tribune*, July 4, 1878.

"*Manhattan from the Bay*" (p. 745). Originally published with the foregoing. This sail was taken with the Sorosis ladies, according to Alma Calder Johnston (wife of William Douglas O'Connor) in her "Personal Memories of Walt Whitman", *Bookman* (New York), December 1917. Cf. "Fancies at Navesink" (pp. 459-462).

"*Human and Heroic New York*" (p. 746). Originally published with the foregoing.

p. 746, ll. 26, 27 : "*the two shall be . . . united*". Since January 1, 1898, Brooklyn has been a borough of the City of New York.

"*Hours for the Soul*" (p. 747). Under the title "An Exceptional Night", this first appeared in the *Critic*, July 15, 1882, with minor changes chiefly in the paragraphing.

p. 749, l. 25 : "*The East*". Cf. "Passage to India" (pp. 372-381).

"*Straw-Color'd and Other Psyches*" (p. 751). Cf. "The Dalliance of the Eagles" (p. 252).

"*Death of Abraham Lincoln*" (p. 752). For discussion concerning the delivery of this lecture, see William E. Barton, *Abraham Lincoln and Walt Whitman*, Chapter XV, Furness, pp. 203-204, and Barrus, pp. 260-269, *passim*.

"*An Egotistical 'Find'*" (p. 763). Published in S.D.C. In the fall of 1879 Whitman had journeyed as far west as the Rocky Mountains. Cf. Letter CXXX (p. 1034).

"*The Prairies and Great Plains in Poetry*" (p. 763). Published in S.D.C.

"*America's Characteristic Landscape*" (p. 764). Published in S.D.C.

"*Earth's Most Important Stream*" (p. 764). Published in S.D.C.

"*Mississippi Valley Literature*" (p. 765). Published in S.D.C.

"*The Silent General*" (p. 767). Published in S.D.C. Cf. "Death of General Grant" (p. 463), and "What Best I See in Thee" (p. 436).

"*President Hayes's Speeches*" (p. 768). Published in S.D.C.

"*Edgar Poe's Significance*" (p. 768). Omitting the date in the first paragraph, this was published in the *Critic*, June 3, 1882.

"*Beethoven's Septette*" (p. 771). Cf. "Letters From Paumanok" (p. 568), "*The Mystic Trumpeter*" (p. 421), and "Proud Music of the Storm" (p. 366).

"*A Contralto Voice*" (p. 771). Published in S.D.C.

p. 772, l. 2 : "*Luther's hymn*". Cf. "Proud Music of the Storm", § 5 (p. 370).

"*Seeing Niagara to Advantage*" (p. 772). Reprinted as part of "Summer Days in Canada", in the London (Ontario) *Advertiser*, June 22, 1880. Whitman was on his way to London, Ontario, where his future biographer, Dr. Bucke, entertained him and then accompanied him on an excursion down the St. Lawrence and up the Saguenay.

"*Tennyson's 'De Profundis'*" (p. 773). First published in "Diary in Canada", pp. 10-11.

"*The Savage Saguenay*" (p. 773). Originally printed as part of

"Summer Days in Canada", in London (Ontario) *Advertiser*, June 22, 1880.

"*Capes Eternity and Trinity*" (p. 774). Printed in S.D.C.

"*Cedar-Plums Like—Names*" (p. 775). Printed in S.D.C.

"*Death of Thomas Carlyle*" (p. 777). Originally printed with some variation (such as the omission of the fourth paragraph and the first two sentences of the fifth) in the *Critic*, February 12, 1881. Republished in S.D.C. For correspondence on the subject of Carlyle's death, see Barrus, pp. 199 ff.

p. 778, l. 39: "*Shooting Niagara*". Cf. "Democratic Vistas" (p. 657), which was in part a reply to Carlyle's essay. For earlier comments on Carlyle, see U.P.P., I, pp. 129-130, and *I Sit and Look Out*, p. 68.

p. 781, l. 16: Cf. "Whitman and Hegel", Mody C. Boatright, University of Texas, *Studies in English*, No. 9, 1929.

"*Carlyle from American Points of View*" (p. 780). Published in S.D.C.

p. 781, l. 6: "*Froude's Memoirs*". Froude's edition of Carlyle's *Reminiscences*, published in New York in 1881.

p. 784, ll. 10, 29: "*His fullest best biographer*", etc. This passage is taken from the Preface (pp. xvi-xvii) of Froude's *Thomas Carlyle. A History of the First Forty Years of His Life*, New York, 1882.

"*A Week's Visit to Boston*" (p. 789). First published with slight variations as "How I Still Get Around at Sixty and Take Notes" No. 3, *Critic*, May 7, 1881.

p. 790, ll. 17, 18: " '*the death of Abraham Lincoln*' *essay*". Given on pp. 752-762.

"*My Tribute to Four Poets*" (p. 791). Under the heading "I Call on Longfellow", this appeared as a section of the *Critic* article immediately preceding. In the original version the first paragraph concluded with the sentence: "I did not see Emerson, and have never seen Whittier."

"*Millet's Pictures—Last Items*" (p. 792). This also appeared with a few changes in the *Critic* article mentioned in the notes immediately preceding, under the caption, "Millet's Pictures— New Suggestions, As wakenings".

"*Custer's Last Rally*" (p. 793). First published in New York *Tribune*, August 15, 1881. Cf. "From Far Dakota's Cañons" (p. 434).

p. 794, l. 25: "*Messieur Crapeau*", i.e. "Johnny Crapaud", or Frogeater.

"*A Visit, at the Last, to R. W. Emerson*" (p. 794). Under the heading "An Early Autumn Side-Bit", and dated "Sept. 17", this was first published in "How I Still Get Around at Sixty and Take Notes", No. 5, in *Critic*, December 3, 1881.

p. 795, l. 32: Here a sentence has been deleted from the original version: "And so, there Emerson sat, and I looking at him."

p. 796, ll. 3, 4: After "Dinner the same", originally appeared in the *Critic* version, the following: "It was not my first dinner with Emerson. In 1857, and along there, when he came to New York to lecture, we two would dine together at the Astor House. And some years after, I living for a while in Boston, we would occasionally meet for the same purpose at the American or Parker's. Before I get through these notes I will allude to one of our CXXXII dinners, following a pretty vehement discussion." Cf. Letter CXXXIV (p. 1038).

"*Other Concord Notations*" (p. 796). Originally printed as a part of the foregoing article.

"*Boston Common—More of Emerson*" (p. 797). Originally printed as a part of the foregoing article.

"*Death of Longfellow*" (p. 798). Originally published in the *Critic*, April 8, 1882. The following paragraphs were omitted in S.D.C.

"Without jealousies, without mean passions, never did the personality, character, daily and yearly life of a poet, more steadily and truly assimilate his own loving, cultured, guiltless, courteous ideal, and exemplify it. In the world's arena, he had some special sorrows—but he had prizes, triumphs, recognitions, the grandest.

"Extensive and heartfelt as is to-day and has been for a long while, the fame of Longfellow, it is probable, nay certain, that years hence it will be wider and deeper."

"*Starting Newspapers*" (p. 799). Originally written for the first number of the Camden, New Jersey, *Daily Courier*, June 1, 1882.

"*By Emerson's Grave*" (p. 802). Originally printed as a signed article in the *Critic*, May 6, 1882. Whitman did not attend the funeral. (Barrus, p, 210.)

"*Final Confessions—Literary Tests*" (p. 802). Published in S.D.C.

"*A Memorandum At a Venture*" (p. 804). First published in *North American Review*, June 1882. Cf. "A Sun-Bath—Nakedness" (p. 740), and "Ventures on an Old Theme" (p. 813).

"*Emerson's Books (the Shadows of Them)*" (p. 810). First published in *Literary World*, May 22, 1880, and republished with a few changes in New York *Tribune*, May 15, 1882. The last five sentences in the first paragraph were added in the *Tribune* revision. In the S.D.C. reprint Whitman omitted the following paragraphs which had appeared in the *Literary World*: "Democracy (like

Christianity) is not served best by its own most brawling advocates, but often far, far better, finally, by those who are outside its ranks. I should say that such men as Carlyle and Emerson and Tennyson —to say nothing of Shakspere or Walter Scott—have done more for political or social progress and liberalization, and for individuality and freedom, than all the pronounced democrats one could name.

"The foregoing assumptions on Emerson and his books may seem—perhaps are—paradoxical, but, as before intimated, is not every first-class artist himself, and are not all real works of art. themselves, paradoxical? and is not the world itself so? As also intimated in the beginning, I have written my criticism in the unflinching spirit of the man's own inner teachings. As I understand him, the truest honor you can pay him is to try his own rules, his own heroic treatment, on the greatest themes, even his own works.

"It remains to be distinctly avowed by me that Emerson's books form the tallest and finest growth yet of the literature of the New World. They bring, with miraculous opportuneness, exactly what America needs, to begin at the head, to radically sever her (not too apparently at first) from the fossilism and feudalism of Europe."

"*Darwinism (then Furthermore)*" (p. 816). Published in S.D.C.

"*The Tramp and Strike Questions*" (p. 817). For a discussion of this projected lecture, see Furness, pp. 54 ff., 222.

"*The Bible As Poetry*" (p. 819). Originally published in the *Critic*, February 3, 1883.

"*A Thought On Shakespere*" (p. 823). Published in the *Critic*, August 18, 1886.

"*Robert Burns as Poet and Person*" (p. 825). First published in the *Critic*, December 16, 1882. The *Critic* version was entitled "Robert Burns" and omitted the first three paragraphs as here given.

"*Walt Whitman in Camden*" (p. 834). First published in the *Critic*, February 28, 1885. Although a pseudonym is used, there is no doubt of Whitman's authorship. (U.P.P., II, p. 58, n. 2.)

p. 834, ll. 35, 36: "*In 1848-9*". Whitman's first and well-known visit to New Orleans lasted but three months, in the spring of 1848; but there are indications that he returned, probably the next year. It appears certain that his first visit did not include "other Gulf States besides Louisiana".

p. 834, ll. 36, 37: "*From 1865 to '73*". Whitman began to live in Washington in January 1863.

p. 835, l. 7: "*prostrated by hospital malaria*". Cf. Letter XXXVI (p. 947), and Letter CIV (p. 1012).

p. 835, l. 17: "*Secretary Harlan dismissed him*". Cf. Letter XCII (p. 1000), and Letter XCIII (p. 1002).

p. 837, l. 12: "*Helen Price*". Cf. Letters VI (p. 886), XXV (p. 926), LIX (p. 972), LXV (p. 978), CI (p. 1010), CVIII (p. 1016), and CXXXIII (p. 1037).

p. 837, l. 13: "*in Dr. Bucke's book*". *Walt Whitman*, published in 1883.

"*The Old Bowery*" (p. 838). First published in the *North American Review*, in 1885. Cf. Letter CXLII (p. 1044).

"*Slang in America*" (p. 845). Printed in Comp. Prose, p. 406. First published in *North American Review*, November 1885. The illustrations in the third paragraph were probably taken from Emerson's *Nature*.

"*A Word About Tennyson*" (p. 850). Originally published in the *Critic*, January 1, 1887.

"*George Fox and Shakspere*" (p. 853). Published in Comp. Prose.

"*The Perfect Human Voice*" (p. 874). First published in Munson's *Illustrated World* (Philadelphia), Vol. I, p. 2, 1890.

"*Old Actors, Singers, Shows, Etc., in New York*" (p. 875). Published in Comp. Prose.

# Letters

Letter I (p. 883): Apparently this is the earliest extant Whitman letter. A *facsimile* copy is in the possession of the Editor.

Letter II (p. 883): In 1849, when Whitman was editing the Brooklyn *Freeman*, his printing office did some of the public printing. The present letter presents a bill for such printing to a member of the city government. (Holloway and Schwarz, *I Sit and Look Out*, p. 7.)

Letter III (p. 884): This letter was written to an unnamed friend of Hector Tyndale.

p. 884, l. 18: "*Mrs. Price and Helen*". Mrs. Abby H. Price and her daughter, close friends of Whitman and his family. Various letters to them are to be found in Glicksberg, pp. 106-118. A long letter about Whitman is quoted in Bucke, pp. 26-32. Cf. Letters V (p. 886), XXV (p. 926), LIX (p. 972), LXV (p. 978), CVIII (p. 1016), and CXXXIII (p. 1037).

p. 885, l. 15: "*Fowler & Wells*". For a discussion of Whitman's relation to Fowler & Wells, anonymous publishers of his Second Edition and of *Life Illustrated*, to which he contributed, see *New York Dissected*, pp. 1-14, and Edward Hungerford, "Walt Whitman and His Chart of Bumps", *American Literature*, January 1931, pp. 350 ff.

Letter IV (p. 886): "*Bardic Symbols*". See "As I Ebb'd with the Ocean of Life" (p. 234).

Letter V (p. 886): Cf. "*Boston Common—More of Emerson*" (p. 797).

Letter VI (p. 887): "*Eighteen Sixty-One*" (p. 258) was not published by the *Atlantic*.

Letter VII (p. 888): Whitman wrote for the New York *Times* a description of his brother's regiment, "The Fifty-First New York City Veterans", U.P.P., II, pp. 37-41; see also Glicksberg, pp. 64-83.

p. 888, l. 9: "*Hannah*", Mrs. Charles L. Heyde, Whitman's sister. Cf. Letters XLVIII (p. 961), and LXIX (p. 982).

p. 888, l. 12: "*Jeff*", Thomas Jefferson Whitman, Walt's brother.

p. 889, l. 15: "*Mat*", Martha Whitman (Mrs. Jefferson Whitman).

p. 890, l. 9: "*Sis*", an affectionate term for Jefferson Whitman's little daughter, Mannahatta.

p. 890, l. 9: "*Andrew*", Andrew Jackson Whitman, another brother.

Letter VIII (p. 892), l. 39): "*Jesse and Eddy*". Jesse and Edward were Walt's other brothers, the oldest and the youngest of the children, and both mentally defective.

Letter XI (p. 895): Cf. This contemporary description of Lincoln with "Abraham Lincoln" (p. 644), and "Death of Abraham Lincoln" (p. 752).

p. 898, l. 22: "*Fred Gray, and Bloom and Russell*". Fred Gray, Nathaniel Bloom and Charles Russell were friends whom Whitman had known in New York before he went to Washington. (Cf. Letter XI, p. 895, and Letter XIX, p. 915.)

In a copy of Frederick H. Hedge's *Prose Writers of Germany* (Philadelphia, 1848) which had been given to Fred Gray by his father in 1856, Whitman wrote several memoranda which throw additional light on his friendship with Gray:

"Aug. 29, '62. F. S. Gray (at Raeffele's, in 6th St.) requested me to keep this book. He goes in a few days on Gen. Smith's staff, down in the Army in Va."                                          W. W.

"Battle of Antietam, Maryland, Sept. '62—F. G. has returned from his battle on a two days furlough—I spent the evening with him (at Pfaffs &c.)—He gave me a fearful account of the battle-field at ½ past 9 the night following the engagement—He crossed it on duty."

"Oct. 1 '62—I have called on Mrs. Gray and heard that Fred is well satisfied with his position & duties."

"Have had this vol. over twenty five years & read it off & on many hours, days & nights—this written Nov. 24, '88 in Maple street Camden N. J.                                          W. W."

Letter XIII (p. 902, l. 30): "*Mr. Lane*", Moses Lane, Chief Engineer of the Brooklyn Water Works, under whom Jefferson Whitman worked as an engineer. His name appears several times in the *Wound Dresser* letters as a contributor of alms to be distributed by Whitman.

Letter XIV (p. 903). In the *Wound Dresser*, whence this letter is taken, the omission at the beginning is made.

p. 904, l. 39: "*Matty*", Martha Whitman.

Letter XVI (p. 908): Compare the description of Lincoln in this letter with "Abraham Lincoln" (p. 644).

Letter XVII (p. 911, ll. 25, 26): "*Copperhead mob*", a term of reproach applied by the Unionists to Northerners who sympathized with the Confederacy.

Letter XIX (p. 915): This letter is printed from the copy retained by Whitman as given by Traubel (III, p. 68). The fourth paragraph was probably not sent. Whitman afterwards said, "It was too damned nonsensical for a letter otherwise so dead serious." (*Ibidem.*) Hugo Fritsch was the son of the Austrian Consul-General (*Wound Dresser*, p. 62). Cf. Letter XXIV (p. 923).

Letter XX (p. 917). Little is known as to who Miss Gregg was, but, like Whitman, she served the wounded soldiers in the hospitals. Cf. Letter XXVIII (p. 930).

Letter XXII (p. 919). This letter is printed by Traubel (II, p. 127) from a draft retained by Whitman, who said: "I don't know for sure who it was written to—probably one of those Boston women—the Curtis people maybe. [Cf. Letters to Mrs. Margaret S. Curtis, pp. 921, 929] . . . I guessed a Massachusetts name because I make a point of mentioning the Yankee boys."

Letter XXIII (p. 922, l. 27): "*Dr. Russell*", Dr. Le Baron Russell of Boston, who was another of those who collected funds for Whitman's hospital ministrations.

Letter XXIV (p. 925, l. 4): "*my newspaper letter*", "Letter from Washington" (U.P.P., II, pp. 29-36).

Letter XXV (p. 928, l. 7): "*W. D. O'C.*", W. D. O'Connor.

p. 928, l. 8: "*C. W. E.*", C. W. Eldridge, who published the 1860 Edition of *Leaves of Grass* and went into bankruptcy on the outbreak of the war.

Letter XXVI (p. 928). This letter is typical of those Whitman wrote to the relatives and friends of wounded soldiers. Cf. "Come Up from the Fields Father" (p. 277 and note).

Letter XXVII (p. 930, l. 29): "*The sisters Wigglesworth*". The Misses Wigglesworth had become interested in Whitman's hospital work when shown a letter from him to Mrs. Hannah Stevenson, mentioned in this letter (MS. in the Bandler Collection).

Letter XXVIII (p. 931, l. 23): "*Oscar Cunningham*". Cf. Letter XXXIV (p. 943), Letter XXXV (p. 945), and "Come Up from the Fields Father" (p. 277).

p. 931, l. 31: "*James Stilwell*". Cf. Letter XXVI (p. 928).

p. 932, l. 6: "*Miss Gregg*". Cf. Letter XX (p. 917).

p. 932, l. 38: "*the Italian Opera*". Cf. "Italian Music in Dakota" (p. 364), "Plays and Operas, Too" (p. 564), and "Old Actors, Singers, Shows, etc., in New York" (p. 875).

Letter XXIX (p. 934). Although the addressee is called "Douglass" in the letter, Traubel says (II, p. 380) that it was sent to Elijah Fox and the date of the letter agrees with the known date of a letter to Fox (Glicksberg, p. 139).

Letter XXX (p. 936). Cf. "*Down at the Front*" (p. 628).

Letter XXXI (p. 938). The note enclosed in brackets is that of the editor of the *Wound Dresser*.

Letter XXXV (p. 945, l. 34): "*poor Oscar Cunningham*". Cf. Letter XXVIII (p. 930), Letter XXXIV (p. 943), and "Come Up from the Fields Father" (p. 277).

Letter XXXVIII (p. 948). George Whitman was captured and imprisoned at Danville, Va. Cf. Letter XL (p. 951), Letter XLII (p. 954), and "[Exchange of Prisoners]" (p. 649). He was exchanged after a few months.

Letter XXXIX (p. 949): This letter is here printed in its entirety for the first time, through the courtesy of Professor Bliss Perry, who owns the manuscript.

p. 949, l. 17: "*Mr. Otto*", Judge William T. Otto, Assistant Secretary of the Department of the Interior, had been induced by J. Hubley Ashton, at O'Connor's suggestion, to further Whitman's application for an appointment in his department. The present letter is a reply to one from O'Connor under date of December 30, 1864. (Traubel, II, pp. 400-403.)

p. 949, l. 33: "*my ambition*", etc. In his letter, O'Connor having just read Whitman's recent letter in the New York *Times* ("The Great Army of the Wounded"), said: "Only it filled me with infinite regret that there is not a book from you, embodying these rich and sad experiences. It would be sure of immortality. No history of our times would ever be written without it, if written with that wealth of details you could crowd into it. Indeed it would itself be history." (*Ibidem*, p. 402.)

p. 950, ll. 33, 34: "*Not a word . . . from my brother*". Cf. Letter XXXVIII (p. 948), Letter XL (p. 951), and Letter XLII (p. 954).

p. 951, ll. 1, 2: "*Mrs. Price's*". Cf. Letter V (p. 886), Letter XXV (p. 926), Letter LIX (p. 972), Letter LXV (p. 978), Letter CI (p. 1010), and Letter CVIII (p. 1016).

p. 951, ll. 4, 5: "*Dr. William F. Channing*", a Whitman admirer who lived in Providence, R.I.

Letter XL (p. 951, l. 22): "*Danville*". George Whitman was imprisoned at Danville, Va. Cf. Letter XLII (p. 954).

p. 952, l. 8: "*the Indian Office*". Cf. "An Indian Bureau Reminiscence", Comp. Prose, p. 411.

Letter XLI (p. 953, l. 38): "*Mr. Shillaber's*", Benjamin Penhalow Shillaber, an editor of the *Saturday Evening Gazette*.

Letter XLII (p. 954): Concerning this letter Whitman said: "We were in much distress of mind about George at that time: my dear mother was terribly exercised: she was heroic, loyal, uncompromising: but she loved George—was profoundly disturbed over the mystery of his movements, whereabouts." (Traubel, III, p. 201.)

Letter XLIII (p. 955, l. 5): "*The grand culminations*", etc. Lee surrendered to Grant at Appomatox Court House two days after Whitman's letter was written.

p. 955, l. 15: *"My book"*: *Drum-Taps*, which had come from the press a week before Lincoln was assassinated; the poems on Lincoln were added in *Sequel to Drum-Taps*, included in most editions.

p. 955, l. 16: *"The commissioner"*. W. P. Dole, Commissioner for Indian Affairs, in whose office Whitman was employed as a clerk.

Letter XLIV (p. 955): From C. P., 64, where the letter is undated, but it was probably sent shortly after the first of May.

Letter XLV (p. 957, l. 19): *"Old Count Gurowski"*. For a picture of the Count and anecdotes concerning him, see Traubel, III, pp. 334-340.

p. 957, l. 30: *"Stevens"*. Thaddeus Stevens, Abolitionist senator, who advocated severe measures in dealing with the states of the defeated Confederacy.

Letter XLVIII (p. 961, l. 20): *"Galaxy of December 1"*. This contained Burroughs' "Walt Whitman and His Drum Taps".

p. 961, l. 27: *"Mr. Conway's Article"*, "Walt Whitman", in *Fortnightly Review*, October 15, 1866.

p. 961, l. 35: *"Lady Audley's Secret"*, a novel by Mary Elizabeth Braddon (on which was based George Robert's play with the same title).

Letter XLIX (p. 962, ll. 18, 19): *"Florence Percy's Poems"*, by Elizabeth Akers ("Florence Percy"), a Vermont poetess. The small 16mo. vol. had been published that year by Ticknor and Fields and contained the well-known "Rock Me To Sleep".

p. 962, l. 21: *"That fool Heyde"*. Hannah Whitman's husband, Charles Heyde, a portrait painter of Burlington, Vt. The original manuscript of Bucke's *Walt Whitman* shows Heyde to have been the critic referred to on page 56. Many letters indicate the low opinion in which this temperamental and erratic artist was held by the Whitman family. (Cf. Traubel, III, p. 498, Letter LXIX (p. 982). Heyde was later confined in an asylum.

Letter L (p. 963): Whitman himself was in doubt as to whether this letter, reproduced from his draft, was ever mailed (Traubel, II, pp. 418-419).

Letter LI (p. 964, l. 22): *"Calamus"*. Cf. the group of poems under this title (pp. 106-208) and *Calamus* letters to Peter Doyle.

Letter LII (p. 965, l. 23): *"Democracy"*. Printed in *Galaxy* December 1867, and later incorporated in *Democratic Vistas*.

p. 965, l. 27: *"Mr. Burroughs' Notes"*, *Notes on Walt Whitman As Poet and Person*, 1867, which Whitman had assisted Burroughs in writing.

Letter LIII (p. 967, ll. 29, 30): *"Mr. O'Connor's Pamphlet"*, "The Good Gray Poet: a Vindication", 1856.

Letter LIV (p. 968): Probably the reference is to the poem-group entitled "Whispers of Heavenly Death" (pp. 399-415), which appeared in *Broadway Magazine*, October, 1868. Cf. Letter LXV (p. 978).

Letter LV (p. 969, ll. 13, 14): "*Grant will be elected*". Cf. "What Best I See in Thee" (p. 436), and "Death of General Grant" (p. 463).

p. 969, ll. 31, 32: "*the Book William Blake*". Swinburne, in his critical study, *William Blake*, 1868, pointed out the kinship of Blake and Whitman as poets. (Cf. the following two letters.) In 1871 he wrote a laudatory poem, "*To Walt Whitman in America*", in *Songs Before Sunrise*. But his "Whitmania" in the *Fortnightly Review*, August 1897, was looked upon as a retraction, though Whitman himself was little disturbed by it. (Traubel, II, p. 154, and *passim*). Yet Swinburne sent Whitman greetings by Edmund Gosse as late as 1887. (Traubel, I, p. 40.)

Letter LVI (p. 970): This letter is a reply to one from Hotten, dated February 5, 1868, promising to send Whitman a copy of the Rossetti selections just coming off the press (Traubel, II, pp. 285-286). In 1872, in a letter to Rudolph Schmidt, Copenhagen, Whitman called Hotten "the English pirate-publisher". (Letter XCII, p. 1000.)

Letter LVIII (p. 971): The article was "Personalism", published in the *Galaxy*, May 1868. It did not appear in the *Fortnightly Review*, but was worked over in *Democratic Vistas*.

Letter LIX (p. 972), l. 27: "*Harlan*", James Harlan, who, as Secretary of the Interior, had dismissed Whitman from his clerkship in 1865.

p. 972, l. 38: "*a poem soon*". "Whispers of Heavenly Death" (pp. 399-415)...

p. 973, l. 1: "*the Impeachment*", i.e., of President Johnson.

Letter LX (p. 973, ll. 12, 13): "*in the book*", *Democratic Vistas*.

Letter LXII (p. 975, l. 19): "*old Mr. Alcott*", A. Bronson Alcott. Cf. Letter LXI (p. 974).

p. 976, l. 11: "*I want the Galaxy folks*", etc. This article, called "Orbic Literature" (cf. Letter LXIII, p. 976), apparently was not published in a magazine.

Letter LXIII (p. 977, l. 10): "*Orbic Literature*". Cf. Letter LXII (p. 974). Probably this was incorporated in "Democratic Vistas" according to Whitman's intention.

Letter LXIV (p. 977): Charles Hine painted a portrait of Whitman in 1859, from which was made the engraving used in the 1860-61 edition of *Leaves of Grass*.

Letter LXV (p. 978, l. 18): "*my piece*". Cf. Letter LIX (p. 972).

Letter LXVI (p. 979, l. 21): "*The R. R. Business*". Doyle was a street-car conductor in Washington.

Letter LXVIII (p. 981, l. 31): "*the enclosed piece*". "Proud Music of the Sea-Storm", which the *Atlantic Monthly* published in February 1869. "After I had written my letter to Emerson", Whitman told Traubel (II, p. 21), "I wondered if I had not overdone my call. But Emerson proceeded without delay: he evidently had no qualms: then Fields took the matter up offhand, writing me at once as you see. The whole business was done in about a week." Whitman declared that in making this use of Emerson's friendship he was acting on the latter's suggestion.

Letter LXIX (p. 982): Cf. Letter XLIX (p. 562). Whitman told Traubel (III, p. 498): "I am always obliged to reach my sister indirectly—through her doctors up there at Burlington, or perhaps a friend or two."

Letter LXX (p. 982): The poem, "Thou Vast Rondure Swimming in Space" (later incorporated in "Passage to India"), was accepted for the *Fortnightly Review*. (See Letter LXXI, p. 983.)

Letter LXXI (p. 983): Fields did not accept the poem for the *Atlantic*, nor was it published in the *Fortnightly Review*.

Letter LXXII (p. 983): First published in its entirety from the manuscript owned by Mr. W. T. H. Howe, by his kind permission.

"*Heyde*". Cf. letter XLIX (p. 962), and Letter LXIX (p. 982).

"*Ashton's*". J. Hubley Ashton. Cf. Letter XXXIX, n., p. 1101.

p. 984, l. 8: "*a very good little photo of me*". Two photographs of Whitman were taken about this time, the excellent one by Frank Pearsall (Brooklyn) reproduced in Holloway, facing p. 198, and the Rice photograph of Whitman with Peter Doyle, a drawing from which was used as a frontispiece to *Calamus*. Of the two, the latter is more probably referred to, since Rice was a Washington photographer.

Letter LXXIV (p. 986): James Parton's wife was "Fanny Fern", the first woman to praise *Leaves of Grass* in print. (*New York Dissected*, pp. 146-154, 162-165.) Both were friends of Whitman, but money matters and perhaps other causes resulted in an estrangement, at least with Parton. Bliss Perry stated the Parton side of the controversy (pp. 123-124), but modified his statement in his second edition (Appendix). Traubel gives in *facsimile* the documents which accompanied the present letter, in which Whitman defends himself (III, pp. 235-239). It seems that gossip made much more of the matter than it signified.

Letter LXXV (p. 987): Through William Rossetti was begun a correspondence between Anne Gilchrist and Whitman, in which she revealed her love for him (cf. Letter LXXXVIII, p. 998). Much of this correspondence was published by Thomas B. Harned in *The Letters of Anne Gilchrist and Walt Whitman*, 1918, where the story of their remarkable friendship is told. Cf. also Hilda M.

Ridley, "Walt Whitman and Anne Gilchrist," *Dalhousie Review*, January 1932.

Letter LXXVI (p. 988): This letter illustrates Whitman's gospel of "adhesiveness" which underlies the group of "Calamus" poems, the letters to Peter Doyle and the political theory in *Democratic Vistas.* "Comradeship—yes, that's the thing: getting one and one together to make two—getting the twos together everywhere to make all: that's the only bond we should accept and that's the only freedom we should desire: comradeship, comradeship." (Traubel, p. 371.)

Letter LXXVII (p. 989): From Whitman's draft of this letter. It was Thomas Dixon, an uneducated but intelligent cork-cutter, who bought from James Grindrod, a book-peddler recently returned from America, the copy of the first edition of *Leaves of Grass,* which had such large influence in England and Ireland. He called it to the attention of William Bell Scott, who in turn gave a copy to William Rossetti. It was Rossetti's volume of selections which fell into the hands of Anne Gilchrist. Dixon organized, with Scott, a School of Art and a Free Library, in Sunderland, and did much to spread the Whitman gospel. (See Harold Blodgett, *Whitman in England*, pp. 15-17.)

p. 989, ll. 28, 29: *"a piece . . . on Democracy"*. "Democracy" in the *Galaxy*, December 1867.

p. 989, l. 31: *"article by an English lady"*. "A Woman's Estimate of Walt Whitman", unsigned, but by Anne Gilchrist, *The Radical* (Boston), May 1870.

Letter LXXVIII (p. 990, l. 27): *"saw the yachts"*. For Whitman's interest in yachting, see "The Fall Regatta", *I Sit and Look Out*, pp. 108-109.

Letter LXXIX (p. 991): Apparently Doyle had been laid off by the street-car company, or feared to be.

Letter LXXXI (p. 993, l. 28): *"I admire and love the French"*. Cf. "O Star of France" (p. 360).

p. 994, l. 4: *"my dear son"*. Whitman was, of course, unrelated to Doyle, but treated him as a son and at times addressed him so. Similarly there is, in the Library of Congress, a letter from William Vandemark, a soldier boy, which addresses Whitman as "father", though another letter from Vandemark makes clear this is intended only in a sentimental sense.

Letter LXXXII (p. 994): First published in its entirety from the manuscript owned by Mr. W. T. H. Howe, by his kind permission.

p. 994, l. 18: *"'Sula"*. Burroughs' wife, Ursula.

p. 994, l. 19: *"Chauncey"*. Chauncey B. Deyo, Burroughs' nephew, who admired Whitman. (Barrus, pp. 88 ff.)

p. 994, l. 22: *"my new edition"*. The fifth edition of *Leaves of Grass* was issued in this year.

p. 994, l. 27: *"a letter from Mrs. Gilchrist"*. Apparently this letter has been lost, since Harned gives none between December 9, 1869 and September 3, 1871. Cf. Letter LXXXVIII n.

p. 994, l. 28: *"Wake Robin"*. By Burroughs.

Letter LXXXIII (p. 995, ll. 20, 21): *"The Poetry of Democracy: Walt Whitman"*. An essay by Edward Dowden.

p. 995, l. 27: *"Wednesday's brush in N.Y."* A parade of Orangemen, though protected by several regiments of soldiers and five hundred police, were attacked by a Catholic mob, and fired upon the crowd. The disturbance was local, as Whitman says, and order was quickly restored; but it created a great stir at the moment, partly because of an attempt to make political capital of it.

Letter LXXXV (p. 997): Cf. "Song of the Exposition" (p. 181).

Letter LXXXVI (p. 997): From Whitman's draft of the letter. Ellis declined to risk an unexpurgated edition of *Leaves of Grass* in England. (Traubel, II, pp. 447-448.)

Letter LXXXVII (p. 998): In July, Dowden had published "The Poetry of Democracy: Walt Whitman" in the *Westminster Review*.

p. 998, ll. 8, 9: *"Mr. Terrell"*. He was Robert Y. Terrell, Professor of Greek in Dublin University, where he had lectured on Whitman (Barrus, p. 59).

Letter LXXXVIII (p. 998): This, the first letter to be written by Whitman direct to Mrs. Gilchrist, is printed from the original manuscript by the kind permission of Mrs. Frank J. Sprague of New York, as are the other letters to Mrs. Gilchrist. A *facsimile* reproduction of the letter is to be seen in Holloway, facing p. 264. Discovering Mrs. Gilchrist's intense interest in his poetry as shown in her letters to William Rossetti, Whitman had, on December 9, 1869, expressed his appreciation to Rossetti (Letter LXXV, p. 987), enclosing an extra photograph for Mrs. Gilchrist and requesting that the letter itself be shown or given to his, as yet, anonymous English admirer. These letters of Mrs. Gilchrist to Rossetti were anonymously published in the Boston *Radical* as "A Woman's Estimate of Walt Whitman", in May 1870. But on September 3, 1871, and again on October 23, Mrs. Gilchrist, having fallen in love with Whitman through reading his poetry, suggested marriage to him (see Harned, pp. 58-66). To these beautiful and impassioned letters the present one is a kindly and delicate reply.

Letter LXXXIX (p. 999): From Schmidt's Whitman essay, "Amerikanske Democratis Digter" (translated in *In Re*), Burroughs got the title for his essay on Whitman, "The Flight of the Eagle". (Barrus, p. 117.)

p. 999, l. 12: *"your poet Björnson"*. Whitman said: "I was particularly interested in the Norwegian Björnson. He sent me his picture once. It is that of a Viking: powerful, inflexible, clean; a face of humanity, purpose; a face of the ideal. Norway has made her best men much bigger than her own size—had made them of world-dimensions: Ibsen, Björnson, the others." (Traubel, II, p. 159.)

Letter XC (p. 999, l. 24): "*saw Mr. Emerson*". For John Burroughs' account of this meeting see Barrus, p. 65. Cf. Letter XCIII (p. 1002).

Letter XCI (p. 1000, l. 18): "*the new edition of my books*". *Leaves of Grass* (1872), and *As A Strong Bird on Pinions Free and Other Poems* (1872).

Letter XCII (p. 1000): From Whitman's draft of the letter.

p. 1001, l. 18: "*ignominiously dismissed*". By Secretary James Harlan. (Cf. Letter XCIII, p. 1002.)

p. 1002, l. 11: "*suspicion of querulousness*". The letter written to Dowden at the same time voices the same complaint. (*Ibidem*.)

Letter XCIII (p. 1002, l. 24): "*What John Burroughs brings*". Burroughs had returned from a trip abroad earlier in the winter.

p. 1003, l. 28: "*Tennyson has written to me*". Cf. Letter XCV (p. 1005), and Letter CIX (p. 1017). Letters from Tennyson to Whitman are reproduced in Traubel, I, facing p. 36, and Donaldson, facing p. 194.

p. 1003, l. 33: "*Emerson has just been this way*". Cf. Letter XC (p. 999).

Letter XCIV (p. 1004, ll. 10, 11): "*your photograph*". Reproduced in Traubel, I, facing p. 406.

p. 1004, l. 20: "*my latest piece*". "The Mystic Trumpeter" (p. 421), in the *Kansas Magazine*, February 1872.

Letter XCV (p. 1005, l. 6): See preceding note.

p. 1005, ll. 9, 10: "*your letter of last summer*". This letter seems to have been lost, since it does not appear in Harned.

Letter XCVI (p. 1005, ll. 36, 37): "*for northern New England*", etc. Cf. Letter XCVIII (p. 1007), and Letter XCIX (p. 1008).

p. 1006, ll. 16, 17: "*a letter I sent you*". This letter was not received. (Harned, p. 77.)

Letter XCVIII (p. 1007, l. 39): "*I delivered my poem*". "Thou Mother with Thy Equal Brood" (p. 410).

Letter XCIX (p. 1008): The omissions in this letter are made in Barrus, pp. 73-74, whence it is taken.

p. 1009, l. 10: "*My sister Martha*", i.e. his sister-in-law, Jeff's wife.

p. 1009, l. 13: "*My sister Hannah*", Mrs. Charles Heyde. Cf. Letter XLIX (p. 962), and Letter LXIX (p. 982).

Letter C (p. 1009): From Whitman's draft of the letter, on the back of which was written, "To Carlyle with Dem Vistas & Am Inst. poem." (Traubel, II, p. 326.)

Letter CI (p. 1010): Whitman suffered a stroke of paralysis on January 23, from which he never completely recovered. His sister-in-law, Martha, died on February 19. (Cf. Letter CII (p. 1010).)

Letter CIV (p. 1012, l. 24): "*a dear sister*". The reference is to Jefferson Whitman's wife.

p. 1013, ll. 5, 6: "*The letters . . . this year*". All of these letters and two others of the period were printed in Harned, but there the letter of July 11 is misdated July 14.

Letter CVI (p. 1015): First published in its entirety from the manuscript owned by Mr. W. T. H. Howe, by his kind permission.

p. 1015, l. 24: "*Eldridge*", Charles W. Eldridge. Cf. Letter XCIX (p. 1008).

p. 1015, l. 27: "*Notes*". John Burroughs' *Notes on Walt Whitman as Poet and Person*, partly written by Whitman, had appeared in 1867.

p. 1015, l. 29: "*a melange*". This was "A Christmas Garland", reprinted in U.P.P., II, pp. 53-58.

Letter CVIII (p. 1017, ll. 18, 19): "*pieces in the Weekly Graphic*". Six papers published under the title, " 'Tis But Ten Years Since", January 24–March 7, 1874, mostly reprinted in Comp. Prose. The title of this series is perhaps reminiscent of the subtitle to Scott's *Waverley*.

p. 1017, l. 24: "*I find myself very lonesome here*". Though treated kindly by his brother George, with whom he boarded, Whitman always felt that the latter was unable to appreciate him as a poet. (Cf. *In Re*, p. 35.) Concerning their home life, see Perry, pp. 312 ff.

Letter CIX (p. 1018, ll. 15, 16): "*Tennyson kindly invited me*", etc. Cf. Letter XCIII (p. 1002).

Letter CX (p. 1018, ll. 26, 27): "*Channy's malady and death*". Chauncey B. Deyo, Burroughs' nephew.

Letter CXI (p. 1019, ll. 24, 25): "*I see the cars and locomotives*", etc. Cf. "To a Locomotive in Winter" (p. 425).

Letter CXII (p. 1020, l. 3): "*a little . . . house*", etc. Whitman did not have a house of his own until 1884, when he bought the one at 328 Mickle Street, which is now a Whitman museum. Cf. Letter CXI (p. 1018.)

p. 1020, l. 17: "*my College piece*". The Tufts College commencement poem, "The Song of the Universal" (p. 209).

Letter CXIII (p. 1020): Cf. "*Emerson's Books (The Shadows of Them)*" (p. 810).

p. 1021, l. 18: "*John Swinton*". As editor of the New York *Times*, Swinton had published some of Whitman's war correspondence (e.g., "The Great Army of the Wounded", p. 632), and remained a staunch friend afterwards.

Letter CXIV (p. 1021): First published in its entirety from the manuscript owned by Mr. W. T. H. Howe, by his kind permission. Whitman had known Stedman in Washington when he was a clerk in the Attorney General's Department. Stedman, through his essay on Whitman in *Poets of America*, did much to overcome the reservations of the conservatives, and in his *Library of American Literature* gave much space to Whitman, whereas Emerson had omitted him entirely from his *Parnassus*. Whitman was full of praise for Stedman the man, but thought his inhibitions prevented his becoming a first-rate writer. (Traubel, I, p. 139 and *passim*.)

Letter CXVI (p. 1022): From Whitman's draft of the letter. The "Einstein" was an acquaintance of the Pfaffian days in New York. "It was to Einstein: but *who* does not matter . . . I was getting a little my old self: certainly was spiritually realizing life once more —tasting the cup to the full." (Traubel, III, pp. 407, 408.)

p. 1023, l. 4: "*my completed writings*", etc. Published together the next year to celebrate the Centennial of the Declaration of Independence.

Letter CXVII (p. 1024, l. 1): "*My new edition*", *Leaves of Grass* and *Two Rivulets*, uniformly bound in the Centennial Edition.

p. 1024, l. 10: "*I do not approve*", etc. In the face of Whitman's warning, Mrs. Gilchrist arrived in Philadelphia with her family in September, where she resided at 1929 North 22nd Street for a year and a half. Whitman was often entertained in her home, as were his friends. In the collection of Mrs. Frank J. Sprague is a large oil painting, by Herbert Gilchrist, showing Whitman at Mrs. Gilchrist's table, with his hostess and one of her daughters.

p. 1024, ll. 16, 17: "*You must not be uneasy*", etc. For a letter she had written to Burroughs concerning her anxiety over the West Jersey *Press* letter (cf. the following note), see Furness, p. 244.

Letter CXVIII (p. 1024): Whitman had written (or certainly he had inspired) an article published anonymously in the West Jersey *Press*, January 26, concerning his neglect and need. This he sent to Rossetti, who gave it publicity through the *Athenæum* (March 11) and accompanied it by an appeal for British support of the poet. This prompted Robert Buchanan to send an article to the London *Daily News* (March 13, cf. Letter CXIX, p. 1025), which started a warm discussion pro and con on both sides of the Atlantic, and greatly stimulated the sales of Whitman's 1876 Edition. For an able discussion of the matter, see Furness, pp. 244-248; see also Holloway, pp. 288 ff.

Letter CXIX (p. 1025): Buchanan's letter is quoted in part, in Barrus, p. 116; quoted in Furness, pp. 245-246.

Letter CXXI (p. 1027): First published in its entirety from the manuscript owned by Mr. W. T. H. Howe, by his kind permission.

p. 1027, l. 26: *"your 'Galaxy' article"*. "A Word or Two on Emerson", *Galaxy*, February 1876. Burroughs referred to Emerson's being hard to please in poetry, finding "too much of the whooping savage in Whitman".

Letter CXXII (p. 1028): From Whitman's draft of the letter.

Letter CXXIII (p. 1029): Whitman wrote from the country, whither he had gone to recuperate.

p. 1029, l. 9: *"the book"*. *Birds and Poets*, by Burroughs, containing a chapter on Whitman entitled "The Flight of the Eagle". The phrase has been taken from an essay on Whitman by Rudolph Schmidt. Cf. Letter LXXXIX, n. (p. 1106).

Letter CXXIV (p. 1029): Published from the manuscript owned by Mr. Alfred F. Goldsmith, by his kind permission.

p. 1029, l. 27: *"22d Street"*, Mrs. Gilchrist and her family lived at 1929 North 22d Street, Philadelphia, where Whitman was a frequent visitor. Cf. Letter CXVII n. (p. 1109).

p. 1029, l. 35: *"Mr. Carpenter"*. Edward Carpenter, author of *Days with Walt Whitman*, 1906.

Letter CXXVIII (p. 1033, l. 2): *"the Creek"*. Timber Creek near the Stafford farm, where Whitman recuperated his strength and wrote many of the nature notes of the period, preserved in *Specimen Days*.

p. 1033, l. 4: *"Brother & Sister"*, Mr. and Mrs. George Whitman, with whom the poet lived.

p. 1033, l. 12: *"Hattie and Jessie"*, daughters of Jefferson Whitman.

p. 1033, l. 19: *"Idle Days & Nights of a Half-paralytic"*, this was an unused title of *Specimen Days*.

p. 1033, ll. 22, 23: *"our young Mrs. Sartoris"*, Nellie Grant Sartoris, the daughter of President Grant, who in 1874 had married Algernon Charles Sartoris, the son of Adelaide Kemble Sartoris and the grandson of the actor, Charles Kemble. On the occasion of her marriage, Whitman had written a poem entitled "A Kiss to the Bride" (p. 497).

p. 1033, l. 26: *"that Cathedral"*, Durham Cathedral, which Mrs. Gilchrist had described in her letter of August 2; *"that baby"*, Mrs. Gilchrist's grandson.

p. 1033, l. 29: *"Bee, Herb, Giddy"*, Mrs. Gilchrist's children, Beatrice, Herbert and Grace.

Letter CXXIX (p. 1033): From Barrus, p. 187, where the place of writing is not given; probably it was Camden, for Whitman was there on August 26, and on September 3. (Comp. Prose, pp. 131-132.)

p. 1033, l. 38: *"the enclosed"*. The paragraphs which Whitman sent Burroughs and the manner in which he used them in "The

Flight of the Eagle" are given in Barrus, p. 111. Whitman's version follows:

"Whitman is not remarkable in details or minute finish. But in spirit, in reverence, in breadth, *ensemble*, and in his vistas he stands unmatched. Through all that fluid, weird Nature, 'so far and yet so near', he finds human relations, human responsions. In entire consistence with botany, geology, science, or what-not, he endues his very seas and woods with passion, more than the old hamadryads or tritons. His fields, his rocks, his trees, are not dead material, but living companions.

"To him all Nature's objectiveness holds a cognizant lurking something, without voice, yet realizing you as much as you realize it. No wonder Addington Symonds, the young Hellenic scholar of England, says, 'Singular as it may appear, Walt Whitman is more thoroughly Greek than any man of modern times!' "

p. 1034, l. 1 : "*the enclosures*". Probably the manuscript of Burroughs' article, "Nature and the Poets", which appeared in *Scribner's Monthly*, December 1879.

Letter CXXXI (p. 1035): First published in its entirety from the manuscript owned by Mr. W. T. H. Howe, by his kind permission.

p. 1035, l. 35 : "*The lecture*". This was the second delivery of Whitman's Lincoln lecture, in Philadelphia, April 15, 1880.

p. 1036, l. 5 : "*in their own apartments*", etc. Though Mrs. Gilchrist's primary motive in coming to America was to be near Whitman, she had other incentives as well. One of her daughters was to study medicine in Philadelphia, and after spending two years there, she travelled to Boston and New York, making contacts with the literary circles in those cities.

p. 1036, ll. 11, 12 : "*Jenny Gilder*". Jeannette Gilder was the "Lounger" who wrote literary gossip for the *Critic*, which published a considerable amount of Whitman's prose and verse. "I have no idea that Joe Gilder cares a fig for me. Jenny is more favorable, though not red-hot at all, nor anywhere near it. My only uncompromising friend in the family is probably Watson [Richard Watson Gilder]—he swears to me—not everything in me, but to me—without shame." (Traubel, II, p. 112.)

Letter CXXXII (p. 1036, l. 33): "*the Staffords*", with whom Whitman lived when he went to White Horse, to seek to restore his health, at Timber Creek.

p. 1037, l. 5 : "*Kennedy*". William Sloane Kennedy.

Letter CXXXIII (p. 1037, l. 25): "*you can write to him*", etc. Helen Price's letter is given in Bucke, pp. 26-32.

Letter CXXXIV (p. 1038): Cf. "A Visit at the Last, to R. W. Emerson" (p. 794).

p. 1038, l. 21 : "*The book*". The Osgood Edition of *Leaves of Grass*.

p. 1038, l. 23: *"Johnston's"*. J. H. Johnston, a jeweler friend whom Whitman often visited in New York. He was active in arranging for Whitman's Lincoln lecture at the Madison Square Theater, in 1879.

p. 1038, l. 24: *"Shall go to Canada"*, etc. Whitman had visited Canada in 1880 (cf. "The Savage Saguenay", *supra* p. 773), but did not go again.

Letter CXXXV (p. 1039, l. 6): *"Beatrice Gilchrist"*, a daughter of Anne Gilchrist, a doctor.

p. 1039, l. 9: *"O. W. Holmes"*. Cf. Letter CLV (p. 1051).

p. 1039, ll. 9, 10: *"old Mr. James"*, Henry James, Sr., father of the novelist.

Letter CXXXVI (p. 1039): Published for the first time from the manuscript in the collection of Captain F. L. Pleadwell, by his kind permission. Mrs. Johnston was the wife of John H. Johnston, the friend whom Whitman often visited at Mott Haven. Their children were Albert ("Ally"), and Kitty and Grace, with whom Whitman was several times photographed. See *Complete Writings*, X, p. 60. She wrote "Personal Memories of Walt Whitman" (*Bookman*, December 1917). Whitman had been the guest of the Johnston's for over six weeks while preparing the Osgood Edition for the press. (Charles N. Elliott, *Walt Whitman as Man, Poet, and Friend*, p. 155.)

Letter CXXXVII (p. 1039): Why Whitman suppressed the name of his correspondent in publishing this letter (Comp. Prose, pp. 311-312) is not known. Dr. P. Popoff published several translations from Whitman poems in the *Zagranichny Viestnik*, March 1883.

Letter CXXXVIII (p. 1040): For a statement of the Osgood difficulty, see Thomas B. Harned, "Walt Whitman and His Boston Publishers" in *Complete Writings*, 1902, vol. 8, pp. 275-300.

p. 1041, ll. 10, 11: *"A Memorandum at a Venture"*, *q.v.* (p. 804). From Barrus, p. 209, where only these two paragraphs are given.

Letter CXXXIX, (p. 1041): Concerning this letter Burroughs said, "That article came out in the 'Century'. I guess I struck out most of what Walt marked—I usually did: He was a wonderful critic." (Barrus, p. 112.) The article seems to have been a review of Froude's *Thomas Carlyle: A History of the First Forty Years of his Life, Century*, June 1882.

Letter CXL (p. 1042, l. 18): *"Mrs. Gilchrist and Herbert."* Mrs. Anne Gilchrist and her artist son, Herbert Harlakenden Gilchrist, whom Burroughs had recently visited at Hempstead.

p. 1042, ll. 14, 15: *"Dr. Bucke . . . his book"*. His biography of Whitman, published the next year.

Letter CXLI (p. 1042): The first paragraph of this letter is omitted.

It contained details concerning the new publishing arrangement, whereby Rees, Wells & Co. were to take over the suppressed Osgood edition.

p. 1042, l. 26: "*Ezra Heywood*". Excerpts from this letter, from the Massachusetts free-lover, are made in Barrus, p. 225. When Heywood came to trial, the court ruled out that part of the indictment which affected *Leaves of Grass*, and Heywood was acquitted. (*Ibidem*.)

p. 1043, l. 11: "*S. D.*": *Specimen Days*.

p. 1043, l. 13: "*Stoddard*": Richard Henry Stoddard. "*Winter*": William Winter. "*The Tribune Letters*". Compare the following paragraph from O'Connor's letter to Burroughs written on October 19: "I shall now gather into a pamphlet (just as soon as my cursed burden of work lifts a little) all that have appeared in the 'Tribune', the Toby letter, and two or three others I have sketched out already (one on Marston and his Joseph Surface Galbraith, and one on 'Sigma', of the catawampous claw variety) and let the fur fly. I mean to make this Comstock crowd memorable, if I can compass it, and they need not imagine that the matter has ended with some stray articles in the newspapers." (Barrus, p. 223.)

Letter CXLII (p. 1044): A letter Whitman wrote to Doyle on the fly leaf of a copy of *Specimen Days* sent to the latter.

Letter CXLIII (p. 1044): James Redpath was editor of the *North American Review*. "The Booth Article" mentioned was probably "The Old Bowery" (p. 838. See Traubel, II, 76; but I do not find it in the *North American Review*). Redpath asked Whitman also to contribute to *Reminiscences of Abraham Lincoln by Distinguished Men of His Time* (1860), edited by Allen Thorndike Rice, owner of the *North American Review*. Whitman's contribution was entitled "Dear to Democracy"; it appears as "Abraham Lincoln" in Comp. Prose, pp. 437-438.

Letter CXLVI (p. 1045): It has been shown that Whitman was not accurate in stating he had not read Emerson before publishing *Leaves of Grass*. (U.P.P., I, p. 132.)

Letter CXLVII (p. 1047, ll. 2, 3): "*Kennedy . . . has a book*". Kennedy's *Reminiscences of Walt Whitman* did not appear until 1896 (Paisley and London).

Letter CXLVIII (p. 1047): First published in its entirety from the manuscript owned by Mr. W. T. H. Howe, by his kind permission. Cf. Letter CXXIV (p. 1029). Carpenter had become an admirer of Whitman through reading his poetry, and in July 1874, had written him a long and cordial letter. From that time on he was an ardent disciple, visiting Whitman in 1877, imitating his style in *Towards Democracy*, and publishing his *Days With Walt Whitman* fourteen years after the poet's death.

Letter CXLIX (p. 1047, l. 28): "*The . . . book*". *Anne Gilchrist, Her Life and Writings*, by Herbert Harlakenden Gilchrist, 1887.

**Letter CL (p. 1048):** Elizabeth Porter Gould had published in the *Critic* (May 28, 1887) a full-page article, "Walt Whitman Among the Soldiers", composed largely of quotations from *Specimen Days*.

**Letter CLI (p. 1048):** John Addington Symonds had written to the *Fortnightly Review* to protest against Swinburne's "Whitmania", published in that magazine (August 1887). Swinburne's defence seemed lukewarm to Kennedy. (Kennedy, Preface.)

**Letter CLII (p. 1048):** This letter was printed by Barrus (p. 270) from a clipping from an unidentified American newspaper.

**Letter CLIII (p. 1049):** First published in its entirety from the manuscript owned by Mr. W. T. H. Howe, by his kind permission.

p. 1049, l. 31: "*O'Connor*". Whitman's Washington friend and staunch champion had been paralyzed for some time, and was to die the following May.

"*Ernest Rhys*" had edited *Poems of Walt Whitman*, in 1886, for the Canterbury Poets Series.

p. 1050, l. 5: "*little Fawcett*". Edgar Fawcett, who wrote "Two Letters Indicating the Con of Whitman". (*Conservator*, September 1895.)

p. 1050, ll. 7, 8: "*little bits in N Y Herald*". Whitman was receiving $100 a month for his frequent brief poems in this paper, later in the year to be collected in *November Boughs*.

**Letter CLIV (p. 1051, l. 11):** "*my bird is singing*", etc. Cf. "My Canary Bird" (p. 456).

**Letter CLV (p. 1051, l. 18):** "*the box of noble books*". Stedman had presented Whitman with a full set of the *Library of American Literature*, 11 volumes, which he had just edited with Miss E. McK. Hutchinson.

**Letter CLVI (p. 1052):** Published in *The Modern School*, April-May 1919.

**Letter CLVII (p. 1052):** Though the two passages given from this letter are the only ones that have been printed or are available (the family of John Addington Symonds preferring to throw no additional light upon his relation to Whitman), one of them has caused so much comment that the editor feels that such a selection as this would be inadequate without its text. This is the reference to Whitman's alleged paternity, which was first published by Edward Carpenter in the *Reformer*, February 1902, and republished in his *Days With Walt Whitman*, 1906. The first paragraph was given in Havelock Ellis' *The Intermediate Sex*. Both were included in a discussion of Whitman and Symonds in *Walt Whitman in England* by Harold Blodgett, pp. 65 ff.

**Letter CLVIII (p. 1052):** In 1890 Dr. J. Johnston of Bolton, Lancashire, visited Whitman, and on his return published *Notes of* *a Visit to Walt Whitman*. The next year, his friend, J. W. Wallace, paid the poet a visit, and in 1917 the two published *Visits to Walt Whitman in* 1890-1891.

p. 1053, l. 3: "*Dr. Holmes*". The article referred to is Chapter X of "Over the Tea Cups", which was in part devoted to Whitman.

Letter CLIX (p. 1053): "*pocket-bk ed'n*". On Whitman's seventieth birthday (May 31, 1889) he had issued a limited autographed and illustrated edition, in leather, in pocket-book style.

p. 1053, l. 19: "*my friend & gillie*". Whitman required the services of a male nurse during the last years of his life.

Letter CLX (p. 1053, l. 28): "*The Notes*". *Notes of a Visit to Walt Whitman*.

Letter CLXI (p. 1054, l. 34): "*J. W. W.*" J. W. Wallace.

Letter CLXII (p. 1055, l. 14): "*W. Sharp's piece*". Sharp had written a criticism of Stedman and Hutchinson's *Library of American Literature* for the *National Review*, London (for March 1891), in which he sought to discredit the opinion that "American literature begins with Walt Whitman, and has as yet got no further".

Letter CLXIII (p. 1055): This letter and later ones sent to the Bolton friends all carried the following printed extract:
"*From the Boston Eve'g Transcript, May* 7, '91.—The Epictetus saying, as given by Walt Whitman in his own quite utterly dilapidated physical case, is, a 'little spark of soul dragging a great lummux of corpse-body clumsily to and fro around'."

Letter CLXIV (p. 1056): First printed in its entirety here, from a manuscript in the Bucke collection, through the kindness of Professor Clifton Joseph Furness, and of the family of Dr. Bucke.

p. 1056, l. 12: "*the burial house*", a lot in Harleigh Cemetery, Camden, had been donated to Whitman, on which he had built a massive family vault for his own resting place, and that of several members of his family.

p. 1056, ll. 15, 16: "*other near relations*". The question of Whitman's paternity was raised when Edward Carpenter (London *Reformer*, February 1902) quoted a passage of a letter from Whitman to John Addington Symonds (cf. Letter CLVII, p. 1052). This is not the place for an adequate discussion of the question whether some of Whitman's friends, like Burroughs and Eldridge, were right in attributing this statement to the fabrications or hallucinations of Whitman's last years. Some writers have advanced the theory that Whitman by means of it sought to defend himself from the persistent queries of Symonds concerning the homosexual implications of the "Calamus" poems. Nearly all Whitman's biographers have dealt with the matter, but not conclusively.

Letter CLXV (p. 1056): "*Epictetus*". Cf. Letter CLXIII, n. (*supra*). Whitman's interest in Epictetus dated back to his early youth; he was about sixteen when he found an *Enchiridion* in a second-hand book shop. "It was like being born again," he said. (Traubel, II, pp. 71-72.) Epictetus' description of a wise man is found in a Whitman notebook of the period 1868-70. (U.P.P., II, p. 94.)

Letter CLXVI (p. 1057): A stenographic report of the conversation at this dinner appears in *In Re*, pp. 297-327.

p. 1057, l. 31: "*Dr. B.*". Dr. R. M. Bucke.

p. 1057, l. 32: "*Horace T.*". Horace Traubel.

Letter CLXVII (p. 1058, l. 7): "*July, Lippincott's*". Traubel printed the stenographic report of Whitman's birthday dinner (cf. Letter CLXVI, p. 1057) in the August number of *Lippincott's Monthly Magazine*, 1891.

p. 1058, l. 9: "*facsimiles*". Too ill to write much, Whitman had several letters of his printed in facsimile and sent by Traubel to his European and American friends. One of these facsimiles is reproduced in Johnston and Wallace, *Visits to Walt Whitman in* 1890-1891, facing p. 235.

Letter CLXVIII (p. 1058): Kennedy reports that Arnold translated parts of *Leaves of Grass* into certain Asiatic languages. (*The Fight of a Book for the World*, p. 272 n.)